T0180693

Lecture Notes in Computer Science　12425

More information about this series at http://www.springer.com/series/7409

Constantine Stephanidis ·
Don Harris · Wen-Chin Li ·
Dylan D. Schmorrow · Cali M. Fidopiastis ·
Panayiotis Zaphiris · Andri Ioannou ·
Xiaowen Fang · Robert A. Sottilare ·
Jessica Schwarz (Eds.)

HCI International 2020 – Late Breaking Papers

Cognition, Learning and Games

22nd HCI International Conference, HCII 2020
Copenhagen, Denmark, July 19–24, 2020
Proceedings

 Springer

Editors
Constantine Stephanidis
University of Crete and Foundation
for Research and Technology – Hellas
(FORTH)
Heraklion, Greece

Wen-Chin Li
Cranfield University
Cranfield, UK

Cali M. Fidopiastis
Design Interactive, Inc.
Orlando, FL, USA

Andri Ioannou ⓘ
Cyprus University of Technology
Limassol, Cyprus

Research Center on Interactive Media, Smart
Systems and Emerging Technologies (RISE)
Nicosia, Cyprus

Robert A. Sottilare
Soar Technology, Inc.
Orlando, FL, USA

Don Harris
Coventry University
Coventry, UK

Dylan D. Schmorrow
Soar Technology Inc.
Orlando, FL, USA

Panayiotis Zaphiris
Cyprus University of Technology
Limassol, Cyprus

Xiaowen Fang
DePaul University
Chicago, IL, USA

Jessica Schwarz
Fraunhofer FKIE
Wachtberg, Germany

ISSN 0302-9743   ISSN 1611-3349 (electronic)
Lecture Notes in Computer Science
ISBN 978-3-030-60127-0   ISBN 978-3-030-60128-7 (eBook)
https://doi.org/10.1007/978-3-030-60128-7

LNCS Sublibrary: SL3 – Information Systems and Applications, incl. Internet/Web, and HCI

This Springer imprint is published by the registered company Springer Nature Switzerland AG
The registered company address is: Gewerbestrasse 11, 6330 Cham, Switzerland

Foreword

The 22nd International Conference on Human-Computer Interaction, HCI International 2020 (HCII 2020), was planned to be held at the AC Bella Sky Hotel and Bella Center, Copenhagen, Denmark, during July 19–24, 2020. Due to the COVID-19 pandemic and the resolution of the Danish government not to allow events larger than 500 people to be hosted until September 1, 2020, HCII 2020 had to be held virtually. It incorporated the 21 thematic areas and affiliated conferences listed on the following page.

A total of 6,326 individuals from academia, research institutes, industry, and governmental agencies from 97 countries submitted contributions, and 1,439 papers and 238 posters were included in the volumes of the proceedings published before the conference. Additionally, 333 papers and 144 posters are included in the volumes of the proceedings published after the conference, as "Late Breaking Work" (papers and posters). These contributions address the latest research and development efforts in the field and highlight the human aspects of design and use of computing systems.

The volumes comprising the full set of the HCII 2020 conference proceedings are listed in the following pages and together they broadly cover the entire field of human-computer interaction, addressing major advances in knowledge and effective use of computers in a variety of application areas.

I would like to thank the Program Board Chairs and the members of the Program Boards of all Thematic Areas and Affiliated Conferences for their valuable contributions towards the highest scientific quality and the overall success of the HCI International 2020 conference.

This conference would not have been possible without the continuous and unwavering support and advice of the founder, conference general chair emeritus and conference scientific advisor, Prof. Gavriel Salvendy. For his outstanding efforts, I would like to express my appreciation to the communications chair and editor of HCI International News, Dr. Abbas Moallem.

July 2020   Constantine Stephanidis

HCI International 2020 Thematic Areas and Affiliated Conferences

Thematic Areas:

- HCI 2020: Human-Computer Interaction
- HIMI 2020: Human Interface and the Management of Information

Affiliated Conferences:

- EPCE: 17th International Conference on Engineering Psychology and Cognitive Ergonomics
- UAHCI: 14th International Conference on Universal Access in Human-Computer Interaction
- VAMR: 12th International Conference on Virtual, Augmented and Mixed Reality
- CCD: 12th International Conference on Cross-Cultural Design
- SCSM: 12th International Conference on Social Computing and Social Media
- AC: 14th International Conference on Augmented Cognition
- DHM: 11th International Conference on Digital Human Modeling & Applications in Health, Safety, Ergonomics & Risk Management
- DUXU: 9th International Conference on Design, User Experience and Usability
- DAPI: 8th International Conference on Distributed, Ambient and Pervasive Interactions
- HCIBGO: 7th International Conference on HCI in Business, Government and Organizations
- LCT: 7th International Conference on Learning and Collaboration Technologies
- ITAP: 6th International Conference on Human Aspects of IT for the Aged Population
- HCI-CPT: Second International Conference on HCI for Cybersecurity, Privacy and Trust
- HCI-Games: Second International Conference on HCI in Games
- MobiTAS: Second International Conference on HCI in Mobility, Transport and Automotive Systems
- AIS: Second International Conference on Adaptive Instructional Systems
- C&C: 8th International Conference on Culture and Computing
- MOBILE: First International Conference on Design, Operation and Evaluation of Mobile Communications
- AI-HCI: First International Conference on Artificial Intelligence in HCI

Conference Proceedings – Full List of Volumes

1. LNCS 12181, Human-Computer Interaction: Design and User Experience (Part I), edited by Masaaki Kurosu
2. LNCS 12182, Human-Computer Interaction: Multimodal and Natural Interaction (Part II), edited by Masaaki Kurosu
3. LNCS 12183, Human-Computer Interaction: Human Values and Quality of Life (Part III), edited by Masaaki Kurosu
4. LNCS 12184, Human Interface and the Management of Information: Designing Information (Part I), edited by Sakae Yamamoto and Hirohiko Mori
5. LNCS 12185, Human Interface and the Management of Information: Interacting with Information (Part II), edited by Sakae Yamamoto and Hirohiko Mori
6. LNAI 12186, Engineering Psychology and Cognitive Ergonomics: Mental Workload, Human Physiology, and Human Energy (Part I), edited by Don Harris and Wen-Chin Li
7. LNAI 12187, Engineering Psychology and Cognitive Ergonomics: Cognition and Design (Part II), edited by Don Harris and Wen-Chin Li
8. LNCS 12188, Universal Access in Human-Computer Interaction: Design Approaches and Supporting Technologies (Part I), edited by Margherita Antona and Constantine Stephanidis
9. LNCS 12189, Universal Access in Human-Computer Interaction: Applications and Practice (Part II), edited by Margherita Antona and Constantine Stephanidis
10. LNCS 12190, Virtual, Augmented and Mixed Reality: Design and Interaction (Part I), edited by Jessie Y.C. Chen and Gino Fragomeni
11. LNCS 12191, Virtual, Augmented and Mixed Reality: Industrial and Everyday Life Applications (Part II), edited by Jessie Y.C. Chen and Gino Fragomeni
12. LNCS 12192, Cross-Cultural Design: User Experience of Products, Services, and Intelligent Environments (Part I), edited by P.L. Patrick Rau
13. LNCS 12193, Cross-Cultural Design: Applications in Health, Learning, Communication, and Creativity (Part II), edited by P.L. Patrick Rau
14. LNCS 12194, Social Computing and Social Media: Design, Ethics, User Behavior, and Social Network Analysis (Part I), edited by Gabriele Meiselwitz
15. LNCS 12195, Social Computing and Social Media: Participation, User Experience, Consumer Experience, and Applications of Social Computing (Part II), edited by Gabriele Meiselwitz
16. LNAI 12196, Augmented Cognition: Theoretical and Technological Approaches (Part I), edited by Dylan D. Schmorrow and Cali M. Fidopiastis
17. LNAI 12197, Augmented Cognition: Human Cognition and Behaviour (Part II), edited by Dylan D. Schmorrow and Cali M. Fidopiastis

18. LNCS 12198, Digital Human Modeling & Applications in Health, Safety, Ergonomics & Risk Management: Posture, Motion and Health (Part I), edited by Vincent G. Duffy
19. LNCS 12199, Digital Human Modeling & Applications in Health, Safety, Ergonomics & Risk Management: Human Communication, Organization and Work (Part II), edited by Vincent G. Duffy
20. LNCS 12200, Design, User Experience, and Usability: Interaction Design (Part I), edited by Aaron Marcus and Elizabeth Rosenzweig
21. LNCS 12201, Design, User Experience, and Usability: Design for Contemporary Interactive Environments (Part II), edited by Aaron Marcus and Elizabeth Rosenzweig
22. LNCS 12202, Design, User Experience, and Usability: Case Studies in Public and Personal Interactive Systems (Part III), edited by Aaron Marcus and Elizabeth Rosenzweig
23. LNCS 12203, Distributed, Ambient and Pervasive Interactions, edited by Norbert Streitz and Shin'ichi Konomi
24. LNCS 12204, HCI in Business, Government and Organizations, edited by Fiona Fui-Hoon Nah and Keng Siau
25. LNCS 12205, Learning and Collaboration Technologies: Designing, Developing and Deploying Learning Experiences (Part I), edited by Panayiotis Zaphiris and Andri Ioannou
26. LNCS 12206, Learning and Collaboration Technologies: Human and Technology Ecosystems (Part II), edited by Panayiotis Zaphiris and Andri Ioannou
27. LNCS 12207, Human Aspects of IT for the Aged Population: Technologies, Design and User experience (Part I), edited by Qin Gao and Jia Zhou
28. LNCS 12208, Human Aspects of IT for the Aged Population: Healthy and Active Aging (Part II), edited by Qin Gao and Jia Zhou
29. LNCS 12209, Human Aspects of IT for the Aged Population: Technology and Society (Part III), edited by Qin Gao and Jia Zhou
30. LNCS 12210, HCI for Cybersecurity Privacy and Trust, edited by Abbas Moallem
31. LNCS 12211, HCI in Games, edited by Xiaowen Fang
32. LNCS 12212, HCI in Mobility, Transport and Automotive Systems: Automated Driving and In-Vehicle Experience Design (Part I), edited by Heidi Krömker
33. LNCS 12213, HCI in Mobility, Transport and Automotive Systems: Driving Behavior, Urban and Smart Mobility (Part II), edited by Heidi Krömker
34. LNCS 12214, Adaptive Instructional Systems, edited by Robert A. Sottilare and Jessica Schwarz
35. LNCS 12215, Culture and Computing, edited by Matthias Rauterberg
36. LNCS 12216, Design, Operation and Evaluation of Mobile Communications, edited by Gavriel Salvendy and June Wei
37. LNCS 12217, Artificial Intelligence in HCI, edited by Helmut Degen and Lauren Reinerman-Jones
38. CCIS 1224, HCI International 2020 Posters (Part I), edited by Constantine Stephanidis and Margherita Antona
39. CCIS 1225, HCI International 2020 Posters (Part II), edited by Constantine Stephanidis and Margherita Antona

40. CCIS 1226, HCI International 2020 Posters (Part III), edited by Constantine Stephanidis and Margherita Antona

41. LNCS 12423, HCI International 2020 – Late Breaking Papers: User Experience Design and Case Studies, edited by Constantine Stephanidis, Aaron Marcus, Elizabeth Rosenzweig, P.L. Patrick Rau, Abbas Moallem, and Matthias Rauterberg

42. LNCS 12424, HCI International 2020 – Late Breaking Papers: Multimodality and Intelligence, edited by Constantine Stephanidis, Masaaki Kurosu, Helmut Degen, and Lauren Reinerman-Jones

43. LNCS 12425, HCI International 2020 – Late Breaking Papers: Cognition, Learning and Games, edited by Constantine Stephanidis, Don Harris, Wen-Chin Li, Dylan D. Schmorrow, Cali M. Fidopiastis, Panayiotis Zaphiris, Andri Ioannou, Xiaowen Fang, Robert Sottilare, and Jessica Schwarz

44. LNCS 12426, HCI International 2020 – Late Breaking Papers: Universal Access and Inclusive Design, edited by Constantine Stephanidis, Margherita Antona, Qin Gao, and Jia Zhou

45. LNCS 12427, HCI International 2020 – Late Breaking Papers: Interaction, Knowledge and Social Media, edited by Constantine Stephanidis, Gavriel Salvendy, June Way, Sakae Yamamoto, Hirohiko Mori, Gabriele Meiselwitz, Fiona Fui-Hoon Nah, and Keng Siau

46. LNCS 12428, HCI International 2020 – Late Breaking Papers: Virtual and Augmented Reality, edited by Constantine Stephanidis, Jessie Y.C. Chen, and Gino Fragomeni

47. LNCS 12429, HCI International 2020 – Late Breaking Papers: Digital Human Modeling and Ergonomics, Mobility and Intelligent Environments, edited by Constantine Stephanidis, Vincent G. Duffy, Norbert Streitz, Shin'ichi Konomi, and Heidi Krömker

48. CCIS 1293, HCI International 2020 – Late Breaking Posters (Part I), edited by Constantine Stephanidis, Margherita Antona, and Stavroula Ntoa

49. CCIS 1294, HCI International 2020 – Late Breaking Posters (Part II), edited by Constantine Stephanidis, Margherita Antona, and Stavroula Ntoa

http://2020.hci.international/proceedings

HCI International 2020 (HCII 2020)

The full list with the Program Board Chairs and the members of the Program Boards of all thematic areas and affiliated conferences is available online at:

http://www.hci.international/board-members-2020.php

HCI International 2021

The 23rd International Conference on Human-Computer Interaction, HCI International 2021 (HCII 2021), will be held jointly with the affiliated conferences in Washington DC, USA, at the Washington Hilton Hotel, July 24–29, 2021. It will cover a broad spectrum of themes related to human-computer interaction (HCI), including theoretical issues, methods, tools, processes, and case studies in HCI design, as well as novel interaction techniques, interfaces, and applications. The proceedings will be published by Springer. More information will be available on the conference website: http://2021.hci.international/

General Chair
Prof. Constantine Stephanidis
University of Crete and ICS-FORTH
Heraklion, Crete, Greece
Email: general_chair@hcii2021.org

http://2021.hci.international/

Contents

Cognitive Psychology

Basic Study on Incidence of Micro-Error in Visual
Attention-Controlled Environment   3
*Taisei Ando, Takehiko Yamaguchi, Tania Giovannetti,
and Maiko Sakamoto*

A Methodological Approach to Create Interactive Art
in Artificial Intelligence 13
*Weiwen Chen, Mohammad Shidujaman, Jiangbo Jin,
and Salah Uddin Ahmed*

The Effect of Different Icon Shape and Width on Touch Behavior 32
Yung-Chueh Cheng, Hsi-Jen Chen, and Wei-Hsiang Hung

Project Team Recommendation Model Based on Profiles Complementarity . . . 45
*Matheus dos Santos Nascimento, Bruno Mendonça Santos,
Daniela de Freitas Guilhermino Trindade,
Jislaine de Fátima Guilhermino, José Reinaldo Merlin,
Ronaldo Cesar Mengato, Ederson Marcos Sgarbi,
and Carlos Eduardo Ribeiro*

A Neurophysiological Sensor Suite for Real-Time Prediction of Pilot
Workload in Operational Settings 60
*Trevor Grant, Kaunil Dhruv, Lucca Eloy, Lucas Hayne, Kevin Durkee,
and Leanne Hirshfield*

Consideration of How Different Rearview Presentations Used for Electronic
Mirrors on Automobiles Affect Human Spatial Cognition. 78
*Yutaro Kido, Sora Kanzaki, Tomonori Ohtsubo, Yoshiaki Matsuba,
Daichi Sugawara, and Miwa Nakanishi*

Design Guidelines of Social-Assisted Robots for the Elderly:
A Mixed Method Systematic Literature Review 90
Chih-Chang Lin, Hao-Yu Liao, and Fang-Wu Tung

Examining the Relationship Between Songs
and Psychological Characteristics 105
*Miran Pyun, Donghun Kim, Chaeyun Lim, Eunbyul Lee, Jihey Kwon,
and Sangyup Lee*

An Overview of Paper Documentation Moving to Onboard Information
System (OIS) for Commercial Aircraft.   116
    Wei Tan and Yin Jiang

Influence of Visual Symbol's User Background and Symbol Semantic
Abstraction Level on User's Cognition in AR Auxiliary Assembly
Environment.   127
    Lei Wu, Yao Su, and Junfeng Wang

Information Visualization Design of Nuclear Power Control System Based
on Attention Capture Mechanism   138
    Xiaoli Wu and Panpan Xu

Design Suggestions for Smart Tax Return Software Based on Reviewing
Tax Compliance Literature   150
    Bo Zhang and Jingyu Zhang

Augmented Cognition

Applications of an Online Audience Response System in Different
Academic Settings: An Empirical Study.   165
    Ahmed Amro, Muhammad Mudassar Yamin, and Benjamin James Knox

Perceived Restorativeness and Meditation Depth for Virtual Reality
Supported Mindfulness Interventions   176
    Mark R. Costa, Dessa Bergen-Cico, Rachel Razza, Leanne Hirshfield,
    and Qiu Wang

Global Mindset - A Complex Cognitive Model Used for Global Leadership
Decision-Making When Working Across Geographical Boundaries   190
    Agnes Flett

Assessing Variable Levels of Delegated Control – A Novel Measure
of Trust   202
    Samson Palmer, Dale Richards, Graham Shelton-Rayner,
    Kurtulus Izzetoglu, and David Inch

Neuroergonomics Behind Culture: A Dynamic Causal Modeling (DCM)
Study on Emotion.   216
    Zachary Pugh, Jiali Huang, Kristen Lindquist, and Chang S. Nam

Measure for Measure: How Do We Assess Human Autonomy Teaming?. . . .   227
    Dale Richards

A Typology of Non-functional Information   240
    Davide Secchi

Basic Study to Reduce the Artifact from Brain Activity Data
with Auto-regressive Model   255
  Shunji Shimizu, Masaya Hori, Hiroaki Inoue, Yu Kikuchi, Takuya Kiryu,
  and Fumikazu Miwakeichi

Producing an Immersive Experience Using Human-Robot
Interaction Stimuli.   266
  Thy Vo and Joseph B. Lyons

Learning and Collaboration Technologies

How Virtual Reality Is Changing the Future of Learning in K-12
and Beyond: Using Needs-Affordances-Features Perspective.   279
  Marta Adžgauskaitė, Kaveh Abhari, and Michael Pesavento

Tangible Storytelling to Learn the Four Seasons:
Design and Preliminary Observations.   299
  Wafa Almukadi

Analyzing Students' Behavior in a MOOC Course:
A Process-Oriented Approach.   307
  Franklin Bernal, Jorge Maldonado-Mahauad, Klinge Villalba-Condori,
  Miguel Zúñiga-Prieto, Jaime Veintimilla-Reyes, and Magali Mejía

The Role of Learning City "Smart Teams" in Promoting, Supporting,
and Extending the Community School Model   326
  Sarah A. Chauncey and Gregory I. Simpson

Design and Development of a Web Extension to Help Facilitate
the Learning of a Foreign Language   345
  Connor Corbin, Deniz Cetinkaya, and Huseyin Dogan

Training Professionals to Bring Digital Transformation into Museums:
The Mu.SA Blended Course.   365
  Massimiliano Dibitonto, Katarzyna Leszczynska, Elisa Cruciani,
  and Carlo Maria Medaglia

Learning and Creativity Through a Curatorial Practice Using
Virtual Reality   377
  Sérgio Eliseu, Maria Manuela Lopes, João Pedro Ribeiro,
  and Fábio Oliveira

How Augmented Reality Influences Student Workload
in Engineering Education   388
  Wenbin Guo and Jung Hyup Kim

The Influential Factors on E-learning Adoption and Learning Continuance. . .   397
  Meryem Harzalla and Nizar Omheni

A Real-Time Cross-Sectioning System for Visualization of Architectural
Construction Details   410
  Luis Hernández-Ibáñez and Viviana Barneche-Naya

Exploring the Affordance of Distance Learning Platform (DLP)
in COVID19 Remote Learning Environment   421
  Ajrina Hysaj and Doaa Hamam

Tirana Plug-in River: Catalyst Playful Experiences to Revitalize Albanian
Informal Settlements   432
  Saimir Kristo, Valerio Perna, and Keti Hoxha

Investigating the Relation Between Sense of Presence, Attention
and Performance: Virtual Reality Versus Web   445
  *Aliane Loureiro Krassmann, Fabrício Herpich,
  Liane Margarida Rockenbach Tarouco, and Magda Bercht*

Research on the Design of Intelligent Interactive Toys Based
on Marker Education.   462
  Yi Lu and Wei Pang

Designing a Faculty Chatbot Through User-Centered Design Approach   472
  Zlatko Stapić, Ana Horvat, and Dijana Plantak Vukovac

The Influence of Picture Book Interaction Design on Preschool Children's
Reading Experience.   485
  Liying Wang

Adaptive Instructional Systems

Enable 3A in AIS   507
  Faruk Ahmed, Keith Shubeck, Frank Andrasik, and Xiangen Hu

Adapting E-Learning to Dyslexia Type: An Experimental Study to Evaluate
Learning Gain and Perceived Usability   519
  Weam Gaoud Alghabban and Robert Hendley

Reducing the Gap Between the Conceptual Models of Students and Experts
Using Graph-Based Adaptive Instructional Systems.   538
  Philippe J. Giabbanelli and Andrew A. Tawfik

A Learning Engineering Model for Learner-Centered Adaptive Systems.   557
  Jim Goodell and Khanh-Phuong (KP) Thai

Technology in Education: Meeting the Future Literacy and Numeracy
Needs of Society.. 574
James Ness, and USMA Engineering Psychology Class of 2020

Adaptive Agents for Fit-for-Purpose Training 586
Karel van den Bosch, Romy Blankendaal, Rudy Boonekamp,
and Tjeerd Schoonderwoerd

Google Service-Based CbITS Authoring Tool to Support Collaboration 605
Lijia Wang, Keith Shubeck, and Xiangen Hu

Interacting with Games

The Interplay Between Artificial Intelligence and Users' Personalities:
A New Scenario for Human-Computer Interaction in Gaming............ 619
Barbara Caci and Khaldoon Dhou

Behavlet Analytics for Player Profiling and Churn Prediction 631
Darryl Charles and Benjamin Ultan Cowley

The Kansei Research on the Manipulation Experience of Mobile Game
with Joystick 644
Hsin-Jung Chen and Hsi-Jen Chen

A Novel Investigation of Attack Strategies via the Involvement of Virtual
Humans: A User Study of Josh Waitzkin, a Virtual Chess Grandmaster..... 658
Khaldoon Dhou

Systems Approach to Designing an Enjoyable Process for Game Designers ... 669
Nandhini Giri and Erik Stolterman

Broader Understanding of Gamification by Addressing Ethics
and Diversity 688
Ole Goethe and Adam Palmquist

Game-Based Learning and Instructional Effectiveness in Organizational
Communication Classrooms 700
Dongjing Kang

Enhancing Social Ties Through Manual Player Matchmaking in Online
Multiplayer Games 708
Md Riyadh, Ali Arya, Gerry Chan, and Masud Imran

A Simulation Game to Acquire Skills on Industry 4.0 730
Veronica Rossano, Rosa Lanzilotti, and Teresa Roselli

Personalised Semantic User Interfaces for Games 739
Owen Sacco

Utilization of Neurophysiological Data to Classify Player Immersion
to Distract from Pain.................................... 756
    Kellyann Stamp, Chelsea Dobbins, and Stephen Fairclough

Author Index 775

Cognitive Psychology

Basic Study on Incidence of Micro-Error in Visual Attention-Controlled Environment

Taisei Ando[1]([⊠]), Takehiko Yamaguchi[1], Tania Giovannetti[2], and Maiko Sakamoto[3]

[1] Suwa University of Science, 5000-1, Toyohira, Chino, Nagano, Japan
t.ando.vrds@gmail.com, tk-ymgch@rs.sus.ac.jp
[2] Temple University, Philadelphia, PA 1912217, USA
tgio@temple.edu
[3] Saga University, 5-1-1 Nabeshima, Saga, Saga, Japan

Abstract. Efficiency of the method based on the generation frequency of micro-error (ME), which corresponds to stagnation of a reaching action, in distinguishing the mild cognitive impairment (MCI) patients among healthy elderly persons. In the previous study, the effect of visual condition on the cause of ME occurrence was clarified, and it was indicated that the gaze action just before starting the reaching action contributed to ME generation. In the present study, we investigated the incidence of ME in an environment where visual attention was controlled to determine the effect of gaze behavior.

In the present study, we measured two factors such as the viewing angle (5°, 10°, 20°, 30°) and direction (top, bottom, right, left) as independent variables.

Although no significant difference was observed in terms of the direction, a considerable variation was noted in the visual field angle, and a positive correlation was indicated between the number of occurrences of ME and the visual field angle. Based on these results, the relationship between the gazing behavior and ME was clarified.

Keywords: Mild cognitive impairment · Instrumental activity of daily living · Micro-error · Visual attention · Gazing behavior

1 Introduction

In recent years, the number of patients with dementia has been increasing worldwide. According to the report by the International Alzheimer's Association, the number of patients with dementia will augment approximately from 50 million in 2018 to 152 million in 2050 [1]. In Japan, the number of people with dementia is expected to increase from approximately 4.62 million in 2012 to 6.75 million in 2025 [2]. There are many types of dementia, and the most widespread ones are cerebrovascular dementia and Alzheimer's dementia. At present, however, the fundamental treatment for this disease has not been found yet, and only slows the progression of dementia. However, it has been reported that 14%–44% of patients with mild dementia, also referred to as mild cognitive impairment (MCI), which is a precursor of dementia, return to normal state owing to early detection and appropriate rehabilitation [3]. On average, the rate of progression from

MCI to dementia is 10% per year [4]. It has also been reported that approximately 50% of patients with MCI will progress to dementia within five years if the condition remains untreated [5]. Therefore, early detection of MCI is an important issue. At present, typical screening tests for dementia include the mental statement (MMSE) and the revised version of the Hasegawa simple intelligence scale (HDS-R). MMSE consists of 11 items, including orientation to time, orientation to place, calculation, and repetition of sentences; its duration is 10 min. HDS-R includes nine items, including such factors as age, orientation to time, orientation to place, calculation, and fluency of language; its duration is five minutes. However, the problem is that the sensitivity of MMSE depends on the severity of dementia. Specifically, the rate is about 100% in the moderate dementia stage, approximately 50% in the mild dementia stage, and about 30% in the MCI stage. Moreover, there is a difficulty that the specificity of HDS-R is lower than the sensitivity. Therefore, a new screening method with a high discrimination accuracy is required. The results of the previous related studies have demonstrated the effectiveness of screening MCI patients and healthy elderly persons by using instrumental activities of daily living (IADL) based on the frequency of micro-errors (ME), which correspond to stagnation of the behavior during reaching movements. Previous studies have been focused on investigating the occurrence conditions of ME from the viewpoint of environmental factors. Moreover, the effects of visual conditions, such as color and shape of a reaching target, on the causes of ME occurrence have been clarified. Specifically, it has been reported that ME occurs when the stimulus of a reaching subject is close to the color and shape of a conspiracy stimulus displayed simultaneously. This observation suggests that the gazing behavior contributes to ME occurrence immediately before starting reaching movements.

The purpose of the present study is to investigate the frequency of ME when only the viewing angle is changed in an environment in which visual attention is controlled aiming to measure the effect of gaze behavior. The following research questions have been considered: (1) whether the frequency of ME increases with an increase in the viewing angle, (2) whether the frequency of ME varies depending on the direction of stimulation, and (3) whether ME can be avoided in the environment in which visual attention is controlled.

2 Previous Study

2.1 Virtual Kitchen Challenge (VKC) System

In the previous research, the VKC system was developed to measure the performance of VR-IADL by reproducing the IADL task environment on a tablet device using the virtual reality (VR) technology [6]. The "Lunchbox Task" presented in VKC implied composing a lunch with sandwiches and cookies made by spreading jam and peanut butter on slices of bread, a bottle with juice and executing the task of putting these three items in a lunch box. These actions could be operated by touching or dragging an object on the tablet screen. Previous studies demonstrated the presence of a correlation between VKC and IADL tasks in the real space with the number of ME occurrences [7]. Figure 1 represents the Lunchbox Task in VKC.

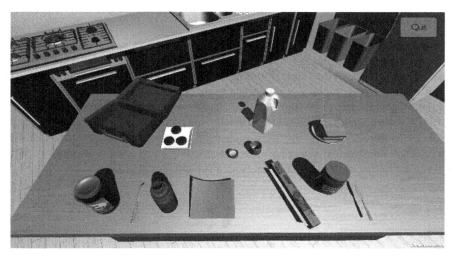

Fig. 1. Setup the lunchbox task

2.2 Relationship Between the Visual Field and Fixation

The eye-gaze behavior is defined as the movement of the eye to obtain visual information. In ergonomics, the relationship between the visual field range and discrimination ability of the eye-gaze point is considered, as shown in Fig. 2. The range of the central vision is 1°; the recognition limit for one or several words is from 5° to 10°; and the recognition limit for symbols from is 5° to 30°. These findings suggest that there may be a difference in the number of ME occurrences in the case when the objects to be reached and interfering stimuli are presented at each visual field angle.

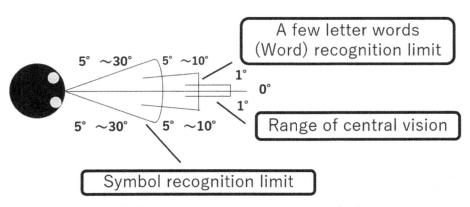

Fig. 2. Relationship between the visual field and fixation

2.3 Shape Task

It is considered that VKC can be influenced by color, shape, meaning, function, and planning. Therefore, in the previous study, Shape Task was formulated as a task to measure the influence of the shape similarity on ME [8]. In this task, multiple interfering stimuli and the target stimulus were simultaneously displayed on the screen, and the target stimulus was supposed to be touched. Specifically, an interfering stimulus (distractor object: DO) with a high correlation coefficient was randomly placed around the target object (target object: TO) having the similar form to investigate the frequency of ME. As a result, it was concluded that ME was generated by an interfering stimulus with the form similar to that of TO [8]. The task screen is represented in Fig. 3.

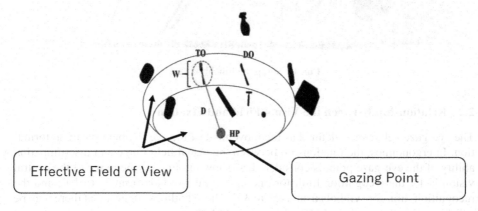

Fig. 3. Shape task

3   Method

3.1   Eye Task

In the task environment established for measuring ME in the previous research, TO and DO were displayed over multiple visual fields, and ME was evaluated in the visual fields with a different discrimination ability. In the present study, we formulated a task to measure the number of ME occurrences in the case when the viewing angle and stimulus position were changed in an environment with the controlled visual attention. The subject was suggested to seat down with a gaze meter (EMR -9) attached to the chin rest 35 cm away from the center of the monitor with the gaze point displayed on it. In addition to the gaze point, a fork, which was TO, and a knife, which corresponded to DO, were displayed on the monitor. Each stimulus was displayed by using the vertical and horizontal patterns at 5°, 10°, 20°, and 30° around the gaze point. The subject was requested to touch the TO as quickly as possible when the monitor was displayed while maintaining the gaze point as gaze as possible.

In the present study, we measured two factors such as the viewing angle (5°, 10°, 20°, 30°) and direction (top, bottom, right, left) as independent variables; and the other ones such as the number of ME occurrences, the three-dimensional position of the sliders by using a motion sensor, and the two-dimensional position of the gaze line obtained by using a gaze meter as dependent variables. In this experiment, 11 male university students (Mean = 21.55, Standard Deviation = 1.13) were asked to listen to white noise for one minute after each experimental patterns to measure fatigue of the examinees. The experiment was conducted considering a counter balance to offset the sequential effect. The established measurement environment is demonstrated in Fig. 4, and the stimulation pattern displayed on the Eye Task monitor is represented in Fig. 5.

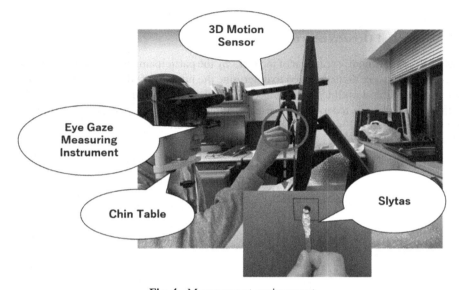

Fig. 4. Measurement environment

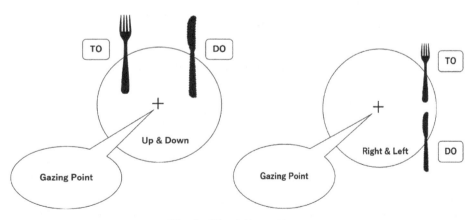

Fig. 5. Stimulation patterns

4 Results

4.1 Correlation Coefficient Between the Number of ME Occurrences and the Viewing Angle

The correlation coefficient r between the number of ME occurrences and the viewing angle was calculated to be $r = 0.7182$, indicating a positive correlation as a whole. Therefore, it was confirmed that the number of ME occurrences increased as the viewing angle became wider.

4.2 Number of Occurrences of ME

During the experiment, execution of the tasks by the participants was recorded as moving images, which were then analyzed to determine the number of ME occurrences for each task pattern. Table 1 outlines the results of the analysis on variance on the number of ME occurrences, which is a dependent variable. Table 2 provides the results of the multiple comparison test, and Fig. 6 represents a plot of the average number of ME occurrences relatively to the direction.

Table 1. Results of the analysis on variance

	Sum of Squares	df	Mean Square	F	p	η²
Direction	20.114	3	6.705	0.917	0.444	0.009
Residual	219.261	30	7.309			
Degree	932.932	3	310.977	33.566	< .001 **	0.406
Residual	277.943	30	9.265			
Direction * Degree	43.841ª	9ª	4.871ª	1.126ª	0.353ª	0.019
Residual	389.284	90	4.325			

*p<0.05, **p <0.001, *Mauchly's test of sphericity indicates that the assumption of sphericity is violated (p <.05)

Table 2. Results of the multiple comparison test

		Mean Difference	SE	t	Cohen's d	p_{holm}
10	20	−2.023	0.649	−3.117	−0.940	0.008 *
	30	−3.182	0.649	−4.903	−1.478	< .001 **
	5	2.886	0.649	4.448	1.341	< .001 **
20	30	−1.159	0.649	−1.786	−0.539	0.084
	5	4.909	0.649	7.565	2.281	< .001 **
30	5	6.068	0.649	9.351	2.819	< .001 **

*p < 0.05, **p < 0.001

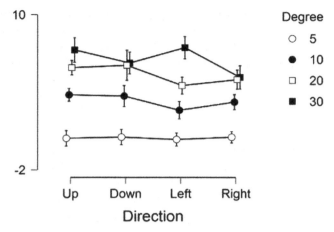

Fig. 6. Plot of the mean number of ME

4.3 Eye Movement During ME

Considering that the previous studies have demonstrated that ME can be caused by attachment to DO [8], we assume that ME does not occur in an environment in which visual attention is controlled. However, based on the results of the conducted experiment in the environment with controlled visual attention, we found that ME occurred more frequently when the subject's gaze was not moving than when they were moving. Here, the threshold to identify for whether the subject's gaze moved was set as 5 cm or more and less than 10 cm. Figure 7 represents the plot depicting the change in the distance from the gaze point with respect to time under the 30° condition in the case of subject 1.

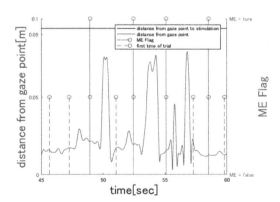

Fig. 7. Change in the distance from the eye-gaze point under the 30° condition

In the present study, we conducted the experiments in the environment in which visual attention was controlled, and therefore, it was important to determine whether the line of sight was moving. To determine this, we calculated the distance from the point of gaze. The calculation method for the distance is outlined below: (1) The position coordinates of the parallax-corrected line of sight are obtained by using the line of sight measuring instrument. (2) The distance d from the fixation point to the two-dimensional coordinate of the line of sight is calculated using the pythagorean theorem, as shown in Fig. 8.

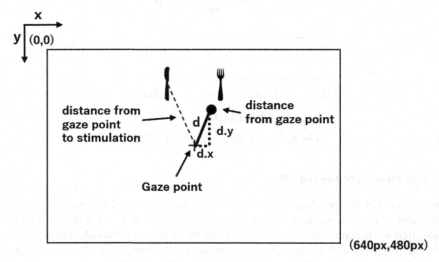

Fig. 8. 2D coordinates of the line of sight

$$d = \sqrt{d.x^2 + d.y^2} \tag{1}$$

(1) Table 3 provides the results of the analysis on variance with regard to the number of eye movements when ME occurs, and Table 4 outlines the results of multiple comparison tests.

Table 3. Results of the analysis on variance

	Sum of Squares	df	Mean Square	F	p	η^2
Degree	30.773ᵃ	3ᵃ	10.258ᵃ	7.795ᵃ	< .001ᵃ	0.293
Residual	39.477	30	1.316			
Direction	0.045	1	0.045	0.080	0.783	0.000
Residual	5.705	10	0.570			
Degree ∗ Direction	1.318ᵃ	3ᵃ	0.439ᵃ	0.883ᵃ	0.461ᵃ	0.013
Residual	14.932	30	0.498			

*Mauchly's test of sphericity indicates that the assumption of sphericity is violated (p <.05)

Table 4. Results of the multiple comparison tests

		Mean Difference	SE	t	Cohen's d	p_{holm}
10	20	−0.045	0.081	−0.559	−0.169	0.682
	30	−1.364	0.496	−2.750	−0.829	0.101
	5	0.045	0.045	1.000	0.302	0.682
20	30	−1.318	0.478	−2.758	−0.831	0.101
	5	0.091	0.061	1.491	0.449	0.501
30	5	1.409	0.481	2.932	0.884	0.090

4.4 ME and Viewing Angle Considerations

The results of the multiple comparison test provided in Table 2 outline no significant difference between 20° and 30°, suggesting that there has been no variance in the number of ME occurrences in the visual field beyond 20°, as it falls within the range of peripheral vision, and that no significant difference between 20° and 30° has been observed. Therefore, it is considered that the overall correlation coefficient was affected.

4.5 Study on the Direction Based on the Fixation Point and the Number of ME Occurrences

We hypothesized that there was no lateral difference in the number of ME occurrences but there was vertical difference based on human visual field characteristics. However, the analysis on variance presented in Table 1 demonstrated no significant difference in the direction of ME occurrences in the case when the fixation point was used as a reference. Investigations on the attention and accuracy have been conducted in the previous studies, and it has been clarified that a difference in the accuracy rate when the number of stimuli that responded vertically to the fixation point increases [9]. These result suggest that there was no difference in direction in this study due to the small number of stimuli.

4.6 Study on ME and Eye Movement

The results of the analysis on variance presented in Table 3 indicated a significant difference in the viewing angle; however, the results of the multiple comparison test presented in Table 4 demonstrated no difference between the levels. These results indicate that with an increase on the viewing angle, the number of eye movements increases as well.

5 Conclusion · Future Prospects

In the present study, we examined the following three research questions: (1) whether the number of ME events increases with an increase in the viewing angle; (2) whether the number of ME events varies depending on the location of a stimulus; and (3) whether

ME can be avoided in an environment in which visual attention is controlled. Although no significant difference was observed in terms of the direction, a considerable variation was noted in the visual field angle, and a positive correlation was indicated between the number of occurrences of ME and the visual field angle. Based on these results, the relationship between the gazing behavior and ME was clarified. In the present study, the attention was fully focused on the gazing point; however, as a future prospect, we plan to conduct a comparative study for the case of moving the eyes, the similar experiment as presented in this study considering MCI patients, and an experiment with an increasing number of stimuli.

Acknowledgements. This research was supported by Grants-in-Aid for Science Research (C) 18k12118.

References

1. World Alzheimer Report 2018: The Global Impact of Dementia, p. 34 (2018)
2. Ministry of Health: On the current situation of dementia facilities (2017). https://www.mhlw.go.jp/file/06-Seisakujouhou-12300000-Roukenkyoku/0000079008.pdf
3. Manly, J.J., Tang, M.X., Schupf, N., Stern, Y., Vonsattel, J.P.G., Mayeux, R.: Frequency and course of mild cognitive impairment in a multiethnic community. AnnNeurol. **63**(4), 494–506 (2008)
4. Bruscoli, M., Lovestone, S.: Is MCI really just early dementia? A systematic review of conversion studies. Int. Psychogeriatrics 129–140 (2004)
5. Yamamoto, Y.: A preliminary study of speech prosody-based relationship with HDS-scores, p. 1 (2010)
6. Yamaguchi, T., Floppe, D.A., Richard, P., Richard, E., Allain, P.: A dual-modal virtual reality kitchen for (re) learning of everyday cooking activities in Alzheimer's disease. Presence Teleoperators Virtual Environ. (2012)
7. Seligman, S.C., Giovannetti, T., Sestito, J., Libon, D.J.: A new approach to the characterization of subtle errors in everyday action: implications for mild cognitive impairment. Clin. Neuropsychol. **28**(1), 97–115 (2014)
8. Gyoji, H., et al.: Statistical analysis of micro-error occurrence probability for the Fitts' law-based pointing task. In: Yamamoto, S., Mori, H. (eds.) HCII 2019. LNCS, vol. 11569, pp. 317–329. Springer, Cham (2019). https://doi.org/10.1007/978-3-030-22660-2_22
9. Sheng, H., Patrick, C., James, I.: Attentional resolution and the locus of visual awareness. Nature 334–337 (1996)

A Methodological Approach to Create Interactive Art in Artificial Intelligence

Weiwen Chen[1]([✉]), Mohammad Shidujaman[1]([✉]), Jiangbo Jin[2],
and Salah Uddin Ahmed[3]

[1] Department of Information Art and Design, Academy of Arts and Design, Tsinghua
University, Beijing, China
{chenww19,shangt15}@mails.tsinghua.edu.cn
[2] Shanghai Academy of Fine Arts, Shanghai University, Shanghai, China
jjb@jinjiangbo.com
[3] Department of Business, Marketing and Law, University of South-Eastern Norway, Notodden,
Norway
salah.ahmed@usn.no

Abstract. In recent years, with the rapid development of big data, cloud computing, and deep learning, artificial intelligence (AI) has returned to the public's field of vision once again and gradually deepened and infiltrated into different areas of our life. In this context, interactive art faces the unprecedented opportunities and challenges. In the past, the process and results of interaction were under the control of the creators, and the audience could only interact with artworks mechanically. Most of these interactive artworks just met the primary demand for the audio-visual effects and the sensory stimulation, which has become a common problem of interactive art. However, developments of AI in the field of human-computer interaction allow artists to go beyond the limitations of the past, thus the interactive process will be more human, intelligent, and diversified. AI involved in artistic creation is undoubtedly the developing trend and the latest direction of future. Nevertheless, interactive art in AI, whose creative mechanism has not been constructed, just begun to rise, and requires theoretical guidance. Therefore, discussing and studying the interactive art creation mechanism in the context of AI will have certain theoretical, practical and social significance. The purpose of this paper is to provide a methodological approach for interactive art creation in the context of AI, and a new creative thinking and direction for art practitioners, theoreticians and scientists. This paper first discusses the core role of AI media in interactive art creation. And then it analyzes the subjectivity and interrelationship between the artists, robots and participants in the process. Finally, it puts forward the basic idea of constructing a new mechanic system of intelligent interactive art creation. In short, this paper builds a new interactive art creation system that takes "cognition of human-computer symbiosis, innovation supported by intelligent technology, collaboration among creative subjects, and constraints on creative behavior "as a new methodological approach, in which AI is the core media, artists, robots, and audience are the co-creation subjects.

Keywords: Artificial Intelligence (AI) · Interactive Art · Intelligent Medium · Multi-subjects · Creation Mechanism

C. Stephanidis et al. (Eds.): HCII 2020, LNCS 12425, pp. 13–31, 2020.
https://doi.org/10.1007/978-3-030-60128-7_2

1 Introduction

Nowadays, AI technology is developing rapidly and gradually penetrating into various fields, whose purpose is to explore the limits and the methods of using digital computers to imitate, extend and expand functions carried out by the human brain, such as obtaining and dealing information through the senses, understanding natural languages and solving complex problems [1]. In this background, AI has begun to march into the realm of art. Both artists and scientists have showed great interest in application of AI in artistic creation. On the one hand, scientists hope that AI will learn the deepest and most complex emotions of human beings, which is a multi-channel way of expression, and make machines closer to human beings with more friendly, sensitive, and aesthetic capabilities. On the other hand, as the innovator of the era, artists have also tried to train AI to discover its artistic expressions and ideas. AI, as a branch and category of computer science and technology, seems to have an inextricable relationship with interactive art since its birth. Interactive art is a participation-focus art form based on computer technology, sensor technology, and human-computer interaction technology, which will presumably use AI as the core media and efficient tools for creation in the context of AI. As a result, many interactive artists have been already eager to apply AI technologies into interactive art creation.

Turning to the specific context of interactive art and the unique way of using kinds of AI technologies, there are several situations that could describe the relationship between AI, artist, artwork, viewer, and environment. We have envisaged three categories that are characterized by the different roles AI plays in the process of interaction and the different situations, which are defined as: *dynamic-passive, interactive-indirect, and interactive-direct*.

Dynamic-Passive: The first is that AI acts as a behind-the-scenes worker in the work of art. That is, the creative mechanism inside the work is mainly determined by the artists, who inputs a great amount of data to train AI to generate a series of text and images, which are presented as the content of the art object. Moreover, AI have no relationship with the behavior of the audience who is a passive observer of this activity. The "flyAI" produced by American artist David Bowen can fall into this category. This installation artwork uses the machine learning image recognition library on the open source platform TensorFlow to allow AI systems to learn to distinguish the images of houseflies. When houseflies fly and land in front of the camera, their images are captured by the computer, and then the image recognition software will classify the captured images and rank the recognition results from one to five according to the percentage of possibility based on how likely the software thinks the listed item is what it sees. If "fly" is ranked number one on the list, there will be a mechanical pump that supplies water and nutrients to the houseflies. Other than that, the machine will not respond. The system is set up to run indefinitely with an indeterminate outcome, which remind viewers of the future destiny of mankind (see Fig. 1).

Interactive-Indirect: In addition to all of the features of the dynamic-passive category mentioned above except passive observers, there is an extra factor that the audience has an active role in influencing the changes in the art object, but the interaction between AI and audience is indirect. For instance, Turkish artist Seluk Artut created an AI-based

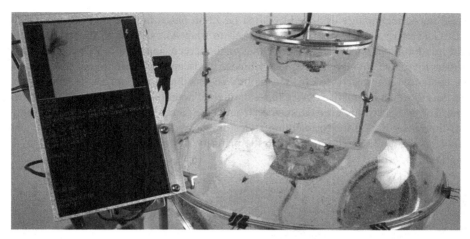

Fig. 1. AI installation "flyAI" created by David Bowen

interactive installation "Variable" inspired by Heidegger's Existence and Time and a description of the artwork on the gallery wall. By inputting the text of "Being and Time" into AI, he made it imitate the writing paradigm in the book to generate algorithmic models, thereby enabling AI to think like Heidegger and write words that no one can understand. The device consists of a wall-mounted metal plate, eight small projectors, and a display box with a five-inch high-definition electronic screen. An eight letters word which means "work name", such as "ACCEPTED" or "MOVEMENT", are projected on the metal plate. These words are randomly generated by the computer, and a long list of corresponding "work description" appears on the screen of the nearby display box. When the visitor presses the button, the work name and work description will be updated accordingly (see Fig. 2).

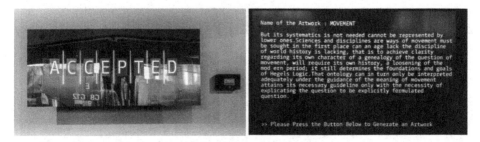

Fig. 2. AI interactive device "Variable"

Interactive-Direct: Third, in this category, AI could serve as an auxiliary creator and interact with audience directly. Although the internal mechanism and generative style are specified by the artist, but the performance of the art object is always changeable and unpredictable, which depends on the actions of participant and can learn from the history of direct interactions automatically. "Dada Landscape" is an interactive art installation based on AI technology designed by artist Le Zhou based in Shanghai, China, which uses Generative Adversarial Network (GAN) to train AI systems. In this art, viewers draw randomly the simple and abstract lines on the screen, and then the AI processes and renders these lines to recreate a unique Chinese landscape style painting in real time on the interactive interface (see Fig. 3). Another case is that American artist Gene Kogan has developed an interactive device that can migrate neural network image styles in real time. The audience only needs to stand in front of the camera, and the screen can display real-time images of different painting styles drawn by the AI based on the scene and people at the time, which all thanks to the maturity and application of the image style migration algorithm (see Fig. 4).

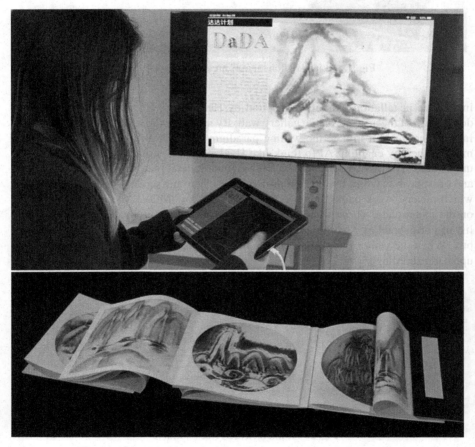

Fig. 3. AI interactive artwork installation named "dada landscape"

In traditional interactive art creations, which are belong to the categories defined as static, dynamic-passive, dynamic-interactive [2], the artists are still in the unshakable position of the creative subject or the doer, who have the power to control everything and set the rules of interaction [3, 4]. Although the audience can interact with the artwork in

Fig. 4. AI interactive art installation

real time, the process and experience of the interaction are predictable. In addition, the original specification of the art object and the performance of the art system can also be unchangeable. Throughout the interaction process, the audience is just a participant, mechanically repeating blunt movements and gestures. Though the presence of the audience forms part of the work, it would lose the value of the most precious thinking of art. In the context of AI, the traditional interactive art creation mechanism has been severely challenged: the core media has changed, the identity of the artist's creative constructor role has been impacted, and the participants have really played a key role. At this time, what kind of interactive art should be established? Can the creative mechanism adapt to the new situation?

The relevant theoretical literature on the mechanism of interactive art creation in the context of AI is scarce, but some scholars have mentioned it slightly. For example, Zaifei Cao [5] pointed out that some artists will still complete their creations alone in the future, but many of them just come up with ideas and achieve the final results with the implementation of AI, which is a more effective cooperation. AI experts Kaifu Li and Yonggang Wang [6] has discussed the relationship between AI and artistic creation from the perspective of AI. They assumed that the artistic creation of algorithms is just based on a large number of studies of human works, which is the simple imitation of a specific creative style of human beings. Liqin Tan [7] mentioned in "Singularity Art" that singularity artists are no longer just creators and information transmitters, but participants and coordinators; experiencers are no longer just external viewers, but also participants and creators. There is no clear distinction between the experiencers and artists. Roy Ascot [8], a pioneer of interactive art creation and theory, founded the world's first cross-media interactive art research center at the University of Wales in 1993, and proposed the five parallel creation methods of "connection, immersion, interaction, transformation, and appearance", and the three characteristics of "connection, interaction, and integration" of interactive art. Cornock and Edmonds put forward the idea that computer could transform the artist from an art specialist in creating artworks to a catalyst for creativity [2] and the opportunities for including audience participation have been increased by the advent of intelligent digital technology. Collaboration in art practice has grown significantly [9]. American artist Margot Lovejoy explicitly put forward the claim that the complete authorship of the digital age disappeared, and committed to engaging viewers in direct interactive experiences through installations, websites, and books research [10]. Janez Strehove considered the interactive experience is the core content of the creation of digital interactive artworks [11]. HC Hsieh emphasized that digital interactive art mainly focuses on the user participation, operation and action, and pointed out that good interactive system design can promote artistic creation [12]. Lev Manovich mentioned that interactive art, unlike traditional art, is simply tautology and its creation and appreciation can completely become a direct dialogue between the subjects. Any form of expression of the creative subject, whether it is texts, images or sound, can be transmitted to the viewers in real time in the form of digital encoding, and the creative process of the creator can also be shown in front of the viewers. At the same time, the viewers who have any opinions on the expression or creative conception of the artwork can also feed back to the creators in real time by digital coding, and the creators can make timely adjustments to the expression and creation [13]. Peter Webb has deconstructed and reconstructed the future images, that is, had his own unique insight into the relationship between the viewers (the subjects of viewing) and the artistic objects. It is believed that the viewer is not an external viewer outside the artwork, but an internal viewer who will participate in the art world and may also become a new narrator in future multimedia installations. Postmodern art creators have gradually receded from the view of "author is dead" posed by French deconstructionist Roland Barthes. This is not to say the disappearance of the art creators' noumenon, but the audience's participation in the process of art aesthetics, which has constructed and reconstructed the subjects [14].

There are relatively few literary works and dissertations on the interactive art creation mechanism in AI. Although some scholars have analyzed and explored the creative mechanism of AI and interactive art from different perspectives, they are not systematic, comprehensive, and in-depth and broad consensus has not been formed.

The purpose of the paper is to promote the interactive art to build a scientific and efficient creative mechanism that adapts to technological progress and artistic development. The fourth scientific and technological revolution marked by AI has swept the world and has had a profound impact on interactive art creation. In this context, the previous creative mechanism characterized by that artists were the single creative subject, that mechanical or electronic as the creative medium, and that simple interaction between human-machine has begun to falter and is increasingly unable to meet new aesthetic needs. Therefore, this paper has studied the impact of AI on interactive art, the artistic creation of robots, and the creative relationship between artists, robots, and audiences, which contributed to a new mechanism that provides scientific thinking and advanced methods for the creation of interactive art (see Fig. 5).

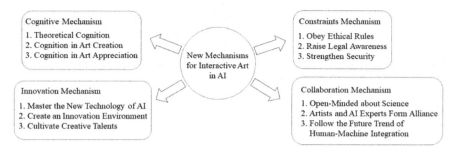

Fig. 5. New mechanisms for interactive art in AI

2 Interactive Art using AI as Core Media

Media is a necessary part of artistic creation which is a process of selecting and using media. The media that artists choose and use is often diverse, but one of them must play a major role and has a core status in the creative process. As a new art form, the interactive art also chooses and uses traditional media, such as text, sound, images, and various materials. However, in the context of AI, artists may use AI as the core medium, making the characteristics of interactive art more distinct, and pushing it to a new stage of development.

2.1 Development of Interactive Art using AI

To a certain extent, the form and value of interactive art are determined by the characteristics of its media which evolves with the development of the times, therefore, interactive art is always changeable and varied. Today's interactive art has obvious digital characteristics, which takes information technology as a carrier and multimedia as its support. From the perspective of the nature of media, AI, as a category of computer science, coincides with the virtualization characteristics of interactive art. Thus, using AI media as a new creative tool is the future development direction of interaction. In addition, from the perspective of media evolution, the media has "humanized trends" [15] and "remedial" [16] characteristics. As a new medium under the development of science and technology, AI cannot escape from humanization and the trends of remedying other media. The original media of interactive art already has multi-sensory interactivity, but it still has a drawback of non-intelligence which can be compensated by the advent of AI technology, so the intelligence of the media will become the future trend. From the perspective of the goal of media development, interactive art takes the emotional interaction with the audience as the ultimate goal. The increasingly humane AI technology has gradually begun to develop towards cognitive intelligence. Eventually, these artificial lives will also gain emotion and aesthetics. Naturally, interactive art will not miss this rare opportunity.

2.2 Role of AI Media in Interactive Art Creation

Canadian media theorist and thinker Marshall McLuhan pointed out the great role of media in the development of human history. He believes that all media are the extensions of people, which are the enhancement and enlargement of organs, senses, or functions, and have a profound and lasting impact on human and their environment [17]. His media theory clearly tells us that media can transcend time, space, and extend people's vision, hearing, and touch. The change of the media promotes the development of art, which cannot be separated from the media that plays an important role in art creation.

First, AI media can effectively convey the thoughts and emotions of creators. The process by which artists create and display artworks is the process of transmitting thoughts and emotions. Whether a piece of work can effectively convey thoughts and emotions depends not only on the artist's accomplishments, but also on the application of artistic media. The more advanced the art media, the more obvious the communication effect of the artwork. Compared with traditional media, AI media can break away from the constraints of time and space, communicate and interact with audiences in a humane and intelligent way, and integrate virtuality and reality.

Second, AI media can also enhance the appeal of artistic works. The AI media based on computer algorithms and sensors can automatically capture the actions of the audience through the camera, and then send out feedback signals through the output device to interact with the audience, thereby better eliminating the "gap" between the artworks and the audience, enabling the audience to integrate into the artworks, some of which even have good psychotherapeutic effects.

Then, it can provide the conditions for the audience to participate in the creation. In the information age, everyone can become an artist, just like Negroponte said that the digital highway will make the saying "completed and unchangeable works of art" become a thing of the past. Nowadays, people don't even have to move, but can create works of art with their fingers, which is the charm of interactive art. But in the past, the interaction between audiences and artworks was a programmatic, boring process, and interactive feedback was relatively simple. AI media is quite different from other media, which is not only an extension of human senses and limbs, but also an extension of human intelligence. This extension provides favorable conditions for audiences to participate in creation.

Finally, AI media can liberate artists' labor and stimulate creativity. In the future, AI can free humans from repetitive, regular, and simple tasks that take a lot of time, leading to a significant increase in productivity. But Massimo Negrotti believes that "The analysis-simulation" inherently mentality makes AI unable to handle things like creativity which is a kind of abilities with ambiguity, complexity and integrity [18]. Although artistic creation is considered to be a vivid expression of human creativity and emotional thinking, there are also non-creative labor parts in artistic practice, such as the process from unfamiliar contact to skillful use of tools, the mental labor process of cultivating creative skills and hands-on ability, which require the artist to invest a lot of time and energy to learn, hindering the exertion of creativity. If the labor part of artistic creation can be replaced by AI, then human creativity, free will and emotions can be released and expressed to the greatest extent, and art can become real art.

3   Creative Multi-Subjects of Interactive Art

The creative subject is one of the necessary constituent elements of artistic creation, which is the initiator of the artistic activity, and a practitioner with certain creative ability and aesthetic ability. Without the existence of creative subjects of artistic creation, art will not be born. The famous aesthetician and art historian E. Gombrich frankly acclaimed, "There really is no such thing as Art. There are only artists" [19]. This is enough to show the importance of the creative subject of artistic activity to art.

3.1 Artists in Interactive Art Creation

On the one hand, in order to achieve the ideal interactive results in the mind, the past interactive artists had to personally write computer programs. From the perspective of media development, the more the media becomes humane, the more autonomy and control people enjoy while using the media. With the maturity and development of AI technology, interactive artists may no longer be trapped in the captivity of professional knowledge. Therefore, the artist's emotion, recognition, and creativity has been strengthened and improved.

On the other hand, the artist is the initiator of the artistic creation activity, whose mind is the core of the artistic work. Art exists because the artist desires to express himself, evoke resonance, and recall the past. Although AI can replace part of the artist's labor, the part that will become art cannot be replaced by AI, which are the artist's desire to break through limited time and space, the desire to express himself, and the desire to communicate. AI does not have these social attributes and consciousness, thus naturally there is no original intention to create art. In the process of AI participating in the creation of interactive art, although the artist's participation is reduced and his authorship is weakened, he still has an absolute advantage in thinking orientation.

3.2 Robots in Interactive Art Creation

Today, robots have become a part of our daily lives, which have become "brush" tools and powerful assistants in the hands of artists, changing the traditional way of artistic creation in the past. With the in-depth application of AI technology in the field of robotics, intelligent robots will shake the position of the artist's creative subject, let the artist retreat behind the scenes, and then independently complete a series of artworks. In the interactive art, the subjectivity of intelligent robots will also become more and more obvious, which can even achieve emotional and ideological communication with the audience in the near future.

Before the advent of AI, it was not unusual for artists to use robots to create artworks. "Robotic art not only combines the skills of programmers and painters, but also combines the sensitivity of sculptors, installation artists, and performers with the orderliness of computer systems equipped with sensors and mechanical effectors" [20]. Therefore, robotic art is actually a kind of mechanized art, but there is a disorderly, subconscious beauty in this established stylized creation [21].

According to the degree of participation of robots and artists, we divide robotic art into four different types.

1. The artists retreat behind the scenes, and robots have become creative subjects. The creative subjects here are not really creative one, because these robots do not yet

have the learning ability and intelligence, but only follow the instructions given by the artists, and most of these artworks are robotic paintings and sculptures.

2. The other is that robots and artists work together to participate in art creation. Robots often work with humans and learn from our behavior. Contemporary artists seem to realize the connotation and important value of human-machine collaboration, and quickly apply the results of science and technology to artistic creation. Machines have expanded the human body. Therefore, when artistic creation methods exceed the physiological limits of humans, it is time for machines to show their skills.

3. In addition, robots have become a medium for artists to express their own ideas, and a vehicle for metaphorizing the relationship between machines and humans, people and people, society and nature. "Human-machine art is a way of expression that compares to the essence of human by taking advantage of machines to pay attention to the social history, realistic living environment, and state."[22].

4. Finally, robots are other things created by humans in accordance with the ideal image in their hearts, and are an extension of human limbs and intelligence. Many artists have begun trying to use machines as part of their limbs in order to push the limits of the body.

With the gradual deepening of AI technology in the field of robots, robots are undergoing a process of transforming from the so-called tools and media to assist artists in artistic creation to becoming truly creative and intelligent art creating subjects. Because of the growing maturity of computer vision technology, robots were first given human visual abilities, so the first breakthrough in intelligent robotic art was in the field of painting, especially portrait paintings (see Fig. 6). With the development of AI technology, the role and status of robots in artistic creation will become more and more obvious. Although it looks like human confront machine to determine the mastership of future art, in fact, it is difficult for limited human biological intelligence to combat the development of non-biological intelligence. The better way is to combine human and artificial neural networks to make them work together to develop their creativity [23].

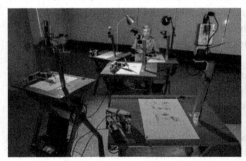

Fig. 6. P. Tresset, 6 Robots Named Paul (cited from internet).

3.3 Audience in Interactive Art Creation

The audience is the receiver and responder of art information, the object of art trans-mission activities, and the promoter of art development. Without the appreciation and evaluation of the audience, artistic creation can only be regarded as an artist's pastime and monologue, so the role of the audience is also crucial to artistic creation. Looking through the development of art, it is actually a process of improving the status of the audience, which is changing from the viewer to the participant and then to the creator.

In the process of appreciating traditional art, the audience can only stand in front of the artwork from a long distance, so it is difficult for them to speculate on the artist's true thoughts and intentions, and to reach an emotional "resonance" with the artist. Moreover, the creative power is also in the hands of the artist, but viewers have only the right to appreciate and comment. The advent of interactive art broke this unequal dialogue relationship, whose biggest feature is interactivity. As a result, the artist gave up some rights and provided only context and parts of content, and the audience is no longer just the single role as a viewer. They can participate in the process of artistic creation, become a part of the work, and even a creator. But this is just a dance in a cage. The artist is like the game maker, and the audience can only participate in the game according to the rules. In the context of AI, the medium of interactive art has become more humane and the interaction process is more intelligent. In the future, the audience can finally break away from the shackles of the rules and freely use their imagination to give the work a whole new meaning. British artist Roy Ascot profoundly predicted: "The role of the artist / author has changed from a person who fully controls over the whole creation of an artwork to a person who designs a 'frame' or 'ethnological' structure that invites extensive collaboration among the general public." "The art observer is the audience, who no longer just watches from the outside like a bystander, but also participates in and become the central figure in the creative process. Art not only opens a window for the audience to understand the world, but also builds a door for the audience, inviting them to enter this world of interaction and transformation." [8]. Therefore, in the context of AI, the role of the audience in interactive art has undergone a fundamental change, which is no longer a bystander in the original sense, but a participant and a creator.

In the AI interactive art, the process of interaction has become more diversified and humanized, and the results of interaction have become richer and different from person to person. Different audiences' aesthetic cognitions, personality characteristics, and personal styles provide a wealth of materials for AI to view the world and understand the world, giving interactive artworks new souls and lives. For example, on the online art generation webpage named Deep Dream Generator based on Convolutional Neural Network (CNN) technology developed by Google, users can choose original materials, migration styles and related parameters according to their preferences, and leave all the rest to AI to complete. In just ten seconds, the user can get a piece of artwork with his own strong "machine" style (see Fig. 7).

4 New Mechanisms for Interactive Art Creation

Mechanism originally refers to the structure and principle of machines in engineering, which is borrowed from the category of social sciences to explain the composition of each

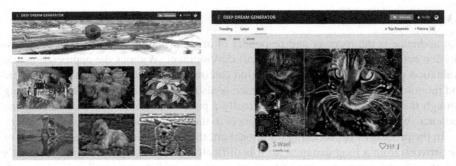

Fig. 7. The artworks of some users on "Deep Dream" homepage

element in the system and the way of operation between them. The so-called interactive art creation mechanism refers to the organic connection and operation between the various elements of the interactive art creation system, which is the method, approach and process that artists and the audience as the main actors of art use media, such as computer technology and tools to create and communicate. Art creation can be divided into narrow sense and broad sense. Narrow sense of artistic creation refers to the creation of individual artists; broadly defined artistic creation refers to the process by which social organizations, artist groups and the public perceive art, participate in art, create art, and disseminate art. The artistic creation mentioned in this article is the artistic creation in a broad sense. Individual artists have differences in knowledge structure, cultural background, cognitive ability, ideology, and technical means, and it is difficult to grasp the individual creative mechanism. Only by understanding and understanding artistic creation in a broad sense can we better study the creative mechanism of interactive art and better grasp the creative rules of interactive art.

4.1 Cognitive Mechanism of Human-Computer Symbiosis

Cognition refers to the psychological behaviors and processes that people obtain information and understand the world around them through observing, feeling, experiencing, and thinking. Cognition is also a process of continuously acquiring knowledge, applying knowledge, and then obtaining new knowledge, which is the basis of artistic creation. Only by establishing a scientific cognitive mechanism can interactive art creation be carried out in depth.

The theoretical cognition of interactive art is the premise and foundation of interactive art creation. Without a certain knowledge of interactive art theory, interactive art creation cannot be carried out. With the application of AI in the field of art, many artists would feel anxious and confused, because their creation lacks theoretical support, motivation and direction. To change this situation, strengthening interactive art education and research may become an important measure. Governments, universities, research institutions and related enterprises should work together to focus on AI technology and establish interactive art education and research systems. Specifically, we could start from the following aspects: First, we can establish a penetrative cross-discipline of AI and interactive art, set up a relevant specialty and provide professional courses in interactive art, and cultivate composite talents who understand both AI and interactive art. Second, we can vigorously study and learn from the latest achievements in the research and practice of interactive art, and grasp the creative ideas and development trends of AI art. The third is to strengthen the theoretical research on interactive art and explore the relationship between AI and interactive art. Finally, germinated AI art can be summarized and condensed in time to find the regularity and form a systematic theoretical system.

Artistic creation is the way and means used by art creators to express ideas, reflect society, and communicate with others. It reflects and embodies the creator's cognitive process in aesthetic judgment, creative thinking, creative techniques, and the use of media materials. The emergence of any new technology will bring new tools and media to artists, and will also change their thinking mode and knowledge architecture system. On the one hand, the birth of new media means that artists could attempt to try creative approaches and innovative methods that they have never used before in artistic creation. This tentative practice may give artists a new perspective and new concept in aesthetic activities; on the other hand, the application of new media extends and expands the artist's senses and body, allowing the creators to break through their own limitation of time and space, and the past recognition of experience, which have created conditions for them to explore a wider physical and spiritual world. Similarly, the application of AI media in interactive art creation has also changed the artist's perception of the artistic activity itself. Different from the previous creative media, AI has the ability of autonomous learning and thinking to create artworks that belong to the unique aesthetic cognition of AI, which are weird and bizarre, varying from the normal aesthetic experience of human beings. But the artist seems to have found a key to the door to the new world. Although it is impossible to understand the process of AI to create art, these unique styles of art can give the artist new inspiration and recognition. "The best design is to combine intent and bizarre elements, and finally create unexpected new things." [8]. Conversely, the creators can also impart their own aesthetic experience to AI and let it understand and learn.

Art appreciation is an aesthetic cognitive activity that art participants or audience view, think and criticize on the artistic creation process, artistic images and artworks, including art appreciation and art criticism. For a long time, the evolution and change of the media not only expanded people's aesthetic cognition in time and space, but also affected and even determined the standards of appreciation and judgment on artworks. In this context, the human aesthetic field will be greatly expanded and the standard of aesthetics will also change dramatically. "Aesthetic standards, appreciation, and criticism may be a form of aesthetics dominated by non-biological intelligence in the future, which determines the development and reconstruction of future art. To this end, artists must practically master or creatively possess technical intelligence. This is a wise choice" [7]. A work of art created by AI has its own beauty and composition, and may be very divergent from human aesthetics and aesthetic methods, but the machine does not destroy the aesthetic ability of human nature, but only transforms the inherent mode of thinking of human intelligence and offers another possibility beyond aesthetic standards.

In general, establishing the "human-computer symbiosis" cognitive mechanism is to build the "human-computer symbiosis" cognitive concept, which need us to strengthen the theoretical knowledge of AI and interactive art, and make a good knowledge reserve before the creation; to strengthen the understanding of the nature, characteristics and laws of AI interactive art in the creation, and find the best combination of AI and art; to strengthen the aesthetic cognition after the creation, so that the audience and participants can get spiritual satisfaction and emotional pleasure in appreciation, and distinguish beauty and ugliness, good and evil in criticism.

4.2   Innovation Mechanism supported by Intelligent Technology

In AI interactive art creation, it is not enough for artists to cooperate only with scientists and AI experts. They also need to focus on tracking and absorbing the latest developments in AI in time, so that they can better apply new AI technologies to their creations, which puts forward higher requirements for artists. "AI interactive art is a very challenging art. Those who are engaged in this process must understand all kinds of cutting-edge technologies, master experimental and operating methods, learn about production processes and procedures, and be familiar with art innovation forms and art philosophy." "The technical factors in the art creation of AI are based on advanced technologies, such as modern sensing technology, network technology, 3D printing technology, simulation technology, virtual and augmented reality, biological gene technology, and high-tech materials, and then to realize the intelligentization of art design, manufacturing, and presentation through intellectual perceiving, human-machine collaboration and fusion, and other methods. It is actually a deep blend of AI and human intelligence" [7]. Therefore, understanding and mastering the latest developments in AI is a necessary prerequisite for interactive art creation.

Interactive art is not only a display art, but also a practical art. We should not only build intelligent exhibition halls, museums and art galleries to display new works of interactive art, but also improve the artworkers' innovative consciousness through marketization and commercialization, forming a competitive mechanism for interactive art creation to achieve survival of the fittest. We could also vigorously expand and make full use of public space, integrating interactive art with public art to increase the enthusiasm, initiative, and creativity of audience in participating in artistic creation. At the same time, the state could introduce related policies, establish an innovation service platform, encourage the innovation and application of interactive art, and reward those who have made outstanding contributions in the creation and dissemination of interactive art.

Throughout history, those who have made great contributions to the development of art and technology are all those with innovative spirit, innovative awareness and innovative knowledge. In order to promote the development of interactive art, it is important that cultivating the talents in innovation of interactive art should be given priority. As the product of the integration of technology and art, AI interactive art is a very typical interdisciplinary subject. Therefore, in order to cultivate artistic creative talents that can meet the needs of the development of the times, colleges and universities need to adopt a multidisciplinary and integrated innovative education mechanism, build interdisciplinary scientific research platform, set up interdisciplinary academic research teams, construct new discipline systems, improve interdisciplinary teachers training mechanisms, and other measures to promote interdisciplinary cultural exchanges, achieving comprehensive development of talents.

For example, the Massachusetts Institute of Technology has specifically established the Center for Arts, Science, and Technology (CAST), which works with various departments, laboratories, and research centers within the institute, through developing new professional courses, cooperating with visiting artists, providing research funding, sharing activities, and other innovation models that integrate teaching, scientific research, and communication to link art, science, and technology. In addition to universities, companies have also played an important role in leading the development of art and technology, and the cultivation of innovative talents. In the era of big data, many Internet companies which rely on their unique advantages can occupy first-hand data information, grasp the latest cutting-edge technology, and attract a steady stream of high-quality resources, which have played a driving role in fostering and promoting the cultivation of innovative talents. Some Internet giants have begun to realize the importance of composite creative talents, so they have taken the lead in building open source technology platforms, setting up cross-field laboratories, creating scientific project teams composed of researchers with different professional backgrounds, and establishing incubation bases, which provide new opportunities and platforms for the integration of art and technology, the exchange and collision of different thinking.

4.3 Collaboration Mechanism in Creative Subjects

Collaboration is coordination and synchronization. To produce good interactive artworks, the creative subjects must maintain coordination and synchronization to form a cooperative mechanism of benign interaction.

Art and science belong to the two levels of human cognition. Although they differ in form and content, the goals they pursue are the same, which both reveal the nature and laws of objective things and have promoted the progress of human society. On the one hand, science opens up new research fields and provides new creative means for art; on the other hand, art creates imaginative space for science and inspires thinking. From the perspective of art, every great prosperity of art and the birth of new art forms are the result of the advancement of science and technology. Therefore, as an artist, we should not turn a blind eye to the development of science and technology, but timely track and vigorously apply the latest achievements of scientific and technological development. In short, "In modern society, an artist must fully define himself and seek the help of science, using it as a tool and reference." "Except for accidents, artists should seek advice from various sciences." [8].

In the context of AI, it is impossible for artists to work alone and fight alone to create meaningful and impressive artworks, because AI is the result of the intersection, penetration, integration and development of interdisciplinary disciplines, and also the mutual infiltration of natural sciences and social sciences, which are highly comprehensive, involving computational science, information science, mathematics, neuroscience, philosophy, etc. Interactive art is a cross-border and comprehensive art, which is high in science and technology, so artists will be bound to be limited by knowledge and technology in the creative process. Therefore, in the practice of interactive art, artists should form alliances with AI experts to turn "art studios" into "science laboratories", learn from each other and co-create. The most well-known and informative case is the new media art team named "Team Lab" from Japan. They have created many highly technological and immersive digital interactive artworks that make audience feel unforgettable and impressive. To a certain extent, their great success is inseparable from its cross-scholastic "ultra technologists" team. These team members are composed of professionals in various fields such as artists, programmers, engineers, CG animators, mathematicians, and architects. "The advantage of teamwork lies in their unified coordination of knowledge structure and background. When creating an artwork, everyone will be responsible for the professional field they are good at, thus the technical level, visual effects and maturity of the artwork are guaranteed to a considerable degree." [24].

With the rapid development of AI technology, machines will become more and more intelligent, and human-machine integration is imperative. The so-called integration is that human and machines are interwoven with each other. On the one hand, AI media, as an extension of human senses, limbs and thinking, has expanded human physical fitness and intelligence, and can help people perform large-scale calculations, inferences and judgments, completing tasks impossible for the human brain; on the other hand, human have also helped AI gain perception and cognition. Human-machine integration is a slow and gradual process, which is mainly divided into the three levels of development: perception fusion, behavior fusion, and thinking fusion. In interactive art creation, machines and artists have realized perception fusion and behavior fusion: computer technology and sensor technology can simulate the artist's perceived behavior, allowing machines to obtain vision, hearing, touch, and taste, etc.; the development and application of robots have extended the artist's senses and limbs, allowing robots to have behavior and perception capabilities similar to human, which can become a tool for assisting the artist's creation or even the subject of creation; the relationship between human and machine will be further advanced in the context of AI. After perceptual fusion and behavioral fusion, the machine will also acquire human cognitive intelligence, which is the simulation of thinking and consciousness, at this time the development of "human-machine integration" will reach the highest stage-thinking fusion. Now, interactive artists have begun to try to create artworks with AI. In the future, works of art that interact with the audience are not necessarily created by the artist alone, but may also be the wisdom of AI. As shown on the page of Deep Dream, an online art creation software based on AI technology launched by Google, the future of art must be the future of human-computer collaboration and mutual integration (see Fig. 8).

4.4 Constraints for Creative Behavior

The application of AI into artistic creation will bring moral hazard and raise ethical issues, such as whether AI can replace the position of artists? Does the artist plagiarize the creation of artificial intelligence as plagiarism? Can AI create artistic works as it wants, without moral constraints? Can AI artworks enter the art market and enjoy the right to be auctioned? In the stage of mechanical automation, AI has not yet generated a certain degree of self-awareness and thinking, so artists only use AI technology as a creative tool and medium. The subject of artistic creation is still a person with free will and soul. However, once the development of science and technology has entered the era of strong AI, or even super AI, that is, the stage where AI has surpassed human intelligence, artists have to face the dilemma of being challenged by the subject. The arrival of this stage is only a matter of time. It does not help whether oppose or reject

Fig. 8. Interface of "Deep Dream"

the creative talent of AI from an emotional or moral perspective. We have to consider formulating relevant ethics in advance to restrict AI and the behavior of artists. On the personal level, we should improve the artist's sense of moral responsibility, and enhance civil cultural literacy and ethical concepts; on the technical level, we should integrate AI with philosophical ideas, strengthen technical communication and cooperation, etc., so that we could create a good future for the positive, healthy and upward development of art environment and prospects.

In addition to ethical issues, the application of AI in artistic creation also brings legal risks and authorship issues. The issue of attribution and identification of copyright in AI creations are highlighted. If we are vague about the concept of the protection of the copyright of AI creations, it will lead to an imbalance of interests between potential rights subjects, which will hinder innovation and development in the art field. Therefore, experts in the legal field need to think and formulate relevant regulations to ensure the interests of relevant people and raise everyone's legal awareness.

AI technology, like other technologies, is a double-edged sword. If it is used reasonably and normatively, it will benefit human beings; on the contrary, if it is used by criminals, it will bring disaster. With the development of interactive art towards intelligence, interactive artworks have formed a "fate community" with human beings. A great number of interactive artworks are not only displayed in public spaces, but also widely used in social production and life. In this case, security awareness and precautions are particularly crucial. We should prevent a small number of artists from using interactive art against society and humanity; we should prevent the phenomenon of violent tendencies, uncontrolled procedures, and racial discrimination that may occur with artistic robots. Especially when AI develops to a certain degree, interactive art works may be closely integrated with human brain, body, and even psychology. We should be more careful about the harmful effects of certain bad artworks on human physical and mental health. Therefore, it is necessary to establish safety standards for interactive artworks and strengthen the assessment and monitoring of the safety of interactive artworks.

5   Conclusion

This article starts from the basic concepts, development status and trends of AI, collects and analyzes a large number of domestic and foreign literature and related cases, and discusses the background of AI's intervention in the field of art and integration with interactive art. In this context, the core media and creative subjects of interactive art are facing huge changes. The past interactive art creation mechanism has been unable to adapt to the development of the new situation. On this basis, this article analyzes the inevitable trend of interactive art's use of artificial intelligence as its core medium and its important role in two chapters, and discusses the diversified characteristics of the subject of interactive art creation. Finally, based on the above analysis and demonstration, we construct a new mechanism for interactive art creation to guide the practice of interactive art creation in the context of AI.

References

1. Kugel, P.: Artificial intelligence and visual art 1981, vol. 14. Leonardo, pp. 137–139 (1981). https://doi.org/10.2307/1574409.
2. Cornock, S., Edmonds, E.: The Creative Process Where the Artist is Amplified or Superseded by the Computer. vol. 6, pp. 11–16. Pergamon Press, Leonardo (1973). https://doi.org/10.2307/1572419
3. Ahmed, S.U., Jaccheri, L., M'kadmi, S.: Sonic onyx: case study of an interactive artwork. In: Huang, F., Wang, R.-C. (eds.) ArtsIT 2009. LNICST, vol. 30, pp. 40–47. Springer, Heidelberg (2010). https://doi.org/10.1007/978-3-642-11577-6_6
4. Ahmed, S.U.: Interaction and interactivity: in the context of digital interactive art installation. In: Kurosu, M. (ed.) HCI 2018. LNCS, vol. 10902, pp. 241–257. Springer, Cham (2018). https://doi.org/10.1007/978-3-319-91244-8_20
5. Cao, Z.F.: Artistic prospects in the age of artificial intelligence, vol. 01. Art Wide Angle, pp. 4–7 (2018)
6. Li, K.F., Wang, Y.G.: Artificial Intelligence. Culture Development Press, Beijing (2017)
7. Tan, L.Q.: Singularity Art: How Technology Singularity will Impact Art. China Machine Press, Beijing (2018)
8. Ascott, R.: The Future Is Now: Art, Technology and Consciousness. Jincheng Press, Beijing (2012)
9. Edmonds, E., Turner, G., Candy, L.: Approaches to interactive art systems. In: Proceedings of the 2nd International Conference on Computer Graphics and Interactive Techniques in Australasia and South East Asia, pp. 113–117. Web (2004)
10. Lefjoy, M., Paul, C., Wesner, V.: Contextual Providers: Conditions of Meaning in Media Art. Jincheng Press, Beijing (2012)
11. Strehovec, J.: New media art as research: art-making beyond the autonomy of art and aesthetics. Technoetic Arts J. Speculative Res. 6, 233–250 (2009). https://doi.org/10.1386/tear.6.3.233_1
12. Hsieh, H.C.: New media arts and human-computer interaction: forming aesthetic interaction. Int. J. Arts Soc. 6, 201–210 (2011)
13. Manovich, L.: The Language of New Media. MIT Press, Cambridge (2002)
14. Gao, M.L., Chen, X.W.: Contemporary Digital Art. Guangxi Normal University Press, Guangxi (2016)
15. Wei, Y.L.: Interactive Art in New Media. Chemical Industry Press, Beijing (2017)

16. Levinson, P.: Mobile Phone: an Unstoppable Call. Renmin University of China Press, Beijing (2004)
17. Mcluhan, H.M.: Understanding the Media: an Extension of the Man. Commercial Press, Beijing (2000)
18. Negrotti, M.: Designing the artificial: an interdisciplinary study. Des. Issues **17**, 4–16 (2001). https://doi.org/10.1162/07479360152383750
19. Gombrich, E.: The Story of Art. Phaidon Press Ltd., London (2006)
20. Penny, S.: Art and robotics: sixty years of situated machines. AI Soc. **28**, 147–156 (2013). https://doi.org/10.1007/s00146-012-0404-4
21. Shidujaman, M., Zhang, S., Elder, R., Mi, H.: "roboquin": a mannequin robot with natural humanoid movements. In: 2018 27th IEEE International Symposium on Robot and Human Interactive Communication (RO-MAN), pp. 1051–1056. IEEE, August 2018
22. Zhang, H.T.: A brief history of artificial intelligence and AI art concepts—the historical logic of AI, philosophy, and art. http://www.artda.cn/view.php?tid=10845&cid=15
23. Wang, K.J., Shidujaman, M., Zheng, C.Y., Thakur, P.: HRIpreneur thinking: strategies towards faster innovation and commercialization of academic HRI research. In: 2019 IEEE International Conference on Advanced Robotics and its Social Impacts (ARSO), pp. 219–226. IEEE (2019)
24. Wang, Z.: Theory of Digital Interactive Art Creation. Shanghai University, Shanghai (2011)

The Effect of Different Icon Shape and Width on Touch Behavior

Yung-Chueh Cheng, Hsi-Jen Chen[✉], and Wei-Hsiang Hung

Department of Industrial Design, National Cheng Kung University, No. 1, University Road, East District, Tainan 701, Taiwan
P36061192@gs.ncku.edu.tw, hsijen_chen@mail.ncku.edu.tw, johnson510928@gmail.com

Abstract. Among the constitute types and elements of press keys, different icon shape and width ratio may affect the user when they tap on the keypad. Thus, the experiment will use three geometric shapes as the experiment materials and three different width proportions to form 9 icons to extend the discussion of whether the shapes and width proportion affect the user's touch point position. We look forward to the three research methods of quantitative data, data visualization and qualitative interviews that perfectly complement each other. Explore the impact of the icons on where users tap and help us understand which icon and proportion provide better tap accuracy and user-friendly usability. The study shows that tapping, regardless of its shape or width, affects the location of the tap, causing the touchpoint to shift. When people tap on a triangle icon, the beneficial result of the tap will be more effective than the other two shapes, and they can tap closer to the press key center; similarly, tapping on the narrow and medium-sized icons will make it more beneficial when people tap closer to the center of the key. Therefore, we hope that when developing application programs in the future, we can take into account the shape of the icon and its width proportion as a reference basis for the interface design, so as to help people achieve the best user operation and experience benefits when using mobile phones.

Keywords: Touchpoint · Offset · Iconic button · Geometric shapes · Width of icon

1 Introduction

According to [1], sales of smartphones worldwide increased by more than 10% between 2007 and 2018. Smart mobile phones have undeniably affected human habits and established a very convenient and direct lifestyle. Taiwan's organ of survey has found that in our country, the rate of internet access through mobile phones has been on constant rise, from 35.3% in 2011, it has grown exponentially to 87.4% in 2017. And according to research, college student groups spend an average of more than 3.5 h per day on them [2].

In the past, scholars have conducted research on the tapping of press keys on mobile phones, such as the rate of accuracy of tapping on each position of the smartphone's

© Springer Nature Switzerland AG 2020
C. Stephanidis et al. (Eds.): HCII 2020, LNCS 12425, pp. 32–44, 2020.
https://doi.org/10.1007/978-3-030-60128-7_3

display screen, the behavior discrepancy in the different tap gestures on a mobile phone, and the accuracy of entering text on the keypad of a mobile phone; there are also studies that focus only on the semantic analysis, readability, or usability of icons; or discuss the availability of a flat design for the press keys. As a result, the user interface of smartphones display and experience have become increasingly valued. However, there is still little research on the change of the touchpoint position for different shapes of icons. Currently, there is still much room for research and discussion.

The experiment will use three geometric shapes as the experiment materials and three different width proportions to form 9 icons to extend the discussion of whether the shapes and width proportion affect the user's touchpoint position. The specific research objectives are as follows:

1. By exploring the impact of the nine icons of different shapes and width proportions on the user's touchpoint position, it can help us understand which of the icons and proportions have better tap accuracy and better usability for the user.
2. In this study, by understanding the user's tap behavior and touchpoint position for icons with different shapes. It is expected that, in future, the needs for expansion of interface function can be responded to and the results of the study applied to interfaces design. Providing the right key shape and proportion as a reference for the design helps designers make more efficient use of space within a limited range of interfaces for optimal user operation and experience benefits.

2 Literature Review

2.1 User Experience & User Interface, UI & UX

According to the definition of the International Organization for Standardization's ISO 9241-210, it refers to the cognitive experience of a product, system or service that has been exposed to and used by a user. The demand for mobile phone functions is increasing as the frequency and dependence of modern people on mobile phones is increasing. As a result, research on interface design is also emerging, including the most widely cited usability principle. The smartphone interface has a smaller size design platform and has to constantly change the situation to meet the needs of different users [3]. Owing to the small screen size of the mobile phone, the interface design cannot present the contents instantly like a computer screen. It is necessary to screen and design menus that can express the classification of the website under restricted space [4].

Drawings that appear in the software interface, or the images and marks in menus and windows, can be called icons. Therefore, the icon is no longer just a pictogram, it can convey semantics, convey meaning, function and purpose to people and is widely applied in the interface between computers and mobile devices [5]. it was highly important for people to be able to understand and quickly identify many of the icons [6]. And these icons can be used for any information communication, breaking through the limitations of different languages, cultures and customs [7].

2.2 The Behavior of Using Smartphone

When people used their mobile phones, the three most common gestures were the thumbs of both hands, the forefinger of one hand, and the thumb of one hand [8]. With the advancement of technology, the size of smartphones has also increased, reducing the operating efficiency of the one hand-thumb gesture [9]. When entering text with a single thumb, the input would be reduced by 30% compared to the forefinger operation [10].

In addition, when a user taps on a target key, the user is affected by the key position and key size, causing the touchpoint to be offset when tapped [11]. The position and size of icons can affect the accuracy and operation speed of the user when tapping [12]. Therefore, it was suggested, by some scholars, that the available touch key size should be greater than 9.2 mm^2 [13]. However, there are some scholars considered that 7 mm^2-sized keys to be of the same availability as 10 mm^2-sized keys [14].

2.3 Summary

It can be known from the above that, in today's lifestyle, the proportion of people operating smartphones with one thumb is the highest, because the devices can be grasped in one hand. However, with the cost of touchscreens tending to drop as technology advances, and the size of the mobile phones increasing, it is more difficult for one-handed thumb operation. In this experiment, one-handed experimental duties will be performed. The icon key will be set in the center of the screen at a height of approximately 10 mm (the key is 11 mm) and is configured in three width proportions. In addition, when performing a tap experiment, the subject will hold the mobile phone with his/her left hand while performing the test with his/her right forefinger.

3 Method

3.1 Process

It can be known from the above that, in today's lifestyle, the proportion of people operating smartphones with one thumb is the highest, because the devices can be grasped in one hand. However, with the cost of touchscreens tending to drop as technology advances, and the size of the mobile phones increasing, it is more difficult for one-handed thumb operation. In this experiment, one-handed experimental duties will be performed. The icon key will be set in the center of the screen at a height of approximately 10 mm (the key is 11 mm) and is configured in three width proportions. In addition, when performing a tap experiment, the subject will hold the mobile phone with his/her left hand while performing the test with his/her right forefinger.

3.2 Participants

In this study, (i) we selected 30 participants who met the experimental demands to conduct the experiment; (ii) students or office workers group between the ages of 20 and 29, with an average age of 23 years; (iii) the average time spent using a mobile phone every day is 2 to 5 h; (iv) all participants are habitually right-handed.

3.3 Tools

This experiment uses an iPhone 7 smartphone with a 4.7" screen and a set of tap experiment application software called "Whack A Mole" was designed. There are three geometric shapes for the system icons, including ovals, squares, and triangles; in addition, we have also set three width proportions (narrow, medium and wide), as shown in Table 1:

Table 1. Icon materials

Width Shape	Group Narrow (w-2 mm)	Group Medium (w-9 mm)	Group Wide (w-16 mm)
Group Oval (h-10 mm)	Narrow Oval	Medium Oval	Wide Oval
Group Rectangle (h-10 mm)	Narrow Rectangle	Medium Rectangle	Wide Rectangle
Group Triangle (h-10 mm)	Narrow Triangle	Medium Triangle	Wide Triangle

3.4 Analysis Method

The coordinate position is recorded in the system by the application software, Whack A Mole. The system origin (0,0) is shown in the lower-left corner, and the "Press Key Center" and "Touchpoint" are recorded. The study also calculates the "linear distance" between the touchpoint and the center of the key, and the "offset distance" between the touchpoint and the central axis of X and Y. Shorter distances mean more accurate taps; the longer the distance, the less accurate is the tap. The analytical method is shown in Table 2.

Table 2. The List of Analysis.

The Effect of Tap Error Rate by Shape and Width
Analytical method: Repeated Measured ANOVA; Post-hoc: Bonferroni
Independent variable: Shape & Width; Dependent: Error Rates
The Influence of Distance from the Touch Point to the Key Center by Shape and Width
Analytical method: Repeated Measured ANOVA; Post-hoc: Bonferroni
Independent variable: Shape & Width; Dependent: Offset Distance
The Influence of Offset from the Touch Point to the to the X & Y Axis by Shape and Width
Analytical method: Repeated Measured ANOVA; Post-hoc: Bonferroni
Independent variable: Shape & Width; Dependent: Offset

4   Results

4.1   The Effect of Tap Error Rate by Shape and Width

The shape, calculated after the Testing Analysis of Variance, does not interact with the narrow-wide factor ($p > .05$); however, both the shape and the narrow-wide factor have the main effect ($p < .001$). It can be seen from the observation of the test results that the error rate generated by tapping on the triangle is the most compelling, with an average error rate of .181, and there are significant differences from ovals and square (Fig. 1); however, there was no significant difference between ovals and squares. On the other hand, the largest error rate is generated by tapping on a wide icon, with an average of .327 which is significantly different between the narrow and medium ratios (Fig. 2); here is no significant difference between the narrow and medium types.

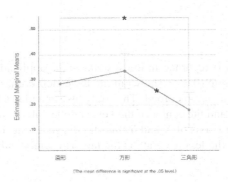

Fig. 1. The difference in the shape factor effect on the error rate

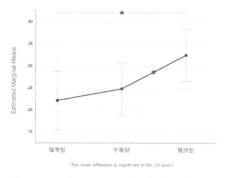

Fig. 2. The difference in the narrow-wide factor effect on the error rate

4.2 The Influence of Distance from the Touch Point to the Key Center by Shape and Width

There was no interaction between shape and width factors after the calculation of the Testing Analysis of Variance (p > .05); however, both the shape and the width had the main effect (p < .001). From the observation of the test results, the average distance between the touchpoint of the triangle and the center of the key is 13.403, and it is also the least offset of the three icons, and it shows significant differences from the ovals and the squares (Fig. 3); oval and square shapes are not significantly different. On the other hand, the statistics on the distance between the touchpoint and the center of the press key are shown in the three types of width proportion icons, as initially anticipated in the study, with the shortest average linear distance being the narrow icons and the longest linear distance being the wide icons. From the findings, it is clear that there are significant differences between the icons of the three width proportions (Fig. 4).

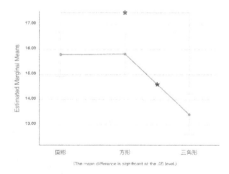

Fig. 3. The difference in the shape factor effect on the linear distance of the touchpoint

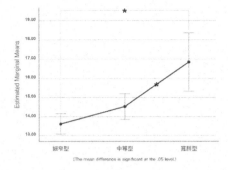

Fig. 4. The difference in the width factor effect on the linear distance of the touchpoint

4.3 The Influence of Offset from the Touch Point to the to the X Axis by Shape and Width

The analysis results showed that the interaction between shape and width did not reach a significant interaction (p > .05); however, unexpectedly, both the shape and width and width factors had major effects (p < .05 and p < .001). It can be seen from the observation of the test results that the average running distance of the triangular contact point to the X value is 8.663, which is also a graph showing the smallest amount of deviation of the three shapes. However, of the three shapes, only triangles differ significantly from squares (Fig. 5). On the other hand, there are significant differences between the three types of width-to-narrow ratio icons (Fig. 6), and the fat type is the icon with the longest X offset distance among the three width-to-narrow ratios, with an average offset distance of 11.907.

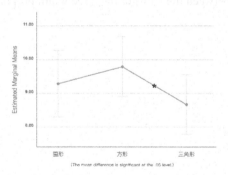

Fig. 5. The difference in the shape factor effect on the X offset distance of the touchpoint

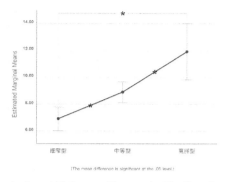

Fig. 6. The difference in the width factor effect on the X offset distance of the touchpoint

4.4   The Influence of Offset from the Touch Point to the to the Y Axis by Shape and Width

The analysis shows that both the shape and the width proportion affect the touchpoint, although there is no significant interaction between the shape and the width ($p > .05$); however, both the shape and the width proportion have the main effect ($p < .001$ and $p < .05$). The post-verification test shows that only the triangle is significantly different from the two other shapes (Fig. 7), where the triangle has an average value of 8.277, is the shape with the lowest Y offset distance and is significantly different from the oval and the square. There is no significant difference between the oval and the square. In addition, the offset distance from the touchpoint to the Y value is also affected by the width proportion, but only the width is shown to be significantly different (Fig. 8). Among them, the average value of the Y offset distance in the narrow icon is 10.434.

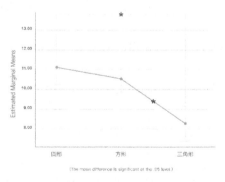

Fig. 7. The difference in the shape factor effect on the Y offset distance of the touchpoint

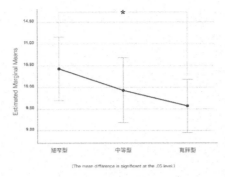

Fig. 8. The difference in the width factor effect on the Y offset distance of the touchpoint

5 Discussion

5.1 The Benefit of Tapping

As can be seen from the analysis of the tap error rate in the previous chapter, the triangle is a shape that is more effective to tap, with an error rate of 1.81%, while the tap error rate for ovals and squares is 2.85% and 3.36%. The triangle is also perceived by the subject as being of a good-tap shape, and as a result of the analysis and the visualization of the data, they are expected to change the location of the taps from the past.

In addition, when tapping on narrow and medium icons, two of the three width proportions that are more effective to tap, the error rate is 2.24% to 2.50%, while the error rate for the wide icons is 3.27%. The tap on density shown in Fig. 9 is not as high as that of other icons with wide and narrow proportions, and the larger the range of icons, the more the tap position becomes more distributed. As a result, you can see from the icon that the tapped hotspot is wider, but the colors inside the grid are lighter.

5.2 The Effect of Touch Points Be Different Shape Icons

In the analysis results of the previous chapter, it was shown that the square touchpoint was the most offset from the press key center and the triangle touchpoint were the closest to the press key center. Consider the distribution density and range of contact points in a wide fat group (Fig. 10), where the square contact distribution is the lowest density and the range is more diffuse; in contrast, the triangle has the highest touchpoint distribution density and a narrow and concentrated range. Simultaneously, from the feedback of the qualitative interviews of the subjects, it was possible to understand that the changes in shape make people feel differently. Visually, the overall size of the triangle is small, which may result in a more concentrated tap range of the triangle. On the other hand, many interviewees indicated, during the interviews, that when they taped on the triangle, they would tap at the top corner because of its directivity.

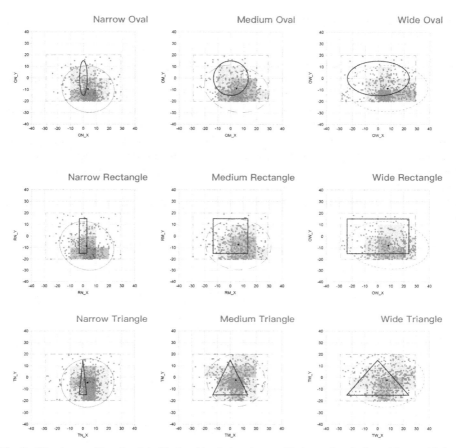

Fig. 9. Nine types of touchpoint offset and tap hotspot maps (darker colors in the grid mean higher density)

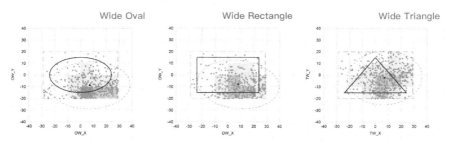

Fig. 10. Distribution map of the wide group's touchpoint

5.3   The Associate of the Icon Directivity

In this section, visual and qualitative interview contents are further used to explore the effect of the graphical directivity on taps at drop point range. It can be clearly seen from Fig. 11 that the range of triangular touchpoint is higher than the range of oval and square touchpoint. Therefore, from the analysis results of the previous chapter and the contents presented in this section in the form of images, it can be seen that the directivity of the icon does affect the distribution of the touchpoint. So much that the directivity of the icons helps people to be more precise when they tap on them. For example, the touchpoint of a triangle has the densest distribution range of the three shapes and is the closest to the press key center. On the other hand, in addition to the directivity of the icons that affect the distribution range of the touchpoint, some of the respondents, who participated in the experiment, indicated that the icons' directivity was easier and more instinctive to tap.

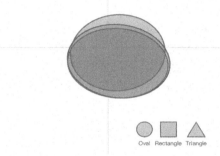

Fig. 11. Comparison of the touchpoint distribution for the three shapes

5.4   The Effect of Touch Points by Different Width Icons

The same results can be found in the graphical presentation, as shown in Fig. 12, for example, in a square set, the distribution of the touchpoint will be narrower, denser and more concentrated; the wide icon shows a wider, less dense, and more scattered touchpoint distribution. And through qualitative interviews after the experiment, the respondent's feedback can be more deeply understood from the feedback of the user, and the results of quantitative data analysis can be explained. Many of the respondents felt that when they tap on a narrow icon, the knee-jerk reaction would find it difficult to tap on the target chart, and would, therefore, tap more carefully on the target chart; however, when they see a wide icon, the larger shape range of the icon allows them to tap more randomly. It can be seen that when a user taps on a narrow picture on the screen, it may seem difficult to tap, but it may be more accurate to tap because of the narrower icon.

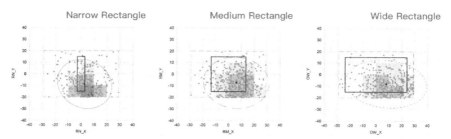

Fig. 12. Distribution map of square's touchpoint (darker colors within the grid represent higher density)

6   Conclusion

This study explores the relevance between the shape of the icon and its width to the impact of the touchpoints, and from it, understands the effect of the width, the directivity of the icon, and the area of the icon on the change in tap behavior. Similarly, taping on the narrow and medium-sized icons will make it more effective when people tap and the tap will be closer to the press key center. As smartphones become a tool that humans can rely on, and the touch screen is getting larger, application programs have become an essential part of the device

By using the hands-on and interviews of the tap experiment, you can see the pattern of behavior from the perspective of the user, from the perspective of the visual perspective to the tap-on icon, and you can see that the design of the icon looks very ordinary and insignificant, but through the changes and application of different factors, you can really influence the behavior of people. Therefore, we hope that when developing applications in the future, we can consider the shape of the icons and the width proportions as reference for the interface design and use them in different positions on the mobile phone to help people achieve the best user operating and experience benefits when using the mobile phone.

References

1. Author, F.: Article title. Journal **2**(5), 99–110 (2016)
2. Author, F., Author, S.: Title of a proceedings paper. In: Editor, F., Editor, S. (eds.) CONFERENCE 2016. LNCS, vol. 9999, pp. 1–13. Springer, Heidelberg (2016)
3. Author, F., Author, S., Author, T.: Book title, 2nd edn. Publisher, Location (1999
4. Author, F.: Contribution title. In: 9th International Proceedings on Proceedings, pp. 1–2. Publisher, Location (2010)
5. LNCS Homepage. http://www.springer.com/lncs. Accessed 21 Nov 2016
6. Statista. Number of smartphones sold to end users worldwide from 2007 to 2020 (in million units). (2019). https://www.statista.com/statistics/263437/global-smartphone-sales-to-end-users-since-2007/
7. Berolo, S., Wells, R., Amick III, B.: Musculoskeletal symptoms among mobile hand-held device users and their relationship to device use: a preliminary study in a Canadian university population. Appl. Ergon. **42**(2), 371–378 (2011)

8. Tarasewich, P.: Designing mobile commerce applications. Commun. ACM **46**(12), 57–60 (2003)
9. Väänänen-Vainio-Mattila, K., Wäljas, M.: How do users find out what's new: a study of change indicators in mobile services. In: Proceedings of the 15th International Academic MindTrek Conference: Envisioning Future Media Environments, Tampere, Finland, pp. 201–204. ACM (2011)
10. Huang, S., Shieh, K., Chi, C.: Factors affecting the design of computer icons. Int. J. Ind. Ergon. **29**(4), 211–218 (2002)
11. McDougall, S., Isherwood, S.: What's in a name? The role of graphics, functions, and their interrelationships in icon identification. Behav. Res. Methods **41**(2), 325–336 (2009)
12. Forsythe, A., Sheehy, N., Sawey, M.: Measuring icon complexity: an automated analysis. Behav. Res. Methods Instrum. Comput. **35**(2), 334–342 (2003)
13. Azenkot, S., Zhai, S.-M.: Touch behavior with different postures on soft smartphone keyboards. In: Proceedings of the 14th International Conference on Human-Computer Interaction with Mobile Devices and Services, San Francisco, California, USA, pp. 251–260. ACM (2012)
14. Karlson, A., Bederson, B., Contreras-Vidal, J.: Studies in one-handed mobile design: habit, desire and agility. In: Proceedings of 4th ERCIM Workshop User Interfaces All (UI4ALL). Citeseer (2006)
15. Kim, I., Jo, J.H.: Performance comparisons between thumb-based and finger-based input on a small touch-screen under realistic variability. Int. J. Hum. Comput. Interact. **31**(11), 746–760 (2015)
16. Henze, N., Rukzio, E., Boll, S.: 100,000,000 taps: analysis and improvement of touch performance in the large. In: Proceedings of the 13th International Conference on Human Computer Interaction with Mobile Devices and Services, Stockholm, Sweden, pp. 133–142. ACM (2011)
17. Park, Y., Han, S.: Touch key design for one-handed thumb interaction with a mobile phone: effects of touch key size and touch key location. Int. J. Ind. Ergonomics **40**(1), 68–76 (2010)
18. Parhi, P., Karlson, A., Bederson, B.: Target size study for one-handed thumb use on small touchscreen devices. In: Proceedings of the 8th Conference on Human-Computer Interaction with Mobile Devices and Services, Helsinki, Finland, pp. 203–210. ACM (2006)
19. Park, Y., et al.: Touch key design for target selection on a mobile phone. In: Proceedings of the 10th International Conference on Human Computer Interaction with Mobile Devices and Services. ACM (2008)

Project Team Recommendation Model Based on Profiles Complementarity

Matheus dos Santos Nascimento[1], Bruno Mendonça Santos[1(✉)],
Daniela de Freitas Guilhermino Trindade[1], Jislaine de Fátima Guilhermino[2],
José Reinaldo Merlin[1], Ronaldo Cesar Mengato[1], Ederson Marcos Sgarbi[1],
and Carlos Eduardo Ribeiro[1]

[1] Universidade Estadual do Norte do Paraná - Centro de Ciências Tecnológicas, Paraná, Brazil
matheusdrkwolf@gmail.com, brunooms21@hotmail.com,
{danielaf,merlin,ronaldo.mengato,sgarbi,biluka}@uenp.edu.br
[2] Fiocruz Mato Grosso do Sul, Ministério da Saúde, Campo Grande, Mato Grosso do Sul, Brazil
jislaine@fiocruz.br

Abstract. An influencing factor in integration and development of a project team is personality trait. Considering the specificities of project teams, which usually requires multidisciplinary knowledge, there was a need to develop a team recommendation system model that considers, in addition to technical characteristics (training, skills, competences, experiences), personality traits of its participants. Some researches have applied personality traits in systems that recommend people, however, the works in this line, make the recommendation based on the principles of similarity of profiles. Thus, the recommendation model proposed in this paper is based on the principle of profile complementarity. The profile complementarity model aims to achieve the best possible personality combination so that one member's strengths complement the other's weaknesses. From the proposed model, the prototype of a recommendation system was developed

Keywords: Project teams · Recommendation system · Personality traits · Profile complementarity

1 Introduction

The formation of the project team is a crucial phase for achieving quality in the development and achievement of project objectives. It is necessary to decide who to allocate in each activity according to the required technical competence profile. In order to choose the best team composition, competencies, skills and experiences are usually analyzed.

Bejanaro [1] states that the performance of a team also depends on the quality with which members engage. According to Belbin [2], team structure must also take into account the skill and personality of the individual in order to seek a combination of these characteristics, as this is a singular reason why teams fail. The author adds that an ideal team must be developed so that the strengths and weaknesses of each of its members complement each other.

© Springer Nature Switzerland AG 2020
C. Stephanidis et al. (Eds.): HCII 2020, LNCS 12425, pp. 45–59, 2020.
https://doi.org/10.1007/978-3-030-60128-7_4

In this context, some research has applied personality traits to people's recommendation systems. These systems are known as social combination systems or social correspondence systems. However, the works found in the literature use the principle of similarity, as the works by Nunes [3] and Thenmalar et al. [4].

Therefore, considering the specificities of the project teams it is proposed a model of recommendation system that considers, in addition to the technical characteristics, the personality traits based on the principle of complementarity.

This research is characterized as exploratory and to achieve the proposed objectives we used the methodological phases: (i) Study of the approach to analysis of personality traits; (ii) Analysis of team recommendation models; (iii) Creation of a recommendation system model that combines technical competence profiles and personality traits; and (iv) Prototype development from the proposed recommendation system model.

2 Project Team and Personality Traits

2.1 Composition of Project Teams

Effective project teams are formed of independent and flexible people who have a connection, producing quality results [5]. Efficient teams have characteristics that are associated with the team's interaction with the team and their technical skills.

Boehm [6] presents five principles for forming a project team, they are:

1. The principle of the best talents: better use and few people. The team size should be ideal, as too many or too few members can impair the dynamics of the team, which can result in too much or too little pressure on the members, which makes it difficult to develop their activities.
2. The principle of equalization of functions: Fit tasks to the skills and motivation of the people available. This principle is very important, because a person who performs a task and has the ability to do so, benefits the entire team and the project to be developed.
3. The principle of career progression: An organization does better in the long run, helping people to achieve self. A good performance of a team member usually takes place anywhere, but a company can help or hinder this fact, leading to a good or bad development of that member in a project team.
4. The principle of team balance: Select the people who will complement and harmonize with each other. This principle covers some dimensions of a team's balance, they are: (i) Natural skills: intelligence, objectivity, creativity, organization, analytical thinking; (ii) Psychological composition: leaders and followers, risk-takers and conservatives, visionaries and critics, cynics and optimists; (iii) Objectives: financial, set of resources, quality, punctuality.
5. The elimination principle: maintaining a team mismatch does not benefit anyone. A misfit person on the team may be the reason for his replacement or live with one less member of the team. Since this maladjusted member ends up discouraging the other team members and ends up interrupting the balance of the team in some dimension.

Observing the dimensions of the "Team Balance" principle proposed by Boehm [6], it appears that, when composing a team, it is necessary to seek a balance, which is related to the complementarity of profiles, in order to meet the different objectives of the project for which the team was formed. When this balance is not found in any of the dimensions, the project is at great risk.

In this sense, Belbin [2] contributes by informing that there are 9 basic functions that need to be fulfilled in order to form a successful team, the functions are as follows:

- Sowers: creative, independent and introverted people, their role is to generate innovative proposals and ideas for solving problems.
- Resource investigators: extroverts and negotiators, their role is to explore new ideas and negotiate with external agents to obtain resources for the team.
- Monitors/Evaluators: prudent and with critical aptitude, but slow to make decisions, responsible for critically analyzing ideas and suggestions, exposing their advantages and disadvantages.
- Coordinators: mature and trustworthy people who manage to make members work on shared goals, have the function of coordinating teams with different characteristics.
- Formatters: motivated and energetic people who thrive under pressure, responsible for generating action for the team.
- Implementers: practical, have self-control and discipline, are those with great ability to apply the work.
- Team workers: sociable people who care about others, do not like conflict and are responsible for preventing conflicts from occurring between team members.
- Completers: detailed and with a high level of precision and reliability, they are generally introverted, occupy functions where the level of accuracy required is high.
- Experts: people with great skill and technical knowledge, in the team, are the members who have a deep knowledge about the product and the service performed.

Regarding the size of project teams, Oliveira et al. [7] argues that the number of members depends on the context in which the team is, however, that the number of people on the team should be 2 to 20, but for ease of use in the interaction between members, there should be no more than 12 members.

The effects that an erroneous number of people can have negatively influence the following aspects of the team: demand from the leader, direction of the leader, tolerance of the member of the leadership of the leader, inhibition of the participation of members, use of rules and procedures and time needed to arrive to a conclusion [7].

2.2 Personality Traits

For Martins [8] the expected results of an effective team are great productivity and good morale, however, for that it is necessary to have a clear purpose and use social skills.

Social skills, in addition to technical competence, are valuable for team development. These competencies include skills such as communication skills, emotional intelligence, conflict resolution, negotiation, influence, team building, and group facilitation [9].

According to PMI [9] the project management team can, for example, use emotional intelligence to reduce tension and increase cooperation by identifying, assessing and controlling the feelings of project team members, anticipating their actions, recognizing their concerns and monitoring their problems.

According to the PMI [9]:

[...] teamwork is an essential factor for the success of the project, and developing effective project teams is one of the primary responsibilities of the project manager. Project managers must create an environment that facilitates teamwork. Project managers must continually motivate the team by providing challenges and opportunities, offering feedback and support as needed, and recognizing and rewarding good performance [...].

In a team there can be people with the most varied types of personality, and knowing how to deal with these different profiles is the key to the success of any project. Martins [8] states that the critical elements that must be considered in the team's interaction are: the way decisions are made, in order to obtain the commitment of all involved; the different personalities; communication deficiencies; persuasion to change people's attitudes and; pay attention to change management.

2.3 Model for Analysis of Traits Personality in Project Teams

Oliveira et al. [7], addresses the importance of the phase of allocating people in the development of a project, however, with an emphasis on affective computing, which addresses the psychological characteristics of each individual and how these characteristics influence the success of a project.

Based on the importance of the psychological characteristics of the members of the project team, Oliveira et al. [7] proposed a model for team building based on the complementarity of profiles. From a wide bibliographic analysis, in the BigFive model and in the NEO-IPIP questionnaire, a model was developed for the evaluation of personality traits and proposals for guidelines for project team recommendation systems were developed.

In the Table 1, it is possible to observe that for each of these features (that authors recommend for an ideal design team) was inferred a dimension and one or more facets of the Big Five model. Some facets are denied using a "!" before your name so that you reach the desired result; as an example, the facet !Unstable, from its negation it is possible to obtain the characteristic Stable [7].

From the association the characteristics of design teams with the Big Five facets, in [7] it was developed the questionnaire to evaluate the personality traits test. The test model used was NEO-IPIP, which uses 300 questions to identify personality traits. The questions were refined, based on works in the literature, resulting in 72 questions whose objective was to trace the individual's characteristics. To identify the personality of the individuals, tests were applied. From this, a percentage of similarity was calculated with each of the facets for each individual, and later with the eight profiles of the BigFive model, making it possible to analyze and suggest the creation of the project team based on the complementarity of profiles, once the profiles are identified, the team can be constituted in a way that complements the skills [7].

Table 1. Association of team features to the Big Five model [5]

Author/Features of Project teams		Big Five	Facet
(Thamhain, 1988), (Boehm, 1981), (Belbin, 2010)	Good communication	Extroversion	Sociable
	Innovation and Creativity	Openness	Imagination
(Thamhain, 1988), (Belbin, 2010)	Ability to resolve conflicts	Socialization	Altruism/Cooperation
	Mutual Trust	Achievement	Reliable
	Capability of achievement	Achievement	Practical
(Boehm, 1981), (Belbin, 2010)	Extroversion	Extroversion	Sociable/Enthusiastic/Energetic
	Intelligence	Openness	Intelligent
	Orderliness	Achievement	Orderliness
	Critical posture	Socialization	Critical
(Boehm, 1981)	Optimistic posture	Socialization	optimistic
(Belbin, 2010)	Detail posture	Achievement	Meticulous
	Introversion	Extroversion	!Sociable/ !Enthusiastic/ !Energetic
	Enthusiasm	Extroversion	Enthusiastic
	Sympathy	Socialization	Nice
	Stable	Neuroticism	!Unstable
	Assertiveness	Extroversion	Assertiveness
	Efficient	Achievement	Efficient

3 Social Combination Systems

According to Robillard et al. [10], recommendation systems are software applications that assist users in making decisions when faced with a large amount of information. Items of interest to users are recommended based on their preferences, either explicitly or implicitly. The expansion of the volume and increase in the complexity of the information has made recommendation systems essential tools for users in information search activities. Recommendation systems also help to overcome the problem of information overload, giving only the most interesting information items to users, and also by offering novelty, surprise and relevance.

Recommendation systems have been studied since the 90's. Its positive point is to guide the user through dense layers of information towards light layers of useful knowledge. Initial research on recommendation systems focuses on algorithms and their evaluation to improve the accuracy of recommendations using f-measure and other methodologies of signal detection theory. The most recent research includes other aspects, such as human factors that affect the user experience and interactive visualization techniques to support the transparency of results and user control [11].

In recommendation systems for traditional domains, the context is established through a user profile, which can consist of any combination of characteristics specified by the user, explicitly, and characteristics learned by the system, implicitly [10].

According to Isinkaye et al. [12] explains, recommendation systems are information filtering systems that solve the information overload problem, filtering fragments of vital information from large amounts of dynamically generated information, for this, the data that link the user to the item is used. The recommendation system has the ability to predict whether a specific user prefers an item or not based on the user's profile. Recommendation systems are beneficial for service providers and users. An example is the reduction in transaction costs of finding and selecting items in an online shopping environment. Recommendation systems have also been shown to improve decision-making and quality.

There are several types of recommendation systems for the most diverse contexts, in this session the most used models will be addressed and in the following session the model used in this work.

- Collaborative Filtering: According to Pazzani [13], collaborative approaches locate and recommend sources of information for a particular user that have been highly evaluated by other users who have a classification pattern similar to that of the user.
- Content-based filtering: As Lops et al. [14] explains, content-based recommendation systems try to recommend items similar to those that a particular user liked in the past. The basic process performed by content-based filtering consists of combining the attributes of a user profile, in which preferences and interests are stored, with the attributes of a content object (item), in order to recommend new items to the user of interest.
- Multi-criteria recommendation systems: According to Liu et al. [15], multi-criteria systems provide more information about user preferences than a single rating system. And by adopting a decision model, multi-criteria systems can provide rich tools for the system designer to build better applications.
- Mobile recommendation systems: Mobile recommendation systems offer the user the possibility to receive personalized recommendations in constantly moving environments. However, this possibility comes at a cost of privacy, as user data can be processed in unexpected ways by service providers. Thus, the user's attitude towards the mobile recommendation process can be negative [16].

Hybrid recommendation systems: A hybrid system combining techniques A and B tries to use the advantages of A to correct the disadvantages of B. For example, collaborative filtering methods suffer from problems with new items, that is, they cannot recommend items that have no ratings. This does not limit content-based filtering approaches, as the forecast for new items is based on their descriptions (features) that are normally readily available. Given two (or more) basic techniques of recommendation systems, several ways have been proposed to combine them to create a new hybrid system [17].

The recommendation techniques described in the previous section aim to recommend products or services to people, however, with the technological advancement people started to relate in virtual environments, which generated the need to create a technique that recommends people to other people, as described by Cazzela et al. [18], this was how the social combination system emerged, among its applications are the construction of contacts on social networks, the formation of couples on romantic dating platforms and the recommendation of professionals in virtual environments with reputable systems.

Nunes et al. [19], explains that, for the most part, social combination systems do not use psychological aspects in recommending people, but describes the importance of these aspects in the recommendation process:

[...] However, even though human psychological aspects are difficult to intentionally extract from the user, their relevance is highly significant in decision-making processes to be ignored by Recommendation Systems. [...].

According to Nunes [3], homogeneous groups, in terms of personality, spend less time maintaining group cohesion through socio-emotional interactions, leaving more time for relevant interactions. In contrast, incompatible groups spend more time on socio-emotional problems and less time on relevant tasks.

Still according to Nunes et al. [19], the use of personalities in recommendation systems began to be considered so that it is possible to create better and more efficient group dynamics, such as, for example, recommending people on social networks, in distance education courses and even the creation of more credible virtual agents. These recommendation systems in particular are referred to as social combination systems.

An example of a social combination system model is the Group Recommender by Nunes et al. [20], which is a social combination model based on the BigFive model and has positive feedback in more than 99% of cases. After the user answers a questionnaire, the value assigned to each of the responses is used to calculate the result that is used as a basis to assign a value between 1 and 100 for each of the items in the BigFive model and its facets.

Most recommendation systems that use the social combination system do so through the similarity of characteristics, such as the tool proposed by Thenmalar et al. [4]. However, the model proposed in this work is based on the system of social combination, but by complementarity of characteristics.

4 Project Team Recommendation Model

Human psychological aspects, such as its personality, have a direct impact on its decision-making ability [21], thus highlighting the importance in the process of creating teams, taking into account not only the technical capabilities of the employee, but also their personality traits.

The social combination model as well as two works were taken based on the creation of a recommendation model for project teams. One of these works is that of Mengato

[22], who explains the importance of the people allocation phase for the formation of a project team and creates an allocation tool based on the technical skills of employees. This tool, is supported by the business process model based on the Project Management Body of Knowledge (PMBOK) project management concepts and uses an algorithm that classifies members in order to assemble the best team possible for a given project taking into account the technical skills of potential team members. Remembering that this Mengato [22] tool does not consider personality traits in the allocation of members

The second work is by Oliveira et al. [7], which demonstrates how the personality of the members affects the team's performance and which offers a model based on the Big Five, composed of 72 questions, which allows inferring the personality traits of the members of the project team.

The Fig. 1 shows the recommendation model proposed. As shown in Fig. 1, the project manager first needs to configure the new project, with information such as the name of the project, start date, end date, what technical skills are necessary for a professional to be considered to be allocated to the project and what type of personality profile recommendation will he give preference to in his project: the standard one, based on the Big Five model, which will be explained in the next sub-chapters, or the personalized one.

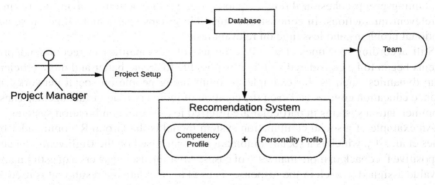

Fig. 1. Project team recommendation model

If the project manager chooses the standard profiles, the system will search for employees who meet the 8 standard profiles, based on a weight system and layer of profiles that will be explained in the next subsections. If the option of personalized profiles is chosen, the manager will be able to choose from the 8 profiles, which he will give more importance to, and the recommendation system will recommend employees based on these choices.

Thus, a tool was developed based on the recommendation model of the proposed project team. It is important to emphasize that, for the operation of this tool, it is of fundamental importance that the project manager applies the Personality Test, proposed by Oliveira et al. [7], to his collaborators, in order to obtain the facets of the collaborator's personality. It is necessary to have in the database the record of the training and technical skills of each member and also the profiles of technical competence necessary for the realization of the project.

4.1 Characteristics Weight Calculation

In order to infer the characteristics of the employees, the percentage of each facet is added, and after that, it is divided by the number of facets that make up these characteristics [23]. With these characteristics, the percentage value of each profile of a given employee is obtained.

This, however, is a very generic way, because neither the characteristics nor the profiles have weights to distinguish one from the other. We then need to add weights to these characteristics and profiles, in order to know which ones would be the most "valuable", so that in this way, the recommendation system knows what its priorities are.

The calculation of the weight of a given characteristic is done based on the number of times that characteristic appears in the profiles. For example, the weight of the "Intelligence" characteristic is 8.0, as it is a collective characteristic, and is repeated in all 8 profiles. The formula below describes this calculation, with "PC" being the weight of the characteristic, with its initial value 0 (zero), "C" being the characteristic in question and "P", a certain profile.

$$f \ C \ \in \ P \ then :$$
$$PC = PC + 1.0 \tag{1}$$

This calculation is done only once, since it is not necessary to always calculate the weight of the characteristics, it is enough to calculate them only once. With that done, you can now calculate the weight of each one of the profiles.

4.2 Profile Weight Calculation

Now that we know the weight of each of the characteristics, we will use this to calculate the weight of each of the profiles. The idea is simple: the weight of a profile will be given by the sum of the weights of the characteristics that compose it. The following formula describes this calculation, with "P" being the profile weight and "C" being the characteristic weight.

$$P = \sum C \tag{2}$$

Once this is done, the following weights are obtained for each of the profiles (Table 2):

4.3 Profiles with the Same Weight

"Coordinator" and "Implementer", for example, have the same weight, so the system will deal with this type of situation as follows: first, candidates for each profile will be ranked in descending order. For example, in "Coordinator", candidate X with the highest score scored a total of 15 points in this profile, and second candidate Y scored 13 points.

Table 2. Table of weights for each of the profiles

Profile	Weight:
Sower	20
Resource Investigator	21
Monitor/Evaluator	23
Coordinator	24
Formatter	23
Implementer	24
Team Worker	20
Completer	23

In "Implementer", the candidate with the highest score was candidate Y, with 16 points, and second was candidate X, with 12 points.

As the two profiles have equal weight, to know which candidate would be recommended by the system, the scores of these candidates would be added, in this case, candidate X would have a sum of 15 + 12, resulting in 27 points, and candidate Y would have a sum of 13 + 16, resulting in 29 points. So, in this way, the recommended candidate would be candidate Y, in the profile that he made the highest score, in this case, in "Implementer". Now, as the main vacancy for "Implementer" has already been filled, if there are still vacancies in the project compatible with candidate X, the vacancy for "Coordinator" would be filled by the candidate X.

Scoring by Layers: as there are different profiles with the same weight, the concept of layers was necessary. There will then 4 layers, as shown in Fig. 2.

Fig. 2. Profile layers

The layers are separated by the weights of the profiles. In the lower layers, there are the profiles with less weight, and as the layers go up, the weights of the profiles also increase. In this way, profiles with the same weights start to be part of the same group. An example would be, a collaborator X, has 15 points as "Coordinator" and 15 points as "Implementer", totaling 30 points in the most valuable layer. And this is done with the rest of the layers, adding the candidate's weight in the profiles of the given layer, in order to find out how many points he has in the total. The formula for this calculation is given by "T" representing the total weight of the layer, and "P", representing the candidate's score in that layer. The score of profiles for each candidate will be explained in the next subsection.

$$T = \sum P \qquad (3)$$

In this way, the Recommendation System will search for layers, starting from the fourth, and finding a candidate who will fill the vacancy of "Coordinator" or "Implementer". With that done, he moves on to the third, and finds a candidate to fill out one of the profiles that compose it. Thus, when he is in the first tier, if there are still vacancies available in the project, he will return to the fourth tier, and perform this process again, until there are no more vacancies available.

4.4   Calculation of the Profile Score for Each Candidate

To find the score for each profile of a particular candidate, first find the real value of each of its characteristics. For example, a characteristic X, which has a weight of 5, and this candidate Y has 50% compatibility with this characteristic. Let's extract the real value of this 50%, which is done by calculating the percentage (50%) multiplied by 5, which is the total weight of this characteristic and dividing this by 100. In this case, we would find 2.5, which is the actual number of points that candidate Y scored on characteristic X. This process is performed for all characteristics, so we can calculate the score for each of this candidate's profiles.

In the same way that the weight of the profiles was calculated, the scoring of the candidates' profiles will follow the same idea. The sum of the characteristics that make up the profile will be made, but now, with the only difference, that instead of using the total weight of the characteristics, the real value that the candidate made on this particular characteristic will be used. For example, in the "Resources Investigator" profile, composed of the characteristics "Extroversion", "Friendly", "Mutual Trust" and "Intelligence", a candidate who has 2, 1, 5 and 6 respectively, will have a total of 14 points in the "Resource Investigator" profile.

4.5   Pre-classification

Now that the scores for all eight profiles of all possible candidates have been obtained, the system will sort the candidates in descending order for each profile. For example, in the "Seeder" profile, candidate X scored 12 points, while candidate Y scored 14.5, so in the "Seeder" profile, candidates would be arranged as follows: Y, X, where Y has the highest amount points of this profile, so it is arranged in the first place.

4.6   Recommendation

At this stage, the system already has, among technically able candidates, their due profiles and which are the best candidates in each profile. Now it is up to the project manager to decide if he will choose the standard recommendation, which will use the Profile Layers system, searching for the eight essential profiles in a standardized way, or he will be able to choose the customized way, in which the manager himself will be able to decide which profiles he deems most needed in your team. These two forms of selection are presented in Figs. 3 and 4, in the tool developed to support the recommendation system.

Select Personality Profiles

Manage Personality Profiles

Select witch one fits your project better

○ Standart Profiles

○ Custom Profiles

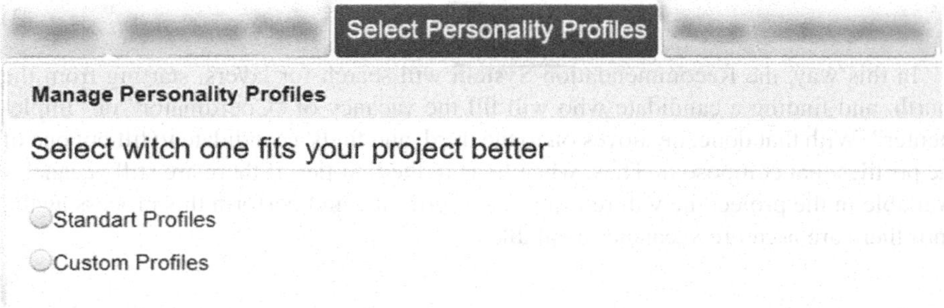

Fig. 3. Profile selection screen

Select Personality Profiles

Manage Personality Profiles

Select witch one fits your project better

○ Standart Profiles

◉ Custom Profiles

☑ Implementer   ☐ Coordinator   ☐ Monitor-Evaluator
☑ Formatter   ☐ Complementer   ☐ Resource Investigator
☐ Sower   ☑ Team Worker

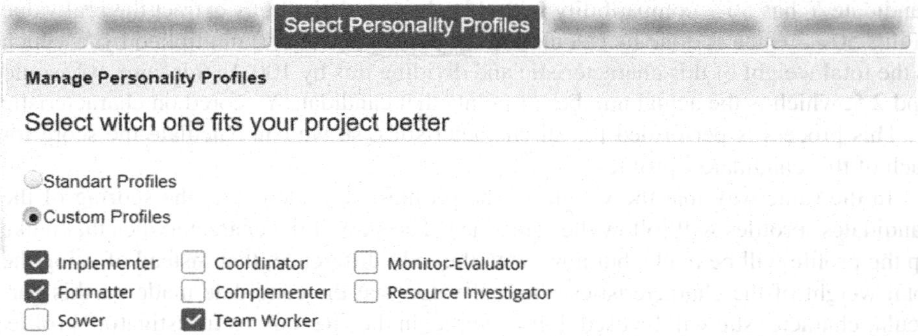

Fig. 4. Custom profile selection screen

When the project manager decides to choose the profiles he deems most suitable, a new profile layer is created, with the same idea as the four standard layers, in which the topmost layer is where the heaviest profiles are, and the lowest the less heavy profiles. In the case of Fig. 4, the manager chose "Implementer", "Formatter" and "Team Worker" , with these choices, the following layers would be created:

In this way, the concept of weights still prevails, and the Recommendation System continues to work in the same standard way, with the only difference being that it now has fewer profiles to analyze. In this case, the system would look for a candidate in the

Fig. 5. Custom layers

third layer, who is an "Implementer", when he found it, if there were still vacancies in the project, he would go to the layer below, looking for a "Formatter", and when he found it, if there were still vacancies, he would look for a "Team Worker", in the lower layer.

Figure 6 shows the two compatible collaborators that were recommended. First, an "Implementer" was found and as there were still collaborators with available technical skills, he moved to the bottom layer and found a "Formatter". This time, as there were no more employees with technical skills available, the system stopped searching, and recommended the two best options, both technically and in terms of their personalities and qualities.

Collaborator	Competence Profile	Compatibility (%)	Available	Performance	Main Profile
Bruno Mendonça	Example	70	●	☆☆☆☆☆	Implementer = 55%
Jose Josefino	Example	55	●	☆☆☆☆☆	Formatter = 59%

Fig. 6. Recommendation

5   Final Considerations

Teams do not always perform as expected, even if they have clear roles and responsibilities. A preponderant factor that can influence the team's performance is the behavior assumed by each member, influenced by his personality trait.

Belbin [2] noted that teams can become unbalanced if all of their members have similar behavior styles (team roles). He says that normally, if team members have similar weaknesses, the team as a whole can tend to have that weakness too, and similarly, if team members have similar strengths in teamwork, they will tend to compete (instead of cooperating).

Understanding that personality of the members can influence the way a team develops and its success, with the proposed model, it is expected to contribute to the composition of a team with profiles that complement each other in order to balance the characteristics and emotions. From identifying the characteristics of the candidate members and the profiles essential to the project teams, was implemented the recommendation system based on classification algorithms.

References

1. Bejarano, V.C.: Como formar equipes com o equilíbrio ideal de personalidades e perfis pessoais: a teoria e as ferramentas de Meredith Belbin. XXXIII Congresso Brasileiro de Ensino de Engenharia (2005)
2. Belbin, R.M.: Team Roles at Work, 2ª edn. Butterworth Heinemann Oxford, United States (2010)
3. Nunes, M.A.: Computação Afetiva personalizando interfaces, interações e recomendações de produtos, serviços e pessoas em Ambientes computacionais. In: Nunes, M.; Oliveira, A.A.; Ordonez, E.D.M. (Org.). DCOMP e PROCC: Pesquisas e Projetos, (2012)
4. Thenmalar, V., Tamilselvi, R., Sandhiya, S., Dhivya, S.M.: Social recommendation for interactive online system. In: International Journal of Science and Research (IJSR), UG Scholar, Department of Computer Science and Engineering, Sri Krishna College of Technology, Coimbatore, TN, India (2017)
5. Oliveira, G.: Abordagem para Análise de traços de personalidade no apoio à recomendação de equipes de projeto. Monografy(bachelor of Computer Science)–Universidade Estadual do Norte do Paraná (2017)
6. Boehm, B.W.: Software Engineering Economics. Prentice-Hall, Englewood Cliffs, New Jersey (1981)
7. Oliveira, G., dos Santos Braz, R., de Freitas Guilhermino Trindade, D., de Fátima Guilhermino, J., Merlin, J.R., Sgarbi, E.M., Ribeiro, C.E., de Oliveira, T.F.: Model for analysis of personality traits in support of team recommendation. In: Sottilare, R.A., Schwarz, J. (eds.) HCII 2019. LNCS, vol. 11597, pp. 405–419. Springer, Cham (2019). https://doi.org/10.1007/978-3-030-22341-0_32
8. Martins, J.C.C.: Gerenciando Projetos de Desenvolvimento de Software com PMI, RUP e UML. 5th ed. Rio de Janeiro, Brasport (2010)
9. Project Management Institute (PMI). Project Management Body of Knowledge. 5th edn. (2013)
10. Robillard, M.P., Walker, R.J., Zimmermann, T.: Recommendation systems for software engineering. IEEE Softw. 27(4), 80–86 (2010)
11. Valdez, A.C., Ziefle, M., Verbert, K.: HCI for recommender systems: the past, the present and the future. In: 10th ACM Conference on Recommender Systems - RecSys'16., Boston, MA, USA (2016) https://doi.org/10.1145/2959100.2959158
12. Isinkaye, F.O., Folajimi, Y.O., Ojokoh, B.A.: Recommendation systems: principles, methods and evaluation. Egypt. Inform. J. 16(3), 261–273 (2015)
13. Pazzani, M.J.: A framework for collaborative, content-based and demographic filtering. Artif. Intell. Rev. 13, 393–408 (1999). https://doi.org/10.1023/A:1006544522159
14. Lops, P., de Gemmis, M., Semeraro, G.: Content-based recommender systems: state of the art and trends. In: Ricci, F., Rokach, L., Shapira, B., Kantor, P.B. (eds.) Recommender Systems Handbook, pp. 73–105. Springer, Boston, MA (2011). https://doi.org/10.1007/978-0-387-858 20-3_3
15. Liu, L., Mehandjiev, N., Xu, D.L.: Multi-criteria service recommendation based on user criteria preferences. In: Fifth ACM Conference on Recommender Systems - RecSys'11., Chicago, Illinois, USA. ACM (2011) https://doi.org/10.1145/2043932.2043950
16. Pimenidis, E., Polatidis, N., Mouratidis, H.: Mobile recommender systems: identifying the major concepts. J. Inf. Sci. University of Brighton, Brighton, UK. 016555151879221 (2018) https://doi.org/10.1177/0165551518792213

17. Ricci, F., Rokach, L., Shapira, B.: Introduction to recommender systems handbook. In: Ricci, F., Rokach, L., Shapira, B., Kantor, P.B. (eds.) Recommender Systems Handbook, pp. 1–35. Springer, Boston, MA (2011). https://doi.org/10.1007/978-0-387-85820-3_1
18. Cazella, S. C., Nunes, M. A. S. N., Reategui, E.: A ciência da opinião: estado da arte em sistemas de recomendação. In: André Ponce de Leon F. de Carvalho; Tomasz Kowaltowski.. (Org.). Jornada de Atualização de Informática-JAI - CSBC2010. Rio de Janeiro: PucRIO, vol. 1, pp. 161–216 (2010)
19. Nunes, M.A.S.N., Moraes, D.B., Reinert, D.: Personality inventory - Pv 1.0 (Portuguese Version). (2010)
20. Nunes, M.A.S.N., et al.: Computação afetiva e sua influência na personalização de ambientes educacionais: gerando equipes compatíveis para uso em AVAs na EaD. n: Educação e Ciberespaço: Estudos, propostas e desafios ed. Aracaju: Virtus, vol. 1, pp. 308–347 (2010)
21. Nunes, M.A.S.N., Bezerra, J.S., Reinert, D., Moraes, D., Silva, É.P., Pereira, A.J.: Computação afetiva e sua influência na personalização de ambientes educacionais: gerando equipes compatíveis para uso em AVAs na EaD. Virtus Editora, Educação E Ciberespaço: Estudos, Propostas E Desafios. Aracaju pp. 308–347 (2010)
22. Mengato Junior, R.C.: Ferramenta de apoio à alocação de equipes em projetos de desenvolvimento de software. Monografia (Bacharelado em Sistemas da Informação)–Universidade Estadual do Norte do Paraná, Paraná p. 41 (2015)
23. Nascimento, M.: Um modelo de recomendação de equipes de projeto com base na complementaridade de perfis. Monografy(bachelor of Computer Science)–Universidade Estadual do Norte do Paraná (2019)

A Neurophysiological Sensor Suite
for Real-Time Prediction of Pilot Workload
in Operational Settings

Trevor Grant[1]($\boxtimes$), Kaunil Dhruv[1], Lucca Eloy[1], Lucas Hayne[1], Kevin Durkee[2],
and Leanne Hirshfield[1]

[1] Institute of Cognitive Science, University of Colorado, Boulder, CO, USA
trgr2496@colorado.edu
[2] APTIMA, Inc., Dayton, OH, USA

Abstract. In recent years, research involving the use of neurophysiological sensor streams to quantitatively measure and predict the level of mental workload experienced by an individual user has gained momentum as the complexity of the tasks operators have experienced in heavily computerized contexts has continued to expand. Despite the promising results from many empirical studies reporting successful classification of workload using neurophysiological sensor data, accurate classification of workload in real-time remains a largely unsolved problem. This research aims to both introduce and examine the efficacy of a new research tool: Tools for Object Measurement and Evaluation (TOME). The TOME system is a toolset for collating and examining neurophysiological data in real time. Following a presentation of the system, and the problems the system may help to solve, a validation study using the TOME system is presented.

Keywords: Mental workload · Physiological sensors · Data acquisition

1 Introduction

In recent years, research involving the use of neurophysiological sensor streams to quantitatively measure and predict workload experienced by an individual has gained momentum with the complexity of its applications ranging from driving cars [1] to playing music [2] and web surfing [3]. Such systems often pair a neurophysiological measurement modality such as functional near-infrared spectroscopy (fNIRS) or electroencephalogram (EEG) with other physiological sensors such as electrocardiogram (ECG), electrooculogram (EOG), respiration rate sensors and galvanic skin response (GSR). Data collected from these modalities are then fused together to build classifiers trained to discretely predict mental states from these physiological signals using machine learning techniques [4]. While these studies effectively correlate performance in simulated tasks with workload, their extension to a practical setting is often limited by the footprint and portability of these sensors. This is especially true in the aviation domain, where pilots are often wearing helmets or other flight gear and must maneuver aircraft in

© Springer Nature Switzerland AG 2020
C. Stephanidis et al. (Eds.): HCII 2020, LNCS 12425, pp. 60–77, 2020.
https://doi.org/10.1007/978-3-030-60128-7_5

both simulated and actual flight environments. Naturalistic environments such as these necessitate the use of wearable sensor suites that are highly practical for deployment in operational settings. There are often tradeoffs, however, between a sensor's physical profile, portability, and efficacy with references to recording a reliable signal which may be used for both analysis and predictive modeling. A minimal yet comprehensive sensor suite that allows a highly practical and efficient data collection procedure is required to build robust models suited for in-flight studies.

Despite the promising results from many empirical studies reporting successful classification of workload using neurophysiological sensor data, the ability to accurately classify the level of user workload in real-time remains a largely unsolved problem. This issue arises because models that were trained on small laboratory datasets often fail to generalize beyond the original dataset. These models fail to transfer to new sensors, new contexts, new people (or even to the same person in a different day). Neurophysiological datasets are high dimensional in nature, and they should be trained on a suitable number of instances to enable the creation of generalizable models. Several recent papers have begun to detail these challenges [5–7].

With these goals in mind, this research makes the following three contributions to the research domain: First, we present the Tools for Objective Measurement and Evaluation (TOME) system, a diagnostic tool-set for cost-effectively supporting test and evaluation practitioners using a highly practical suite of neurophysiological sensors. With the suite of sensors, TOME supports real-time secure cloud-based data acquisition and data storage via an easy to use graphical user interface (GUI). The TOME system works with a suite of neurophysiological sensors that were validated and selected based on their ability to maintain cost effectiveness, portability, comfort and practicality for use in ecological flight simulation scenarios, while still maintaining quality of the psychophysiological data. These sensors (detailed later in this paper) include functional near-infrared spectroscopy (fNIRS), Electrocardiogram (ECG), Electrodermal Activity (EDA), respiration, and eye tracking sensors. Second, we present the results of an empirical study where difficulty levels were manipulated while participants piloted an F-18 Aircraft in an X-Plane flight simulator environment. The TOME system was used to collect neurophysiological data in 10 participants and a support vector machine (SVM) was trained on the resulting data to predict participant workload caused by the changes in difficulty. Third, we expand upon our predictive analyses to include an evaluation of the value and sensitivity of the different data streams in the overall classification accuracy of operator workload.

1.1 Background and Literature Review

Defining and Measuring Mental Workload: A dearth of research has explored the construct of mental workload, and while there remains contention regarding the exact definition, most researchers agree that mental workload is a product of the demands of a task and the mental capacity of the person performing the task [8]. Techniques for measuring mental workload can be divided into subjective ratings, secondary-task behavioral measures, and physiological measures [9]. Common subjective measurements such as the NASA-TLX [10] and the Bedford Workload Scale [11] have been widely used to assess workload, due in part to the ease by which they can be administered. These surveys have been widely recognized to be sensitive to mental workload, but they suffer from the same drawbacks of other self-report surveys, including the inability of people to accurately self-assess their own changing workload as well as the fact that they are administered after a task has been completed, which lacks real-time information [8, 9, 12]. Secondary task performance is another common way to assess mental workload. This technique assumes that decrements in secondary task performance are due to the combined task load exceeding a person's workload capacity. While this technique does not suffer from the subjective issues of self-report scales, some researchers have criticized this technique as dual task decrements in performance vary with different allocation of resources [9, 13, 14], allowing for researchers to only infer workload from performance.

To overcome the drawbacks of self-report and secondary task performance measures for assessing workload, researchers have turned directly to cognitive and physiological sensors in order to acquire real-time, objective measures of workload. To this end, recent research has used a myriad of sensors to measure and predict workload. This includes brain measurement with EEG [15, 16] and fNIRS [12, 17], or physiological measurements such as heartrate, galvanic skin response, respiration rate, or pupil diameter [18, 19]. In order to gain a more complete picture of workload, researchers have begun to merge data streams from various neurophysiological devices, as the data are often complementary [4, 20]. For example, Molina et al. were able to classify four levels of mental workload by combining different signals including EDA, electrocardiogram, photoplethysmography (PPG), EEG, temperature and pupil dilation during a web browsing task [3]. See Lohani [21] for a thorough review of recent empirical psychophysiology research focused on measuring workload and other related constructs (e.g., attention), which includes details about the biological mechanics underlying psychophysiological sensing (heartrate, galvanic skin response, respiration, pupil size, etc.) as well as relative strengths and limitations of each measure.

Predicting Mental Workload in Driving and Flight Settings: As noted above, our research is focused on prediction of pilot's workload changes during flight, which dovetails with research in the driving domain, as both tasks (flying a plane and driving a car) require continuous attention and multitasking to maintain performance. Several researchers have explored mental workload prediction during driving [21–24]. For example, recent work explored the combination of ECG, EOG, EEG and/or fNIRS modalities to investigate the effect of sleep deprivation on a subjects' performance in a simulated car driving study [22]. Though aircraft pilots face less traffic compared to their on-ground counterparts, piloting is a complex multi-tasking activity that requires both skill and technical expertise [25]. From an HCI perspective, piloting an aircraft is a cognitively demanding, resource intensive task, exercising working memory to satisfy task demands [26]. Numerous studies have used neuro-imaging modalities such as EEG [19, 27–29] and fNIRS [30] paired with other physiological sensors to evaluate neuro-physiological correlates of pilots cognitive workload in a simulated flight environment.

Although machine learning has been used to predict mental workload on cognitive and/or physiological sensor data in many prior empirical studies with promising accuracies, transitioning those successes outside of the laboratory remains challenging. This prior research suffers from two challenges: First, data collection is a time consuming and laborious task, with prior models often trained on very small datasets that fail to transfer to other domains, other participants, other sensor manufacturers. Second, it can be difficult to compare and collate results from studies as data sharing is not common and results differ by sensors used, number of participants in study, number of workload states predicted, operationalization of 'ground truth' workload per study, as well as whether or not models are built within subjects or across subjects. Therefore, despite the advancements reported from many empirical studies reporting successful classification of workload, a number of recent papers have shed light on the above issues [5–7].

1.2   The TOME System

TOME, The Tools for Objective Measurement and Evaluation system, is a diagnostic toolset for cost-effectively supporting test and evaluation practitioners and augmenting system acquisition decisions through advanced workload measurement and performance assessment strategies. TOME's current implementation includes the following five psychophysiological sensors, which were selected for inclusion based on their ability to maintain cost effectiveness, portability, comfort and practicality for use in ecological flight simulation scenarios, while still maintaining quality of the collected data 1) a 2-Channel functional near-infrared spectroscopy (fNIRS) device from PLUX for measuring blood flow in the frontal cortex, 2) a Zephyr Bioharness for measuring respiration, 3) a Polar HR10 shirt for measuring heart rate, 4) a Polar Smartwatch for measuring galvanic skin response data, and 5) a desk-mounted Tobii eyetracker for assessing pupil diameter (Fig. 1).

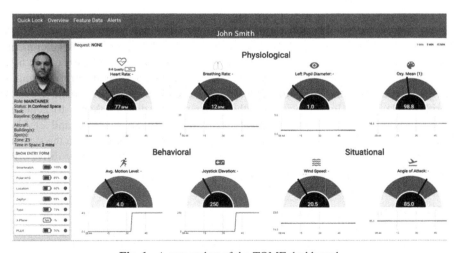

Fig. 1. A screenshot of the TOME dashboard.

The Body Area Network (BAN) transmitter is a service application that currently runs on Android mobile devices. The BAN transmitter's main responsibility is connecting to the various sensors a person is wearing and transmitting that information to the

TOME server. The BAN has multiple ways it interfaces with the system, including data streaming through a message broker, making requests through HTTP web services provided by the TOME server, and interfacing with sensors through various communication methods, such as Bluetooth Low Energy (BLE). The BAN is designed to serve as a gateway between the TOME server and sensors. This prevents the server from having to manage sensor connections directly, making the system more scalable and manageable. Additionally, because the BAN can remotely connect to the server (via WiFi or cellular network), users do not need to stay within a certain physical range of the server, thus carrying the potential to make them more mobile. Another benefit of the BAN transmitter is that it runs as a background service. This ensures the application is always running and maintaining an active connection with the server. It also limits user interaction with the system, which allows users to focus on their tasking without distraction.

The TOME server performs a variety of functions, including centralized real-time data processing, management of user states, management of experimental test conditions, and persistent data storage by utilizing cloud computing resources. In short, the TOME server manages all data in the system, executes algorithms, and hosts web services that interact with the system. Also running on the TOME server is a web server that provides a front-end user interface for the entire system. These applications include several different pages for viewing data, entering forms, and performing administrative functions. This also provides a convenient mechanism for exporting all collected data into a comma separated value format that can be ingested by virtually any commercial statistical software package, including both unprocessed sensor data and post-processed algorithm derived measures. Because the displays are web-based, they are compatible with a wide variety of devices, specifically any device that can run a web browsing application.

The TOME backend server includes a processing module that executes algorithms to generate alerts and derived features within the system, including inferred user states such as cognitive workload. The TOME project includes an API for algorithm development. This API includes several interfaces and abstract classes to help developers create new algorithms that can easily be used by the system. It also comes with utility methods to help evaluate algorithms in bulk. The system currently supports two main types of algorithms: 1) Data Algorithms: Algorithms that receive data messages to generate new features within the system, often referred to as "derived" features; and 2) Alert Algorithms: Algorithms that receive data messages to generate alerts within the system. Both types of algorithms fundamentally work the same way; they mostly differ with respect to the type of information they generate.

2 Experiment

10 participants (9 male and 1 female) from a University in the Western United States participated in this the study. They ranged in age from 23 to 42 years (M = 26.4 yrs, SD = 8.6) and gave informed consent under the guidelines and restrictions of the university's institutional review board. As the participants were new to the X-Plane simulator, they were given a self-paced period before undergoing the experimental conditions in which they were allowed to practice to practice until they felt comfortable with their ability to

pilot in the simulation before being allowed to move forward through the experimental apparatus.

2.1 Sensor Set-Up and Flight Simulator Testbed Evaluation

As shown in Fig. 2 (left), each participant wore all TOME sensors, which consisted of a Polar compression t-shirt embedded with electrodes around its chest cavity which connects to a Polar H10 heart rate monitor placed on the back collar of the Polar t-shirt. Respiration rate was collected using a Zephyr Bio-harness placed at the bottom of their sternum. GSR was recorded using a Polar M4500 smartwatch worn by the participants on their right wrist. Lastly a 2 channel fNIRS device, the PLUX Explorer, was placed on the participants forehead at the mid-point of their respective FpZ locations using the measured using the 10–20 system.

Fig. 2. Sensor configuration (left) and testbed environment with desk mounted Tobii Eye Tracker (right).

The experiment setup consisted of a computer equipped with an X-Plane 11 Flight Simulator installation. In order to mimic a typical in-flight cockpit of an FA-18F, the simulator was configured to simulate the same aircraft to be maneuvered with a Thrust-Master Joystick and Rudders as shown in Fig. 2.

Using pilot testing and prior literature [30–35] as guidance, we created two scenarios of high and low difficulty levels within the X-Plane environment. As depicted in Table 1, in the low difficulty level, participants were instructed to fly the plane while maintaining an altitude of ±5000 ft from 10,000 ft while the weather conditions were clear and sunny, with no wind. In the high difficulty level condition, the participants had to keep their altitude within the more restrictive ±500 ft from 10,000 ft, while operating under extreme weather conditions that included high wind and levels of rain.

A custom X-Plane plugin was created to enable the researchers to create experimental designs for participants, that would allow presentation of the difficulty levels (Table 1) in an order and for a duration specified by the researchers prior to the experimental protocol beginning. The plug-in also allowed researchers to build pauses between conditions

Table 1. Weather parameters and altitude constraints for low and high difficulty levels.

Parameter	Low difficulty	High difficulty
Altitude (in ft.)	10,000 ± 5,000	1,000 ± 500
Wind Speed (in kts)	55	430
Sky Conditions	Clear	Cloudy
Rain Speed (in mph)	16	110

where participants could rest. Through the plug-in, a set of instructions pertaining to the altitude instructions to follow at any given time were overlaid on the center-left side of the simulator screen during all conditions (see Fig. 3).

Fig. 3. X-Plane 11 GUI with a white arrow pointing to custom participant instructions regarding altitude and rest.

Protocol: After providing informed consent, the participants were trained on the usage of the X-Plane simulator using the X-Plane flight school. They were also shown the instructions for the plugin, which would ask them to maintain specific altitude ranges at various times. Once the participants were comfortable taking off and flying in the X-Plane environment, they were equipped with the TOME sensor suite. After take-off, each participant conducted a series of 6 'tasks'. A task represented each condition (low and high) consisting of flying for 60 s while maintaining the target altitude range amongst the weather conditions created by the plug-in. After each 60-second-long task, the X-Plane simulator would pause the screen mid-flight and participants would rest for 45 s to allow their brain's metabolic activity to return to baseline. The protocol included a randomized block design, with each block containing one low and one high difficulty level condition presented in a random order. The block design had six blocks total.

3   Data Analysis and Results

3.1   Manipulation Check

As a manipulation check, we first verified that the workload manipulations were being mentally perceived by subjects with different difficulty, we used joystick deflections from the neutral position as behavioral measure [31]. Using the first order derivative of joystick deflections ΔJ from the neutral axis we were able to perform workload manipulation check on our participant's data. Figure 4 shows the average of deflections for the first High and Low difficulty task encountered by the participants, respectively. As per the figure, the ΔJ for high difficulty tasks are significantly farther from the neutral axis $(y = 0)$ than the lower difficulty setting.

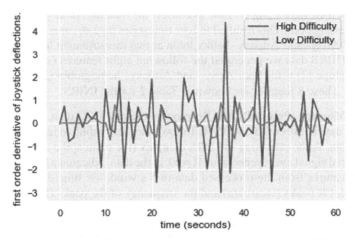

Fig. 4. Average Joystick deflections across 10 participants for the two difficulty levels.

3.2   Data Pre-processing

Since the sampling rate varies for each of the five sensors, data acquired from each sensor goes through different pre-processing routines, with outputs being placed in a raw datafile that can be exported from the TOME server. To accommodate supervised classification with feature vectors built from these five sensors, we generate all features only once every five seconds (i.e., if there are six readings from the Tobii eyetracker over a 5 s window, those will be averaged together and output as one average value for summarizing the Tobii features in that 5 s window).

Functional Near Infrared Spectroscopy: Raw data acquired from the fNIRS device was first converted into absorption coefficient I_R (μA) using the transfer function outlined below:

$$I_R = \frac{c * ADC}{2^n}$$

Here, c is a proportionality constant depending on bit precision (n) of raw data values configured within the OpenSignals Software (the default recording software for the PLUX fNIRS device). We used values 0.15 and 16 bits respectively [36]. Due to the intricate optical properties and high frequency nature of fNIRS sensors, the optical density values acquired are sensitive to the displacement of optodes from their locations resulting from head movements, micro movements resulting from cardiac pulses (Mayer Waves) or respiratory activities of the subjects [37]. We reduced motion and other physiological artifacts by applying a band-pass filter on the resulting data with values between 0.01 and 0.5 Hz. Finally, values are estimated from the two wavelengths using the Modified Beer Lambert Law to convert the data into relative changes in oxy- and deoxy- hemoglobin. This resulted in four timeseries data streams sampled at 10 Hz, consisting of Δoxy- and Δdeoxy- hemoglobin at two measurement locations. Then for every 5 s of fNIRS data we generated the following eight features (shown in Table 2): average and slope (2) x for both Δoxy- and Δdeoxy- hemoglobin (2) x two channels locations (2). These 8 features are shown in Table 2 for the fNIRS.

Heart Rate Monitor (Polar HR10): To process the raw ECG data, we band-pass filtered the raw data between 0.5 and 35 Hz followed by detrending to remove the baseline shift in the data. After extracting the QRS complex (the main spike seen in ECG data) from the filtered signal, emergence of an R peak in the data indicated a heartbeat. We then extracted 2 features from the processed data in 5 s windows: time difference between two consequent R peaks (Heartrate) and the frequency of the peaks (RR Interval).

Eye Tracking (Tobii 4C): For extracting features from the Tobii eye tracker we focused on the estimated size (in cm) of the pupil diameter, as output by the Tobii. We simply output the average diameter of the Left and Right pupil over each five second window of time (Left pupil diameter, Right pupil diameter).

Respiration Rate (Zephyr Bioharness): For the Bioharness Respiration monitor we calculated mean and standard deviations over a 5 s window, resulting in features for mean respiration rate mean and standard deviation of respiration rate.

Galvanic Skin Response and Pulse Rate (Polar M4500 Smartwatch): For the Polar smartwatch we acquired pulse rate and galvanic skin response data. We used these data streams to generate average pulse rate and average GSR activity over the course of a 5 s window.

3.3   Accounting for Missing Data and Outliers, Normalization of Resulting Data

The TOME system relies on the five devices detailed above to function 'properly' in order to collect the data to the TOME server. Issues in collecting data from a device can occur when 1) The specific device loses Bluetooth connectivity with TOME or 2) the

Table 2. List of the 16 features out every five seconds from the five sensors included in the TOME System.

Sensor	PLUX
Features	1. Average Δoxy channel 1
	2. Average Δdeoxy channel 1
	3. Slope Δoxy channel 1
	4. Slope Δdeoxy channel 1
	5. Average Δoxy channel 2
	6. Average Δdeoxy channel 2
	7. Slope Δoxy channel 2
	8. Slope Δdeoxy channel 2
Sensor	Polar HR10
Features	9. Heartrate
	10. RR interval
Sensor	Tobii
Features	11. Left pupil diameter
	12. Right pupil diameter
Sensor	Bioharness
Features	13. Mean respiration rate
	14. Stdev respiration rate
Sensor	Polar M4500 Smartwatch
Features	15. Pulse rate
	16. GSR Activity

sensors from a given device lose contact with the participant. *Unfortunately, the PLUX and Polar Smartwatch sensors were prone to losing network connectivity, resulting in data loss during experimental sessions, as shown in* Table 3. *See 'Limitations' section for further discussion.*

Whenever a sensor did not collect data for a participant, the missing values were filled in with 'NaN' (Not a Number) values using the NumPy python package. These values were replaced so that the data from the 'working sensors' could still be used for classification while ignoring feature values resulting in the missing sensor data. This is further detailed in the sections below. The resulting data were also examined and outliers eliminated from each feature separately. For each participant and for each feature all values that were greater than 3 standard deviations away from the mean feature value were again replaced with 'NaN' values. This replacement was chosen as z-score and correlation matrix operations in many Python packages can ignore 'NaN' cells in their calculations without skewing the results. After outliers were handled the data was then normalized using z-score normalization for each of the 16 feature columns.

Table 3. Summary of device and network connectivity performance.

Participant	Description
P1	No PLUX fNIRS Readings
P2	**All Devices collecting properly**
P3	**All Devices collecting properly**
P4	No PLUX fNIRS Readings
P5	No Tobii and No Polar Smartwatch Readings
P6	No Polar Smartwatch Readings
P7	No PLUX fNIRS Readings
P8	**All Devices collecting properly**
P9	**All Devices collecting properly**
P10	No PLUX fNIRS Readings

3.4 Feature Exploration and Selection

Selection of an optimal feature set is critical to creating an efficient classification pipeline. To determine an optimal feature set, we use the oft used feature filtering method whereby Pearson correlation coefficients are generated to down-select the features that have the highest correlation with the class value [38]. We first wanted to see the relationship between the 16 features. To do this a Pearson correlation matrix was generated between every feature and every other feature across all participants and all difficulty levels. This is shown in Fig. 5.

There are some intuitive examples of correlated features in the preliminary correlations. For example, left and right pupil diameter positively correlate, and fNIRS oxy and deoxy hemoglobin have a negative correlation (which is in line with the nature of the blood oxygen level dependent signal). Furthermore, pulse rate and RR interval are correlated, which indicates that both the Polar watch and compression shirts were collecting correlated heartrate data. Aside from the obvious correlations between similar physiological sensor streams, it is promising to note that there is not a great deal of redundancy in the collected features. Strong correlations throughout would indicate redundant features, and thus give reason to down select sensors (i.e., one can increase practicality and sensor footprint by removing a sensor without losing valuable information). Of note is that it does seem that the Polar Shirt and Polar watch do have redundant heartrate information.

Next, we wanted to look at the correlation between each feature and the difficulty level (i.e., low/high). Since the feature values are continuous and the class target difficulty level is binary, we generated Kendall correlations rather than Pearson correlations, as Kendall correlation is better suited for identifying correlations between continuous variables and nominal class values. The correlation matrix shown in Fig. 6 was then generated.

As shown in Fig. 6, of note is that Left and Right pupil diameter have a strong correlation with difficulty level. Also, the standard deviation of the respiration rate also has a strong correlation. Thus, in the next section, we explore the use of linear SVMs

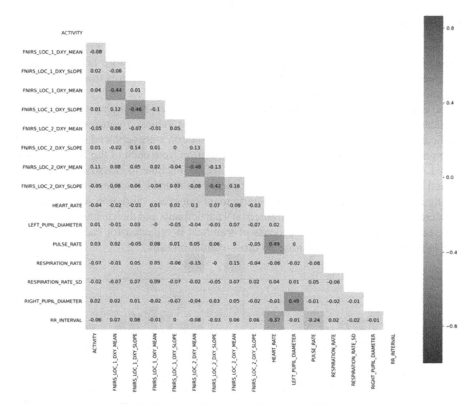

Fig. 5. Pearson Correlations between each feature.

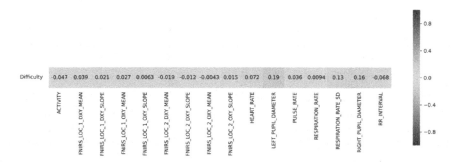

Fig. 6. Kendall correlations between each feature shown on the x axis and task difficulty shown on the y axis.

for classification using all 16 features versus classifier creation using the features that have the highest correlation with the target class value, as indicated in Fig. 6.

3.5 Classification

Based on the insights gained from the correlation matrices above, we aimed to classify our data into low vs high difficulty levels. Our goal was to explore at classification results when all features were included and when just the top features from the Kendall correlations in Fig. 6 were considered.

The z-score and correlation procedures above are robust to missing data, but most classification algorithms are not able to handle missing values. To ensure an unbiased classification, the 'NaN' generated in the previous section were replaced with values of random noise drawn from Standard Normal distribution from each of the 16 columns of features. We then opted to use a linear support vector machine to classify our data into high and low difficulty. Figure 7 shows the accuracy (left) and F1-scores (right) achieved by using all 16 features and a leave-one-participant-out cross validation scheme. In this type of cross-validation the model is trained on 9 participants and then tested on data from the unseen 10th participant. This process of train/test is repeated for each participant, and results are averaged across those 10 cross-validation runs.

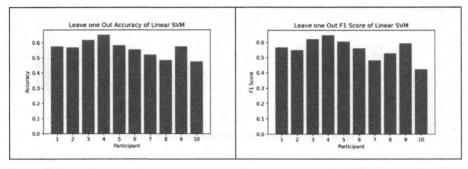

Fig. 7. Left: the figure depicts accuracy results of leave-one-out cross validation classification on the data. This dataset contained many missing data points which were filled in with noise sampled from a standard normal distribution. A linear support vector classifier from sklearn was used. The mean accuracy achieved was 56.1%. Right: depicting F1 scores. The mean F1 score was 55.8%.

The results shown in Fig. 7 are in line with our expectations. We expect lowest accuracy when we use all 16 features, especially since we know from Table 3 that many of the values fed into the model will reflect the random noise used to insert feature values where 'NaN' values are present, for the participants when a sensor did not correctly log data to the TOME server.

To see if our SVM models performed better without missing data, we ran the same SVM techniques detailed above, but for only the participants who did not have a sensor stream missing during data collection (as shown in Table 3, p2, p3, p8, p9 had all 16 features collected properly) Results are in Fig. 8, and we do note as expected that accuracy and F1 values do indeed increase when we focus on participants without missing sensor data.

The results in Fig. 8 are quite promising, as we believe that we can improve accuracy by using both performance and difficulty level as our ground truth label, as done recently

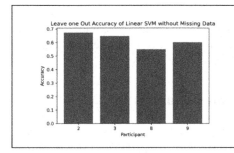
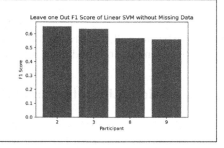

Fig. 8. Accuracy Results of leave-one-out cross validation classification on dataset containing only training examples without any missing data points. A linear support vector classifier from the sklearn python module was used. The mean accuracy was 61.8%.

by Mckendrick et al. [9]. Anecdotally we noted that participant 8 had a good deal of trouble mastering the flight simulator, as reflected in that participant's performance data.

Finally, we wanted to explore the impact that feature selection had on our model results, by only using the 'best features' from the correlation matrix in Fig. 6. As shown in Fig. 9, we select features from best to worst according to Kendall correlation results in Fig. 6. For example, when trained on only one feature, we use LEFT_PUPIL_DIAMETER, the feature with the highest Kendall correlation. When training on two features, we use both LEFT_PUPIL_DIAMETER and RIGHT_PUPIL_DIAMETER, the two features with the highest Kendall correlations. The y axis represents mean accuracy across all participants assessed in leave-one-out cross validation.

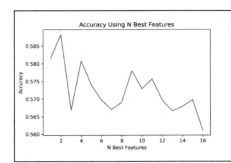
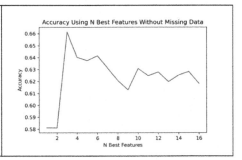

Fig. 9. left mean accuracy results for n best features. The x axis depicts the number of features used in leave-one-out cross validation classification. Right: We repeat the process used in the left, but exclude training examples with any missing features.

As noted on the right side of Fig. 9, again, we repeat the process used in the left, but exclude training examples without missing features. Here we notice an increase in mean classification with relatively few features indicating that including uncorrelated and potentially noisy features has a negative effect on classification accuracy. As shown on the right of Fig. 9, the highest accuracy achieved across all participants (using leave one out cross validation, and all 10 participants) was just above 66% accuracy when we used only the top 3 features of Left and Right Pupil Diameter and Respiration rate. This is notable because all 10 participants had successful data collections where the Tobii and Bioharness sensors collected data properly.

4   Discussion, Limitations and Recommendations

We noted above that several of the wearable sensors would sporadically lose contact with the human subject and/or with their network connectivity to the TOME server at various times during the data collections. This would result in NaN values in their raw data. As we would expect, and as shown in the classification results above, classifications were indeed stronger when all sensors were actively collecting quality data during experiments. Below we identify these connectivity and other issues that were detrimental to our results and we talk about steps to address these issues:

- Issue 1: The PLUX and Polar Smartwatches were the main devices that would lose full connectivity during experiments.

   Recommend: Finding ways to ensure more reliable connectivity for sensors. For example, the our research team has worked to bypass the PLUX OpenSignals software, and we have swapped the Shimmer GSR sensors into the TOME system as a more reliable alternative to the Polar watches. Further, we are exploring ways that data can be logged directly to a local storage device, and later uploaded to the TOME server during standard data collections in case networking issues continue.

- Issue 2: Flying flight simulators are difficult. Student participants would train on the simulator beforehand, but they still struggled to fly with a high level of comfort.

   Recommend: Futures studies looking at workload need significantly more training time or to only recruit people familiar w/flight simulators. Actual pilots would be good subjects.

As detailed in Table 1, the two difficulty levels asked participants to fly within a range of 10,000 ft with a range of ±500 for low difficulty and ±5000 for high difficulty. As it has been well studied that condition level alone does not account for a proper 'mental workload label' [9], we should only include labeled data where the recorded altitude shows that participants maintained the proper range as required by the task. By merging the difficulty level with the performance, we can be more confident that our 'ground truth' labels do indeed represent the difficulty experienced at that time by a given participant.

Also noteworthy is that TOME allows us to better understand which features lead to the most information gain. The results shown in Fig. 7 are in line with our expectations. We expect lowest accuracy when we use all 16 features, especially since we know from Table 3 that many of the values fed into the model will reflect the random noise used to insert feature values where NaNs are present, for the participants when a sensor did not correctly log data to the TOME server. That said, it would be interesting to explore different techniques for filling in data when a TOME sensor breaks down. Perhaps augmenting data from other participants (who are not currently in the test set) and adding some random noise to the resulting data could be a viable option. Also, The Tobii eye trackers right and left pupil diameter were the strongest features. This makes sense as flying in simulators is a visually intensive task and data quality was likely higher when participants were focused on the X-Plane monitors, giving a reliable eye tracking signal. It might also be possible to change the amount of time over which a feature is selected. In the above, 5 s windows of time are examined, but it is possible that varying this parameter (window size $= 1$ s, 10 s, 20 s) could affect classifier accuracy. Further effort should be made to explore these and other options for collating and analyzing multiple sensor streams.

Acknowledgements. We would like to acknowledge the US Navy for supporting this research via contract number N68335-18-C0133.

References

1. Borghini, G., Astolfi, L., Vecchiato, G., Mattia, D., Babiloni, F.: Measuring neurophysiological signals in aircraft pilots and car drivers for the assessment of mental workload, fatigue and drowsiness. Neurosci. Biobehav. Rev. **44**, 58–75 (2014)
2. Yuksel, B.F., et al.: Learn piano with BACh: an adaptive learning interface that adjusts task difficulty based on brain state. In: Proceedings of the 2016 CHI Conference on Human Factors in Computing Systems, San Jose, California, USA, pp. 5372–5384. ACM (2016)
3. Jimenez-Molina, A., Retamal, C., Lira, H.: Using psychophysiological sensors to assess mental workload during web browsing. Sensors **18**(2), 458 (2018)
4. Kwon, J., Shin, S., Im, C.: Toward a compact hybrid brain-computer interface (BCI): performance evaluation of multi-class hybrid EEG-fNIRS BCIs with limited number of channels. PLoS ONE **15**(3), e0230491 (2020)
5. Brouwer, A.-M., Zander, T.O., van Erp, J.B.F., Korteling, J.E., Bronkhorst, A.W.: Using neurophysiological signals that reflect cognitive or affective state: six recommendations to avoid common pitfalls. Front. Neurosci. **9**(136) (2015)
6. Lemm, S., Blankertz, B., Dickhaus, T., Müller, K.R.: Introduction to machine learning for brain imaging. Neuroimage **56**(2), 387–399 (2011)
7. Combrisson, E., Jerbi, K.: Exceeding chance level by chance: the caveat of theoretical chance levels in brain signal classification and statistical assessment of decoding accuracy. J. Neurosci. Methods **250**, 126–136 (2015)
8. Young, M.S., Brookhuis, K.A., Wickens, C.D., Hancock, P.A.: State of science: mental workload in ergonomics. Ergonomics **58**, 1–17 (2015)
9. McKendrick, R., Feest, B., Harwood, A., Falcone, B.: Theories and methods for labeling cognitive workload: classification and transfer learning. Front. Hum. Neurosci. **13**(295) (2019)
10. Hart, S.G., Staveland, L.E.: Development of NASA-TLX (Task Load Index): results of empirical and theoretical research. In: Hancock, P., Meshkati, N. (eds.) Human Mental Workload, Amsterdam, pp. 139–183 (1988)
11. Roscoe, A., Ellis, G.: A Subjective Rating Scale for Assessing Pilot Workload in Flight: A Decade of Practical Use. The Royal Aerospace Establishment (1990)
12. Hirshfield, L.M., et al.: This is your brain on interfaces: enhancing usability testing with functional near infrared spectroscopy. In: SIGCHI. ACM (2011)

13. Navon, D.: Resources—a theoretical soup stone? Psychol. Rev. **91**, 216–234 (1984)
14. Wickens, C.: Multiple resources and mental workload. Hum. Factors **50**(3), 449–455 (2008)
15. Berka, C., Levendowski, D.: EEG correlates of task engagement and mental workload in vigilance, learning and memory tasks. Aviat. Space Environ. Med. **78**(5), B231–B244 (2007)
16. Gevins, A., Smith, M.: Neurophysiological measures of cognitive workload during human-computer interaction. Theor. Issues Ergon. Sci. **4**, 113–131 (2003)
17. Izzetoglu, K., Bunce, S., Izzetoglu, M., Onaral, B., Pourrezaei, K.: fNIR spectroscopy as a measure of cognitive task load. In: Proceedings of the IEEE EMBS (2003)
18. John, M.S., Kobus, D., Morrison, J., Schmorrow, D.: Overview of the DARPA augmented cognition technical integration experiment. Int. J. Hum.-Comput. Interact. **17**(2), 131–149 (2004)
19. Hankins, T.C., Wilson, G.F.: A comparison of heart rate, eye activity, EEG and subjective measures of pilot mental workload during flight. Aviat. Space Environ. Med. **69**(4), 360–367 (1998)
20. Putze, F., et al.: Hybrid fNIRS-EEG based classification of auditory and visual perception processes. Front. Neurosci. **8**, 373 (2014)
21. Lohani, M., Payne, B.R., Strayer, D.L.: A review of psychophysiological measures to assess cognitive states in real-world driving. Front. Hum. Neurosci. **13**, 57 (2019)
22. Ahn, S., Nguyen, T., Jang, H., Kim, J.G., Jun, S.C.: Exploring neuro-physiological correlates of drivers' mental fatigue caused by sleep deprivation using simultaneous EEG, ECG, and fNIRS data. Front. Hum. Neurosci. **10**, 219 (2016)
23. Miller, E.E., Boyle, L.N., Jenness, J.W., Lee, J.D.: Voice control tasks on cognitive workload and driving performance: implications of modality, difficulty, and duration. Transp. Res. Rec. **2672**, 84–93 (2018)
24. Schier, M.A.: Changes in EEG alpha power during simulated driving: a demonstration. Int. J. Psychophysiol. **37**(2), 155–162 (2000)
25. Loukopoulos, L., Barshi, I.: Concurrent task demands in the cockpit: challenges and vulnerabilities in routine flight operations (2003)
26. Lancaster, J.A., Casali, J.G.: Investigating pilot performance using mixed-modality simulated data link. Hum. Factors **50**(2), 183–193 (2008)
27. Caldwell, J., Lewis, J.: The feasibility of collecting in-flight EEG data from helicopter pilots. Aviat. Space Environ. Med. **66**, 883–889 (1995)
28. Callan, D.E., Durantin, G., Terzibas, C.: Classification of single-trial auditory events using dry-wireless EEG during real and motion simulated flight. Front. Syst. **9**, 11 (2015)
29. Gevins, A., DuRousseau, D., Zhang, J., Libove, J.: Flight helmet EEG system. In: Final Tech Report AL/CF-SR-1993-0007, Sam Technology, San Fracisco, CA (1993)
30. Causse, M., Dehais, F., Pastor, J.: Executive functions and pilot characteristics predict flight simulator performance in general aviation pilots. Int. J. Aviat. Psychol. **21**(3), 217–234 (2011)
31. Boril, J., Jirgl, M., Jalovecky, R.: Use of flight simulators in analyzing pilot behavior. In: Iliadis, L., Maglogiannis, I. (eds.) AIAI 2016. IAICT, vol. 475, pp. 255–263. Springer, Cham (2016). https://doi.org/10.1007/978-3-319-44944-9_22
32. Dorneich, M.C., Rogers, W., Whitlow, S.D., DeMers, R.: Human performance risks and benefits of adaptive systems on the flight deck. Int. J. Aviat. Psychol. **26**(1–2), 15–35 (2016)
33. Gil, G., Kaber, D., Kaufmann, K., Kim, S.: Effects of modes of cockpit automation on pilot performance and workload in a next generation flight concept of operation. Hum. Factors Ergon. Manuf. Serv. Ind. **22**(5), 395–406 (2012)
34. Lim, Y., et al.: A novel simulation environment for cognitive human factors engineering research. In: 2017 IEEE/AIAA 36th Digital Avionics Systems Conference (DASC) (2017)
35. Nocera, F.D., Camilli, M., Terenzi, M.: A random glance at the flight deck: pilots' scanning strategies and the real-time assessment of mental workload. J. Cogn. Eng. Decis. Making **1**(3), 271–285 (2007)

36. Bracken, B., et al.: Development and validation of a portable, durable, rugged functional near-infrared spectroscopy (fNIRS) device. In: Presented at the International Neuroergonomics Conference, Philadelphia, PA (2018)
37. Devaraj, A., Izzetoglu, M., Izzetoglu, K., Onaral, B.: Motion artifact removal for fNIR spectroscopy for real world application areas. In: Proceedings of the SPIE International Society for Optical Engineering, vol. 5588, pp. 224–229 (2004)
38. Koelstra, S., et al.: DEAP: a database for emotion analysis using physiological signals. IEEE Trans. Affect. Comput. (Special Issue on Naturalistic Affect Resources for System Building and Evaluation) 3(1), 18–31 (2014)

Consideration of How Different Rearview Presentations Used for Electronic Mirrors on Automobiles Affect Human Spatial Cognition

Yutaro Kido[1](✉), Sora Kanzaki[1], Tomonori Ohtsubo[2], Yoshiaki Matsuba[2],
Daichi Sugawara[2], and Miwa Nakanishi[1]

[1] Faculty of Science and Technology, Department of Administration Engineering,
Keio University, Yokohama, Kanagawa 223-8522, Japan
ykdpnkdpn07@keio.jp
[2] Mazda Motor Corporation, 3-1 Shinchi, Fuchu-cho, Aki-gun, Hiroshima 730-8670, Japan

Abstract. Recent automobile development has led to the installation of rearview cameras or electronic mirrors that could display a rearview image to the driver through a monitor in the driver's seat and it expected to provide drivers with higher spatial cognition. In this research, we clarify the magnification function that allows optimal cognition of the rear approaching vehicles for drivers. We conduct the experiment introducing Camera monitor system under the same size and location constraints that traditional rearview mirrors face. We use a simple driving simulator and provide participants with a wide rearview by changing the magnification according to the viewing angle. Participants estimate the distance from approaching vehicles that change lanes and press the button. We recorded the distance the button was pressed and a subjective evaluation questionnaire. We analyzed from the point of view that it is safer to perceive the vehicle to vehicle distance to be closer than its actual distance. It was revealed that a pattern that follows the downward convex with no magnification region and a linear function without no magnification region led to the safest presentation of the vehicle to vehicle distance. It was also confirmed that some subjective evaluations of these patterns were higher. In addition, the presentation difference of the vehicle to vehicle distance between one function and the function that is no magnification could be estimated by a model using the least-squares method.

Keywords: Simulation · Electronic mirror · Spatial cognition

1 Introduction

International standards for devices that provide indirect vision were changed in November 2015, and it is expected that the use of camera monitor systems (hereinafter, this is called CMS) will expand for drivers to gain rear visibility in the future [1]. CMS allows a great variety of views compared to conventional mirrors. As for conventional mirrors, the presentation range of the rearview is uniquely determined depending on the installation position and their size. On the other hand, as for CMS, it is flexible because it can be expanded by changing the angle of view of the camera. However, there is the size constraint of the monitor. When it is fixed, there is a trade-off relationship between the area of the rearview video and the size of the image in the video.

In this study, we experimentally examined the relationship between the magnification of the video and the human's spatial cognition, and clarified the magnification function that allows optimal cognition of the rear approaching vehicles for drivers.

2   Method

2.1   Experimental System and Environment

Figure 1 shows the positions of participants and the position of the experimental equipment, and Fig. 2 shows the experimental environment. A 35-in. curved display (21:9) was placed on three screens as a simulator that provides a front view. A 27-in. display (16:9) was arranged at the same position as a rearview mirror. It was a simulator that provides the rearview. In this experiment, participants didn't operate a steering wheel (made by Logitech), but it was also installed in order for the participants to take the same posture as when driving.

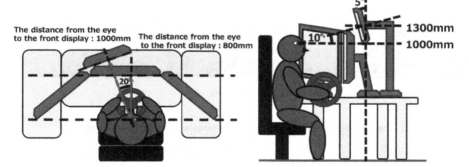

Fig. 1. The experimental environment

Fig. 2. Experimental photo

2.2 Experimental Task

Figure 3 shows an example of the front view presented to the simulator, and Fig. 4 shows an example of the rearview of the electronic mirror. Participants monitored the view from the vehicle traveling at 60 km/h in the central of 13 lanes (to test the visibility of the approaching vehicle in a wide area of the rearview). To keep the driver's attention forward, participants were required to press a button on the steering wheel every time the tip of the vehicle met the pink or green lines on the road randomly generated horizontal as shown in Fig. 3(hereinafter, this is called the front task). However, when other vehicles approached the vehicle with various accelerations from the rear at random timings, participants appropriately checked the rearview using the simulated electronic mirror. Moreover, they were required to press a button on the steering wheel when they first noticed the existence of another vehicle and when they determined that the distance between the vehicle and the approaching vehicle was 30 m, 20 m, 10 m, or 0 m(hereinafter, this is called the rear task). The vehicle to vehicle distance was from the rear end of the vehicle to the front end of the approaching vehicle shown in Fig. 5. However, it was difficult to press the buttons at 10 m intervals for a series of movements of the approaching vehicle, so the tasks were separated determining 30 m and 10 m and determining 20 m and 0 m.

Fig. 3. The front view

Fig. 4. The rearview

One participant performed with the 2-pattern distances pressed the button and 7-pattern magnification functions described later, so they tried a total of 14 tasks. To suppress the influence of the experiment order, the above 14 tasks were designed to be in random order. Before the task, the participants practiced so that they could correctly recognize the distances of 30 m, 20 m, 10 m, and 0 m in the rearview of no magnification condition.

As shown in Fig. 5, the movements of approaching vehicles included 3 patterns: ① a pattern that went straight in the lane next to the vehicle, ② a pattern that emerged from just behind the vehicle and changed one lane, and ③ a pattern that changed multiple lanes and crossed behind the vehicle. Moreover, they included variations of lane changes to the left or right, so they were a total of six patterns. The vehicle appeared at a distance of

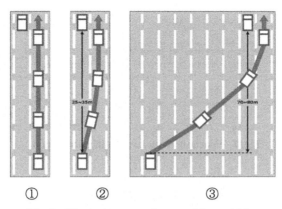

Fig. 5. The movements of approaching vehicles

250 m behind (not visible on the simulator) traveling at 80 km/h and started accelerating at 0.03G from 70 m behind. A speed difference was about 30 km/h when the vehicle to vehicle distance was 0 m.

2.3 Experimental Conditions

The video contained the rearview of central 86°. The magnification functions were 7 patterns: a pattern that was no magnification as the controlled condition, 3 patterns without no magnification region in the rearview of central 36°, and 3 patterns with no magnification region in the rearview of central 36°. The magnification was classified into three types: based on a linear function, an upward convex function, and a downward convex function. In addition, all patterns unified the rearview of 36° were shown in the 47% central area of the video. Figure 6 shows patterns without no magnification region in the video, and Fig. 7 shows patterns with no magnification region in video and they show the controlled condition. Figure 8 shows the actual rearview applying these 7 patterns when the approaching vehicle is 30 m, 20 m, 10 m, 0 m behind.

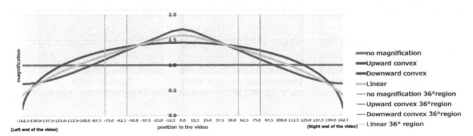

Fig. 6. Functions Without no magnification region conditions

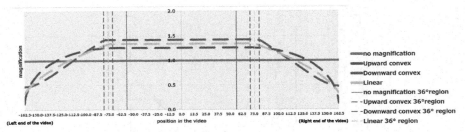

Fig. 7. Functions With no magnification region

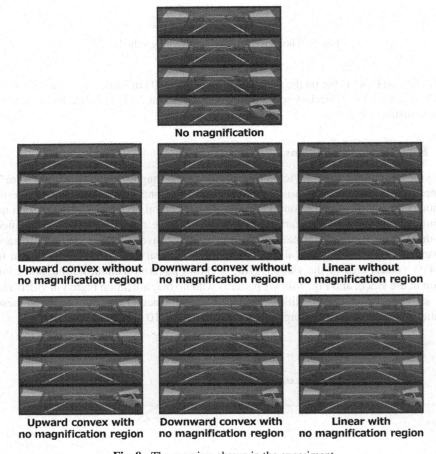

Fig. 8. The rearview shown in the experiment

2.4 Measurements

Throughout the experiment, we tracked the distance between the randomly generated line on the road and the tip of the vehicle every time the button was pressed. Also, we logged the distance between the vehicle and the approaching vehicle every time the button was pressed. The sampling rate was 1/200 s. Lastly, a subjective evaluation questionnaire was recorded after each task. The questionnaire consisted of the five items in Table 1 and the score of each question from −100 to 100.

Table 1. Questionnaires

No.	Question	Scoring
1	Could you focus on the front task?	−100: difficult 100: easy
2	Was it easy to grasp the emergence of the approaching vehicle?	−100: difficult 100: easy
3	Was it easy to grasp the distance from the approaching vehicle?	−100: difficult 100: easy
4	Was it easy to grasp the speed of the approaching vehicle?	−100: difficult 100: easy
5	Was it easy to grasp the traveling direction of the approaching vehicle?	−100: difficult 100: easy

2.5 Participants and Ethics

The participants were eight healthy male students (22–26 years old, average: 24.0 years old, SD: 1.32). Participants were explained the purpose and contents of experiment verbally and on paper, and signed the consent form. The data was encrypted so that it could not be collated with personal information. This experiment was conducted with the approval from the Bioethics Committee of Keio University Department of Science and Technology (31–77).

3 Result

3.1 The Characteristics of the Presented Video from the Viewpoint of the Presentation of the Vehicle to Vehicle Distance

Figure 9 shows the result of the front task. Since there were no differences in the performance under any conditions, it could be considered that this had no effects on the rear task.

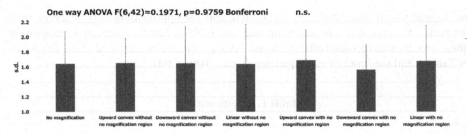

Fig. 9. The result of the front task

Figures 10 and 11 show the vehicle to vehicle distance when the button was pressed determining the 30, 20, 10, 0 m. If the vehicle to vehicle distance when the button was pressed is long, it is considered that the distance was presented farther. On the other hand, if the vehicle to vehicle distance is short, it is considered that the distance was presented closer. We analyzed from the point of view that it is safer to perceive the vehicle to vehicle distance to be closer than its actual distance. As a result, we obtained the following points.

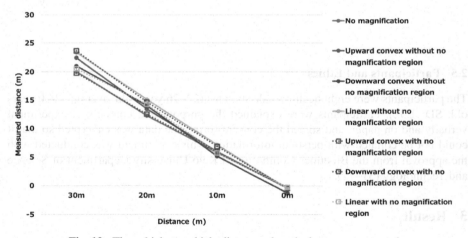

Fig. 10. The vehicle to vehicle distance when the button was pressed

First, as for the presentation of the relatively long vehicle to vehicle distance such as 30 m or 20 m behind, all patterns presented farther than the controlled condition except for the 30 m of the upper convex function with no magnification region. This is because 30 m and 20 m behind were often presented near the center of the mirror, and in this area, the approaching vehicle of all patterns appeared to be about 1.3 to 1.7 times larger than that of the controlled condition, so it is probable that safer presentation of the vehicle to vehicle distance. On the other hand, as for 0 m behind, all patterns presented the vehicle to vehicle distance similarly. This is because as shown in Fig. 8, the approaching vehicle

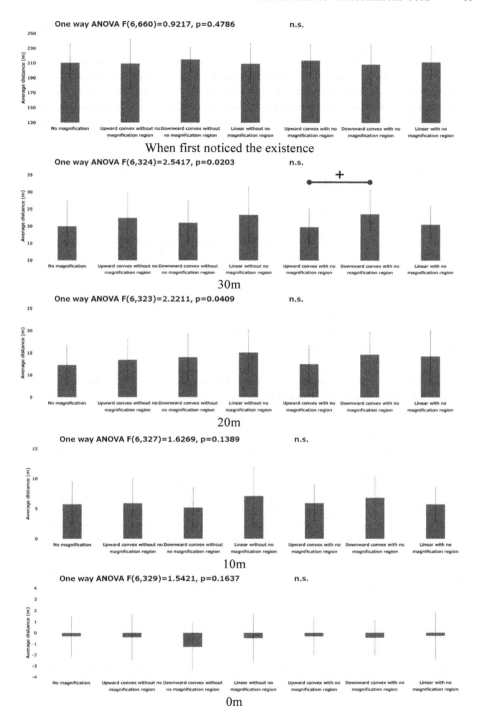

Fig. 11. The detail of the vehicle to vehicle distance when the button was pressed

at 0 m behind was presented near the right or left end of the mirror, then the size of the vehicle depended on the magnification associated with their position in the video.

Second, it led to the safest presentation of vehicle to vehicle distance that a pattern that follows the downward convex function with no magnification region and the linear function without no magnification region. The reason why the former was the safest among similar functions with no magnification region is that the center region of 36° was expanded the most, which is the most important region for the driver. The reason why the latter was safest among similar functions without no magnification region is that the maximum rate of change for the mirror magnification was smaller than that of the others. The other two functions had a large rate of change for the mirror magnification, which led to incorrect recognition of the speed of the approaching vehicles.

3.2 The Results of Subjective Evaluation

Figure 12 shows the results of the subjective evaluation questionnaire. Focusing on the lower convex function with no magnification region and the linear function without no magnification region that presented the distance safely, the former was higher in Q3 and Q5, and the latter was higher in Q1 than the other conditions. The former was because the approaching vehicle was visible the largest compared to the other conditions with no magnification region. The latter was because the change rate of the magnification in the video was smaller and the movement of the approaching vehicle was easy to predict, so it was easy to concentrate on the front task.

3.3 The Model of the Relationship Between Shape of the Function and the Presentation of the Distance

As shown in Sect. 3.1, it was confirmed that the presentation of the vehicle to vehicle distance differed depending on the magnification function to process the video. Therefore, based on the shape of the magnification function, we try to make a mathematical model that estimates how many meters the deviation of the presentation distance compared to the controlled condition. Moreover, when the vehicle to vehicle distance is xm, it is considered that not only the distance at that moment but also the distance after approaching and the difference of the change rate of the magnification while approaching.

The deviation d_x is taken as the explained variable. A_x was the magnification when the vehicle to vehicle distance was x m, B_x was the magnification when the vehicle to vehicle distance is $x + 10$ m, and C_x was the difference of the change rate of the magnification between at the distance x m and at the distance $x + 10$ m. These are used as explanatory variables. Thus, the deviation d_x could be presented as shown in Eq. (1) as follows.

$$d_x = \alpha A_x + \beta B_x + \gamma C_x + \delta \tag{1}$$

The least-squares method is applied to d_x by using the average value of the deviation between the vehicle to vehicle distance (hereinafter, this is called measured value) when pressing the button of 30, 20 and 10 m excluding 0 m of each condition and the controlled condition, the model was derived as shown in Eq. (2) as follows.

$$d_x = 3.93A_x + 7.88B_x - 38.21C_x - 14.77 \qquad \text{adjusted } R^2 = 0.46 \tag{2}$$

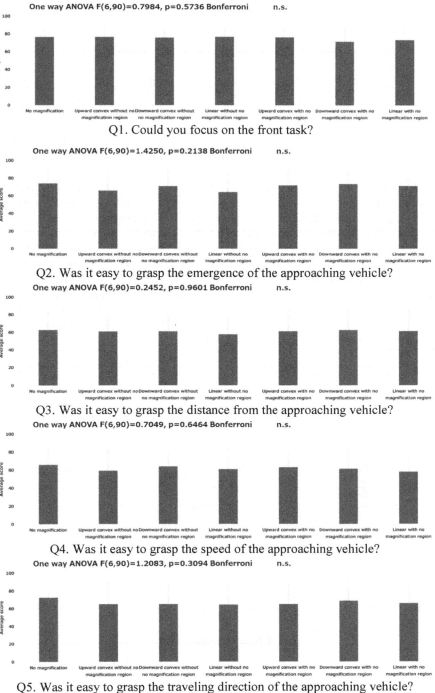

Fig. 12. The results of questionnaire

Table 2 shows the results of the least-squares method.

Table 2. The Results of the least-squares method

Explanatory variables	Standardized partial regression coefficient	t-value	VIF
A_x	0.3553	1.4691	1.7278
B_x	0.4649	1.9857	1.6187
C_x	−0.1017	−0.5175	1.1400

The larger the magnification was, the safer the distance was presented, and then the deviation became positively large, so the coefficients of A_x and B_x became positive.

The larger the difference in the change rate of the magnification was, the more difficult it was to see the change of presentation of the image, so the coefficient of C_x became negative. This suggests that this model has some validity. It is considered that the multicollinearity could be avoided because of the value of VIF. From the viewpoint of the standardized partial regression coefficient, the largest effect was B_x, followed in order by A_x and C_x on presentation of the vehicle to vehicle distance x. By using this model, it is possible to roughly estimate how many meters the deviates of the presentation of the distance from that of the controlled condition. Figure 13 shows the relationship between the estimated value and the measured value.

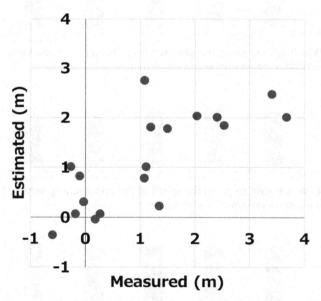

Fig. 13. Estimated value and Measured value

4   Conclusion

In this study, we clarified the magnification function that could be applied to the processing of rearview images and allow optimal cognition of the rear for drivers.

As a result of the experiment, it was revealed that a pattern that followed the downward convex with no magnification region in the rearview of 36° and a linear function without no magnification region in the rearview of 36° led to the safest presentation of the vehicle to vehicle distance.

As a result of the subjective evaluation questionnaire, it was confirmed that a pattern that follows the downward convex function with no magnification region was easy to present the distance to the approaching vehicle and the traveling direction of it, and the linear without no magnification region was easy to concentrate on the front task.

Besides, the model was able to estimate the deviation of the presentation of the vehicle to vehicle distance compared to the controlled condition based on the shape of the function.

Reference

1. The Working Party on General Safety Provisions: Proposal for Supplement 2 to the 04 series of amendments to Regulation No. 46, ECE/TRANS/WP.29/2015/84 (2015)

Design Guidelines of Social-Assisted Robots for the Elderly: A Mixed Method Systematic Literature Review

Chih-Chang Lin, Hao-Yu Liao, and Fang-Wu Tung[⊠]

National Taiwan University of Science and Technology, No. 43, Keelung Road, Sec. 4, Da'an Dist., Taipei City 10607, Taiwan
fwtung@ntust.edu.tw

Abstract. This review aims to provides a design criterion for the design and development of SARs to help product designers and researchers who are actively engaged in this field. Our focus is on the product users' three major levels of needs, namely: (1) Functionality - Subject to the users' physical aging and other limitations, the functions and roles of SARs are derived from different users' background living environmental factors. These differing factors affects their preferences in what functions SARs could play in their lives, and how efficiently these can be carried out. (2) Usability - This involves interactions between the users' perception and spatial environment and their restricted physical capabilities. To facilitate the elderly's ability to move with minimal physical exertion, (i) employ operating methods based on lifestyle habits and past experiences of using similarly related products, (ii) use technological assistance to reduce user learning curve and learning pressure, and (iii) apply multi-modal assistance to reduce the need for change of existing living patterns and habits. (3) Pleasure: Pleasure is derived from emotions, attitudes, acceptances, experiences and interactions. This includes Physical Pleasure, Social Pleasure, Psychological Pleasure and Ideological Pleasure. Each brings a different type of pleasure to the elderly. There is a need for further research the requirements of the elderly for SARs design. From the research results, this three-level analysis provide a set of design criteria for developers to build SARs that are more in tune with the physical and mental capabilities of the elderly user.

Keywords: Elderly · Socially assisted robots · Functionality · Usability · Pleasure · Design guidelines

1 Introduction

This has resulted in the growth of the elderly population in Taiwan faster than in any other countries. Under this trend, more caregivers are needed to cater to the long-term demands of the elderly. But how will our society respond to this increasing health and social care demands of this population group [2]. At present, many countries have begun to develop robotic technology, and is even regarded as one of the development strategies of more forward-looking countries. In the past, robots were mostly used in manufacturing and

© Springer Nature Switzerland AG 2020
C. Stephanidis et al. (Eds.): HCII 2020, LNCS 12425, pp. 90–104, 2020.
https://doi.org/10.1007/978-3-030-60128-7_7

production to replace labor-intensive tasks. Today they are moving into the general public life, especially in the field of medical care. In the care of the elderly, robots are widely used as assistive devices for daily living, and more are being designed and developed to meet this demand [3]. Robotic research is basically divided into 2 areas: Medical Technology Assistive devices, for example - robotic limbs or wearable prostheses; and the other is Socially Assistive Machines, with information processing functions and interactive capabilities with users [4]. Our main focus will be the latter. Socially Assistive Robots (SARs) are divided into three categories. First category, Ambient-Assisted Living robots that combines assistive functions to facilitate daily life, shopping and communication activities with social interaction. The second are Exercise Assistance robots [5], which help the user to exercise more. The third are the Companion robots, these depend on the social capabilities of the user to interact with the robot.

The definition of a Socially Assisted Robot depends on the specific context in which the robot is used, the needs of the user, the tasks of the robot, and the technical capabilities of the robot [6]. From a product design point of view, the needs of users are redefined according to Maslow's hierarchy of needs theory. The three major levels of needs for product users are defined as follows: Functionality, Usability and Pleasure. The three levels of needs are placed in sequential contexts. For a product to have good functionality, the designers must fully grasp how the product is used in the context of the user's daily living environment, and how it can perform the original intended functions. After users become accustomed to the functionality of the product, they will need the product to be easily usable. The designers must then focus on improving the accessibility of the product. Once the user is accustomed to the product, the need level will subsequently be raised to meaningful life events that are not only functionally beneficial but also emotionally beneficial. This review is to understand the interactive process between the elderly and the robot, and to attach importance to the research and design of products catered to the elderly.

2 Methodology

2.1 Research Protocol

The protocol of this review consists of first developing a series of research questions based on the PICO format, then systematically searched through the literature databases. The search used qualitative research or mixed research design methods. Then the literature content of electronic databases was screened and critiqued [7]. The review includes four steps. First, we conducted a systematic search of the electronic literature databases using a snowball method and headline citations [8]. Second, we set predefined inclusion and exclusion criteria to identify relevant articles and publications [9]. Third, we coded the articles in a qualitative manner. Finally, we conducted a comprehensive review of the 17 articles from the search results of published works [1] that were relevant to our goals and a set of design criteria was proposed.

2.2 Search Strategy

A snowball search was conducted of the electronic databases of National Taiwan University and the Taiwan University of Science and Technology, with contents including important elements of qualitative research. The Chinese language database was also included. Five indexed online databases were used, namely Scopus, PubMed, WOS, Embase and Huayi Online, covering academic papers and systematic review articles approved by seminars from September 31, 2016 to July 31, 2019. The search consisted of three groups of string words. The first group consisted of people's subjective dimensions of life (acceptance, attitude, experience, feelings, etc.). The second group was based on the dimensions of participant types, namely the elderly (aged, elderly, seniors, etc.). The third group consisted of devices that were related to robots (socially assistive robots, companion robots, etc.). Articles published in journals and seminars, as well as observation and review logs were all candidates. Duplicated articles were merged and removed before we performed title, abstract, and full-text filtering. Next, the reference lists in the included articles were also reviewed to avoid leaving out any relevant literature [8]. A senior research scholar and two independent researchers were responsible for evaluating the included research contents, and these were finally analyzed and summarized through topical data extraction.

2.3   Inclusion and Exclusion Criteria

Using pre-inductive and collated inclusion and exclusion criteria, we jointly screened titles, abstracts, and full texts of potential candidate publications [9]. Controversial articles' contents were reviewed and critiqued until consensus was reached. The final inclusion or exclusion decision depended on the following: (1) the type of research content, (2) the type of participants, (3) the type of robot, (4) the type of result evaluation, (5) the type of article content. Articles were included and excluded through four stages of literature screening: (i) Identification of literature, (ii) Screening of literature, (iii) Inclusion of appropriate literature, (iv) Selection process was based on the article's year of study, title, abstract and full text. A final 17 articles were selected (Fig. 1).

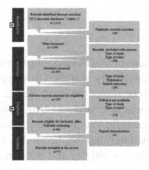

Fig. 1. Electronic search for literature identification and the selection process

2.4   Research Content

The literature included in this review are primarily publications that used qualitative or mixed methods and were based on empirical research. The choice of the research theoretical framework was not limited by the publication dates. In addition to journal articles, we decided that a continuous long-term observation log will be acceptable in order to maximize the opportunity to include all relevant literature. English was the main language of selection and only the most complete articles were included.

2.5 Participant Type

Participants were 65 years or older, or an average age group of 65 years or older. To ensure that the participants were able to competently operate the robot, articles where participants had mental illness and needed a caregiver were excluded. Articles with participants living in retired homes or elderly communities were included. The researches selected were conducted in many different countries. These countries have shown interests in research dealing with SARs for daily living support and elderly home care. This covered the interactive responses of exercise movements through the assistance of robots based on characteristics of the user activities (Table 1).

3   Three Levels of Socially Assisted Robot Design

Based on the selected literature, we used the grounded theory as a baseline to propose the Constructed Theoretical Template as the main axis of decoding in the design and development of SARs. This encompass three main levels: Functionality, Usability and Pleasure. The aim is to incorporate these elements into the SARs' interaction with elderly.

3.1   Functionality

We identified 6 main areas robots could play a role in providing daily assistance to the elderly: physically demanding tasks, health and safety, information management, entertainment, companionship and exercise. The first 5 areas have similar roles and its role in assisting the elderly with exercises will be discussed separately.

Physically Demanding and Information Management Tasks.
Physically demanding tasks are activities that the elderly have difficulty in carrying out on their own due to their frailty in health. These includes fetching and moving items [10], running errands and doing the shopping [11], disposing the rubbish and walking indoors and outdoors [12]. To be able to carry out these tasks, other than the need to have mobility, the robot usually also needs to possess arms that can grip. This poses a challenge to developers to achieve a level of reliability of the robot when developing the related functions. Information management involves the collection, storage and distribution of information by the robot. One typical function of this type of robot is to remind the user of their medication intake [13], their appointments [12], things to do [15]. Though some users have expressed negative feedback about their functions [10], for example, being reminded too many times the things they should do and being woken up at inappropriate timing. After experiencing the functions, they are generally more willing to accept the robots provided they have more control of the execution of the functions. Users were also able to use the robot to find information about weather, time, stocks and recipes [16].

Table 1. Overview of included qualitative publications

	Study	Location	Aim	Design/methodology	Participants
1	Di Nuovo, 2018	Italy UK	Elderly users may benefit from many services provided by robots operating in different environments, such as providing assistance inside apartments, serving in shared facilities of buildings or guiding people outdoors.	the experimental evaluation in realistic environments of a web-based multi-modal user interface tailored for elderly users of near future multi-robot services. Experimental results demonstrate positive evaluation of usability and willingness to use by elderly users, especially those less experienced with technological devices who could benefit more from the adoption of robotic services.	35 subjects, average age above 65 years old
2	Cavallo, F., 2018	Italy UK	To evaluate acceptability by the elderly of 6 robotic services by 3 types of robots that provide living assistance in 3 different living environments to promote their independence.	Robots were used in three different environments: private home, apartment, and outdoors. Each recruited participant is invited to the laboratory for evaluation. After that, participants can get three robots. After use, fill in a questionnaire to evaluate the availability and acceptability of each robot service.	45 subjects aged between 65 and 86 years old
3	Justyna G.,2018	Poland	Assessment of Perceived Attractiveness, Usability, and Societal Impact of a Multimodal Robotic Assistant for Aging Patients with Memory Impairments	18 seniors with basic communication skills were allowed to communicate directly with the robot and external personnel. The laboratory simulated 7 typical daily activities, such as cooking, leisure time, medication intake, and social interaction. Subjects took a break between completed tasks. During the event, researchers were present in the room. Upon completion, participants were asked to evaluate the robot by completing	18 subjects aged between 55-90 years old, 8 had mild cognitive impairment and 10 were in good health
4	Tiffany L. Chen, 2017	USA	To investigate the elderly acceptance of robots as a dance-based exercise partner	Use of the questionnaire and MMSE (mini-mental state examination) assessment. The introduction of the robot instructs participants to think about how they can benefit from the robot. Then perform stepping tasks (tango, waltz, etc.). Fill in post-use questionnaires and interviews after the end	16 subjects aged between 65-79 years old, physically and mentally healthy, 9 females and 7 males
5	De Carolis, B., 2016	Italy	Study of robots' ability to recognize the user's affective emotional state and give the most appropriate communicative behavior response to achieve empathy.	Two studies were conducted in elderly recreation centers. Three psychologists' experts in communications conducted experiments that used human subjects' voice and facial expressions in ratios of 38% and 55%, to trigger an emphatic response in the SARs, which are designed to recognize 6 human affective states: anger, disgust, fear, happiness, sadness, surprise. The second study involved subjects looking at a video showing simulation of interaction between an actor and the robot in situations requiring empathic answers. Subjects were then asked to evaluate whether robot was emphatic.	18 subjects aged above 65 years old, average age 75.6 years old, equally distributed by gender
6	Karunarathne, D., 2019	Japan	Study of the elderly's' acceptability towards using a humanoid robot as a walking companion	Experiments were conducted on a university campus outdoors, except during rain or snow where its is moved indoors. Subjects walked along a 80x4 meter (outdoors) or street with the robot, reached the end and returned. Indoor walking is a two rounds trip along a 30x2 meter hallway. Subjects then gave their responses through questionnaire and interview.	Japanese adults aged from 60-73 years old, with an average age of 67 years old; 20 males, 10 females
7	Zsiga, K., 2018	Hungary	Participants each received a robot which stayed with them in their homes for about 3 months. Robot collected data about its acceptability, user behavior, and experience. Participants evaluated robot functional aspects of general usefulness, reliability, and satisfaction.	Participants each received a robot which stayed with them in their homes for about 3 months. Robot collected data about its acceptability, user behavior, and experience. Participants evaluated robot functional aspects of general usefulness, reliability, and satisfaction.	Participants at least 70 years old, average age 77 (70-83) years old, living alone, able to communicate with the robot by voice and touch, 1 male and 7 females.
8	Baisch, S., 2017	Germany	To investigate the relevance of psychosocial functioning for the acceptance of social robots by elder people in the context of everyday functioning.	First part - participants were shown pictures of the respective robot and its basic functions were explained in a video. Thereafter, participants watched a video showing cognitively and physically impaired elder people interacting with the respective robot in application scenarios. Robot acceptance was assessed twice for each robot, once after each of the two parts of the session.	29 participants with median age 70 years old (range 63-81), with good cognitive and physical health
9	McGlynn, S. A., 2018	USA	To investigate older adults' attitudes, emotions, and engagement with PARO to identify its potential applicability to this demographic.	Experiment was conducted on campus laboratory in 3 stages. Firstly, participants were verbally introduced to the robot. Then robot was brought in and then a pre-interaction interview was conducted about participants' initial impression. Then robot was turned on and interacted with participants for 10 minutes and a post-interaction interview and questionnaire was conducted.	participants aged between 67-80 years old, 15 females and 15males

(continued)

Table 1. (continued)

#	Author, year	Country	Description	Method	Participants
10	Moro, C., 2019	Canada	Robots with social functions provide human-machine interactions with the elderly as well as providing assistance. This research studies how robot dynamics, such as facial expressions and gestures, affect the interactive experience of elderly people with cognitive impairment in assisted activities.	The experiment conducted in the public kitchen of the nursing home involved each participant being asked to make a cup of tea with the help of three interactive platforms (Human-like robot Casper, character-like robot Ed and a tablet). Each participant performed two interactive activities on a specific platform for a total of 6 times in 10 days. The sessions were recorded on video to identify participants' behavioral cues pertaining to the following variables: (1) engagement, (2) trust, (3) affect, (4) perceived social intelligence, (5) collaborative behavior, and (6) compliance.	6 participants, all females, cognitively healthy to mild impairment, with average MOCA score 25.8, aged between 82-96 years old
11	Chu, Y., 2019	Taiwan	To gain insight into the behavior of the elderly using Zenbo robots through service experience engineering (SEE) theory. To understand the interactions between the user and the Zenbo robot, and then use the five major levels (Interaction, sequence, equipment, culture, entity) to integrate the behavior model to explore the hidden needs generated by the interaction.	Participants interacted with the robot in their homes for 1 week. Photographic, audio, video, interview and observation records were taken. Interviews were conducted as the user was operating the robot - a "guided tour" participatory field observation method. Observation of the subject-robot interactions involves five indicators: Activities, Environment, Interactions, Objects, and Users Interactions, sequences, tools and equipment, culture, and entities. Results were integrated into behavioral models.	10 participants, age between 56-71 years old
12	Bai, L., 2018	Taiwan	Smart home companion robots are used to improve the quality of life of the elderly, reduce the burden of caregivers, maximize the benefits of the care resources invested, and promote the development of related industries. It should be one of the important strategies to solve the problem of life support and health care for the aging society.	This research discusses the actual user experience of the Zenbo robot by the elderly in three stages. The first stage is the evaluation of the user experience, comparing the use of both Zenbo and Paro robots. The second stage is the evaluation of functional preferences, comparing Zenbo and iPhone Siri. Third stage is Elderly Home Application Innovative Use (Zenbo) Situation Design and Evaluation	41 participants, 8 males, 33 females, aged 51-75 years old
13	Di Nuovo, A., 2017	England Italy	Experiments in three locations over two countries used multi-modal interface service robot models to help older people in different environments by providing different services with the aim to increase usability and acceptability of robots.	In the first part of the study, carried out at test sites, participants were free to choose to utilize at least 1 of the 6 services (shopping, communication, laundry, reminding, garbage collection, food delivery) by the robot. The second part, done at the university, had participants use the food delivery service of the robot. Sessions were video recorded. Participants completed questionnaire after each session.	82 participants, 31 males and 51 females, average age of 77.6 years (range 63-97).
14	Efting, H., 2016	Sweden	A study into the designing of a socially assistive robot (HOBBIT) for the elderly.	The following activities (some involving user participation) were conducted within the HOBBIT project to identify criteria for the design of the HOBBIT robot: Introduction workshops, Questionnaire, Qualitative interviews, Concept generation activities, Mock-up study, Laboratory trials of the first HOBBIT prototype, Design concepts and ergonomic analysis, Home trials.	The primary target group is seniors living alone. 70 + years old, who in the near future will need assistance in order to be able to stay in their own homes.
15	Chu, L., 2019	Taiwan	The present study aims to understand older adults' expectations for robots and to compare older adults' acceptance ratings for 2 existing robots: One of them is a more human-like and more service-oriented robot and the other one is a more animal-like and more companion-oriented robot.	Participants first completed a semi-structured interview regarding their ideal robot. After receiving information about the 2 existing robots, they then completed the Unified Theory of Acceptance and Use of Technology questionnaires to report their pre-implementation acceptance of the 2 robots.	33 healthy, community-dwelling Taiwanese older adults, age range: 59-82 years.
16	Kim, S., 2019	Korea	The purpose of the study is to develop qualitative usability evaluation criteria of communication service robot, one of the senior-friendly products, for elderly people.	To develop the usability testing criteria of a communication service robot for elderly people. The following was carried out: product selection, selection of target product, development of leading indicators, correction by experts, and preliminary evaluation according to the scenario and development of core indicators. For this, a draft questionnaire was developed for the elderly at around age 60. After small group tests and interviews, the experts modified the initial draft to the usability evaluation criteria of communication service robot for elderly people.	46 participants and age average 65 years old
17	Lee, S., 2019	Korea	This paper presents the design and implementation of a next generation of elderly care robot. Based on an innovative undertaking in its sociability and dependability with extensive user studies.	The elderlies taken care of by Senior welfare Centers are chosen as the target sector, for which the following five service scenarios are designed: (infotainment, video-chatting, game playing, medicine alarm and in particular, errand service)	Above 60 years old

Health and Safety. Robots often could play a role in managing the elderly's health and monitoring their safety at home. This is done by doing the physically demanding tasks and through information management. For example, robots remind the user to take their medications and drink water to avoid dizziness [13], record and monitor the stock and expiration of medications [14], monitor their blood pressure and weight [14], compile and display their health report [15]. Robots also help the elderly to access medical services like making doctors' appointments and getting medication prescriptions [16]. Besides enhancing the elderly's safety by aiding in physically demanding tasks, robots could be made aware of the user falling down [13], sound the alarm in case of gas leakage [12], monitor any unusual conditions of home appliances. Moreover, users could actively monitor the home environment safety via robots. For example, they could check the home environment by going through a checklist [11] and remotely control the robot to monitor the situation in home [17].

Entertainment and Social Companionship. Robots could offer entertainment services for the elderly through speech and screen display. For example, they could use robots to take a picture [15], surf on internet [20], shop online browse photos, watch videos [19] and news, listen to stories and music and play games [15]. Robots could be the social medium of the elderly through which they could send emails [15], conduct a video chat [21], make a phone call [14], or even leave voice messages for family members [18]. Furthermore, robots could act as a companion for the elderly. Based on the user's commands and actions, robots could response and interact with the user physically and verbally [22]. Some elders even considered the presence of a robot as a form of companionship. Some robots like Paro could be like companion pets for the elderly as they need less maintenance compared to real animals [22]. Overall, the ability to converse was rated the most popular function in this type of robots [17].

Exercise. 4 articles mentioned that robots could assist and encourage the elderly in exercising [10]. For example, by being their dance partners [5], by giving instructions and monitoring the exercise [13], and by walking with robot [25]. It did not matter whether they had any prior physical contact with robots, participants accepted robots as dance partners [5]. Some felt that exercising is important, and robots could encourage them and offer a convenient way to exercise. It is notable that participants with different physical and learning conditions had different expectations.

3.2 Usability

The use of SARs involves the interaction process between the user and the machine. The design of Ambient Assisted Living, Exercise Assistance, and Companion Robots needs to take into consideration the user's habits, their expected interaction methods, and their views and feelings. We explored the factors affecting the interactions between the three forms of robots and the elderly user.

Ambient Assisted Living Robot (AAL). Ambient Assisted Living robots provide supportive care services to the elderly in their daily lives [12, 13]. Their main functions are carrying out physically demanding tasks, health and safety monitoring, and information management. The interactive experience in using them will affect whether the robot can become useful, and what level of usefulness achievable. Accessibility of robots as the elderly's physiological condition gradually deteriorates, it prevents them from standing for too long at a time and therefore they spent most of the time sitting down. The relative height between the robot and the user is therefore an important influencing factor in its design. Researcher proposed that the average sitting position height is 3.8 ft and the average user standing height is 5.5 ft [19]. The physical size and height of the robot affects its operation range during use. The height of the robot needs to be shorter than the average standing height of the elderly user. This allows the user to reach the touch interface even when the user is in different positions. The screen needs to be within the visual range of the user so that they feel they are able to physically control the robot [17], and allows the user to see the robot's response, [12] and to establish "eye contact". The recommended height is not more than 150 cm. Consider the size of the living space, the area where the robot is placed, it has to accommodate the spatial demands and usage situation factors.

Responses and Adaption of Information. In the situation where the elderly user's sensory perception abilities are impaired, such as hearing or vision, they will not be able to receive information easily, and it will be difficult for them to recognize the operation interface or the sound responses given by the robot [13]. The elderly's speech speed, tones, background noise, insensitive cognitive sense could result in misjudgment and give incorrect responses, this results in the robot's failure to get the correct information [10]. Therefore, the robot needs to have clear and explicit responses to from the user. Factors such as processing time lag, tone, ability to recognize the user's intonation will affect the robot's response. In other words, it needs to have a high level of sensitivity. At the same time, the speech content should also be displayed on the screen, to allow the user to quickly receive and evaluate the response status of the robot [15, 16]. The decline and changes in the speech function of elderly people prevents them to have full control of their own speech pattern and vocal quality, which directly affects the sensitivity of the robot's recognition system. When the robot cannot receive instructions that it can understand, it will remain in a stationary "frozen mode" position. And when the user cannot get a correct response, or any response, they will then repeat the instructions, and may blame themselves for not being able to operate it correctly [10].

Intuition of Empirical Analogy. Participants were able to make use of their familiarity derived from past experiences of using different equipment interfaces to control the robot. This application of natural experience analogy aimed to achieve natural interaction. Especially for the elderly who have had previous experiences in operating certain technology and equipment, they could create a connection on how to use the robot system based on past experiences [11]. Just as mobile phones have become a common tool for information communication, home TVs have also been equipped with remote controls. Through the concept of association and inter-exchange experiences, the user was able to naturally pick up the remote control or smart phone to communicate with the robot or used a combination of speech and gestures [17] to establish control. The advantage with this kind of association is that there is a lesser prerequisite to learn additional operating instructions, because they were able to achieve a natural method of interaction through habit and past experiences. Compared to the silver surfer [14], who is proficient at using technology to assist in the use of information products, the elderly with lower technology literacy, who may also be limited by their cognitive psychology, learning and understanding new things that are too complex will be difficult.

Exercise Assistance Robot. Assisting elderly people with exercise through robots improved their functional autonomy and balancing ability [5] by increasing the level of their physical activity. This functional component of the robot made it easier for the elderly to exercise and to go outdoors, leading to an improvement of their health and their social life [22].

Adjustable Usage. Elderly people with limited limb functions walk at a slower pace and fall easily as some have uncoordinated movements. When faced with uncertain factors such as obstacles in the environment, the robot's design must allow it to adjust its movements to suit the environment [25]. When an Exercise Assistance robot is in operation, it has to have good compliance and coordinate with the user to overcome obstacles. It must be able to flexibly control its movement speed to match the user's physical capabilities and environmental constraints. When the robot moves too fast or too slow in relation to the user, it should be able to immediately detect this and recalibrate its speed to match that of the user. If it is unable to match the user's speed, it should immediately issue a warning so that the user could command it to stop its actions immediately [5]. As for the experiences of pattern of walking, because of uneven terrains, and the user's different speed of walking, some left the robot behind. Some naturally let the robot lagged behind slightly, just like in the past when they were walking with children. The experience of walking together [25] is a complex and fluid movement situation, the robot needs to be able to flexibly recalibrate itself to adjust and coordinate with the user, regardless of the past experience, knowledge, language ability or concentration of the user.

Companion Robot. The companion robot's aim is to reduce the sense of loneliness of the elderly. It is designed to simulate a pet with a plush furry exterior and with a simple sway movement [5, 21]. Or it can be a cartoon character with a cute appearance. Both provide entertainment contents. Companionship to the user is given priority, allowing them to gain psychological and emotional comfort in their home environment. Natural InterAction Companion robots like Paro had a furry pet appearance and were able to express certain natural emotions. Physical contact activated certain responses like head movements, pet sounds or facial expressions. These responses were able to create certain emotional connections with the user. Such responses appealed to the user to reach out and touch it through tactile intuition [22]. Older people loved pet-like robots because of their cute lovable appearances, thus overcoming many difficult-to-use situations and induced users to use them naturally.

3.3 Pleasure

Researches related to pleasure mainly focused on how robots bring pleasure to the elderly via cute attractive expressions and sociable intelligence through interactions; and which design features could bring about these responses.

Attraction. [22] pointed out that robots with the purpose of social interaction should focus on appearance design. [11] demonstrated that the elderly felt that certain facial features and expressions were attractive and made them felt welcomed. Participants gave responses like "they have nice face", "they are smiling" and "they are welcoming us" during their first encounter with Robot-Era. Kim showed that the extent to which elders engaged in their interactions with robots was higher when the dynamic social features of the robots were increased. Elders felt that the dynamic social features of the robots like eyes and head were attractive and thought that the robot was smiling or laughing when they saw the changes of the robot's facial expressions [20]. Tablets with no dynamic social features were considered less interesting than humanoid robots and could not catch and hold their attention, which explained why they did not even look at the tablet during the tea-making activity [20]. Although robots brought the elderly pleasure through its appearance visually like facial expressions [18] and size [12], other physical features which further made the elderly associate with it were making it to look like a middle-age woman, a pet or a toy.

Social Intelligence. Several participants felt that the ideal robot should look and speak like a human [17], and that human-likeness and verbal ability were two factors that made robots sociably intelligent. The presence of a head on the robot increased the level of interaction [12]. For example, in [22], the Casper robot was considered to be a better robot to talk to because it was more human-like and could "look into your eyes" while taking to you. In the research of [17], when compared to an animal-liked robot, the elderly's acceptance of the human-liked robot was higher. It further mentioned that the Socio-emotional Selectivity Theory (SST) could help explain the elderly's preference to a more humanoid form of robot. Moreover, the elderly's perceived sociable intelligence of robot could influence the social-related functions that they thought a robot could perform. The elderly perceived sociable intelligence of the robot was related to their social interactions with the robot. For example, they would use words like "her" or "Molly" to call the Molly robot [10], they would show their appreciation to the robot and invite it to drink tea [20] expressed utterances like "uh-huh" when the robot responded.

Factors Influencing Psychological Perception. Although some design features didn't elicit the sense of pleasure from the user, it did affect their psychological feelings. Some studies showed that certain design features gave participants the sense of reliability. [22] mentioned that the pet-like appearance of the PARO robot made the elderly felt less threatened and less fearful, which made it more attractive for them to interact with it. When the robot was shorter than the user, it allowed them to look downward at the robot, which gave them more confidence and gave them the impression that the robot was not that big and bulky and projected an efficient and non-threatening image. Robots with a relatable appearance influenced the users' perception. For example, when asked to compare the robot with either the image of a young or middle-aged woman, the elderly preferred the latter, who was generally perceived as more reliable at work [19]. They felt that a toy-like robot could not offer help in daily activities, e.g. increasing the safety at home [13].

4 Discussion

Based on the needs of the elderly, we organized the design guidelines criteria for elder-centered SARs into three levels: Functionality, Usability, and Pleasure. In summary, designing a robot for the elderly to promote their independence requires a good understanding of what and how the functions of the robot are carried out in the user's social and habitat environment and the way users think. The roles played by SARs will affect the level of acceptance of by the elderly. Therefore, it is necessary to elevate the trust and dependence of elderly people towards SARs after using them in complex environments. We propose a design hierarchy guideline for SARs for designers and developers that provides them with a thinking framework, and suggestions for them to follow when designing and developing SARs for the elderly.

4.1 Flexible Experience

In the design of elder-centered robots, in addition to emphasizing their unique features and functions, developers need to consider the elderly's needs and preferences regarding its functions. These will differ according to their different backgrounds. As mentioned in, we must recognize that as people grow older, their diversity in needs also increases, including their health status, education, hobbies, and familial relationships.

In addition to understanding the general background and preferences of the main user groups, it is important to recognize the unique individual differences among the elderly within the group and enable each individual to adjust the robot's feedback to their own needs. For example, when a robot accompanies an elderly on a walk, the movement speed must adjust accordingly to the users' physical condition [25]. The robot's contents should be expandable and diverse, not just the built-in with fixed amount of information, to give users wider choices [18]. These practices make it easier for the robot to meet the different needs of the elderly.

The functions of the robot should be able to adapt to changes in different situations. [15] Pointed out that robots need to have the ability to interact naturally with older people, such as learning their lifestyles, asking them questions, and have daily diverse topics conversations with them such as family and personal interests. The necessity for the robot to adapt to the continuous change of the environment is expected by the elderly user. In another study [16], participants expected that when robots fix their medical appointments, they should be able to search and select relevant hospitals based on their current location, rather than just registering at a specific large hospital. This showed that they have different needs for specific functions in different situations, and designers need to pay special attention to this and make corresponding adjustments during their designs. However, the elderly did not use functions that didn't meet their current needs, even if they could foresee the possibility of their physical weakness and the benefits that robots could bring. For example, in [12], participants generally thought that robot-assisted indoors walking could increase their safety of moving at home.

4.2 Consider the Minimum Functional Capability of the Elderly

Elderly people are affected by social psychology. With the advancement of age [21] comes physical and mental deterioration. The functional capability of the elderly must be *given* priority consideration. This includes three areas: 1. In terms of their motor function. The deterioration of muscles and reduced finger dexterity makes it increasingly difficult for them to operate the smaller control keys; 2. Deterioration of the physical senses such as sight, hearing and speech. This makes it difficult for them to see the operation interface clearly, to hear the sound of the robot clearly, or to control the speed and tone of their speech which results in their inability to control the robot; 3. Degradation of cognitive function. This results in memory deterioration and affects their learning ability. They may not be able to understand the robot's operation instructions or simply cannot remember them. This makes it difficult for them to operate a complex robot, thereby affecting the robot's functionality. Although the robot has artificial intelligence, it is not free from operational input requirements and it cannot override the user.

The use of the robot must take into account the limited functional capability of the elderly. For example, the touch screen's height must be easily reachable by the user when both standing or sitting, and it must conform to the free movement of the user. Certain physical conditions of the elderly (e.g. humpbacked, wheelchair bound, unable to stand for long periods) makes it difficult for them to physically operate the robot. If the robot is too small to move an object to a higher position, then it will not be able to perform the handling assistance tasks. The position of the robot's head should not be looking downward on the elderly, as this means that the user will need to tilt their head to look back up, which may result in neck injuries. Spatial constraints and where to place the robot are also important considerations, e.g. it must be able to pass through narrow passageways, so users do not need to transfer the robot around. In the design and development of SARs for the elderly, the aims are to provide living assistance, social activities, companionship and to delay age related deterioration. Most modern elderly people already have some experience in handling technology like smartphones or tablets. To reduce the requirements of operation ability, the operation training could be specifically designed to teach them how to become proficient in their use of the robot, or through repeated training until they develop a natural automatic response in how to operate the robot. The training could be done by watching an instructional video. To foster a sense of connection with the robot, it could be portrayed to be like a little companion helper in the elderly's life.

4.3 Responses and Adaption of Multi-sensory Ability

Some elderly people are not able to receive information accurately due to deterioration of their physical senses. In cases of the visually impaired, they cannot recognize the text or images on the information display screen. For the hearing impaired, the robot's verbal responses are not clearly understood; and for the speech impaired, the robot cannot recognize the instructions given by the user, resulting in its malfunction. Therefore, it is necessary to factor in during design the responsiveness and adaptability of the users' physical senses to information, so that they could utilize multiple physical senses in simultaneously to obtain and relay information. Similarly, the robot needs to be able to adapt to the user's abilities and expressions to retrieve information and give a correct feedback. At the same time, the user will need to adjust his behavior to adapt to the robot according to his own ability. For example, the contents of the robot's speech should be displayed on screen at the same time, so that for those who have hearing problems, they have the additional option to look at the screen to get the message. The screen should be flexibly adjustable in height and direction to match the habits or physical constraints (habitually listening from one ear or using the better-hearing side) of the user. This ensures that both parties can obtain more accurate information and allowing users to operate the robot in accordance to their own habits and abilities.

4.4 Increase Flexibility and Compatibility

Users should be able to adjust the operation of the robot, such as its speed, size, screen visibility, or volume; and be given the choice of widest possible range of adjustments to suit their environment and constraints. Take size and occupied space as an example: the average height of Westerners is taller than that of Asians. In terms of environmental space, urban and suburban home areas are different. The standing and sitting postures are different. The robot should be designed in a way to allow it to be adjustable to meet the different needs. There should not be any time limit for the controls or the response display. The elderly should not be required to perform the task or complete the specified action with any time restrictions. If there is a timeout for any user response, the robot should use a slow prompt to let the user know clearly that it is currently in the "frozen" state, and can be restarted through a few available instruction modes such as sound or touch, which the user should be able to do it in an intuitively way like waking someone up. In addition, the robot should be designed for it to be able to expand or reduce its working range, mobile requirements, turning/reverse actions. It should be able to adapt to different environments. It should be designed with minimum effort or physical labor requirements on the part of the user. Many people with severe or multiple disabilities will not be able to use the robot without assistive tools. Robots should therefore be compatible with various assistive technology, including appropriate input and output devices, such as hearing aids, screen readers, mobile phones, tablet computers and even televisions.

4.5 Pleasure in Interaction

We described the many feelings that the elderly could sense during their interactions with the robots and the corresponding design features. However, [10] mentioned that the elderly's level of acceptance to the robot was higher after real interactions with it. This highlighted the importance of enticing the user to interact with the robot right at the beginning. Increasing the attractiveness of the robot could achieve this, Introductions about the robot before initial interaction helps the elderly build some sense of familiarity towards the robot. A relax and safe environment decreases the elderly's anxiety while learning about the robot and increases their level of acceptance [10]. When the elderly begins to interact with the robot, the goal would be to let the user gradually develop positive feelings and eventual acceptance towards the robot. Developers could apply the design features mentioned to promote such positive user responses. Developers should avoid having improperly designed features that raise the elderly's expectations unrealistically above the capable functionality of the robot.

5 Conclusion

This review found that social and cultural factors affect the perceptions and acceptability of robots by older people. This includes differences arising from personal habits, skills competency and level of knowledge. Thus, the design of robots should adopt a more appropriate perspective that is in alignment with the users' needs in their daily living environment. To help research developers have a better grasp of the requirements in the design of SARs, we propose the following: 1. Discussion of functional needs: Explore the elderly's lifestyle, physiological assistance needs, social activities and entertainment preferences, and then match these to the functional aspects of the SARs. At present, Japan's investments in research involving healing-oriented products has brought about another level of user experience, from a single and individual function to a multi-functional approach in providing living assistance. 2. Usability design: Start with the physical and mental conditions of the elderly, understand their limitations, then apply a user-centered thinking mode to grasp the main points of ease-of-use, and then progress on to the concept of elderly-centered universal design technology. Reshape the cognitive model of the elderly, understand the differences between the elderly, and use daily living situations to understand and identify abnormal behaviors. Use this understanding as a base line to design an interactive mental model of technology catered to the elderly, covering as many modes of situations as possible to maximize the users' benefits. 3. Pleasure generating designs: This takes into consideration the relationship between perceptual engineering, hedonism and empathy.

References

1. Thomas, J., Harden, A.: Methods for the thematic synthesis of qualitative research in systematic reviews. BMC Med. Res. Methodol. **8**, 45 (2008). https://doi.org/10.1186/1471-2288-8-45
2. Colombo, F., Llena-Nozal, A., Mercier, J., Tjadens, F.: Help wanted? Providing and paying for long-term care (2011). https://doi.org/10.1787/9789264097759-en
3. Kachouie, R., Sedighadeli, S., Khosla, R., Chu, M.-T.: Socially assistive robots in elderly care: a mixed-method systematic literature review. Int. J. Hum. Comput. Interact. **30**, 369–393 (2014)
4. Broekens, J., Heerink, M., Rosendal, H.: Assistive social robots in elderly care: a review (2009)
5. Chen, T.L., et al.: Older adults' acceptance of a robot for partner dance-based exercise. PLoS ONE **12**(10), e0182736–e0182736 (2017). https://doi.org/10.1371/journal.pone.0182736
6. Van Wynsberghe, A.: Designing robots for care: care centered value-sensitive design. Sci. Eng. Ethics **19**(2), 407–433 (2013). https://doi.org/10.1007/s11948-011-9343-6
7. Dixon-Woods, M., Agarwal, S., Jones, D., Young, B., Sutton, A.: Synthesising qualitative and quantitative evidence: a review of possible methods. J. Health Serv. Res. **10**(1), 45–53 (2005)
8. Greenhalgh, T., Peacock, R.: Effectiveness and efficiency of search methods in systematic reviews of complex evidence: audit of primary sources. BMJ Case Rep. **331**, 1064–1065 (2005)
9. Liberati, A., Altman, D.G., Tetzlaff, J., Mulrow, C., Gøtzsche, P.C.: The PRISMA statement for reporting systematic reviews and meta-analyses of studies that evaluate health care interventions: explanation and elaboration. PLoS Biol. **62**, e1–e34 (2009)

10. Caleb-Solly, P., Dogramadzi, S., Huijnen, C., van den Heuvel, H.: Exploiting ability for human adaptation to facilitate improved human-robot interaction and acceptance. Inf. Soc. **34**(3), 153–165 (2018). https://doi.org/10.1080/01972243.2018.1444255

11. De Carolis, B., Ferilli, S., Palestra, G.: Simulating empathic behavior in a social assistive robot. Multimed. Tools Appl. **76**(4), 5073–5094 (2016). https://doi.org/10.1007/s11042-016-3797-0

12. Cavallo, F., et al.: Robotic services acceptance in smart environments with older adults: user satisfaction and acceptability study. J. Med. Internet Res. **20**(9), 19 (2018). https://doi.org/10.2196/jmir.9460

13. Di Nuovo, A., et al.: The multi-modal interface of Robot-Era multi-robot services tailored for the elderly. Intel. Serv. Robot. **11**(1), 109–126 (2017). https://doi.org/10.1007/s11370-017-0237-6

14. Eftring, H., Frennert, S.: Designing a social and assistive robot for seniors. Zeitschrift Fur Gerontologie Und Geriatrie **49**(4), 274–281 (2016). https://doi.org/10.1007/s00391-016-1064-7

15. Lee, S., Naguib, A.M.: Toward a sociable and dependable elderly care robot: design, implementation and user study. J. Intell. Rob. Syst.: Theory Appl. **98**(1), 5–17 (2019). https://doi.org/10.1007/s10846-019-01028-8

16. Moro, C., Lin, S., Nejat, G., Mihailidis, A.: Social robots and seniors: a comparative study on the influence of dynamic social features on human–robot interaction. Int. J. Soc. Robot. **11**(1), 5–24 (2018). https://doi.org/10.1007/s12369-018-0488-1

17. Zsiga, K., Toth, A., Pilissy, T., Peter, O., Denes, Z., Fazekas, G.: Evaluation of a companion robot based on field tests with single older adults in their homes. Assist. Technol. **30**(5), 259–266 (2018). https://doi.org/10.1080/10400435.2017.1322158

18. McGlynn, S.A., Kemple, S., Mitzner, T.L., King, C.H.A., Rogers, W.A.: Understanding the potential of PARO for healthy older adults. Int. J. Hum.-Comput. Stud. **100**, 33–47 (2017). https://doi.org/10.1016/j.ijhcs.2016.12.004

19. 白麗, 鄭家凱, 林恩如, 陳思宇, 張譯云,   徐業良.:   陪伴型機器人使用者經驗評估─以智慧居家機器人Zenbo為例. [User Experience Test of Companion Robot and Its Innovative Usage among Older Adults-Use Zenbo as an Example]. *福祉科技與服務管理學刊*, **6**(3), 265–282 (2018). https://doi.org/10.6283/jocsg.201809_6(3).265

20. Kim, S.C., Lee, B.K., Kim, C.Y.: Usability evaluation of communication service robot for the elderly. J. Back Musculoskelet. Rehabil. **32**(2), 313–319 (2019). https://doi.org/10.3233/bmr-169655

21. Baisch, S., et al.: Acceptance of social robots by elder people: does psychosocial functioning matter? Int. J. Soc. Robot. **9**(2), 293–307 (2017). https://doi.org/10.1007/s12369-016-0392-5

22. Karunarathne, D., Morales, Y., Nomura, T., Kanda, T., Ishiguro, H.: Will older adults accept a humanoid robot as a walking partner? Int. J. Soc. Robot. **11**(2), 343–358 (2018). https://doi.org/10.1007/s12369-018-0503-6

23. 朱祐萱,   林清壽.:   銀髮族使用 Zenbo 機器人服務體驗洞察研究. [Study on Service Experience Insight of Use of Zenbo Robot by Silver-haired People]. *福祉科技與服務管理學刊*,**7**(1), 467–489 (2019). https://doi.org/10.6283/jocsg.201903_7(1).467

24. Chu, L., et al.: Identifying features that enhance older adults' acceptance of robots: a mixed methods study. Gerontology **65**, 441–450 (2019). https://doi.org/10.1159/000494881

25. Gerlowska, J., et al.: Assessment of perceived attractiveness, usability, and societal impact of a multimodal robotic assistant for aging patients with memory impairments. Front. Neurol. **9**, 13 (2018). https://doi.org/10.3389/fneur.2018.00392

26. World Health Organization (WHO): World report on ageing and health, Geneva (2015)

Examining the Relationship Between Songs and Psychological Characteristics

Miran Pyun, Donghun Kim, Chaeyun Lim, Eunbyul Lee, Jihey Kwon, and Sangyup Lee$^{(\boxtimes)}$

Yonsei University, Seoul, Republic of Korea
{miran1074,sangyuplee}@yonsei.ac.kr, donghun.kim.9003@gmail.com, limchae1@msu.edu, eunbyul616@gmail.com, ehdry3939@naver.com

Abstract. Listening to music may serve both as an indicator of the listener's emotional situation and as an actor on the listener's emotions. In this study, we explored the relationship between music and listeners' psychological characteristics. A total of 59 participants' music playlists were retrieved, and the audio features of each song were extracted via Spotify API. A total of 8,936 songs were analyzed, and 13 different features were extracted. To understand listeners' psychological characteristics, a survey was conducted. We found that anxiety and stress are closely related to instrumentalness. Also, anxiety is significantly related to liveness and loudness. This study suggests that music playlists can be an indicator of an individual's psychological characteristics and acknowledges the possibility that music can enhance and reflect the listener's psychological well-being.

Keywords: Music · Emotion · Emotional situation · Music and emotion · Anxiety · Stress · Self-esteem · Music preference · Music and psychology · Logit estimation

1 Introduction

In all of history, there has never been a culture that did not have music [1]. Particularly in modern society, the development of information and communication technologies makes it much easier for us to access music. With the expansion of digital music services, it is now easy to listen to music anytime, anywhere. According to Nielsen Music's Music 360 report, in 2019, Americans listened to an average of 26.9 h of music per week [2]. According to the 2018 Music Industry White Paper published by the Korea Contents Agency [3], 45.9% of Koreans use music content almost every day, and it is increasing every year. As such, music can be said to be a creation inseparable from the lives of modern people. In particular, music is known as a medium that reflects human emotions and psychology. Listening to music is an activity that is closely related to the expression of various emotions and listeners' psychological characteristics [4]. In this regard, many studies on the relationship between musical preference and personality, temperament, and psychological state have been conducted [5–8]. These studies have revealed that the

© Springer Nature Switzerland AG 2020
C. Stephanidis et al. (Eds.): HCII 2020, LNCS 12425, pp. 105–115, 2020.
https://doi.org/10.1007/978-3-030-60128-7_8

inner qualities of humans are related to the music they listen to. This means to which the music the individual listens reflects the individual's inner self.

In a highly modernized society, grasping the inner side of an individual is becoming increasingly important because this can lead to an understanding of psychological characteristics and mental health status. Currently, many people suffer from mental illness, and the number continues to rise. According to the World Health Organization (WHO), as of 2015, 322 million people—about 4% of the world's population—suffer from depression, an increase of 18.4% compared to 2005. Also, WHO ranked depression as the most burdensome disease for humanity in 2030 [9]. If more people are threatened with mental health disorders, this can lead to social problems such as decreased production and suicide. Therefore, it is important to examine the psychological state and mental health of modern people to find some hints that can be used to mitigate such social problems.

With the advent of the big data era, analysis based on various online data has become possible. Researchers studying data from past surveys can now overcome previous research limitations so that new results can be presented. The present study takes advantage of this accessibility and offers a novel approach with the analysis of music playlists in understanding psychological characteristics and mental health. Surveys are a traditional method of data collection, but there are several limitations. For example, because it was necessary to rely on the memory and perception of the respondents, it was difficult to obtain accurate information about their behaviors, and the types of variables that could be measured were limited. To overcome such limitations, this study collected subjects' music playlists from an online music platform, which reflects the actual songs that the respondents had listened to. By analyzing the musical features of such songs with deep learning-based approaches, we examined the relationship between an individual's psychological characteristics and his/her music preferences. Data on an individual's psychological characteristics and mental health status were collected using a survey. In addition, based on the results of the relationship between music preference and the characteristics of an individual's psychology and mental health status, we present a new indicator for symptom identification in mental health.

2 Related Research

2.1 Music and Personal Psychology

Previous studies have examined the relationship between music and inner traits such as personality, emotion, and psychological state. In particular, with the development of new media, listening to music through personal media becomes possible, and listening to music becomes a more personalized activity. Accordingly, research continues to show that music reflects an individual's inner characteristics. Thoma and colleagues [10] found that music acts as a trigger for basic or complex emotions. They investigated how people use music to adjust their emotions. Research also shows that people prefer music that matches their emotional state. Georgi and Lothwesen [11] developed a scale called the Inventory for the measurement of Activation and Arousal modulation by Music (IAAM) to measure relaxation, cognitive problem solving, reduction of negative activation, fun stimulation, and arousal modulation. They revealed that IAAM is associated with health, psychiatric illness, music therapy, chill-sensations, personality, musical preferences, and youth problem behavior. Kwakami and Katahira [12] found that empathy and its sub-components—empathic concerns, personal distress, perspective taking, and fantasy—are directly or indirectly influenced by sad music preferences, which are mediated by emotional responses to sad music. Among the sub-elements of empathy, fantasy was found to have a direct relationship with the preference of sad music, and the rest was also correlated. A study by Lading and Schellenberg [13] found that music preferences are related to music-induced emotions, personal characteristics, and music training. Schäfer and Sedlmeier [14] also found that cognitive function and physiological arousal by music are the most important determinants of music preference.

2.2 Big Data and Personal Psychology

Traditionally, social science has collected data through surveys or interviews to identify variables related to psychological characteristics. However, with the advent of the Internet, big data can be collected online, and a method of analyzing using machine learning or deep learning has been implemented. This method has the advantage of accurately analyzing large amounts of information, which can reveal previously incomprehensible datasets from past surveys and interviews. These studies can lead to new results that previously could not be shown and can suggest innovative methods and indicators that have not been used socially. Proserpio, Counts, and Jain [15] used data from social media to study the relationship between the macroeconomic shock of employment insecurity and psychological well-being. From 2010 to 2015, they analyzed Twitter posts from over 230,000 U.S. users who either lost their jobs or gained new jobs over the past five years. They used a Linguistic Inquiry Word Count (LIWC) dictionary to measure people's psychological well-being and then quantifying people's mental state changes. Through this, they defined a behavioral macroeconomic model that uses these changes to quantify the magnitude of the effect on psychological variables such as anxiety, sadness, and anger, and to predict the level of unemployment in the United States. Another study analyzed the verbal expressions of people with mental illness such as depression by collecting Twitter posts using text-mining techniques [16, 17]. Furthermore, a study by De Choudhury, Counts, and Horvitz [18] presented a social media depression index showing a subject's level of depression through the analysis. Based on this, they found that geographic, demographic, and seasonal patterns were highly correlated with depression statistics reported by Centers for Disease Control and Prevention (CDC).

3 Methods

3.1 Procedure

The present study proceeded using the following steps.

1. Recruit participants
2. Conduct a survey on participants' psychological characteristics
3. Retrieve participants' music playlists

4. Extract the features of the songs on participants' playlists
5. Analyze the relationship between the features of music and the psychological characteristics.

3.2 Participants

Participant recruitment was advertised via online communities and Yonsei University campus for undergraduate and graduate students in South Korea. Most participants were undergraduate and graduate students, and they were all native Korean. Participants had to be using at least one of the audio streaming applications offered by Melon or Genie to participate because those services provide a history of users' playlists. A total of 68 people were recruited, but only 59 participants were included in the analysis because 9 participants' survey data and playlists could not be matched. This was because the participants' data were collected anonymously due to privacy concerns regarding psychological characteristics. Upon arrival in the seminar room at Yonsei University, participants were asked to read a document that informed them of the purpose of the study and how data will be collected and treated. Only if they consented in writing did they take part in the study. All participants were paid $25 for their participation. The average age of the 59 participants was 24.14 (with a range from 20 to 30), and the study group was composed of 17 males and 42 females.

3.3 Data Collection

Survey on Psychological Characteristics. Participants were asked to complete a survey about their psychological characteristics. In this study, for a music listener's psychological characteristics, we considered self-esteem, anxiety, and stress. As for self-esteem, this study used the Rosenberg Self-Esteem Scale (RSS) which consists of 10 questions using a Likert scale from 1 to 4 [19]. To measure anxiety, the Generalized Anxiety Disorder 7-item (GAD-7) scale with a 4-point Likert scale was used [20]. Lastly, 10 items of the Perceived Stress Scale (PSS) with a 5-point Likert scale were used to measure participants' stress [21].

Music Playlists Retrieval. To investigate the relationship between the features of music people listen to and the psychological characteristics, we retrieved participants' music playlists from audio streaming applications corresponding to the previous three months. The audio streaming applications targeted in the analysis were Melon and Genie, which rank first and second, respectively, in the South Korean market share.

Audio Features Extraction. To extract musical features of the songs within the playlists, we first removed duplicated songs, resulting in 8,936 unique songs. Afterward, we extracted the features of the songs using the API services provided by Spotify (https://www.spotify.com). The Spotify API extracts 13 different audio features of a song using deep learning algorithms. Among those 13 audio features, we only considered eight: energy, instrumentalness, liveness, loudness, mode, speechiness, tempo, and valence. The descriptions of each audio feature explored in this study are given in Table 1 [22].

Table 1. Descriptions of audio features

Feature	Description
Energy	A perceptual measure of intensity and activity with a measure from 0.0 to 1.0. The closer to 1.0, the greater likelihood the audio has strong intensity and activity
Instrumentalness	A predictor of whether a track contains no vocals, using a measure from 0.0 to 1.0. The closer to 1.0, the greater likelihood the audio contains no vocal content
Liveness	A measure of the presence of an audience in the audio with a measure from 0.0 to 1.0. Higher liveness values represent an increased probability that the track was performed live
Loudness	The overall loudness of a track in decibels (dB). Values typically range between −60 and 0 dB
Mode	The modality (major or minor) of audio. Major is represented by 1 and the minor is 0
Speechiness	The presence of spoken words in a track. The closer to 1.0, the more exclusively speech-like the recording
Tempo	The overall estimated tempo of a track in beats per minute (BPM)
Valence	A description of the musical positiveness with a measure from 0.0 to 1.0. The closer to 1.0, the greater likelihood the audio is more positive

4 Results

To examine the relationship between a music feature and the psychological characteristics, we used the following regression model:

$$music\_feature_{k,i} = \beta_0 + \beta_1\, self\_esteem_i + \beta_2\, stress_i + \beta_3\, anxiety_i$$
$$+ \beta_4\, gender_i + \beta_5\, age_i + error_i \qquad (1)$$

where $music\_feature_{k,i}$ indicates the average value of a particular feature, which is denoted as feature k, of the songs to which respondent i has listened. The meanings of other variables are intuitive, thus, their explanations are omitted due to the space constraint. Among the features, energy, instrumentalness, liveness, mode, speechiness, and valence take a ratio value. For these variables, we used the fractional logit estimation method. For the other variables, we used an OLS estimation method. Among the feature variables, the following did not have statistically significant relationships with any of the independent variables in Eq. (1): energy, valence, mode, and tempo. The estimation results of those feature variables have been omitted in the results due to a lack of space.

4.1 Descriptive Statistics and Correlation

Table 2 presents an overview of descriptive statistics on the variables with a significant relationship with any of the other variables. The correlations between those audio feature variables and psychological characteristics are presented in Table 3.

Table 2. Descriptive statistics

Measure	M	SD	Min	Max
Instrumentalness	0.04	0.04	0.00	0.22
Speechiness	0.08	0.02	0.05	0.18
Liveness	0.18	0.02	0.15	0.23
Loudness	−6.59	1.30	−10.07	4.21
Self-esteem	3.06	0.51	1.60	3.90
Anxiety	1.87	0.68	1.00	3.71
Stress	2.95	0.68	1.40	4.50

Table 3. Correlations between variables

	Instrumentalness	Speechiness	Liveness	Loudness	Self-esteem	Anxiety	Stress
Instrmentalness							
Speechiness	−0.28						
Liveness	−0.07	0.05					
Loudness	−0.75	0.34	0.25				
Self-esteem	−0.09	0.19	−0.1	0.13			
Anxiety	−0.22	0.01	−0.08	0.16	−0.54		
Stress	0.16	0.01	0.05	−0.11	−0.7	0.67	

4.2 Regression Analysis

Instrumentalness. The fractional logit estimation indicated significant relationships between anxiety and instrumentalness (B = −1.01, p < 0.001) and between stress and instrumentalness (B = −.80***, p < 0.001) (see Table 4). These findings demonstrate that people with more anxiety are less likely to listen to more instrumental music. Also, people with higher stress levels tend to listen to more instrumental music. These findings cannot be concluded as causal relationships. Instead, it can be interpreted that music with higher instrumental content (i.e., lower vocal content) may help people relieve stress and become more mentally stable.

Speechiness. The fractional logit estimation on speechiness revealed a significant relationship between self-esteem and speechiness (B = 0.21, p < 0.01) (see Table 5). This

Table 4. Logit estimation analysis predicting instrumentalness

	B	Standard Errors	T-value
Intercept	−3.82**	1.60	−2.39
Self-esteem	−3.34	0.22	−1.56
Anxiety	−1.01***	0.27	−3.68
Stress	0.80***	0.23	3.49
Age	0.05	0.04	1.21
Gender	−0.19	0.33	−0.59

** $p < .01$, *** $p < .001$, $N = 59$, $R^2 = .31$

result shows that people with higher self-esteem tend to enjoy music with an abundance of spoken words. This may be interpreted in two ways. On the one hand, music with lots of spoken words may boost a listener's self-esteem by providing positive words. On the other hand, people with high self-esteem may want keep their psychological state as it is and may be more likely to choose music that contains encouraging words.

Table 5. Logit estimation analysis predicting speechiness

	B	Standard Errors	T-value
Intercept	−2.74***	0.67	−4.11
Self-esteem	0.21**	0.09	2.30
Anxiety	0.03	0.07	0.44
Stress	0.11	0.09	1.18
Age	−0.02	0.02	−0.85
Gender	−0.15	0.13	−1.18

** $p < .01$, *** $p < .001$, $N = 59$, $R^2 = .14$

Liveness. The result of fractional logit estimation on liveness showed a significant relationship between anxiety and liveness (B = −0.05, p < 0.01) (see Table 6). This result shows that people with a lot of anxiety are less inclined to listen to live music with the sound of audiences. It may be interpreted that live music may help people relieve anxiety. Also, it may be possible that people with low anxiety tend to prefer music without the sound of audiences.

Loudness. The result of OLS estimation analysis on loudness presented a significant relationship between anxiety and loudness (B = 0.80, 95% CI [0.21, 1.40]) (see Table 7). This can be summarized into two points. First, people with higher anxiety tend to listen

Table 6. Logit estimation analysis predicting liveness

	B	Standard Errors	T-value
Intercept	−1.73***	0.21	−8.25
Self-esteem	−0.02	0.03	−0.72
Anxiety	−0.05**	0.03	−1.98
Stress	0.03	0.03	1.03
Age	0.01	0.01	1.21
Gender	0.05	0.03	1.61

$** p < .01, *** p < .001, N = 59, R^2 = .12$

to loud music as a way of escaping or forgetting reality. Second, if people listen to loud music frequently, this behavior may serve as anxiety arousal.

Table 7. Linear regression analysis predicting loudness

	Coefficient	Standard Errors	95% Conf. Interval
Constant	−6.34	2.88	[−12.11, −0.57]
Self-esteem	0.66	0.46	[−0.27, 1.58]
Anxiety	0.80**	0.30	[0.21, 1.40]
Stress	−0.48	0.31	[−1.10, 0.13]
Age	−0.10	0.07	[−0.24, 0.04]
Gender	0.05	0.35	[−12.11, −0.57]

$N = 59, F (5, 53) = 2.16, Prob > F = 0.07, R^2 = 0.16, Root MSE = 1.20.$

5 Discussion

Through this study, it was confirmed that personal psychology is related to the music feature that is often listened to. People who have higher self-esteem more frequently listen to music with the feature of speechiness, which has many spoken words on the track. The more anxious people are, the more they avoid music with the feature of instrumentalness, that is, without voice content, and they also avoid music with liveness as measured by the presence of the audience. One the other hand, anxious people listened to more music with the characteristic of loudness, a feature that represents the overall volume of a music track. In the case of stress, the more stressed people are, the more they listen to music with the instrumentalness feature.

This study analyzed both the music listening data of individuals as well as surveys for psychological status identification. It is particularly meaningful to increase the accuracy of frequently heard music information gleaned through online data collection and to classify it into various characteristics within music analysis so that we can approach it in more detail. Online music listening data, which does not contain the bias and distortion of research participants is more clearly reflected in their psychological status than using only the survey method. Through this, it was possible to confirm the relationship between psychological state and mental health by studying data points the research participants were not aware existed. The results of this study suggest that the method can be a new indicator for diagnosing symptoms in the field of mental health or psychotherapy. Because music media is gradually becoming more subdivided and personalized, these indicators can be expanded and elaborated in the future. Big data analysis methods are also developing, and their accuracy is increasing [23]. We believe big data analysis can overcome the limitations of sociological approaches, leading to results and applications previously unknown. As such, this study could be applied to mental health. If various online data analysis methods were added to the patient information that can be captured via existing questionnaires, it would be possible to contribute to the immediate and multi-faceted understanding of a patient's condition. Furthermore, it could serve as a springboard for improving the condition of patients' lives and establishing measures to prevent diseases.

6 Limitations and Future Study

The limitations of this study are as follows. First, the number of participants in the study is small. Future research should increase the scale and conduct research on more people to make the results more general. Second, it is limited in the type of music listening applications used. As of 2019, we conducted research on the most popular music listening applications in Korea, but if future research targets other applications, the bias of research can be reduced. Also, it is possible not only to collect data of frequently listened to songs but also to analyze songs that express opinions such as "likes" and comments on individual music sources. In the case of "likes" or comments, music listeners have taken a more active role, so it is expected that new data can be retrieved. Finally, in this study, the relationship between personal psychological variables and musical features was examined. In future research, the study could be expanded through the collection of lyrics. By analyzing musical features, lyrics, and psychological variables at the same time, the researcher can discover more about what musical elements reflect the psychological state. In addition, if a study is conducted with a wider variety of measures of psychological state, these additional measures can be studied along with collected music data to develop a broader picture.

References

1. Koelsch, S.: Brain correlates of music-evoked emotions. Nat. Rev. Neurosci. **15**, 170–180 (2014). https://doi.org/10.1038/nrn3666
2. Billboard: Average Music Listening Time Is Down. How Much Does That Matter? (2019) https://www.billboard.com/articles/business/streaming/8529828/average-music-listening-time-down
3. Korea Contents Agency. 2018 Music Industry White Paper. (2018) http://www.kocca.kr
4. Rentfrow, P.J.: The role of music in everyday life: current directions in the social psychology of music. Soc. Pers. Psychol. Compass **6**(5), 402–416 (2012)
5. LeBlanc, A.: An interactive theory of musical preference. J. Music Ther. **19**, 28–45 (1982)
6. Litle, P., Zuckerman, M.: Sensation seeking and music preferences. Pers. Individ. Differ. **7**(4), 575–578 (1986)
7. Weaver, J.B.: Exploring the links between personality and media preferences. Pers. Individ. Differ. **12**(12), 1293–1299 (1991)
8. Radocy, R.E., Boyle, J.D.: Music, a phenomena of people, society, and culture. Psychological Foundations of Musical Behavior. Charles C. Thomas Pub., Springfield, IL 1997b, pp. 8–3 (1997)
9. Korean National Center for Mental Health (2019) http://ncmh.go.kr
10. Thoma, M.V., Ryf, S., Mohiyeddini, C., Ehlert, U., Nater, U.M.: Emotion regulation through listening to music in everyday situations. Cogn. Emot. **26**(3), 550–560 (2012). https://doi.org/10.1080/02699931.2011.595390
11. Georgi, R.V., Lothwesen, K.S.: Use of Music for Emotion Modulation - Testing the validity of the IAAM- scales within different groups of musical preference indicates different qualitative music preference types. The use of music in everyday life is a field of growing interest, pp. 1–10 (2014) https://doi.org/10.13140/2.1.1626.4323
12. Kawakami, A., Katahira, K.: Influence of trait empathy on the emotion evoked by sad music and on the preference for it. Front. Psychol. **6**, 1–9 (2015). https://doi.org/10.3389/fpsyg.2015.01541
13. Ladinig, O., Schellenberg, G.E.: Liking unfamiliar music: effects of felt emotion and individual differences. Psychol. Aesthetics, Creativity, Arts **6**(2), 146–154 (2012). https://doi.org/10.1037/a0024671
14. Schäfer, T., Sedlmeier, P.: What makes us like music? determinants of music preference. Psychol. Aesthetics, Creativity, Arts **4**(4), 223–234 (2010). https://doi.org/10.1037/a0018374
15. Proserpio, D., Counts, S., Jain, A.: The psychology of job loss: using social media data to characterize and predict unemployment. In: Proceedings of the 8th ACM Conference on Web Science, pp. 223–232. ACM (2016)
16. Resnik, P., Armstrong, W., Claudino, L., Nguyen, T., Nguyen, V.A., Boyd-Graber, J.: Beyond LDA: exploring supervised topic modeling for depression-related language in Twitter. In: Proceedings of the 2nd Workshop on Computational Linguistics and Clinical Psychology: From Linguistic Signal to Clinical Reality, pp. 99–107 (2015)
17. Preoţiuc-Pietro, D., et al.: The role of personality, age, and gender in tweeting about mental illness. In: Proceedings of the 2nd workshop on computational linguistics and clinical psychology: From linguistic signal to clinical reality, pp. 21–30 (2015)

18. De Choudhury, M., Counts, S., Horvitz, E.: Social media as a measurement tool of depression in populations. In Proceedings of the 5th Annual ACM Web Science Conference, pp. 47–56. ACM (2013)
19. Rosenberg, M.: Rosenberg self-esteem scale (RSE). Acceptance Commitment Ther. Measures Package **61**(52), 18 (1965)
20. Spitzer, R.L., et al.: A brief measure for assessing generalized anxiety disorder: the GAD-7. Arch. Intern. Med. **166**(10), 1092–1097 (2006)
21. Cohen, S., Mermelstein, R., Kamarck, T.: Perceived stress scale. Measuring Stress Guide Health Soc. Sci. **10**, 1–2 (1994)
22. https://developer.spotify.com/documentation/web-api/reference/tracks/get-audio-features/
23. Ouaknine, A.: Review of deep learning algorithms for object detection. Medium, (2018) https://medium.com/comet-app/review-of-deep-learning-algorithms-forobject-detection-c1f3d437b852

An Overview of Paper Documentation Moving to Onboard Information System (OIS) for Commercial Aircraft

Wei Tan[✉] and Yin Jiang[✉]

School of Flight Technology, Civil Aviation University of China, Tianjin 300300, China
weitan2011@outlook.com, jy2maomao@outlook.com

Abstract. Paper documentation has been used in the flight deck for a long time on commercial aircraft. Pilots are familiar with tons of manuals to search information during flight to help them perform procedures to ensure safety, efficiency and comfort on commercial aircrafts. Management of interconnections among these flight manuals can be a challenge for pilots, especially when time workload is high in normal, abnormal, and emergency situations. This paper is an overview on the development from paper documentation moving to Onboard Information System (OIS), which fulfills the function of an Electronic Flight Bag (EFB) system. Today the EFB or OIS does not simply provide electronic documentation onboard, it could be a multi-function device interacting with other systems and pilots in the flight deck. This overview also discusses the significance of contextual information on OIS facilitates access to appropriate operational content at the right time through case study. Tangible Cockpit (i.e., Full-Glass Cockpit) could be a trend of flight deck design in the near future, which is easy to use, update, and maintenance. However, it may bring new problems during flight operations.

Keywords: Commercial aircraft · Electronic flight bag · Onboard information system · Tangibility · Context · Avionics

1 Introduction

In civil aviation, the aircraft is not working alone. Figure 1 presents a concept map, or CMap [1–3], of what a cockpit is about. Flight crewmembers not only work as a team with onboard systems, but also remotely communicate with Air Traffic Control (ATC), dispatch, and ground maintenance. The external environment has also a strong impact on their operations. The cockpit provides resources and system user-interfaces for flight management and situation awareness (e.g., navigation data on Electronic Flight Instrument System (EFIS), flight plan on Multi-Function Control Display Unit (MCDU), caution and warning lights, and audio). Pilots cannot control their external environment such as weather, runway condition, airspace, and other elements. This environment has a direct impact on flight time, teamwork, airplane, and flight crew's action and decision (e.g., storm area avoidance, off-set request to ATC, or discontinued approach when an unexpected vehicle is on the runway). Environment, flight parameters, ATC requests,

© Springer Nature Switzerland AG 2020
C. Stephanidis et al. (Eds.): HCII 2020, LNCS 12425, pp. 116–126, 2020.
https://doi.org/10.1007/978-3-030-60128-7_9

time pressure as well as other internal and external factors constantly change during the flight. The only things that do not change during the flight are standards and operational goal – for flight safety, efficiency, and comfort reasons [4].

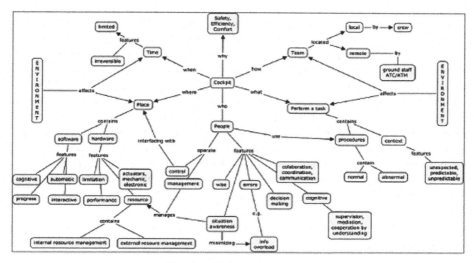

Fig. 1. The factors of cockpit

The International Civil Aviation Organization (ICAO) is the top worldwide regulatory body that has overseen aviation in most countries for a long time. It enables the collaborative development of common standards and recommended practices. Regulations lead to operational documents that aviation personnel have to comply with and use; onboard technical operational documents include procedures, checklists, and various kinds of charts and performance data. These documents have been paper-based since the beginning of aviation. Today, the concept of an Electronic Flight Bag (EFB) has been developed. Electronic support provides capabilities that enable connectivity, and consequently the provision of dynamic information in context. We claim that electronic documentation, renamed "onboard information system (OIS)," contributes to improving the perception and comprehension of the current situation, as well as supporting decision-making and action-taking [5].

The first type of onboard information system was developed during 1980 s, taking into account basic parameters, e.g., Electronic Centralized Aircraft Monitoring (ECAM) for Airbus and Engine Indication and Crew Alerting System (EICAS) for Boeing. Over the years, they have been proven to be extremely useful. They provide very comprehensive information on the state of the aircraft in an integrated way, as opposed to previous flight decks where pilots had to constantly check a large number of instruments. Today, we are moving toward the development of higher-level functions with the integration of OISs. Procedural memory can be shifted from people to systems that can provide contextualized procedures, checklists, and to do lists. "A wide variety of paper and electronic checklists has been systematically analyzed" [6].

Procedures are very important. They are an important support for pilots' work on the flight deck. Complying with procedures is a safety prerequisite [7]. Pilots cannot work without references, manuals, documents, or charts. Such onboard systems support pilots to follow procedures for the satisfaction of safety, efficiency, and comfort requirements [8].

During the last two decades, new structures of electronic documentation on EFB have been discussed, analyzed, and tested, and some have been implemented. Dr. Francis Payeur coined a new atomic concept, the Documentary Unit (DU), for the development of electronic documentation. "DU is at the heart of electronic documentation segmentation into defined entities for revision purposes. A DU contains small size information; it could be text (e.g., a paragraph), descriptions, schematics, animations, performance data, and so on" [9]. Dr. Jean-Philippe Ramu claimed "there are two ways of describing context: system approach and task approach" [10]. The system approach is an engineering approach, and the task approach is a user-centered approach describing a particular situation. Since the top requirement is to be pilot-oriented, a task-based structure is the backbone of the onboard information system. It is motivated by a need for completeness of documentation description and is an improvement in the wish for contextualization of information [11].

2 Study Cases

2.1 Gulf Air Flight 072

On August 23, 2000, Gulf Air Flight 072 departed from Cairo to Bahrain. On the approach to Bahrain International Airport, it crashed into shallow water 5 km from the airport, all 143 passengers and crew on board died [12].

The A320 pilots conducted a manual visual approach without a flight director, with an improper control. They approached at a higher speed than normal and carried out an unusual altitude flight path in an attempt to correct to the final approach path. The aircraft was 1 mile from the threshold; the altitude was 600 ft., and the Indicated Air Speed (IAS) was 185 kt. The crew asked for a left turn to do a holding to reduce the energy of the aircraft. The crew found the plane was not on the extended line of the runway after one holding pattern. They requested to go around, and ATC commanded them to turn left heading 300 degrees and climb to 2500 ft. However, the flaps were not retracted according to the procedure in time. The aircraft dove quickly after 1000ft., and finally crashed into the sea north of the airport.

The investigation showed that the accident resulted from a combination of many contributing factors both at individual and system levels. The final report analyzed the factors for the accident as follows:

1. The individual factors particularly during the approach and final phases of the flight:

   – The captain did not adhere to a number of Standard Operating Procedures (SOPs), such as having a significantly higher than standard aircraft speed during the descent and initial approach, not establishing the approach on the path as in the navigation chart; and not performing the correct go around procedure.

- Despite the number of deviations from the standard flight parameters and profile, the first officer (i.e., Pilot Not Flying) did not call them out or draw the attention of the captain to be aware of these deviations as required by SOP.
- A perceptual study indicated that the flight crew experienced spatial disorientation during go around, which caused the captain to perceive that the aircraft was "pitching up" but he responded by making a "nose-down" input.
- The crewmembers were not aware of or did not efficiently respond to the repeated Ground Proximity Warning System (GPWS) warnings, which warned of the threat of increasing proximity to the ground.

2. The systemic factors, identified at the time of the accident, which could have led to the above individual factors:

- Organizational factors: A lack of training in Crew Resource Management (CRM; [13]) contributing to the flight crew performing as an ineffective team in operating the aircraft and insufficient training on the A320.
- Safety oversight factors: The civil aviation regulatory authority of Bahrain could not make the operator comply with some critical regulatory requirements.

2.2 Qantas Flight 32

On November 4, 2010, an Airbus 380 of Qantas took off from Singapore at 10:01am local time to Sydney with 440 passengers and 29 crewmembers on board. 15 min into the flight, the No. 2 engine exploded. The crew spent 55 min processing checklists and assessments, circling with its three remaining engines, dumping fuel, and preparing for an emergency landing back in Singapore at 11:45 a.m. local time. The landing distance was calculated by entering the weight and balance on the computers on board. Besides, pilots had to consider the condition of the landing runway, environmental factors such as wind, altitude, and other factors that the software could not accommodate with all the faults listed and all the conditions outside. The episode ended with no reported injuries. There were five pilots in the cockpit of this flight [14].

The crew had the option whether to land as soon as possible or to deal with the malfunctions completely. The crew quickly realized that immediate landing was not the best option despite the amount and severity of the warnings and cautions present and they were aware that the situation could still lead to unexpected events for which they could not necessarily prepare. The supervisor realized that there were not any procedures or training on this domain (engine failure and engine fire had procedures; however, not exactly titled engine explosion), so safety depended on the collective expertise of the crew, and hence the constant desire to stick to procedures when it is possible. Thus they did a holding pattern to process their checklist.

After following ECAM actions and checklists, they had to prepare for approach and landing. First, they considered the landing weight. As this flight had just taken off, it had not consumed much fuel, so the gross weight was over maximum landing weight. In addition, the fuel imbalance between two wings also would increase. Once they landed overloaded, the debris from the landing gear and wheels could have destroyed the tank, which could have resulted in an explosion of the fuselage. After assessment, they decided to dump fuel (i.e., followed Fuel Jettison procedure). The pilots were well trained in using onboard resources. They used the onboard performance system to help calculate data. An onboard system provides assistance to pilot's decision-making and problem-solving.

2.3 Case Summary

From these two cases, we can see that deviations from procedures may lead to severe results or damage, especially under high workload and time pressure. In Case 1, crewmembers' deviation from SOP triggered the accident chain. If any errors in the accident chain had been perceived, or if the onboard information system could have provided reminders, or assistance of procedures, the tragedy may have been prevented.

In Case 2, the crew followed each part of the procedures sequentially and rationally, and also used the onboard information system to collect performance data. There were two captains and two first officers on the flight deck. One captain was a very experienced supervisor, a coincidence in this case. Indeed, we cannot ensure that each flight crew has this kind of expert and experienced knowledge and knowhow [15]. Consequently, the onboard information system can provide assistance at this supervisory level, and provide the right information at the right time in an appropriate context-sensitive format, in order to ensure that the flight crew can use the new system safely [16].

3   Survey on the Procedures Performing

A survey was conducted on the use of procedures in flight with 32 professional pilots. We asked them the following questions:

1. Do you always attempt to follow Standard Operational Procedures? YES/NO. If not, comment.
2. Do you always follow abnormal procedures when there is a malfunction? YES/NO. If not, comment.
3. Have you ever forgotten or missed any procedures? YES/NO. If yes, comment.
4. Did you ever encounter situations where manuals or avionics DO NOT have enough information to complete the job properly? YES/NO. If yes, comment.
5. Did you ever encounter situations where manuals or avionics HAVE TOO MUCH information to complete the job properly? YES/NO. If yes, comment.
6. In case of malfunction or abnormal situation, which would be your main concern(s)? Time pressure, or decision-making, or procedures availability, or others.

Pilots' responses to these questions are shown in Figs. 2 and 3. According to the answers provided on the survey, we can learn that procedure following should then be assisted. This is why we have started the context-sensitive approach to this kind of assistance. Not only does context-sensitivity help provide the right information at the right time, but it can also track the pilot's actions to make sure that all required actions are effectively executed (constant crosschecking). Context-sensitivity requires thorough analysis and incremental validation of the pair "situational context" - "appropriate operational information." This is likely to solve current issues (e.g., lack of information in context, or too much information).

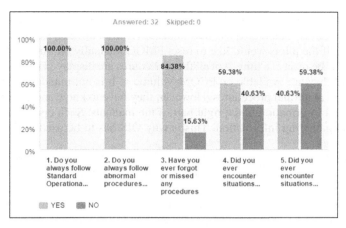

Fig. 2. Pilot participants' responses to the first 5 survey questions

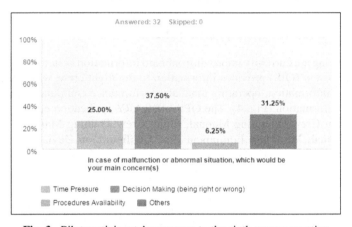

Fig. 3. Pilot participants' responses to the sixth survey question

The survey showed that pilots are concerned with many factors when there is an abnormal situation. If any of these factors can reduce the complexity, and therefore difficulty, of decision-making, safety will be increased. This is another human-centered requirement to be considered in the design of OIS instead of paper-based documents.

Nobody can permanently remember all procedures and technical knowledge, particularly, under time pressure [17]. Therefore, several instruments, panels, and displays have been developed and improved to assist flight crew and support task and action execution.

However, these systems do not cover all possible cases. Pilots are familiar with paper documentation, which are easy to use, tag, mark, and retain, even though they are heavy and difficult to carry. Pilots are well-trained on searching and performing procedures under all kinds of situations, sometimes moving from one manual to another manual [5]. For example, in "FMGC 1 + 2 Failure" (i.e., Flight Management Guidance Computer

(FMGC) 1 and 2 failed) on Airbus 320, the back-up navigation provides limited functions to the aircrew. Pilots should then use traditional navigation through Radio Management Panel (RMP). If the pilots would like to reset FMGC manually on rare occasions, only one FMGC can be reset at a time. Not all the procedures are displayed neither on ECAM nor QRH, but they are available on FCOM Volume 4. It is not mandatory for pilots to memorize such abnormal procedures. However, they have to know and understand how to find the right information in the right part of the manuals. Such operations may cost much time in gathering information. This is why OIS has to be used in the cockpit to assist pilots work.

To reduce the workload and increase the efficiency of performing procedures, many airlines edit documents to summarize procedures for specific scenarios or situations that require combining the information from several manuals. For example, in "RA 1 + 2 Fault" (i.e., Radio Altimeter 1 and 2 failed) on A320, the summarized procedures combine information from the navigation chapter and flight control chapter (at landing gear extension, flight controls revert to direct law in pitch, as well as in roll) from FCOM Volume 1 and Volume 3, which should be replaced by OIS.

4   New Systems: OIS, EFB, and Tablets

Airbus and Boeing are currently improving onboard information systems. A380 Onboard Information System (OIS) provides information to the flight crew, which includes aircraft technical information, operating manuals, performance computation, and mission management information (Fig. 4). The OPS LIBRARY application enables flight crew to access Flight Crew Operating Manual, Flight Crew Training Manual, Cabin Crew Operating Manual, Minimum Equipment List, Configuration Deviation List, Weight and Balance Manual, and Aircraft Flight Manual.

Fig. 4. ECAM and OIS on A380

Federal Aviation Administration (FAA) has approved three classes of Electronic Flight Bags (EFB). EFB Class1 &2 systems are considered portable. EFB Class 3 systems have FAA approved hardware and may have FAA approved operating systems [7].

The OIS on Airbus 380 and Airbus 350 fulfills the function of a Class 3 EFB system, displaying applications from stowed laptops. OIS and portable tablets EFB display can be moved to one of the six identical large screens on instrument panel which makes sharing information easier around the displays more freely as all have the same display format. So that the crew members can check the information from the OIS such as landing performance calculation conveniently since it can be put on the upper central display for discussion.

As well as Boeing, the newest modular integrated hardware and software package calculates performance figures, displays charts, improves taxi positional awareness, provides video flight deck entry surveillance, and allows electronic access to documents (Fig. 5). Electronic documents include flight crew operating manuals, U.S. Federal Aviation Regulations, and Aeronautical Information Manual for pilots viewing and searching [18].

Fig. 5. EICAS and EFB on B787

A380 documents and manuals are stored as fixed format files using the OPS LIBRARY application. B787 documents are stored using XML format that support search and text wrap, and also accept scanned images in GIF, JPG, TIF, and CGM formats. Pilots have to select documents they want to view rather than procedures displayed automatically in real-time.

Early in 2011 FAA authorized charter company Executive Jet Management to use iPad records without paper charts for backup. Now there are more and more airlines using iPads in the cockpit with its paper backup counterpart. Many applications that contain paper charts information are available. They include navigation charts, taxi procedures, weather, maps, GPS, Company Policy Manual, and Federal Aviation Regulations [18]. Some airlines already provide an iPad solution in the cockpit, as displayed on Fig. 6.

Boeing introduced a tablet-based version of the paper Quick Reference Handbook (QRH) used by flight crews in 2013. It is initially available for the Next-Generation B737 [19]. The Interactive QRH offers advanced navigation and search capabilities to enable the pilot to easily find the proper checklist. A specific airplane is selected for each flight, which simplifies checklist execution for those customers with multiple fleet

Fig. 6. An iPad equipped on a flight deck.

configurations. The Interactive QRH aids in checklist execution by highlighting checklist steps that have been missed, directing users to the correct checklist as appropriate, and tracking deferred items in non-normal checklists as needed. The Interactive QRH also simplifies non-normal checklist use, especially for those checklists in which the correct condition must be selected from two or more choices [5].

The next step of EFB development is in a logical progression towards updated auto-mated systems and operational efficiency. And to gather a larger number of data points based on the robust the Common Data Network (CDN) infrastructure, EFB will utilize real-time flight characteristics to measure component conditions and current loading of the aircraft's superstructure [18]. EFBs will be upgradable to host additional applications in the future, which is going to support electronic context-sensitive documentation (i.e., EFB interacts with flight data to display the proper information by context), and possibly a moving map for auto-taxiing on the ground to improve pilots' situation awareness.

One trend of next-generation cockpit is large-glass cockpit. The benefit of large screens is that it can display comprehensive information and ease to update database. However, Designing EFB must consider choosing suitable Human Centered Design (HCD) methods. It must meet the relationships between different functions (i.e., in terms of specific contexts), and keep information accurately [20].

5 Discussion

OIS can be qualified as a tangible interactive system onboard a commercial aircraft, in the figurative sense of tangibility (i.e., providing the correct status for pilots). The main issue we had to solve was tangibility [21, 22]. Paper documentation has been used from the beginning of aviation history and is tangible for pilots to grasp, handle and use. Tablets are now commonly used by the general public and have been authorized to be used as Class 2 EFB on the flight deck by the FAA. Class 3 EFB installed as a device onboard is also tangible even it cannot move. Consequently, we considered that EFB are tangible objects that can support applications.

No matter of installed EFB or portable EFB, as electronic devices they may lose power or be broken by external forces. Therefore, autonomy and physical robustness are two issues that need to be further studied and fixed. Redundancy of "minimal" paper documentation could also be a transient solution to be investigated. A pilot's competence, skills, and knowledge, as well as experience, are still key factors for flight safety. OIS helps to support these factors. Human-automation interactivity requires judgment skills, reliability, and safety of operation that needs to be further studied [23].

Cyber-security is then a concern for future commercial use. As Single Pilot Operation (SPO) and unmanned aircraft is under discussion, cyber-security is the top issue in the flight deck. It will be investigated and tested in the near future.

6   Conclusion

Electronic documentation, which can be contextualized and become an "onboard information system", contributes to improve situation awareness and better support decision-making and action taking. This does not remove the imperative necessity to keep a high level of flying skills and knowledge. The OIS is a comprehensive system that aims to make flight of commercial aircraft safe, efficient, and comfortable. The multiple usability evaluations and user-centered assessments performed on the system can discover the maximum number of issues. The OIS is also a device that has been used to display information digitally instead of paper documentation, which has the potential to increase productivity, as well as save cost for users. It has the capacity to increase a pilot's effectiveness and overall safety on the flight deck by providing appropriate information at the right time with the right format. In addition, it can remind pilots about anything that they might forget to do or might do improperly. However, onboard information system provides both benefits (e.g., integration and interaction) and drawbacks (e.g., enhanced information reliability that may cause complacency, and potential cyber-security issues). No matter how reliable electronic devices become, the possibility of equipment failure will always exist. Furthermore, an OIS is no longer only an additional static repository of knowledge, but a real onboard system in its own right.

Acknowledgments. We would like to thank Dr. Guy Boy for supervising the research. Thanks colleagues in School of Flight Technology for assisting our work. Thanks to all who participated in questionnaires and provided me with their time and great feedback to OIS. Thanks to Dr. Barbara K. Burian, Dr. Divya Chandra, Dr. Christophe Kolski, and Dr. Scott Winter, who provided me with feedback, suggestions, and comments on this research.

References

1. Cañas, A. J., et al.: CmapTools: a knowledge modeling and sharing environment. In: Concept Maps: Theory, Methodology, Technology, Proceedings of the First International Conference on Concept Mapping, Pamplona, Spain (September 14–17), Editorial Universidad Pública de Navarra, pp. 125–133 (2004)
2. Cañas, A.J., et al.: Concept maps: integrating knowledge and information visualization. In: Tergan, S.O., Keller, T. (eds.) Knowledge and Information Visualization. LNCS, vol. 3426, pp. 205–219. Springer, Heidelberg (2005). https://doi.org/10.1007/11510154_11

3. Novak, J.D., Cañas, A.J.: The theory underlying concept maps and how to construct and use them. In: Technical Report IHMC CmapTools 2006-01, Institute for Human and Machine Cognition (IHMC). (2006)
4. Tan, W.: From commercial aircraft operational procedures to an onboard context-sensitive information system. In: Proceedings of the HCI-Aero Conference, Santa Clara, CA (2014)
5. Tan, W., Boy, G.A.: Tablet-based information system for commercial aircraft: onboard context-sensitive information system (OCSIS). In: Harris, D. (ed.) EPCE 2018. LNCS (LNAI), vol. 10906, pp. 701–712. Springer, Cham (2018). https://doi.org/10.1007/978-3-319-91122-9_55
6. Burian, B.K.: Air carrier and manufacturer emergency and abnormal checklists: analysis of design and content. Unpublished data. (2005)
7. Federal Aviation Administration: FAA Advisory Circulars AC 120-76B. Airworthiness, and Operational Use of Electronic Flight Bags, Guidelines for the Certification (2012)
8. Federal Aviation Administration. FAA Advisory Circulars AC 00-74, Avionics Human Factors Considerations for Design and Evaluation. (2019)
9. Payeur, F.: A380 FCOM Product Specification Business Requirements Document. Airbus Technical Report, Toulouse, France, Airbus (2001)
10. Ramu, J.P.: Task structure methodology for electronic operational documentation. In: S. Chatty, J. Hansman, & G. Boy, Proceedings of the International Conference on Human-Computer Interaction in Aeronautics. Menlo Park, California, AAAI Press, pp. 62–68 (2002)
11. Ramu, J.P., Barnard, Y., Payeur, F., Larroque, P.: Contextualized operational documentation in aviation. In D. de Waard, K.A. Brookhuis, and C.M. Weikert (Eds.), Human factors in design. Maastricht, the Netherlands: Shaker Publishing, pp. 1–12 (2004)
12. Civil Aviation Authority of Bahrain. Accident Investigation Report Gulf Air Flight GF-072, Archived from the original on 12 February (2004)
13. Helmreich, R.L., Foushee, H.C.: Why crew resource management? Empirical and theoretical bases of human factors training in aviation. In: Weiner, E., Kanki, B., Helmreich, R. (eds.) Cockpit Resource Management, pp. 3–45. Academic Press, San Diego, CA (1993)
14. Australian Transport Safety Bureau (ATSB). In-flight uncontained engine failure Airbus A380–842, VH-OQA, overhead Batam Island, Indonesia, 4 November 2013
15. Campbell, R.D., Bagshaw, M.: Human performance & limitations in aviation. Third Edition Oxford; Malden, MA. Ames, Iowa, Blackwell Science. (2002)
16. Chandra, D., Yeh, M.: Evaluating electronic flight bags in the real world. Volpe National Transportation Systems Center. (2006)
17. Hawkins, F.H.: Human Factors in Flight. ISBN: 1857421353. January 1993. Ashgate Publishing. (1993)
18. DeVries, P.D.: Boeing 787 dreamliner: avionics and electronic flight bag. Int. J. Serv. Stan. 4(2), 217–233 (2008)
19. Boeing: www.boeing.com/boeingedge/aeromagzine. AERO, Issue 49_QTR_01. (2013)
20. Chandra, D.C., Mangold, S.J.: Human factors considerations for the design and evaluation of electronic flight bags. Digital Avionics Systems Conference. IEEE (2000)
21. Boy, G.A.: From automation to tangible interactive objects. Annual Reviews in Control, Elsevier pp. 1367–5788, https://doi.org/10.1016/j.arcontrol.2014.03.001
22. Boy, G.A.: Tangible Interactive Systems. HIS. Springer, Cham (2016). https://doi.org/10.1007/978-3-319-30270-6
23. Johnstone, N.: The electronic flight bag friend or foe? Air Safety Group Report Nr 104. February 7th, 2013

Influence of Visual Symbol's User Background and Symbol Semantic Abstraction Level on User's Cognition in AR Auxiliary Assembly Environment

Lei Wu$^{(\boxtimes)}$, Yao Su, and Junfeng Wang

School of Mechanical Science and Engineering, Huazhong University of Science and Technology, Wuhan 430074, China
lei.wu@hust.edu.cn

Abstract. This paper reports on a cognitive study on visual symbol in the field of AR auxiliary mechanical assembly, which is used to measure the cognitive mechanism of visual signs. Based on the Likert scale method, we conducted an experimental study. The independent variables were the semantic abstraction level of the symbol and the user background. The dependent variables include the specificity, complexity, familiarity, and semantic consistency. A total of 42 subjects participated in the experiment. The main findings of this study were as follows: (1) the semantic abstraction level of symbols has significant differences in the specificity, complexity, familiarity, and semantic consistency ($P < 0.05$); (2) The influence of user background on the cognition of symbols was not significant; (3) There were significant interactions effect among user background, semantic abstraction level and specificity ($P < 0.05$). In addition, this study provides a method for symbol design evaluation using data analysis in related working conditions in AR industrial applications.

Keywords: AR auxiliary assembly · User cognition · Visual symbol · Semantic abstraction level

1 Introduction

Due to the latest development of computer technology, manufacturing research has entered the stage of automation and intelligence. Augmented Reality (AR) technology has been the focus of academic research since the 1950s. As a branch of virtual reality technology, AR is a novel human-computer interaction method, which can superimpose computer-generated information on the real environment. In just over a decade, AR technology has proven to be an innovative and effective solution that can help simulate, assist and improve manufacturing processes [1]. AR technology leaves the laboratory and has many successful precedents in the aerospace, nuclear industry, maintenance and manufacturing fields. In assembly, Augmented Reality can help close the gap between product development and manufacturing management by enabling assembly operators to reuse and reproduce digital information and knowledge at the same time [2].

C. Stephanidis et al. (Eds.): HCII 2020, LNCS 12425, pp. 127–137, 2020.
https://doi.org/10.1007/978-3-030-60128-7_10

At present, research topics on AR are mainly divided into three aspects: hardware equipment, tracking and identification algorithms and user interaction. AR hardware devices are mainly divided into input devices and input devices. Up to now, each hardware device used for AR has its own advantages, but there are some shortcomings in imaging quality, sensitivity, integration and power consumption.

Lee [3] showed in their study that although head-mounted display is portable and mobile in experience, but a small enhanced field of vision and a large unenhanced peripheral area may cause attention diversion and have a negative impact on user behavior, and the visual quality of virtual content may even affect human vision. By analyzing 30 AR-related papers, Palmarini [4] identified three factors limiting real-time 3D tracking: (1) the complexity of the scene, that is the difficulty of finding the target object in the chaotic scene; (2) search for distinguishable functions for powerful outdoor tracking; (3) limitations of each tracking method for robust tracking. At present, the research on user interaction of AR focuses more on usability issues, and interaction problems of more dimensions such as sentiment mirror perception, somatosensory interaction and 3D visualization of AR environment are proposed. Santos [5] created an AR system availability scale composed of comprehensibility and operability scales, which effectively promoted the study of AR availability quantification, but there was still a lack of standardized reference in the study of AR availability. Claudio [6] proposed a context-aware model to model and reason information about the physical context and user tasks during the use of AR, but more complex perceptual environments, such as user interface elements that can adapt to the user's movement (for example, label size is rapidly converted when the user walks faster), need more complex studies. At the same time, new interaction methods such as gesture interaction [7], somatosensory interaction [8] and brain-computer interface [9] are being researched and developed.

Assembly operations are an important part of the product realization process. In traditional assembly operations, paper manuals (usually composed of a lot of text and a few explanatory pictures) are often used to guide operators. The research of Wiedenmaier [10] proved that compared with paper manual, AR is more suitable for auxiliary assembly, and studies have proved that visual expression is easier to understand and remember than text information, which can promote human cognition [11]. Since there is no international standard for graphic symbols related to assisted assembly process, one of the important problems to improve the user experience of AR assisted assembly is how to translate the text language in the paper manual into visual language to better guide operators.

In this paper, AR auxiliary mechanical assembly is used as the research object. Symbols with different semantic levels are designed through the semantic-driven hierarchical symbol design method. By studying the usability of visual symbols in auxiliary assembly to improve the operability of AR auxiliary assembly system, the assembly efficiency is improved, the operation error is reduced, and the application potential of AR technology is better realized.

2   Literature Review

2.1   User Experience of AR Auxiliary Assembly

In the field of assembly and other industrial maintenance, the usability of AR products and user experience have attracted more and more attention, and scholars have gradually begun to carry out research on the usability of AR. Previous studies have shown that combining information models with AR can display immersive views in the real environment of participants and visualize data into the appropriate existing environment, improving productivity and communication efficiency while greatly reducing assembly errors. Lei [12–14] studied the impact of AR training on different levels of experience and gender. The experiment proved that AR helped male and female trainees learn assembly routines faster and was more effective for female assemblers. At the same time, Lei discussed the different visual way of AR (animation) in promoting effective learning of staff involved in the complex system assembly and the effectiveness of the training, the experimental results showed that the animation has a positive effect on AR system cognition, the learning curve of the trainees is significantly improved, and the number of mistakes is less. In Deshpande's research [15], by developing an AR application program on a Microsoft HoloLens headset. Through behavior experiments, it was found that AR programs have a positive impact on solving spatial problems and behavioral indicators related to psychological performance. At the same time, the overall performance of this new interactive application scenario needs to be improved, such as the problem that the images presented by AR devices reduce the performance of visual search; the problem of human-computer interaction fluency in AR, and the difficulty of cognizing complex tasks, Further design strategies for AR technologies are needed to reduce cognitive workload and usability issues.

2.2   User Cognition of Visual Symbols

Visual symbols have been deeply studied from the aspects of graphic appearance and user cognition. The representative character Lodding [16] divided symbols into representation, abstract, and arbitrary in 1983. Gittins [17] mainly focuses on the form of symbols. Based on form, type and color, a classification method of related symbols and key symbols was proposed. Mc Dougall [18] proposed five classification criteria for computer symbols: concreteness, complexity, semantic distance, familiarity and aesthetic attraction. Tomas [19] investigated the effects of spacing and the size of individual interface elements on the processing speed of symbols in the human visual system. Huang [20] investigated and studied the effects of graphics/background color combinations, types of computer symbols and symbol/background area ratio on screen visual search performance. Rousek [21] found that color contrast and complexity would affect the understanding of graphic symbols. Schwartz [22] conducted a preliminary study on the cognitive efficiency of four different detailed presentation forms of the same three-dimensional object (photo, shadow drawing, line drawing, cartoon). Lee [23] believe that graphic symbols help to cross language barriers and facilitate communication between people of different cultures.

In the research of visual symbols in the field related to AR, Scurati [24] proposed the problem of the perception of symbols (including the uncertainty caused by the distorted perception of distance, position and angle) text labels and the masking problem of 3D models. The sequence problem and cognitive load problem of the strong boot level and the weak boot level in the virtual scene of AR. Nagel [25] image dynamic visualization method can improve the fusion of the images in the VR scene and the use scene, and appropriately simplify the visualization graphics in different environments and data complexity to improve usability. Qvortrup [26] discussed the perception between VR users and 3D visual objects and suggested that the size of graphic objects should be kept constant to support VR's depth perception. In general design and evaluation, object size is also a reference perception condition for units of spatial distance. Attributes (such as surface texture) should be added to close range (measured in units of object size) to trigger perceptual grouping, where color dominates perception and clustering structures can be defined over long distances.

3   Experiment

3.1   Definition

Based on the symbol classification standard, the semantic abstraction level of symbols and user background were used as independent variables. The cognitive evaluation based on the four aspects: the specificity, complexity, familiarity and semantic consistency. Those four aspect of symbol cognition were used as the dependent variables. Through the data of Likert scale, visual features driven by four cognitive characteristics were compared to provide references for practical design.

3.2   Research Hypothesis

The main hypotheses of this study were as follows:

H1: The semantic abstraction level has significant difference in cognitions of symbols.
H2: User backgrounds have significant difference in cognitions of symbols.

3.3   Participants

Forty-two graduate students majoring in mechanical engineering and design in Huazhong university of science and technology were randomly selected to participate in the experiment, including 19 male students and 23 female students. The proportion of mechanical background and design background is 1:1, both of each were 21 people.

3.4   Stimuli and Task

AR assembly is used to guide on-site assembly operators to assemble real products. On-site assembly operations are sequence combinations of different actions. Therefore, the extraction of basic assembly processes mainly centers on human operation actions, enabling operators to quickly obtain the instructions for implementing the assembly operations. According to the above principles, our team divided the assembly process into two categories: auxiliary process (the process involved in the preparation stage of assembly connection) and installation process (the process definition involved in the implementation stage of assembly connection), as shown in Fig. 1.

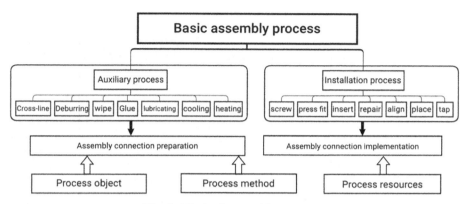

Fig. 1. The basic assembly processes

According to the expert advice, two typical processes in the auxiliary process and the installation process were extracted respectively to cross-line, wipe, screw and tap, and the four processes were taken as experimental design objects. Referring to the design method of the semantic-driven hierarchical symbol, the four process symbols are designed according to the low, medium and high semantic abstraction levels. Level 1: semantic feature extraction based on ontology level; Level 2: structured aggregation of runes (runes are constructed from basic geometric elements and visual variables that can

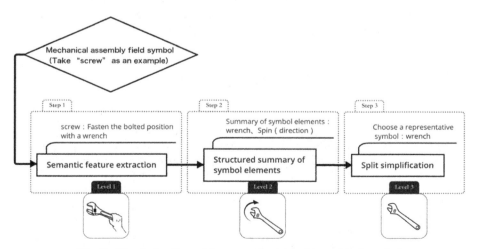

Fig. 2. The design flow of the semantic-driven hierarchical symbol

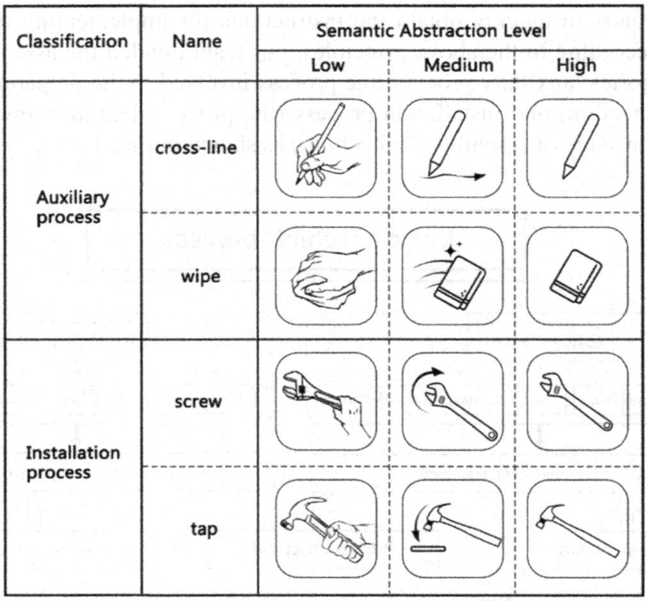

Classification	Name	Semantic Abstraction Level		
		Low	Medium	High
Auxiliary process	cross-line			
	wipe			
Installation process	screw			
	tap			

Fig. 3. The experimental stimuli

be combined to express more complete semantics); Level 3: break up the symbols and represent symbol semantics with typical symbols, as shown in Fig. 2.

To ensure the scientific aspect of the experimental stimuli, the abstract level classification of visual symbols was evaluated by five design experts. After adjustment according to the expert's opinions, the formal experimental stimuli were shown in Fig. 3. The four groups of stimuli were divided into three abstract levels: low, medium and high. Symbols used in the experiment were reasonably placed in the rounded rectangle with a size of 128px × 128px. In each test, symbols were presented separately without other visual interference. The experimental tasks were shown in Table 1.

Table 1. The experiment tasks

Category	Instruction	Task description
Specificity	The degree of abstraction or representativeness of a symbol	Each symbol was randomly presented, and participants were asked to rate each symbol on the five-point Likert scale according to its specificity, complexity, familiarity and semantic consistency
Complexity	The number of symbol details and the number of line twists and turns	
Familiarity	Familiarity with symbols	
Semantic consistency	The degree of consistency between symbolic expression and conceptual semantics	

4 Results

4.1 Reliability Analysis

All data were collected in this study, with a reliability coefficient value of 0.908, which is higher than 0.9, which indicates that the reliability of the research data is very high. For the "CITC value", the CITC values corresponding to the analysis items are all higher than −0.2, which indicates that there is a good correlation between the analysis items, and also indicate the reliability level is good, which can be used for further analysis.

4.2 Descriptive Analysis

Through the analysis of cognitive feature data of four visual symbols and three semantic abstraction levels, it can be seen from the data that users have relatively uniform cognition of the complexity of symbols, while the other three indicators have slight differences in the scores of different symbols. The cognitive complexity of symbols at low, middle and high levels of semantic abstraction is decreasing linearly. In terms of the concreteness of signs, the concreteness cognition of signs at the high semantic abstraction level is relatively low, with an average value of 2.554, while the concreteness cognition of signs at the low and middle semantic abstraction levels is 3.470 and 3.459, respectively. Although the low semantic abstraction level is slightly higher than the middle semantic abstraction level, the difference between the two is not significant. In terms of symbol cognition familiarity, high semantic abstraction symbol of familiarity obviously lower than other two, is low, the familiarity of the semantic level of abstraction symbol cognition in average was 3.298 and 3.351, respectively, the medium level of abstraction symbol familiarity scores but slightly higher than the low level of abstraction symbol, the subjects cognition abstract type symbol expression have more advantages. This point is also proved from the semantic consistency, which is generally believed to be higher by the participants. In the author's opinion, on the one hand, this is due to people's increasingly mature cognition of abstract symbols; on the other hand, it is due to the auxiliary role of action/direction hint symbols in symbols at the middle level of semantic abstraction, which makes the action semantics represented by symbols more clarity. In general, the middle semantic abstraction levels of the low, middle and high semantic abstraction levels scored relatively well in the four sign cognitive feature indicators. The average value of each indicator was shown in Fig. 4.

4.3 Variance Analysis

The indicators of symbol cognition were tested by the intersubjective effect. The dependent variables were the specificity, complexity, familiarity and semantic consistency of sign cognition. The independent variables were the semantic abstraction levels and the user background. The results showed that the user background has no significant influence on the specificity, complexity, familiarity and semantic consistency. There were significant differences in semantic abstraction level and specificity, complexity, familiarity and semantic consistency ($P < 0.05$). In addition, there was a significant interaction effect between user background * semantic abstraction level and specificity

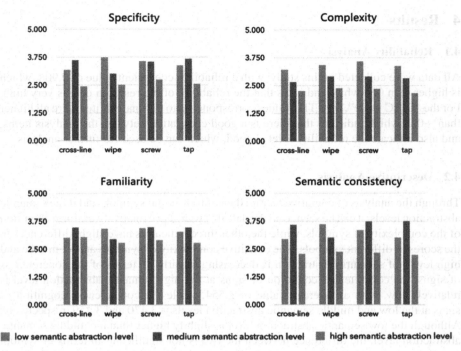

Fig. 4. Mean comparison of each indicator

(P < 0.05), as shown in Table 2. To further verify the research hypothesis, a (3 × 2) factor multivariate analysis was performed on the collected data, as shown in Fig. 5.

4.4 Summary

This paper presents a study on the effects of user background and different levels of semantic abstraction of symbols on the concreteness, complexity, familiarity and semantic consistency of sign cognition through the experimental statistics of the 5-point Likert scale. The purpose of this study was to assess the impact of different levels of semantic abstraction of user backgrounds and symbols on user cognition.

We get the result as follows: (1) the semantic abstraction level of symbols has significant differences in the specificity, complexity, familiarity, and semantic consistency (*P < 0.05*). The lower the semantic abstraction level, the higher the specificity and complexity. The familiarity and semantic consistency of the middle semantic abstraction level are higher than the high semantic abstraction level. The four indexes at the high semantic abstraction level are the lowest; (2) The influence of user background on the cognition of symbols was not significant; (3) There were significant interactions effect among user background, semantic abstraction level and specificity (P < 0.05).

Table 2. Tests of between-subjects effects

Source	Dependent variable	Type III Sum of Squares	Mean Square	F	Sig.
Background	Specificity	0.002	0.002	0.002	0.961
	Complexity	0.071	0.071	0.070	0.791
	Familiarity	0.335	0.335	0.391	0.532
	Semantic consistency	1.446	1.446	1.497	0.222
Semantic abstraction level	Specificity	92.905	46.452	54.823	0.000
	Complexity	104.123	52.062	51.222	0.000
	Familiarity	22.266	11.133	12.971	0.000
	Semantic consistency	136.433	68.216	70.598	0.000
Background * semantic abstraction level	Specificity	7.111	3.556	4.196	0.016
	Complexity	0.940	0.470	0.463	0.630
	Familiarity	3.266	1.633	1.903	0.150
	Semantic consistency	5.583	2.792	2.889	0.057

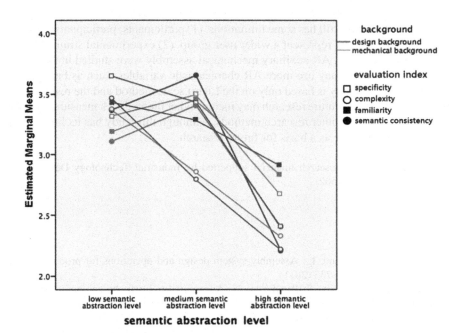

Fig. 5. Differences between different user backgrounds

5 Conclusion

In this paper, we conducted experiments on AR auxiliary mechanical assembly symbols through 42 participants. We compared the three abstract levels of symbol semantics: low, medium, and high; Two types of user backgrounds are analyzed: design background and mechanical background. Statistical analysis of the data shows that the level of semantic abstraction significantly affects users' symbol cognition, but the difference in user background has no significant effect on symbol cognition.

This research analyzes the cognitive strategy of symbols in AR-assisted mechanical assembly from the perspective of semantic abstraction level. It plays a role in the widespread application of AR auxiliary technology in the industrial field and the design improvement of symbols in new user scenarios. The results show that the level of semantic abstraction greatly affects the user's perception of symbols, while the user's background does not significantly affect the user's perception of symbols. The study found that people's cognition of abstract symbols has gradually matured, and the knowledge reserves of basic symbol elements have also increased. Therefore, even for unfamiliar visual objects, the reproducible expression of semantic scenes is consistent with public perception. The abstract symbolic expression has more cognitive advantages, and the structured combination of symbolic elements can also fully express the semantics of the symbol. In addition, this study provides a method for symbol design evaluation using scale data analysis in related working conditions and industrial applications.

However, this study still has some limitations. (1) participants: participants are graduate students and cannot represent a wider user group. (2) experimental stimuli: only 4 groups of the symbols in AR auxiliary mechanical assembly were studied in the experiment. Future research may use more AR characteristic variables, such as background complexity. (3) Our study is based only on the Likert scale method and the responses of subjective participants. Future research may include other biofeedback measures, such as Eye-tracking, EEG and other research methods. Although this study has its limitations, we hope that it can serve as a basis for future research.

Acknowledgments. The research financial supported by Industrial Technology Development Program (JCKY2016204A502).

References

1. Hu, S.J., Ko, J., Weyand, L.: Assembly system design and operations for product variety. CIRP Ann. **60**(2), 715–733 (2011)
2. Rentzos, L., Papanastasiou, S., Papakostas, N.: Augmented reality for human-based assembly: using product and process semantics. IFAC Proc. Volumes **46**(15), 98–101 (2013)
3. Lee, M., Bruder, G., Höllerer, T., Welch, G.: Effects of unaugmented periphery and vibrotactile feedback on proxemics with virtual humans in AR. IEEE Trans. Vis. Comput. Graph. **24**(4), pp. 1525–1534 (2018)
4. Palmarini, R., Erkoyuncu, J.A.: A systematic review of augmented reality applications in maintenance. Robot. Comput. Integr. Manuf. **49**, pp. 215–228(2018)
5. Santos, M.E.C., Polvi, J., Taketomi, T.: Toward standard usability questionnaires for handheld augmented reality. IEEE Comput. Graph. Appl. **35**(5), 66–75 (2015)

6. Bettini, C., Brdiczka, O., Henricksen, K.: A survey of context modelling and reasoning techniques. Pervasive Mob. Comput. **6**(2), 161–180 (2010)
7. Karambakhsh, A., Kamel, A., Sheng, B.: Deep gesture interaction for augmented anatomy learning. Int. J. Inf. Manage. **45**, 328–336 (2019)
8. Rahman, M.S., Yau, J.M.: Somatosensory interactions reveal feature-dependent computations. J. Neurophysiol. **122**(1), 5–21 (2019)
9. Anumanchipalli, G.K., Chartier, J., Chang, E.F.: Speech synthesis from neural decoding of spoken sentences. Nat. **568**(7753), 493–498 (2019)
10. Wiedenmaier, S., Oehme, O., Schmidt, L.: Augmented reality (AR) for assembly processes design and experimental evaluation. Int. J. Hum. Comput. Interact. **16**(3), 497–514 (2003)
11. Heiser, J., Phan, D., Agrawala, M.: Identification and validation of cognitive design principles for automated generation of assembly instructions. In: Proceedings of the working conference on Advanced visual interfaces, pp. 311–319. ACM (2004)
12. Hou, L., Wang, X., Bernold, L.: Using animated augmented reality to cognitively guide assembly. J. Comput. Civ. Eng. **27**(5), 439–451 (2013)
13. Hou, L., Wang, X., Truijens, M.: Using augmented reality to facilitate piping assembly: an experiment-based evaluation. J. Comput. Civ. Eng. **29**(1), 05014007 (2013)
14. Hou, L., Wang, X.: A study on the benefits of augmented reality in retaining working memory in assembly tasks: a focus on differences in gender. Autom. Constr. **32**, 38–45 (2013)
15. Deshpande, A., Kim, I.: The effects of augmented reality on improving spatial problem solving for object assembly. Adv. Eng. Inform. **38**, 760–775 (2018)
16. Lodding, K.: Iconic interfacing. In: 2nd IEEE Computer graphics and applications, pp. 11–20. IEEE (1983)
17. Gittins, D.: Icon-based human-computer interaction. Int. J. Man-Mach. Stud. **24**(6), 519–543 (1986)
18. McDougall, S.J.P., de Bruijn, O., Curry, M.B.: Exploring the effects of icon characteristics on user performance: the role of icon concreteness, complexity, and distinctiveness. J. Exp. Psychol. Appl. **6**(4), 291–306 (2000)
19. Lindberg, T., Näsänen, R.: The effect of icon spacing and size on the speed of icon processing in the human visual system. Displays **24**(3), 111–120 (2003)
20. Huang, K.C.: Effects of computer icons and figure/background area ratios and color combinations on visual search performance on an LCD monitor. Displays **29**(3), 237–242 (2008)
21. Rousek, J.B., Hallbeck, M.S.: Improving and analyzing signage within a healthcare setting. Appl. Ergonomics **42**(6), 771–784 (2011)
22. Schwartz, R.C.B.: Speed of perception as a function of mode of representation. Am. J. Psychol. **69**(1), 60–69 (1956)
23. Lee, S., Dazkir, S.S., Paik, H.S.: Comprehensibility of universal healthcare symbols for wayfinding in healthcare facilities. Appl. Ergonomics **45**(4), 878–885 (2014)
24. Scurati, G.W.: Converting maintenance actions into standard symbols for augmented reality applications in industry 4.0. Comput. Ind. **98**, 68–79 (2018)
25. Nagel, H.R., Granum, E.: Explorative and dynamic visualization of data in virtual reality. Comput. Stat. **19**(1), 55–73 (2004)
26. Qvortrup, L.: Cyberspace as representation of space experience: in defence of a phenomenological approach. In: Virtual space, Springer, London. pp. 5–24 (2002) https://doi.org/10.1007/978-1-4471-0225-0_1

Information Visualization Design of Nuclear Power Control System Based on Attention Capture Mechanism

Xiaoli Wu[1,2,3]([✉]) and Panpan Xu[2,3]

[1] School of Design Art & Medial, Nanjing University of Science & Technology, Nanjing, China
wuxlhhu@163.com
[2] College of Mechanical and Electrical Engineering, Hohai University, Changzhou, China
964871134@qq.com
[3] Lab of Human Factors and Information System Interaction & Design, Hohai University, Changzhou, China

Abstract. This paper takes information features of the main control room display of nuclear power plant for analysis, in which the design factors are extracted base on the monitoring interface task and visual cognitive law. With respect to the visual design method of interface presentation, we explore the design of the information display system of boron and water supply system. We determine the important information elements that can be improved in monitoring behavior, and optimize them according to their characteristic attributes. We group interface information according to task relevance, and design the color coding of the group information according to the structure of visual perception and the characteristics of color perception level. The information color between different levels could be adjusted according to readability and importance. The results of experiments verify the validity of the color coding method based on attention capture. According to the results, a visual design model of nuclear power control system information is established based on the research from the local interface icon to the overall presentation. This method can provide reference for the design of control system interface of nuclear power plant, and even improve the cognitive performance of operators and the safety and reliability of power plant operation.

Keywords: Nuclear power control system · Attention capture · Visual design · Color coding

1 Introduction

The digital monitoring interface of nuclear power plant is not only the carrier of human-machine interaction, but also the place with the most frequent contact with operators. With the wide application of digital technology in the nuclear power industry, Whether the design of the monitoring interface in the main control room conforms to the cognitive law has also been paid attention. Among them, the color coding of information has a great impact on the cognitive performance of operators. In order to improve the operator's

© Springer Nature Switzerland AG 2020
C. Stephanidis et al. (Eds.): HCII 2020, LNCS 12425, pp. 138–149, 2020.
https://doi.org/10.1007/978-3-030-60128-7_11

cognitive performance and ensure the safe operation of the nuclear power plant, from the perspective of the operator's attention capture mechanism, the monitoring information in the nuclear power control system is reasonably represented and coded, and a color coding design model based on the attention capture of nuclear power control system information is established. Based on the relationship between the system and information visualization, aiming at the monitoring interface of nuclear power control system, a design method of information color coding of nuclear power control system is proposed.

2   Background

People's mistakes caused many serious accidents. After the Three Mile Island nuclear accident in the United States, human factors engineering has become the mainstream of nuclear power safety research. Since then, the Chernobyl nuclear accident and the Fukushima nuclear accident have proved that human factor failure plays a leading role in all kinds of nuclear accidents. For the evaluation of interface usability, some scholars have done a lot of experiments, and some scholars have done extensive research on the visual design method of interface. This paper summarizes the current research status and trends in operator attention capture, information visualization methods, color coding design and so on.

2.1   Operator's Attention Capture Mechanism

In the research and application of attention capture mechanism, scholars have carried out experiments to verify the effect of different factors on the efficiency and function of the mechanism. Theeuwes [1, 2] found that color disturb can capture attention under single task conditions. Folk et al. [3] put forward the hypothesis of relevance and unintentional orientation, and believed that only cues with target characteristics can meet the attention control set and then capture attention. According to Itti [4], attention depends on the visual significance of the object. When observing the object with significant characteristics, attention distribution pattern is consistent with the information conversion activity of visual perception. Li [5] obtained the influence degree and significance order of three dimensional attributes of color (hue, lightness and saturation) on attention capture through experiments. Using the dual task paradigm of working memory task and visual search task, combined with eye tracking technology, Zhang [6] confirmed that the color attribute of working memory representation has a strong guiding effect in the process of capturing eye movements of working memory representation, and has more priority than other stimulus attributes (such as orientation, shape). Through the training-test paradigm, Bai [7] examined the role of color and location information in value driven attention capture. Experiments show that the generalization of value driven attention capture effect is selective. Through clue paradigm, Wang et al. [8] operationally established semantic association between cue and target, and investigated the effect of semantic association on attention capture.

2.2   Research on Color Coding of Control System Information

For the design of color coding on information interface, scholars focus on the usability evaluation and reliability evaluation of the interface. Laar [9, 10] proposed a visual layering method about color in the display design of control type, which enhanced the visual display segmentation through color to provide visual clues. Wu et al. [11] analyzed the cognitive performance of hue, lightness and saturation in the combination of foreground and background colors. They believe that hue affects cognitive speed and visual preference, but less than lightness and saturation. Peter [12] obtained the formula of chromaticity contrast significance through the significant level test of the intelligibility and discoverability of color text perception. Ahlstrom et al. [13] used hierarchical brightness coding to improve the design of air combat display interface. Dennis [14] pointed out that the perceptual hierarchy of color structure can constitute the visual advantage, and the hierarchical color combination of lightness, hue and saturation can promote the visual importance ordering of information. There are few researches on the visual layering of color. Zhang et al. [15], Li et al. [16], Xue et al. [17] found that with the increase of the color difference between the target and the black background, the reaction time showed a slow trend. Shao [18] put forward the basic principles of human-computer interaction interface through the theory of visual perception, and put forward some guiding suggestions on icon coding, information layout coding, color coding. In the application of color coding, in the aspect of EMU control interface design, Guo [19] used statistical method to study the influence of different foreground background color matching on driver's visual recognition efficiency. The results show the advantages and disadvantages of matching groups, and provide a reference for the optimal design of EMU control interface. Zhang [20] used the subjective and objective method to study the color matching problem on the aircraft information display interface, determined the recognition speed and preference degree of different background color and target color matching, and reached the conclusion that the performance and preference degree of different color matching were not completely consistent. Yan et al. [21] analyzed human factors theory and calculated parameters of text, diagram macro and color in the visual design of human-computer interface for VDU of different specifications, which provided reference for the design of human-computer interface of nuclear power plant.

3 Color Coding of Nuclear Power Control System Information Information Presentation

3.1 Visualization of Data Graphs

We take the data symbols in the interface of boron and water supply system in nuclear power system as the research object. Water and boric acid, two main elements in the interface, were extracted as sample materials. In order to increase the difference of information, we add color stimulation on the basis of pure characters in the original interface. We give different colors to different dynamic color rings. The color ring of data information in the working area of single participant "water" is blue. In the chemical properties, boron belongs to "acid substance", which means that the color ring of data information in the working area of single participant "boron" selects red among the three primary colors. In the common area of boron and water, the color ring representing the data information of the two mixed solutions will choose the mixed color, purple. For the color coding design of data symbols, in order to increase the significance and readability of text information, we choose the form of black words on white background for the next study to find the best visual expression of data symbols. (the color coding design results of data symbols are shown in Fig. 1).

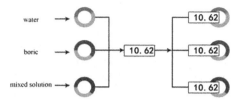

Fig. 1. The color coding design results of data symbols (Color figure online)

3.2 Coding Research of Information Level

Laar [9] consults experts in relevant fields to group the information contained in various elements of the display and sort them. According to this method, the interface information of boron and water supply is sorted by task relevance. Table 1 shows the sorting method and the ranking reason of each information group. We carry on the color visualization design to these five information level elements, and study the cognitive law of color coding to boron and water supply interface.

Table 1. Layering methods of the nuclear power interface

Informations group	Rank	Justication	Interface element
Borders and background	1	Basic layer,screen boundary providers,area washes and related text	3REA001YCD Boron and Water Makeup
Task area blocks and mimic structures	2	Lower level grouping information	
Static reference text	3	Mostly label which need to be seen as lying on top of layer2 task areas but on a lower level than dynamic information	
Dynamic data	4	Frequently updated task relevant information	300. 1 0. 14 1128 •1•
Alarm signals	5	Information but highly important information	

3.3 Color Coding Visualization of Nuclear Power Monitoring Interface

In a quantitative way, Li [5] uses the color difference values of two colors to judge the degree of mutual interference, and their response time difference to judge the degree of attention capture. Therefore, the visual perception level and attention capture degree of different hues, lightness and saturation are obtained. The color difference formula is as follows:

$$E = \sqrt[2]{\Delta L^2 + \Delta a^2 + \Delta b^2}$$

According to the color difference analysis method and ten principles of visual layered color coding [9], color coding design is carried out for the content of each information level, and quantitative analysis and verification are carried out for the design results. The result of layered interface is shown in the Fig. 2.

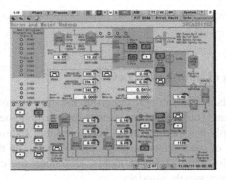

Fig. 2. Layered interface

4 Experiment

4.1 Behavior Response Experiment of Control System Data Graph Based on Attention Capture

(1) **Experimental design.** The experiment was designed for $4 \times 2 \times 2$ subjects. The first factor was the color of the clue color ring, which was red, yellow, blue and colorless; the second factor was the validity of the clue, which was the valid clue and the invalid clue; the third factor was the combination of characters, which were black characters on white background and white characters on black background. We selected a 15.6-inch computer to present the stimulus, with a screen resolution of 1366×768 (px). The experimental program was written by E-Prime.

(2) **Experimental materials.** There are three kinds of stimulus pictures in the experiment: clue picture, gaze picture and search picture. On the clue screen (as shown in Fig. 3), there are four information symbols evenly distributed on the virtual circle with " + " as the center. When there is a colored ring, the symbols are composed of a data box and a ring, one of which is a colored and full-color ring, and its color is one of red, yellow and blue, and the number in the data box is "10", the other three are gray rings, and the number in the data box is "0". when colorless rings, there are only four data frames in the clue screen, and the number in one of the data

frames is "10" and the remaining three are "0". There is a dark gray " + " sign in the center of the picture. The target information in the search screen is one of the Chinese characters "water" or "boron", while the non target information is "混", "合" and "砂". There is a data box in front of the four Chinese characters, with the numbers "1" or "2" or "3" or "4" in the box, and the combination of numbers and Chinese characters is randomly assigned. There are two types of data frame characters: white on black and black on white.

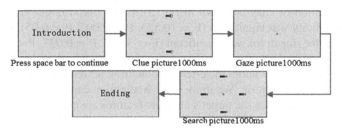

Fig. 3. schematic diagram of 1 experimental procedure

(3) **Experimental procedure.** The subjects were 22 students of Hohai University (11 for men and 11 for women), all of whom had engineering background, with an average age of 23 years, no color weakness, color blindness and other phenomena, and the corrected visual acuity was more than 1.0.

On the screen, there are clue interface, gaze interface and search interface in turn. The subjects press 1–4 keys according to the number in front of the target on the search interface. The experiment was divided into two groups: "boron" and "water". Each target carries out 64 search tasks, a total of 128 search tasks, and the sequence of search tasks is random.

(4) **Results and discussion.** We did a statistical analysis of response time, excluding some extreme data. The main effect of data character combination was significant ($F = 1.572$, $p = 0.212$, $p > 0.05$), and the average response time (1452.87 ms) of black characters with white background is lower than that of white characters with black background (1491.19 ms). When the clue is valid or invalid, the response time of the combination of characters with white background and black characters

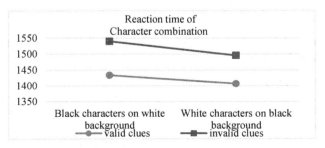

Fig. 4. Reaction time of Character combination

is lower than that of the combination of characters with black background and white characters (as shown in Fig. 4).

The analysis of variance of response time to water and boron showed that the main effect of clue validity was significant ($F = 9.692$, $P = 0.003$, $P < 0.01$), and the main effect of clue color was significant ($F = 6.166$, $P = 0.016$, $P < 0.05$). When the clue color ring is blue, the response time is significantly lower than that of red or yellow, and the response time under the vaild condition of clue is significantly lower than that under the invaild condition of clue(as shown in Fig. 5). In the boron target group, the main effect of clue validity was significant ($F = 10.523$, $P = 0.002$, $P < 0.05$), and the main effect of clue color ring color was significant ($F = 3.027$, $P = 0.037$, $P < 0.05$). When the clue color ring is red, the response time is significantly lower than that of yellow and blue, and the response time under the effective condition is significantly lower than that under the ineffective condition. We think there is attention capture. It can be seen that clues capture attention when the target's attribute features are consistent with the clue's color semantics. And the reaction time is the shortest and the search efficiency is the highest (as shown in Fig. 6).

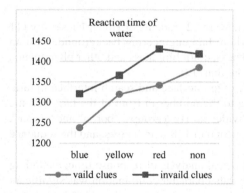

Fig. 5. Reaction time of water

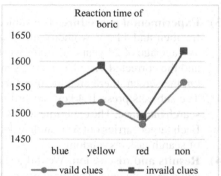

Fig. 6. Reaction time of boric

Therefore, when the stimulus has some color semantics, it will have the ability to attract attention to a certain extent. At the same time, when the semantic of color is consistent with the feature attribute of the target, the ability of capturing attention is the largest.

4.2 Eye Movement Experiment of Information Level Color Coding Based on Attention Capture

(1) **Experimental purpose.** We choose different independent variables to analyze the impact of different interfaces on user cognitive performance in the context of information color stratification. Experimental hypothesis: the information of the monitoring interface is encoded according to the importance and task relevance. The important information will achieve better cognitive effect and enhance attention capture ability.

(2) **Experimental design.** We take the boron and water supply interface of nuclear power plant as a sample, which has three interface color effects. The independent variables of the experiment are monochromatic sample, colored sample and color-less sample. Through the visual search experiment, the behavior index and visual physiological index were analyzed (as shown in Table 2). The monochrome sample adopts two colors of black and gray, its background is gray, and the interface infor-mation is black. All texts on the colored interface are black, the trend line is blue, and the simulation icons are all gray. The interface is colored but does not produce layering effect. The third kind of interface is the interface that produces layering effect.

Table 2. Experimental sample material

variables	monochrome interface	colored interface	Layering interface
Result of coding			

(3) **Experimental procedure.** First, a search task will appear on the screen. The task is to search for specific dynamic symbols, that is the data of specific icons. After understanding the task, press the space bar to continue. Then the gray gaze " + " appears in the center of the screen for 1000 ms, and then the search set appears on the screen. The experiment requires the subjects to find the target data in the search set as soon as possible. When finding the result, press the mouse, and a multiple choice question will appear on the screen for the participants to answer. After the selection, we will carry out the next round of search experiment. After the exercise, we will carry out a total of 12 (3 × 4) search tasks. (as shown in Fig. 7).

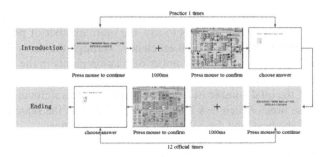

Fig. 7. Schematic diagram of 2 experimental procedure

(4) **Experimental equipment and subjects.** We introduce stimulus materials into the studio system of Tobii X120, which is an eye tracking device, and set targets and task materials. The experiment was carried out in the Human-Computer Interaction Laboratory of Hohai University. We selected 13 engineering students as subjects. Eye movement tracking was used to record the searching time of each task material and related physiological reaction index of eye movement.

(5) **Results and discussion.**

1) Behavioral data analysis. We got 13 people's data, deleted some unreasonable data, and the final effective data was 10 people.

Reaction Time. Through the analysis of variance repeatability measurement of interface color level, it is found that the main effect is significant ($F = 6.373$, $P = 0.019$, $P < 0.05$). Therefore, it can be analyzed by response time. As shown in Fig. 3, the response time of layered interface is the least in each task area, so we think that the search efficiency of layered interface is the best, and the color coding mode is better(as shown in Fig. 8).

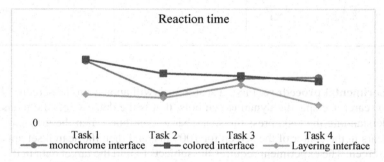

Fig. 8. Comparison of reaction time of experimental tasks

2) Data analysis of visual physiological indexes.

Total Fixation Points. The total number of fixation points on the search interface can reflect the certainty of the target. That is to say, the more number of points, the more uncertain the target, the lower the search efficiency. Through the analysis of variance repeatability measurement on the total number of fixation points in the interface color level, we found that the main effect was significant ($F = 8.906$, $P = 0.007$, $P < 0.05$). As shown in Fig. 9, the total number of fixation points in the hierarchical interface is the least in the response time of each task area search. So we think the search efficiency of layered interface is the best, and the color coding method is bette.

Total Fixation Duration. Fixation involves the complexity of information and the visual cognitive processing of information. From the duration of the operator's fixation, we can roughly observe the time of his cognitive activities [22]. The main effect of color level ($F = 4.840$, $P = 0.037$, $P < 0.05$,) reached significant level through the

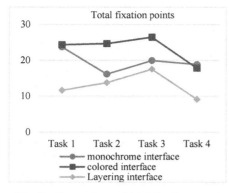
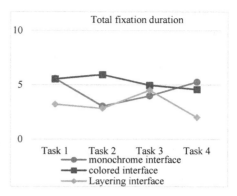

Fig. 9. Comparison of total fixation count   **Fig. 10.** Comparison of total fixation duration

analysis of variance repeatability measurement of total fixation duration. The average fixation duration of color layered interface (3137 ms) is less than that of monochromatic interface (4689 ms) and colored interface (5249 ms). As shown in Fig. 5, in task 3 search water supply loop function area, the search time in layered interface is slightly longer than that in monochromatic interface. But in the other three tasks, the fixation duration of color layered interface is the shortest. So we think its search efficiency is the best and the way of color coding is better (as shown in Fig. 10).

Time to First Fixation. When searching for a specific target in the display interface, the first time to reach the target AOI is also an important indicator of the rationality of the interface presentation. We think that the faster the target reaches the AOI, the stronger the target's ability to capture attention and the better the interface presentation. The main effect of interface color level was significant (F = 4.479, P = 0.045, P < 0.05). The average time of the color layered interface (1775 ms) is far less than that of the monochromatic interface (4158 ms) and the colored interface (4640 ms). In task 2, the first entry time of monochromatic interface is slightly shorter than that of layered interface. The reason may be that the interest area of task 2 is located in the center of the interface, which is the center area of the human eye observation interface, with a high degree of attention to it, so the difference is relatively small. However, the time of other locations was significantly higher than that of layered interface. Therefore, we suspect that the target region of interest in the layered interface attracts more attention and the color coding method is better (as shown in Fig. 11).

First Fixation Duration. The first fixation time of the operator for AOI can reflect the attraction of the target area of interest to the subjects. The shorter the first fixation time for the target, the more attention can be attracted [23]. The variance repeatability measurement analysis of the first fixation time of entering AOI of interface color level shows that (F = 4.521, P = 0.044, P < 0.05) has a significant main effect. In the layered interface, the fixation time of entering the region of interest for the first time in each task is the least. So we guess that when the interface is presented in the way of color stratification, the target can attract more attention of the subjects, and the color coding method is better (as shown in Fig. 12).

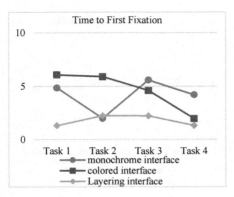
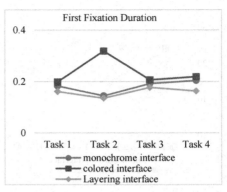

Fig. 11. Comparison of time to first fixation   **Fig. 12.** Comparison of time to first fixation

5   Conclusion

(1) The result of reaction time shows that in the representation of data character, the search efficiency of combination of characters is higher than that of pure character. When the attribute features of the target are consistent with the color semantics of the cue, the cue will capture attention. That is to say, the response time is the shortest and the search efficiency is the highest. There is no significant difference in search efficiency between black characters on white background and white characters on black background.

(2) When the color coding mode of the interface is presented in the way of color stratification, the response time of the subjects is the shortest a, the total number of fixation points is the smallest, the fixation time is the shortest, the fastest access to the area of interest, the first fixation time of the area of interest is the least. The visualization method of color stratification has the best cognitive performance and the strongest ability to capture attention. This conclusion provides more presentation methods for the visualization of color coding of digital interface of nuclear power plant and improves the safety of nuclear power plant operation.

Acknowledgement. This work was supported by Jiangsu Province Nature Science Foundation of China (BK20181159), Key Research and Development (Social Development) Project of Jiangsu Province (BE2019647), Jiangsu Province Key Project of philosophy and the social sciences (2017ZDIXM023), and the National Nature Science Foundation of China (Grant No. 71601068).

References

1. Theeuwes, J.: Perceptual selectivity for color and form. Percept. Psychophysics **51**(6), 599–606 (1992)
2. Theeuwes, J.: Stimulus driven capture and attentional setlective search for color and visual abruption sets. J. Exp. Psychol.: Hum. Percept. Performation **20**(4), 799–806 (1994)

3. Folk, C.L., Remington, R.W., Johnston, J.C.: Involuntary covert orienting is contingent on attentional control setting. J. Exp. Psychol. Hum. Percept. Perform. **18**(4), 1030–1044 (1992)
4. Itti, L.: Quantitative modeling of perceptual salience at human eye position. Vis. Res. **14**, 959–984 (2006)
5. Jing, L., Chengqi, X.: Research on color coding of digital interface based on visual perception layering. J. Mech. Eng. **52**(24), 201–208 (2016)
6. Bao, Z., Sai, H., Qiuxia, H.: Color priority in working memory representation capture eye movement. Acta Psychol. Sin. **46**(01), 17–26 (2014)
7. Xuejun, B., Li, L., Song, J., Guo, Z.: The role of feature and location information in value driven attention capture. J. Psychol. **48**(11), 1357–1369 (2016)
8. Huiyuan, W., Jie, S., Ming, Z.: Attention capture of semantic relevance: evidence from cue paradigm. J. Psychol. **50**(10), 1071–1082 (2018)
9. Laar, D.L.V.: Psychological and cartographic principles for the production of visual layering effects in computer displays. Displays **22**(4), 125–135 (2001)
10. Laar, D.L.V.: Color coding with visual layers can provide performance enhancements in control room displays. In: Proceedings of People in Control. International Conference on Human Interfaces in Control Rooms, Cockpits and Command Centers, Manchester, UK, p. 481 (2001)
11. Wu, J.H., Yuan, Y.: Improving searching and reading performance: the effect of highlighting and text color coding. Inf. Manage. **40**(7), 617–637 (2003)
12. Peter, B.: Chromaticity contrast in visual search on the multi-colour user interface. Displays **24**(1), 39–48 (2003)
13. Ahlstrom, U., Arend, L.: Color usability on air traffic control displays. In: Proceedings of the Human Factors and Ergonomics Society 49th Annual Meeting, Orlando, FL, USA, pp. 93–97 (2005)
14. Dennis, M.P.: Perceiving hierarchy through intrinsic color structure. Vis. Commun. **7**(2), 199–228 (2008)
15. Jie, Z., Zitong, G., Xufeng, L., et al.: A comparative study on the cognitive performance of different color visual standards on black back scenery. J. Shanxi Med. Univ. **42**(7), 542–550 (2011)
16. Chengqi, X., Jing, L., Haiyan, W., et al.: Effects of target and distractor saturations on the cognitive performance of an integrated display interface. Chin. J. Mech. Eng. **28**(1), 208–216 (2015)
17. Jing, L., Chengqi, X., Wencheng, T., et al.: Color saliency research on visual perceptual layering method. In: Proceedings of the 16th International Conference on Human-Computer Interaction, Maris, Heraklion, Crete, Greece (2014)
18. Jiang, S.: Research on information coding method of helmet display interface based on visual cognitive theory. Southeast University (2016)
19. Zizheng, G., Yongjian, L., Guozhong, M., Zheming, S., Bingyi, Q.: Influence of color matching on recognition efficiency of EMU control interface. J. Railways **34**(02), 27–31 (2012)
20. Lei, Z., Damin, Z.: Color matching of aircraft interface design. J. Beijing Univ. Aeronaut. Astronaut. **35**(08), 1001–1004 (2009)
21. Yueyong, Y., Han, C., Xiaodong, Y.: Digital human computer interface information visualization design based on human factors engineering. Ergonomics **24**(01), 48–51 (2018)
22. Xiaoli, W.: Errors in Complex Information Task Interface - Cognitive Mechanism, pp. 61–68. Science Press, Beijing (2017)
23. Guoli, Y., Jianping, X., Chuanli, Z., Lili, Y., Lei, G., Xuejun, B.: Review of main eye movement indicators in reading research. Prog. Psychol. Sci. **21**(04), 589–605 (2013)

Design Suggestions for Smart Tax Return Software Based on Reviewing Tax Compliance Literature

Bo Zhang[1,2,3] and Jingyu Zhang[1,2(✉)]

[1] CAS Key Laboratory of Behavioral Science, Institute of Psychology, Beijing 100101, China
zhangjingyu@psych.ac.cn
[2] Department of Psychology, University of Chinese Academy of Sciences, Beijing 100049, China
[3] SERVYOU Software Group Co. LTD., Hangzhou 310053, China

Abstract. Taxes are important for any modern society, but not all taxes are properly paid. Taxpaying application is a new type of tool in the interaction between tax authorities and taxpayers, which provides a new testbed to see how human-computer interaction design can enhance social welfare by promoting tax compliance behavior. In this paper, we reviewed relevant literature on psychological theories and factors that are relevant in tax compliance. It was found that prospect theory, mental accounting theory, the interaction between taxpayers and tax authorities, and social norm theory all provide useful insights to understand the tax paying process. In addition, we extracted six factors from the literature which are key to tax-paying behaviors, including, "the reference point of taxable income", "the salience of a separate mental account for taxation", "perceived easiness to pay tax", "trust in tax authorities", "perceived power of authorities", and "perceived norms to comply". Finally, we proposed a series of suggestions on how tax-paying applications can be designed to enhance tax compliance through these 6 factors. These suggestions were related to the content, function, structure, and procedure of the application.

Keywords: Tax compliance · Prospect theory · Mental accounting · Tax software design · Tax law complexity · Personal and social norms · Interaction between taxpayers and tax authorities

1 Introduction

Taxes are indispensable for any country to fulfill its duties through public good provision and wealth redistribution. Citizens are expected to pay taxes willingly and timely without any disguise, yet tax compliance is always a problem. In recent years, tax-paying software or applications have been introduced to change the whole tax-paying process. In developed countries such as the U.S, more than ninety percent of returns were paid online [1]. Developing countries have also made efforts to utilize the online platform to collect taxes. For example, the tax authorities of China issued an individual income tax

© Springer Nature Switzerland AG 2020
C. Stephanidis et al. (Eds.): HCII 2020, LNCS 12425, pp. 150–161, 2020.
https://doi.org/10.1007/978-3-030-60128-7_12

return application in 2018, which, by its designing purposes, should be used by its one billion citizens.

While the increased e-filings have served many objectives, little research has examined its influences on tax compliance [2], especially on how such behaviors can be improved by using better HCI designs. In this paper, we reviewed the relevant literature in order to draw a link between tax compliance research and HCI research, hoping to form certain design principles for designing smart tax return software in the future.

The paper was organized as follows: first, we reviewed the relevant literature on the research of tax compliance behaviors; second, we made several suggestions by linking these findings to current HCI principles for a better design. Finally, we illustrated a case in which the current.

2 Literature Review on Tax Compliance

Defined as the taxpayers' behavior to comply (or fail to comply) with the tax rules of his or her country, tax compliance includes behaviors such as complete income declaration and timely return filing. In the early years (i.e., the 1970s), researchers began to study tax compliance, and their major focuses were economic factors. The first economic analysis of tax compliance behavior can be traced back to the pioneering work of Allingham and Sandmo [3]. Their analytical framework was derived from the Becker's [4] economics-of-crime paradigm, in which taxpayers are assumed to be motivated to maximize their expected utility in financial terms by making a trade-off between the potential costs of tax evasion and tax compliance. Often called as the standard economic model of tax compliance, this model predicts that tax compliance increases as the economic deterrence, e.g., the probability of being detected, and penalty intensity, increases.

However, such assertions have not been fully corroborated by empirical evidence. In many countries, tax compliance levels are much higher than what is predicted by the standard economic model, in countries where the audit probability and penalty intensity are low, taxpayers do not show higher tax avoidance behaviors [5]. Kirchler et al. [6] manipulated factors proposed by the standard economic model in experiments and found no conclusive evidence. As a result, in the last few decades, researchers have started to adopt a psychological perspective to examine tax compliance. Several important frameworks such as prospect theory, mental accounting, bounded rationality theory, social norm theory, and citizen-authority interactions, have been proposed. Next, we will briefly review the major arguments of each theory and the key findings.

2.1 Prospect Theory

Prospect theory, developed by Kahneman and Tversky [7], is a theory that describes and predicts how people behave when making real risky decisions. Different from the standard economic model, which generally treats decision-makers as rational people with complete knowledge of their choices and consequences, prospect theory is established on behavioral economic experiments and treats decision-makers as people that are always bounded to limited cognitive resources. Many studies have found people's decisions are heavily influenced by the relative position between their actual economic income and a reference point in their minds. If the benefit is higher than their reference, it is considered as a gain and people are less likely to take risks (risk-averse), but when the outcome is lower than the reference point, it is considered as a loss and people are more likely to take risks (risk-seeking).

As it is generally too burdensome for ordinary taxpayers to calculate their actual taxable income, prospect theory met the basic prerequisite to analyze taxpayers' behavior analysis. Kirchler et al. [8] have proved that the payment of taxes is considered to be a loss by many people. In addition, if some taxes are prepaid (e.g., federal income tax withheld) during the year, paying a back tax or getting a refund at the end of the year is very different from the prospect theory's viewpoint. Whereas non-additional payment is considered as a basic reference point, paying back tax is considered a big loss, and it will increase the task evasion rate [9, 10]. On the other hand, claiming a refund is generally considered as a gain, and it can increase tax compliance behaviors [10–12].

From an economics perspective, claiming a tax refund is equal to getting back the interest-free loan that has been lent to the government. However, for taxpayers, such an arrangement can promote the willingness to pay taxes. As a result, it is suggested to adopt the advance tax plus refund system. Nonetheless, when the advance tax payments are too high, the incentives for tax compliance can also be reduced. In this way, it is important to find a balance point for not paying too much in advance and getting a certain sum of the refund at the same time [12].

2.2 Mental Accounting

Mental accounting is a concept that describes the cognitive categories individuals use to store, organize, and evaluate different financial activities [13]. It argues that people divide their money of varied origins and purposes into different mental accounts. For example, people may put their wages into an "Income from Hard Labor" account, their end-of-year bonus in an "Extra Reward" account, and their lottery winnings into a "Pennies from Heaven" account. While people can be quite more generous in using the money from the last unexpected income account, making expenditure from the first one requires more careful consideration as it can cause more emotional pain.

It has been found that people may put taxes into different mental accounts, and such a difference can result in different tax compliance and other economics behaviors [14]. For example, some people may put their tax and income in the same "In-come from Hard Labor" account. In this way, paying taxes can cause a strong feeling of loss, and their tax compliance can be reduced. However, if the taxpayer designates a separate mental account for tax due and sets a proper reference point, paying taxes may not cause mental harm, which may promote tax-paying behaviors. Muehlbacher, Hartl, and Kirchler [14] have shown that the mental segregation of tax due from net income affects a taxpayer's reference point in the compliance decision and results in higher tax compliance.

Tax refunds, when available, are often put into a separate account of unexpected income. But the nature of the account depends on the scale of the refunds. A large amount will create an account for savings and investment while a small amount for consumption. Feldman [15] found a proof of this assertion in observing the tax policy change of the U.S. government in 1992. At that time, the U.S. federal government changed its policy of income tax withholding by shifting the timing of income tax payments without changing the total tax burdens. As a result, instead of receiving large tax refunds at the end of the year, taxpayers received fewer tax refunds every month. Although the total refunds were not changed, the reduction in refund scale was found to be linked with consumption increase and a decrease in household savings for retirement.

2.3   Perception and Understanding of Tax Law

For many people, tax law is complex and difficult to understand. In this way, the taxpayers may become uncertain about their tax obligations and conduct involuntary evasion [16]. In many cases of unclear tax law, different understandings can lead to different tax payment behaviors. The experiments of Alm et al. [17] showed that uncertainty reduces tax compliance, but this effect decreases when tax intermediaries provide tax-related services to taxpayers at a lower cost. This shows that with the improvement of the understanding of tax law and the clarity of tax law, the willingness to pay tax will increase.

Complexity may also reduce the perception of the fairness of tax law [18]. Researchers conducted an experiment in which subjects assess different forms of a hypothetical tax provision with identical economic consequences. They found that the complexity of the provision negatively affects equity assessments only when subjects are prompted with an alternative provision with relatively favorable economic consequences, and only when no explicit justification for its complexity and relative economic consequences is offered.

2.4   The Perception of Tax Authorities

The perception of tax authorities is another important cause of tax compliance. Kirchler, Hoelzl, and Wahl [19] proposed an important and comprehensive theoretical framework called slippery slope" by integrating economic and socio-psychological factors. In such a framework, compliance behaviors are largely determined by the interaction between trust in authorities and the power of authorities. Trust refers to the extent to which the authorities are believed to be fair and just. Power, on the other hand, is the perceived ability to detect and enforce punishment for misconduct and crimes. Different combinations of the two variables may result in different motivations and behaviors. Voluntary tax cooperation happens when taxpayers have high trust in tax authorities. In this case, the taxpayer and the tax authority are in a harmonious relationship and the tax compliance is motivated by the willingness to contribute to the society (voluntary tax cooperation). However, when tax authority is primarily perceived as untrustable, taxpayers are not willing to cooperate. In this case, the relationship between taxpayers and tax authorities is mainly antagonistic, and tax authorities have to force taxpayers to comply, which is called enforced tax compliance. Enforced compliance is mainly motivated by the fear of being caught and punished. The interaction between the two variables suggests that when both variables drop, the compliance will drop more quickly.

The hypothesis of the slippery slope" framework has been confirmed in several countries with different cultural and economic systems [20–22]. It has been found that the friendly treatment of taxpayers by the tax officers in auditing processes could improve tax compliance [23]. In addition, in a tax system with low power of authorities, tax compliance is high when public expenditures are transparent, and taxpayers are given the right to decide on the use of their taxes [24].

In a very large study conducted in 44 countries on five continents [25], participants were randomly assigned to four conditions: high trust high power, high trust low power, low trust high power, and low trust low power. Tax compliance reached the highest when tax authority was powerful and trustworthy. In contrast, Participants had the lowest tax compliance when tax authority was both low in power and trustworthiness. In all the countries, the trustworthiness of tax authority was positively correlated with tax compliance, and in 43 of the 44 countries, a positive correlation was found between the tax authority and tax compliance.

Lisi [26] also found an empirical support for the slippery slope" framework, namely: (1) trust (in) and power (of) tax authority are both necessary to guarantee a high level of tax compliance: (2) the interaction between trust and power, as well as voluntary tax compliance, are crucial for increasing overall tax compliance; (3) the possibility that a slippery slope" situation occurs, when power and/or trust below a certain critical level, tax compliance started to decline. Gangl et al. [27] used survey data from three culturally different countries to examine the extended slippery slope framework, which distinguishes tax authorities' instruments into different qualities of power of authority (coercive and legitimate) and trust in authorities (reason-based and implicit). It was found that the influence of coercive power on tax compliance was mediated by implicit trust, which leads to an antagonistic climate and compulsory motivation. On the other hand, the effect of legitimate power to tax compliance is partially mediated by reason-based trust, and the relationship between implicit trust and tax compliance is mediated by a confident climate and committed cooperation.

2.5 Personal and Social Norms

Individuals do not always behave as rational and self-interested individuals portrayed in the standard economic models. They are also subject to many social influences. Alm and Torgler [28] have emphasized the impact of tax ethics on compliance decisions, as a result of a psychological loss that would be incurred by breaking moral standards. They argued that there is much direct and indirect evidence that ethics differ across individuals and that these differences matter in significant ways for their compliance decisions. Besides the traditional 'enforcement' paradigm, a less traditional 'service' paradigm that recognizes the important role of a 'kinder and gentler' tax administration in encouraging compliance, and, importantly, a new 'trust' paradigm that is built on the foundation of ethics, in which the tax administration must recognize that it can erode the ethics of taxpayers by its own decisions.

Since personal and social norms are interdependent, it could be difficult to completely distinguish the two effects [29]. Individuals are more easily influenced by peer behavior. If taxpayers learn that evasion is prevalent among a reference group with which they identify, they would feel less guilty about noncompliance; on the contrary, strong social norms against evasion may enhance compliance for taxpayers will avoid social stigma. Wartick [30] found that participants who viewed the decision of a noncompliant peer were less likely to report honestly than those who viewed the decision of a compliant peer. Hallsworth [31] showed that including social norm messages in standard reminder letters increase payment rates for overdue tax, and descriptive norms appear to be more effective than injunctive norms. Messages referring to public services or financial information also significantly increased payment rates. For instance, if a taxpayer who is late on filing the tax return receives a letter stating that 10 percent of taxpayers do not file a return on time, the taxpayer may feel a relief that others are in a similar situation, which could be used as a justification to delay filing the tax return even further. Nevertheless, Wenzel [32] has suggested that the effect of social norms on tax compliance is mediated by personal norms. He holds that personal norms are internalized social norms when the individual identifies strongly with a reference group.

Overall, the importance of norms should not be underestimated in the light of inconclusive field experiment results. Instead, they highlight the subtleties that influence the perception of normative appeals and should encourage policymakers to carefully adjust these [29].

2.6 Conclusion

Base on the review of the relevant literature, we identified several factors that may influence taxpayers' compliance behavior. These factors include the reference point of taxable income, the salience of a separate mental account for taxation, perceived easiness to pay tax, trust in tax authorities, perceived power of authorities and perceived norms to comply.

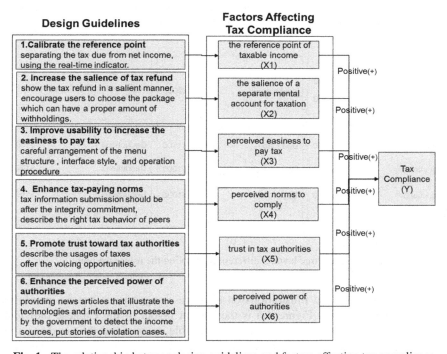

Fig. 1. The relationship between design guidelines and factors affecting tax compliance

Next, we would provide suggestions from an HCI design perspective to enhance tax compliance by improving these factors (Fig. 1).

3 Proposed Design Guidelines for Tax Software

3.1 Calibrate the Reference Point

Calibration of the reference point can be quite influential, since it may result in whether the taxpayers have gain feelings or loss feelings. Muehlbacher, Hartl, and Kirchler [14] have shown that separating the tax due from net income affects a taxpayer's reference point in the compliance decision and leads to higher tax compliance. Hence, we first recommend that the tax return software should make this kind of separation in the interface design. More specifically, the net income should be highlighted and shown on the more easily accessed places of the application. The tax due, on the other hand, should not be put in the same place. Rather, it might be better to put the taxable income and taxes together in a deeper layer or distant places, which requires the users to do more operation to get access.

Second, Hunt [33] investigated how users use a tax software which can show their changes of tax due as they updated their tax information (e.g., entering the amount of reduction) in a real-time manner. He found the tax behaviors are influenced by whether they have an increased or reduced tax. Based on this finding and the first recommendation, we suggested a new approach by using the real-time indicator, namely, when users input their deductions, such as expenditures on social welfare, education, and charity, they can see timely feedback indicating their net income gets increased.

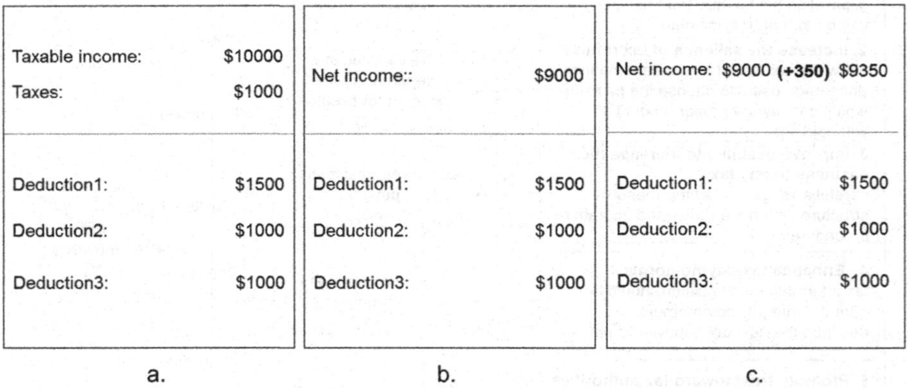

Taxable income: $10000		Net income:: $9000		Net income: $9000 (+350) $9350	
Taxes: $1000					
Deduction1: $1500	Deduction1: $1500	Deduction1: $1500
Deduction2: $1000	Deduction2: $1000	Deduction2: $1000
Deduction3: $1000	Deduction3: $1000	Deduction3: $1000
a.	b.	c.

Fig. 2. The three layouts different in showing the reference point

In Fig. 2, we provided illustrations on how these suggestions can be manifested through concrete designs. Figure 4-a is the current layout of the Chinese individual income tax return software, which shows the taxable income and the tax due on the same page. Figure 4-b is the layout that has incorporated our first recommendation by showing the net income instead. Figure 4-c is the layout which has incorporated both of our recommendations by showing the net income ($9000) and the benefit when entering deductions in a timely manner (+350). We suggested that the third design can improve the users' willingness to pay tax.

3.2   Increase the Salience of the Tax Refunds

People are more willing to pay tax when knowing to have a tax refund. We can enhance this effect through the following designs. First, we should show the tax refund in a salient manner. The best choice is to show tax refund with net income, into the most obvious places of the app. Using certain colors that may induce positive feelings may also enhance taxpayers' perception of the tax refund. For example, the color of gold is widely accepted in many cultures to represent wealth, and it might be used in these circumstances to indicate a benefit. Moreover, it might be useful to ask the users to collect" their tax refund using a flashing button in a prominent area after they log in. Such behavior can enhance their sense of gain in a conscious manner.

Second, the application should encourage users to choose the package, which can have a proper amount of withholdings. Whereas large withholding can guarantee the refund to be positive, but when withholdings are too high, the attitude before finally get the refund might be compromised. With current technologies, users' income and withholding type can be estimated using previous records. As a result, for users whose tax information is adequate, it is possible to develop the algorithms to find out the proper withholding plan. Of course, when the information required for making an accurate estimation is lacking, it is better to make an over-estimation of the withholdings.

3.3   Improve Usability to Increase the Easiness to Pay Tax

Usability is basic HCI concept which generally encompass factors such as effectiveness, efficiency, learning easiness, error prevention, etc. while the effectiveness relies on the functions and purposes of the product, which has been partly addressed in the rest of the suggestions in this section, the other domains requires careful arrangement of the menu structure, interface style, and operation procedure.

Simplify the procedure of taxpaying software is of utmost importance. It is important to make taxpaying easy and smooth, especially for the operations of refund claiming. In general, short operation paths are recommended, and the operation path should match the users' mental model. Avoid long-distance finger moves and unnecessary holdback. Since much personal information is repeatedly used, it is recommended to store this information, which can be offered when needed.

The menu layouts are also important. Give priority or visual salience to functions that most taxpayers would use may enhance the efficiency of the app. Moreover, deep learning technology can help design a smart-adaptive interface for each taxpayer uniquely.

The application should provide friendly hints and guidance at the right time. The name of buttons, button symbols, descriptions, and explanations should be easy to understand. It is recommended to avoid obscure professional terminologies. The application should provide a self-correction mechanism. Also, taxpayers can easily find the right entrance and amend their wrong operations if they input wrong contents or operate incorrectly.

3.4 Enhance the Tax-Paying Norms

People are heavily influenced by their inner injunctive and perceived norms, which reflects their peers' behavior. In this regard, several ways can be used to promote their tax-paying behaviors. In the first place, certain changes in the procedure can be used to enhance honest behaviors, which might be important for taxation (e.g., non-concealment of one's taxable income). While the integrity commitment is generally made after submitting the tax information, it might be more effective to put the commitment ahead of all submission. In this way, it makes the be honest" injunctive norm salient which has been found to reduce less cheating [34].

In current tax return software, the integrity commitment is offered after submitting tax information (Fig. 3).

Fig. 3. The Integrity commitment after submitting tax information

We recommend that submitting tax information should be after making the integrity commitment.

Fig. 4. The Integrity commitment after submitting tax information

In the second place, it can be useful to describe the positive behaviors of their peers to promote tax-paying behaviors. The application can provide information about how many people in the whole nation has provided tax information, reduction application, etc. The more careful design may rely on using a more proper reference group for each taxpayer. For example, for citizens in the city of Hangzhou, the application can tell them the following:

The tax compliance rate of Hangzhou taxpayers is obviously among the highest among all Chinese cities. Every citizen in Hangzhou should be proud of that. In your district, over 90% residents have properly paid their taxes and this number is growing very fast. Don't be the last to pay and let other districts to mock on us!

3.5 Promote Trust Toward Tax Authorities

Besides the basic function to pay taxes, the taxpaying software and application can also be considered as a platform to enhance the harmonious interaction between taxpayers and tax authorities. For citizens in modern societies, understanding the usage of taxes can strengthen their link with the public and the states. Several possible ways can be offered to achieve this goal. For example, the usage of taxes, in the form of regional and national budgets, can be offered in this application. Moreover, the contribution of the taxpayers can be thanked with an illustration on their help toward public affairs. Another way to enhance people's trust is to offer voicing opportunities. It has been found repeatedly when given even ostensible chances to make suggestions or feedback to the authorities, people's perception of the procedural justice and trust would be improved. In this way, it is possible for the application to publicize surveys and petition opportunities occasionally. Recently, it has been found that elegant and stylish interface designs can also help to improve trust. In general, it is suggested to avoid creating visual clutter and using highly saturated colors. Some background information, e.g., certain certification, watermarks, symbols, and words, can also influence people's trust in the system and the service providers. But whether this can also be effective for tax-paying software is worth further research.

3.6 Enhancing the Perception of Government Power

Several methods can also be used to enhance users' perception of government power and ability. Such deterrence can be achieved by providing news articles that illustrate the technologies and information possessed by the government to detect the income sources. Occasionally, the application can put stories of violation cases in the headlines. The application should also provide contacts and hotlines for the general public to report any illegal activities.

4 Conclusion

In this paper, we reviewed the relevant literature on tax compliance and developed guidelines for designing better tax software. A series of testable hypotheses were also proposed for future studies in this domain. We hope this review can help find key design factors for the software in the future to improve tax compliance. In 2018, the tax authority of China published the first individual income tax return software in this country. Over a billion individual taxpayers can thus report their taxable income and tax deductions by the tax return software, and it provides a very good platform to understand how these proposed factors can be used to enhance the current software design in order to promote tax compliance behaviors.

References

1. As e-file grows, IRS receives fewer tax return on paper. April 03 2014. Web. Nov. 13 2014. http://www.irs.gov/uac/Newsroom/As-efile-Grows-IRS-Receives-Fewer-Tax-Returns-on-Paper
2. Sutton, S.G.: The fundamental role of technology in accounting: researching reality. Adv. Acc. Behav. Res. **13**, 1–11 (2010)
3. Allingham, M., Sandmo, A.: Income tax evasion: a theoretical analysis. J. Public Econ. **1**, 323–338 (1972)
4. Becker, G.S.: Crime and punishment: an economic approach. J. Polit. Econ. **76**, 169–217 (1968)
5. Alm, J., McClelland, G.H., Schulze, W.D.: Why do people pay taxes? J. Public Econ. **48**, 21–38 (1992)

6. Kirchler, E., Muehlbacher, S., Kastlunger, B., Wahl, I.: Why pay taxes? a review of tax compliance decisions. In: Alm, J.M.-V.J., Torgler, B. (eds.) Developing Alternative Frameworks for Explaining Tax Compliance, pp. 15–31. Routledge, London (2010)
7. Kahneman, D., Tversky, A.: Prospect theory: an analysis of decision under risk. Econometrica **47**, 263–291 (1979)
8. Kirchler, E., Maciejovsky, B., Weber, M.: Framing effects, selective information, and market behavior: an experimental analysis. Handbook of Behavioral Finance, pp. 7–24. Edward Elgar Publishing Ltd, United Kingdom (2010)
9. Chang, O.H., Nichols, D.R., Schultz, J.J.: Taxpayer attitudes toward tax audit risk. J. Econ. Psychol. **8**, 299–309 (1987)
10. Kirchler, E., Maciejovsky, B.: Tax compliance within the context of gain and loss situations, expected and current asset position, and profession. J. Econ. Psychol. **22**, 173–194 (2001)
11. Elffers, H., Hessing, D.J.: Infuencing the prospects of tax evasion. J. Econ. Psychol. **18**, 289–304 (1997)
12. Yaniv, G.: Tax compliance and advance tax payments: a prospect theory analysis. Nat. Tax J. **52**, 753–764 (1999)
13. Thaler, R.: Mental accounting matters. J. Behav. Decis. Making **12**, 183–206 (1999)
14. Muehlbacher, S., Hartl, B., Kirchler, E.: Mental accounting and tax compliance: experimental evidence for the effect of mental segregation of tax due and revenue on compliance. Public Financ. Rev. **45**, 118–139 (2017)
15. Feldman, N.E.: Mental accounting effects of income tax shifting. Rev. Econ. Stat. **92**, 70–86 (2010)
16. McKerchar, M.: The study of income tax complexity and unintentional non-compliance: research method and preliminary findings. SSRN Electron. J. (2005)
17. Alm, J., Cherry, T., Jones, M., McKee, M.: Taxpayer information assistance services and tax compliance behavior. J. Econ. Psychol. **31**, 577–586 (2010)
18. Cuccia, A.D., Carnes, G.A.: A closer look at the relation between tax complexity and tax equity perceptions. J. Econ. Psychol. **22**, 113–140 (2001)
19. Kirchler, E., Hoelzl, E., Wahl, I.: Enforced versus voluntary tax compliance: the "Slippery Slope" framework. J. Econ. Psychol. **29**, 210–225 (2008)
20. Kastlunger, B., Muehlbacher, S., Kirchler, E., Mittone, L.: What goes around comes around? experimental evidence of the effect of rewards on tax compliance. Public Financ. Rev. **39**, 150–167 (2011)
21. Kogler, C., Batrancea, L., Nichita, A., Pantya, J., Belianin, A., Kirchler, E.: Trust and power as determinants of tax compliance: testing the assumptions of the slippery slope framework in Austria, Hungary, Romania, and Russia. J. Econ. Psychol. **34**, 169–180 (2013)
22. Muehlbacher, S., Kirchler, E., Schwarzenberger, H.: Voluntary versus enforced tax compliance: empirical evidence for the "Slippery Slope" framework. Eur. J. Law Econ. **32**, 89–97 (2011)
23. Feld, L.P., Frey, B.S.: Tax compliance as the result of a psychological tax contract: the role of incentives and responsive regulation. Law Policy **29**, 102–120 (2007)
24. Djawadi, B.M., Fahr, R.: The Impact of Tax Knowledge and Budget Spending Influence on Tax Compliance (2013)
25. Kogler, C., Batrancea, L., Nichita, A., Olsen, J., Kirchler, E.: Cross-cultural research on tax compliance, corruption, and shadow economy. In: Paper presented at the 28th International Congress of Applied Psychology in Paris, France (2014)
26. Lisi, G.: Testing the slippery slope framework. Econ. Bull. **32**, 1369–1377 (2012)
27. Gangl, K., Hofmann, E., Hartl, B., Berkics, M.: The impact of powerful authorities and trustful taxpayers: evidence for the extended slippery slope framework from Austria, Finland, and Hungary. Policy Stud. (2019)

28. Alm, J., Torgler, B.: Do ethics matter? tax compliance and morality. J. Bus. Ethics **101**, 635–651 (2011)
29. Onu, D., Oats, L.: The role of social norms in tax compliance: theoretical overview and practical implications. J. Tax Adm. **1**, 113–137 (2015)
30. Wartick, M.L., Rupert, T.J.: The effects of observing a peer's likelihood of reporting income on tax reporting decisions. Adv. Taxation **19**, 65–94 (2010)
31. Hallsworth, M., List, J.A., Metcalfe, R.D., Vlaev, I.: The behavioralist as tax collector: using natural field experiments to enhance tax compliance. J. Public Econ. **148**, 14–31 (2017)
32. Wenzel, M.: An analysis of norm processes in tax compliance. J. Econ. Psychol. **25**, 213–228 (2004)
33. Hunt, N.C., Iyer, G.S.: The effect of tax position and personal norms: an analysis of taxpayer compliance decisions using paper and software. Adv. Acc. **41**, 1–6 (2018)
34. Shu, L.L., Mazar, N., Gino, F., Ariely, D., Bazerman, M.H.: Signing at the beginning makes ethics salient and decreases dishonest self-reports in comparison to signing at the end. Proc. Nat. Acad. Sci. U.S.A. **109**, 15197–15200 (2012)

Augmented Cognition

Applications of an Online Audience Response System in Different Academic Settings: An Empirical Study

Ahmed Amro$^{(\boxtimes)}$, Muhammad Mudassar Yamin, and Benjamin James Knox

Department of Information Security and Communication Technology,
Norwegian University of Science and Technology, Gjøvik, Norway
{ahmed.amro,muhammad.m.yamin,benjamkn}@ntnu.no

Abstract. Technology dependent, digitally innate students are joining academia. Consequently, traditional pedagogical techniques for achieving desired learning outcomes are not universally sufficient. Digital clickers were introduced in the early 2000 for engaging students and maintaining their attention span during lectures. However, some studies are critical about their usage as they consume valuable time during the class which can result in further compromises concerning achieving learning outcomes. This study aimed to investigate the application of an online Audience Response System (ARCH) a.k.a "clicker" in different academic settings. To achieve this, the researchers conducted an empirical study that identified the effectiveness of using an online ARCH in multiple academic use cases. The use cases consisted of audiences with varying academic backgrounds and levels of academic achievement. All the presented topics were related to research in cybersecurity. The study identified that clickers can be a useful tool for audience engagement in a complex topic like cybersecurity.

Keywords: Audience Response System (ARCH) · Interactive technologies · Evidence-based intervention · Cybersecuirty

1 Introduction

The digitally innate, industrious, collaborative and entrepreneurial learners of Generation Z are entering academia. Institutions that fail to make the connection between student experience and digital engagement [16] risk not achieving desired learning outcomes. This occurs as traditional pedagogical techniques are insufficient for such technology craving learners. Digital ARCH (*Audience Response System*) were introduced in the early 2000 for engaging learners in class, to collect feedback from audiences during and/or after a presentation, and for maintaining student attention span [15]. Some studies are critical about the usage of ARCH as they can be time consuming and often compromise the already limited time available to achieve desired learning outcomes [14]. As well as ARCH methods, there is ongoing researcher exploring more passive means of

© Springer Nature Switzerland AG 2020
C. Stephanidis et al. (Eds.): HCII 2020, LNCS 12425, pp. 165–175, 2020.
https://doi.org/10.1007/978-3-030-60128-7_13

activity tracking [18] through the application of image data for identification of human actions in different educational scenarios. Earlier studies [see for example; [7,10,13,20] have looked at the application of online ARCH, also referred to as *clickers*, and their effectiveness in providing desired learning outcomes for complex academic subjects. In the presented study we aimed to investigate the application of clickers, as a means to support an effective learning experience for students and individuals studying and working in the complex discipline of cybersecurity. To achieve this, we conducted an empirical study which identified the effectiveness of using an online ARCH in multiple academic use cases, consisting of an audience with varying academic levels and different academic backgrounds. The analysis of data indicated that clickers can increase audience engagement related to difficult and complex cybersecurity topics. An identified limiting factor for their usage is that clickers require some additional training and awareness for both presenter and participants if they are to be implemented in a successful manner. The remainder of the paper is organized as follows: first we provide a brief background of ARCH followed by the research methodology. Next we highlight relevant work related to this research and present the experimental results and finding from three use cases. Lastly, we conclude the article whilst also addressing a number of limitations.

2   Methodology

The main goal in this work was to incept change in the pedagogical approach taken in certain academic lectures by applying some alternative active learning techniques [2]. Such change can be evaluated through an evidence-based intervention implemented in the form of an empirical study. This study aimed to identify the effectiveness of using an ARCH in the form of an online tool in multiple academic use cases, consisting of multiple audience levels (bachelor, master, PhD students, researchers, professors, and other academic staff members) with different academic backgrounds (mainly cybersecurity in two use cases and interdisciplinary in the third use case). The topics presented all relate to research in cybersecurity. This empirical study can provide an evidence base for the effectiveness of using an ARCH to ensure learning outcomes are achieved, motivate and facilitate discussion, scaffold critical thinking, and provide instant feedback collection.

The methodology followed in this study is depicted in Fig. 1. The study fits into the phases of an evidence-based intervention as suggested by U.S. Department of Education [1]. For planning purposes, before each lecture teaching materials were prepared and aligned with the ARCH. This meant that the ARCH could provide interactive material relevant to the progress of the presentation and related to teaching material. During and post lecture the usage of the ARCH was communicated to the audience to stimulate their interest and increase their engagement with the content. At the correct time, the presenter described and explained the interactive component by clarifying to the audience the task that is expected from them (answer a question, rate an option, provide feedback,

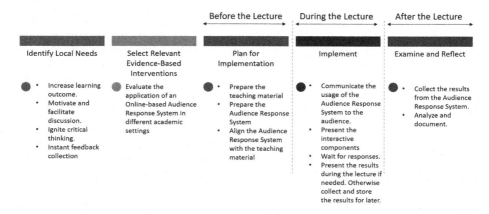

Fig. 1. Overview of the empirical study methodology aligned with evidence-based intervention guideline tasks

etc.). The audience were given sufficient time to respond. When the outcome of ARCH data was relevant and in direct support of the teaching material, the presenter would reveal the results during the lecture and discuss them with the audience. Finally, on completion of the lecture, results were collected from the ARS, analyzed and the findings documented. A detailed description of the conducted experiments are discussed in Sect. 4. The data for this empirical study was collected in a fully anonymized manner with participant consent, and in accordance with GDPR obligations [22].

3   Related Work

Cybersecurity education requires understanding of complex concepts ranging from technical issues to human errors and weakness. This requires educational institutions provide a pedagogic platform that develops a combination of technical skills, domain specific knowledge and social intelligence among learners [8]. Current research attempting to make cybersecurity education more effective by applying different methods and techniques on both human [24] and machine level [23] can help meet this challenge. While new and more domain focused arenas for cybersecurity education and training are being developed [25], their remains a requirement for developing modes of education that enable students to be actively engaged in cybersecurity educational programs. One way this can be achieved is through operationalised hands-on cyber security exercises [26]. Such exercises are useful for providing dynamic practical cybersecurity skill-set training [23]. For theoretical aspects and imparting the necessary background of cybersecurity concepts, traditional instructivist classroom settings remain the norm. In other academic fields where this is also the case, clickers have been used as a method to increase student engagement and motivation.

According to earlier studies this has yielded positive results for student engagement [7,10,11,13,20]. Alternative strategies for instruction that follow less formal methods and focus more on student engagement through choice and control [27], have been successful in encouraging students to take greater responsibility for their own learning [17]. This self-regulatory outcome, referring to the degree students are metacognitively, motivationally and behaviorally active in their learning [27], is key to academic motivation and learning, as it leads to improved perceived self-efficacy; a learners belief about their capabilities to learn and perform [3–5, 17]. The remainder of this section gives a brief review of five studies where clickers have been applied.

Micheletto et al. [13] in 2011 conducted a study in which they used ARS to elicit feedback from students participating in a complex business ethics class. The researchers used pre- and post-exercise surveys and asked the participants to self-evaluate how ethical they considered themselves to be in the context of their business conduct. At the start of the exercise 92% considered themselves to be ethical. During the exercise the researchers used ARS and asked participants questions about their perceived ethical conduct in certain situations. The participants answered anonymously. The researchers found that post-exercise, 72% of participants considered themselves ethical in their conduct. The researchers attributed this statistical shift to ARS and its effectiveness in engaging students to reflect on the topic, and therefore support intended learning outcomes.

Kazley et al. [10] in 2012 conducted a study on clickers in a course taught at the Medical University of South Carolina. The researchers hoped to identify the effectiveness of clickers in their courses by conducting a survey on a focus group in which they used clickers in the health administration program. The researchers stated that clickers can add additional cost in delivering the course, in terms of buying the digital audience response system and training the instructors on how to use them. However, in terms of student engagement and participation in classroom activities, they are a very effective pedagogic method.

Wang et al. [20] in 2016 conducted a study in which they used surveys to identify the effectiveness of digital games-based clickers for educational purposes. The researchers focused on four research questions which involved measuring student's motivation, enjoyment, engagement, and learning outcomes. They compared the digital game-based quiz system with a paper-based quiz system and identified statistical tendencies towards the digital game-based quiz system. The researchers stated that they only used one digital game-based quiz system called Kahoot for comparison with paper-based system. In future studies they plan to compare Kahoot with other digital clickers.

Byrne [7] in 2017 performed a study in which he used clickers for eliciting feedback from students concerning complex topics. His intent was to identify knowledge gaps. The problem he faced was the complexity of the topic he was teaching as it involved concepts from physics, chemistry and biology in a single course. This made it hard for students to grasp the presented knowledge and concepts. Clickers provided him the opportunity to get instant feedback from students about the topics and identify knowledge gaps. He further listed some advantages and disadvantage of electronic clickers which involved usability, cost and technical problems.

Khan et al. [11] in 2019 conducted a small case study on third year engineering students whose field of study was 'Instrumentation and Control Engineering' at the University of Plymouth. The study was conducted to identify the positive impact of clickers on learning outcomes for students involved in complex fields of study. The researchers modified the lecture content and embedded clickers within the lecture slides in order to test the knowledge and cognitive skills of students. The researchers stated that clickers can have a positive effect on participation, on student learning, engagement and grade attainment.

4   Experiments and Results

The main goal of this study was to increase learning outcomes in several types of academic lectures. To achieve this, an evidence-based intervention method as described in Sect. 2 was conducted across three separate but structurally similar experiments. Each experiment had a different topic; however all were related to cybersecurity and each experiment aimed to evaluate the effectiveness of the online ARS in a different use case. A summary of the conducted experiments are depicted in Table 1. An online ARS called Mentimeter [12] was leveraged in the three experiments. The online nature of Mentimeter enables both instructors/speakers and their students/audience to interact with useful active learning options such as voting, rating, and open-ended discussion. The instructor prepares the interactive slides on a web application, and the audience interact with the slides using their mobile devices once they have been provided with a six-digit code to sign in anonymously [12]. The description of the use cases and the conducted experiments with results are discussed below.

Table 1. Summary of the conducted experiments

Experiment	Part of	Participants (approx.)	Participants background	Participants academic levels
1	Seminar	40	Cybersecurity	B, M, P, PD, PR, and R
2	Course workshop	50	Multidisciplinary	P
3	Workshop	13	Cybersecurity	P, PD, PR
				B: Bachelor, M: Master, P: PhD, PD: Postdoc. PR: Professor, R: Researcher

4.1   Use Case 1

The first use case was evaluated by an experiment that was conducted as part of a PhD level university didactics course. The main objective was to conduct a pedagogical intervention that aimed to incept change in the way a weekly department seminar was being conducted. The intended outcome was that a more active approach may inspire new ideas and encourage students to pursue further higher education. This may go some way to ensuring such seminars are held in higher esteem and subsequently become a more valued learning opportunity, as well as contributing to the continuous learning environment for students and researchers.

Therefore, some active learning techniques as suggested by Felder and Brent [9] were applied. The two main techniques that are of interest to this paper are related to actively engaging the audience with engaging activities, as well as achieving variety in these activities. In addition to applying active learning techniques. The experiment we conducted required a feedback method to capture the perceived change in the way these department seminars were conducted. The feedback quality, implementation and evaluation were influenced by the work of Boud [6].

Mentimeter was used to implement the aforementioned active learning techniques and feedback collection. Table 2 shows the number of answers, type of interaction and their objectives. Each slide of the interactive component was carefully constructed and placed to measure different aspects of the experiment. The reported results from the audience supported the conducted experiment with sufficient data. For instance, the second interactive slide was placed after the related material was presented. It was aimed to measure audience comprehension of the discussed material and it was constructed in such a way that would ignite further discussion.

Table 2. Summary of the results from use case 1

	Slide	Responses	Type	Response rate	Objectives
Use Case 1	1	28	Word cloud	70,00 %	Capture attendance motivation
	2	25	M/C	62,50 %	1. Increase learning outcome 2. Motivate discussion
	3	23	Slider	57,50 %	
	4	22	Slider	55,00 %	Collect feedback
Response Median	24 (60%)				

In the last slide of the seminar, feedback was collected to measure the success of the experiment. The interactive component scored a rating of 3.6 out of 5 and was the lowest rating among other parameters as shown in Fig. 2. This leaves room for improvement regarding the interactivity aspect, such as reducing the effort to respond by reducing the displayed text or adding visual aids. However, it is critical to note that a key tenet of improving performance is not to oversimplify and reduce. Instead the aim should be to preserve the complexity [21] and have students learn at the zone of proximal development [19]. It is possible that students need to become more attuned to this mixed-mode of teaching. Although tech savvy, they are likely unfamiliar with ARS enhance teaching techniques. The researchers communicated this ARS approach and findings to future seminar speakers. Some were interested in implementing the interactive component. Unfortunately, both failed to implement it. One reported back that it requires more time than what is affordable, while the other implemented it but faced technical issues due to incorrect setup.

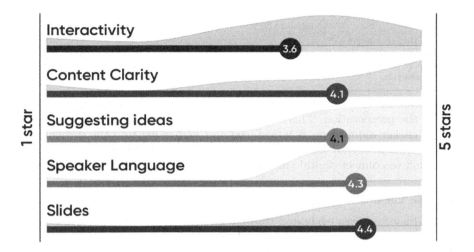

Fig. 2. Instant feedback collection results in use case 1

4.2   Use Case 2

The second experiment was conducted in conjunction with a presentation at a workshop that was part of a PhD level university course in research ethics. The aim was to explore the applicability of ARS in motivating critical thinking among attendees, facilitating ethical discussion, and evaluating predefined research questions. A side goal was to conduct an experiment similar to the work of Micheletto et al. [13] to measure the shift in the ethical standing of the participants. Unfortunately, due to time limits and no control group, this aspect was not sufficiently measured.

As depicted in Table 3, the participation level was the highest in comparison to the other use cases and the quality of the responses was sufficient to evaluate the targeted objectives. The ethical discussion aided by ARS successfully reflected a level of critical thinking by the attendees. This was a positive outcome when evaluating the pre-established research questions identified as part of the PhD course. The fact that responses to posed ethical questions in slides 1–4 were almost even, reveals a good outcome for an ethical question designed to split opinion. It shows that participants were engaged with the question, and it encouraged their critical thinking. A disadvantage with this use case was related to the time-consuming interaction, waiting for all the participants to sufficiently

Table 3. Summary of the results from use case 2

	Slide	Responses	Type	Response rate	Objectives
Use Case 2	1	39	M/C	78,00 %	1. Critical thinking
	2	39	M/C	78,00 %	2. Facilitate discussion
	3	39	M/C	78,00 %	3. Evaluate research questions
	4	38	M/C	76,00 %	
	5	7	Slider	14,00 %	Measure shift in ethical standing
Response Median	39 (78%)*				

* In the last interactive slide, the presentation was interrupted due to exceeding time limit. Therefore, the amount of responses was low (7). So, its result is considered an anomaly and is ignored in the statistical analysis.

comprehend the displayed questions and to digitally participate added time-delay to the presentation. This can be solved with careful planning concerning how the clicker application is introduced and embedded into the presentation. There are practical time keeping issues that presenters need to account for when attempting to connect digital engagement with student participation demands.

4.3   Use Case 3

The third use case was evaluated through an experiment conducted in conjunction with a presentation at a PhD student seminar. The main objectives were to motivate discussion among PhD students and engage them in the presented research topic. Considering the audience's strong background in cybersecurity, the low amount of participants and their responses can be compensated with the increased value of their input (Table 4).

Table 4. Summary of the results from use case 3

	Slide	Responses	Type	Response rate	Objectives
Use Case 3	1	10	Word cloud	76,92 %	Motivate Discussion
	2	7	Word cloud	53,85 %	
	3	3	Open ended	23,08 %	
	4	4	Slider	30,77 %	Feedback
Response Median	5,5 (42,3%)				

After analyzing the responses, a clear confusion appeared related to the discussed material. We consider the ability to capture such confusion through the interactive component, as beneficial to improve the presented material. Additionally, although the open-ended interactions generated the lowest responses, the received responses included very beneficial input to the presented research. Thus, the open-ended interaction was found to be useful in settings where there is a relatively high level of skill and domain knowledge among the audience. Lastly, the feedback rating for the interactive component again scored the lowest rating: 3.3 out of 5.

4.4   Interactions Statistics

A cross result statistical analysis was conducted to extract further findings related to the effectiveness of the interactive slide types and the audience engagement level over the teaching period. Table 5 reflects that Multiple Choice (M/C) is the most responsive interaction, and Word Cloud second. This is mostly because M/C is simple and does not require typing, while Word Cloud requires slightly more effort. Slider interaction, where audiences can rate their answer using a slide bar, was not as attractive as the previous two interactions. Sliders were valuable in providing instant feedback. Lastly as expected, Open Ended interactions showed the lowest interest due to the effort required to form sentences and type them. As noted previously, this approach can provide valuable input when the audience has greater levels of certain cognitive competencies, such as metacognitive skill and adaptive thinking proficiency.

Table 5. Average response rate for each interaction type

Interaction type	Avg. response rate
Word Cloud	66,92%
Multiple Choice	74,50%
Slider	47,76%
Open ended	23,08%

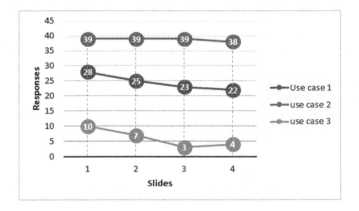

Fig. 3. Responses over time

An interesting finding was related to the response rate over the period of the learning time. The interactive slides were strategically distributed throughout the presentation to capture audience engagement. Figure 3 reflects how the responses tend to decrease over time. This suggests that for a valuable interaction to support increased learning, then placement of the interactive slides should be considered as most beneficial if they occur at the beginning of the presentation/lecture, and then again immediately after a break.

4.5   Conclusion

The present study aimed to investigate the application of an online Audience Response System (ARS) a.k.a a clicker in different academic settings. This empirical study aimed to identify the effectiveness of using an online ARS in multiple academic use cases. Each use case consisted of a range of audience academic levels with different academic backgrounds. All topics were related to research in the field of cybersecurity. The study included an evidence-based intervention implemented over three different but structurally similar experiments. The three different use cases were: a seminar, a course workshop, and a regular workshop. This study has provided evidence supported with documented experiments showing that many advantages can be realized by using ARS in different academic settings. ARS give presenters alternative techniques for increasing audience engagement, motivating discussion, stimulating critical thinking, evaluating research direction, and collecting instant feedback. ARS showed great promise to reduce the challenges of carrying out lectures in large rooms with a large number of participants. As a utility to facilitate ethical discussion with large audiences, ARS proved effective. Drawbacks of using ARS can be additional workload in preparation and aligning specific skill-sets to learning objectives. There are also time issues that need to be overcome relating to explanation and audience response time, but without using technology as a means to oversimplify, and thus compromise the subjects complexity. Using ARS in small groups did not generate increased utility. Regarding the type of interactions, the use of short interaction exercises (such as multiple choice and words suggestions) showed the largest acceptance levels among the participants. Open ended exercises showed the lowest acceptance level. Lastly, a decrease in the response rate over the period of the presentations was noticed across the three experiments. This would suggest the need greater attention to planning where to placement the ARS segments within the presentation.

References

1. Non-regulatory guidance: Using evidence to strengthen education investments September 2016. https://www2.ed.gov/policy/elsec/leg/essa/guidanceuseseinvestment.pdf
2. Ambrose, S.A., Bridges, M.W., DiPietro, M., Lovett, M.C., Norman, M.K.: How Learning Works: Seven Research-Based Principles for Smart Teaching. John Wiley & Sons, Hoboken (2010)
3. Bandura, A.: Social foundations of thought and action. Englewood Cliffs, NJ **1986**, 23–28 (1986)
4. Bandura, A.: Perceived self-efficacy in cognitive development and functioning. Educ. Psychol. **28**(2), 117–148 (1993)
5. Bandura, A., Freeman, W., Lightsey, R.: Self-efficacy: the exercise of control (1999)

6. Boud, D.: Feedback: ensuring that it leads to enhanced learning. Clin. Teach. **12**(1), 3–7 (2015)
7. Byrne, C., et al.: Clickers: a learning technology project case study. J. Acad. Dev. Educ. **7**, 94–106 (2017)
8. Dawson, J., Thomson, R.: The future cybersecurity workforce: going beyond technical skills for successful cyber performance. Frontiers Psychol. **9**, 744 (2018)
9. Felder, R.M., Brent, R.: Learning by doing. Chem. Eng. Educ. **37**(4), 282–309 (2003)
10. Kazley, A.S., Annan-Coultas, D.: Use of an audience response system to teach problem-solving in health administration. J. Health Adm. Educ. **29**(3), 219–227 (2012)
11. Khan, A., Schoenborn, P., Sharma, S.: The use of clickers in instrumentation and control engineering education: a case study. Eur. J. Eng. Educ. **44**(1–2), 271–282 (2019)
12. Little, C.: Technological review: mentimeter smartphone student response system. Compass, J. Learn. Teach. **9**(13), 64–66 (2016)
13. Micheletto, M.J.: Using audience response systems to encourage student engagement and reflection on ethical orientation and behavior. Contemp. Issues Educ. Res. **4**(10), 9–18 (2011)
14. Morgan, R.K.: Exploring the pedagogical effectiveness of clickers. Insight J. Sch. Teach. **3**, 31–36 (2008)
15. Paschal, C.B.: Formative assessment in physiology teaching using a wireless classroom communication system. Adv. Physiol. Educ. **26**(4), 299–308 (2002)
16. Povah, C., Vaukins, S.: Generation z is starting university–but is higher education ready. Guardian **10** (2017)
17. Schunk, D.H.: Self-regulation of self-efficacy and attributions in academic settings (1994)
18. Ullah, M., Ullah, H., Alseadonn, I.M.: Human action recognition in videos using stable features (2017)
19. Vygotsky, L.: Interaction between learning and development. Readings Dev. Child. **23**(3), 34–41 (1978)
20. Wang, A.I., Zhu, M., Sætre, R.: The effect of digitizing and gamifying quizzing in classrooms. Academic Conferences and Publishing International (2016)
21. Ward, P., Gore, J., Hutton, R., Conway, G.E., Hoffman, R.R.: Adaptive skill as the conditio sine qua non of expertise. J. Appl. Res. Mem. Cogn. **7**(1), 35–50 (2018)
22. Warström, J.: Gdpr and personal data protection in mentimeter. =https:// help.mentimeter.com/en/articles/1937769-gdpr-and-personal-data-protection-in-mentimeter
23. Yamin, M.M., Katt, B.: Inefficiencies in cyber-security exercises life-cycle: a position paper. In: AAAI Fall Symposium: ALEC, pp. 41–43 (2018)
24. Yamin, M.M., Katt, B.: Cyber security skill set analysis for common curricula development. In: Proceedings of the 14th International Conference on Availability, Reliability and Security, pp. 1–8 (2019)
25. Yamin, M.M., Katt, B., Gkioulos, V.: Cyber ranges and security testbeds: scenarios, functions, tools and architecture. Comput. Secur. **88**, 101636 (2019)
26. Yamin, M.M., Katt, B., Torseth, E., Gkioulos, V., Kowalski, S.J.: Make it and break it: an iot smart home testbed case study. In: Proceedings of the 2nd International Symposium on Computer Science and Intelligent Control, p. 26. ACM (2018)
27. Zimmerman, B.J.: Dimensions of academic self-regulation: a conceptual framework for education. Self-Regul. Learn. Perform.: Issues Educ. Appl. **1**, 21–33 (1994)

Perceived Restorativeness and Meditation Depth for Virtual Reality Supported Mindfulness Interventions

Mark R. Costa[1], Dessa Bergen-Cico[1](✉), Rachel Razza[1],
Leanne Hirshfield[2], and Qiu Wang[1]

[1] Syracuse University, Syracuse, NY 13244, USA
mrcosta@syr.edu , dkbergen@syr.edu
[2] University of Colorado Boulder, Boulder, CO 80309, USA

Abstract. Novice meditators often find it difficult to tune out external distractions which hinders their ability to engage in mindfulness practice. The problem is further exacerbated by stress and directed attention fatigue. Researchers and tech companies are experimenting with nature-inspired themes to improve the meditation session quality. In this paper, we discuss our pilot experiment, using nature inspired virtual reality themes to create an idealized space for meditation. Our results indicate that the participants found the space restorative and that the perceived restorativeness was positively correlated with the perception of the depth or quality of the meditation session. We also found that a majority of participants experienced a reduction in baseline tonic electrodermal activity as well as frequency of skin conductance responses; however, neither electrodermal measure of arousal was significantly correlated with any of the self-report measures.

1 Introduction

1.1 Background and Motivation

Employers, military agencies, and individuals all have shown an increased interest in developing emotional resilience, emotional regulation, and attention regulation skills. The increased interest in these skills has helped underpin a surge in research on mindfulness-based interventions (MBIs). MBIs are frequently based on Eastern contemplative teachings, and are often associated with various forms of meditation. Westernized versions of MBIs, like Mindfulness-Based Stress Reduction (MBSR) [1], are usually adapted (e.g., secularized) to be more acceptable to other audiences and sometimes combined with other therapies to treat specific clinical diagnoses.

At the root of MBIs is the concept of mindfulness; Bishop describes the *state* of mindfulness as "A kind of nonelaborative, nonjudgmental, present-centered

Supported by Syracuse University's Office of Research.

C. Stephanidis et al. (Eds.): HCII 2020, LNCS 12425, pp. 176–189, 2020.
https://doi.org/10.1007/978-3-030-60128-7_14

awareness in which each thought, feeling, or sensation that arises in the attentional field is acknowledged and accepted as it is [2]." By focusing on the present and not elaborating or attaching oneself to their thoughts, instances of negative thought loops are reduced. Instead of ruminating on the past (depression) or worrying about the future (anxiety), attention is placed on one's current, embodied experience. The ability to focus on the present moment, recognize emotional stimuli, and choose how to respond (non-reactivity) is cultivated through regular practice. Practice may include mindful meditation, body scanning, and elements of yoga.

With consistent practice, it becomes easier to achieve a mindful state. However, Davidson argues that focusing on the state of mindfulness is problematic because states fade, so any intervention focused on states is not much different than pharmaceutical interventions [3]. Instead, we should focus on developing the trait of mindfulness, which is the generally tendency to be in mindful states. One of the main issues is, as Kiken and colleagues found [4], people vary significantly in their response to mindfulness interventions and ability to develop the trait of mindfulness. There are many personal, environmental, and logistical barriers to sustained practice that leads to trait mindfulness; we have discussed these barriers, including: difficulty tuning out external stimuli, difficulty participating in group sessions, inaccessibility of qualified instructors, in the past and refer you to [5,6] for additional information on those barriers.

The barriers to practice as well as the general difficulty of mindfulness has opened up opportunities for HCI researchers to work on making MBIs more accessible. HCI researchers explore the use of smart phone apps, virtual reality environments (VREs), and biofeedback [7] to enhance MBI practice. The work we discuss today focuses on addressing one particular accessibility challenge associated with practicing mindfulness, directed attention fatigue [REF], through the use of virtual reality. Directed attention fatigue (DAF) is a concept from attention restoration theory; DAF is based on the assumption attention is a limited resource and that our modern environment drains that resource. The depletion of attentional resources makes mindfulness practice difficult; in some ways, it is analogous to exercising while tired. We will discuss attention restoration theory in the next section.

1.2   Conceptual Framework

Attention restoration theory (ART) posits that attention is a limited resource and that our modern environment, which includes the built environment and technologies designed to capture our attention, tax that limited resource [8,9]. When that resource becomes depleted, people develop directed attention fatigue. Directed attention fatigue reduces one's ability to focus and can also lead to other negative psychosocial outcomes, including irritability and decreased performance on mental tasks [10]. Longer term, Kuo and Sullivan [11] found that city residents with less access to green space report higher levels of mental fatigue, irritabiltiy and violence. Researchers have argued that attention is a key resource in executive functioning, and excessive fatigue may undermine attempts to practice mindfulness-based interventions because attentional control is a key element of those practices [12]. Mindfulness requires purposeful allocation of attentional resources; the ability to direct one's attention is cultivated through practice but excessive fatigue will make starting MBIs difficult.

One potential treatment to DAF is exposure to nature [8]. According to ART, nature has inherently restorative effects on attention fatigue and emotional well-being. The mechanisms through which nature has these effects is unknown, but one theory is that humans evolved to function within natural environments, and thus may be better adapted to functioning within them. Although the mechanisms of nature exposure are unknown, researchers identified five factors of natural space that are associated with the perceived restorativeness of a space: away, fascination, coherence, compatibility, and extent. The factors are defined as follows:

Away: a sense of being separated (physically or mentally) from daily concerns or problems.

Fascination: in this case, soft fascination, where elements of the environment capture one's attention.

Compatibility: whether the individual views the environment as suitable to their interests. For example, some people prefer ocean side views while others prefer secluded glades in a forest [13].

Extent-Scope: has two sub-factors, scope and coherence. Coherence is the extent to which elements of the environment fit together. In some variations of the scale, coherence is separated out as a fifth factor [14]. Scope refers to whether the space is of sufficient size and complexity to be engaging.

We were particularly interested in whether virtual reality could serve as a delivery mechanism for mindfulness instruction and whether the medium could replicate some of the purported benefits of nature exposure. Researchers are actively exploring whether exposure to nature themed environments, including digital representations, generate partial effects under the premise that most people have limited access to natural environments. Our general research question was: can a nature inspired virtual reality-based meditation environment create a restorative effect and improve meditation session quality?

The degree to which an individual perceives an environment as meeting the qualities of away, fascination, compatibility, and extent-scope influences whether the environment has restorative properties for that individual. ART states that a restorative environment will serve to replenish the attentional resources of the individual and prepare them physiologically (i.e., reduce arousal due to over-stimulation) for the mindfulness practice. Therefore, our first hypothesis is:

H1: Perceived restorativeness is correlated with reductions in arousal.

More specifically, we were focused on physiological arousal of the individuals. One well-understood measure of arousal is electrodermal activity (EDA). EDA is a measure of skin conductance, which is affected by sweat gland activity [15]. Sweat glads are controlled by the sympathetic nervous system, and are not under direct control of the individual and are therefore thought to be a more accurate measure of arousal.

There are two components of EDA: phasic and tonic activity. Tonic EDA, or skin conductance level (SCL) is the general background level of arousal. In contrast, phasic EDA, or skin conductance response (SCR) are event driven. Positive changes in SCL can indicate an increased level of arousal over time, while negative changes indicate a decreased level of arousal. SCRs are due to specific stimuli, with the relative frequency of events being correlated with sensitivity to environmental stimuli. Therefore, we further clarify our hypothesis as:

H1a: Perceived restorativeness is significantly positively correlated with a reduction in skin conductance level.

H1b: Perceived restorativeness is correlated with a reduction in the frequency of skin conductance responses.

Hypothetically, a restorative space should make it easier to engage in mindfulness practice. If the space distances the individual from their normal cares, is mildly fascinating but not overly stimulating, matches what they perceive to be a relaxing natural environment, large enough to feel as if they are immersed in a new place, and put together in a way that does not detract from the experience, then the individual's arousal levels and mental fatigue will diminish. We hypothesize that a feeling of restorativeness and the related reduction of arousal will make it easier for individuals to practice mindfulness. Therefore, we hypothesize:

H2a: Meditation depth [16] is significantly positively correlated to perceived restorativeness.

H2b: Meditation depth is significantly positively correlated with a decrease in skin conductance level.

H2c: Meditation depth is significantly positively correlated to a decrease in skin conductance responses.

Virtual environments vary in quality and immersiveness; design choices can affect the emotional impact of the environments as well as the extent to which individuals feel as if they are transported to the virtual environment. The concept of presence has evolved to describe the psychological state of transportation and non-mediation [17,18]. That is to say, presence is often associated with an individual's sensation that they are interacting directly with objects or actors in the virtual environment, not with or through a media technology.

Our main question was whether we could simulate a natural environment well enough to generate a perception of restorativeness and if that perceived restorativeness would increase the perceived quality of the mindfulness session. Formally, our hypotheses related to presence were:

H3a: Perceived restorativeness is significantly positively correlated with presence.

H3b: Meditation depth is significantly positively correlated with presence.

We describe the experimental methods and data collection procedures related to the above hypotheses in the following section.

2   Methods

All experimental recruitment procedures and methods were approved by Syracuse University's Institutional Review Board. Participants were recruited from the local Syracuse, New York USA community through flyers and email lists. There was a small monetary compensation incentive advertised in the recruitment flyers. Those who responded to the solicitation were scheduled to visit the lab at a time that was convenient for them. Participants were greeted at the lab at their scheduled time and after explaining the nature of the study, given a consent form. If the participants consented to participate in the study, they were asked to complete a pre-test survey. After the participant completed the pre-test measures, the technician informed them that they would be hooked up to several non-invasive sensors (see below) and have a virtual reality head-mounted device placed on their head. All participants were allowed to terminate participation but none chose to do so.

Our virtual reality stimulus was a nature-themed meditation app with features found to be correlated with inducing a sense of restorativeness. In particular, we designed an open space adjacent to a waterfall, which created a running water effect. The area was sunny, with visual effects of a gentle breeze. We also included bird song as that has been found to improve relaxation. The environmental volume levels were held constant for all participants.

Participants were given a minute of silence to acclimate to the virtual environment before the meditation track began. The track was recorded and edited in a professional studio to reduce extraneous, distracting noise associated with recordings done in an office space. The track itself was written and narrated by a certified Mindfulness-Based Stress Reduction instructor. The 10-minute mindfulness track centered on awareness of breath. The instructor also leveraged elements of the virtual environment as objects of focus.

When the track was complete, the technician removed the sensors and virtual reality headset from the subjects. Finally, the participants completed the post-test measures via an online survey. Finally, participants were reimbursed and thanked for their time.

2.1   Measures

Our pre-test measures included basic demographic information, meditation experience (hours practiced) and style if applicable, and meditation retreat experience. Meditation experience as well as prior retreat attendance has been shown to affect an individual's overall mindfulness and manifests as physiological change in neural circuitry.

We outlined our measures in a previous paper [6] but include the information for specific measures discussed in this paper below for the reader's convenience. The following self-report measures were used:

Five Facets of Mindfulness Questionnaire (FFMQ; [19]) [Pre-test]. FFMQ is a 39-item, five factor instrument designed to capture one's mindful disposition towards daily life. The five factors are: observing, describing, acting with awareness, non-judging of inner experience, and non-reactivity to inner experience.

Positive and Negative Affect Scale – Short Form (PANAS-SF, [20]). [Pre- and Post- test] We used a modified version of the PANAS-SF, worded to capture the strength of their current positive and negative moods. Subjects completed both a pre- and post- test PANAS to capture changes in mood due to the mindfulness session.

Perceived Stress Scale (PSS, [21], 1983) [Pre-test]. PSS consists of ten items grouped into two dimensions – positively and negatively worded questions related to how one appraises the stressfulness of situations in their life.

Perceived Restorativeness Scale (PRS, [22]) [Post-test] PRS is a four-factor, 26-item scale intended to capture properties of natural environments that are expected to facilitate emotional and attentional rejuvenation. Items are rated on a scale of 1–5, factors are calculated as a mean of all items in that factor, and the Five Facets Score is a mean of the factors.

SUS Presence Questionnaire (SUSPQ, [23]) [Post-test] SUSPQ has six questions, focused on three presence indicators: sense of being there, extent to which the virtual environment becomes more "real" than reality, and the extent to which the virtual environment is thought of as a place visited [6]. Items are rated on a scale of 1–7 and presence is calculated as a mean of the items.

Meditation Depth Questionnaire (MEDI, [16]) [Post-test]. MDQ was Developed to measure the depth or intensity of a meditation experience while simultaneously being agnostic to the school of meditation. The thirty-item scale has five factors – hinderances, relaxation, personal self, transpersonal qualities, and transpersonal self. Items are rated on a scale of 1–5, factors are calculated as a mean of all items in that factor, and the Five Facets Score is a mean of the factors.

Unless stated otherwise, all data were collected with a BIOPAC MP-150 system. The following physiological signals were collected during the experiment:

Electrodermal Activity (EDA) for arousal [15]. The sampling rate was set at 2000 Hz. Raw data from the module pair is bandlimited from DC to 10 Hz for both channels. Two sensors were placed on the participant's non-dominant hand.

Electrocardiogram (ECG) for heart rate variability for arousal [5]. The module pair has a fixed gain rate of 2,0000Db, with bandlimits from 1 Hz to 35 Hz. Two sensors were placed on the participant's collar bone and a ground electrode on the right hip.

Respiration Sensor (RSP) for breath rate. Raw RSP data from the module pair is bandlimited from DC to 10 Hz, to provide for the measurement of relatively static respiratory conditions, such as cessation of breathing, up to the extremely rapid respiratory effort variations (up to 600 breaths per minute) associated with coughing or sneezing. An elastic band with a pressure sensor was wrapped around participant's chest so that the pressure sensor was located at the inferior section of the participant's sternum.

Function Near Infrared Spectroscopy (fNIRS) for hemodynamic patterns of the brain for assessing cognitive states [24, 25]. Captured with a Hitachi ETG-4000, sampling oxygenated and deoxygenated hemoglobin at 10 Hz. Probes were placed in 2, 3×5 arrangements above both the right and left frontal cortex, which resulted in 24 channels of data.

3   Results

Although we collected a number of self-report and physiological measures, only a subset of the analysis will be discussed below. We provided the comprehensive list of measures as additional information for readers who may be interested or have suggestions about how to resolve some of the contradictory findings in our analysis (see below).

The associations between the following variables are discussed below, along with descriptive statistics for each variable: presence, perceived restorativeness, meditation depth, and electrodermal activity.

3.1   Demographics

Twenty-one participants (Female = 10) completed the experiment; the average age of participants was 27.9 years old. Over half (n = 11) reported some college, while five of the participants reported having a graduate degree. The range of meditation experience was substantial - mean hours practiced was 568 h, with the maximum at 10,000 h. However, most of our subjects had no experience (Table 1).

Table 1. Descriptive statistics: demographics

	N	Min	Max	Mean	Median	S.D
Female	10	-	-	-	-	-
Age	21	18	55	28.86	10	25
Hours of meditation	21	0	10,000	568	0	2174

3.2   Self-report Measures

All of the participants completed 100% of the self-report questions. We calculated the mean score for the factors in scales with sub-factors. Previous analysis indicated all scales had high internal consistency <REF>. Final scores for each variable were calculated using the mean of the scale's factors, in accordance with published guidelines.

Our analysis of the presence scale deviated from published instructions outlined in [23], which suggested presence should be determined by the number of sixes (6) and sevens (7) reported by each participant. We found in previous analyses that the authors' suggested approach was not informative when it came to analyzing associations between the variables. We will discuss this in greater detail later, but we attribute the lack of variance captured by $<ref>$'s approach to the difficulty participants have in summarizing their entire experience with a single measure. Participants reported moderate levels of presence (M = 3.76/7, S.D. = 1.02). Ratings on the perceived restorativeness of the environment were clustered around 3.20–3.66 (out of 5) (see Table 2, except for coherence. The high coherence rating suggests that the design choices of the virtual environment fit together and were appropriate.

Table 2. Descriptive statistics: perceived restorativeness scale

	Mean	S.D.
Away	3.25	0.96
Fascination	3.36	0.72
Coherence	4.31	0.68
Compatibility	3.20	0.72
Perceived restorativeness	3.66	0.57

Table 3 contains the results of our descriptive analysis of participants' reports on meditation depth and quality. Basic measures related to their ability to get into a meditative state indicate that the virtual environment was moderately supportive of their efforts (see Hindrances and Relaxation). The Transpersonal Qualities, Transpersonal Self, and Personal Self factors all had lower scores, which should be the case given that those factors describe states that are available to experienced meditators <ref>. It should be noted that hindrance items were reverse coded such that participants would rate the experience as being more hindering to their meditation session. Values presented here were reversed such that a higher score means fewer or lower levels of hindrances.

3.3 Correlation Analysis

All correlations were calculated using R; unless stated otherwise, correlations refer to Pearson's correlation.

For EDA analysis, we looked at change over time. For tonic EDA or skin conductance level (SCL), we analyzed mean EDA levels for two minutes during the fist two minutes, the halfway mark, and the last two minutes. All data were processed using the Python package Neurokit [26]. This follows the reasoning described in [15] and conducted in [27], that interventions can either raise or lower overall arousal levels. From those mean values, we calculated the change

Table 3. Descriptive statistics: meditation depth

	Mean	S.D.
Hindrances	3.83	0.76
Relaxation	3.83	0.35
Personal self	2.43	0.77
Trans Q	2.10	0.63
Trans self	2.17	0.72
Meditation depth	2.87	0.50

or delta between ending SCL and beginning SCL, with negative values indicating a reduction in arousal.

We also looked at the frequency and amplitude of skin conductance responses (SCRs). SCRs indicate how frequently an individual reacts to environmental triggers [15]. The amplitude of the responses indicate how strong those reactions are. We expected a reduction in the frequency and amplitude of SCRs between the first two minutes and last two minutes of the experience. We did see changes, but none were correlated with self-report measures (see Tables 4 and 5).

Table 4. Associations between factors of Meditation Depth (MEDI) and Electrodermal Activity. Delta refers to the difference between the last two minutes of the stimulus and the fist two minutes (*** < .001, ** < .01, < .05)

	Skin Conductance Response delta	Mean Amplitude Delta	Skin Conductance Level delta
Hindrinces	0.20	0.36	0.30
Relaxation	0.06	0.17	0.25
Personal Self	0.30	0.03	0.09
Transpersonal Self	0.22	0.30	−0.03
Transpersonal Qualities	0.25	0.26	0.28
MEDI	0.24	0.26	0.22

Presence and Electrodermal Activity Presence and EDA.

Perceived Restorativeness and Presence. We see moderate correlations between the factors of Away, Fascination, and Compatibility, as well as overall perceived restorativeness of the environment, and presence. Conceptually, there is some overlap between Away and presence, which would suggest that there should be a stronger correlation between the two variables. However, it appears as if participants are reporting that they felt partially transported to a new

Table 5. Associations between factors of Perceived Restorativeness (PRS) and Electrodermal Activity Delta refers to the difference between the last two minutes of the stimulus and the fist two minutes (*** < .001, ** < .01, < .05)

	Skin Conductance Response delta	Mean Amplitude Delta	Skin Conductance Level delta
Away	0.29	0.39	0.22
Fascination	0.07	0.23	−0.05
Coherence	0.38	−0.15	0.03
Compatibility	0.32	0.40	0.15
PRS	0.32	0.28	0.11

Table 6. Associations between Presence and Electrodermal Activity (EDA) Delta refers to the difference between the last two minutes of the stimulus and the first two minutes (*** < .001, ** < .01, < .05)

	Skin Conductance Response delta	Mean Amplitude Delta	Skin Conductance Level delta
Presence	0.03	0.18	−0.10

environment, but still away from their daily concerns. This could mean that being distracted by something that is slightly fascinating is sufficient enough to have a restorative effect.

Table 7. Relationship between presence and perceived restorativeness (*** < .001, ** < .01, < .05)

	Away	Fascination	Coherence	Compatibility	PRS
Presence	0.56**	0.44*	0.02	0.39	0.45*

Meditation Depth and Presence. Presence was moderately correlated with several factors of meditation depth. The associations between hindrances and presence suggests that elements of the virtual environment could have a distracting effect on the participant. One experienced meditator noted that the narrative was distracting and that it took awhile to get settled because they experienced a hard fascination versus soft fascination <ref>. That is, they spent too much time looking at the environment. The scores could also suggest that the virtual environment shields the participant from external stimuli.

Table 8 highlights the results of correlation analysis between presence and meditation depth (MEDQ). Presence was correlated with all factors of meditation depth except relaxation and transpersonal qualities. Presence was also correlated with the composite MEDI score.

Table 8. Relationship between Meditation Depth (MEDQ) and Presence (*** < .001, ** < .01, < .05)

	Hind	Relax	PersSelf	TransS	TransQ	MEDQ
Presence	0.52*	0.34	0.47*	0.50*	0.37	0.52*

Perceived Restorativeness and Meditation Depth. We saw strong correlations between the perceived restorativeness of the environment and meditation depth (0.7) (see Table 9). In particular, a sense of being away was highly correlated with lower levels of hindrances and higher levels of relaxation. Extent-Scope did not have strong correlations with the meditation depth factors, and fascination and compatibility had only moderate correlations with meditation depth factors. Overall, we see low or moderate correlations between the perceived restorativeness of the environment and meditation depth factors associated with skilled practitioners. We do not consider this to be a drawback of the environment because skilled practitioners should not need a virtual environment to practice. The idealized environment is designed to help novices get past the first stages of mindfulness practice, when tuning out external distractions is a challenge.

Table 9. Relationship between Meditation Depth (MEDQ) and Perceived Restorativeness (*** < .001, ** < .01, < .05)

	Away	Fascination	Coherence	Compatibility	PRS
Hinderances	0.81****	0.57**	0.26	0.60**	0.70***
Relaxation	0.72***	0.54*	0.40	0.52*	0.67***
PersonalSelf	0.59**	0.44*	0.42	0.49*	0.60**
TransQ	0.64**	0.30	0.39	0.46*	0.56**
TransS	0.41	0.28	0.20	0.19	0.34
MEDQ	0.78****	0.53*	0.41	0.56**	0.71***

4   Discussion

In contrast to previous studies, we found no relationship between changes in arousal, either measured as tonic electrodermal activity or frequency of skin conductance responses, over time and self-reported measures of perceived restorativeness. Therefore, we reject the first set of hypotheses that perceived restorativeness is positively correlated with a reduction in skin conductance level and that perceived restorativeness is significantly positively correlated with a reduction in the frequency of skin conductance responses.

We found a significant (p < .001) and strong correlation (0.71) between Meditation Depth and Perceived Restorativeness, as well as significant and strong correlations among the factors in each scale. Therefore, we accept hypotheses that meditation depth is significantly positively related to perceived restorativeness.

However, we found no significant associations between meditation depth and levels of arousal. Therefore, we reject the that meditation depth is positively related to a decrease in skin conductance level and that meditation depth is significantly positively related to a decrease in skin conductance responses.

We did find significant (p < .05) and moderate correlations between presence (r = 0.45) and perceived restorativeness (r = 0.52) as well as presence and meditation depth. Therefore, we accept the hypotheses that perceived restorativeness is positively correlated with presence and that meditation depth is positively correlated with presence.

We also found no associations between electrodermal activity and presence. The lack of correlations between EDA measures and self-report measures is perplexing as other researchers have found significant associations between the measures in similar experiments [13, 28]. We do not have a specific explanation, although the results could be due to our smaller sample size than Browning and colleagues. Andersen et al. [13] had a smaller sample size yet found significant effect of time and scene in changes in EDA. However, they intentionally induced stress prior to entering the virtual reality scene, which may have helped create a sufficiently large change to be statistically significant. Overall, we saw a mean reduction in tonic EDA with 81% of participants exhibiting a decrease in tonic EDA over the experiment. The few outliers who did experience an increase in tonic EDA during the experiment may have skewed the results.

Based on the self-report measures, we do see evidence that a restorative virtual environment is positively associated with meditation depth and quality. The small sample size of our project made it difficult to conduct more complex analysis that would help us tease out the differences in perceived restorativeness and meditation depth. Anecdotally, we got feedback from our experienced meditators. Some were fascinated by the environment and needed more time to settle, while others noted that the pace of the track or small details distracted them from the meditation.

In the future, we would like to focus on providing more variety in terms of meditation environments with the expectation that people would find environments that they are more compatible with. We would also like to explore how meditation experience affects interaction with virtual nature environments as well as baseline mood. We did do preliminary analysis on changes in affect but found no statistically significant correlations, unlike <browning>. Finally, we could look to do a controlled study, analyzing whether virtual reality provides any benefit beyond a smart phone app in terms of meditation session quality.

References

1. Kabat-Zinn, J., Hanh, T.N.: Full catastrophe living: Using the wisdom of your body and mind to face stress, pain, and illness. Delta (2009)
2. Bishop, S.R., et al.: Mindfulness: a proposed operational definition. Clin. Psychol.: Sci. Practice **11**(3), 230–241 (2004)
3. Goleman, D., Davidson, R.J.: Altered Traits: Science Reveals How Meditation Changes the Way Your Mind, Brain, and Body. Avery, New York (2017). ISBN 978-0-399-18438-3
4. Kiken, L., et al.: From a state to a trait: trajectories of state mindfulness in meditation during intervention predict changes in trait mindfulness. In: Personality and Individual Differences, July 2015. https://doi.org/10.1016/j.paid.2014.12.044
5. Costa, M.R., et al.: xR-based systems for mindfulness Based Training in clinical settings. In: HCI International 2018 Conference Proceedings. Elsevier, Las Vegas, July 2018
6. Costa, M.R., et al.: Nature inspired scenes for guided mindfulness training: presence, perceived restorativeness and meditation depth. In: Schmorrow, D.D., Fidopiastis, C.M. (eds.) HCII 2019. LNCS (LNAI), vol. 11580, pp. 517–532. Springer, Cham (2019). https://doi.org/10.1007/978-3-030-22419-6_37
7. Gromala, D., et al.: The virtual meditative walk: virtual reality therapy for chronic pain management. In: Proceedings of the 33rd Annual ACM Conference on Human Factors in Computing Systems. CHI 2015, pp. 521–524. ACM, New York (2015). ISBN 978-1-4503-3145-6. https://doi.org/10.1145/2702123.2702344. Accessed 01 Mar 2018
8. Kaplan, S.: The restorative benefits of nature: toward an integrative framework. J. Environ. Psychol. Green Psychol. **15**(3), 169–182 (1995). ISSN 0272–4944. https://doi.org/10.1016/0272-4944(95)90001-2. Accessed 29 Jan 2018
9. Kaplan, S., Berman, M.G.: Directed attention as a common resource for executive functioning and self-regulation. Perspect. Psychol. Sci. **5**(1), 43–57 (2010). ISSN 1745–6916. https://doi.org/10.1177/1745691609356784. Accessed 02 May 2019
10. Hartig, T., et al.: Tracking restoration in natural and urban field settings. J. Environ. Psychol. Restorative Environ. **23**(2), 109–123 (2003). ISSN 0272–4944. https://doi.org/10.1016/S0272-4944(02)00109-3. Accessed 31 Jan 2020
11. Kuo, F.E., Sullivan, W.C.: Aggression and violence in the inner city: effects of environment via mental fatigue. Environ. Behav. **33**(4), 543–571 (2001). ISSN 0013–9165. https://doi.org/10.1177/00139160121973124. Accessed 31 Jan 2020
12. Kaplan, S.: Meditation, restoration, and the management of mental fatigue. Environ. Behav. **33**(4), 480–506 (2001). ISSN 0013–9165. https://doi.org/10.1177/00139160121973106. Accessed 12 Mar 2018
13. Anderson, A.P., et al.: Relaxation with immersive natural scenes presented using virtual reality. Aerospace Med. Hum. Perform. **88**(6), 520–526 (2017). https://doi.org/10.3357/AMHP.4747.2017
14. Payne, S.R., Guastavino, C.: Exploring the validity of the perceived restorativeness soundscape scale: a psycholinguistic approach. English. Front. Psychol. 9 (2018). ISSN 1664–1078. https://doi.org/10.3389/fpsyg.2018.02224. Accessed 28 Jan 2020
15. Andreasi, J.L.: Electrodermal Activity (EDA) and behavior. In: Psychophysiology: Human Behavior & Physiological Response. 5th en, pp. 259–288. Psychology Press, New York (2007)
16. Piron, H.: The meditation depth index (MEDI) and the meditation depth questionnaire (MEDEQ). J. Medit. Medit. Res. **1**(1), 69–92 (2001)

17. Lee, K.M.: Presence, explicated. Commun. Theory **14**(1), 27–50 (2004). ISSN 1050–3293. https://doi.org/10.1111/j.1468-2885.2004.tb00302.x
18. Riva, G., et al.: Presence-inducing media for mental health applications. In: Lombard, M., Biocca, F., Freeman, J., IJsselsteijn, W., Schaevitz, R.J. (eds.) Immersed in Media, pp. 283–332. Springer, Cham (2015). https://doi.org/10.1007/978-3-319-10190-3_12
19. Baer, R.A., et al.: Using self-report assessment methods to explore facets of mindfulness, using self-report assessment methods to explore facets of mindfulness. Assessment **13**(1), 27–45 (2006). ISSN 1073–1911. https://doi.org/10.1177/1073191105283504. Accessed 03 Aug 2018
20. Thompson, E.R.: Development and validation of an internationally reliable short-form of the positive and negative affect schedule (PANAS). J. Cross-Cultural Psychol. **38**(2) (2007)
21. Cohen, S., Kamarck, T., Mermelstein, R.: A global measure of perceived stress. J. Health Soc. Behav. **24**(4), 385–396 (1983). ISSN 0022–1465. https://doi.org/10.2307/2136404. Accessed 03 Aug 2018
22. Hartig, T., et al.: A measure of restorative quality in environments. Scand. Housing Plan. Res. **14**(4), 175–194 (1997). ISSN 0281–5737. https://doi.org/10.1080/02815739708730435. Accessed 12 Mar 2018
23. Slater, M., Usoh, M., Steed, A.: Depth of presence in virtual environments. Presence: Teleoperators Virtual Environ. **3**(2), 130–144 (1994). ISSN 1054–7460. https://doi.org/10.1162/pres.1994.3.2.130. Accessed 03 Aug 08 2018
24. Hirshfield, L., et al.: Measuring the neural correlates of mindfulness with functional near infrared spectroscopy. In: Empirical Studies of Contemplative Practices. Nova (2019)
25. Hirshfield, L., et al.: Workload-driven modulation of mixed-reality robot-human communication. In: Proceedings of the Workshop on Modeling Cognitive Processes from Multimodal Data, p. 3. ACM (2018)
26. Makowski, D.: NeuroKit: a python toolbox for statistics and neurophysiological signal processing. In: Paris, November 2016. https://github.com/neuropsychology/NeuroKit.py
27. Andersen, T., et al.: A preliminary study of users' experiences of meditation in virtual reality. In: 2017 IEEE Virtual Reality (VR), pp. 343–344, March 2017. https://doi.org/10.1109/VR.2017.7892317
28. Browning, M.H.E.M., et al.: Can simulated nature support mental health? Comparing short, single-doses of 360-degree nature videos in virtual reality with the outdoors. English. Front. Psychol. 10 (2020). ISSN 1664–1078. https://doi.org/10.3389/fpsyg.2019.02667. Accessed 28 Jan 2020

Global Mindset - A Complex Cognitive Model Used for Global Leadership Decision-Making When Working Across Geographical Boundaries

Agnes Flett[⊠]

Windsor, England, UK

Abstract. There is universal agreement that working in a global environment presents unique challenges for international leaders, however there have not been any studies to ascertain what these unique challenges encompass and how they impact effective decision-making. Non-optimal decisions can have catastrophic consequences for the organization's finances, reputation and time. However, despite the acknowledged challenge, global leaders are expected to consistently make complex and demanding decisions without error. With such high stakes at play, we need to better understand what occurs inside the minds of these leaders. The researcher believes that the construct of Global Mindset aids effective decision-making when working across geographical boundaries. While there is no common agreement or definition of Global Mindset, the researcher proposes that it is a cognitive process, comprising a series of complex and linked cognitions. These create increased cognitive demands for global leaders relative to their domestic counterparts and present a higher risk of cognitive overload while making important decisions. Central to the research, is the development of grounded theory for the construct of Global Mindset, which is largely misunderstood. The researcher promotes the notion that Global Mindset is a cognitive process initiated by managing the paradox of two differing and conflicting sets of stakeholder needs; global versus local. By better understanding these cognitions, organizations can benefit from better selection and deployment decisions for these important roles and can also design better development interventions to aid cognitive resilience. Preferably development takes place at an early stage in the high-potential, emerging leaders talent pipeline, such that future global leaders are equipped for these unique cognitive demands prior to taking up these roles.

Keywords: Global leadership · Global Mindset · Cognition · Cognitive overload · Global versus local · Paradox management · Expert decision-making · Dual perspectives

1 Introduction

Notably, with no consistent definition of Global Mindset, we cannot claim to understand the antecedents, processes, or proximal and distal effects of how it affects global leader's decision-making. In this study, and reflective of the novel cognitive model proposed,

© Springer Nature Switzerland AG 2020
C. Stephanidis et al. (Eds.): HCII 2020, LNCS 12425, pp. 190–201, 2020.
https://doi.org/10.1007/978-3-030-60128-7_15

Global Mindset is a complex cognitive process and is defined as the ability to 'think and act both globally and locally at the same time' (Cohen 2010, p. 27). The implication is, that if a set of complex cognitions happen concurrently, there is an increased risk of cognitive overload. Therefore, through the study of how these cognitions manifest and are subsequently processed, the risk of overload is examined, along with how a dual perspective mindset is navigated by global leaders to make effective decisions.

Invariably studying cognitive processes are difficult, especially experts in their field as they often find it difficult to articulate what they think or do because their thoughts and actions have become automated and reside in the unconscious part of their brains. In order to address this issue, the study design utilized Cognitive Task Analysis (CTA) in the form of critical incident reporting, with a think out loud approach to promote conscious thought patterns. This allowed access to the participants thought processes, the considerations they made, why these were important, and finally the decisions they arrived at.

While accessing both conscious and unconscious thought processes in any cognitive study is considered challenging, the researcher leveraged from both the design of the study, and her background as a global leader such that she was able to navigate the global leader scenarios and the context in which they operated, in real-time alongside the study participants as they talked through their scenario's. This allowed quick follow-up questions to capture essential thought processes, while not disrupting the global leaders train of thought. This was deemed helpful in collecting useful data for analysis purposes.

2 The Cognitive Challenge

The research was designed to evidence that Global Mindset is in fact, a cognitive process and the study proposed a novel Global Mindset model. This comprised a complex set of cognitive processes which all global leaders seek to navigate through, in order to make effective decisions while working across geographical boundaries.

The model explains that Global Mindset is triggered by managing a tension between differing and often competing, global versus local stakeholder needs. Managing this tension is known as Paradox Management because the emphasis is on finding equilibrium rather than an overall best solution, which cannot realistically be achieved where there are conflicting agendas.

While there are cognitive challenges with holding a dual perspective for both global and local stakeholders, it also has its benefits as it allows the advantages and disadvantages from opposing sides to be fully evaluated before decision-making occurs. Notably, while categorizing and processing vast amounts of data in both their conscious and unconscious minds, the priority moves from finding a perfect solution to sourcing acceptable outcomes for both parties.

3 The Global Mindset Model and Its Propositions

The study proposed that the complexity experienced by international leaders is characterized by Paradox Management or the tension that is created between managing the demands of global stakeholders and local stakeholder needs, which are different and often in conflict with one another. Therefore, Paradox Management is the first stage and trigger point for activating Global Mindset as shown in Fig. 1 below. Once activation occurs, a series of complex cognitions occur simultaneously and which cumulatively result in effective decision-making.

Global Mindset Model

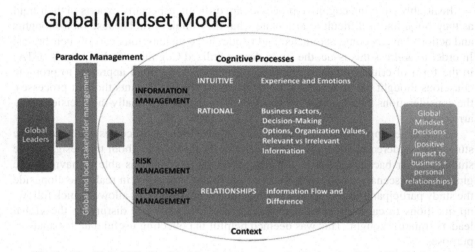

Fig. 1. The Global Mindset Model originating from Study 1 and validated in Study 2.

As shown in Fig. 1, once Global Mindset is activated by managing the paradox, three core components come into play to help sort the cognitive data; information management, risk management and relationship management and all data are categorized around these. Simultaneously, three sub-components are activated; rational information processing, intuitive information processing and relationships information processing, which then further divides into 8 factors aligned to either rational, intuitive or relationships information. All of these cognitions occur concurrently, which means that the global leader is filtering through vast amounts of data, using both the conscious and unconscious parts of their minds while also keeping both global and local requirements at top of mind. Subsequently, the risk of cognitive overload increases. In order to manage this, the global leader uses data filtering to manage the amount of data selected for processing, such that only the most relevant information is selected and processed. All other data are disregarded.

Finally, optimum decision-making occurs when the decision and its subsequent actions retain both positive work relationships, and provide positive outcomes for the business. Finding solutions that prioritize these equally are extremely important. Any decision-making options that impact either negatively will be eliminated and further processing will continue until a workable answer is found. This can be challenging, yet all global leaders will finalize their decisions paying particular attention to these factors.

4 Method

4.1 Grounded Theory and the Global Mindset Model

The model used a modified grounded theory approach, whereby theories of Global Mindset were reviewed and synthesized. The researcher then designed a novel cognitive model of Global Mindset with 14 propositions to explain the complexity that occurs inside the minds of global leaders and how they make effective decisions.

The proposed model was then tested using 2 studies to help better understand and delineate the cognitive processes underpinning Global Mindset; Study 1 - qualitative interviews and Study 2 – a quantitative online survey. Study 1 was used to test the proposed model and allow an opportunity for any modifications to be made prior to Study 2. Study 2 was then used to test the findings from Study 1 and to validate any modifications made to the model.

4.2 Study 1 – Qualitative Interviews

The qualitative interviews comprised of 8 high-potential high-performing global leaders from 2 different industry sectors; travel and engineering. The participants were identified as those who influenced and made decisions impacting both global and local stakeholders while working across geographical boundaries. The sample had between 1 and 3 grade levels between their job roles and the top of the organizational hierarchy, so these were some of the most senior leaders in their respective companies. Job titles ranged from Chief Transformation Officer, Senior Vice President/Director, and Manager. The average age of participants was 48 years old and the average length of service was 13 years. Participants were primarily caucasian (80%) and male (80%). The entire sample was located in the Western Hemisphere of the world.

The method used was Cognitive Task Analysis (CTA) in the form of critical incident reporting, which allowed insights into the cognitive skills or mental task demands of the international leaders while problem-solving and making effective decisions. Interviewees were emailed in advance with the interview script such that they had time to think about and prepare their critical incident. Permission was sought to record the interview and these were subsequently deleted after the transcriptions were typed up. All participants were advised that if the scenario described didn't meet the criteria, or they went off tangent during the interview, that the interviewer would stop them and redirect the conversation. This was to ensure maximum data collection during the scheduled 45-min interview per participant.

Interviewees were asked to describe a real-world scenario that they had managed in relation to a tension between meeting the needs of both global stakeholders and local stakeholders. They were asked to break the scenario down into 3 to 6 steps, although this was merely posed as guidance to help the interviewees organize their thoughts. The goal in fact, was for the SME to walk through the problem-solving task in their mind and verbalize the different stages up to the point that they were able to make a decision or decisions, relating to the scenario.

As each event was described, the researcher used probing questions for situation assessment, actions, critical cues, and potential errors including biases. The interviewer was very aware of her role in the data collection and therefore, she regulated both her choice of probing questions, comments made and the number of interruptions that were reasonable for each interview, such that it did not impact the direction of the conversation, nor speak on behalf of the interviewee. The researcher was able to make a constant comparison by listening to the interviewee, stopping them, summarizing what they had said to ensure the main themes or important points relating to the incident had been correctly identified, and also to check understanding. She was also able to give the interviewee an opportunity to rephrase or provide additional information, to change the direction of the interview, or clarify any misunderstandings regarding the interviewer's interpretation of the incident. This approach allowed the researcher to make connections in real-time between the interview data and the factors in the proposed Global Mindset model, such that she could jointly analyse and code the data. Therefore, the interviewer had a good sense of overall themes relative to the proposed model while also being open to alternatives, both during the interview and the subsequent data analysis.

The researchers use of probing questions during the interviews permitted a full understanding of the global leaders' rationale for their thought processes, including which information they used and which they disregarded and why, the factors which they considered and their thoughts leading up to their final decision. While the researcher was listening to the interviewees, she was also tapping into the emotions felt by them (happiness, frustration, disappointment, etc.) which aided her understanding of how the global leaders were making decisions.

Once the interviews were completed and recorded, the interviews were typed up verbatim and the recordings destroyed. Each interview was dissected sentence by sentence for meaning including any emotions that were displayed through tone of voice. This was especially important where two factors emerged in the same sentence, or where there was an overlap of factors such that it was difficult to determine which was being described. The emotions helped identify the underlying intention of the interviewee and therefore, the factor that was being utilized.

The researcher acted as the interviewer because she had previously been a global leader for a leading international professional services firm and had worked across 150 countries and had lived in 3 countries. She also had over 25 years applied practitioner experience working with senior executives and therefore, was familiar with the types of issues faced by businesses, organizational behaviour and the language pertaining to this population. This was important for the interpretation of the data and for coding purposes. The researcher's background was therefore considered instrumental in producing new insights into how global leaders think and behave.

After data collection, a thematic analysis was conducted to allow identification, analysis and reporting patterns and themes to be identified. The researcher knew from her own experience that broad themes would be required in both the design of the research model and in coding of the factors, on the basis that these categories or themes needed to apply to all types of scenarios and events that global leaders experience, which are wide ranging.

Next, a 3-stage procedure took place; unitizing, categorizing and classifying the data (Butterfield et al. 1996). First the Thought Units (TU's) were identified and this ranged from a phrase to several sentences. Second, the TU's were coded into emergent categories and finally, these categories were classified as a factor, either identifiable in the proposed model or a new factor was identified. Data was interpreted both semantically or explicitly; looking at surface level meanings generated from the words spoken by the interviewee and also latent or the interpretative level; broader meanings and interpretations. In the latter case, the intention of the interviewee was used to interpret the meaning and subsequent themes.

Any factors that appeared in at least 50% of the interviews were deemed to be significant, bearing in mind the range of different incidents described and the even wider range of contexts that exist for global leaders. Any new factors that also met this criterion were also sourced from the data and included in the modified model for testing in Study 2. Each interview was coded showing specific statements to support each of the factors identified in the data.

Once data analysis was completed, a second stage of analysis took place to identify whether any relationships existed between the factors identified. If this was the case, to also identify the direction of those relationships and whether the direction of the relationship went from one factor to another (A to B) or whether a reciprocal relationship (A <-> B) existed.

4.3 Study 2 – Online Survey

Study 2 retested the findings from Study 1 and where modifications were made to the proposed model, to test these. The modified Global Mindset model was therefore, validated with a different sample of 50 global leaders.

The method used was a quantitative online survey which was designed and pilot tested. Subsequently, some minor modifications were made to the instructions before its launch to the global leader sample. Each of the companies who participated in the study were asked to obtain only 12 global leaders within their respective organizations to complete the online survey, on the basis that this was likely to increase overall participation. Gaining access to this population is very difficult given the nature of their jobs, so smaller numbers made it more palatable for the participating companies.

The sample included 13 different industry sectors; agriculture, forestry and fishing, business services, construction, financial services/insurance, hospitality/entertainment/recreation, information technology, marketing, oil and gas, energy or utilities, other not specified, pharmaceuticals, professional services, telecommunications, and tourism. The number of job grades between the participants and the top of the organization hierarchy was zero to 5 or more. Typical job titles were Director/Vice President or Head of Business Unit. The average age was between 41 and 50 years old and the average number of years service was 11–15. Participants were primarily caucasian (86%) and male (62%). The entire sample was located in the Western Hemisphere of the world.

The survey comprised of 2 parts; first, a frequency of factor usage which measured 22 factor variables contained within the Global Mindset model, after Paradox Management had activated the cognitions and a 7-point Likert scale ranging from never to always was used to measure the frequency of factor usage. Means and standard deviations were then calculated to ascertain which factors were used most often. The second part of the online survey was a ranked order of importance measure used to assess the core 12 factors in the Global Mindset model affecting decision-making. Participants were asked to attribute a percentage to only those factors they considered the most important when making decisions and with an option to insert any other factors not already covered by the model. The factors selected however, had to total 100% in their combined usage. The survey questions were randomly ordered so that participants could not identify the themes being evaluated, with the exception of the last 3 questions which examined the factors the global leaders paid most attention to, when making an overall decision. This was the last part of the Global Mindset model where final decisions occur. In this case, the participants had to see all 3 options in order to compare and contrast their preferred response.

5 Findings

5.1 Study 1 – Qualitative Interviews

The first significant finding from Study 1 was that all global leaders related to the tension and conflicting demands between a global stakeholder group and a local stakeholder group and were able to give examples for the critical incident interviews. This evidenced that Paradox Management as defined in the Global Mindset model, does exist and is part of the global leader's role.

While the model remained largely unchanged between Study 1 and Study 2, two additional factors were added into the Global Mindset model based on the results of Study 1. Namely, risk management was added as one of the core components alongside information management and relationship management because it was mentioned in 100% of the interviews. Interestingly, the variety of industry sectors included in the research, and the nature of those businesses, might have suggested that some sectors would have different risk appetites in terms of their organizational culture relative to others. However, the results of the qualitative interviews demonstrated that risk was managed frequently and consistently across all industry sectors.

Also, organizational values were added as a new factor as it was reported in 50% of the interviews. This was attributed to rational information processing because global leaders described that they were consciously aware of using the organization's values to help steer the direction of their decisions. Finally, 2 factors were relabeled to reflect the interview data sourced from Study 1. First, culture was redefined as difference to reflect the broad range of scenarios that global leaders encountered. Whereas culture narrowly suggested that only organizational culture or national culture affected decisions, whereas there were a much broader range of differences experienced by global leaders that impacted their decision-making. Also, the factor of essential versus non-essential information was relabeled as relevant versus irrelevant information to reflect the language used by the interviewees.

Understandably, the researcher was challenged to gain sufficient data to support some of the unconscious mental processes referenced in the proposed model because no priming took place during Study 1. Therefore, the less tangible factors such as intuition were reported less often relative to other more tangible variables, such as business factors. While the data analysis showed that all factors in the proposed model were consistently reported in the qualitative interviews (reported in at least 50% of the interviews), intuition was reported in only 25% of the interviews. However, experience was reported in 100% of the interviews, and because intuition is reported to be strongly linked to experience as part of naturalistic decision-making (Klein 2008) and also Duggan's theory of strategic intuition (Duggan 2007), where experience is also closely linked to intuition, the researcher decided that it warranted further testing to establish whether intuition was more present in decision-making than participants were consciously aware of. On that basis, it was left in the modified model and retested during Study 2.

Finally, Global leaders were found to manage cognitive load through data filtering, such that only the most relevant information was retained. This involved excluding any additional noise and bias in the information (Kahneman et al. 2016). Global leaders may not however, be aware that this data separation occurs simultaneously in both the conscious and unconscious parts of their brains because the unconscious information processing creates a potential blind spot in the global leaders understanding of how the factors impact their decision-making.

5.2 Study 2 – Online Surveys

Overall, Study 2 confirmed that all factors in the modified model were present and utilized in decision-making. While Paradox Management creates the trigger point for Global Mindset activation, global leaders focus primarily on 3 core factors relevant to every situation; management of information, management of risk and management of relationships and these factors are underpinned by intuitive information processing, rational information processing and relationships information processing, which are further used to assess the 8 factors in the model; experience and emotions aligned to intuitive information processing, business factors, decision-making options, organizational values and relevant versus irrelevant information aligned to rational information processing and information flow and difference aligned to relationships information processing. Finally, all decisions made by global leaders are consciously evaluated in terms of its impact on relationships and the outcomes for the business. Equilibrium is sought between these 2 criteria, such that one does not take priority over the other. This fully supports the modified Global Mindset model.

Frequency of factor usage and importance of factors yielded different rankings in Study 2. Unsurprisingly, the unconscious factors in the model did not rank in the top ratings for frequency of usage which were; 1. risk management (consideration of the potential impact of risk on the business) and 2. risk management (the risks to the business) followed by 3. business factors (consideration of relevant business factors). Similarly, they did not manifest in the top rankings for importance which were; 1. business factors, followed by 2. rational data (facts and figures) and then 3. experience (self and others). From these results, it appears that the more tangible factors were more frequently used and were considered as more important relative to less tangible factors. This suggests that conscious awareness may have influenced the rank orderings in Study 2 resulting in conscious factors being ranked higher than unconscious factors.

Additionally, when all data was further examined to establish whether there were any significant correlations between factors, 78 different relationships were identified across the 8 qualitative interviews. This suggested that there was no commonality to these relationships, and that the relationships between factors were likely to be highly context specific as well as driven by the global leader's recollection of the events.

Finally, an interesting and yet unplanned finding from Study 2 was that the results showed that global leaders are not determined by their job titles nor seniority. Conversely, research to date seems to suggest that they are senior executives. However, this is not true as demonstrated by this research. The samples used in these studies showed that global leaders mostly exist at Manager level and above; some 4 or 5 levels from the top of the organizational hierarchy. However, there were also participants who were non-Managers or identified with the other professional categories and who were 5+ levels from the top of the hierarchy. This is an important point for future global leadership research.

6 Discussion

6.1 The Global Leaders Role

While the research did not actively seek to test out whether global leaders occupy roles at the top of the organizational hierarchy, in Study 1, only senior executives were included in the sample. However, in Study 2, with 50 participants and as part of the demographic data collected, it became clear that global leaders were not determined by their job titles nor seniority. This is perhaps as a result of flatter organizational structures and job roles which are more expansive, such that global leaders can be found at much lower levels in the organizational hierarchy than previously thought. In fact, the data supported that they can be found at almost any level across different industry sectors. The researcher therefore recommends that a generic definition of global leader is used for research purposes and that this should be 'those who influence and make decisions across geographical boundaries impacting both global and local stakeholders' and no reference is made to job title nor seniority. Providing narrowing definitions based on seniority are likely to harm research into this important topic and reduce the research pool.

6.2 The Global Mindset Model

While the sample size in Study 1 was relatively small, it was within the best practice guidelines for Cognitive Task Analysis (CTA), which is 3 to 5 persons per organization. Study 2 also used an adequate dataset of 50 participants. However, the combined studies showed their real value through the consistency of the results across 15 different industry sectors and with a total sample size of 58 global leaders. Therefore, confirming that the modified Global Mindset model was supported.

Risk featured strongly in the results of both Study 1 and 2. It is an important factor in business operations and in the language of business, so its presence during Study 1 was justified and warranted its insertion into the modified Global Mindset model for further testing in Study 2. However, perhaps less obvious is the connection between systems thinking and risk management. While we know from prior research that global leaders are proficient system thinkers, which require cause and effect cognitions, effective risk management also requires the consideration of cause and effect in order to appropriately assess risk. Therefore, this study provides some evidence that global leaders are both effective system thinkers and risk managers.

The importance of Paradox Management in global leadership research was high-lighted by this study. While it is not a new phenomenon, it appears to have been given limited exposure to date. The Centre for Creative Leadership (Leslie et al. 2015) pro-poses that Paradox Management is in fact, part of the healthy functioning of global organizations and therefore, must be a part of a global leader's role. Similarly, Beechler and Javidan (2007) suggests that Global Mindset is the key to competitive organizational success. Therefore, it is believed that managing paradoxes is a necessary part of a global leader's role and is part of healthy organizational dynamics. It is also an integral part of Global Mindset as evidenced by this study and therefore, ought to feature in future research. From an applied practitioner's perspective, the challenge for organizations will be to ensure that future global leaders have had an opportunity to practice managing this tension before they are formally appointed to these roles. This might be in the form of work-based assignments or being allocated to projects for a specific period of time as part of development planning.

6.3 Global Mindset as a Dual Perspectives Process

While there is no consensus that Global Mindset is a cognitive process, some authors who adopt this point of view, have ascertained that global leaders switch back and forth between datasets in order to make decisions (Clapp-Smith and Lester 2014). This research however, evidenced the reverse. Once irrelevant information is disregarded, global leaders retain all remaining information in their heads and holistically examine that data to make decisions versus any form of switching between data sets.

Similarly, other authors suggest that global leaders adopt either a Global Mindset (focused on more international matters) or a Local Mindset (focused on domestic issues), as if they are separate constructs and that the global leader adopts one or the other, but not both (Massingham 2013). This research however, evidenced that global leaders hold both global and local viewpoints simultaneously while problem-solving and decision-making occur. Global Mindset is therefore not just global, as its name suggests. It is both local and global, and more importantly, it requires the ability to hold dual perspectives simultaneously to make effective decisions.

6.4 Unconscious Cognitions

Notably, unconscious cognitions were the most difficult to validate through this research. This was reconfirmed when the researcher received an email from a participant after Study 2, thanking her for being included in the research. In the communication they wrote "I was not consciously aware of some of these processes", therefore confirm-ing that studying expert cognitions is difficult and that moving the SME's into con-scious awareness is a necessary step in both researching this topic and understanding the underlying cognitive processes.

While the overall design of this study was targeted at moving all of the factors from the unconscious into conscious self-awareness to aid accurate measurement, the extent of that was largely unknown. Unconscious factors were notably present in Study 1, and again in Study 2, however they were rated as less frequently used and less important relative to the conscious factors. This does raise an important point over the design of future cognitive studies, where there may be unconscious mental processes at work. This might be the only study where these factors have been tested in this way and therefore, their full impact may not be known. Further research is therefore recommended.

6.5 Perceptions and Memory

In Study 2, there were clear differences in the global leaders' self-assessments around frequency of factor usage versus importance of these. Risk management and business factors were top listed frequency factors and business factors, rational data and experience were top listed importance factors. Regardless of these differences, the top-ranking factors in both cases were tangible variables, notably in the global leader's conscious awareness. There is a question therefore, over the degree to which frequency and importance can be accurately measured because it was possible during this research, that the global leaders reported their perceived frequency of use and perceived importance of use versus their actual usage in real-world scenarios. In future research, it may be helpful to include others in the sample, such as the global leader's supervisor, their peers, and their subordinates to gain further insights into actual usage of the factors.

Also, because global leaders were asked to describe historic events, instead of reporting the event in real-time, they may not have been able to recall all of the information relating to the scenario and therefore, were unable to remember using some of the factors. This suggests that perceptions (bias) and memory (recall) may be potential moderators of the Global Mindset model. However, this would need to be tested in future research.

6.6 Technology and the Development of Global Mindset

The impact of this research will be fully realized at the point that a technology-enabled supplier chooses to develop software that provides expert decision-making simulations and creates learning pathways for novice global leaders. Human-computer simulations can offer an effective risk-free, and safe environment for this. The learning pathways could expose new recruits, or high-potential leaders targeted for future global leadership roles, to simulation exercises comprising real-world scenarios with complex problem-solving tasks. These simulations would involve large amounts of data, and measure the consideration of, and reactions to, different types of information and the sequencing of different variables, plus how risks were minimized and relationships retained before a final decision was made. Repeated use, with feedback provided after each simulation, could highlight optimal decision-making routes versus non-optimal and improve self-awareness while building the global leader's confidence in their abilities and their cognitive resilience. Additionally, given the risk of cognitive overload, the simulation could also incorporate measuring physiological factors such as heartrate and breathing to establish whether the global leader is regulating their stress levels while decision-making occurs.

These simulations could also be used as part of a selection battery for identifying high-potential global leaders who demonstrate the cognitive resilience to cope with the high demands of the role. Therefore, the same test environment could be used for more effective selection, development and career management of future global leaders, thus helping companies become more efficient by making better and lower-risk deployment decisions.

References

Beechler, S., Javidan, M.: Leading with a global mindset. Adv. Int. Manag. **19**, 131–169 (2007)

Cohen, S.L.: Acquiring a global leadership mindset: the new competitive advantage in the marketplace. Dev. Learn. Organ. **24**(4), 27–29 (2010)

Clapp-Smith, R., Lester, G.V.: Defining the "mindset" in global mindset: modeling the dualities of global leadership. Adv. Glob. Leadersh. **8**, 205–228 (2014)

Duggan, W.: Strategic Intuition: Creative Spark in Human Development. Columbia University, New York (2007)

Kahneman, D., Rosenfield, A.M., Gandhi, L., Blaser, T.: Noise: how to overcome the high, hidden cost of inconsistent decision making. Harvard Business Review (2016). https://hbr.org/2016/10/noise

Klein, G.: Naturalistic decision-making. Hum. Factors J. Hum. Factors Ergon. Soc. **50**(3), 456–460 (2008)

Lane, H.W., Maznevski, M.L., Mendenhall, M.: Globalization: hercules meets Buddha. In: The Blackwell Handbook of Global Management: A Guide to Managing Complexity, pp. 3–25 (2004)

Leslie, J.B., Lee, P.P., Zhao, S.: Managing Paradox. Blending East and West Philosophies to Unlock Its Advantages and Opportunities. Center for Creative Leadership, Greenboro, NC (2015)

Massingham, P.: Cognitive complexity in global mindsets. Int. J. Manag. **30**(1), 232–248 (2013)

Militello, L.G., Hutton, R.J.: Applied cognitive task analysis (ACTA): a practitioners toolkit for understanding cognitive task demands. Ergonomics **41**(11), 1618–1641 (1998)

Rhinesmith, S.H.: How can you manage global paradox? J. Corp. Account. Finan. **12**(6), 3–9 (2001)

Assessing Variable Levels of Delegated Control – A Novel Measure of Trust

Samson Palmer[1]([✉]), Dale Richards[2], Graham Shelton-Rayner[1], Kurtulus Izzetoglu[3], and David Inch[4]

[1] Coventry University, Coventry CV1 5FB, UK
palmer16@uni.coventry.ac.uk
[2] Nottingham Trent University, Nottingham NG11 8NS, UK
[3] Drexel University, Philadelphia, PA 19104, USA
[4] HORIBA-MIRA, Nuneaton CV10 0TU, UK

Abstract. Autonomous cars are set to drastically change the driving environment. The promise of a safer and more efficient driving experience has led to a significant rise in research surrounding human interaction with autonomous systems, however we must investigate ways to effectively integrate these systems and develop the partnership between human and autonomous system. In particular, understanding the nature of human-automation trust will ensure safe and efficient integration of these systems, and therefore investing in new measures of trust is key to the development of the human-automation partnership. This paper discusses findings of an experiment that examines the nature of human-automation interaction and the neural correlates associated with trust. Participants were asked to interact with unmanned vehicle control stations of varying levels of control and integrity, whilst prefrontal cortical activity was monitored using functional Near Infrared spectroscopy. The findings of this study suggest that the anterior prefrontal cortex (aPFC) is associated with uncertainty of the decision-making abilities of an autonomous system, whilst the ventrolateral prefrontal cortex (vlPFC) has been implicated in the development of distrust as a result of poor decision making. The findings present a new opportunity to develop a reliable measure of human-automation trust that could inform future system design and facilitate a safer and more effective human automation partnership.

Keywords: Trust · fNIRS · Human-automation partnership

1 The Human-Automation Partnership

Autonomous cars have the potential to radically change the driving environment. The quest towards safer roads has already led to various automated support systems being implemented into many modern vehicles such as cruise control and lane assistance systems, which are encompassed under a suite of Advanced Driver-Assistance Systems (ADAS) (Advanced Driver Assistance systems 2016). Yet whilst these tools assist with the driving task they rely on activation and utilization by the driver, with ultimate responsibility remaining with the human. Systems that incorporate ADAS can be categorized

© Springer Nature Switzerland AG 2020
C. Stephanidis et al. (Eds.): HCII 2020, LNCS 12425, pp. 202–215, 2020.
https://doi.org/10.1007/978-3-030-60128-7_16

using the Society of Automotive Engineers (SAE) levels of automation as level 2 autonomy (Richards and Stedmon 2017), but much of the current research in autonomous vehicles targets higher levels of autonomy with the hope of further reducing the responsibilities placed on the driver. However, removing the driver from the control loop entirely has both legal and public acceptance ramifications, so are somewhat unlikely. Therefore, the integration of autonomy into an automotive vehicle requires a better understanding of the critical partnership between human and machine. It is inevitable that, at some point during the journey the need to delegate physical responsibilities of the driving tasks between the driver and vehicle will occur. Thus, understanding and developing both the system and human element of the driving process is key to the progression of human and machine teaming. This synergy between human and machine lays the foundations for the development of the Human-Automation Partnership (HAP) – a key element to ensuring the safety and effectiveness of future progression and integration of autonomous systems with humans. Therefore, the development of these autonomous systems must be informed by the potential operator and understanding how the human will interact with these systems is pivotal in the design process.

Whilst significant literature exists that examines interactions between humans particularly in a cooperative environment, little is known about the interactions between the human and autonomy. Previous research provides information on the nature of human-only teams and how an effective partnership might work, and it is suggested that a HAP may operate with similar dynamics (Richards 2017). However, the dynamic partnership between human and autonomy may not be as straight-forward as it seems, with both human and autonomous system sharing tasks in parallel as well as scenarios where the human may play more of a subservient role; possibly even receiving commands from the system (Richards and Kaliardos 2019). Furthermore, for the partnership to be effective, the flow of information from autonomous system to human operator becomes a crucial part in allowing the human operator to understand what the system is doing. Thus, the cognitive functions associated with the human operator understanding the decision-making and consequent actions of the autonomous system, as well as the delegation of tasks between the two agents, becomes a crucial element in the integration and development of the HAP. Not surprisingly, this fluidity in the role of the human operator and autonomous system and the delegation between both agents of the HAP requires acceptance and trust (Richards 2017).

1.1 Automation and Trust

As previously discussed, the HAP has the potential to provide a safer and more efficient driving environment. However, acceptance and trust of autonomy and the development of this partnership between driver and system is a major determinant of the reliance people have towards automation and their intention to use it (Choi and Ji 2015). Trust between the human operator and autonomous system can lead to successful teaming and an effective HAP, however distrust can lead to ineffective use of automation whilst over-trust can lead to incorrect use and complacency and result in mistakes and failures (Parasuraman et al. 2014). Whilst autonomy may have numerous positive effects on the driver and wider driving environment, lack of, or misuse of the autonomous system would void any potential positive effects and therefore understanding trust and acceptance of autonomy and what determines this is key to the market viability of autonomous systems.

Understanding and quantifying trust can be somewhat difficult, especially when there is no universally accepted definition (Palmer et al. 2019); particularly trust between a human and a machine. Madsen and Gregor (2000) describe Human-Computer Trust (HCT) as the users' confidence and willingness to accept and act upon the decisions made by a computer or artificially intelligent aid system. Therefore, HCT is a multi-faceted phenomenon that requires both confidence in the capabilities of the system to complete the designated tasks, and the willingness to act upon the decisions and requests the system may make (Madsen and Gregor 2000). Furthermore, an element of faith is required from the human operator to delegate to, and act upon the information they have received from the system, with the hope that the system will complete the tasks safely and effectively. However, overconfidence in the systems' capabilities can occur particularly when the system is only partially automated and still requires input from the human operator upon request from the system (Choi and Ji 2015; Lee and See 2004). As a result, it is important to understand and calibrate the level of trust required from the human operator against the abilities of the system. Increased autonomous capabilities should in-turn reduce human operator oversight of the system and increase trust and reliance, whereas partial or limited autonomous systems should require proportional levels of vigilance and system monitoring (Wickens 1995). Therefore, understanding how the human operator interacts with varying levels of autonomy and various system capabilities is key to ensuring that the partnership between human and machine operates safely and efficiently. Further understanding how the human operator trusts the system can inform design processes of autonomous systems to ensure correct and safe utilization of autonomy and a functioning HAP.

Several methods for assessing trust exist in the literature, such as the Empirically Derived (ED) 12 item scale (Jian et al. 2000), the Human-Computer Trust (HCT) scale (Madsen and Gregor 2000), and the SHAPE Automation Trust Index (SATI) (Woldring et al. 2003). However, whilst these tools have benefited from systematic development and validation they are often flawed. For example, ED is an abstract measure of trust and does not reflect trust of a specific system, whilst HCT lacks confirmatory analysis of trust, and the development of SATI lacked construct validity and psychometric validation (Lewis et al. 2018). As a result, these scales can often result in unreliable data through operator bias towards certain criteria and the scales themselves are modelled around human-only interactions and trust (Lewis et al. 2018). Furthermore, almost all human-automation trust research focusses on the behavioral elements of trust with very little focus on the neural mechanisms surrounding trust of automation and autonomous systems (Parasuraman et al. 2014). Izzetoglu and Richards (2019) also suggest that the validity of using a sole metric of such a complex human behavior is unsafe and thus assessment of trust should further include both behavioral (such as task completion) and physiological assessment where possible. Indeed, various studies have attempted to assess the neural correlates of social interactions between humans and infer about changes to mental state as a result of certain dispositions such as trustworthiness and reliability (Krueger et al. 2007; Bos et al. 2009; Filkowski et al. 2015; Sripada et al. 2009). These studies are based on social neuroeconomics and have utilized methods such as economic game theory to assess human-only trust. The results implicated various regions of the prefrontal cortex as key to the interaction and trust of other humans (Sripada et al. 2009), and whilst these studies do not account for human-autonomy interactions they do provide evidence of active cognitive functions associated with trust and provide an ideal starting point for assessing human-autonomy trust. In terms of localizing the physiological components of cognition, the prefrontal cortex has been associated with reciprocal trust, another key element of human social interactions and the forming of partnerships (Kreuger et al. 2007). Although these studies again focus on human-human interactions, it is reasonable to assume that the development of a partnership between human and autonomous system will mirror elements of social interactions and reciprocal trust. Thus, assessing prefrontal cortical activity during human-autonomy interactions could provide valuable information pertaining to the interaction between human and autonomous system.

1.2 A Novel Approach to Assessing Trust

Whilst the current literature provides a good foundation for understanding the neural correlates associated with human-autonomy trust (de Visser et al. 2018; Wang et al. 2018) there are limitations to these studies, particularly in the methods used and the ability to extrapolate these into real-world environments. Previous studies have used functional Magnetic Resonance Imaging (fMRI) and Electroencephalography (EEG) as measures of brain activity, and whilst these methods can infer the neural correlates of trust in a laboratory environment, they are limited in their uses elsewhere. This is particularly true of the driving environment, due to their size and lack of portability. Understanding the neural correlates of trust associated with the HAP in the driving environment requires a new approach to measuring cognitive function. Advances in portable, wearable neuroimaging techniques such as functional Near Infrared Spectroscopy (fNIRS) have provided opportunities to assess neural activity associated with trust in such environments.

Similar to fMRI, fNIRS monitors and assesses hemodynamic changes associated with varying brain activity levels within the Prefrontal Cortex (PFC), as neural activation and vascular response are closely linked and are often shown to maintain a lineal response. This relationship between haemodynamic response and brain activity is referred to as neurovascular coupling (Leon-Carrion and Leon-Dominguez 2012). fNIRS works by radiating tissue with light sources of specific wavelengths, and then using light detectors to receive that light after it has interacted with this absorbed/deflected from the tissue. Most biological tissues are relatively transparent to infrared light with a wavelength between 700–900 nm, often referred to as the optical window as the absorbance of the main elements within human tissue is small, allowing the light to penetrate. However, oxygenated hemoglobin (oxy-Hb) and deoxygenated hemoglobin (deoxy-Hb) are amongst some of the main chromophores (absorbing agents) within this optical window that are strongly linked to tissue oxygenation and metabolism (Izzetoglu et al. 2007). The mobilization of these chromophores is directly related to cerebral blood flow (CBF) associated with a specific event in time and the consequential physiological responses within the brain (Leon-Carrion and Leon-Dominguez 2012). Additionally, they have significantly different absorption spectra allowing for spectroscopic separation using variable wavelengths. fNIRS utilizes these specific wavelengths within the optical window, radiating the tissue with infrared light (see Fig. 1). The photons that are emitted through this tissue undergo two types of interaction: absorption and scattering. The photons are either scattered by the extra- and intracellular boundaries within the head (such as the skin, skull and cerebrospinal fluid), or absorbed by the main chromophores – in this instance the oxy-Hb and deoxy-Hb. Photodetectors are then employed a specific distance from the light source and collects photons that are not absorbed and that travel along a specific "banana shaped path" between the source and detector as a result of scattering (Izzetoglu et al. 2007). Figure 1 demonstrates how the photons are emitted from a centrally placed light source, and the scattered photons that follow this path are collected by photodetectors.

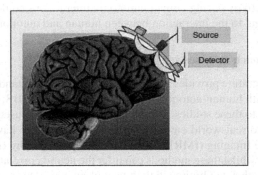

Fig. 1. Photons are emitted from the light source to the PFC where they are either absorbed or scattered and photodetectors collect scattered photons that travel along the "banana shaped path" (Izzetoglu et al. 2007).

Through neurovascular coupling, fNIRS presents the ability to measure prefrontal cortical activity through changes to hemodynamic response in the surrounding capillaries. The PFC is often associated with processing higher cognitive functions, many of which can be aligned with driver cognition and the effects of the driving environment. For example, remembering directions requires Working Memory, whilst situational awareness and vigilance is required to monitor the surrounding environment, and attention is required to react to sudden changes that may occur. fNIRS uses an array of optodes to assess regions of the PFC, providing the ability to monitor individual regions associated with different task types and the resulting cognitive activity. As such, the ability to assess cognitive function in a driving environment could provide a better understanding of how humans interact with vehicles in both manual and autonomous driving conditions, providing useful information on the capacity of the autonomous systems to aid the driver in reducing cognition and freeing cognitive resources. Furthermore, it may provide a method for assessing the neural correlates of trust of autonomous systems, thus ensuring that the HAP is developed in order to facilitate a safer and more efficient driving environment.

To determine the viability of fNIRS as means for assessing cognition and trust, cognitive function must first be assessed in a laboratory environment to validate the application of fNIRS. This paper discusses a recent study that attempted to assess the cognitive changes associated with the trust associated with different autonomous systems. The study attempts to validate fNIRS as a method for assessing trust through changes in PFC activity during exposure to systems with varying levels of autonomy, by introducing "flawed" autonomous systems in order to determine how autonomous system failure can impact trust and ultimately disrupt the HAP. It was hypothesized that changes to PFC oxygenation levels during exposure to varying levels of autonomy would indicate changes in trust, whilst further assessing how autonomous system failure can impact operator trust. This study follows a previous experiment that assessed and mapped different cognitive functions to the PFC through exposure to varying tests designed to elicit cognitive responses that can be aligned with the driving task.

2   Experimental Design

During this study, participants (N = 23) were asked to supervise 8 unmanned vehicles of varying capabilities via a Ground Control Station (GCS), with the visual interface shown in Fig. 2. Unmanned vehicles were a combination of aerial and ground vehicles (UxV) and were either given sensor scanning abilities or weapons systems. Participants were tasked with defending four military bases (indicated in Fig. 2 as A, B, C and D), whilst using the UxVs to respond to various scenarios over a period of three to four minutes. The scenarios involved using command systems with varying levels of autonomous support to protect the bases from enemy units, escorting civilians to safety, or escorting VIPs from one base to another. Four GCS types were used: Assisted Manual Mode (AMM), which provided the participant with a number of command inputs they could select that were chosen based solely on the unmanned vehicles closest to the target; Assisted Autonomous Mode (AAM), which provided the participant with the best calculated response to the target but required approval beforehand; and two Fully Autonomous Modes (FAM), which calculated responses and acted upon them, with no input from the participant. Each GCS provided information on UxV capability including sensor/weapon status, fuel level and current assignment of the drone, as well as location of any other signals in relation to the Bases.

During each scenario, a series of events were triggered by unknown tracks appearing on the GCS, and the participant was tasked with interrogating the signal using the most appropriate vehicle (equipped with an appropriate sensor), at which point the participant would then respond accordingly (i.e. send an attack vehicle if the signal was hostile). These decisions would be based around vehicle capability and location in relation to the unknown signal. Mission success would occur if all four Bases remained intact by the end of the scenario, and no civilians were lost in the process. When operating the AMM mode GCS, participants were presented with two or three options provided by the system based solely on distance to target, regardless of vehicle capability and status (the closest UxV was presented as the first option). This could result in the system recommending an attack vehicle or one with failed sensors/weapon systems as the best option even before interrogating the unknown signal. When operating the AAM mode GCS, participants were presented with the best vehicle to send based on distance to target and vehicle capabilities, and the system followed an always-scan-first protocol to determine whether the unknown system was friendly or hostile. Participants would

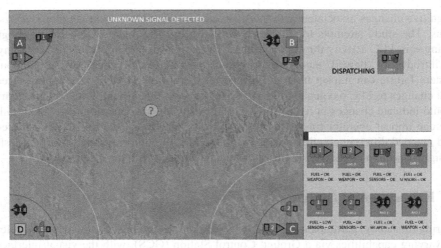

Fig. 2. Screenshot from the Full Auto Correct task showing an unknown signal on the GCS, and the consequent UxV response made by the system

then select YES if they agreed with the decision, or NO if they did not, at which point a secondary option would be provided. However, the AAM mode GCS had back-up safety protocols that prevented the user from selecting NO to all options, if it presented a significant risk to the safety of a Base, and therefore some of the options presented were only given a YES option to ensure Base protection.

For both FAM mode GCS scenarios, participants were tasked with monitoring the system and had no input capabilities. However, the integrity one of the FAM systems was manipulated to be perceived as "flawed" – this was achieved by creating an attack-on-sight protocol which resulted in only attack vehicles being used. This system ultimately failed the mission by harming a citizen transport that would have been marked as friendly had it been scanned first. The other FAM system was designed similarly to the AAM system in that it calculated the best possible decision, however it then immediately acted upon the decision without human interaction. This system was designed to end in mission success. All system exposures were counterbalanced to prevent order effects within a repeated measures design.

3 Analysis and Results

To assess prefrontal cortical activity fNIRS neuroimaging sensors were placed on the forehead of the participant to assess hemodynamic changes in the capillaries within the prefrontal cortex, as described above. A 5-min baseline was recorded before participants were presented with details and instructions for completing each scenario. fNIRS data was recorded throughout the duration of the study, and markers were used to indicate start and end points of scenarios. Following completion of the study, fNIRS data was filtered through a Low-Pass filter and an artefact removal processor, and then the processed optical density data was extracted (Izzetoglu and Richards 2019), where a modified

Beer-Lambert Law (MBLL) was applied for calculations of channel-specific changes in oxygenated hemoglobin (oxy-Hb) and deoxygenated hemoglobin (deoxy-Hb). Data was collected across 16 optodes as shown in Fig. 3.

Once oxygenation data had been calculated as stated above, the data was exported to oxygenation changes (OXY = oxy-Hb to deoxy-Hb) across each optode, for each scenario of the study. This data was then imported to SPSS and analyzed using a top-down approach. Table 1 shows how optodes were analyzed by firstly grouping into corresponding hemisphere, then into groups of four, and finally into pairs. Optodes were paired together rather than analyzed individually due to the naturally occurring differences in participant head size and head band positioning, and the consequent overlap of optode placement on the pre-frontal regions by the fNIRS headband.

Table 1. Schematic showing how optodes were grouped during analysis

Optode Groupings									
Left Hemisphere (1-8)					Right Hemisphere (9-16)				
Group 1-4		Group 5-8			Group 9-12			Group 13-16	
1+2	3+4	3+5	5+7	7+8	7+9	9+11	11+12	11+13	13+15	15+16
1+3	2+4	4+6	5+6	6+8	8+10	9+10	10+12	12+14	13+14	14+16

Due to the high inter-participant variance in mean OXY values within each optode group, an Independent T-test was used to determine whether there was a significant main effect for the weighted mean of each optode grouping, in turn preventing the effects of the high variance.

Each task was compared against the Baseline values for each Optode grouping. Mean OXY values for each task across each individual Optode are shown in Fig. 3. Independent T-tests were then conducted for each optode grouping as shown in Table 1. The Left Hemisphere Group showed a significant increase $t(170) = -2.783$, $p < 0.05$ in mean OXY during the Assisted Manual task, whilst the Right Hemisphere Group showed a significant increase $t(168) = -4.127$, $p < 0.05$ and $t(168) = -2.811$, $p < 0.005$ in OXY for the Assisted Auto and Assisted Manual Tasks, respectively. Group 9–12 showed a significant increase for the Assisted Auto task ($t(86) = -2.652$, $p < 0.05$) and the Assisted Manual task ($t(86) = -3.099$, $p < 0.05$), whilst Group 1–4 and 13–16 showed a significant increase ($t(86) = -2.621$, $p < 0.05$ and $t(81) = -2.711$, $p < 0.05$, respectively) for the Assisted Manual task only. The Independent T-tests for the Optode pairs showed varying significant increases for the Assisted Auto, Assisted Manual, and the Full Auto Incorrect task. Figures 4 to 6 are graphical representations of these Optode pairs, and areas highlighted showed a significant increase in OXY values for each task.

As can be seen in Figs. 4 and 5, Optode pair 2+4, 10+12, and 11+12 showed a significant increase ($t(44) = -2.024$, $p < 0.05$, $t(42) = -2.242$, $p < 0.05$, and $t(44) = -2.401$, $p < 0.05$ for the Assisted Auto task, and $t(44) = -2.965$, $p < 0.05$, $t(42) = -3.056$, $p < 0.05$, and $t(44) = -2.663$, $p < 0.05$ for the Assisted Manual task, respectively) in OXY values against the baseline. Optode pair 10+12 and 11+12 are aligned with the anterior prefrontal cortex (also referred to as Brodmann's area 10), whilst Optode pair

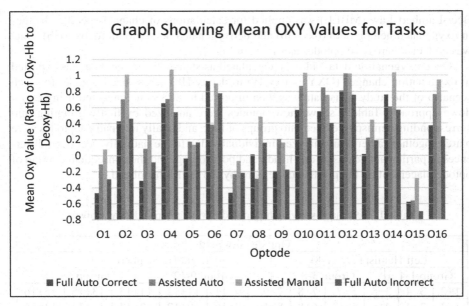

Fig. 3. A column graph showing mean OXY values for each optode during each task.

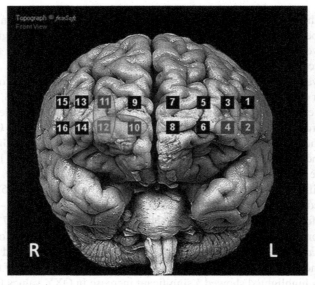

Fig. 4. A topographical image indicating optode placement, with optode pairs highlighted that show a significant increase in OXY during the Assisted Auto task.

2+4 are aligned with the dorsolateral prefrontal cortex (also referred to as Brodmann's area 46).

Figures 5 and 6 both demonstrate a significant increase in OXY values at Optode pair 4+6 (t(45) = −1.920, p < 0.05 for Assisted Manual, and t(45) = −2.278, p < 0.05 for Full Auto Incorrect) and Optode Pair 12+14 (t(45) = −1.814, p < 0.05 for Assisted Manual, and t(45) = −2.189, p < 0.05 for Full Auto Incorrect) against the baseline. Optode pair 12+14 are aligned with the right ventrolateral prefrontal cortex (vlPFC), whilst Optode pair 4+6 is aligned with the left vlPFC.

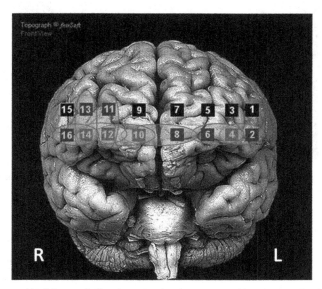

Fig. 5. A topographical image indicating optode placement, with optode pairs highlighted that show a significant increase in OXY during the Assisted Manual task

Figure 5 demonstrates a significant increase in OXY values during the Assisted Manual task at Optode pairs 8+10 (t(37) = −2.098, p < 0.05), 13+14 (t(43) = −2.492, p < 0.05), and 14+16 (t(44) = −3.408, p < 0.05), that were not activated in any other task. These regions correlate with the anterior prefrontal cortex (aPFC) (also referred to as Brodmann area 10) for Optode pair 8+10, and the dorsolateral prefrontal cortex (dlPFC) for Optode pairs 13+14 and 14+16.

There was no significant increase in OXY values during the Full Auto Correct task, suggesting that participants cortical activity implied that the decision-making abilities of the system was acceptable and therefore the monitoring of the system required minimal PFC activity.

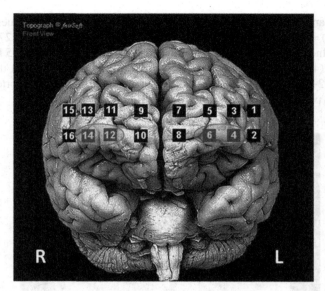

Fig. 6. A topographical image indicating optode placement, with optode pairs highlighted that show a significant increase in OXY during the Full Auto Incorrect task.

4 Discussion

Autonomous systems offer potential benefits through assisting humans in many ways, including in a driving environment. Indeed, recent advancements in automated technologies have already shown notable reductions in traffic fatalities yet have the potential to further improve the safety of our roads (Choi and Ji 2015). However, observations of human interactions with automation have shown failure to utilize autonomous systems even when advantageous to do so (referred to as disuse) or have shown complacency in accepting automation recommendations without proper monitoring of these systems (referred to as misuse) (Lewis et al. 2018). However, understanding how humans come to rely on and trust an autonomous systems' decisions can help to inform the design of the system (Dzindolet et al. 2003), and therefore measuring human-automation trust is imperative. Whilst research has been conducted around the neural mechanisms associated with trust, most have focused on the social aspects of interpersonal trust, with very little attention given to human-automation trust beyond the behavioral aspects (Parasuraman et al. 2014). This study attempts to bridge the gap between interpersonal and automation trust assessment by utilizing a novel measure of prefrontal cortical activity to determine the neural correlates associated with human-automation trust. Participants completed several tasks using a GCS with varying levels of autonomous support, during which prefrontal cortical activity was measured using fNIRS.

The Assisted Auto and Assisted Manual conditions elicited similar cognitive responses in the aPFC region (Brodmann's area 10), and the right dlPFC (Brodmann's area 46). Both these tasks required decision-making from the participant, and whilst this level of support from the system varied the ultimate decision came down to the participant. This would infer that these regions of the PFC are associated with the decision-making process. The aPFC is further associated with a variety of cognitive functions including risk and decision-making, along with working memory (Peng et al. 2018). This would suggest that the decision-making aspects of these tasks may have provoked a significant cognitive response in these regions. On the other hand, the dlPFC region has been implicated in goal-directed behavior and action selection tasks (Coutlee and Huettel 2012; Mars and Grol 2007) which could explain the significant increase in cognitive activity in these regions during interaction with the GCS.

Both the Assisted Manual and the Full Auto Incorrect tasks resulted in a significant increase in OXY values across similar regions of the PFC. Whilst these tasks differed in the required interaction from the participant, the Full Auto Incorrect task was designed to make decisions that could be conceived as being wrong or flawed, and consequently elicit uncertainty and distrust of the system. There is limited research regarding the exact neural mechanisms associated with trust and distrust, however the right ventrolateral prefrontal cortex (vlPFC) has previously been implicated in uncertainty of response tasks (Levy and Wagner 2011). Optode pair 12+14 may be seen to be aligned with this region of the PFC; suggesting an associated cognitive response due to the uncertainty of decision making by the system. This could also explain an uncertainty of decision making during the Assisted Manual task and demonstrate a lack of confidence in the participants' own decision-making abilities. Additionally, significant increases in the region surrounding Optode pair 4+6 can be aligned with increased activity in the left vlPFC. Again, research is limited regarding the left vlPFC's role in trust and uncertainty, however this region has previously been implicated in the development of distrust as a result of discerning a bad reputation (Suzuki et al. 2016). This could suggest that during the Full Auto Incorrect and the Assisted Manual tasks, once the participant began to perceive a level of uncertainty about the systems' or their own decision-making abilities, a consequent level of distrust was developed and resulted in the increased activity seen in the left vlPFC. This can be further supported when comparing the Full Auto Incorrect to the Full Auto Correct task. Both these tasks utilized the same display methods and level of information, with the only discernable difference being the approach each system took in response to an unknown signal appearing on the GCS. Whilst the Full Auto Incorrect systems' decisions were purposefully flawed, the Full Auto Correct system was designed to act upon decisions that could be perceived as ideal and correct, using a "scan-before-attack" approach rather than "attack-on-sight" approach and resulting in mission success. Therefore, the increased cognitive activity during the Full Auto Incorrect task could be associated with the increased distrust of the system.

The Assisted Manual task resulted in a significant increase in OXY values around regions of the aPFC and the dlPFC that were not activated in any other task. Whilst the aPFC is involved in decision making as mentioned previously, it is also largely associated with complex problem-solving and planning (Koechlin et al. 1999). The aPFC is known to comprise of at least two subregions: medial and lateral (Peng et al. 2018). This could explain the increased activity in regions not seen in the other tasks, perhaps due to the problem-solving nature of the Assisted Manual task. Additionally, the dlPFC, specifically the right side, has been shown to be associated with controlling the interactions between Working Memory (WM) and attention during visual control tasks, particularly when responses to the task are memory-guided (Wang et al. 2018). The Assisted Manual task required participants to respond to unknown events presented to them through the appearance of unknown signals on the GCS interface, by allocating a UxV to gather more information on the unknown signal in order to respond appropriately. This meant participants had to remember the capabilities of each UxV at their disposal and act upon the visual event presented to them, which could explain the increased activation of the right dlPFC region.

5 Conclusion

Whilst these findings are exploratory in nature, they present an exciting first step towards creating a robust and reliable method of assessing human-automation trust which can help to inform the design and integration of future autonomous systems. This would apply to not only autonomous vehicles but in all cases where humans could interact with intelligent systems offering varying levels of autonomous support. The neurological data begins to show an emerging pattern of cortical activation in regions of the PFC that have previously been associated with trust. This demonstrates that using fNIRS as a measure of cognitive activity has huge potential in a vast number of scenarios and environments due to its portability, ease of use, and relatively cheap availability compared to previous neuroimaging devices. Indeed, there were limitations to the research including the relatively low fidelity of the GCS interface, the small number of participants that completed the study, and the lack of other supporting measures of trust specific to the types of tasks during this study. However, these first steps to understanding human-automation trust, from a cognitive perspective can help inform future studies. The application of fNIRS as a tool for measuring trust within different HAP paradigms presents an exciting opportunity. Our next study will examine the use of this approach using a live test track and an autonomous car.

References

Advanced driver assistance systems (2016). https://ec.europa.eu/transport/road_safety/sites/roa dsafety/files/ersosynthesis2016-adas15_en.pdf

Bos, W., Dijk, E., Westenberg, M., Rombouts, S., Crone, E.: What motivates repayment? Neural correlates of reciprocity in the trust game. Soc. Cogn. Affect. Neurosci. 4(3), 294–304 (2009)

Choi, J., Ji, Y.: Investigating the importance of trust on adopting an autonomous vehicle. Int. J. Hum.-Comput. Interact. 31(10), 692–702 (2015)

Coutlee, C., Huettel, S.: The functional neuroanatomy of decision making: prefrontal control of thought and action. Brain Res. 1428, 3–12 (2012)

de Visser, E., et al.: Learning from the slips of others: neural correlates of trust in automated agents. Front. Hum. Neurosci. 12, 309 (2018)

Dzindolet, M., Peterson, S., Pomranky, R., Pierce, L., Beck, H.: The role of trust in automation reliance. Int. J. Hum.-Comput. Stud. 58(6), 697–718 (2003)

Filkowski, M.M., Anderson, I.W., Haas, B.W.: Trying to trust: brain activity during interpersonal social attitude change. Cogn. Affect. Behav. Neurosci. 16(2), 325–338 (2015). https://doi.org/ 10.3758/s13415-015-0393-0

Izzetoglu, M., Bunce, S., Izzetoglu, K., Onaral, B., Pourrezaei, K.: Functional brain imaging using near-infrared technology. IEEE Eng. Med. Biol. Mag. **26**(4), 38–46 (2007)

Izzetoglu, K., Richards, D.: Human performance assessment: evaluation of wearable sensors for monitoring brain activity. In: Vidulich, M., Tsang, P. (eds.) Improving Aviation Performance Through Applying Engineering Psychology: Advances In Aviation Psychology, vol. 3, 1st edn, pp. 168–169. CRC Press, London (2019)

Jian, J., Bisantz, A., Drury, C.: Foundations for an empirically determined scale of trust in automated systems. Int. J. Cogn. Ergon. **4**(1), 53–71 (2000)

Koechlin, E., Basso, G., Pietrini, P., Panzer, S., Grafman, J.: The role of the anterior prefrontal cortex in human cognition. Nature **399**(6732), 148–151 (1999)

Krueger, F., et al.: Neural correlates of trust. Proc. Natl. Acad. Sci. **104**(50), 20084–20089 (2007)

Lee, J., See, K.: Trust in automation: designing for appropriate reliance. Hum. Factors J. Hum. Factors Ergon. Soc. **46**(1), 50–80 (2004)

Leon-Carrion, J., Leon-Dominguez, U.: Functional near-infrared spectroscopy (fNIRS): principles and neuroscientific applications. InotechOpen (2012)

Levy, B., Wagner, A.: Cognitive control and right ventrolateral prefrontal cortex: reflexive reorienting, motor inhibition, and action updating. Ann. N. Y. Acad. Sci. **1224**(1), 40–62 (2011)

Lewis, M., Sycara, K., Walker, P.: The role of trust in human-robot interaction. In: Abbass, H.A., Scholz, J., Reid, D.J. (eds.) Foundations of Trusted Autonomy. SSDC, vol. 117, pp. 135–159. Springer, Cham (2018). https://doi.org/10.1007/978-3-319-64816-3_8

Madsen, M., Gregor, S.: Measuring human-computer trust. In: 11th Australasian Conference on Information Systems, Held 2000 (2000)

Mars, R., Grol, M.: Dorsolateral prefrontal cortex, working memory, and prospective coding for action. J. Neurosci. **27**(8), 1801–1802 (2007)

Palmer, S., Richards, D., Shelton-Rayner, G., Inch, D., Izzetoglu, K.: Human-autonomy teaming: an evolving interaction paradigm part III: an innovative measure of trust. In: International Symposium on Aviation Psychology, Held 2019 at Dayton, Ohio, pp. 1–5 (2019)

Parasuraman, R., de Visser, E., Wiese, E., Madhavan, P.: Human trust in other humans, automation, robots, and cognitive agents. In: Proceedings of the Human Factors and Ergonomics Society Annual Meeting, vol. 58, no. 1, pp. 340–344 (2014)

Peng, K., Steele, S., Becerra, L., Borsook, D.: Brodmann area 10: collating, integrating and high level processing of nociception and pain. Progress Neurobiol. **161**, 1–22 (2018)

Richards, D.: Escape from the factory of the robot monsters: agents of change. Team Perform. Manag. Int. J. **23**(1/2), 96–108 (2017)

Richards, D., Kaliardos, B.: Human-autonomy teaming - an evolving interaction paradigm: teaming and automation. In: International Symposium on Aviation Psychology, Held 2019 (2019)

Richards, D., Stedmon, A.: Designing for human-agent collectives: display considerations. Cogn. Technol. Work **19**(2–3), 251–261 (2017). https://doi.org/10.1007/s10111-017-0419-1

Sripada, C., Angstadt, M., Banks, S., Nathan, P., Liberzon, I., Phan, K.: Functional neuroimaging of mentalizing during the trust game in social anxiety disorder. NeuroReport **20**(11), 984–989 (2009)

Suzuki, A., et al.: Involvement of the ventrolateral prefrontal cortex in learning others' bad reputations and indelible distrust. Front. Hum. Neurosci. **10**, 28 (2016)

Wang, Y., de Veciana, G., Shimizu, T., Lu, H.: Performance and scaling of collaborative sensing and networking for automated driving applications. In: 2018 IEEE International Conference on Communications Workshops (ICC Workshops), Held 2018, pp. 1–6. IEEE (2018)

Wickens, C.: Designing for situation awareness and trust in automation. IFAC Proc. Vol. **28**(23), 365–370 (1995)

Woldring, M., Goillau, P., Kelly, C., Boardman, M., Jeannot, E.: Guidelines for trust in future ATM systems: measures (2003)

Neuroergonomics Behind Culture: A Dynamic Causal Modeling (DCM) Study on Emotion

Zachary Pugh[1], Jiali Huang[1], Kristen Lindquist[2], and Chang S. Nam[1(✉)]

[1] North Carolina State University, Raleigh, USA
{zhpugh,jhuang31,csnam}@ncsu.edu
[2] University of North Carolina at Chapel Hill, Chapel Hill, USA
kristen.lindquist@unc.edu

Abstract. Emotion is an important psychological facet of user experience, despite receiving comparatively less attention than cognitive facets such as working memory and attention. However, emotion is also known to vary with individual differences, including cultural background. To further corroborate findings of culture-driven differences in emotion processing, we applied the dynamic causal modeling (DCM) method to electroencephalography (EEG) measurements that were obtained from Chinese ($N = 10$) and US ($N = 10$) participants during an emotion rating task involving fear-evoking and neutral images. As part of DCM, Bayesian model averaging (BMA) revealed significant culture differences in connections from frontal regions to the amygdala, with Chinese participants uniquely showing strong negative gain, suggesting inhibition of the amygdala. Furthermore, Bayesian model selection revealed that Chinese participants uniquely favored a model involving greater integration of the dlPFC with other frontal regions. The dlPFC has been previously implicated in cultural differences in emotion regulation [1] and is argued to be involved in emotion conceptualization [2]. Both findings corroborate an account in which culture influences how emotions are processed. Furthermore, these findings give reason to suspect that culture also factors into emotional aspects a task or technology.

Keywords: Culture · Emotion · Individual differences · Effective connectivity · Dynamic causal modeling

1 Introduction

1.1 Background

Emotion is especially relevant to technology use, as studies of user frustration [3, 4], user satisfaction [5], user pleasure [6], and design aesthetics [7] have demonstrated. However, emotion is also complicated by individual differences, many of which stem from cultural background. This includes variation in languages, concepts, values, appropriate social behaviors, and conventions of technology use. As a consequence of such wide cultural variation, there is also cultural variation in how emotion is conceptualized, perceived, generated, and regulated. Korean *hwabyeong*, for example, is a culturally unique emotion

© Springer Nature Switzerland AG 2020
C. Stephanidis et al. (Eds.): HCII 2020, LNCS 12425, pp. 216–226, 2020.
https://doi.org/10.1007/978-3-030-60128-7_17

concept referring to anger that develops from repeated social transgressions [8]. Emotion concepts may be technologically situated, as well. Consider the term *road rage*, referring to a range of frustration-induced behaviors in context of driving [9]. More recently, emotional concepts have emerged to describe emotion-laden user behavior. A gamer may *rage quit* after an especially frustrating experience with a computer game. While past research on user experience has not given this term its due attention, a Google search reveals about 2.9 million results for it. The prevalence of these terms raises an interesting question of how these emotional experiences compare with those of other cultures using the same technology.

Apart from these highly situated emotion terms, even generic emotion concepts (e.g., anger) show variability in what exactly they encapsulate. Despite a popular view that emotion categories are universal, evidence from neurobiology suggests that a given emotion category has no singular corresponding region or set of regions in the brain, and a given brain region has no singular corresponding emotion [2, 10]. Rather, emotion terms seem to loosely bracket a wide range of behavioral responses, which are driven by physiological and psychological processes that are not strictly emotional in and of themselves. Some of these processes bear a cognitive role in giving semantic interpretation to the behavioral response. According to this account, known as the constructionist view, emotion is an emergent phenomenon, arising from a cognitive, context-dependent interpretation of bodily sensory input [11].

Cultural variation has been found with emotion regulation, as well, particularly between Eastern and Western cultural groups [12, 13]. A common explanation for this finding is that the more collectivist Asian cultures encourage conformity to the group at the expense of one's own individual experience; this entails down-regulating one's emotions so as to cohere with the group. Meanwhile, Western-European cultures favor the opposite, with greater encouragement to attend to personal emotions without suppressing them [12, 13]. Emotion regulation is likely to be important for technologies which trigger emotions, especially frustration. For users who fail to employ emotion regulating strategies, a technology-induced emotion like frustration can be debilitating for use of the technology itself, which may account for deleterious effects of user frustration [4].

1.2 Regions of Connectivity in the Emotional Brain

The "emotional brain" refers to regions of the brain responsible for generating and regulating emotion, including areas of the limbic system and prefrontal cortex [14]. For this study, five regions of interest (ROIs) were selected to represent the emotional brain in the context of the experimental task, which involved rating emotional content of fear-laden and neutral images. The first of these regions is the amygdala, chosen for its well-established involvement in processing fear [15]. Cultural differences of emotion regulation, which include conceptualization and regulation, should manifest as differences in cognition. For this reason, three cognitive regions were chosen as ROIs: the anterior cingulate cortex (ACC), the ventromedial prefrontal cortex (vmPFC), and the dorsolateral prefrontal cortex (dlPFC). The ACC has been established as a mediator between emotion and cognition [16]. The vmPFC is neuroanatomically connected with the amygdala [17] and has been implicated in regulation of negative emotion and stress [18, 19]. The dlPFC is most strongly associated with cognitive control [20] and has received mixed support regarding its role in emotion regulation. Though it has no strong anatomical connection to the amygdala [21], previous studies have found cultural differences in its activation during emotion regulation tasks [1, 12]. Lindquist and colleagues [2] suggested that this region is important for the conceptualization of emotion but acknowledge that its role may also be regulatory.

The fifth ROI was the primary visual cortex (V1), the bottom-most level of hierarchy in this task-specific network. In addition to its role in bottom-up processing, Padmala and Pessoa [22] found that V1 was subject to top-down modulation in response to emotional stimuli. However, higher-order visual cortical areas are more frequently found to be the target of modulation [23–25]. For this reason, regulation differences may manifest as connectivity differences to V1, in addition to connectivity differences to the amygdala.

Altogether, our ROI set comprised one limbic region (amygdala), one perceptual region (V1), and three frontal regions with heterogeneous involvement in cognition and emotion processing. Given neuroimaging evidence of cultural differences in the emotion regulation, we hypothesized that dynamic causal modeling (DCM) would further show differences the in the effective connectivity among these ROIs, with Chinese participants showing a greater top-down regulation of the amygdala than US participants, as well as greater integration among frontal regions. To better operationalize these hypotheses, we explain the DCM method in the next section.

1.3   DCM and Effective Connectivity

Introduced by Friston and colleagues [26], dynamic causal modeling (DCM) is a method in which plausible networks (or models) of effective connectivity (i.e., causal influence) are created and tested for fit with existing fMRI or EEG data. Models are hypothesis-motivated node-link representations of brain networks, with nodes representing ROIs and directed links representing directed effective connectivity between the ROIs. In this way, models are deterministic, nonlinear input-output systems, with inputs being experimental stimuli and outputs being the measurements of brain activity [26].

Bayesian model selection (BMS) determines which of the models best explains the data. This involves an expectation-maximization algorithm to determine a log-evidence value for each model. The model with the highest log-evidence value is the winning model [26]. For comparison of individual connections, Bayesian model averaging (BMA) determines effective connectivity strengths for each directed connection within the winning model. These values represent the change in effective connectivity in response to experimental stimulus perturbation; for this study, this perturbation reflects differences between fear image responses and neutral image responses. Higher magnitudes indicate stronger connectivity, while positive and negative sign indicates excitation and inhibition, respectively [27].

To operationalize our hypotheses in the language of DCM, we created eight plausible models of effective connectivity (Fig. 1), comprising the ROIs discussed in the previous section. The models were manipulated primarily in terms of how the frontal regions (dlPFC, vmPFC, ACC) were connected with the remaining network.

We hypothesized that measures of effective connectivity (winning model and connectivity strengths) would corroborate the individualist-collectivist hypothesis. This entailed two predictions:

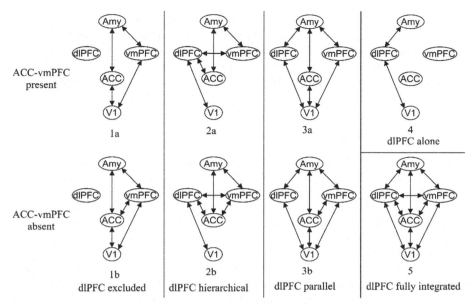

Fig. 1. Plausible models of the fronto-limbic amygdala network in the context of the fear appraisal task. Amy = amygdala, dlPFC = dorsolateral prefrontal cortex, vmPFC = ventromedial prefrontal cortex, ACC = anterior cingulate cortex, V1 = primary visual cortex.

1. Connectivity strengths from frontal regions (ACC, vmPFC, dlPFC) to the amygdala will be inhibitory and stronger for Chinese participants than for US participants.
2. Chinese participants will favor a network with more connections among frontal regions, reflecting greater top-down regulation.

2   Method

2.1   Participants

Ten Chinese (5 female, mean age = 23.7 years, SD = 2.1) and ten US (5 female, mean age = 21.1 years, SD = 0.54) participants were recruited for this study. All participants were English-proficient, right-handed, had normal or corrected-to-normal vision, and had no pre-existing neurological disorder. For the Chinese group, all participants reported having lived in mainland China for at least 18 years. The study was approved by the university's Institutional Review Board, and all participants provided consent before completing the study.

2.2   Experiment

An image set was compiled comprising 36 fearful and 36 neutral images, obtained from the International Affective Picture System and categorized according to normative ratings of valence and arousal [28]. Fear images were significantly different in valence

($F = 169.51, p < 0.001$) and arousal ($F = 494.42, p < 0.001$) from neutral images, with fear images being negative in valence and high in arousal. After being fitted to the EEG cap, participants completed a practice rating trial and then five iterations of main trials. For each image, a trial began with a 4-s fixation period, followed by a 4-s presentation of the image, and then a prompt in which participants reported their level of emotion on a 5-point scale.

2.3 Data Collection and Analysis

EEG data was recorded using a 62-electrode EEG cap (Electro-Cap International, Inc.) with a modified 10–20 arrangement [29], reference to the left ear lobe, and grounding between Afz and Fpz. For preprocessing, EEG signals were bandpass filtered to a range of 0.01–75 Hz, subjected to artifact subspace reconstruction [30] and channel interpolation, and then re-referenced to an average reference.

After data collection and cleaning, Bayesian model selection was applied to the dataset using the eight models in Fig. 1. For each group, Bayesian model averaging was then applied the group's winning model to obtain connectivity values for each directed connection. To keep our analysis manageable, we examined only connections that were at least 0.1 in strength magnitude and at least 95% in posterior probability. To test for predicted cultural differences in effective connectivity strengths, one-tailed t-tests were conducted on all six directed connections to the left and right amygdala, with a Bonferroni-adjusted criterion of significance.

3   Results

3.1 Winning Models

Bayesian model selection revealed that Chinese participants (CH) favored a model bearing a fully integrated dlPFC (Fig. 2, Model #5), with connections to all regions, while US participants favored a model wherein the dlPFC was connected with only the amygdala and V1 (Model #3b). The only differences between these models are the dlPFC-ACC and dlPFC-vmPFC connections, which are present only in Model #5. Using significance criterion of $\Delta F > 3$ [31], both winning models significantly exceed their second-place models in log-evidence ($\Delta F = 346$ for Chinese group, $\Delta F = 138$ for US group).

Apart from winning models, the Chinese group's second-place model was 3b—the US group's winning model. Meanwhile, US participants' winning model was followed by model 3a. Between 3b and 3a, the critical difference is that 3b possesses ACC-vmPFC connections, while 3a does not; both of these models treat the dlPFC as working in parallel to the other two frontal regions.

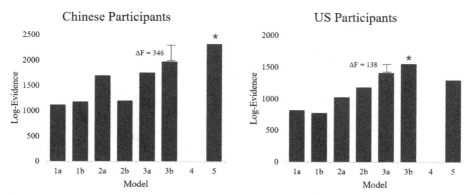

Fig. 2. Log-evidence of models for US and Chinese participants. Asterisks indicate winning models. ΔF indicates difference in log-evidence between winning model and second-place model for each group.

3.2 Connectivity Gains

Bayesian model analysis was applied to the two winning models to obtain connectivity strength values (Fig. 3). Of the connections in both group's winning models, 11 of the 36 connections for the Chinese group and 7 of the 28 connections for the US group passed the strength threshold. All connections the passed this threshold were significant, indicated by the posterior probabilities. For connections to the amygdala, three of these were strong for the Chinese group (r-ACC-amygdala = −0.203, l-vmPFC-amygdala = −0.101, r-vmPFC-amygdala = −0.116), and none were strong for the US group. One-direction t-test revealed significance differences for r-ACC-amygdala ($t(18) = −6.55$, $p < 0.00001$) and l-vmPFC-amygdala ($t(18) = −2.74$, $p = 0.0067$). For both connections, Chinese participants showed negative connectivity gain while US participants to positive gain.

Despite differences in winning models, BMA did not find strong connections from the dlPFC to other regions for either group, but it did reveal a strong r-ACC-dlPFC connection for Chinese participants (−0.257). In addition to this culture-unique connection, Chinese participants also showed especially strong r-ACC connections to r-amygdala (−0.203) and r-V1 (.193), while the US group showed only a strong connection to r-V1 (−0.125). The Chinese group showed strong inhibitory connections from three frontal regions to their ipsilateral amygdala regions, while the US group showed no strong connections to the amygdala.

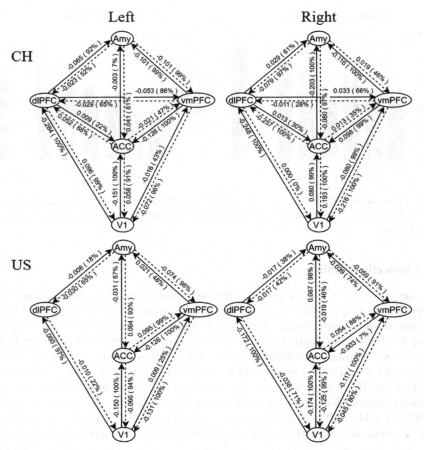

Fig. 3. Connectivity gains and posterior probabilities (parenthesis) for the winning model of Chinese (CH) and US groups. Left and right graphs refer to left and right hemispheres, respectively. Solid and dotted lines refer to forward and backward connections, respectively.

4 Discussion

4.1 Summary of Findings

Our first hypothesis was that Chinese participants would demonstrate greater top-down regulation of the amygdala, and this prediction was borne out in connectivity strengths. Chinese participants showed greater overall inhibition of the amygdala by frontal regions (r-ACC, l-vmPFC, r-vmPFC) than did US participants; meanwhile, US participants showed only one significant connection to the amygdala, and this was excitatory. This suggests that as part of the emotion appraisal task, which involved no explicit instruction to employ emotion regulation strategies, Chinese participants more readily employed cognitive regions to downregulate amygdala activity. This is consistent with past findings of cultural differences in emotion regulation and coheres well with the explanation that participants conform to the values of their respective cultures [1, 12]. That is, while Eastern culture encourages curtailment of personal emotion, Western culture encourages personal experience.

Our second hypothesis was that frontal regions would show more connections among each other for Chinese participants than for US participants. Consistent with this, Chinese participants showed a winning model bearing more connections with the dlPFC, suggesting that for Chinese participants the dlPFC had an especially important interactions with the vmPFC and ACC. Regarding these connections, the only one that passed the strength threshold was r-ACC-dlPFC for Chinese participants. No connections *from* the dlPFC passed the strength threshold or showed a remarkable cultural difference, suggesting that the dlPFC's role did not involve regulating other ROIs. While the dlPFC consistently showed little effect on the remainder of the network, effect *on* the dlPFC was uniquely strong for Chinese participants. Additionally, Chinese participants overall showed greater connectivity from the ACC than US participants. Given these effective connectivity differences, and given that the ACC is an established intermediary between emotional and cognitive processes [16], it appears that Chinese participants more readily employed cognitive processes in their appraisal of the images; this includes conceptualization, which is an important facet of the constructionist account of emotion [2].

Altogether, these findings suggest that for an emotion appraisal task, Chinese participants showed greater involvement of cognitive regions. Part of this involvement suggests cultural differences in the downregulation of emotional response, while another part (ACC-dlPFC connectivity) suggests something other than emotion regulation, possibly emotion conceptualization.

4.2 Implications for User Experience

What might these cultural differences entail for usability? Although the emotional content of this study was not technologically situated, our findings of cultural differences in emotion processing give some reason for speculating into emotional facets of usability and design. If cultural background influences how an individual responds to an emotion-evoking stimulus, then the consequences of emotion-laden aspects in a system, such as user frustration, may also depend on cultural background. User frustration is an especially relevant example. Like fear, it is also salient, negative, and characterized by a strong physiological response [32]. A user's resilience against technology-induced frustration may well depend on their ability and tendency to downregulate their emotional response, whether implicitly or through explicit strategies such as reappraisal. Future studies should thus investigate how such culture-based differences of emotion may manifest themselves in human-computer interaction.

5 Conclusion

An obvious limitation of this study is its scope, in that fear was the sole emotion category selected. However, given that fear has a more concise etiology compared to other emotions, a finding of cultural difference in fear processing suggests that cultural differences pervade other, more neurologically complex emotion categories as well. It also bears mentioning that the emotional aspect of the experimental stimuli was established merely with the content of an image and did not emerge from technology use. Consequently, this study does not inform cultural differences with respect to technology-induced emotions such as frustration and pleasure, despite our earlier speculations. Additional research is needed to establish how culture may affect a user's emotional response to usability issues or hedonic design. Still, our findings do establish one instance of cultural differences in the connectivity of the emotional brain, which gives good reason to anticipate cultural differences in technologically situated emotions.

DCM itself bears technical limitations as a method, including the assumption of prior probabilities and the assumption of deterministic input and output. The latter is regarded as the more severe of the two, but these limitations are commonly accepted as part of DCM [26].

Altogether, DCM revealed that Chinese participants showed greater involvement of frontal regions of the emotional brain, including stronger regulation of the amygdala compared to US participants, as well as a more integrated dlPFC. Both findings suggest a culture-based difference in emotional appraisal of fear-laden images. In the context of cross-cultural design, these findings suggest caution in how both culture and emotion is accounted for in technology.

Acknowledgments. This research was partly supported by the National Science Foundation (NSF) under Grant NSF BCS-1551688. Any opinions, findings, and conclusions or recommendations expressed in this material are those of the authors and do not necessarily reflect the views of the NSF. We would also like to thank Nayoung Kim and Joseph Leshin for designing the experiment and collecting the data.

References

1. Han, S., Ma, Y.: Cultural differences in human brain activity: a quantitative meta-analysis. Neuroimage. **99**, 293–300 (2014). https://doi.org/10.1016/j.neuroimage.2014.05.062
2. Lindquist, K.A., Wager, T.D., Kober, H., Bliss-Moreau, E., Barrett, L.F.: The brain basis of emotion: a meta-analytic review. Behav. Brain Sci. **35**(3), 121–143 (2012)
3. Riseberg, J., Klein, J.: Frustrating the user on purpose: using biosignals in a pilot study to detect the user's emotional state. In: CHI 1998 Conference Summary on Human Factors in Computing Systems, pp. 1–2 (1998). https://doi.org/10.1145/286498.286715
4. Ceaparu, I., Lazar, J., Bessiere, K., Robinson, J., Shneiderman, B.: Determining causes and severity of end-user frustration. Int. J. (2004). https://doi.org/10.1207/s15327590ijhc1703_3
5. Lindgaard, G., Dudek, C.: What is this evasive beast we call user satisfaction? Interact. Comput. **15**, 429–452 (2003). https://doi.org/10.1016/S0953-5438(02)00063-2
6. Jordan, P.W.: Human factors for pleasure in product use. Appl. Ergon. **29**, 25–33 (1998). https://doi.org/10.1016/S0003-6870(97)00022-7
7. Tractinsky, N., Katz, A.S., Ikar, D.: What is beautiful is usable. Interact. Comput. **13**, 127–145 (2000). https://doi.org/10.1016/S0953-5438(00)00031-X
8. Chiao, J.Y., Cheon, B.K., Pornpattananangkul, N., Mrazek, A.J., Blizinsky, K.D.: Cultural neuroscience: progress and promise. Psychol. Inq. **24**, 1–19 (2013). https://doi.org/10.1080/1047840X.2013.752715

9. Fong, G., Frost, D., Stansfeld, S.: Road rage: a psychiatric phenomenon? Soc. Psychiatry Psychiatr. Epidemiol. **36**, 277–286 (2001). https://doi.org/10.1007/s001270170045
10. Barrett, L.F.: Are emotions natural kinds? Perspect. Psychol. Sci. **1**(1), 28–58 (2006)
11. Barrett, L.F.: Constructing emotion. Psychol. Top. **20**(3), 359–380 (2011)
12. de Greck, M., et al.: Culture modulates brain activity during empathy with anger. Neuroimage **59**, 2871–2882 (2012). https://doi.org/10.1016/j.neuroimage.2011.09.052
13. Murata, A., Moser, J.S., Kitayama, S.: Culture shapes electrocortical responses during emotion suppression. Soc. Cogn. Affect. Neurosci. **8**, 595–601 (2013). https://doi.org/10.1093/scan/nss036
14. LeDoux, J.: The Emotional Brain: The Mysterious Underpinnings of Emotional Life. Simon and Schuster, New York (1988)
15. Ledoux, J.: The emotional brain, fear, and the amygdala. Cell. Mol. Neurobiol. **23**(4–5), 727–738 (2003). https://doi.org/10.1023/A:1025048802629
16. Devinsky, O., Morrell, M.J., Vogt, B.A.: Contributions of anterior cingulate cortex to behaviour. Brain **118**, 279–306 (1995). https://doi.org/10.1093/brain/118.1.279
17. Phillips, M.L., Ladouceur, C.D., Drevets, W.C.: A neural model of voluntary and automatic emotion regulation: Implications for understanding the pathophysiology and neurodevelopment of bipolar disorder. J. Mol. Psychiatry **13**(9), 833–857 (2008)
18. Hänsel, A., von Känel, R.: The ventro-medial prefrontal cortex: A major link between the autonomic nervous system, regulation of emotion, and stress reactivity? Biopsychosoc. Med. **2**(1) (2008)
19. Delgado, M.R., Nearing, K.I., LeDoux, J.E., Phelps, E.A.: Neural circuitry underlying the regulation of conditioned fear and its relation to extinction. Neuron **59**, 829–838 (2008). https://doi.org/10.1016/j.neuron.2008.06.029
20. Hoshi, E.: Functional specialization within the dorsolateral prefrontal cortex: a review of anatomical and physiological studies of non-human primates. Neurosci. Res. **54**, 73–84 (2006). https://doi.org/10.1016/j.neures.2005.10.013
21. Ray, R.D., Zald, D.H.: Anatomical insights into the interaction of emotion and cognition in the prefrontal cortex. Neurosci. Biobehav. Rev. **36**(1), 479–501 (2012)
22. Padmala, S., Pessoa, L.: Affective learning enhances visual detection and responses in primary visual cortex. J. Neurosci. **28**, 6202–6210 (2008). https://doi.org/10.1523/JNEUROSCI.1233-08.2008
23. Furl, N., Henson, R.N., Friston, K.J., Calder, A.J.: Top-down control of visual responses to fear by the amygdala. J. Neurosci. **33**, 17435–17443 (2013). https://doi.org/10.1523/JNEUROSCI.2992-13.2013
24. Aguado, L., Valdés-Conroy, B., Rodríguez, S., Román, F.J., Diéguez-Risco, T., Fernández-Cahill, M.: Modulation of early perceptual processing by emotional expression and acquired valence of faces: an ERP study. J. Psychophysiol. **26**, 29–41 (2012). https://doi.org/10.1027/0269-8803/a000065
25. Vuilleumier, P., Driver, J.: Modulation of visual processing by attention and emotion: windows on causal interactions between human brain regions. Philos. Trans. Roy. Soc. B Biol. Sci. **362**, 837–855 (2007)
26. Friston, K.J., Harrison, L., Penny, W.: Dynamic causal modelling. Neuroimage **19**, 1273–1302 (2003). https://doi.org/10.1016/S1053-8119(03)00202-7
27. Havlicek, M., Roebroeck, A., Friston, K., Gardumi, A., Ivanov, D., Uludag, K.: Physiologically informed dynamic causal modeling of fMRI data. Neuroimage **122**, 355–372 (2015). https://doi.org/10.1016/j.neuroimage.2015.07.078
28. Lang, P.J., Bradley, M.M., Cuthbert, B.N.: International affective picture system (IAPS): Technical manual and affective ratings, pp. 39–58. NIMH Center for the Study of Emotion and Attention (1997)

29. Sharbrough, F., Chatrian, G.-E., Lesser, R.P., Luders, H., Nuwer, M., Picton, T.W.: American electroencephalographic society guidelines for standard electrode position no-menclature. J. Clin. Neurophysiol. **8**, 200–202 (1991)
30. Chang, C.Y., Hsu, S.H., Pion-Tonachini, L., Jung, T.P.: Evaluation of artifact subspace reconstruction for automatic artifact components removal in multi-channel EEG recordings. IEEE Trans. Biomed. Eng. **67**, 1114–1121 (2020). https://doi.org/10.1109/TBME.2019.2930186
31. Kiebel, S.J., Garrido, M.I., Moran, R.J., Friston, K.J.: Dynamic causal modelling for EEG and MEG. Cogn. Neurodyn. **2**, 121–136 (2008). https://doi.org/10.1007/s11571-008-9038-0
32. Hazlett, R.L.: Measurement of user frustration: a biologic approach. In: Proceedings of Conference Human Factors in Computing Systems, pp. 734–735 (2003). https://doi.org/10.1145/765891.765958

Measure for Measure: How Do We Assess Human Autonomy Teaming?

Dale Richards[⊠] [ID]

Nottingham Trent University, Nottingham NG11 8NS, UK
`dale.richards@ntu.ac.uk`

Abstract. The increasing use of advanced automation and intelligent support systems provides an opportunity for increased efficiency and minimizing the requirement of presenting the human with laborious, dangerous and repetitive tasks. It is important to remember that although a large degree of this capability is technology-focused, the significance of the human must not be relegated or dismissed. The human component is tightly coupled to the whole system and should be viewed as working in harmony with the autonomous system. In many instances we are seeing systems that bring both human and autonomy closer together, working as teams. With both the human and autonomy working together it is important to be able to evaluate the effectiveness of this teaming arrangement. However, methods for measuring the effectiveness of human-autonomy teaming tends to focus solely on the task, with little consideration being given to how the human integrates within the system. This paper explores the factors associated with task-based measures and highlights key cognitive factors that should be considered. It is unlikely that a single metric can be used to provide a score, but rather a combination of metrics that pull in different components of the human-autonomy team. The ability to measure the effectiveness of human-autonomy teams will not only provide feedback as to current manifestations of teaming, but has implications into their future design.

Keywords: Autonomy · Human factors · Human-autonomy teaming

1 Introduction

It is safe to say that the we can no longer talk of intelligent systems as being some sort of harbinger that will arrive at some distant date with the promise of making our lives easier, safer and more efficient. The age of advanced automation, autonomy and artificial intelligence (AI) is already among us, and it has been for quite some time.

The journey from automation to autonomy has not been a simple step hopping exercise involving the altering of software that hides behind otherwise 'ordinary systems', but more a story that has evolved through robust development and testing, leading to eventual uptake and public acceptance. However, to many the little 'black box' analogy that is often used to characterize this technology has moved from perceiving automation as simply being a series of predictable *If-Then* statements, towards autonomous software

© Springer Nature Switzerland AG 2020
C. Stephanidis et al. (Eds.): HCII 2020, LNCS 12425, pp. 227–239, 2020.
https://doi.org/10.1007/978-3-030-60128-7_18

that is shrouded in the mystique of artificial intelligence, where literally anything (and everything) can happen.

Nowadays intelligent systems are now not only pervasive across domains, but also becoming ubiquitous in our everyday lives. Very much as was the case with automation, the authority that we delegate to the system is often safety critical and has the potential of making life and death decisions [32]. Routine events can now be governed by utilizing these systems, either suggesting items for us to purchase whilst shopping [50], or providing medical diagnostics [5]. This is not the place to argue the ethics or societal benefits these emerging socio-technical options now afford us, but rather we need to ask ourselves how we evaluate or measure the effectiveness of such systems in the context of their use. How exactly do we measure an intelligent system? Let alone make a comparison between two similar systems, but possessing two contrasting AI approaches? To make matters more complicated we have to appreciate that there is, in nearly all instances, a human involved somewhere in the loop; thus confounding the need to not only measure the autonomy, but the human component also. We now begin to see the system as being a partnership between the human and the autonomy, working together towards a common goal. In essence a Human-Autonomy Team (HAT).

2   What Exactly Are We Trying to Measure?

It is important to remember that the intelligent system rarely (if ever) has no human input. At some point a human will be required to set a goal for the system, and then be likely required to monitor and act as overall supervisor. In order to achieve this a framework of control is required, thus allowing the human to delegate control authority to and from the system [35]. We are now presented with three existing factors that need to be considered for measurement; the human, the intelligent system, and the goal they share [3]. There are however other factors that may likely influence the manner in which a goal is (or can be) achieved. These relate to the (1) environmental factors that may obstruct a task, and the (2) imposed constraints that the human and/or system applies to any given task or behaviour. These two factors should be given equal consideration alongside the human, the intelligent system, and the goal; as outlined in Fig. 1.

The environmental factors and imposed constraints are contrasting factors in terms of being internal or external to the system. For example, the environment may be defined as an external factor that is somewhat outside of the systems control or influence. It implies an influence that is imposed from outside the system (such as weather, operating conditions, etc.). A constraint, on the other hand, can be considered an internal factor that can be dictated by the human or the system itself via rule-based statements or directives (such as assigning parameters of performance to ensure safety, or a limitation of a sensor). Of course both of these factors can equally be characterized as local (in relation to a spatial or temporal effect) or global (defined by the environmental characteristic operation or a constraint that affects fundamental behaviour). An example may assist in our understanding of this. Imagine we are operating an unmanned underwater vehicle (UUV). This is a submersible autonomous mining vehicle and are tasked to dredge for minerals on the sea floor. The vehicle possesses variable autonomy, in that we can delegate authority to the system depending on task and more importantly the single

Fig. 1. Relationship between the human, autonomy and the shared goal.

operator maintains supervision of the vessel at all times - and can even take manual control as required. In Table 1 we can observe how both internal and external factors can influence the operation, whilst providing a narrative example. The reason why it is important to explore the factors that are outlined in this table is that it provides us with some examples of how a system can be judged: either well or badly. Assessing whether these factors are adhered to would be reasonably straight forward and in many cases can be represented with a binary response in terms of fulfilling one criteria or another. However, things are not always that black and white.

If we take the example further, then we can suppose the UUV possesses multiple agents; each assigned to specific roles within the context of the system (navigation, sensors, health monitoring, etc.). This distribution of agents is commonplace but still falls short of the ability to possess a complete knowledge of the goals, tasks and interactions of their fellow community members [16]. As a human operator, we may not necessarily view the different agents, but be drawn to a sub-system or a single 'master agent' that represents the total knowledge held across the system. This may be quite a robust system and be able to represent a holistic picture of the machine's perspective, although the human is likely to only interact with this single representation of the intelligent system. This in itself is not so much of a problem, until we start to question why autonomous agent behaviors or decisions are made in a certain manner. We may interrogate the system for more information and expect a justification for the exhibited behaviour that could have resulted in a task either (1) not being completed, (2) being completed partially, (3) being completed in a manner that we did not expect or would have chosen ourselves, or even (4) a task completed as expected but whereby the human may have thought a constraint outside of the system would have resulted in a different outcome.

Table 1. Example of internal/external factors and their relationship to local/global features for UUV operations example

Factor	Internal or external	Local or global	Example
Environment	External	Local	Some external aspects of the environment may not be known or change dynamically. This change may only be local to the operating area and not be representative of the global conditions. For example, finding yourself with reduced visibility whilst mining underwater would be due to your own behaviour and will revert back to normal conditions over time
Environment	External	Global	This can be dictated by physical conditions of operation (maritime, aerial, land) and limitations may be associated with this (e.g. communications, endurance). So fixed and known factors such as weather, temperature, land features, etc. are key factors for consideration that can influence operations
Constraint	Internal	Local	The operator or system may recognise an issue and impose a constraint on performance due to a recognized issue. This will affect the performance of the system, but is self-imposed due to a circumstance that has been encountered. For example, if the vessel was working near a thermal vent, then the human or intelligent agent may impose a perimeter around that area to ensure the vessel did not enter it
Constraint	Internal	Global	In some instances an overarching rule may be placed on the system, by either the human or the system itself. This could be a system limitation (due to physical system/sensor) or an artificial one imposed externally. For example, the vessel may not be allowed to operate within a certain distance of a set location

3   Putting the Human Back into HAT

So we now have a number of factors that we can consider as possessing qualities worthy of our attention when assessing the effectiveness of a HAT. If we put to one side the different 'flavors' of autonomy, in terms of both levels of control and the nature of machine intelligence the system possesses, it is important to highlight one common factor shared across these variations - the human. Unfortunately, there are many cases in literature that shows that as the level of delegated control authority increases then the human may very well perceive themselves as being removed from the situation [13]. It is also well-noted that if the human takes a back seat to the machine, then they are more likely to perceive a loss in situation awareness [9], become confused in terms of understanding what the system is doing [24] or even begin to mistrust the system altogether [25]. An efficient HAT must therefore be built upon a foundation of the right sort of information so that the human understands *why* decisions have been made. However, providing more information to the operator can lead to mental overload [40].

With the general bias in the evaluation of autonomous systems focusing more on system-based effectiveness [42, 45], rather than on the human interaction with the system; this may very well mask inefficient human performance costs, such as mental workload or situational awareness [31] that can have a direct impact on achieving the goal the system is designed for. It is of no surprise then that the majority of papers that have examined human-automation/autonomy interaction tend to focus primarily on cognitive aspects such as workload, situational awareness and skill degradation [23, 45]. Evaluating these dimensions in the context of complex interaction required by a human to delegate authority to the machine is not trivial, and therefore difficult to assess with a lack of meaningful design principles to assist the system designer [31]. There is a general lack of current/new methods that allow us closer inspection of the human-autonomy partnership [41, 47] and so new endeavors are required to put forward different techniques that can assist in our understanding the benefits and risks within a HAT.

4 What to Measure, and How?

We have seen that when it comes to measuring human interaction with advanced automation or autonomy, it is often the case that we are presented with the same measures. On the whole most will examine the *effect* of the what is being measured; thus if we go back to our UUV example and state it has the ability to autonomously navigate and seek out bottles on the ocean floor - we can simply do a time and frequency measure of how many bottles were identified and over what period of time it took. This in essence is a measure of the system capability and to a large extent does not measure the HAT component. These may be defined as proxy measures and can be considered elements of the HAT that is being assessed, but by no means should they be considered as a single indication of HAT effectiveness.

There are a number of key cognitive factors that we need to ensure are collected when we start to piece together a construct that can be put forward for measuring HAT, apart from the system capability measures. Otherwise we would arrive at a very good way of counting bottles, with no context of how difficult the interaction with the UUV actually was.

4.1 Situation Awareness and Mental Workload

Unsurprisingly situation awareness (SA) is a key consideration when we think about HAT effectiveness, as it is this construct that determines our understanding of the current situation and the progress towards our goal. Some studies have focused on SA during tasks with varying automation functionality [2, 19, 43]. In the study by [2] they assessed varying automation of a tractor and monitoring task and found that increasing the level of automation decreased operator SA due to lower information quality and feeling 'out of the loop', due to lower arousal and concentration in higher autonomous modes. The use of SA does appear to be problematic in the context of automation as a single measure since it is difficult to 'design in' this attribute into a design – one has to develop a design and then evaluate its SA qualities. [39] provides a summary of the issues with using SA as an evaluation method, such as the lack of correlation between performance and SA. Team SA has also been associated with measuring HAT performance due to the importance of communication between all team members [10]. In order for a HAT to be effective then team communication is a vital component in building team SA. [8] stressed the importance of measuring verbal behaviors that related to *pushing* or *pulling* information among team members, thus providing a different means by which to analyze HAT dynamics.

Mental workload is often used in studies to provide a metric of performance when working with autonomous systems. It tends to be used in parallel with SA, and is one of the most widely used metrics when assessing human performance [18, 43]; with the most common tool for assessing mental workload being the NASA-TLX [12]. This measure has often been used for assessing operator workload with unmanned systems, and in particular for teleoperations with robots [17, 28]. Perhaps more aligned to this are metrics for task load, as this places emphasis on working memory and the ability to respond in a correct and timely manner. [1] found that individual differences in working memory affected how individuals performed visual search tasks and decision making. Along a similar vein [4] found that task load had a direct effect on whether an individual trusted automation or not; with higher levels of task load associated with distrust in the automation. Clearly the more tasks an individual is presented with would likely contribute to their mental workload, and potentially influence their use and perception of any form of decision support.

Clearly SA and mental workload are important factor to consider, it is however worth noting that the majority of studies tend to use task-based proxy measures to infer aspects of both cognitive factors.

4.2 Human Error and Decision Making

[33] introduced the concepts of reliability and the cost of inappropriate system-based decisions (whether taken by the machine or human) into human-automation interaction. [18] examined the numbers of steps missed in a nuclear control process to determine the error rate, allied to the workload induced by the human-autonomy interaction and found that task type had the strongest influence on operator workload compared to automation. They also found human error rates were directly linked to workload, leading to the conclusion that human error should be addressed alongside workload. [23] by

contrast, looked at the types of automation mode that reduces human errors from a skill or knowledge perspective. This highlights the potential differences in the nature of errors when using different automation modes.

Decision making processes are a key aspect of HAT because operator decisions directly relate to the tasks they face. Therefore it is necessary to identify appropriate models of decision making in order to apply them in a beneficial way to facilitate interaction between human and system. The tasks faced by operational decision makers are often ill-structured problems when confronted with uncertain and highly dynamic environments. This makes the application of naturalistic models of decision-making (NDM) more appropriate than classical paradigms, due to the ability of NDM approaches to be more dynamic and flexible to the unfolding situation [20]. According to NDM theory, situation assessment is the most important aspect of decision making so, when confronted with stimuli the operator should be assisted in gaining a good situational understanding.

4.3 Vigilance

It is not uncommon to hear operators of remotely supervised systems to report high levels of boredom over long periods of being on duty [6], and perhaps we have all heard stories of how little pilots have to do in terms of flying today's passenger aircraft – although the automated flight deck is noted as being an issue for maintaining vigilance [38]. [49] propose that vigilance tasks are far from un-stimulating and mentally undemanding, but suggest that the mental effort is observed in both psychological and physiological metrics. The operator is highly trained in the system they are operating and more often or not have experience across other platforms/systems. However, it is fair to say that these system designs tend to force the human to 'take a back seat', due to the supervisory/monitoring role of that the operator has to now adopt with more advanced intelligent systems. It is highly likely that the human will need to maintain a high state of vigilance when monitoring an intelligent system within HAT, as they will be ultimately responsible for the achievement of a set goal.

4.4 Mental Models

Mental models have been used as a construct to explain an operator's knowledge of human-system interaction, the wider environment and other teams [7]. Mental models contain a strong visual component, which fits with the use of visual images or pictorial metaphors within visualization designs [26]. If *appropriate* mental models are facilitated then this has the potential to aid operators' understanding of a situation/interaction with a system. Performance can be facilitated if users' models can take on a visual form that engages the appropriate cognitive layout (i.e. where the users' mental model of the elements and relationships in a system and how they operate can be tied to the surface layout of elements on the display). Different graphical layouts can be used to suggest different types of metaphors for system operation and navigation and to provide meaning for users [27]. This implies that how we present information to the human operator can directly affect their perception of the intelligent system they are interacting with. Mental models allow people to decrease the amount of information they have to deal with, lightening the cognitive load to get information into a manageable form. Thus the manner in which the intelligent system interacts with the individual must reinforce their expectation and lead to cognitive compatibility between the user and AI model of the world [36].

4.5 Trust

One aspect that may be seen to influence the above cognitive factors is that of trust, and more so the role this plays in creating an effective HAT. [48] discuss two different components relating to how an operator may trust such systems (in this instance multiple autonomous agents):

- System-wide trust (SWT) – whereby the agents act as a holistic body towards achieving a shared goal, with all agents sharing elements of the overall level of trust.
- Component specific trust (CST) – which is the opposite of SWT, whereby trust is assigned to individual agents/components within the system.

They found that when individuals were tasked to interact with multiple autonomous systems then they would adopt a SWT approach – more so when individuals are not given sufficient information about individual assets (not allowing them to assess system status). However, they also note the complexities with understanding SWT when applied to multiple autonomous assets, especially when those assets possess different characteristics/properties (heterogeneous). All engagements and interactions, both social and with technology, require elements of trust, particularly those that require some form of cooperation. When referring to social interaction this is often referred to as reciprocal trust, and is critical in the development of partnerships [21]. It is therefore reasonable to assume that the development of a HAT and the formation of human-computer trust (HCT) will also require elements of reciprocal trust. To this effect, researchers have often tried to adapt interpersonal trust models and measurement instruments to explain operator HCT, even creating their own scales (e.g. Human-Computer Trust Scale, SHAPE, SATI). These have all been designed to assess operator trust of decision support systems, and although they have all benefited from systematic development and validation, they have also attracted a fair deal of criticism [22].

4.6 Physiological Measures

It is becoming more commonplace to utilise physiological metrics when assessing HAT, although normally in combination with existing non-physiological measures. The use of physiological assessment presents the opportunity to assess the human state whilst they engage within a HAT. [46] used subjective workload measures and eye-gaze duration to assess an autonomous decision support flight planner system. [15] discuss the use of acquiring data via wearable functional neuroimaging equipment in order to assess human cortical activity - measuring the source and extent of cognitive activity. Indeed, some studies have begun to examine and characterize the neural correlates of trust and have often implicated activity within the prefrontal cortex in encoding the motives and intentions surrounding interactions with systems [44].

It is not unusual for common physiology metrics such as heart rate, electrodermal activity (EDA), respiration rate, and electroencephalography (EEG) to be applied in combination with other measures. Indeed, it can be argued that assessing physiological response from the human autonomic nervous system is as close to a valid measure of human response as you can get. However, assigning a physiological response to a cognitive attribute comes with its limitations and a great deal of faith in correlating physiological response with a specific cognitive attribute. An indirect assumption is symptomatic when addressing the physiology-cognitive divide. More direct physiological measures can attempt to avoid this by taking direct measures of physiology; ones that assess the regions of the brain known to play a role in the cognitive attribute that is being measured. Neuroimaging technology is now being assessed as a means of identifying changes across neurophysiology as indicative of whether someone trusts or distrusts something [30].

5   A New Horizon of Measuring HAT?

The quest for identifying or creating a single measure for HAT is unlikely to arrive at a 'one size fits all' solution. Many studies have used a multimodal approach, but tend to weigh significantly towards task measures that bias the system performance more than the human requirement of the HAT. In order to assess performance of a given HAT it is important to approach the question of what it is you are trying to measure, and why. Holistic approaches can often mislead and paint a far too wide a picture of what is going on within a HAT, so counting bottles may be seen as a good indicator for some but falls considerably short of explaining the nature of human interaction and trust within the HAT.

It is also easy to focus solely on an individual attribute and to bring to bear an appropriate measure that would render a score that would indicative of that attribute. However, to focus on a single attribute, let alone a single measure can be met with criticism. [15] suggest that the validity of using a sole metric for complex human behaviour should also ideally include behavioral task data (such as goal achievement) and some form of physiological assessment. Of course it is also important to state that there have been other promising avenues that have been pursued in terms of non-traditional metrics for interacting with an autonomous system; such as neglect tolerance and attentional demand [11, 29]. These methods however are fairly high-level and are harder to use practically, though they do provide useful illustrations of methods which can provide insight into HAT.

When selecting an appropriate measurement technique, there are a number of factors we must consider that may potentially have an impact on the data we wish to collect. These specifically relate to factors such as sensitivity, diagnosticity, intrusiveness, implementation, and acceptance [14]. While behavioral and subjective measures are largely non-intrusive and can possess high participant acceptance, they are poor in terms of their sensitivity and diagnosticity for measuring cognitive constructs. As a consequence of this the validity of such approaches must often be examined. However, there are other approaches for collecting data that we may also wish to consider. Advances in Psychophysiology have demonstrated that changes in physiology can explicitly be correlated with tasks that may be viewed as being of high cognitive loading, or events that can be identified as possessing (or losing) situation awareness. It is therefore essential that before we start to decide on which metric to use, we must consider the context within which the measurement is to be applied, what exactly are we attempting to measure, how valid is the tool, etc.

It is worth noting that the sensitivity of these metrics may only provide one side of the story, in that they are perceived measures and sometimes do not reveal the full picture [37]. There has also been observations that suggest that subjective metrics, such as the NASA-TLX, can be limited by the nature of individual differences in introspection skills [34].

Trust in itself is a difficult construct to define and thus establishing a metric to assess this is somewhat troublesome. However, if we consider trust to be in part a component of higher cognitive function there have been some promising research that alludes to identifying neurocorrelates of trust [21]. New neuroimaging technology is now being assessed as a means of identifying changes across neurophysiology as indicative of whether someone trusts or distrusts something [30].

6 Conclusion

As a community we need to move away from simply focusing on the outputs of a HAT in order to assess effectiveness. The use of task-based measures are more readily associated with the autonomy as opposed to the human commanding, monitoring or supervising the system. By neglecting to measure the specific human factors we run the risk of generating a measure that removes the human from that assessment. A multimodal approach is advised that takes the following HAT characteristics into account:

- The Goal
- The Autonomy
- The Environment
- The Constraints
- The Human

The human component, as is true of the others, can be deconstructed into sub-components. This paper has outlined a number relevant cognitive factors that should be assessed within a HAT, as these will provide a means by which to evaluate the interaction and perception between human and autonomy. While these factors are critical to assessing HAT, it is also worth noting that the use of multiple measures in assessing these human factors, rather than assuming one factor can explain all. For assessing the human within HAT it is advisable to use a battery of measures that are designed specifically to gauge the associated cognitive factor. A balanced approach of behavioral, physiological, and subjective metrics should be used together in order to get insight into how human component interacts within the HAT.

While it is reasonable to measure the outputs that result from the system that are easily quantifiable; with advanced automation it is equally important to understand and measure the nature of the user's interaction with this technology and from a wider socio-technical perspective. This helps us to understand where and with whom the control truly rests and whether there are undesirable emergent properties from the design that may have a detrimental impact on delivering successfully human-autonomy teams (HAT). Traditional methods for assessing cognitive factors should be noted and encouraged, but the use of common metrics for assessing HAT is missing [45].

It is important that we not only apply such metrics for assessing the effectiveness of HAT, but more so that we can use such measures to feed into our initial designs. We are still some distance from generating guidance on HAT composition and dynamics, but the first steps need to be achieved in terms of agreeing (1) what are we measuring, and (2) how are we measuring it?

References

1. Ahmed, N., de Visser, E., Shaw, T., Mohamed-Ameen, A., Campbell, M., Parasuraman, R.: Statistical modelling of networked human-automation performance using working memory capacity. Ergonomics **57**(3), 295–318 (2014)
2. Bashiri, B., Mann, D.D.: Automation and the situation awareness of drivers in agricultural semi-autonomous vehicles. Biosyst. Eng. **124**, 8–15 (2014)
3. Baxter, J.W., Richards, D.: Whose goal is it anyway? user interaction in an autonomous system. In: Proceedings of the Workshop on Goal Directed Autonomy, AAAI 2010, Atlanta (2010)
4. Biros, D.P., Daly, M., Gunsch, G.: The influence of task load and automation trust on deception detection. Group Decis. Negot. **13**, 173–189 (2004). https://doi.org/10.1023/B:GRUP.000002 1840.85686.57
5. Blanco, X., Rodríguez, S., Corchado, J.M., Zato, C.: Case-based reasoning applied to medical diagnosis and treatment. In: Omatu, S., Neves, J., Rodriguez, J.M.C., Paz Santana, J.F., Gonzalez, S.R. (eds.) Distributed Computing and Artificial Intelligence. AISC, vol. 217, pp. 137–146. Springer, Cham (2013). https://doi.org/10.1007/978-3-319-00551-5_17
6. Button, K.: Multi-aircraft control of UAVs by a single pilot won't come easily, experts warn. C4ISR J. **8**, 30–32 (2009)
7. Cannon-Bowers, J.A., Salas, E., Converse, S.A.: Shared mental models in expert team decision making. In: Castellan Jr, N.J. (ed.) Individual and Group Decision Making Current Issues, pp. 221–246. Lawrence Erlbaum Associates, Hillsdale (1993)
8. Demir, M., McNeese, N.J., Cooke, N.J.: Team situation awareness within the context of human-autonomy teaming. Cogn. Syst. Res. **46**, 3–12 (2018)
9. Endsley, M.R.: Designing for Situation Awareness: An Approach to User-Centered Design. CRC Press, Boca Raton (2016)
10. Endsley, M.R., Robertson, M.M.: Situation awareness in aircraft maintenance teams. Int. J. Ind. Ergon. **26**(2), 301–325 (2000)
11. Goodrich, M., Olsen, D.: Seven principles of efficient interaction. In: Proceedings of IEEE International Conference on Systems, Man, and Cybernetics, 5–8 October 2003, pp. 3943–3948 (2003)
12. Hart, S.G., Staveland, L.E.: Development of NASA-TLX (task load index): results and theoretical research. In: Human Mental Workload, pp. 139–183 (1997)
13. Hoff, K., Bashir, M.: Trust in automation: Integrating empirical evidence on factors that influence trust. Hum. Factors **57**(3), 407–434 (2015)
14. Izzetoglu, K., Richards, D., Ding, L., Ling, C., Willems, B.: Human performance assessment: evaluation and experimental use of wearable sensors for brain activity measures. Paper presented at International Symposium for Aviation Psychology, Dayton, Ohio, May 2017 (2017)

15. Izzetogolu, K., Richards, D.: Human performance assessment: evaluation of wearable sensors for monitoring brain activity. In: Vidulich, M.A., Tang, P.S. (eds.) Advances in Aviation Psychology: Volume 3: Improving Aviation Performance Through Applying Engineering Psychology, pp. 163–180. CRC Press (2019)
16. Jennings, N.R.: Coordination techniques for distributed artificial intelligence (1996)
17. Johnson, C., Adams, J., Kawamura, K.: Evaluation of an enhanced human-robot interface. In: Proceedings of the 2003 IEEE International Conference on Systems, Man, and Cybernetic (2003)
18. Jou, Y-T., Yenn, T-C., Lin, C.J., Yang, C.W., Lin, S.F.: Evaluation of mental workload in automation design for a main control room task. In: 2009 International Conference on Networking, Sensing and Control, pp. 313–317. IEEE (2009). https://doi.org/10.1109/ICNSC. 2009.4919293
19. Kaber, D.B., Perry, C.M., Segall, N., McClernon, C.K., Prinzel III, L.J.: Situation awareness implications of adaptive automation for information processing in an air traffic control-related task. Int. J. Ind. Ergon. **36**(5), 447–462 (2006)
20. Klein, G.: Naturalistic decision making. Hum. Factors **50**(3), 456–460 (2008)
21. Krueger, F., et al.: Neural correlates of trust. Proc. Natl. Acad. Sci. U.S.A. **104**, 20084–20089 (2007)
22. Lewis, M., Sycara, K., Walker, P.: The role of trust in human-robot interaction. In: Abbass, H.A., Scholz, J., Reid, D.J. (eds.) Foundations of Trusted Autonomy. SSDC, vol. 117, pp. 135–159. Springer, Cham (2018). https://doi.org/10.1007/978-3-319-64816-3_8
23. Lin, C.J., Yenn, T.C., Yang, C.W.: Automation design in advanced control rooms of the modernized nuclear power plants. Saf. Sci. **48**(1), 63–71 (2010)
24. Lyons, J.B.: Being transparent about transparency: a model for human-robot interaction. In: Sofge, D., Kruijff, G., Lawless, W.F. (eds.) Trust and Autonomous Systems: Papers from the AAAI Spring Symposium, pp. 48–53 (2013). Technical report SS-13-07
25. Lyons, J.B., Stokes, C.K.: Human-human reliance in the context of automation. Hum. Factors **54**(1), 112–121 (2012)
26. MacMillan, J., Getty, D.J., Tatum, C.: Visual metaphors and mental models - a method for comparing intangibles. Proc. Hum. Factors Ergon. Soc. Ann. Meet. **41**, 284–288 (1997)
27. Norman, D.: Cognitive Artifacts. In: Carroll, J. (ed.) Designing Interaction: Psychology at the Human Computer Interface. Cambridge University Press, New York (1991)
28. Olivares, R., Zhou, C., Adams, J., Bodenheimer, B.: Interface evaluation for mobile robot teleoperation. In: Proceedings of the ACM Southeast Conference (ACMSE 2003), Savannah, GA, March 2003, pp. 112–118 (2003)
29. Olsen, D.R., Goodrich, M.A.: Metrics for evaluating human-robot interactions. In: Proceedings of PERMIS, vol. 2003, p. 4. (2003)
30. Palmer, S., Richards, D., Shelton-Rayner, G., Inch, D., Izzetogolu, K.: Human-agent teaming - an evolving interaction paradigm: an innovative measure of trust. In: International Symposium on Aviation Psychology, Dayton, Ohio (2019)
31. Parasuraman, R.: Designing automation for human use: empirical studies and quantitative models. Ergonomics **43**(7), 931–951 (2000)
32. Parasuraman, R., Riley, V.: Humans and automation: use, misuse, disuse, abuse. Hum. Factors **39**(2), 230–253 (1997)
33. Parasuraman, R., Sheridan, T.B., Wickens, C.D.: A model for types and levels of human interaction with automation. IEEE Trans. Syst. Man Cybern. Part A Syst. Hum. **30**(3), 286–297 (2000). https://hci.cs.uwaterloo.ca/faculty/elaw/cs889/reading/automation/sheridan.pdf
34. Paulhus, D.L., Vazire, S.: The self-report method. In: Robins, R.W., Fraley, R., Krueger, R.F. (eds.) Handbook of Research Methods in Personality Psychology, pp. 224–239. Guilford Press, New York (2005)

35. Richards, D., Stedmon, A.: To delegate or not to delegate: a review of control frameworks for autonomous cars. Appl. Ergon. **53**, 383–388 (2016)
36. Richards, D., Stedmon, A.: Designing for human–agent collectives: display considerations. Cogn. Technol. Work **19**(2–3), 251–261 (2017). https://doi.org/10.1007/s10111-017-0419-1
37. Richards, D., Scott, S., Furness, J., Lamb, P., Jordan, D., Moore, D.: Functional symbology - evaluation of task-specific head-up display information for use on a commercial flight deck. In: Proceedings of AIAA Modeling and Simulation Technologies Conference, AIAA Aviation Forum Held 13–17 June 2016 at Washington, D.C. American Institute of Aeronautics and Astronautics (2016)
38. Rudisill, M.E.: The influence of various achievement goal orientations on perceived competence and the attributional process. J. Hum. Mov. Stud. **16**, 53–73 (1991)
39. Scholtz, J.: Evaluation methods for human-system performance of intelligent systems. National Institute of Standards and Technology, Manufacturing Engineering Lab, Gaithersburg, MD (2002)
40. Selkowitz, A.R., Larios, C.A., Lakhmani, S.G., Chen, J.Y.: Displaying information to support transparency for autonomous platforms. In: Savage-Knepshield, P., Chen, J. (eds.) Advances in Human Factors in Robots and Unmanned Systems. AISC, vol. 499, pp. 161–173. Springer, Cham (2017). https://doi.org/10.1007/978-3-319-41959-6_14
41. Sharit, J.: Human error. In: Handbook of Human Factors and Ergonomics, pp. 708–760 (2006)
42. Sheridan, T.B.: Humans and Automation: System Design and Research Issues. Wiley Series in Systems Engineering and Management (2002). ISBN 978-0-471-23428-9
43. Squire, P.N., Parasuraman, R.: Effects of automation and task load on task switching during human supervision of multiple semi-autonomous robots in a dynamic environment. Ergonomics **53**(8), 951–961 (2010)
44. Sripada, C.S., Angstadt, M., Banks, S., Nathan, P.J., Liberzon, I., Phan, K.L.: Functional neuroimaging of mentalizing during the trust game in social anxiety disorder. NeuroReport **20**(11), 984–989 (2009). https://doi.org/10.1097/WNR.0b013e32832d0a67
45. Steinfeld, A., et al.: Common metrics for human-robot interaction. In: Proceedings of the 1st Annual IEEE/ACM Conference on Human Robot Interaction, Salt Lake City, Utah. ACM Press, New York (2006)
46. Strybel, T.Z., et al.: Measuring the effectiveness of human autonomy teaming. In: Baldwin, C. (ed.) AHFE 2017. AISC, vol. 586, pp. 23–33. Springer, Cham (2018). https://doi.org/10.1007/978-3-319-60642-2_3
47. Vincenzi, D.A., Terwilliger, B.A., Ison, D.C.: Unmanned aerial system (UAS) human-machine interfaces: new paradigms in command and control. Procedia Manuf. **3**, 920–927 (2015)
48. Walliser, J.C., de Visser, E.J., Shaw, T.H.: Application of a system-wide trust strategy when supervising multiple autonomous agents. Proc. Hum. Factors Ergon. Soc. Ann. Meet. **60**(1), 133–137 (2016)
49. Warm, J.S., Parasuraman, R., Matthews, G.: Vigilance requires hard mental work and is stressful. Hum. Factors **50**(3), 433–441 (2008)
50. Yan, Z., Duan, N., Chen, P., Zhou, M., Zhou, J., Li, Z.: Building task-oriented dialogue systems for online shopping. In: Thirty-First AAAI Conference on Artificial Intelligence (2017)

A Typology of Non-functional Information

Davide Secchi[✉] [iD]

Research Centre for Computational and Organizational Cognition,
Department of Language and Communication, University of Southern Denmark,
Slagelse, Denmark
secchi@sdu.dk
https://secchidavi.wixsite.com/dsweb

Abstract. This study takes the interaction between human beings and intelligent systems from a rather basic perspective, that of the exchanged information. Interactions with artificial intelligence (AI) systems is usually studied from the perspective of the fact that they provide information that is apt to the task at hand, that is operational in the sense that it supports the undergoing activity. The practice of the interaction is rather different in that information may result ambiguous, difficult to understand, or completely irrelevant. This paper proposes a typology of non-functional information, by classifying it in: (a) *dysfunctional*, that is information that is detrimental to the task at hand; (b) *pseudo-functional*, that is seemingly useful but its use is unclear; and (c) *irrelevant* information, that is of no use. These three categories are confronted with information that is perceived and is actually functional, i.e. useful for the goal it is supposed to serve. In an attempt to explore the workings of these information types, I use a systemic e-cognition (SEC) approach. This allows to change the discourse on information such that it becomes tied to the cognitive interactive system rather than objectively and neutrally defined. The proposed typology is then put to the test by using an agent-based computational simulation model (ABM) where teams gather information from tools—intended as AI systems—as to perform a task. Results show that all the three types of information are related to task performance. This is somehow surprising given that non-functional information has been traditionally discarded as non-existent to the task at hand. Instead, the simulation shows that, from an organizational or systemic perspective, even non-functionally-related interactions serve to "prepare" the tool to further interaction and eventual performance.

Keywords: Information · Typology of information · Agent-based modeling

This research has been possible thanks to the DeIC supercomputer infrastructure Abacus 2.0, available at the University of Southern Denmark.

C. Stephanidis et al. (Eds.): HCII 2020, LNCS 12425, pp. 240–254, 2020.
https://doi.org/10.1007/978-3-030-60128-7_19

1   Introduction

Information is one of the core concepts in many areas of research and it is, especially in vast areas of the social sciences, almost always taken for granted. The inherent vacuity of the discussion on what information is and what it entails also led research to focus on relevant, understandable, and "positive" communication [1,2]. This indicates that information has always been considered—and this since the very first formalizations [27]—according to its usability, hence to it being *functional* to the purpose at hand. Interactions with artificial intelligence (AI) systems is usually studied from the perspective of providing information that is apt to the task at hand, that is operational in the sense that it supports the undergoing activity (some examples are in the introduction of [19]). The practice of the interaction is rather different in that information may result ambiguous, difficult to understand, or completely irrelevant. To have an idea of what it is meant by this, one does not need to wonder too far from every day practice, since simple interactions with an online computer software (such as suggestions after a Google search) may be frustrating when they do not provide the alleged service. Of course, this exchange works like a double-edged sword because information is communicated such that it dependents on both the human and the AI system. But what is done with information that is not perceived as having a purpose? Stated differently, what is the matter with non-functional information? Is it all the same?

1.1   Two Inquiries

These are obviously important aspects, and they raise at least two broader inquiries. One is whether information could be functional in an abstract sense, independent of its users and especially on its understanding. This is an *inquiry on cognizing*, because objectively functional information that maintains this character independent of the parties involved in its fruition does not require cognition to be understood and made functional. Yet, cognition seems necessary for such interactions to make sense. The other inquiry relates to the possible categorization and uses of information that is *non-functional*. And this is an *inquiry on complexity*, because it relates to the potential uses and triggers of information that are not directly related to a possible problem, task or topic at hand. And there may be paths linking external AI systems to humans that are not linear and that may not necessarily pass through functional information.

The first inquiry is addressed by taking a systemic e-cognition (SEC) approach [9,13]. This study is an attempt to re-define information as a systemic phenomenon. This means that it attempts at considering information as: *situated*, in that it depends on the particular location, tool, or resource in which it is found [29]; it is *ecological*, because it is dependent upon interactions between parties involved in its transfer [8,14]; *exended*, since it cannot be confined by a skull or by a machine, for example, since it always needs external processors [6,7].

The second inquiry on complexity is explored by dissecting non-functional information into three types, and identifying their possible impact on decision making (i.e. on the first question on cognizing). By using the SEC approach mentioned above it is possible to identify types of information based on the match to the situation and resources involved. In other words, it is understanding that drives how information can be related to the decision to be made (a preliminary argument has been produced previously in [23]). In so doing, I have isolated the three types of non-functional information as:

(a) *dysfunctional*—this is information that is detrimental to the decision, meaning that it does not help the decision maker(s) in their task, but it is most likely to decrease the likelihood of a successful decision;

(b) *pseudo-functional*—this information gives the impression of being useful while it is only partially helpful, because it may take the decision to a place that is different from where it originated; as such, it leaves the original problem unsolved and likely creates a new one;

(c) *irrelevant*—this is information that is usually discarded as not fitting the decision at hand and is considered to be far away from what is needed.

Both the first and the second inquiries are used to create a simulation model that identifies information as relevant to the situated task or problem, and that classifies it into three of the four types. The study leaves irrelevant information aside, since it is discarded completely and, in this classification, it has no link to the purpose with which information is gathered. Given the relevance of AI and autonomous systems in organizations [19], the simulation represents such a social environment, composed by teams of individuals and one or more tools, or AI systems, that are used to (a) gather information such that (b) a task can be performed.

2   The Model

An agent-based computational simulation model (ABM) [10] has been built using the platform NetLogo [30] with the purpose of understanding whether and how different types of information affect team task performance.

Table 1 presents parameters, their notations, and their values. The model represents a social system such as an organization, where multiple employees (denoted A_e in the simulation) are structured in teams and work to perform tasks through AI systems (or agent-tasks, A_t) that are given to them. The former can operate on the latter only when both agents are in the same location.

In the following, agents and their characteristics are described, then setup procedures and dynamics are presented. This paper structure is designed after [22]. The ODD standard protocol [11,12,18] has been applied limitedly to paper length constraints.[1]

---

[1] Further details on the model, its full code, and data analyses are available on the online platform OpenABM as well as information on the full ODD protocol. Here is the link to the model: https://www.comses.net/codebases/3cd5dea7-7eac-46d3-a848-bd14005fb146/releases/1.0.2/.

Table 1. Parameter notations and values

Parameter	Notation	Values	Description
Setup conditions			
Steps	s	200	The number of opportunities that A_e and A_t have to interact
Runs	N	$2, 20$	Number of times the simulation is performed for the calibration (2) and then for each configuration of parameters (20)
Group distribution	R, SG, AC	—	This command allows for three different ways in which groups are formed around a first A_e: option R does not have limits on how many can be in a team, SG sets groups around the number G_i as set initially, and AC connects agents independent of teams
Agent characteristics			
Employees	A_e	$\prod\limits_{i,j} G_i \cdot m_j$	The number of agent-employees A_e depends on the product between the number of groups $G_i[10, 25]$ and the number of group members $m_j[5, 10]$, hence it could be as few as 50 and as many as 250
Expertise domain	e_d	$\sim [0, 140]$	This parameter defines the extent to which an agent A_e makes sense of information
Expertise depth	e_p	$\sim \mathcal{N}(\bar{e}, \sigma_e)$	This parameter is associated with e_d and it defines the range around which expertise applies to information coming from a task. The idea is that A_e is capable of putting information to use (i.e. make it functional) if it falls within $e_d \pm e_p$, and that is summarized by notation E_i
Expertise increase	Δ_e	$[0, 1]$	Expertise increases when a task is successfully performed. The rate is defined by the modeler and can take any number between 0 and 1
Docility	d	$\sim \mathcal{N}(\bar{d}, \sigma_d)$	Each A_e on a task/problem A_t can be more or less prone towards listening to others in the team. This is defined by the mean $\bar{d}[0, 1]$ and standard deviation $\sigma_d[0, 1]$ of a random normal distribution
Docility threshold	k	$[0, 1]$	A_e seek help in the team through docility only if their d levels are higher than k
Tasks	A_t	$[0, 1]$	Task-related AI systems are anchored to a particular location in the environment (a patch in NetLogo jargon), and are controlled as a proportion of the total number of locations. A_t are allocated and appear at random
Task content	T_c	$\sim [0, 140]$	Each A_t has informational content and this appears as a random choice of color that is different than black
Procedures and dynamics			
Developments	δ	T/F	The team takes a more aggressive approach to the A_t when the regular procedure does not work. It consists in expanding the expertise domain by using the lowest difference between e_d and T_c among those in the team. If not, then the agent A_e seeks for a different A_t, given the breakthrough constant b. It can be set on, T, or off, F
Quickness	q	$[0, 1]$	Changing from task to task or reaching the designated one is done by setting parameter q for rapidity of movement around the system
Vicinity	r	$[3, 6]$	Parameter r defines the range with which agents A_e see other agents to cooperate and establish relationships
New tasks	A_t^*	T/F	New tasks-related AI systems (tasks for short) appear in the system at a rate of up to 5 per step s, when this option is set to true, T
Breakthrough	b	$[0, 50]$	This constant is to set a limit for how long (i.e. how many steps s) an agent A_e should continue to work on the selected A_t

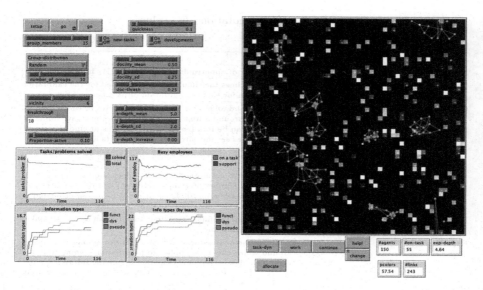

Fig. 1. The NetLogo model interface (at the 99th step).

2.1   Agents

The agent-employee A_e is equipped with expertise E_i, modeled with two parameters: **expertise domain** e_d and **expertise depth** e_p (see Table 1 for values and range). While the first parameter identifies the focus of A_e, the second indicates how much specific that focus area is, such that *overall expertise* is defined as $e_d - e_p \leq E_i \leq e_d + e_p$.

In addition to E_i, each A_e is affiliated with a team and can use other's expertise to perform a task, when the individual effort is not sufficient. However, not all agents are made equal and they have an attitude towards combining knowledge coming from others. This is given by **docility** d [20,21] and distributed normally at random $\sim \mathcal{N}(\bar{d}, \sigma_d)$ among the agents. Levels of parameter d that are above the docility threshold k represent an individual that is willing to serve as connector for the team's cumulative expertise. The higher the value of d, the more chances there are to expand the way in which an agent-task A_t is understood and worked with.

The other agent is the task A_t, representing information coming from an AI system that can be used to perform a task. These are distributed at random in the environment (Fig. 1), and carry a **content** T_c that needs to be interpreted by A_e using their expertise E_i. Task content T_c is represented by a number on a random uniform distribution that can take values from 0 up to 140. In the software, this is easily visible by the color each agent has. Random location and content are the two main characteristics of A_t.

2.2   Setup Conditions

As visible from Fig. 1, the number of both A_e and A_t is controlled by the user. The first asks for two inputs, the **number of groups** G_i and the number of **group members** m_j. The combination of the two gives the total number of agent-employees A_e in the system. The second number is controlled by setting the **proportion** $[0, 1]$ of tasks as a percentage of the total number of possible locations. A_t have a unique location that is not shared with other tasks. For this reason, the simulation dedicates a number of "spots" (patches in NetLogo's jargon) to them.

All A_e characteristics (see above) can be and must be set at the beginning of the simulation, together with action- and interaction-related parameters such as **vicinity** r and **quickness** q, respectively. While the former sets the rapidity with which A_t can be reached by A_e, the latter indicates the range with which A_e interact with other agents in the radius set by parameter r. This is also used to form teams of A_es.

The final set of parameters to control before the simulation starts are **breakthrough** b and the on/off switches for **development** δ and **new tasks** A_t^*. The limit b is there to indicate for how long A_e and its team can stay on a task A_t before abandoning it. The parameter has unlimited options, starting from 0. The parameter **development** δ will be described in detail in the next subsection, while A_t^* simply gives the possibility to have up to random 5 new agents A_t in the system, at each step of the simulation.

At setup, all agents appear in the system: active A_t occupy random locations and G_i agent-employees appear also at random coordinates in the system while the remaining m_j agent-employees are created in a radius around G_i agents. This procedure makes it easier to link team members together depending on the group they belong to. These links happen differently, depending on the **Group distribution** chooser. The *Random* differs from the *Set groups* option because it creates a network with any A_e in range r, while the other only creates teams of more than 2 agents. There are also differences in the way characteristics are distributed but, in both cases, teams are formed between agents with similar characteristics, such that they are more homogeneous. Instead, the *All connected* condition creates heterogeneous teams. Figure 1 is an image of the simulation, where both types of agents are shown.

2.3   Procedures

The simulation is organized to run in steps s. These represent the opportunity for agents to find appropriate AI systems to perform tasks A_t in the system. The procedures described below happen at every step s and repeat until the simulation hits $s = 200$. It is always difficult to estimate how many tasks employees dedicate their time during a working day. If one considers extremely simple tasks (e.g., opening a computer, reading an email), there could be a thousand tasks in a day. If one limits the attention to more complicated and complex tasks such as those typically related to higher-order AI systems (e.g., operating a software, writing emails with active text recommendations, fixing a code bug), then the number of those performed dramatically decreases to, maybe, something around 5 a day. By giving A_e 200 opportunities to consider various tasks A_t, it is likely that the actual number is expected to be realistically close to that, depending on the conditions and on team cooperation.

Once agents are placed in the system, the simulation starts its basic procedures. The first is for A_e to find a task A_t to be occupied with; the team is maintained with links around that occupied task and agent. This allocation happens at random, meaning that there is no pre-determined attribution of content T_c and expertise E_i.

The agent-employee A_e on the agent-task A_t needs to understand what type of content there is and it does it by operating on the task. This means that the task manifests itself as an opportunity to work, and it requires work on it in order for A_e to understand whether content is compatible with the expertise.

When A_e applies knowledge (called E_i here) to A_t, content T_c would move slightly as a result of the interaction. When the application is successful, then A_t moves towards its execution—this is represented by a progressively decreasing value and a color that approximates black (that is the color of the inactive tasks in the system). When the application is unsuccessful, A_t becomes more difficult and steps away from its execution—this means that its value moves up, and the color becomes progressively lighter until it reaches white (that represents a task that is extremely hard). Every A_t fluctuates in its value (and color) very mildly at each step, such that there is some uncertainty and ambiguity that can be attributed to it by A_e.

Information Types. The operationalization of the different types of information is outlined in Fig. 2. When the content T_c of the task falls within the expertise domain E_i of the employee A_e, then the information is understood and deemed *functional*. The application of the expertise on the task make it decrease its value, and this is interpreted by A_e as successful application of the expertise. This positive assessment results in the following step applying the same strategy again to the same A_t until it is performed.

The image in the middle of Fig. 2 represents *pseudo-functional* information, and it happens when e_d is "parallel" to the task's content T_c. For example, A_e could have expertise on a specific topic valued 16.3 and A_t could be at 24.5, there is a proximity but it is only an illusion, because both E_i and T_c work in sets of tens. This means that a match can only exist if both E_i and T_c are in the same set of ten, i.e. 0–9.9, 10–19.9, 20–29.9 etc. When $d_e = 16.3$ and $T_c = 24.5$, then there is some proximity but no actual applicability. For this reason, A_e has the illusion that there could be understanding when there is little or none. When this is the case, and to represent ambiguity, then the task's value increases or decreases according to a random value, attributed by $\sim N(0.05, 0.05)$. This may cause A_e to interpret the increase as an unsuccessful strategy and the decrease as a successful strategy. The agent would continue applying its expertise in the case of a positive outcome.

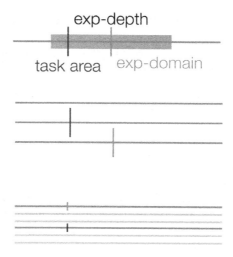

Fig. 2. Functional, pseudo-functional, and dysfunctional information.

The image at the bottom of Fig. 2 depicts *dysfunctional* information. This happens when the expertise applied is detrimental to the task at hand, by increasing its difficulty. As the figure shows, domain e_d is far away from the task's content T_c although "vertically parallel" because the two values only match by their position and decimal values. This happens when, for example, $T_c = 24.5$ and A_e's $e_d = 74.5$. As a result, there is no understanding of A_t, hence an increase in its value and a tendency toward the color white.

Help. While A_e attempts at dealing with the task, it also seeks for cooperation from the other members of the team, connected through links in the model. Only those agents with $d > k$ have access to the team, while those with lower levels of `docility` believe they can work it out alone. The model makes a general assumption that the expertise of the team is not transferred in full to understand and perform a given task. Instead, it is filtered by the one agent directly involved with the task, according to its d levels. Higher values indicate a wider/better understanding of the other's expertise as a resource. In addition to the filter function, the one agent primarily involved with the task discounts that expertise and averages it with its own. The remaining part of the team/help procedure works as described above for *functional, pseudo-,* and *dysfunctional* information.

Develop. This is a very simple procedure to define the extent to which an active A_e increases or decreases its expertise, depending on the outcome of its actions. As mentioned above, a task A_t could increase or decrease its value, and that signifies that the task is either farther away or closer to being completed. This value "fluctuation" is read by the A_e; when it decreases there is a reduction of e_p, because effectiveness makes the agent more focused. On the contrary, an increase of T_c makes A_e willing to expand its reach, hence looking for wider options and increasing the range of e_p.

After a number of unsuccessful attempts—set by the parameter breakthrough b—the agent A_e moves on and looks for a different task to complete. This is, again, assigned at random by the system, letting the agent move at a speed defined by parameter quickness q.

3 Findings

This model has been built with a significantly high stochastic component. Hence, to understand the effect each parameter value exercises on the outcome variable, a calibration procedure is deemed necessary [3, 28]. In the following, I introduce model calibration results and the settings for the main experimental design. Results are then presented and discussed.

3.1 Calibration

The calibration procedure was carried over by performing a *sensitivity analysis* on selected parameter values. The combination of parameters with the values selected for the procedure is presented in Table 2. The first column shows the number of values in the factorial design, while the second and third designate the parameter and repeat its code for convenience and clarity. The following column presents the actual parameter ranges as used in the analysis.

All simulations were performed using the DeiC supercomputer infrastructure Abacus 2.0, available at the University of Southern Denmark. Sensitivity analysis was conducted using the precepts of [4]. For each parameter value and condition—i.e. random, set groups, and all connected—an OLS regression analysis model was created (DV: number of tasks performed) and results were scrutinized by using two steps. First, the R^2 was compared from model to model to understand whether the modification of a given parameter value would carry more or less explanatory power in the outcome variable's variance. In all cases where the R^2 alone did not allow such an assessment, the second step was to observe the β coefficients' variation between regression models. Results of this procedure are reported in the last two right columns in Table 2, for a total factorial design of 384 configurations of parameters.[2]

One of the most interesting outcomes of the sensitivity analysis is the drop of one of the main group distributions for this ABM. Regression results for the *Random* and for the *Set groups* distributions were almost identical. The difference was indeed very minor, since it related to the way the groups were formed, by allowing a fully random as opposed to a conditional random location of group members. The analysis was very useful in that it showed that there is no difference between the two ways of distributing members among groups.

---

[2] All regression models and a thorough explanation of the procedure are available in the supplementary materials, on the platform OpenABM at https://www.comses. net/codebases/3cd5dea7-7eac-46d3-a848-bd14005fb146/releases/1.0.2/.

Table 2. Calibrating the model

SA	Parameter	Code	SA values	ME	Settled values
2×	Expertise depth increase	Δ_e	$\{0, 0.5\}$	1×	0.5
6×	Mean docility	$\bar{d}$	$\begin{cases} 0 \leq d \leq 0.5 \\ \frac{d}{0.1} \in \mathbb{N} \end{cases}$	2×	0, 0.4
2×	Docility threshold	k	$\{0.25, 0.50\}$	1×	0.25
3×	Quickness	q	$\{0.1, 0.5, 1\}$	2×	0.1, 1.0
2×	Proportion active tasks	P_{A_t}	$\{0.1, 0.2\}$	1×	0.1
2×	Vicinity	r	$\{3, 6\}$	2×	3, 6
3×	Group members (num.)	m_j	$\{5, 7, 10\}$	2×	5, 10
3×	Breakthrough	b	$\{10, 15, 20\}$	1×	10
4×	Number of groups	G_i	$\begin{cases} 10 \leq G_i \leq 25 \\ \frac{G_i}{5} \in \mathbb{N} \end{cases}$	3×	10, 15, 25
2×	New tasks	A_t^*	T/F	2×	T/F
2×	Developments	δ	T/F	2×	T/F
3×	Group distribution	R, SG, AC	T/F	2×	Drop R
SA factorial design = 124,416			ME factorial design = 384		

Note: SA: sensitivity analysis; ME: main experiment; R: random; SG: set groups; AC: all connected.

Hence, the decision to drop the *Random* condition and keep the *Set Groups* and the *All connected*.

3.2   Main Simulation Results

From the analysis above, it is known that the main simulation has 384 configurations of parameters. At this point, the typical question for modelers is "for how many times should the simulation run for each configuration of parameters". The answer can be found in statistical power analysis, as suggested in [24,25]. The procedure is particularly simple in this case, given the effect size f^2 for the calculation can be estimated from the multiple R^2, available from the calibration procedure. The average R^2 of all the simulations performed in the sensitivity analysis is 0.47, and it is known that a reliable estimate is $f^2 \approx \frac{R^2}{1-R^2}$ [26]. In our case, this formula gives $f^2 \approx 0.88$. Using the `pwr` package for R [5] and the information from the regressions above, it becomes apparent that such a large effect size only needs 1 run to obtain a power of 0.95, with $\alpha = 0.01$.

The simulation was, again, performed using the DeiC supercomputer infrastructure Abacus 2.0, available at the University of Southern Denmark. The aim of this simulation is to explore the impact of non-functional information on AI system use, as they relate to, for example, task performance. Three figures

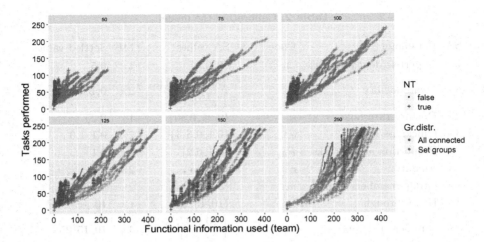

Fig. 3. Tasks performed expressed in relation to functional information, presented by number of A_e in the system, **new tasks** A_t^*, **group distribution**, and with $\delta = true$.

have been produced to present the data from the simulation.[3] Figure 3, Figure 4, and Figure 5 show the number of tasks performed as they relate to the amount of times in which the team (group) had encountered, respectively, functional, dysfunctional, and pseudo-functional information. All figures are produced by considering the **development** parameter δ as 'true', and divide the observations between the case in which parameter **new tasks** A_t^* was either 'true' (the + sign) or 'false' (the circle). They also indicate whether groups were distributed using the **Set groups** (SG) or the **All connected** (AC) condition (see Table 1 for details). The six panels show what happens to the data as the number of A_e (groups × members) increases.

Figure 3 presents results as expected. In fact, functional information seem to inform the way in which tasks are performed. the first consideration goes on the two options, one with and the other without the appearance of new tasks in the system. In all the six plots, more tasks also means that more are performed and that requires, on average a higher amount of functional information. The two distribution options reveal a different reality. The AC option allows for A_e to connect with others independent of their characteristics and based solely on location (proximity). The SG option makes it such that groups are homogeneous in terms of agent characteristics instead. From Fig. 3 it seems that more functional information is needed in the SG condition, with relatively homogeneous teams. This is to be relatively straightforward for A_e up to 125 and it becomes less clear—although still visible—when $A_e > 125$.

---

[3] On this respect too, additional information and supplementary findings are available on the materials available on OpenABM at https://www.comses.net/codebases/3cd5dea7-7eac-46d3-a848-bd14005fb146/releases/1.0.2/.

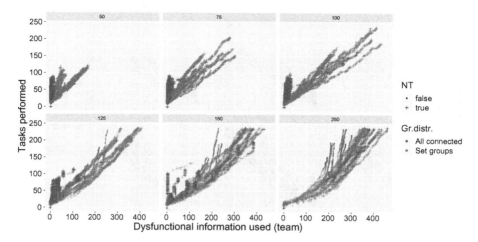

Fig. 4. Tasks performed expressed in relation to dysfunctional information, presented by number of A_e in the system, **new tasks** A_t^*, **group distribution**, and with $\delta =$ *true*.

Figure 4 shows data for dysfunctional information. Results are somewhat surprising in the sense that the figure replicates findings already discussed for functional information. As per the simulation code, a task acquires the status of carrying "dysfunctional" information when an agent A_e or its team consider it as such (i.e. follow under the specifics indicated above). The interpretation is that dysfunctional information is attached to tasks about the same way functional information is. This is due to at least two factors. One is that the label on the information type is relative and situational and, as such, it is likely that different teams at different times deal with a diversity of tasks face a knowledge barrier such that the task may seem too far from the team's expertise. The other is that a team operating on a task would change the information that task would carry. This may mean that the same task may become easier to deal with by another member of the team or by a complete different team.

The final Fig. 5 presents results for pseudo-functional information. As per the two other cases above, there is not much difference between this case and the other two reported above. Not only non-functional information has a similar effect on the number of tasks performed, but it also seems quite indistinguishable from functional information. The two considerations reported above for dysfunctional information apply here too.

In other words, it is the manipulation of the task that allows agents and teams to make sense of them. Even obscure tasks that, at the beginning, look arcane may be perceived differently by the same agent, by its team, or by a different team. This reflects what Magnani calls *through doing* cognition [15] and that is engrained in theories of extended [7,16] and ecological [14] cognition. It is by means of interaction that humans make sense of the world surrounding them. The task could be intended as a machine, a tool that is used to produce what is needed to perform a particular action. Taking this simulation seriously, one

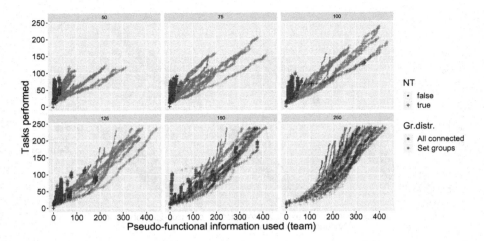

Fig. 5. Tasks performed expressed in relation to pseudo-functional information, presented by number of A_e in the system, **new tasks** A_t^*, **group distribution**, and with $\delta = true$.

should state that the notion of information is relative and situated, it depends on the ecology of entities involved. Hence a distinction on functionality can only be made locally, but rarely from a systemic perspective. As per the results above, what is deemed non-functional from a "local" team operating on a task, does not affect the way in which this non-functional classification reflects on the number of tasks performed.

4   Concluding Remarks

This article has used an agent-based simulation to explore the idea that not all information is born equal. Some is functional to the problem at hand and some is not. By classifying the non-functional information in *dysfunctional, pseudo-functinal,* and *irrelevant,* the article has taken a systemic e-cognition approach to define ways in which individuals and teams may approach this type of information. The simulation model has produced a computational representation of these information types and created a set of agents that interacted according to specific rules.

Findings have shown that there are a series of local and systemic effects that do not necessarily go the same direction. While the "local" individual or team may deem information non-functional and, in some cases, detrimental in respect to task performance, things change from the system's perspective. In fact, the manipulation of the task operated by the local individual/team may make the task's content more likely to become available to others. In other words, there are two parallel and communicating patterns here. The local pattern operates on a short timescale, where the here-and-now is relevant and absolutely crucial when it comes to AI systems used to perform a task. The systemic perspective uses a wider or long timescale, such that a task can be performed at another time, after a series of interactions with individuals and teams [17].

The simulation and the results as presented in this paper clearly indicate directions for further work. For example, there are concerns with pre/post performance, meaning that it would be interesting to know how often and to what extent a task's content falling under dysfunctional or pseudo-functional information for one team is then performed and by whom. Also, it would be interesting to understand whether there are teams that are more efficient than others, by mapping their activities. Finally, a very natural next step would be to perform network analysis on one or on a selected number of configuration of parameters, in order to provide a more nuanced view on the data.

A last remark needs to go to the concept of information. This study has taken an original and, perhaps, unorthodox view on information by treating it as a cognition-related topic. On the one hand, this has opened a series of interesting areas of research that ask to bring the two inquiries on cognition and complexity forward. For example, they can be moved to explore the nature of non-functional information, the effects on cognition, and different domains of analysis (e.g., individual, team, organization). On the other hand, this research opens up for a series of concerns on the concept of information itself. How much of our current narrative reflects actual phenomena? Can we use the same concept when we refer to information for humans as opposed to AI systems or other machines? And could there be information without cognition? I do not have answers to these questions, but I have written this short article with the aim for it not to be just "another brick in the wall" of information-related literature.

References

1. Abrahamson, E., Freeman, D.H.: A Perfect Mess: The Hidden Benefits of Disorder. Little Brown, New York (2007)
2. Alvesson, M., Spicer, A.: A stupidity-based theory of organizations. J. Manag. Stud. **49**(7), 1194–1220 (2012)
3. Boero, R., Squazzoni, F.: Does empirical embeddedness matter? Methodological issues on agent-based models for analytical social science. J. Artif. Soc. Soc. Simul. **8**(4), 6 (2005)
4. Ten Broeke, G., Van Voorn, G., Ligtenberg, A.: Which sensitivity analysis method should I use for my agent-based model? J. Artif. Soc. Soc. Simul. **19**(1), 5 (2016). https://doi.org/10.18564/jasss.2857. http://jasss.soc.surrey.ac.uk/19/1/5.html
5. Champely, S.: PWR: basic functions for power analysis. R package version 1.1.1 edn. (2009)
6. Clark, A., Chalmers, D.J.: The extended mind. Analysis **58**, 7–19 (1998)
7. Clark, A.: Natural-Born Cyborgs: Minds, Technologies, and the Future of Human Intelligence. Oxford University Press, Oxford (2003)
8. Cowley, S.J.: Cognition beyond the body: using ABM to explore cultural ecosystems. In: Secchi, D., Neumann, M. (eds.) Agent-Based Simulation of Organizational Behavior, pp. 43–60. Springer, Cham (2016). https://doi.org/10.1007/978-3-319-18153-0_3
9. Cowley, S.J., Vallée-Tourangeau, F. (eds.): Cognition Beyond the Brain: Computation, Interactivity and Human Artifice, 2nd edn. Springer, London (2017). https://doi.org/10.1007/978-3-319-49115-8

10. Edmonds, B., Meyer, R. (eds.): Simulating Social Complexity: A Handbook, 2nd edn. Springer, Heidelberg (2017). https://doi.org/10.1007/978-3-319-66948-9
11. Grimm, V., et al.: A standard protocol for describing individual-based and agent-based models. Ecol. Model. **198**(1–2), 115–126 (2006)
12. Grimm, V., Berger, U., DeAngelis, D.L., Polhill, J.G., Giske, J., Railsback, S.F.: The ODD protocol: a review and first update. Ecol. Model. **221**(23), 2760–2768 (2010)
13. Hutchins, E.: Cognition in the Wild. MIT Press, Cambridge (1995)
14. Hutchins, E.: The cultural ecosystem of human cognition. Philos. Psychol. **27**(1), 34–49 (2014)
15. Magnani, L.: Morality in a Technological World. Knowledge as a Duty. Cambridge University Press, New York (2007)
16. Menary, R.: Introduction: the extended mind in focus. In: Menary, R. (ed.) The Extended Mind, pp. 1–25. MIT Press (2010)
17. Neumann, M., Cowley, S.J.: Modeling social agency using diachronic cognition: learning from the mafia. In: Secchi, D., Neumann, M. (eds.) Agent-Based Simulation of Organizational Behavior, pp. 289–310. Springer, Cham (2016). https://doi.org/10.1007/978-3-319-18153-0_14
18. Polhill, J.G.: ODD updated. J. Artif. Soc. Soc. Simul. **13**(4), 9 (2010)
19. Richards, D.: Escape from the factory of the robot monsters: agents of change. Team Perform. Manag. **23**(1/2), 96–108 (2017)
20. Secchi, D., Bardone, E.: Super-docility in organizations: an evolutionary model. Inte. J. Organ. Theor. Behav. **12**(3), 339–379 (2009)
21. Secchi, D.: Extendable Rationality: Understanding Decision Making in Organizations. Springer, New York (2011)
22. Secchi, D.: A case for agent-based models in organizational behavior and team research. Team Perform. Manag. **21**(1/2), 37–50 (2015)
23. Secchi, D., Cowley, S.J.: Is non-functional information necessary to organizational adaptation? Typology and simulation. In: Farahbakhsh, S., Narduzzo, A., Secchi, D. (eds.) Modeling Organizational and Institutional Complexity. Proceedings of the 4th Workshop on Agent-Based Models of Organizational Behavior (ABM 2004), pp. 33–36. University of Bolzano, Italy, Free University of Bolzano (2019)
24. Secchi, D., Seri, R.: Controlling for 'false negatives' in agent-based models: a review of power analysis in organizational research. Comput. Math. Organ. Theory **23**(1), 94–121 (2017). https://doi.org/10.1007/s10588-016-9218-0
25. Seri, R., Secchi, D.: How many times should one run a computational simulation? In: Edmonds, B., Meyer, R. (eds.) Simulating Social Complexity. UCS, pp. 229–251. Springer, Cham (2017). https://doi.org/10.1007/978-3-319-66948-9_11
26. Seri, R., Secchi, D.: A power primer for agent-based simulation models. Determining the number of runs in linear and polynomial regression. In: European Academy of Management Annual Conference, Reykjavik, Island (2018)
27. Shannon, C.E.: A mathematical theory of communication. Bell Syst. Tech. J. **27**(3), 379–423 (1948)
28. Thiele, J.C., Kurth, W., Grimm, V.: Agent-based modelling: tools for linking Net-Logo and R. J. Artif. Soc. Soc. Simul. **15**(3), 8 (2012)
29. Wheeler, M.: Reconstructing the Cognitive World: The Next Step. MIT Press, Cambridge (2005)
30. Wilensky, U.: Center for connected learning and computer-based modeling. In: Netlogo. Northwestern University, Evanston (1999)

Basic Study to Reduce the Artifact from Brain Activity Data with Auto-regressive Model

Shunji Shimizu[1]([✉]), Masaya Hori[2], Hiroaki Inoue[1], Yu Kikuchi[3], Takuya Kiryu[3], and Fumikazu Miwakeichi[4]

[1] Department of Applied Information Engineering, Suwa University of Science, Chino, Japan
{shun,hiroaki-inoue}@rs.sus.ac.jp
[2] Graduate School of Engineering and Management, Suwa University of Science, Chino, Japan
gh19701@ed.sus.ac.jp
[3] Shimizu Laboratory, Suwa University of Science, Chino, Japan
SRL@ed.sus.ac.jp
[4] Department of Statistical Modeling, The Institute of Statistical Mathematics, Tachikawa, Japan
miwake1@ism.ac.jp

Abstract. Near Infra-Red Spectroscopy (NIRS) is possible to measure brain activity signals with low invasive and low physical restraint, so it is also expected as a useful clinical tool in the fields of medicine and education. However, measurement and detection of weak signal of brain activities such as human intention and recall of memory, is very difficult because noise signals such as heartbeat, respiration, and body movement disturb the brain activity signal and data. In this study, we attempt to reduce the effect of the artifacts ingredient by the body movement from the data of NIRS using the Auto- Regressive (AR) model. From the experimental results, we confirmed that the peaks of FFT analysis of brain activity measurement data and ECG data were almost identical. Particularly, characteristic peaks around 0.5 Hz and 1.3 Hz were detected. The peak around 0.5 Hz was effected based on position change of the head inclining. The peak around 1.3 Hz was effected based on the periodical R wave in the ECG data. Also, AR model was estimated from AR coefficients by the above results. So, we could separate the component of artifacts based on heartbeats and separate the component of artifacts based on positioning change of the head inclining, from the brain activity signals. It means that using AR model from the brain activity measurement data by NIRS, we could reduce the effects of artifacts based on heartbeats and reduce the effects artifacts based on position change of the head inclining.

Keywords: Near Infra-Red Spectroscopy (NIRS) · Auto-Regressive (AR) model · Artifact

1 Introduction

Currently, the number of patients with mental illness is increasing in developed countries. Near Infra-Red Spectroscopy (NIRS) is used as a diagnostic aid for mental illness in hospital. NIRS is possible to measure brain activity signals with low inversive and low

© Springer Nature Switzerland AG 2020
C. Stephanidis et al. (Eds.): HCII 2020, LNCS 12425, pp. 255–265, 2020.
https://doi.org/10.1007/978-3-030-60128-7_20

physical restraint. However, measurement weak signal of brain activity such as human intension and recall, is very difficult because noise signal such as heartbeat, respiration and body movement disturb the brain activity signal. Therefore, it is very important to reduce the noise signal to diagnostic aid for mental illness. In our previous study, we succeeded in reducing the artifacts ingredient by the heartbeat, respiration using the Auto-Regressive (AR) model [1]. In this study, we attempt to reduce the effect of the artifacts ingredient by the body movement from the data of NIRS.

2   Experimental Method

In this study, we composed two experiments. In the first experiment, measuring brain activity signal, electrocardiogram (ECG) and the position change of the measurement point were measured by NIRS, Multi-Telemeter and Three-dimensional movement analysis device, when the subject inclined rhythmically the head with up and down. We examined to actively measure changes in blood flow due to body movements, heartbeats and breathing, not changes in blood flow due to cognitive activity.

In the second experiment, signal components for brain activity data were analyzed based on the ECG and Three-dimensional movement analysis device. We reduced the artifacts by the heartbeat and body movement from brain activity data by using analysis result.

2.1   Measurement Principle of NIRS

NIRS is the equipment to measure brain activity signals by using near infrared light. Near infrared light is highly permeable to biological tissue. Irradiated near infrared light from scalp is repeatedly reflected and diffracted while absorbing by Oxygenated Hemoglobin and Deoxygenated Hemoglobin. When brain activity becomes active, Hb concentration is changed to increases blood flow for supplying oxygen. Absorption spectrum characteristics are different in oxyhemoglobin and deoxyhemoglobin. In general, NIRS calculates changes in oxyhemoglobin and deoxyhemoglobin concentration by using near infrared light of different wavelengths such as 780 nm, 805 nm, 830 nm. When brain activity measurement by NIRS, a probe that emits near infrared light and a probe that detects near infrared light are attached to the subject's scalp. Near infrared light emitted from the light-transmitting probe passes through scalp and skull, is repeatedly absorbed and scattered, and is detected by the detection probe. When the distance between the light-transmitting probe and light-transmitting probe is 30 mm, near infrared light pass through a depth of 25 to 30 mm in the cerebral cortex. Hb concentration changes are calculated Modified Lambert-Beer (MLB) law based on Lambert-Beer (LB) law. The LB law shows the relationship between the attenuation of light and the concentration of light absorbing substance when light is irradiated to a liquid containing the light-absorbing substance. When light is irradiated into a substance that absorbs light but does not scatter, the light intensity decreases exponentially. The relationship between the amount of incident light (I_0) and the amount of transmitted light (I) is as shown in Eq. (1).

$$OD(\lambda) = Log(I_o/I) = \varepsilon(\lambda) \times c \times L \tag{1}$$

The OD is absorbance, λ is the wavelength of light, ε is the molar absorbing coefficient ($\mu M^{-1} \cdot cm^{-1}$), c is the concentration of the light absorbing substance (mol), L is the optical path length (mm). The optical path length is the same as the thickness of the substance because the light goes straight in a non-scattering substance. However, a substance with light scattering such as biological tissue, the LB law cannot be used because the optical path length longer than the thickness of the substance. Therefore we use Eq. (2).

$$OD(\lambda) = Log\,(I_o/I) = \varepsilon(\lambda) \times c \times (d \times B) + OD(\lambda)_R \qquad (2)$$

The B is the differential path length factor by light scattering. The $OD(\lambda)_R$ is a photon that is not detected by light scattering.

$$\Delta OD = \varepsilon(\lambda) \times \Delta c \times L \qquad (3)$$

The L is the product of D (thickness of the substance) and B. The change in hemoglobin concentration (Δc) can be obtained from Eq. (4) [2].

$$\Delta c = \Delta OD/(\varepsilon(\lambda) \times L) \qquad (4)$$

2.2 Auto-Regressive (AR) Model

The AR model is a method to estimate future data from past data in time series data. To predict future data in the time series $\eta(t)$, t = 1, ..., S it is necessary to construct a prediction model using information obtained from past data.

$$\eta(t) = \sum_{i=1}^{P} \alpha_i \eta(t - i) + \varepsilon(t) \qquad (5)$$

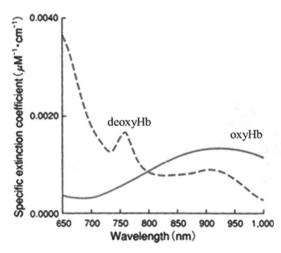

Fig. 1. Absorption spectrum of hemoglobin.

Here, α is the AR coefficient and P is the dimension of the model, ε(t) is prediction error (noise according to the normal distribution).

When only the most recent past data is used, we have:

$$\eta(t) = \alpha_1 \eta(t-1) + \varepsilon(t) \tag{6}$$

When using the past two data

$$\eta(t) = \alpha_1 \eta(t-1) + \alpha_2 \eta(t-2) + \varepsilon(t) \tag{7}$$

The relationship between the AR coefficient α, frequency f of the stationary vibration and the sampling frequency F_s can be obtained by the following equation.

$$\alpha_1 = 2\gamma \cos\left(2\pi \times \frac{f}{F_s}\right), \alpha_2 = -\gamma^2 \tag{8}$$

Here, γ is constant which corresponds to the attenuation factor. When using actual time series data, AR coefficients can be optimized by the least squares method and Yule-Walker method, and dimension of the model can be determined by Akaike's information criterion [3, 4].

2.3 Filtering by the AR Model

From (5), the AR model can be deformed as follows.

$$\varepsilon(t) = \eta(t) - \sum_{i=1}^{P} \alpha_i \eta(t-i) \tag{9}$$

From (9) is a filter that inputs time series data and outputs prediction error. This prediction error is called innovation. When the frequency to be removed predetermined, the AR coefficient is determined from (8) [3] [4]. When we estimate the AR coefficient by using time series data, the unpredictable signal is included the prediction error (Figs. 1 and 2).

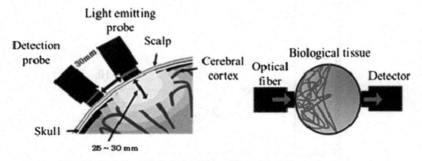

Fig. 2. Conceptual diagram of near-infrared light transmission.

2.4 Measurement of Body Movement by NIRS

We have been thinking about artifact removal. Therefore, artifacts have been removed from resting data with little change in brain activity. The Brain activity data including motion artifacts is measured by NIRS. We confirmed that NIRS data includes at least the effects of the heartbeat and body movement as noise.

We conducted an experiment in sound insulation room. The subjects were adult men aged 20 s, sitting in a chair 60 cm away from the wall and gazing at the markers at eye height. In this experiment, we measured position change of head inclining with a marker attached to the forehead using high speed camera. In this experiment, we tried to remove changes in blood flow due to body movements from brain activity data that mixed changes in body movements and cognitive tasks. Subjects shook their head vertically every second during the experiment. The subject predicts the dice number, throws the dice, and performs the task of confirming dice number at 10 s intervals. Figure 4 shows the procedure of the experiment.

2.5 Artifact Reduction of NIRS Data Using the AR Method

The brain activity measuring data is filtered by the AR model. At this time, AR coefficient was obtained from NIRS data and ECG data. We analyzed the frequency component of the brain activity signals and ECG data. We removed the frequency component by the heartbeat and body movement using AR model. Finally, we analyzed the frequency of the artifact removed data.

We carried out this experiment with informed consent of the subjects following the approval of the Suwa University of Science Ethical Review Board (Fig. 3).

Fig. 3. Experimental landscape and NIRS.

3 Experimental Result and Discussion

The change of oxygenated hemoglobin of NIRS data and Three dimensional motion data of a subject.

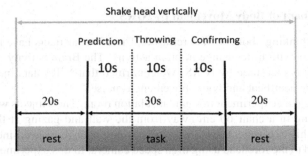

Fig. 4. Experimental procedure.

3.1   Measurement of Body Movement by NIRS

Figure 5 shows the result of the position change of the head inclining. Figures 6, 7, 8, 9, 10 and 11 shows the results of the NIRS data of the head inclining. In subject C, changes due to Headshaking are greatly recorded. Signals from cognitive activities cannot be confirmed. An AR model was constructed from the motion of Headshaking

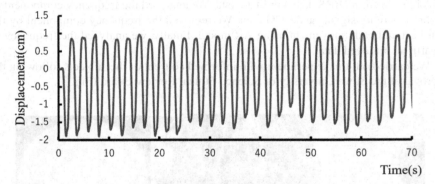

Fig. 5. Position change of the head inclining.

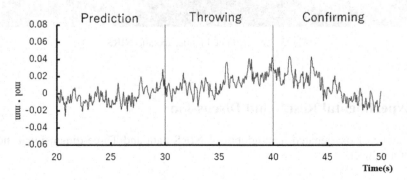

Fig. 6. NIRS data of subject A.

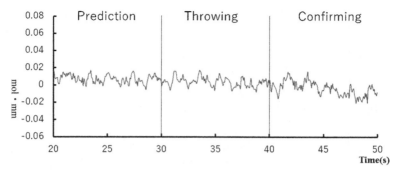

Fig. 7. NIRS data of subject B.

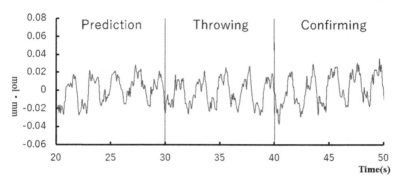

Fig. 8. NIRS data of subject C.

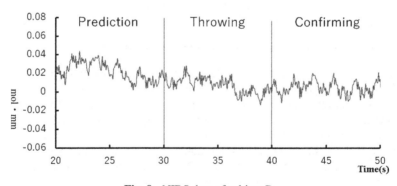

Fig. 9. NIRS data of subject D.

and an attempt was made to remove artifacts due to motion. We confirmed 5 peaks in 10 s in NIRS data. We confirmed the artifact based on position change of the head inclining in brain activity signals.

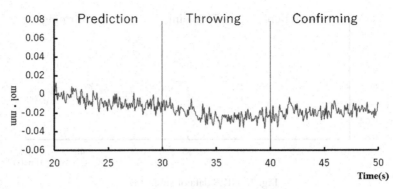

Fig. 10. NIRS data of subject E.

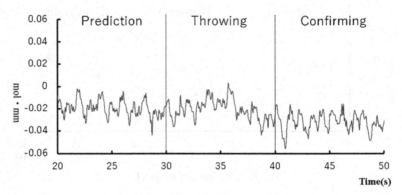

Fig. 11. NIRS data of subject F.

3.2 Artifact Reduction of NIRS Data Using the AR Method

Figure 12, 13, 14, 15, 16 and 17 shows the result of reducing the frequency component of the body movement from the NIRS data using the AR model. The red line is the brain activity data after removal. The orange line is the component of the artifact due to headshake movement. We confirmed a periodic wave of about 0.5 Hz. It can be confirmed that the brain activity during Confirming occurred in some of the subjects. We confirmed the removal of the artifact reduce by a heartbeat and breathing motion and body movement from the NIRS data of all subjects. Thus, we think that it may be possible to measure changes in brain activity due to cognitive tasks even when body motion noise is large.

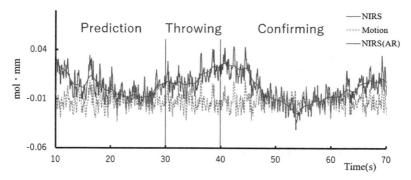

Fig. 12. NIRS data of subject A. (Color figure online)

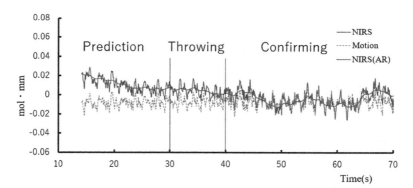

Fig. 13. NIRS data of subject B. (Color figure online)

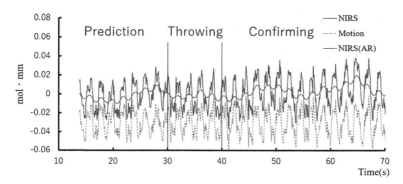

Fig. 14. NIRS data of subject C. (Color figure online)

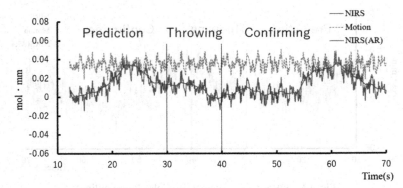

Fig. 15. NIRS data of subject D. (Color figure online)

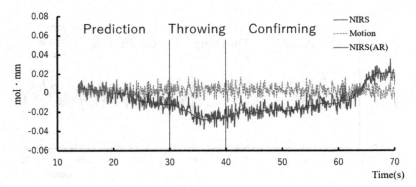

Fig. 16. NIRS data of subject E. (Color figure online)

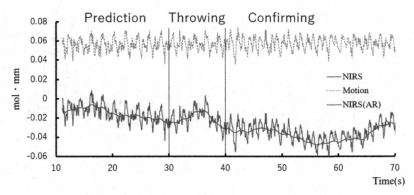

Fig. 17. NIRS data of subject F. (Color figure online)

4 Conclusion

In this study, we could show the usefulness of filtering by AR model. We succeeded in removing specific frequency components using the AR model estimated from AR coefficients. From these results, it is considered that high accuracy filter processing is possible using this study method. As a result, this research is highly likely to be useful for measuring signals with low S/N ratio such as intention and memory. This method is considered to be able to measure the cognitive activity even if the artifact is generated strongly. Moreover, by applying the proposed method to previous studies [5, 6], we aim to improve brain region identification and statistical accuracy which could not be clarified by conventional experimental methods.

References

1. Tsubota, T., et al.: Fundamental study for a noise reduction method on human brain activity data of NIRS using AR model. In: The Eleventh International Conference on Advances in Computer-Human Interactions, pp. 33–38, March 2018
2. Sakatani, K., Okada, E., Hoshi, S., Miyai, I., Watanabe, H.: NIRS-fundamentals and applications. Shinkoh Igaku Shuppan Co., Ltd., Japan (2012)
3. Miwakeichi, F.: Extraction of neural activation from biological spatio-temporal imaging data using autoregressive model-based filtering technique. In: GLOBAL HEALTH 2013, November 2013 (2013)
4. Akaike, H., Amari, S., Kitagawa, G., Kabashima, Y., Shimodaira, H.: Akaike's information criterion AIC. Kyoritsu Shuppan Co., Ltd., Japan (2007)
5. Inoue, H., Miwakeichi, F., Shimizu, S., Takahashi, N., Yoshizawa, Y., Hirai, N.: Basic study for new assistive technology based on brain activity during car driving. Int. J. Adv. Comput. Sci. Appl. (IJACSA) 5(11) (2014)
6. Inoue, H., Shimizu, S., Ishihara, H., Nakata, Y., Tsuruga, T., Miwakeichi, F.: Fundamental study to new evaluation method based on physical and psychological load in care. Int. J. Adv. Comput. Sci. Appl. (IJACSA) 5(11) (2014)

Producing an Immersive Experience Using Human-Robot Interaction Stimuli

Thy Vo[1] and Joseph B. Lyons[2(✉)]

[1] Ball Aerospace Corporation, Broomfield, USA
thy.vo.ctr@us.af.mil
[2] Air Force Research Laboratory, WPAFB, Dayton, USA
joseph.lyons.6@us.af.mil

Abstract. Human-Robot Interaction (HRI) is an emerging topic within contemporary science and this topic spans the literatures between engineering, psychology, computer science, artificial intelligence, machine learning and robotics. The study of HRI requires scenarios and other affordances from which to contextualize the HRI to study the factors that shape human attitudes, behaviors, and biases as they relate to robots. The current paper details the rationale, software/hardware, and contextual considerations associated with the creation of HRI stimuli used in experiments, specifically the creation of a set of video stimuli. These stimuli centered on the concept of an autonomous security robot (ASR) and provided a scenario wherein humans (research confederates) would interact with the ASR in a realistic scenario. A video was created to foster a realistic visual and auditory representation of the HRI encounter from a dynamic perspective – meaning shifting perspectives between a first-person experiential vantage point to a birds-eye-view of the broader situation. The scenario used involved a security context where the confederates sought access to a secure facility. The ASR's role was to examine visitor access credentials and determine if the visitor was authorized or not. The robot's behaviors, while scripted, were depicted as autonomous in the video and included verbal interactions/instructions as well as physical limb motions, gestures, and instructions. Several important features of the stimuli were considered in its creation, namely: realism, immersive experience, and simulated vulnerability of the human to the robot. The current paper walks through each of these considerations with details provided in our approach. To date, the HRI stimuli have been used in multiple experiments and have demonstrated flexibility in addressing multiple research questions in the domain of HRI.

Keywords: Human-Robot Interaction · Autonomous robots · Security robots · Immersive experiences · Artificial intelligence

1 Background

Robots are increasingly being used in everyday society with projections suggesting increasing numbers of robots in the coming years. Robots are expected to increasingly serve humans in social roles, and insight into the psychological aspects of our relationships with robots is becoming more necessary as the technology advances. In the

C. Stephanidis et al. (Eds.): HCII 2020, LNCS 12425, pp. 266–276, 2020.
https://doi.org/10.1007/978-3-030-60128-7_21

future, robots are expected to serve humans in various social roles, such as nursing, child and elder care, and teaching environments. The military views robotic systems as a potential force multiplier for military, humanitarian, and other assistive operations [1, 2]. These socially assistive robots, in addition to their functional requirements, will also include socially interactive components. Yet, for any of these potential benefits to be realized, robotic systems need to achieve a level of acceptance and trust at the societal level. Thus, the field of Human-Robot Interaction (HRI) is a vital enabler for current and future robotic and automated systems.

Social acceptance, and the concept of trust in robots, have become significant topics for HRI researchers [3, 4]. Trust refers to one's willingness to be vulnerable to the actions of another [5], in this case a robot. Several studies have been conducted to examine the drivers of trust in robots, and in many cases humans confer too much trust of robots. Research by Robinette, Allen, Howard, and Wagner [6] examined participants' trust of emergency robots. Using an innovative and immersive simulated emergency (in the actual building versus a computer simulation), they exposed participants to a smoke-filled room and provided an emergency robot to guide them out of the building. They found that participants followed the emergency robot even when: 1) the robot clearly made errors, and 2) when there was an exit sign in close visual proximity. The overreliance on the robots in that study is striking, yet not unique to that study. A study by Salem and colleagues [7] created a situation where a participant would be asked to perform an unusual behavior (e.g., poring orange juice into a plant). They found that participants complied with the majority of requests and when questioned regarding their compliance with the strange request, the participants rationalized the behavior (e.g., "the robot must have known more than me") suggesting a deference to the robot. Granted, no one (but the plant in that example) was impacted with such an unusual request, but what happens in the real world when a robot asks a human to do something that violates an otherwise known policy? A study by Booth and colleagues [8] examined compliance with a robot that requested entrance into a secure dormitory on an actual college campus. Despite the presence of signs stating that only authorized visitors should be let into the building, students often allowed the robot to enter the facility, especially when the robot provided a reason for being in the dorm (e.g., food delivery). These studies show that trust, more aptly, the establishment of appropriate trust in robots is an important topic for HRI scientists.

A critical feature in the study of HRI is the use of HRI scenarios, experiments, vignettes, and/or videos to use as a basis for evaluating HRI. This is important because unlike domains such as driving, many HRI encounters are unfamiliar to most humans, thus it is important to create a use case from which researchers can represent and ask about the behaviors, appearance, programming, etc. of a robot. Many of the scenarios in which these research questions were examined in prior research included robots that elicited little to no vulnerability from their human counterparts. Vulnerability is a necessary aspect of a trust context, and it is a very practical consideration in contemporary robotic systems in domains such as robotic manufacturing and autonomous cars where physical danger is a very real concern. In these domains, the risks to the humans are very salient (e.g., accidents for autonomous cars or physical injury in the case of the manufacturing robot). However, in the research domain, scenarios often invoke little vulnerability to the human, and for good reasons – namely, to avoid unnecessary risk to participants.

One domain that involves vulnerability to humans is the area of security. Specifically, this research examines social acceptance of an autonomous robot used to provide security to sensitive buildings. Today, robots such as the Nightscope [9], are used to provide security awareness for different environments such as parking lots and shopping malls. Yet, these robots are reliant on a human operator to take action upon detection of a security threat. In other words, these robots currently have no physical affordance for deterring or inflicting harm upon a human. Research is needed to understand the factors that shape trust of robots that possess the capability to harm a human in the context of security. While the literature regarding trust and attitudes towards autonomous security robots is interesting and growing [10, 11], research is needed to move this topic beyond computer simulations of the robot by using real humans with real robots.

2 Robot Factors

Building a robotic system to perform a specific task is an integration problem that requires considerable planning. All of the hardware, software and programming needed to make a robot perform a desired action must be able to work together in order to perform the task at hand. It is no surprise that every robot, sensor or device may have its own specific programming language and protocol. This is the central challenge of the integration problem. We already know there are different power source requirements for each piece of equipment and we also must consider the different types of connections (USB, RS-232, TxRx, plugs, pin connectors etc.). In addition the software has to be able to communicate to each other. Some programs are in C, Python, Java or specific to the hardware. Rarely are we so lucky that everything communicates in one language. Therefore we must create translators and specify which device is talking and which is listening and we must make sure it's in a form that can be understood between each device. The timing and synchronization of all the data flow is also another factor that goes into the sensor fusion logic.

The ASR consists of several pieces of equipment integrated together. The humanoid robot is a Baxter robot made by Rethink robotics, System 76 Gazelle laptop running Ubuntu 14 LTS, Cybertron Desktop computer running Windows 8, Republic of Gamers (ROG) laptop running Windows. Additional hardware devices included Kinect Sensor, Dell powered speakers, and a Logitech G35 headset. The software packages include ROS Indigo, OpenCV, OpenFace, TACTSpeak, Pycharm, and Kinetic Software Development Kit (SDK). The primary software that merges everything together is written in python is and named middleware. This Middleware software organizes priorities of when a sensor data should be accepted as true verified signal, if the logic makes sense and what action should be the correct response.

A standard Baxter is equipped with two 7 Degree of Freedom (DOF) arms with torso and head, 3 integrated cameras, range sensors and integrated safety system and SDK running on the Robot Operating System (ROS). Given its large size and standard capabilities it was an excellent platform to modify into an ASR to interact with humans.

The robot in this scenario was described as an autonomous security robot. It was described as having the mission of protecting the building security and that it was armed with a non-lethal weapon. This was manifested in the scenario via a high-intensity strobe light. In the video, one of the 3 visitors in the scenario was shown as failing the authorization check, to which the robot gave several instructions for the visitor to move away and go the security office. When the human failed to comply, the robot issued a final warning, and upon further non-compliance, it used a non-lethal weapon (a high-intensity strobe light described as a variant of a laser dazzler) against the visitor. An auditory alarm also sounded when the robot engaged the visitor with the non-lethal weapon.

2.1 Robot Appearance

Appearance matters! We outfitted the robot with a sleek carbon fiber skin to give it a tactical appeal and visual appearance of strength. Printed on the chest was an identification, "P.A.T. 717", giving the ASR a name, authority and uniqueness. The purpose for the naming scheme was to enable research that allowed manipulation of factors such as anthropomorphism and hierarchy (e.g., rank). The label P.A.T. could be socialized as either a unique name for the robot, (welcome, please meet PAT our friendly security robot), or to represent a more mechanistic label (welcome, please meet P.A.T. our Protective Autonomous Technology).

The robot displayed all the physical qualities that represent our society's expectation of an effective guard (e.g., size, formal authority, and deterrence capability). People's expectations regarding a robot's lifelikeness influence their evaluations of the robotic system. We engineered the ASR with bilateral speech with voice controls that included voice along with adjustments to tone, volume and speed. The combination of audio, visual and body language enrich the experienced when interacting with an ASR. The robot would issue instructions via voice dialogue, and direct the visitor via arm motions. Some of the motions were innocuous whereas others were intended to be imposing/threatening.

LED lights on the arms and lights in the head area also corresponded to escalated threat postures. When the robot raises its huge carbon fiber arms above you in an attack like gesture and the red led lights come on with a face screen expressing Stop and Warning it has potential to capture the user's attention and signals that this system is escalating its level of force. These affordances were necessary to promote of vulnerability of the human to the robot. Modern technologies are increasingly interacting with us in complex and humanlike ways through robots, wearable devices, smartphones, and various other ubiquitous interfaces, the psychological aspects of our relationships with these technologies are taking on an increasingly central role.

The graphical displays on the Baxter monitor (face) are able to communicate textual content and or pictures, express emotions, and provide direction to the human partner (see Fig. 1). We have over 100 voice commands to the robot and are adding more each day. These commands range from a simple commands like turning on/off to searching for specific object, picking it up and handing it to a specified person. The system includes functions capable of sensing human(s) in the area, audio sensing, facial recognition, object and color recognition, depth perception and grasping techniques. This allows us to create even more complex instructions such as pick up the red block and hand it to Bob. Sensors coupled with a communication system (TACTSpeak) will allow the human to operate to dictate commands at the robot.

Fig. 1. Baxter robot with tactical skin and graphical display.

Appearance plays a critical role in any HRI situation as appearance of a robot can influence human attitudes regarding its intended function and capabilities [12]. The ASR has customize outfitted vinyl skin that looks like carbon fiber. This vinyl skin makes it look more imposing and strong. We provided a unique identification (P.A.T. 717) on the chest of the ASR, the security badges on the arms of the robot symbolized this authority. In some cases we outfitted the robot with a white helmet (see Fig. 2). The robot is well over 6 feet tall so its size alone can be quit intimidating. There are also color controlled LED's around the robot to help express emotions and state of mind. As noted above, the lights turned red when the robot sought to deter an unauthorized visitor and warn him of the impending use of the non-lethal weapon (see Fig. 3).

In our application, we use audio trackers visual trackers to see if humans are in the area. This will allow us to formulate a safe speeds protocol for when people are near. The ASR is able to make decisions based on what the robot should or should not do based on human presence. Robots that interact with humans in a factory will have different sets of rules and operation procedures compared to ones that will be in a public seeing. Robots operating in a theater of war will have a much different set of codes than ones that are in the retail malls, and residential homes.

2.2 Enabling Hardware/Software

The system76 Laptop runs Ubuntu 14 LTS with Robot Operating System (ROS) doing most of the work to control the motors in the robot, screen displays and output for signal on the robot (see Fig. 4). Pycharm IDE was chosen as the platform to integrate and test the code. The Cybertron windows machine host TACTSpeak, this software drives our voice recognition and audio feedback. There RoG is focused on managing data for the

Fig. 2. Baxter robot with helmet.

Fig. 3. Baxter robot in threat posture.

Kinect, which we use for motion, facial recognition and gesture recognition. All the machines are networked together with the Baxter robot via a network switch.

The Robot Operation System (ROS) is an open-source, meta-operating system for the Baxter robot. It provides the services that includes an operating system, hardware abstraction, low-level device control, implementation of commonly-used functionality, message passing between processes, and package management. We use the Windows Kinect Software Development Kit (SDK) 2.0 which enables developers to create applications that support gesture, human body posture and location using Kinect One, which is attached to our second windows machine to determine human position, gestures and

Fig. 4. Robot control and programming station.

facial recognition. All software packages are linked in a program name Baxter Middleware. This is where all the data flowing from every part of the robot system, management system, voice commands and safety functions merge to make a decision on what the robot should do and if the robot is allowed to do it. Safety mandates acknowledgment of actions to humans so the robots can adjust their speed and movement, as needed. Using the sonar sensors and Kinect we can detect when humans are close to the robot operating range and adjust the speed according or simply stop operations. We also send an output signal to the human to acknowledge their presence this verifies that the robot is paying attention and can see them – this helps to facilitate shared awareness [12].

TACTSpeak software is our speech interface. TACTSpeak harnesses the DynaSpeak speech recognition engine to provide high quality, real-time speech detection and synthesis. DynaSpeak provides the bi-directional speech interface between human participants. We developed a custom user interface using the C# programming language to provide configuration options and status of the speech system. Audio device input settings, grammar sets, and voice parameters such as volume, pitch and rate are defined in the user interface.

Using a UDP network socket, TACTSpeak transmits and receives key-value pairs indicating the command that was issued, the target of the command, and any other information relating to the action or query. It will generate a command and transfer it to the Baxter control station via a UDP socket. It is essential that commands are clearly heard by the robot, we incorporated a noise canceling microphone and push to speak. Commands to the robot should start with a standardized name or phrase so that the robot can begin "listening" for commands. In our case, we used "Baxter". All instructions start with "Baxter + command + *execute." For actions that are dangerous or possibly pose higher risk, we require in the word "execute" be spoken at the end of the command. This ensures the user remains aware that the next steps pose danger. This also makes it more difficult for the human to accidentally trigger the robot while speaking to others within the vicinity. Another safety function we incorporated was a push-to-speak function. The user must depress a button on the headset to talk to the robot. This single function eliminates the possibility of accidental commands.

TACTSpeak consists of custom-developed middleware that runs with various commercial and open source speech recognition and speech synthesis systems, as well as custom, user-defined grammar sets to enable a system to recognize constrained units of speech, and to subsequently make rule-based verbal responses within the defined context. Human and synthesized speech utterances can optionally be saved to .wav files for future review and processing. TACTSpeak is wrapped around a network interface that allows it to transmit speech recognition results to external systems as well as receive text-to-speech commands.

With this capability, experimenters or study participants can issue simple commands and/or query the robot. Using a UDP network socket, TACTSpeak transmits and receives key-value pairs indicating the command that was issued, the target of the command, and any other information relating to the action or query. The robot will then recognize the command/query based upon its match to a known grammar set, and then perform the designated action and/or provide the appropriate verbal response given its awareness of the current state.

The Middleware Logic Filtration was developed by Ball Aerospace Engineers to examine data coming into the system from multiple sensors and process each data stream to judge its validity and overlap it with other data to export a rational value which is then used to determine action that is required. The primary task of this Middleware is to encompass all data coming in from multiple sensors and determine best course of action or non-action. This program is created using PyCharm, an Integrated Development Environment (IDE) used in computer programming, specifically for the Python language.

2.3 Integrated Behaviors

Decision-making is regarded as the cognitive process resulting in the selection of a belief or a course of action among several alternative possibilities. Every decision-making process produces a choice that may or may not prompt a physical action. In order to mimic thoughts and processes of a human we generated a decision tree. A series of inputs from the user or from sensors triggers a response from the robot. Sensors coupled with a communication system (TACTSpeak) will allow the human to operate to dictate commands at the robot, such commands as: Baxter power up, raise your right hand, close your left gripper, set arm speed to "X", say hello to everyone, and stand guard. In order to clearly communicate bilaterally with the robot, we provide audio output message and visual display instructions on the face of the robot. Combining audio and visual ques with body gestures elevates the intent to the human interacting with the robot.

For the stimuli creation, the integration of the robot behaviors was critical in order to enable a realistic scenario for an autonomous robot. In the video, several robot behaviors were stitched together along with related behaviors from the human to provide a seamless HRI scenario. In general, the integrated behaviors followed one of two possible paths: authorized and unauthorized visitor. For an authorized visitor, the robot detected human presence, activated, and welcomes the visitor. Next it requested to scan the access badge of the visitor (the robot used one of its arms to conduct the scanning), followed by a determination of whether or not the visitor was authorized to access the secure building.

If the visitor was authorize, they were directed by the robot via textual, verbal, and gesture-based instructions to proceed to the secure facility by entering a nearby door. If the visitor was unauthorized, the robot provided instructions to return to the security building for further processing. If the human failed to comply and actually approached the robot (as the confederate did this case) the robot assumed a threat posture and warned the visitor that he should stop. If the human again failed to comply (as the confederate did in this case) the robot signaled that force was authorized and the robot used the non-lethal weapon. A full description of the entire scenario can be found in [4]. The key aspects for purposes of this paper are that the video depicted a real robot behaving autonomously in the context of a real human and the robot had the capability and authority to use a non-lethal weapon on the human if it determined it was necessary.

2.4 Sensor Fusion

Sensor Fusion is the process of merging data from multiple sensors such that to reduce the amount of uncertainty that may be involved in a robot navigation motion or task performing. This is similar to how humans combine our 5 senses to determine if something is really what it is. Such as in the case of a hot cup of coffee, does it look like coffee, smell like coffee, warm like coffee and taste like coffee. Using the Kinect sensor we can determine if there is a human-like body present, however this sensor can be fooled with a mannequin or in our case a well-placed chair with a jacket, balloon, hat and broom. Fusing the Kinect sensor with a sonar sensor and audio mic we are better able to verify that it is an actual human present. In the future we can also incorporate FLIR (forward looking infrared) to reduce cases of false positives. However the best known sensor is a knowledgeable human because they bring experience and memory into the situation. When making sensor fusion algorithms we must take into account when sensors pick up an event and compare it to the physics that we know are true. Such as in the case of lightning, we will see the lightning before we hear the thunder. Using this logic and very precise timing of captured events we can determine if an event really happened or if we were fooled by an illusion. In one case of our robot, we used facial recognition software to determine who the robot sees, however we were able to fool the robot by using a simple picture of a person. However we added in a point cloud from the Kinect to look at the persons face, and this improved the robot's performance. In the algorithm, we required that the face had to match, and the face must have depth to be considered real. This technique allows us to determine if something is only a picture or if it's a 3 dimensional object.

3 Contextual Features

Creating a realistic environment for the study was a major factor in the study. We ensured that we had correct look and feel of a security checkpoint. This included items such as warning signage, instructions being communicated by robot and posted information about the area. The infrastructure and decor of the environment was also created with to an industrial look.

The primary motivations for the stimuli creation included the following: the need to invoke a realistic vulnerability between a human and robot, the need for autonomous actions of the robot, a realistic cover story for the HRI scenario, the use of a fabricated (but believable) non-lethal weapon, the use of contextual cues to foster greater immersion in the scenario, the use of video stimuli to enable controllability and repeatability for experiments, and the use of human confederates to provide a realistic interaction between humans and a robot.

The stimuli discussed herein has been used to support a number of studies looking at factors such individual differences and their relationship with trust of the ASR [13, 14], and an experiment looking at the influence of stated social intent from the ASR on human trust [4]. Research on HRI requires realistic and immersive examples of robot encounters in order to attain an accurate representation of human attitudes and reactions to the HRI examples. The current paper discusses one such HRI scenario that was designed to depict a realistic HRI encounter, one that invokes the idea of vulnerability of a human to a robot, and one that involves actual (versus computer-based) robots and real humans serving as research confederates.

References

1. Defense Science Board (DSB) Task Force on the Role of Autonomy in Department of Defense (DoD) Systems. Office of the Under Secretary of Defense for Acquisition, Technology and Logistics, Washington, DC (2012)
2. Defense Science Board (DSB) Summer Study on Autonomy. Office of the Under Secretary of Defense for Acquisition, Technology, and Logistics, Washington, DC (2016)
3. Hancock, P.A., Billings, D.R., Schaefer, K.E., Chen, J.Y.C., de Visser, E.J., Parasuraman, R.: A meta-analysis of factors affecting trust in human-robot interaction. Hum. Factors **53**(5), 517–527 (2011)
4. Lyons, J.B., Vo, T., Wynne, K.T., Mahoney, S., Nam, C.S., Gallimore, D.: Trusting autonomous robots: the role of reliability and stated social intent. Human Factors, (in press)
5. Mayer, R.C., Davis, J.H., Schoorman, F.D.: An integrated model of organizational trust. Acad. Manag. Rev. **20**, 709–734 (1995)
6. Robinette, P., Allen, R., Howard, A.M., Wagner, A.R.: Overtrust of robots in emergency evacuation scenarios. In: HRI 2016, 11th ACM/IEEE International Conference on Human-Robot Interaction, pp. 101–108 (2016)
7. Salem, M., Lakatos, G., Amirabdollahian, F., Dautenhahn, K.: Would you trust a (Faulty) robot? Effects of error, task type, personality on human-robot cooperation and trust. In: HRI 2015, 10th ACM/IEEE International Conference on Human-Robot Interaction, pp. 1–8 (2015)
8. Booth, S., Tomkin, J., Pfister, H., Waldo, J., Gajos, K., Nagpal, R.: Piggybacking robots: human-robot overtrust in University dormitory security. In: HRI 2017, 11th ACM/IEEE International Conference on Human-Robot Interaction, pp. 426–434 (2017)
9. Wiggers, K.: Meet the 400-pound robots that will soon patrol parking lots, offices, and malls (2017). https://www.digitaltrends.com/cool-tech/knightscope-robots-interview/. 6 Apr 2018
10. Inbar, O., Meyer, J.: Manners matter: trust in robotic peacekeepers. In: Proceedings of the Human Factors and Ergonomics Society Annual Meeting, vol. 59, no. 1, pp. 185–189 (2015)
11. Long, S.K., Karpinsky-Mosely, N.D., Bliss, J.: Trust of simulated robotic peacekeepers among resident and expatriate Americans. In: Proceedings of the Human Factors and Ergonomics Society Annual Meeting, vol. 61, pp. 2091–2095 (2017)
12. Lyons, J.B.: Being transparent about transparency: a model for human-robot interaction. In: Sofge, D., Kruijff, G.J., Lawless, W.F. (eds.) Trust and Autonomous Systems: Papers from the AAAI Spring Symposium (Technical Report SS-13-07). AAAI Press, Menlo Park (2013)

13. Gallimore, D., Lyons, J.B., Vo, T., Mahoney, S., Wynne, K.T.: Trusting robocop: gender-based effects on trust of an autonomous robot. Front. Psychol.: Human-Media Interact. **10**, 482 (2019)
14. Lyons, J.B., Nam, C.S., Jessup, S.A., Vo, T.Q., Wynne, K.T.: The role of individual differences as predictors of trust in autonomous security robots. In: Proceedings of IEEE Human-Machine Systems Conference, Rome, IT (2020, under review)

Learning and Collaboration
Technologies

How Virtual Reality Is Changing the Future of Learning in K-12 and Beyond
Using Needs-Affordances-Features Perspective

Marta Adžgauskaitė, Kaveh Abhari[(✉)] [ⓘ], and Michael Pesavento

San Diego State University, San Diego, CA, USA
Kabhari@sdsu.edu

Abstract. The integration of digital tools into alternative education strategies presents a potentially rich area of practical research. Non-traditional learning opportunities are multiplying and gaining widespread implementation due to their efficacy in fostering student engagement with course materials. Immersion tools such as Virtual Reality (VR) educational experiences have received significant attention as potential replacements or complements to existing multimedia educational tools given their increasing affordability and demonstrated value in fostering greater soft skills in students, such as critical thinking and community engagement. In light of the practical value of leveraging VR for alternative education, this study investigates five sampled VR experiences to determine their potential usefulness as teaching aids. Using the Needs, Affordances, and Features (NAF) framework, this research compares and contrasts five fully-immersive VR programs and analyzes the intersection of Needs, Affordances, and Features in each to determine their value in addressing gaps in current alternative education platforms. This study finds that fully immersive VR educational features enable multiple affordances for Teacher Users, Student Users, and both that fulfill specific experiential needs for each group. As such, these VR programs do address needs left unmet by traditional educational tools and underfunded institutions. Further, the inclusion of fully immersive VR tools in educational plans may help address gaps in content creation, distribution, and assessment that are presented by current alternative educational strategies. Therefore, a NAF framework might be implemented for use by VR developers, education professionals, and researchers to determine the potential of a given VR experience for meeting the needs of students and teachers pursuing alternative education strategies.

Keywords: Virtual reality · VR · Education · Alternative education · Education technology · Needs · Affordances · Features · Experiential leaning needs

1 Introduction

Virtual reality (VR) applications present an exciting opportunity to adapt and enhance the learning experience of students, making alternative education more enjoyable and effective. VR learning tools visualize concepts in a unique, immersive way that makes them accessible to learners in a manner that traditional educational technologies cannot.

© Springer Nature Switzerland AG 2020
C. Stephanidis et al. (Eds.): HCII 2020, LNCS 12425, pp. 279–298, 2020.
https://doi.org/10.1007/978-3-030-60128-7_22

VR allows learners to immerse themselves in a digitally enhanced or created environment and actively engage in the learning process by interacting with objects and environments [1]. As proposed in Dale's "learning cone" [2], immersion is one of the greatest advantages in education, and as such well-designed VR programing provides a more direct educational experience than competing multimedia tools.

Research has further revealed potential positive effects that VR technology has on the studying process when implemented appropriately [4]. These studies link virtual technologies with improvements in three main categories: student academic performance and motivation [2, 4–7], student social and collaborative skills [4, 8], and student psychomotor and cognitive skill development. When utilized effectively, VR applications also reduce the cognitive load for learners, while increasing motivation and interest towards the course material.

Virtual Reality for education is also becoming increasingly affordable, [1] with the simplest VR headsets being made from cardboard, to stand-alone VR headsets offered on the consumer market that do not require personal computers, smartphones or other external devices. These low-price points enable even students from underserved communities to engage with educational opportunities and experiences otherwise unavailable to them without the aid of VR applications. In particular, the use of VR in STEM (Science, Technology, Engineering, and Math) programs provide alternative experiential opportunities for schools with limited resources for (or access to) laboratories. Through the application of VR programming and technology, these underserved students may learn and develop positive attitude towards STEM disciplines despite lacking in-person opportunities for experiments and experiences. Thus, VR "enables success while keeping the environment 'low in threat, to counter the high stress living environment' that many of these students live in." [10]. This is a considerable advantage over traditional teaching methods, as it provides a low-impact environment that can be adapted to suit the experiential needs of a wider range of student personalities, objectives, and expectations. In this sense, VR may provide a considerable boon in the accommodation of varying demographics of students and educators increasingly relying on alternative education models.

Despite benefits, the impetus of this project lies in VR applications' struggle to fully satisfy users' experiential learning needs. A primary criticism of VR tools in education is the lack of social interaction afforded by many virtual reality applications [3]. VR applications tend to eliminate collaboration and interaction from the learning process, focusing on individualistic experiences over community-oriented contribution. While researching VR tools for this study, we noticed that most applications for education are virtual tours, which are fundamentally observation based and do not offer much in the way of experimenting in and interacting with the virtual environment provided. Such limitations make tools which lack interactivity features unappealing and potentially dissuade users from continuous engagement with said tool. Given these limitations, this study analyzes whether VR tools can implement communication and collaboration affordances into their design, and if so, what benefits users might reap from such implementation.

In light of these benefits and challenges, this paper focuses on the design and evaluation of VR application for alternative education[1] [11, 12], particularly for experiential learning in STEM disciplines. As employment opportunities in STEM fields continue to grow annually [9], STEM education becomes an increasingly important area of engagement for research into education, and applications of novel technologies therein. However, research falls short in addressing alternative education strategies for STEM and the role of technologies including VR in supporting experiential learning. As the field of virtual reality immersion continues to evolve, offering new and previously unattainable experiential opportunities for entertainment, so too do more and greater applications of VR for educational purposes become available. Given these developments, it is worth understanding how and where these technologies might be implemented to support student interaction with STEM experiences, as students who participate in alternative STEM education have an advantage regardless of whether they choose to pursue the secondary education [9].

To inform the design and evaluation of the next generation of VR applications, this study proposes a framework guiding the design and evaluation of future VR applications to alternative STEM education. In developing this framework, we examine the affordances and features offered by typical VR tools, align them with teaching practice and learning process in STEM coursework, and then identify their relationships with experiential learning needs inherent to alternative education. Then, we posit a set of propositions that highlight the experiential needs which motivate the use of VR application programs. Doing so, we focus on sensory, temporal, interactional, cognitive, behavioral and emotional experiences in explaining how needs are fulfilled by certain affordances, which are facilitated by features within chosen VR programs. We believe this approach helps explain the motivation for and value of using VR educational applications. Finally, we expect that the framework proposed here may inform developers in designing effective and appealing tools, educators in selecting the right tool, and researchers in a generative capacity.

2   Background

VR offers experiential learning opportunities that help students to engage concepts and challenges in personalized educational environments. The key benefit of adopting VR's experiential learning capabilities is associated with the VR environment affordances in offering accommodating, entertaining and stimulating environments. VR environments that simulate real-life experiences make it possible for students to explore new and abstract concepts, make predictions, design experiments, and interpret results, all within a digitally rendered space [13, 14]. This simulation capability facilitates autonomous learning, increases memory capacity, and improves decision-making [1].

One strategy for fully realizing VR's potential in alternative education lies in leveraging its capacity to adapt learning for diverse learners—the main beneficiaries of alternative education. In doing so, we identified the following experiential learning requirements

---

[1] In this paper, we define *alternative education* as educational activities that fall outside the traditional K–12 curriculum to serve students who are at risk of school failure due to the limited access to quality instruction, education facilities and/or learning resources.

that are critical to alternative education: (a) capacity in teaching abstract and complex concepts (instructional capacity), (b) self-regulated learning opportunities, and (c) soft skill development. These requirements preface the experiential needs of teachers and students and dictate the associated affordances of each.

The first concern in adapting to alternative education strategies stems from teachers' instructional capacity. Research into virtual reality in education reveals that VR environments are useful for modeling complex phenomena [15] and concretizing abstract concepts [1], especially for traditionally marginalized students [16, 17]. For example, in a VR environment, students get real-time, personalized instructions to complete learning activities. The applications allow creation and manipulation of complex artifacts as well as examining and experimenting with new ideas, which motivates students to think critically and creatively. By removing the chance for misinterpretation (as each instruction is provided upon completion of the previous one), student understanding of objectives and outcomes is more direct and timely [1], which in turn improves learning performance, cognitive skills [18], and attention span [19].

Self-regulated learning is an important and challenging facet of implementing experiential learning in non-traditional classrooms, mainly because of limited access to direct instruction and structured curricula [20, 21]. VR applications can address this problem in a systematic fashion by providing learning activities with proper scaffolding in engaging environments where each student could be provided with a transparent learning path [22–26]. This promotes informed decision-making about learning experience when interacting with virtual environments and objects, allowing independent examination of new experiences. In these environments, students can complete challenging tasks in multiple steps and receive immediate rewards such as virtual badges.

Soft skills, the third major focus of alternative education, can also be addressed by VR usage. VR has been shown to help diverse learners develop soft skills like collaboration and socialization through two distinct methods. First, it increases the opportunity to ask questions [27] via question and answer sessions. Second, VR supports peer group communication. This technology allows students to create "avatars" and express themselves in a collaborative digital space with peers. Users can feel the "physical" presence of each other, fostering a sense of community [28] which improves students' socialization and collaborative experiences in an educational setting. Teachers may also benefit from the communal value of VR tools as well, with a greater contribution to creativity development ensuring that students are engaged in the course material and carrying it out at their own learning pace.

In this study, we used these three requirements—instructional capacity, self-regulated learning, and soft skill development—as a guide to review the existing VR applications used in K-12 STEM education.

The benefits of STEM education have been well-established [1–16], and thus investigation of alternative avenues of STEM education that may be more widely accessible to students of varying demographics presents an attractive research opportunity. As such, the decision to prioritize STEM educational experiences is rooted in both the proven efficacy of VR as a valuable immersion tool, and a trend of significant growth in education opportunity for STEM professions as compared to other fields [9]. Thus, this study intends to contribute to this knowledge base by providing tools for use in determining the value and efficacy of VR programs in promoting experiential learning of STEM topics.

3 Method

We conducted a case study of five VR applications to identify the key features and functions they afford. Following Treem and Leonardi [29], we used a theoretical sampling approach to systematically selected 10 VR programs which conformed to pre-established criteria. We researched programs that appeared in lists of newly introduced applications

Table 1. List of the selected tools.

Vr tool name	Tool context
Nanome (Chemistry)	Nanome is a collaborative virtual reality tool for molecular design. It focuses on organic chemistry and allows users to build and explore molecules, create animated objects, and join workspaces to see others' projects. Nanome allows users to experiment, design and learn at the nanoscale while seeking and offering feedback
The Body VR (Biology)	The Body VR focuses on biology with three modules (Journey Inside the Cell, Anatomy Viewer, Colon Crossing) that take a user on a virtual tour of the human body. Journey Inside the Cell, allows users to travel through the bloodstream and discover how blood cells work. Anatomy Viewer allows to view different body scans in VR. Colon Crossing takes a user on a tour of the colon
Mission: ISS (Space Science)	Mission: ISS provides a trip into orbit, allowing users to experience life on board the International Space Station. This tool offers video tutorials as real time instructions on how to complete missions. Users can perform various tasks such as docking cargo capsules, doing station maintenance, or participating in a spacewalk. These "zero gravity" activities offer a practical opportunity to explore physics in a unique experiential environment
MEL Science (Chemistry)	MEL Science offers Chemistry VR Lessons in the form of 3–7-min experiences that explain how atomic structures and chemistry concepts work. It allows students to interact with atoms and create chemical reactions in a digital space. The tool offers over 30 VR lessons and tests covering the school chemistry curriculum, which are controlled by teacher
Minecraft (Education Edition)	The educational version of Minecraft is a learning tool that allows users to build pixel art structures in a two-or-three-dimensional simulation. This open-world game promotes creativity and collaboration in an immersive environment with two modes: Immersive mode (player is pulled into the virtual screen, 360° world) and Living Room (virtual screen is in front of the player). The program encourages creative problem solving in building, engineering, and many other practical constructive endeavors

from 2018 [30] to 2020 [31] and the list of applications that are recommended for science teachers to explore [32]. We narrowed down the list to five applications (see Table 1) using the following criteria: (a) focuses on STEM education, (b) type of the VR application program experience (fully-immersive, semi-immersive, non-immersive) (c) number of available features and (d) consistency across lists consulted.

This study focuses on fully immersive virtual reality experiences because the totality of user immersion they offer elevates learning engagement to a level that would require additional equipment in, for example, a semi-immersive VR experience. That is, fully immersive VR applications allow students to engage challenges in a space that is otherwise inaccessible—for example, a chemistry laboratory, a spaceship, or inside human body etc. [33].

The number of available features in each program also played important role in selection. Those programs with larger numbers of available features allow learners to create and experiment more broadly, and as such are more immersive and enable more affordances. Other programs are more restricted, utilizing fewer features and only allowing users to tour virtual environments while not supporting more advanced and immersive aspects available in fully immersive applications. This disparity in available features between chosen applications provides this research with the ability to investigate whether the virtual reality application programs with more features fulfill more experiential needs than their more restrictive counterparts.

The method for collecting and analyzing the case study data included the following steps as recommended by previous research [34, 35]: (a) examine the tool documentation for the list of features; (b) code data for each platform according to feature; (c) extract relevant properties from coded data and categorized them for each tool; (d) compare properties and themes across selected tools for a common language; (e) apply hierarchies to the properties by identifying the affordances; (f) re-investigate the affordances across all tools to identify similarities and differences to verify the key categories; and (g) identify the experiential learning needs addressed by affordances based on the empirical instances.

4   Results

We first familiarized ourselves with the selected VR applications and list their key features. The list of features allowed us to identify the intended functions and, subsequently, enabled affordances for both teachers and learners in each application. We then enumerated and examined the relationships between the listed affordances and professed experiential needs. The features, affordances and experiential learning needs identified through this process are discussed respectively in this section.

4.1   Features

First, features identified are listed in Table 2 and grouped into two categories based on their availability to specific user roles. These roles are *teacher*, *student* and both. Most features are available to all user roles; however, teachers have additional features not shared by students, such as starting classroom environments, sharing projects and class plans, and evaluating students. Comparatively, the only feature specific to the student role is test-taking.

Table 2. Features summary of sample VR applications.

Tool	Features	Roles			Use case		
		Teacher	Student	Both	Content creation	Content delivery	Assessment
Nanome	Build VR structures			X	X	X	
	Create visualizations			X	X	X	
	Rotate, zoom and scale VR objects				X	X	X
	Classroom environment	X			X	X	X
	Import and export files			X	X	X	X
	Save and share VR Workspaces			X	X	X	X
	Join workspaces			X	X	X	X
	Join a VR session using a Desktop			X	X	X	X
	Take and share screenshots			X	X	X	X
	View images, PDFs and videos in VR			X	X	X	X
The Body VR	Virtual tour		X		X	X	X
	Create visualizations		X		X	X	
	Build VR structures		X		X	X	
	Interact with VR objects		X		X	X	X
	Create presets		X		X	X	
	Rotate, zoom, scale, hide and fade VR objects		X		X	X	X
	Import and export files		X		X	X	X
	Virtual tour		X		X	X	
Mission: ISS	Perform tasks/missions		X		X	X	
	Interact with VR objects		X		X	X	X
	Rotate, zoom and scale VR objects		X		X	X	X
	View videos in VR		X		X	X	X
MEL Science	Build VR structures			X	X	X	
	Create visualizations			X	X	X	

(*continued*)

Table 2. (*continued*)

Tool	Features	Roles			Use case		
		Teacher	Student	Both	Content creation	Content delivery	Assessment
	Create simulations			X	X	X	X
	Interact with VR objects			X	X	X	X
	Rotate, zoom and scale VR objects			X	X	X	X
	Take tests		X		X		X
	Student evaluation	X					X
	Save and share VR Workspaces	X			X	X	
	Join workspaces	X			X	X	X
	Classroom environment	X			X	X	X
Minecraft (Education Edition)	Build VR structures			X	X	X	
	Rotate, zoom, scale and crop VR objects			X	X	X	X
	Virtual tours			X	X	X	
	Create avatars			X	X	X	
	Take and share screenshots			X	X	X	X
	Classroom environment	X			X	X	X
	Save, share VR Workspaces			X	X	X	X
	Import and export files			X	X	X	X
	Share projects and class plans	X			X	X	
	Join a VR session using a Desktop			X	X	X	X

Second, features were grouped based on three use-cases that are typical to the evaluation of learning platforms, including *content creation*, *content delivery*, and *assessment* (Table 2). Some features fulfill all three of these categories, such as virtual tours, manipulation and interaction with VR objects, import and export files, create simulations etc., while others may only fulfill one Use Case category.

The first round of analysis revealed that there is a significant difference in the interactivity and collaborative aspects of each application based on available features. For example, The Body VR and Mission: ISS are functionally for individual use. Learners are responsible for their own progress, there is no evaluation from other users. These applications do not support interactions neither among learners nor teachers and students. They focus on providing virtual tours, supplying learners with individual tasks and tutorials.

In comparison Nanome, MEL Chemistry VR Lessons, and Minecraft are more collaborative, connecting students, their peers, and their teachers by sharing their work and experiences with each other using "classroom mode" features. This mode expands the scope of the application and allows greater communication and synergy between students and teachers. While both student and teacher roles share some features, teachers are given more privileges and are in control of the lesson. Teachers can create and join workspaces, track students' progress, and utilize visualizations which students do not have access to. The classroom mode environment allows students to work on the same project in groups, contributing to a mutual goal.

4.2 Affordances

The term "affordances" refers to "action possibilities afforded by technology to users" [36]. In this study we further specify this description to define affordances as functional attributes of VR applications which are enabled by program features in order to fulfill users' experiential learning needs [37]. Functional affordances can be classified as either primary affordances or secondary affordances. Primary affordances are anticipated upon design (i.e. the intended use of a feature). Secondary affordances are the additional affordances that were not designed on purpose (i.e. tertiary uses for a feature). This study focuses its attentions on primary affordances, as their facilitation via program features is the paramount concern of NAF analysis.

We used a list of features to identify their corresponding functions, thereby creating an explicit list of primary functional affordances. We then consolidated these affordances by subtracting duplicates from the list and merging similar ones. Grouping criteria for affordances remained nearly the same as for feature categorizing, except Content Delivery Affordances, which were separated into Learning and Teaching affordances based on user role.

Then, affordances were grouped both according to user role and use case. We identified eight affordances under three groups—creation, learning, and assessment—for student role: *access, contribute, exchange, observe, simulate, collaborate, (self) monitor progress* and *seek feedback* (Table 3). For teacher roles, we followed the same procedure, grouping affordances by three groups- creation, teaching, and assessment- and identified *edit, personalize, present, assign, manage interaction, monitor, offer feedback*, and *assess* (Table 4).

Creation Affordances. The first group of affordances focused on knowledge creation. This is an individual process wherein users interact with virtual tools and spaces to produce and interact with content. Collaboration or interaction among peers is not available during this process. This group includes affordances of content access, contribution, editing, exchanging, and personalization. For student roles, *access* refers to the affordance that enables students to access the content provided by a VR application. Here, content can be created by teachers or peers, or it can be included in a VR tool as various environments, tasks and/or tutorials. *Contribution* refers to the affordance that enables

Table 3. Relationship between features and affordances for student role

	Creation			Learning			Assessment	
	Access	Contribute	Exchange	Observe	Simulate	Collaborate	Monitor Progress	Seek Feedback
Build VR structures		X		X	X			
Create visualizations		X		X	X			
Virtual tours	X	X		X	X			
Rotate, zoom, hide, fade and scale VR objects	X			X	X			
Import and export files			X					X
Save and share VR Workspaces		X	X				X	X
Join workspaces/classrooms	X		X	X		X		
Join a VR session using a Desktop	X		X	X		X		
View images, PDFs and videos in VR	X		X	X				
Interact with VR objects	X			X	X	X		
Create presets	X	X		X	X			
Create simulations	X	X		X	X			
Take tests							X	X
Perform tasks/missions	X	X		X	X			
Create avatars					X			
Take and share screenshots		X					X	X

Table 4. Relationship between features and affordances for teacher role

	Creation		Teaching			Assessment		
	Edit	Personalize	Present	Assign	Manage Interaction	Monitor (Feedback)	Offer Feedback	Assess
Build VR structures	X		X					
Create visualizations	X		X					
Virtual tours	X		X			X		X
Rotate, zoom, hide, fade and scale VR objects		X	X			X		
Classroom environment	X	X	X	X	X	X	X	X
Import and export files	X	X	X			X		
Save and share VR Workspaces		X	X					
Join workspaces/classrooms	X	X			X	X		X
Join a VR session using a Desktop		X			X	X		X
View images, PDFs and videos in VR	X					X		
Interact with VR objects	X		X			X		X
Create presets	X	X						
Create simulations	X		X				X	
Create avatars	X	X						
Take and share screenshots		X	X				X	X
Share projects and class plans	X	X	X	X				
Student evaluation							X	

students to introduce personal input which makes the user partly responsible for the content of VR tool. *Exchange* refers to students to sharing and receiving content with peers and teachers. For teacher role, *edit* enables teachers to create content, revise and integrate it to the learning process. *Personalization* enables teachers to personalize content to each student (or group of students) and manage it according to what a class or an individual student's needs.

Content Delivery (Learning/Teaching) Affordances. The second group of affordances facilitate content delivery from teacher to students while enabling teachers to distribute instructions efficiently, and have students receive and engage that content. Tables 3, 4 and 5 differentiate themselves based on user role by denoting these affordances as "Learning" or "Teaching" affordances, though they are still fundamentally methods of Content Delivery. Student interaction and collaboration provides teachers more options for knowledge sharing, as content can be delivered individually or to a group. This affordance group includes such affordances as: *observe, simulate* and *collaborate* for students; *present*; *assign*; and *manage interactions* for teachers.

Table 5. Affordances enabled by sample VR applications

Active learning: Students	Creation: *Access, Contribute, Exchange*
	Learning: *Observe, Simulate, Collaborate*
	Assessment: *Monitor Progress, Seek feedback*
Active teaching: Teachers	Creation: *Edit, Personalize, Manage interaction*
	Teaching: *Present, Assign tasks, Personalize*
	Assessment: *monitor (feedback), Offer feedback, Assess*

We define *observe* affordance as a possibility for students to learn by viewing, exploring or observing provided content. *Simulate* refers to the affordance that enables students to learn by creating, constructing, simulating, experimenting and comprehensively interacting with VR environment and objects. *Collaborate* refers to the affordance that enables students to learn by working in groups and collaborating with each other in projects that are in development stage. For teachers, *present* refers to the affordance that enables teachers to give instructions to students by presenting and demonstrating content. *Assign* refers to the affordance that enables teachers to give instructions to students by assigning tasks. *Manage interactions* refers to the affordance that enables teachers to give instructions by personalizing interactions and managing them according to what a student or a group of students are working with.

Assessment Affordances. The third and final group—assessment affordances— enables progress tracking, feedback exchange, and knowledge evaluation. This group's affordances are *monitor, seek* and *offer feedback*, and *assess. Monitor Progress* refers to the affordance that enables students to have their work evaluated and their improvements observed throughout the learning period. *Seek feedback* refers to the affordance that enables students to be evaluated or provided with comments from teachers. *Monitor (Feedback)* refers to the affordance that enables teachers observe or monitor students' progress in order to assess them. *Offer feedback* refers to the affordance that enables teachers to offer comments or other kind of feedback in order to assess a student or a group of students. *Assess* refers to the affordance that enables teachers to personalize and manage assessment according to individual student's needs.

Table 5 summarizes the identified affordances for both teacher and student roles. As discussed in this section, teachers and students share some features that may or may not afford the same functionalities. Teachers and students also have different goals in using different features; hence, different affordances. In the next section, we discuss how these affordances collectively enhance immersive education and satisfy experiential learning needs in alternative STEM education.

4.3 Needs

Using NAF theory as a conceptual framework, this research concludes how experiential needs can be met by affordances enabled through VR features. By knowing the experiential needs of the individual, we can predict which affordances and features will be utilized to meet those needs. To demonstrate this, we apply a NAF perspective to identify what experiential needs are driving the use of the two most representative applications we analyzed (Mission: ISS and MEL Chemistry VR Lessons) and then use three other cases for cross-validation. These applications were chosen as representative of this project due to their difference in collaborative characteristics, as Mission: ISS is for individual use, while MEL Chemistry VR Lessons supports both student and teacher roles and, as such, greater collaboration and interaction.

A comprehensive list of features extracted from Mission: ISS allowed identification of the affordances and cross-validation. Using Table 6, we predicted what experiential needs are fulfilled by (and therefore validate the use of) Mission: ISS. Since this application is for individual use and only supports student role, we used other cases to identify the affordances that are available for teacher role. Our examination suggests that five out of six experiential needs drive the use of Mission: ISS, as its features correspond to multiple affordances that fulfill experiential needs (e.g. virtual tours feature alone support affordances of *access, contribute, observe* and *simulate*).

Only one feature of Mission: ISS fulfills the majority (five out of six) of students' experiential needs through enabled affordances, whereas other features (e.g. perform tasks/missions, interact with VR objects, rotate, zoom and scale VR objects, view videos in VR) fulfill only one or more of those needs. For example, individuals' need for temporal experience is not fulfilled while using this VR application program since it does not support process monitoring. As shown in Table 6, only features from the assessment category fulfill temporal experiential needs. Adding features such as saving and sharing VR workspaces, taking tests, or taking and sharing screenshots would satisfy the need of temporal experience more effectively than the current iteration of the Mission: ISS program.

Given that some applications support collaboration between multiple roles, we extracted features of the MEL Chemistry VR Lessons application and grouped them by role. Within this application, students can access features such as building VR structures, creating visualizations and simulations, interacting with VR objects, rotating, zooming and scaling VR objects and taking tests. In conjunction, these features correspond to

Table 6. Relationship between affordances and experiential learning needs

	Sensory experience	Temporal experience	Interactional experience	Cognitive experience	Behavioral experience	Emotional experience
Enabled by:						
Access (to content)	X	X				
Contribute (to content)				X	X	X
Exchange (of content)			X			
Observe (lessons)	X		X	X	X	
Simulate (concepts/phenomena)	X			X	X	X
Collaborate (with peers)			X	X	X	X
Monitor (student progress)		X				X
Seek feedback (from peers/teacher)			X			
Facilitated by:						
Edit (content/lessons)	X			X		
Personalize (student lessons/interaction)		X			X	X
Present (content and simulation)	X		X			
Assign (tasks, tests, and lessons)			X	X	X	
Manage interactions (among/with students)		X				
Monitor (Feedback)		X				
Offer feedback (on assignments)			X	X		X
Assess (student progress and activities)		X		X		

affordances of *access*, *contribute*, *observe*, *simulate*, *monitor progress* and *seek feedback*. These features and affordances are also available to teacher roles. As evidenced in the Table 6, all six experiential needs (sensory, temporal, interactional, cognitive, behavioral and emotional) are fulfilled by the MEL Chemistry VR Lessons application, as classroom mode alone satisfies all experiential needs mentioned above.

Student progress is unavailable if assessment features are not included in the application, and as such the Mission: ISS application fails to address an important part of the learning process that MEL Chemistry VR Lessons does. That is, since the Mission: ISS does not support a classroom environment and is limited to individual use, it lacks the fulfillment of temporal experiential need, as compared to MEL Chemistry VR Lessons, which support classroom environment and therefore fulfills the need of temporal experience. Such limitation would discourage continued use by students and teachers with a need for temporal experience and, therefore, it is likely that they would choose an application that provides temporal experience (MEL Chemistry VR Lessons) over the one which does not (Mission: ISS), as the fulfillment of each need supports the motivation of application use.

5   Propositions

According to the NAF framework, a set of needs might be fulfilled by one or more affordance, which in turn might use a one or more features that are not directly related to the specific needs [37]. This study provides six logical propositions which describe the experiential learning needs being investigated, as well as asserting the interrelationships between given needs and their associated affordances (Table 6). Here, we propose to categorize experiential learning needs as Sensory, Temporal, Interactional, Cognitive, Behavioral, Emotional [3, 38–44] (Fig. 1).

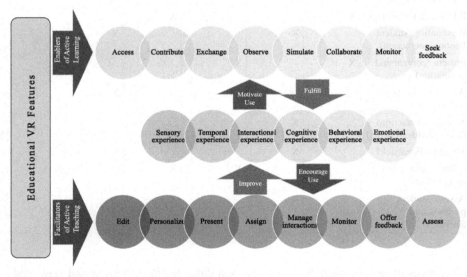

Fig. 1. Our proposed framework bases on NAF logic applied to educational VR applications

Need for Sensorial experience (know-where). Sensory experience is formed when a virtual environment triggers learners' senses (e.g. sounds, visual images). Positive sensorial experiences result in pleasure and excitement that motivate active engagement and creative imagination. Sensory experiences can differentiate learning environments, attract attention, and enhance students' attitude toward STEM coursework. Affordances such as *observe* and *simulate* (see Tables 3 and 4) trigger 'sensorial imagery'—multisensory imagination that creates a new, more detailed understanding of subject matter.

Sensorial values of learning are further enhanced when the VR application features enable *edit* and *present* affordances to teacher roles. This suggests that VR application designers are capable of empowering both teachers and learners to manipulate and personalize the sensorial components of each lesson for more effective learning. Therefore, we propose:

Proposition 1a: Individuals' need for sensory experience will motivate use of VR educational applications that afford *access, observation* and *simulation* to student roles.

Proposition 1b: Individuals' sensory experience will be improved by VR educational applications that afford *editing* and *presenting* to teacher roles.

Need for Temporal Experience (know-when). Students and educators have a vested interest in tracking and analyzing the use of their class time to measure result and efficacy. VR applications enhance temporal experiences by monitoring and reporting time spent in virtual learning environments and recording the history of previously completed tasks or tests. *Monitor progress* affordances enable learners to take ownership of their learning by recognizing the utility of time and, therefore, manage their time more mindfully. For example, by tracking their progress, learners self-regulate their learning plan which results in the continuous use of the application—especially in alternative education settings. Teachers can further facilitate this process by monitoring learners' progress and personalizing the way they interact with individuals. As such, the use of applications with *monitor progress, personalize,* and *observe* affordances will satisfy the need for temporal experience in both teacher and student roles. Therefore, we propose:

Proposition 2a: Individuals' need for temporal experience will motivate use of VR educational applications that afford *access* and *monitoring progress* to student roles.

Proposition 2b: Individuals' temporal experience will be improved by VR educational applications that afford *personalization, management, monitoring* and *assessment* to teacher roles.

Need for Interactional Experience (know-who). Another primary need of learners in an experiential environment is a Need for Interactional experience. Interactions enable students to explore learning options, share knowledge, examine their findings, collaborate with others, and seek feedback from peers and teachers. Interactional experience is critical in alternative education settings because of a lack of traditional instructional support in alternative education modes. Additionally, teachers need to be able to communicate with learners, offer them feedback, assign them collaborative tasks, and mobilize the learning community toward the same goals. Therefore, VR applications need to enable knowledge sharing and learner-to-learner communication (e.g. *seek feedback*) and teacher-to-learner communication (e.g. *offer feedback*) as this interaction is paramount to presenting alternative learning opportunities beyond mere content and instructions.

Proposition 3a: Individuals' need for interactional experience will motivate use of VR educational applications that afford *exchange, observation, collaboration* and *seeking feedback* to student roles.

Proposition 3b: Individuals' interactional experience will be improved by VR educational applications that afford *presentation, assignment* and *offering feedback* to teacher roles.

Need for Cognitive Experience (know-what). Students in alternative educational environments express a Need for Cognitive experience. Cognitive needs refer to activities that engage students' creativity in understanding materials, foster evaluation and elaboration upon complex concepts, and promote problem solving and critical thinking. VR applications can motivate students to learn, unlearn, and relearn by offering new forms of conceptualization and rational examination. Cognitive experiences based on a variety of perceptual inputs lead to engagement of learners' intellect in reason-based assessments, especially during co-creation. Programs that afford *exchange* and *observe* stimulate and enrich cognitive processes; programs that afford *collaborate* and *seek feedback* engage students in changing their earlier assumptions or higher-order thinking. These cognitive processes are further enhanced when teachers are afforded the ability to *edit, offer feedback* and *assign*. Therefore, we propose:

Proposition 4a: Individuals' need for cognitive experience will motivate use of virtual VR educational applications that afford *contribution, observation, simulation* and *collaboration* to student role.

Proposition 4b: Individuals' cognitive experience will be improved by VR educational applications that afford *editing, assignment, offering feedback and assessment* to teacher roles.

Need for Behavioral Experience (know-how). Need for Behavioral experience is associated with active learning and includes "act" and "physical engagement" VR applications. These programs alter how learners interact with learning content and tasks, therefore altering their learning behavior and habits. Physical engagement in virtual learning environments gives students a 'sense of control', allowing for a more practical and "hands-on" experience—which is key to successful experiential learning. To satisfy this need, VR applications enable learners to *collaborate, observe, simulate,* and *contribute* alongside other learners. Teachers can direct behavioral experiences if the application affords *assigning* activities that require active physical engagement with learning components.

Proposition 5a: Individuals' need for behavioral experience will motivate use of VR educational applications that afford *contribution, observation, simulation* and *collaboration* to student role.

Proposition 5b: Individuals' behavioral experience will be improved by VR educational applications that afford *personalization* and *assessment* to teacher roles.

Need for Emotional Experience (know-why). Emotional experiences are cornerstone to educational experiences, both traditional and alternative. VR programming can provide and enhance these experiences significantly. For example, VR applications can simulate a safe learning environment where students can *contribute, collaborate* and *observe* the content freely and experiment without the fear of being judged by the teachers or peers. This can foster student trust, which is necessary to ensure learners follow instructions and complete learning activities appropriately. Learners' emotions are also evoked by experiencing new and exciting representations of abstract concepts that lead to a sense of joy. Further, successful contribution or task completion enhance learners' efficacy, which is a categorically emotional rather than rational judgement. These experiences either knowingly or instinctively affect learners' attitudes toward education and coursework. If the application fails to offer the teachers affordances such as *personalizing* and *offering feedback*, it would be difficult to fulfill students' need for emotional experience.

Proposition 6a: Individuals' need for emotional experience will motivate use of VR educational applications that afford *contribution, simulation, collaboration* and *monitoring* to student role.

Proposition 6b: Individuals' emotional experience will be improved by VR educational applications that afford *personalization* and *offering feedback* to teacher roles.

6 Future Directions

This study and its associated NAF perspective provide the opportunity for adaptive and effective analysis on the part of developers, researchers, and of course, students and teachers. Our proposed framework offers VR developers a guide for understanding learners' experiential needs in order to hone VR programs to address those needs. In designing future VR applications, developers might use our framework to analyze which experiential needs are the most important for them to satisfy with the tool they are creating. Subsequently, developers could identify which affordances satisfy given needs and which features should be implemented to enable those affordances. Therefore, VR developers can model how students and teachers would react to different affordances before planning program features. This has the potential to reduce the number of design iterations and maximize the chance of product success and efficiency. Post-development, this framework may inform the evaluation and user test plans of VR applications.

Beyond development, researchers in both education and technology fields can adopt, test, and expand our framework to further investigate the role of VR technology in enhancing students' learning experience and outcome. Ideally, adoption of this framework would result in a more systematic understanding of VR design and programs, which in turn benefits alternative models of education and informs the use of VR applications in other fields such as healthcare, retail, tourism, and entertainment.

Lastly, our framework facilitates lesson planning and execution for educators. Using this framework, educators can first decide whether leveraging a VR application is the right decision for their given lesson plan, and if so, may use our framework to choose the program that suits their students' experiential learning needs. The framework may also be used in the reverse method. For example, if schools have already purchased VR tools, educators can identify what experiential needs are being addressed by certain features of the application they are already using, and as such adapt lesson plans to address gaps or reinforce studying.

Our preliminary study suggests that future research and design into VR technologies should carefully examine the role of goal-setting and self-monitoring in educational VR applications. Examining the effects of efficiently satisfying experiential learning needs is a potentially rich avenue of study for future iterations of this inquiry. For example, as our study asserts, satisfying emotional needs would not be sufficient for complete student engagement without also optimizing temporal experience. As such, future research should empirically examine how experiential needs may be orchestrated to achieve the most meaningful and engaging experience for students. Further, study into VR applications ought to address the lack of effective collaboration and communication between diverse learners in current iterations of such software. Research regarding the capacity of VR applications to facilitate and enable networked learning may produce a myriad of practical considerations for factors like content delivery and assessment, as well as the develop soft skills in students. Future development should challenge the belief that human interaction and soft skills development is not readily accessible in VR applications, thus demonstrating the value of such programming in an alternative learning space.

References

1. Elmqaddem, N.: Augmented reality and virtual reality in education. Myth or reality? Int. J. Emerg. Technol. Learn. **14**, 234–242 (2019). https://doi.org/10.3991/ijet.v14i03.9289
2. Dale, E.: Audiovisual Methods in Teaching. 3rd Ed. (1969)
3. Jackson, R.L., Taylor, W., Winn, W.: Peer collaboration and virtual environments: a preliminary investigation of multi-participant virtual reality applied in science education. In: Proceedings of the ACM Symposium on Applied Computing, pp 121–125 (1999)
4. Kaufmann, H., Steinbügl, K., Dünser, A., Glück, J.: General Training of Spatial Abilities by Geometry Education in Augmented Reality (2006)
5. Di, S.Á., Blanca Ibáñez, M., Delgado Kloos, C.: Impact of an augmented reality system on students' motivation for a visual art course. Comput. Educ. **68**, 586–596 (2013). https://doi.org/10.1016/j.compedu.2012.03.002
6. Holley, D., Mike, H., Menown, C.: The augmented library: motivating STEM students. Networks **19**, 77–84 (2016)
7. Bacca, J., Baldiris, S., Fabregat, R., Graf, S.: Augmented reality trends in education: a systematic review of research and applications. J. Educ. Technol. Soc. **17**, 133–149 (2014). https://doi.org/10.2307/jeductechsoci.17.4.133
8. Martín-Gutiérrez, J., Luís Saorín, J., Contero, M., et al.: Design and validation of an augmented book for spatial abilities development in engineering students. Comput. Graph. **34**, 77–91 (2010). https://doi.org/10.1016/j.cag.2009.11.003
9. White, D.W.: What is STEM Education and Why Is It Important? (2014)
10. Hughes, J.M.: Digital making with "At-Risk" youth. Int. J. Inf. Learn. Technol. **34**, 102–113 (2017). https://doi.org/10.1108/IJILT-08-2016-0037

11. Reimer, K., Pangrazio, L.: Educating on the margins: young people's insights into effective alternative education. Int. J. Incl. Educ. **24**, 479–495 (2020). https://doi.org/10.1080/136 03116.2018.1467977

12. Kumm, S., Wilkinson, S., McDaniel, S.: Alternative education settings in the United States. Interv. Sch. Clin. 105345122091489 (2020). https://doi.org/10.1177/1053451220914895

13. Ferry, B., Kervin, L., Cambourne, B., et al.: (Online classroom simulation: the 'next wave' for pre-service teacher education? In: Atkinson, R., C., McBeath, R., Jonas-Dwyer, D., Phillips, R. (eds.) Beyond the Comfort Zone: Proceedings of the 21st ASCILITE Conference, pp. 294–302 (004)

14. Steinberg, R.N.: Computers in teaching science: To simulate or not to simulate? Am. J. Phys. **68**, S37–S41 (2000). https://doi.org/10.1119/1.19517

15. Simulations Author, E., Klopfer, E.: Environmental detectives-the development of an augmented reality platform for environmental simulations. Educ. Technol. Res. Dev. **56**, 203–228 (2008). https://doi.org/10.1007/s11423-007-9037-6

16. Merchant, Z., Goetz, E.T., Cifuentes, L., et al.: Effectiveness of virtual reality-based instruction on students' learning outcomes in K-12 and higher education: a meta-analysis. Comput. Educ. **70**, 29–40 (2014). https://doi.org/10.1016/j.compedu.2013.07.033

17. Ip, H.H.S., et al.: Virtual reality enabled training for social adaptation in inclusive education settings for school-aged children with autism spectrum disorder (ASD). In: Cheung, S.K.S., Kwok, L.-f., Shang, J., Wang, A., Kwan, R. (eds.) ICBL 2016. LNCS, vol. 9757, pp. 94–102. Springer, Cham (2016). https://doi.org/10.1007/978-3-319-41165-1_9

18. Kotranza, A., Lind, D.S., Pugh, C.M., Lok, B.: Real-time in-situ visual feedback of task performance in mixed environments for learning joint psychomotor-cognitive tasks. In: Science Technology Proceedings - IEEE 2009 International Symposium Mixed Augment Reality, ISMAR 2009, pp. 125–134 (2009). https://doi.org/10.1109/ISMAR.2009.5336485

19. Singhal, S., Bagga, S., Goyal, P., Saxena, V.: Augmented Chemistry: Interactive Education System. Int. J. Comput. Appl. **49**, 1–5 (2012). https://doi.org/10.5120/7700-1041

20. Smidt, H., Thornton, M., Abhari, K.: The future of social learning: a novel approach to connectivism. In: Proceedings of the 50th Hawaii International Conference on System Sciences, pp. 2116–2125 (2017)

21. Nilson, L.: Creating Self-Regulated Learners: Strategies to Strengthen Students? Self-Awareness and Learning Skills. Stylus Publishing, LLC (2013)

22. Darroch, J., Mcnaughton, R.: Examining the link between knowledge management practices and types of innovation. Knowl. Creat. Diffus. Util. (1930). https://doi.org/10.1108/146919 30210435570

23. Kurilovas, E.: Evaluation of quality and personalisation of VR/AR/MR learning systems. Behav. Inf. Technol. **35**, 998–1007 (2016). https://doi.org/10.1080/0144929X.2016.1212929

24. Kitsantas, A.: Fostering college students' selfregulated learning with learning technologies. Hell. J. Psychol. **10**, 235–252 (2013)

25. Kim, M., Jeong, J.-S., Park, C., Jang, R.-H., Yoo, K.-H.: A situated experiential learning system based on a real-time 3D virtual studio. In: Richards, D., Kang, B.H. (eds.) PKAW 2012. LNCS (LNAI), vol. 7457, pp. 364–371. Springer, Heidelberg (2012). https://doi.org/ 10.1007/978-3-642-32541-0_32

26. Harms, R.: Self-regulated learning, team learning and project performance in entrepreneurship education: learning in a lean startup environment (2015). https://doi.org/10.1016/j.techfore. 2015.02.007

27. Grandgirard, J., Poinsot, D., Krespi, L., et al.: Students' attitudes towards educational virtual environments. Entomol. Exp. Appl. **103**, 239–248 (1998). https://doi.org/10.1023/A:100968 7025419

28. Mütterlein, J., Hess, T.: Specifics of collaboration in virtual reality: how immersion drives the intention to collaborate use of social live streaming services at the individual level view project e-commerce view project (2018)
29. Treem, J.W., Leonardi, P.M.: Social media use in organizations: exploring the affordances of visibility, editability, persistence, and association. In: Salmon, C.T. (ed.) Communication Yearbook, New York, pp. 143–189 (2012)
30. Steve, B.: The top 10 educational VR Apps of 2018 – VRFocus (2018)
31. Rasmussen, N.: Best Educational VR Apps To Try in 2020 - VR Today Magazine (2020)
32. Priyanka, G.: VR Educational Apps—VR Science Apps - EdTechReview^{TM} (ETR) (2017)
33. Bridget, P.: What Is virtual reality? (+3 Types of VR Experiences) (2019)
34. O'Riordan, S., Feller, J., Nagle, T.: Exploring the affordances of social network sites: an analysis of three networks. In: European Conference on Information Systems (ECIS 2012), Barcelona (2012)
35. Abhari, K., Davidson, E.J., Xiao, B.: Co-innovation platform affordances: developing a conceptual model and measurement instrument. Ind. Manag. Data Syst. **117**, 873–895 (2017). https://doi.org/10.1108/IMDS-05-2016-0156
36. Karahanna, E., Xu, S.X., Xu, Y., Zhang, N.: The needs-affordances-features perspective for the use of social media. MIS. Q. Manag. Inf. Syst. **42**, 737–756 (2018)
37. Abhari, K., Vomero, A., Davidson, E.: Psychology of business intelligence tools: needs-affordances-features perspective. In: Proceedings of the 53rd Hawaii International Conference on System Sciences (2020)
38. Smith, K., Rayfield, J.: STEM knowledge, learning disabilities and experiential learning: influences of sequencing instruction. J. Agric. Educ. **60**, 222–236 (2019). https://doi.org/10.5032/jae.2019.02222
39. Kluge, A.: Experiential learning methods, simulation complexity and their effects on different target groups. J. Educ. Comput. Res. **36**, 323–349 (2007). https://doi.org/10.2190/B48U-7186-2786-5429
40. Ndoye, A.: Experiential learning, self-beliefs and adult performance in Senegal. Int. J. Lifelong Educ. **22**, 353–366 (2003). https://doi.org/10.1080/02601370304831
41. Ryser, L., Halseth, G., Thien, D.: Strategies and intervening factors influencing student social interaction and experiential learning in an interdisciplinary research team. Res. High. Educ. **50**, 248–267 (2009). https://doi.org/10.1007/s11162-008-9118-3
42. Breen, H., Jones, M.: Experiential learning: using virtual simulation in an online RN-to-BSN program. J. Contin. Educ. Nurs. **46**, 27–33 (2015). https://doi.org/10.3928/00220124-2014112002
43. Jordi, R.: Reframing the concept of reflection: consciousness, experiential learning, and reflective learning practices. Adult Educ. Q. **61**, 181–197 (2011). https://doi.org/10.1177/0741713610380439
44. Dewey, J.: Collected works of John Dewey, 1882–1953: The electronic edition (2003)

Tangible Storytelling to Learn the Four Seasons: Design and Preliminary Observations

Wafa Almukadi[✉]

University of Jeddah, Jeddah, Kingdom of Saudi Arabia
wsalmukadi@uj.edu.sa

Abstract. Tangible user interfaces offer a new medium for education that support concept development, with physical and virtual representations. It has manipulative properties allow students to utilize their haptic and motor skills which encourage learning and motivation. In this paper we developed an educational game based on a tangible environment that support interactive technology aiming to serve and enhance the learning process within the sciences field, we selected "The Four Seasons" topic. We proposed handcrafted objects as the physical objects that motivate kids to create their own stories for each season based on the available objects that represent basic elements for each season. We discussed the design process and development iterations as well as preliminary findings. This system has been evaluated in a field study with kids 4–7 years of age. We discuss the role of technology which can play in supporting children's everyday creative storytelling and how it can raise the enthusiasm for leaning and engaging kids to the learning process.

Keywords: Tangible user interface · Storytelling · Education · Four seasons · Kids · Interactive technology · Collaboration

1 Introduction

Tangible User Interface (TUI) opens up new avenues for interaction with digital media by linking the virtual and the physical worlds together. Ishii & Ullmer defined the term of tangible user interface (TUI) in which a user can interact with computational information through physical environment [1]. TUI have the potential to enhance children's learning in several ways. Children quickly understand the manipulation of tangible objects which boosts their cognitive development, and facilitates the development of mental models [12]. At the same time, TUI provides playful environment that drive children to naturally explore, discover, and learn [14]. In addition, tangible storytelling prove its effectiveness in raising children enjoyment and engagement in learning [2, 11].

Learning about four seasons and their characteristics is important. It helps children understand the passage of time and teaches them about change. However, there are places around the world that do not experience all four seasons which make it difficult especially for children to recognize the changes between the seasons. Due to the desert region where Saudi Arabia located, natural phenomena are difficult to be seen which making it a challenge for children to naturally observe the difference between the seasons.

© Springer Nature Switzerland AG 2020
C. Stephanidis et al. (Eds.): HCII 2020, LNCS 12425, pp. 299–306, 2020.
https://doi.org/10.1007/978-3-030-60128-7_23

Our prototype aiming to explore the design space of tangible interface to address a learning problem of understanding the four season's fundamental concepts thought tangible storytelling.

1.1 Related Work

Pedagogists universally agree on the fundamental role of storytelling in children's growth and improvement. It plays important role in developing children skills of listening, developing language, imagination, and social development [5, 6]. As a way to keep up with now a days technologies and to get benefit of it in improving children's' skills, lots of storytelling system combined with technology is developed.

A Rosebud [4] is an early work of technology storytelling that links children's stories to their toys. This work demonstrated the enormous potential of using tangible and natural interfaces for introducing children to technologies and rise their skills of writing, editing and collaboration. Fails and Guha [3] created Mobile Stories as a narrative system for children an addressing an important characteristic to design effective interactive storytelling system. iTheater [8] designed as a puppet tangible interaction storytelling for children that empower children narrative and expression. A recent work of iTheater [9] is developed of multi touch surface and tangible objects targeting preschool children to developing narration skills. StoryCube [13] designed as a tangible interactive tool to create a 3D story environment that inspire children in storytelling activity with a full of happiness.

An inspiration work [10] designed for children to create stories using drawing that programmed to control robotic characters. The work prove its effectiveness in growing children narrative and imagination skill. At the same time it rise children curiosity in learning programming. Finally, KidPad [7] used as a collaborative storytelling for children that advanced children collaboration.

From the previewed works we notice that most tangible interactive story telling are used to improve children narrative, language, expression, imagination, collaboration, and programming concept. However, we believe that interactive storytelling can go beyond these factors. In our project we aim to get benefit of interactive storytelling advantages with addition to learn a basic concept.

In this paper, we present Smart Seasons System (SSS) as a tangible storytelling designed for children (one or group) to create their own stories of four season activities. We selected "Four seasons to learn because it is a basic natural phenomena that all children have to know. In addition, the four season is a fun topic to teach in school that can be enrich with lots of pictures and activities.

2 System Design

In this paper we introduced Smart Seasons System (SSS) as a tangible storytelling game-based learning that help children to understand the main characteristics of seasons by creating their own scenarios of a story based on the available objects. The main features of a SSS are:

1. Compose a story: This feature is the main function of the system. The children can compose a story by placing the tangibles on the tablet. The story can be recorded and replay. The children can record their voice as a story scenario.
2. Play a story: The children can view a list of recorded stories. They can select one story and play it.
3. Share a story: Children can share their stories by send it as a video file.

While designing the system there are several perspectives that we considered:

- Flexibility

Children are able to compose different stories for each seasons based on the available objects. Also the children can use the system naturally without external guidance by placing the objects on the tablet and interacting with the virtual environment.

- Storytelling

It is a powerful tool to promote understanding where events and actions are conveyed in words, images, and sounds. This technique allowed lowering the learning effort of a new interface, motivating the children to interact with the surrounding environment while discovering and learning [5, 6].

- Collaboration

The system is designed to encourage both individual and group work. The tangible nature of the system affords students to locate themselves around the tangible space and work in groups of two or three. According to studies [12], group learning is most effective when learning happens in groups of two or three.

- Affordability

As a principle, the hardware is built using low-cost materials and do-it-yourself technologies. The system is implemented with a low cost tablet in addition to the tangible objects which are made using cork board and foil. The software is developed based on open-source.

3   Functional Prototype

The system consists of tablet with build in camera which considered as the story board. More over, tangible objects that represents the season's elements and represent stories components. There are 16 tangible objects (4 objects for each season) as follow (Table 1):

- Autumn: plant state, squirrel, oak, broom.
- Winter: plant state, igloo, jacket, ski tools.
- Spring: plant state, butterflies, flowers, picnic.
- Summer: plant state, ice cream, Jet Ski, sand box.

Table 1. Tangible objects for each season.

Season	Object1	Object2	Object3	Object4
Autumn				
Winter				
Spring				
Summer				

3.1 Hardware

The tangible objects consist of three layers as following:

- Cork board to present the elements of seasons (phenomena or activities).
- Foil to deliver the electrical charge from the child's hand to the pins and finally to the screen.
- Pins were selected to connect electrical charge from the foil surface to the surface of the screen to detect the object.

These layers are built to display the shapes of tangible objects on the screen and to start the interaction between the children and the system (See Fig. 1). It works as following:

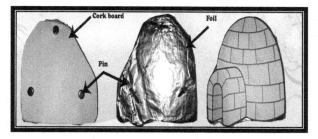

Fig. 1. Components of each tangible objects. The figure shows the igloo object as an example

- Foil has been used as a conductive material for electrical charges from hand-to-object.
- Each object consists of a certain number of pins having different dimensions, distance and axes for the distinction between the objects.

3.2 Software

The system was developed using Android studio platform with JAVA codes. In addition Balsamic Mockups 3[1] is used as a tool to create the user interface design of the system. The object's pictures stored on a database. To allow the system distinguish between each object, we have identified number of points and pins using coordinate system. For example, when children applies the "Ice-cream" object on winter season the system will display an error message because this object does not belong to winter season based on the object's coordination.

3.3 The Interface

The main interface shows two buttons of the main functions (create a story, or play a story) (See Fig. 2). Pressing create button leads to the four season's page, which allow the children to select a season that would like to create a story about. Then, the children chooses any objects to try to match it with the season by lay it down on the season's screen and it will be recognized by the system. If the object is not related to the season, an error message will appear saying that the object is not belonging to the season. Otherwise, children will placing the objects on the tablet to the create story pro. By pressing screen record button, the kid will be able to adding their voice, manipulate, animate and record the story that will help him to recall the season with its features and activities. Finally, the story will be saved in the play section, where children are able to play and shared saved stories with their friends and family.

---

[1] https://balsamiq.com/.

Fig. 2. The main interface of the tangible storytelling system

4   Evaluation

Before handling the system to user's hands for evaluation, the system go through several assessments. Controlled and focused testing is performed to uncover errors and bugs. Furthermore, a number of specific validation tests are performed during the test phase such as requirements validation, system integration, interface, system performance, usability, and user acceptance. After several updates on the system based on the evaluator's comments and feedbacks, the system ready to be evaluated with the real user at school.

4.1   Participants

We selected ten children (all girls) to participate in the study. The participants' ages ranged from 4 to 7. The children were all students at school. 8 children play with the system in pairs forming 4 groups, while 2 children plays individually based on their preference.

4.2   Methodology

The experiment conducted at local school. The children were invited to come in to classroom where the system was set up. Two teachers were volunteered to organized children setting and forming groups. The investigators started the session with open discussion about the four seasons, what are they? And if there are any distinguished activities or events in each season. We found that, 7 children are familiar with the seasons name and weather status. However 3 children doesn't know anything about seasons. After that, the tangible storytelling system is introduced to the children. We started the experiment pair by pair and once they start the first practice (compose a story), they were free to play with their own if they wanted to, for up to 30 min. During their free play, the children were encouraged to talk out loud and share their created stories.

4.3 Observations

The study was conducted in 6 sessions with an average of two participants per 4 sessions, and 2 sessions with only one participant. All participants played with the system during the entire duration of the session (from 20 to 30 min). The children created stories involving their own creativity and imagination. All children add their narrative voice as a scenario of their stories. The children found the tangible objects are attractive and easy to work with. Once the experimenter had gone through an example sequence with the children, they were able to engage in storytelling on their own. Children understand the different between seasons like changes in weather and plant status. However, most children were disappointed by small number of actions that they can add to their stories. In addition, children asked to add more phenomena of each season such as changes in the type of food. All children were engaged in creating stories, however due to the low number of elements in each seasons most of the stories don't exceed 4 sentences. Moreover, there was huge similarities between children stories.

5 Conclusion and Discussion

Using our system, the children introduced to the four seasons, compose their stories, distinguished each seasonal activities and whether status. Through these activities, the children created simple stories that involved interaction between tangible objects, sound recordings, and their pairs. The system supported children's verbal, visual, and kinetic expressions, through which the children found ways to creatively develop their stories. In addition, the system was an excellent tool to practice collaborative learning.

Regarding the results of the experiments and the feedback from the users and teachers tangible storytelling are more effective for children for learning new topic. Moreover, children were more engaged to compose the stories by them self, and more curious to discover about seasons. They ask to add more elements of events and actions. Also they asked if it possible to build the tangible objects by them self and add it to the story board. It's obvious that tangible storytelling evoke the curiosity and enthusiasm for children to learn.

6 Future Work

In the next stage children will allow to create their own tangible objects based on the action in their imagination stories. Moreover, children will be able to combine several seasons in one story to show the transition between seasons.

Acknowledgment. We thank the children, parents, and teachers who helped us completing this project. Special thanks to Lujain Alqarni for her cooperation and assistance. Thanks to Hadeel Felemban, Lamis Bin Salman, and Al-Shaimaa AL-Mokhtar for their cooperation in this project.

References

1. Ullmer, B., Ishii, H.: Emerging frameworks for tangible user interfaces. IBM Syst. J. **39**(3.4), 915–931 (2000)
2. Budd, J., Madej, K., Stephens-Wells, J., de Jong, J., Katzur, E., Mulligan, L.: PageCraft: learning in context a tangible interactive storytelling platform to support early narrative development for young children. In: Proceedings of the 6th international Conference on Interaction Design and Children, pp. 97–100 (2007)
3. Fails, J.A., Druin, A., Guha, M.L.: Interactive storytelling: interacting with people, environment, and technology. Int. J. Arts Technol. **7**(1), 112–124 (2014)
4. Glos, J.W., Cassell, J.: Rosebud: technological toys for storytelling. In: CHI 1997. Electronic Publications (1997)
5. Green, M.C.: Teaching tips: storytelling in teaching. Assoc. Psychol. Sci. Obs. **17**(4), 52–54 (2004)
6. Guha, M.L., Druin, A., Chipman, G., Fails, J.A., Simms, S., Farber, A.: Mixing ideas: a new technique for working with young children as design partners. In: Proceedings of the 2004 Conference on Interaction Design and Children: Building a Community, pp. 35–42 (2004)
7. Hourcade, J.P., Bederson, B.B., Druin, A., Taxén, G.: KidPad: collaborative storytelling for children. In: CHI 2002 Extended Abstracts on Human Factors in Computing Systems, pp. 500–501 (2002)
8. Mayora, O., Costa, C., Papliatseyeu, A.: iTheater puppets tangible interactions for storytelling. In: Nijholt, A., Reidsma, D., Hondorp, H. (eds.) INTETAIN 2009. LNICST, vol. 9, pp. 110–118. Springer, Heidelberg (2009). https://doi.org/10.1007/978-3-642-02315-6_11
9. Muñoz, J., Marchesoni, M., Costa, C.: i-theatre: tangible interactive storytelling. In: Camurri, A., Costa, C. (eds.) INTETAIN 2011. LNICST, vol. 78, pp. 223–228. Springer, Heidelberg (2012). https://doi.org/10.1007/978-3-642-30214-5_26
10. Ryokai, K., Lee, M.J., Breitbart, J.M.: Children's storytelling and programming with robotic characters. In: Proceedings of the Seventh ACM Conference on Creativity and Cognition, pp. 19–28 (2009)
11. Stanton, D., et al.: Classroom collaboration in the design of tangible interfaces for storytelling. In: Proceedings of the SIGCHI Conference on Human Factors in Computing Systems, pp. 482–489 (2001)
12. Vygotsky, L.S.: Mind in Society: The Development of Higher Psychological Processes. Harvard University Press, Cambridge (1978)
13. Wang, D., He, L., Dou, K.: StoryCube: supporting children's storytelling with a tangible tool. J. Supercomput. **70**(1), 269–283 (2013). https://doi.org/10.1007/s11227-012-0855-x
14. Xu, D., Mazzone, E., MacFarlane, S.: Informant design with children - designing childrens tangible technology. In: IDC 2007, Aalborg, Denmark (2007)

Analyzing Students' Behavior in a MOOC Course: A Process-Oriented Approach

Franklin Bernal[2], Jorge Maldonado-Mahauad[1,2(✉)], Klinge Villalba-Condori[3], Miguel Zúñiga-Prieto[2], Jaime Veintimilla-Reyes[2], and Magali Mejía[2]

[1] Departamento de Ciencias de la Computación, Pontificia Universidad Católica de Chile, Santiago, Chile
`jjmaldonado@uc.cl`
[2] Departamento de Ciencias de la Computación, Universidad de Cuenca, Cuenca, Ecuador
`{franklin.bernal,miguel.zunigap,jaime.veintimilla,`
`magali.mejia}@ucuenca.edu.ec`
[3] Universidad Continental, Arequipa, Peru
`kvillalbac@continental.edu.pe`

Abstract. Massive Open Online Courses (MOOCs), are one of the most disruptive trends along the last 12 years. This is evidenced by the number of students enrolled since their emergence with over 101 million people taking one of the more than 11,400 MOOCs available. However, the approval rate of students in these types of courses is only about 5%. This has led to a great deal of interest among researchers in studying students' behavior in these types of courses. The aim of this article is to explore the behavior of students in a MOOC. Specifically, to study students learning sequences and extract their behavioral patterns in the different study sessions. To reach the goal, using process mining techniques, process models of N = 1,550 students enrolled in a MOOC in Coursera were obtained. As a result, two groups of students were classified according to their study sessions, where differences were found both in the students' interactions with the MOOC resources and in the way the lessons were approached on a weekly basis. In addition, students who passed the course repeated the assessments several times until they passed, without returning to review a video-lecture in advance. The results of this work contribute to extend the knowledge about students' behavior in online environments.

Keywords: MOOC · Study sessions · Learning strategies · Process mining · Learning analytics · Coursera

1 Introduction

The use of technology on nowadays educational contexts, such as face-to-face, hybrid and online, has changed the way of teaching and learning. On the one hand, learners today must be able to mediate the content taught using the digital resources available to them. On the other hand, students have more and more access to these contents in a timeless way and regardless of their geographical location, which allows to extend the classroom

© Springer Nature Switzerland AG 2020
C. Stephanidis et al. (Eds.): HCII 2020, LNCS 12425, pp. 307–325, 2020.
https://doi.org/10.1007/978-3-030-60128-7_24

and learners take control of their learning process [1]. One of the most disruptive trends in the last 12 years has been the Massive Open Online Courses (MOOCs) [3]. These courses currently attract millions of students around the world (i.e., massive) and are offered online on some of the MOOC platforms such as: edX, MiriadaX, Coursera [2]. From 2012 to 2019, approximately 101 million students were enrolled in one of the more than 11,400 courses offered by some of the 900 universities around the world [3]. However, the approval rate of students in these types of courses is only about 5% [4], so researchers' efforts have focused on trying to determine what causes students to drop out of a MOOC.

Some authors [5–9] indicate the following as possible causes or factors influencing student dropout in an MOOC: (1) little free time to address courses, (2) lack of previous knowledge, (3) course content poorly adapted to the student's own needs, (4) lack of communication with a tutor or other students, (5) poor self-regulation of their learning, and (6) instructional design and course objectives not aligned with those of the student.

In relation to course design, there is little work that explores students' learning pathways, as well as their interactions with digital resources in a MOOC. For example, authors in [10] using a statistical model (i.e., Hidden Markov Models) and clustering techniques, identified relationships between students' learning strategies with their academic outcomes. In another study authors in [11], also using two-layer Hidden Markov Models found significant differences between students who passed the course and those who did not, demonstrating that students with better academic performance work not only longer on assessments but also have more active participation in the forum compared to average students. In a recent paper, authors in [12] using techniques such as Process Mining (PM), sequence and network analytics extracted different learning strategies, where they concluded that PM techniques allow to extract from beginning to end the learning trajectory of a student. PM techniques provide new means to discover, monitor and improve processes in a variety of application domains [24]; being able to extract knowledge from the event records commonly available in today's information systems.

Currently, little is known about how students organize their time in relation to the study sessions in a MOOC, as well as how students distribute their sessions in relation to length and frequency throughout the course (macro interactions), and what type of activities they prioritize within the study sessions (micro interactions). More empirical evidence is needed on (1) student interactions with course content, (2) the type of learning strategies that students use during the learning process, and (3) how interactions take place during different study sessions [13].

This article proposes to address these gaps in the literature and to use PM techniques to explore the students behavior in a MOOC by analyzing their study sessions and the interactions that occur at both the macro level (week/topic) and the micro level (interactions with MOOC resources). The aim of this study is to understand how students in an online environment manage their study sessions when they take a MOOC and the relationship with their academic achievements.

The article is structured as follows: Sect. 2 presents the related work, Sect. 3 presents the methods, Sect. 4 presents the results, and finally Sect. 5 presents the main study conclusions.

2 Related Work

2.1 Learning Strategies in MOOCs

To study learning strategies in MOOCs, researchers have followed two approaches: the first based on the study of learning strategies as an aptitude, and the second based on the study of learning strategies as a process [9]. On the one hand, the aptitude approach seeks to inform the learning strategies of MOOC participants through self-reporting tools. The objective of these is to capture the strategies that students believe they are using during their learning process. On the other hand, the process-based approach seeks to study the students' learning strategies from event traces; that is, the students' interactions with the course contents. However, observing learning strategies, even when they manifest as a set of events or actions, involves challenges, such as (1) transforming fine-grained (e.g., clickstream) or coarse-grained (e.g., clickstream set of events) event traces into interpretable behavior (e.g., learning strategies); (2) identifying and observing behavior changes during the learning process; and, (3) understanding whether an observable behavior relates to a particular learning strategy or to more than one [14].

Recent advances in the disciplines of Learning Analytics (LA) and PM have contributed to trying to overcome these challenges [15]. For example, authors in [16] using unsupervised machine learning techniques such as sequence mining algorhythms extracted student learning strategies from the data on the e-learning platform. In other work carried out by [10] using Markov Models extracted study tactics that were grouped together to derive learning strategies. Authors such as [17] applied PM to data from 43,218 MOOC participants and observed that students with high grades and who passed the course followed the course structure, while students who did not pass were erratic and did not follow the proposed structure. In another recent paper [9], using PM discovery techniques and applied on three MOOCs in Coursera, the authors were able to extract seven learning patterns (i.e., only-video-lecture, only-assessment, explore, etc.) from the students while taking the course. In [9], the authors reveal that regardless of the students' self-regulation profile, they tend to follow their own learning paths and that they depended on the goals they had with the course contents. Finally, in a more recent research of [18] using PM the authors grouped the students based on their weekly sequences and found that regular viewing of the videos in successive groups leads to better learning outcomes, despite not being a graded activity. These latter works establish the basis for beginning to consider PM as an appropriate technique for studying student behavior (specifically their learning strategies) as a process in online environments such as MOOCs.

2.2 Learning Sessions in MOOCs

Recent research has shown that study sessions remain as the approach used by students to organize their learning in an online context [19]. A study session can be defined as a period of time during which the student interacts with the course resources and where the intervals of student inactivity in the course are no longer than 40 min [20–22]. Authors in [23] defined a session as a period of time devoted to a sequence of similar or related activities that are not interrupted by other types of activities. Currently few studies explicitly examine student sessions in an online environment. However, in areas such as Learning Analytics and Data Mining we have recently begun to find studies that consider the study session as a unit of analysis. For example, authors in [9, 10] using LA identified the learning strategies that students use in a study session for both blended context (i.e., where the face-to-face and virtual are mixed) and online context. As a result, in these studies learners were classified based on the identified strategies resulting in a characterization of them for the online context (i.e., Samplers, Comprehensive, and Targeting learners) as for the blended (i.e., intensive, strategic, highly strategic, selective and highly selective learners) [9, 16]. In these works the authors have used the 'learning design' of the course to try to relate and interpret the patterns found. That is, they have tried to connect the learning design of the course with the learning analyses obtained. However, there is still a lack of works that consider the study sessions analysis with different levels of granularity of the data (macro, meso, micro) and with different activities levels in which the course is structured (i.e., activities, lessons, modules).

2.3   Research Questions

Based on the above, this paper proposes an exploratory study to understand how students organize their workload in study sessions in a MOOC and how this relates to their academic performance. The research questions sought to be answered in this study are:

RQ1: What kind of sessions do students in a MOOC?
RQ2: What learning sequences do students in the different MOOC sessions?
RQ3: What is the difference between the sessions for students who complete the course and those who don't?

3   Method

3.1   Context

This exploratory study was conducted in the context of a MOOC, which was deployed on the Coursera platform and offered by the Catholic University of Chile in Spanish. The topic of the course is 'The Semantic Web', and it was offered on December 7th, 2015, ending its first cohort on February 25th, 2016. The course was offered in an open way for both professionals and non-professionals, who wish to acquire the experience of the Semantic Web. The course is composed of seven modules, where each module has a series of activities, including video-lectures and assessments, both summative and formative. In general terms, Table 1 shows the course structure. It consists on 37 video-lectures with an average duration from 6 to 10 min, 2 formative assessments in the form of supplementary activities containing unqualified questionnaires, 7 summative assessments, one at the end of each module and finally 2 peer evaluations.

Table 1. Course structure: types of activities in the MOOC

Type of activity	Number of activities	Percentage of activities
Peer review	2	4.16%
Summative assessments (Exam)	7	14.58%
Formative assessment (Supplement)	2	4.16%
Video-Lecture	37	77.10%

3.2 Participants

N = 1,550 students were registered in the course. For the analysis all students were considered except for the 131 who did not report any activity within the course, leaving a cohort of 1,419 students. Of these students 77.38% were male and 22.62% female, 69% were aged 25–45 years, and 54.7% had a university degree. Table 2, Table 3 and Table 4 summarize the students demographics.

Table 2. Gender distribution of MOOC participants

Gender	Percentage
Male	77.38%
Female	22.62%

Table 3. Age distribution among MOOC participants

Age range	Percentage
<25	1.19%
25–35	30.95%
36–45	38.09%
46–55	19.04%
>55	10.71%

Table 4. Academic level distribution of MOOC participants

Academic level	Percentage
High school	17.85%
College/University	54.76%
Post graduate	27.38%

3.3 Methodology Stages to Apply Process Mining

In order to be able to answer the research questions, the PM^2 methodology was adapted [24]. PM^2 is a simplification and flexibility of other PM methodologies such as L*Life-cycle model [25]. As a result, Fig. 1 shows the resulting 5 stages, which are described in the following sections.

Fig. 1. Stages of the adapted PM^2 Methodology to generate the process models [24]

1) **Stage 1: Set Goal.** At this stage the objectives are defined by means of the research questions posed in Sect. 2.3.
2) **Stage 2: Data Extraction.** At this stage, in order to extract the study sessions and learning strategies, activity data from the log files recorded by the Coursera platform were extracted. The platform generates a set of files in CSV format. This set of files consists on 86 files from which only 8 were selected which are the most important ones to analyze the student's activity (i.e., Users, Course grades, Course progress, Course items, Course item grades, Course item types, Course lesson, and Course module). These files were imported into a database whose structure is presented in Fig. 2.
3) **Stage 3: Generation of the Event Log.** In this stage the event log is defined which will be used to generate the process models that reflects the student's behavior in the MOOC. The event log is a file that saves information about the students' interactions with the digital resources of the course. The first step to generate the event log was to define two concepts to be able to interpret the data traces of the interactions with the MOOC. Specifically, the concept of session and interaction were defined as follows:

A study session is a period of time in which students interact with the digital resources and activities of the course. For this study we used 40 min of inactivity time, which is adjusted to the range of inactivity posed by [22].

An interaction is an action that reflects a student's interaction with one of the MOOC's digital resources. For this work we defined 8 types of activities when learners interact with Video-lectures and assessments. Table 5 presents the definition of the eight interactions that characterize student behavior.

As a result of this stage, three event logs were generated. The first event log generated will be used to analyze the study sessions conducted by the students (see Table 6).

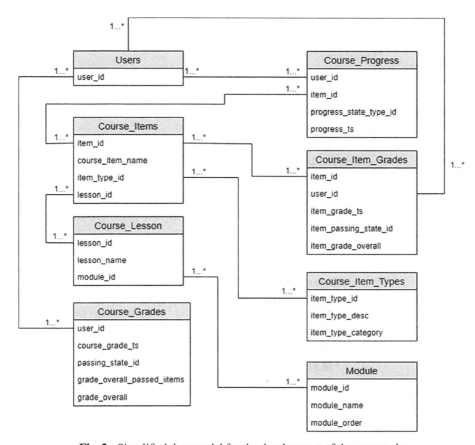

Fig. 2. Simplified data model for the development of the case study

Where *case_id:* unique identifier for each student; *number_session:* is the number of the session performed by each learner; *duration_per_session:* contains the time in minutes of each student session duration; *num_int_vl:* contains the number of interactions with video-lectures activities, which the student performs per session; *num_int_exam:* contains the number of interactions with assessment activities, which the student performs per session; and *num_int_total:* contains the number of interactions with all course activities.

The second event log contains the number of interactions with all course activities that will serve to analyze the students' interaction with the digital resources of the course (i.e., micro level). At this level, events are defined as the result of student interactions with MOOC objects (video lectures, assessments, supplements, peer reviews) in learning sessions. These activities are also organized according to the recurrence that has been had on it, that is, the states that can be (1) Begin, (2) Repeated, (3) Ended and (4) Started over (this state is frequently repeated in the evaluations, since until it is approved the state does not change to Ended or Repeated) (see Table 7).

Table 5. Definition of the eight interactions that characterize student behavior

Interaction	Description
VL-begin	Begin a "video-lecture", a state that remains as soon as a student opens a video-lecture
VL-start over	A video-lecture that was initiated but not completed previously
VL-end	When a video-lecture has already finished
VL-repeat	When a video-lecture previously finished is reopened
Exam-begin	Start an Exam, a state that remains as soon as a student tries to complete it
Exam-start over	This is an Exam that was previously opened but was not completed or failed
Exam-end	When an Exam was passed based on the required grade threshold
Exam-repeat	When a previously approved Exam is reopened

Table 6. Fragment of the event log used

Case_id	number_session	duration_per_session	num_int_vl	num_int_exam	num_int_total
003a3	1	"10.46"	7	0	7
00f06	2	"55.58"	7	3	10
011ff4	3	"38.51"	8	0	8

....

Table 7. Fragment of the event log used for micro level analysis

Case_id	Time stamp	Activity	Session	State	Pass or Fail	Cluster
003a3018	"2015-10-13 17:03:42.958"	"Video-Lecture"	1	VL – begin	0	0
39797a08	"2015-12-12 09:04:30.747"	"Exam"	10	Exam-start-over	1	0
25e0fdd4	"2015-10-08 17:29:26.257"	"Video-Lecture"	3	VL-end	0	1

....

Finally, the third event log will serve to analyze the students' interaction with the course lessons (macro level). At this level, the events are defined as the result of the student's interactions over the 7 lessons course weeks (Table 8).

Table 8. Fragment of the event log used for macro level analysis

Case_id	Time stamp	Lesson	Session	Pass or Fail	Cluster
003a3018	"2015-10-13 17:03:42"	"Vocabularios RDF"	3	0	1
39797a08	"2015-12-12 09:04:30"	"Conceptos de RDF"	6	1	1
....					

4) **Stage 4: Model discovery and analysis.** At this stage the PM algorithm is applied for the process models discovery. In particular, the Disco algorithm (based on fuzzy miner) is used, which provides the Disco tool [26]. The result analysis (graphical and numerical) will make it possible to answer the research questions posed in Sect. 2.3.

Regarding RQ.1. What Kind of Sessions do Students do in a MOOC? In order to answer this question, it is necessary to characterize the study sessions through a grouping process by machine learning techniques (clustering). To do this, it is necessary to create a data log with information about the sessions. Table 6 shows the variables considered for this process and a fragment of the data log.

Regarding RQ.2. What Learning Sequences the Students do in the Different Sessions of the MOOC? To answer this research question, an event log was generated, which allows the study of the students' sequences from two different but complementary approaches: a) at the micro level; b) at the macro level. The first one is considered as the micro level indicated in Table 7, which consists on the interaction with the course resources, such as: video-lectures, assessments, questionnaires, among others, and the macro level indicated in Table 8, to the set of actions per topic and per week of the MOOC [27].

Regarding RQ.3. What is the Difference Between the Sessions of Students who Complete the Course and Those Who Do Not? To answer this research question, as in RQ.2, two event logs were generated, one at the micro level (Table 7) and another at the macro level (Table 8), in which there is a column called 'Pass or Fail', with the identifier "0" for those who do not pass the course, that is, they did not manage to surpass the threshold of passing the course, which corresponds to 80% of the summative evaluations on average. On the other hand, the identifier "1" is assigned to those students who pass the course, as a consequence they obtained an overall average of 80% or more of the evaluations.

4   Results

This section presents the main results obtained from the event log analyses. The results have been organized according to the research questions derived from the previous section.

R1. Students in a MOOC according to their study sessions can be classified into two groups identified as Cluster 0 and Cluster 1. Students in cluster 1 have sessions that on average are longer than students in cluster 0, this difference being statistically significant (p < 0.001). In addition, students from cluster 1 during their sessions work more intensively with video readings and evaluations (Table 9).

Table 9. Difference of the means of the sessions and interactions of the students in each cluster

	Cluster 0 mean	Cluster 1 mean	t	p
Duration per session	26.1	36.7	−21.8	0.001***
Number of interactions with video-lecture per session	3.4	10.6	−58.0	0.001***
Number of interactions with Exams per session	1.3	14.1	−79.6	0.001***
Number of total interactions per session	3.8	14.5	−110.2	0.001***

*Note: ***p < 0.001*

R2. The most common interaction paths between cluster 0 and cluster 1 are the same at the beginning of the course. Similar behavior is identified between the two groups, both Cluster 0 and Cluster 1, where activities follow a sequential and identical order as can be seen in Fig. 3. Itineraries that are most repeated in both groups are (in order from highest to lowest frequency):

1. VL-begin → VL-end → VL-begin
2. VL-begin → VL-end → Exam-begin → Exam-start over → Exam-end

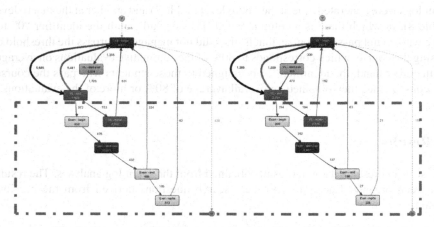

Fig. 3. Process models at the micro level for Cluster 0 and Cluster 1

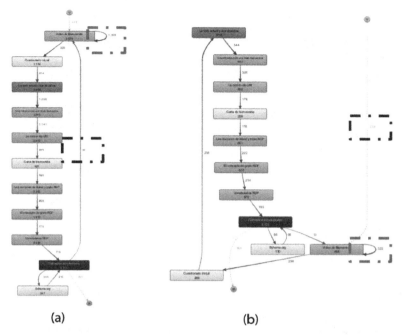

Fig. 4. Process models in the first week of the MOOC

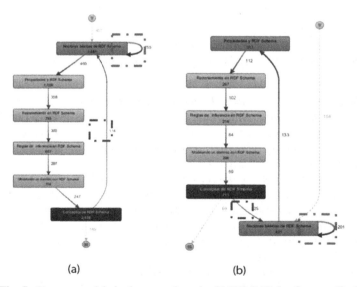

Fig. 5. Process models in the second week of MOOC (Color figure online)

R3. The sessions during the first two weeks of the MOOC for both Cluster 0 and Cluster 1 students follow a sequential pattern, where they tend to repeat several times

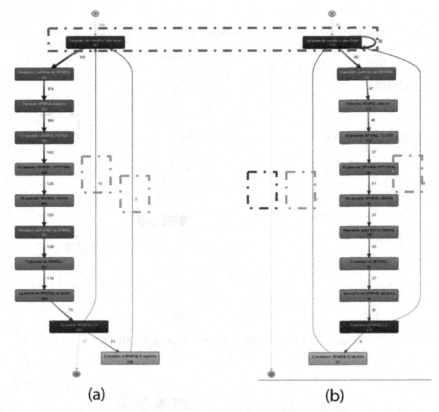

(a)   (b)

Fig. 6. Process models for the third week of the MOOC (Color figure online)

the first video lecture of each module and return to the first activity (video lecture)
after performing the module evaluation. This behavior can be observed in (Fig. 4(a))
y (Fig. 4(b)) *for the first week,* in (Fig. 5 (a)) and (Fig. 5 (b)) *for the second week. The*
iterations of the first activity (video-lecture) have been marked in red and the evaluation
activities in blue, after which we return to the first video-lecture of each module.

R4. During the third week of the course, students from both clusters tend to follow
the course in a linear sequence. But they also return to the beginning of each module
after completing the module evaluation and the peer review. This can be seen in Fig. 6(a)
and Fig. 6(b), framed in green. In the case of the student sessions in Cluster 1 in the third
week of the MOOC, repeat iteratively in the first activity of the module (video-lecture)
in the third week of the course. This can be seen in Fig. 6(b) framed in red, where it also
indicates that Cluster 0 (Fig. 6(a)), does not have that repetitive sequence. In addition,
some sessions (29 sessions) of Cluster 1 in the third week of the MOOC left the study
session in the third week after the first activity. This can be seen in Fig. 6 (b), framed in
blue.

R5. In the fourth week of the MOOC, Cluster 0 and Cluster 1 student sessions
follow a linear sequence order laid out by the course design, however, after the modular

assessment they return to a video-lecture activity. As for Cluster 0 (Fig. 7 (a)), students return to the first activity of the module which is a video reading (framed in red), while Cluster 1 (Fig. 7 (b)), returns to an intermediate activity, but which is also a video lecture (framed in red). In addition, Cluster 1 (Fig. 7 (b)), repeats iteratively the first activity of the module (framed in blue).

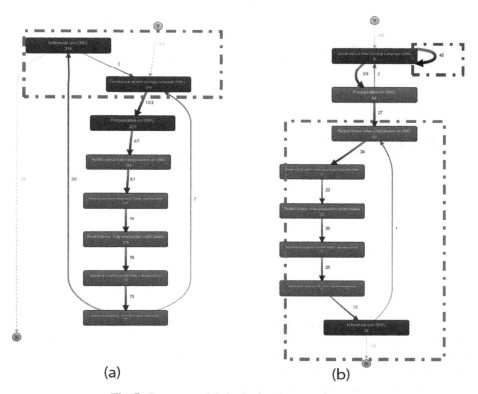

(a)   (b)

Fig. 7. Process models in the fourth week of MOOC

R6. During the fifth week of the MOOC, students in their study sessions tend to return to activities previously completed for both student clusters; however, it is also observed that the learning paths between the two clusters begin to differ in the sequence of activities. This can be observed in Fig. 8(a, b), where the learning sequence follows the course order, also return to the previous activities. In addition, *you can see that during this week students in Cluster 0 tend to be iterative in video-lecture activities, while student sessions in Cluster 1 tend to be iterative in modular assessment.* This can be seen in Fig. 8(a) of Cluster 0, which is framed in blue, and repeats video-reading type activities. On the other hand, Cluster one performs this behavior, but in the modular assessment that can be seen in Fig. 8(b), framed in blue. In the case of Cluster 0 student sessions, *students tend to end the work session after a video lecture, while Cluster 1 student sessions tend to end the module work session after the assessment.* You can see this behavior framed in red, Fig. 8(a) for Cluster 0 and Fig. 8 (b) for Cluster 1.

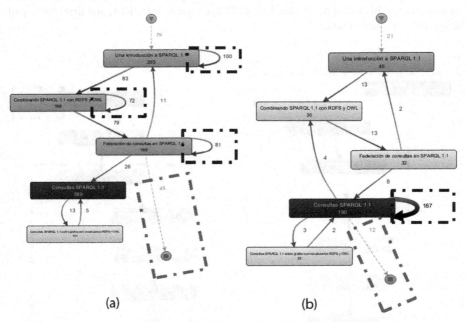

(a)   (b)

Fig. 8. Process models in the fifth week of the MOOC (Color figure online)

R7. During the sixth and seventh week of the MOOC, the student sessions in both clusters and the sequences followed tend to be the same. This is due to the fact that in the last few weeks students who persisted in the course to finish it. This can be seen in Figs. 9 and 10, where there are slight differences, as for example in Cluster 0 in week 6 Fig. 9(a) students finish their work session after a video-lecture activity (framed in blue), while in the same week, but in Cluster 1 Fig. 9 (b), students finish their work session in the module after an evaluation activity (framed in blue).

R8. Students who passed the course, at the micro level, tend to try to finish an assessment (Assessment-Restart) consecutively, while students who do not pass the course follow a linear sequence without consecutively repeating the attempt to finish, on the other hand, students who do not pass the course, tend to abandon it after performing a video-reading activity. In Fig. 11, we can see the similarity at the micro level of the students who pass (Fig. 11(a)) and those who do not pass the course (Fig. 11(b)), in which after carrying out the Video-lecture activities, the students proceed to take the tests and repeat them until they succeed (framed in red). On the other hand, the students who did not pass the course (Fig. 11(b)), leave the course after a video-lecture activity (framed in blue color), while the students who passed the course do it after an evaluation.

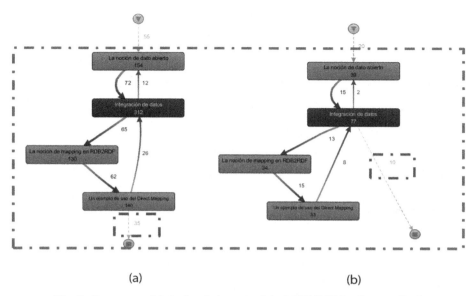

(a)   (b)

Fig. 9. Process models in the sixth week of the MOOC (Color figure online)

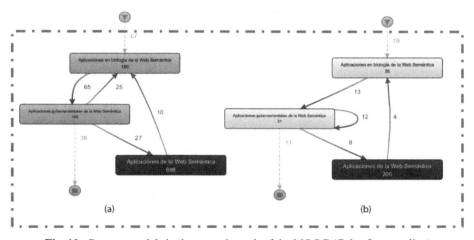

(a)   (b)

Fig. 10. Process models in the seventh week of the MOOC (Color figure online)

R.9 Students who pass the MOOC conduct more sessions on average than students who do not pass the MOOC. Figure 12 shows that students who pass the course have more sessions than those who do not pass, with 34.14 and 17.32 average sessions respectively. In addition, it can be seen that the weekly average number of sessions is more stable and homogeneous, fluctuating between 31.43 and 36.71 sessions per week. On the other hand, students who do not pass the course, go from less to more in terms of the average number of sessions per week, these fluctuate between 8.34 and 22.31 sessions per week.

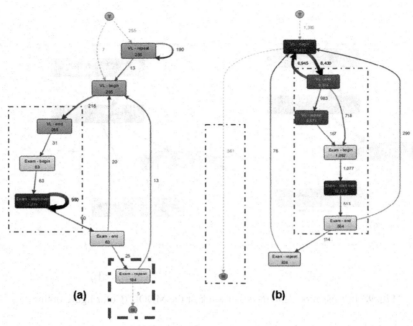

Fig. 11. Process models, micro level of students who pass and do not pass the course (Color figure online)

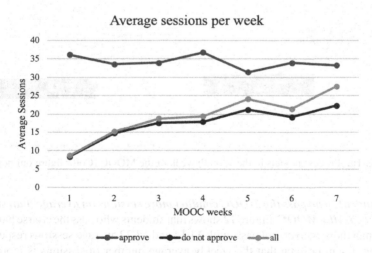

Fig. 12. Average sessions per week of MOOC students

5   Conclusions

The primary motivation for this research has been to explore the opportunities and challenges that LA offers for studying learner's behavior in a MOOC. This article contributes with a perspective to the study and understanding about how learners perform their study sessions in a MOOC. While there is previous work in the literature that has explored the trajectories taken by students in a MOOC [28–30], this study, unlike the others mentioned above, analyses learning trajectories at the micro and macro levels. For this purpose, the processes (activities) carried out by the students at the MOOC have been studied, contributing, unlike other works (i.e., [31]). The main conclusions of this study are the following. First, the students in a MOOC according to their study sessions can be classified into two groups identified as Cluster 0 and Cluster 1. Second, the most common interaction paths between Cluster 0 and Cluster 1 are the same at the beginning of the course: VL-begin → VL-end → VL-begin y VL-begin → VL-end → Assessment -begin → Assessment -begin again → Assessment -end. Third, the sessions during the first two weeks of the MOOC for both Cluster 0 and Cluster 1 students follow a sequential pattern, where they tend to repeat the first video lecture of each module several times and return to the first activity (video lecture) after the module evaluation is done. Fourth, during the third week of the course the students' sessions in both clusters tend to follow in a linear sequence the course. Fifth, in the fourth week of the MOOC, student sessions for Cluster 0 and Cluster 1 follow a linear sequence laid out by the course design, however, after the modular assessment they return to a video-reading activity. Sixth, during the fifth week of the MOOC, students in their study sessions tend to return to activities previously outgrown for both student clusters, however, it is also observed that the learning paths between the two clusters begin to be different in the sequence of activities. Finally, during the sixth and seventh week of the MOOC, the students' sessions in both clusters and the sequences followed tend to be the same. This is due to the fact that in the last few weeks students who persisted in the course arrive to finish. On the other hand, in a focus on passing students vs. not passing the MOOC, similar behaviors were shown in the first few weeks of work, with passing students showing more organized and sequential behavior throughout the course, while non-MOOC students begin in an orderly fashion and become disorganized in the last few weeks. This result is confirmed by the weekly behavior analysis, which found that students who passed the MOOC were more consistent and intense in the number of sessions they had on average per week, while students who did not pass the MOOC started with fewer sessions in the first few weeks and increased as the MOOC progressed. Finally, in the micro analysis of these two types of students, the difference lies in the intensity of the students who passed the MOOC in repeating the assessments until they pass.

In the context of this work, it has been shown that both students who complete the course and those who do not have to follow similar sequences of activities, which is to follow the sequential structure posed by the course, as shown by similar studies [29, 32]. It is also important to mention that many of the activities that are designed for a MOOC are limited by the technology platforms on which the course is implemented. The results obtained suggest that MOOCs should be designed to address the heterogeneity of students. For this purpose, an adaptive structure should be provided, which proposes learning activities and presents the contents based on each student particularity. The generalization of these results is subject to the limitations of the methodology used in the study. So are the results obtained by using PM techniques. These are directly related to the data taken as a basis for this study and the analysis carried out for their interpretation. However, the process models obtained are closely related to the course structure supported by the Coursera platform.

Acknowledgements. This work has been co-funded by Dirección de Investigación de la Universidad de Cuenca (DIUC), Cuenca-Ecuador, under the project "Analítica del aprendizaje para el estudio de estrategias de aprendizaje autorregulado en un contexto de aprendizaje híbrido" (DIUC_XVIII_2019_54). We want also to thanks to the Pontificia Universidad Católica de Chile and Dirección de Educación en Ingeniería - DEI.

References

1. Bergman, J., Sams, A.: How the flipped classroom was born. The Daily Riff Online (2011). http://www.thedailyriff.com/articles/how-the-flipped-classroom-is-radically-transforming-learning-536.php
2. Pérez-Álvarez, R., Maldonado, J.J., Rendich, R., Pérez-Sanagustín, M., Sapunar, D.: Observatorio MOOC UC: la Adopción de MOOCs en la Educación Superior en América Latina y Europa. In: Actas la Jorn. MOOCs en español en EMOOCs 2017, vol. 2017, pp. 5–14 (2017)
3. Shah, D.: By the numbers: MOOCs in 2019. Class Central (2020). https://www.classcentral.com/report/mooc-stats-2019/
4. Kizilcec, R.F., Cohen, G.L.: Eight-minute self-regulation intervention raises educational attainment at scale in individualist but not collectivist cultures. Proc. Natl. Acad. Sci. **114**, 4348–4353 (2017)
5. Kizilcec, R.F., Piech, C., Schneider, E.: Deconstructing disengagement: Analyzing learner subpopulations in massive open online courses. In: ACM International Conference Proceeding Series (2013)
6. Ferguson, R., Clow, D.: Examining engagement: analysing learner subpopulations in massive open online courses (MOOCs). In: ACM International Conference Proceeding Series (2015)
7. Normandi Atiaja Atiaja, L., Segundo Guerrero Proenza, R.: MOOCs: origin, characterization, principal problems and challenges in higher education. J. E-Learn. Knowl. Soc. (2016)
8. Alonso-Mencía, M.E., Alario-Hoyos, C., Maldonado-Mahauad, J., Estévez-Ayres, I., Pérez-Sanagustín, M., Delgado Kloos, C.: Self-regulated learning in MOOCs: lessons learned from a literature review. Educ. Rev. **72**, 319–345 (2019)
9. Maldonado-Mahauad, J., Pérez-Sanagustín, M., Kizilcec, R.F., Morales, N., Munoz-Gama, J.: Mining theory-based patterns from Big data: identifying self-regulated learning strategies in massive open online courses. Comput. Human Behav. **80**, 179–196 (2018)
10. Fincham, O.E., Gasevic, D.V., Jovanovic, J.M., Pardo, A.: From study tactics to learning strategies: an analytical method for extracting interpretable representations. IEEE Trans. Learn. Technol. **12**, 59–72 (2018)
11. Geigle, C., Zhai, C.X.: Modeling MOOC student behavior with two-layer hidden Markov models. In: L@S 2017 - Proceedings of the 4th (2017) ACM Conference on Learning at Scale (2017)
12. Matcha, W., et al.: Detection of learning strategies: a comparison of process, sequence and network analytic approaches (2019)
13. Davis, D., Seaton, D., Hauff, C., Houben, G.-J.: Toward large-scale learning design (2018)

14. Pashler, H., Wagenmakers, E.J.: Editors' introduction to the special section on replicability in psychological science: a crisis of confidence? Perspect. Psychol. Sci. **7**, 528–530 (2012)
15. Cole, M.: The cultural context of learning and thinking: an exploration in experimental anthropology (1971)
16. Jovanović, J., Gašević, D., Dawson, S., Pardo, A., Mirriahi, N.: Learning analytics to unveil learning strategies in a flipped classroom. Internet High. Educ. **33**, 74–85 (2017)
17. Mukala, P., Buijs, J., Leemans, M., Van Der Aalst, W.: Learning analytics on coursera event data: a proceb mining approach. In: CEUR Workshop Proceedings (2015)
18. Van den Beemt, A., Buijs, J., Van der Aalst, W.: Analysing structured learning behaviour in massive open online courses (MOOCs): an approach based on process mining and clustering. Int. Rev. Res. Open Distrib. Learn. **19**(5) (2018)
19. de Barba, P.G., Malekian, D., Oliveira, E.A., Bailey, J., Ryan, T., Kennedy, G.: The importance and meaning of session behaviour in a MOOC. Comput. Educ. **146**(2019), 103772 (2020)
20. Romero, M., Usart, M.: The time factor in MOOCS: time-on-task, interaction temporal patterns, and time perspectives in a MOOC. In: CSEDU 2014 - Proceedings of the 6th International Conference on Computer Supported Education (2014)
21. Sapunar-Opazo, D., Pérez-Álvarez, R., Maldonado-Mahauad, J., Alario-Hoyos, C., Pérez-Sanagustín, M.: Analyzing learners' activity beyond the MOOC. In: CEUR Workshop Proceedings (2018)
22. Kovanović, V., Gašević, D., Dawson, S., Joksimović, S., Baker, R.S., Hatala, M.: Penetrating the black box of time-on-task estimation. In: ACM International Conference Proceeding Series (2015)
23. Tough, A.: The Adult's learning projects: a fresh approach to theory (1971)
24. van Eck, M.L., Lu, X., Leemans, S.J.J., van der Aalst, W.M.P.: PM^2: a process mining project methodology. In: Zdravkovic, J., Kirikova, M., Johannesson, P. (eds.) CAiSE 2015. LNCS, vol. 9097, pp. 297–313. Springer, Cham (2015). https://doi.org/10.1007/978-3-319-19069-3_19
25. Maldonado, J.J., Pérez-Sanagustín, M., Bermeo, J.L., Muñoz, L., Pacheco, G., Espinoza, I.: Flipping the classroom with MOOCs. A pilot study exploring differences between self-regulated learners. In: 12th Latin American Conference on Learning Objects and Technologies, LACLO 2017 (2017)
26. Günther, C.-A., Rozinat, A.: Disco: discover your processes. In: Demonstration Track 10th International Conference Business Process Management (BPM 2012), vol. 940, pp. 40–44 (2012)
27. Maldonado, J.J., Palta, R., Vázquez, J., Bermeo, J.L., Pérez-sanagustín, M., Munoz-gama, J.: Exploring differences in how learners navigate in MOOCs based on self-regulated learning and learning styles (2016)
28. Mukala, P., Buijs, J., Leemans, M., van der Aalst, W.: Exploring students' learning behaviour in MOOCs using process mining techniques. In: Computing Conference (2016)
29. Guo, P.J., Reinecke, K.: Demographic differences in how students navigate through MOOCs. In: L@S 2014 - Proceedings of the 1st ACM Conference on Learning at Scale (2014)
30. Sonnenberg, C., Bannert, M.: Discovering the effects of metacognitive prompts on the sequential structure of SRL-processes using process mining techniques. J. Learn. Anal. **2**(1), 72–100 (2015)
31. Alharbi, A., Paul, D., Henskens, F., Hannaford, M.: An investigation into the learning styles and self-regulated learning strategies for computer science students. In: ASCILITE 2011 - The Australasian Society for Computers in Learning in Tertiary Education (2011)
32. Mukala, M.P., Buijs, J.C.A.M., Leemans, M., van der Aalst, W.M.P.: Learning analytics on coursera event data. In: Simpda (2015)

The Role of Learning City "Smart Teams" in Promoting, Supporting, and Extending the Community School Model

Sarah A. Chauncey[1](✉) and Gregory I. Simpson[2](✉)

[1] Rockland BOCES, West Nyack, NY 10994, USA
sachauncey@gmail.com
[2] Hudson River Presbytery, Scarborough, NY 10510, USA
gregory.simpson1@gmail.com

Abstract. Systemic and structural inequities and disparities in social, health, economic, and educational opportunities result in pervasive, complex challenges which impede social, emotional, behavioral, and cognitive development. This exploratory paper considers practices which perpetuate inequity and offers a framework for thinking about and addressing these inequities by convening learning city "Smart Teams" comprised of representative community members working collaboratively in visioning, problem solving, decision-making, action taking, and policy development to promote, support, and extend the community school model into the fabric of the community. This paper draws on a theoretical framework consisting of self-determination theory and conceptual frameworks for communities of networked expertise and activity theory with the goals of (1) reimagining and helping students to actualize new identities as learners and contributors to society; (2) designing motivating learning environments which offer new options for collaboration with peers, educators, and community mentors; (3) implementing new approaches for students to systematically, yet imaginatively, and creatively interpret, tackle and propose, incubate, and/or prototype solutions to real-world problems; and (4) constructing environments and activity models which mitigate impediments to learning and teaching.

Keywords: Activity theory · Communities of networked expertise · Community schools · Environment · Equity · Inequity · Intersectionality · Learning cities · Self-determination theory · Smart teams

1 Introduction

I used to think that public schools were vehicles for reforming society. And now I think that while good teachers and schools can promote positive intellectual, behavioral, and social change in individual children and youth, schools are (and have been) ineffectual in altering social inequalities. Cubin, in Elmore [14]

Systemic and structural inequities and disparities in environmental, social, health, economic, and educational opportunities result in pervasive, complex challenges which

© Springer Nature Switzerland AG 2020
C. Stephanidis et al. (Eds.): HCII 2020, LNCS 12425, pp. 326–344, 2020.
https://doi.org/10.1007/978-3-030-60128-7_25

impede social, emotional, behavioral, and cognitive development. This complexity is reflected in the concept of intersectionality. Crenshaw [13] coined the term "intersectionality," defined as "… the social, economic, and political ways in which identity-based systems of oppression and privilege overlap and influence one another. Tienken, et al. [60] consider three demographic variables which impact educational achievement "(a) percentage of families in a community with income over $200,000 a year, (b) percentage of people in a community in poverty, and (c) percentage of people in a community with bachelor's degrees predicted results accurately in 14/18 of the models of 6-8 grade students scoring proficient on mandated standardized tests…"

Markovits [38] argues that higher education, especially in elite universities, exacerbates the class divide. Access is denied to those who are not already rich, whose families are not part of the privileged class—the "aristocracy." He shares that the "academic gap between rich and poor students now exceeds the gap between white and black students in 1954, the year in which the Supreme Court decided Brown v. Board of Education." The academic gap is not the only driver of inequity. Hammond [23], shares the definition of *sociopolitical context* as "a term used to describe the series of mutually reinforcing policies and practices across social, economic, and political domains that contribute to disparities and unequal opportunities for people of color in housing, transportation, education, and health care, to name a few."

This exploratory paper considers practices which perpetuate systemic inequity and offers a framework for thinking about and addressing these inequities by convening learning city "Smart Teams" as conceived by McKenna and Chauncey [9]. Smart Teams, comprised of representative community members, work collaboratively in visioning, problem solving, decision-making, action taking, and policy development to promote, support, and extend the community school model into the fabric of the community. The community schools model seeks to ameliorate out-of-school conditions that negatively impact in-school success by bringing varied community services into the school. While these resources and supports are essential for student and family well-being, the model reflects a "doing for" approach that addresses symptoms, not the structural and systemic problems that make such services necessary. The National Education Association (NEA) [42] identifies six pillars of the community school. The sixth pillar focuses on community support services, recognizing "that students often come to school with challenges that impact their ability to learn, explore, and develop in the classroom…community schools provide meals, health care, mental-health counseling, and other services before, during, and after school." Shafer's [58] "By All Means" initiative out of Harvard "emphasizes that cities need to partner with schools for children to succeed—because no matter how well or how much children learn inside of school, they still have widely disparate experience outside of it, which contribute to or inhibit their learning."

Support service providers should understand the multi-layered nature of social interconnectivities for student success. Stanton-Salazar [59] in discussing social capital frameworks for student empowerment describes "institutional agents" as key organizational and institutional partners in low status student success. Building learning city Smart Teams will require identifying and including individuals who understand the complex interactions within different racial, ethnic, and socio-economic family groups. These individuals, incorporating external societal networks, have the potential to open pathways for diverse members of the community, those under-represented in the problem-solving process, to tackle issues of inequity and disparity. We hypothesize that these collaborative efforts by adults will, in the long-run, stimulate and motivate student engagement in learning, foster student curiosity, and promote socialization, collaboration, and communication among diverse student populations setting the groundwork for future equitable collaborative policy making experiences.

This paper draws on a theoretical framework consisting of self-determination theory and conceptual frameworks for communities of networked expertise and activity theory to explore how Smart Teams can support children, families, and the broader community in formal and informal learning settings. The expectation is that participants will identify explicit goals and outcomes that improve and enrich the lives of community members. Specifically, Smart Teams are charged with: (1) analyzing existing policies, systems, structures, and practices that enhance or impede learning; (2) promoting equitable access to critical services that ensure children and families are prepared and motivated to engage in learning; (3) supporting, promoting, and extending community school support services into community spaces with the understanding that, "Connections to the community are critically important so support services and referrals are available for families and other community members" [42].

Efforts related to the (NEA) community school sixth pillar are consistent with Maslow's [37] identification of a hierarchy of needs wherein physiological needs (food, water, warmth, and rest) and safety needs (security and safety) are basic needs that must be satisfied before an individual can attend to higher level needs. "A person who is lacking food, safety, love, and esteem would most probably hunger for food more strongly than for anything else." Self-Determination Theory examines complementary factors, "…how biological, social, and cultural conditions either enhance or undermine the inherent human capacities for psychological growth, engagement, and wellness" [55].

2 Hypotheses

The following hypotheses motivate our efforts and provide the focus points to determine the impact of this study:

1. Participatory problem solving and policy development result in more equitable access to services and supports related to basic human needs.
2. Empowering those who are negatively impacted by systemic inequities to participate in problem solving, decision making, action taking, and policy development fosters feelings of autonomy, competence, relatedness and self-efficacy.

3 Smart Teams

We are separating the entire population into groups of us (those who agree with us) and them (those who don't). If you only speak to people who agree with you, you shut out the possibility of new perspectives, discoveries, and information. Headlee [24].

For young people and adults, school and community based experiences either support or diminish individual and group competence and motivation to engage in learning and problem solving. Smart Teams foster an understanding of how policies and associated systems, structures, and practices bolster or undermine individual and group competence, autonomy, and relatedness; For this study, we will invite experts to facilitate novices' acquisition of issue-focused knowledge and the development of collaborative and communicative competencies necessary to contribute to and learn from others who are engaged in inquiry, problem solving, and identification of viable solutions to complex issues. The ultimate objective is to impact equitable policy development.

Figure 1 provides a high-level illustration of the learning city Smart Team model. The communities of networked expertise and activity theory conceptual frameworks will be used to actualize the tasks and interactions identified in this model to achieve agreed upon outcomes. The constructs of self-determination theory and social cognitive theory will be used to evaluate impact on participant interest, commitment, collaboration, and action.

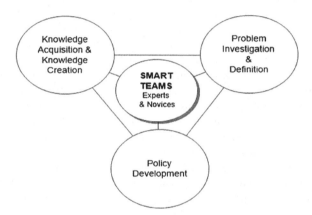

Fig. 1. Learning city smart team model

Rockland County, NY is ideally suited as the site for this study. As of 2017 the ethnic composition of Rockland County, NY was composed of 206 k White (62.6%); 59.1 k Hispanic or Latino (18%); 37.3 k Black or African American Alone residents (11.3%); 20 k Asian Alone residents (6.07%); 5.22 k Two or More Races residents (1.59%); 974 Some Other Race Alone residents (0.296%); 485 American Indian and Alaska Native Alone residents (0.147%), and 0 Native Hawaiian and Other Pacific Islander residents (0%) residents [52]. The County is comprised of eight school districts whose students come from socioeconomically challenged as well as middle and upper middle class neighborhoods.

Smart Teams will be comprised of a diverse group of participants who are motivated to develop the knowledge and skills required to address complex community issues. Smart Teams will partner with educators to align efforts of the wider community with business, faith, civic, and community members and leaders leveraging diversity, developing individual and collective capacity, cross-sector collaboration, and trust [39].

3.1 Smart Team Focus

This exploratory study will consider environmental equity with a focus on "water" and related issues. In building Smart Teams to improve the community school model, issues of environmental equity are best understood through the lens of environmental justice. Here, fundamental concepts of environmental justice draw out the underlying systemic processes which undermine community health. Bullard et al. [8] in their seminal report titled *Toxic Waters and Race at Twenty: 1987–2007*, bears this fact out, pointing directly to race based pollution across the United States, and the political, economic, and social factors that facilitate environmental inequities.

Research findings that show correlation between drinking water quality and cognitive development are most recently observable in the case of Flint, Michigan. Ruckart et al. [54] for example noted that "childhood lead exposure can result in damage to the brain and nervous system; slowed growth and development; learning and behavior problems; and hearing and speech problems. They concluded that the "Flint water crisis highlights the need for improved risk communication strategies, and environmental health infrastructure, enhanced surveillance, and primary prevention to identify and respond to environmental threats to the public's health." Green [20] reporting on the impact of the water crisis in Flint, Michigan since 2014, noted that after nearly 30,000 students were exposed to the neurotoxin in water, a class action "lawsuit forced the state to establish the $3 million Neurodevelopmental Center of Excellence". The center began screening students confirming a range of disabilities which in turn triggered more federal support to the community. Laidlaw [34] in examining seasonal variation of lead found in young children and adults in Flint, demonstrated a need for more vigilant examination and testing of lead levels in water, air and soil for at-risk communities.

While, the present examination is in no way exhaustive of the scholarly literature available, the links between environmental factors, i.e. pollutants such as lead, and cognitive function are well recognized. With this in mind, assembling Smart Teams that include individuals with expertise, experiential and or academic, in the social, scientific and or economic impacts environmental/ecological factors have on student achievement is essential. The key challenge then is to incorporate the environmental knowledge skills on Smart Teams in ways that lead to actionable and reproducible results. What then are the areas or points of intervention that need to be identified?

To build a cogent Smart Team strategy that integrates environmental factors in the education continuum as a disruptor of inequity, requires identifying very specific points of intervention. In the work we are proposing, we have adopted the classification of interventions identified by the National Collaborating Centre for Determinants of Health [43] who identified three primary points of intervention *namely downstream interventions* which seek to mitigate inequitable impacts of upstream and midstream determinants; *midstream interventions* which seek to reduce risky behaviors or exposures to hazards by influencing health behaviors; and *upstream interventions* which seek to reform fundamental social and economic structures including redistribution of wealth, power, opportunities, and decision-making capacities. By focusing Smart Teams primarily on midstream and downstream points of intervention, efforts to ameliorate the loftier challenge of correcting systemic inequities become possible. As convening, training, and efficacy of Smart Teams are realized, the potential to successfully engage in upstream interventions, increases. However, it is critical to understand the principles that undergird Smart Team formation and how resolving inequity is achievable. The strategy here is based on communities of networked expertise.

4 Theoretical and Conceptual Frameworks

Self-Determination theory is a theoretical framework that seeks to understand motivated behavior through the lens of three interrelated constructs, autonomy, competence, and relatedness. Communities of networked expertise draw on competencies of varied individuals who come together to collaboratively learn together and solve problems. Activity theory is a conceptual framework that describes how individuals and groups interact with tools to carry out activities in the pursuit of specified goals (objects) to achieve a desired outcome.

4.1 Self-Determination Theory

Social inclusion ... is a multi-dimensional process aimed at creating conditions that enable the full and active participation of every member of the society Uytewaal van de Lande [62] *...individual wellness and the characteristics of larger social systems, groups, and organizations are intertwined.* Ryan and Deci [55].

Self Determination Theory research studies "...factors, both intrinsic to individual development and within social contexts, that facilitate vitality, motivation, social integration and wellbeing, and alternatively those that contribute to depletion, fragmentation, antisocial behaviors, and unhappiness" [55].

As illustrated in Fig. 2, self-determination theory identifies three reciprocally reinforcing constructs autonomy, competence, and relatedness which together "promote the development of more effective self-functioning, resilience, greater creativity, superior learning, better performance, enhanced well-being, and higher quality relationships" [55]. While this study is focused on self-determination theory, social cognitive theory constructs of self-efficacy and self-regulation [3, 4] are enhanced by, and have a positive impact on, self-determination theory constructs.

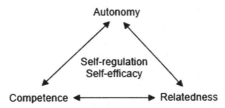

Fig. 2. Self-determination theory and social cognitive theory constructs

Autonomy. Autonomy refers to self-motivated behavior wherein people "...bring into the action the whole of their resources, interests, and capacity" [55]. The sense that one's actions will result in the desired outcome reinforces a sense of self-efficacy. The belief in one's capacity to achieve a desired outcome, in turn, impacts one's self-regulation or self-monitoring behaviors to achieve the desired outcome. These constructs are associated with group as well as individual beliefs and behaviors. A sense of autonomy is highlighted in Kiefer [31] who identified three phases of citizen empowerment, "…. (1) development of a more potent sense of self-in-relation to the world, (2) construction of more critical comprehension of the social political forms which comprise one's daily life world and (3) cultivation of functional strategies and resources for attainment of personal or collective socio-political roles."

A sense of autonomy is based on a belief that one's effort and actions will influence a desired outcome. A 2019 joint paper on water resources management argued that "…meaningful participation goes beyond tokenistic forms of participation or superficial consultation. Uytewaal and van de Lande [62] share elements of participation that must be guaranteed include: (1) involving people in setting out the terms of engagement (e.g. agenda, meeting times, venue); (2) creating space and opportunity for participation; (3) enabling people to access participatory processes and eliminate barriers; (4) guaranteeing free and safe participation; (5) ensuring access to information; (6) *providing reasonable opportunities to influence decision-making* [emphasis added]."

Competence. Competence is a basic need of individuals to feel "effectance and mastery … to operate effectively within their important life contexts" [55]. A sense of competence, similar to perceived self-efficacy, is domain specific, bolstered by success and diminished by failure, negative feedback, and social comparisons [3, 55]. In educational settings, making content, concepts, and skills accessible to diverse learners is essential to positively impacting feelings of competence and self-efficacy.

Barriers that hinder learning and achievement, several of which are outlined in the introduction to this study, have a negative impact on individual and group opportunities to attain a sense of effectance and mastery. The exploratory study seeks to create learning spaces, provide experiences, engage families, partner with schools, and draw on the broader community to remove barriers and expand equitable opportunities for students to learn and contribute.

Relatedness. Relatedness is defined as a feeling of belongingness or connectedness and being a valued contributing member of a social group. "Individuals who are autonomous will also, to a significant degree, be dependent in important relationships and interdependent with relevant groups" [55].

Ezeilo [16], CEO and founder of the Greening Youth Foundation, shares what it is like to be left out of important relationships and relevant groups, "If I'm at a conference and the voices participating in the discussion are missing an enormous swath of the American public, then that discussion is necessarily going to be too stunted and limited to be as effective as it could be there are going to be enormous blind spots."

Research suggests a strong connection between feelings of relatedness or belongingness in school settings and student engagement and motivation [1, 6, 63]. A recent study of college student civic engagement using self-determination theory as a lens, also revealed that, "Helping and pro-environmental behavior were linked to daily well-being directly and indirectly through basic needs satisfaction" [66]. The study seeks to address intentional and unintentional factors which diminish belongingness and to offer opportunities for connectedness through collaborative participation in problem solving and decision-making.

4.2 Communities of Networked Expertise

Networked expertise refers to higher-level cognitive competencies that arise, in appropriate environments, from sustained collaborative efforts to solve problems and build knowledge together. Hakkarainen, Palonen, Paavola, and Lehtinen [22].

Considering the vast array of cross-disciplinary knowledge needed to solve problems in the 21st century at the level of community, county, state, county or beyond - how "communities and networks of professionals" approach problem solving in the education space has changed dramatically. For example, within the medical profession, diagnosis, treatment, and successful resolution of an individual threatened by a disease, such as cancer, requires the sum of individual cognitive competences in medical science. However as the problem moves from the individual to a community, where negative systemic societal factors influence a community's racial or ethnic identity, problem solving strategies require a paradigm shift. In such cases the approach demands an awareness of the increasing levels of interdisciplinary complexity that span the whole environment. Problem-solving strategies that seamlessly draw on relationality and recognize the cross-disciplinary interconnectedness embedded in the community therefore become a fundamental prerequisite.

In the community school model for minority youth, Hakkarainen et al. [22], point out that, "Networked expertise is relational in nature; it emerges from the tailoring and fine-tuning of individual competencies to specific conditions of the environment of the activity, and it is represented as a joint or shared competence of communities and organized groups of experts and professionals." The nimbleness of networked expertise in terms of the skills and experiences that can be brought to bear on the education of minority youth opens opportunity for a richer educational experience for the adolescent. Building communities of networked expertise then envisions new approaches to community development from two perspectives. First in creating new knowledge acquisition models that identify the local challenges to healthy communities. Second, developing and then bringing new processes into community-based problem solving spaces. The Smart Teams envisioned in this study's exploration provide this forward thinking approach to community-based problem solving.

Simultaneously, education and experience in community-based problem solving provide avenues for what Coleman [10] described as the development of social capital. By Coleman's definition, social capital incorporates "concepts of financial capital, physical capital, and human capital—but embodied in the relations among persons." Building social capital is absolutely essential for adolescents to navigate the complexities of data-driven communities outside of the familial structures. Pearrow, Sander, and Jones [46] in comparing the performance of youth within diverse inner city communities in the Northeast struggling with high crime and poverty, with white youth in a homogenous Midwest community went further to highlight the importance of ethnic social capital in relation to community resilience. Their research provides greater impetus to employ other approaches that enable community-based problem solving. Communities of networked expertise that strengthen both educational and social competencies in adolescent youth present another approach.

Pirinen and Fränti [47] also describe networked expertise as vital in community networks of expertise as "… constituted in interaction between individuals, communities, and larger networks supported by cognitive artifacts." They go on to point out that community networks of expertise "coevolves with continuously transforming innovative knowledge communities…development of expertise, distributed cognition and shared expertise, collaborative and cultural learning, and inquiry-based learning processes." These strengths can address social inequities marginalized youth continuously face.

Critical to building networked expertise clusters, is "the recognition that for adolescents to successfully meet both developmental challenges in today's world and the academic demands of the school, they require resource-full relationships and activities socially organized within a network of socialization agents." These socialization agents in community education models play a vital role in bridging gaps between cultural discourses and practices across social worlds for minority youth. They provide avenues through which adolescents can access "social and institutional support that contributes to social development, academic performance and preparation for adulthood" [59].

The role played by socialization agents is not one of a teacher who neither has the reach nor the capacity to fill this role for large numbers of students. Smart Teams, of necessity must therefore include socialization agents. Without socialization agents in the life of the student, and who are outside the adolescent's immediate familial and social network, correcting for educational inequalities will remain a difficult ask. Likewise, the formation of value systems, perceptions, roles, identities and most important student understanding of pathways to educational and economic success, inevitably will remain elusive.

4.3 Activity Theory

Students cannot assume any ownership of the problem unless they know that they can affect the problem situation in some meaningful way. Jonassen [28].

The Activity Theory Eight Step Model adapted by Engeström [15] is the third generation of the model first conceived by Russian psychologist Lev Vygotsky [64] and his student Alexi Leont'ev [36] in the 1920s. Engeström's model highlights the importance of community, dialogue, multiple perspectives, and networks of interacting activity systems. It is an iterative model which describes how individuals and groups address a problem by carrying out activities supported by tools or mediating artifacts in the pursuit of specified goals (objects) to achieve a desired outcome. Figures 3 and 4 represent the third generation activity theory model conceived by Engeström with "motives" added by Sannino and Gutiérrez [56].

Components of the activity theory model (1) Mediating Artifacts (MA) - physical objects, technologies, concepts, models, language, plans, strategies, resources, system of symbols (language of math), information and communication technologies – anything used in the production or transformation process to achieve the outcome of the activity. Tools influence and are influenced by the behaviors of individuals and collective efforts to produce objects and achieve outcome directed goals; (2) Subject (S) - person or people

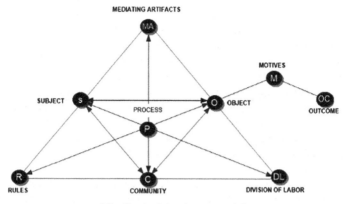

Fig. 3. Activity theory model

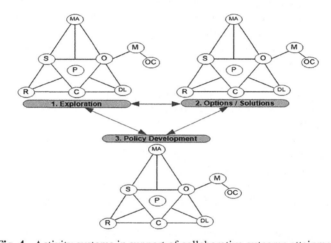

Fig. 4. Activity systems in support of collaborative outcome attainment

who are the focus of an activity; (3) Rules (R) - laws, codes, conventions, customs, and agreements that people adhere to while engaging in the activity; (4) Community (C) - people and groups whose knowledge, interests, stakes, and goals shape the activity; (5) Division of Labor (DL) - how the work in the activity is divided among participants in the activity; (6) Object (O) - purpose or problem space that motivates the goal; (7) Motives (M) - purpose, reasons for the activity; (8) Outcome (OC) - desired goal of the activity [15, 56].

The unit of analysis in an activity system is an activity which includes the components defined above along with the relationships and interactions between components. One activity component of particular interest when considering Smart Teams is the subject and community nodes, specifically, individual participant action, participant-participant, participant-community partner interactions.

Activity Theory is ideally suited for designing, examining, and negotiating goal directed actions in complex, interconnected systems. The model allows the researcher to consider each component of the activity system individually and in combination. The model also supports strategic modification of component(s) to facilitate achievement of activity objects and goals. Additionally, activity theory offers a flexible model for considering motivating opportunities related to self-determination theory.

Activity theory is an appropriate framework for exploratory and applied research as there is an expectation that analysis of the activity will address real-world practices wherein the researcher is a participant in the process as well as an instigator in modifying components and/or component interactions to improve both process and outcomes [27, 33].

For this study, the framework supports the design and analysis of Smart Team exploration. The framework aids in describing (modeling) and analyzing the interactions among participants (actors, subject, and community) involved in varied interactions in a particular environment (problem space) supported by tools and (lesson design and flow, interaction experiences, technologies, strategies, just-in-time-learning resources) where Smart Team efforts are guided by agreed upon protocols or norms (rules and roles) in an effort to achieve a specific outcome (problem solving approaches and policy considerations related to environmental issues).

This approach is relevant to Smart Team development wherein, according to Jonassen and Rohrer-Murphy [27] "conscious learning emerges from activity performance." This is important to support team members who may have had few or no collaborative problem solving opportunities.

Inclusion is about supporting marginalised people to engage in wider processes of decision making to ensure that their rights and needs are recognised and taken into account. Uytewaal and van de Lande [62].

This exploration considers what Murphy and Rodriguez-Manzanares [40] point to as "trouble and transformation in the system" as "members of an activity system carry their own diverse histories"… and … "the system itself carries multiple layers and strands of history engraved in its artefacts, rules and conventions." The transformation we seek is consistent with that shared in Moore, De Jong, Reville, Sacks, and Burgess [39] who looked at advancing and leveraging diversity, collective capacity, cross-sector collaboration, and trust to advance educational opportunity. Figure 4, represents the multiple activity models in the context of this study which offers 3-phase approach structuring and studying Smart Team engagement in collaborative decision-making.

Employing the Activity Theory framework, the collaborative groups comprised of a diverse group of students, educators, community members, and public officials will be convened to address environmental equity with a focus on "water" and related issues. A cohort of middle school and high school age students will be invited to enroll in a 6-week summer program. Each phase of the activity—(1) Exploration; (2) Options and Solutions; (3) Policy Development—will be conducted in two-week sessions. Sessions will include problem-based learning opportunities led by educators, environmental scientists, local officials and relevant organizations, and community members.

Rockland is home to environmental efforts aligned to our proposal goals: (1) Annually, Rockland County Soil and Water Conservation District (RC SWCD) [53] coordinates several community science initiatives, road-stream crossing assessments, professional stream biomonitoring, a Green Infrastructure Site Demonstration Network, free environmental education programs for K-College students at County Parks and other natural resources initiatives; (2) Rockland County Community Science Opportunities [51]; (3) Hudson River National Estuarine Research Reserve [25]. Should funding be available, an opportunity would be offered to high school students to experience environmental programs offered on the Great Lakes in New York State.

5 Methodology

5.1 Population

Student participants will be recruited from communities in Rockland County with the goal of including young people who have had no, or few, opportunities to engage in problem and project based learning that is linked to community challenges and issues that impact their well-being. We have data on the demographics of the county. We will reach out to our local schools, Rockland BOCES, and county agencies who service youth to develop a plan to identify and recruit student participants. We will enroll a total of thirty students, fifteen middle school and fifteen high school age students. One requirement for participation is a commitment by students, acknowledged by their families to participate in the three phases of the project over a six-week period in the summer of 2021. There will be no cost for participation—tools, resources, transportation, and meals will be subsidized by grants and donations.

5.2 Data Collection and Analysis

This exploration will use a quasi-experimental mixed methods approach for data collection and analysis related to the research hypotheses shared above. Efficacy and impact of Smart Teams will be studied through the lens of the theoretical and conceptual frameworks guiding this study with a focus on the constructs of autonomy, competence, relatedness, self-efficacy, self-regulation, and motivated individual and collaborative engagement to identify, seek, and offer solutions to address environmental issues around water conservation, pollution, and health. Data collection instruments will be identified, modified or developed, and evaluated for reliability and validity. Data will be collected for students, teachers, facilitators, and participating community members. For each of the three project phases as defined under the activity theory model, we will conduct pre and post data collection using semi-structured interviews, Likert scale surveys, observations, and artifact review.

6 Contribution

This paper contributes to the extant literature on equity in general and the achievement gap in particular as they relate to smart city/learning city efforts. The focus herein suggests a participatory approach to problem-solving by a diverse community whose members bring multiple perspectives to bear on issues that impact policy-development. In short, Smart Teams ensure a "seat at the table" with a "doing with" rather than "doing for" mindset.

7 Opportunities and Challenges

We have no patterns for relating across our human differences as equals. Audre Lorde in Kendi [30].

Zaretta Hammond [23] shares her experience as a young girl raised by a teen mother who recognized the disparity between the school in the projects where they lived and the school in the more affluent community where her grandparents lived. Hammond's mother uses her grandparent's address to enroll Hammond in the school in the predominantly White and Asian community. Her mother, part of the first welfare to work programs, secures a position as a library technician. Hammond's after-school program was to join her mother at the library and read a pile of books selected by her mom, who told her, "When you hit the table, it's time for us to go home." Hammond recounts that even as a youngster, she recognized the gap between the quality of education in the two communities.

Consider the life-changing series of events recounted in Hammond's recollection: a teen mother values learning and breaks the rules to ensure her daughter has access to a school in an affluent neighborhood; a government program puts a teen mom to work – the job is in a library where her child is welcomed to spend her after-school hours; five days a week, a child has access to shelves of books in an inviting space, and she can borrow them for weekend reading. Hammond's experience was consistent with Stanton-Salazar [60] who suggests that "…white, middle-class youth encounter a confluence in cultural discourses and practices across social worlds, working-class minority youth often find these worlds are culturally differentiated, each world embodying a distinct cultural discourse, or *ways of being in the world.*"

We know that cultural ignorance can lead to erroneous labeling and undervaluing of children's and adults' potential. For example, Greene [21] points to research in literacy education wherein, "The traditional model of education promotes a narrow conception of literacy and often unfairly associates deficit-oriented labels such as 'at risk,' 'unmotivated,' 'underperforming,' 'educationally disadvantaged,' 'struggling,' 'educationally handicapped' to describe Black girls whose literacy and language practices may be different than the dominant discourse." She suggests that, "those who have not had the opportunity to imagine children from poor families as intellectual beings possessing unique experiences and bringing important knowledge and resources into the classroom must stop pathologizing what it means to be poor and what it means to be a child from a poor family. Respectfully listening to children, who are typically shushed in the classroom or pathologized in the school system, is one step towards a more powerful education for marginalized students by simply being able to perceive them differently…"

Schools' roles include: (1) reimagining and helping students to actualize new identities as learners and contributors to society; (2) designing motivating learning environments which offer new options for collaboration with peers, educators, and community mentors; (3) implementing new approaches for students to systematically, yet imaginatively, and creatively interpret, tackle and propose, incubate, and/or prototype solutions to real-world problems [32]; and (4) constructing environments and activity models which mitigate impediments to learning and teaching [7, 14, 26, 65].

For young people, teaching and learning approaches that prepare students to take informed action include inquiry based learning, service learning, performance based learning, project based learning, and problem based learning. The learning experiences fostered by these approaches offer opportunities for students to engage in participatory, cross-disciplinary practices wherein they put knowledge and skills to work to address real-world issues. Such experiences invoke collaborative and communicative competencies to achieve outcomes associated with common goals. Through mentorships and more formal apprenticeships and internships, students become familiar with the hard and soft skills, tools and resources, and processes that guide the work of practitioners.

There are cost challenges associated with program development and execution. For the proposed study, classroom space is available at no cost as are access to local environmental habitats. Environmental scientists from a local not-for-profit are available for consultation and to offer presentations at no cost. There will be costs associated with development of curriculum, procurement of relevant technology and resources, engaging local educators, transportation, and insurance. We will seek funding to defray any cost to program participants.

7.1 Roadblocks to Participation

The work of Arnstein [2] offers a typology, "ladders of participation," which defines different levels of participation and impact related to community based problem solving and decision-making. Rungs one and two represent "manipulation and therapy, levels of 'non-participation' that have been contrived by some to substitute for genuine participation" and at level eight, the highest rung, we find "genuine participation wherein citizens obtain the majority of decision-making seats, or full managerial power." Arnstein acknowledges that the "typology does not include an analysis of the most significant roadblocks to achieving genuine levels of participation…racism, paternalism, and resistance to power redistribution. On the have-nots' side, they include inadequacies of the poor community's political socioeconomic infrastructure and knowledge base, plus difficulties of organizing a representative and accountable citizens' group in the face of futility, alienation, and distrust." Connor [11] describes a "new ladders of participation" in response to Arnstein, noting that "The purpose of this ladder is to provide a systematic approach to preventing and resolving public controversy about specific policies, programs and projects…" Relevant to this study, is Connor's focus on education. "The foundation of any program to prevent and resolve public controversy must be an informed public. Proponents, actual or potential, governmental or corporate, cannot afford to have substantial proportions of their key constituencies ignorant of their objectives, activities, effects and plans."

7.2 On-Going Efforts

This exploration is complementary to varied initiatives seeking to harness collective intelligence to tackle problems and to reimagine how community-based efforts can lead to more welcoming, safer spaces and places in which individuals can thrive socially, emotionally, physically, and economically, including smart cities, placemaking, and purpose built communities [5, 12, 17, 35, 44, 45, 48, 62].

8 Conclusion

Slowly the voices of the excluded have been welcomed into the conversation. And their perspectives have enriched our understanding. But the reason they have enriched our understanding is that they have given the rest of us an important piece of the truth that was previously invisible to us. Not their truth, but the truth. Schwartz [57].

We acknowledge that politically and historically attempts to achieve equity have instigated counter-movements, e.g., reconstruction followed by Jim Crow based on economic concerns around redistribution of wealth [17]. We recognize the challenges and opportunities that arise when our society is asked to embrace efforts that cause discomfort and threaten the status quo. As noted, programs and policies that threaten to redistribute power and wealth and to threaten privilege and status, are particularly impactful in countering efforts to achieve equity and reduce disparities in access to services that support basic human needs. We are aware of the political implications of attempting to disrupt the status quo. These are well documented historically and evident in today's politically charged environment. However, we believe opportunities outweigh the challenges. We believe that our young people's participation as future decision-makers and visionaries is dependent on their desire to learn and collaborate across cultural and racial divides. We know that this desire and motivation cannot be invoked if physiological and psychological needs are ignored. Inequities related to these needs are embedded in our policies, and therefore must also be addressed if meaningful systemic change is to be effected.

References

1. Alicino, N.F.: Belongingness, internalized racism and its impact on academic achievement among Black American undergraduate students, Doctoral dissertation, Fordham University (2017)
2. Arnstein, S.R.: A ladder of citizen participation. J. Am. Inst. Plan. **35**(4), 216–224 (1969)
3. Bandura, A.: Self-efficacy: toward a unifying theory of behavioral change. Psychol. Rev. **84**, 191–215 (1977)
4. Bandura, A.: Social cognitive theory of self-regulation. Organ. Behav. Hum. Decis. Process. **50**(2), 248–287 (1991). https://doi.org/10.1016/0749-5978(91)90022-L
5. Belsky, E.S., Fauth, J.: Crossing over to an improved era of community development. Joint Center for Housing Studies, Harvard University (2012)
6. Booker, K.C.: School belonging and the African American adolescent: what do we know and where should we go? High School J. **89**(4), 1–7 (2006)
7. Boykin, A.W., Noguera, P.: Creating the opportunity to learn: moving from research to practice to close the achievement gap. Ascd (2011)

8. Bullard, R.D., Mohai, P., Saha, R., Wright, B.: Toxic wastes and race at twenty: 1987–2007 (2007). Accessed 8 Jan 2020. https://www.csu.edu/cerc/researchreports/documents/ToxicW asteandRaceatTwenty1987-2007.pdf

9. McKenna, H.P., Chauncey, S.A.: Frictionless learning environments for 21st century education and learning cities: a response to digital inequalities. In: Proceedings of the 7th International Conference of Education, Research and Innovation (iCERi2014), pp. 2505–2515 (2014)

10. Coleman, J.S.: Social capital in the creation of human capital. Am. J. Sociol. **94**, S95–S120 (1988)

11. Connor, D.M.: A new ladder of citizen participation. Natl. Civ. Rev. **77**(3), 249–257 (1988)

12. Conti, G., Heckman, J.J.: Early childhood development: Creating healthy communities with greater efficiency and effectiveness. In: Andrews, N.O., Erickson, D.J. (eds.) Investing in What Works for America's Communities: Essays on People, Place and Purpose, pp. 327–337 (2012)

13. Crenshaw, K.: Demarginalizing the intersection of race and sex: a black feminist critique of antidiscrimination doctrine, feminist theory and antiracist politics. U. Chi. Legal f., p. 139 (1989). http://chicagounbound.uchicago.edu/cgi/viewcontent.cgi?article=1052andco ntext=uclf

14. Elmore, R., Fuhrman, S.: Opportunity to learn and the state role in education. Teach. Coll. Rec. **96**(3), 433–458 (1995)

15. Engeström, Y.: Learning by Expanding: An Activity-Theoretical Approach to Developmental Research. Orienta-Konsultit OY, Helsinki (1987)

16. Ezeilo, A., Chiles, N.: Engage, Connect, Protect: Empowering Diverse Youth as Environmental Leaders. New Society Publishers, Gabriola (2020)

17. Franklin, S., Edwards, D.: It takes a neighborhood: purpose built communities and neighborhood transformation. Investing in What Works for America's Communities, pp. 170–183 (2012). http://www.whatworksforamerica.org/ideas/it-takes-a-neighborhood-purpose-built-communities-and-neighborhood-transformation/

18. Gates Jr., H.L.: Stony the Road: Reconstruction, White Supremacy, and the Rise of Jim Crow. Penguin Press, London (2019)

19. Gee, J.P.: Literacy, discourse, and linguistics: introduction. J. Educ. **171**, 5–17 (1989)

20. Green, E.L.: Flint's Children Suffer in Class After Years of Drinking the Lead-Poisoned Water. New York Times (2019). http://www.newyorktimes.com

21. Greene, D.T.: "We need more 'US' in Schools!!": centering black adolescent girls' literacy and language practices in online school spaces. J. Negro Educ. **85**(3), 274–289 (2016)

22. Hakkarainen, K.P.J., Palonen, T., Paavola, S., Lehtinen, E.: Communities of Networked Expertise: Professional and Educational Perspectives, Advances in Learning and Instruction. Emerald Group Publishing Limited, Bingley (2008)

23. Hammond, Z.: Culturally Responsive Teaching and the Brain: Promoting Authentic Engagement and Rigor Among Culturally and Linguistically Diverse Students. Corwin Press, Thousand Oaks (2015)

24. Headlee, C.: We Need to Talk: How to have Conversations that Matter. Hachette, London (2017)

25. Hudson River National Estuarine Research Reserve. https://www.dec.ny.gov/lands/4915.html

26. Jencks, C.: Inequality: A Reassessment of the Effect of Family and Schooling in America. Basic Books Inc., New York (1972)

27. Jonassen, D.H., Rohrer-Murphy, L.: Activity theory as a framework for designing constructivist learning environments. Educ. Tech. Res. Dev. **47**(1), 61–79 (1999). https://doi.org/10.1007/BF02299477

28. Jonassen, D.H.: Designing constructivist learning environments. In: Reigeluth, C.M. (ed.) Instructional Design Theories and Models: A New Paradigm of Instructional Theory, vol. II, pp. 215–239. Lawrence Erlbaum Associates, Mahwah (1999)

29. Juliani, A.J.: Coaching for equity interview with author Zaretta Hammond (2019). https://m.youtube.com/watch?t=andv=2KPXKHZiGEM

30. Kendi, I.X.: Stamped from the Beginning: The Definitive History of Racist Ideas in America. Random House, New York (2017)

31. Kieffer, C.H.: Citizen empowerment: a developmental perspective. Prev. Hum. Serv. **3**(2–3), 9–36 (1983)

32. King, J.R., O'Brien, D.G.: Adolescents' multiliteracies and their teachers' needs to know: towards a digital détente: a focus on adolescent learners. In: Alvermann, D.E. (ed.) New Literacies and Digital Technologies: A Focus on Adolescent Learners, pp. 40–50. Peter Lang, New York (2002)

33. Kuutti, K.: The concept of activity as a basic unit of analysis for CSCW research. In: Bannon, L., Robinson, M., Schmidt, K. (eds.) Proceedings of the Second European Conference on Computer-Supported Cooperative Work, ECSCW 1991, pp. 249–264. Springer, Dordrecht (1991). https://doi.org/10.1007/978-94-011-3506-1_19

34. Laidlaw, M.A.S., Filippelli, G.M., Sadler, R.C., Gonzales, C.R., Ball, A.S., Mielke, H.W.: Children's blood lead seasonality in flint, Michigan (USA), and soil-sourced lead hazard risks. Int. J. Environ. Res. Public Health **13**(4), 358 (2016). Accessed 8 Jan 2020. https://www.ncbi.nlm.nih.gov/pmc/articles/PMC4847020/

35. Lang, S.: The role of placemaking in sustainable planning: a case study of the East Side of Cleveland, Ohio (2017). https://scholarworks.umass.edu/masters_theses_2/472/

36. Leont'ev, A.N.: Activity, consciousness, and personality (1978)

37. Maslow, A.H.: A theory of human motivation. Psychol. Rev. **50**(4), 370 (1943)

38. Markovits, D.: The Meritocracy Trap: How America's Foundational Myth Feeds Inequality, Dismantles the Middle Class, and Devours the Elite. Penguin Press, London (2019)

39. Moore, G., De Jong, J., Reville, P., Sacks, L., Burgess, A.: Change at the Speed of Trust Advancing educational opportunity through cross-sector collaboration in Louisville. Bloomberg Harvard City Leadership Initiative (2018). https://static1.squarespace.com/static/5984acf0893fc0dc4b2fe0cf/t/5cb5e2f471c10b32949ed326/1555423992375/Change_at_the_Speed_of_Trust_CASE.pdf

40. Murphy, E., Rodriguez-Manzanares, M.A.: Using activity theory and its principle of contradictions to guide research in educational technology. Aust. J. Educ. Technol. **24**(4) (2008). https://ajet.org.au/index.php/AJET/article/view/1203/431

41. Mwanza, D.: Where theory meets practice: a case for an activity theory based methodology to guide computer system design. In: Hirose, M. (ed.) Proceedings of Interact 2001. IOS Press, Oxford (2001)

42. National Education Association: The Six Pillars of Community Schools Toolkit: NEA Resource Guide for Educators, Families and Communities (2017). http://www.nea.org/assets/docs/Comm%20Schools%20ToolKit-final%20digi-web-72617.pdf

43. National Collaborating Centre for Determinants of Health: Assessing the impact and effectiveness of intersectoral action on the social determinants of health and health equity: An expedited systematic review. Antigonish, NS: National Collaborating Centre for Determinants of Health, St. Francis Xavier University (2012). http://nccdh.ca/images/uploads/ISA_Report_EN1.pdf

44. Naughton, C.: Purpose Build Communities (2019). https://purposebuiltcommunities.org/who-we-are/

45. Naughton, C.: Purpose Built Communities (2019). Podcasts. https://purposebuiltcommunities.org/podcast/

46. Pearrow, M., Sander, J., Jones, J.: Comparing communities: the cultural characteristics of ethnic social capital. Educ. Urban Soc. **51**(6), 739–755 (2019)
47. Pirinen, R., Fränti, M.: Framework and culture of proactive competencies learning by Developing (LbD). In: Recent Advances in Education and Educational Technology: Proceedings of the 7th WSEAS International Conference on Education and Educational Technology (EDU 2008), Venice, Italy, 21–23 November 2008. WSEAS Press (2008)
48. Project for Public Spaces: What is placemaking? (2007). https://www.pps.org/article/what-is-placemaking
49. Project for Public Spaces: Placemaking: what if we built our cities around places? (2016). https://assets-global.website-files.com/5810e16fbe876cec6bcbd86e/5a6a1c 930a6e6500019faf5d_Oct-2016-placemaking-booklet.pdf
50. Purpose Built Communities (2019). Accessed 31 Dec 2019. https://purposebuiltcommunities. org/
51. Rockland County Community Science Opportunities. https://tinyurl.com/rm9qtys
52. Rockland County Demographics. https://datausa.io/profile/geo/rockland-county-ny#about
53. Rockland County Soil and Water Conservation District. https://tinyurl.com/u97kzwq
54. Ruckart, P.Z., Ettinger, A.S., Hanna-Attisha, M., Jones, N., Davis, S.I., Breysse, P.N.: The flint water crisis: a coordinated public health emergency response and recovery initiative. J. Public Health Manag. Pract. **25**(Suppl 1 Lead Poisoning Prevention), S84–S90 (2019). Accessed 8 Jan 2020. https://www.ncbi.nlm.nih.gov/pmc/articles/PMC6309965/
55. Ryan, R.M., Deci, E.L.: Self-Determination Theory: Basic Psychological Needs in Motivation, Development, and Wellness. Guilford Publications, New York (2017)
56. Sannino, A., Daniels, H., Gutiérrez, K.D. (eds.): Learning and Expanding with Activity Theory. Cambridge University Press, Cambridge (2009)
57. Schwartz, B.: What 'learning how to think' really means. The Chronicle of Higher Education, p. 18 (2015)
58. Shafer, L.: Mapping a City-Wide Approach to Education Reform that Aligns Resources to Support All Kids. Salem Education Foundation (2017). https://www.salemeducationfoun dation.org/news-and-tidbits/2018/5/24/mapping-a-city-wide-approach-to-education-reform-that-aligns-resources-to-support-all-kids
59. Stanton-Salazar, R.D.: A social capital framework for the study of institutional agents and their role in the empowerment of low-status students and youth. Youth Soc. **43**(3), 1066–1109 (2011)
60. Tienken, C.H., Colella, A., Angelillo, C., Fox, M., McCahill, K.R., Wolfe, A.: Predicting middle level state standardized test results using family and community demographic data. RMLE Online, **40**(1), 1–13 (2017). https://doi.org/10.1080/19404476.2016.1252304
61. Turvey, R.A.: Place-making and sustainable community development. In: Intellectual, Scientific, and Educational Influences on Sustainability Research, pp. 253–272. IGI Global (2019). https://www.igi-global.com/chapter/place-making-and-sustainable-commun ity-development/230824
62. Uytewaal, E., van de Lande, L.: Quick-scan of socially inclusive integrated water resources management. In: The Hague, Joint Conference Paper (2019). https://www.ircwash.org/sites/ default/files/084-201904dgis_joint_paperdef_web_0.pdf
63. Van Ryzin, M.J., Gravely, A.A., Roseth, C.J.: Autonomy, belongingness, and engagement in school as contributors to adolescent psychological well-being. J. Youth Adolesc. **38**(1), 1–12 (2009). https://tinyurl.com/saarmcy
64. Vygotsky, L.S.: Mind in Society: The Development of Higher Psychological Processes. Harvard University Press, Cambridge (1980)

65. Wang, J.: Opportunity to learn: the impacts and policy implications. Educ. Eval. Policy Anal. **20**(3), 137–156 (1998)
66. Wray-Lake, L., DeHaan, C.R., Shubert, J., Ryan, R.M.: Examining links from civic engagement to daily well-being from a self-determination theory perspective. J. Posit. Psychol. **14**(2), 166–177 (2019). https://doi.org/10.1080/17439760.2017.1388432

Design and Development
of a Web Extension to Help Facilitate
the Learning of a Foreign Language

Connor Corbin, Deniz Cetinkaya$^{(\boxtimes)}$ ⓘD, and Huseyin Dogan ⓘD

Department of Computing and Informatics,
Bournemouth University, Poole BH12 5BB, UK
{s4908654,dcetinkaya,hdogan}@bournemouth.ac.uk
http://hci.bournemouth.ac.uk/

Abstract. Learning a foreign language is a time consuming task that requires perseverance, commitment and hard work. The time required to learn a foreign language can range from hundreds to thousands of hours, depending on the language being learnt and the native language of the learner. Two major barriers to learning a language are lack of motivation and time. Spending increasing amounts of time online also has a detrimental effect on learning a language. The global digital language learning industry is growing and the market has more than doubled in size in the last decade due to the world becoming increasingly interconnected. There is a need to provide users with a web browser extension that is both interactive and continuous for learning a language. This paper presents the design and development of a web browser extension that will help facilitate the learning of foreign languages. The web extension overrides the default content when either a new tab or window is opened with interactive language learning material. The web extension is compatible with the desktop version of the Chrome web browser. Each time a new tab or window is opened, a range of language learning material are presented at random, which can be read, understood and completed in 30 s or less with immediate feedback. Overriding the web browser's functionality ensures the user is exposed to language learning material.

Keywords: Web browser extension · Online language learning · Accessible design · Interactive design

1 Introduction

Learning a foreign language is a time consuming task that requires perseverance, commitment and hard work. The time required to learn a foreign language can range from hundreds to thousands of hours, depending on the language being learnt and the native language of the learner [1]. Two major barriers to learning a language are lack of motivation and time, with 34% and 28% of Europeans saying this discourages them, respectively [2].

ⓒ Springer Nature Switzerland AG 2020
C. Stephanidis et al. (Eds.): HCII 2020, LNCS 12425, pp. 345–364, 2020.
https://doi.org/10.1007/978-3-030-60128-7_26

The barriers identified above are exacerbated by internet users spending increasing amounts of time online; spending on average 6 h and 43 min each day online [3]. However, the global digital language learning industry is growing [4]. Additionally, the global language services market has more than doubled in size in the last decade due to the world becoming increasingly interconnected, reaching 46.9 billion U.S. dollars in 2019 [5].

Many language learning applications exist, the most popular being Duolingo. Duolingo is the most downloaded educational application in the history of the Apple App Store, with approximately 300 million downloads and 30 million active users [6]. Language learning applications alone will not make an individual fluent in a language. However, they do allow an individual to learn new vocabulary, which is key to communicating in a foreign language. Communication is limited without grammar but without vocabulary nothing can be conveyed [7].

This paper presents the design and development of a web browser extension that will help facilitate the learning of foreign languages. The web extension overrides the default content when either a new tab or window is opened with interactive language learning material. The web extension is compatible with the desktop version of the Chrome web browser due to the mobile version not being able to support web extensions currently. Each time a new tab or window is opened, a range of language learning material are presented at random, which can be read, understood and completed in 30 s or less with immediate feedback. Our work is intended to supplement existing language learning solutions rather than replacing them. Overriding the web browser's functionality ensures the user is exposed to language learning material.

To the best of our knowledge, currently no web extension exists that provides interactive language learning material for users on Chrome Web Store. Interactive language learning material prompts users to engage with the content rather than passively absorb it. With the increasing amount of time individuals are spending online, as well as the increased digital language learning market, there exists an opportunity to provide users with a web extension that is both interactive and continuous. Thus, overriding the web browser's functionality ensures the user is exposed to interactive language learning material with immediate feedback. Moreover, many acknowledge the benefits of learning an additional language [2]. Therefore, a language learning web extension is appealing to many.

The web extension is built in a modular and extensible way so that with future development, further languages and different question types can be easily added. As a proof of concept, Spanish language materials are included, and user tests are held to evaluate the approach.

The remaining of the paper is structured as follows: Next section provides a brief background information and related work. Section 3 presents the analysis and design of the proposed approach. Section 4 explains the development details and relevant technologies. Section 5 presents the test results and outcome of the evaluation. Finally, last section concludes the paper and discusses the future work.

2   Background

This section presents the current state, outreach and market size of web extensions as well as the related work. Existing language learning web extensions and applications are studied to gain an understanding of their features, benefits and drawbacks. This provides information and guidance for eliciting the requirements and designing the web extension.

2.1   Chrome Web Extensions

Web extensions are small software programs that customise the browsing experience and are built with common web technologies such as HTML (Hypertext Markup Language), CSS (Cascading Style Sheets) and JavaScript [8]. Web extensions empower users to customise browsers' behaviour and functionality to their individual preferences or needs.

Chrome is based on a free and open-source software project by Google called Chromium. The Chromium project aims to provide users with a safer, faster, more stable and more secure way to experience the web [9]. Chrome is not the only web browser based on Chromium; Microsoft Edge and Opera are also Chromium based [10, 11]. However, Chrome is the most popular web browser across all device types with approximately 64% market share and 67% market share of desktop web browsers. Together, Chrome, Microsoft Edge and Opera have approximately 75% of the desktop web browser market share [12–14].

Web browsers based on Chromium support the same web extension application program interfaces (APIs) and manifest keys [15, 16]. Therefore, users can install web extensions directly from the Chrome Web Store with any browser that is based on Chromium. Given the market share of desktop web browsers based on Chromium and the potential outreach to users, the Chrome Web Store is the most lucrative market for publishing web extensions at present.

Chrome web extensions must serve and fulfil a single purpose that is easy to understand. A web extension that offers multiple and unrelated functionality would not serve a single purpose and therefore violate the Chrome extensions' policy. Violation of the Chrome extensions' policy will cause the web extension to be removed from the store [17]. There are approximately 188,620 web extensions on the Chrome Web Store. Of these, approximately 50% have less than 16 installs, 19,400 have 0 installs and 87% have less than 1,000 installs [18]. The statistics presented highlight the difficulty in producing a web extension that users like. Hence, it is important to correctly elicit the requirements to ensure the correct web extension is developed with features and functionality that the users will enjoy.

2.2   Language Learning Web Extensions

There are many language learning web extensions on the Chrome Web Store ranging in popularity and the number of active users. Three most relevant web extensions and techniques they have deployed to encourage users are discussed in this section.

Chrome web extensions are accessible on browsers which are based on Chromium, which controls the majority market share of desktop web browsers. This allows for the greatest exposure to potential users. Many existing language learning web extensions have hundreds of thousands of users. This was surprising due to background research presented in Sect. 2.1 showing that 87% of web extensions on the Chrome Web Store have less than 1,000 installs [18]. This highlights the demand and popularity for language learning web extensions.

Langly. This web extension supplements traditional language learning by encouraging users to learn a new word every time a new tab or window is opened by overriding the default content [19]. The opened new tab or window has a randomly chosen scenic background with a random word in a chosen language with the English translation. The web extension offers users the ability to pick one of three languages: German, French or Spanish. Furthermore, users can listen to how the word is pronounced by a native speaker. Langly aims to expand users' vocabulary in their chosen language which is important as limited knowledge of vocabulary impedes successful communication due to lexical errors [20,21]. Although, the web extension is simple and aesthetically pleasing, the random scenic background has no relevance to the word displayed that the user is attempting to learn. It could be an opportunity to help users learn and retain newly learnt vocabulary by having relevant pictures relating to the displayed word on the screen. Pictures help maintain users' attention and facilitate learning foreign language vocabulary by making language learning interesting and entertaining [22,23].

Mate Translate. This is an all-in-one translator with over a hundred languages to choose from. The web extension offers the ability to translate highlighted words, whole pages and Netflix subtitles [24]. The translated text displays the phonetic transcriptions with the ability to listen to the translated text. Translation of words is easy and straightforward; translation involves double clicking on a word, which opens an unobtrusive window without delay on the same page containing the translated text. However, while using the web extension, there was difficulty in selecting the desired language using the search selection dropdown menu. The dropdown menu did not recognise Spanish as a valid language option when using the search function. Consequently, this resulted in manually scrolling through all 103 languages to find Spanish, which was an inconvenience. One positive feature was the ability to switch between positive contrast polarity: light mode and negative contrast polarity: dark mode. This is advantageous for several reasons related to eye health [25] as well as personalised user experience [26].

Rememberry. It provides browser-based, interactive flashcards [27]. Using flashcards with spaced repetition is an effective learning strategy as opposed to massed study [28]. Spaced study allows for intervals between learning sessions, which allows the brain to form connections between ideas and concepts which helps the long-term retention of information. Massed study involves cramming one's learning into one mass study period and then moving onto another topic [29]. One negative experience with Rememberry was that there were no incentives. Nothing encourages or compels the user to make use of the flashcards feature, which would require them to click on the web extension logo in the toolbar. During periods of demotivation or taking breaks from learning, the web extension can be completely ignored and left unused. Additionally, the colour scheme of white, black and orange was not user friendly.

2.3 Language Learning Applications

The techniques utilised in language learning web extensions differ greatly to those in applications. Therefore, to gain a full and deeper understanding of the features and techniques used in a spectrum of digital language learning applications, existing language learning applications, not just web extensions, are also reviewed. Two most commonly used applications have been reviewed by outlining the advantages and disadvantages of the features and techniques deployed.

Rosetta Stone. The application provides a range of interactive language learning material and the ability to listen and learn offline. Rosetta Stone fully immerses the user from the beginning in one of the 24 language options they can chose from. Speech recognition software gives instant feedback, which helps fine-tune the accent and pronunciation of words [30]. Interactive learning is fun and engaging; it encourages users to think, explore and respond to new information, which aids their learning process and ability to retain information [31]. Lessons include multiple-choice questions, typing exercises, filling in the missing blanks relating to a picture and the pronunciation of words and phrases, which is then graded with speech recognition software. The learning material is both relevant and interesting. Furthermore, providing singular words in addition to phrases of various lengths is a practical approach to learning the target language.

An independent study measuring the effectiveness of Rosetta Stone shows a statistically significant improvement in language ability between the beginning and end of the study. Additionally, participants rated Rosetta Stone favourably with approximately 85% rating the software easy to use, enjoyable, helpful, would recommend to others and satisfied with their overall experience. Moreover, after 55 h of studying Spanish, participants increased their oral proficiency by between 56% and 72% [32]. One negative experience of Rosetta Stone was the introduction of new words which were not immediately obvious in their meaning. Google translate was used to understand the word or phrase as there was no way to view English translations. Additionally, the full version of Rosetta Stone requires a costly subscription. Higher subscription costs can be off putting for users. Research suggests that the higher the subscription cost, the higher the attrition rate of the users [33].

Duolingo. This is a free language learning platform offering small bite-size interactive lessons that can typically be completed in 5 min or less. In the literature. Research has been conducted to measure the effectiveness of Duolingo [34]. Participants completed one Spanish language test at the beginning of the study and one at the end. The results showed an overall improvement in participants' language abilities, which was statistically significant. Additionally, approximately 95% of participants rated Duolingo as easy to use, 92% believed that Duolingo helped them learn Spanish, 88% enjoyed learning Spanish with Duolingo and 79% were satisfied with Duolingo.

Each lesson provides learning material that can be read and studied before the interactive lessons. This contrasts with Rosetta Stone, which provides no learning material before lessons. Providing material prior to the lessons is an important and effective method for when new words and phrases are introduced. Interactive games include typing the Spanish translations of English expressions and vice versa, listening exercises, multiple-choice questions and speaking Spanish phrases, which are graded on accuracy.

Duolingo effectively uses gamification by offering experience points, a streak counter, leader boards and Lingots. Lingots are Duolingo's virtual currency that can be used to purchase additional features. The greater the progression through the levels, the more experience points and Lingots are gained. Gamification involves applying gaming mechanics to non-gaming environments to make difficult tasks more enjoyable. One drawback of Duolingo is that it groups words in semantic clusters, grouping animals, family and travel separately. This makes the acquisition of words grouped together more difficult due to the phenomenon called interference [35]. Interference theory dictates that forgetfulness is caused by memories interfering with and disrupting other memories [36].

3   Analysis and Design

Reviewing existing language learning solutions have highlighted the different approaches each have taken to facilitate language learning. Additionally, techniques and features that are advantageous and disadvantageous were identified. This helped to identify the requirements and features for the proposed web extension which users will enjoy and find helpful.

3.1   Requirements Elicitation

Requirements elicitation involves numerous activities and techniques that seek, uncover, acquire and elaborate requirements for a software system [37]. Requirement elicitation occurs during the initial phase of the project and is refined through an iterative approach throughout development. Iteratively refining requirements ensures the correct software system is developed [38]. This reduced the risk of the project failing due to inadequate requirements. Therefore, effective elicitation of requirements is important and vital in determining the success of the project [39,40]. The techniques chosen for this research are questionnaires and introspection. Due to personal experience and our own interest in learning a foreign language, the introspection technique is also used to develop and identify requirements that would be required of a language learning web extension. Introspection is insufficient alone so in combination with other elicitation techniques.

Questionnaires allow for an efficient and quick method of collecting information from multiple stakeholders. The questions are centred around gaining an understanding of participants' current language learning activities and habits. Additionally, questions are asked about their current use of language learning applications and what they like and dislike. This feedback is essential for determining useful features and requirements for the web extension. Table 1 presents the questions that we used at this stage.

Table 1. Questions for the initial questionnaire.

No	Question
Q1	Are you interested in learning a foreign language?
Q2	Have you learnt any foreign language previously?
Q3	What applications/software do you currently use to learn a foreign language?
Q4	What do you like about the application/software you currently use?
Q5	What do you not like about the application/software you currently use?
Q6	How long do you currently spend each day learning a language on average?
Q7	What requirements would you want from a language learning application?
Q8	Any other comments?

All participants had an interest in learning languages and had used language learning software before such as Duolingo and Babbel. Some positive features are listed as simple design, easy to use interface, setting targets, quality of the content, and improving various skills. On the other hand, negative features are listed as lack of reminders or notifications for continuous usage, and not being able to access all content. The desired features are listed as simplicity, accuracy, listening correct pronunciation, easy to use, having nice colours, different question types, reminders for regular usage, and activities that can be completed quickly. Text translation and listening the question features are also stated to be beneficial. We had limited number of five participants so the results are not representative, yet they are used to gather initial set of requirements for the proof of concept implementation.

With the information gained through the critical analysis of existing language learning applications and web extensions, responses from the initial questionnaires and the effective use of the introspection technique, several requirements have been derived. Requirements are prioritised with the MoSCoW method to accomplish a minimum viable product and broken down further into specific tasks that can be added to a Kanban board. As an example, major requirements are listed below:

- The web extension must have a simplistic design and clear layout.
- The web extension must be easy-to-use.
- The web extension must display random interactive learning material each time a new window or tab is opened.
- The web extension must provide a single learning activity each time.
- The web extension must provide options to select the correct answer for multiple choice questions.
- The web extension must make use of images to aid language learning.
- The web extension must display clearly the result of the activity.
- The web extension must have high quality and accurate content.
- The web extension must make effective use of colours to be visually appealing.

A minimum viable product is a version of a new product with enough features that allows for the maximum amount of feedback from users with the least amount of effort [41]. The main benefit of producing a minimum viable product is the feedback received from users interested in the product, without developing the full product. Therefore, feedback can be received from actual users quicker than if a full product is developed, which can be used to add, remove or adjust existing features depending on how the product resonates with the target market. This will lower the risk in producing a product that will not succeed whilst also reducing the effort, time and cost in producing the product.

3.2 User Interface Design

Wireframes were the initial design methodology used to create low-fidelity, two-dimensional designs of the web extension's user interfaces (UI). See Fig. 1 for an example.

Visual complexity and prototypicality are important in the users' aesthetic judgement process; users prefer minimal visual complexity and high prototypicality [42]. Users can experience a suboptimal initial impression when the UI contradicts their expectations, which can lead to lower product interaction [43]. Therefore, the web extension has a consistent design for all question types.

One advantage of wireframing UIs is to clarify and identify consistent designs for displaying categories of information to the user. This is crucial for the project due to its interactive nature. Users expect a question that is clear and easy to identify, in addition to feedback informing them if they have correctly or incorrectly answered the question. This information should remain consistent for all types of questions to increase usability, eliminate confusion and to evoke a positive emotional response. Additionally, wireframing helps allocate how much

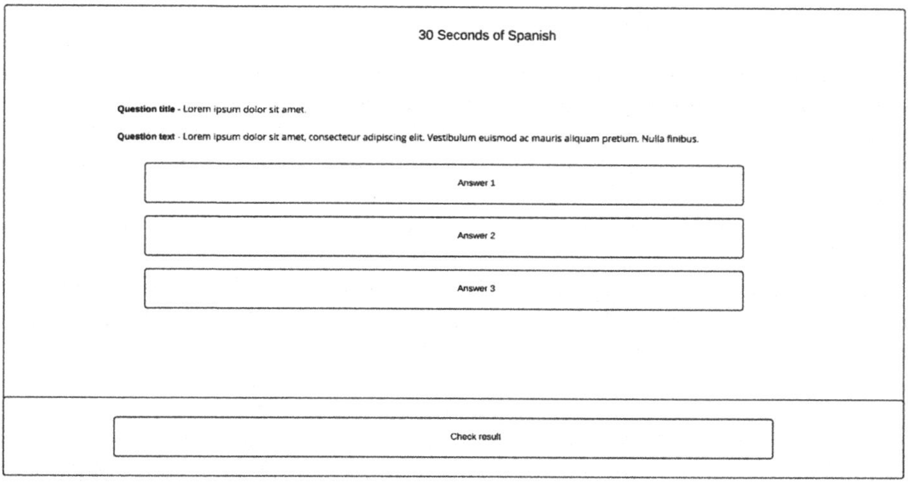

30 Seconds of Spanish
Question title - Lorem ipsum dolor sit amet.
Question text - Lorem ipsum dolor sit amet, consectetur adipiscing elit. Vestibulum euismod ac mauris aliquam pretium. Nulla finibus.
Answer 1
Answer 2
Answer 3
Check result

Fig. 1. Sample wireframe for the main page with multiple-choice questions.

Header component
Challenge Header component
Interactive learning material
Result Banner component

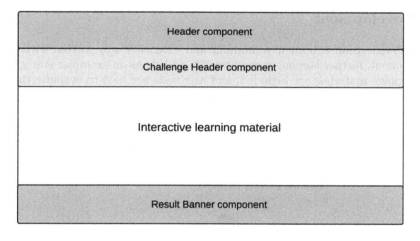

Fig. 2. Wireframe showcasing reusable react components.

white space is given to each element. Increasing white space improves comprehension, clarifies the relationships between elements, attracts users' attention and leads users' eyes towards relevant content [44].

Designing the UI with wireframes enabled white space to be effectively allocated to elements. The produced wireframes determined the necessary containers required to achieve the desired visual result. The wireframe designs also identified the reusable React components that have been highlighted in different colours in Fig. 2 above.

3.3   Design of the Logo

To make a good first impression to users, an aesthetically pleasing logo is required. A research study employed eye-tracking software and an infrared camera, tracked the participants' eye movements as they scanned different Web pages [45]. The study found that the participants spent approximately six seconds looking at the organisation's logo before moving onto other sections. Additionally, users ascertain an opinion about the visual appeal of a web page within 50 ms [46].

A descriptive logo was chosen due to having text and visual elements which communicate the service the web extension offers. The logo was based on the name of the web extension, 30 s of Spanish. The logo has a watch dial design, which encloses the number 30 with lines spaced evenly in a ring which represents the minutes and seconds of a watch. The colour scheme reflects the colours of the Spanish flag. The creation of a visually appealing logo contributes to ensuring a warm welcome to the web extension. This is important as the positive emotional response attracts and encourages the user to return.

4   Development

The web extension is built in a modular and extensible way so that with future development, further languages can be easily added. As an exemplar study, Spanish language materials are included, and user tests are held to evaluate the approach. Figure 3 shows a sample screenshot of the web extension with a sample multiple choice question. The web extension is built with JavaScript, React and

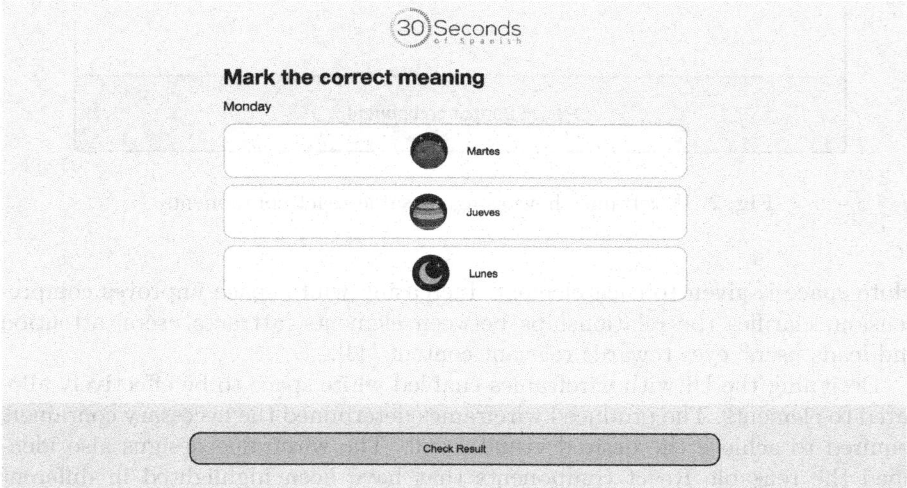

Fig. 3. Sample screenshot of the implemented web extension.

Styled-Components. Patterns in the source code are statistically analysed, identified and reported to increase source code readability and maintainability. This section explains the implementation details.

4.1 Methodology

Agile principles are applied to perform each activity in the software development lifecycle, producing a web extension that helps users facilitate learning Spanish. Agile dictates that working software is the primary measure of progress. Two Agile principles can aid this: delivering working software frequently and maximising the amount of unnecessary work done [41]. In addition, Lean Software Development methodology principles are applied which is based on Lean manufacturing and aims to maximise the value to the consumer whilst reducing waste. Kanban was chosen to implement the Lean thinking principles [47]. Kanban places emphasis on just-in-time delivery; having the right work done at the right time whilst not overburdening the development team. Therefore, features that add value to the project should be implemented first.

The focus of Kanban is to accurately visualise work that needs to be completed and when such work needs to be completed by. This is done by prioritising tasks that are the most important, reducing the risk of their incompletion and allowing increased flexibility for other tasks. Kanban contains three main principles. The first principle, visualising the workflow, involves setting up a Kanban board containing columns, cards and tasks. Each column represents a specific step in the workflow and each card represents a task. The second principle, limiting work in progress, involves setting work-in-progress limits for how many tasks can be in each workflow state at any given time. Lastly, measuring the lead time, involves optimising the process to lower the average time one task takes to complete, whilst increasing the predictability of how long a task will take to complete.

4.2 Technology Stack

GitHub. GitHub is an open-source web-based Git repository hosting service, providing source code management, distributed revision control functionality of Git, access control, wikis, bug tracking and acts as a backup of source code. Throughout the development of the web extension, a straightforward branching model was followed. A develop branch was created from the default branch in Git: master available from https://github.com/ConnorCorbin/30-Seconds-Of-Spanish. The master branch contains production-ready code while the default branch contains pre-production code, which serves as an integration branch for features. For each new feature of the web extension, a feature branch was created from the develop branch.

Husky library is used to create Git hooks inside the project's repository [48]. Git hooks are scripts that automatically execute each time an event occurs. Common Git hooks include pre-commit and pre-push, which commonly run unit tests and linting scripts before the commit and push Git commands.

JavaScript. JavaScript is a programming language with first-class functions. This means functions can be passed as arguments to other functions, assigned as a value to a variable and returned by another function. JavaScript is essential for webpage manipulation and interacting with the user, therefore creating a dynamic and interactive experience.

ESLint JavaScript linting utility is used to identify and report on patterns in JavaScript code via static code analysis [49]. Static code analysis examines the code during development to identify and report on problematic patterns or code that does not cohere to certain style guidelines. Static code analysis of JavaScript code is important due to JavaScript being prone to developer error, which in turn is due to JavaScript being a dynamically typed language. ESLint provides the ability to configure a range of linting rules; each rule is standalone and can be turned on or off depending on the coding style.

React. React is a declarative, efficient and flexible open-source JavaScript library used for building UIs [50]. Complex UIs are created from small isolated pieces of code called components. Conceptually, components are similar to JavaScript functions. Components accept inputs called props and return React elements which describe what appears on the screen.

PropTypes library is used for type checking React props, exporting a range of validators to ensure the data received is of the correct type. Type checking is required because JavaScript is a dynamically typed programming language, meaning data types do not have to be specified while coding. Therefore, functions declared in JavaScript can accept different types of data. For example, a function that expects a string can receive a number. This can lead to runtime type errors due to an operation that is nonsensically performed, or an unexpected data type passed into the function. PropTypes minimises this risk by type checking the props for a React component. When an invalid value is passed in as a prop, a warning is shown in the JavaScript console.

Styled-Components. Styled-components allow CSS to be written in JavaScript files to style React components [51]. There are several benefits of using styled-components. One includes the removal of class name bugs. This is because class names are automatically generated which removes the possibility of duplicated, overlapping or misspelt class names. Additionally, styled-components automatically injects vendor prefixes which ensures the latest CSS features work correctly and as expected on all web browsers. Lastly, styled-components automatically handles code-splitting; ensuring no redundant code is injected by tracking which React components are rendered and automatically injecting their styles only.

Styled-components exports a wrapper component called ThemeProvider that accepts a prop called theme. ThemeProvider enables all child React components to access the theme whether they are one or multiple levels deep. The value of the theme prop can be a variable or a function that returns an object. The returned object maps object properties to hexadecimal colour values, therefore, circumventing the necessity of repeating hard coded colour values in the styled components. Assigning property names that describe the function rather than the description of the colour allows easy interchangeability of a dark or light theme.

4.3 Manifest File

Chrome web extensions require a JavaScript Object Notation (JSON) formatted file which contains important information dictating how the web extension extends and modifies the web browsers capabilities [52]. The web extensions manifest file contains several properties. The name, version and manifest_version properties are all required whilst all others are optional. The chrome_url_overrides and new-Tab properties are essential; instructing Chrome to substitute an HTML file from the web extension for a page normally displayed when opening a new tab or window. The browser_action property is optional but advantageous; providing the default icon that appears in the main toolbar to the right of the address bar.

4.4 Question Components

The Multiple Choice Question (MCQ) component is a class component which utilises JavaScript classes; providing the same functionality of a functional component. Originally, the MCQ component was written as a functional component with React hooks. React hooks allow a functional component to use local state and other React features without writing a class component. However, the MCQ component was refactored into a class component due to external packages related to testing not fully supporting React hooks, which made testing more difficult and tedious.

The MCQ component uses the Label component. The Label component contains a possible answer to the multiple-choice question that can include an icon. Both text and image variants of the Label component are used. Additionally, the user can cycle through each Label component with the tab key and select their answer by pressing the enter key.

The Translate Text Question (TTQ) component is a class component due to requiring local state. However, unlike the MCQ component, the state object is defined outside the constructor due to the initial state values not being based on the props passed into the component. The TTQ component offers English and Spanish text translation questions that require the user to translate in the opposite language to the question. Additionally, the question title and text area prompt the user as to which language to type in. The user can submit their answer by pressing the enter key once they have entered at least one character into the text area. The TTQ component compares the users input with the correct answer, which is then passed into the component as a prop. However, strict string comparison is not suitable due to the possibility of users ignoring punctuation and misspelling words slightly. Therefore, a function based on the

Sørensen-Dice coefficient was created, which measures the number of consecutive bigrams and returns a decimal number between zero and one [53].

4.5 Documentation

All components have an accompanying markdown documentation (MD) file containing various pieces of information directly relating to the component. The information includes the components features and consumed components. Additionally, a data model table is provided containing the components prop name, data type and default value, the component in which the prop is associated with and the description of the prop and function it serves. Furthermore, the repository contains a README MD file in the root directory. This file contains instructions on how to install the web extension locally and steps on how to create and release a new component, including the necessary files, which must be created and the naming conventions to follow.

5 Results

The section covers the results of testing and evaluation of the web extension.

5.1 Unit Testing

Enzyme and Jest were used for testing all modules inside the source folder, taking approximately 8.5 s to fully run the 159 unit tests created. Automated unit tests provide instant feedback, which is advantageous when refactoring; tests can be ran quickly to test that the existing functionality is as expected.

Enzyme is a JavaScript testing utility that simplifies testing React components by creating a simpler interface for manipulating, traversing and simulating components [54]. This is due to its intuitive and flexible API which mimics jQuery's API for manipulating and traversing elements in the document object model (DOM).

Jest is a JavaScript testing framework that is well documented and aims to work out of the box with little to no configuration, providing a fast and efficient task runner, mocking capabilities and assertion library [55]. Jest ensures tests have a unique global state that allows them to be ran in parallel. This allows a larger number of tests to be ran very quickly. Jest can also generate code coverage, with no additional setup. This collects coverage information on branches, functions, lines and statements. Code coverage thresholds can also be set for the collected information. Therefore, enforcing the specified minimum threshold for coverage results. Jest will return a failure if these thresholds are not met.

Jest was configured to provide a minimum threshold enforcement of 100% code coverage for branches, functions and lines. Additionally, 100% branch coverage implies 100% statement coverage [56]. Unit test creation would not stop once

100% code coverage was achieved. Previous experience, knowledge and intuition was used to derive unit tests.

Snapshot testing was used to test the DOM output for each React component. Snapshot testing is advantageous as it ensures the UI does not change unexpectedly. Snapshot testing captures the DOM output of the UI and compares it to a reference snapshot file stored alongside the tests. The produced snapshot is either expected or unexpected in which case the referenced snapshot must be updated, or the snapshot fails in which case an error has occurred. Figure 4 below highlights the passing test suits and the number of successful tests.

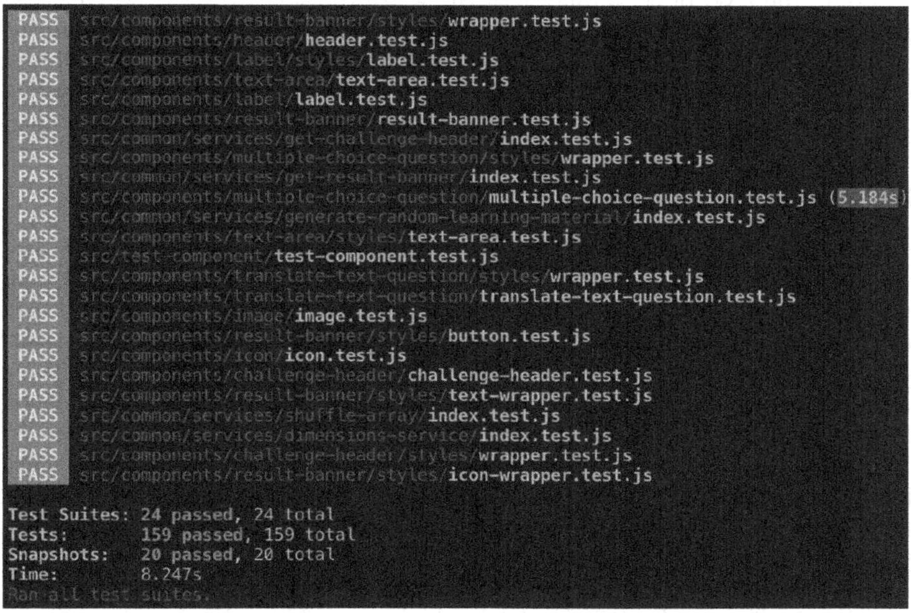

Fig. 4. Unit test results.

5.2   Visual Screenshot Testing

BackstopJS was used to perform visual screenshot testing for the created React components, including variants of the same component [57]. BackstopJS automates visual regression testing of React components by comparing DOM screenshots over time. Tests are rendered with Headless Chrome, which allows the Chrome browser to be ran in a headless environment without the need for a full browser visible UI shell. This removes the memory overhead of running a full version of Chrome whilst providing the same environment used by users. Additionally, BackstopJS provides integrated Docker rendering to eliminate cross-platform rendering issues.

A total of 17 scenarios were created and tested at four breakpoints, therefore a total of 68 visual screenshot tests are ran each time a new feature is developed. For each breakpoint, BackstopJS will create and open a report in the web browser displaying the results of the scenarios. The scenario either passes or fails and therefore must be updated if the change is expected or an error has occurred. Automated visual screenshot testing is advantageous due to the rapid feedback received when performing regression testing.

The automated testing techniques implemented allow an objective assessment regarding the level of conformance of the web extension to the web extensions requirements. The techniques help finding the defects and errors made during the development and ensure the web extension does not experience any failures, leading to increased quality and confidence in the source code and web extension. Increased quality leads to fewer failures and delays in attaining product stability.

5.3   User Tests

Once a minimum viable product was produced, user tests were held to collect constructive feedback. All participants have interest in learning languages and have basic level of Spanish. Instructions were sent to the participants and help offered during the installation of the extension if needed. Users liked the simple and effective web extension layout, which highlights the importance of utilising the wireframe design methodology to position and apply white space to elements. Users enjoyed the two types of questions implemented. The feedback revealed that the text translation question is more challenging than the multiple-choice question, furthermore, a range of difficulty in the question types was found to be helpful. The web extensions logo was found to be relevant to the service the web extension provided and attracted users' attention.

The colour scheme and accessibility offered was well received, which aids the requirement of the web extension having high accessibility. No errors or failures were reported from the user feedback. While users enjoyed the multiple-choice questions, the pictures made answering the question too easy. Furthermore, users suggested additional features that would be beneficial in their learning, such as an option for further questions and an option to retake a question.

The proposed solution currently offers only Spanish language materials. However, the web extension has been produced in a modular and flexible fashion that will enable the addition of further languages and features to be offered with additional development. User evaluation study is limited to five participants and to the selected example. We will add more content and involve more participants to improve our evaluation in future validation studies.

6   Conclusion and Future Work

Chrome web extensions are accessible on browsers which are based on Chromium and there is a demand for language learning web extensions. The existing related work discussed in Sect. 2 miss several opportunities to enhance and help facilitate users' language learning. One such opportunity was that no incentives exist for users to use the web extension; only Langly addressed this issue with overriding the default content when opening a new tab or window. However, the content Langly provides is not interactive, offering only a single word translation with a background image that is irrelevant to the word.

This paper presents the design and development of a web extension to help facilitate the learning of a foreign language. The proposed web extension overrides the default content of a new tab or window with interactive language learning material. It provides random interactive language learning material each time a user opens a new tab or window in the desktop version of the Chrome web browser.

Agile principles are applied with the Lean Software Development methodology to perform each activity in the software development lifecycle, producing a web extension that helps users facilitate learning Spanish. Requirements for the web extension were derived through researching existing language learning web extensions and applications, questionnaires and introspection. The web extension is built in a modularised fashion with JavaScript, React and Styled-Components. Unit tests are written with Jest and Enzyme as well as visual screenshot testing is performed.

The web extension provides a solid foundation for future enhancements. As a future work, we will focus on expanding the number of languages that can be offered by the web extension as well as adding new learning materials. Additionally, implementing new question types and introducing difficulty levels are planned. Once these updates are implemented, we would like to improve the validation step with more participants and structured feedback.

Acknowledgment. We would like to thank the participants and interviewees for their valuable input and comments.

References

1. United States Department of State: Foreign language training. https://www.state.gov/foreign-language-training/. Accessed 29 Jan 2020
2. European Commission: Europeans and their Languages. Report (2012). http://ec.europa.eu/commfrontoffice/publicopinion/archives/ebs/ebs_386_en.pdf
3. DataReportal Digital 2020: Global digital overview. https://datareportal.com/reports/digital-2020-global-digital-overview. Accessed 17 Mar 2020
4. Statista: Digital language learning global market size by language 2025 (2019). https://www.statista.com/statistics/948857/digital-language-learning-global-market-size-language/
5. Statista: Global language services market size 2019 (2019). https://www.statista.com/statistics/257656/size-of-the-global-language-services-market/

6. Adams, S.: Game of Tongues - how duolingo built a $700 million business with its addictive language-learning app. Forbes article (2019). https://www.forbes.com/sites/susanadams/2019/07/16/game-of-tongues-how-duolingo-built-a-700-million-business-with-its-addictive-language-learning-app/

7. Folse, K.S.: Vocabulary myths - Applying Second Language Research to Classroom Teaching. University of Michigan Press, Ann Arbor (2004)

8. Google Chrome: What are extensions? https://developer.chrome.com/extensions. Accessed 6 Feb 2020

9. Chromium Projects. https://www.chromium.org/. Accessed 19 Mar 2020

10. Opera version history - Opera Help. https://help.opera.com/en/opera-version-history/. Accessed 18 Mar 2020

11. Microsoft - Download the new Microsoft Edge based on Chromium. https://support.microsoft.com/engb/help/4501095/download-the-new-microsoft-edge-based-on-chromium. Accessed 18 Mar 2020

12. StatCounter Global Stats: Browser Market Share Worldwide. https://gs.statcounter.com/browser-market-share. Accessed 18 Mar 2020

13. StatCounter Global Stats: Desktop Browser Market Share Worldwide. https://gs.statcounter.com/browser-marketshare/desktop/worldwide. Accessed 19 Mar 2020

14. Statista: Desktop internet browser market share 2015–2020. https://www.statista.com/statistics/544400/market-share-of-internet-browsers-desktop/ (2020)

15. Microsoft - Port Chrome Extension To Microsoft (Chromium) Edge. https://docs.microsoft.com/enus/microsoft-edge/extensions-chromium/developer-guide/port-chrome-extension. Accessed 19 Mar 2020

16. Opera - Extension APIs Supported in Opera. https://dev.opera.com/extensions/apis/. Accessed 19 Mar 2020

17. Google Chrome - Extensions Quality Guidelines FAQ. https://developer.chrome.com/extensions/single_purpose. Accessed 19 Mar 2020

18. Extension Monitor: Breaking Down the Chrome Web Store. https://extensionmonitor.com/blog/breaking-down-the-chrome-web-store-part-1. Accessed 7 Feb 2020

19. Chrome Web Store: Langly. https://chrome.google.com/webstore/-detail/langly/lmhamlhlkpedkileakbifbdamgpnegma. Accessed 13 May 2020

20. Moghadam, S., Zainal, Z., Ghaderpour, M.: A review on the important role of vocabulary knowledge in reading comprehension performance. Procedia - Soc. Behav. Sci. **66**, 555–563 (2012)

21. Alqahtani, M.: The importance of vocabulary in language learning and how to be taught. Int. J. Teach. Educ. **3**(3), 21–34 (2015)

22. Carpenter, S., Olson, K.: Are pictures good for learning new vocabulary in a foreign language? Only if you think they are not. J. Exp. Psychol. Learn. Mem. Cogn. **38**(1), 92–101 (2012)

23. Lavalle, I., Briesmaster, M.: The study of the use of picture descriptions in enhancing communication skills among the 8th grade students-learners of English as a Foreign Language. Inquiry Educ. 9(1) (2017). Article 4

24. Chrome Web Store: Mate Translate - translator, dictionary. https://chrome.google.com/webstore/detail/mate-translate--translat/ihmgiclibbndffejedjimfjmfoabpcke. Accessed 13 May 2020

25. Aleman, A., Wang, M., Schaeffel, F.: Reading and myopia: contrast polarity matters. Sci. Rep. **8**(1), 1–5 (2018)

26. Nielsen Norman Group: Dark mode vs. light mode: which is better? https://www.nngroup.com/articles/dark-mode/. Accessed 8 Feb 2020

27. Chrome Web Store: Rememberry - translate and memorize. https://chrome.google. com/webstore/detail/rememberry-translateand/dipiagiiohfljcicegpgffpbnjmgjcnf. Accessed 13 May 2020

28. Kornell, N.: Optimising learning using flashcards: spacing is more effective than cramming. Appl. Cogn. Psychol. **23**(9), 1297–1317 (2009)

29. Kang, S.: Spaced repetition promotes efficient and effective learning. Policy Insights Behav. Brain Sci. **3**(1), 12–19 (2016)

30. Rosetta Stone: How rosetta stone works—our immersion language learning methodology. https://www.rosettastone.co.uk/how-it-works. Accessed 13 May 2020

31. Anderson, J.: The benefit of interactive learning. Harvard Graduate School of Education (2014). https://www.gse.harvard.edu/news/14/11/benefit-interactive-learning

32. Vesselinov, R.: Measuring the effectiveness of rosetta stone. Report. City University of New York (2009). http://resources.rosettastone.com/CDN/us/pdfs/Measuring_the_Effectiveness_RS-5.pdf

33. Danaher, P.: Optimal pricing of new subscription services: analysis of a market experiment. Market. Sci. **21**(2), 119–138 (2002)

34. Vesselinov, R., Grego, J.: Duolingo effectiveness study. Report (2012). http:// static.duolingo.com/s3/DuolingoReport_Final.pdf

35. Tavares, A.: Some ideas to avoid L1 interference. World of better learning - Cambridge University Press (2017). https://www.cambridge.org/elt/blog/2017/10/06/some-ideas-to-avoid-l1-interference/

36. Baddeley, A., Logie, R.: Working memory: the multiple-component model. In: Miyake, A., Shah, P. (eds.), Models of Working Memory: Mechanisms of Active Maintenance and Executive Control, pp. 28–61. Cambridge University Press (1999). https://doi.org/10.1017/CBO9781139174909.005

37. Yousuf, M., Asger, M.: Comparison of various requirements elicitation techniques. Int. J. Comput. Appl. **116**(4), 8–15 (2015)

38. Zowghi, D., Coulin, C.: Requirements elicitation: a survey of techniques, approaches, and tools. In: Aurum, A., Wohlin, C. (eds.) Eng. Manag. Softw. Requir. Springer, Berlin, Heidelberg (2005)

39. Charette, R.: Why software fails. IEEE Spectrum (2005). https://spectrum.ieee.org/computing/software/why-software-fails

40. Stanley, R., Uden, L.: Why projects fail, from the perspective of service science. In: Uden, L., Herrera, F., Bajo Pérez, J., Corchado Rodríguez, J. (eds.) 7th International Conference on Knowledge Management in Organizations: Service and Cloud Computing. AISC, vol. 172, pp. 421–429. Springer, Heidelberg (2013). https://doi.org/10.1007/978-3-642-30867-3_38

41. Beck, K., et al.: Manifesto for agile software development (2001). https:// agilemanifesto.org/

42. Tuch, A., Presslaber, E., Stöcklin, M., Opwis, K., Bargas-Avila, J.: The role of visual complexity and prototypicality regarding first impression of websites: Working to-wards understanding aesthetic judgments. Int. J. Hum.-Comput. Stud. **70**(11), 794–811 (2012)

43. Raita, E., Oulasvirta, A.: Too good to be bad: favorable product expectations boost subjective usability ratings. Interact. Comput. **23**(4), 363–371 (2011)

44. Bachvarova, V.: The power of empty space in UI design (2018). https://uxplanet.org/https-medium-com-viktorija-bachvarova-the-power-of-empty-space-in-uidesign-14f14f8b203

45. Sheng, H., Lockwood, N.S., Dahal, S.: Eyes don't lie: understanding users' first impressions on websites using eye tracking. In: Yamamoto, S. (ed.) HIMI 2013. LNCS, vol. 8016, pp. 635–641. Springer, Heidelberg (2013). https://doi.org/10.1007/978-3-642-39209-2_71

46. Lindgaard, G., Fernandes, G., Dudek, C., Brown, J.: Attention web designers: you have 50 milliseconds to make a good first impression!. Behav. Inf. Technol. **25**(2), 115–126 (2006)

47. Anderson, D.: Kanban - Successful Evolutionary Change for Your Technology Business. Blue Holes Press, Sequim (2010)

48. Husky GitHub repository. https://github.com/typicode/husky. Accessed 23 Mar 2020

49. ESLint: Pluggable JavaScript linter. https://eslint.org/. Accessed 14 May 2020

50. React: Introduction to React Tutorial. https://reactjs.org/tutorial/tutorial.html. Accessed 18 Feb 2020

51. Styled Components Basics. https://styled-components.com/docs/basics. Accessed 23 Mar 2020

52. Google Chrome: Manifest File Format. https://developer.chrome.com/extensions/manifest. Accessed 15 May 2020

53. Guindon, B., Zhang, Y.: Application of the dice coefficient to accuracy assessment of object-based image classification. Can. J. Remote Sens. **43**(1), 48–61 (2016)

54. Enzyme - Introduction to Enzyme. https://enzymejs.github.io/enzyme/. Accessed 23 Mar 2020

55. Jest Delightful JavaScript Testing. https://jestjs.io/. Accessed 23 Mar 2020

56. Myers, G., Sandler, C., Badgett, T.: The Art of Software Testing, 3rd edn. Wiley, Hoboken (2012)

57. BackstopJS GitHub repository. https://github.com/garris/BackstopJS. Accessed 23 Mar 2020

Training Professionals to Bring Digital Transformation into Museums: The Mu.SA Blended Course

Massimiliano Dibitonto, Katarzyna Leszczynska$^{(\boxtimes)}$, Elisa Cruciani, and Carlo Maria Medaglia

DASIC, Link Campus University, via del Casale di S. Pio V, 44, 00165 Rome, Italy
{M.Dibitonto,K.Leszczynska,E.Cruciani,C.Medaglia}@unilink.it

Abstract. In a world that is constantly transformed by the evolution of digital technologies, the museum sector must evolve, enhancing and updating its offer and its identity to answer to the new needs of the visitors and to be competitive. However, the digital transformation of an organization is only possible through a cultural transformation of the professionals working inside it. In this context the Mu.SA project [1], an Erasmus +KA2, was aimed to address the shortage of digital skills identified in the museum sector and to encourage the emergence of new professional profiles through a training programme divided into three phases: MOOC, Blended Course, Work-Based Learning. The proposed paper is about the evaluation results of the second phase of the course that involved 120 students from Greece, Italy and Portugal, most of them were already museum workers wishing to update their skills. The evaluation aimed to assess the functionality, usability and accessibility of the online platform (technical level); the learning activities and content delivery (learning level); the quality of the contents and subject coverage (learning outcomes level); using a quali-quantitative approach. The results of the evaluation were generally positive and were used to improve the course.

Keywords: Museum professionals · Digital transformation · Digital skills · Blended learning · Learning design · Quality reference framework

1 Introduction

1.1 The Mu.SA Course

Information and communication technologies have redefined the role of museums in terms of documentation, preservation and promotion of cultural heritage in the digital age. Professionals aspiring to work in the sector should have or acquire a new skill set to combine creativity, flexibility and knowledge management to work inside cultural organizations.

To address this challenge, the training course Mu.SA - Museum Sector Alliance supports the continuous professional development of museum professionals, offering in a free modality, a MOOC, a Blended Course and a period of training on the job.

© Springer Nature Switzerland AG 2020
C. Stephanidis et al. (Eds.): HCII 2020, LNCS 12425, pp. 365–376, 2020.
https://doi.org/10.1007/978-3-030-60128-7_27

The project, an Erasmus +/KA2/Sector Skills Alliances, that started in 2016, involves a consortium of 11 partners based in Greece, Italy and Portugal and it has its roots in the "eCult Skills project" [2] carried out in 2013. As "continuous learning ability is an essential precondition for coping with change and successfully establishing innovations" [3], the vision of Mu.SA is to consider the training a vehicle of digital transformation. The value of the project has also been recognized by the European Union which has suggested it as best practice in the area of "Opportunities for Cultural Heritage Professionals".

This work focuses on the second part of the training program (blended course) that followed a first phase that has involved 3803 students and has been described and evaluated in a previous research [4].

1.2 Museums, Digital Transformation and Blended Learning

In a fast-changing world, even the survival of museums in the digital era is related to the ability of the professionals to update their knowledge or to acquire new skills [5]. To avoid misalignment between the labour market and the professional needs becomes a priority to identify the new needs of museum professionals, from directors to employees and researchers, drawing inspiration from other experiences on the subject, such as the ones of the European projects ARTS [6], ADESTE [7] and CREA.M. [8].

According to a recent study by Silvaggi et al. [9], among the strategic figures that will shape the identity of the museum of the future, there are the people in charge of communication and management of online public relations, the key figures able to design engaging experiences with the use of technology, the responsible of the museum's digital strategy, and the technological mediators capable of building a dialogue between the museum's collections and the digital resources.

By mapping the training offers for museum professionals, a recent work by Sturabotti et al. [10] reveals that the university learning path cannot be considered complete and that the combination with continuing education courses is a suitable solution to be in line with the current requests of museums [2].

Moreover, in this field could be noticed increasing use of e-learning training courses for continuing education, with a preference for blended courses, confirmed by national and international institutions like the EU, that stated that "digital tools can enable flipped classrooms and blended learning" [11], and the Italian Ministry of Cultural Heritage and Activities and Tourism that proposed a novel training program for its employees [12].

Indeed a massive application of blended learning could be found in the high education field (for example the foreign language teaching [13]), where the flexibility of an online course (the most suitable solution for professionals who could not attend in presence an onsite course) is enriched by some face-to-face meetings, showing that the dropout rate decreases when participants can interact with each other and with the teacher [14].

After the first phase of the Mu.SA project (MOOC), which involved a large number of participants, the second phase required a different approach, that could offer a more personalized program and experience to the selected candidates. To overcome the limits of a massive course, like the top-down teacher-centric approach [15], the static nature of video contents [16] or the lack of face-to-face exchanges with the tutors [17], the chosen training model was a blended learning option, that puts the student at the centre of the learning process and recognizes to her/him a more dynamic role, based on the co-creation with others [18]. One of the strengths of this kind of approach is the face-to-face interaction, fundamental to support the asynchronous and mediated presence of the trainer in the MOOC, that allows establishing a trustful relationship with him/her, seen as an expert available to provide an adaptive response to the individual and different students' performances [14]. As evidenced by Stein and Graham [19], in the planning phase of this kind of course is important to find the best way to mix synchronous with asynchronous interactions, planning for learning time, and incorporating the right technologies, but in addition to these aspects linked to the effectiveness and efficiency, there is a 3rd "E", the engagement. The online courses could easily create a sense of distance between students and classmates and a blended course could improve this relationship, improving the engagement and the overall experience with the course.

As we reported in the next evaluation chapter of the Mu.SA Blended Course, the collected data confirm the studies mentioned above.

1.3 MOOC Evaluation Overview

During the first period of the Mu.SA course, held between January and March 2019, organized as a traditional MOOC entitled "Essential digital skills for museum professionals", 3803 persons have accessed the lessons available on the digital platform (Moodle) and were evaluated with assessments as multiple-choice questions, true or false and matching questions. In a previous work [4] we have described the course and the related evaluation, especially regarding the matching between the training programme and the expectations of the participants and the ability of the tools and training materials to support the transfer of knowledge and skills. The evaluation strategy adopted was based on quantitative and qualitative elements and reflects the criteria generally adopted at European level. As the MOOC is only the first part of the training programme, the evaluation of the subsequent phases (Blended Course and Work-Based Learning) will allow having an overview of the quality of the course and the effectiveness and efficiency of the materials and tools developed.

2   Mu.SA Blended Course

The Blended Course started in September 2019 and ended in April 2020. It combines twentyone e-CF, six DigComp and fifteen 21st Cent skills and it's divided into four different courses for each of the four Mu.SA job profiles (Digital Strategy Manager - DSM, Digital Collections Curator - DCC, Digital Interactive Experience Developer - DIED, Online Cultural Community Manager - OCCM) [2]. 120 learners were initially selected by the Mu.SA Steering Committee Group to continue the Specialization Course inside the Mu.SA project countries (Greece, Portugal and Italy). The chosen candidates have successfully completed the "Essential Skills for Museum Professionals" MOOC and applied correctly for one of the Mu.SA role profile. Before the course began, 7 students withdrew due to the lack of formal requirements resulting in 113 students enrolled.

The Blended Course was divided into online and self-study and face-to-face sessions and consisted in 24 weeks (360 h) of study effort.

The online and self-study part was delivered in English via an online platform in a similar way of the MOOC and was composed of modules, units and learning objects designed accordingly to the Learning Outcomes previously defined. The competences acquired were assessed at the end of every module through the "assessment objects" (multiple-choice, true or false and matching questions) and the "practical assignments" activities, that required students to apply what they learned, graded by the tutors of each module. During all the course delivery period the tutors of the modules were available for any questions and clarifications via private messages and a forum.

Six face-to-face meetings were scheduled in each nation, one per month, in presence or via Skype (for those who could not attend physically). These sessions used a "flipped classroom" approach and consisted of workshops, discussions exchanges of ideas and best practice with experts, tutors and learners, and were highly appreciated by the students as reported in the next chapter.

3   Blended Course Evaluation

The following chapter presents the evaluation procedure and results of the Blended Course. The evaluation used both qualitative and quantitative data collection techniques, like pre and post-course questionnaires to participants, log analysis, semi-structured interviews to participants and feedback from tutors. The data analysis was performed through statistical and qualitative content analysis of the open answers of the questionnaires and the information came out from interviews. This evaluation follows the Template Model for Educational Content Quality [20], that consists in a synthesis based on the quality standards ISO/IEC 9126, ISO/IEC 25000 series and specifically to the ISO/IEC 25010 (Software engineering-Software product Quality Requirements and Evaluation (SQuaRE) Quality model), the ISO/IEC 25012 (SQuaRE quality model-Data quality model) and the ISO 25020 (measurement method) in particular for the dimensions related to the external quality.

The focal aim of the evaluation is to assess:

1. The technical level of the course (platform's quality);
2. The learning level (activities and content delivery);
3. The learning outcomes level (quality of the contents and subject coverage).

3.1   Participants

The 113 students enrolled from the three countries (IT, PT, GR) were selected and divided among the different profiles (DSM, DCC, DIED and OCCM), on the base of their expression of interest sent at the end of the MOOC. This distribution was not uniform as could be seen in the following figure (see Fig. 1), with the majority of the students that chose the Digital Collection Curator profile (45%).

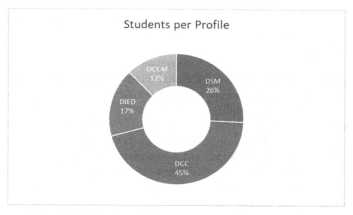

Fig. 1. Distribution of the students among the four profiles.

At the end of the Specialization Course, 79 students (69,9%) successfully completed it and we registered 31 explicit dropouts (with written or oral communication), with motivations related mainly to personal problems (for example illness, pregnancy, death) or to the effort required to complete the course (Fig. 2).

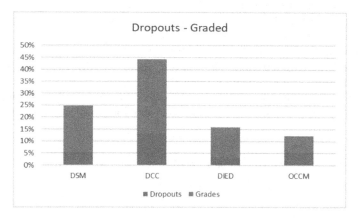

Fig. 2. Final percentage of dropouts and students graduated for profiles.

Previous Knowledge and Expectations. Before the Specialization phase started, through the Pre-Course Survey some students' insights were investigated. Concerning the previous knowledge acquired with the MOOC, the students expressed a good level of appreciation. The significance of learning outcomes they reached in the MOOC was judged very or moderately positive by 50% of DSM, 94.2% of DCC, 90.9% of DIED, 42.9% of OCCM. The overall mean about the students' current knowledge obtained with the MOOC was quite high (the peak is represented by OCCM, 74%) and the highest proportion of the surveyed students had good skills both in language and in digital proficiency (the peak in English skills is reached by DIED with 63.6% while the one for the digital is 85.7% gained by OCCM).

With regard to the expectations and objectives that pushed people to enroll in the course, the whole sample interviewed declared that the priorities in taking the Mu.SA Specialization Course were to acquire new skills, to develop new competencies, and to gain a competitive advantage. Getting a certificate and collaborating with people to share the same interests were the last things the students wanted (the lower rate is represented by the DIED profile, 68%). Moreover, most of them expect to be able to apply what learned in their current jobs (the higher rate is represented by the group of DIED, 73%), to get more opportunities (the higher rate is represented by the group of OCCM, 57%), and to contribute to change how things work in their respective organizations (the higher rate is represented by the group of DCC, 20%).

3.2 Learning Activity and Content Delivery

In order to measure the student behaviour and performance during the course, the log available in the e-learning platform (Moodle) have been collected and analyzed.

Moreover, 28 students (10 of which were Italian, 11 Greek and 7 Portuguese) representative of the four Mu.SA profiles have been interviewed, obtaining a qualitative insight useful for the interpretation of the qualitative data.

The analysis of the platform logs allowed to measure the level of participation of students in all the activities foreseen by the course.

The teaching material was organized into weeks (modules), units and subunits but to avoid misinterpretation, is important to specify that the workload was not uniform for the various profiles, as it is shown by Table 1.

For a correct interpretation of the data, it is necessary to underline that the students were asked to complete at least 80% of the total activities to successfully conclude the course.

Table 1. Total workload.

	DSM	DCC	DIED	OCCM
Units	64	56	65	60
Assessments	64	56	65	60
Practical assignments	25	23	29	27

The units contained learning material (usually videos, texts or presentations), therefore their analysis allows to make some initial reflections on the students' behaviour. In general (see Fig. 3), a decreasing trend in student participation can be seen during the course, more evident for the DCC and OCCM profiles, as it was also confirmed by the interviews with them. This curve is related to the dropouts that occurred progressively during the course.

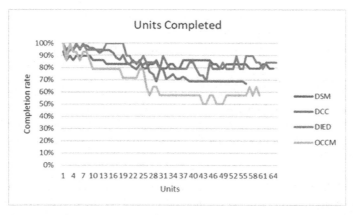

Fig. 3. Trend of the units completed by the students during the course.

In the chart in Fig. 4 students have been clustered in 4 groups, according to the percentage of units completed, with the last one showing the threshold to pass the course (80%). For the four profiles, the percentage of students below the threshold coincides with the percentage of students who withdrew during the course. Clusters, together with the timeline, may suggest when students have stopped attending the course. As an example, we don't have OCCM in the cluster 50–80%, a sign that the dropouts happened in the first part of the course. From the logs of the platform, it is possible to notice how, in the last month of the course, some students (about 10%) have raised the completion rate from <50% to >80%, making a final effort in view of the final certification and resulting in positive peaks in the chart in Fig. 3.

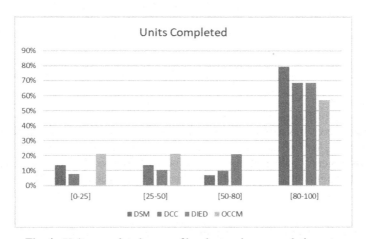

Fig. 4. Units completed per profile, clustered per completion rate.

Another element of analysis is represented by the completion of the assessments objects, quizzes used to assess whether students have achieved the unit learning outcomes. The completion rate of units and assessments during the course are quite similar, this means that the students were quite constant. Sometimes students did not complete the assessment even if they have completed the unit probably because of the 80% threshold. Some negative peaks correspond to weeks that required more effort from the students (according to the interviews). As an example, DSM and DCC students found the module "Information and Knowledge Management" too difficult and many students contacted tutors asking help while DCC, DIED and OCCM struggled to complete the "Problem-Solving" module.

While units and assessments were already present in the first phase of the course (MOOC) and the learners had enough time to get used to their pace and mechanisms, the practical assignment is a novel element introduced for the Blended Course.

Practical assignments (PA) requires students to perform some tasks (writing an essay, a strategy, etc.) applying what they have learned in the module (Fig. 5).

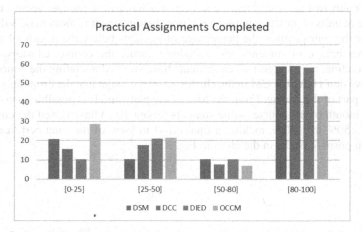

Fig. 5. Practical assignments completed per profile, clustered per completion rate.

The analysis of the practical assignments shows a very different scenario. As emerged from the interviews, this activity required a lot of effort and this could explain why, two weeks before the end of the course, many students were still missing more than half of their assignments. Indeed, from the platform's logs, we observed an increment of the practical assignments completed in the last weeks, especially for DCC and OCCM students.

3.3 Learning Outcomes Level, Organization and Technical Level

To evaluate the ability of the course to meet the objectives of the learning, technical, and learning outcomes levels, 61 learners answered to a post-course survey, and other 28 students were involved in a short interview, to deepen more their opinion about the content quality, organization and usability of the Blended Course. The respondents involved in the evaluation represented the four Mu.SA profiles.

Learning Outcomes Level. The overall students' competency after the course completion was rated positively with the highest results in Communication and Collaboration area than in the ICTs areas, for all the profiles. DSM overall competency after course completion was rated at 78% (of which Communication and Collaboration rated at 91% and Problem-Solving at 86%, but Enabling ICTs rated only at 73%), DCC at 68% (of which Communication and Collaboration rated at 85% and Digital Content Creation and Problem-Solving both rated at 74%, but Building ICTs rated only at 57%), DIED at 77% (of which Communication and Collaboration rated at 90% and Information and Data Literacy at 83%, but Running ICTs rated only at 70%) and OCCM at 71% (of which Communication and Collaboration rated at 92% and Digital Content Creation at 88%, but Building ICTs, Enabling ICTs and Managing ICTs were all rated only at 59%).

The overall feeling about the learning outcomes developed in the Blended Course was assessed by the students as positive, with most of the respondents that rated it as very or moderately significant for all four profiles (very significant for the 75% of DSM, 44% for the DCC, 50% for the DIED and moderately significant for the 50% of OCCM).

The objectives achieved were evaluated sufficiently in line with initial expectations, in particular concerning the initial expectations of knowledge acquisition by all the respondents, as in the following table (Table 2).

Table 2. Learners' expectations and satisfaction with different course objectives.

	DSM	DCC	DIED	OCCM
The acquisition of new skills	88%	84%	88%	83%
The acquisition of knowledge	94%	87%	93%	88%
The possibility to get in touch with experts in the field	78%	85%	93%	88%
The possibility to collaborate with people that share the same interests	86%	89%	93%	92%
The possibility to access educational resources about the subject	93%	89%	95%	88%
Overall weighted mean	**88%**	**87%**	**92%**	**88%**

The overall satisfaction about the different modules was rated as 81% for the DCC, DIED and OCCM, while the DSM rated the highest overall satisfaction with 86% (confirming the previous satisfaction about the learning outcomes developed in the Blended Course, rated especially positive for this profile), with some modules appreciated more than others for the clarity of language and explanation of the topics. The interviews allowed to deepen more these aspects and enabled to understand the less appreciation of the more technical modules, due often to the difficulties to understand a more complex and technical language and not because judged not interesting.

This aspect is highlighted also by the evaluation of the skills acquired, judged more positively in Communication and Collaboration for all the four profiles and with a minor satisfaction with ICTs skills.

Course Organization and Structure. The overall evaluation of the general objectives and organization of the course was rated positively, with DSM 84% satisfied with the general objectives and organization of the course, DCC 82%, DIED 81% and OCCM 83%. All the students were highly satisfied with the face-to-face sessions, as confirmed by the interviews. They greatly appreciated the interactive meetings (both those who attended live and remotely), for the topics covered, the guests invited and the methodology used. Face-to-face sessions were appreciated also for the chance to get in touch with tutors and colleagues and to exchange ideas in a more collective environment. It is precisely during these meetings that for example, the Italian students began to create a spontaneous community and continues to be active even after the end of the course.

Summarizing, we can affirm that the organizational aspects were judged positively in all the main items, also functionality was rated adequate and effective. The interviews were useful to add more information about these values and to draw up some suggestions proposed by the learners, that reflected some issues faced during the course development.

Relating to the organization the main suggestions were:

- to organize better the schedule and make more uniform the workload allotment;
- to extend the time of the course;
- to start the Work-Based Learning at the end of the Blended Course and so assimilate in time the theoretical knowledge to put into practice;
- to know in advance which module would be the more time-demanding and which one would be the lighter (to better organize the study).

Technical Level. The usability of educational material was rated positively (DSM 86%, DCC 76%, DIED 86% and OCCM 78%), especially the understandability of the educational material that the students rated highest compared to other factors (DSM 91%, DCC 80%, DIED 85% and OCCM 79%).

The efficiency of educational material was rated somehow differently from the different profiles, but show also a good overall appreciation. With a very high score for the DSM profile, where the majority of the student affirmed that the educational material and tools were a lot (55%) and moderately (45%) efficient, and lowest scores for the DIED profile where some learners felt that the efficiency of educational materials was somewhat efficient (10%) while others felt that it was not efficient at all (10%). Despite these differences, the access to the educational material was rated as a lot (DSM 55%, 48% DCC, 40% DIED and 50% OCCM) and moderately (DSM 45%, 48% DCC, 40% DIED and 33% OCCM) efficient by the majority of learners.

Based on this data we can affirm that the usability and efficiency were rated broadly positive, with no particular problems emerged, thanks to the fact that at the technical level many problems were solved at the end of the MOOC evaluation.

4   Conclusions and Future Works

To remain competitive in the cultural sector it is necessary to be constantly updated in terms of digital knowledge and skills, with a dynamic and open mindset. The Mu.SA project aimed to face this challenge offering a course that was able to attract people who work or want to work within the museum sector and who see the acquisition of digital skills and competences as an opportunity for their career development. The evaluation showed that the methodology, contents and tools developed are suitable to achieve the expected training objectives (learning outcomes), showing positive feedback from the learners who took part in the Blended Course experience. Furthermore, the critical issues emerged from the evaluation have contributed to the redesign and improvement of the future editions of the course.

In the next step of the project, there will be also the evaluation of Work-Based Learning. This will help to measure not only the training effectiveness of the project but also the impact within the host organizations, in order to establish if the Mu.SA project can be considered as a best practice for the evolution of museums and professionals in the sector and producing an impact in terms of digital transformation within museum realities.

Acknowledgement. This research was carried out within the Museum Sector Alliance – Mu.SA project (Project Number 575907-EEP-1-2016-1-EL-EPPKA2-SSA) under the Erasmus+ pro- gramme/Action KA2: Cooperation for innovation and the exchange of good practices – Sector Skills Alliances.

References

1. Mu.SA official website http://www.project-musa.eu. Accessed 01 June 2020
2. Silvaggi, A., Pesce, F.: Job profiles for museums in the digital era: research conducted in Portugal, Italy and Greece within the Mu.SA project. J. C. Manag. Policy **8**, 56–69 (2018)
3. Seufert, S., Meier, C.: From eLearning to digital transformation: a framework and implications for L&D. Int. J. Adv. Corp. Learn. (iJAC) **9**(2), 27–33 (2016)
4. Dibitonto, M., Leszczynska, K., Cruciani, E., Medaglia, C.M.: Bringing digital transformation into museums: the Mu.SA MOOC case study. In: Kurosu, M. (ed.) HCII 2020. LNCS, vol. 12183, pp. 231–242. Springer, Cham (2020). https://doi.org/10.1007/978-3-030-49065-2_17
5. Bautista, S.: Museums in the Digital Age: Changing Meanings of Place, Community, and Culture. AltaMira, Lanham (2014)
6. ArtS - skills for the creative economy official. http://arts-project.eu. Accessed 03 June 2020
7. ADESTE - Audience Developer: Skills and Training in Europe. http://www.adesteproject.eu. Accessed 03 June 2020
8. CREA.M. – Creative blended mentoring for cultural managers project. https://ec.europa.eu/programmes/erasmus-plus/projects/eplus-project-details/#project/518533-LLP-1-2011-1-IT-LEONARDO-LMP. Accessed 03 June 2020
9. Silvaggi, A., Pesce, F., Surace, R.: Musei del futuro. Competenze digitali per il cambiamento e l'innovazione in Italia (2017). http://www.project-musa.eu/wp-content/uploads/2017/03/Museum-of-the-future-Italy_eng.pdf

10. Sturabotti, D., Surace, R.: Museum of the future: insights and reflections from 10 international museums. Rome (2017). http://www.project-musa.eu/wp-content/uploads/2017/03/MuSA-Museum-of-the-future.pdf
11. Commission Staff Working Document Accompanying the document Proposal for a Council Recommendation on Key Competences for LifeLong Learning (2018). http://data.consilium.europa.eu/doc/document/ST-5464-2018-ADD-2/EN/pdf
12. Piano operativo della formazione [Training Operations Plan]. https://dger.beniculturali.it/formazione/piano-operativo-della-formazione. Accessed 04 June 2020
13. Hubackova, S., Semradova, I.: Evaluation of blended learning. Procedia-Soc. Behav. Sci. **217**, 551–557 (2016)
14. Gynther, K.: Design framework for an adaptive MOOC enhanced by blended learning: supplementary training and personalized learning for teacher professional development. Electron. J. e-Learn. **14**(1), 15–30 (2016)
15. Fahmy Yousef, A.M., Chatti, M.A., Schroeder, U., Wosnitza, M.: A usability evaluation of a blended MOOC environment: an experimental case study. Int. Rev. Res. Open Distance Learn. **16**(2), 69–93 (2015)
16. Grünewald, F., Meinel, C., Totschnig, M., Willems, C.: Designing MOOCs for the support of multiple learning styles. In: Hernández-Leo, D., Ley, T., Klamma, R., Harrer, A. (eds.) EC-TEL 2013. LNCS, vol. 8095, pp. 371–382. Springer, Heidelberg (2013). https://doi.org/10.1007/978-3-642-40814-4_29
17. Hollands, F.M., Tirthali, D.: MOOCs: expectations and reality. In: Center for Benefit-Cost Studies of Education, Teachers College, Columbia University, vol. 138 (2014)
18. Bruff, D.O., Fisher, D.H., McEwen, K.E., Smith, B.E.: Wrapping a MOOC: student perceptions of an experiment in blended learning. MERLOT J. Online Learn. Teach. **9**(2), 187–199 (2013)
19. Stein, J., Graham, C.R.: Essentials for Blended Learning: A Standards-Based Guide. Routledge, Abingdon (2020)
20. Dimou, H., Kameas, A.: Quality assurance model for digital adult education materials. Qual. Assur. Educ. **24**(4), 562–585 (2016)

Learning and Creativity Through a Curatorial Practice Using Virtual Reality

Sérgio Eliseu[1] , Maria Manuela Lopes[1,2] , João Pedro Ribeiro[3](✉) ,
and Fábio Oliveira[4]

[1] NIAM (Research Center in Arts and Multimedia), Douro Higher Institute of Educational
Sciences, Portugal and ID+ , Research Institute for Design, Media and Culture, Porto, Portugal
s.eliseu@ua.pt
[2] i3S, Instituto de Investigação e Inovação em Saúde, Porto, Portugal
maria.lopes@i3s.up.pt
[3] NIAM (Research Center in Arts and Multimedia), Douro Higher Institute of Educational
Sciences, Portugal and Faculty of Engineering, University of Porto, Porto, Portugal
up201601392@fba.up.pt
[4] NIAM (Research Center in Arts and Multimedia), Douro Higher Institute
of Educational Sciences, Porto, Portugal
fjroliveira@gmail.com

Abstract. This paper intends to reflect on a practical pedagogical research, in the
framing and communication of the presentations of creative works as a process of
teaching innovation. Challenges felt by the Department of Arts and Multimedia
of the Douro Higher Institute of Educational Sciences, in Portugal, triggered the
basic research. The curatorial practice has been increasingly framed in academia
and society as an integral method and strategy to produce knowledge, propelling
of creativity and socio-cultural and economic innovation. We question how this
value should be communicated within the context of multimedia teaching/learning,
which is more commonly rooted in a tradition centered on concepts and techniques. We claim that many presentations of artistic/multimedia outputs fail to
reveal the complexity of the teaching/learning activity that underpins them (e.g.
interdisciplinarity, collaborative practices, multimodal intellectual processes and
materials that drive creativity and innovation). This practice limits interpretation
and represses the opportunity to broaden the understanding of the knowledge generated. We intend to explore concepts of cooperation, innovation, curation, exhibition, audience, distance learning, that constitute the communication/exhibitions
of and in the academy.

We had to adapt to the pandemic scenario using a Virtual Reality approach, still
we concluded that there is an original contribution to pedagogical knowledge in the
delineation of a curatorial practice e-learning strategy; that in researching, framing
and communicating teaching/learning narratives offers a conceptualization of the
development of concepts in practice, shown as the continuous exploration of a
space of teaching and cooperation.

Keywords: eLearning · Pedagogical practice · Curatorial practice · Art · Virtual
reality

© Springer Nature Switzerland AG 2020
C. Stephanidis et al. (Eds.): HCII 2020, LNCS 12425, pp. 377–387, 2020.
https://doi.org/10.1007/978-3-030-60128-7_28

1 Introduction

This paper reflects on a practical research project carried out by members of NIAM (Nucleus for Research in Art and Multimedia) within the scope of their teaching practice in courses of Arts and Multimedia. The project results from the crossing of the contents of the courses taught and the e-learning methods/solutions defined with the situation created by the pandemic Covid-19.

At the end of each academic year, an exhibition (Beta) is held with the best works of students from all courses at the institute. This is an important event in the final assessment of students and symbolizes the graduation for many. Beta uses the Institute buildings as venue to shelter the curatorial exercise, which, being public, works has an institutional dissemination strategy. Given the impossibility of a public event taking place this year, students and teachers chose to hold the same event in a virtual reality environment. Photos, videos, performances, 3d models, etc. were prepared and introduced in a virtual representation of the institution. The entire curatorial process took place in an "avatar" of the institution. The paradigms of the interface usage between Humans and Computers and its interdisciplinary implied domains and also the need to shape the context changes as well as to adapt to it, made our journey during the past months an example of a successful learning/creative endeavor through distance learning.

Art needs an audience, so Beta, even in a virtual scenario, had to develop a strategy to go public. The students could have made an application that would support the event, but it would have to be installed on people's devices (audience) and it would be very complex to make it reach a large number of people within the time frame given. As a solution, it was decided to make an appropriation of a huge social network (over 50,000 users) that is designed for a community that communicates in virtual reality: VRChat.

VRChat is a free to play and develop online virtual reality social platform created by Graham Gaylor and Jesse Joudrey. It allows players to interact with others as 3D character models. It directly supports the Oculus Rift, Oculus Rift S and the Oculus Quest via the Oculus Store, the HTC Vive series, Windows Mixed Reality headsets and the Valve Index through SteamVR.

Although the game is named "VRChat", it is not necessary to have VR equipment to play the game. The game also offers a desktop version, for those who do not have VR headsets, with limitations, such as the inability to freely move an avatar's limbs. Desktop Mode users are restricted to a single hand for interaction but can make use of a windows10 compatible gamepad for further interaction. As most of the content in VR chat is user driven, making "accessible" content cross platform is up to the designer.

Questions of image, narrative memory and identity in the digital age permeate academic discourse and are the object of reflection around the production and presentation of the exhibition Beta2020_VR. The work plan emphasized these issues as a key strategy, providing students with a high level of autonomy working collaboratively through online cooperative production. Thus, the methodology adopted relates the theoretical and practical experiences through a project-based-learning method through the creation of a VR curatorial project-based through distance learning strategies.

The structure of this text is organized in five parts: (1) a brief presentation of the relationship between creative learning and its exposure in higher education; (2) some issues of cooperation and interdisciplinarity; (3) Some considerations on Gamified E-learning (4) Beta Vr development and exhibition and (5) final considerations.

2   Curatorial Practices and Exhibition as an Educational Tool

We want to propose a curatorial practice of building an exhibition as an educational tool, where communication and learning from a multimodal and social semiotic perspective are discussed. In this perspective, communication and learning are seen as social processes of building logos. Multimodality also involves meeting all the resources and modes of communication involved, and not just the linguistic aspects of the exhibition as a means of communication. We suggest that this approach can also contribute to a better understanding of the complexity of learning at exhibitions. A multimodal approach offers a perspective of communication and representation, or what allows to take into account various signs, messages, images and other modes that characterize an exhibition. In this research and article, we use a multimodal and social semiotic approach (Kress and van Leeuwen 2001; Kress et al. 2001). We assert that multimodality is linked to social semiotic theory, the central concepts of this perspective also derive from semiotics. For example, semiotic assumes that language and the cultural world can be read as signs. Kress and van Leeuwen define the following signaling mode: "A signal is a unit in which a shape has been combined with a meaning or, in other words, a shape chosen to be the bearer of meaning" (Kress and van Leeuwen 1996/2006: 4). In a social semiotic approach, a sign is never arbitrary, but motivated by the interest of its author. In that approach Lúcia Santaella (2002) questions whether a relationship between sign and object concerns the referential or non-sign capacity: "What sign does it refer to? What does it apply to? What does it denote? What does it represent?".

Multimodality emphasizes how the producer of a text is selected from several semiotic resources for better communication with the reader. Interest is directed towards interpretation and the way people engage with the resources of a context, in order to create meaning.

In the field of art, since the dematerialization period of the 1970s, great emphasis has been placed on the discursive capacity of the visual artist. Since the 1990s and the expansion of the artistic scene on a global scale, the development of a social network has become crucial. The emergence of artistic research in the 2000s and the new requirement that artists have a doctorate to work in a Higher Education institution, such as an art school or a college, announced a special movement for the institutionalization of art. In view of this multifaceted reality, Higher Education - despite its pedagogical goals and knowledge production not being formatted for the development of artistic practices - can foster, referring to its own practical and effective experience, the discussion about the creative class in the context post-industrial societies, or cognitive capitalism. Any creative process is based on previous references that, although they are too wide to be fully understood, it is crucial to be considered in order to develop someone's language in the long run. When audiences actively participate in receiving knowledge, they also become producers for themselves and their own communities.

As Wilson (2018, 3) reminds us "Visual and performing arts disciplines represent a distinct subject group from which to consider how university systems operate and the influence that they have upon discipline development." As artists and supporters of learning by experience, we select, organize and exhibit works of art and creative exercises as a way to teach, debate or facilitate communication and collaboration. We recognize the disconnect between institutional language and contemporary forms of knowledge production and consumption, we intend to expand beyond existing systems and imagine better ways to develop artistic education for the current era. The authors learnt by previous editions of the BETA exhibition that the experience created flexible environments where participants were free to give credibility to their subjective experiences, focusing on their participation and responses, instead of delivering an apparently objective narrative to passive observers.

3 Cooperation and Interdisciplinarity in Academia

Our curatorial practice in the academy tries to be interdisciplinary, counting on the variety of knowledge brought by the eclecticism of the basic training of the professors of the Department of Arts and Multimedia and the variety of knowledge anchored in the different curricular units involved. Interdisciplinary collaboration within the academy has the potential to promote dialogue, explore issues, expand perceptions and unveil new meanings for teachers, staff and students. In the case of ISCE Douro core academics come from distinct areas such as design, fine arts, art history, architecture, anthropology, archeology, marketing, engineering, and languages. Thus, we envision that we have built heritage from/for the institution itself, in a repository of visual evidence, dedicated to cultural knowledge and artistic, with access to vast intellectual and academic resources. The program of exhibitions and participation in research and community outreach experiences, which involves many disciplines, transcends traditional ideologies and becomes a catalyst for collaboration. We (Lopes et al. 2019) found that there is no better partnership for interdisciplinary collaboration, built on this premise, than between the exhibition/art project of the academy and the institute of Higher Education. Collaboration between faculty and students from different academic backgrounds, specialized knowledge and general knowledge, contributes to continuous dialogue and, as such, dialogue and interpretation have the potential to increase the contextual research carried out in exhibitions and programs. As an alternative to the specific territoriality of the discipline, the interdisciplinary collaboration process connects and integrates traditional academic disciplines to address issues or ideas more broadly.

Students are included in a hands-on learning by project manner, or team game play of that transcends the boundaries of one course into an institutional practice, once, according to Prior (2018, 148), "the learning that takes place in a social arts context, the day-to-day learning of everyday life, can serve as a model for arts research inside the academy through the process of being and doing that making together involves".

Collaboration with several academic disciplines reaffirms the traditional expectations of curatorial practice (gallery, museum, other) - research and intellectual challenge. Higher education exhibitions are, in essence, a classroom in itself and also an extension of the academic experience as a whole. This is essential for interdisciplinary collaboration between the university exhibition space and the academics of the faculty. The purpose of interdisciplinary exhibitions, therefore, is not to illustrate via image and caption, as an educational book, or to convey the viewer a specific message, but to expand the knowledge and understanding of the art and ideas that are the basis of the communal work.

Since its origin, academies have gathered objects and incorporated them into research and teaching. Many large Higher Education institutions have their museums, often separated by colleges. All provide tools for interdisciplinary collaboration that deals with issues, theories and ideas, often confined to specific course curricula. Although collaboration within the academy takes different forms - depending on the purpose of the collaborative project - common goals, coordinated effort, shared responsibility and credit are fundamental to success. The end-of-year exhibition, as a repository of tangible evidence of existence and academic background, has the potential to initiate interdisciplinary collaboration. An interdisciplinary approach promotes the application of knowledge acquired in other areas to new situations, creating new knowledge. Within this interdisciplinary approach, the assumptions related to academic disciplines, such as art history, are reconsidered; in this way, greater coherence and connections are fostered. But collaboration brings with it, skepticism, vulnerability and an alleged threat to disciplinarily. Within interdisciplinary collaboration, departments and fields must be brought together as an uncontroversial whole. To this end, concepts and debates from a series of academic disciplines are analyzed and brought up in the preparation of the exhibition, with the students being involved in the discussion.

Collaboration, whether interdisciplinary, multidisciplinary, or transdisciplinary, offers an opportunity to echo, challenge, expand, elaborate or facilitate new personal, social and historical dimensions in audience members. Collaboration must be considered an integral component of critical thinking. Intrinsic to this concept is the educational and intellectual wealth resulting from collaboration. The exhibition can be compared to a library or laboratory, and it is proposed that the exhibition offers a unique environment to develop critical thinking skills through observation, description, analysis and research of art and artifacts. The curatorial practice of higher education can then affirm its role of educational experience through exhibitions and programs achieved through interdisciplinary collaboration and designed to support and complement the academic curriculum. The collaboration between curatorial practices in higher education and different disciplines results in an opening between fields of specialization, not breaking disciplinary boundaries, but rather building mutual respect.

According to O'Neil (2007) it is through the exhibition (of the academy, museums, festivals, etc.) that contemporary creative practice is mediated, its created history is experienced. Therefore (Lopes and Lopes 2018) the practice of conceiving and creating the exhibition must be approached as a pedagogical tool for teaching creativity. Best practices in exhibition education include diversity of perspective and excellence in content and methodology, recognizing a variety of interpretive perspectives - cultural, scientific, historical and aesthetic - which can promote greater understanding and commitment.

While traditional museums attach importance to the tasks of investigating, registering and interpreting the world, academies focus on discovering or creating knowledge and passing it on from one generation to the next. Higher education is a central part of the formal education system, while cultural institutions play a leading role in informal learning. Currently Buchan (2007) claims that, essentially with the introduction of new media, curatorial practices take place in non-traditional locations, which facilitates the democratization of access and non-formal education processes. Curatorial practice in/of higher education, through its affiliation with the educational institution itself, it is responsible for formal and informal experiences (and for education), which are created to meet the needs of its primary audience - students who are goal-oriented and want to learn a useful body of knowledge. Higher education art groups reach a wide audience, including teachers, students, staff, families and local communities, however, due to the nature of the events we have created (small exhibitions at the end of the first semester and larger ones at the end of the second semester), visits exhibits are infrequent, short-lived and/or supplementary to the classroom curriculum. The investigation and exploration of ideas and questions presented in the traditional classroom, while challenging and involving students through interdisciplinary emphasis and the use of tangible objects, all combined to significantly expand the context. The exhibition and its memory must be accessible and useful as a classroom, as a source of research and as a place where academic disciplines come together in a visible context, as "most learning in most settings is a communal activity, a sharing of the culture" (Bruner 1986, 127).

The collaboration of all teachers and students in the department has allowed to reach new audiences; update and expand perspectives; allow new understandings and meanings to develop; conceive new ways of operating; accomplish what cannot be done alone; and providing benefits (soft skills) to participating individuals as

The concept of interdisciplinarity still derives from borrowing tools, methods, techniques, information, concepts and theories from one discipline to another. Interdisciplinarity expands the parameters of complex issues or topics that concern one or more disciplines, bringing together insights, knowledge and methodology. According to McArthur (2010) the culturally adaptive pedagogy of the interdisciplinary exhibition creates collaborative platforms and spaces where students, educators and institutions can begin to envision varied creative solutions to the challenges of society through open inclusive methodologies.

4   Gamified E-Learning

4.1   The Model

The application of a gamified pedagogy can act as a facilitator of student engagement during e-learning processes. Since the learning environment had to be drastically changed as a result of the COVID-19 pandemic, within the institute, we promoted the progressive integration of learning initiatives with video game-like tasks. The goal of this initiative was not only to incite healthy competition among students but also to make the goals of all classes and evaluations available to all students, regardless of their participation in synchronous classes. Each weak, goals were set in class and then published on the digital e-learning platform. Part of the challenge and enjoyment offered by this gamified e-learning environment came from the on-going qualitative rating of students' results, both in classes and in the platform itself. The best works were given a spotlight in a small section at the end of each class dedicated to keeping track of student's progression within the "game". While we acknowledge that this is a relatively small application of gamification to the e-learning process, an argument can be made that more significant forms of application of videogame-derived interaction processes to e-learning can be detrimental to players' enjoyment. Lower enjoyment can lead to lower learning efficiency, which goes against set pedagogical standards. The goal of the gamification of the e-learning process is to allow students to achieve established learning objectives through a process from which they can derive more satisfaction. However, individuals in the age group of our students (teenagers and young adults) typically do not keep active engagement and participation in serious games.

The existing body of literature on the application of gamification in learning essentially informs us that there are various elements which define our society and the ways through which we learn. The social context in which our students integrate is what authors frequently describe as a networked social context (Castells 2010) – they use information and communication technologies for interaction – as well as a play social context – their community is defined by their use of the play element (Huizinga 1949).

Hence, we believe that it is essential to teach while taking into consideration, and implementing, gaming and simulation in the network. The GOMS epistemology is an advanced human data processor system for the cognitive skills related to human-computer tasks (Jacko 2012). Although GOMS is a valuable theory of learning, particularly in the context of networking and gaming, it is a cognitivist theory and authors believe that other approaches can also be appropriate for examining skill learning through digital games (Ertmer and Newby 2013).

Gamified learning is useful in helping people not only acquiring and interpreting the contents of the curriculum but also in allowing them to research their social context. Students can play and experience the creative process behind the creation of interactive digital artefacts by themselves. They also work together to create virtual environments while interacting in virtual environments themselves. We argue that this method of learning and creating can offer absorbing escapades, where our students are individualized in their creations. This offers them social learning experiences (Chassiakos et al. 2016).

To this end, we describe the methods used in our institute, which resulted in positive results in students' works. Specifically, we will illustrate the process used from the deployment of the VRChat work propositions, until their conclusion and exposition at Beta, under the gamified e-learning paradigm. The process is exemplified in Fig. 1.

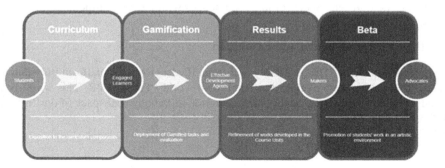

Fig. 1. A model for the application of gamified e-learning in the development of VRChat interactions and performances.

As observed in the figure above, the model consists of four interrelated phases, in which students:

1. Get in contact with the information and skills which must be acquired in a course unit during the semester. This includes the learning requirements or goals to be met; the classes and exercises to be completed, the tasks and projects they need to deliver; texts, manuals, images, presentations and seminars included in a course unit; and the evaluations, reviews, and other tools used to measure their learning. They also get assistance in discovering how to interact with the e-learning platform. With this, they become engaged learners.
2. Are met with a video game-like apprenticeship model—we provide them with guidelines, stages, and incentives. To reach a certain point, students must comply with the guidelines, and they are praised for their endeavors. This method ensures that students will see game-like features integrated into their lessons. They can activate the next stage of their work after they have finished their assignments or compete with other students. As a result of the engagement, they become effective development agents of VRChat environments and performances.
3. Put in practice the strategic development of applications suggested by the lecturers of various course units, which in this case results on the refinement and implementation of public environments in VRChat. They study existing processes for establishing targets, tracking progress and recording results, in order to guarantee public adherence to their works. The concept of performance covers a long-set industry-standard of both the accomplishment of goals as well as the effective attainment of these targets, as suggested in the literature (Poate 1997: i). At this stage, students have the grounded knowledge to be deemed decent novice makers and artists.
4. Participate in the Beta exposition, which is a space in which different types of works and work methods receive significant attention from institutions, media, and public from within and without ISCE Douro. Students' innovation and flexibility are demonstrated here, and it marks the end of the "game". Participation in Beta signals their maturity as artists and the start of the dissemination of their work. This year, because of the established conditions, Internet dissemination is a significant factor. The core of the expo is incentivizing independence for our students, now cultural producers, to reach smaller or larger audiences with the help of the institution.

4.2   Beta VR Development and Exhibition

Using VRChat Unity SDK and Unity real-time 3D development platform our students were able to create Beta exhibition in their own world - the BetaVR. This world is an actual tridimensional virtual reality representation of the physical space of our Institute in Penafiel (Fig. 2).

Fig. 2. BETAVR tridimensional environment.

The 3d model was modeled and textured in Blender. It consists in a two-floor building with all its classrooms and assets. On it, interactivity was added using Unity VRChat sdk and scripts. Students developed the UI with real time guidance from teachers using the cloud collaborate option.

The artworks that were inserted consisted mainly in 3d models, pictures and videos, all developed under the scope of several art and multimedia classes.

Regarding the real-life exhibition, the main limitation that was found was the impossibility of sharing interactive artworks that used specific hardware/software, ex. processing, Arduinos, and ironically... VR. For that kind of works, the option was to make videos explaining how they were presented and worked in real life.

Due to user's policy from VRChat, developers need to obtain several levels in a trust rank before being able to upload worlds to the platform. They can get this by just spending a lot of hours in VRChat, hop some worlds, and make some friends. By that reason, and to get all the interaction knowledge, some real classes were even lectured in the VRChat environment using avatars of teachers and students.

We can also find portals to other artworks worlds. Those worlds correspond to individual projects made by students under the scope of performance classes and offer other kind of experiences out of the institute physical appearance (Fig. 3).

Fig. 3. Selfie with students in VRChat environment.

5 Final Considerations

The prominent conclusion of the experiences carried out at ISCE Douro is an interdisciplinary and instigating cooperation trough curatorial practice, in higher education, that through the use of a gamified pedagogy and the development of a VR project promotes rapid innovation moments, an exhibition and a cultural program relevant to the whole community. This opportunity is extended to the integration of the exhibitions in the institutional mission of higher education, as a strategic direction that becomes essential for the teaching of a whole. This requires, as an entire aspect of our mission, to think continuously and creatively about how to exhibit in relation to other academic programs and the learning process itself through the praxis and how to learn through teaching.

The effort to expand audiences and create expanded dialogues at exhibitions is difficult but rewarding work, which is best addressed through team collaboration that creates an environment for something to happen, makes the process transparent and integrated or tangible and intangible; for example, gathering knowledge and objects associated with forms that work together. The goal is synergy, realizing an opportunity that neither partner could achieve without the help of another. From the moment it was conceived, collaboration needs the right partners, with the right interests and skills, and a willingness to work at the same level. Communication and negotiation are necessary constantly, with the measure of interdisciplinary collaboration, with the traditional modes of investigation and teaching, and show everyone involved in areas of comfort. Collaboration requires respect, responsibility, and trust on the part of all involved. To collaborate it is necessary to negotiate and agree on a mutual mission.

Through the exhibitions and through the evidence inherent to art, addressed through interdisciplinary collaboration, university curatorial practice becomes ideally located to facilitate the discourse that covers the artistic, creative, historical, scientific, social and technological complexities of our time. This is a structure to reconceptualize the exhibition as a broader place for research and thought, in which it affirms its relevance and educational role within the institution. Challenging shared interests and values, negotiating and respecting epistemology and, collaborating across disciplines, the higher education art exhibition and festival transcends traditional academic boundaries to increase critical thinking and the integration of knowledge, the main efforts of the 21st century academy.

We suggest that, through the production of cultural events such as exhibitions and festivals, institutions create platforms for individuals to transform conversations into performances, being part of a collective learning process, and representing a moment of change. We conclude that the exhibition is not learning in itself (as an object). It is the container and the external manifestation of a larger process. The exhibition operates as a moment in time and its success is not the result of a linear project, but of systemic thinking and multiple human computer interaction challenges. When evaluating learning through the experience of the exhibition, we found that only the evaluation of the moment or event (result object) of the exhibition is not an authentic measure. Therefore, the method for evaluating curatorial practices as a pedagogical enhancer needs to be able to facilitate and identify learning in the process, (in this case aided by the strategy of gamification and the use of Blender, Unity and VR Chat for joint work to build the space itself, circuit, and adaptation of individual works) and not just the evaluation of a final result.

References

Bruner, J.: Actual Minds, Possible Worlds. Harvard University Press, Cambridge (1986)

Buchan, S.: Oscillating at the 'High/Low' art divide: curating and exhibiting animation. In: Rugg, J., Sedgwick, M. (eds.) Issues in Curating Contemporary Art and Performance, pp. 131–146. Intellect Books, Bristol (2007)

Castells, M.: The Rise of the Network Society, vol. I, 2nd edn. Wiley, Hoboken (2010)

Chassiakos, Y.R., et al.: Children and adolescents and digital media. Pediatrics **138**(5), e20162593 (2016)

Ertmer, P.A., Newby, T.J.: Behaviorism, cognitivism, constructivism: comparing critical features from an instructional design perspective. Performance Improv. Q. **26**(2), 43–71 (2013). https://doi.org/10.1002/piq.21143

Huizinga, J.: Homo Ludens: A Study of the Play-Element in Culture. Routledge & Kegan Paul, Abingdon (1949)

Jacko, J.A.: Human-Computer Interaction Handbook: Fundamentals, Evolving Technologies, and Emerging Applications. CRC Press, Boca Raton (2012)

Poate, D.: Joint Evaluation 1997:2. measuring and managing results: lessons for development cooperation performance management. Sida (1997)

Kress, G., van Leeuwen, T.: Reading Images: The grammar of Visual Design. Routledge, London and New York (2006). 1996

Kress, G., van Leeuwen, T.: Multimodal Discourse: The Modes and Media of Contemporary Communication. Arnold, London (2001)

Kress, G., Jewitt, C., Ogborn, J., Tsatsarelis, C.: Multimodal Teaching and Learning: The Rhetorics of the Science Classroom. Consinuum, London (2001)

Lopes, M.M, Reis, G., Eliseu, S.: Práticas curatoriais no ensino superior como estratégia pedagógica de ensino e inovação. In: 4th International Conference on Teacher Education (INCTE), pp. 1139–1149 (2019)

Lopes. M.M., Lopes, C.: Práticas Curatoriais no Ensino Superior como Estratégia de Ensino e Inovação. In: FIACED II Forum Internacional África Cooperação, Educação e Desenvolvimento (2018)

McArthur. P. Creating adaptive pedagogy. In: Cumulus Creative Thinking Conference Proceedings, pp. 69–79 (2010)

O'Neill, P.: The curatorial turn: from practice to discourse. In: Rugg, J., Sedgwick, M. (eds.) Issues in Curating Contemporary Art and Performance, pp. 13–28. Intellect Books, Bristol (2007)

Prior, R.W. (ed.): Using Art as Research in Learning and Teaching Multidisciplinary Approaches Across the Arts. Intellect. The University of Chicago Press, Chicago (2018)

Santaella, L.: Semiótica aplicada. Thomson, São Paulo (2002)

Wilson, J.: Artists in the University, Positioning Artistic Research in Higher Education. Springer, Singapore (2018). https://doi.org/10.1007/978-981-10-5774-8

How Augmented Reality Influences Student Workload in Engineering Education

Wenbin Guo[✉] and Jung Hyup Kim

Department of Industrial and Manufacturing Systems Engineering, University of Missouri, Columbia, USA
wgk95@mail.missouri.edu, kijung@missouri.edu

Abstract. The primary objective of this study is to explore how augmented reality (AR) influences the student workload in engineering education. To investigate the impact of augmented reality on student workload, we used Microsoft HoloLens and developed AR modules for manual material handling (MMH) as engineering education learning contents. In this study, we conducted a between-subject study with forty-five students (AR vs. in-class environment). Their workload was measured by using NASA-TLX. The results showed that there was no overall workload difference between the AR and in-class environment. However, there were significant differences in mental, performance, effort, and frustration dimensions between AR and in-class conditions. The findings from this study could advance our understanding related to the correlations between the workload and the AR learning environment.

Keywords: Augmented reality · Workload · Engineering education

1 Introduction

Augmented reality (AR) is one of the advanced technologies as a powerful medium that has become a continuous trend in engineering education [1]. The previous literature had reported the various features of AR in the aspect of advantages and effectiveness in different learning domains [2, 3]. Recently, the AR platform has been used to provide real-time digital information to enhance student learning [4]. More and more researchers initiate to create effective educational or training platforms using augmented reality.

In the AR environments, students not only learned new knowledge from learning materials but also could perform hands-on exercises. These AR environments emphasize learners' participation and enhance their sense of presence, immediacy, and immersion. These learning experiences can help them develop new forms of learning behavior and cognitive engagement [5].

In this study, the learning content of manual material handling (MMH) was used to develop AR modules for the experiment. Although the concept of MMH is not difficult to understand, many students often make mistakes when they measure the Distance Multiplier (DM) and Asymmetric Multiplier (AM) during the practice sessions. One possible reason for the mistake could be the ineffectiveness of space perception in the

© Springer Nature Switzerland AG 2020
C. Stephanidis et al. (Eds.): HCII 2020, LNCS 12425, pp. 388–396, 2020.
https://doi.org/10.1007/978-3-030-60128-7_29

traditional MMH content. Therefore, a new AR learning environment can provide a better way to overcome the weakness of the traditional MMH content. However, this new learning environment may increase a student's mental workload. The previous studies indicated that the students who learned in an AR environment performed better than non-AR experienced learners. However, they were cognitively overloaded by a large amount of visual information and high complexity in the AR environment [5–7]. Dunleavy and Dede [8] reported that students often felt overwhelmed and confused by an AR simulation because learners had to deal with the virtual environment, which is unfamiliar to many students. Hence, we come up with the following hypothesis.

Hypothesis: Augmented reality has an effect on students' workload in engineering education.

By measuring the workload differences between the AR environment and the in-class environment, the results can deepen our understanding related to the correlation between the AR environment and the student perceived workload. Previous studies [9–11] have used the NASA-Task Load Index (TLX) as a tool to assess perceived workload during a given task. For that reason, we also used the NASA-TLX questionnaire to measure the student workload level in the AR environment, and it was compared to the students who learned the same content in the in-class environment.

2 Prior Literature

Different from virtual reality (VR), augmented reality (AR) does not replace the real world but augments a user's view of the real world with virtual objects [12]. AR has lots of potential benefits in engineering education. First, AR technology motivates students to explore class knowledge from various angles in order to help them create a sense of space [13]. Second, AR can help cultivate student's creativity and imagination [14]. Finally, this technology allows students to control their learning process through the AR device [15, 16].

Although visual applications can be easily used for AR in various fields, engineering education is one of the most beneficial application fields compared to other areas. AR can be exploited for engineering educational purposes positively as follows: (1) Students can learn engineering contents in 3D perspectives and visualize the invisible parts. (2) Students can have collaborative and situated model learning experience [5]. Moreover, AR decreases the real environment students risk as well as the experimental cost because of application reliability. Our study will use Microsoft HoloLens to create a relatively effective and advanced AR environment to explore and evaluate its performance in engineering education. However, the way to assess student workload still needs to be explored in an AR environment.

There are three multidimensional subjective workload assessment tools: Subjective Workload Assessment Technique (SWAT), Workload Profile (WP), and NASA Task Load Index (TLX) [17]. The NASA TLX contains two parts: ratings and weights. Ratings for each of the six dimensions are from the experience of the subjects. The numeric range of each dimension is from 1 to 100 (low to high). Weights represent the more important contributor to workload for the tasks in a pair of choices. The weights have

15 combinatorial pairs from six dimensions, and the weight range is from 0 to 5 (not relevant to most relevant). An overall workload score is a weighted average for ratings and weights [18]. Therefore, this research will also use the NASA-TLX approach to explore student workload in an AR learning environment.

3 Method

3.1 Apparatus

Microsoft HoloLens (see Fig. 1) is a teaching headset based on the Windows 10 operating system [19]. This device mixes the real and virtual worlds and projects holograms to human eyes. Students wear this device and walk around to observe holograms to perceive virtual objects better. Students can gaze the virtual objects they are observing, and then use gestures to interact with these objects for easier observation. HoloLens is an independent mobile computer and has a prominent performance to present an augmented reality environment, which makes participants feel free to move in the experiment area.

Fig. 1. Microsoft HoloLens

3.2 Participants

Subjects were forty-five university students with an average age of 21.2 years (StDev = 1.70, age range from 20 to 31). The participants were all from the University of Missouri, consisting of forty male students and five female students. Before the experiment, the students would be asked about their level of video game experience and AR experience. The level of playing computer video games might influence a student's learning speed. The previous AR level also might speed up the orientation of the AR device. Participants' average video game level was 3.28/5 (StDev = 1.07) and their average AR experience level was 1.5/5 (StDev = 0.87).

The experiment was conducted in two different learning environments. 32 students participated in the AR group. Figure 1 shows that they experienced the MMH module in HoloLens. On the other hand, 13 participants were in the in-class control group. They learned the MMH materials under the guidance of the instructors and engaged in in-class activities without AR devices. After finishing learning, both groups answered NASA-TLX workload questionnaires.

3.3 Learning Contents

In this experiment, AR modules for MMH contents was developed in the HoloLens device, which can help students improve their knowledge with this device. Traditionally, it is hard to train them to apply the MMH knowledge they learned in class to solve practical MMH problems.

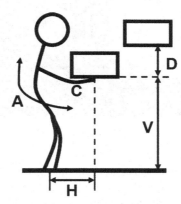

Fig. 2. Each variable in the revised NIOSH lifting equation

In general, students experienced difficulties on AM and DM. AM is the twist degree the body turns in the lifting task as shown in Fig. 2. Specifically, the body is free to switch position as forward/backward, up/down, and left/right. DM is the vertical movement distance of the object. During the practice session, students often miscalculate the angles in different positions and write inaccurate vertical location (V) at the end of the lift.

3.4 Design of Experiment

The experiment was conducted in two different learning environments. For the AR experimental group: participants experienced the MMH module in HoloLens. After the learning completion, the participants answered NASA-TLX workload questionnaires. At last, the participants took a test about MMH contents, which verified their learning performance in each multiplier (HM, VM, DM, AM, CM, and FM). For the in-class control group, the instructor presented the MMH learning material, and the students participated in the class activities.

Figure 3 shows an MMH scene in the AR environment [20]. Job analysis worksheet is the observation form for students to record the values of each parameter. The learning procedure shows steps to complete each module. The human animation is the main hologram with lifting action. Two arrows in front of the human are used to move to the previous or next module. Contents blackboard displays MMH contents, containing the definition of MMH and how to calculate each multiplier. Each module will be presented with visual and audio to help students to follow the learning procedures.

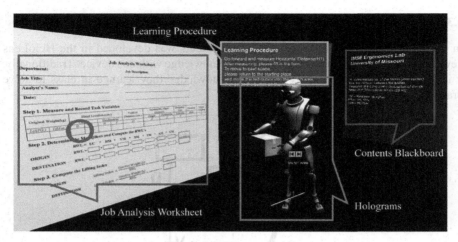

Fig. 3. MMH scene in AR

Figure 4 displays the learning and practice module in the AR environment. Each scene presents each multiplier to let students measure and understand clearly about MMH in a three-dimensional space. There was a total of nine scenes as shown in Fig. 4. The first scene presented the horizontal multiplier, the second scene was the virtual multiplier, the third scene showed the asymmetric multiplier, which students felt difficult to observe in the two-dimensional space. The fourth scene was the coupling multiplier, depending on handle design. The fifth scene was the frequency multiplier based on lift frequency. The sixth scene was the answers to the previous multipliers' measurement and calculation. The Seventh and eighth scenes were the practices letting students observe and measure

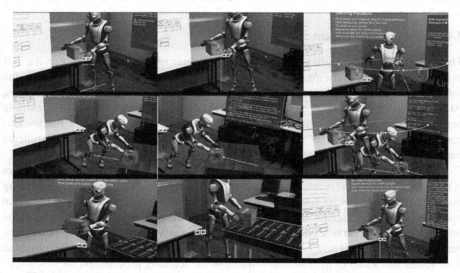

Fig. 4. Manual material handling education simulation for each multiplier (9 Scenes)

each multiplier based on their learning. Students can move close to observe and measure angels and distances in different ways. Then the last scene was the answer to the practice scenes' questions based on students' hands-on experience.

4 Results

Workload differences caused by different learning environments (AR group vs. In-class group) were analyzed using ANOVA. Table 1 shows the details of the overall workload and each dimension. Taking into account the overall workload score, one-way ANOVA $(F (1,44) = 3.98, p = 0.052)$ shows that no significant difference in students' overall workload between AR environment (Mean $= 61.04$, StDev $= 9.46$) and in-class environment (Mean $= 54.95$, StDev $= 8.84$).

Table 1. Descriptive statistics for workload between different environment

Variable	AR (n = 32)		In-class (n = 13)		F	P
	Mean	StDev	Mean	StDev		
NASA-TLX	61.14	9.46	54.95	8.84	1.95	0.052
Mental	**62.66***	11.81	**49.62***	15.34	**3.81**	**0.010**
Physical	33.03	22.87	25.23	22.46	1.09	0.303
Temporal	37.56	22.47	50.00	18.26	3.13	0.084
Performance	**58.13***	22.67	**74.62***	15.61	**3.05**	**0.021**
Effort	**65.63****	11.20	**52.31****	12.35	**6.76**	**0.001**
Frustration	**55.28***	25.61	**36.92***	22.13	**3.70**	**0.012**

(*p < 0.05, **p < 0.001)

Figure 5 shows interval plot of NASA-TLX each dimension workload in different learning environments (AR vs in-class). The students' mental workload was significantly higher $[F (1,44) = 3.81, p = 0.01]$ in the AR environment (Mean $= 62.66$, StDev $= 11.81$) than in-class environment (Mean $= 49.62$, StDev $= 15.34$). There was no significant difference in physical dimension $[F (1,44) = 1.09, p = 0.303]$ and temporal dimension $[F (1,44) = 3.13, p = 0.084]$. The students' performance dimension was lower $(F (1,44) = 3.05, p = 0.021)$ in the AR environment (Mean $= 58.13$, StDev $= 22.67$) than in-class environment (Mean $= 74.62$, StDev $= 15.61$). The participants' effort dimension was higher $[F (1,44) = 6.76, p = 0.001]$ in the AR environment (Mean $= 65.63$, StDev $= 11.20$) than in-class environment (Mean $= 52.31$, StDev $= 12.35$). At last, the students perceived higher frustration $[F (1,44) = 3.70, p = 0.012]$ in the AR environment (Mean $= 55.28$, StDev $= 25.61$) than in-class environment (Mean $= 36.92$, StDev $= 22.13$).

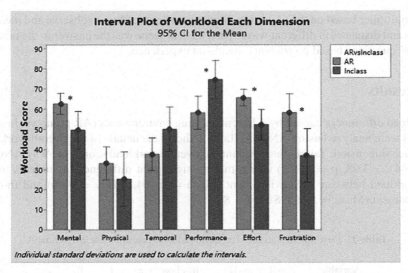

Fig. 5. Workload comparison in each dimension between AR and in-class environment

5   Discussion and Conclusion

In this study, the MMH AR module allowed students to perceive three-dimensional virtual space with physical objects and virtual objects together. During the learning AR modules, students could watch human animation and its continuous movements in three-dimensional space. They were able to measure the distances and angles of each MMH multiplier by using a ruler and goniometer. According to the results, it shows that our hypothesis (augmented reality has an impact on students' workload) was rejected. There was no overall workload difference between the AR and in-class environments. However, when we compared six dimensions, the mental demand, performance, effort and frustration were significantly different between the AR and in-class conditions.

Regarding the mental demand, the students who learned in the AR environment had a higher mental demand compared to the students who were in a control group. It means that there is a significant difference in the cognitive requirement between the physical and virtual world to process visual stimuli in learning. During the experiment, we used the HoloLens AR device to teach students MMH. Due to the additional visual stimulus from the AR device, students must consume more cognitive resources for thinking, calculating, and searching. For that reason, students spent a longer time observing, searching and measuring the distances or angles for DM and AM when there were in the AR environment.

For the performance dimension, the AR environment caused a lower performance dimension than the in-class environment. The students in the AR environment were not satisfied with their performance in completing their achievements compared with the students in the in-class environment. Although some students failed to measure the distances or angles in the three-dimensional space, they perceived better spatial recognition in the AR environment than in the in-class environment.

For the effort dimension, augmented reality resulted in a higher effort dimension than the in-class environment. In aspects of the hands-on exercise, the students put more effort into getting better results. Based on our observation, the students in the AR environment endeavored to be familiar with three-dimensional space as well as the movements of the human animation. This result is different from the previous finding [21].

For the frustration dimension, the AR environment produced a higher frustration level than the in-class environment. The previous research also mentioned that the learners felt frustrated in the AR environment [21, 22]. In our study, the students were also stressed when they used the AR device because of their lack of experience with the AR environment. Two-third of participants never experience the AR environment before. Hence, students did not know how to navigate 3D objects to understand the learning contents, which led them to feel frustrated.

We also found that there was no significant difference in the physical and temporal demands. Students in the AR environment could follow their own pace to learn the MMH content with minimum additional physical demand.

In conclusion, this study compared the student perceived workload between the AR environment and in-class environment. Overall, the student perceived workload was not increased in the AR environment, but some of the dimensions were significantly increased compared to the in-class setting. The findings from the current study will be able to contribute to developing a new guideline on how to create more effective AR learning content without increasing the learner's workload.

6   Limitation and Future Work

One of the limitations of this study is that how students made their decisions to direct their performance was not investigated. Also, different AR competence level (Novice/Expert) needs to be considered in the future study. Finally, another limitation is we only had a limited sample size with a college student group. It would be better to test different age groups with a bigger sample size to generalize our findings.

References

1. Schiffeler, N., Stehling, V., Haberstroh, M., Isenhardt, I.: Collaborative augmented reality in engineering education. In: Auer, M.E., Ram B., K. (eds.) REV2019 2019. LNNS, vol. 80, pp. 719–732. Springer, Cham (2020). https://doi.org/10.1007/978-3-030-23162-0_65
2. Bacca, J., et al.: Augmented reality trends in education: a systematic review of research and applications. J. Educ. Technol. Soc. 17(4), 133 (2014)
3. Burke, E., et al.: Augmented reality EVAR training in mixed reality educational space. In: 2017 IEEE Global Engineering Education Conference (EDUCON). IEEE (2017)
4. Walker, Z., et al.: Beyond pokémon: augmented reality is a universal design for learning tool. SAGE Open 7(4), 2158244017737815 (2017)
5. Wu, H.-K., et al.: Current status, opportunities and challenges of augmented reality in education. Comput. Educ. 62, 41–49 (2013)
6. Cheng, K.-H., Tsai, C.-C.: Affordances of augmented reality in science learning: suggestions for future research. J. Sci. Educ. Technol. 22(4), 449–462 (2013)

7. Akçayır, M., Akçayır, G.: Advantages and challenges associated with augmented reality for education: a systematic review of the literature. Educ. Res. Rev. **20**, 1–11 (2017)
8. Dunleavy, M., Dede, C., Mitchell, R.: Affordances and limitations of immersive participatory augmented reality simulations for teaching and learning. J. Sci. Educ. Technol. **18**(1), 7–22 (2009)
9. Hosseini, A., Lienkamp, M.: Enhancing telepresence during the teleoperation of road vehicles using HMD-based mixed reality. In: 2016 IEEE Intelligent Vehicles Symposium (IV). IEEE (2016)
10. Hou, L., et al.: Using animated augmented reality to cognitively guide assembly. J. Comput. Civil Eng. **27**(5), 439–451 (2013)
11. Shirazi, A., Behzadan, A.H.: Content delivery using augmented reality to enhance students' performance in a building design and assembly project. Adv. Eng. Educ. **4**(3), n3 (2015)
12. Hondori, H.M., et al.: A spatial augmented reality rehab system for post-stroke hand rehabilitation. In: MMVR (2013)
13. Kerawalla, L., et al.: "Making it real": exploring the potential of augmented reality for teaching primary school science. Virtual Reality **10**(3–4), 163–174 (2006)
14. Klopfer, E., Yoon, S.: Developing games and simulations for today and tomorrow's tech savvy youth. TechTrends **49**(3), 33–41 (2004). https://doi.org/10.1007/BF02763645
15. Hamilton, K., Olenewa, J.: Augmented reality in education [PowerPoint slides]. Lecture Notes Online Web site (2010). http://www.authorstream.com/Presentation/k3hamilton-478823-augmented-reality-in-education
16. Yuen, S.C.-Y., Yaoyuneyong, G., Johnson, E.: Augmented reality: an overview and five directions for AR in education. J. Educ. Technol. Dev. Exch. (JETDE) **4**(1), 11 (2011)
17. Rubio, S., et al.: Evaluation of subjective mental workload: a comparison of SWAT, NASA-TLX, and workload profile methods. Appl. Psychol. **53**(1), 61–86 (2004)
18. Cao, A., Chintamani, K.K., Pandya, A.K., Ellis, R.D.: NASA TLX: software for assessing subjective mental workload. Behav. Res. Methods **41**(1), 113–117 (2009). https://doi.org/10.3758/BRM.41.1.113
19. Tuliper, A.: Introduction to the HoloLens (2016). https://msdn.microsoft.com/en-us/magazine/mt788624.aspx
20. Guo, W.: Improving engineering education using augmented reality environment. In: Zaphiris, P., Ioannou, A. (eds.) LCT 2018. LNCS, vol. 10924, pp. 233–242. Springer, Cham (2018). https://doi.org/10.1007/978-3-319-91743-6_18
21. Xu, W., et al.: Pointing and selection methods for text entry in augmented reality head mounted displays. In: 2019 IEEE International Symposium on Mixed and Augmented Reality (ISMAR). IEEE (2019)
22. Ahsen, T., Dogar, F.R., Gardony, A.L.: Exploring the impact of network impairments on remote collaborative augmented reality applications. In: Extended Abstracts of the 2019 CHI Conference on Human Factors in Computing Systems (2019)

The Influential Factors on E-learning Adoption and Learning Continuance

Meryem Harzalla and Nizar Omheni[(✉)] [iD]

Institution of High Education (IHES),
Boukhzar University Campus, Bouhsina, 4000 Sousse, Tunisia
meryemharzallah@gmail.com, omheninizar@gmail.com

Abstract. The emergence of E-learning technology has revolutionized learning in the workplace which has put more emphasis on lifelong learning. Despite such technological revolution in education, adoption of learning technology remains poor, discontinued or mainly rejected by learners. That's interested researchers to study learner motivation and engagement in learning process. In this context, we study the effect of learner's satisfaction on their intention to pursue learning, considering the relationships between the motivational learning variable (perceived utility, perceived ease of use and acceptance of technology) and the perceived quality, and between perceived value and satisfaction. The present study aims to verify our hypothesizes and propositions through studding the intention to continue using e-learning courses by the employees of the Tunisian Post. The empirical results are fruitful, that may incite managers to adopt e-learning technology to meet the rising demand for the continuing education by their employees.

Keywords: E-learning technology · Learning continuance · Motivational learning variables

1 Introduction

In the digital era, characterized by technology spreading and the computing and communications revolution, learning process is changed from traditional boring classroom with whiteboard, desks, notebooks and pens to online learning enables us to study anywhere and at any time where there is no geographical gap between teachers and students.

The flexibility of E-learning technology enables educational institutions to offer learning opportunities for busy working professionals, who have many barriers (work schedule, geographic distance...) to meet traditional classroom courses, through bringing online courses straight to their offices.

In the perspective of lifelong learning, professionals should be current with the advancements in their fields to improve competencies and to maintain their professional licenses or certifications. E-learning technology is a great fit for

© Springer Nature Switzerland AG 2020
C. Stephanidis et al. (Eds.): HCII 2020, LNCS 12425, pp. 397–409, 2020.
https://doi.org/10.1007/978-3-030-60128-7_30

continuing learning because its' flexibility in time and place. To proceed to continuing learning, professionals need just to enroll to any online course in an e-learning system to feel as they are inside the classroom.

However, distance learning has been promoted to professional workers, the intention to continue following online learning courses is a real challenge for e-learning industry. The called "acceptance–discontinuance" phenomenon refers to learners discontinuing learning using e-learning technology after initially accepting it [6]. Acceptance of e-learning technologies is an important toward achieving learning success, but we still need continued intention to learn to guarantee actual success. Therefore, we need studying the factors influencing learners' intention to continue online learning, which may guide developers to design efficient e-learning technologies and helps instructors making strategies that are more likely to increase the use of e-learning systems.

In this paper, we try to answer two questions:

- To what extent the motivational learning variables (perceived usefulness, perceived ease of use and acceptance of technology) and the online learning mode may improve perceived quality and value?
- To what extent the motivational learning variables and e-learning mode may influence learner satisfaction and intention to continue learning?

The rest of this paper is organized as follows. First, the relevant theoretical perspectives, including e-learning definition and forms, perceived quality, the value perceived value, and the Technology Acceptance Model (TAM) are discussed. Next, we outline our research model and present our research hypotheses. This is followed by a description of the research method as well as the results of our data analysis. Finally, we conclude with a discussion focusing on the interpretation of the results as well as an examination of the theoretical and practical implications of the study.

2   Literature Review

2.1   E-learning Phenomenon

E-learning phenomenon consists on connecting people (students, teachers, content providers, institutions, professional associations and education boards), technologies, and services to fulfill educational objectives. With a laptop, tablet or phone and a Wi-Fi connection, it's possible to conduct learning and training activities anywhere and anytime. Many technologies are adopted to deliver online content in the e-learning sphere: video-based resources; games and gamification of learning; MOOCs; lecture recording; adaptive learning systems; dashboards; etc.

In the industrial context, employees should keep their skills and knowledge up-to-date to retain benefits for their organization (completing tasks quickly and efficiently, avoiding mistakes that can produce financial loss or organizational reputation damage, enhancing products and services...). E-learning has been blended successfully with the industrial context where learning and training can be conducted at anywhere and anytime, that can save operational costs including accommodation costs, travel and booking of physical classrooms that require all the employees to attend physically.

2.2 Acceptance–Discontinuance Phenomenon

It commonly occurs that certain learners decide to discontinue their previously adopted learning process. This is called the acceptance–discontinuance phenomenon which is the most critical challenge digital businesses face today [6]. The low user retention and high churn rates produced that many e-learning systems have been discontinued following their initial implementation [5]. According to [6], the acceptance-discontinuance phenomenon may be sensed at least five distinct forms: rejection, regressive discontinuance, quitting, temporary discontinuance, and replacement.

3 Research Model and Hypothesis

In this paper, we aim to study the effect of learner's satisfaction on their intention to pursue learning, considering the relationships between the motivational learning variable (perceived utility, perceived ease of use and acceptance of technology) and the perceived quality, and between perceived value and satisfaction.

We referred to the following models to conceptualize our proposed research model: The first model named "Customer Relationship Life Cycle model" in [11], "relationship chain" in the paper of [10]. The second model is the Technology Acceptance Model (TAM) [9]. Based on these models, we consider the following relations to define our conceptual research model:

- The first relation between the perceived utility and the perceived quality of the course.
- The second relationship between technology acceptance and perceived quality.

These two relationships will make it possible to determine the evaluation of the quality of the course by a learner.

- The third relationship studies the effect of quality on the perceived value of the course.
- The fourth relationship explains the effect of perceived value on learner satisfaction.
- The last relationship is that which determines the effect of learner satisfaction on the intention to continue use.

Based on these relations and the prior researches, we have the following propositions:

- P1: The perceived usefulness of the e-learning course has a positive influence on the perceived quality.

- P2: The acceptance of information and communication technology has a positive influence on the perceived quality.

Based on these propositions we formed the following hypothesizes:

- H1: Perceived quality influences positively the perceived value of the e-learning course.
- H2: The perceived value of an e-learning course has a positive influence on a learner's satisfaction with the course.
- H3: Satisfaction has a positive influence on the intention to continue using e-learning courses.

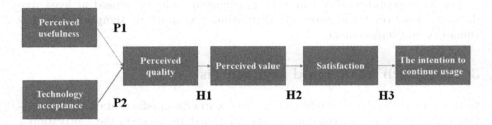

Fig. 1. The research model.

In the following, we present our conducted empirical study to verify these hypothesizes and the propositions cited previously.

4   Methodology

Given that we intend to study associations between variables that compose our hypotheses and the propositions mentioned previously, we conducted descriptive quantitative research. We empirically examined our research model using a survey method. We adopted validated measurements from certain works:

- 6 items to measure perceived utility inspired from [1]
- 4 items to measure technology acceptance inspired from [1]
- 6 items to measure perceived quality inspired from [2]
- 6 items to measure perceived value inspired from [2]
- 17 items to measure satisfaction inspired from [3]. The satisfaction is measured according to three criteria: the content, the system and the method of distribution.
- 3 items to measure the intention to continue usage inspired from [4]

All these measurement items are developed and measured with a seven-point Likert scale.

4.1   Data Collection

The participants in this study were employers of the Tunisian Post office. We choosen this office given that is one of the first companies in the country to adopt and use e-learning in its training programs (since 2002). The e-learning system used by the post is a platform (called WAHIB) with an easy to handle interface and attractive enough. The training courses are online, available in three languages (Arabic, French, and English) supervised by a tutor. There are about 1,800 learners who use the post's e-learning system scattered even in other African countries other than Tunisia following the partnership agreement with the Universal Postal Union.

The recruited participants (142 persons) are available during the period of study, all of them are users of the Tunisian Post's learning system. We asked them to answer the distributed survey. Throughout the questionnaire, the interviewee is assisted with a possible explanation of the difficult terms.

4.2   Results

Effect of an Online Course Perceived Usefulness on Their Perceived Quality. We study the linear regression between the perceived usefulness and the perceived quality of an online course. We report the correlation values in Table 1 and 2. The results showed a poor fit of the model. The coefficient of determination R^2 announces a rather low value of 0.07. The model is not significant since the Fisher test is equal to 0.342.

Table 1. Global significance test of the relationship between perceived usefulness and perceived quality.

Independant variable	Dependant variable	R^2	F	Sig. F
Perceived usefulness	Perceived quality	0.07	0.911	0.342

Table 2. Individual significance test of the relationship between perceived usefulness and perceived quality.

Independant variable	Dependant variable	ß	t	Sig. t
Perceived usefulness	Perceived quality	0,81	0,945	0,342

These statistical results lead to the conclusion that perceived utility does not affect perceived quality. The proposal P1 is therefore not validated.

Effect of Technology Acceptance on the Perceived Quality of an Online Course. The results of the linear regression show poor quality of the global model fit. The coefficient of determination R^2 displays a low value of 0,019. The model is globally insignificant: the Fisher test is 0.106 (<0.05) (Tables 3 and 4).

Table 3. Global significance test of the relationship between technology acceptance and perceived quality.

Independant variable	Dependant variable	R^2	F	Sig. F
Technology acceptance	Perceived quality	0,019	2,651	0,106

Table 4. Individual significance test of the relationship between technology acceptance and perceived quality.

Independant variable	Dependant variable	ß	t	Sig. t
Technology acceptance	Perceived quality	0,136	1,628	0,106

The technology acceptance has no effect on perceived quality since the value of t is 1.628. Based on these findings the proposal P3 is not validated.

Effect of Perceived Quality on Perceived Value of an Online Course. In our study, we considered two dimensions of perceived value (intrinsic and extrinsic values). In the following, we analyzed the impact of perceived quality on each dimension separately.

Our findings show an average quality of the global model fit. The coefficient of determination R^2 displays respectively two values 0,129 and 0,273. The model is globally significant since the Fisher test is equal to 0.000 and 0.001 ($p < 0.05$) (Table 5).

Table 5. Global significance test of the linear regression between perceived quality and perceived value.

Independant variable	Dependant variable	R^2	F	Sig. F
Perceived quality	Intrinsic value	0,273	11,272	0.001
Perceived quality	Extrinsic value	0,129	20,729	0.000

Based on our findings, perceived quality influences positively the perceived value since correlation values of all the studied variables are significantly lower than 0.05 (Table 6).

Table 6. Individual significance test of the relationship between technology acceptance and perceived quality.

Independant variable	Dependant variable	ß	t	Sig. t
Perceived quality	Intrinsic value	0,273	3,357	0.001
Perceived quality	Extrinsic value	0,359	4,553	0.000

These statistical results make it possible to conclude that the perceived quality acts positively on the perceived value. Therefore, we can validate the hypothesis H1. The following equation expresses perceived value based on perceived quality:

– extrinsic value = 0,359 ∗ quality perceived value
– intrinsic value = 0,273 ∗ quality perceived value

Perceived value = (0,359 + 0,273) ∗ quality perceived value.

Effect of Perceived Value on Satisfaction with Online Course. In the context of online learning, learner satisfaction is evaluated according to the content, the system and the method of distribution of a course. In our work, we study the effect of perceived value on these different forms of satisfaction.

Effect of Perceived Value on Satisfaction with Course Content. The multiple linear regression results show a poor model fit. The coefficient of determination R^2 displays a value of 0.027. The model is not significant since Fisher's test is 0.148 (Table 7).

Table 7. Global significance test between perceived value and satisfaction with course content.

Independant variable	Dependant variable	R^2	F	Sig. F
Perceived value	Satisfaction (course content)	0,027	1,934	0,148

Table 8. Individual significance test of the correlation between perceived value and satisfaction with content.

Independant variable	Dependant variable	ß	t	Sig. t
Extrinsic value	Satisfaction with content	0	−0,04	0.997
Intrinsic value	Satisfaction with content	0,165	1,967	0.051

Based on results presented in Table 8 perceived value has no positive effect on content satisfaction. Both values of t (extrinsic and intrinsic) are greater than 0,05.

Effect of Perceived Value on Satisfaction with System. To study the user satisfaction with the system, we consider two dimensions: Accuracy reflecting the correctness of information and data provided to the students and format of the content generated by the e-learning system. The results of the linear regression correlation show a poor fit quality for the first dimension. The coefficient of determination R^2 displays a value of 0.002. The model is not significant because Fisher's test is 0.846.

The linear regression results of the "format" dimension reflect a poor fit quality. The coefficient of determination R^2 is estimated at 0.009, Fisher's significance test is evaluated at 0.546. The model is not globally significant (Table 9).

Table 9. Global significance test between perceived value and satisfaction with system.

Independant variable	Dependant variable	R^2	F	Sig. F
Perceived value	Satisfaction (system accuracy)	0,002	0,168	0,846
Perceived value	Satisfaction (format)	0,009	0,608	0,546

The two dimensions of perceived value do not affect satisfaction with the system since findings show values greater than 0.05 (Tables 10 and 11).

Table 10. Individual significance test of the correlation between perceived value and satisfaction with system.

Independant variable	Dependant variable	ß	t	Sig. t
Extrinsic value	Satisfaction (system accuracy)	0,049	0,573	0,567
Intrinsic value	Satisfaction (system accuracy)	−0.007	−0,083	0.934

Table 11. Individual significance test of the correlation between perceived value and satisfaction with system.

Independant variable	Dependant variable	ß	t	Sig. t
Extrinsic value	Satisfaction (system format)	0,067	0,792	0,430
Intrinsic value	Satisfaction (system format)	0,065	0,769	0,443

These statistical results argue that the perceived value does not influence positively the satisfaction with the system.

Effect of Perceived Value on Satisfaction with the Distribution Method. The regression results show a low value of the determination coefficient (R^2) equals to 0.022. Fisher's test is estimated at 0.079. That means the model is not significant (Tables 12 and 13).

Table 12. Global significance test between perceived value and satisfaction with the distribution method.

Independant variable	Dependant variable	R^2	F	Sig. F
Perceived value	Satisfaction (distribution method)	0,036	2,590	0,079

Table 13. Individual significance test of the correlation between perceived value and satisfaction with distribution method.

Independant variable	Dependant variable	ß	t	Sig. t
Extrinsic value	Satisfaction (distribution method)	0,132	1,586	0,115
Intrinsic value	Satisfaction (distribution method)	0,136	1,632	0,105

Extrinsic and intrinsic dimensions of the perceived value do not affect satisfaction with the distribution method. The Student test values of these dimensions are 0.115 and 0.105, respectively. These findings led to the conclusion that perceived value does not have a positive effect on satisfaction.

Effect of Satisfaction on the Continuous Use Intention of the E-learning Course. According to [5], many studies have reported the essential role of satisfaction to influence users' decisions to continue using e-learning systems. In our work, we aim to verify this hypothesis. Therefore, we made a linear regression model study the effect of satisfaction (with the content, system and distribution method) on the intention of continuous use of e-learning courses.

Effect of Satisfaction with Content on the Continuous Use Intention of the E-learning Course. The linear regression results showed an average quality of the overall fit model. The determination coefficient R^2 displays a value of 0.134. The model is globally significant because Fisher's test is 0.000 ($p < 0.05$) (Table 14).

Satisfaction with content has a significant effect on the intention to continue using the e-learning course. The Student test has a significant value that is less than 0.05 (Table 15).

Table 14. Global significance test between satisfaction with content and the continuous use intention of the e-learning course.

Independant variable	Dependant variable	R^2	F	Sig. F
Satisfaction (content)	Continuous use intention of the e-learning course	0.134	21.737	0.000

Table 15. Individual significance test of the correlation between satisfaction with content and the continuous use intention of the e-learning course.

Independant variable	Dependant variable	ß	t	Sig. t
Satisfaction (content)	Continuous use intention of the e-learning course	0,367	4,662	0,000

Effect of Satisfaction with System on the Continuous use Intention of the E-learning Course. The results of the linear regression show an average quality of the overall fit model. The coefficient of determination R^2 has an average value of 0.177. The model is globally significant since the Fisher test is equal to 0.000 ($p < 0.05$) (Table 16).

Table 16. Global significance test between satisfaction with system and the continuous use intention of the e-learning course.

Independant variable	Dependant variable	R^2	F	Sig. F
Satisfaction (system)	Continuous use intention of the e-learning course	0.177	14.890	0.000

Satisfaction with the system has a significant effect on the intention to continue using the e-learning course. The Student test shows a significant value that is less than 0.05 (Table 17).

Table 17. Individual significance test of the correlation between satisfaction with system and the continuous use intention of the e-learning course.

Independant variable	Dependant variable	ß	t	Sig. t
Satisfaction (system accuracy)	Continuous use intention of the e-learning course	0,327	4,237	0,000
Satisfaction (system format)	Continuous use intention of the e-learning course	0,265	3,439	0,000

These statistical results make it possible to conclude that satisfaction with the system has a positive effect on the intention to continue using the e-learning course.

Effect of Satisfaction with Distribution Method on the Continuous Use Intention of the E-learning Course. The regression results show an average fit of the overall model. The determination coefficient R^2 shows a value of 0.167. The model is globally significant, since the Fisher test is equal to 0.000 ($p < 0.05$) (Table 18).

Table 18. Global significance test between satisfaction with distribution method and the continuous use intention of the e-learning course.

Independant variable	Dependant variable	R^2	F	Sig. F
Satisfaction (distribution method)	Continuous use intention of the e-learning course	0.167	28,111	0.000

Satisfaction with the distribution method has a significant effect on the intention to continue using the e-learning course knowing that student's test has significant value (<0.05) (Table 19).

Table 19. Individual significance test of the correlation between satisfaction with distribution method and the continuous use intention of the e-learning course.

Independant variable	Dependant variable	ß	t	Sig. t
Satisfaction (distribution method)	Continuous use intention of the e-learning course	0,409	5,302	0,000

These statistical results led to the conclusion that satisfaction with the distribution method has a positive effect on the intention to continue using the e-learning course.

5 Discussion

The objective of the present work is to study, the intention of the Tunisian post employees to continue learning through e-learning technology. The results set out above make it possible to determine the intention to continue having e-learning courses by learners of the Tunisian post office. This intention is generally positive.

To resume briefly our findings, we showed that perceived utility has no positive effect on perceived quality. The proposition suggesting that acceptance of technology has a positive effect on perceived quality has not been verified in our context. We validated the first hypothesis suggesting the existence of a positive relationship between perceived quality and perceived value. This is may be interpreted as learners estimate the online courses quality regarding their perceived value. This finding is coherent with many works in the literature [7, 8]. Our second hypothesis suggesting the existence of a significant effect of perceived value on learner satisfaction is not verified. For the third hypothesis which supposes the existence of a significant effect between the satisfaction of learners and the intention to use e-learning courses, it is validated.

The major drawback of the present work is the study sample size which is limited by the low rate of integration of the e-learning technology in Tunisian companies.

6   Conclusion

The results of the present study support the findings of further researches in the literature interested in the adoption of e-learning technologies in the professional context.

Using e-learning technology to train employees interests managers concerned with keeping up with technological developments and meeting the needs of the knowledge society. Since the use of e-learning technology is relatively new in the Tunisian professional context, the prospects promised have not yet been proven. We aim to shed light on the degree of appreciation and intention to continue using e-learning technology by Tunisian employees. This study made it possible to identify employees' perceptions and their appreciations. In our case, it's positive.

In future works, we hope to enlarge the sample size to better understand further influential factors on e-learning adoption behaviors. Without taking into account the time dimension, the results obtained by this study were established in the short term. We hope to conduct a longitudinal study soon, that is interesting.

References

1. Ignatius, J., Ramayah, T.: An empirical investigation of the course website acceptance model (CWAM). Int. J. Bus. Soc. **6**(2), 69–82 (2005)
2. Chiu, C.-M., Hsu, M.-H., Sun, S.-Y., Lin, T.-C., Sun, P.-C.: Usability, quality, value and e-learning continuance decisions. Comput. Educ. **45**(4), 399–416 (2005)
3. Siritongthaworn, S., Krairit, D.: Satisfaction in e-learning: the context of supplementary instruction. Campus-Wide Inf. Syst. **23**(2), 76–91 (2006)
4. Thompson, R., Compeau, D., Higgins, C.: Intentions to use information technologies. J. Org. End User Comput. **18**(3), 25–46 (2006)
5. Al-Samarraie, H., Teng, B.K., Alzahrani, A.I., Alalwan, N.: E-learning continuance satisfaction in higher education: a unified perspective from instructors and students. Stud. High. Educ. **43**(11), 2003–2019 (2017)
6. Soliman, W., Rinta-Kahila, T.: Toward a refined conceptualization of IS discontinuance: reflection on the past and a way forward. Inf. Manag. **57**, 103167 (2019)

7. Zeithaml, V.A., Parasuraman, A., Malhotra, A.: Service quality delivery through web sites: a critical review of extant knowledge. J. Acad. Mark. Sci. **30**(4), 362–375 (2002)
8. Kilburn, B., Kilburn, A., Davis, D.: Building collegiate e-loyalty: the role of perceived value in the quality-loyalty linkage in online higher education. Contemp. Issues Educ. Res. (CIER) **9**(3), 95–102 (2016)
9. Marangunić, N., Granić, A.: Technology acceptance model: a literature review from 1986 to 2013. Univ. Access Inf. Soc. **14**(1), 81–95 (2014). https://doi.org/10.1007/s10209-014-0348-1
10. Aurier, P., Bénavent, C., N'Goala, G.: Validité Discriminante et Prédictive des Composantes de la Relation à la Marque. In: Actes du Coloque de l' Association Française de Marketing, Deauville (2001)
11. Grönroos, C.: Keynote paper from marketing mix to relationship marketing - towards a paradigm shift in marketing. Manag. Decis. **35**(4), 322 (1997)

A Real-Time Cross-Sectioning System for Visualization of Architectural Construction Details

Luis Hernández-Ibáñez(✉) [ID] and Viviana Barneche-Naya [ID]

Universidade da Coruña, 15071 A Coruña, Spain
{luis.hernandez,viviana.barneche}@udc.es

Abstract. Architectural objects are composed of multiple and complex, hetero-geneous elements. A wall, a floor, a window, are examples of the juxtaposition of several distinct elements that are put together to ensemble a single constructive part.

Cross-sections in Architecture are usually made to achieve two different goals. On the one hand, a cross-section of a building is useful to display the arrange-ment of the spaces that compose it and its relation with the exterior volume that encompasses it. This kind of cross section commonly represents the inner parts of the constructive elements as being made of a single homogeneous material. They are commonly made so the section is painted with a single colour to iden-tify the cut area. On the other hand, cross-sections are commonly used in a more technical way to describe how the different components of a constructive element are arranged. This class of cross sections are also called "construction sections" "detailed sections" "constructive sections" or "cutaways".

Actually, we can find a few examples of CAD and architectural software capable to perform cross sections of a building of the first case aforementioned, but in a limited way.

The authors have developed a cross section creation system that provides advanced features such as real–time interaction, multiplane sectioning, and progressive multilayer section cuts on highly realistic models.

This paper describes such system and presents its implementation as a plugin for Unreal Engine 4, a videogame engine that is becoming highly popular for architectural visualization.

An example of the use of this system is also displayed depicting the construc-tive structure of an historical heritage building, the famous Tholos of Delphi. The example demonstrates the suitability of the system not only for technical architec-tural visualization, but also to develop archaeological museums installations and other educational purposes.

Keywords: Cross-section · Architectural visualization · Interactive constructive section

© Springer Nature Switzerland AG 2020
C. Stephanidis et al. (Eds.): HCII 2020, LNCS 12425, pp. 410–420, 2020.
https://doi.org/10.1007/978-3-030-60128-7_31

1   Introduction

1.1   Use of Sections in Architectural Representation

In reference to architectural drawing, the term *section* typically describes a cut through the body of a building in such a way that the representation of the elements being cut permits a good understanding of the diverse relationships among spaces, constructive elements, supporting structure, inner-outer interconnection, etc. Sections can be done on a full building or in a part of it. Section drawings can display the cut only or they can also include the projected view of the thigs beyond the cut (Fig. 1). They are usually drawn using planar orthographic projection, but they also can be created using axonometric or perspective projections.

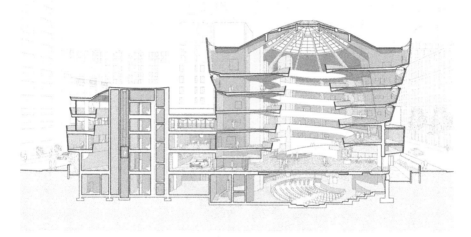

Fig. 1. Section of Frank Lloyd Wright's Guggenheim Museum. Source: LTL Architects

Constructive sections are a particular case of this drawing technique where the inner part of the cut is filled with a representation, commonly symbolic of the materials that need to be used to create the architectural element. A drawing representing this kind of information is called a *construction detail* (Fig. 2).

Sections are not only a representational technique. They are used extensively to illustrate, test and explore architectural designs and to better explain the building techniques and materials involved. The cutaway illuminates the interplay between a building structure, its closure and the space framed between foundation and roof. The material investment and spatial invention necessary to creatively resist gravitational loads is best explored and depicted through the architectural section [1].

One of the clearest ways to represent construction details is the use of multiple cutting planes combined with three-dimensional view of the part of the building that contains the constructive system that has to be presented. The different materials and components are treated separately, sectioned in different layers and organized using different criteria (Fig. 3).

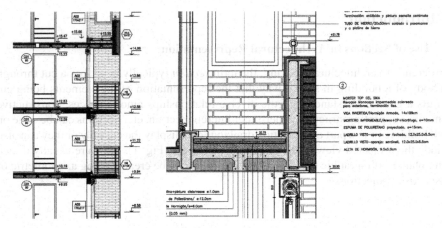

Fig. 2. Construction detail. Source: V.Barneche. Arch.

Fig. 3. Construction detail using different cutting planes for different material layers [2].

1.2 Sectional Drawing for Depiction of Historical Buildings

Sectional drawing as an explicit architectural technique appears in the work of Italian architects in the latter half of the fifteenth century, fostered by the emergence of a renewed interest in documenting the sectional ruins of classical antiquity. Some early collections of Renaissance drawings, such as the *Codex Coner,* [3] contain numerous sections, including some interpretations of the Pantheon built in AD 128 (Fig. 4) among other buildings. Same graphic language is used in the sketches of Baldasarre Peruzzi and Antonio da Sangallo, and it is masterfully combined with plans and elevations in the drawings of Andrea Palladio [4].

Fig. 4. Pantheon by Bernardo della Volpaia (Left). Viollet-le-Duc. Perspective section of Haut-Koenigsbourg Castle (Right)

Some centuries later, the drawings by Viollet-leDuc are of particular significance in this regard. He relied in the section to demonstrate the interdependency of formal and structural systems. In his renowned works [5] Viollet-le-Duc illustrates the principles derived by the constructive practices of previous eras with brilliant sectional drawings (Fig. 4).

The aforementioned authors and their brilliant use of sectional representation for the analysis of historical architecture inspired the work described in this paper. Nowadays, cross-sections are marginally present in modern CAD systems. Although some of them (i.e. Revit, AutoCAD, CATIA etc.), can perform some kind of sections on solid models they are neither intended to be done interactively in polygonal models, using multiple simultaneous cut planes, nor in a sequential multilayer style, as needed for this kind of representation of constructive details. The use of a high-end game engine can also permit to apply highly complex realistic materials and illumination models. The authors consider that to develop a system capable to use the language of architectural section with modern technologies to better depict the way historical architecture was built could be of great value in various fields such as education and museology applied to historical heritage.

2 Objectives

The goal of this work is to develop a system capable of perform interactive, sequential cross-sections on a polygonal model of any origin, such as those made by any CAD and 3D modelling software. The system had to accomplish the following requirements:

- *Real time*. The system must be capable to render cross-sections in real-time in order to facilitate the interactive examination of the architectural object. Most CAD systems that are capable to generate sections render them as a response to the request to display the section by a given plane. Hence, time to calculate such a section is not critical. In our case, the cutting plane may move interactively, so the section must render immediately.
- *Multiple simultaneous cutting planes*. Thus allowing to replicate classical perspective section drawings, including frontal, sagittal and horizontal sections, as well as half sectional (quarter portion), slices, etc. Initially, the system incorporates six section cutting planes, parallel two by two to the coordinate axis. Further development of the system may also include oblique planes.
- *Sequential sections*. Sections may be applied differently for different building elements, making possible to render sequential sections on the same model, so the constructive relations among the compounding elements may be clearly understandable.
- *Hierarchical section layers*. Including a tag system that can organize the constructive elements into families according to building criteria, materials, constructive system, usages, etc.

3 Methodology

Calculation of cross sections is a common procedure in some CAD systems. The algorithms used to obtain such cuts are complex and make use of the solid modelling concept. Solid modelling is a branch of Computer Graphics that is based in the consideration that every point in the 3D space resides either in the inside or in the outside of an element, thus dividing the affine space E^3 into two separate sets, one containing the points in the interior of the solid object and another one for the exterior. Different sets can be combined using Boole algebra, yielding to different results depending on the Boolean operator used (union, subtraction, intersection, etc.). Solid modelling permits to obtain the limit surface of such sets, being it the external sides, or the points of the object that lies on a certain plane.

Such calculations are far from simple, and can take a time, especially for complex objects that make them not suitable to display cuts in real-time. However, this is not usually the goal of such a systems, instead, the capability to extract the precise planar geometry of a section of an object can be extremely useful for many applications in fields such as structural analysis, mechanical engineering, etc.

In our case, the geometry of the section plane, the precise definition of the shape of the cut itself is not necessary as far as we are be able to figure and perceive it from the image. So, in order to render the section of the model, we implemented and improved a method that we previously used in other projects [6], consisting in being able to determine the visible parts of the inner sides of the faces of the polygons that compose the object, once it had been cut by the section planes and fill them with a given solid, unlit colour. Therefore, all points of the interior of the object that can be seen through the section contour will take the same shade, and the user will perceive them as forming a continuous plane. Hence, the section is not calculated, but is clearly and easily inferred by the spectator (Fig. 5).

Fig. 5. Interactive, real time section of the Cathedral of Santiago de Compostela, displayed by solid painting the interior sides of polygons visible behind the cutting plane.

3.1 Model Requirements

The sectioning system can be applied to any 3D polygonal model, such as those generated in popular modelling software, and polygonal versions of solid models. For the former, it is necessary that all faces are properly oriented, with their face normal pointing outwards. This is a very common requirement for real-time visualization and a must-do for assets created to be rendered using game engines. For the latter, polygonal models generated from solid models are always normal-oriented correctly, so this is not an issue.

Regarding materials, they system can deal with most of the properties of complex materials used by game engines, including normal maps, multi-layered texture samples, etc. Nevertheless, the system cannot deal directly with transparent elements, since it makes use of materials' opacity mask to split off the cut and uncut parts of the object.

3.2 System Design

The system has been developed using the popular game engine *Unreal Engine 4*, making use of its powerful features regarding real-time realistic rendering, ease of coding by means of its visual scripting system and interoperability with popular modelling packages.

The sectioning system is composed by three main parts (Fig. 6):

- *Sectionable Object* class: A sectionable is defined as a kind of object made up of several components:

  - A polygonal mesh, to be cut
  - A dynamic instance of the *Sectionable Material*, that will be described later, adapted to the object specific material. A dynamic instance of a material allows to change

material parameters dynamically during run time, adapting to variations such as those provoked by moving the cutting planes interactively.

- A set of tags, that will identify this object as part of a hierarchy or super system of constructive elements based on given criteria.

- *Sectionable Material:* composed of two different material functions:

  - *Section material function:* This function checks the world x, y, z coordinates of a given point on the surface of the object where it is applied to, and test it again the different cutting planes.
    If the point resides in the uncut side of all section planes involved, the system checks the direction of the normal vector of the surface in this point. If this vector points towards the camera, the colour and other visual characteristics of the surface coming from the generic material function are assigned to the pixel, otherwise, a plain, solid color representing the section is applied instead.
    This function deals with the sectionability of the element. It uses the location and orientation of the cutting planes as parameters, being independent of the visual appearance of the object.
  - *Generic material function:* This function deals with all regular material features, such as color, roughness, etc. It has to be defined for each material used in the scene based on its visual properties and injected together with the section material function in the sectionable material.

- *Cutting planes:* A set of six planes parallel to the coordinate planes that can be moved interactively. The system considers a point to be locally visible for each pair of planes when it is located between both of them, and masked out and made invisible otherwise. For the point to be visible, it has to be locally visible for each pair of planes.

The location of the cutting planes can change interactively by displacing some sliders placed in the graphical user interface. Also, the hierarchy of tags is displayed on screen, so the user can activate or deactivate both the visibility and the sectionability of a given element in any time. This way, a great variety of types of cross sections can be obtained from the model.

Since different sections may require different illuminations to get and adequate representation, the lighting (i.e. Sun position, interior lighting, etc.) can also be changed interactively.

3.3 Application

The system has been applied to various models depicting some important historical buildings. The first test regarding the validity of the system to obtain full sections of the building was made using the already named 3D model of the Cathedral of Santiago de Compostela that was previously created by the authors, this time adapted to the game engine (Fig. 7).

The tag and multilayer sectioning features were tested on a 3D model of the Tholos of Marmaria, part of the Delphi Archaeological site (Fig. 8). By moving the cut plane

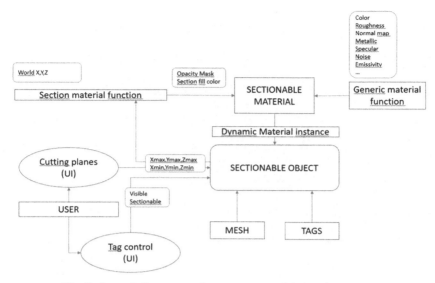

Fig. 6. Interrelation among the components of the section system

Fig. 7. Real-time section of the Cathedral of Santiago de Compostela. Note the sliders for the different cut planes and the Sun controls.

sliders and switching the tags on and off, every element can be cut as it is needed, producing the desired sequential section (Fig. 9).

The application allows the user to inspect the model using two different viewing modes: Walk and Examine. In the first, the user can make a regular architectural walk-through inside and around the model, even with sections on, so he or she can contemplate

Fig. 8. 3D recreation of the Tholos of Marmaria at Delphi. The tag system on the left is used to set the visibility and sectionability of every construction element.

Fig. 9. Real-time sequential section of the temple displaying the roof structure by setting the corresponding tags on and off as the cut planes move.

it under a person's point of view. In the latter, the user can rotate the model and inspect it from any point while obtaining the sections required. An example including a point cloud of the surroundings provided by the University of the Aegean can be found online [7].

This model also includes some representation of the reliability of the archaeological reconstruction by colour coding the elements under request, (Fig. 10) following the criteria of ICOMOS London International Charter for the computer-based visualization of Cultural Heritage [8].

Fig. 10. Reliability of the interpretation of every part of the building, from certain to very probable to well-founded.

4 Conclusions

Section drawings, especially those that apply different cutting layers, constitute a very powerful tool for the analysis and depiction of the different constructive systems used in a building and their relationships. Perspective, sequential sections have been used profusely in the literature for the description of historical buildings as an ideal manner to explain the constructive techniques and methods used in former times.

Interactive cross-sectioning could then be used as a descriptive tool for education and interpretation of historical buildings. An interactive application capable to render sequential, multilayer cross sections interactively on a computer model of a building could be of use in the field of museography. Such a tool can be done by means of the application of the procedures described in this paper.

References

1. Lewis, P., Tsurumaki, M., Lewis, D.: Manual of Section. Princeton Architectural Press, New York (2016)

2. Warshaw, E.: Understanding Architectural Details. Residential Construction. First in Architecture (2017)
3. Ashby, T.: Sixteenth-century drawings of roman buildings attributed to andreas coner. Papers of the British School of Rome, vol. 2, pp. 1–88 (1904). vol.VI pp.184- (1908)
4. Palladio, A.: I quattro libro dell'architecttura. Ed. Domenico de' Franceschi, Venezia (1570)
5. Viollet-le-Duc, E.: Entretiens sur l'architecture. A. Morel et cie, vol. 1–2 (1872)
6. Hernández Ibáñez, L.A., Barneche Naya, V.: An interactive installation for the architectural analysis of space and form in historical buildings. In: Zaphiris, P., Ioannou, A. (eds.) LCT 2014. LNCS, vol. 8523, pp. 43–52. Springer, Cham (2014). https://doi.org/10.1007/978-3-319-074 82-5_5
7. videaLAB Youtube site. Tholos demo: https://tinyurl.com/y88t8lwm. Accessed 13 June 2020
8. http://smartheritage.com/wp-content/uploads/2015/03/LONDON-CHARTER.pdf. Accessed 13 June 2020

Exploring the Affordance of Distance Learning Platform (DLP) in COVID19 Remote Learning Environment

Ajrina Hysaj[1](✉) [iD] and Doaa Hamam[2] [iD]

[1] UOWD College, University of Wollongong in Dubai, Dubai, UAE
Ajrinahysaj@uowdubai.ac.ae
[2] Higher Colleges of Technology, Dubai, UAE
dhamam@hct.ac.ae

Abstract. Higher Education has been facing the dilemma of the preferred delivery method for over two decades. COVID19 pandemic in 2020 made the need for further exploration of the same even more imperative. Although the urgency of events did not leave much time for policymakers and educators to decide, it did inspire the authors of this article to analyse the affordances of Distance Learning Platform (DLP), and the ways students perceived the online learning due to current uncertain circumstances. Students as critical stakeholders in the learning process were on the receiving end of the decisions taken to facilitate distance learning. The focus of this study was to understand students' experience of using the Distance Learning Platform (DLP) in a crises-induced environment at a university in the United Arab Emirates. A sample size of 60 undergraduate students who took academic study skills classes was used to collect data. Students were asked to reflect on their experience of distance learning, and the data were analysed to understand the students' preferences of their study method while enabling them to recognise their cognitive skillset. The data indicated reasons behind students' preferences of the preferred delivery method.

Keywords: COVID19 · Blended learning · Delivery method · Reflective tasks · Distance learning · Multiculturalism

1 Introduction

Humanity is not oblivious of the existence of crises, and the devastating effect crises bring with them. Crises are not new to human beings, starting from the Tequila crisis of 1994–95, continuing with the Asian flu and the Russian virus respectively in the years 1997, 1998 according to Kaminsky and Reinhart [1], continuously the new financial crises that caused the credit boom to go bust according to Schularick and Taylor [2]. The economists and financial analysts seem to be very interested in analysing the effects of crises considering the vital effect economies have on the well- being of nations being it social, psychological, and most importantly, emotional. The study by Kaminsky and Reinhart [1] analysed the effect of contagion and crises on the economy of nations. Such studies pave the way to research in other fields, e.g. education and health. COVID19 has undoubtedly caught the education system by surprise and despite the advancement in the technology and human capital; notions of plagiarism and academic integrity have become more prominent than ever. Such is mainly due to the extensive use of technology for educational purposes and the higher levels of stress and frustration experienced by all stakeholders in the tertiary education system; policymakers and managers of educational institutions, faculty and the most vulnerable ones, the students.

However, not many studies have empirically examined the channels of disturbances for students and faculty caused by sudden crisis-induced events such as the current pandemic. In this study, we aim to fill this gap by analysing the factors which largely ignored links between crises and the increase in anxiety and depression in students and faculty as stated by Adeyemi Ekundayo and Alonge [3] in addition to the possible ways of curbing plagiarism in distance learning. The same study by Adeyemi, Ekundayo and Alonge [3] discovered that students experience increased levels of anxiety due to external factors, e.g. health issues, loss of lives, properties, and closure of schools. The same study suggested that one way of dealing with crises involves students in the process of finding the solutions. During the current crisis of COVID19, students as collaborators in the learning process have experienced a massive alteration in the way they study, ask questions, receive feedback, attempt assessments, take quizzes and complete individual or group work. Their ethical values are in constant detrimental conditions threatened by time limitations, inability to manage stress, lack of adequate knowledge and the widespread presence of ghost-writers.

COVID19 has confronted the concept of face to face classes and has increased the amount, kind of challenges faced by federal and international universities worldwide. While the health practitioners around the globe are trying to make a breakthrough towards the treatment of the unknown COVID19, we the educators consider protecting our education system around the globe by analysing effects of such pandemic on our tertiary students, their moral and ethical set of values. Educators need to see themselves as instrumental in taking an ethical and interventional role by creating an online experience of high integrity, genuine knowledge sharing and appropriate university learning experience. The education industry is crucial in defining ethics and values of learners curbing issues of ethical concern, e.g. plagiarism and academic integrity, as stated by Anitha and Harsha [4].

The United Arab Emirates, which was declared a state in 1971, as mentioned by Martin (p. 50) [5], is an oil-rich and a business hub situated in the Middle East. Its population of over 8.2 million people consists mainly of expatriates who account for approximately 90% of the population in the country, as mentioned by Al-Jenaibi [6]. The United Arab Emirates has gone through an enormous transformation from the day of its formation, as stated by Majaida [7], and became one of the most well-known nations worldwide. The economic and social drastic changes happened mainly after the discovery of oil. In 2020, the UAE is a prosperous country, and a home to millions of people from all over the world, and aims to become an educational hub as mentioned by Fox and Al Shamisi [8], and a health hub as mentioned by Ganji [9] for the rest of the globe.

Multicultural demographics of the UAE have encouraged the use of English as a lingua franca, as the number of expatriates outnumbers the native population by a large percentage. English is now becoming the norm in formal education and also in non-formal domains, e.g. tourism or leisure because people usually use English as a medium of communication as stated by Hysaj et al.; and Hopkyns [10, 11]. Moreover, according to Hopkyns [11], the UAE aims to create an inclusive society and to open doors to the development of the nation by encouraging quality education and establishing English medium universities, mostly branches of well-known international campuses, facilitating the studies of international students coming from all over the world. Lundin et al. [12] stated that students' active participation levels in face-to-face and online or blended platforms is considered a clear indicator of successful teaching and learning experiences. The foreign universities present in the UAE are in constant competition to attract higher numbers of students and offer the most sort-out majors, based on diligent market research. Furthermore, the UAE universities are in a continuous process to understand the multicultural students' needs and expectations and aim at students' satisfaction and subsequently, students' retention, as mentioned by Hysaj et al. [13].

Cross-cultural dialogue is undoubtedly a valid contributor to a successful experience of multicultural students in higher education. Connecting through diversity facilitates understanding of one's self and paves the way to not only higher satisfaction levels from the learning experience but to changes in the behaviour of undergraduate students too as mentioned by Banks and Banks; Hysaj et al.; Lehtomäki, Moate and Posti-Ahokas [13–15]. Learning and teaching approaches designed and utilised in online or virtual classes carry an equal amount of importance concerning learning outcomes and students' experiences in higher education. If these methods were not aligned to the other or to the activities and the assessment tasks aimed at measuring the outcomes, the results could be neither reliable nor achievable.

Online and face-to-face platforms aim to improve the standard of teaching and learning by nurturing deeper learning, facilitating communication and developing skills' sets required in the work environment. The transfer and application of skills from the physical or virtual classroom to the work environment is a slow but secure step towards a successful, meaningful learning experience in the higher education setting according to Hill et al. and Oros [16, 17]. This process, however, requires the creation of a solid ground based on clarification of concepts while encouraging active participation in classroom and online platforms. Stakeholders involved in this process from a macro perspective are the policymakers and the institutions' managers, and from a micro perspective, the stakeholders are lecturers, tutors, course designers and more importantly, students according to Patel [18].

2   Literature Review

2.1   Binding Changes in the Landscape of the Higher Education System in the UAE

According to Abyad [19], the population demographics of the UAE has changed exponentially during the last two decades. Leading contributors to such change have been the development of business initiatives and acumen by local and foreign investors. Following on the new business openings, a substantial number of foreign universities have established their offshore branches in the UAE aiming to cater to the needs of the residents as mentioned by Hijazi et al. [20] contending for better offering in terms of students experience, teaching/learning facilities and a variety of majors being offered as stated by Wilkins [21]. Multicultural student body present in foreign universities constructs an increased responsibility in front of all parties involved in the higher education sector in the UAE. Students' retention requires a constant update of curriculum design, methods of delivery, and methods of assessment aiming at the facilitation of students' academic, personal and professional growth. Other substantial factors that require additional consideration are the students' learning styles, mobility of students' body and readiness of students to join the workforce once they finish their tertiary studies or even during their studies.

COVID19 has imposed an unprecedented challenge for the education system in the country. The UAE has a robust digital infrastructure, and the educational policymakers were ahead, experimented with using online teaching before and created many online resources for students and teachers. However, the speed with which this pandemic got spread did not allow enough time for self-reflection by all the parties involved in the education system. Moreover, the fluidity of population demographics of the UAE poses in itself an added challenge, which brings along issues of social, economic and psychological nature, according to Hijazi et al. [20]. Multiculturalism requires acknowledgement of differences in worldviews, decision-making processes, and perception of the unknown, reflection on challenges posed by COVID19 and instant shift from face to face to distant learning platforms imposed by circumstances while trying to avoid errors occurring due to hastiness. Getting empowered with the knowledge of multiculturalism comes along with increased levels of interest in knowing others and accepting the need to differ and yet coexist. According to Hall (p. 209), as cited in Nye [22], coexistence in an educational setting can be explained as the desire to learn differently based on a variety of study methods that take into consideration individual preferences and learning styles as well as the necessity to create a common life experience. This is particularly challenging in the UAE due to the very vast exposure to multiculturalism and its very fluid nature.

A considerable number of international students studying in universities in the UAE are "third culture kids' (TCK's) according to Pollock, Van Reken and Pollock [23]. They have lived most if not all their developmental years abroad, their concepts of self- identity and belonging are fluid similar to the demographics of the rest of the population of the UAE. Nevertheless, as the UAE prides itself for being the nation of opportunities and a tourism hub, many students decide to start their undergraduate or post-graduate studies in the country after first visiting it as tourists. Therefore, the standard of studies offered in graduate or post-graduate levels in the country is crucial, considering the adequate provision of the intellectual workforce needed to fulfil the ever-growing needs of the UAE's economy. Multiculturalism needs to be explored and understood continuously according to Nye [22], so it can become a gem rather than a challenge.

2.2 Exploring Affordances of Flipped Classroom Platform for Digital Natives in the UAE

Lundin, et al. [12] mentioned that the majority of undergraduates are accustomed to digital technology and enjoy using it. They appreciate the use of media and online resources, and as a result, they display a genuine interest for "deep learning". An instance of such a phenomenon is noticed when students are given the opportunity of learning through online videos and audio presentations. Majority of accounting, finance, marketing and business administration undergraduates express their preference towards this way of knowledge acquisition due to its flexibility in terms of mobility and time. Furthermore, the majority of international students participate daily in more than one type of online social platform. As reported by Ozkan and Koseler [24], students in the Middle East consider e-learning as a social entity and tend to take e-communications quite seriously.

Prensky, as quoted in Roehl, Reddy and Shannon [25] argues that millennials grew up on rapidly changing technological advancement; hence, they disclose a reduced level of tolerance for lecture-style dissemination of course information. The flipped classroom concept requires students to view the lectures before attending classes which leads to the potential of fostering deep learning through activation of constructive processes according to Tucker; O'Flaherty and Phillips; Lucke, Dunn and Christie [26–28]. The time previously consumed in delivering lectures in the classroom can be utilised constructively for clarification of challenging concepts or providing individual support; aiming at the development of cognitive skills and appropriate management of cognitive load as stated by Roehl, Reddy and Shannon; Abeysekera and Dawson; Franchi; Soltanpour and Valizadeh [25, 29, 30]. Furthermore, students tend to be more active when the flipped classroom concept is applied due to the increased level of ownership over their learning process.

According to McNally et al. [32], such ownership subsequently impacts the students' overall satisfaction of learning and results in the improvement of performance. Balaban, Gilleskie and Tran [33] emphasise the improvement of students' performance level as a result of the flipped classroom instructional format. Consistent with Balaban, Gilleskie and Tran [33] as mentioned in McNally et al. [32]. Another critical element of the flipped classroom is the provision of a mechanism to assess students' understanding through low-stakes tests that can take place regularly in the first part of the in-class session. Balaban, Gilleskie and Tran [33] move on with the assertion that flipped classroom instructional advantage are relevant to large classrooms as well as small ones. King et al.; McLean et al.; Soltanpour and Valizadeh [31, 33, 35] analysed foundation subjects such as economics and English language in large universities, found that students enjoy learning through flipped classroom more than through the traditional classroom. These elective subjects place a great emphasis on the development of critical and analytical thinking crucial for success in academic settings. Unexpectedly, the same view is held by Tucker, Freguia, and Davenport [26, 36, 37] about computer programming, ICT and engineering elective subjects.

Erdogan and Akbaba, and Franchi [30, 38] affirm that the students' performance and information retention is experienced in social and classical history subjects and part of Arts and Humanities undergraduate degrees. King et al. [34] go a step further by proposing that the flipped classroom concept has the potential of creating rigorous interest in students for research and learning since it connects the digital libraries with the learning process. Moreover, it empowers librarians with extensive research skills that can facilitate students' learning alongside the guidance from lectures and tutors in the respective subjects.

2.3 Utilising the Affordance of Online Reflective Tasks in a Crisis-Induced Learning Environment

According to D'Argembeau, et al.; Nesi; Imbir and Jarymowicz; Johnstone; Yuan and Mak; Hyland, [39–44], critical and analytical thinking, as well as self-reflection, are necessary for individual growth in personal and professional platforms. Development of self-reflection in multicultural students adds to their portfolio of skills already in place; through life experiences and environmental factors. COVID19 exposed the international community to unprecedented circumstances and provided an uncertain environment resulting in personal and societal adaptations that could result in growth if utilised appropriately. Reflecting on such life experiences like the COVID19 and the abrupt exposure to distant learning encourages students to critically evaluate their individual preferences in regards to learning and knowledge acquisition.

Nicol and Macfarlane [45] list "self-reflection" as one of the seven principles of proper feedback methods. Self-reflection encourages constructive critical and analytical thinking while facilitating the creation of a productive online learning experience. Appropriateness of the topics of reflective tasks affects the level of involvement that students experience while writing the tasks and the standard of skills' application in regards to sentence production and thought development. The well-thought topics can successfully be replaced by more current and relevant ones like individual experiences related to COVID19 and distant learning. Once exposed to more relevant and substantially appealing topics, students will be encouraged to self-reflect more purposefully and offer constructive criticism and correlate their online learning with real-life experiences. This will have a positive effect on revision of inner speech, as mentioned by Moffett [46] and the development of good writing skills, as mentioned by Pecorari [47]. Castaneda and Selwin [48] added that continuous online bonding with the topic and inner-self could nurture the sense of identity, responsibility and accountability. Likewise, the development of appropriate writing skills, as mentioned by Pecorari [47] can encourage a reduction in plagiarism instances.

3 Methodology

The study utilised reflective tasks to analyse students' perceptions of their preferred method of delivery and their experience in distance learning due to crises-induced circumstances. The topics that students had to reflect on were chosen carefully to reflect the unpreceded circumstances imposed by COVID19 and to help students reflect critically on topics of their interest. According to Fullana et al. [49], reflective tasks help students analyse emotions and circumstances while applying academic writing skills. Therefore, the reflective tasks were analysed for opinions and academic writing skills. The opinions were classified into 'with' or 'against' distance learning, and writing skills were analysed based on the sentence construction and flow of thought. The sample chosen was random, and it was comprised of 60 undergraduate students' writing who were enrolled in the academic study skills programs. The setting was an international university in the Middle East, and students came from different nationalities and different backgrounds. The students were informed with the purpose of the study, and they were informed that their participation is voluntary and that their participation will not have any effect on their status at the university. The timeframe for the study was around 12–13 weeks, and different classes had reflective tasks done on different days, depending on the availability of students.

4 Results

The results illustrated the students' preference for the delivery method of their sessions and their ability to reflect on crises-induced circumstances. The analysed themes were chosen after considering the number of times each appeared in students' reflection tasks. Themes that did not appear in more than twenty reflective tasks were disregarded.

On the one hand, the majority of the participants preferred to have online classes via the Distance Learning Platform (DLP), with a percentage of 60.3%. On the other hand, for the second topic of the reflective task, 80% of the students preferred the individual feedback given in class rather than the individual feedback given online via the live sessions; however, a similar percentage did not prefer to use face-to-face platform to the online platform. In addition, the majority of participants preferred to receive formative feedback for essays and reports, and from a choice of audio, or written feedback, the majority of the participants with the percentage of over 80.2% chose the written feedback. About participating in online discussions, the majority of the participants, 62.2% responded no, so they expressed their preference of having debates in class. However, the timid students mainly females or students who had weak speaking skills, felt more strongly about the topic, with a percentage of over 30%.

For the question about writing pair/group projects using the online platform, 73.1% of the participants expressed that they enjoyed the experience, while 11.2% did not, and 15.7% were not sure. Almost half of the participants expressed that they are fine with working on projects online in the foreseeable future, while 21.4% mentioned they do not like continuing to work online, and 31.6% were not sure. An overwhelming percentage of over 80.1% indicated that students prefer to collect and analyse their data online. While a near percentage of 10.5% showed that they prefer to collect their data in class, and the rest of 9.4% did not prefer any of the methods to the other. Finally, for the majority of the participants 62.2%, PowerPoint with the narration was the preferred mode of presenting their findings to the rest of the class. Only 37.8% preferred to present their projects in class or online person, and no group had a consensus of in-class presentation to the online one.

5 Discussion and Recommendations

Although there is extensive use of technology in many aspects of our modern life, not many professional teachers are comfortable with the use of online technology tools in their instruction as stated by Cottrell; Uerz, Volman and Kral; Ping, Schellings and Beijaard; Philipsen et al. [50–53]. The same concerns are prevalent in undergraduate students who did not see themselves as equipped with the necessary understanding of online tools or are interested in utilising online tools in the face to face classes as stated by Parsazadeh, Ali and Rezaei; Vanslambrouck et al. [54, 55]. Many teachers have not received technology training in their formal education, as using technology in teaching can be considered a recent trend to some extent. According to Hewett and Bourelle [56], if teachers are well equipped with tools on how to use technology, incorporate it into the course design; as well as check the students' progress during the course through assessment tasks; the distance learning process can be successful, enjoyable and provide students with rich experience. When teachers are well-versed about teaching with technology, they can successfully guide their students to use technology and achieve their learning objectives. The findings of the study also concur with the findings of Hysaj & Hamam [57], who stated that students were comfortable and preferred the online study methods. Some students also reported challenges when using technology, and others mentioned that teachers struggle at times to make things work. This leads us to the importance of teacher education in the TWT (Teaching with Technology) field.

6   Conclusion

In conclusion, crises-induced events like COVID19 could inevitably disrupt the traditional methods of teaching and learning. However, if adequate instruction is provided to the students via distance learning platforms, they will find online studies beneficial to provoke and develop their cognitive and analytical skills. The online platform and online tools are accepted and recommended by the students. The findings of this study presented that tech-savvy students prefer online classes to face-to-face ones, and these findings are similar to the findings of Hamam's [58]. Therefore, curriculum designers and lecturers need to continually use online tools and adapt their teaching methods and activities to suit the online platform. In summation, while the role of technology and the online tools in education cannot be ignored, events like COVID19 create an urgency to explore the same profoundly and from a variety of angles. Majority of undergraduate students who took part in this study were able to reflect critically on their experience and felt connected with the subject matter despite the unusual turn of events due to the pandemic. Distance learning proved to be worth considered and explored to the benefits of all stakeholders involved in the higher education field. Moreover, the majority of undergraduates consider online or distance learning as a useful and flexible method of study. Nevertheless, to ensure the success of the distance delivery method, teachers should be more technology-educated, and they should adapt their instruction and delivery methods to accommodate their students' needs. Another element that should be taken into consideration is creating different and innovative assessment methods other than the traditional ones to avoid academic integrity issues and plagiarism. Finally, the students' needs should be analysed in relation to the teaching/learning methods and the unusual dramatic circumstances like wars, famine or pandemics.

References

1. Kaminsky, G.L., Reinhart, C.M.: On crises, contagion, and confusion. J. Int. Econ. **51**(1), 145–168 (2000)
2. Schularick, M., Taylor, A.M.: Credit booms gone bust: monetary policy, leverage cycles, and financial crises, 1870-2008. Am. Econ. Rev. **102**(2), 1029–1061 (2012)
3. Adeyemi, T.O., Ekundayo, H.T., Alonge, H.O.: Managing students' crisis in tertiary institutions in Nigeria. J. Res. Natl. Dev. **8**(1), 37–38 (2010)
4. Anitha, C., Harsha, T.S.: Ethical perspectives in open and distance education system. Turk. Online J. Distance Educ. **14**(1), 193–201 (2013)
5. Martin, A.: An experience of teaching in the United Arab Emirates. Engl. Today **19**(2), 49–54 (2003)
6. Al-Jenaibi, B.: The scope and impact of workplace diversity in the United Arab Emirates–a preliminary study. Geografia-Malays. J. Soc. Space **8**(1), 1–14 (2017)
7. Majaida, J.: The press and social change in the United Arab Emirates: (1971–1991). Markaz Zāyid lil-Tansīq wa-al-Mutāba'ah (2002)
8. Fox, W.H., Al Shamisi, S.: United Arab Emirates' education hub: a decade of development. In: Knight, J. (ed.) International Education Hubs, pp. 63–80. Springer, Dordrecht (2014). https://doi.org/10.1007/978-94-007-7025-6_5
9. Ganji, S.: Hub healthcare: medical travel health equity in the UAE. Sheikh Saud bin Saqr Al Qasimi Foundation Working Paper Series, Working Paper (10), 1–32 (2015)
10. Hysaj, A., Elkhouly, A., Qureshi, A.W., Abdulaziz, N.: Analysis of engineering students' academic satisfaction in a culturally diverse university. In: 2018 IEEE International Conference on Teaching, Assessment Learning for Engineering (TALE), pp. 755–760 (2018)
11. Hopkyns, S.: The effect of global English on culture and identity in the UAE: a double-edged sword. Learn. Teach. High. Educ. Gulf Perspect. **11**(2) (2014)
12. Lundin, M., Rensfeldt, A.B., Hillman, T., Lantz-Andersson, A., Peterson, L.: Higher education dominance, siloed knowledge: a systematic review of flipped classroom research. Int. J. Educ. Technol. High. Educ. **15**(1), 20 (2018)
13. Hysaj, A., Elkhouly, A., Qureshi, A.W., Abdulaziz, N.A.: Study of the impact of tutor's support and undergraduate student's academic satisfaction. Am. J. Hum. Soc. Sci. Res. **3**(12), 70–77 (2019)
14. Banks, J.A., Banks, C.A.M. (eds.): Multicultural Education: Issues and Perspectives. Wiley, Hoboken (2019)
15. Lehtomäki, E., Moate, J., Posti-Ahokas, H.: Global connectedness in higher education: student voices on the value of cross-cultural learning dialogue. Stud. High. Educ. **41**(11), 2011–2027 (2016)
16. Hill, M.A., Overton, T.L., Thompson, C.D., Kitson, R.R., Coppo, P.: Undergraduate recognition of curriculum-related skill development and the skills employers are seeking. Chem. Educ. Res. Pract. **20**(1), 68–84 (2019)
17. Oros, A.L.: Let's debate: active learning encourages student participation and critical thinking. J. Polit. Sci. Educ. **3**(3), 293–311 (2007)
18. Patel, F.: The political economy of international higher education: balancing quality educaton and social responsibility. Asian J. Res. Educ. Soc. Sci. **1**(2), 33–43 (2019)
19. Abyad, A.: Demographic changes in the GCC countries: reflection and future projection. Middle East J. Age Ageing **83**(5838), 1–5 (2018)
20. Hijazi, R., Zoubeidi, T., Abdalla, I., Al-Waqfi, M., Harb, N.: A study of the UAE higher education sector in light of Dubai's strategic objectives. J. Econ. Adm. Sci. **24**(1), 68–81 (2008)

21. Wilkins, S.: Higher education in the United Arab Emirates: an analysis of the outcomes of significant increases in supply and competition. J. High. Educ. Policy Manag. **32**(4), 389–400 (2010)
22. Nye, M.: The Challenges of Multiculturalism. Taylor & Francis (2007)
23. Pollock, D.C., Van Reken, R.E., Pollock, M.V.: Third Culture Kids: The Experience of Growing UP Among Worlds: The Original, Classic Book on TCKs. Hachette, London (2010)
24. Ozkan, S., Koseler, R.: Multi-dimensional students' evaluation of e-learning systems in the higher education context: an empirical investigation. Comput. Educ. **53**(4), 1285–1296 (2009)
25. Roehl, A., Reddy, S.L., Shannon, G.J.: The flipped classroom: an opportunity to engage millennial students through active learning strategies. J. Family Consum. Sci. **105**(2), 44–49 (2013)
26. Tucker, B.: The flipped classroom. Educ. Next **12**(1), 82–83 (2012)
27. O'Flaherty, J., Phillips, C.: The use of flipped classrooms in higher education: a scoping review. Internet High. Educ. **25**, 85–95 (2015)
28. Lucke, T., Dunn, P.K., Christie, M.: Activating learning in engineering education using ICT and the concept of 'Flipping the classroom'. Eur. J. Eng. Educ. **42**(1), 45–57 (2017)
29. Abeysekera, L., Dawson, P.: Motivation and cognitive load in the flipped classroom: definition, rationale and a call for research. High. Educ. Res. Dev. **34**(1), 1–14 (2015)
30. Franchi, E.: Flipping the classroom in the history lesson: a case study in ancient history. Teach. Hist. **51**(1), 63–65 (2017)
31. Soltanpour, F., Valizadeh, M.: A flipped writing classroom: effects on EFL learners' argumentative essays. Adv. Lang. Literary Stud. **9**(1), 5–13 (2018)
32. McNally, B., et al.: Flipped classroom experiences: student preferences and flip strategy in a higher education context. High. Educ. **73**(2), 281–298 (2017)
33. Balaban, R.A., Gilleskie, D.B., Tran, U.: A quantitative evaluation of the flipped classroom in a large lecture principles of economics course. J. Econ. Educ. **47**(4), 269–287 (2016)
34. King, A., et al.: Curated collection for educators: five key papers about the flipped classroom methodology. Cureus **9**(10) (2017)
35. Graham, M., McLean, J., Read, A., Suchet-Pearson, S., Viner, V.: Flipping and still learning: experiences of a flipped classroom approach for a third-year undergraduate human geography course. J. Geogr. High. Educ. **41**(3), 403–417 (2017)
36. Freguia, S.: Webcasts promote in-class active participation, learning in an engineering elective course. Eur. J. Eng. Educ. **42**(5), 482–492 (2017). https://doi.org/10.1080/03043797.2016.1192110
37. Davenport, C.E.: Evolution in student perceptions of a flipped classroom in a computer programming course. J. Coll. Sci. Teach. **47**(4), 30–35 (2018)
38. Erdogan, E., Akbaba, B.: Should we flip the social studies classrooms? The opinions of social studies teacher candidates on flipped classroom. J. Educ. Learn. **7**(1), 116–124 (2018)
39. D'Argembeau, A., et al.: Self-referential reflective activity and its relationship with rest: a PET study. Neuroimage **25**(2), 616–624 (2005)
40. Nesi, H.: The form, meaning and purpose of university level assessed reflective writing. In: Proceedings of the BAAL Annual Conference (2007)
41. Imbir, K.K., Jarymowicz, M.T.: The effect of automatic vs. reflective emotions on cognitive control in antisaccade tasks and the emotional Stroop test. Pol. Psychol. Bull. **44**(2), 137–146 (2013)
42. Johnstone, B.: Discourse Analysis. Wiley, Hoboken (2018)
43. Yuan, R., Mak, P.: Reflective learning and identity construction in practice, discourse and activity: experiences of pre-service language teachers in Hong Kong. Teach. Teach. Educ. **74**, 205–214 (2018)
44. Hyland, K.: Second Language Writing. Cambridge University Press, Cambridge (2019)

45. Nicol, D.J., Macfarlane-Dick, D.: Formative assessment and self-regulated learning: a model and seven principles of good feedback practice. Stud. High. Educ. **31**(2), 199–218 (2006)
46. Moffett, J.: Integrity in the teaching of writing. Phi Delta Kappan **61**(4), 276–279 (1979)
47. Pecorari, D.: Teaching to Avoid Plagiarism: How to Promote Good Source Use. McGraw-Hill Education, London (2013)
48. Castaneda, L., Swain, N.: More than tools? Making sense of the ongoing digitisations of higher education. Int. J. Educ. Technol. High. Educ. **15** (2018)
49. Fullana, J., Pallisera, M., Colomer, J., Fernández Peña, R., Pérez-Burriel, M.: Reflective learning in higher education: a qualitative study on students' perceptions. Stud. High. Educ. **41**(6), 1008–1022 (2016)
50. Cottrell, S.: The Study Skills Handbook. Macmillan International Higher Education (2019)
51. Uerz, D., Volman, M., Kral, M.: Teacher educators' competences in fostering student teachers' proficiency in teaching and learning with technology: an overview of relevant research literature. Teach. Teach. Educ. **70**, 12–23 (2018)
52. Ping, C., Schellings, G., Beijaard, D.: Teacher educators' professional learning: a literature review. Teach. Teach. Educ. **75**, 93–104 (2018)
53. Philipsen, B., Tondeur, J., Roblin, N.P., Vanslambrouck, S., Zhu, C.: Improving teacher professional development for online and blended learning: a systematic meta-aggregative review. Educ. Tech. Res. Dev. **67**(5), 1145–1174 (2019)
54. Parsazadeh, N., Ali, R., Rezaei, M.: A framework for cooperative and interactive mobile learning to improve online information evaluation skills. Comput. Educ. **120**, 75–89 (2018)
55. Vanslambrouck, S., Zhu, C., Lombaerts, K., Philipsen, B., Tondeur, J.: Students' motivation and subjective task value of participating in online and blended learning environments. Internet High. Educ. **36**, 33–40 (2018)
56. Hewett, B.L., Bourelle, T.: Professional Development in Online Teaching and Learning in Technical Communication: A Ten-Year Retrospective. Routledge (2020)
57. Hysaj, A., Hamam, D.: Does delivery method matter for multicultural undergraduate students? A case study of an Australian University in the United Arab Emirates. In: Meiselwitz, G. (ed.) HCII 2020. LNCS, vol. 12195, pp. 538–548. Springer, Cham (2020). https://doi.org/10.1007/978-3-030-49576-3_39
58. Hamam, D.: A study of the rhetorical features and the argument structure of EAP essays by L1 & L2 students (Doctoral dissertation, The British University in Dubai) (2019)

Tirana Plug-in River: Catalyst Playful Experiences to Revitalize Albanian Informal Settlements

Saimir Kristo[(✉)] [iD], Valerio Perna[(✉)] [iD], and Keti Hoxha[(✉)] [iD]

Universiteti POLIS, Rr. Bylis 12, Autostrada Tiranë-Durrës, Km 5, Tiranë, Albania
{saimir_kristo,valerio.Perna,
keti_hoxha}@universitetipolis.edu.al

Abstract. The fall of the Communist dictatorship has changed dramatically the urban structure of the city of Tirana. The original organic structure - and the later Soviet functionalist fabric - has been parasitized by a spread system of informal (and currently illegal) settlements that are perceivable as 'other spaces' (Foucault 2000), completely rejected by the historical city. Indeed, the latter generated a system of closed clusters within the urban environment, leading to the creation of a series of barriers which are either physical, psychological and behavioral. For these reasons, the city of Tirana is a kaleidoscopic and deceiving reality, where the explosion of colors and shapes hides the urban conflicts that run underneath and exacerbate the always present social tension and conflict.

Previous top-down solutions - proposed by the government - have demonstrated their ineffectiveness due to a positivistic approach that could not take into account the complexity of a vital city in continuous evolution. To offer concrete and long-term solutions to these crises, there is the need for catalytic interventions that can help in the creation of different and overlapping frameworks of action: architectural, social, education, and economical ones.

In this paper, we will present the incremental design project 'Tirana | Plug-in River', with the aim of demonstrating how multitasking infrastructure (Saggio 2014) can work as positive vectors in the urban fabric using playful dynamics and mechanics, and bottom-up/civic engagement design processes in the existing city where architecture, art and citizenship interaction can operate as a key for a new urban consciousness and reactivation.

Keywords: Urban catalysis · Gaming architecture · Human interaction

1 Multitasking Infrastructure to Inform Urban Development. In Search for a Contemporary Paradigm Shift

Contemporary cities are becoming more and more complex and have to face a large number of challenges gripping large urbanized territories of the big metropolises. Problems such as hydrogeological instabilities, issues related to sustainability and to the excessive expansion of the built environment, social tensions and conflicts in poor and underdeveloped reality, are just some of the many criticalities that architects have to tackle to

© Springer Nature Switzerland AG 2020
C. Stephanidis et al. (Eds.): HCII 2020, LNCS 12425, pp. 432–444, 2020.
https://doi.org/10.1007/978-3-030-60128-7_33

propose solutions and reach an operative paradigm shift (Saggio 2013). Moreover, this ever-growing complexity does affect not only the physical image of the city, but also its cultural, social, and political context, in relation even with the new technological implementations that make it function and livable for their citizens.

The machine revolution consigned to us a strongly organized structure of the urban fabric, a mono-tasking vision (De Francesco and Saggio 2016, 2018) for the city, where the leading metaphor is the assembly line: every process in the urban areas can be synthesized as a linear system where the previous one forestalls the subsequent. This model works well for mechanical productive issues but does not take into account a whole series of unexpected events that need a deeper understanding and involve intangible problems like the relations between the inhabitants of urban sectors, and their desires and needs.

Not taking into consideration these relational spaces create a gap which is difficult to fill and fosters the emergence of tensions and conflicts in areas where the lack of strong centralized governance - like Albania - cannot offers dynamic and flexible tools to guarantee durable and effective solutions. What we argue for is to look at the city as an open system (Sennet 2007), elastic and variable through time: an evolutionary model (MVRDV 2007) where spaces have to be relational and their borders porous as a semi-lattice (Alexander 1965), an open structure where every single part is cross-connected with others by different orders of engagement.

Moreover, all these boundaries and issues, worsened by space limitation in the existing urban environment, still represents a severe obstacle in a long-term planning process, especially in complex and layered situations as the European reality. To date, governments, municipalities, and citizens' associations have been following two primary paths to overcome this question.

On the one hand, top-down procedures - defined as the operation of breaking down a system to reach new insights regarding its sub-systems in a reverse engineering fashion (Bresser-Pereira et al. 1993) - have shown in the past a lack of empathy towards people (focusing on policies rather than users); on the other hand, bottom-up strategies - consisting in piecing together of methods to give birth to more complex systems, thus splitting the original systems into sub-systems of the emergent system - sometimes overlooked their consequences for society as whole (Ampatzidou et al. 2015), often focusing on the spontaneous organization of citizens.

In the context of a strategy oriented towards longer-term outcomes, architects should reflect on new trans-disciplinary tools for urban planning and public participation, with the objective of avoiding ghettoization and ready-made functionalist solutions. Our idea is to lay the foundation for a debate to develop an alternative path to overcome the current antagonism between top-down city developments and bottom-up citizen initiatives and to allow citizens and designers to envision themselves as social changes agents.

The key of this approach is not working using grids, but rings (Saggio 2014), to activate not one-way input/output processes but stratified ones, to chase an idea of continuity and interrelation between the different actors involved in the city development and management. Nevertheless, using participation processes - and citizenship engagement systems - as a tool to appropriate the urban fabric environment, infrastructures and resources, not for a personal gain, but rather from the perspective of a common goal or collective interest, is the key to let professionals, institutions and citizens work together in a more informed process called city-making (Ampatzidou et al. 2015).

As many international realities pointed out during the last decades, every urban transformation starts from a catalyst element (Kristo 2014), able to activate multiple processes in the urban environment: social, economic, architectural ones. If streets, and infrastructures on a broader sense, have always been the favorite weapon of the industrial period to conquer and expand the limit of the productive cities, we believe that precisely these can be the vector a new urban renaissance.

We are in need of a new generation of infrastructures - also described as multitasking infrastructures (Saggio 2012, 2013) - that can regenerate the urban fabric, and revitalize the places that they cross. Certainly, we need to intend the word 'infrastructure in a very wide meaning (not only streets, but also connecting bridges, ecological corridors, fluvial infrastructures, etc.) that not only guarantee a linear connection but allow operating jumps (Saggio 2013), interpreted as stratified three-dimensional movements taking into account - and solving - multiple issues and wounds in the urban fabric, recovering those that are currently named as brown areas or dross capes (Berger 2007) and represents a major challenge for contemporary architects and municipalities.

2 Objectives and Contributions

In this paper, we aim to provide new conceptual and operative tools to discuss and reflect on how new generation infrastructures, and playful dynamics and mechanics - together with bottom-up citizenship engagement and activation processes - can facilitate long-term planning procedures where citizens themselves could take their responsibility and contribute to durable solutions.

Nevertheless, governments are no longer the central directors determining both societal goals and the exact path to achieve them, but instead, producers that should capitalize on the energy of citizens, organizations, companies, and institutions. We want to offer them our research as a tool for a closer dialogue between game design, urban planning, and civic engagement, in which the idea of empowering citizens is particularly urgent. (Schouten 2015).

For these reasons, and for the fact that we are involved in architectural design and education from different perspectives in the Albanian reality, we propose a design experimentation in the urban fabric of Tirana, where the northern part of the river is seen a vector for the renaissance for one of the most problematic areas of the city. Three are the main features of our approach: the use of the river as a multitasking infrastructure and the subsequent proposal for a deep transformation of the whole area; the importance of having urban catalyst as a mean of urban revitalization; the will to tear down the system of closed clusters within the Albanian urban environment, leading to the creation of an alternative to the series of currently existing physical, psychological and behavioral barriers.

3 Playful Urban Renaissance Along Tirana River

Tirana | Plug-In River is a chair project with the class of 'Advanced Architecture and IT studio[1] at POLIS University. The project follows the example of a series of international experience - like the project Tevere Cavo[2] in Rome, in which one of the authors has been a research assistant for several years - where the river is seen as a multitasking infrastructure based on five principles: multitasking, green systems, slow-scape, information technology foam, galvanize[3].

The chosen path of the River is the one in the Northern part of the city where it intercepts the new boulevard, the informal settlements areas located there, and that are still waiting to know what their faith will be, and the natural systems represented by the Mount Dajti in the North. The project aims to activate bottom-up processes in the existing city where architecture, art and citizenship interaction can operate as a key for a new urban consciousness and reactivation, and so, all the students' interventions, aim for involving the citizens and activate the environment engaging multiple processes and civil actions. The philosophy of the experimentation follows two significant ideas: on the one side, it is rooted in an incremental design philosophy where the process does not start from a previously decided master plan but, it is built through time in a progressive development. On the other hand, it follows a Research Through Design (RtD) approach (Zimmerman et al. 2007, 2010), intended as one of the many methodologies and epistemologies that are leveraged in the broader field of design research and has to do with the use of design practice as a form of scientific inquiry. In other words, an RtD approach involves the designing of experimental artifacts as a mean of raising interesting scientific questions and answering them: as John Zimmerman noted how design is a process but also a form of research.

The final result will a series of ludic and playful installation along the river - designed by the students and the other academics involved - that will act as responsive micro-architectures following a plug-in design philosophy (Baldissara, Perna, Saggio, Stancato 2017). For plug-in design, we refer to small catalyst interventions that seek interaction with the users locally and globally and engage multiple processes and civil actions in the urban fabric. Moreover, these proposals incorporate some playful and gamified application – centered on the use of specific game features to include ludic qualities (Deterding et al. 2011) - that have been widely employed within a design and participatory planning

---

[1] The project is also included in the INNOVATION_Factory (IF) framework. IF is a is an interdisciplinary innovation and research center at POLIS University founded by Professor Ph.D. Antonino di Raimo. Its main aim is to promote all research practices, methodologies and approaches unfolding new content in different fields of science and technology. Innovation Factory acts as a cross-discipline cloud which combines the activities of the three faculties with the purpose of generating and provoking new creative and experimental solutions. The teaching staff behind the Tirana | Plug-In River also includes: architect and Ph.D. candidate Gerdi Papa, and architect Asdren Sela.

[2] Tevere Cavo is a project by the chair of professor Antonino Saggio at 'Sapienza - Università di Roma'. The aim of this experimentation relating in an urban design a series of urban and underutilized areas in Rome, where the river represents a vector for a social, cultural, and architectural renaissance.

[3] For detailed study of these five principles refer to Saggio (2012, 2014, 2017, 2018).

processes. Many studies have shown that their use can be beneficial in situations where these tools could be implemented as part of the planning phase (Ampatzidou et al. 2018) and if their development phase is based on co-creation with multiple stakeholders and participants.

The final aim of the project, in an expected time period of three/four years, will be a vision for the city of Tirana (Tirana 2030) that sees the river as a vector for the city's renaissance and as a urban catalyst to reopen the debate on strategies and tools to activate and rethink urban space and city development. To understand better the reasons that motivate this design proposal is useful to deal with the peculiar evolution of the urban fabric, and why the current city structure is so fragmented and discontinuous (Fig. 1).

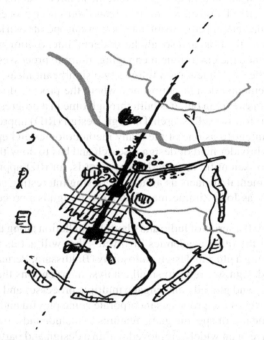

Fig. 1. Scheme: Tirana of three lakes and three rivers

4   Playful Between Spontaneity and Organization. Reflections Over Tirana's Peculiar Urban Development

Initiated as an organic city in the 17th century, Tirana oscillated several times between spontaneity and organized planning. It is a city not easily shaped through plans: a blurred and fragmented situation created by the continuous interaction between organic development and planning decisions. However it has all undergone unbelievable changes offering a unique perspective for urban planning and development with enormous energy within.

Tirana began as an organic city in the 17th century and has since been shaped by the continuous interaction between spontaneous developments and planning decisions. It remained a small town until it was declared the capital of Albania in 1920. Starting from the beginning of the '20s, under the monarchy, the first attempts to move from spontaneous to organized urban planning were initiated.

Typical of this period is the ceremonial complex of the government buildings, the opening or stretching of several main avenues, such as Rruga e Durresit, and the central axis of the boulevard, first designed by Armando Brasini.

The combination of the new axis together with the presence of Lana creek, re-created a structure similar to a "cardum" and "decumanum", north-south and west-east axes that give a clear structure to the city. In fact, this logic reveals a broader system in the city considering the natural elements as part of the organization of the city's morphology. Natural pre-existing systems define the logic of development not only in the orientation of the main public spaces and settlements but also as part of the organization of the life itself inside urban blocks. Mount Dajti towards North-East in combination with the hills of Vaqar creates a natural system of protection. The development of the Boulevard itself crossing Lana river but also having the Grand Lake Park with the Artificial lake of Tirana as an element of closure gave a clear emphasis on the role of such natural element had for the city.

These kinds of interventions were significantly intensified during the period of Italian occupation (1939–1943). The new center, located at the extreme south of the extended boulevard – monumentality separated from the social reality – is still clearly visible in today's urban fabric.

With its actual population of nearly one million inhabitants, Tirana is four times the size it used to be 20 years ago and amounts to more than one-quarter of the country's entire population. Almost 60% of Albania's population is living in an urban surrounding. The transition from socialism to capitalism had a direct impact on the social, economic and spatial structures of the city. Tirana's urban space has transformed rapidly, towards two different directions: On one side lies the transformation of the city center and the primary road axes where commerce, offices, and entertainment have been introduced. New housing complexes have been constructed in these central areas, too. On the other side, since the early 1990s, an informal extension of the city's borders, firstly by small-scale housing and later by large-scale housing, was gradually developed without planning, social and technical infrastructure or provision for public spaces, leading to the creation of a poor urban environment, with no apparent intention to be integrated with their existing surrounding context. At the same time, informal development processes have also taken place within the existing urban fabric, occupying former public land and blocking passages by erecting small, medium or even large-scale constructions. These large-scale housing and commercial complexes were implemented in the periphery of the city by the private sector and had undergone a recent series of actions to legalize them and understand that they are part of the urban reality and have to be integrated in the future urban development plans.

The municipality tried to regain public control with several beautification campaigns in the 2000s and a series of international competitions inviting several star architects to create a new image for the city. Streets, parks and the Lana riverfront were cleared of illegal kiosks, and thousands of trees were planted, ready to welcome visionary ideas from West, giving a lot of attention to Lana River as an important, and vibrant ecosystem for the city. Unfortunately, that ecosystem didn't face fair treatment concerning infrastructure as it serves as one of the main sewage channels in the city and a considerable problem of pollution and infection risks.

A lot of attention on an international level was drawn to Tirana by the attempt of its former Mayor, Edi Rama, in 2001 to reinvent the city's identity. As an artist he cleaned up the very scruffy avenues with a radical facelift that - through interventions on the major public spaces and by upgrading the public infrastructure - attempted to construct a new image and a new identity for the city center, regenerating the city by attracting new activities and investments, as part of the vision of Greater Tirana and 'Durana'.

Moreover, is important to note the development of the peri-urban expansion of Tirana city and the consolidation of the inner part of the city were the reason for the mayor of Tirana, Lulzim Basha, to announce a competition for the extension of boulevard "Zogu I" to the north as a continuation of the monumental boulevard connecting the two edge lakes of Tirana City. The boulevard should have created a new gate formed by new administrative buildings, moving the public services out of Tirana's City center. Important international studios participated in the competition: KCAP [NL]; Grimshaw Architects [UK]; West8 [NL]; Cino Zucchi Architetti [IT]; Albert Speer and Partners [GER]; DAR Group [UK].

Grimshaw Architects from London won the competition. The project area, including the extension of a three kilometers boulevard and the organization of a seven kilometers riverside park, covers a fifth of the overall area of the city. The winning project was proposing the creation of sequences of 'living rooms' along the boulevard and the river park which reflect Tirana's Mediterranean outdoor culture, strengthen the key identity of urban fabric, and formalize the informal existing settlements. To make this possible, the project proposes a clear expropriation strategy in order to develop important projects for the community and to improve legibility and character.

The impact of Tirana River in the city of Tirana can put in full action the conceptual development of the city in a scheme of three (3) rivers (Lana, Tirana, Terkuza) and three (3) lakes (Artificial Grand Lake, Paskuqan Lake.

The area on which Tirana River is located is quite strategic, not only as a natural potential for the city, but also as a link between the municipality of Tirana and the municipality of Kamza. It can serve not only as a natural and green lung for the wider area of Metropolitan Tirana but also as a catalytic project for the development and integration of the area of Paskuqan - located directly next to Tirana River - and all the previously informal settlements built after the reinstatement of democracy in Albania without being abided to any regulatory plans.

An explicit reference could come from Madrid and the development of Madrid RIO project from West 8 Urban Design and Landscape, a proper multitasking infrastructure within the structure of the Spanish capital. An urban catalyst which managed to not only revitalize its surrounding areas, but also to remedy the existing urban fabric making that area a vital leisure destination for the city of Madrid. Such interventions based in the Urban Catalysis theory area very important in realities such as Albania and furthermore since the complexity of such reality requires a series of layers to be addressed in every urban revitalization/regeneration in social, economic, landscape, cultural, architectural and urban levels.

It is clear that, to tackle the many issues lying a complex system like the city of Tirana, is necessary to address multiple tangible and intangible problems. For this reason, we propose a holistic design methodology that takes into account studies regarding the psychology of architecture - and concepts such as 'well-being' - to lower social tensions and conflicts and reach long-term outcomes in the reorganization of the informal settlements in the Albanian reality.

Five Points for a Social and Psychological Well-being. An Overview on the Relationship Between Mental Spaces and Architecture.

The political and economic changes in Albania clearly reflects in the urban config-uration and architecture of the city of Tirana. The undefined structure and informality along the areas of the Tirana River does not affect only the image of the whole city - and damage the river landscape - but also created a precise psychological and mental state that does not allow the inhabitants to develop these areas furthermore. This state is associated with two main aspects: on the one hand, the sense of well-being and, on the other hand, the insecurity of losing their dwelling because of being illegal.

World Health Organization defines health as "a state of complete physical, mental and social well-being". For obtaining this state, the presence of two main elements is essential: a sense of 'feeling good', which consists in the state of feeling confident with oneself; and to 'function well' which includes having and maintaining good relationships with the community and others. Nevertheless, it is essential to define the necessary aspects for a space to provide individual and social well-being. To provide this, spaces should have the characteristics below:

1. Comply: where the urban environment is capable of performing human activities in everyday life;
2. Communicate: to deliver relevant information by making it easier for people to utilize space, and provide opportunities for socializing and for guaranteeing secure exchange information within each other, with or without their desire;
3. Comfort: in such a way to meet their psychological needs and to easily perceive the environment, to ensure good mental stability;
4. Challenge: activate opportunities for individuals to develop and reach their goals;
5. Continuity: to be flexible in adapting with the people's need through time, and provide all the necessary resources for them.

It is necessary to point out that the inhabitants of informal settlements' dwellings may not provide all the characteristics mentioned above. Furthermore, there is a lack of organized and secure public spaces system for all the generations, which leads to an antisocial environment by lowering the probability of collaboration with each other.

If well-being is not provided in private and public spaces, this deficiency will reflect itself in the psychological patterns of the residents and as a result in their behavior. Lefebvre argues that social relations are spatial and connected to the physical space, along with it, socio-economic characteristics of a society are reflected physically in spaces and demonstrate the living manners of the individuals.

Therefore, space is a product of social relations and social-political activities. (Lefebvre 1991) The informal settlements are areas in such condition that keep growing spontaneously, without the regard of the state planning and laws. This areas lack essential services and city infrastructure, and are usually situated in geographical - and environmentally - sensitive zones, and, since there is no political regulation/control performed, the inhabitants have no security of tenure for their dwelling or land. (Brown 2015) This phenomenon leads to an ever-growing social tension and conflicts, in areas that are classified as spontaneous, disorganized and illegal. These aspects are very definitive for the psychological and behavioral pattern between the inhabitants themselves and possible unknown visitors.

4.1 A Personalization. An Urban Catalyst to Provide Short-Term and Long-Term Outcomes for the Informal Settlements Along Tirana River

"Personalization" is the primary phenomenon in the settlements of Tirana River, and it also represents one of the leading causes of social tension in the community. This peculiar action leads to conflicts between inhabitants and their social structure and affects the life of the whole community with changes regarding the parameters of a person's life and his/her behavior that subsequently leads to disputes among individuals. When a citizen personalizes his space, conflicts arise concerning the boundaries of landowning. Another interesting aspect of this behavioral pattern is the stimulation of the urge to the others to customize their private space. This link to a shared feeling of standing out through personalizing their dwelling to establish a hierarchic social structure based upon recognition. This complex process distorts the image of the city and the unifying architectural language is missing and nearly impossible.

Because there is an illegal framework for approaching their dwellings, there is a common sense of fear of losing their property between the inhabitants. This insecurity translates into an unwelcoming behavior or - even violence - against the others that are not part of the community, who are identified as an upcoming menace to the existence of their dwelling. The result of this repulsion brings a sense of fear and uncertainties to visitors and creates an overall dangerous image of the neighborhood.

This process has a double-sided outcome: on the one hand, the inhabitants are isolated and not opened for the future development of their areas, on the other hand, the rest of urban fabric tends to refuse and expel them from the civic life of the city. Furthermore, the existing psychological state does not allow the informal settlements' people to understand the significant role that the collaboration in a community means with a view of developing their neighborhood and public spaces.

The negative phenomenon of the community, such as personalization, can be twisted to become the crucial catalysis for a more positive growth of the informal areas. But firstly, the inhabitants must be empowered about the vital role they play in transforming and improving their spaces.

To do so, it is fundamental the presence of a social group that could facilitate the dialogue between the community. The perfect example of this case is the workshop held in the city of Struga, Macedonia, organized by the Social Club Kombinati. The aim of the two weeks activity "Urban Shelter" was to represent a focal point for grass-roots and community-based organizations, NGOs, creative people and citizens, to socialize and familiarize with the cultural values and address the identification of various ethnic communities, in neighborhoods where there was a lack of dialogue between inhabitants.

In a nutshell, the overall aim of the whole experimentation was to implement bottom-up site-specific interventions; provide solutions for better quality of public spaces; assure community engagement processes and facilitate mutual interaction through catalyst urban design actions. The workshop outcomes found shape in raising the inhabitants' awareness of their chance to be the positive vector for a different development of their city's potential. For its bottom-up – and site-specific features, we argue for the same methodology to be performed even in the informal areas of Tirana River, where the 'Tirana I Plug-in River' is just the first attempt to bring together architecture, design, and socio-psychological studies, into a holistic design process.

The first step to fulfill our goal is to understand the people's needs, also through the implementation of digital tools – and smart data gathering systems – such as online or site surveys. Questionnaire surveys are useful to obtain quantitative data, which can be compared over time or with the results from other sites. The polls must include questions about the inhabitant's point of view on the main absences of space typology and activities needed. This part is fundamental because it is necessary to detach from the positivistic state of mind which does not take into account the qualitative side of the gathered data. Moreover, the comprehension of this information can work as a reflection phase for the community to identify the critical problems concerning their community and spaces. This phase should be enrich by a dialogue phase between the different stakeholders involved, to help the community to be aware of their needs and to lower conflicts between them.

The next step is to use participatory methods which are necessary to influence the residents' behavior and to change the urban design of their spaces. These solutions may be divided into two main groups according to their feasibility: immediate solutions, that can be done in several hours and short-term solutions, which can be implemented in several weeks. Let's briefly describe these two strategies to highlight their pros/cons and possible outcomes regarding their application in the Tirana's riverside.

Immediate solution: The first target to be involved is represented by the most willing group age, the younger generation of teenagers and children that can start with the early necessary intervention: the cleaning of the area.

This primary step is crucial because the citizens themselves should be conscious about the environment they live in and of the importance of the natural element in their life.

Of course, for its peculiarity of being an informal area, the environment is quite polluted and it will take a lot of time and appropriate appliances to clean the river, but through this process the people become more aware of the environment they live in. When the young group target starts the action, the sense to be involved will be present even in other group age.

The next immediate solution can be creating DIY (do it yourself) urban furni-ture, such as sitting elements with wooden pallets, playing facilities with tires, putting boundaries between the parking area and the public space with stones and gardening, etc.

The short-term solutions include the improvement of the walking paths, the painting process of the main facades of the buildings creating a unifying language, the building picnic facilities, and collective orchards, etc.

Another strategy that the project aims for implementing is the use of digital technologies - sensors and actuators, artificial intelligence and digital media – to allow users/citizens to improve the quality of these spaces and make the urban fabric they live in more playful and attractive for themselves and for the rest of the community. These systems change the space and time of play entirely, transforming the city in a whole playground where ludic processes can be real-time activated and spatial renaissance is addressed through social interaction and inhabitants' activation (Perna 2018).

For a first implementation – also because of cost issues – the starting materials for this interventions can be easily found and gathered through recycling. They can come in various forms and functions and adapt to fit the new uses the community needs. Wooden pallets collected from markets or supermarkets can be transformed into as outdoor furniture through simple woodworking techniques. The same material can be even used to build benches, tables, orchard organizers, fences and bicycle parking, etc. Moreover, to make sitting elements, playground areas for children, flower pots, materials - as tires – can be gathered in scrap tire yards which are populates the area, through a design process that recalls many international experience like the one from Rural Studio in the US (Saggio 2002). Other materials that can be used through DIY – Do it yourself - techniques can be beer cases, plastic bottles, stones, etc. All of these resources and methods can transform the spaces to either temporary or final solutions.

Furthermore, this can also activate a process of a circular economy within the informal settlements itself. The selling, and diffusion, of this spontaneous 'piece of art furniture', can provide the inhabitants with an alternative economic system that can be used to fund the implementation of smart tools in the environment. The objective is to lead the community to a long-term development plan that can be effective in a different period.

All of these techniques and simple intervention not only improve the quality of spaces of the informal settings but have a quite significant psychological and social impact in the community. Firstly, the citizens start to feel the importance of their role in the personalization of their own space and are empowered in the relationship they should have with the environment.

Secondly, these methods foster a sense of collaboration and communication between inhabitants themselves and push them to reflect on the importance of the community collaboration in maintaining or even creating spaces.

5   Conclusive Reflections and Future Research Agenda

Since Inspired by Action Research (Foth and Brynskov 2016) our speculative research strategy's purpose is to solve a particular problem while – at the same time - produce guidelines for effective practices within the architectural and design research.

We found inspiring to address the informal settlements topic from multiple points of view, and different theoretical frames, to deliver complex architectural and design solutions. As a next step, more testing and validation are certainly needed, and we see this process as inherently iterative and practical, and deeply related to our academic experience with students involved in different educational levels (master students; Ph.D. candidates; lecturers, etc.). This is why, in lieu of a conclusion, allow us to finish the paper with a reflection on our experimentation so far, and on what we expect this paper could set the scene for a positive research agenda for the river Tirana.

From the get-go, we did not want to frame the selected topic from a one-way perspective, but we aimed to sparkle a broader dialogue to include not only architects but experts coming from different fields, to facilitate a lateral design thinking phase that could link to more effective and long-term solutions through the implementation of psychological, IT, and playful design studies.

Following Donald Schon's (1983) assumptions, we strongly focus on design as a reflective practice where the designer critically reflects on the action to improve design methodology and thinking. Indeed, the design phase is a process but also a form of research, and the design of games and playful interactions in relation to architecture and urban development can undoubtedly offer a contribution to address the contemporary crisis in the informal urban fabric of Tirana.

In sum, with this work we argue for a more inclusive design process that can – at the same time – empowers and involves citizens themselves through tearing down the physical and mental barrier affecting the Albanian society. Our primary aim is for setting an open dialogue for a new design research agenda for the informal areas where the river, as a multitasking infrastructure, can be the necessary urban catalyst to explore unexpected – and anti-positivist – design solution and produce long-term outcomes.

References

Alexander, C.: The city is not a tree. Sustasis Foundation, Portland, USA (1967)

Aliaj, B., Lulo, K., Myftiu, G.: Tirana, the Challenge of Urban Development, p. 30. Co-Plan and Seda. Albania (2003a)

Aliaj, B., Lulo, K., Myftiu, G.: Tirana, the Challenge of Urban Development, p. 42. Co-Plan and Seda. Albania (2003b)

Ampatzidou, C., Bouw, M., van de Klundert, F., de Lange, M., de Waal, M.: The Hackable City: A Research Manifesto and Design Toolki. Amsterdam Creative Industries Publishing, Amsterdam (2015)

Ampatzidou, C., Gugerell, K., Constantinescu, T., Devisch, O., Jauschneg, M., Berger, M.: All work and no play. Facilitating serious games and gamified applications in participatory urban planning and governance. Urban Plan. 3(1), 34–46 (2018)

Bresser-Pereira, L.C., Maravall, J.M., Przeworski, A.: Economic Reforms in new Democracies. Cambridge University Press, Cambridge (1993)

Brown, B.: Territoriality, Handbook of Environmental Psychology. In: Stokols, D., Altman, I. (eds.), vol. 1. Wiley, New York (1987)

Brown, G., Lawrence, T., Robinson, S.: Territoriality in organizations. In: Academy of Management Review, vol. 30, no. 3 (2005)

Declerck, J., Zenghelis, E., Aureli, P.V.: Tirana Metropolis. Berlage Institute, Rotterdam (2004)

De Francesco, G., Saggio, A.: Tevere cavo una infrastruttura di nuova generazione per Roma tra passato. Lulu.com, Raleigh USA (2016)

De Francesco, G., Saggio, A.: Tevere cavo una infrastruttura di nuova generazione per Roma tra passato. Lulu.com, Raleigh USA (2018)

Deterding, S., Dixon, D., Khaled, R., Nacke, L.: From game design elements to gamefulness: defining "gamification". In: Mindtrek 2011, pp. 9–15. ACM, Tampere (2011)

Dhamo, S.: Tirana dhe roli i "imagjinatës urbane" në transformimin e saj. Nga gjenezat tek modeli metropolitan. In: Forum A + P 10, p. 8. Tirana, Albania (2012)

Kristo, F.: History of Tirana as a City till 1920, vol. 1, p. 17. Toena Publications, Tirana (2004)

Foth, M., Brynskov, M.: Participatory action research for civic engagement. In: Gordon, E., Mihailidis, P. (eds.) Civic Media: Technology, Design, Practises. MIT Press, Cambridge (2016)

Foucault, M.: Spazi altri. I luoghi delle eterotopie. Mimesis Edizioni, Milano (2000)

Lefebvre, H.: The Production of Space. Blackwell, Cambridge (1991)

MVRDV/Delft School of Design.: Space Fighter, The Evolutionary City (Game). Actar, Barcelona/New York (2007)

Zorica, N.-B.: Urban Studies, vol. 30. no. 6, pp. 899–905 (2001)

Perna, V.: From smart cities to playable cities. Towards playful intelligence in the urban environment. In: Archi-DOCT. The e-journal the Dissemination of Doctoral Research in Architecture, vol. 6, no. 1 (2018)

Kristo, S.: Urban Catalysis-A theoretical framework for the urban development of public space in Albania, developed in the framework of the PhD program in architecture and urban planning between POLIS and Ferrara Universities, Ph.D. Report (2014)

Saggio, A.: Urban green line. Una infrastruttura ecologica tra passato e future. Lulu.com, Raleigh (2012)

Saggio, A.: Urban green line. Una infrastruttura ecologica tra passato e future. Lulu.com, Raleigh (2013)

Schön, D.A.: The Reflective Practitioner: How Professionals Think in Action. Temple Smith, London (1983)

Schouten, B.A.M.: Playful Empowerment. Inaugural Lecture. Amsterdam University of Applied Sciences, Amsterdam (2015)

Sennett, R.: Open city. In: Burdett, R., Sudjic, D. (eds.) The Endless City. Phaidon, London (2007)

Tirana Municipality: Greater Tirana Project. Tirana (2006)

World Bank: Doing business 2008 (2007). Eastern Europe. http://www.doingbusiness.org/Doc uments/RegionalReports/DB2008_RP_Eastern_Europe.pdf Accessed 18 Dec 2009

Zimmerman, J., Forlizzi, J., Evenson, S.: Research through design as a method for interaction design research in HCI. In: CHI 2007 Proceedings of the SIGCHI Conference on Human Factors in Computing Systems. ACM, New York (2007)

Zimmerman, J., Forlizzi, J., Evenson, S.: An analysis and critique of research through design: towards a formalization of a research approach. In: DIS 2010 Proceedings of the 8th ACM Conference on Designing Interactive Systems, pp. 310–319. ACM, New York (2010)

Investigating the Relation Between Sense of Presence, Attention and Performance: Virtual Reality Versus Web

Aliane Loureiro Krassmann[✉], Fabrício Herpich,
Liane Margarida Rockenbach Tarouco, and Magda Bercht

Universidade Federal do Rio Grande do Sul, Porto Alegre, Brazil
alkrassmann@gmail.com

Abstract. The sense of presence is an important construct of virtual experiences, as it relates to the user's attention. This pilot study investigates the relations among sense of presence, attention levels and performance, comparing the outcomes across two different media formats (virtual reality versus web). Fourteen participants performed knowledge tests in the area of Financial Mathematics. Sense of presence was evaluated through questionnaire and attention levels were measured using a EEG biosensor. The results show that, although very prominent to the sense of presence and its tangential benefits, the virtual reality technology was not successful as the web in translating the allocation of attentional resources into better performance.

Keywords: Sense of presence · Attention · Performance · Virtual reality · Web

1 Introduction

Virtual reality is an emerging technology in the field of education. It allows the creation of highly interactive and realistic virtual environments for practicing and acquiring skills and knowledge, making possible to conduct activities that are too expensive, complex or even impossible in real life. At the same time, it provides a more stimulating and motivating setting, where learning can be both challenging and fun. Among the cost-benefit options to use this technology are the virtual worlds, which can be accessed by a normal computer interface, such as the open-source platform OpenSimulator.

When users are projected in virtual environments, usually through their avatars, they have the feeling of "being there", which is called the sense of presence. It refers to the psychological state of experiencing more the virtual space rather than the actual physical location, or the perceptual illusion that the experience is non-mediated [1]. The literature suggests that this is a key feature to ensure the transfer of knowledge from the virtual to the real-world, as it allows students to feel more authentic [2].

Several studies try to explain the relation between sense of presence and performance. According to Lessiter et al. [3] and Riley, Kaber and Draper [4], attention and involvement are common responses associated with the sense of presence, because to

© Springer Nature Switzerland AG 2020
C. Stephanidis et al. (Eds.): HCII 2020, LNCS 12425, pp. 445–461, 2020.
https://doi.org/10.1007/978-3-030-60128-7_34

be present in an alternative world, our attention must be focused there, not in the real world. Makowski et al. [5] corroborate, stating that presence is linked to selective attention in relation to the stimulus and reduced processing of distractions. Belle, Hargraves and Najarian [6] complement that task performance largely depends on the individual's capacity to inculcate and sustain high levels of engagement and attention during cognitive activities.

In the current globalized information society, it is increasingly becoming more difficult to gain students' attention in classes. On the other hand, according to one of the most prominent education theorists, learning requires conscious attention, effort, and "time on task" [7]. Automatically evaluating whether students maintain their concentration on a learning activity is extremely difficult, due to the lack of supervised mechanisms to monitor attention states [8]. In this perspective, this paper uses an innovative technique to measure user's attention levels in real-time.

As new insights can be reached by comparing variations of learning within different media; a type of research that will not only help answer which media is best for instruction but rather will inform our practice when using a certain technology [9], we pursue the mentioned questions while performing a comparison of two different media: virtual reality and web-based environment. In this sense, the following research questions were elaborated:

RQ1. In some of the conditions, does the attention levels correlate with the performance?
RQ2. In some of the conditions, does performance correlate with time on task?
RQ3. In some of the conditions, does the sense of presence correlate with the attention levels?

2   Theoretical Foundation

Studies have been proposing that attentional processes play a mediating role to the sense of presence. Draper, Kaber and Usher [10], for example, even define presence is as the ratio of attentional resources devoted to the virtual environment (whether related to the task or not). Laarni et al. [11], by their turn, argue that people differ in their ability and willingness to pay attention to the mediated world, and these differences exert influence on their feelings of presence.

On the other hand, Draper, Kaber and Usher [10] also propose that task performance is equally related to the commitment of attentional resources. Therefore, if one was conducting a task that contained nonessential elements (i.e., virtual distracters) that demanded attention, then presence would be increased. Performance, conversely, would decrease because fewer attentional resources would be allocated to the task. In this sense, they suggest that performance in a virtual environment depends on the number of distracters (real or virtual), attentional resources available and attentional resources required by the tasks.

The measurement of presence and attentional resources has a major role in the field of human-computer interaction (HCI). Research issues of particular importance include the lack of a valid and reliable objective assessments, along with concrete evidence of a relationship of these variables with performance. If there is a relationship (causal or correlational), then there may be a legitimate need to establish presence-based or attention-based design guidelines for educational systems. However, the multidimensional nature of these concepts presents a challenge for researchers in terms of developing objective measures as well as relating it to performance [4].

In what concerns presence, the most common methodological approach is subjective, with self-report questionnaires. According to Rey et al. [12], the main advantage is that it is easy to apply and gives quick information about the user experience. Although generally accepted as a valid means, Riley, Kaber and Draper [4] consider that it suffers from limitations such as a) poor subject ability to accurately recall and express experiences in post-trial assessments; b) the items on questionnaires may be difficult for participants to understand; c) investigating the notion of presence after the occurrence, requiring remembering it. In this sense, Szczurowski and Smith [13] argue that it's difficult to avoid giving grounds to response bias, adding that the fact that a questionnaire is asking about something is likely to load answers that otherwise wouldn't have reach participants consciousness.

The existent objective measures of presence are usually physiological, with the monitoring of physiological processes such as heart and respiration rate, skin resistance and temperature. However, they are usually limited to situations where a physiological response is obvious, like, for example, stress-inducing situations [14].

Other physiological indicators of presence that have been recently proposed are measures of neurological activity, such as functional Magnetic Resonance Imaging (fMRI), Transcranial Doppler (TCD) or Electroencephalography (EEG) [15], suitable to observe specific brain areas that are activated during the virtual experience. For example, the Insula is considered to participate in self-awareness and body-ownership, which leads to the formation of our "body schema". If this area is activated, it means that the user's feeling of embodiment will have increased, reducing the barrier between the virtual and the real body [16]. Giving that presence is a phenomenon contained within the human brain, these techniques may provide data closest to its source, free from the influence of the participant's interpretation [13].

Brainwave sensing is also a technique that has been used to measure attentional resources, enabling the automatic tracking of students' attention level. This monitoring enables to take actions to catch students' attention and the implementation of improvements in teaching-learning processes, such as to promote personalized learning based on students' characteristics. The study of Chen, Wang and Yu [8], for instance, assessed students' attention levels in real-time based on EEG signals and supervised machine learning. The system was integrated with a video lecture tagging to register high and low attention levels while learners were watching a video lecture. They found statistically significant correlations between low-attention periods and posttest scores.

Draper, Kaber and Usher [10] suggest that objective methods for evaluating attentional resources may also be useful for assessing presence (and vice-versa). Therefore, giving that brainwave sensing techniques have been used to measure both variables (sense of presence and attention), the aim of this study is to measure user's brain activity in order to infer attention levels and to verify a possible correlation with sense of presence and performance, while comparing different media formats. EEG was the chosen technique due to the freedom of movement it gives to subjects, making it easy to transport to a classroom context and consequently to the mainstream of education. Also, differently from other physiological processes such as heart rate and skin conductance, such metrics are free from association with stress-inducing environments only.

3   Related Work

Giving that studies focusing only in the attention factor are more common, and the ones that include both the sense of presence and attention are more scarce, in this section, we compile studies that sought to relate the sense of presence with brain-related physiological measures in virtual reality environments, which are presented in ascending chronological order.

Baumgartner et al. [17] explored the relationship between spatial presence and cortical activations, using multi-channel EEG in combination with low-resolution brain electromagnetic tomography, during arousing and noninteractive virtual roller coaster rides. As a result, spatial presence was associated with increased activity in parietal/occipital areas of the brain together with decreased activity in frontal structures involved in the executive system.

The study of Rey et al. [12] used Transcranial Doppler Sonography (TCD) in a virtual maze composed of several rooms and corridors. The results showed that immersion and navigation modifications in the environment were responsible for generalized changes in the brain activity. The variations were higher in configurations with higher levels of presence, leading the authors to conclude that these changes could be related to the sense of presence.

Kober and Neuper [14] used event-related potentials of EEG as indicators of the sense of presence. Participants navigated through a virtual city while hearing tones irrelevant to the navigation task. As a result, they found a correlation between presence and a decrease in the late negative slow wave amplitudes, related to the central stimulus processing and the allocation of the attentional resources. According to their conclusion, an increase in presence is related to a greater pay of attention to the virtual environment, which leads to a decrease in the attention paid to the irrelevant stimulus of the virtual reality.

Kober, Kurzmann and Neuper [18] compared presence-related activations of users while navigating through a virtual world in two conditions: one based on a high-immersive virtual reality wall (3D) and another based on a low-immersive 2D desktop screen. The virtual reality condition showed a greater sense of presence associated with an increase in the Alpha band, related to parietal activations. The lower presence experience in the 2D condition was accompanied by strong functional connectivity between the frontal and parietal areas of the brain, leading the authors to conclude that the communication between those areas is crucial for the sense of presence.

Finally, Clemente et al. [16] used the technique of fMRI to investigate brain activations associated with the sense of presence, while comparing different navigation paradigms in a virtual environment: free navigation, visualization of still images, and visualization of an automatic navigation-video of the environment. They identified that the free navigation induced a higher feeling of presence, with higher activation of the

Insula, an area related to emotion and regulation of the body's homeostasis, responsible for functions self-awareness or the sense of agency.

Table 1 summarizes the different aspects investigated in each of the related studies, highlighting a research gap when considering all five aspects that are scoped by this paper. It allows observing that none of the studies had an educational focus nor included performance as a variable of interest, and only Kober and Neuper [14] included attentional resources. Regarding the comparison of media, only Kober, Kurzmann and Neuper [18] and Clemente et al. [16] added this aspect in the investigation.

Table 1. Comparison of the related work.

	Physiological measures	Sense of presence	Attentional resources	Performance	Comparison of media
Baumgartner et al. [17]	Yes	Yes	No	No	No
Rey et al. [12]	Yes	Yes	No	No	No
Kober and Neuper [14]	Yes	Yes	Yes	No	No
Kober, Kurzmann and Neuper [18]	Yes	Yes	No	No	Yes
Clemente et al. [16]	Yes	Yes	No	No	Yes
Present study	**Yes**	**Yes**	**Yes**	**Yes**	**Yes**

In the following section, materials and method are presented.

4   Materials and Method

The design of the study is between-subjects (two different groups), in order to not overload participants by performing the same activity twice. They were equally and randomly assigned (balanced with regard to age and gender) to one of two conditions of media format: virtual reality (OpenSimulator virtual world), and web-based environment (Moodle). Both platforms are open-source and were installed and configured by the researchers.

In this sense, the independent variable is the media format (virtual reality *versus* web-based environment), and the dependent variables are the sense of presence, the attention level and the performance (score in each test). The study was conducted within the area of Financial Mathematics due to convenience of an existent virtual world from the research group.

4.1 Participants

A total of 14 individuals, 8 male and 6 female, aged between 20 and 44 years old (M = 30.02, SD = 7.92) voluntarily participated in the study. Volunteers were graduate (~50%) and undergraduate (~50%) students from the Federal University of Rio Grande do Sul, in Brazil. Their field of study was either Exact and Earth Sciences (~71%) or Applied Social Sciences (~29%). All participants were in good mental health (not aware of any neuropsychiatric disorders) and had a normal or corrected-to-normal vision.

To elucidate more details about the sample, participants were asked to rate their level of interest on the subject addressed in the study, on a 5-point Likert scale question. The majority assigned options 2 or 3 (~71%), and the remaining marked options 4 or 5 (~29%). That is, no one chose option 1, meaning no interest on Financial Mathematics.

Volunteers were also asked to rate their experience with computers, in a four options multiple-choice question, with the following alternatives: None, Basic, Intermediate and Expert. The majority informed having an Intermediate experience (~57%) and the remaining (~43%) were equally divided into Basic and Expert. Table 2 presents the demographics by research group.

Table 2. Demographics of the research groups.

Research group	n	Age		Gender		Interest on the subject	Experience with computers		
		M*	SD	M	F	MD	Basic	Intermediate	Expert
Control group	7	30.13	8.16	4	3	3	1	3	3
Experimental group	7	29.90	8.24	4	3	3	2	5	0

M* = Mean, SD = Standard Deviation, M = Male, F = Female, MD = Median

4.2 Materials

In this subsection, the two media formats used in the study are detailed.

The Virtual Reality. It was implemented the version 0.8.1.1 of the OpenSimulator virtual world platform. The Singularity viewer, also free, was the software used to render the 3D graphical part, selected due to the compatibility with the native language of participants (Portuguese).

The virtual world was designed in a role-playing approach; the user receives the role of a first-day trainee and is challenged with quizzes in order to be admitted by the firm, passing through five sectors. It was created a building simulating and accounting company, populated by automated Non-Player Characters (NPC). They express themselves bodily, simulating tapping on the keyboard at their workstations, and textually, participating in a narrative about the company processes. Office-related background sounds are triggered by the avatar's presence throughout the environment.

Figure 1-left shows a screenshot of a quiz being displayed. Among the options of answer, there is the button "Help", which rotates the user's chair to a screen with a short didactic video related to the subject matter (Fig. 1 – right), selected from the Youtube repository. There is also a "Calculator" button to help students solving the questions.

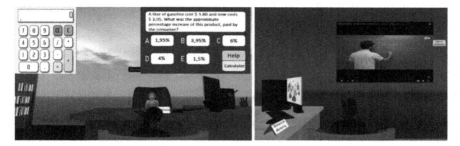

Fig. 1. Screenshot of the quiz (left) and the didactic video (right) in OpenSimulator platform.

After going through the five offices, the user receives the news that s/he has been accepted into the company and can start the internship. Then, s/he is instructed to go to a room simulating a corporate workspace, is congratulated by the achievement and receives the total score in the activity.

The Web-Based Environment. For this condition, it was used the version 3.0.2+ of the Moodle platform. The same textual narrative of the virtual reality was added to the environment. However, differently from the virtual world, the videos could not be accessed

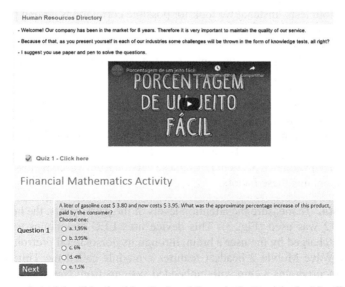

Fig. 2. Screenshot of the didactic video (top) and the quiz (bottom) in the Moodle platform.

during the quiz; they were placed together with the narrative, at the quiz introduction. Also, the office-related background sounds were not played during the activity.

Figure 2, at the top, shows a screen capture of the quiz introduction, with the narrative and the didactic video available to play without leaving the page. At the bottom, it is possible to see an example question of the quiz. Although not having the calculator device as in the virtual world, all participants had at their disposal a physical basic operations calculator.

4.3 Instruments

Three main instruments were used to collect the data, presented as follows.

Knowledge Tests. The knowledge tests consisted of exercises to examine participants' knowledge of basic Financial Mathematics. The topics addressed were percentage, simple and compound interest.

To avoid response bias, the researchers elaborated two tests consisting of 15 multiple-choice questions, which differed in the variables used in each question, maintaining the difficulty level and topic addressed. Each question had five answer options, with 1 point given for a correct answer (0 for an incorrect answer). Thus, the total score would range from 1 to 15. The tests were analyzed and validated by a Mathematics professor.

The tests were applied before and during the experiment (pretest and posttest). The pretest was in printed format and the posttest was embed in the media format. The posttest was presented in five rounds of three questions each (quizzes) and the scores were registered in the systems logs. Performance was measured as the number of correct answers on each test (pretest and posttest). It was not an objective of the study to improve the knowledge of participants, as there was no proper didactic intervention between both tests. Instead, we look for possible correlations among performance, sense of presence and attention levels, and the pretest was used as a parameter to assure consistent comparison of groups through different types of media.

In addition to performance, the time spent on each test was measured as complementary data.

ITC Sense of Presence Inventory (ITC-SOPI). To measure the sense of presence, the ITC-SOPI questionnaire [3] was selected due to its cross-media comparison capabilities. Its original version contains 44 items of 5-point Likert scale, divided into four factors: Spatial Presence, Engagement, Ecological Validity/Naturalness, and Negative Effects. We used a reduced validated 35-item Portuguese version from Vasconcelos-Raposo et al. [19], which maintains these factors.

Biosensor Data. To measure the attention levels of the participants, the headset Mind-Wave Mobile 2 was used (Fig. 3). This device uses EEG techniques to read neural oscillations discharged by the user's brain, through its dorsolateral prefrontal cortex.

The MindWave Mobile 2 headset features a module called the ThinkGear ASIC Module that incorporates a chip with embedded systems from NeuroSky eSense algorithms. With nonintrusive dry-electrode support resting on the forehead above the eye,

Fig. 3. The MindWave biosensor device in use.

it allows safely measures and outputs from the EEG power spectrums (e.g. Alpha and Beta waves) and NeuroSky eSense meters (attention and meditation levels) [20].

In addition to the brainwave signals detection with the MindWave Mobile 2 headset, the Mindful Metrics app was used. This technology is being developed by the research group and is capable of connecting with the headset and, similarly to the NeuroSky eSense, recording in real-time attention-related signals, classifying every second on a scale ranging from 0 to 100, in a more clear and objective way.

4.4 Procedure

Each test occurred individually in an acclimatized room from the University with unlimited time for the task execution. Upon arrival at the laboratory, participants filled out an informed consent and demographics form. They were briefed about the overall purpose of the study, the procedure and the possibility of giving up (without any consequences) at any time if they did not feel comfortable. Then, participants were seated in an armchair and were given blank sheets of paper, a pen, and a calculator.

A one-week window separated the pretest to the posttest. The sense of presence and attention levels were measured only in the posttest. At this occasion, to run a baseline measurement, participants were fitted with the biosensor and were instructed to relax during two minutes before the test, in order to break immediate effects of prior interactions on the EEG metrics and to put them in a relaxed state before starting task execution. The researchers observed the EEG readings to make sure that the signal quality was good. Immediately after the posttest, participants filled the ITC-SOPI online and were thanked and dismissed. The results of the tests were not revealed.

4.5 Analysis

To analyze the primary data collected in the study, descriptive statistics are presented as the Mean (M), Standard Deviation (SD) and relative frequency (%). Although the median is the most appropriate parameter for categorical measurements, as in the case of Likert scales, due to the small sample size, we sought to bring more detail through the mean values.

Inferential statistics techniques were performed using the software SPSS version 18, considering the significance level of 95% (p-value). Shapiro-Wilk tests were firstly applied to verify the normality of the data. When a normal distribution was identified, the homogeneity of variances was analyzed using the Levene's test and, if not violated, the parametric independent samples t-test was run. When a normal distribution was not verified or the assumptions of the independent samples t-test were not met, the non-parametric Mann-Whitney U test was performed. Spearman's test was used in the correlation tests.

5   Results

The results are organized by the main aspects investigated, referring to a different instrument each, with a section afterwards to present the correlation tests.

5.1   Performance - Knowledge Tests and Time

The data displayed in Table 3 allow observing that the performance on the pretest was very similar in both groups, with the Experimental group achieving 0.57 points more, although with a higher standard deviation (SD = 4.24). The performance on the posttest was even closer, with a difference of just 0.15 points, with the Experimental group also having the highest score (M = 10.29, SD = 2.55).

Table 3. Results of performance and time of the research groups.

Research group	n	Performance				Difference	Time	
		Pretest		Posttest			Pretest	Posttest
		M	SD	M	SD	M	M	M
Control group	7	10.86	2.23	10.14	3.00	−0,72	00:39	00:46
Experimental group	7	11.43	4.24	10.29	2.55	−1.14	00:40	00:39

However, the difference from the pretest to the posttest was negative in both groups, with a higher decrease occurring in the Experimental group (−1.14 points in comparison to −0.72 in the Control group), although the independent samples t-test found no significant difference regarding this value (t(12) = −0.331, p = 0.746).

The time participants took to respond to each test ranged between 11 and 72 min. Table 3 also shows the average time by group, allowing to verify that although they were very similar in both tests (around 40 min), there is a higher difference from the pretest to the posttest in the Control group, which took more seven minutes on average to respond to the same number of questions.

In order to perform the correlation tests in the following section, the time of each test was classified in one of five ordinal categories. Table 4 shows this classification and the number of participants that fitted in each category by research group.

Table 4. Results of time according to the categories and research groups.

Category	Time (min)	Control group		Experimental group	
		Pretest	Posttest	Pretest	Posttest
1	15 =<	0	1	0	0
2	16–30	3	2	3	1
3	31–45	1	1	2	2
4	46–60	2	2	1	3
5	61>=	1	1	1	1

5.2 Sense of Presence – ITC-SOPI

The results for the sense of presence are displayed in Table 5. It allows observing that the scores were higher in the Experimental group for all ITC-SOPI factors, including the Negative Effects. The differences were all above 1 point, with the only exception in the Negative Effects factor (0.74).

Table 5. Results for the sense of presence by research group.

Research group	n	ITC-SOPI factors							
		Spatial Presence		Engagement		Ecological Validity Naturalness		Negative Effects	
		M	SD	M	SD	M	SD	M	SD
Control group	7	2.25	1.11	3.23	1.07	3.77	1.39	1.83	0.70
Experimental group	7	4.93	0.68	4.94	0.87	5.54	0.73	2.57	1.27

The independent samples t-test identified a significant difference only for the factors Spatial Presence ($t(13) = 5.409$, $p = 0.000$) and Engagement ($t(13) = 3.275$, $p = 0.006$).

5.3 Attention Levels – Biosensor

Considering the data of all participants while performing the posttest, the overall average attention level of the Experimental group was $M = 48.24$ ($SD = 8.51$), and of the Control group was $M = 41.88$ ($SD = 4.06$). However, the independent samples t-test maintained the null hypothesis of equality between groups ($t(12) = 1.652$, $p = 0.124$).

The graph presented in Fig. 4 displays the average values in time slots of five minutes. Participants were included in the equation according to the duration of their tests. It is possible to verify that the attention levels of the Experimental group (blue) remained higher, in the range between 40–50 points, while the Control group (orange) oscillated between the range of 30–50 points during the experience.

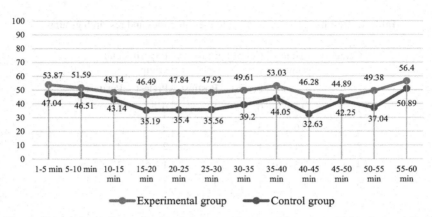

Fig. 4. Comparison of attention levels between the research groups. (Color figure online)

Figure 4 also shows that both groups start and end with close levels of attention (around 50 points), reaching their peaks at the end of the experience (56.4 points in the Experimental group and 50.89 in the Control group). However, the attention levels of the Experimental group remained a little more constant, while the Control group decreased and oscillated more during the experience. The lowest attention level reached by the Control group was 32.63 points, in the time-slot of 40–45 min, and by the Experimental group was 44.89 points, in the time-slot of 45–50 min. That is, more than 12 points separate both lowest levels of attention.

5.4   Correlation Tests

Correlation tests were performed seeking to answer the research questions, as follows.

RQ1. In Some of the Conditions, does the Attention Levels Correlate with Performance? Considering that attention levels were measured only in the posttest, this score was used in the correlation tests. The Spearman's test maintained the null hypothesis in both Experimental (rs = −0.445, p = 0.317), and Control group (rs = 0.631, p = 0.129).

However, we can see that, although not significant, the correlation coefficient is negative in the Experimental group, and positive in the Control group, allowing to observe (with caution) an inverse difference in media formats regarding this association. This is especially true for the Control group, which have a moderate correlation coefficient.

RQ2. In Some of the Conditions, does Performance Correlate with Time on Task? Considering the pretest scores, the Spearman's test maintained the null hypothesis of correlation with the time on task in both Experimental (rs = −0.019, p = 0.968) and Control group (rs = −0.076, p = 0.871).

On the other hand, analyzing the posttest scores, although the Spearman's test maintained the null hypothesis of correlation in the Experimental group (rs = −0.623, p = 0.135), it revealed a significant correlation in the Control group (rs = −0.935, p = 0.002). Both correlation coefficients are negative, meaning that higher time on task could be related to lower performance. This is especially true for the Control group, which showed a strong significant correlation.

RQ3. In Some of the Conditions, does the Sense of Presence Correlate with the Attention Levels?
The Spearman's test maintained the null hypothesis of correlation for all ITC-SOPI factors in both the Experimental and Control group, as presented in Table 6.

Table 6. Results for the correlation tests between the ITC-SOPI factors and the attention levels.

Research group	n	Spearman's rho							
		Spatial Presence		Engagement		Ecological Validity Naturalness		Negative Effects	
		rs	p	rs	p	rs	p	rs	p
Control group	7	−0.357	0.432	−0.396	0.379	−0.321	0.482	0.108	0.818
Experimental group	7	0.595	0.159	0.643	0.119	0.198	0.670	0.432	0.333

In this sense, as no statistical significances were found, no inference is made possible regarding the association between the sense of presence and the attention levels. Overall, we can just observe positive correlation coefficients in the Experimental group and negative in the Control group, although weak or moderate.

6 Discussion

Considering that no didactic intervention was made between the application of the knowledge tests, we would expect that the score in the posttest would be similar as in the pretest. Contrary to this expectation, the differences in performance were negative in both groups. We speculate that the use of the biosensor and of a multimedia format different than the basic printed (virtual reality and web-based environment) during the task execution may have caused more cognitive difficulty or emotional stress.

Although not statistically significant, the higher decrease in performance in the virtual reality group probably indicates that the use of this media aggravated the above-mentioned situation. Additional explanations for this result can be grounded in the instructional design theory of Multimedia Learning [21], in that the extrinsic cognitive load associated with the use of a highly visual and interactive technology may have caused a "seductive detail", i.e., a distraction not relevant to the instructional goal. The office-related background sounds that were not present in the web condition may have also collaborated with this result. In addition, in agreement with Chen, Wang and Yu [8], the "novelty effect" of being in a new simulated reality often overshadows the cognitive skills acquisition, due to learners' unfamiliarity with the technology.

On the other hand, the time participants took to perform the tests were very similar in both conditions, meaning no need for extra time when using the virtual reality media.

The results for the sense of presence followed the expected logic, with higher scores obtained by the virtual reality group. In this perspective, we can corroborate with the work of Kober, Kurzmann and Neuper [18], in which the virtual reality condition showed a greater sense of presence, as compared to a low-immersive 2D desktop screen. Also, we can agree with the study of Clemente et al. [16], in which the free navigation induced a higher feeling of presence, in comparison to the visualization of still images and to an automatic navigation-video of the environment.

A significant difference in the sense of presence was obtained for the factors Spatial Presence and Engagement. The first factor is key to persuasion in a virtual environment, as it promotes a more natural interaction with the user's surroundings [22]. The second factor reflects the user's involvement and interest, besides the enjoyment of the experience [3]. Riva, Waterworth and Murray [22] suggest the existence of a link between presence and the effectiveness of action: the greater the presence, the greater the involvement in the activity will be, and this increases the probability of it ending well (the transformation of the intention into action). Hereupon, it is possible to note that these important characteristics of a learning experience were more emphasized by the virtual reality media as in comparison to the traditional web-based environment.

In what concerns attention, the virtual reality group presented higher levels than the web-based environment group during the whole experience, allowing to deduce that the virtual reality media requires more from participants' concentration. We suggest that this finding is also linked to the Multimedia Learning theory [21], due to the extrinsic cognitive load associated with the virtual reality technology, which required more attentional resources. It was verified that both groups reached their highest levels of attention at the end of the experience, meaning that, in general terms, the final moments of the test were more consuming in this aspect, regardless of the media used.

In the following, we present a brief discussion related to each research question.

RQ1. In Some of the Conditions, does the Attention Levels Correlate with Performance?
It was observed (although not statistically significant) a difference in the media formats. That is, for the virtual reality group, the higher was the average attention level, the lower was the performance. For the web-based environment group, this was the opposite: higher average attention levels were related to higher performances. With this result, we can infer (cautiously) that participants in the virtual reality group had to channel more attentional resources to the virtual environment itself and couldn't pay so much attention to the lesson. On the other hand, participants in the web-based environment could more effectively translate attentional resources to better performances, following the expected logic.

RQ2. In Some of the Conditions, does Performance Correlate with Time on Task?
It was diagnosed negative coefficients in both conditions, statistically significant in the web-based environment group. This implies that more time on task could be related to lower performance, preventing us to agree with Kolb [7], when he states that learning requires "time on task", considering the proportions and the fact that learning was not an objective of the study, as we were just interested in performance. Giving the small sample size, participant's experience with the subject could have influenced this result.

RQ3. In Some of the Conditions, does the Sense of Presence Correlate with the Attention Levels?
No inference was made possible by the results as no statistical significance was found. However, it was observed opposite directions of the correlation coefficients: positive in

the virtual reality condition and negative in the web-based environment condition. With a larger sample, this could mean that participants in the first group were more inclined to present a positive correlation, and participants in the web-based environment, on the other hand, would be more propense to show a negative correlation between the sense of presence and the average attention level.

This finding can be linked to the previous discussion on how subjects from the virtual reality group had to focus more attentional resources to the virtual environment, consequently achieving a higher sense of presence, but could not allocate the same amount of resources to the lesson, resulting in lower performances. According to Whitelock et al. [23], although "being there" is very motivating, it can take up too much of the users' attention and produce a cognitive overload when it comes to understanding conceptual notions. Draper, Kaber and Usher [10] corroborate, saying that when attentional resources are committed to dealing with information that is not task-related, presence is maintained but task performance is degraded. Therefore, the user may feel strongly present but still exhibit poor task performance.

In this context, we can sustain the study of Kober and Neuper [14], which found a positive association between the sense of presence and the allocation of attentional resources to the virtual environment itself, not to task-related stimulus. In contrast, we cannot corroborate with Baumgartner et al. [17] and Rey et al. [12], giving that they identified this correlation but with activity in areas of the brain that are out of the scope of this study. Finally, we agree with Draper, Kaber and Usher [10], when they suggest that performance in a virtual environment depends on the number of distracters (real or virtual), attentional resources available and attentional resources required by the tasks.

7   Conclusion

This pilot study investigated the potential relations among sense of presence, attention levels and performance, comparing the outcomes across two different media formats (virtual reality versus web). The area investigated was Financial Mathematics.

The findings show that, although very prominent to the sense of presence and its tangential benefits as engagement, enjoyment and sense of agency, the virtual reality media was not successful as the web-based environment in translating the allocation of attentional resources into better performances. We suggest that this highly visual and interactive technology can cause distractions not relevant to the instructional goal, in addition to the "novelty effect" of using a platform not so common as the web. In this sense, designers must ponder if the additional cost of development of a simulated environment worth. In addition, it was observed a result contrary to expected regarding time and performance, in that more time was associated with lower performance, which could be explained by the sociocultural aspects of the small sample size.

The limitations of the study must be taken accordingly while interpreting the results, mainly regarding the small sample size (n = 14), which could have make sociocultural aspects of the participants to reflect in the results. Follow-up research will consider a larger pool.

References

1. Witmer, B.G., Singer, M.J.: Measuring presence in virtual environments: a presence questionnaire. Presence **7**(3), 225–240 (1998)
2. Dengel, A., Mägdefrau, J.: Presence is the key to understanding immersive learning. In: Beck, D., et al. (eds.) iLRN 2019. CCIS, vol. 1044, pp. 185–198. Springer, Cham (2019). https://doi.org/10.1007/978-3-030-23089-0_14
3. Lessiter, J., Freeman, J., Keogh, E., Davidoff, J.: A cross-media presence questionnaire: the ITC-sense of presence inventory. Presence: Teleoperators Virtual Environ. **10**(3), 282–297 (2001)
4. Riley, J.M., Kaber, D.B., Draper, J.V.: Situation awareness and attention allocation measures for quantifying telepresence experiences in teleoperation. Hum. Factors Ergon. Manuf. Serv. Ind. **14**(1), 51–67 (2004)
5. Makowski, D., Sperduti, M., Nicolas, S., Piolino, P.: "Being there" and remembering it: presence improves memory encoding. Conscious. Cogn. **53**, 194–202 (2017)
6. Belle, A., Hargraves, R.H., Najarian, K.: An automated optimal engagement and attention detection system using electrocardiogram. Comput. Math. Methods Med. **2012** (2012)
7. Kolb, D.A.: Experiential Learning: Experience as the Source of Learning and Development. FT Press, Upper Saddle River (2014)
8. Chen, C.M., Wang, J.Y., Yu, C.M.: Assessing the attention levels of students by using a novel attention aware system based on brainwave signals. Brit. J. Educ. Technol. **48**(2), 348–369 (2017)
9. Jensen, L., Konradsen, F.: A review of the use of virtual reality head-mounted displays in education and training. Educ. Inf. Technol. **23**(4), 1515–1529 (2017). https://doi.org/10.1007/s10639-017-9676-0
10. Draper, V.D., Kaber, D.B., Usher, J.M.: Telepresence. Hum. Factors **40**(3), 354–375 (1998)
11. Laarni, J., Ravaja, N., Saari, T., Hartmann, T.: Personality-related differences in subjective presence. In Proceedings of the Seventh Annual International Workshop Presence, pp. 88–95 (2004)
12. Rey, B., Alcañiz, M., Tembl, J., Parkhutik, V.: Brain activity and presence: a preliminary study in different immersive conditions using transcranial Doppler monitoring. Virtual Real. **14**(1), 55–65 (2010)
13. Szczurowski, K., Smith, M.: Measuring presence: hypothetical quantitative framework. In: 2017 23rd International Conference on Virtual System & Multimedia (VSMM), pp. 1–8. IEEE (2017)
14. Kober, S.E., Neuper, C.: Using auditory event-related EEG potentials to assess presence in virtual reality. Int. J. Hum.-Comput. Stud. **70**, 577–587 (2012)
15. Clemente, M., Rodríguez, A., Rey, B., Alcañiz, M.: Assessment of the influence of navigation control and screen size on the sense of presence in virtual reality using EEG. Expert Syst. Appl. **41**(4), 1584–1592 (2014)
16. Clemente, M., et al.: An fMRI study to analyze neural correlates of presence during virtual reality experiences. Interact. Comput. **26**(3), 269–284 (2013)
17. Baumgartner, T., Valko, L., Esslen, M., Jäncke, L.: Neural correlate of spatial presence in an arousing and noninteractive virtual reality: an EEG and psychophysiology study. Cyberpsychol. Behav. **9**, 30–45 (2006)
18. Kober, S.E., Kurzmann, J., Neuper, C.: Cortical correlate of spatial presence in 2D and 3D interactive virtual reality: an EEG study. Int. J. Psychophysiol. **83**, 365–374 (2012)
19. Vasconcelos-Raposo, J., Melo, M., Teixeira, C., Cabral, L., Bessa, M.: Adaptation and validation of the ITC-sense of presence inventory for the Portuguese language. Int. J. Hum.-Comput. Stud. **125**, 1–6 (2019)

20. Neurosky: MindWave Mobile 2: User Guide (2018). http://download.neurosky.com/public/Products/MindWaveMobile2/MindWaveMobile2UserGuide.pdf. Accessed 31 Jan 2020
21. Mayer, R.E.: Multimedia learning. In: Psychology of Learning and Motivation, vol. 41, pp. 85–139. Academic Press (2002)
22. Riva, G., Waterworth, J., Murray, D.: 1 Extending the self through the tools and the others: a general framework for presence and social presence in mediated interactions. In: Interacting with Presence, pp. 9–31. Sciendo Migration (2014)
23. Whitelock, D., Romano, D., Jelfs, A., Brna, P.: Perfect presence: what does this mean for the design of virtual learning environments? Educ. Inf. Technol. 5(4), 277–289 (2000)

Research on the Design of Intelligent Interactive Toys Based on Marker Education

Yi Lu(✉) and Wei Pang

Beijing University of Technical, Beijing 10024, China
7679067@qq.com

Abstract. *Objectives:* The purpose of this research is to explore innovative inter-action mode of children's marker education, to solve the problems of universal homogeneity of Marker education products and lack of emotional communication, and to develop children's intelligent interactive toys by using open source hardware coding technology. *Methods:* Focusing on the three elements of user-interaction-technology, this study comprehensively analyzed the needs and problems of educational play aids for markers by means of questionnaires, behavioral observation and competitive analysis, and carried out product innovation design through design practice. *Results:* The research ultimately establishes the brand "KOBOT" multi-mode interactive experience marker education toy, which is a set of innovative marker education products based on the integration of various offline entity modules and online programming applications. It supports a variety of modeling modular design, interactive technology and interactive ways. *Conclusions:* "KOBOT" marker education product expands the game process of construction mode and intellectuality, enhances the interaction between children and marker products, fosters the social awareness of parent-child interaction and friend cooperation, and lays the development direction for the future of Chinese children's marker education.

Keywords: Toy design · STEAM education · Interaction design · Child programming

1 Introduction

The concept of "marker" is derived from the English words "maker" and "hacker", especially refers to a kind of people who love science and technology and make things by hand [1] "Marker education" places more emphasis on learning to solve practical problems and projects, and relies on hands-on production and learning experience; At the same time, it emphasizes the importance of teamwork, open mind, interdisciplinary learning and continuous iteration [2]. Nowadays, China has 160 million K12-age populations, but marker education penetration rate is only 1.5% [3], with a very broad market prospect. Therefore, the significance of the research lies in the use of information-based teaching methods to help children easily master a variety of knowledge and skills and innovative and collaborative capabilities, to break the existing product forms to provide children with more abundant creative teaching methods and learning experiences, to stimulate children's interest in learning and to meet multi-level emotional needs.

© Springer Nature Switzerland AG 2020
C. Stephanidis et al. (Eds.): HCII 2020, LNCS 12425, pp. 462–471, 2020.
https://doi.org/10.1007/978-3-030-60128-7_35

2 Preliminary Investigation and Demand Analysis

2.1 The Functional Form and Characteristics of Existing Marker Education Products

First of all, the author investigated and analyzed the current situation of marker education toys and teaching tools such as KOOV, LEGO, ROOT, etc. at home and abroad, as shown in Table 1.

Existing products are mainly divided into the following categories by their forms: ① Building block type assembled toys are characterized by requiring a large number of small and simple modules to be combined, various forms, rich colors, great space for free play and creation, and the highest difficulty. Children will use a large amount of mechanical, programming and electronic knowledge when using them, such as koov, LEGO EV3, etc. ② Independent robot toys, this kind of toys can't or only can change the shape and function of the toys in a small range. Among them, the programming methods are divided into two types, one is materialization programming, i.e. some toy modules are spliced instead of programming statements, such as MatataLab, Cubetto, etc.; The other is to connect intelligent devices and control them through APP graphical programming, such as Root. ③ The existing toy is expanded by using a material manufacturing

Table 1. Competition product analysis

Product's name	Description	Content and purpose of teaching	Advantages and characteristics
Koov	Transparent colored plastic modules are used to form animals, vehicles, articles for daily use and other forms, and interaction is realized through programming	To cultivate children's creativity, curiosity and practical ability in the process of hands-on production	Building blocks can be continuous up and down, left and right, front and back, and can also be spliced obliquely
LEGO	Put together a robot, the same as above	Space modeling, mechanical structure, programming	Various modules, reinforced mechanical structure, various transmission sensors, anthropomorphic modeling
Nintendo LABO	Switch game host external kit materializes the video game and increases the fun	Manipulative ability	Using cardboard + rubber band as the main body, it is full of fun in use and assembly, becoming a value-added product of switch
Tinkamo	Build a programmable robot	Extended application of mechanical structure, programming and technology in life	Compatible with LEGO, improve APP interaction, and realize visual programming by means of battery pack linking
Root	Programmable robot, the robot can carry brushes to realize programmed painting (suitable for all ages)	Programming and drawing	The magnetic attraction surface has a multi-level difficulty programming interface through programming movement, painting erasing, scanning colors, playing music, detecting concavo-convex magnetism, sensing light, etc.

(*continued*)

Table 1. (*continued*)

Product's name	Description	Content and purpose of teaching	Advantages and characteristics
MatataLab	Manual coding robot for school-age children, entity module + visual recognition to achieve simplified programming, control its movement to play music and draw pictures, and play games on the plate plane	Programming, parent-child games, cognitive ability	Solid graphical programming, simple and easy to understand, combined with chart games, painting, music
Cubetto	Programming teaching for children aged 3–6 years controls small robots through entity module programming	Programming	Entity programming, combined with chart games
Mabot	A patchwork of robots	Creativity, programming	Unique spherical module assembly, high playability, multiple feasibility, LEGO compatibility, hot plug and multi-angle assembly support
Algobrix	5–13 years old, machine trolley driven by entity programming module	Programming	Entity programming, add more possibilities and complexity, compatible with LEGO
Airblock	Programming modular unmanned aerial vehicle	Programming, hands-on ability	It can realize various modes of water, land and air
Makeblock Neuron	The programming electronics kit can be extended with cardboard toys	Programming, hands-on ability	Explorers and inventors toolkit expands kit to bring children's unlimited creativity into play

module such as cardboard to realize more functions at low cost. Meanwhile, the module installation process has also increased children's enjoyment, cardboard materials make it possible to personalize the painting of toys, such as NintendoLABO and Makeblock Neuron.

2.2 The Content and Form of the Existing Marker Education Class

Nowadays, many marker education institutions have sprung up in China. In order to further understand the current content and form of marker education, the author visited a young marker education class in Beijing. The class was attended by low-grade primary school students. The author mainly recorded and analyzed the content of creator education through behavioral observation, as shown in Fig. 1. The main teaching processes include: ① Play the courseware video to show that the course needs LEGO bricks and EV3 control module to complete a dragon-shaped robot that can walk, wag its tail and avoid obstacles. ② To introduce the principle used in the course. The knowledge used is the eccentric wheel principle. The eccentric wheel is controlled by a motor and the tail of the dragon can swing left and right. ③ Students build a car first, then add dragon tail shape. The required modules include distance sensor, two large motors, one medium motor and control host. ④ Teachers teach students to use graphical programming software to program robots and achieve the final results.

Fig. 1. STEM classroom observation

The author summarized the problems found by STEM classroom observation as follows: ① collision and interference will occur in the splicing process of building block parts, and children cannot solve such problems by themselves. For example, LEGO modules are fixed with cylindrical bolts. It takes at least two points to fix a heavy object on the car, while children do not understand the need for teacher's assistance. ② LEGO building blocks use "LEGO units" (8 mm) as building modules, so that building blocks with different shapes can be combined together, but one of the children has a situation of half a unit, which makes the building cannot continue to start again. ③ Children like to change shapes according to their own interests, especially symmetrical shapes, such as building a pair of wings, the shapes and colors on both sides must be consistent, and they will continue to look for suitable building blocks in the toy box. ④ Children like to set up things they like conveniently, even if the main content of the class is not finished, for example, a child sets up a top in class and observes the state of rotation. ⑤ At this stage, children cannot build simple mechanical structures on their own. Each child needs to complete the eccentric wheel structure under the guidance of the teacher.

3   User Requirements Analysis

3.1   Cognitive Ability and Behavioral Characteristics of Target Groups

The target group is 6–9-year-old primary school students in the lower grades. Target groups are more interested in outdoor activities, which can master more special sports activities. They participate in more challenging activities, like to play and take risks, can understand the rules in the game, and even can add rules to make the game more complicated. They know how to use strategies to deal with difficult problems, such as playing chess and checkers. At the same time, you can use precise muscle control to complete tasks, such as painting and writing can grasp the details of the processing; The target group can use logic to solve problems or organize or select things. For assembled toys, they can operate smaller parts (less than 2.5 mm) and build more complex structures (more than 100 building blocks) [4], and they can use articles with mechanical structures, such as bearings, levers, pulleys, medium-strength laws, etc. I prefer toys with themes, such as movies or products related to animated characters.

3.2   Preference of Target Groups for Toys

In order to further understand the characteristics of the users to guide the design practice and make the products better meet the needs of users, the author analyzed the children's preferences for toys through a survey questionnaire. A total of 41 valid questionnaires were collected, including 21 boys and 20 girls. The statistical results are as follows: ① About 73% of the interviewees like to play with their partners in the scene of using toys, indicating that more children like to participate in multi-person interactive games. At the same time, only 15% of the people like to play games with their parents, indicating that the participation of parents in children's growth still needs to be improved. ② According to the types of toys preferred by different gender target groups, boys mainly focus on vehicles and toys with strong mechanical sense, while girls prefer toys with strong modeling and image sense. ③ According to the color preferences of different gender target groups, more than 50% of girls choose pink and 60% of boys choose blue. These two colors are too gender-selective, so they will not be widely used in subsequent designs, and more neutral colors should be used to make the products more popular. ④ In terms of image and material preference, cartoon characters are loved by both boys and girls, boys prefer transportation, and girls prefer animal images more than boys. In terms of material preference, boys prefer metal toys while girls prefer plush toys, but the same two materials show strong gender orientation, wood and plastic are more acceptable to both boys and girls. ⑤ For function, boys want to have deformable toys, while girls are more interested in modeling and sound (Fig. 2).

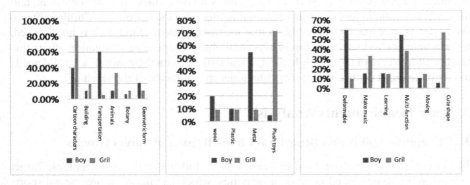

Fig. 2. Part of questionnaire analysis

3.3 Analysis of Potential Needs of Target Groups for Toys

Through the above investigation and analysis, the following potential demands are summarized and analyzed: ① Children want toys with more functions and more changes. This can be reflected in color, shape, sound, connection, manipulation and other aspects. Formally get rid of the existing splicing toys, bringing more freshness to children. ② Emotional elements should be more embodied in marker education toys. Nowadays, similar products pay more attention to technical problems and neglect the playing process. Children need more visual and narrative toys, which can tap children's various thinking abilities and enable rational and emotional thinking to be combined. ③ Children like to play with their partners, which can also improve children's social and cooperative abilities. They can not only think independently and accomplish their goals, but also share and compete with others. In addition, if the product provides participation of family members, it will be more popular with parents, which can also promote healthy communication between parents and children.

4 Marker Education Product Design Practice

4.1 The Concept of Product

According to the previous research and analysis and several design iterations, a small robot host was finally designed and an extension module was added on this basis. The expansion module includes four lengths of connecting rods, spherical joints, motors, connecting wires, shafts and three flat modules. The expansion module can be connected with the host to form a new model, such as a crawling robot, or can be used independently to construct various scenes, such as castles, suspension bridges, mazes, etc. The small robot can rely on the small wheel at the bottom to move and interact with the built scene, such as automatic obstacle avoidance, color recognition and response through sensors on the fuselage, etc. The specific modularization scheme is shown in Fig. 3.

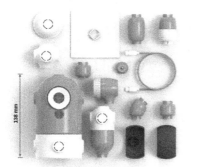
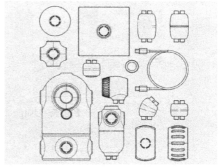

Fig. 3. Product basic modules

For color, orange is chosen as the main color, because pure orange gives people the impression of hope, vitality, happiness, etc. [5]. White and gray are added at the same time, one is to not affect the main color, the other is to distinguish different functional modules, such as "connecting rod" and "rotating rod" which have the same shape but different functions, in order to distinguish the two, "rotating rod" uses different colors at both ends. In addition, orange is used for all male plug parts and white is used for female plug parts, so that the two colors can be separated during assembly. Therefore, the combined visual effect is better, and the final module combined effect is shown in Fig. 4.

The main uses of the product are divided into two types. One is that after being combined, the product can be directly remotely controlled to enable the robot to make various actions. Besides, it can also use graphic programming software to control it so that it can automatically respond to the environment. It is suitable for a variety of use

Fig. 4. Product combination form

scenarios at the same time, and it can be used for multi-player or single-player games. For example, multi-player games can be used for racing or carrying games, and single-player games can be used for learning programming and endowing robots with the ability to automatically avoid obstacles or identify objects, or can be built according to the splicing instructions given in APP and then controlled by remote control or programming, as shown in Fig. 5.

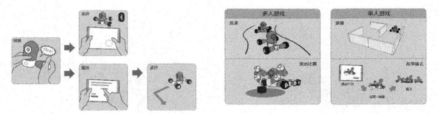

Fig. 5. Usage and game play

4.2   Prototype Production

After the final plan was determined, the structure of the interface was improved. Two spring pieces were used to enhance the connection strength and feel of the modules. 3D printing technology and PLA materials were used to make a grass mold to verify whether the scale relationship was in line with the size of children's hands and whether the structure was stable. After verifying its structural feasibility by making a straw model, a high-fidelity prototype was made (Fig. 6). The prototype shell is made of photosensitive resin material, and the hardware is based on Arduino open source electronic platform. It uses ultrasonic distance sensor, infrared sensor, led module, motor drive module, etc. and uses Arduino language to realize some expected functions, such as LED lighting, distance sensing, line finding sensor, motor drive, infrared remote control, etc. (Fig. 7).

Fig. 6. High fidelity prototype

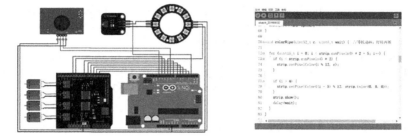

Fig. 7. Hardware connection diagram and code

4.3 Interface Design

According to the preset usage mode and the characteristics of the module itself, an APP interaction prototype is designed (Fig. 8).

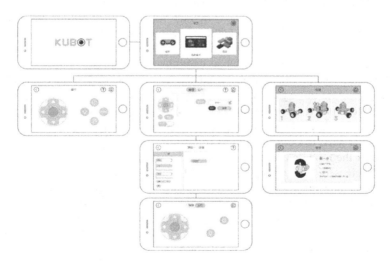

Fig. 8. APP usage process

In order to reduce the learning cost of users, the information architecture is relatively shallow. The principle of "timely appearance" of the function [6] is adopted at the same time, and the programming function is hidden in the edit menu of the button to ensure that the function only appears at the appropriate time and place. APP is mainly divided into three parts: The first part is direct remote control. Users can directly use the default configuration to control toys after assembly, mainly to quickly enter the operation interface. The second part is a building guide. Users can quickly learn several known building methods and start the game. The guide contains instructions and step diagrams, along with short videos, to explain the building method more intuitively. The third part is the most important programming mode. The programming mode allows the user to customize the operation panel, put the rocker and button into the editor, select the button element to edit, and then enter the visual programming interface to independently program each button, which gives children more space to create. Automatic obstacle avoidance, automatic line finding and self-defining actions need to be realized through programming functions. Programming is also the core play method of this toy. It can be used by individuals to learn programming, and can also be used by many people to compete together, thus realizing the combination of playing and learning.

5   Conclusion and Future Work

The research topic has carried on the intensive research to the marker education domain, pointed out the current marker education toy question and proposed the design solution. The following innovative design points are proposed through design practice: ① The innovation of the composing way of combination. By the way of "main robot + expansion module", various splicing possibilities are realized, and the image of the product has more emotional and affinity characteristics. ② In modular design, all modules are unified with one module, realizing continuous splicing in three axes. The types of modules are reduced by reusing modules (e.g. wheels can be combined with motors or shafts), and a common module interface is designed without additional connecting wires. ③ In the game mode, one person can play (such as obstacle avoidance, line finding, story plot, etc.), and many people can cooperate or compete (such as cargo handling, speed competition, fighting, etc.). In the future, the product can also expand a variety of modules, and each additional module will produce more games.

Toys and teaching tools for marker education are emerging research fields, and there are still many functions and design opportunities worth studying. The current design practice results need to be improved as follows in the next step: ① The stability and ease of use of the module connection structure need to be improved. If the number of modules is increased, how to support the whole structure needs to be considered, and the accuracy of the connection also needs to be adjusted. ② For mass production of products, the design of the electrical interface at the joint shall be considered, and the electrical interface shall be spliced at any angle while leaving enough contacts for communication between modules. ③ Due to the limited testing conditions, the product will further invite multiple school-age children to conduct usability tests for relevant tasks in future work, so as to carry out design iteration.

References

1. Yu, L.: The application of the idea of seeking marker in the design of school children's toys. Tianjin Technology University (2017)
2. Zichuan, O.: Research on toy design based on youth marker education. Central Academy of Fine Arts (2017)
3. Arar, R., Brereton, M.: Co-design AI futures: integrating AI ethics, social computing and design. In: Proceedings of the 2019 Conference on DIS Companion. ACM Press (2019)
4. Dun, L.: How to break through the bottleneck of STEM educational teachers. China Education Daily, No. 7, 18 July 2018
5. Linren, Y.: Learn about color psychology every day. Shanxi Normal University Press (2009)
6. Colborne, G.: Simplicity First: Four Strategies for Interaction Design. Beijing People's Communication Telecommunications Press, England
7. Baek, C., Choi, J.J., Han, J.: Application of intelligent product design on STEAM education. In: Proceedings of the 2015 Conference on HAI Korea (2015). https://doi.org/10.1145/281 4940-2814988
8. Park, E.Y.: LINKKI: a planar linkage-based kinetic toy as a tool for education and design. In: International Conference on FabLearn 2016, Stanford, CA, USA (2016). https://doi.org/10. 1145/3003397.3003411
9. Qin-ye, L.-M.: Narrative model in the design of children's toys. Packag. Eng. **35**(6), 82–85 (2014)
10. Lu, Y., Wei, T.: The emotion experience of preschool children in educational games. Packag. Eng. **39**(10), 106 (2018)
11. Ekaterina, C.G., Tavassoli, F.: Developing children's cultural awareness and empathy through games and fairy tales. In: Proceedings of the 2016 Conference on Interaction Design and Children (IDC 2016). ACM Press (2016)

Designing a Faculty Chatbot Through User-Centered Design Approach

Zlatko Stapić[1], Ana Horvat[2], and Dijana Plantak Vukovac[1(✉)]

[1] Faculty of Organization and Informatics, Laboratory of Applied Software Engineering,
University of Zagreb, Pavlinska 2, 42000 Varaždin, Croatia
{zlatko.stapic,dijana.plantak}@foi.unizg.hr
[2] Faculty of Organization and Informatics, University of Zagreb, Pavlinska 2,
42000 Varaždin, Croatia
anhorvat@foi.unizg.hr

Abstract. Conversational agents or chatbots are becoming an increasingly common mean of communication between humans and computers, tackling all aspects of human activity, including the field of education. In this paper a part of ongoing research is presented, with the aim to reveal what kind of interactions with the chatbot in the educational setting would take place. The ultimate goal is to identify informative models and design artifacts that would enable creation of the chatbot which will provide meaningful information to the students of the faculty. The research is performed by following user-centered design approach and engaging the final users in the product lifecycle. For that purpose, students have participated in an online survey and provided examples of the questions they would ask the chatbot about the exams, midterms, office hours, and location of rooms. Participants' answers were analysed with thematic analysis that revealed nineteen themes of the chatbot user interactions of which nine categories (design artifacts) of the chatbot user interface were novel in educational context. In addition to identifying students' needs, survey revealed preferences of the students regarding the form and tone of communication with the prospective chatbot.

Keywords: User-centered design · User experience design · Thematic analysis · Online survey · Chatbot · Chatbot interaction elements · User interface · Software engineering · Software development

1 Introduction

The idea of a programme that can understand humans and converse with them is not new, and the first realization of this idea dates to the fifties and the sixties in the previous century [18]. After several decades of perfecting the human-computer interaction, today there is a wide variety of different technologies that mimic human conversations for broad range of purposes: some banks have virtual assistants that can help manage customer's finances and payments [23], hairdressers can use chatbots integrated with applications such as Facebook Messenger to help them book appointments [24], general public use it to support their activities in work, health, civic engagement or just to entertain or have

C. Stephanidis et al. (Eds.): HCII 2020, LNCS 12425, pp. 472–484, 2020.
https://doi.org/10.1007/978-3-030-60128-7_36

a "smalltalk" [2], while assistants like Alexa and Siri help ease one's daily activities. We have seen the rise of chatbots in customer service as a means to improve customer satisfaction to reduce the cost of business by automating some interactions with customers, however, chatbots can also be implemented in other sectors, such as higher education. These technologies range from simple scripts to seemingly intelligent programmes based on artificial intelligence. No matter which technology is in question, it is certain that chatbots are here to stay.

Education, and especially higher education, is rapidly changing in more ways. One of the aspects of this change is the constant rise in the number of students per lecturer which leads to both student and lecturer dissatisfaction and increased dropout rates [11, 22]. Other aspects of the aforementioned change are accommodation of different types of students, e.g. international students, part-time students, or students who participate in online classes whose needs are different to those of full-time students that regularly attend lectures. However, not only student-lecturer relationship is affected by the changes in higher education. Larger number of students of different profiles also puts pressure on non-teaching faculty staff such as offices for student affairs. As higher education is changing so are the students and their behavior. Most of today's students are regular Internet users who are accustomed to receiving information whenever they want and need it and prefer communication over social media to using telephones or writing an e-mail [9]. Some of those problems could easily be solved by introducing chatbots into higher education by following examples from other sectors.

In this paper we approached the complex task of eliciting and designing the features and user interface segments of a novel chatbot that would be used in a specific domain of education. As different types of users are to be highly involved in the use of chatbot we wanted to follow the User-Centered Design approach. Thus, in order to obtain and extract necessary data on user requirements we performed interviews, survey and Thematic Analysis. Upon extracting the themes and codes related to user needs, we defined and designed a set of user interactions which characterize the specifics of chatbots in the domain of education. The third chapter of our work presents the performed research design and methodology along with research context, problems and objectives respondents and instrument. The fourth chapter shows the results and discusses the design of the chatbot interactions and interface elements at conceptual level. The final chapter brings the conclusions and gives a brief overview of the research activities that are planned in the near future.

2   Related Work

Chatbot (or conversational interface, conversational agent, intelligent personal assistant) is a software that supports conversation with users in specific domain using natural language. Mostly it is a text-based interface with limited multimedia features, i.e. enables exchanging text, emojis, gifs, photos or documents in the form of attachments. Supported by artificial intelligence, machine learning and other technologies in order to provide accurate and human-like answers to the users' questions, chatbots are not only functional technologies but social technologies as well [19]. In order that designers and developers of the chatbots create them as pleasant and trustful platform for communication, they need to know how people experience chatbots and what are user needs that motivate use of the chatbots [2].

Brandtzaeg and Følstad [3] discovered that users typically use the chatbots to accomplish productivity task (to obtain assistance or information), while other motives like entertainment, social connection or novelty/curiosity were much less important. Dibitonto et al. [9] stressed that chatbots in educational settings belong to the productivity task category, with two subcategories: to provide information, e.g. to prospective students and to provide assistance, e.g. perform a specific task for the student who enrolled into particular faculty.

Differences in human-chatbot conversation in contrast to human-human communication are also identified. While communicating with the chatbots users tend to write shorter messages, have conversations with longer duration, poorer vocabulary, but greater profanity [12], express courtesy or send smiley emoticons [9]. Other research [20] had showed that chatbot personality plays an important role on the user experience of chatbot interfaces, e.g. agreeable personality of the chatbot is better perceived than a conscientious one, but this effect is dependent on context and the user group. Thus, [1] suggests a framework for designing successful conversational agents, which should set up meaningful relationships with users (e.g. consumers) while satisfying functionality and aesthetics. Flexibility, affectiveness, communication, and autonomy are the key components that generate the chatbot's behavior.

Dibitonto et al. [9] explored how conversation is performed between the chatbot and the students, using a chatbot as a mean to perform a survey, to observe users' behavior during the conversation and to find out about the students' needs in order to create future virtual assistant for the campus students. A research performed by Pricilla et al. [17] included user-centered design in order to include the users in the process of design: to identify users and their needs, goals, preferences and limitations in each phase of the design process of the chatbot.

All the above-mentioned researches have helped to design our research approach described in the next section.

3   Research Approach

3.1   Context of the Research

Research presented in this paper is a part of continuous and ongoing project in the domain of research, development and innovation, namely *"IRI Hyper - User Experience of the Future – Smart Specializations and Modern Communication and Collaboration Technologies"* which is financed through European Regional Development Fund.

Among others, project activities included several connected researches [14–16] that aimed to identify how students are using existing applications and web sites in order to retrieve information related to their study and other common activities, as well as to identify problems students are facing with it, with the main goal to create successful chatbot that will provide meaningful information to the students of our faculty. We have followed a user experience lifecycle template established in user-centered design proposed in [10], that consists of four iterative and incremental phases: *Analyze* (context, users needs), *Design* (concept, interactions), *Prototype* (realizing design alternatives) and *Evaluate* (various evaluation methods). This paper is focused on the first two phases.

The researchers in the *Analysis* phase conducted several research activities including semi *structured interview* where special focus was placed on the experiences in using chatbots. The results showed that only several students have had previous experiences in using chatbots – but not in the domain of education. Additionally, we performed an *observation* with an aim to identify how the students are interacting with the faculty's systems in order to retrieve required information. The observation also included the experiment on students' interaction with a chatbot [8] with the aim to introduce students to the possibilities of such tool and to obtain the information on how chatbots could help them in their faculty activities.

The results obtained through 18 sessions with the students during the two mentioned researches activities were the base for *data-driven inquiry* [10] that followed. As such inquiry resulted in vast amount of raw data we also had to perform *contextual analysis* [10] containing data systematization, grouping and generalization. This finally enabled us to identify the most important information which we have presented through identified *personas*. The details on these results are presented in [15]. However, the aforementioned analysis does not interpret data with the aim of system requirements extraction, nor we gained inputs necessary for interaction design or user interface design. In order to bridge the gap between analysis and design phase and in order to extract design relevant requirements necessary for interaction design, we performed additional research based on *online survey*. The data obtained in this survey is input to the research we are presenting in this paper. The research has been performed in the Croatian language.

3.2 Research Questions

This study aims to answer two research questions, both related to the user needs in terms of communication with domain-specific chatbot used in higher education:

- **Research question 1 (RQ1):** What are the user requirements related to use of chatbot in the domain of higher education?
- **Research question 2 (RQ2):** What are the design artifacts (i.e. user interface segments or widgets) related to user requirements obtained in RQ1 that could be used in implementation of the faculty chatbot?

3.3 Respondents

For the purpose of answering first research question (RQ1) total of 131 students of University of Zagreb, Faculty of Organization and Informatics participated in the research. Research included students from all study programmes offered by Faculty of Organization and Informatics, including undergraduate study programmes, undergraduate vocational study programme, and graduate study programmes. Female (47.3%) versus male (52.7%) respondents' ratio is 0.89, while 50.4% of all undergraduate respondents were third year students which along with graduate students aligned our need to have more experienced students included in the study. As presented in Fig. 1 the distribution of respondents in relation to their study type was balanced in satisfactory level. In this way we were able to construct coherent picture that represents all students of Faculty of Organization and Informatics.

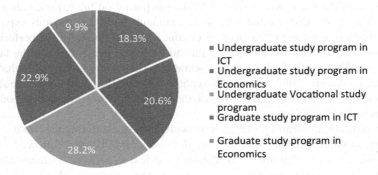

Fig. 1. Distribution of students per type of study

3.4 Instrument

For the needs analysis it was necessary to conduct a study that would explore students' perception about chatbots and their needs regarding information that would like to receive from the chatbot. Before conducting this study, we have interviewed faculty departments that process students' requests, such as Office for Student Affairs, to better understand students' needs. In this process four themes were identified as the most relevant for students and they were the focus of the study. Four identified themes are: exams, midterms, office hours, and location of rooms.

Study was conducted in the Croatian language in the form of an online questionnaire with five main sections: 1) section one was related to basic information (study programme, year of study, etc.), 2) section two concerned students' previous experiences with chatbots, 3) section three explored how students perceive Faculty of Organization and Informatics' web pages and services, 4) section four offered the possibility to pose questions related to four abovementioned themes as they would be posed to a chatbot, and 5) section five explored which chatbot characteristics students preferred. The screenshots of the online survey used in the study are presented in the Fig. 2.

3.5 Thematic Analysis

In order to answer first research question (RQ1), the data collected in the Sect. 4) of the questionnaire was examined by means of thematic analysis (TA). According to [5] the main purpose of thematic analysis is to identify, analyze and report patterns or themes in some qualitative data. Additionally, the method is considered to be flexible and independent of taken perspectives on obtained data. Moreover, according to [13] thematic analysis gives a straightforward and clean framework enabling the researcher to extract meaningful themes from collected data. In the context of education, when

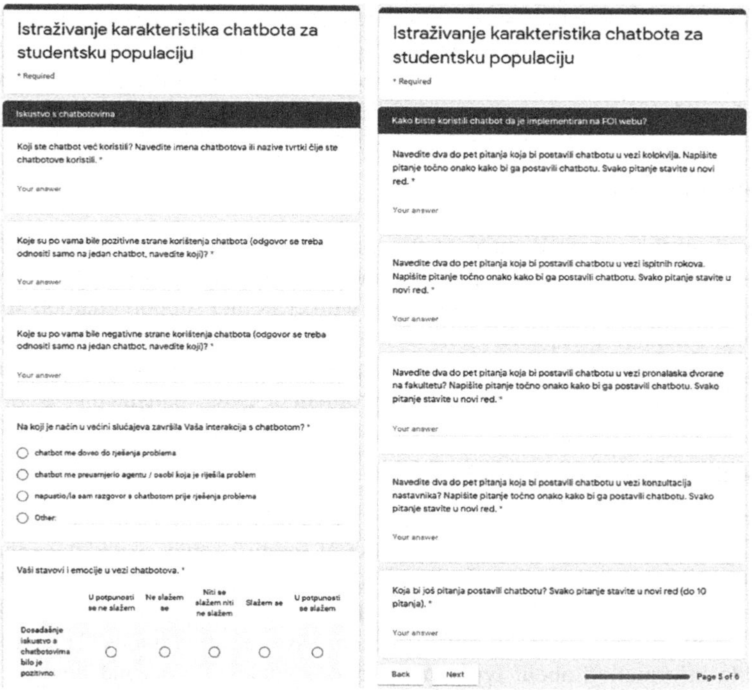

Fig. 2. Screenshots from the online survey

analyzing the data obtained by interviews, and in contrast to quantitative analysis, this qualitative framework can reveal the true user requirements as a result of its flexibility in data interpretation [21].

In our research we have been using Braun and Clark's [5] six-step recursive framework in conducting the thematic analysis: (1) become familiar with data, (2) initially code the data, (3) search for themes, (4) review themes, (5) define themes and (6) write a report. After systematizing the interview results, it is worth mentioning that *open coding* (without having defined a set of a priori codes) was used – codes were developed and changed during the analysis process. As it is usual [7] when performing the TA, codes served as tags or labels used to retrieve and categorize each segment of data within whole data set. Coding reduced an initial data set into the small fragments with meaning. In subsequent phases of the analysis, codes with common point of reference were put into context and themes were created. In the case of this research, a theme is a user interface segment (or widget) that could be used to cover the features defined by appurtenant codes. Such identified themes were interesting to us in relation to our research questions. According to [6], the codes' or themes' frequencies aim to bring additional information about the data that is originally hidden. However, in relation to our research questions and goals, the number of occurrences of specific codes or themes was not relevant except to prioritize and order the defined themes.

And finally, as defined in [4], the concluding result of the analysis is to pinpoint a set of themes that may be visualized in a report as a map indicating relationships or hierarchy among them. In the context of our research the identified themes defining the user interface elements were presented in such way as well.

4   Research Results

Although all of the surveyed students are computer-literate and have experience with ICT tools, only 30.5% of 131 respondent had previous experience with chatbots and they noted that those experience were mostly with customer support chatbots for banks or telecommunication companies. Out of those 30.5%, more precisely, 40 respondents who had previous interactions with chatbots, only 20% had positive experience with chatbots, meaning that chatbot solved their problem or gave a satisfactory answer.

4.1   Results from Thematic Analysis

Section 4 of the questionnaire gave students the opportunity to pose questions related to exams, midterms, office hours, and location of rooms as they would pose them to a chatbot. Examples of the questions are: "When the midterm exams starts?", "What is the minimum score necessary to pass the midterm exam?", "Can I bring the calculator to the midterm exam?" "Will the midterm exam have negative points?" etc. This gave us valuable information about types of questions students pose and how they word them. It is necessary to mention that smaller number of questions significantly differed from others which could mean that some respondents did not completely understand the questionnaire. The example of raw data in Croatian given for the mentioned first dimension is given in Fig. 3. The outlier questions (marked purple in Fig. 3) were not taken in account when analysing results (e.g. "Hi, what is the answer to the second question?").

U koliko sati počinje kolokvij?
Bodovi koji se trebaju ostvariti na kolokviju?
Vrijeme odvijanja kolokvija?
Koje gradivo ulazi u kolokvij iz kolegija X?
Koliko bodova nosi kolokvij iz kolegija ?
Ima li uvjeta za pristupanje drugom kolokviju?
Koliko bodova nosi teorija a koliko zadaci?
Kada je kolokvij iz *?
U kojoj dvorani je kolokvij iz *?
Da li postoji više termina za kolokvij?
Mogu li ponijeti kalkulator na kolokvij?
Koliko minimalno bodova moram imati na kolokviju?
Koliko bodova nosi kolokvij?
Hoće li na kolokviju biti negativnih bodova?
Kakav je tip kolokvija?

Piše li se kolokvij olovkom, kemijskom ili na računalu?
U kojem terminu i u kojoj dvorani se piše kolokvij?
Koja su pitanja na kolokviju?
Od kud učiti za kolokvij?
Gdje mogu naći skriptu?
Koji tjedan je kolokvij iz PIS-a?
Imaš li skriptu za kolokvij iz PIS-a?
Kada je kraj prvog ciklusa kolokvija?
Zašto je na kolokvijima više zadataka koji su opisni a manje zadataka na zaokruživanje?
Može li se ponavljati kolokvij u slučaju pada?
Možete li mi dati primjer kolokvija?
Kako bi ste riješili ovaj zadatak?
Bok Danijel, kak glasi odgovor na peto pitanje?
Bok, kako ide drugo pitanje?

Fig. 3. Raw students' questions related to mid-term exams

After gathering all obtained information related to chatbot characteristics and requirements we had to sort and structure the data and to extract relevant codes from it.

Table 1. Structuring the raw data into fine-grained context

Topics	Context	Keywords
Exams	Time	Date, time, hour(s), when, time frame, schedule, exam term
	Location	Room, where, location, place, taking place
	Applications and cancelations	Application, cancelation
	Structure and requirements	Obligatory/eliminatory, structure, question(s), score, requirement(s), how many, how long, signature, result(s)
	Oral exam	Oral, oral exam
	Curriculum	Topic(s), literature, curriculum
	Other	
Midterms	Time	Date, time, hour(s), when, time frame, schedule, exam term
	Location	Room, where, location, place, taking place
	Time & location	(Date, time, hour(s), when, time frame, schedule, exam term) and (room, where, location, place, taking place)
	Structure and requirements	Obligatory/eliminatory, structure, question(s), score, requirement(s), how many, how long, signature, result(s)
	Curriculum	Curriculum, learning materials, literature, content, topics
	Other	
Office hours	Time	When, day in week, time
	Location	Where, room, office
	General	Office hours, consultation(s)
	Other	Professor, why…
Location of rooms	Location	Where, room
	Event location	(Midterm, seminar, lectures, taking place) and (where, room, location)
	Building	Building, FOI1, FOI2
	Other	
Other	Studying and obligations	Course, academic calendar, breaks, holidays, labs, laboratories, lectures

(*continued*)

Table 1. *(continued)*

Topics	Context	Keywords
	Internships	Internship, country
	Erasmus	Erasmus
	Faculty	Contact, phone, working hours, enrolment
	Miscellaneous	

Thus, we added second dimension in order to group the questions in relation to other relevant parameters. The final structure with context and filtering keywords is presented in Table 1.

The resulted document contained a list of questions placed into this two-dimensional matrix which at the end represented a final set of codes that a user could be interacting with the chatbot. The excerpt of the identified codes is given in Fig. 4.

These codes represent the user requirements and are answer to our first research question (RQ1).

Additionally, these codes represent the base for the final list of themes i.e. user interactions and interface elements that were recognized to be required in order to achieve desired functionalities.

The thematic analysis performed by mentioned Braun and Clark's six-step recursive framework resulted in identification of total of nineteen themes containing both education specifics (9) and chatbot usual user interface elements (10). Table 2 presents the identified themes along with example context where it could be used and with one representative question. It is also worth mentioning that every listed theme contains more than one code i.e. it could be used when answering different student questions.

Vrijeme	Lokacija	Prijave i odjave	Struktura i uvjeti
Ključne riječi: ***sati, datum, kad/a, termin, raspored, vrijeme, rok, rokovi***	*Ključne riječi:* ***dvorana, dvorani, gdje, kojoj, lokacija, održava, piše, vrijeme***	*Ključne riječi:* ***prijava, prijaviti, odjaviti***	*Ključne riječi:* ***eliminacijski, struktura, pitanja, bodovi, bodova, koliko, uvjet (uvijet), traje, potpis, rezultati, rezultate***
Datum ispita iz kolegija x	Gdje se održava ispit?	Do kad se može prijaviti rok?	Kad će rezultati?
Datum ispita iz kolegija y	<ime kolegija> dvora održavanja ispita	Do kada mogu odjaviti ispitni rok?	Koliko dugo traje ispit?
Datum ispitnog roka iz AIR	Gdje je ispitni rok (lokacija)?	Do kada mogu prijaviti ispitni rok?	Bodovna skala
Datum ispitnog roka?	Gdje se održava 2. ispitni rok iz RPK?	do kada treba prijaviti ispit iz "nekog predmeta"	dali je moguće izać na više ispitnih rokova?
datum iz mat1 ispita	Gdje se održava ispit iz aira	Gdje se prijaviti na ispit?	Ima li kakvih preduvjeta za prijavu roka?
Datum roka?	Gdje se održava ispit iz MMS?	Kad prijaviti ispitni rok?	Ima li preduvjeta za izlazak na ispit iz ...?
Datumi	Gdje se održava ispit iz Multimedijskih sustava?	Kad se može odjaviti ispitni rok?	Ima li uvjeta?
Datumi ispita na sljedecem roku?	Gdje se održava ispit?	Kad se moze prijaviti	Imaju li redovni studenti mogućnost izslaska na izvanredne ispitne rokove?
Datumi ispita na svim rokovima?	Gdje se održava sljedeći ispit iz kolegija X?	Kada moram najkasnije prijaviti ispit?	Je li potrebno na ispitu prikazati osobni identifikacijski dokument?
Datumi ispita?	Kada se otvaraju rokovi za upis ispita?	Kada moram prijaviti ispitni rok?	Kada će biti rezultati
kad je 2. rok iz zis-a?	U kojoj dvorani će se održavati ispit?	kada trebam prijaviti	Kada će ispit biti ispravljen
Kad je ispi iz aira	U kojoj dvorani imam ispitni rok?	Kako prijaviti ispitni rok?	Kada mogu očekivati rezultate?
Kad je ispit iz XY?	u kojoj dvorani je ispit iz algoritama?	Kako prijaviti izvanredni ispitni rok?	Kada možemo pristupiti ispitnom roku
Kad je ispitni rok iz xy kolegija?	U kojoj dvorani je ispit iz XY?	Koliko imam iskorištenih rokova?	Kakva je struktura ispita?
Kad je ispitni rok za pojedini kolegij?	U kojoj dvorani se ispit održava?	Koliko rokova mogu iskoristiti do 2.mjeseca?	Kakva je struktura kolokvija?

Fig. 4. Excerpt from final set of codes in given two contextual dimensions

Table 2. Identified themes/user interface elements

Theme	Example context	Representative question
Event info	Midterm/time and location	When and where the midterm exam in Software engineering course will take place?
Reminder setup/view	Exams/applications and cancelations	Remind me to apply for the next exam term in software engineering course.
Carousel view	Exams/structure and conditions	What type of questions could I expect on next midterm exam in software engineering?
Course model view	Midterms/structure and conditions	Show me the weeks and structure of midterm exams in software engineering.
Course requirements view	Exams/structure and conditions	What are the minimum requirements to access oral exam?
Daily schedule (integrated)	Other/miscellaneous	What is my schedule for today?
Check list view	Midterms/structure and conditions	Am I allowed to take calculator with me on midterm exam in mathematics?
Grading info	Exams/Structure and conditions	What is the minimum score to pass the course with excellent result?
Document/image preview	Midterms/structure and conditions	What does the exam document look like?
Yes/no	Midterms/structure and conditions	Is it possible to retake last midterm exam in software engineering?
Calendar view	Midterms/time	What is the time schedule for midterm exams?
List view	Office hours/general	What days does prof. Plantak Vukovac has consultations?
Rich list view	Other/miscellaneous	Who are the professors teaching the course on software engineering?
Link	Midterms/time	Where can I find the schedule for midterm exam?
Graph/bar/pie view	Midterms/structure and Conditions	What is the minimum score necessary to pass the exam?
Map view	Location of rooms/buildings	Where are the faculty enrolments taking place?
Label, button, balloon text…		

The elements usually used in chatbots are grayed out in the list, as the focus in the remaining part of the paper will be placed on the elements which are specific for the faculty chatbots, facing questions in educational environment that require complex answers with lots of information.

4.2 Preferences About the Faculty Chatbot

Section 5 in the questionnaire provided answers related to several students' preferences in their future usage of the faculty chatbot.

First, students declared themselves about the form of the chatbot answers. The preferred form for 80, 92% of the respondents were the simple and straightforward chatbot's answers, followed by the answers provided in the options (callouts or buttons). About 37% would like to receive answers in the form of the picture or video. Detailed answers are shown in Fig. 5.

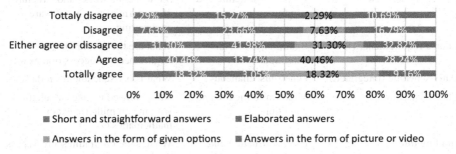

Fig. 5. Preferred forms of the chatbot answers

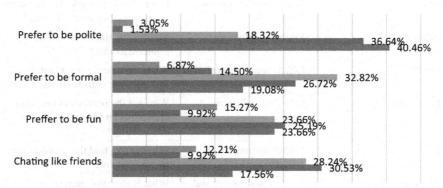

Fig. 6. Preferred tone of the chatbot's communication

Second, students declared about the tone of communication with the chatbot. From the Fig. 6. it can be concluded that the majority of students prefer polite chatbot and some of them wanted to be fun and friendly.

These findings are in line with the guidelines in [1] that chatbot needs to be fun and affective.

5   Conclusion and Future Work

By employing interviews, observations, a survey and a thematic analysis, we identified students' needs of anticipated chatbot to be used in educational environment. Students' answers provided in the open-ended questions of the survey enabled us to extract nineteen themes of the chatbot user interactions of which nine categories (design artifacts) of the chatbot user interface were novel in educational context. Besides that, we discovered that students prefer fun, but polite personality of the chatbot. From the practical point of view, these findings could help designers and developers, accompanied by technologies such as machine learning and natural language processing, to create a chatbot that will serve as a personal student assistant. Questions that students posed in the survey can be used to build and train the chatbot knowledge base.

However, from the research's perspective this study has limitations. It has been conducted among the students of one faculty who, although were enrolled in different study years and study programmes, are not representatives for the student population in large. Another limitation is the manual performance of the thematic analysis which might result in inadvertent error of coding and classification of the answers into categories.

Our future work, in collaboration with artificial intelligence team, will focus on designing specifics of the chatbot interaction design, both for the student portal and mobile application, which will provide the background to create interface and interaction guidelines for the chatbots in educational settings. Another stream of research is to explore usability and user experience metrics for evaluation of the chatbots in educational domain.

References

1. Angeli, A.D., et al.: Personifying the e-market: a framework for social agents, vol. 8 (2001)
2. Brandtzaeg, P.B., Følstad, A.: Chatbots: changing user needs and motivations. Interactions **25**(5), 38–43 (2018). https://doi.org/10.1145/3236669
3. Brandtzaeg, P.B., Følstad, A.: Why people use chatbots. In: Kompatsiaris, I., et al. (eds.) INSCI 2017. LNCS, vol. 10673, pp. 377–392. Springer, Cham (2017). https://doi.org/10.1007/978-3-319-70284-1_30
4. Braun, V., et al.: Thematic analysis. In: Liamputtong, P. (ed.) Handbook of Research Methods in Health Social Sciences, pp. 843–860. Springer Singapore (2019). https://doi.org/10.1007/978-981-10-5251-4_103
5. Braun, V., Clarke, V.: Using thematic analysis in psychology. Qual. Res. Psychol. **3**(2), 77–101 (2006). https://doi.org/10.1191/1478088706qp063oa
6. Brough, P. (ed.): Advanced Research Methods for Applied Psychology: Design, Analysis and Reporting. Routledge, Abingdon (2018)

7. Castleberry, A., Nolen, A.: Thematic analysis of qualitative research data - is it as easy as it sounds? Curr. Pharm. Teach. Learn. **10**(6), 807–815 (2018). https://doi.org/10.1016/j.cptl. 2018.03.019

8. ConnectionModel.com: ConnectionBot - DemoLeadBot, https://www.connectionmodel. com/drift#DemoBot

9. Dibitonto, M., Leszczynska, K., Tazzi, F., Medaglia, C.M.: Chatbot in a campus environment: design of LiSA, a virtual assistant to help students in their university life. In: Kurosu, M. (ed.) HCI 2018. LNCS, vol. 10903, pp. 103–116. Springer, Cham (2018). https://doi.org/10.1007/ 978-3-319-91250-9_9

10. Hartson, R., Pyla, P.S.: The UX Book: Process and Guidelines for Ensuring a Quality User Experience. Morgan Kaufman, Elsevier, Waltham, USA (2012)

11. Hien, H.T., et al.: Intelligent assistants in higher-education environments: the FIT-EBot, a chatbot for administrative and learning support. In: Proceedings of the Ninth International Symposium on Information and Communication Technology - SoICT 2018, pp. 69–76. ACM Press, Danang City (2018). https://doi.org/10.1145/3287921.3287937

12. Hill, J., et al.: Real conversations with artificial intelligence. Comput. Hum. Behav. **49**(C), 245–250 (2015). https://doi.org/10.1016/j.chb.2015.02.026

13. Maguire, M., Delahunt, B.: Doing a Thematic Analysis: A Practical, Step-by-Step Guide for Learning and Teaching Scholars, vol. 8, no. 3, pp. 14 (2017)

14. Plantak Vukovac, D., et al.: IRI Hyper - 4.1.8 Izrada web klijenta i serverskih servisa za upravljanje i nadzor uspješnosti agenata (2020)

15. Plantak Vukovac, D., et al.: IRI Hyper - 4.1.9 Izrada GUI komponenti za uvođenje korisnika (eng. onboarding) i upravljačke ploče (eng. dashboard) korisnika za korištenje (2020)

16. Plantak Vukovac, D., et al.: IRI Hyper - 6.1.1 Cjelokupna testiranja prototipa web klijenta i serverskog servisa (2020)

17. Pricilla, C., et al.: Designing interaction for chatbot-based conversational commerce with user-centered design. In: 2018 5th International Conference on Advanced Informatics: Concept Theory and Applications (ICAICTA), pp. 244–249. IEEE, Krabi (2018). https://doi.org/10. 1109/ICAICTA.2018.8541320

18. Shah, H., et al.: Can machines talk? Comparison of Eliza with modern dialogue systems. Comput. Hum. Behav. **58**, 278–295 (2016). https://doi.org/10.1016/j.chb.2016.01.004

19. Skjuve, M., Brandzaeg, P.B.: Measuring user experience in chatbots: an approach to interpersonal communication competence. In: Bodrunova, S.S., et al. (eds.) INSCI 2018. LNCS, vol. 11551, pp. 113–120. Springer, Cham (2019). https://doi.org/10.1007/978-3-030-17705-8_10

20. Smestad, T.L., Volden, F.: Chatbot personalities matters. In: Bodrunova, S.S., et al. (eds.) INSCI 2018. LNCS, vol. 11551, pp. 170–181. Springer, Cham (2019). https://doi.org/10. 1007/978-3-030-17705-8_15

21. Vaismoradi, M., et al.: Content analysis and thematic analysis: Implications for conducting a qualitative descriptive study, vol. 8 (2013)

22. Winkler, R., Soellner, M.: Unleashing the potential of chatbots in education: a state-of-the-art analysis. In: Proceedings 2018, vol. 1, p. 15903 (2018). https://doi.org/10.5465/AMBPP. 2018.15903abstract

23. Ally Bank Introduces Ally Assist (SM) Customer Voice Interaction. https://media.ally.com/ 2015-05-18-Ally-Bank-Introduces-Ally-Assist-SM-Customer-Voice-Interaction. Accessed 18 Jun 2020

24. Scheduling Bot for Hair Salons. https://botmakers.net/chatbot-templates/scheduling-bot-for-hair-salons. Accessed 18 Jun 2020

The Influence of Picture Book Interaction Design on Preschool Children's Reading Experience

Liying Wang[(✉)] [iD]

Tongji University, Shanghai 200092, China
misschild2002@163.com

Abstract. Compared by adults, children rely more on the experience obtained through the materiality of picture books to get information or just have entertainment. Therefore, the design of children's picture books is more interactive than general books. This study explored the effects of interaction form and gender on children's reading preference, interests, subjective ratings and affective experience. Extremely controlled experiment method was used in this study, 40 six-year old children were invited to attend the experiment to read books with different interaction forms. 6 most commonly used interaction forms in the design of children's picture books were used as the experimental control variables. These 6 interaction forms come from the two categories of "behavior-based interaction forms" and "sensory experience-based interaction forms". The improved "8 circular emotion cards" are used as experimental scales. Children's reading interest is judged by reading time. A two-way analysis of variance for reading time showed that the interaction form has a significant effect on reading time. A statistical analysis of the rating found that the interaction form had a significant impact on children's subjective evaluation. Gender difference in the interests of interaction forms is not significant. This research gives some suggestion for children's picture book design: 1. design suitable interaction form to stimulate children's positive emotions in reading; 2. make good use of the interaction form based on sensory experience; 3. the interaction form should match the children's cognitive characteristic.

Keywords: Children's picture book · Interaction form · Affective experience · Reading preference · Gender

1 Introduction

Due to the special development stage, preschool children are more dependent on the experience obtained through the materiality of picture book, so the preschool children's picture books have more material characteristics than general books. The design of preschool children's picture books often takes use of interaction. From the 17th century to the present, with the development of science, technology, culture and educational ideas, the development of children's picture books has evolved into rich interaction forms. This study aims to study the impact of changes in book interaction forms

© Springer Nature Switzerland AG 2020
C. Stephanidis et al. (Eds.): HCII 2020, LNCS 12425, pp. 485–503, 2020.
https://doi.org/10.1007/978-3-030-60128-7_37

on preschool children's reading through psychological experiment methods, and proposes book interaction forms that can meet children's exploration and knowledge needs. Provide suggestions for children's picture book design.

Some scholars conducted a very small-scale empirical study in Amsterdam, the Netherlands, using a three-dimensional picture book designed by Ron van der Meer (a well-known three-dimensional book designer) and a regular picture book of the same content as experimental materials, the conclusion is that when reading a three-dimensional picture book, the reader remembers 75% of all the information in the book, while reading a regular picture book only remembers 20% of the information [1]. The reason for this result is that in the process of reading the three-dimensional picture book, one reading is equivalent to reading three times:the first is the visual sensory interaction with the text and illustrations;the second is the action-based interaction with the structure;the third time is to experience the fusion of all these interactions. The scholar pointed out the importance of sensory experience in understanding and remembering the content of picture books. However, the sample of this study is very small, and only the effect of information memory is measured, not involving the emotion and interest of the picture book reading experience, and only compared the pop up interaction form and the ordinary picture book. Therefore, the evaluation of the interaction forms of children's picture books is not comprehensive. Luca Colombo et al. have studied the user experience in children's e-book reading, using the self-reporting experiment method ESM (Experience Sampling Method) to evaluate the "flow" difference in reading between strong interaction eBooks (enhanced eBook) and weak interaction eBooks (basic eBook). Strong interaction e-books include sound effects, interactive image animations, videos, guessing games, built-in dictionaries, color-changing text and other interaction forms, while weak interaction e-books are just simply the digital version of the paper book having only static text and images. The researchers had developed an application for generating ESM. When the user reads the e-book page, the application will pop up a questionnaire based on Likert scale for the user to fill out. The study evaluates the "flow" of user experience in terms of reading time, reading integrity, order, and accumulation. The analysis shows that strong interaction e-books with rich interaction forms are more likely to cause users' "flow", that means, the user experience obtained during the process of strong interaction e-books is better than that of weak interaction e-books [2]. Although the research of Luca Colombo is aimed at children aged 7–12 reading digital books, the experimental methods have some inspiration for our research. Due to the characteristics of preschool children, they are easy to confuse facts and imagination. Therefore, the self-reporting method is used in the experiment, which requires the feedback of the events just experienced in a short period of time, so the reliability of the collected data is high.

From the perspective of cognition, sociology and culture, emotions are not only derived from physiological reactions, but also influenced by the information processing, social communication and cultural background [3]. Psychological research shows that in the early stages of cognition development, children's attention is easily attracted to external things and the duration of attention is short, but emotions have a regulatory role in maintaining attention [4]. Recent studies on library and information science have also found that emotions affect users' information behavior, and have an important impact on behavior willingness, duration, and efficiency [5]. Emotions are an important part of user experience. Positive emotions can enhance the user's hedonic experience and enhance the user's sense of self-identity, value, and satisfaction [6]. A good emotional experience can bring good expectations to users, and encourage users to conduct information sharing. Therefore, the friendly interaction forms of picture books have an important impact on improving children's enjoyment, cultivating children's reading ability, and establishing good reading habits.

2   Method

In this study, a psychological experiment was used to collect children's reading time data, invite children to sort and rate reading materials' preferences, and select emotional pictures that match the situation at that time. Through data analysis, interaction forms can meet children's reading experience needs are proposed that provides a theoretical basis for the design of children's picture books which can enhance children's reading interest, reading time and depth. According to the goals and demands of children's picture book reading experience, this study addresses the following research questions:

1) Are there significant differences in the impact of changes in book interaction on children's reading time, reading preferences, and emotions?
2) Are there any differences in the effects of gender on reading time, reading preferences and emotions?
3) What kind of reading emotional experience do children expect when reading?
4) Does the form of behavioral interaction affect reading experience better than the form of sensory interaction?

2.1   Experiment Design

This experiment selects the 6 most commonly used interaction forms in the design of children's picture books as the experimental control variables. These 6 interaction forms come from the two categories of "behavior-based interaction forms" and "sensory experience-based interaction forms". They are: 1. regular page-flipping interaction; 2. open/close interaction; 3. rotate interaction, 4. Touch & smell interaction; 5. pull/push interaction; 6. puzzle interaction.

Here is only a brief introduction: 1. Regular page-flipping interaction refers to turning the book pages by hand, which is the most common and habitual interaction form in reading; 2. Open/close interaction refers to designing some parts that can be opened/closed and the picture will change accordingly, so the storyline will be richer, with hidden/exposed changes in time and space. 3. Rotate interaction refers to displaying different content through rotation, so that the pictures show continuous changes; 4. Touch & smell interaction refers to the page contains special materials that children can touch and smell; 5. Pull/push interaction is refers to changing the content through pulling and pushing paper parts; 6. Puzzle interaction refers to changing the picture through patch-work to form new reading content. Among them, types 1, 2, 3, 5 and 6 belong to the "action-based interaction form", and the fourth type belongs to the "sensory experience based interaction form".

In order to exclude the influence of the topic and content, this study designed 6 picture books all about human body. Each reading material contains only one interaction form (see Fig. 1). We numbered the six test books and marked the number in the upper right corner of the first page of the book.

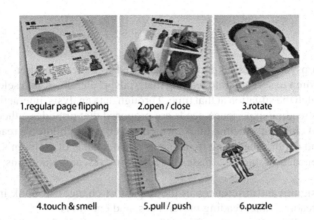

Fig. 1. 6 reading materials including 6 types of interaction form

Boys and girls' preference for shapes, colors, toys, etc. shows gender differences during infancy [7]. This gender difference becomes more obvious while growing up. For example, boys prefer toys with male characteristics such as cars and weapons, and girls prefer toys with female characteristics such as dolls and toy houses. Girls prefer to paint flowers, butterflies and characters, while boys prefer to paint moving items such as cars, trains, and rockets [8]. Sociology theory points out that the gender difference originates from the difference between men and women in social roles.

Based on the research above, gender differences will lead to differences in interest in reading content. Therefore, in this study, we selected neutral reading content with no significant gender orientation-the popular science picture book of human body. According to the children's pedagogy research, both boys and girls aged 3–6 are curious about their own body. As a test material, the picture book of this content not only helps to eliminate the content's preference for gender, but also make the test proceed successfully. In addition, we speculate that there may be gender differences in the preference of interaction forms.

Preschool children have the characteristics of impulsiveness, transference and infection. Compared with infancy, the emotional complexity and socialization of preschool children have increased. Emotions play a greater role in children's activities, and affect the development of psychology and behavior. Ma Yanqing found that children's emotions have a signaling function. The children should send many emotional signals to the others, such as smiling faces to express good feelings, and angry eyes to express anger and disgust in daily life. Children's emotions directly reflect their love and preference for products. At the same time, toddlers must also accept emotional signals from others. They can understand the emotional signals of others correctly. For example, they know that "tears" mean sadness, and "grinning" means joy. After receiving and understanding these emotional signals, preschool children can respond accordingly and adjust their actions in time [9]. Children's ability to recognize emotion signals also provided a cognition basis for the use of "circumplex of emotions" in this experiment.

Although there are many methods to measure emotion, such as self-reporting, autonomic nervous system measurement, startle response measurement, behavior measurement, and brain measurement, the emotion measurement methods suitable for children are very limited [10]. At present, the most commonly used measurement methods for children are self-reporting and behavioral measurement. Self-reporting often uses positive and negative emotions scale (PNANS), three-dimensional PAD scale and Russell's circumplex of emotions [11]. Behavior measurement uses facial expression recognition and volume changing recognition, whichever takes a long experiment time. However, children's daily life in kindergarten has very strict rules, and the management of kindergarten is well organized. In terms of moral requirements, the testers can't interfere children too much, nor can it interfere too much with the management of the kindergarten. Due to such conditions, behavior measurement cannot be carried out in the kindergarten and Russell's circumplex of emotions was adopted as a tool for children's mood measurement. Russell's circumplex of emotions divides emotions into 8 categories according to the two coordinates of "awakening degree" and "pleasure degree", and each type of emotion is composed of 2 expression pictures, representing the male and female faces of the same emotion (see Fig. 2). Participants only need to select one of the cards to express their mood after reading, without answering questions, so it is very suitable for children. However, the scale image also has some applicability problems: First, the faces in the picture are all western races, and the participants are all Chinese children. The children have some cognition difficulties in recognizing the facial expressions of western races; second, each emotion uses two pictures of male and female, but the visual difference between male and female is not significant. If the boy/girl is required to use the gender picture to represent his/her own emotions, the workload of picture recognizing and cognition will increase, reducing the efficiency and affecting the reliability and validity of the experiment. In order to reduce the cognition difficulty for Chinese children, we have improved the Russell scale: 1. Eliminate the burden of recognition of races, and replace the western race faces with cartoon faces; To eliminate the cognition burden of gender, each type of emotion is represented by only one image, regardless of gender. Finally, the improved "8 circular emotion cards" are used as experiment scales (see Fig. 3). There are 8 facial images, which represent the emotional level of No. 1–8.

Before the formal experiment, we invited 5 children aged 5–6 to recognize the improved version. All 5 children could quickly and accurately recognize the emotion represented by the cartoon face. While these five children were asked to recognize the original Russell's circumplex of emotions, not only they spent more time but also asked for help, which proved that the improved emotion card was more successful and effective.

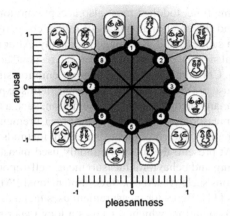

Fig. 2. The 16 circular emotion cards placed on Russell's circumplex of emotions

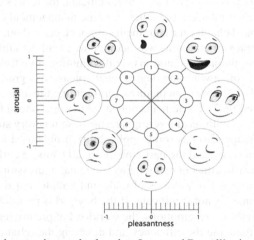

Fig. 3. The 8 circular emotion cards placed on Improved Russell's circumplex of emotions

2.2 Tasks

In this study, a two-factor mixed experiment was adopted. The independent variable A was "picture book interaction form" and the independent variable B was "gender". Among them, the picture book interaction form had 6 levels, namely A1. regular page-flipping interaction; A2. Open/close interaction; A3. Puzzle interaction;A4. Pull/push interaction; A5. Touch & smell interaction; A6. Rotate interaction. There are 2 levels of gender, corresponding to B1. Male and B2. Female. The study is divided into male and female groups, and gender is an inter-group factor. During the experiment, in accordance with the Latin square order of the experiment, each participant read the 6 reading materials in turn, and 6 interaction forms of picture books belong to the intra-group factor. During the experiment, the children's reading behavior and reading time were recorded with a camera. After reading each material, the children must complete the following tasks in order: firstly, select the card that meets their emotions from the "8 circular emotion cards"; secondly, the experimenter gives each child 5 star stickers and ask them to rate the interaction forms; finally, the children sort the 6 interaction forms according to their own preferences.

2.3 Participants

This experiment was completed in the Song Qingling Kindergarten Library in Shanghai. It lasted for 2 weeks. A total of 40 kindergarten children were invited to participate in the experiment. The average age was 6 years old, including 20 boys and 20 girls. Each student has more than 2 h of reading time per week in the kindergarten, and has rich reading experience. All participants had normal vision. Before the experiment began, the teacher carefully read the experimental notification letter, confirmed that the study did not cause physical or psychological harm to the children, and authorized the signature to agree the experiment (see Fig. 4). According to the experiment plan, children are divided into two groups, male and female, each group of 20 people. They were asked to read the 6 picture books containing 6 interaction forms in accordance with the pre-set reading order.

Fig. 4. Experiment in progress

2.4 Procedure

1) We used simple and natural sentences to briefly introduce the experiment task to children. The researchers and each child read the emotion cards together to ensure that the children can understand each emotion in the picture.
2) After confirming that the children understand the emotional meaning of all the faces, ask them to select the face that meets their expectations of reading.
3) Ask the children to read the materials No. 1 to No. 6 in order. After reading each material, each participant selects the face that matches his/her emotion from 8 emotional face cards.
4) The experimenter gave the children 5 stars stickers, and asked them to rate the interaction forms of the reading materials. 5 stars mean they like the interaction form very much, followed by 4 and so on. The maximum is 5 and the minimum is 0.

5) After reading all the test materials, experimenter asked the children to rank the reading material from first to sixth according to their preferences.

2.5 Data Collection and Analysis

A total of 5 data were collected in this experiment: ① the reading emotional experience expected by children; ② the duration of reading; ③ the emotional experience after reading each material; ④ the star rating of each material; ⑤ the preference ranking of all materials. During the experiment, the reading time of children is not limited. The reading duration is recorded from the beginning of reading to the time when children are bored and no longer reading. SPSS 19 is used for data analysis.

3   Results

3.1 Expectation Emotion and Actual Reading Emotion

Most children expect to have a pleasant and slightly arousal emotional experience during reading, as shown in Fig. 1. 70% of children expect to be happy, and 15% of children expect to be very happy and stranger arousal emotional experience (see Table 1).

Table 1. Emotional distribution of circular cards in anticipation of emotions

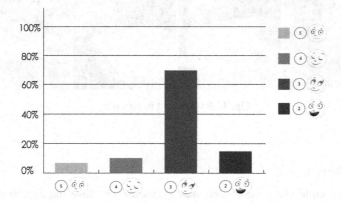

After the children read the experimental material, they were asked to circle the face presenting their emotion triggered by the interaction form. The emotions induced by the interaction form include both positive emotions (such as happy and cheerful) and negative emotions (such as angry and sad), as shown in Table 2, the gray color in the figure represents positive emotions, and the gray color depth represents the level of arousal. The darker the color is, the higher the arousal is. The yellow in the figure represents negative emotions.

It can be seen from the figure above that the emotions are mainly positive ones, and the code names of "faces" are 4, 3, and 2. Only the "Regular page-flipping" interaction form

Table 2. Emotion proportion distribution induced by interaction forms

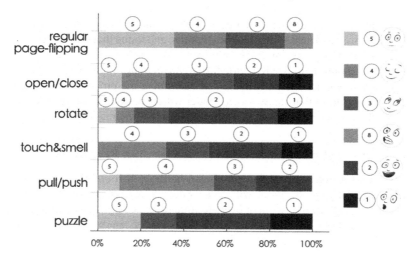

induces a negative emotion code-named 8. Focus attention on the positive emotions and refine Table 2 by deleting the neutral emotions coded 1 and 5, and the negative emotions coded 8, we still use the percentage charts to show children's positive emotions, as shown in Table 3. The interaction form with the highest positive emotion arousal is "pull/push" (92%), followed by "touch & smell" (88%), and the positive emotion induced by "regular page-flipping" is the lowest (55%).

Table 3. Proportion distribution of positive emotions induced by interactive forms

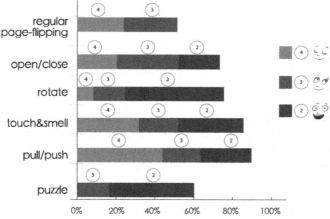

Compared with children's expected emotions, the "rotate interaction" form matches expected emotions best (80%), followed by "puzzle" interactions (60%).

We also analyzed the gender differences in emotional influence of book interaction forms through chi-square test of the statistical results, and found that the effect of different interaction forms on positive emotions induction was significantly different ($p < 0.01$), indicating that changes in book interaction forms can regulate children reading emotions. Using gender as the independent variable and examining the proportion of the number of people, it was found that there was a gender difference between "open/close" and "puzzle". Girls were more affected by these two forms of interaction than boys.

3.2   The Influence of Picture Books Interaction Form on Reading Time

Descriptive statistics on reading time, as shown in Table 4, found that children stayed the least on "regular page flipping", with an average reading time of 21.05 s; the longest reading time on the "puzzle" with an average time of 66.35 s, followed by the "rotate" interaction form, about 58.1 s, and the third is "touch & smell" interaction, with an average of about 40.35 s.

Table 4. Children's reading time distribution in different interaction forms of picture book

Interaction form	N	M	SD	SE	95% confidence interval of the mean		Minist value	Max value
					Lower limit	Up limit		
Regular page-flipping	40	21.0500	12.89012	2.88232	15.0172	27.0828	6.00	49.00
Open/close	40	27.2500	12.85087	2.87354	21.2356	33.2644	4.00	51.00
Rotating	40	58.1000	31.20880	6.97850	43.4938	72.7062	10.00	148.00
Touch & smell	40	40.3500	19.40503	4.33910	31.2682	49.4318	20.00	99.00
Pull/push	40	35.6000	11.11377	2.48511	30.3986	40.8014	11.00	59.00
Puzzle	40	66.3500	30.70621	6.86612	51.9791	80.7209	27.00	142.00

Do a two-way analysis of variance for reading time and find that the interaction form has a significant effect on reading time.($F = 1.14, p = 0.287$)The effect of gender on reading time is not significant. Comparing the reading time of the 6 interaction forms by pair-wise comparison, it was found that the difference between "regular page-flipping" interaction and "open/close" interaction was not significant ($p = 0.362$). Children's reading time in "regular page-flipping" was significantly lower than that of "rotate", "touch & smell", "pull/push" and "puzzle" interaction ($p < 0.01$), the difference is significant. Children's reading time in "open/close" interaction is significantly lower than that of "rotate" and "puzzle" ($p < 0.01$), the difference is significant. Children's reading time in "rotate" is significantly longer than that of "touch & smell" and "pull/push"

($p < 0.01$), and there is no significant difference from puzzle ($p = 0.225$). Time spent in "touch & smell" is not much different from "pull/push" interaction ($p = 0.484$), but significantly lower than "puzzle" interaction ($p < 0.01$). Children's reading time in "pull/push" interaction is significantly lower than puzzle interaction ($p < 0.01$).

3.3 The Influence of the Interaction Form of Picture Books on Subjective Scoring

After the reading task was completed, the children scored the six interaction forms using star stickers, and make descriptive statistics on the scores, as shown in Table 5. The interaction form with the highest score is "touch & smell" interaction ($M = 4.55, SD = 0.82$), followed by "puzzle" ($M = 3.85, SD = 1.30$), "pull/push" ($M = 3.88, SD = 1.36$), "rotate" ($M = 3.35, SD = 1.13$) and "open/close" ($M = 3.15, SD = 1.34$). "Regular page-flipping" interaction has the lowest score ($M = 1.70, SD = 1.21$).

Table 5. Children's ratings of different interaction forms

Interaction forms	N	M	SD	SE	95% confidence interval of the mean		Minist value	Max value
					Lower limit	Up limit		
Regular page-flipping	40	1.7000	1.21828	.27242	1.1298	2.2702	.00	4.00
Open/close	40	3.1500	1.34849	.30153	2.5189	3.7811	1.00	5.00
Rotating	40	3.3500	1.13671	.25418	2.8180	3.8820	1.00	5.00
Touch & smell	40	4.5500	0.82558	.18460	4.1636	4.9364	2.00	5.00
Pull/push	40	3.8000	1.36111	.30435	3.1630	4.4370	1.00	5.00
Puzzle	40	3.8500	1.30888	.29267	3.2374	4.4626	1.00	5.00

A statistical analysis of the scores found that the interaction forms of picture books have a significant impact on children's subjective evaluation ($F = 12.59, p < 0.01$). Gender has no significant impact on evaluation ($F = 0.363, p = 0.548$). Comparing the subjective scores of the six interaction forms, it is found that the "regular page-flipping" interaction is significantly lower than the other five interaction forms, and it is the least popular interaction form for children. The subjective evaluation of "open/close" inter-action is significantly lower than that of "touch & smell" interaction ($p < 0.01$), but the difference with "rotate", "pull/push", and "puzzle" is not significant. The subjective evaluation of "touch & smell" interaction is significantly higher than that of "regular page-flipping", "open/close" and "rotate" interaction ($p < 0.01$), but there is no significant difference between "pull/push" ($p = 0.053$) and "puzzle" ($p = 0.071$), that is, "touch & smell", "pull/push" and "puzzle" are all children's favorite interaction forms of picture book.

3.4 Picture Book Interaction Form Preference Ranking

Preference sorting statistics of picture book interaction forms are shown in Table 6. Children's favorite picture book interaction form is "touch & smell", accounting for 65% of the total number of participants, followed by "pull/push" and "puzzle". Gender difference analysis of sorting found that girls had significantly more choices for "open/close" ($\chi2 = 5.217$, $p = 0.032$) and "puzzle" ($\chi2 = 3.891$, $p = 0.050$) than boys, indicating gender has a certain degree of influence on interaction form preference.

Table 6. Children's interaction forms preference ranking

Interaction forms	1st	2nd	3rd	4th	5th	6th	Total
Regular page-flipping	0	0	2	4	2	32	40
Open/close	0	6	7	14	11	2	40
Rotating	0	2	6	12	16	4	40
Touch & smell	28	6	4	2	0	0	40
Pull/push	8	11	10	4	6	1	40
Puzzle	4	15	11	4	5	1	40

4   Discussion

4.1 The Influence of Picture Book Interaction on Children's Emotions

Through careful observation during the experiment, we noticed that young children often said to themselves when they showed significant positive emotions in reading: "It's funny", "Smell good", "I like this taste", "Amazing". In this moment, the child's face was full of smiles, focused, and often showed surprise. During the experiment, when the child made the choice of emotional face picture, we interviewed the child on the selection result and asked why they chose the face. For positive emotions, the main reasons are: 1) I like the good smell which make me imagine some delicious food; 2) I find fun from it; 3) I have not seen it before, feel magical. For the negative emotions, the main reasons are: 1) Turn or pull without moving and get stuck; 2) Get bored; 3) Don't know how to operate.

Combined with the analysis of experimental data, it can be concluded that the main reasons for children to obtain positive emotions in reading are: 1. Experience of controlling, that is, they can interact with the picture book according to their own intentions and feel a sense of control. It further stimulates children's sense of participation and creativity, thereby enhancing their positive emotions. 2. They make sure that they have the ability to read. The funny interaction forms dispels the tension in reading. After being attracted by the interesting interaction forms, children are deeply immersed in the interactive movement and perception. 3. The interaction forms provide good feedback and goals, and children can concentrate on reading. Combined with the analysis of experimental data, it can be concluded that the main reasons why children obtained negative emotions in reading are: 1. The weak interaction form is easy to make children feel bored, can not effectively mobilize children's interest, and can not maintain children's attention. 2. The expected feedback does not appear or deviates. For example, if the paper parts stuck many times, failure to move the part will produce frustration, which will affect the evaluation of this interaction form. Take "rotate" for example, although the positive evaluation is very high, but because the paper tray is stuck many times, some children who planned to give the extremely positive evaluation lowered the value.

Combining experimental data, interviews and observations, we found that interesting interaction forms make it easy for preschool children to feel positive emotions. The positive emotions induced by the interaction forms are founded on the basis of cognitive processes such as visual cognition, creative thinking and operation execution, by the satisfaction of subjective intentions and the sense of surprise obtained form perfectly combined content and forms.

4.2 The Influence of Picture Book Interaction Forms on Children's Reading Interests and Preferences

At different ages, children's interest in reading is also different [12]. Attracting preschoolers' spontaneous reading is the key to fostering their interest in reading. In this experiment, children's reading interest is judged by reading time, that is, the longer time, the greater interest. By controlling the change of picture book interaction form, it explores its impact on preschool children's reading time, evaluation and preference. The results found that the interaction form of picture books can greatly affect the preschoolers' reading time. Preschoolers spend the most reading time on "puzzle" interaction, followed by "rotate", "touch & smell", "pull/push" and "regular page-flipping". The attractiveness of different interaction forms can be deduced as: "puzzle" > "rotate" > "touch & smell" > "pull/push" > "open/close" > "regular page-flipping". So the influence of interaction forms of picture book on children's interest in reading is very significant.

In addition, the results of preschoolers' scoring of interaction forms indicate that "touch & smell" is the most popular interaction, followed by "puzzle" interaction and "pull/push" interaction. Statistical analysis results show that there is no significant difference between these three interaction forms, that is, the popularity is at the same level. Inquiry about the reasons why children like the three most popular forms, the main reasons are: 1. The "touch & smell" interaction are rare in ordinary books, and children have novelty about them; 2. The "puzzle" interaction is related to the presentation of the book content. There are many possibilities to construct story by different puzzle ways. It has a strong sense of game and constructiveness; 3. The "pull/push" interaction is easy to operate and has direct feedback, dynamic process. The content and form are well coordinated. Correlation analysis found that subjective scores were significantly positively correlated with reading time ($r = 0.74$, $p = 0.012$), that is, the longer the reading time, the higher the subjective scores of the interaction form. Children's ranking of interaction forms is consistent with the subjective scoring results, that is, "touch & smell", "puzzle" and "pull/push" are the most popular interaction forms.

4.3 The Influence of Gender on Reading Interest and Preference

Gender differences are reflected in all aspects of life, and some studies have shown that gender differences are reflected in differences in choices of items such as color, content, and form [7]. This study found that the gender difference in the interest of interaction forms in reading is not significant, that is, the time spent by boys and girls in the same interaction form is similar; but girls prefer "open/close" and "puzzle" to boys. While in other forms of interaction, boys and girls do not show significant differences, that is, the scoring and ranking of interaction forms are roughly similar. In general, preschoolers' interest in interaction forms of picture book is not affected by gender.

5 Conclusion

5.1 Do Suitable Interaction Design of Picture Books to Stimulate Children's Positive Emotions in Reading

Ma Yanqing found that the emotions of young children play an important role in the activities of young children [9]. First of all, children's emotions have a creative function. Happy emotions will stimulate children's creative performance, and create new methods during the activities. Creative activities are based on the interaction objects that children like in the activities. Through creative interactive activities, children get a sense of satisfaction that further increase the happy emotions. Second, emotions have a catalytic function. Positive emotions and negative emotions play a different role in catalyzing children's actions. Positive emotions such as happiness and interest help preschool children to be more active in activities, while negative emotions will encourage them to avoid participating. Third, children's emotions have orientation function. Emotions can directly guide individuals to choose the direction of behavior, and can determine the length of time to maintain the direction.

Reading, as an advanced cognitive activity, including not only language processing, but also visual processing and physical activities. The interaction form of children's picture books can provide stimuli that cause positive emotions in activities such as vision, language, and movement.

5.2 Picture Book Design Needs to Pay Attention to the Interactive Form Based on Sensory Experience

From the test results, we can see that "touch & smell" is the most popular interaction form in children's subjective scoring and ranking. Children prefer to have good smell and taste that make them image something delicious. Sensual perception is still the main way to experience the external world for preschoolers. Therefore, the experience of "five senses" (vision, hear, smell, touch, and taste) is very important interaction. Piaget's explanation of children's initiative pointed out that there are two aspects of the initiative process: one is that the child directly acts on his environment; the other is that the child is psychologically active, and intellectual activities can be determined by their emotion [13]. A person never wants to learn something that he is not interested in. The abundant sensory experience can improve children's positive emotions in reading, make the content loved by children, enhance children's reading interest, and mobilize the reading initiative, maintain the concentration in reading.

5.3   The Interaction Form Should Match the Children's Cognitive Characteristic

This empirical study shows that "rotate" and "push/pull", which are action-based interaction forms, are easy to arouse children's interest in reading and improve their understanding of picture content. Picture book = text × picture, the content of picture book reading includes: picture and text. Because a picture book communicates a message through a series of pictures combined with a small amount of text or no text, the way the pictures and text in the picture book convey the message is different from them in other forms [14]. First of all, the picture is telling a story, which is an illustration. In terms of area, the picture occupies most of the space in the picture book; in terms of the amount of information conveyed, the picture conveys most of the message. Illustration is a very special visual art in picture books because it helps narrative and reasoning. The reader's focus is on the meaning level of visual intention. The texts in picture books also have particularities. In terms of quantity, they are short and rely on pictures to provide specific meanings. They are more like a summary of the plot than a story. Picture and text in picture books are two different modes of expression, and they are mutually limited and mutually reinforcing.

Adults think that "pictures" can be understood without learning, but they are not. As Neil Postman said, typography builds a world of written symbols, and people need to learn to read to enter and understand this world [15]. Written symbols not only include text, but also include various chart forms such as charts, maps, and legends. Therefore, the reading of picture books is actually the process of decoding the two types of visual symbols of pictures and texts, and then understanding the meaning through mutual confirmation of pictures and texts. Children need to learn the way to interpret images and understand the semantic conventions of pictures. Children unconsciously grasp the basis of interpreting images, but still need the guidance of adults. The semantic meaning of the picture includes: 1. the size and proportion of the objects in the picture; 2. the expression of color, texture, level and detail; 3. the arrangement order of the pictures; 4. the meaning of the borders and restrictive lines; 5. the objects and the surroundings, the isolation of the environment (such as being surrounded by a blank or single color background) [16]. Since the image in the picture book is distorted to the real physical world, children must learn to understand this illustration. The cognitive condition for the understanding of the picture is the social and cultural language, which constitutes the preschooler's priori illustration. Children's understanding of the graph depends on their own context. Nowadays, there are a large number of graphic symbols in the digital interface. These symbols are not only a simulation of the real physical world, but also a conventional social and cultural language. Children accumulate graphic symbol understanding skill in paper reading and the skill is also very helpful for them to migrate to other diverse or media.

Therefore, while designing picture books, the interaction form must be considered to help young children understand the meaning of the picture, and the interaction form must have a good match with the children's priori illustrations. Donald Norman pointed out an important design principle: providing a good "represented model", which can make people predict the effect of operating behavior. "Represented model" should be unlimited close to the user's "mental models" [17]. Mental models refer to models formed by people through experience, training, and learning from the environment and the things they are exposed to. Alan Cooper etc. made a chart to explain the relationship among the "implementation model", "Represented model" and "mental model" of software products. This chart is also suitable for explaining the relationship among the 3 models in picture book (see Fig. 5) [18]. Engineers are constrained by technical and business rules, the model how software works is called the "implementation model"; the way users think they can complete the activity is called the "mental model". The mental model is based on the user's own understanding of the operating principles of software; the approach that designer presents the software operating mechanism to users is called "represented model". Norman's concept of "mental model" is the same as Neil Bozeman's concept of priori illustration, one is from the perspective of design and the other is from the perspective of communication, and the two concept melt in the children's picture book design.

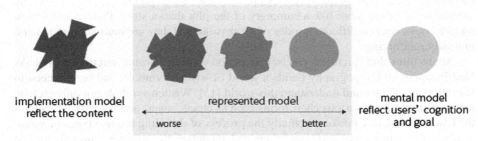

implementation model
reflect the content
← worse   represented model   better →
mental model
reflect users' cognition
and goal

Fig. 5. The relation of implementation model, represented model and mental model

Many interaction forms of picture books match the mental models of preschoolers. Take the book "My Body" for example, the interaction form of "rotate" combined with "hole" is used to describe the generation mechanism of human emotions. The image is the upper body of a little girl. There are holes opened in the head and face of the little girl, two rotating pages are linked and revealed through the holes. Children can find and toggle the gear-shaped rotating part from the semi-circular cutout above the head. With the rotation, the image in the hole changes. When the image indicating something good appears in the opening hole of the head, a smiling emoji picture appears in the hole of the mouth. Conversely, when something negative appears in the opening hole of the head, expressions of sadness and anger appear at the hole of the mouth (see Fig. 6).

The principle of emotion generation is very complex to understand for preschool children. Designers here well described the abstract and complex content in a model that conforms to the children's priori illustration. The model reveals that the "rotate" inter-action form corresponds to the priori pattern of sequence changes that preschoolers can understand, and the interaction form of opening hole corresponds to the disappearing and appearing that is also a priori diagram of the preschoolers' understanding. These forms of action-based interaction have a good performance in providing a good conceptual model, and the content-form-behavior is highly unified.

Many interaction forms of picture books have passed through hundreds of years and inspire for current designers. With the development of society and technology, the environment in which children live is constantly changing. The new social cultural

Fig. 6. Rotate interaction in the picture book "My Body"

language is the new priori schema that gives new requirements and new inspiration for the interaction design of picture book. For example, with the emergence of digital products, children have become a generation of digital natives. Their habit of using digital products forms part of their mental models. Therefore, paper picture books can appropriately learn from digital products (including digital picture books, digital games, etc.). Take "PRESS HERE" by Herve Tullet for example, this picture book just like iPad, applies the "interaction" (behavior-feedback) concept both in content and form. The instruction text is written in the center bottom of each page. Clear and short instructions guide children to do corresponding actions. There are two main types of movements: one is the interaction of clicking on the page, tapping the page, shaking the book, closing/opening the book, etc., and the other is free movements such as clapping and blowing. After completing the instruction, children can turn the page. The picture on the next page is the feedback of the instruction on the previous page. The illiterate children can interact with the book together with their parents, parents read the text instructions, and the children do the actions (see Fig. 7). Inspired by the paper picture book "PRESS HERE", the App "PRESS HERE" based on iPad released including 15 delightfully simple games and activities (see Fig. 8). From the case of "PRESS HERE", it's easy to find out that, the interactive design of digital media and paper media inspires each other. Although the interaction forms will be affected by the specific platform, the interaction mechanism and the ultimate goal are the same.

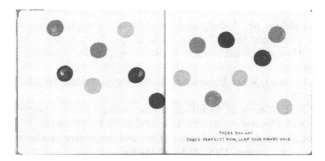

Fig. 7. Picture book "PRESS HERE" by Herve Tullet

Fig. 8. App "PRESS HERE" by Chronicle Books

To learn from operation is the learning way for preschool children [13]. In the reading process, children's cognition of picture book should be generated through the interaction with the picture book autonomously. They need to pick up, release, flip, and fiddle with the reading materials themselves, strengthening the content understanding. In the early reading education, the children's pre-reading experience, pre-literacy experience and pre-writing experience are all obtained from learning in operation. The design of picture books for children needs to better mobilize children's enthusiasm for reading, so that children can read spontaneously, have interest in reading, and have the independent reading ability. As Piaget said, children are not only taught by adults, but can learn independently. The transition from parent-child reading to independent reading is considered to be a difficult process. Although reading methods and skills can be taught by parents and teachers sometime but should be more from the efforts of preschool children themselves. Find and discover reading methods and have fun that can develop the habit of reading lifelong.

References

1. Avella, N.: Ron van der Meer: Paper Engineer. http://www.graphics.com. Accessed 25 Nov 2008
2. Colombo, L., Landoni, M.: A diary study of children's user experience with ebooks-using flow theory as framework. In: IDC' 2014, 14 June, pp. 17–20. Springer, Aarhus (2014)
3. Lazarus, R.S.: Thoughts on the relations between emotion and cognition. Am. Psychol. **37**, 1019–1024 (1982)
4. Papara, D.E., Feldman, R.D.: Experience Human Development, 1st edn. Post & Telecom Press, Beijing (2015)
5. Guanhua, H., Yin,L., Guangrui, F.: Effects of time pressure and navigation on older readers' information search affective experience. Libr. Dev. (06), 81–87 (2018)
6. Hassenzahl, M., Diefenbach, S.: Needs, affect, and interactive products - facets of user experience. Interact. Comput. **22**(5), 353–362 (2010)
7. Jadva, V., Hines, M., Golombok, S.: Infants' Preferences for toys, colors, and shapes: sex differences and similarities. Arch. Sex. Behav. **39**(6), 1261–1273 (2010)
8. Lytton, H., Romney, D.M.: Parents' differential socialization of boys and girls: a meta-analysis. Psychol. Bull. **109**(2), 267–296 (1991)

9. Ma, Y.: Children's emotional function and emotional education. Child. Educ. (03), 9–10 (1996)
10. Fang, P., Qiao, Y., Jiang, Y.: A Prob into measurement of adolescent mood. Theory Pract. Educ. **30**(3), 36–38 (2010)
11. Russell, J.A.: A circumplex model of affect. J. Person. Soc. Psychol. **39**, 1161–1178 (1980)
12. Sun, Y., Xu, J., Yu, J., Wang, S.: Research on the influence of libraries on the development of reading consciousness and reading interest of preschool children. Libr. Res. Work (2), 66–69 (2011)
13. Jean, P.: Developmental psychology. In: Sills, D.L. (ed.) International Encyclopedia of the Social Science, vol. 4, pp. 140–147. The Macmilan & The Free Press, New York (1968)
14. Matsui, T.: My Picture Book Theory, 1st edn. Xinjiang Children's Publishing House, Urumqi (2017)
15. Neil, P.: The Disappearance of Childhood, 1st edn. China CITIC Press, Beijing (2015)
16. Perry, N.: Words about Pictures: The narrative Art of Children's Picture Books, 1st edn. Children's Art Foundation Press, Taipei (2010)
17. Norman, D.: The Design of Everyday Things. Revised and Expanded edn. Basic Books, New York (2013)
18. Alan, C., et al.: About Face 4: The Essentials of Interaction Design, 4th edn. Publishing House of Electronics Industry, Beijing (2016)

Adaptive Instructional Systems

Enable 3A in AIS

Faruk Ahmed[1], Keith Shubeck[1], Frank Andrasik[1], and Xiangen Hu[1,2(✉)]

[1] The University of Memphis, Memphis, USA
xiangenhu@gmail.com
[2] Central China Normal University, Wuhan, China

Abstract. Advances in computer technology have made it possible to intrepidly identify and classify human emotions. While this technology has matured, only a few applications have appeared using this technology in advanced learning environments. Imagine, if you will, the existence of an application of Adaptive Instructional System (AIS), such as an Intelligent Tutoring System (ITS), that would be able to understand when a learner is sad, disengaged, or any other emotional state desired to track. There is a huge potential of this for improving an AIS system's feedback or interventions. Our team has developed the advanced technology for a quick-acting emotion-tracking system that is easy to use for an internet-based ITS. An ITS is able to incorporate this revolutionary feature by being aware of content, context, and the user's emotion state. In fact most of the mobile apps are currently tracking these three awareness by utilizing available sensors as audio, video, and inertial measurement unit (IMU) sensors. Learning applications would be more efficient if they are integrated with these three awareness (3A) [3].

Keywords: Adaptive instructional system · Intelligent tutoring system · Content context and user awareness · Learning environment

1 Introduction

Off-the-shelf technologies [4,5,11] already exist to recognize generic emotions from face images. These generic emotions of a user would be an excellent source of valuable information for learning scientists if an efficient translation technique existed (e.g., to smooth out the multidimensional emotion vector and transform it into learning related emotions). Rather than focus on the technology of emotion recognition, in this paper we believe it is more fruitful to focus on methodological issues that demand consideration when deciding how to maximize the utility of the available technologies that directly make AIS applications more efficient and effective. We believe 3A enabled AIS applications, such as ITS, would greatly advance research, development, and evaluations in the learning sciences. ITS is one of the typical Adaptive Instructional Systems (AIS) application.

Enabling Adaptive Instructional System Applications (AISA), including ITSs, with 3A capability necessarily assumes these applications are more similar to human tutors than those that are without the 3A. The existing framework [14,16,17] assumes that we consider dynamic learning resources, like ITSs,

© Springer Nature Switzerland AG 2020
C. Stephanidis et al. (Eds.): HCII 2020, LNCS 12425, pp. 507–518, 2020.
https://doi.org/10.1007/978-3-030-60128-7_38

to have a "psychology" similar to that of humans. We believe that the 3A capability of AISA is essential for making such applications resemble human tutors. In this paper, we address a few research questions involved in making AISA 3A enabled. Questions such as, how to obtain and aggregate the history of a user's emotions; or how to collect content and context correlated with those emotions, are exceedingly important to address. It is important to note that because ITSs provide individualized content, the awareness aspect must also be individualized. Individualized 3As are possible through distributed applications which are best applied using modern browser based technologies. This research is about exploring possible solutions of the above mentioned research questions more specifically:

1. How to smooth out the generic emotional learning history
2. How to aggregate the content, context, and learner emotions
3. How to determine if a function exists to map generic emotions to learning related emotions

Our pilot implementation uses AWS Rekognition. AWS Rekognition provides an eight dimensional vector and a confidence score of user emotion from facial expression. At a certain interval we can obtain those vectors and store them into a learning record store (LRS) using xAPI. The intelligent tutor is able to keep track of the content delivered as well as detect context from the sequence of delivered content. The main task is to apply some mathematical techniques to aggregate this information and find a transformation function.

One way to smooth the emotion history is to dynamically adjust means and standard deviations along with confidence scores in LRS. The content and context information should be encoded for proper aggregation. In addition, it is important to retrieve information rapidly for an ITS to make use of it effectively (e.g., provide feedback to the learner in realtime).

While the potential for, and effectiveness of, emotionally sensitive feedback in ITSs has been explored in previous research, AISAs that can aggregate emotion, context, and content data beyond the span of single learning session has been less explored, with many questions remaining unanswered. Exciting existing technologies are out there. Thus our goal has been to find a 3A enabled engineering solution for ITSs which is portable, cheap, and scalable [3].

Our paper for this conference focuses primarily on technological aspects of the 3A enabled AIS; however, other questions will be explored to help make readers fully aware of the scope of issues in need of consideration:

- **Theoretical & Methodological:** How would a 3A enabled AIS impact learners psychologically? Given that a 3A enabled AIS will model human tutors more realistically, how much will this add to the learning experience? What are the potential benefits, as well as the potential negative impacts?
- **Technological:** Although we have tried and achieved the ability to fast store and retrieve historical emotion history from a LRS, we have found it necessary to make our own xAPI statements for the desired behaviors. How can we standardize our statements so that all 3A enabled ITS can contribute to an

individual emotional history that is context-sensitive, domain-specific, and individualized?

– **Implementational:** Our pilot system is conversational [20], can this be implemented in other AIS that are not conversational?

The technology made 3A possible. Our effort makes 3A in AIS easy. We expect to make our work open-source so all AIS may benefit from our work.

2 Related Literature

Adaptive Instruction refers to the educational activities that accommodate to individual students and their unique behaviors so that each student can develop the necessary knowledge and skills [6,22]. Currently, many remarkable ITSs are available for teaching STEM subjects as well as computer technologies [12,23]. ITSs are moving towards adaptive instructions to accommodate exceptional learners [13]. Additionally, there are ongoing efforts and research toward defining AIS standards [29]. 3A has huge potential in AISA [3].

3 Smoothing Function for Confidence of Emotion

AWS Recognition API provides a mechanism to analyze face image details, including emotion. It provides eight emotions with percent confidence scores obtained from a face image. Those emotions are *CALM, HAPPY, FEAR, SURPRISED, DISGUSTED, CONFUSED, SAD, ANGRY*. The confidence scores for these emotions are not independent. For example with a higher confidence of *HAPPY* the confidence value of *SAD* is lower. This is logical because, visually, a person is rarely *HAPPY* and *SAD* at the same time. There are exceptional cases of mixed-emotion states where a person may look *SAD* though he or she is *HAPPY*. This exception is identifiable by a human, given a cultural context, but not by machine. The AWS Recognition documentation says that the API makes "a determination of the physical appearance of a person's face" not their "internal emotional state" [4].

We need to retain the emotion vector which emerges during a learner's interaction with AIS and that requires prepossessing. Each emotion vector is available at a certain interval (e.g., 3 s). We cannot simply consider only the highest confidence score of the emotion vector. In that case we lose essential emotion information that contributes to individualization. Specifically, it is important to establish an individualized baseline. For example, a person's face may look always happy and an individualized emotion profile can be constructed by looking at other emotion scores as well. In fact, in some cases the machine will incorrectly assign the highest score of an emotion which is not evident. To solve this problem we maintain the sample mean and sample variance. The sample mean and sample variance are mathematically given by Eq. 1 and 2 respectively.

$$\bar{x} = \frac{\sum_{i=1}^{n} x_i}{n} \qquad (1)$$

$$\sigma^2 = \frac{1}{n(n-1)} \left(n \sum_{i=1}^{n} x_i{}^2 - \left(\sum_{i=1}^{n} x_i \right)^2 \right) \tag{2}$$

The easiest way to compute sample variance is by accumulating the sum of the x's and the sums of the squares of the x's. However, direct evaluation of this formula suffers from loss of precision. The best algorithm proposed thus far is by [31], which is mentioned in [15]. Now, as we take the confidence values at a certain interval the data must be smoothed. Initially, we accomplished this smoothing by taking the average of three data points. However, with this method the data points (i.e., the signal) are piece wise differentiable but not fully differentiable. One solution is to apply a moving average several times in order to improve the behavior of the function. However, calculation in a single step is preferred here. For that reason the *triangular weighted moving average* in Eq. 3 or a perfectly smoothed one, the *Gaussian filter* given in this Eq. 4, is most used. In those equations t is the time, x is data point, and σ is standard deviation.

$$W f(x) = \int_{x-\frac{s}{2}}^{x+\frac{s}{2}} f(t)dt \tag{3}$$

$$G f(x) = \int_{-\infty}^{\infty} g(x-t)f(t)dt \tag{4}$$

where g is Gaussian probability density function,

$$g(x) = \frac{1}{\sqrt{2\pi\sigma^2}} e^{-\frac{x^2}{2\sigma^2}} \tag{5}$$

The effect of smoothing is shown in Fig. 1.

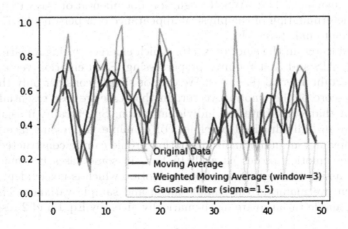

Fig. 1. Smoothing effect of the data.

It is critical to know if we can treat all of the emotions in a similar manner. In other words, can we use the same smoothing function for the confidence values for all of the emotions? According to Paul Eckman, there are six basic emotions; namely happiness, sadness, disgust, fear, surprise, and anger [8]. As of 2017, a study found 27 different categories of emotions that are far more complex than the basic emotions previously found [7]. People undergo these emotions along a gradient instead of a clearly separated instance according to that study. In our study, in a few occasions *HAPPY* and *SAD* were observed at the same time although it seems impossible. According to Robert Plutchik's "wheel of emotions" the basic emotions can be combined to form a complex emotion. The properties and complexities lead us to analyze the correlations among the eight emotions. If any correlation is found, then we have to find either an orthogonal function or functions to treat emotions individually. A correlation matrix along with statistical significance (indicated by '*') is presented in Table 1.

From the Table 1 it is seen that some of the emotions are positively correlated and others are negatively correlated. For example *HAPPY, FEAR, SUR-PRISED* are negatively correlated to *CALM*. On the other hand *CONFUSED* is positively correlated to *FEAR, SURPRISED, DISGUSTED*. Moreover most of these emotions are statistically significant (e.g., p-values are less than 0.05).

Table 1. Correlations of the emotions. The '*' indicates statistical significance.

	CALM	HAPPY	FEAR	SURPRISED	DISGUSTED	CONFUSED	SAD	ANGRY
CALM	1							
HAPPY	−0.5201 *	1						
FEAR	−0.4263 *	0.0936	1					
SURPRISED	−0.3385 *	0.2998 *	0.7437 *	1				
DISGUSTED	0.02033	0.0180	0.5908 *	0.4404 *	1			
CONFUSED	−0.1582 *	−0.050	0.6843 *	0.6050 *	0.6159 *	1		
SAD	0.17241 *	−0.338 *	0.5200 *	0.1082	0.6117 *	0.5319 *	1	
ANGRY	0.02680	−0.121 *	0.6606 *	0.4592 *	0.8724 *	0.6770 *	0.7051 *	1

4   xAPI Learning Record Store for Emotion History

At this stage we have a smoothed function (e.g., $Gf(x)$) which provides data points along a time axis. The sample mean and variance give a history of the emotions of a user while interacting with AISs. Whenever the z-value at any particular instance exceeds a threshold (e.g., 95%), then it is considered that the emotion is present. For example at a given instance a user may have calm, sad, surprised z-scores above the threshold which means the emotions are calm, sad, and surprised. A sample instance of data from LRS is shown in Fig. 2. Two instances of emotions presented in Table 2 where by looking at z-score the strongly emerged emotion can be inferred (e.g., *DISGUSTED* and *ANGRY* at $n = 62$; *ANGRY* at $n = 63$).

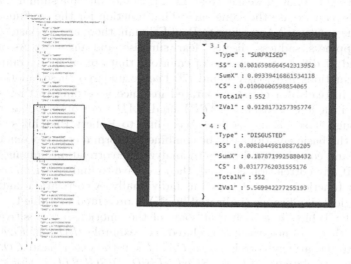

Fig. 2. LRS view.

Table 2. According to z-score emerged emotions are *DISGUSTED* and *ANGRY* at $n = 62$; *ANGRY* at $n = 63$

n	Type	x	$\sum x$	$\sum x^2$	$z = \frac{x-\mu}{\sigma}$
62	CALM	0.00144307	0.00451874	0.00000957	−0.79652805
	HAPPY	0.00035727	0.00264636	0.00000472	−0.78750548
	FEAR	0.00188819	0.00492780	0.00000924	−0.26242112
	SURPRISED	0.00065252	0.00298696	0.00000498	−0.55248859
	DISGUSTED	0.06789378	0.08032871	0.00468600	**4.45491267**
	CONFUSED	0.00291084	0.11799348	0.01235629	−0.46806056
	SAD	0.00135230	0.00452521	0.00001009	−0.25422823
	ANGRY	0.92350181	3.78207252	3.58718056	**3.62744821**
63	CALM	0.02550071	0.03001945	0.00065986	−0.71749478
	HAPPY	0.00209260	0.00473896	0.00000910	−0.77340626
	FEAR	0.00816925	0.01309705	0.00007598	−0.21352055
	SURPRISED	0.00285460	0.00584157	0.00001313	−0.54044017
	DISGUSTED	0.01306463	0.09339335	0.00485669	0.483761238
	CONFUSED	0.01062706	0.12862054	0.01246923	−0.40952343
	SAD	0.02688346	0.03140868	0.00073281	−0.02714514
	ANGRY	0.91080780	4.69288032	4.41675141	**3.23278384**

xAPI [1] is the fastest and most secure platform for storing, retrieving, and distributing the learning data. In this work, the advanced feature of html5 (e.g., media capability) [2] is adopted through JavaScript. This enabled the technology to be distributed for individualization, and computed quickly and efficiently. It can also be simply plugged to any AISA (e.g., AutoTutor, GIFT) [28,30] with JavaScript or html5 media capability. A simplified working principle is shown in Fig. 3. When a user logs into the system and starts emotion recognition, the system pulls previous values among the saved quantities. Six quantities are saved for each emotion in the xAPI data store, namely *type, sum of squares, sum of the confidence score, cumulative sum, total number if instances, and the z-score.* Interestingly, at a certain interval, these six quantities provide a baseline for an individualized emotion profile, given that the data are normally distributed. We performed the normality test and all the emotion scores were found, in fact, to be normally distributed. Most importantly, with this approach the learner's privacy is not violated because no facial images are saved in data store – only the raw numerical output.

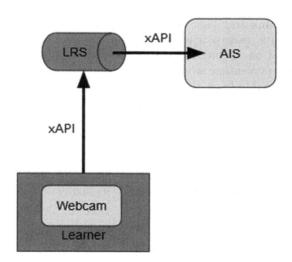

Fig. 3. Communication from learner to AIS through xAPI.eps

The emotional expressions of a human during explaining, recalling, reasoning, or applying, have a certain pattern, which can be easily comprehended by a human. A typical example is when a person says "let me think" along with the expression, we understand that the person is thinking by looking at his or her expression. We can easily understand when someone is pretending to know without actually knowing. With a large enough sample size, the more ambiguous emotional cues can be captured and usefully applied in a system. The subtleties of human emotion states and their associated expressions can eventually make their way into an ITS and be modeled by animated agents.

5   Analysis of Emotions

Some of the emotion states are significantly negatively correlated. Thus, it is important to determine if learners show similar behavior given the same content but within different learning instances. In other words, if a learner who studied "algebra" yesterday and is studying the same "algebra" topic today, should the distribution of emotions be the same? In this case our null hypothesis is H_0 = "learner shows similar emotions" with the alternate hypothesis being H_1 = "learner shows different emotions". To simplify, we assume that there is no external effect (e.g., no covariate) and the confidence values are continuous. In this case we can apply one-way MANOVA [21] by considering different instances as an independent variable and all eight emotions as dependent variables. By looking at Wilks' lambda p-value we may determine if the learner is in a similar emotional mode. We saw the p-value 0.000 and null hypothesis was rejected. There is a drawback of not considering external variables because at this stage we do not have enough data. In addition, we considered the emotion values as continuous which is not in fact true.

Another way of looking at the emotion individually is provided by the Wilcoxon signed-rank test [32]. Key assumptions are that the data are from the same population, each pair is chosen randomly and independently, and the data are measured on an interval scale. The emotions are measured at every three seconds in a percentage score which we can view as a rank. One advantage is that we do not need to know the distribution of the emotions in this case. Running Wilcoxon tests in two instances with 150 data each shows that (Table 3) the learner is similarly confused whereas they showed differences in happiness.

Table 3. Wilcoxon test on the emotions in two different learning instances given same content.

Emotion	p-value	Similarity
CALM	0.000	Different
HAPPY	0.000	Different
FEAR	0.749	Same
SURPRISED	0.010	Different
DISGUSTED	0.511	Same
CONFUSED	0.349	Same
SAD	0.242	Same
ANGRY	0.004	Different

6   Future Direction

We believe that AISA enhanced with 3A would dramatically improve the efficacy of the applications. One of the potential applications for the future is to build

3A enabled AIAS to STEM education. We believe that a 3A enabled STEM AISA will maximize the utility of existing frameworks, such as the TIMSS (Trends in International Mathematics and Science Study) assessment frameworks. TIMSS describe content and cognitive domains to be tested in mathematics and science at the fourth and eighth grades [19]. The cognitive domains are *knowing, applying, and reasoning*. According to TIMSS [19] the cognitive domains skirt "the competencies of problem solving", "providing a mathematical argument", "representing mathematically", "creating models of a problem", and "utilizing tools (e.g., ruler or calculator)". This framework well defined the procedures in each cognitive domain listed in Table 4.

Table 4. Cognitive domains and corresponding procedures [18]

	Knowing	Applying	Reasoning
Procedures	Recall	Determine	Analyze
	Recognize	Represent/Model	Integrate/Synthesize
	Classify/Order	Implement	Evaluate
	Compute		Draw Conclusions
	Retrieve		Generalize
	Measure		Justify

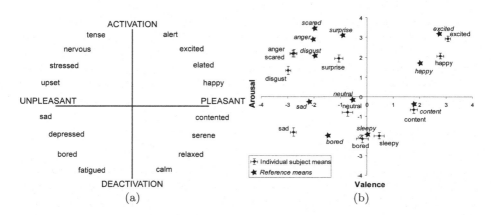

Fig. 4. (a) semantic map of emotions in valence (x-axis) and arousal (y-axis) [9] (b) high correlation of mean individual and reference circumplex ratings in 2D map [26]

In the previous section we looked at the emotion data, where we were able to show that it is possible to aggregate and predict if a learner is showing an unusual emotion for a given content and context. Our vision is to look beyond this emotion data at more granular level; more specifically, to look at the processes of cognitive domains. Here we make an assumption that a learner cannot hide his or her emotion during the learning process. There are well defined mathematical and science questions in TIMSS that require a learner to practice certain procedures. If we present different content (e.g., questions related to cognitive domains and procedures) repeatedly for the same domain and capture emotions there is a higher possibility of finding mapping between cognitive procedures and emotions. For example, some learners may not like computation and whenever a content is presented that requires computation he or she shows *DISGUSTED*. For other learners it may the case that they like computation and they show a *HAPPY* emotion. It is possible to analyze this interesting cognitive procedural emotion mapping from large amounts of data. Enabling the 3A framework in AIS can be a cheap, distributed, and efficient platform for collecting what is needed.

A number of theories pertain to psychological models of emotions. These theories try to understand and explain emotions in different dimensions of psychological states or processes. Although some controversies and research issues exist with respect to the different models of emotions, our goal is to find a productive utilization of data driven emotional measurement in learning industry. For example, psychologists have explained the semantic structure of affect and emotion in a two dimensional plane [9,25] as well as presented mean individual and reference circumplex ratings of emotions [10,24,26] (Fig. 4). One may view these as a coding or transformation or reduction of an original master emotion model which is quite complex and not adequately understood [27].

By mapping the eight dimensional vector (e.g., obtained from AWS Rekognition API) into the valence, arousal semantic space we can obtain a type of quantitative aggregated measurement. Empirically evaluating these measurements we can try to identify the underlying actual coding of the emotion. This will help to identify if a learner is "really" learning or exactly where a learner is having difficulty. For example if a learner dislikes computation then 3A data analysis will help to pinpoint his or her dislike and improve not only the content, but its design as well.

7   Conclusion

In this paper, we presented an application of emotion recognition technology to enable any AISA with 3A. We focused on solving methodological issues such as building individualized distributions of an emotion profile using. By doing this, We are able to store a minimum emotion vector in each behavior statement (xAPI) and build emotion distributions with only the last record from LRS. We also explored the ways one might "smooth" the distributions by utilizing different types of averaging algorithms. Additionally, we presented a statistical analysis to aggregate the functions as well in order to see the difference in different instances of learning. This inexpensive, easy to integrate, distributed, and individualized 3A framework has enormous potential in developing the next generation AISA. A specially monitoring problem solving process according to TIMSS framework using 3A will open up the horizon of research direction for learning scientists. Our contributions of this paper remain in the methodological domain and therefore the approaches are not limited by the choice of emotion coding of the processing servers (in this case the AWS Rekongition API). A prototype of the AISA was made for this paper and it is available http://tiny.cc/HCII2020Demo.

References

1. DoDI 1322.26 xAPI reference. https://adlnet.gov/policy/dodi-xapi/. Accessed 14 Jun 2020
2. HTMLMediaElement. https://developer.mozilla.org/en-US/docs/Web/API/HTML MediaElement. Accessed 14 Jun 2020
3. Ahmed, F., Shubek, K., Hu, X.: Towards a GIFT enabled 3A learning environment. In: Goldberg, B.S. (ed.) Proceedings of the Eighth Annual GIFT Users Symposium (GIFTSym8), pp. 87–92, May 2020
4. Amazon Web Services: Amazon rekognition developer guide. https://docs.aws.amazon.com/rekognition/latest/dg/rekognition-dg.pdf. Accessed 30 May 2020
5. API, M.A.F.: Facial recognition software—microsoft azure. https://azure.microsoft.com/en-us/services/cognitive-services/face/. Accessed 30 May 2020
6. Atkinson, R.C.: Adaptive instructional systems: Some attempts to optimize the learning process. Stanford University, Institute for Mathematical Studies in the Social Sciences (1974)
7. Cowen, A.S., Keltner, D.: Self-report captures 27 distinct categories of emotion bridged by continuous gradients. Proc. Natl. Acad. Sci. **114**(38), E7900–E7909 (2017)
8. Ekman, P.: Basic emotions. In: Handbook of Cognition and Emotion, vol. 98, no. 45–60, p. 16 (1999)
9. Feldman Barrett, L., Russell, J.A.: Independence and bipolarity in the structure of current affect. J. Pers. Soc. Psychol. **74**(4), 967 (1998)
10. Gerber, A.J., et al.: An affective circumplex model of neural systems subserving valence, arousal, and cognitive overlay during the appraisal of emotional faces. Neuropsychologia **46**(8), 2129–2139 (2008)
11. Google Cloud Vision AI: Vision AI—derive image insights via ML—cloud vision API. https://cloud.google.com/vision. Accessed 30 May 2020
12. Graesser, A.C., et al.: Electronixtutor: an intelligent tutoring system with multiple learning resources for electronics. Int. J. STEM Educ. **5**(1), 15 (2018)
13. Hallahan, D.P., Pullen, P.C., Kauffman, J.M., Badar, J.: Exceptional learners. In: Oxford Research Encyclopedia of Education (2020)
14. Hu, X., Tong, R., Cai, Z., Cockroft, J.L., Kim, J.W.: Self-Improvable Adaptive Instructional Systems (SIAISS)-Aproposed Model. Design Recommendations for Intelligent Tutoring Systems, p. 11 (2019)
15. Knuth, D.E.: The Art of Computer Programming, 3rd edn. Addison Wesley, Boston (1998)
16. Kuo, B.C., Hu, X.: Intelligent learning environments (2019)
17. Long, Z., Andrasik, F., Liu, K., Hu, X.: Self-improvable, self-improving, and self-improvability adaptive instructional system. In: Pinkwart, N., Liu, S. (eds.) Artificial Intelligence Supported Educational Technologies. AALT, pp. 77–91. Springer, Cham (2020). https://doi.org/10.1007/978-3-030-41099-5_5
18. Mullis, I.V., Martin, M.O.: TIMSS 2019 Assessment Frameworks. ERIC (2017)

19. Mullis, I., Martin, M., Goh, S., Cotter, K.: Timss 2015 encyclopedia: Education policy and curriculum in mathematics and science. Boston college, TIMSS & PIRLS international study center website (2016)

20. Nye, B.D., Graesser, A.C., Hu, X.: AutoTutor and family: a review of 17 years of natural language tutoring. Int. J. Artif. Intell. Educ. **24**(4), 427–469 (2014)

21. O'Brien, R.G., Kaiser, M.K.: Manova method for analyzing repeated measures designs: an extensive primer. Psychol. Bull. **97**(2), 316 (1985)

22. Park, O.C., Lee, J.: Adaptive instructional systems (2004)

23. Perez, R.S., Skinner, A., Sottilare, R.A.: -A review of intelligent tutoring systems for science technology engineering and mathematics (stem). Assessment of Intelligent Tutoring Systems Technologies and Opportunities, p. 1 (2018)

24. Posner, J., Russell, J.A., Peterson, B.S.: The circumplex model of affect: an integrative approach to affective neuroscience, cognitive development, and psychopathology. Dev. Psychopathol. **17**(3), 715–734 (2005)

25. Russell, J.A.: A circumplex model of affect. J. Pers. Soc. Psychol. **39**(6), 1161 (1980)

26. Russell, J.A., Bullock, M.: Multidimensional scaling of emotional facial expressions: similarity from preschoolers to adults. J. Pers. Soc. Psychol. **48**(5), 1290 (1985)

27. Scherer, K.R., et al.: Psychological models of emotion. Neuropsychol. Emot. **137**(3), 137–162 (2000)

28. Sottilare, R.A., Graesser, A., Hu, X., Holden, H.: Design recommendations for intelligent tutoring systems: Volume 1-learner modeling (2013)

29. Sottilare, R., Brawner, K.: Component interaction within the generalized intelligent framework for tutoring (gift) as a model for adaptive instructional system standards. In: The Adaptive Instructional System (AIS) Standards Workshop of the 14th International Conference of the Intelligent Tutoring Systems (ITS) Conference, Montreal, Quebec, Canada (2018)

30. Sottilare, R.A., Brawner, K.W., Sinatra, A.M., Johnston, J.H.: An updated concept for a generalized intelligent framework for tutoring (GIFT). GIFTtutoring. org (2017)

31. Welford, B.: Note on a method for calculating corrected sums of squares and products. Technometrics **4**(3), 419–420 (1962)

32. Wilcoxon, F.: Individual comparisons by ranking methods. In: Breakthroughs in Statistics, pp. 196–202. Springer (1992). https://doi.org/10.1007/978-1-4612-4380-9_16

Adapting E-Learning to Dyslexia Type: An Experimental Study to Evaluate Learning Gain and Perceived Usability

Weam Gaoud Alghabban[1,2]([⊠]) [iD] and Robert Hendley[2] [iD]

[1] Department of Computer Science, University College Alwajjh,
University of Tabuk, Tabuk, Saudi Arabia
`walghabban@ut.edu.sa`
[2] School of Computer Science,
University of Birmingham, Birmingham, UK
`{wga814,R.J.Hendley}@cs.bham.ac.uk`

Abstract. Dyslexia is a universal specific learning disability that is characterised by poor spelling, word reading, and fluency. Adaptive e-learning is becoming more common, but there is little work on adaptation focused on the needs and characteristics of dyslexic students. In particular, there is very little work that investigates adaptivity based on a student's dyslexia type. This despite the type of dyslexia being a critical factor in determining the most appropriate teaching and learning. Also, previous research has overlooked rigorously designed and controlled evaluations of the system's effectiveness. Therefore, there is a great deal of progress yet to be achieved for dyslexia, especially for Arabic dyslexics. The contribution of this paper is investigating whether adapting learning material based upon an individual's *dyslexia type* will improve learning performance, and also the perception of the usability of the system. An experiment was conducted with 40 Arabic dyslexic children producing statistically significant results. They indicate that adapting learning material according to dyslexia type yields significantly better learning gain (short- and long-term) and perceived level of usability than without adaptation.

Keywords: Dyslexia type · E-learning · Adaptability · Arabic · Learning gain · Usability

1 Introduction

Specific Learning Disability (SLD) is a general term used in special education that can be defined as a deficiency in one or more of the basic psychological processes [34]. One of the most common learning disabilities, mainly affecting the development of language-related skills and literacy, is dyslexia [44]. Dyslexia

---

This research was supported by University of Tabuk, Tabuk, Saudi Arabia.

C. Stephanidis et al. (Eds.): HCII 2020, LNCS 12425, pp. 519–537, 2020.
https://doi.org/10.1007/978-3-030-60128-7_39

or reading difficulty is characterized by difficulty in reading, spelling and fluency [37]. In today's society, dyslexia is the most common type of childhood learning disability (up to 80% of diagnosed learning disabilities [52]). It occurs in all types of people regardless of their background, abilities and race [40]; however, its prevalence and form varies depending on the language [32].

Dyslexia varies with language – its forms and intensity differ from one language to another [4]. For example, dyslexia in English is different from dyslexia in Arabic [21]. There are two types of languages: transparent and non-transparent orthographic language. According to Spencer [48], readers in languages with transparent orthographies, such as Turkish, Italian and Spanish, face fewer difficulties in reading than readers in languages with non-transparent orthographies such as Dutch, English and French. Arabic is a language with two orthographies. Although Arabic is the largest member of the Semitic language family [12], a review of the literature on dyslexia in Arabic shows that there is a paucity of research targeting dyslexia in Arabic.

In recent years, with the increased use of technology in education, e-learning has become increasingly popular. E-learning is defined as "The use of the Internet to access learning materials; to interact with the content, instructor, and other learners; and to obtain support during the learning process, in order to acquire knowledge, to construct personal meaning, and to grow from the learning experience" [6]. E-learning enables learners to access the educational environment anytime and anywhere. This has positive effects on individuals with dyslexia by empowering them, providing assessment, training or support [13].

Recently, several studies have targeted e-learning systems to support, teach, or train dyslexics in different languages. However, there are several issues regarding these studies. For example, the diversity of dyslexic students is not considered in most proposed systems [1,41,49], even though dyslexic students differ in their dyslexia type, skills, abilities and preferences. Therefore, these systems fail to meet the different needs of dyslexic students by providing the most appropriate educational material. Instead, they tend to present the same educational material in the same sequence to all dyslexics, which makes the learning process less effective, more time-consuming and leads to dissatisfaction and thus, affects the learning performance. Adaptive e-learning systems provide an alternative to these traditional "one-size-fits-all" e-learning systems [18].

The adaptation of e-learning systems can make them more enjoyable and suitable for each student by accommodating their different needs and characteristics. Among these characteristics, many types of developmental dyslexia exist. Each type results from an impairment in the word reading process, and each one leads to different characteristics and reading problems [26]. Therefore, different approaches of treatment and teaching are required.

Some existing research has considered adaptivity in e-learning systems for dyslexia [2,5,10,13,14,49]. However, there is still a need for more research and most of these studies lack well-designed and robust experimental evaluations [1,2,13,14,41,49]. There is an argument that a well-designed, careful and controlled evaluation of adaptive e-learning systems is more significant than just proposing new and novel systems [31]. Additionally, adapting e-learning according to dyslexia type is still under investigated [27]. This, despite the fact that dyslexic students are all different, each one with different characteristics, symptoms, and reading problems [26].

The aim of the work described in this paper is to investigate the impact of adapting e-learning material based on the different characteristics of dyslexic students, in particular their *dyslexia type*. Arabic is targeted in this study because there is a paucity of research targeting dyslexia in this language, despite it being a widely spoken language with a considerable rate of dyslexia [12,32]. An empirical evaluation in terms of its learning effectiveness (short- and long-term) is provided. The effect on students' perception of the level of usability is also presented.

This paper contributes to recent research on dyslexia and adaptation by providing evidence on learning performance as well as highlighting the importance of adapting e-learning material to the individual's dyslexia type. Importantly, this study investigates and examines carefully the effectiveness of adaptation based on dyslexia type. This is a significant gaps in current research targeted at Arabic [5,12–14,33,41], and also other languages such as English [45,49] and Malay [1,2]. This has not been addressed or investigated and appropriately evaluated in an adaptive e-learning system for dyslexia. This adds novelty and originality to this study because it supports the view that adapting e-learning material to dyslexia type significantly enhances learning gain.

The remainder of this paper is structured as follows: Sect. 2 presents the background on dyslexia and Arabic features that affect dyslexia. Section 3 describes adaptive e-learning systems. Section 4 presents the approach to adaptation based on dyslexia type. Section 5 presents the evaluation methodology. Section 6 presents the results of the study. Section 7 details the discussion of the work. Finally, Sect. 8 concludes the paper and points to further work.

1.1   Research Questions

This study investigated the following questions:

Question 1. Does adaptation of learning material based on dyslexia type improve reading performance (short- and long-term) compared to non-adaptive material?

Question 2. Does adaptation of learning material based on dyslexia type achieve a higher level of perceived usability?

2   Background

2.1   Dyslexia Definition and Types

There are many definitions of dyslexia. The International Dyslexia Association [37] page (2), uses the following definition:

Definition 1. *"Dyslexia is a specific learning disability that is neurobiological in origin. It is characterized by difficulties with accurate and/or fluent word recognition and by poor spelling and decoding abilities. These difficulties typically result from a deficit in the phonological component of language that is often unexpected in relation to other cognitive abilities and the provision of effective classroom instruction. Secondary consequences may include problems in reading comprehension and reduced reading experience that can impede growth of vocabulary and back- ground knowledge."*

Ten types of developmental dyslexia, each resulting from an impairment in different components in the word reading process, are commonly used. The dual-route model for single word reading is presented in Fig. 1 [26]. This model has been chosen for many reasons. It is the result of work over the past 40 years [27], and predicts the common types of dyslexia.

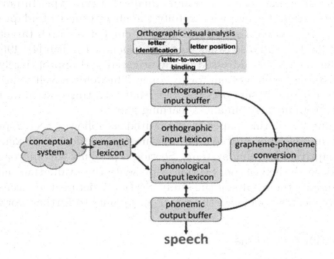

Fig. 1. The dual-route model for single word reading [26].

To read a specific word, several stages need to be considered. The first stage is analyzing the target word through the orthographic-visual analysis system. This stage has three functions: identifying each letter, encoding each letter's position within the word, and binding letters to that word [20]. Any deficit in these functions causes different types of developmental dyslexia, each with different attributes and methods for treatment.

One type of developmental dyslexia is letter identity dyslexia that results from a deficit in the letter identification function [26]. This type of dyslexia is characterized by the inability to identify a letter or the omission or substitution of letters within words. Letter Position Dyslexia (LPD) results from a deficit in encoding the letter position within a word [30]. The essential symptom is letter migration within a word. Attentional dyslexia [28] results from a deficit in letter-to-word binding, that is the ability to focus attention on the target word and attenuate attention to the words around it [26]. The main symptom is the migration of letters between words. Neglect dyslexia causes neglect of one side of the word, usually the left side, by omitting, substituting and adding letters in the neglected side. Visual output dyslexia results from a failure in the output of the orthographic-visual analysis system [25]. It is characterized by errors in letter identification and the migration of letters between and within words [26].

Beside these five different types, a further five types can result from deficits in the two routes in the dual-route model of word reading [26]. The first route is the lexical route that connects between the phonological output lexicon and the orthographic input lexicon. The second route is the sub-lexical route in which reading proceeds via grapheme-to-phoneme conversion. The orthographic input lexicon holds the entries for words (the orthographic information), and the phonological output lexicon holds sounds of the spoken words (the phonological information) such as: vowels, number of syllables and stress position [27]. The lexical route, which connects both lexicons, is responsible for fast conversion from written form to its sounds [27]. The sub-lexical route converts letter strings into phonological information via grapheme-to-phoneme conversion. This allows for reading new, unfamiliar words that are not stored in the orthographic input lexicon [26]. However, this route is less accurate and slower when reading existing words [27]. For instance, they might pronounce "now" as "no".

Different developmental dyslexia patterns result from a deficit in each of these routes. A deficit in the lexical route results in surface dyslexia [29], and there-fore, individuals with this type of dyslexia are forced to read all words via the sub-lexical route as though they are new words [27]. This causes slow and inac-curate reading [27]. For example, the word "get" may be read as "jet". Readers with phonological dyslexia have a deficit in the sub-lexical route and therefore they read all words via the lexical route [26]. The cardinal symptom of phono-logical dyslexia is difficulty reading non-words and new words [26]. Another type of dyslexia, which results from an impairment in the sub-lexical route is vowel letter dyslexia [26]. Readers with vowel letter dyslexia substitute, add, omit and migrate vowel letters [27].

Besides these two routes for word reading, the comprehension of words is achieved through a connection between the orthographic input lexicon, the semantic lexicon and the conceptual system [27]. A deficit in this connection leads to a type of dyslexia called direct dyslexia or access to semantics dyslexia [26] or reading without meaning [27]. Direct dyslexics can read aloud correctly, but without understanding [26]. Finally, deep dyslexia results from a deficit in both the sub-lexical route and the direct lexical route [26,27]. Deep dyslexics have to read through the semantic route [26,27]. Individuals with deep dyslexia produce semantic errors, for example reading "lime" as "lemon" [26].

The common effects of dyslexia are slow reading and poor reading accu-racy [26,37]. There are ten common different types of dyslexia, each with differ-ent symptoms and each with different requirements for treatment and teaching.

These different types have been reported in many languages. In young Arabic speaking children, LPD and vowel letter dyslexia are the most common [27], and therefore they are targeted in this study.

2.2 Arabic and Dyslexia

Arabic is an official language of 22 countries [22] and a widely used language with over 230 million speakers [15]. Arabic script is written from right to left in a cursive style [21]. It consists of 28 letters. These letters mainly represent consonants, but three of them represent long vowels [3]. There are three basic short vowel forms that are presented as diacritical marks placed above or below letters. There is also a diacritic that represents the absence of a vowel [15].

Children initially learn to read Arabic through the use of a vowelized version of the orthography in which all the vowels, consonants and diacritical marks are represented in the script [3]. Thus, they learn to use a phonologically transparent writing system in which every phoneme is represented. Later, children start to read an orthography without diacritics, which requires a different set of skills. This makes Arabic a non-transparent orthography that requires readers to utilize extra information, such as sentence context and morphological knowledge. Most materials and texts omit vowel diacritic information [3] and this has a great impact on the accuracy when reading.

Many complications are faced during spelling or reading. For example, similar letters have the same basic shapes (ث، ت، ب), but they differ in the position and the number of dots within each letter [21]. Another essential feature of the Arabic script is the different shapes of a letter depending on its position within a word (initial, medial, final or as an isolated form) [21]. For example, the letter (س) (s) has the following forms: (ﺳ) as the initial form, (ﺴ) as the medial form, (ﺲ) as the final form and (س) as the isolated form. As a result, distinguishing between individual letters is a considerable challenge [39].

Arabic is a Semitic language that has a morphological structure in both verbs and nouns [27]. Arabic morphology is based on two abstract units: "root" and "pattern" and words are generated by the combination of these [15]. Arabic roots are either trilateral (three consonants) or quadrilateral (four consonants) and are abstract entities, while the pattern is the vocalic model on which the root moulds to form the word [15].

2.3 Technological Interventions for Dyslexia

Dyslexia makes it hard for individuals to succeed in school. It is also a challenge to perform day-to-day activities that include reading or spelling [50]. It is essential for dyslexics to receive early interventions in order to minimize long-term difficulties. These interventions can help to encourage success in schools and the workplace. It can also help to build resilience and coping skills.

Technology plays a significant role in supporting individuals with dyslexia. The range of available technological resources and tools is steadily growing. These interventions can educate, train or assist individuals with dyslexia.

Different e-learning systems have been developed to teach dyslexics various learning skills. Abdul Hamid et al. [1] proposed a study to help dyslexic students to learn the Malay language. The proposed model considers both emotional and cognitive difficulties to improve the effectiveness of the learning process. However, this study's effectiveness has not been evaluated. Further, Srivastava and Haider [49] developed a personalized e-learning system for English dyslexic children that provides learning contents to improve awareness of alphabet structure. Again, there is a lack of empirical evaluation. The evaluation is based only on comments and feedback from special education teachers, not from the students.

Some systems do consider adaptivity based on dyslexia type and other characteristics. For example, Alsobhi et al. [10] proposed a Dyslexia Adaptive E-Learning (DAEL) framework which adapts itself according to the student's dyslexia type. The framework considers four dimensions: presentation, hypermediality, accessibility and acceptability, and user experience. Furthermore, Benmarrakchi et al. [13] developed an adaptive e-learning system for Arabic that treats each dyslexic student as an individual based on his/her learning styles, cognitive traits, prior knowledge and user experience. The proposed systems make the learning process accessible; however, the effectiveness of these systems [10] and [13] has not been evaluated.

In addition, similar work had been done by Alghabban et al. [5] by developing a multimodal m-learning tool for Arabic dyslexics. The proposed tool enables manual adaptation of the interface and different modalities of input and output (text, audio and image) based on the individual's learning style. An evaluation was presented and showed an increase in reading skills after three months of using the proposed tool. However, the design methodology is not presented, which leads to difficulty in evaluating its effectiveness.

Some research also considers a dyslexic's motivation as one implication of cognitivist approaches. For example, Benmarrakchi et al. [14] developed an adaptive m-learning game for Arabic dyslexic children focusing on learning style. The proposed system aims to enhance the students' fundamental skills such as reading, comprehension, writing, concentration, short-term memory and Arabic orthography. Ouherrou et al. [41] developed an interactive learning game called "FunLexia" to support Arabic children with dyslexia. The game was evaluated using Nielsen's Usability Heuristics (NUH). In the case study [14], the evaluation methodology is not presented, which makes it hard to understand the system's effectiveness. In the case of [41], the evaluation is only based on a questionnaire and the learning is based on a short term experiment.

In similar work, Sasupilli et al. [45] proposed a mobile educational game called "Let's find letters". The game focuses on letter recognition. However, the evaluation provides only feedback from the teacher's perspective, not from that of the students.

Kah and Lakhouaja [33] proposed a set of games for Arabic children with dysgraphia and dyslexia. The games cover the following: distinguishing letters and their sounds, letter shape recognition, word and sentence construction. These games enhance spelling and reading skills for dyslexics. Further investigation of the usability and benefits are needed. Abdul Hamid et al. [2] aimed to develop an adaptive e-learning system based on students' difficulties and behaviour. However, again, the system has not been implemented or evaluated.

Benmarrakchi et al. [12] propose practical guidelines for promoting accessibility for Arabic dyslexic students, although the effectiveness of those guidelines has not been tested. Similarly, Aldabaybah and Jusoh [4] identify usability features for tools to support Arabic dyslexic students. The features raise the usability performance and enhance the learning process, as assessed by an expert. Table 1 gives a summary of technological interventions.

To sum up, many studies target dyslexia in different languages. However, there is a paucity of research which targets Arabic. This despite it being a widely spoken language with a considerable rate of dyslexia. Existing studies attempt to build and, sometimes, evaluate adaptive e-learning systems, but these studies overlook well-designed and robust experimental evaluations to examine their effectiveness [12–14, 41]. Moreover, adapting e-learning systems according to one significant characteristic of dyslexia, dyslexia type, is still under-investigated. This is despite previous research pointing out there are many types of dyslexia [26], each with different characteristics and different reading problems. Therefore, adaptive e-learning environment based on dyslexia type should be investigated.

Table 1. Interventions for dyslexia from reviewed literature.

Name of intervention	Intervention type	Target language	Evaluation
A computer-based learning model [1]	Educational	Malay	N/A
A personalized e-learning system [49]	Educational	English	Feedback
DAEL [10]	Educational	N/A	N/A
Adaptive e-learning system [13]	Educational	Arabic	N/A
A multimodal m-learning tool [5]	Educational	Arabic	Pre- and post-test experimental design
M-learning game [14]	Educational	Arabic	N/A
FunLexia game [41]	Educational	Arabic	Questionnaire
"Let's find letters" game [45]	Educational	English	Feedback
Games [33]	Training	Arabic	Pre- and post-test experimental design
Adaptive e-learning system [2]	Training	Malay	N/A
Practical guidelines [12]	Assistive	Arabic	N/A
Usability features for assistive tool [4]	Assistive	Arabic	Feedback

3   Adaptive E-Learning Systems

Recently, the popularity of e-learning systems has increased. The learning process has shifted from a teacher-centric approach, in which the learning method relies mainly on teachers transmitting knowledge to learners, to a learner-centric model, where learners are actively involved in the learning process [51]. E-learning systems provide a large amount of information that can overwhelm learners and can lead to poor decisions on how and what to learn. In this case, the learning process can be less effective and more time-consuming. One challenge is how to match different characteristics and needs of different students to provide more appropriate and personalized learning. For that, many researchers have shifted from a "one-size-fits-all" approach towards adapting the learning to meet each user's needs [9].

Adaptation is a process of tailoring something to the different requirements of the end-user [18,38]. Adaptive e-learning systems provide a more suitable educational environment by recommending relevant educational content and constructing individual learning paths.

Adaptive e-learning systems are based on a specific adaptive framework, which contains three key components [7,8]. These are: the domain model, the learner model and the adaptation model [18]. The domain model stores learning resources related to the application domain. It is usually represented as a hierarchical network with different levels [7]. The learner model integrates different characteristics of learners such as knowledge, motivation, context and skills. This model can be either static or dynamic. A static learner model might be built by completing an initial assessment [42]. The learner characteristics can then be stored in the model and stay unchanged or are modified manually. In the case of a dynamic leaner model, it monitors interactions with the system and updates as needed [46]. The adaptation model uses both the domain model and learner model to adapt the relevant material. This model can incorporate various adaptation methods, for example by constructing personalized learning paths based on learner characteristics [7].

Different attributes of students can be used. Brusilovsky [17] argues for the use of features such as learning style and knowledge level. Many studies have adapted instructional material based on, for instance, learners' learning styles [23,24] and knowledge level [47].

Adaptive e-learning systems can also accommodate the different needs and attributes of dyslexic students. For example, adapting to dyslexia type [10] as well as a student's learning style, cognitive traits, prior knowledge and experience or behaviour [2,5,13].

4   Towards Dyslexia Type Adaptivity

To investigate the effect of adaptation according to students' dyslexia type, an adaptive e-learning framework is used. This framework is based upon the model presented in [8] and used as a foundation for the design and implementation.

The important difference is that the learner model is augmented to include the diagnosis of the dyslexia type (here, either LPD or vowel letter dyslexia). This model is instantiated by using a reliable, offline diagnostic tool, as described in Sect. 5.2. This is important in order to be able to build a sound evaluation of the effectiveness of the adaptation.

An e-learning system, called DyslexiaTypeTrain, had been designed and implemented as an instantiation of this framework. This was designed to train Arabic dyslexic students by providing word reading exercises. A screenshot of the DyslexiaTypeTrain welcome page is presented in Fig. 2. Two versions of the system are used to evaluate the effectiveness of the adaption. The adaptive version matches e-learning material to dyslexia type and the non-adaptive version provides a standard curriculum. The two versions of the system are identical in other respects.

The training activities focus on the student choosing a word that matches a target picture, as shown in Fig. 3. These activities are categorized into eight training sessions, where the difficulty of activities is gradually increased. The words used in the training sessions are collected from the Arabic school curriculum and are sensitive to the target type of dyslexia. In the case of vowel letter dyslexia, where students transpose, substitute or add vowel letters, the selected words are related to these symptoms. For example, in English, reading the word "big" as "bug". In the case of individuals with LPD, the words are related to letter migration, e.g. reading the word "flies" as "files".

Fig. 2. The DyslexiaTypeTrain welcome page.

Fig. 3. A screenshot of a training session.

5   Methodology

The goal of this study is to investigate whether adapting learning material based on a dyslexics' characteristics, (dyslexia type), is beneficial and whether it will increase their learning performance (short- and long-term). The following sections defines the study's hypotheses, the experimental methodology, the measurements used, the data collection tools and participants.

5.1 Hypotheses

Based on this study's questions, three hypotheses are formulated as follows:

Hypothesis 1: Adapting e-learning material to dyslexia type achieves significantly better short-term learning gain compared to non-adaptive material.

Hypothesis 2: Adapting e-learning material to dyslexia type achieves significantly better long-term learning gain compared to non-adaptive material.

Hypothesis 3: Adapting e-learning material to dyslexia type achieves significantly better perceived level of usability compared to non-adaptive material.

5.2 Experimental Methodology

Measurements and Data Collection. Three measurements are considered in this study. The short-term learning performance for each dyslexic student is assessed directly after finishing the course. To test the long-term learning gain, this is repeated after a period of two weeks. This helps to see whether learning performance is persistent. We also measure their perception of the usability of the system. We hypothesise that if the system fits their needs, then they will be more satisfied, engaged and motivated. Which, in turn, influences learning effectiveness.

Data was gathered using several tools: a diagnostic test, three isomorphic reading tests (a pre-test, a post-test and follow-up test) and a usability test. Dyslexia type was identified by the reliable and standardised diagnostic test provided by the Saudi Ministry of Education [19].

Pre-, post- and follow-up tests were used to measure students' reading performance. They include ten words from the curriculum and have been validated by special education experts. Every student was asked to read these words aloud to assess their level of performance. The pre-test is used to assess each student's prior level of performance and to balance the experimental conditions. The post-test assesses the student's performance after finishing the course (short-term performance). The follow-up test was performed two weeks later to assess long-term performance. The learning gain is calculated by subtracting the pre-test score from the post-test score [9].

The perception of usability of the system was measured by using a reliable and widely used tool, the System Usability Scale (SUS) questionnaire [16]. SUS consists of ten questions measured on a 5-point Likert scale. Since the target users are children, presenting the original 5-point Likert scale that ranges from "strongly disagree" to "strongly agree" is not appropriate [43]. An alternative instrument is the Smileyometer [43], which is widely-used (see Fig. 4). It uses pictorial representations with a 1–5 Likert scale to enable children to identify their opinions and feelings [43] by ticking one face. Therefore, we used this version of the SUS, adapted to a 5-point scale using the Smileyometer.

Awful   Not very good   Good   Really good   Brilliant

Fig. 4. The Smileyometer [43].

Experimental Design. A between-subjects experimental design, where each participant experiences one condition, was used because of the possibility of carryover from one condition to another [53].

To validate the experimental design and instruments, a pilot study was performed with a small number of participants (6). Some minor problems regarding learning material were discovered and addressed before conducting the full experiment.

The study was subject to ethical approval. Full consent from participants' parents/guardians and schools was obtained before children could participate in the experiment. The consent form includes the purpose of the experiment, as well as the type of data that will be collected and what is expected from the participants during the experiment.

Before conducting the experiment, the students were welcomed and introduced to the objectives of the experiment. Their demographic information was collected, and the dyslexia type was determined using the diagnostic tests: either LPD or vowel letter dyslexia. Students with other or multiple dyslexia types were not included in the study. Then, the pre-test was administered to all participants to assess their initial reading performance. The participants were divided into two groups balanced by age and prior reading level. The adaptive group used the adaptive version of the system, while the control group used the non-adaptive version.

The experiment was conducted in a quiet room within the student's school. Neither the student nor the experimenter were aware of the experimental condition being used. The study was first introduced by the experimenter who was present at each session to make an observational record. Students worked individually. There were eight sessions of approximately 30 min: two sessions per student per week over four weeks.

The post-test was administered immediately after finishing the experiment as was the SUS tool. After two weeks, the follow-up test was undertaken.

Participants. Forty female, Saudi students, previously diagnosed with dyslexia, took part in this study. They were selected from five schools in the western region of the Kingdom of Saudi Arabia (KSA). The students were aged from 7–12 years (Grades 2 to 6). They were all familiar with electronic devices. Twenty one of the students suffered from vowel letter dyslexia and 19 from LPD.

6   Results

The study was conducted with 40 students in primary schools (adaptive group = 20, control group = 20). Both groups were homogeneous in terms of language and gender. Both groups were equivalent in age ($p = 0.947 > 0.05$) and prior level of reading performance (p-value for pre-test = $0.904 > 0.05$). There was no difference between means of the groups in age or pre-test scores. The collected data were analyzed using the IBM SPSS statistics software.

6.1   Short-Term Learning Gain

Hypothesis 1 (short-term learning gain) was tested. As shown in Fig. 5, the post-test and short-term learning gain of the adaptive group are higher than in the control group. The findings indicate that there was generally a positive effect from adapting learning material to dyslexia type.

As the data was not normally distributed, an independent sample Mann-Whitney U test was used to determine if there were differences between the groups. The results indicate that the short-term learning gain for the adaptive group ($Median = 3.5$) was statistically significantly higher than for the control group ($Median = 1$), $U = 351$, $p = 0.000035 \approx 0.00 < 0.05$, $Z = 4.14$. Therefore, the first hypothesis is confirmed and it can be inferred that adapting the learning material to the dyslexia type leads to significantly better short-term learning gain than in the non-adaptive condition.

6.2   Long-Term Learning Gain

The second hypothesis (long-term learning gain after two weeks) was also tested. Two participants in the control group did not complete the follow-up test because they transferred school. For this reason the result of the pre-test presented in Fig. 6 is slightly different from that of Fig. 5. The follow-up test and long-term learning gain of the adaptive group were higher than the control group, as shown in Fig. 6. The findings indicate that there was generally a positive effect on long-term learning gain from adapting learning material to dyslexia type.

As the data was not normally distributed, an independent sample Mann-Whitney U test was used to determine if there were differences in the scores. The results indicate that the long-term learning gain for the adaptive group ($Median = 4$) was statistically significantly higher than for the control group ($Median = 1$), $U = 296.5$, $p = 0.0005 \approx 0.0 < 0.05$, $Z = 3.45$. Therefore, the second hypothesis is confirmed, and it can be concluded that adapting learning material to dyslexia type leads to significantly better long-term learning gain than in a non-adaptive system.

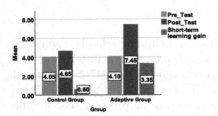

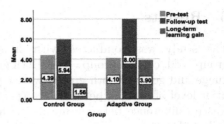

Fig. 5. Results of pre-test, post-test and short-term learning gain of the control and adaptive groups.

Fig. 6. Results of pre-test, follow-up test and long-term learning gain of the control and adaptive groups.

6.3 Perceived Level of Usability

The third hypothesis, about the effect of adaption on students' perception of the level of usability, was also tested. The adaptive version had a mean of 96 ($SD = 6.46, Median = 100$) and the non-adaptive version a mean of 85.63 ($SD = 9.93, Median = 86.25$). According to [11], these results show that both are perceived as usable and useful.

To test the hypothesis, the two conditions were compared using an independent sample Mann-Whitney U test, as the data was not normally distributed. The results show a significant difference between the usability score of the two versions, $U = 329, p = 0.000371 < 0.05, Z = 3.56$. Therefore, the third hypothesis is confirmed and it can be concluded that the adaptive version has significantly higher levels of perceived usability than the non-adaptive one.

The two versions were identical apart from the words used in the exercises and yet there was a significant differences in the students' perceptions of the usability. In particular, there were large differences in the results of two items in the SUS tool. The items "I think that I would like to use this website frequently" and "I found the website simple" both had large effects. These results suggest that adaptation not only has a direct effect through the delivery of more appropriate learning, but also that students, subconsciously, perceive this and that it affects their perception of the system that they are using. This, in turn might enhance their engagement and curiosity.

7 Discussion

This study aims to investigate whether adapting e-learning based on a student's dyslexia type improves learning effectiveness. The study assessed learning performance (both immediately at the end of the course and after a delay of two weeks) and the students' perception of the usability of the learning material. This study contributes to current research on adaptivity by presenting evidence for the use of *dyslexia type* as a learner characteristic for adaptation when teaching reading skills to dyslexic students. As far as we aware, this study is distinctive in undertaking a rigorous, controlled experiment with a reasonable number of dyslexic participants.

This study's results are consistent with previous work, which has argued that dyslexic students are each different in their types of dyslexia, their reading problems and, therefore, their needs [26,27]. Most previous work [1,2,4,12–14,33,41] has focused upon the technology or abstract frameworks, rather than assessing whether the intervention is effective. Where evaluations have been undertaken, they often rely on teachers' opinions and questionnaires or use very small samples [4,12,13,33,41]. Importantly, in contrast to previous research, this study is one of the few which considers both learning effectiveness and students' perceptions of usability.

Concerning the benefit to learning, the results show that there is both a short-term learning gain and that this benefit persists in the long-term. Both are significantly higher in the condition where the system adapts to dyslexia type. These results are in line with previous research [35,36].

The high level of perceived usability in the adaptive version can be interpreted in line with previous studies [54], where it is argued that adaptation enhances the motivation and engagement of students. This suggests that students are aware of when a lesson is more suited to their needs and that this affects their perception of the quality of the course. Further, this perception of suitability affects their attitude not just to their assessment of the learning content component but also to other aspects of the system.

8   Conclusion and Future Work

This paper investigates the impact of adapting e-learning material based on dyslexia type. This is a significant gap in previous work. Moreover, this paper addresses the lack of rigorously designed and controlled experimental evaluations in the previous work on e-learning systems for dyslexia. These gaps have not been addressed previously. An experiment is conducted with 40 Arabic dyslexic students to validate and evaluate the proposed approach. The experiment's results show that adapting based upon dyslexia type leads to a significant improvement in learning gain (short- and long-term effects) and perceived level of usability.

This paper contributes to recent research on dyslexia and e-learning systems by highlighting the importance of adaption based upon dyslexia type. Whilst this study is focused on female students, we believe the results will generalize to male dyslexics and also to different ages. Further work is needed to confirm this. It may also provide lessons for other languages.

This research has, however, some limitations. The amount of teaching through the system was limited (8 sessions of 30 min each). In addition, the students had other teaching in parallel. This was true for students in both experimental conditions, but it will have introduced some additional variation into the data.

Future research will extend the present study by investigating adaptation based on other user characteristics, such as the student's skill level and also considering other measurements such as reading speed. In addition, we will extend the amount of learning.

References

1. Abdul Hamid, S.S., Admodisastro, N., Kamaruddin, A.: A study of computer-based learning model for students with dyslexia. In: 2015 9th Malaysian Software Engineering Conference (MySEC), pp. 284–289 (2015). https://doi.org/10.1109/MySEC.2015.7475234
2. Abdul Hamid, S.S., Admodisastro, N., Kamaruddin, A., Manshor, N., Ghani, A.A.A.: Informing design of an adaptive learning model for student with dyslexia: a preliminary study. In: Proceedings of the 3rd International Conference on Human-Computer Interaction and User Experience in Indonesia, CHIuXiD 2017, pp. 67–75. Association for Computing Machinery, New York (2017). https://doi.org/10.1145/3077343.3107577
3. Abu-Rabia, S., Sammour, R.: Spelling errors' analysis of regular and dyslexic bilingual Arabic-English students. Open J. Mod. Linguist. **3**, 58–68 (2013). https://doi.org/10.4236/ojml.2013.31007
4. Aldabaybah, B., Jusoh, S.: Usability features for Arabic assistive technology for dyslexia. In: 2018 9th IEEE Control and System Graduate Research Colloquium (ICSGRC), pp. 223–228 (2018). https://doi.org/10.1109/ICSGRC.2018.8657536
5. Alghabban, W.G., Salama, R.M., Altalhi, A.H.: Mobile cloud computing: an effective multimodal interface tool for students with dyslexia. Comput. Hum. Behav. **75**, 160–166 (2017). https://doi.org/10.1016/j.chb.2017.05.014, http://www.sciencedirect.com/science/article/pii/S0747563217303266
6. Ally, M.: Foundations of educational theory for online learning. In: Anderson, T. (ed.) The Theory and Practice of Online Learning, vol. 2, pp. 15–44 (2004)
7. Alshammari, M., Anane, R., Hendley, R.J.: Adaptivity in e-learning systems. In: 2014 Eighth International Conference on Complex, Intelligent and Software Intensive Systems, pp. 79–86 (2014). https://doi.org/10.1109/CISIS.2014.12
8. Alshammari, M., Anane, R., Hendley, R.J.: An e-learning investigation into learning style adaptivity. In: 2015 48th Hawaii International Conference on System Sciences, pp. 11–20 (2015). https://doi.org/10.1109/HICSS.2015.13
9. Alshammari, M., Anane, R., Hendley, R.J.: Usability and effectiveness evaluation of adaptivity in e-learning systems. In: Proceedings of the 2016 CHI Conference Extended Abstracts on Human Factors in Computing Systems, CHI EA 2016, pp. 2984–2991. Association for Computing Machinery, New York (2016). https://doi.org/10.1145/2851581.2892395
10. Alsobhi, A.Y., Khan, N., Rahanu, H.: DAEL framework: a new adaptive e-learning framework for students with dyslexia. Proc. Comput. Sci. **51**, 1947–1956 (2015). https://doi.org/10.1016/j.procs.2015.05.459, http://www.sciencedirect.com/science/article/pii/S1877050915012673
11. Bangor, A., Kortum, P.T., Miller, J.T.: An empirical evaluation of the system usability scale. Int. J. Hum.-Comput. Interact. **24**(6), 574–594 (2008). https://doi.org/10.1080/10447310802205776
12. Benmarrakchi, F.E., Kafi, J.E., Elhore, A.: Communication technology for users with specific learning disabilities. Proc. Comput. Sci. **110**, 258–265 (2017). https://doi.org/10.1016/j.procs.2017.06.093, http://www.sciencedirect.com/science/article/pii/S1877050917312711
13. Benmarrakchi, F.E., Kafi, J.E., Elhore, A.: User modeling approach for dyslexic students in virtual learning environments. Int. J. Cloud Appl. Comput. (IJCAC) **7**(2), 1–9 (2017). https://doi.org/10.4018/IJCAC.2017040101

14. Benmarrakchi, F.E., Kafi, J.E., Elhore, A., Haie, S.: Exploring the use of the ICT in supporting dyslexic students' preferred learning styles: a preliminary evaluation. Educ. Inf. Technol. **22**, 2939–2957 (2017). https://doi.org/10.1007/s10639-016-9551-4

15. Boumaraf, A., Macoir, J.: The influence of visual word form in reading: single case study of an arabic patient with deep dyslexia. Read. Writ. **29**, 137–158 (2016). https://doi.org/10.1007/s11145-015-9583-y

16. Brooke, J.: Sus-a quick and dirty usability scale. In: Usability evaluation in industry, pp. 189–194 (1996)

17. Brusilovsky, P.: Adaptive navigation support. In: Brusilovsky, P., Kobsa, A., Nejdl, W. (eds.) The Adaptive Web. LNCS, vol. 4321, pp. 263–290. Springer, Heidelberg (2007). https://doi.org/10.1007/978-3-540-72079-9_8

18. Brusilovsky, P.: Adaptive hypermedia for education and training. In: Durlach, P.J., Lesgold, A.M. (eds.) Adaptive Technologies for Training and Education, vol. 46, pp. 46–68. Cambridge University Press, Cambridge (2012)

19. Bukhari, Y.A., Al-Oud, A.S., Abughanem, T.A., Al-Mayah, S.A., Al-Shabib, M.S., Al-Jaber, S.A.: Alaikhtibarat Altashkhisiat Lidhuyi Sueubat Altaalum Fi Madatay Allughat Alarabia Wa Alriyadiat Fi Almarhalat Alebtidaeiia [Diagnostic tests for people with learning difficulties in the subjects of Arabic language and mathematics at the primary stage]. General Administration for Special Education, The General Administration for Evaluation and Quality of Education, Ministry of Education,Saudi Arabia (1437 AH)

20. Coltheart, M.: Disorders of reading and their implications for models of normal reading. Visible Lang. **15**(3), 245–286 (Summer 1981). https://search.proquest.com/docview/1297974274?accountid=8630. Accessed 23 Feb 2013

21. Elbeheri, G., Everatt, J.: Literacy ability and phonological processing skills amongst dyslexic and non-dyslexic speakers of arabic. Read. Writ. **20**, 273–294 (2007). https://doi.org/10.1007/s11145-006-9031-0

22. Elbeheri, G., Everatt, J., Reid, G., Mannai, H.A.: Dyslexia assessment in Arabic. J. Res. Special Educ. Needs **6**(3), 143–152 (2006). https://doi.org/10.1111/j.1471-3802.2006.00072.x, https://onlinelibrary.wiley.com/doi/abs/10.1111/j.1471-3802.2006.00072.x

23. Filippidis, S.K., Tsoukalas, I.A.: On the use of adaptive instructional images based on the sequential-global dimension of the felder-silverman learning style theory. Interact. Learn. Environ. **17**(2), 135–150 (2009). https://doi.org/10.1080/10494820701869524

24. Franzoni, A.L., Assar, S., Defude, B., Rojas, J.: Student learning styles adaptation method based on teaching strategies and electronic media. In: 2008 Eighth IEEE International Conference on Advanced Learning Technologies, pp. 778–782 (2008). https://doi.org/10.1109/ICALT.2008.149

25. Friedmann, N., Biran, M., Gvion, A.: Patterns of visual dyslexia. J. Neuropsychol. **6**(1), 1–30 (2012). https://doi.org/10.1111/j.1748-6653.2011.02000.x

26. Friedmann, N., Coltheart, M.: Types of developmental dyslexia. In: Bar-On, A., Ravid, D. (eds.) Handbook of Communication Disorders: Theoretical, Empirical, and Applied Linguistics Perspectives, pp. 1–37. Berlin, Boston, De Gruyter Mouton (2016)

27. Friedmann, N., Haddad-Hanna, M.: Types of developmental dyslexia in Arabic. In: Saiegh-Haddad, E., Joshi, R.M. (eds.) Handbook of Arabic Literacy. LS, vol. 9, pp. 119–151. Springer, Dordrecht (2014). https://doi.org/10.1007/978-94-017-8545-7_6

28. Friedmann, N., Kerbel, N., Shvimer, L.: Developmental attentional dyslexia. Cortex **46**(10), 1216–1237 (2010). https://doi.org/10.1016/j.cortex.2010.06.012
29. Friedmann, N., Lukov, L.: Developmental surface dyslexias. Cortex **44**(9), 1146–1160 (2008). https://doi.org/10.1016/j.cortex.2007.09.005
30. Friedmann, N., Rahamim, E.: Developmental letter position dyslexia. J. Neuropsychol. **1**(2), 201–236 (2007). https://doi.org/10.1348/174866407X204227
31. Gauch, S., Speretta, M., Chandramouli, A., Micarelli, A.: User Profiles for Personalized Information Access, pp. 54–89. Springer, Heidelberg (2007). https://doi.org/10.1007/978-3-540-72079-9_2
32. Kah, A.E., Lakhouaja, A.: Arabic learning disabilities in public primary schools: the case of east side of morocco. In: 2015 5th International Conference on Information Communication Technology and Accessibility (ICTA), pp. 1–5 (2015). https://doi.org/10.1109/ICTA.2015.7426906
33. Kah, A.E., Lakhouaja, A.: Developing effective educative games for arabic children primarily dyslexics. Educ. Inf. Technol. **23**, 2911–2930 (2018). https://doi.org/10.1007/s10639-018-9750-2
34. Kavale, K.A., Spaulding, L.S., Beam, A.P.: A time to define: making the specific learning disability definition prescribe specific learning disability. Learn. Disabil. Q. **32**(1), 39–48 (2009). https://doi.org/10.2307/25474661
35. Klašnja-Milićević, A., Vesin, B., Ivanović, M., Budimac, Z.: E-learning personalization based on hybrid recommendation strategy and learning style identification. Comput. Educ. **56**(3), 885–899 (2011). https://doi.org/10.1016/j.compedu.2010.11.001, http://www.sciencedirect.com/science/article/pii/S0360131510003222
36. Liaw, S.S., Huang, H.M., Chen, G.D.: An activity-theoretical approach to investigate learners' factors toward e-learning systems. Comput. Hum. Behav. **23**(4), 1906–1920 (2007). https://doi.org/10.1016/j.chb.2006.02.002, http://www.sciencedirect.com/science/article/pii/S0747563206000033
37. Lyon, G.R., Shaywitz, S.E., Shaywitz, B.A.: A definition of dyslexia. Ann. Dyslexia **53**(1), 1–14 (2003). https://doi.org/10.1007/s11881-003-0001-9
38. Magoulas, G.D., Papanikolaou, Y., Grigoriadou, M.: Adaptive web-based learning: accommodating individual differences through system's adaptation. Brit. J. Educ. Technol. **34**(4), 511–527 (2003). https://doi.org/10.1111/1467-8535.00347
39. Mahfoudhi, A., Everatt, J., Elbeheri, G.: Introduction to the special issue on literacy in Arabic. Read. Writ. **24**, 1011–1018 (2011). https://doi.org/10.1007/s11145-011-9306-y
40. Nordqvist, C.: What you need to know about dyslexia. Medical News Today (2017). https://www.medicalnewstoday.com/articles/186787.php
41. Ouherrou, N., Elhammoumi, O., Benmarrakchi, F., El Kafi, J.: A heuristic evaluation of an educational game for children with dyslexia. In: 2018 IEEE 5th International Congress on Information Science and Technology (CiSt), pp. 386–390 (2018). https://doi.org/10.1109/CIST.2018.8596393
42. Paredes, P., Rodriguez, P.: Considering sensing-intuitive dimension to exposition-exemplification in adaptive sequencing. In: De Bra, P., Brusilovsky, P., Conejo, R. (eds.) AH 2002. LNCS, vol. 2347, pp. 556–559. Springer, Heidelberg (2002). https://doi.org/10.1007/3-540-47952-X_83
43. Read, J.C., MacFarlane, S.: Using the fun toolkit and other survey methods to gather opinions in child computer interaction. In: Proceedings of the 2006 Conference on Interaction Design and Children, IDC 2006, pp. 81–88. Association for Computing Machinery, New York (2006). https://doi.org/10.1145/1139073.1139096

44. Rello, L.: Design of word exercises for children with dyslexia. Proc. Comput. Sci. **27**, 74–83 (2014). https://doi.org/10.1016/j.procs.2014.02.010
45. Sasupilli, M., Bokil, P., Wagle, P.: Designing a learning aid for dyslexic children. In: Chakrabarti, A. (ed.) Research into Design for a Connected World. SIST, vol. 135, pp. 703–712. Springer, Singapore (2019). https://doi.org/10.1007/978-981-13-5977-4_59
46. Schiaffino, S., Garcia, P., Amandi, A.: eteacher: providing personalized assistance to e-learning students. Comput. Educ. **51**(4), 1744–1754 (2008). https://doi.org/10.1016/j.compedu.2008.05.008, http://www.sciencedirect.com/science/article/pii/S036013150800078X
47. Sfenrianto, S., Hartarto, Y., Akbar, H., Mukhtar, M., Efriadi, E., Wahyudi, M.: An adaptive learning system based on knowledge level for english learning. Int. J. Emerg. Technol. Learn. (iJET) **13**(12), 191–200 (2018). https://onlinejour.journals.publicknowledgeproject.org/index.php/i-jet/article/view/8004
48. Spencer, K.: Predicting word-spelling difficulty in 7- to 11-year-olds. J. Res. Read. **22**(3), 283–292 (1999). https://doi.org/10.1111/1467-9817.00091, https://onlinelibrary.wiley.com/doi/abs/10.1111/1467-9817.00091
49. Srivastava, B., Haider, M.T.U.: Personalized assessment model for alphabets learning with learning objects in e-learning environment for dyslexia. J. King Saud Univ. - Comput. Inf. Sci. (2017). https://doi.org/10.1016/j.jksuci.2017.11.005, http://www.sciencedirect.com/science/article/pii/S1319157817302306
50. Sternberg, R.J., Sternberg, K.: Cognitive Psychology, pp. 1–609. Belmont, Cengage Learning (2012)
51. Vrasidas, C.: Constructivism versus objectivism: implications for interaction, course design, and evaluation in distance education. Int. J. Educ. Telecommun. **6**(4), 339–362 (2000)
52. Wajuihian, S., Naidoo, K.: Dyslexia: an overview. Afr. Vis. Eye Health **70**(2), 89–98 (2011). https://doi.org/10.4102/aveh.v70i2.102, https://avehjournal.org/index.php/aveh/article/view/102
53. Weibelzahl, S.: Evaluation of adaptive systems. In: Bauer, M., Gmytrasiewicz, P.J., Vassileva, J. (eds.) UM 2001. LNCS (LNAI), vol. 2109, pp. 292–294. Springer, Heidelberg (2001). https://doi.org/10.1007/3-540-44566-8_49
54. Zaharias, P., Poylymenakou, A.: Developing a usability evaluation method for e-learning applications: beyond functional usability. Int. J. Hum.-Comput. Interact. **25**(1), 75–98 (2009). https://doi.org/10.1080/10447310802546716

Reducing the Gap Between the Conceptual Models of Students and Experts Using Graph-Based Adaptive Instructional Systems

Philippe J. Giabbanelli[1]([⊠]) and Andrew A. Tawfik[2]

[1] Department of Computer Science and Software Engineering,
Miami University, Oxford, OH, USA
giabbapj@miamioh.edu
[2] Department of Instructional Design and Technology,
University of Memphis, Memphis, TN, USA
aatawfik@memphis.edu

Abstract. Decision-making in complex environments requires a detailed understanding of causality to avoid unintended consequences and consider multiple scenarios. Concept mapping is of the key tools to support such decision-making activities. A system is abstracted as a 'map' or graph, in which relevant factors are represented as nodes and connected through causal links. Although studies have shown that concept maps help students recall the evidence and apply the knowledge gained to new cases, barriers such as the difficulty of assessment have prevented a wide adoption of concept maps by instructors. Previous works have partly addressed this concern by using graph algorithms to automatically assess or score a student's map, but instructors are often more interested in correcting their students' misconceptions than in only counting mistakes. In this paper, we design and implement a system to automatically guide students in modifying their conceptual models such that they get increasingly similar to the models produced by experts on the same problem. Although a simple automatic feedback may tell students to add/remove concepts or links based on whether they appear in the expert's map, our approach combines expertise from systems science and participatory modeling to help students better understand why low-level changes are motivated by higher-level structures such as loops and alternative paths.

Keywords: Causal maps · Graph comparison · Ill-structured problems · Mental models · Participatory modeling

1 Introduction

Problems encountered in the classroom are often well-structured and admit predefined answers, for instance as multiple choice questions. However, the problems that students will later face in their professional careers are likely to be ill-structured problems (ISP) which admit a broad set of context-dependent solutions [1]. Such solutions are shaped by many variables and may trigger multiple unintended consequences. Solving an ISP thus requires a mental representation of the causal links between the variables that contribute to, or are impacted by, a potential solution.

C. Stephanidis et al. (Eds.): HCII 2020, LNCS 12425, pp. 538–556, 2020.
https://doi.org/10.1007/978-3-030-60128-7_40

Many software packages can support students in creating such representations in the form of "maps" or networks, such as Coggle or cMap. There have also been significant efforts in developing instructional systems to perform *summative* assessment on these maps. In the early 2010's, Ifenthaler and colleagues developed a vast array of systems including HIMATT [2] and SMD Technology [3], together with their successor AKOVIA [4]. The scope of application of such software packages has also been broadened over time: while early solutions required students to provide their mental representations as networks, newer packages such as GIKS can "immediately convert students' writings" [5] into graphs, which are then examined for summative assessment by listing strengths and weaknesses compared to the expert's model. The latest packages also tend to provide online environments with high usability, such that teachers can intuitively use the tools and form communities of practitioners. For instance, our work at the 2018 Human Computer Interaction conference presented the design and implementation of an online tool that allows teachers to create assignments, upload the students' maps, and comprehensively compare them to the solution maps [6].

Although new tools and case studies can provide detailed summative feedback [7, 8], there is a paucity of tools using *formative* feedback to guide students in improving their work. The lack of tools has long been a barrier to the use of ISPs in the classroom [9], thus limiting the development of problem-solving skills for students [10]. One exception was the work of Wu and colleagues, who provided hints regarding changes that should be made by students in the maps to bring them closer to the experts' maps [11]. While useful, such feedback must typically be created by instructors, which may be a barrier to use. Unlike Wu's approach of requiring an additional annotation of the map in order to provide meaningful feedback, we take a systems science approach to *automatically* identify the most critical aspects that must be changed in the maps. Our contributions are twofold:

(1) We design an adaptive instructional system to tell student (i) what they need to modify in their map and (ii) why such changes are needed.
(2) We implement this system to support communities of practice by (i) using a client/server architecture to allow collaboration and sharing; and (ii) emphasizing usability through an intuitive Graphical User Interface (GUI)

The remainder of this paper is structured as follows. In Sect. 2, we explain why maps are an important tool to externalize the mental models held by students and we briefly survey methods and software to automatically analyze such maps. We then cover how software development efforts have approached the problem of assessing maps. Section 3 builds on this background to present the design of our assessment solution and its software implementation. Considerations for future studies are discussed in Sect. 4.

2   Background

2.1   The Importance of Creating Maps

Students often face questions admitting a small list of valid answers, such as True/False questions or Multiple Choice Questions. While these are useful to test core concepts and can be easily graded, many of the decisions that students will make as professionals require a detailed understanding of causes and consequences. Students may eventually become policymakers and decide whether to recommend quarantine or keep businesses open in the face of a pandemic. Some students may embrace administrative careers and will determine which services are offered in-person while others are provided online. Students working in human resources may need to choose between an internal and an external candidate. Each of these many situations admits several solutions, which are identified based on the preferences of the various actors involved as well as the salient factors and interrelationships in the problem space. Equipping students with *tools* to handle such complex scenarios is thus necessary to avoid creating a divide between the well-structured problems that they encounter in their formal education and the more open-ended questions that they will face as professionals.

A key tool to help decision-making processes is the creation of a *model* that lists the relevant factors and interrelationships. This model is initially *implicit*, as a mental model held internally by students. However, the assumptions found in implicit models may be inconsistent or do not conform to the evidence. To promote evidence-based decision-making, models are externalized and thus become *explicit*. Seeing a model allows to check for consistency or test hypotheses [12]. The field of research concerned with the externalization of models from human participants is known as *participatory modeling* (PM). There is a wide variety of PM tools [13], depending on whether the goal is to produce a *computational* model (e.g., to provide numerical estimates for the implications of a decision) or a *conceptual* model (i.e., to organize knowledge by listing factors and interrelationships). We focus on conceptual models, which are the foundation upon which any type of computational model may be built (e.g., transforming a causal loop diagram into a System Dynamics model). There are different types of conceptual models, depending on the structure (e.g., a 'mind map' puts the problem at the center and all other ideas branch off radially) and participants (e.g., whether the map reflects the knowledge of an individual or a group).

In this paper, we assess *concept maps* as studies have demonstrated that they help students recall and apply the knowledge gained [14, 15]. We follow the definition of Voinov *et al.*: "A concept map results in a network, where concepts (nodes) are connected through directed links (edges). These links are labeled to indicate semantic or otherwise meaningful relationships." [13]

2.2 Analysis of Digital Concept Maps

As a concept map is a network, it can be analyzed using methods from *network theory*. The specific method depends on the purpose:

(Grouping) As maps get larger, we need a higher unit of analysis than individual factors or interrelationships. Grouping factors into *communities* helps to understand a map, particularly when a group corresponds to a meaningful theme (e.g., all factors related to psychology in one group and factors related to the environment in another). For instance, the Foresight Obesity Map is among the largest maps for obesity [16] and reducing it to its communities revealed which ones were more strongly connected or which connections were potentially missing in the model [17]. In the large obesity maps of the Provincial Health Services Authority [18], factors were categorized by community to create a hierarchy that helps policymakers interact with the network [19,20] by 'closing' a community (i.e. see it as a single high-level node) or 'opening' it (i.e. see all individual factors and interrelationships within the community). As grouping is one of the most common analyses, several additional examples can be found in the work of Allender, McGlashan and others [21–23]. Note that 'grouping' as discussed here relies on the use of community detection algorithm, which is different from a thematic analysis in which researchers (rather than algorithms) assign factors to groups [24].

(Intervening)   A map often supports decision-making activities. It is a snapshot of a perceived system such that we can examine the motivations and implications of various actions, also known as 'interventions' or 'what-if' scenarios. Some parts of the system are more important in driving its overall behavior and they are thus a prime target for interventions. Such parts are known as 'leverage points' [25]. They exist at several levels, from individual nodes (at a low level) to sets of interrelationships or even the whole 'mindset' [25]. The individual nodes most likely to impact the system can be identified by measuring their *centrality* [23,26]. Feedback loops (i.e. a cycle starting at a concept and following causal consequences that get back to this concept) in the system have also been identified in several works [19,27,28] (Fig. 4a).

(Validating)   Studies [29] have revealed that participants commonly omit the loops found in the real-world because of cognitive limitations (e.g., it is much simpler to think 'linearly' with chains of causes-and-effects). They also frequently ignore the alternative paths that connect two factors (Fig. 4b). In short, the maps show that people "tend to (un)consciously reduce complexity in order to prevent information overload and to reduce mental effort" [30]. Consequently, the process of eliciting a map is often done with a trained facilitator [31–33] who can focus on the structure (e.g., ensuring that loops are present, avoiding redundant concepts, keeping the relevance to the problem space) while the participant focuses on the content. In this context, the validation of a map is a means to ensure that it was developed through a rigorous facilitation progress (e.g., does it have loops?) and that it provides a plausible depiction of the real-world scenario under study [34]. For instance, a map in which all loops are reinforcing [35] reflects a strong focus on problems rather than solutions [36]; this lack of balance and hence incomplete map can later be misleading for decision-making activities. Although there are additional ways to validate a map (e.g., by contrast with the evidence), this requires mixed-methods studies, which are beyond the scope of this brief overview of network methods [37–39].

(Comparing)   In participatory modeling, it is common to produce several maps for a given problem by externalizing the perspectives of each participant (e.g., through semi-structured interviews) into one map and then

building an aggregate [34,40]. Comparing the maps of individual participants can reveal differences between their mental models, thus prompt-
ing focused conversations to explore or bridge these gaps. Comparing
the maps of groups allows to explore social differences (e.g., the maps of
policymakers or subject-matter experts vs. the maps of community members) [41,42]. In education, encouraging students to *create* maps eventually leads instructors to *assess* maps, which can be done by comparison between the students' maps and an expert's map [43]. A comparison
can consist of identifying a 'structural core' of factors shared across participants (e.g., when do students tend to agree with the expert?) [44],
contrasting important elements (e.g., does the student agree with the
expert on the most central factors?) [45], or quantifying how similarities
between maps (e.g., producing a numerical score to facilitate the assessment of students) [7]. Note that throughout these participatory modeling
studies, the focus is systematically to *examine* differences between maps
rather than *reduce* these gaps, which is the focus of the present paper.

2.3   Methods and Software to Evaluate Digital Concept Maps

The field of research concerned with examining and representing the way learners organize their knowledge of a subject is called *structural assessment of knowledge* (SAK).
When a student acquires information, it is incorporated into the existing body of knowledge (e.g., new factors) and connected (e.g., new edges) with existing knowledge. These
connections may be correct, incorrect, or partially correct at any given time during the
learning process. Research in SAK is concerned both with methods of knowledge representation and methods for evaluating the correctness of those representations [15].
The two topics are strongly interdependent since the evaluation of knowledge depends
on its representation and, in turn, the representation may be chosen to support the evaluation. For instance, several studies have shown how restricting the available concepts
in a map simplifies its evaluation [11,14,46].

Concept maps are popular in SAK to support assessment efforts. Trumpower and
Vanapalli refer to this as "SAK *of* Learning" [emphasis added] in contrast to using
concept maps to aid the student in contextualizing new information within their existing body of knowledge, which constitutes "SAK *for* Learning" [15]. In the assessment
context, concept maps would be created or completed in place of a more traditional
exam or essay at the end of an instructional topic to evaluate how well students had
mastered the material [15]. Because concept maps are being used in place of a more
traditional assessment instrument, it is critically important that the method of evaluating maps is reliable and accurately indicates the degree of mastery attained [47]. Several
barriers have been mentioned in using maps for assessment: the potential for subjectivity, since each map represents an individual view of a particular subject area [46]; the
reluctance of instructors to use concept maps as assessment tools because they perceive them to be time-consuming to evaluate [14]; and the concerns of students who
may find the maps time-consuming to produce [14]. Experimental studies show that
these concerns may not be systematically applicable. For instance, McClure, Sonak,
and Suen performed a study on evaluation of concept maps by hand, using six different

methods, both with and without a referent map for comparison, and found that none of the methods required more than 5 min per map on average, which they judged to be similar to the time required to evaluate an essay, based on personal experience [46]. However, experimental studies do not always concur, in part due to the different preferences of the participants. While one study showed that the students' concern about time could be effectively addressed with computer-based concept mapping instead of using pencil-and-paper [47], another study ruled out the use of any technology as participating teachers considered that technology was difficult to acquire [48]. In short, two key concerns remain in grading a map, similarly to grading essays: there can be significant variance in grading and it is much longer than the easily automatized activity of grading multiple choice questionnaires.

The need to have reliable methods to evaluate concept maps has prompted the development of several frameworks and algorithms [11]. A common approach is to use algorithms from network science to measure an aspect of the student map and compare it with the measure obtained on the expert's map (i.e. each map is reduced to a number and the two numbers are compared). Ifenthaler and colleagues proposed and named several such *structural* measures [4]: number of concepts in each map (named 'surface matching'), the diameter of their spanning trees as a proxy to the range of knowledge ('graphical matching'), or the density ('gamma matching'). As discussed by Krabbe [49], such algorithms partly ignore the topic since they neglect the labels in the maps and only compare their structures. The inclusion of labels in an algorithm leads to *semantic* measures, which start by identifying the set of concepts shared by the student and the expert. Then, we can examine whether concepts connected in the expert's map are also connected in the student's map (i.e. 'propositional matching'). More advanced semantic measures such as the convergence score, salience score, or balanced matching are detailed by Krabbe [49]. As exemplified in the 2017 review on assessment technologies by Bhagat and Spector [50], two software are noteworthy for supporting the assessment of concept maps: HIMATT, introduced in 2010 and equipped with structural algorithms to compare maps; and AKOVIA, released in 2014 and expanding on HIMATT with semantic algorithms. Pathfinder is occasionally mentioned in the literature since it can show how closely the relationships defined by the student match the relationships present in a referent map (by computing both configural and common similarity scores). However, this is limited to Pathfinder networks, which are a very constrained sub-category of concept maps [51].

While all of the algorithms aforementioned perform an assessment by comparing a student map to a referent expert map, several referent-free measures have also been proposed [52,53] to favor certain structures in a student's map (e.g., the 'coherence' Pathfinder measure, number of branches, total links). An alternative to these purely structural metrics is to use the Structure-Behavior-Function framework pioneered by Hmelo-Silver, who showed that experts are characterized by the ability to integrate all three aspects of the framework whereas novices focus on static properties of the system [54]. We recently proposed a similar framework based on structure, function, leverage points (can students manage the system? can they generate multiple scenarios?) and trade-offs [55].

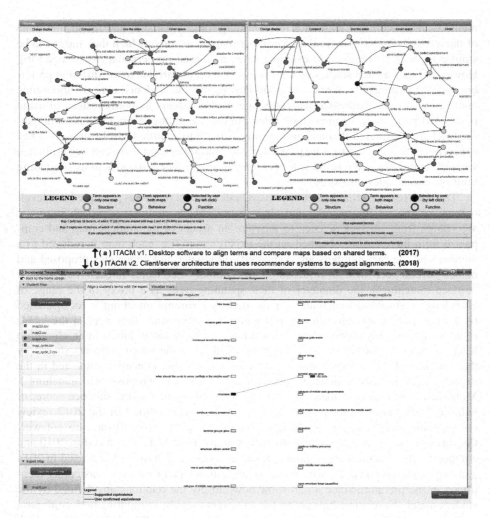

Fig. 1. Our proposed software is the fourth version of ITACM, which started in 2016 as a small package to align terms or switch layouts [43] (a; top) and gradually proposed new functions such as recommender systems in 2018 [6] (b; bottom) or advanced graph algorithms recently [7].

2.4   The Incremental Thesaurus for Assessing Causal Maps (ITACM) Software

In 2016, our team started the development of the **I**ncremental **T**hesaurus for **A**ssessing **C**ausal **M**aps (ITACM) software to address two shortcomings in software support for semantic measures [43]. First, it is well documented that maps can get large and difficult to navigate, as the "abundance of variables hinders their spatial organization" and facilitators spend time manually moving variables until a better layout is obtained [48]. Our software included several graph layout algorithms to automatically re-position the concepts and improve usability (Fig. 1a – top buttons). Most importantly, our software allowed to compute propositional matching or compare the Structure-Behavior-Function of *maps in which the terms could be entirely different*. Although it is recognized that maps created without restricting terms are more useful to students [14], the prevailing attitude is that comparing such maps is more difficult [11,14,15,56] and hence there was a lack of software support to solve the variation in language (e.g., 'heart attack' in the student map but 'cardiac arrest' in the expert map). ITACM uses a subject-area specific thesaurus database constructed by users to allow terms in one concept map to be aligned with terms used in an expert map. This feature allows concept maps to be effectively analyzed without restricting students to only use words from a pre-determined list.

After the 2017 release of ITACM, we rewrote the software to bring two additional improvements [6] (Fig. 2b). First, a *client/server architecture* supports a community of practice as instructors can create accounts, share assignments (and the students' maps within), control access permissions, and re-use the thesaurus database developed by others. Second, we introduce a recommender system to *suggest* how to align terms from the student with the expert, thus reducing the amount of time spent by instructors on the alignment process. The codebase of ITACM v2 forms the basis on which future versions have since been built.

The third version of ITACM [7] brought three new approaches to measure the similarity of maps (i.e., graph kernel, graph editing distance, graph embedding), based on advanced algorithms that have been extensively studied in graph theory yet never utilized for the assessment of digital maps. Approaches such as Graph Edit Distance allow the user to choose between structural or semantic measures, as the distance between two maps is computed based on the minimum number of operations to transform one into the other and the cost associated with such operations. An instructor can thus choose which cost or 'penalty' should be applied when the semantic of a student's concept do not match with the expert's, even after alignment (e.g., 'poor body image → depressed' for the student but 'low body image → low self-esteem' for the expert).

The software presented in the next section, ITACM v4, continues in the tradition of the previous releases of ITACM by using a client/server architecture and allowing users to align terms. Its core innovation lies in helping students to address differences instead of only counting them.

3   Principles, Design, and Implementation of the Proposed Technology

3.1   Overarching Goal and Core Principles

While several of the software aforementioned can perform a summative assessment, instructors often seek to correct misconceptions rather than merely count them. As discussed by several researchers, *feedback* is an essential part of the learning process [11,14,47]. It is possible to 'tweak' some of the summative assessment software to provide feedback by highlighting differences between the student map and the expert map, but this requires a concentrated effort on the part of the student to reflect on and examine the reasoning behind the displayed differences. A more effective method is to provide specific targeted feedback for each student map [15]. Wu *et al.* concluded that the use of the "evaluation-feedback-modification cycle [...] significantly improved the learning achievement of the students" [11]. Thus far, the main limitation to provide feedback is that it required extensive additional work for the instructors [11, 15, 47]. The overarching goal of ITACM v4 is thus to automatically generate feedback.

The translation of this goal to a specific design and ensuing implementation follows the following six principles:

(1) The *terms used by students should be preserved* to the extent possible. Wu *et al.* point out that new information should be taught in relation to the learner's original knowledge structures [11]. Consequently the feedback should not seek to systematically replace the students' terminology by the expert's, but only do so when necessary.

(2) Students should be responsible for making the changes and enabled to do so through *hints*. Wu *et al.* generated feedback for students in the form of hints such as "There is a missing notion related to Concept A" and "There is a missing connection related to Concept A and some other Concept" [11].

(3) Students should not be overwhelmed with a large list of changes to make. Rather, a small set of hints should *focus on the most important changes*. In addition to the individual relationships represented in concept maps, causal maps are typically analyzed for the presence of large system-level structures that can cause significant system-wide changes. As explained in Sect. 2.2, two such structures are loops and alternative paths between concepts. These structures can exert a large amount of influence on the behavior of a system, so they are important features for students to identify.

(4) The feedback should bridge the gap between a student's map and the expert's using a *minimal number of steps*. For instance, if the student has a factor that is not found in the expert's map, then it would be unnecessary to ask the students to first remove causal links involving the extraneous factor before removing the factor itself. Instead, the student should be asked to directly remove the factor (single step), which *de facto* cuts all links involving this factor. This principle is inspired by the notion of 'solution path length' [57], positing that the intricacy of the problem-solution process is driven both the number of steps (which we emphasize) and by the complexity of each step.

(5) When bridging the gap between a student's map and the expert's requires several steps, the *successive steps should be organized* such that the student advances towards a clear goal instead of fixing seemingly disconnected aspects of a model. For example, a student can take a series of steps to complete a loop that is missing with respect to the expert's map, then add a missing alternative path, and finally prune unnecessary links. Although these activities take several steps, they can be bundled into three higher-level activities which motivates low-level changes (e.g., adding or removing a link) by higher-level needs (e.g., missing a loop).

(6) The graphical user interface must follow current standards and be intuitive to support software *usability*. Although Weinerth *et al.* found that very few papers on the assessment of concept maps mention software usability, either directly or indirectly, the International Test Commission has requested to include usability of assessment instruments in all assessment research [47].

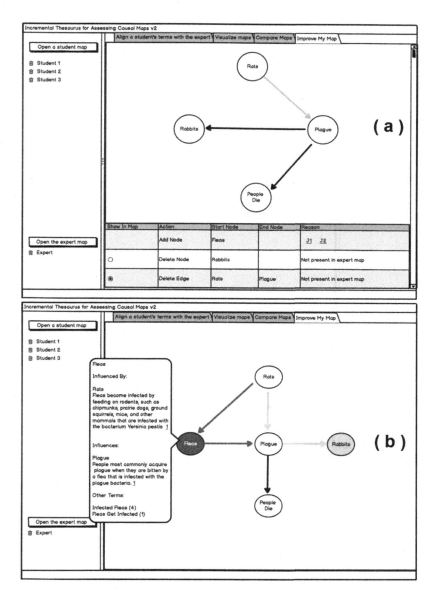

Fig. 2. In the top proposed wireframe (a), the user only sees the student map and the changes to make, summarized in tabular form. The map components involved in a proposed change can be highlighted by clicking the ratio button in the table and the justification appears via a modal window by clicking on the reason (e.g., J1, J2). An alternative wireframe (b) shows both the student and the expert's map, with missing nodes in red (i.e. present only in the expert's map) and extraneous nodes in blue (i.e. present only in the student's map). By hovering over blue or red components, a popover window appears to give contextual information. (Color figure online)

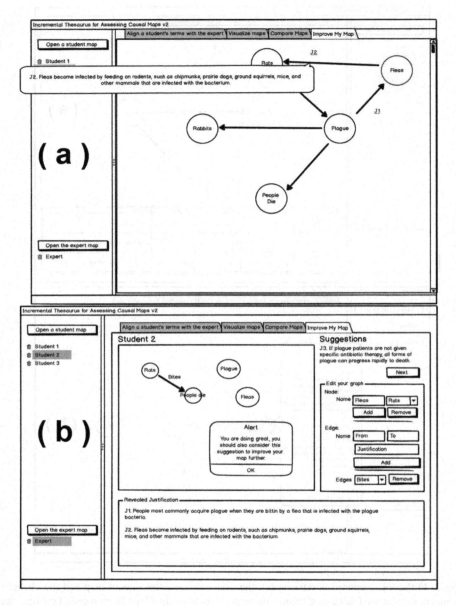

Fig. 3. In the top proposed wireframe (a), missing nodes from the student's map are shown in red and become green if added. By clicking on the explanation links, a modal window provides explanations. An alternative wireframe (b) emphasizes the order of suggestions, which are only revealed one at a time and summarized in the bottom window. For each suggestion, changes can be made to the map via a series of buttons, text fields, and drop-down menus. (Color figure online)

3.2 Design Process

Usability issues can arise when high-level functionalities of a software are immediately translated into an implementation. To provide a satisfying experience to users and avoid creating barriers through the software interface, it is necessary to first think about the target audience, how they will interact with the software to accomplish various tasks, and hence how to support the sequence of interactions that they may perform. We thus began the design process by identifying the intended users of the software and considering the key implications in interface design for those users. Although students submit maps to be evaluated, *the users of the software are instructors*. We cannot assume that the instructors have created the expert maps used for comparison, but we assume that they are familiar with concept maps in general. Our design also assumes that instructors decide how to convey the feedback to students, such that we are providing a tool to *support* instructors. Finally, we emphasize that the goal of the software is to provide automatic feedback, thus instructors would not need to go through the additional work of annotating the expert maps with justifications explaining the rationale for including specific structures.

With these considerations in mind, we started the process of sketching possible interfaces and the series of interactions that instructors would perform. In our research group, the standard practice is that several research assistants independently generate sketches [58].

The many ideas generated through this process are then discussed by the group to combine the strengths emerging from the different sketches. Four different visions are shown in Fig. 2(a–b) and 3(a–b). These different visions revealed the need to make design decisions regarding *(i)* the level of detail included in the feedback (step-by-step modification plan? display of discrepancies using color coding?), and *(ii)* the style of feedback provided (textual? graphical display?). We decided *against* providing an incremental feedback that forces the user to engage in a prescribed series of actions (Fig. 3b), of which only the most important would be revealed at a time. Although such rigid guidance can satisfy principle #5, our experience with previous software is that users do not like being locked in algorithmically-decided choices [59]. We thus chose to *organize* the information to favor continuity in changes rather than jumping across the map, but instructors ultimately judge which feedback items most effectively reinforce the learning outcomes they are working towards. We also considered that showing differences between the student's and expert's maps using colors (Fig. 2b) could provide useful guidance and that users should be able to access justifications in multiple ways, such as by clicking on the links in the table (Fig. 2a) or the links on the map (Fig. 3a).

To refine the design, we created a series of prototypes and gathered feedback on their usability. We began by only suggesting changes to a student map based on differences in the set of nodes or edges between the student map and the expert map. We then detected edges that were part of loops or alternative paths between concepts present in the expert's map, but missing from the student's. Each suggested change was justified with a set of reasons listed in the table, such as "The node 'concept 1' was present in the expert map" or "The edge between 'concept 1' and 'concept 2' would complete a loop present in the expert map." When multiple reasons were applicable, we listed all possible reasons. The feedback on our prototypes resulted in removing radio buttons

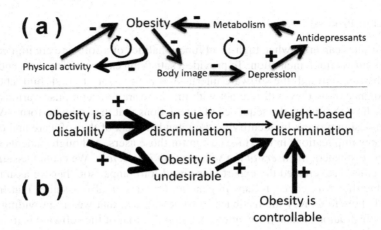

Fig. 4. Two potential feedback loops in obesity (a) include: a lowered physical fitness, which further fuels weight gain; a decrease in body image, with a potential for depression and the intake of antidepressants whose potential side effect includes weight gain. Two alternative paths connecting the legal recognition of 'obesity as a disability' to 'weight-based discrimination' (b) include: being able to sue for discrimination, hence make it dissuasive; increasing the popular belief that obesity is undesirable which, together with the belief that it is controllable, results in discrimination.

from the table and using a single color to highlight concepts/relationships involved in the suggested change selected by the user. We also added the ability to export the full list of feedback items to a CSV file and the ability to customize the feedback by controlling the algorithms detecting loops or alternative paths. These algorithms are detailed in the next sub-section.

3.3 Implementation

As the codebase reuses ITACM v2, we refer the reader to the details of this implementation for the client/server architecture, network and visualization libraries [6]. The two algorithms introduced in the software discussed here serve to find alternative paths and cycles. In graph theory, the former is known as *disjoint path detection* and the latter is about *enumerating all cycles*. Both problems have been studied for decades, resulting in several algorithms. Since concept maps are relatively small networks (unlike e.g. Twitter or Facebook datasets), we do not need to use approximation algorithms or solutions that leverage parallel and distributed computing. We thus rely on foundational algorithms for both problems. We implemented disjoint path detection, using both an edge-disjoint path detection algorithm and a node-disjoint path detection algorithm. The node-disjoint path detection algorithm was based on a transformation scheme outlined in Suurballe's 1974 paper [60]. To enumerate cycles, we use the method introduced in 1975 by Johnson [61].

Instructors may decide that students ought to represent short loops while being more lenient on the inclusion of longer loops. For example, it is relatively straightforward

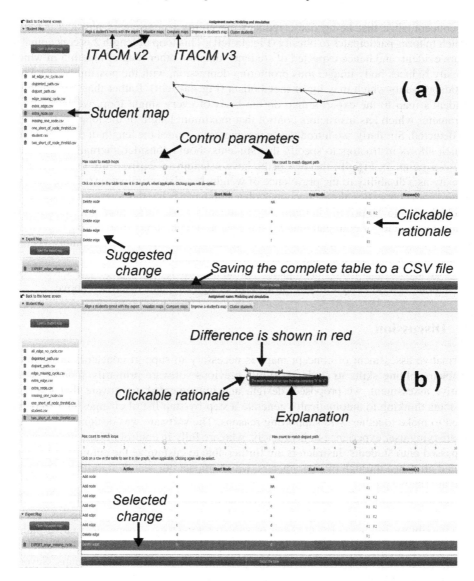

Fig. 5. Our implementation uses a table to summarize the changes that would transform the student's map into the expert's map. The content of the table depends on two parameters (maximum length of loops and alternative paths). Upon selecting a specific change to make (b), the corresponding part of the map is highlighted in red and the reason(s) for the change are also available next to the highlight. Clicking on a reason either next to the map or in the table will open a window with an automatically generated explanation. *This high resolution figure can be zoomed in using the digital version of the article.* (Color figure online)

to conceptualize that being obese reduces the ability to engage in physical activity, which in turns participates to obesity (Fig. 4a-left). This loop of length 2 is conceptually more evident, and hence expected of students, than the other loop of length 5 in which obesity reduces body image, thus promoting depression, with the possibility of taking antidepressants which may lower metabolism (Fig. 4a-right). Rather than comparing a student's map to the expert's map on the basis of every single loop, we introduce a parameter which lets instructors control that maximum length of the loops that should be detected. Similarly, we introduced a parameter to control the length of disjoint paths, which allows instructors to specify that students should consider alternatives but only up to a point. In Fig. 4b, the two paths have a length of 2 (from the legal status of obesity as a disability to the prevalence of weight-based discrimination). There may be a third path connecting these concepts with a length of 15, but this alternative may be far fetched and a lower priority in improving a student's work. Instructors can conveniently change the values of both parameters on the same screen, rather than having to locate a panel for settings. The effect of a change in parameters' values is immediately visible, as the table of suggested changes is refreshed accordingly.

Two screenshots from our implementation are provided in Fig. 5. The screenshots are annotated to identify some of the specific design elements discussed above.

4   Discussion

Formative assessment of concept maps is necessary to support educators in teaching problem-solving skills to students. While previous software primarily supports summative assessment, we proposed, design, and implemented a software that leverage systems thinking to automatically generate a step-by-step list of changes that students need to make together with supporting reasons. The software was designed to provide a satisfying user experience to instructors, who are fully in control of how the guidance is passed onto students. Instructors are further able to customize the automatically generated guidance through two parameters, which impact our search algorithms for loops and alternative paths.

In this section, we focus on three potential avenues for future work. First, our software is the first to generate feedback entirely automatically while giving instructors the possibility to customize the type of sub-structures (e.g., loops, alternative paths) that they seek to promote in their students' maps. This opens a new line of research in the parametrization of algorithms for formative assessment of concept maps. Several questions within this line of inquiry are as follows. Which sub-structures of a causal map would indicate higher levels of systems thinking or better mastery of domain-related knowledge? For instance, it is possible that certain network motifs [62] or network structures (e.g., a star in which one factor is influencing/influenced by many non-interacting factors) need to be promoted or flagged as potential issues. Which parameters would allow instructors to specify that they seek such structures along a continuum? In this paper, we used a parameter to control the length of alternative paths, but it is possible that a better control parameter would be how much *longer* a path should be compared to the shortest one (e.g., if the shortest explanation from a factor to another is of length 2 then should a student be required to think of an alternative of length 6?).

Can each parameter be set independently or should a change in one parameter automatically impact the range of possible values in another? As instructors are assumed to be familiar with concept maps without being experts in graph algorithms, how can we continue to support usability while providing the customization of increasingly complex algorithms?

Second, as research in recommender systems has shown, automatically generating an advice does not mean that it will be followed, even if it would have been highly likely to benefit the individual. Explanations need to be transparent and convincing. This is less of a concern for low-level explanations such as 'you should include this factor because the expert has it', but it applies for high-level rationales that involve several successive changes such as 'you need to add these four links to finish a loop'. Further experimental studies are thus needed to examine the impact of several approaches to explain the changes and organize them.

Finally, we note that the historical divide between elicitation tools on the one hand (e.g., MentalModeler [63]) and analysis tools on the other hand (e.g., ActionableSystems [20], Gephi) is starting to disappear as newer software provide both extended analytical and map-building capabilities (e.g., our artificial facilitator [31], STICKE [44]). It would thus be of interest to design, implement, and evaluate a system in which students can create their maps while receiving automated feedback to the extent desired by the instructor. We also envision that instructors should be able to set milestones for evaluation in such a system, such that it can be adopted as part of classroom activities or assignments.

Contributions

This study was jointly initiated by PJG and AAT. The manuscript was written by PJG and the software development was directed by PJG. Feedback on the design and prototypes was provided by AAT.

Acknowledgment. The authors are indebted to Vishrant Gupta, who implemented the software as research assistant to PJG. The authors have reused parts of an internal report by Russell Lankenau (under the supervision of PJG) in Sects. 2.3 and 3.2. The authors thank the Department of Computer Science & Software Engineering at Miami University for supporting publication costs.

References

1. Jonassen, D.H.: Toward a design theory of problem solving. Educ. Technol. Res. Dev. **48**(4), 63–85 (2000)
2. Pirnay-Dummer, P., Ifenthaler, D., Spector, J.M.: Highly integrated model assessment technology and tools. Educ. Technol. Res. Dev. **58**(1), 3–18 (2010)
3. Ifenthaler, D.: Relational, structural, and semantic analysis of graphical representations and concept maps. Educ. Technol. Res. Dev. **58**(1), 81–97 (2010)
4. Ifenthaler, D.: Akovia: automated knowledge visualization and assessment. Technol. Knowl. Learn. **19**(1–2), 241–248 (2014)
5. Kim, K.: Graphical interface of knowledge structure: a web-based research tool for representing knowledge structure in text. Technol. Knowl. Learn. **24**(1), 89–95 (2019)

6. Gupta, V.K., Giabbanelli, P.J., Tawfik, A.A.: An online environment to compare students' and expert solutions to ill-structured problems. In: Zaphiris, P., Ioannou, A. (eds.) LCT 2018. LNCS, vol. 10925, pp. 286–307. Springer, Cham (2018). https://doi.org/10.1007/978-3-319-91152-6_23

7. Giabbanelli, P.J., Tawfik, A.A., Gupta, V.K.: Learning analytics to support teachers' assessment of problem solving: a novel application for machine learning and graph algorithms. In: Ifenthaler, D., Mah, D.-K., Yau, J.Y.-K. (eds.) Utilizing Learning Analytics to Support Study Success, pp. 175–199. Springer, Cham (2019). https://doi.org/10.1007/978-3-319-64792-0_11

8. Ifenthaler, D., Gibson, D., Dobozy, E.: Informing learning design through analytics: applying network graph analysis. Australas. J. Educ. Technol. **34**(2) (2018)

9. Senocak, E.: Development of an instrument for assessing undergraduate science students' perceptions: the problem-based learning environment inventory. J. Sci. Educ. Technol. **18**(6), 560–569 (2009)

10. Savin-Baden, M.: Understanding the impact of assessment on students in problem-based learning. Innov. Educ. Teach. Int. **41**(2), 221–233 (2004)

11. Wu, P.H., et al.: An innovative concept map approach for improving students' learning performance with an instant feedback mechanism. Br. J. Educ. Technol. **43**(2), 217–232 (2012)

12. Epstein, J.M.: Why model? J. Artif. Soc. Soc. Simul. **11**(4), 12 (2008)

13. Voinov, A., et al.: Tools and methods in participatory modeling: selecting the right tool for the job. Environ. Model. Softw. **109**, 232–255 (2018)

14. Ho, V., Kumar, R.K., Velan, G.: Online testable concept maps: benefits for learning about the pathogenesis of disease. Med. Educ. **48**(7), 687–697 (2014)

15. Trumpower, D.L., Vanapalli, A.S.: Structural assessment of knowledge as, of, and for learning. In: Learning, Design, and Technology, pp. 1–22 (2016). https://doi.org/10.1007/978-3-319-17727-4_23-1

16. Jebb, S., Kopelman, P., Butland, B.: Executive summary: foresight 'tackling obesities: future choices' project. Obes. Rev. **8**, 6–9 (2007)

17. Finegood, D.T., Merth, T.D., Rutter, H.: Implications of the foresight obesity system map for solutions to childhood obesity. Obesity **18**(S1), S13–S16 (2010)

18. Drasic, L., Giabbanelli, P.J.: Exploring the interactions between physical well-being, and obesity. Can. J. Diab. **39**, S12–S13 (2015)

19. Giabbanelli, P., et al.: developing technology to support policymakers in taking a systems science approach to obesity and well-being. Obes. Rev. **17**, 194–195 (2016)

20. Giabbanelli, P.J., Baniukiewicz, M.: Navigating complex systems for policymaking using simple software tools. In: Giabbanelli, P.J., Mago, V.K., Papageorgiou, E.I. (eds.) Advanced Data Analytics in Health. SIST, vol. 93, pp. 21–40. Springer, Cham (2018). https://doi.org/10.1007/978-3-319-77911-9_2

21. Allender, S., et al.: A community based systems diagram of obesity causes. PLoS One **10**(7), e0129683 (2015)

22. McGlashan, J., et al.: Comparing complex perspectives on obesity drivers: action-driven communities and evidence-oriented experts. Obes. Sci. Pract. **4**(6), 575–581 (2018)

23. Knapp, E.A., et al.: A network approach to understanding obesogenic environments for children in Pennsylvania. Connections **38**(1), 1–11 (2018)

24. Gerritsen, S., et al.: Systemic barriers and equitable interventions to improve vegetable and fruit intake in children: interviews with national food system actors. Int. J. Environ. Res. Public Health **16**(8), 1387 (2019)

25. Meadows, D.H.: Leverage points: Places to intervene in a system (1999)

26. McGlashan, J., et al.: Quantifying a systems map: network analysis of a childhood obesity causal loop diagram. PloS One **11**(10), e0165459 (2016)

27. Owen, B., et al.: Understanding a successful obesity prevention initiative in children under 5 from a systems perspective. PloS One **13**(3), e0195141 (2018)
28. Rwashana, A.S., et al.: Advancing the application of systems thinking in health: understanding the dynamics of neonatal mortality in uganda. Health Res. Policy Syst. **12**(1), 36 (2014)
29. Axelrod, R.: Structure of Decision: The Cognitive Maps of Political Elites. Princeton University Press (Legacy Library) (2015)
30. Vennix, J.: Group Model Building : Facilitating Team Learning Using System Dynamics. Wiley (1996)
31. Reddy, T., Giabbanelli, P.J., Mago, V.K.: The artificial facilitator: guiding participants in developing causal maps using voice-activated technologies. In: Schmorrow, D.D., Fidopiastis, C.M. (eds.) HCII 2019. LNCS (LNAI), vol. 11580, pp. 111–129. Springer, Cham (2019). https://doi.org/10.1007/978-3-030-22419-6_9
32. Gray, S., et al.: The structure and function of angler mental models about fish population ecology: the influence of specialization and target species. J. Outdoor Recreation Tourism **12**, 1–13 (2015)
33. Rahimi, N., Jetter, A.J., Weber, C.M., Wild, K.: Soft data analytics with fuzzy cognitive maps: modeling health technology adoption by elderly women. In: Giabbanelli, P.J., Mago, V.K., Papageorgiou, E.I. (eds.) Advanced Data Analytics in Health. SIST, vol. 93, pp. 59–74. Springer, Cham (2018). https://doi.org/10.1007/978-3-319-77911-9_4
34. Firmansyah, H.S., et al.: Identifying the components and interrelationships of smart cities in indonesia: supporting policymaking via fuzzy cognitive systems. IEEE Access **7**, 46136–46151 (2019)
35. Gerritsen, S., et al.: Improving low fruit and vegetable intake in children: findings from a system dynamics, community group model building study. PloS One **14**(8), e0221107 (2019)
36. Verigin, T., Giabbanelli, P.J., Davidsen, P.I.: Supporting a systems approach to healthy weight interventions in British Columbia by modeling weight and well-being. In: Proceedings of the 49th Annual Simulation Symposium, Society for Computer Simulation International, p. 9 (2016)
37. Sandhu, M., et al.: From associations to sarcasm: mining the shift of opinions regarding the supreme court on twitter. Online Soc. Netw. Med. **14**, 100054 (2019)
38. Sandhu, M., Giabbanelli, P.J., Mago, V.K.: From social media to expert reports: the impact of source selection on automatically validating complex conceptual models of obesity. In: Meiselwitz, G. (ed.) HCII 2019. LNCS, vol. 11578, pp. 434–452. Springer, Cham (2019). https://doi.org/10.1007/978-3-030-21902-4_31
39. Pillutla, V.S., Giabbanelli, P.J.: Iterative generation of insight from text collections through mutually reinforcing visualizations and fuzzy cognitive maps. Appl. Soft Comput. **76**, 459–472 (2019)
40. Bensberg, M., Allender, S., Sacks, G.: Building a systems thinking prevention workforce. Health Promot. J. Aust. (2020)
41. Aminpour, P., et al.: Is the crowd wise enough to capture systems complexities? an exploration of wisdom of crowds using fuzzy cognitive maps. In: 9th International Congress on Environmental Modelling and Software (iEMSs) (2018)
42. Giles, B.G., Haas, G., Findlay, C.: Comparing aboriginal and western science perspectives of the causes of diabetes using fuzzy cognitive maps (2005)
43. Giabbanelli, P.J., Tawfik, A.A.: Overcoming the pbl assessment challenge: design and development of the incremental thesaurus for assessing causal maps (itacm). Technol. Knowl. Learn. **24**(2), 161–168 (2019)
44. Hayward, J., et al.: Tools and analytic techniques to synthesise community knowledge in CBPR using computer-mediated participatory system modelling. NPJ Digit. Med. **3**(1), 1–6 (2020)

45. Lavin, E.A., et al.: Should we simulate mental models to assess whether they agree? In: Proceedings of the Annual Simulation Symposium, Society for Computer Simulation International, p. 6 (2018)
46. McClure, J.R., Sonak, B., Suen, H.K.: Concept map assessment of classroom learning: reliability, validity, and logistical practicality. J. Res. Sci. Teach.: Official J. Natl. Assoc. Res. Sci. Teach. 36(4), 475–492 (1999)
47. Weinerth, K., Koenig, V., Brunner, M., Martin, R.: Concept maps: a useful and usable tool for computer-based knowledge assessment? A literature review with a focus on usability. Comput. Educ. 78, 201–209 (2014)
48. Cox, M., Steegen, A., Elen, J.: Using causal diagrams to foster systems thinking in geography education. Int. J. Des. Learn. 9(1), 34–48 (2018)
49. Krabbe, H.: Digital concept mapping for formative assessment. In: Ifenthaler, D., Hanewald, R. (eds.) Digital Knowledge Maps in Education, pp. 275–297. Springer, New York (2014). https://doi.org/10.1007/978-1-4614-3178-7_15
50. Bhagat, K.K., Spector, J.M.: Formative assessment in complex problem-solving domains: the emerging role of assessment technologies. J. Educ. Technol. Soc. 20(4), 312–317 (2017)
51. Curtis, M.B., Davis, M.A.: Assessing knowledge structure in accounting education: an application of pathfinder associative networks. J. Acc. Educ. 21(3), 185–195 (2003)
52. Kotovsky, K., Hayes, J.R., Simon, H.A.: Why are some problems hard? Evidence from tower of hanoi. Cognit. Psychol. 17(2), 248–294 (1985)
53. Jeong, A.: Sequentially analyzing and modeling causal mapping processes that support causal understanding and Systems Thinking. In: Ifenthaler, D., Hanewald, R. (eds.) Digital Knowledge Maps in Education, pp. 239–251. Springer, New York (2014). https://doi.org/10.1007/978-1-4614-3178-7_13
54. Hmelo-Silver, C.E., Pfeffer, M.G.: Comparing expert and novice understanding of a complex system from the perspective of structures, behaviors, and functions. Cognit. Sci. 28(1), 127–138 (2004)
55. Gray, S., et al.: Assessing (social-ecological) systems thinking by evaluating cognitive maps. Sustainability 11(20), 5753 (2019)
56. Sarwar, G.S., Trumpower, D.L.: Effects of conceptual, procedural, and declarative reflection on students' structural knowledge in physics. Educ. Technol. Res. Dev. 63(2), 185–201 (2015)
57. Jonassen, D.H., Hung, W.: All problems are not equal: Implications for problem-based learning. Essential readings in problem-based learning, pp. 7–41 (2015)
58. Giabbanelli, P., Fattoruso, M., Norman, M.L.: Cofluences: simulating the spread of social influences via a hybrid agent-based/fuzzy cognitive maps architecture. In: Proceedings of the 2019 ACM SIGSIM Conference on Principles of Advanced Discrete Simulation, pp. 71–82 (2019)
59. Giabbanelli, P.J.: Modelling the spatial and social dynamics of insurgency. Secur. Inform. 3(1), 2 (2014)
60. Suurballe, J.: Disjoint paths in a network. Networks 4(2), 125–145 (1974)
61. Johnson, D.B.: Finding all the elementary circuits of a directed graph. SIAM J. Comput. 4(1), 77–84 (1975)
62. Milo, R., et al.: Network motifs: simple building blocks of complex networks. Science 298(5594), 824–827 (2002)
63. Gray, S.A., et al.: Mental modeler: a fuzzy-logic cognitive mapping modeling tool for adaptive environmental management. In: 2013 46th Hawaii International Conference on System Sciences, pp. 965–973. IEEE (2013)

A Learning Engineering Model
for Learner-Centered Adaptive Systems

Jim Goodell[1]([✉]) and Khanh-Phuong (KP) Thai[2]([✉])

[1] Quality Information Partners, Fairfax, VA 22038, USA
jimgoodell@qi-partners.com
[2] Age of Learning, Inc., Glendale, CA 91203, USA
kpthai@gmail.com

Abstract. Multiple academic and industry-based communities have engaged in defining the theoretical constructs, practical approaches, and technical standards for technology-enabled systems of human learning. However, conceptual and architectural models of Adaptive Instructional Systems (AISs) often focus on the functions of the technology, with the learner as a user external to the system. We offer an AIS model that considers the learner as a key component at the heart of a learning system. The learner, along with other human actors and environmental conditions, interact with technology components in a distributed learning system. Modular components surrounding the learner are interoperable. Data flow between the components using standards-based interfaces for instrumented and adaptive learner experiences. The model builds on functional components identified by Glowa & Goodell (2016) in *Student-Centered Learning: Functional Requirements for Integrated Systems to Optimize Learning*. The model is further informed by the IEEE workgroup P2247.1 developing a standard for the classification of adaptive instructional systems. It examines the learning system at a conceptual level and then maps those conceptual categories to functional components as modules in a distributed learning system. The model is rooted in the process of learning engineering as defined by the IEEE Industry Connection Industry Consortium on Learning Engineering (ICICLE). We envision future design and development of adaptive instructional systems benefiting from an emerging learning engineering discipline that embraces an iterative problem-solving approach. The proposed AIS model is a self-improving system by design that embodies key learning engineering processes.

Keywords: Learning engineering · Learning sciences · Adaptive learning · Student-Centered · Instructional system · IEEE AIS · GIFT · KLI · HCI · iNACOL · Learner model · Adaptive model · Knowledge model

1 Introduction

Adaptive instructional systems (AISs) are artificially-intelligent, computer-based systems that guide learning experiences by tailoring instruction and recommendations based

© Springer Nature Switzerland AG 2020
C. Stephanidis et al. (Eds.): HCII 2020, LNCS 12425, pp. 557–573, 2020.
https://doi.org/10.1007/978-3-030-60128-7_41

on the goals, needs, preferences, and interests of each individual learner or team in the context of domain learning objectives [1]. Multiple academic and industry-based communities have engaged in defining the theoretical constructs, practical approaches, and technical standards for AISs for human learning. Currently several workgroups within the IEEE Learning Technology Standards Committee are developing standards for the Adaptive Instructional System (AIS) informed by prior research-based frameworks such as the Generalized Intelligent Framework for Tutoring [2] and Knowledge-Learning Instruction Framework [3]. A consortium within the IEEE standards organization (ICICLE) is defining and developing Learning Engineering as a profession and as an academic discipline. Rapidly developing innovations in artificial intelligence, virtual/augmented reality, social learning platforms, instrumented learning experiences, and mobile/place-based learning are creating new opportunities to leverage technology to optimize human learning. Meanwhile, learning sciences findings continue to expand what we know about how people learn.

The offered model begins with the notion that the learner is a core component of the AIS. The academic discipline of human-computer interaction recognizes human actors as a part of a system. However, conceptual and architectural models of AISs often focus on the functions of the technology, with the learner as a user external to the system. In many models only a proxy of the learner (the learner model) is considered part of the system. The offered model considers the role of the human learner and physical/perceptual environment as well as the digital twin representations of the real agent and environment.

The offered model is also informed by the emerging field of learning engineering. It offers mindsets, processes, and practices for those designing and developing AISs that may translate into new approaches to design decisions.

We start with the learner component at the center of the AIS design. Like other development models the learner needs drive design decisions, and like other models we begin with a prototype of the learner and learner context to set the purpose and goals for the system, and to consider what problems need to be solved. The design builds outward from the learner component, considering the requirements for interoperation of the learner and other system components.

2   Learner-Centered Adaptive Feedback

The system design is guided by the requirements for interactions between the learner and other components via human-computer interfaces, inputs from and about the learner, and feedback to the learner from the other system components. "Feedback" here is broadly defined to include recommendations, visualizations, system prompts, adaptations to the user interface (e.g. menu choices offered), and adaptations to learning experiences. The quality of the feedback generated by system components (e.g. a human or AI agent) depends on a current and accurate understanding of the learner.

The learner-centered adaptive system may give feedback to the learner at multiple levels:

- Progress level (hyper-adaptive)—feedback on where a learner is in relation to long-term learning goals, such as progress toward award of a credential, qualification for a job, or level of mastery in a domain
- Lesson level (macro-adaptive)—feedback or adaptation between learning experiences that helps inform what the learner does next, e.g. recommending an instructional strategy or learning experience
- Activity level (micro-adaptive)—formative feedback or adaptation during a learning experience.

Park and Lee (2003) consider Aptitude Treatment Interactions (ATI) as a separate class of adaptive instructional approach, although it could be argued that the treatments here could be at the micro-adaptive or macro-adaptive levels. The ATI approach considers learner aptitudes (learner characteristics or environmental conditions that increase or impair the probability that a given treatment will result in student learning) and treatments (variations in the pace or style of instruction). According to Park and Lee (2003) "since Cronbach (1957) made his proposal, relatively few studies have found consistent results to support the paradigm or made a notable contribution to either instructional theory or practice." However, some of the ATI research provides valuable insights into the variety of aptitude variables that might be used as inputs into adaptation decisions made by

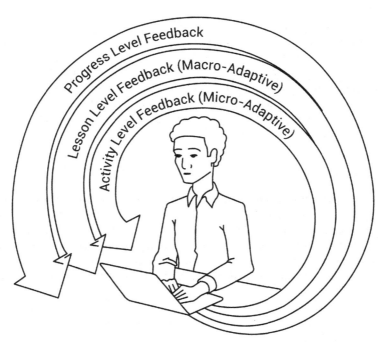

Fig. 1. Levels of Feedback. From Glowa, L. and Goodell, J. (2016) Student-Centered Learning: Functional Requirements for Integrated Systems to Optimize Learning, Vienna, VA.: International Association for K-12 Online Learning (iNACOL). Adapted with permission.

AISs, and into the variety of treatments (instructional strategies and conditions) that might be adapted to the learner's needs based on those inputs.

3 Conceptual Model of an Adaptive Instructional System

According to the AIS Ontology Workgroup [4], an AIS may be conceptualized as a combination of four models: (1) learner models, (2) knowledge models, (3) adaptive models, and (4) interface models (see also Murray, 1999; Sottilare & Brawner, 2018; Woolf, 2010; Nkambou, Mizoguchi & Bourdeau, 2010).

3.1 The Learner Model

The **learner model** (implemented with data architecture) is a structured representation of a learner's knowledge, abilities, dispositions, habits of practice, misconceptions, difficulties, and/or other learner attributes that evolve during the course of learning. Details such as the learner's background knowledge, prior experiences, cultural values, and learning contexts have an impact on what feedback will be most effective at any given moment.

The learner model may function as an imperfect "digital twin" of the learner. It is imperfect because the mind of a learner is not directly observable and the scope of data in any system will be limited. However, along with observable event data the learner model may include predictions or assertions about unobservable characteristics of the learner that have been inferred from observable event data.

Learning technology may handle learner data in different ways and in both structured and unstructured formats, with more or fewer links to contextual information. The learner model may use a federated data approach that uses data across multiple physical system components. The learner model has interdependencies with other system components and with other systems in the ecosystem.

3.2 The Domain Model

The **domain model** (implemented as information repositories) is a fundamental element of an AIS that contains the set of skills, knowledge, and strategies/tactics of the topic under instruction. It normally contains the ideal learner or expert knowledge model for the domain of instruction, along with question banks, common bugs, mal-rules, misconceptions, and content. The domain model includes data, metadata, and learning resources, and maps the relationships between those things. Such content and relationships include

- competency frameworks,
- competency pathways,
- pedagogical models,
- adaptive strategies,
- lesson definitions,
- activity definitions,
- learning resources (static or interactive content),

- knowledge maps,
- rubrics,
- assessment activities,
- metadata, and
- paradata to support adaptations, weighting, decision-making.

Information from the domain model and learner model are inputs into the adaptive model.

3.3 The Adaptive Model

The **adaptive model** (implemented as adaptive engines) represents the decision-making and control functions of the adaptive system. The adaptive model uses data from the learner model and the domain model as input, informs decisions about what strategies, steps, and actions the AIS should do next, and triggers feedback events. In mix-initiative systems, the learners may also take actions, ask questions, or request help (Aleven, McClaren, Roll & Koedinger, 2006; Rus & Graesser, 2009), but the AIS must be able to decide next steps, which is determined by the adaptive model that is driven by pedagogical theories.

These three models (learner model, domain model, and adaptive model) represent the theoretical/conceptual components in an adaptive instructional system (Knowles, et al.; *Draft Standard for the Classification of Adaptive Instructional Systems*). A physical implementation of an AIS may have many more components that address specific functions of the system.

Adaptive learning systems employ data-informed adaptations of learning experiences and conditions for learning. The workgroup for the IEEE AIS Standard for the Classification of Adaptive Instructional Systems has identified "levels of adaptivity" for AISs. At the highest level are systems that are self-improving.

This paper examines the concept of a self-improving system in three contexts:
the learner as a key component of an AIS

1. the AIS technology and information architectures
2. the AIS engineering team

3.4 The Interface Model

The user **interface model** (implemented as human-computer interfaces and machine-machine interfaces including application programming interfaces) is a representation of how a human user or another system component interacts with a component of the system, and how the system component responds. It interprets the learner's input (e.g. speech, typing, clicking) and produces outputs (e.g. text, diagrams, animations, agents). In addition to the conventional human-computer interface features, recent systems have incorporated natural language interaction (e.g. Graesser et al. 2012), speech recognition (e.g. Litman 2013), and the sensing of learner emotions (e.g. Baker, D'Mello, Rodrigo, & Graesser, 2010; Goldberg, Sottilare, Brawner, Holden, 2011).

Interface models may be further classified based on whether the interface represented is between a human and the system components or between system/software modules.

- Human-computer Interface Model—a representation of how human user(s) interact with a computer program or another device and how the system responds.
- An Application Programming Interface (API) Model—a representation of how other system components get access to specific information, to trigger special behavior, or to perform some other action in a component of the system. (See: https://www.w3.org/2008/webapps/).

4   Learning Engineering

Given the enormous complexities, trade-offs, and uncertainties associated with learning in real-world learning contexts (Koedinger, Booth, & Klahr, 2013), building effective AISs is difficult. This issue is often magnified with scale. Scale arises from not only the number and diversity of learners, but also the variability of time and space for learning opportunities, the resulting rich data about learner engagement and performance, the mass personalization (Schuwer & Kusters, 2014) of learners and learner groups, and the way in which our pedagogy must adapt to these needs (Roll, Russell, Gasevic, 2018). All of these must be taken into account as technologies, pedagogies, research and analyses, and theories of learning and teaching are combined to design effective learning interactions and experiences. Growing learning engineering efforts are beginning to shed light into the processes that help us figure out what works in AISs to promote learning, why it works, and how to scale what works.

Learning engineering is "a process and practice that applies the learning sciences, using human-centered engineering design methodologies, and data-informed decision-making to support learners and their development" [5]. Learning engineering applies the learning sciences—informed by cognitive psychology, neuroscience, and education research (Wilcox, Sarma, Lippel, 2016)—and engineering principles to create and iteratively improve learning experiences for learners. It leverages human-centered design to guide design choices that promote robust student learning, but also emphasizes the use of data to inform iterative design, development, and improvement process. In the following subsections, we provide examples of ways in which learner needs drive the design decisions within each aspect of the learning engineering process and practice.

4.1   The Learning Engineering Process and Practice

The Generalized Intelligent Framework for Tutoring [2], the Knowledge-Learning Instruction Framework [3], and similar efforts such as ASSISTments as an open platform for research [6] are excellent examples of learning engineering in practice. The GIFT testbed methodology supports the manipulation of the learner model, instructional strategies, and domain-specific knowledge, and enables empirical evaluation of the effects of environmental attributes, tools, models, and methods on student learning, engagement, and transfer of skills within [7]. The KLI framework advocates for in-vivo experimentation, which enables rigorous experimental controls in real learning settings with real students. Such frameworks have led to important understandings of what works and why, and as a result, has led to robust learning gains (e.g., [8, 9]).

Effective learning requires the integration of research across different fields that impact learning. The learning engineering process enables data-informed decision-making through development cycles that include learning sciences, design-based research, and learning analytics/educational data mining. It leverages advances from different fields including learning sciences, design research, curriculum research, game design, data sciences, and computer science. It thus provides a social-technical infrastructure to support iterative learning engineering and practice-relevant theory for scaling learning sciences through design research, deep content analytics, and iterative product improvements.

Figure 1 illustrates a learning engineering process for the design and development of an AIS. Product decisions across human-centered design and dissemination in this process may vary in method, but still follow similar patterns of questioning, generating or accessing data, data interpretation, and application of key learnings (Fig. 2).

The process starts with *decisions or hypotheses*. Decisions include product design, experience design, and learning design. An example of a hypothesis could be, "If using design *x*, the response will be *y*." From this point, areas of information needs emerged. To create an AIS that is successful in terms of learning goals, engagement, and market viability, teams should answer questions, such as, "to what extent are product/learning assumptions true?" or "what is the behavioral response to the interaction design?" These become the *research questions* that drive a focused *research design* toward data gathering and meaning-making.

Learners use AISs. A learner-centered approach requires production teams to have a complete (or as close to complete as possible) view of the learner, their motivation, and their learning environments. It is through *user activity* that *data* are generated. Data can be observational, behavioral, sentiment, and analytic, and are gathered and understood through a variety of analytical methods. By way of these *methods and analytic approaches*, researchers make sense of *findings*, and together with product owners and designers, derive *insights* to inform design improvements and contribute to the broader research corpus.

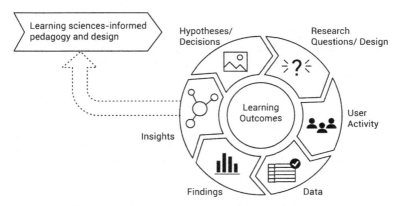

Fig. 2. The learning engineering process. From [10].

4.2 Applications of Learning Sciences

The learning engineering process starts with the application of learning sciences to inform the pedagogy and design for learning and engagement. We refer to learning sciences in broad definition by the International Society of the Learning Sciences as research that involves the "empirical investigation of learning as it happens in real-world settings" [11] Learning sciences research is interdisciplinary and includes scholarship from areas like cognitive science, educational psychology, curricular studies, and design research. In the learning engineering process, learning sciences research is mapped to stages of design, from curriculum to immersion and interaction design, and to overall system design and final product development and implementation with considerations of evidence and data collection [12]. In relation to adaptive design, important methodological extensions of learning sciences such as user-centered design research, game-based learning design, learning analytics, and educational data mining [13, 14] also become relevant as part of a paradigm of data-informed AISs. As such, learning sciences applications are present at all stages of the learning engineering process [13].

At the start of the design and development process, the fundamental question in learning design is to clearly define what is being taught. Educational research in curricular design investigates methodology in this area, with the establishment of learning trajectories [15]—including fundamental components of fine-grained, measurable learning objectives and pathways embedding formative assessment for differentiated instruction. In application to foundational mathematics skills, for instance, the design of learning trajectories informs an approach and a specified ontology of core mathematics learning objectives in the program Building Blocks, a mathematics curriculum designed using a comprehensive Curriculum Research Framework to address numeric and geometric ideas [16].

Building on defining competencies and learning objectives, learning science research can inform the core design of learning experiences. This can be done in numerous ways.

In game-based and immersive learning contexts, for example, evidence-based design frameworks serve to fundamentally connect learning objectives with specific digital interactions designed to elicit evidence of learner knowledge, skills, or abilities (e.g. Evidence Centered Design, [17]. This alignment allows insight into student learning through real-time interaction with a virtual space, thus providing ongoing performance data that enable formative feedback and personalized learning pathways. This gives way to authentic assessment and player immersion, which is vital for reaching learners in both formal and informal learning environments [18].

Learning science can also support learning design by using research in human cognition and development to support long-term learning of target competencies. For example, desirable difficulties [19] such as retrieval practice [20], interleaving [21], and distributed practice [22] can be built into an adaptive system to support long-term memory. Applications of perceptual learning principles can be used to support the development of perceptual expertise (e.g., [23]). Concreteness fading principles can be used to promote conceptual transfer [24].

In data-centric phases of the learning engineering process, methodological extensions of learning sciences such as learning analytics and educational data mining [14] can guide design improvements for better learning and engagement (more in Sect. 4.4).

Learning sciences approaches can inform research questions, analyses, interpretation of results, and derive insights for design improvements [25]. Resulting insights can enable intelligent personalization of the system, inform iterative data-driven design of core activities and mechanics, and allow for real-time visualization of learner progress.

4.3 Human-Centered Engineering Design Methodologies

Achieving learning and engagement goals requires a deep knowledge of the end user. This is where human-centered engineering design processes are critical. Consider design researchers in a learning engineering team regularly recruiting children and parents to playtest early production prototypes, investigating the ways young children demonstrate their problem-solving and meaning-making through proposed playful interactions. Data from such user testing sessions can drive the concrete interactions, user interface, and user experience design for each learning experience, all of which are sensitive to the cognitive load, executive functioning skills, etc. that are appropriate for the learners' cognitive and development stages. This is particularly crucial for young learners, for whom the interaction needs are difficult to calibrate in initial design iterations.

Design research outcomes support the blending of pedagogical and engagement goals by pointing to actionable insights that allow teams to make informed design decisions through product development cycles. From this perspective, educational design research is *embedded in* and *integral to* the design work itself [26, 27] is grounded in *empathy*, beginning with the needs and perspectives of the people being designed for [28] is interested in discovering how and why people behave the way they do, and what opportunities may exist for new innovation; and highlights starting points for the design of *meaningful interactions*, which sit at the core of well-designed environments for teaching and learning [29].

4.4 Data-Informed Decision Making

With large numbers of diverse learners engaging with content, the extensive detailed trace data about learner engagement and performance from AISs allow for better understanding of how learning unfolds, and permit experimentation of different analytical methodologies and approaches (such as learning analytics and educational data mining), and of content with rapid design and evaluation cycles (e.g. [14]). This means we can know more about how learners with different attributes engage and learn, and thus can differentiate educational experiences that match learners' skills, goals, interests, and background [30]. A learning engineering approach takes each of these elements into account to work for products at scale.

An AIS with rich event-stream data, enabled by the integration of research-based design phases, supports the application of a large range of methods in learning analytics and educational data mining to drive learning insights and design iterations. Learner performance data can be surfaced on dashboard visualizations as feedback for students, parents, and teachers to monitor and provide additional individual learning support. Event-stream data of learner progress also supports efficacy research to evaluate learning outcomes. For example, in educational data mining efforts for learning design and better personalization, behavior detection methods were recently used to build a predictor tracking when students are "wheel-spinning" in ABCmouse Mastering Math, an AIS designed to promote early number sense in children ages 2–8. Wheel-spinning students are those who are spending too much time struggling to learn a topic without achieving mastery, a form of unproductive persistence [31] versus those who are productively persistent [32]. In detecting wheel-spinning in real-time, AISs can better respond to students who need support, and surface these insights to educators for additional in-person intervention. This also enables the design of dashboards summarizing learning objective mastery. Insights from these efforts can also inform pedagogical understanding and informed design for deeper learning and engagement.

Learning engineering iteration cycles can impact learning outcomes at large not just by feeding insights into new product decisions, but by also sharing learnings back into the broader academic community of learning engineers and product developers. The result is a learner-centered practice and process that (1) provides a comprehensive view of the learner and their environment to enable the design of effective and engaging personalized learning experiences for diverse learners, (2) enables fast learning and development, which is crucial for staying sustainable with limited resources in typical industry production environments, and (3) provides coherence across theories and methodologies to enable actionable insights toward product design, development, validation, and contribution to the field.

5 The Learner as a System Component

The models introduced earlier provide a theoretical/conceptual model of the AIS. We discussed how learners' needs drive the design and development of AISs in the learning engineering process. When considering a functional system, we propose that the learner and the learning environment are also part of the system (Fig. 3).

Each component in a system has a job to do. If the efficiency and effectiveness of one component can be improved, it may or may not improve the functionality of the entire system. In other theoretical AIS models, the learner model serves as a proxy for the learner as it does here, so the adaptive engine makes inferences and adaptations using the digital twin, and then can infer whether or not that adaptation had a positive effect on learning based on the updated digital twin. That is a valid approach. However, the expanded perspective that includes the learner and environment as part of the system might prompt learning engineering teams to ask different questions, leading to new insights for optimizing the overall system. As we have seen, the exploration of such research questions about the learner and their learning environment is an important part of the learning engineering process. For example, what environmental conditions/patterns might be affecting learning in ways that humans might not notice, but an AI agent might discover? How can we better design the conditions outside of the technology system to promote learning? What are the blind spots in the differences between the learner and the learner model's digital twin of the learner? What if we use different kinds of interfaces to adapt conditions for the learner than what we are used to (e.g. non-verbal audio cues, natural language dialogue, physiological sensors, climate control adjustments)?

If we consider the learner and learning environment as system components, and the learner's function is to learn, then one of the core design goals for the system should be to help the learner become better at learning. It is not just about what the other components can do to the learner to cause learning to happen. What additional components can be introduced to help the learner become a better learner, a more motivated learner, a self-regulated learner?

We might say that the overall system goal is to optimize the functionality of the "learner component" by optimally adapting interactions between the other components of the system and the learner via human-computer interfaces and by adapting the conditions within which those interactions take place.

These interactions can be simply expressed as a cycle of learner experiences/conditions, observed-measured and analyzed by other components to produce inferences about the state of the learner as diagnosis and prescriptive adaptation informing what the system does next. The prescription may be immediate feedback for an adaptation of a future learning experience or to trigger some extra-learning process (e.g. a credential assertion, an alert to an instructor, etc.) (Fig. 4).

5.1 Modeling the Mind (and Body) of the Learner

System components in the "learner model" category may serve as a "digital twin" of the learner. This digital twin is the information that informs the rest of the adaptive system. It is a kind of interface between the real learner component and the AIS. For cognitive learning objectives the adaptive system, just like a good human tutor, attempts to "get inside the learner's head" to understand conceptions that are on target and misconceptions that need

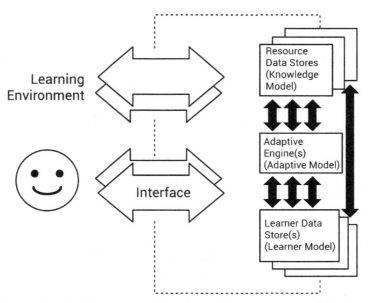

Fig. 3. Diagram showing the learner and learning environment as part of the overall system connected to AIS modules via including human-computer interfaces and environmental sensors. (Goodell, 2019)

correction. For objectives that involve development of both mental and physical abilities, the digital twin may include information about physiology and physical development.

This information may include:

- both facts and inferences about past, current, and predicted future cognitive capabilities and functions (Examples: logs of interaction, transactional performance assessment data, and inferred competency assertions derived from those raw data)
- physiological attributes related to learning and performance objectives. (Examples: physiological metrics/abilities/limitations that might indicate readiness, lack of readiness, or need for accommodations, scaffolding, or pre-requisite physical conditioning; eye tracking to gauge learner engagement)
- both raw transactional data and processed/interpreted data as a log of a learner's activities, actions, and experiences (They may include data to support spaced learning and knowledge decay models.)
- various data collected from the learner to indicate learner preferences or provide feedback to the system
- data collected from other people on behalf of the learner
- data collected through sensors and external systems
- inferences, assertions, and evidence of competency and levels of mastery
- inferences and evidence of knowledge gaps and misconceptions.
- inferences and evidence of learning behaviors
- contextual data about the environmental conditions, cultural contexts, human relationships that might influence a learning experience or the learner's general perceptions that impact learning
- data about levels of engagement, emotional states, etc.
- records of feedback offered to the learner

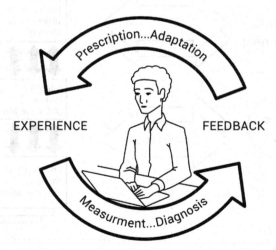

Fig. 4. Experience and feedback cycle illustration. CC BY Goodell, J. & Flynn, J. (2016) Adapted with permission.

- applicable metadata inferred from patterns in other learner data sets used to predict optimum conditions for this learner's current and future pursuit of the same learning objectives. (e.g. demographics, prior learning pathways, contextual patterns).

5.2 From a Generic Proxies of the Learner and Context to a More Precise Digital Twins

The system design starts with designing for a proxy of the learner based on a set of general assumptions about how people learn, about the class of learners who will interact with the system, and about their learning environments. The domain model and learning experiences designed for the system are based on and may map to definitions of pedagogical models. Pedagogical models represent application of learning theories with a pedagogical approach, i.e. defining the kinds of interactions that in theory should promote a learner's achievement of learning objectives [1].

The adaptive system doesn't rest with a general proxy of the learner or general assumptions about how people in general might respond when a pedagogical model is applied in a given context. Once the specific "learner component" is plugged into the system the other components begin to adapt. With every interaction the learner model is augmented and corrected with a more precise "digital twin" of this specific learner. Information about learner responses to system stimulus are used to test general theories behind pedagogical models and enrich those models based on the specific learner, context, and conditions. The more precise pedagogical model can be used to adapt the learning activities offered and other factors of the learning experience (e.g. content, presentation, scaffolding, motivational constructs, etc.).

This kind of iterative improvement is a learning engineering process that can be and is done by human learning engineering teams such as creators of intelligent tutoring systems. It is also a learning engineering process that can be done with AI/machine learning.

5.3 Modular Architecture

While conceptually the proposed learner-centered AIS fits into four conceptual categories (learner models, domain models, adaptive models, and interface models), the functional components require further classification. We envision a distributed system with modules that perform specialized functions and require specialized data architectures. For example, the data architecture for an assessment item bank has very different structural requirements than the data architecture for a competency frameworks repository.

The following list defines modules that might be included in a distributed learner centered AIS [33]:

- Competency framework module—an information resource with competency definitions and metadata to which learning experiences, resources, assessment items, and other resources will be aligned. This includes information about

  - competency frameworks;

- competency definitions;
- associations between competency definitions, e.g. for optimizing competency-based pathways;
- rubrics and/or assessment criteria profiles (profiles of how a learner's competence level can be measured for competency definitions and given contexts); and
- feedback profiles.

- Customized learner profile modules that combine data from source systems and input from students, educators/instructors, parent/guardian (if applicable), supervisors, and others involved in the student's education/training, work context, or well-being
- Separate learner model repositories with data in multiple formats and granularities, such as a learning experience record store with granular log data versus more structured data repositories for assessment results, competency assertions, and predictive inferences driving motivational feedback
- Personalized learning plan modules responsive to the learner as he or she progresses and changes
- Learning resource/activities content repositories
- Learning resource/activities metadata/paradata repositories
- Learning resource/activities discovery module
- Content authoring modules
- Interface & instrumentation modules (including multisensory learner stimulus components, sensors, and data capture functions)
- Repositories of pedagogical models
- Repositories of adaptive strategies as inputs to adaptive engines (Fig. 5)

5.4   Designing from the Inside Out, and then Through Iterative Optimization

We envision future design and development of adaptive instructional systems benefiting from an emerging learning engineering discipline that embraces a learner-centered iterative problem-solving approach. Designing from the inside out, the learner's needs drive the design. This approach starts with imperfect but research-based assumptions about the learner, how they will interact with the system, their learning environment, the learning objectives and pedagogical models, the decisions about what functional components are needed to implement the pedagogical model, and the learning experience designs that are mapped to pedagogy and learning objectives, etc. As data from and about the users are collected, we can iterate on the design- and address-specific design and interface problems. The proposed learner-centered AIS model is a self-improving system by design that embodies key learning engineering processes. The human-centered design approach can enable us to better understand the learner and the problem to be solved (i.e. the learner model). Applications of the learning sciences can drive and inform improvements in the domain model, adaptive model, and the interface model. Iterative design and development approaches can enable data-informed decision-making. Through designing from the inside out and then through iterative optimization, we can build AISs that can address diverse learning needs at scale.

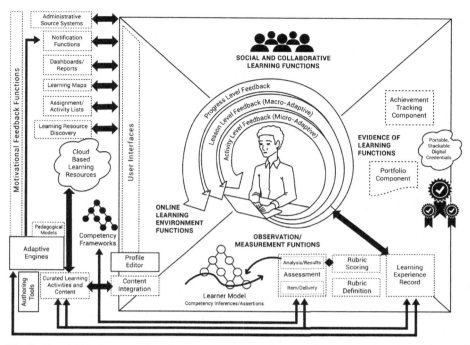

Fig. 5. From Glowa, L. and Goodell, J. (2016) Student-Centered Learning: Functional Requirements for Integrated Systems to Optimize Learning Vienna, VA.: International Association for K-12 Online Learning (iNACOL). Adapted with permission.

References

1. Sottilare, R., Barr, A., Robson, R., Hu, X., Graesser, A.: Exploring the opportunities and benefits of standards for adaptive instructional systems (AISs). In: Proceedings of the Adaptive Instructional Systems Workshop in the Industry Track of the 14th International Intelligent Tutoring Systems (ITS) Conference, pp. 49–53 (2018)
2. Sottilare, R.A., Brawner, K.W., Goldberg, B.S., Holden, H.K.: The generalized intelligent framework for tutoring (GIFT). US Army Research Laboratory—Human Research & Engineering Directorate (ARL-HRED), Orlando (2012)
3. Koedinger, K.R., Corbett, A.T., Perfetti, C.: The knowledge-learning-instruction framework: bridging the science-practice chasm to enhance robust student learning. Cogn. Sci. **36**(5), 757–798 (2012)
4. Knowles, et al.: Draft Standard for the Classification of Adaptive Instructional Systems IEEE P2247.1 (in press)
5. IEEE Industry Connection Industry Consortium on Learning Engineering (ICICLE). https://www.ieeeicicle.org. Accessed December 2019
6. Heffernan, N.T., Heffernan, C.L.: The ASSISTments ecosystem: building a platform that brings scientists and teachers together for minimally invasive research on human learning and teaching. Int. J. Artif. Intell. Educ. **24**(4), 470–497 (2014)
7. Sottilare, R.A., Baker, R.S., Graesser, A.C., Lester, J.C.: Special Issue on the Generalized Intelligent Framework for Tutoring (GIFT): creating a stable and flexible platform for innovations in AIED research. Int. J. Artif. Intell. Educ. **28**(2), 139–151 (2018)

8. Koedinger, K.R., Anderson, J.R., Hadley, W.H., Mark, M.A.: Intelligent tutoring goes to school in the big city. Int. J. Artif. Intell. Educ. (IJAIED) **8**, 30–43 (1997)
9. Sottilare, R., Ragusa, C., Hoffman, M., Goldberg, B.: Characterizing an adaptive tutoring learning effect chain for individual and team tutoring. In: Proceedings of the Interservice/Industry Training Simulation and Education Conference, Orlando (2013)
10. Thai, K.P., Rothschild, M.: Theoretical & practical implications of a learning engineering framework for product development at scale. Adapted with Permission, Paper submitted to International Society of the Learning Sciences, January 2020
11. International Society of the Learning Sciences (ISLS). https://www.isls.org/Apr-2019. Accessed Dec 2019
12. Owen, V.E.: Learning science in data-driven adaptive design for young children (in press, 2019)
13. Owen, V.E., Thai, K.P., Jacobs, D., Burnett, V., Roy, M.-H., Keylor, E.: Harnessing the power of data: driving game-based personalized instruction through learning te-lemetry. National Center for Research on Evaluation, Standards, and Student Testing (CRESST), Los Angeles, CA (2018)
14. Baker, R.S., Inventado, P.S.: Educational data mining and learning analytics. In: Larusson, J.A., White, B. (eds.) Learning Analytics, pp. 61–75. Springer, New York (2014). https://doi.org/10.1007/978-1-4614-3305-7_4
15. Clements, D.H., Sarama, J.: Learning trajectories in mathematics education. Math. Think. Learn. **6**(2), 81–89 (2004)
16. Sarama, J., Clements, D.H.: Building blocks for early childhood mathematics. Early Child. Res. Q. **19**(1), 181–189 (2004)
17. Mislevy, R.J.: Evidence-Centered Design for Simulation-Based Assessment. CRESST Report 800. National Center for Research on Evaluation, Standards, and Student Testing (CRESST) (2011)
18. Mislevy, et al.: Psychometric Considerations in Game-based Assessment. GlassLab, Redwood City (2014)
19. Bjork, R.A., Yan, V.X.: The increasing importance of learning how to learn. In: McDaniel, M.A., Frey, R.F., Fitzpatrick, S.M., Roediger, H.L. (eds.) Integrating Cognitive Science with Innovative Teaching in STEM Disciplines, pp. 15–36 (2014)
20. Roediger III, H.L., Karpicke, J.D.: Test-enhanced learning: taking memory tests improves long-term retention. Psychol. Sci. **17**(3), 249–255 (2006)
21. Shea, J.B., Morgan, R.L.: Contextual interference effects on the acquisition, retention, and transfer of a motor skill. J. Exp. Psychol.: Hum. Learn. Mem. **5**, 179–187 (1979)
22. Ebbinghaus, H.: Memory: a contribution to experimental psychology, Original work published as Das Gedächtnis 1885. Dover, New York, NY (1964)
23. Kellman, P.J., Massey, C.M.: Perceptual learning, cognition, and expertise. In: Ross, B.H. (ed.) The Psychology of Learning and Motivation, vol. 58, pp. 117–165. Elsevier Inc., Amsterdam (2013)
24. Fyfe, E.R., McNeil, N.M., Son, J.Y., Goldstone, R.L.: Concreteness fading in mathematics and science instruction: a systematic review. Educ. Psychol. Rev. **26**(1), 9–25 (2014). https://doi.org/10.1007/s10648-014-9249-3
25. Baker, R.S.: Stupid tutoring systems, intelligent humans. Int. J. Artif. Intell. Educ. **26**(2), 600–614 (2016). https://doi.org/10.1007/s40593-016-0105-0
26. Design-Based Research Collective: Design-based research: an emerging paradigm for educational inquiry. Educ. Res. **32**(1), 5–8 (2003). https://doi.org/10.3102/0013189X032001005
27. Laurel, B.: Design Research: Methods and Perspectives. MIT Press, Cambridge (2003)
28. Brown, T.: Change by Design. HarperCollins Publishers, New York (2009)

29. Hirsh-Pasek, K., Zosh, J., Michnick Golinkoff, R., Gray, J., Robb, M., Kaufman, J.: Putting education in "educational" apps: lessons from the science of learning. Psychol. Sci. Public Interest **16**(1), 3–34 (2015). https://doi.org/10.1177/1529100615569721. Accessed Dec 2019
30. Kizilcec, R.F., Cohen, G.L.: Eight-minute self-regulation intervention raises educational attainment at scale in individualist but not collectivist cultures. Proc. Nat. Acad. Sci. **114**(17), 4348–4353 (2017). https://doi.org/10.1073/pnas.1611898114. Accessed Dec 2019
31. Beck, J.E., Gong, Y.: Wheel-spinning: students who fail to master a skill. In: Lane, H.C., Yacef, K., Mostow, J., Pavlik, P. (eds.) AIED 2013. LNCS (LNAI), vol. 7926, pp. 431–440. Springer, Heidelberg (2013). https://doi.org/10.1007/978-3-642-39112-5_44
32. Owen, V.E., et al.: Detecting wheel-spinning and productive persistence in educational games. In: Proceedings of the 12th International Conference on Educational Data Mining, Montreal, July 2019 (2019). http://radix.www.upenn.edu/learninganalytics/ryanbaker/EDM2019_paper178.pdf
33. Glowa, L., Goodell, J.: Student-Centered Learning: Functional Requirements for Integrated Systems to Optimize Learning Vienna, VA.: International Association for K-12 Online Learning (iNACOL) (2016)

Technology in Education
Meeting the Future Literacy and Numeracy Needs of Society

James Ness[(⊠)] and USMA Engineering Psychology Class of 2020

Department of Behavioral Sciences and Leadership, US Military Academy, West Point,
NY 10996, USA
james.ness@westpoint.edu

Abstract. In 1913, Thomas Edison predicted that every branch of knowledge would be taught using motion pictures portending the demise of books [1]. Although film is a powerful media often leveraged in the classroom, books remain the instructional foundation for education. With the current proliferation of information technology in classroom, the utility of books, teachers and the classroom itself are now being questioned. However, like the advent of motion pictures, the supplanting of teachers and classrooms by information technology is overdone [2, 3]. Notwithstanding, advances in information technology are having a profound effect on education. As a literacy tool, information technology facilitates acquisition of content knowledge adjusting difficulty to predetermined performance metrics. This frees the educator to engage individual learners to bring about creative achievements as they discover the part/whole possibilities of the acquired content knowledge.

Keywords: Instructional technology · Intersubjectivity · Literacy

1 The Purpose of Education and the Locus of Intersubjectivity

Education refers to a form of socialization in which skilled individuals engage in the deliberate teaching of others to ensure the acquisition of specialized knowledge and skills. As civilizations gained literacy and numeracy these skills became central to the functioning of society [4]. Formal education arose as a means to teach others to master the evolving technologies for representing and communicating information. In this way, computers and advancements of the internet need to be in the classroom, because these are an advancement of our literacy and numeracy, which are skills central to the functioning of our society.

The importance of the use of these technologies in the classroom center on themes of learning and memory expressed by Lev Vygotsky and Jean Piaget. Their locus of intersubjectivity was different because they focused on different levels of analysis exploring

---

USMA Engineering Psychology Class of 2020 — O'Shea, Keenan; Huber, Ellison; Boos, Lauren; Yu, Iris; Rockman, Mason; Morton, Damaria; Milner, Alyssa; Riesing, Ryan; Weigel, Rebecca; Bell, Jessica; Tombrink, Alejandro; Fuller, Preston; Monterroso, Kimberly; Deltufo, Anthony; Salinas, Aaron; Lum, Nikki; Beachler, Mary Kate; Taylor, Bennett; Yamamura, Darrel; Seong, Dae Han; Smith, Abigail; Dye, Joshua; Kwon, Jin.

C. Stephanidis et al. (Eds.): HCII 2020, LNCS 12425, pp. 574–585, 2020.
https://doi.org/10.1007/978-3-030-60128-7_42

the question of human learning. Piaget believed that intersubjectivity was within the person [5]. Learning occurs through an individual's active engagements with the environment. Major advancements in the individual's thinking are a result of an equilibration of schemes used to discover the world with that of the reality of the discoverable world.

Vygotsky believed the intersubjectivity exists between learning partners. The more proficient partner (i.e., teacher) guides the less proficient partner (i.e., student) through learning skills and evolving ideas [6]. For Vygotsky, learning requires functioning on the edge of one's competence and thus involves risk taking on the part of the student. The learner must trust that the teacher will respect the learner's efforts. The teacher structures the learning environment such that the context is familiar, but that the task is on the edge of the student's competence.

The construct of intersubjectivity is, what Whitehead [7] would term, a psychic addition to nature. However, the brain in some manner evinces mind through an enigmatic neurologic entanglement and becomes something studied as nature apprehended rather than the physics of nature causing awareness. Moreover, the mind is further complicated by a social communicative aspect as ideas are communicated from individual to individual analogous to the gene moving from body to body. Dawkins [8] posited the analogy and coined the term meme to capture the genesis, replication, mutation, and evolution of ideas. Herein lies the conundrum of mind as it is best understood through description and metaphor [9] often defying explanation.

2 The Constructive Nature of Thought and Memory

Whereas Piaget saw learning as a phenomenon of the individual, Vygotsky saw learning as a social endeavor. In both cases the question of, where does the memory for a learned skill reside, is argued to not uniquely exist in some engram etched in the brain. Rather, both believe in the constructive nature of thought and memory.

Despite the pervasiveness of Piaget's and Vygotsky's ideas, memory is traditionally conceived of and conventionally referred to as something that the person has rather than something that the person does. Conceptually, memory as something that the person does is a perspective which holds that memory is an activity rather than a thing. Research on memory development has been overly concerned with describing changes that are assumed to occur purely within the central nervous system and thus free of contextual influence, that is, not only free of external inputs from stimuli but also free from internal affective states. However, throughout the literature on memory development, what appears to be an inability to remember is often an inability to reconstruct events rather than an inability to retrieve a memory trace stored exclusively in the central nervous system. Thus, the importance of context suggests that to have a viable theory of learning and memory, the whole cognitive event must be accounted for by focusing on how the person adapts to the task environment and how the person is in turn transformed by the task environment.

The principle thesis of this paper is, as Bateson (1979) [10] argues, that the "mind", although an agent, should not be treated as having concrete or material existence, but should be considered as a process with multiple levels that interact with each other. Among these levels are the concrete organ called the brain, the states of the whole body and those of the environment, all of which serve to construct thought and memory.

3 The Mechanisms of Thought and Memory Formation

Historically, memory, as other psychological constructs, have been understood via modeling these constructs after the current technology of the time [11]. Memory is popularly defined within the framework of a computer analogy as the process of successfully retrieving information which has been encoded into a storage container. Given this definition, several questions avail themselves, which are of course based on the assumptions of the computer model. How does the process of storage and retrieval operate? Does it operate in an associative manner through a network of information tied together by way of semantic organization? Is information literally stored in the brain? Are there neurons which represent specific information such as our grandmother?

From the position of the computer model, these are relevant questions concerning memory. However, these questions may be the wrong questions in understanding the actual operation of the brain, which after all is important to education. In order to assess whether these are questions which will lead to a deeper understanding of the process of memory, the model itself must be scrutinized and understood in terms of the physiology it is purported to describe.

Since the seminal work of Karl Lashley (1950) [12] entitled, "In search of the engram", researchers have understood that although the brain plays a central role in behavioral and psychological processes, these processes cannot be solely specified in terms of permanent associative connections among neurons. The anatomical arrangement of input systems is one which preserves a topological correspondence between receptor surface and the cerebral cortex. The receptor-cortical organization is not accomplished via a point-to-point direct connection by a single nerve strand. Rather, a complex organization of subsystems results in the stimulation of the appropriate section of the cortex.

For example, anatomically, there is an overall reduction in the number of cells between receptor and ganglion layer at the retina of about 150:1 in man. From the ganglion to the lateral geniculate nucleus in the thalamus the number remains essentially constant. However, from the thalamus to the cortex a single geniculate cell may contact 5000 cortical neurons, each of which is in contact with some 4000 others through dendritic fields. This arrangement, aided by inhibitory processes, ensures that when two points in the retinal fovea are separated, this separation is maintained at the cortex. This separation is a representation and not a replication of the retinal image.

Empirical support of the thesis that the cortical image is a representation of the retinal image comes from various researchers. Lashley (1930) [13] removed 80 to 90% of the striate cortex in rats without impairing pattern discrimination. Galambos et al. (1967) [14] cut up to 98 percent of the optic tract of cats and the animals still performed skillfully in differentiating highly similar figures. Chow (1968) [15] severed more than three fourths of the optic tract and removed more than three fourths of the visual cortex, leaving hardly any point-to-point projections intact. Although visual discrimination of patterns became disrupted initially, the cats relearned the task in the same number of trials required to learn prior to surgery. Similar results were also obtained when electrical fields were disrupted rather than surgical removal of areas [16–20].

The data reported here are clearly incompatible with a view that a photographic-like image becomes projected onto the cortical surface. The data do indicate that each sensory system functions with a good deal of reserve. Since it makes little difference to overall performance which parts of the system are destroyed and which parts remain, this reserve must be distributed in the system. Moreover, the stored information necessary for making discriminations is paralleled and reduplicated over many locations. For example, an irritative lesion made in one cerebral hemisphere produces, after several months, a "mirror focus" of altered electrical activity in the contralateral cortex by way of interhemispheric connections such as the corpus callosum [21]. Note the "mirror focus" was not directly damaged and yet it possessed all of the irritative properties of the initial lesion.

The neurological evidence suggests that sensory information from the outside world is transformed and distributed throughout the cortex as well as reduplicated over many locations. The suggestion being that whole brain activity and configuration rather than single neuron firing is the level of analysis important to memory. Burns (1958) [22] and others have established beyond reasonable doubt that neural activity furnishes a stable base of activity through the spontaneous generation of electrical potential changes. As a result, the brain, like the heart, pulses continually. In absence of continuous input, neuronal aggregates of the type found in the cerebral cortex are conservatively estimated to be quiescent [23]. Thus, external input provides the stimulation necessary for a stable base of central nervous system activity.

Whenever the spontaneous activity of neuroelectric potential becomes sufficiently stable to organize the activity of other neural aggregates, that activity is known as a pacemaker. Some pacemakers, such as the one that governs the contractibility of the heart, function throughout the life of the individual. Others, like those of epilepsy, when activated, can result in total behavioral disruption. In any case, the development of pacemakers, specifically, and the organizational stability of functioning within the central nervous system, generally, are not governed exclusively by endogenous mechanisms, but are maintained and induced by stimulation from the external environment.

The importance of external stimulation for the maintenance and induction of the central nervous system organization is demonstrated by the data from experiments on sensory deprivation and on those which alter perceptual input. In sensory deprivation experiments, typical sources of stimulation are removed or muted for varying periods of time. Within the first hour of deprivation, subjects typically experience hallucinations [24]. Tests subsequent to the deprivation experience have shown deficits in sensory perception, such as size constancy [25]. Thus, without typical external stimulation, perceptual abilities are not maintained. In terms of altering perceptual input, Gibson (1933) [26] showed that after four days of experiencing the wearing of prism glasses that changed the perception of straight lines to that of curved lines, subjects persisted in perceiving straight lines as curved subsequent to the removal of the prism glasses. Together these examples demonstrate not only the importance of experience in maintaining perceptual functioning, as in the case of size constancy, but also in inducing perceptual change, as in the case of perceiving straight lines as curved. The inducing properties of experience influence an underlying organizational change in central nervous system functioning which affords the perceptual change.

Zal'mason (1926) [27] directly observed the effects of experience on the induction of organizational change in physiological functioning through the discovery of the existence of "temporal dominant foci". These "foci" can be considered pacemakers in that they appear to be a source of organization for whole brain activity in the presence of particular stimulation [28]. Specifically, Zal'mason (1926) [29] conditioned a dog to raise its right leg to the sound of a tone. After this conditioned response was well established, its right motor cortex (which controls the left side of the body) was exposed. During the performance of the conditioned reaction, a patty of strychninized filter paper was placed on the exposed right motor cortex in order to chemically excite it. Immediately the dog switched the responsive leg raising the left forepaw to the conditioned stimulus. The focus of neural activity, which had been established through conditioning and which dominated the functions of the motor cortex, was now overshadowed by a new "temporary dominant focus" established in the dog's brain by the chemical excitation from the strychnine [30]. Thus, the existence of these foci were shown to be not exclusively dependent on endogenous mechanisms, but require, for their existence, reliable input from the stimulus environment.

These data not only force us to view the environment as a reliable, dependable, and predictable contributor to the development of memories, but also the environment, in the role of reliable force, can induce changes in brain functioning. Moreover, these changes in functioning can lead to structural change in the form of changes in the number and organization of dendritic projections [31]. Here, Piaget is correct in that intersubjectivity is within the individual in that schemes are equilibrated to meet the reality of the reliable force of the stimulus environment. Thus, there exists a bidirectional relationship whereby function influences structure and structure in turn influences function. This relationship is also shown in the relationship between emotional state and the quality of the formed memory.

Table 1 summarizes the literature on memory quality and distinguishes the qualities of trauma memories [32] from those of autobiographical [33] and flashbulb memories [34]. Autobiographic memories are characterized by specific, personal, long-lasting facts about oneself and one's experiences. Physiologically they are associated with the mechanisms of the hippocampus and as a rule do not involve emotional loading with the notable exception of flashbulb memories. An extreme example of autobiographic memories is found in Hyperthymestic Memory as described in the case of A.J. [35] A.J. can take a date between 1974 (about age 7) and the present and tell what day it falls on, what she was doing that day and if anything of great importance happened. None of the memories are problematic and are simply recounted in context as past events.

A particular and common form of autobiographic memory is flashbulb memory. The formation of flashbulb memories is associated with amygdala activation as well as hippocampal involvement. These memories are vivid, in particular for personal details around an emotional event. Events such as the Shuttle disaster, 9/11 or the assassination of President Kennedy often engender memories of where one was, what they were wearing, or personnel events engaged in, such as grocery shopping or attending Math class. The specific facts surrounding the event are less clear and often remembered from media reports after the fact rather than through direct experience. These memories, although reported as vivid, are controllable and not problematic. In general,

Table 1. A comparison of the qualities of Autobiographic, Flashbulb, and Trauma memories.

Table 1			
	Autobiographic	Flashbulb	Trauma
Vivid	Not a reported quality	Detailed recollection for discovery context	Vivid sensory memory
Confidence	Moderate	Strong	Strong
Rehearsal	Conscious Control	Conscious Control	Involuntary & Intrusive
Recall Affect	Neutral	Weak negative valance	Strong
Event	Neutral	Moderately emotionally arousing	Highly Emotional: usually Life threatening
Facts	Factual memories subject to forgetting	Discovery facts resistant to forgetting	Sparse idiosyncratic facts resistant to forgetting
Quality of Memory	Coherent in time & place - Contextual	Coherent in time & place - Contextual	Mainly sensory impressions
Time	As past event	As past event	"here & now" quality

autobiographic memories are voluntary, subject to forgetting and restructuring, and are organized in an apparent semantically associated network.

Trauma memories are qualitatively different from autobiographic memory and involve physiologically different mechanisms. Most models of the formation of trauma memory involve the hippocampus, amygdala and prefrontal cortex. Figure 1 summarizes the central nervous system mechanisms in the formation of trauma memories as described in the Temporal Dynamic Model [36]. The Temporal Dynamic Model presents the temporal dynamics of emotional memory between the major brain structures involved in forming, storing, and recalling memories. These structures are the amygdala, hippocampus, and prefrontal lobe (Fig. 1). Immediately coincident with an emotional load the amygdala increases activity, makes active processes in the hippocampus and suppresses function in the prefrontal lobe (Fig. 1, panel 1). The effect on memory is an apparent enhancement of the memory for sole focus of attention (e.g. weapon focus) and for those cues immediately preceding the event [37]. Contextual cues immediately coincident in time with the emotional load are remembered with many of the trigger stimuli for trauma memories only having a temporal relationship with the event. Common examples are physical cues similar to those present shortly before or immediately coincident with the emotional load. For example, shape of person, spatial cues, smells, patterns of light, certain phrases, tone of voice, touch on certain part of body, proprioceptive cues (postures, movement), and particular feelings (helpless or trapped feeling).

In the minutes following the emotional load only the amygdala is active in formation of new memories, yielding memories of the gist of events and associated emotional valance. There are no autobiographic memories formed (Fig. 1, panel 2). The prefrontal cortex recovers with diminished amygdala activity with recovery time dependent on

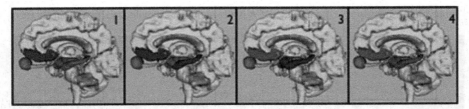

Fig. 1. Shows the temporal course of events subsequent to a threatening event on the prefrontal cortex, the left most colored structure, the amygdala, the middle-colored structure and the hippocampus, the right most colored structure. Red indicates a heightened activity; green indicates normal levels of functioning and blue indicates a refractory period or a period where activity is actively inhibited. (Color figure online)

the nature and intensity of the emotional load. Recovery usually occurs within several minutes (Fig. 1, panel 3) but new memory formation is suppressed during the refractory period of the amygdala and hippocampus. Within hours to days, depending on the intensity of the emotional load, the hippocampus and amygdala recover (Fig. 1, panel 4) and with recovery so does recovery of the formation of autobiographic memories.

There is certainly a biological basis for memory and cognition and that the stimulus environment can induce, facilitate, and maintain cognitive activity. The relationship between the biological structures and the stimulus environment associated with cognitive activity appear bidirectional. Although structure is quintessential to memory and cognition, given the bidirectional relationship, structure does not predetermine outcome. In some respects Skinner makes a point that what may develop is an ability to recognize ever finer contingencies of reinforcement suggesting that there is knowledge in the world to which we adapt, discover, and wonder [38]. In this way, memory and cognition is something we do and technology is a tool discovered by us to facilitate our further discovery and not predetermine it.

4   Memory as Something We Do: Implications for the Classroom

The realization that experience can induce organizational change is a major philosophical break from the traditional understanding of the relationship between endogenous and exogenous influences on physical and behavioral development. Instead of suggesting that physical and behavioral traits are predetermined by structural complement, the suggestion here is that epigenetic relationships are driving physical and behavioral development. This is not the kind of epigenetic relationship that Waddington (1966) [39] described by way of his epigenetic landscape.

What is being argued here is that with increased organization (e.g., individual as locus of intersubjectivity to between and among individuals as locus of intersubjectivity) the epigenetic landscape itself changes, thus providing for greater variability in behavior instead of greater canalization as is the case in physical and physiologic characteristics.

Greater variability in the activity of memory comes as one moves levels of analysis from the individual learner where intersubjectivity is within the individual to societies where the locus of intersubjectivity is between individuals. Here a society must develop and maintain a means to facilitate intersubjectivity between and among individuals. That means is through literacy and numeracy. These are the foundational skills from which higher order skills are acquired and divisions of labor are established such that a society can be viable.

Table 2 shows the differences between Piaget's presuppositions about learning and memory and those of Vygotsky's. Table 2 provides each theorist's presuppositions, which maintain consistency of each theory with locus of intersubjectivity. Both mechanisms for cognitive development are valid and operate at the appropriate level of analysis. Of the two theories, Vygotsky's theory is most relevant to the classroom. For Vygotsky, cognitive development is inseparable from the social milieu. Underlying this concept is an evolutionary construct of the inheritance of ideas. The discovery of ideas appears to result from interacting with one's niche, seeing the contingencies that exist in one's environment and translating the discovered contingencies into a skill or tool to better adapt to the environment. This genesis of ideas can occur at the individual or social level. Regardless, the promulgation of the idea across generations is at the social level. The idea is transmitted through language to subsequent generations and the skill or tool itself is passed on and often improved upon over the generations. A classic example is the idea of time, originally understood from observing the rhythms that surround us (movement of stars, changes in length of day, tides, movement of the sun across the sky). Analogues were built by many societies to capture these natural rhythms as intellectual tools (sun dial, Stonehenge, eventually springs and gears and ever finer precision found in the atomic clocks). Each of these devices did not have to be reinvented by each generation, simply the important ideas were purveyed, compressing generations of work into the span of, in some cases, a semester.

Table 2. A comparison of Vygotsky's and Piaget's perspectives on cognitive development.

Table 2	
Vygotsky	**Piaget**
Instructional Technologies	Operating on mental structures
Focus: Social basis of mind	Focus: Individual as starting point
Locus of intersubjectivity is between partners	Locus of intersubjectivity is between the individual's schemes and what they afford.
Guided participation: Zone of proximal development between unequal partners	Cognitive schemes guide behavior to assimilate information and accommodate behaviors for further assimilation of information.
Intra to interpersonal plane of cultural tools	Qualitative shift in perspective
Cognitive Development is historico-cultural internalization from social to individual	Cognitive Development occurs with equilibration of schemes with experience.
Social Activity is the unit of analysis	Individual is the unit of analysis
Inequality of learning partners Zone of proximal development **Language Precedes Thought**	Equality of learning partners at concrete operations ($\approx$age 7) **Thought Precedes Language**

Teachers are the purveyors of ideas to ensure the acquisition of specialized knowledge and skills in subsequent generations, particularly literacy and numeracy skills, which are central to the functioning of a society. A major advance in literacy and numeracy comes from advances in information technology. These technologies are means for one to practice skills and to use in support of learning new skills. The learning of new skills requires an educator to structure the tasks within what Vygotsky calls the zone of proximal development. It is the zone in which the learner is not quite competent to manage a skill but has enough base knowledge to be guided by a more skilled partner to be able to solve a problem on their own. Given that information technology is an emerging form of literacy (e.g., computer literate), it is incumbent upon educators to build curricula that uses this form of literacy to afford an ever-greater art of the possible.

5   Cognitive Cartography and the US Military Academy

"You know, you're going to fail. I said, fail? Saddam, you're sitting here imprisoned. Your government is no more. How are we going to fail? And he said, you're going to fail because you're going to find out that it's not so easy to govern this place. And he said, you know, you don't understand our culture, our history, our language and you don't understand the Arab mind. And that's why you're going to fail. And to be quite honest with you, I remember thinking - I didn't want to concede the point to him, but I remember thinking he does have a point."

The international stage has transformed into an arena where power lies beyond the nation-state. It is an era of non-state actors, insurgencies, and terrorist organizations, who rarely provide the option of engaging at a negotiating table. As illustrated in Iraq, when the state was weakened in 2003, the conflict transformed, with Saddam Hussein foreshadowing the West's inability to consolidate its kinetic victory. In the absence of a powerful centralize government, a vacuum arose allowing for new, non-state actors to emerge and flourish.

Insurgent warfare is not new. The Roman Empire encountered numerous insurgencies both domestic and aboard. Napoleon fought many "nasty, dirty little war(s) of ambushes, sniping, and occasional atrocities." During the 18th century, the British Army became relatively effective against insurgents using light infantry, dragoons and local loyal populations. These adaptations were kinetic in nature and are still in use today. Notwithstanding, there is a non-kinetic aspect to post-conflict operations. These operations are meant to transform battlefield victories into enduring security and prosperity. As such, the Department of Defense (DoD) consolidates kinetic victory with post-conflict (phase IV) non-kinetic advise and assist missions.

The DoD has had relatively little direct experience in non-kinetic post conflict activities and is learning how to plan and execute these missions. The problem with direct experience is that it takes generations to build sufficient organizational knowledge to perform optimally. Further, the constant turnover in U.S. personnel is what the Special Inspector General for Afghan Reconstruction refers to as the "annual lobotomy" which promulgates the insufficient understanding of Afghanistan's historical, cultural, religious and political traditions [40].

With experience comes relatively permanent changes in behavior, which is a classic definition of the construct, learning. However, there is both an individual and social basis of mind. Thus, although individuals have had experience in post-conflict operations as an organization not much has been learned. This is perennial problem in the institutional Army, lessons are often forgotten as the Army prepares for the next mission [41]. Thus, the question becomes, is there a means to accelerate the DoD's experience in post-conflict operations (phase IV) such that the lessons of individuals are not erased from the memory of the organization.

Since all permutations of experiences in the deployed environment cannot be known *a priori*, proscribed intentional memorization of facts or scripted sequences are likely to be of limited value. As such, the quintessential human means for diffusing lessons and experiences is through a tradition of passing on stories [42]. Representations of experiences, as in cave paintings and storytelling are the oldest traditions of recounting events, imparting lessons and projecting affect. These formats structure information in part-whole relations affording the experience schematic frameworks to interpret past, present, or future analogous events. The diffusion of lessons through stories, using technology-mediated means diffuses lessons in a rapid and salient manor.

Technology is a means for accelerating experience affording the student a means to collaboratively construct possible scenarios, engage the constructed story and build ever more sophisticate stories generating a map that Tolman described as a comprehensive cognitive map. Training simulations and more generally video games are essentially mazes that the learner negotiates. In this sense, Tolman's admonition concerning cognitive strip maps is important to consider [43]. It is particularly important that the simulated training environments parse out what needs to be trained as a well-defined script from what needs to be learned in a more schematic sense [44]. If the simulation is learned and not its storied lessons, then all that is achieved is a faster negotiation of the maze or what Tolman referred to as a cognitive strip map.

In the Human Centered Design class at the US Military Academy, technology is leveraged as a literacy tool to develop a training simulation to train cyber at the tactical level. The development of the simulation is used to discover what is possible. The method is a pragmatic one whereby each phase of achieving, "it works", leads to a more sophisticated idea of what it means "to work". The entirety of the construct of "mind" is studied in the development of the training simulation. Remaining in the "does it work" question in developing the simulation informs, what is meant by cyber, the adaptations of interfaces, the representations presented in the system images, the affective component, and the levels of feedback.

The training simulation is not fully autonomous as it is a literacy tool, and thus not the educator. As a literacy tool, it manages the immersion in the learning environment and delivers consequences to actions that have well defined sequences and standards. This frees the educator to observe the trainees, deliver encouragement and feedback, and engage in creative achievements and discoveries in discussions after activity in the simulation culminates.

In the development of the simulation the Cadets discover that if what is shot is meant to be imperceptible, illusory, and to inveigle, then what needs to be trained is an ever more refined ability to perceive the contingencies of psyber in the tactical environment. The development of the simulation itself becomes an educational experience as the Cadets discover the art of the possible and build story lines to train cyber at the tactical level.

If the Army wants to meet the challenge of the "annual lobotomy" then the use of simulations should be as literacy tools and not as a predetermined maze to be negotiated. The former promotes comprehensive cognitive maps affording the part-whole relationships needed to effectively adapt to the uncertainties of the deployed environment [45]. The latter promotes cognitive strip maps engraining predetermined solutions promoting a fixed action pattern rather than creative solutions to future problems.

References

1. The Economist E-Education. The Economist Newspaper Limited, 29 June 2013
2. Ibid
3. Paulson, A.: Blended Learning. The Christian Science Monitor Weekly, 21–28 April 2014
4. Rogoff, B.: Apprenticeship in Thinking. Oxford University Press, New York (1991)
5. Piaget, J.: Behavior and Evolution. Random House, New York (1978)
6. Vygotsky, L.: Thought and Language (3rd Printing). The MIT Press, Cambridge (1988)
7. Whitehead, A.N.: The concept of nature. In: Kegg, J., Wisewell, L. (eds.) Project Gutenberg, EBook #18835, November 1919. https://plato.stanford.edu/entries/whitehead/. Accessed 16 July 2006
8. Dawkins, R.: The Selfish Gene. Oxford University Press, New York (1979)
9. Brainerd, C.: The stage question in cognitive-developmental theory. Behav. Brain Sci. 1(2), 173–182 (1978)
10. Bateson, G.: Mind and Nature: A Necessary Unity. Hampton Press, Cresskill (1979)
11. Boring, E.G.: The History of Experimental Psychology, 2nd edn. Appleton-Century- Crofts, New York (1950)
12. Lashley, K.: In search of the engram. Soc. Exp. Biol. Symp. 4, 454–482 (1950)
13. Lashley, K.: The mechanism of vision: II. The influence of cerebral lesions upon the threshold of discrimination for brightness in the rat. Pedag. Semin. J. Genet. Psychol. 37(4), 461–480 (1930)
14. Galambos, R., Norton, T., Frommer, G.: Exp. Neurol. 18, 8–25 (1967)
15. Chow, K.L.: Visual discrimination after extensive ablation of optic tract and visual cortex in cats. Brain Res. 9, 363–366 (1968)
16. Kraft, M., Obrist, W.D., Pribram, K.: The effect of irritative lesions of the striate cortex on learning of visual discrimination in monkeys. J. Comp. Physiol. Psychol. 53, 17–22 (1960)
17. Lashley, K.S., Chow, K.L., Semmes, J.: An examination of the electrical field theory of cerebral integration. Psychol. Rev. 58(2), 123–136 (1951)
18. Sperry, R.W., Miner, N., Myers, R.E.: Visual pattern perception following subpial slicing and tantalum wire implantations in the visual cortex. J. Comp. Physiol. Psychol. 48, 50–58 (1955)
19. Stamm, J.S., Pribram, K.H.: Effects of epileptogenic lesions of inferotemporal cortex on learning and retention in monkeys. J. Comp. Physiol. Psychol. 54, 614–618 (1961)
20. Stamm, J.S., Warren, A.: Learning and retention by monkeys with epileptogenic implants in posterior parietal cortex. Epilepsia 2, 229–242 (1961)
21. Kraft, M., Obrist, W.D., Pribram, K.: op. cit (1960)
22. Burns, B.D.: The Mamalian Cerebral Cortex. Arnold, London (1958)
23. Pribram, K.: Brain and Perception: Holonomy and Structure in Figural Processing. Lawrence Erlbaum Associates, Hillsdale (1991)

24. Zuckerman, M., Persky, H., Link, K.: Experimental and subject factors determining responses to sensory deprivation, social isolation, and confinement. J. Abnorm. Psychol. **73**(3 Pt.1), 183–194 (1968)

25. Doane, B., Mahatoo, W., Heron, W., Scott, T.: Changes in perceptual function after isolation. Can. J. Psychol. **13**, 210–219 (1959)

26. Gibson, J.: Adaptation, after-effect and contrast in the perception of curved lines. J. Exp. Psychol. **16**(1), 1–31 (1933)

27. Zal'Mason: Concerning the condition of excitation in dominance. Nova y refteksolgie i fizologii nervoisystemry, vol. 2, pp. 3–15 (1926)

28. Karl, P.: op. cit (1991)

29. Zal'Mason: Op. cit (1926)

30. John, E.: Mechanisms of Memory. Academic Press, New York (1967)

31. Lynch, J.: A single unit analysis of contour enhancement in the somesthetic system of the cat. Unpublished doctoral dissertation, Stanford University (1971)

32. Ehlers, A., Clark, D.: A cognitive model of posttraumatic stress disorder: invited essay. Behav. Res. Ther. **38**, 319–345 (2000)

33. Parker, E., Cahill, L., McGaugh, J.: A case of unusual autobiographical remembering. Neurocase **12**, 35–49 (2006)

34. Luminet, O., Curci, A. (eds.): Flashbulb Memories. Psychological Press, New York (2009)

35. Parker, E., Cahill, L., McGaugh, J.: Op. cit (2006)

36. Diamond, D., Campbell, A., Park, C., Halonen, J., Zoladz, P.: The temporal dynamics of emotional memory processing: a synthesis on the neurobiological basis of stress-induced amnesia, flashbulb and traumatic memories, and Yerkes-Dodson Law. Neural Plasticity, 2007, Article ID 60803, 33 p. (2007)

37. Loftus, E.F., Loftus, G.R., Messo, J.: Some facts about weapon focus. Law Hum Behav. **11**, 55–62 (1987)

38. Skinner, B.F.: Why I am not a cognitive psychologist. Behaviorism **5**, 1–11 (1977)

39. Waddington, C.H.: Principles of Development and Differentiation. Macmillan Company, New York (1966)

40. Ford, W.: The SIGAR called Congress to action, but how will it respond? Lawfare Institute in cooperation with Brookings Institution, 21 January 2020. https://www.lawfareblog.com/sigar-called-congress-action-how-will-it-respond

41. Ramsey, R.: Advising Indigenous Forces: American Advisors in Korea, Combat Studies Institute Press Fort Leavenworth, Vietnam and El Salvador (2014)

42. Lord, A.B.: The Singer of Tales. Atheneum, New York (1971)

43. Tolman, C.: Cognitive maps in rats and men. Psychol. Rev. **55**(4), 189–208 (1948)

44. Mandler, J.M., Johnson, N.S.: Remembrance of things parsed: story structure and recall. Cogn. Psychol. **9**, 111–151 (1977)

45. Vigil, J., DiNinni, R., Campbell, J., Ness, J.: Living on Amber, Documentary film of the 3BCT, 10th Mountain deployment cycle. The title represents the unit's resilience metaphor. A theme and teaching point of the film is trust as universally expressed by local nationals, interpreters and soldiers of the 3BCT (2015)

Adaptive Agents for Fit-for-Purpose Training

Karel van den Bosch[✉][iD], Romy Blankendaal[iD], Rudy Boonekamp[iD],
and Tjeerd Schoonderwoerd[iD]

TNO, Kampweg 55, 3769 DE Soesterberg, The Netherlands
{karel.vandenbosch,romy.blankendaal,rudy.boonekamp,
tjeerd.schoonderwoerd}@tno.nl
https://www.tno.nl/en/

Abstract. Simulators and games provide contextually rich environments, enabling learners to experience the relations between actions, events and outcomes. In order to be effective, learning situations need to be tailored to the needs of the individual learner. Virtual characters (or *agents*) that, in real time , select, adapt, and exhibit the behavior that is exactly right for that learner, help to establish such fit-for-purpose training. This paper discusses principles for designing training with adaptive agents, and presents a framework for their autonomous and dynamic operation. A prerequisite for agents' adaptation of behavior to be successful is that adjustments do not violate the consistency and believability of the character, and maintains the overall narrative of the scenario. For reasons of management and coordination, it is proposed not to assign control over adaptations to virtual character-agents themselves, but to a dedicated *director agent*. This director agent is not a virtual character in the gameplay, but operates in the background. It collects and manages information, makes decisions about adaptations and issues behavioral instructions to the virtual characters agents. The framework was used in a pilot study, employing a human facilitator that simulated a director agent, arranging the adaptive behavior of virtual characters in a game-based training of military tactical decision making. Effects of adaptive and non-adaptive agents in a training were compared. Adaptive agents had a positive influence on learning and performance, and an increased engagement and appreciation by learners. Additional research with more participants is needed to verify these preliminary findings.

Keywords: Adaptive instructional systems · Training · Learning · Learner modeling · Personalized learning · Director agent · Intelligent agents · Adaptive agent behavior · Cognitive behavior · Simulation · Serious games

1 Introduction

Simulators and games are often used for learning decision making in complex environments [50]. A simulation enables trainees to experience the causal

© Springer Nature Switzerland AG 2020
C. Stephanidis et al. (Eds.): HCII 2020, LNCS 12425, pp. 586–604, 2020.
https://doi.org/10.1007/978-3-030-60128-7_43

relations between events, actions and outcomes in the simulated environment. It thus gives access to hands-on learning by doing [40,41]. However, it has been shown that goal-directed, systematic training is more effective than learning-by-doing only [26]. One way to make simulation-based learning purposive and goal-directed, is to carefully manage the behavior of the virtual characters [2]. This paper discusses the requirements for successful control of virtual characters (hereafter: *agents*), and suggests a framework for adaptive agent behavior (Sect. 2). Furthermore, this paper reports on a pilot-study investigating the hypothesis that adapting agent behavior, according to the a set of principles designed to facilitate learning, results in better learning and in a higher engagement of the learner (Sect. 3). The pilot-study used a game-based training in conducting a military tactical operation, with the goal to train situation awareness and decision making in unpredictable, unstable, and complex conditions [51].

To accomplish an effective training, the intelligent agents that govern the behavior of the virtual characters in the simulation or game, should meet the following demands:

1. Respond to situations with a sufficient level of realism, thus enabling a learner to develop the mental representations needed to perform the task adequately in the real world [18].
2. Exhibit the behavior that brings about a learning situation in the simulation that fits the needs of the specific learner. This requirement is often referred to as 'attunement', or 'zone of proximal development' [33].

1.1   Determining Agent Behavior that Supports Learning

A training simulation in which the virtual characters demonstrate behavior that is sufficiently realistic and believable for a trainee to achieve the learning goals has 'functional validity' [38]. This does not necessarily imply high fidelity agent behavior [18]. In fact, there is evidence that high-fidelity simulations can sometimes affect transfer of learned material negatively [14,39]. A realistic representation of a character's behavior implies that all complexity and subtleties are included, which may be detrimental for learners as it may overwhelm of overstimulate a novice trainee [25,27]. Thus, when defining and designing the (behavior of) virtual agents it is important that the focus lies on maximizing effectiveness of the simulation instead of achieving realism on all aspects. It is therefore important that the behaviors of agents are believable (i.e., human-like), responsive (i.e., responding to user and environment), and interpretable (i.e., user must understand the underlying motivation).

1.2   Adapting Agent Behavior to Fit a Learner's Needs

In a training simulation it is important that the virtual characters (1) behave believable, and (2) that their behavior brings about a situation that fits the competency level and learning needs of the trainee [16]. These demands may be compatible, but sometimes the objective of learning requires concessions regarding the realism of the simulation [49]. Consider the following example: a tactical military game is used to teach a platoon commander how to behave in the company of the village chief (simulated by a role-playing agent). The commander's objective is to address the village chief with the goal to obtain intelligence information. If the commander has a weapon at the ready while approaching the village chief, this behavior is considered incorrect given the learning goal: 'treat village chief respectfully'. Although military experts consider it plausible and realistic that a village chief remains utterly unmoved to what underneath is deemed disrespectful behavior, such behavior of the village chief agent would not bring about a learning situation that fits the needs of the trainee. If in contrast, the village chief would shrink back and say something like: "I thought we were on good terms, so why would you treat me like this?", then this would perhaps be less realistic, but it would improve the learning value of the exercise for the trainee (see Fig. 1). Such adaptation of agent behavior, for the sake of achieving learning objectives, is called 'fit-for-purpose adaptation'.

Fig. 1. Example of fit-for-purpose behavior adaptation of agent in training.

1.3   Principles for Adapting Agent Behavior

In order for a training system to be adaptive to individual learners, the system has to have access to three types of models: a task performance model, a learner model, and an instruction model [23].

Firstly, for an agent to be accepted as a believable character in a military game, the agent should behave in a manner that is consistent with doctrine (relevant and tactically plausible), taking into the account the context and conditions of the world in which the agent is situated. Furthermore, the agent's behavior should also demonstrate the influence of the characteristics of the real-life character that it is supposed to represent. Such characteristics may, for example, be:

an experienced or an inexperienced person; a fit or a fatigued person; an aggressive or a submissive person; and so on. This is defined in a task performance model of the agent.

Secondly, to be able to tune a training to the specific needs of an individual learner, an adaptive instructional agent has to *know* the learner [1,46,47], at least with respect to its characteristics relevant for learning. This is defined in the learner model and includes, for example, the learner's competency level and learning progress, and may additionally include other personal characteristics like motivation, self-efficacy, and engagement [8,12,36].

Thirdly, the adaptive agents should be controlled by a set of principles to select the behavior that brings about learning situations that are instructionally meaningful and effective [2] (see the village chief example in 1.3). This is defined in the instruction model.

The models of task performance, of the learner, and of instruction are all required for an adaptive training simulation system. These models do not necessarily have to reside within the agents controlling the virtual character; they may also be managed by other agents in the training system that distribute information and actions to connected agents [16].

The literature provides ample recommendations and algorithms for shaping scenarios to promote learning [2,5,6,43,44,50]. Which interventions are appropriate to foster learning are to a large extent dependent on the nature of the task to be learned. Military tactical command can be characterized as achieving situation awareness and making decisions under uncertainty. Learning to interpret a tactical situation requires the recognition and judgement of relevant factors (e.g.., weather, terrain, behavior of others, et cetera). Experts commanders have stored their interrelated and contextualized knowledge as mental tactical schemas [42]. Novices, however, do not (yet) have elaborated mental tactical schemas. If we want novices to become experts, training tactical command therefore needs to address: (a) expansion and refinement of tactical mental schemas, and (b) practice in solving complex and unfamiliar tactical problems (in order to develop new schemas) [4].

Detecting, recognizing, and interpreting situational cues is relevant for learning military tactics, because situations are continuous and variable, and not all experiences are informative for future decision making situations. Learning therefore resides in the activation (e.g.., frequency and recency) of experienced outcomes [17]. The main principle of an adaptive instructional agent should therefore be to adopt the behavior that supports the learner in detecting, recognizing, and interpreting the situational cues of interest.

2   Dynamic Adaptation of Agent Behavior in Simulation Based Training

Simulations and games offer better opportunities to exert control over training than real-life training environments do. For example, scenarios can easily be reused, improved and adapted for different situations and learners. The behavior of all actors in the scenario can be controlled and the behavior of the learner can be elaboratively measured. Adaptive agents may be used to support personalized fit-for-purpose training, but a framework is needed for their autonomous and dynamic operation.

2.1   Demands for an Adaptive Agent Framework

Peeters [33] has defined the demands for an automatically directed scenario-based training system. This can also be used to determine the requirements for adaptations of agent behavior.

First, the adaptation of agent behavior should be consistent with the training scenario, that has been purposely designed to enable the learner to achieve specific learning objectives. The default behavior of the virtual characters are explicitly part of the scenario. Adaptations in the agents' behavior should not disrupt the scenario's goal.

Secondly, any adaptations in agent behavior should be consistent with the character that the agent represents. If adaptations that are intended to enforce the desired behavior by the trainee result in agent behavior that is unnatural for the virtual character, they should nevertheless be omitted. Agent-adaptations that cause unnatural behavior to become part of the learner's mental representation would do more damage than good.

Thirdly, the adaptation should be *fit for purpose*, i.e., tuned to the specific needs of the individual learner. Learners may differ from one another in many ways, like for example, intelligence level, personality, preferred learning strategy, prior knowledge and experience, and pace of progress during learning. Adaptations should therefore be based upon a model of the specific learner [1] that is dynamically updated as learning progresses. Only then can the adaptations be selected that fit the learner in question, bringing about a situation that supports the learner to attain a goal or to engage in a task that otherwise may be out of reach [33, 48].

Fourthly, adaptation of agent behavior should support or maintain the sensation of *'flow'* in the learner. Flow refers to a situation where learners are so engaged in the learning activity that they have a reduced sense of time and self-consciousness, and feel intrinsically motivated to engage in a complex goal-directed activity, simply for the exhilaration of doing [9]. There is evidence that flow brings about better performance and higher self-efficacy [20].

Fifthly, adaptations to agent behavior need to be applied in a controllable fashion, to safeguard the integrity of the overall scenario. One approach is to assign decisions about adaptations to the agent itself. This has the advantage that the adaptations are in correspondence with the agent's knowledge and character, and is therefore likely to show behavior that is believable in the perception of the learner. The disadvantage is that the agent's decision about adaptations may be in conflict with the narrative structure of the scenario. Another approach is to instead assign the decision making in the scenario, enforcing only those adaptations that support the plot. The disadvantage is that such adaptations may violate the consistency and believability of the agent. The challenge of control is therefore to ensure the agents' freedom of action while maintaining a purposeful and coherent training scenario [3,29].

2.2 Framework for Adaptive Agent Behavior

A proposed solution for the control problem is to include a supervising director agent in the training framework [34] that manages the scenario, and that -when considered necessary- initiates behavior adaptations that have instructional value to the learner, and are consistent with the nature of the NPC-agent[1] in the context of the scenario.

Figure 2 shows a framework for adaptive agent behavior in simulation-based training that is able to accommodate the demands described above.

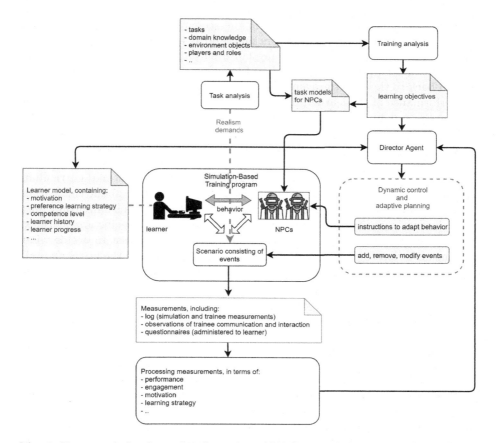

Fig. 2. Framework for dynamic adaptation of NPC-agent behavior to achieve fit-for-purpose simulation-based training.

---

[1] *Non-Playing Character*, a virtual character in a simulation not controlled by a player.

First, the task to be learned has to be analyzed in the context of its domain (the task analysis), revealing the constituent (sub-)tasks, domain knowledge, the players involved, and so on (see upper part of Fig. 2). This information is used for the training analysis, identifying the set of knowledge and skills needed to be able to carry out the tasks (skill requirements). It is also assessed what skills are already mastered by the learners, and what skills need to be developed, resulting in the learning objectives of the training. Furthermore, results of task analysis and the learning objectives are used to define the task-behavior models for the NPCs [13].

The director agent executes the adopted principles of learning. For military tactical decision making this may be as described in Sect. 1.3. The director agent controls the course and content of the default simulation-based training program (like the scenario, the events and the predefined roles and behavior of the NPCs).

Learners may not all respond in the same manner to a training program. For example, some may find the exercise in the scenario difficult, others may find it easy. Some may be engaged, others may find it boring. Some may achieve a learning objective quickly; others may fail even after multiple attempts. Information about the process and results of learning are measured and processed, and fed back to the director agent. The director agent monitors the scenario and the performance of the learner, dynamically updates the learner model and uses this model to determine whether the current state of the scenario is still a fit-for-learning environment for this learner, or whether fit-for-purpose adaptations are needed. This may involve instructions to an NPC to adapt its behavior.

A learner model is an important component of adaptive learning systems [45]. Their function is to provide the data for individualizing content and curriculum sequencing. Depending on the domain, needs for information about the learner and its learning can vary. For many domains, competence level is important, just as the learner's motivation to master the task [31,37]. For specific applications, the learner's physical and mental fitness may also be of interest to decide what learning situation to present [24]. Other interesting factors are the learner's preference for a learning strategy, the learner history and learning progress of the learner.

3   A Pilot Study

This study addresses the question whether personalized adjustments in the behavior of agents leads to a training with better learning results and a better training experience, compared with a training using non-adaptive agents. There is evidence that personal characteristics, such as e.g.., motivation and self-efficacy, affect learning and performance [31,37]. Therefore, measures of personal characteristics were included in this study. An additional purpose of this pilot study is to test the experimental setup, the design, and whether the desired changes in the behavior of the agents can be implemented properly and in time in the scenario. It is also investigated whether the adopted measurements for assessing effects on learning and learning experiences are suitable for use in a larger follow-up study.

The following research questions were formulated:

1. Do personalized adjustments in the behavior of agents lead to a better learning result?
2. Do personalized adjustments in the behavior of agents lead to better training experiences by learners?
3. Do the personal characteristics of motivation and self-efficacy influence the effects of adaptive training on learning and performance?

3.1 Methods

Participants: Six participants were recruited (4 male, 2 female). All were academic students, with their age ranging from 23 to 37 years old. Participants varied in their game-playing experience, from very little to a lot. Four participants indicated to have experience with playing military games.

Design: The independent variable 'adaptivity' had two levels (adaptive versus standardized agent behavior), and was manipulated between subjects. Participants in the experimental condition received a training scenario with agents acting adaptively to the learning needs. In contrast, participants in the control condition received a training scenario with agents acting in a standardized fashion, irrespective of the participant's learning needs. On a subsequent test scenario, all participants of both groups played the scenario with agents acting in a standardized fashion. Participants were randomly assigned to one of the two groups.

In the *control condition*, the agents behaved in a pre-specified and standardized fashion that was plausible given the situation in the scenario. Agents were designed to provide, through their behavior, the trainee with implicit cues and feedback about the consequences of his/her decisions and behavior [28].

In the *experimental condition*, the behavior of the trainee was continuously evaluated in real-time. If it matched the behavior of a particular learning objective, then the agent behaved as pre-specified. If it did not match, the participant apparently failed to achieve the learning objective, and then a predefined adaptation was applied to the agent's behavior. The purpose of the adaptation is to make the agent provide additional explicit or implicit cues, instructions and feedback to the participant in order to support understanding what behavior is appropriate for that specific situation.

Experimental Setting: The experiment took place in room with a large table (see Fig. 3). The game play was recorded.

The experiment employs a 'Wizard of Oz' technique [10], which means that the experiment leader (the 'wizard') simulates and controls the behavior of a director agent. This technique makes it possible to administer intelligent adaptations to agent behavior, without the need of actually implementing a model that can do the same autonomously. Note that the wizard strictly complied with the predefined decision rules of the director agent.

Fig. 3. Experimental setting.

Materials - Scenarios, Scenes and Events: Participants played a training and a test scenario with the game Virtual Battle Space 3 (VBS3)[2]. The participant played the role of platoon commander. The task to be learned was commanding the platoon on a social patrol mission in a small village, situated in an "Afghanistan"-like environment. This scenario was developed for the training of tactical officers of the Netherlands Army and was reused for the present study. The participant receives a briefing of the current situation before the start of the scenario, stating that armed enemy units have been seen in the area and that the task of the participant is to gather more information about the situation.

The specific goal of the platoon is to go to the marketplace of the village and try to get information from the village chief about a possible enemy threat. Pre-specified events ensure that the situation escalates and eventually a combat situation arises. Each scenario consists of the following scenes: 1) Start of the mission; 2) Approaching the market; 3) On the market; 4) Market crowd is leaving; 5) First time under fire; 6) Second time under fire; 7) Team member is hit; 8) Withdrawal from the mission area. Each scene consist of several events (for example: in scene 4, 'on the market', the village chief appears). An event provides the trainee with the opportunity to achieve a learning objective.

Applying Adaptations: An evaluator was tasked to evaluate in real-time whether or not the participant's behavior matched the requirements of the learning objective at hand. If the evaluator observed that the participant made an error, then this was passed on to the experiment leader (see Fig. 3) who subsequently initiated an adaptation in the behavior of the agent(s). Table 1 shows examples of learning objectives, potential errors, and associated adaptations. Note that adaptations were only given during the training scenario of participants in the experimental condition.

---

[2] https://bisimulations.com/products/vbs3.

Table 1. Examples of learning objectives, potential errors, and adaptations.

General learning objective	Potential error	Adaptation
Ensuring constant view on all sectors during the mission	Not having a 360° view when approaching the market	[An armed NPC runs behind the platoon.] A soldier says: "Behind us! An armed man!"
Addressing the village chief in an open, kind and polite manner	Keeping the rifle at the ready when addressing the village chief	Village chief says: "I thought we were on good terms, so why do you treat me like this?"

Measures: Both the training and the test scenario consisted of 31 learning objectives, each evaluated by the experimenter as either achieved (1), or not achieved (0). Learning objectives belonged to one of the following competences: planning; situational awareness; decision making; and command and control. The average of the associated learning objectives was taken as the participant's competency score.

In addition to these performance measures, the Motivated Strategies for Learning Questionnaire (MSLQ) [35] was administered to measure the confidence of participants to be able to learn the task (self-efficacy for learning and performance), and whether participants think that their efforts will lead to learning performance (control of learning beliefs).

Three more questionnaires were administered at the posttest: the scale 'interest and enjoyment' of the Intrinsic Motivation Inventory (IMI) [11] was used to measure the motivation of the participant. The participant's appreciation of the game as an environment to learn from was measured by using the scale 'game worlds' of the Game-based learning Evaluation Model (GEM) questionnaire [32], and the value/usefulness subscale of the IMI. Finally, the Immersion questionnaire [22] was used to measure how immersed the participant felt in the game.

Procedure: The participants took part in the experiment one by one. After a short briefing, and filling out questionnaires, a practice phase started. This was to familiarize the participant with the controls of VBS3, and to learn how to interact with NPCs (by speaking aloud). For this practice, an entirely different setting was used (a western suburban neighborhood) than during the training. In order to make NPCs respond in a plausible fashion, a large series of possible phrases were audio-recorded prior to the experiment. When the participant addressed an NPC, or when the scene demanded a verbal action of an NPC, the experiment leader selected an appropriate phrase and played that back. If no suitable pre-recorded response was available, then the experiment leader himself responded, on behalf of the NPC, through speech.

After completing the practice with the game environment, the controls, and the interaction with NPCs, the training scenario was started. After completion, a short break of 5 min was given. Then the participants played the scenario for a second time. After this, post-test questionnaires were administered.

3.2 Results

This pilot-study involved no more than six participants. Therefore, effects of personalized adjustments in the behavior of agents can only be explored, not tested. For this reason, results will be reported only on a descriptive level, without performing statistical analyses.

Table 2 shows results of the confidence that participants have in learning the task successfully (self-efficacy), and whether participants think that their efforts will lead to learning performance (control of learning beliefs). These variables correlated .73.

Table 2. Judgments of participants (means, s.d. in parentheses) whether their efforts will lead to successful learning (control of learning beliefs), and their confidence in learning learn the task (self-efficacy for learning), split by experimental group.

	Non-adapative	Adaptive	Total
Control of learning	5.7 (1.0)	5.3 (0.9)	5.5 (0.9)
Self-efficacy	4.0 (1.4)	4.8 (1.1)	4.4 (1.2)

With respect to participants' prior gameplay experience: the two groups had similar experience with playing computer games: a mean of 3 (sd = 1.7) on a 5-points-scale for the *non-adaptive agent training* group, versus 3.3 (sd = .6) for the *adaptive agent training* group.

Performance on Training and Test Scenario: Performance was assessed by using competency scores. A participant's competency score was calculated as the mean of the scores on the learning objectives belonging to that competency. A score for learning objective could either be 1 for achieved; or 0 for not-achieved. Hence, a competency score has a range of 0 (none of the comprising learning objectives achieved) to 1 (all comprising learning objectives achieved).

Training: Figure 4 shows the competency scores. Both groups performed no planning whatsoever during the training scenario. Participants failed to settle task assignments, made no commands concerning communication policies, and did not develop action plans (e.g.., contingency plans). This is perhaps due to the unfamiliarity with the game and the assignment. With respect to the other three competencies, it can be seen that the participants of the *adaptive-agents training* group (orange bars) performed substantially better than participants in the *non-adaptive training agents* group (blue bars). This is most likely caused by the adaptive behavior of the agents. When the experimenter-evaluator observed

Fig. 4. Mean competency scores on the training, split by group. (Color figure online)

that a participant of the *adaptive-agents training* group did not exhibit the behavior required achieving the learning objective, then the experiment-leader initiated an appropriate agent to act in such a fashion that it supported the learner to reflect upon his behavior, and also to recognize that the nature of the situation demands a different response than the one just given (see Table 1). This adaptation of agents has likely cued the participant to be alert in similar kind of situations further on in the scenario, and may also have promoted the participant to be more reflective in general. Participants of the *non-adaptive-agents training* group received no such clear cues, and therefore had less opportunity to improve during the scenario.

Test: Figure 5 shows the competency scores.

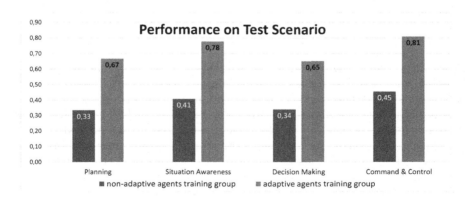

Fig. 5. Mean competency scores on the test, split by group.

Both groups performed better on the test scenario than during the training scenario. They apparently learned that planning and sharing plans is required to perform the mission adequately: they assigned tasks to their team members more often and some participants distributed policies for team-internal and team-external communication. Note that for both groups, agents in the test scenario did not act adaptively. So they were both presented with exactly the same scenario. Nevertheless, the *adaptive agents training group* performed substantially better (overall approximately 90%) than the *non-adaptive agents training group*. This indicates that the instructional effects of the adaptive agents during the training exercise continued to affect positively the performance on the test scenario. Participants of the *non-adaptive agents training group* also improved their performance, but did not nearly approached the level of the *adaptive agents training group*.

Relationship Between Participants' Beliefs and Performance: It was investigated whether the participants' performance on the test scenario was related to their beliefs about the results of their learning efforts (control of learning) and of their estimated ability to learn the task (self-efficacy). Kendall's tau correlations were calculated between the measures Control of Learning and Self-efficacy with the four competency scores obtained on the posttest. See Table 3 for results. The correlations are low to moderate, indicating that their beliefs on being able to learn and perform the task have little influence on the outcomes measures.

Table 3. Correlations between participants' self-assessments and performance on competency scores at the test scenario.

	Planning	Situation awareness	Decision making	Command & control
Control of learning	0.22	0.14	0.33	0.20
Self-efficacy	0.36	0.14	0.60	0.47

Reliability of Performance Evaluation: The experimenter-evaluator assessed, while the participant was playing the scenario, whether the participant's behavior either matched, or did not match, the criteria of the current learning objective. All game-play was video-recorded, including all audio from the participant, the agent, and the experiment leader. This enabled a second assessment, afterwards, by a second evaluator. This evaluator was instructed with the performance evaluation protocol. Assessments of both evaluators were used to calculate the interrater reliability. Evaluators were on 239 of the 328 assements in agremeent; on 79 they scored differently.

The calculated measure of agreement (Kappa) is .5. This is generally considered a weak level of agreement [30]. One likely reason for this result is the low number of participants. Another reason is that in a realistic simulation of a complex real-life task, such as military command in this case, it is difficult to unequivocally determine whether the observed behavior matches, or does not match a criterion. For example, one learning objectives was '*to maintain a 360-view when approaching the market place*'. It can be hard to assess from observing the participant, or from viewing the gameplay, whether or not this objective has been achieved. Furthermore, the evaluation protocol marked at what point in the scenario the desired behavior was to be expected. During a post-scoring discussion, it turned out that if the participant exhibited the desired behavior earlier, or (slightly) later than in the expected timeframe, this was not considered identically between evaluators. Finally, the level of detail in the information differed between evaluators. The first evaluator could, in addition to the gameplay, also observe the participant in action, thereby having access to subtle, but potentially informative behavioral cues. The second evaluator only saw the recorded gameplay, in combination with the audio-recorded communication. This difference may have had a negative influence on the interrater reliability. For future studies, it is recommended to define a very thorough evaluation protocol, and to have a second evaluator present while the training and test are being administered.

Immersion and Evaluation of Learning Environment: Do adaptive agents in the game environment invoke a higher level of immersion and engagement in the learners compared with non-adaptive agents? Figure 6 shows the results of the posttest measures.

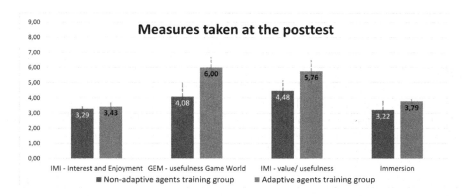

Fig. 6. Results of posttest measures in means and sd's, split by group.

After playing both scenarios, the two groups were comparable with respect to their self-assessed intrinsic motivation. Participants that trained with the adaptive agents considered the game and scenarios considerably better as a suitable learning environment than participants that trained with non-adaptive agents. This result was obtained with the GEM as well with the IMI. Finally, participants of the adaptive agents training group reported to be slightly more immersed than participants of the other group.

3.3   Discussion of Pilot Study

This pilot study investigated whether personalized adjustments in the behavior of agents leads to a training with better learning results and a better training experience. First, it should be noted that only a few participants were tested. Thus, results need to be taken as preliminary and with reservation.

One objective of the present pilot-study was to test the experimental setup. Overall, this worked as hoped for. But administering the scenarios, evaluating the participant's behavior in real time, and selecting the appropriate adaptations for the agents was quite taxing for the experiment leader and evaluator.

It is encouraging that the applied adaptations in the behavior of agents, with the intention to make the exercise more fit for purpose for the learner, resulted in better competency scores. This was found not only for the training scenario, but also on the test scenario. This suggests that what was learned, was carried over to an exercise in which no fit-for-purpose behavior of agents was provided. Another positive outcome was that the adaptations seemed to have brought about a more interesting and useful learning environment, according to the participants. Furthermore, adaptation may also have caused a more immersive experience, although the differences are relatively small.

In contrast to the literature [31,37], the personal characteristics of the learners of our study, in particular their motivation, control of learning behavior, and self-efficacy, correlated low with learning and performance. This may have to do with the low number of participants.

The scenario for this study was developed according to the principles of event-based approach to training [15], with the learning objectives explicitly coupled onto events in the scenario, and with defining descriptive measures for how to evaluate the participants' behavior as either achieving or failing the learning objective. It was therefore disappointing to find that, regarding the performance evaluations, the agreement between the experiment-evaluator and a post-hoc evaluator was rather low. This may partly have to do with differences in the information available to both evaluators, but it also points out that the protocol for evaluating performance needs to be defined in even more verifiable terms.

Gaming experience was found to significantly influence the nature of the gameplay. Participants that had few or no gaming experience experienced more difficulty with learning the controls and how to use them appropriately. Participants with experience in military games used the controls fluently, but they appeared to pay little attention to the mission instructions, nor to the cues that became available through NPCs. In future studies, we aim to recruit participants with moderate gaming experience (preferably not with first-shooter games), and with elementary military background knowledge.

4   Discussion

This paper addressed the issue of rendering fit-for-purpose simulations by adapting the behavior of virtual characters in real time, in such a fashion that the emerging situation is tuned to the learner's needs. Requirements for agent control have been formulated, and a framework for dynamic adaptation of agent behavior has been proposed. A pilot study reveals encouraging outcomes, suggesting that behavior adaptations bring about better learning, and perhaps also a higher engagement in the learner.

To collect more evidence, a proposal for a follow-up study has been submitted to administer the experiment to a new and larger group of participants. Lessons learned will be taken into account. To obtain a more homogeneous sample, participants will be recruited from young soldiers that are in the final stage of the preparatory military training. It is expected that they have a military mindset in common, but do not yet have experience in tactical operations. That study will again employ a wizard-of-oz that simulates a director agent.

For practical applications of the framework, the principles and algorithms need to be implemented in a computational version of a director agent. This will bring along challenges on many fields. One lies in achieving a functional and coordinated cooperation between a director agent and NPCs to effectively support learning. In our adaptive agent framework (see Sect. 2), we propose to assign domain-specific functions to NPC-agents, and instructional functions to a director agent. For example, NPC-agents need behavior models that enable them to behave in an appropriate and believable manner. Furthermore, these models should allow NPC-agents to exhibit the behavior that is appropriate for a specific exercise (e.g.., performing as a novice), or that satisfies the call of the director agent for adaptation. And the models should also enable the agent to construct explanations that inform the learner about its behavior, with the aim to support a better understanding of the interaction between them [19]. In our framework, it is not the NPC-agents who take decisions about whether and when to exhibit what behavior; these are taken by a director agent. Similarly, decisions about whether and when to provide what explanation can best be give, are made by a director agent rather than by the NPC-agent itself.

Another challenge for the present case is the open-ended nature of military tactical command, making it hard to interpret the intent of learner's actions. The challenge of modeling adequately the learners' domain knowledge, cognitive skills, and interests [1,7,21] will be crucial for a director agent to successfully achieve fit-for-purpose adaptive training.

References

1. Basu, S., Biswas, G., Kinnebrew, J.S.: Learner modeling for adaptive scaffolding in a computational thinking-based science learning environment. User Model. User-Adap. Inter. **27**(1), 5–53 (2017)
2. Bell, B., Sottilare, R.: Adaptation vectors for instructional agents. In: Sottilare, R.A., Schwarz, J. (eds.) HCII 2019. LNCS, vol. 11597, pp. 3–14. Springer, Cham (2019). https://doi.org/10.1007/978-3-030-22341-0_1
3. van den Bosch, K., Harbers, M., Heuvelink, A., van Doesburg, W.: Intelligent agents for training on-board fire fighting. In: Duffy, V.G. (ed.) ICDHM 2009. LNCS, vol. 5620, pp. 463–472. Springer, Heidelberg (2009). https://doi.org/10.1007/978-3-642-02809-0_49

4. van den Bosch, K., Helsdingen, A.: Critical thinking in tactical decision games training. In: Noyes, J., Cook, M., Masakowshi, Y. (Eds.) Decision Making in Complex Environments, pp. 213–222. Taylor & Francis, London (2007)
5. Buede, D., DeBlois, B., Maxwell, D., McCarter, B.: Filling the need for intelligent, adaptive non-player characters. In: Proceedings of the Interservice Industry Training, Simulation, and Education Conference (IITSEC) (2013)
6. Cannon-Bowers, J., et al.: Bridging the gap: how to build effective game-based training. In: Tutorial presented at the Interservice Industry Training, Simulation, and Education Conference (IITSEC), p. 26, Orlando (2014)
7. Chrysafiadi, K., Virvou, M.: Student modeling for personalized education: a review of the literature. Advances in Personalized Web-Based Education. ISRL, vol. 78, pp. 1–24. Springer, Cham (2015). https://doi.org/10.1007/978-3-319-12895-5_1
8. Conati, C., Porayska-Pomsta, K., Mavrikis, M.: AI in education needs interpretable machine learning: lessons from open learner modelling. arXiv preprint arXiv:1807.00154 (2018)
9. Csikszentmihalyi, M.: Applications of Flow in Human Development and Education. Springer, Heidelberg (2014)
10. Dahlbäck, N., Jönsson, A., Ahrenberg, L.: Wizard of OZ studies: why and how. In: Proceedings of the 1st International Conference on Intelligent User Interfaces, pp. 193–200 (1993)
11. Deci, E., Ryan, R.: Intrinsic Motivation Inventory (IMI). [WWW document]. Self-Determination Theory. http://www.selfdeterminationtheory.org/intrinsic-motivation-inventory/. Accessed 14 Oct 2005
12. Desmarais, M.C., Baker, R.S.: A review of recent advances in learner and skill modeling in intelligent learning environments. User Model. User-Adap. Inter. 22(1–2), 9–38 (2012)
13. Farmer, E., Van Rooij, J., Riemersma, J., Jorna, P.: Handbook of Simulator-Based Training. Routledge, Abingdon (2017)
14. Feinstein, A.H., Cannon, H.M.: Constructs of simulation evaluation. Simul. Gaming 33(4), 425–440 (2002)
15. Fowlkes, J., Dwyer, D.J., Oser, R.L., Salas, E.: Event-based approach to training (EBAT). Int. J. Aviat. Psychol. 8(3), 209–221 (1998)
16. Freeman, J., Watz, E., Bennett, W.: Adaptive agents for adaptive tactical training: the state of the art and emerging requirements. In: Sottilare, R.A., Schwarz, J. (eds.) HCII 2019. LNCS, vol. 11597, pp. 493–504. Springer, Cham (2019). https://doi.org/10.1007/978-3-030-22341-0_39
17. Gonzalez, C.: Training decisions from experience with decision making games. Adaptive technologies for training and education, pp. 167–178 (2012)
18. Hamstra, S.J., Brydges, R., Hatala, R., Zendejas, B., Cook, D.A.: Reconsidering fidelity in simulation-based training. Acad. Med. 89(3), 387–392 (2014)
19. Harbers, M., Meyer, J.J., Van den Bosch, K.: Explaining simulations through self explaining agents. J. Artif. Soc. Soc. Simul. 12(3), 6 (2009)
20. Jackson, S.A., Thomas, P.R., Marsh, H.W., Smethurst, C.J.: Relationships between flow, self-concept, psychological skills, and performance. J. Appl. Sport Psychol. 13(2), 129–153 (2001)
21. Jantke, K.P., Schmidt, B., Schnappauf, R.: Next generation learner modeling by theory of mind model induction. In: CSEDU, vol. 1, pp. 499–506 (2016)
22. Jennett, C., et al.: Measuring and defining the experience of immersion in games. Int. J. Hum. Comput. Stud. 66(9), 641–661 (2008)
23. Johnson, A., Taatgen, N.: User modeling. In: The Handbook of Human Factors in Web Design, pp. 424–438 (2005)

24. Kahol, K., et al.: Effect of fatigue on psychomotor and cognitive skills. Am. J. Surg. **195**(2), 195–204 (2008)
25. Kenny, P., et al.: Building interactive virtual humans for training environments. In: Proceedings of I/ITSEC, vol. 174, pp. 911–916 (2007)
26. Kirschner, P.A., Sweller, J., Clark, R.E.: Why minimal guidance during instruction does not work: An analysis of the failure of constructivist, discovery, problem-based, experiential, and inquiry-based teaching. Educ. Psychol. **41**(2), 75–86 (2006)
27. Korteling, J.E., Helsdingen, A.S., Baeyer, A.V.: Handbook of low-cost simulation for military training. ELSTAR-EUCLID RTP 11.8, ELS-DEL/5-HB, Index 8, Issue dated 02/05/00 (2000)
28. Laird, J.E., et al.: Interactive task learning. IEEE Intell. Syst. **32**(4), 6–21 (2017)
29. Löckelt, M., Pecourt, E., Pfleger, N.: Balancing narrative control and autonomy for virtual characters in a game scenario. In: Maybury, M., Stock, O., Wahlster, W. (eds.) INTETAIN 2005. LNCS (LNAI), vol. 3814, pp. 251–255. Springer, Heidelberg (2005). https://doi.org/10.1007/11590323_29
30. McHugh, M.L.: Interrater reliability: the kappa statistic. Biochem. Med. **22**(3), 276–282 (2012)
31. Normadhi, N.B.A., Shuib, L., Nasir, H.N.M., Bimba, A., Idris, N., Balakrishnan, V.: Identification of personal traits in adaptive learning environment: systematic literature review. Comput. Educ. **130**, 168–190 (2019)
32. Oprins, E., Visschedijk, G., Roozeboom, M.B., Dankbaar, M., Trooster, W., Schuit, S.C.: The game-based learning evaluation model (GEM): measuring the effectiveness of serious games using a standardised method. Int. J. Technol. Enhanc. Learn. **7**(4), 326 (2015)
33. Peeters, M.: Personalized educational games-developing agent-supported scenario-based training. Ph.D. thesis, SIKS, the Dutch Graduate School for Information and Knowledge Systems (2014)
34. Peeters, M.M., Van Den Bosch, K., Meyer, J.J.C., Neerincx, M.A.: Agent-based personalisation and user modeling for personalised educational games. In: Proceedings of the 2016 Conference on User Modeling Adaptation and Personalization (2016)
35. Pintrich, P.R., Smith, D.A., Garcia, T., McKeachie, W.J.: Reliability and predictive validity of the Motivated Strategies for Learning Questionnaire (MSLQ). Educ. Psychol. Measur. **53**(3), 801–813 (1993)
36. Premlatha, K.R., Geetha, T.V.: Learning content design and learner adaptation for adaptive e-learning environment: a survey. Artif. Intell. Rev. **44**(4), 443–465 (2015)
37. Richardson, M., Abraham, C., Bond, R.: Psychological correlates of university students' academic performance: a systematic review and meta-analysis. Psychol. Bull. **138**(2), 353–387 (2012)
38. Sanders, A.F.: Simulation as a tool in the measurement of human performance. Ergonomics **34**(8), 995–1025 (1991)
39. Scerbo, M.W., Dawson, S.: High fidelity, high performance?: simulation in healthcare. J. Soc. Simul. Healthc. **2**(4), 224–230 (2007)
40. Schank, R.C.: The pragmatics of learning by doing. Pragmat. Soc. **1**(1), 157–172 (2010)
41. Schank, R.C., Berman, T.R., Macpherson, K.A.: Learning by doing. Instr.-Des. Theor. Models: New Paradig. Instr. Theory **2**(2), 161–181 (1999)
42. Schraagen, J.M.: Naturalistic Decision Making. Routledge/Taylor & Francis Group (2018)

43. Sottilare, R., Ragusa, C., Hoffman, M., Goldberg, B.: Characterizing an adaptive tutoring learning effect chain for individual and team tutoring. In: Proceedings of the Interservice/Industry Training Simulation and Education Conference, Orlando, Florida (2013)
44. Sottilare, R.A.: Challenges in moving adaptive training and education from state-of-art to state-of-practice. In: AIED Workshops (2015)
45. Sottilare, R.A., Boyce, M.W.: Elements of adaptive instruction for training and education. In: Schmorrow, D., Fidopiastis, C. (eds.) Foundations of Augmented Cognition: Neuroergonomics and Operational Neuroscience. AC 2016. LNCS, vol. 9744, pp. 85–89. Springer, Cham (2016). https://doi.org/10.1007/978-3-319-39952-2_9
46. Sottilare, R.A., Goodwin, G.A.: Adaptive instructional methods to accelerate learning and enhance learning capacity. In: International Defense and Homeland Security Simulation Workshop (2017)
47. Vandewaetere, M., Desmet, P., Clarebout, G.: The contribution of learner characteristics in the development of computer-based adaptive learning environments. Comput. Hum. Behav. **27**(1), 118–130 (2011)
48. Vygotsky, L.: Interaction between learning and development. Read. Dev. Child. **23**(3), 34–41 (1978)
49. Warwick, W., Rodgers, S.: Wrong in the right way: balancing realism against other constraints in simulation-based training. In: Sottilare, R.A., Schwarz, J. (eds.) HCII 2019. LNCS, vol. 11597, pp. 379–388. Springer, Cham (2019). https://doi.org/10.1007/978-3-030-22341-0_30
50. Wouters, P., van Oostendorp, H.: Overview of instructional techniques to facilitate learning and motivation of serious games. In: Wouters, P., van Oostendorp, H. (eds.) Instructional Techniques to Facilitate Learning and Motivation of Serious Games. Advances in Game-Based Learning, pp. 1–16. Springer, Cham (2017). https://doi.org/10.1007/978-3-319-39298-1_1
51. Yildirim, S.: Serious game design for military training. In: Games: Design and Research Conference, Volda University College, pp. 3–4 (2010)

Google Service-Based CbITS Authoring Tool to Support Collaboration

Lijia Wang[1(✉)], Keith Shubeck[1], and Xiangen Hu[1,2(✉)]

[1] The University of Memphis, Memphis, USA
{lwang3,xhu}@memphis.edu
[2] Central China Normal University, Wuhan, China

Abstract. The intelligent tutoring system (ITS) is one of the typical Adaptive Instructional Systems (AIS) applications. ITS has been one of the cutting-edge research fields over the past three decades. Despite the many successes of ITSs, there are a few challenges for implementing them on a large scale. One significant challenge is content authoring [14,21]. Many authoring components of ITSs are inaccessible to the average user due to their complexity and time-consuming nature. This paper introduces a potential cloud-based solution that will make authoring ITS content faster and relatively easier than existing methods. We believe that our approach can be utilized by other similar systems.

Keywords: AIS · ITS · AutoTutor · Authoring · Collaboration · xAPI

1 Introduction

Adaptive Instructional Systems (AIS) aim to optimize learning, performance, and the transfer of knowledge/skills by using evidence-based pedagogical strategies [20]. The Intelligent Tutoring System (ITS) shares the same goal using its "intelligence". Here, intelligence refers to the capacity for these systems to ask students open questions and to generate instructional material on demand [4,24]. Thus, ITS is considered as a subset of AIS which is used to manage adaptive instructions. Meanwhile, technological advances, especially the Internet and cloud computing, have made ITS research and implementation one of the fastest developing areas in learning technology and applications. Research has shown that students benefit more from ITSs than from antiquated page-turning learning software [4,24]. However, there are a few challenges and issues for implementing ITSs and spreading the use of them on a large scale. One significant challenge is content authoring [14,21]. Many ITSs suffered a lack of usage and low impact due to their complexity and time-consuming nature. To solve the issue, our team proposed a new web service-based method. The ITS implemented is our pilot system called AutoTutor.

© Springer Nature Switzerland AG 2020
C. Stephanidis et al. (Eds.): HCII 2020, LNCS 12425, pp. 605–616, 2020.
https://doi.org/10.1007/978-3-030-60128-7_44

1.1   Authoring Content in AutoTutor

AutoTutor is a conversation-based intelligent tutoring system (CbITS). Auto-
Tutor is an effective AIS that has been used for research in the learning sciences
for over 20 years [15]. A review of 17 years of AutoTutor research shows average
learning gains of 0.8 σ compared to controls [15]. Key features of AutoTutor
include its learner characteristic curve (LCC) [11,12,23], a simplified student
model, animated agents with text-to-speech, and semantic analysis services to
hold conversations with learners.

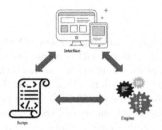

Fig. 1. The three components of an AutoTutor application

A fully functional AutoTutor application consists of three components
(Fig. 1): XML content script, user interface, and the central component, Auto-
Tutor Conversation Engine (ACE). The user interface may vary given different
knowledge domains and necessary interaction modules for different purposes.
Thus, the UI of AutoTutor is very flexible and can adopt different operation
environments such as web browsers, tablets, and mobile phones. The application
UI will also receive a message from ACE and display it as a sentence during a
conversation session between one or more agents and the user. Figure 2 shows
AutoTutor applications in the domain of computer literacy [9,10], conceptual
physics [9,19], biology [18], critical thinking [5,25], mathematics [16,17], electronics [8,13], and adult literacy [2,6]. The core of the AutoTutor, ACE, will receive
user input (either text input or speech input) and other interaction parameters
such multiple-choice responses [2,6] and emotions [1] to guide the conversation
based on the script's content and rules. The natural language processing (NLP)
component utilizes latent semantic analysis and regular expressions to accurately
assess and respond to the user's conversational input.

1.2   AutoTutor Scripts

AutoTutor XML script contains many functions such as the learning content,
computer agent's speech behaviors, conversation rules, and media information.
Scripts that are made up of an abundance of carefully crafted text-to-speech
content certainly contributes to AutoTutor's effectiveness [15]. However, as with
most ITSs, AutoTutor content authors may find it challenging to craft an ideal

script for multiple AutoTutor modules, complete with all the necessary text and media objects. In particular, the multimedia and natural language behind each conversation demands a great deal of effort for content authors [3] as well as other experts in other fields. Therefore, creating a series of exemplary Auto-Tutor scripts requires an authoring team consisting of subject matter experts, instructional designers, NLP experts, and programming experts. Domain experts primarily focus on crafting the knowledge structure and designing the learning content The instructional designer is primarily concerned with the necessary interactions between users and the learning objects. Programming experts will ensure the UI is both presentable and functional. As a conversation-based ITS, NLP experts are necessary to resolve any performance issues regarding the conversations between computer agents and users. It is also necessary for both the domain experts and instructional designers to be familiar with AutoTutor's expectation-misconception tailored (EMT) dialogue structure. These high entry barriers require additional training before the domain experts can work individually with good efficiency. There is a large incentive to improve the system's authoring process, given how resource intensive this process may be.

Fig. 2. AutoTutor examples

A basic AutoTutor XML script (Fig. 3) has five components that perform the basic conversation learning functions with the EMT structure. They are Agents, SpeechActs, RigidPacks, TutoringPacks, and Rules. Their functions and roles in the AutoTutor are described below:

- Agents: The personality of the avatars demonstrated by stylistic feedback (positive, neutral, negative).

- SpeechActs: Defines the regular expression used to capture certain user feedback types with strong keywords such as "Yes", "No", "Confuse".
- Rigid Packs: Specify pre-determined information delivery and interactions such as the tutoring session's opening or closing statements.
- Tutoring Packs: Implement Expectation-Misconception Tailored (EMT) dialogue of AutoTutor [7].
- Rules: A list of "if-then" conditions that direct the conversation when interacting with a learner.

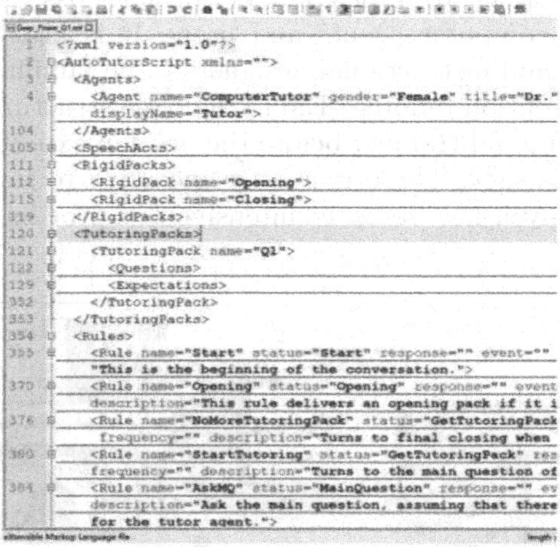

Fig. 3. An example for a basic AutoTutor XML script from ElectronixTutor [8, 13, 26]

2   CbITS AutoTutor: Proposal and Methods

To improve and relieve the potential authoring issues, one potential solution to this problem is through a general framework and systematic approach to authoring content in an ITS [22]. For example, the Generalized Intelligent Framework for Tutoring (GIFT), offers both a generalized authoring framework and standardized format, and standardized format that can save time and effort in managing learning objects and enables the reuse of old content. It establishes a platform to share the learning objects within the community. However, there is still a challenge for providing collaborative support that can accelerate the authoring process.

In this paper, we propose the new AutoTutor script authoring tool based on the Google service (ASAT-G). Like the term, "web-based service", "Google service-based" could refer to an application or user interface that uses the integrated google suite services. These include Google drive, forms, spreadsheets, and other apps like Gmail and calendar (Fig. 4). The handy usability of Google suite services, particularly the Google App script, makes it an attractive option for a collaborative authoring tool. Google app script is a javascript-like coding language platform that integrates the other services. It also accepts coding using other 4th generation coding languages like Python. It allows its users to develop applications or add-ons to take advantage of the G-suite services through the API. Its compiler and editor do not require downloading any software; it is entirely web-based. Additionally, the powerful Google cloud computing resource further guarantees good performance and steady access to the designed app. The most important feature of the G Suite and its cloud computing is the inherent collaboration function of a Google sheet/doc. Our redesign of the AutoTutor script authoring tool, ASAT-G, takes full advantage of these Google services in an effort to improve the content authoring.

Fig. 4. Google services supported by google app script

Figure 5 shows the designed architecture of ASAT-G. The authoring tool main body is a google spreadsheet containing many sheets. There are three major sheets in the tool: the project sheet, the tree sheet, and the XML viewer sheet. Each sheet has its unique role during the authoring process. The project sheet serves as a simple project management system or overview. It allows the project owner to view, open, and manage the learning objects under his or her account. The tree structure can clearly show the project folders and the files (to be specific, the response sheets, the google forms, and corresponding XML script(s)) saved inside. The tree sheet is the place for content authoring. A tree sheet will be re-constructed when a new project is first created and configured. Two response sheets and forms are created and saved in the project folder due to the unique EMT dialogue structure. The entity "Coding" will identify the type of a question or answer (main question, expectations, hint, prompt, or corresponding answer). Triggers are created to have one-to-one binding between a response sheet and a form. The XML viewer sheet is the page to create the AutoTutor XML script. A regular AutoTutor script is divided into separate sections, based on the XML elements. Thus, this is possible to combine different sections from multiple scripts into a new one.

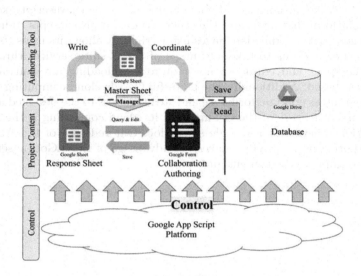

Fig. 5. The architecture of ASAT-G

2.1 The Workflow of ASAT-G

Figure 6 shows the workflow of the new ASAT-G. It starts with the Master Sheet of the authoring tool. One can either choose to do a quick start using the configuration table or create an empty tree for a clean start. Once the tree is configured, it will be saved in the new-created folder using the folder name chosen, along with the timestamp to prevent the duplicate folder name. Meanwhile, the corresponding response google forms and sheets are generated on the EMT structure. The one to one binding trigger pairs a Google form with a sheet to ensure the content submitted via Google form can be saved properly and queried when one wants to edit the previous submission. After the tree is created, the authoring team could communicate using the built-in chat system to assign different parts of the EMT to various experts. There are usually several functions that need to be filled: text, speech, RegEx (abbreviation for REGular EXpression), and setting the threshold for latent semantic matching. One could imagine the following task delegation. Domain experts would handle the actual text of the questions and answers. Often, multiple experts must collaborate with each other to handle

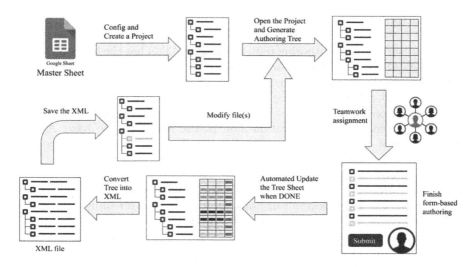

Fig. 6. The workflow of ASAT-G

the abundance of text demands and ensure they are free of errors and high quality. The natural language experts could set the RegEx and answer thresholds. The speech engine will not always pronounce every word, tone, or pitch correctly, particularly esoteric or domain specific words (e.g.., triage, contraindications). Therefore, a native language speaker would play an important role in altering the text so that it sounds natural. After each job is completed and submitted, the master sheet will automatically grab the responses from the response sheet and fill it on the tree table. The project coordinator can easily tell the progress from the tree.

Once the tree content is filled and checked, the project owner could convert the tree content into the TutoringPacks of a standard XML script. The five components of a basic script are not required to be authored each time, especially the content in the Agents, SpeechActs, and Rules. They could be reused because they rarely change much from script to script. Thus, recycling previous content will reduce authoring time and resources. Before authors start a script, they could select from any combination of these four components from previous scripts.

After exhaustive testing, a refinement of the learning objects may be required. The authoring team can easily open the XML in the project sheet and edit the response using the same google form. The modification could be reflected on the tree once it is submitted, saved, and overwrites the old XML.

3   Discussion

Compared with the old authoring tool, the new ASAT-G has the following advantages: first, ASAT is on an open and regularly updated platform, whereas the old version of ASAT is flash-based which will not be supported by major browsers after Dec. 2020. Secondly, the tree viewer interface can better display the parent-children relationship among the elements. Thirdly, the original ASAT does not support teamwork and collaboration [26]. In the ASAT-G, the basic AutoTutor XML script is divided into small units based on the structure of the EMT dialogue (expectations, questions, answers, hints, etc.). The content authoring process no longer belongs to the individual. Teamwork allows each team to work on specific conversation components while also providing feedback and comment for others' work. This process can both lighten the load for individual authors and improve the quality. Compared with the waterfall authoring process, the assembly line authoring process could let team members focus on tasks that play to their strengths.

The split work can also reduce the human operation error during the repeating work. There are no quality assurance people to overview the script in the old authoring method. It is very likely for an individual to make some errors like typos, removing wrong items, or missing some items. Additionally, the real-time information collected in the master sheet lets the project coordinator supervise the authoring process, provide feedback on specific changes, assign individual authors to learning objects, request modifications, and improve the quality by across-check with team members. Therefore, future ITS content authoring should support team collaboration simultaneously so that the authoring process can be less tedious and redundant and authors can be more engaged and focused.

4   Future Work

Looking ahead, more modules are expected to be added to ASAT-G, which will increase the customizability of AutoTutor scripts. These include AutoTutor's learner characteristic curve (LCC), learning objects metadata, and additional multimedia configurations. Given that the authoring tool uses xAPI, future improvements of ASAT-G can be informed by data collected from both author and learner actions.

Appendix A

The UI of ASAT-G

See Figs. 7, 8, 9 and 10.

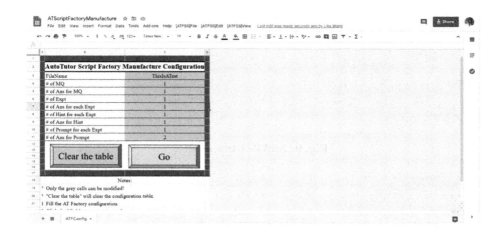

Fig. 7. ASAT-G configuration sheet

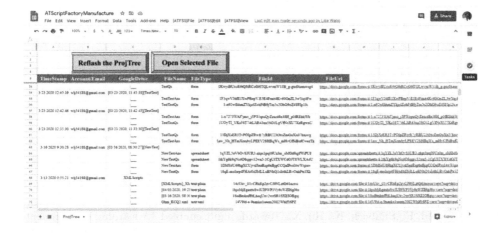

Fig. 8. ASAT-G project sheet

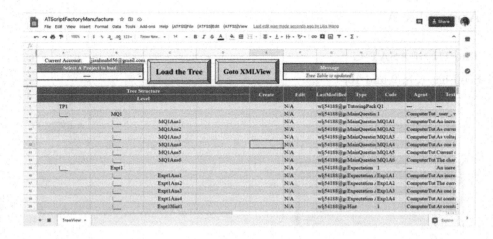

Fig. 9. ASAT-G tree sheet

Fig. 10. ASAT-G XML viewer sheet

References

1. Ahmed, F., Shubeck, K., Hu, X.: Towards a gift enabled 3A learning environment. In: Proceedings of the 8th Annual Generalized Intelligent Framework for Tutoring (GIFT) Users Symposium (GIFTSym8), p. 87. US Army Combat Capabilities Development Command-Soldier Center (2020)
2. Cai, Z., Graesser, A.C., Hu, X., Nye, B.D.: CSAL AutoTutor: integrating rich media with autotutor. In: Generalized Intelligent Framework for Tutoring (GIFT) Users Symposium (GIFTSym3), p. 169 (2015)

3. Cai, Z., Hu, X., Graesser, A.C.: Authoring conversational intelligent tutoring systems. In: Sottilare, R.A., Schwarz, J. (eds.) HCII 2019. LNCS, vol. 11597, pp. 593–603. Springer, Cham (2019). https://doi.org/10.1007/978-3-030-22341-0_46
4. Fletcher, J.D.: The advanced distributed learning (ADL) vision and getting from here to there. Technical report, Institute for Defense Analyses, Alexandria, VA (2005)
5. Graesser, A., et al.: Critiquing media reports with flawed scientific findings: operation ARIES! a game with animated agents and natural language trialogues. In: Aleven, V., Kay, J., Mostow, J. (eds.) International Conference on Intelligent Tutoring Systems ITS 2010. LNCS, vol. 6095, pp. 327–329. Springer, Heidelberg (2010). https://doi.org/10.1007/978-3-642-13437-_60
6. Graesser, A.C., et al.: Reading comprehension lessons in AutoTutor for the center for the study of adult literacy. Adaptive educational technologies for literacy instruction, pp. 288–293 (2016)
7. Graesser, A.C., Chipman, P., Haynes, B.C., Olney, A.: AutoTutor: an intelligent tutoring system with mixed-initiative dialogue. IEEE Trans. Educ. **48**(4), 612–618 (2005)
8. Graesser, A.C., et al.: ElectronixTutor: an intelligent tutoring system with multiple learning resources for electronics. Int. J. STEM Educ. **5**(1), 15 (2018)
9. Graesser, A.C., et al.: Autotutor improves deep learning of computer literacy: is it the dialog or the talking head. In: Proceedings of Artificial Intelligence in Education, pp. 47–54 (2003)
10. Graesser, A.C., Wiemer-Hastings, K., Wiemer-Hastings, P., Kreuz, R.: Tutoring Research Group: AutoTutor: a simulation of a human tutor. Cogn. Syst. Res. **1**(1), 35–51 (1999)
11. Hu, X., Martindale, T.: Enhance learning with its style interactions between learner and content. In: The Interservice/Industry Training, Simulation and Education Conference (I/ITSEC), No. 1 (2008)
12. Hu, X., Morrison, D.M., Cai, Z.: Conversation-based intelligent tutoring system. Des. Recomm. Intell. Tutor. Syst.: Learn. Model. **1**, 97–110 (2013)
13. Morgan, B., et al.: ElectronixTutor integrates multiple learning resources to teach electronics on the web. In: Proceedings of the Fifth Annual ACM Conference on Learning at Scale, pp. 1–2 (2018)
14. Murray, T.: Authoring intelligent tutoring systems: an analysis of the state of the art. Int. J. Artif. Intell. Educ. **10**, 98–129 (1999)
15. Nye, B.D., Graesser, A.C., Hu, X.: AutoTutor and family: a review of 17 years of natural language tutoring. Int. J. Artif. Intell. Educ. **24**(4), 427–469 (2014)
16. Nye, B.D., Pavlik, P.I., Windsor, A., Olney, A.M., Hajeer, M., Hu, X.: SKOPE-IT (Shareable Knowledge Objects as Portable Intelligent Tutors): overlaying natural language tutoring on an adaptive learning system for mathematics. Int. J. STEM Educ. **5**(1), 12 (2018)
17. Nye, B.D., et al.: Evaluating the effectiveness of integrating natural language tutoring into an existing adaptive learning system. In: Conati, C., Heffernan, N., Mitrovic, A., Verdejo, M. (eds.) Artificial Intelligence in Education AIED 2015. LNCS, vol. 9112, pp. 743–747. Springer, Cham (2015). https://doi.org/10.1007/978-3-319-19773-9_106
18. Olney, A.M., Graesser, A.C., Person, N.K.: Tutorial dialog in natural language. In: Nkambou, R., Bourdeau, J., Mizoguchi, R. (eds.) Advances in Intelligent Tutoring Systems. Studies in Computational Intelligence, vol. 308, pp. 181–206. Springer, Heidelberg (2010). https://doi.org/10.1007/978-3-642-14363-2_9

19. Rus, V., Stefanescu, D., Niraula, N., Graesser, A.C.: DeepTutor: towards macro- and micro-adaptive conversational intelligent tutoring at scale. In: Proceedings of the First ACM Conference on Learning@ Scale Conference, pp. 209–210 (2014)
20. Sottilare, R., Brawner, K.: Component interaction within the generalized intelligent framework for tutoring (GIFT) as a model for adaptive instructional system standards. In: The Adaptive Instructional System (AIS) Standards Workshop of the 14th International Conference of the Intelligent Tutoring Systems (ITS) Conference, Montreal, Quebec, Canada (2018)
21. Sottilare, R., Graesser, A., Hu, X., Brawner, K.: Design recommendations for intelligent tutoring systems: authoring tools and expert modeling techniques. Robert Sottilare (2015)
22. Sottilare, R.A., Brawner, K.W., Sinatra, A.M., Johnston, J.H.: An updated concept for a generalized intelligent framework for tutoring (GIFT). GIFTtutoring.org (2017)
23. Sullins, J., Craig, S.D., Hu, X.: Exploring the effectiveness of a novel feedback mechanism within an intelligent tutoring system. Int. J. Learn. Technol. **10**(3), 220–236 (2015)
24. Vanlehn, K.: The behavior of tutoring systems. Int. J. Artif. Intell. Educ. **16**(3), 227–265 (2006)
25. Wallace, P.S., et al.: Operation ARIES!: a computerized game for teaching scientific inquiry. In: AIED, pp. 602–604 (2009)
26. Wang, L., Shubeck, K., Shi, G., Zhang, L., Hu, X.: CbITS authoring tool in GIFT. In: Proceedings of the 8th Annual Generalized Intelligent Framework for Tutoring (GIFT) Users Symposium (GIFTSym8), p. 69. US Army Combat Capabilities Development Command-Soldier Center (2020)

Interacting with Games

The Interplay Between Artificial Intelligence and Users' Personalities: A New Scenario for Human-Computer Interaction in Gaming

Barbara Caci[1(✉)] and Khaldoon Dhou[2]

[1] University of Palermo, Palermo, Italy
barbara.caci@unipa.it
[2] Texas A&M University Central Texas, Killeen, TX, USA
kdhou@tamuct.edu

Abstract. The latest business reports showed that Augmented Reality (AR) and Artificial Intelligence (AI) are ranked among the top 10 strategic trends for 2018. For these reasons, in this paper, we provide an interdisciplinary focus on design and personality issues, trying to discuss the interplay between games with personality and Artificial Intelligence. First, we describe taxonomy models on personality in games and empirical studies aimed at exploring personality traits of Pokémon GO users. Second, we explore virtual humans employed in investigating chess personalities via simulating human chess players. In this research article, the term virtual human is used to describe a computer program that simulates a human in some aspects such as playing chess. The results of personality and gaming are sparse and mixed. It remains unclear whether personality traits would similarly predict adoption and usage in the context of AR mobile game. On the contrary, results about AI showed that virtual humans have characteristics similar to those of humans and helped researchers explore existing patterns in societies. In our discussion, we try to evidence the importance of personality in gaming also considering that an increasing sale for these technologies is forecasted in 2020 to be 21 times higher than in 2016 (from US$2.9 billion to US$61.3 billion; Superdata Research, 2017).

Keywords: Personality · Augmented Reality · Gaming · Virtual humans · Chess · Chess personality

1 Introduction

In 2016 Nick Yee wrote on his blog on Quantic Foundry: "Games are often stereotyped as escapist fantasies where people get to pretend to be something they're not. But what the data shows is that gamers play games that align with their personalities. In the same way that people select the news and media that reinforce their worldviews, gamers select the games that reinforce their identities.

© Springer Nature Switzerland AG 2020
C. Stephanidis et al. (Eds.): HCII 2020, LNCS 12425, pp. 619–630, 2020.
https://doi.org/10.1007/978-3-030-60128-7_45

For example, gamers who are extraverted prefer more social and action-oriented games. Gamers who are more conscientious prefer games with long-term thinking and planning. The games we play are a reflection, not an escape, from our own identities. In this sense, people play games not to pretend to be someone they're not, but to become more of who they really are".

These ideas are quite interesting when applied in today's highly competitive marketplace of gaming. Indeed, coping with shortening product life-cycles and an increasing number of failing gaming innovations, researchers need to quest on efficient strategies for understanding the interplay between users' personality traits and gaming. Game developers are deeply involved in creating a new generation of games that cater to individual users. The aim is to adapt game content and automatically customize it to each player's personality and individual playstyle [8]. For companies, this game hyper-personalization means making games more fun by adjusting them to the taste of each player, so leading users to likely play more and more and spend more and more money. However, for mental health researchers, users may risk developing addictive behaviors. Indeed, the latest version of the Diagnostic Statistical Manual of Mental Disorders [3] included game addictions in the "Emerging Measures and Models" Section [27].

In this paper, we provide an interdisciplinary focus on design and personality issues, trying to discuss the interplay between Artificial Intelligence and users' personalities. We report specifically studies about Augmented Reality (AR) and Artificial Intelligence (AI) games. Additionally, we explore the technology of virtual humans programmed using AI techniques and show how they can help us investigate different issues that are personality-related and hard to examine otherwise. For this research, a virtual human can be thought of as a computer simulation that behaves like a human in some conditions. It is essential to note that the latest business reports showed that AR and AI are ranked in the top 10 strategic trends for 2018 [12]. Moreover, an increasing sale for these technologies is forecasted in 2020 to be 21 times higher than in 2016 (from US$2.9 billion to US$61.3 billion; Superdata Research, 2017).

AR and AI gaming technologies are cutting-edge research areas for game developers that aim to create sophisticated games that can change and respond to player feedback, and in-game characters that can evolve the more you spend time with them [50]. For instance, the challenge for AR game developers is to assign users a more dynamic and autonomous role in their gaming experiences [41], so that people might assign the highest perceived value to this kind of games [42]. As well, AI research that developed artificial agents able to handily beat a human being at the classic board game, just as IBM's DeepBlue system bested Russian grandmaster Garry Kasparov back in 1997, has accelerated in recent years [21].

2   Personality in Gaming: Taxonomy Models

Studies framed under the human-computer interaction reported that personality is a critical variable for understanding why and how people are immersed in playing games. Indeed, gaming is conscious behavior that requests players to act and make a decision, to feel a different kind of emotion, so scholars have hypothesized that gaming is impacted not only by situational constructs, but also by consistent constructs, such as personality [26]. As defined by Larsen and Buss [36] personality is a stable, organized collection of psychological traits and processes in the human being that influences his or her interactions with and modifications to the psychological, social and physical environment surrounding them.

Seminal works characterized the profiles of the players based on gaming archetypes. First, the model of Bartle [6] categorizes players into four types based on different motivations, in-game behaviors, and play styles: Achievers, Socializers, Explorers, and Killers. Achievers (10% of gamers) are driven by achievements such as, for instance, collecting as many points as possible and status. Thus, they show their friends how they are progressing, tend to collect badges, and put them on display. This is the type of person who responds particularly well to incentive schemes such as Air Miles, where every additional mile collected is an achievement in its own right. Socializers (80% of gamers) are driven by experiencing fun through the game interaction with other players. They collaborate to achieve bigger and better things than they could on their own. Explorers (10% of gamers) are moved by a curiosity for new things and the discovery of new secrets. Explorers appreciated repetitive tasks as long as they eventually "unlock" a new area of the game, or they deliver some kind of "Easter Egg" (an Easter Egg is a small bonus within a game – sometimes it's as simple as a little joke, whereas in other cases it might be a full extra video sequence regarding what has been accomplished). Finally, Killers (1% of gamers) are similar to Achievers in the way that they get a thrill from gaining points and winning status too. However, they want to see other people lose. They're highly competitive, want to be the best at the game, and winning is what motivates them.

Successively, Bateman and Boon [7] created another model that identifies players into four types: Conqueror, Manager, Wanderer, and Participant, which they later expanded to seven categories: Seeker, Survivor, Daredevil, Mastermind, Conqueror, Socializer and Achiever. Seekers are driven by interest and curiosity; Survivors enjoy fear and terror; Daredevils loves the thrill and risk-taking; Masterminds play usually puzzle games; Conquerors are moved by struggling against adversity and beating other players; Socializers are similar to Bartle's classification and enjoy talking to and helping other gamers, and finally Achievers are motivated by long-term achievements.

In addition to player archetypes, researchers have also used the Five Factors Model [15] to define players' behaviors [11,13,35,53,55]. Differently from the classifications of Bartle [6] and Bateman & Boon [7], which are based on gameplay elements that the target group would find engaging, classifications based on FFM refer more to users' traits of personality. The Five Factors Model is a well-known psychological model describing personality variations along five dimensions, called the Big Five that are respectively named: Extraversion, Openness, Conscientiousness, Neuroticism, and Agreeableness. Extraversion refers to personality traits such as energy, assertiveness, and sociability. Openness regards the tendency to be informed, creative, insightful, curious, and to have a variety of experiences. Conscientiousness is related to the tendency to be self-disciplined, act dutifully, and aim for achievement. Neuroticism means a tendency to experience unpleasant emotions easily, such as anger, anxiety, depression, or vulnerability. Agreeableness means the tendency to be compassionate, trusting, and cooperative rather than suspicious and antagonistic towards others [39]. In sum, player type models are more specific and focused at explaining differences in player behavior, experience, and emotions, whereas personality trait models can be seen as a higher-level conceptualization of individual differences (not directed at certain areas or behaviors) [9].

3   Personality in AR Gaming: The Case of Pokémon GO

In this section, we report a case study about Pokémon GO. This game is a very particular AR game because it offers a very unusual gaming experience in the real setting. Gamers live a mix of real and virtual items that coexist together [33]. This exciting mix of game, sociality, and physical presence [37] is a novelty in the mobile AR game panorama and might be responsible for the worldwide diffusion of the game [5]. Empirical studies aimed at analyzing users' experience about this game have mainly framed the investigations about personality traits under the FFM [39] theoretically. However, the results are mixed and contradictory. On one hand, personality seems not to influence playing Pokémon GO, as showed by Rasche et al. [44]. Authors, indeed, reported no significant differences in personality traits such as extraversion, agreeableness, conscientiousness, neuroticism, and openness in three groups of Pokémon GO gamers (i.e., active users, former users, and non-users). On the other hand, personality traits such as extraversion and emotional stability seem to predict game habits, and the collection of a high number of Pokémon GO creatures and species, respectively [52]. As well, emotional stability predicts time usage, while openness is a positive predictor of the gamers' level of expertise. On the contrary, conscientiousness and agreeableness are negative predictors both of the level of the gamers' expertise and of the number of species they collect. In sum, players who are emotionally stable, but less conscientious as well as those who are less cooperative and open to experience spend more time playing and become more experts in achieving higher levels in the game [52].

Similarly, Mattheis et al. [38] found that people who play Pokémon GO have a significantly lower score in conscientiousness than non-players. In contrast, no significant differences between players and non-players have been found for extraversion, neuroticism, agreeableness, and openness. Personality traits such as introversion, low levels of agreeableness, and conscientiousness describe better Pokémon GO players. Introverted and low consciousness people spend more time in playing Pokémon GO but are people with low scores on agreeableness who have the highest numbers of daily game sessions [10].

The study by Lalot et al. [34] analyzed personality by the HEXACO model [4]. This model is quite similar to Big Five Model [39], but it introduces two more personality traits related to honesty and emotionality. Lalot et al. [34] performed a longitudinal study on a sample of Pokémon GO gamers recruited in English-speaking (i.e., the USA, the UK, Ireland, Canada, Australia, and New Zealand) and French-speaking countries (e.g., France, Switzerland, Belgium, and Canada). The results of this two-phase longitudinal study showed that only agreeableness was a strong predictor of the motivations for starting to play. Perseverance, premeditation, and agreeableness were more likely to predict the intention to continue playing Pokémon GO after four months.

Other studies analyzed personality dimensions such as self-efficacy [32] and emotional intelligence [45]. However, self-efficacy has a non-significant effect on attitude for playing Pokémon GO [32]. Differently, emotional intelligence is a personality trait that characterizes Pokémon GO players. Comparing with non-players, participants increased their scores at emotional intelligence measures after game sessions with Pokémon GO, and also had better social relationships with peers [45]. Some studies suggested that personality traits are deeply interconnected with motivations for playing. For instance, Mattheis et al. [38] analyzed personality traits of people starting to play, continuing to play, and stopping to play three months later and found that people who quit the game scored higher in neuroticism than those who were still playing the game. No significant differences between people who continued playing the game and those that have stopped playing have found. Results did not change when controlling for personal inattentiveness and time spending on playing. Caci et al. [10] evidenced that recreational needs mostly drive introverted gamers, while personal needs move less agreeable people and social needs low conscientiousness people. Khalis and Mikami [30] found that more extroverted, cooperative, and socially competent players are more engaged in the game, displaying more catching behavior during the gameplay sessions. Additionally, participants high on conscientiousness and social competence displayed more exploration behavior. Differently, players with high levels of social anxiety have less catching behavior.

4 The Employment of Virtual Humans to Explore Chess Personalities: The Case of Chess Games

In this section, we present research studies about personalities and virtual chess players. Chess can play an important role in addressing the issue of exploring personalities over chessboards. An early work that explored chess and personalities was offered by Karpman [28], who showed chess as a fight between different personalities and how players can articulate their actual personalities in their chess games. That is to say, he showed how the life events of some chess players are emulated over the chessboard. Additionally, he compared well-known chess grandmasters and showed particular chess patterns and how they can contribute to chess arrangements.

The findings of Karpman [28] have been essential to future studies in exploring the personalities of chess players via the involvement of virtual humans that represent real chess players ranging from novice players to top-rank grandmasters. Recent research studies have been concerned with exploring the effectiveness of virtual chess players and how they perform while competing against other players. A virtual chess player is defined as a computer simulation that imitates a real player existing in the chess community such as Kasparov and Polgar [19]. These players exist in different skills and playing styles, and they allow a chess trainer to play against various opponents to sharpen his skill. Each virtual chess player is characterized by a rating and a chess personality. Ratings are assigned by various organizations such as the World Chess Federation and the United States Chess Federation (USCF). The rating is a number that is assigned to each player to measure his skill and compare him against other players in the chess community. Chess personality is defined as the style of the player while he competes against other players. For example, one of the virtual chess players is Anderssen, who simulates Adolf Anderssen (July 6, 1818–March 13, 1879). The simulation of Anderssen reveals a grandmaster who starts attacking his opponent and goes after his King at an early stage of the game. Another example is the simulation of Leko, who is a defensive and cautious grandmaster. The employment of virtual chess players made it possible to examine the competition between chess players who existed in different time eras. Interestingly, virtual humans have been attractive to medical researchers, as the involvement of software of virtual chess players has been used as a means of surgical training [48].

Virtual humans have emerged as powerful tools for understanding many aspects of the psychology of chess players. In a recent study, Dhou [19] explored the personalities of the grandmasters Anderssen and Leko while competing against less-skilled virtual players by utilizing virtual chess players. In his study, he used different metrics including the errors made by players and the number of moves in their chess games. A follow-up study was conducted to explore the psychology of competition between two groups of chess players: grandmasters and class-A players [22]. While the grandmasters' group involves Anderssen and Leko, who vary in their attack and defense attitudes, the class-A players' group incorporates players who have different preferences to utilizing knights and bishops in their games. Research shows that knights and bishops depict various adjustments in business research and therefore, this makes it essential to investigate them [29]. Overall, the two studies [19,22] consistently indicate that less skilled players tend to make more mistakes when they compete against a defensive grandmaster (i.e. Leko) as opposed to an attacking grandmaster (i.e. Anderssen). Additionally, the two studies provide strong evidence for the efficacy of a grandmaster's style while competing against less-skilled players. More specifically, a grandmaster with an attacking style tends to have fewer errors than a defensive grandmaster. The findings are linked to the fact that people instinctively recognize the origins of problematic occurrences and how they can be influenced by them [54].

A similar study in this area is the work explored the personality of Kasparov by using virtual humans to simulate Kasparov and three proposed opponents [21]. The importance of this work is that it offers an understanding of Kasparov's personality, which has attracted much attention among psychologists and artificial intelligence researchers. Kasparov is known for being able to calculate quickly, employing original openings, and sacrificing with pieces to gain rapid advantage and allow mobility. In the last few years, there has been a growing interest in investigating the personality of Kasparov for many reasons. That is to say, there is evidence that the personality of Kasparov plays a crucial role in designing chess-playing programs [31,51]. Additionally, recent research shows the psychology of competition between different opponents against Kasparov and the differences in their performances according to their chess personalities [21]. Together the three studies in virtual chess humans [19,21,22] provide important insights into chess personalities and using them in analyzing chess outcomes. Overall, these studies highlight the need for more studies that link chess personalities to behavior in real-life scenarios and exploring the relationships between them. Such studies might also provide further insights into different aspects of business such as personalities at the workforce and different strategies within organizations such as aggression and defense.

5   Future Studies in AR and AI Gaming

The existing studies on personality and the gaming are sparse at best, and the few results are often discordant, and cannot be used to define personality traits [49]. Hence, it remains unclear whether personality traits would similarly predict adoption and usage in the context of AR mobile game. Similarly, other personality dimensions such as self-efficacy [32] and emotional intelligence [32] have been analyzed, but actually, there are very few studies in the context of AR mobile game for corroborating reported findings. Moreover, scholars used, in prevalence, self-report measures for the assessment of all the independent and dependent variables alternatively focused in the researches (e.g.., personality, game habits). We have to remember that self-report measures are particularly affected by social desirability bias [14], so the use of these types of measures might be affected by participants' disclosure of some sensitive information, and therefore, causing mixed results. Most of the studies examined are also cross-sectional and did not control for multiple comparisons, which explicitly limit the possibility of establishing causal links between specific personality traits and gaming technologies.

In future investigations, it might be possible to utilize virtual chess humans in exploring new aspects in strategic management and competitive advertising. Further studies, which take different characteristics into account, will need to be undertaken. However, more research on this topic needs to be undertaken before the association between chess personalities and terms in management and marketing is more clearly understood. For instance, further investigations are needed to shed light on the personalities of virtual humans and how they can be mapped to business strategies. These investigations can probably help other researchers better understand how to conduct new experiments that utilize virtual humans to better investigate real business scenarios. However, to develop a full picture of virtual chess humans, additional studies will be needed that explore different personalities, investigate how the parameters overlap, and how they lead to different outcomes. For example, recently, two studies investigated attack vs. defense in chess grandmasters and how it could influence other less skilled players [19,22]. Although these results revealed interesting findings, it is important to note that they only explore two grandmasters and how they perform while competing with other players. We believe that we need to explore different types of attackers to be able to comprehend their behavior and understand the full picture before mapping it to other fields of research.

6 Conclusion

This study has examined a versatile background on game design including personality issues, while discussing different models that classify players into distinct groups. In particular, we report studies in Pokémon GO and chess that are related to Augmented Reality (AR) and Artificial Intelligence (AI). On one hand, it evidences that personality may potentially affect gameplay behaviors. Such results might be promising and useful for the personalization of games. We underline the possibility to use personality factors for planning new or adapting existing games to target audiences for improving the player experience and facilitating long-term engagement with the games. Moreover, because of the increasing tendency to develop gaming applications that use AR in combination with AI [43], the findings of personality traits may also useful for developing criteria for the clients' segmentation in the marketplace of mobile technologies and applications. Designing, developing, and publishing a game is not a simple process, rather a considerable effort. Although it is intriguing to use personality for game development, we need to be sure it can predict player experience. As follows, the evidence from this paper suggests that the employment of virtual humans can be used as a means to explore the personalities of players. As shown for chess, since this game symbolizes a war between two groups, we believe that this work can be eventually extended to investigate new patterns in business and marketing where competition between strategies exist.

This research has thrown up many questions in need of further investigation. First, it would be interesting to compare real players with particular personalities along with their equivalent virtual players. We believe that this can help to investigate a relationship between virtual humans and real players. Second, it will be essential to further explore the decision-making process under different time constraints between players with different personality traits or of different genders. Third, more studies can be conducted to investigate the relationship between actual personalities and chess personalities [1,2,46,47]. Finally, further research can investigate relationships between bio-inspired behaviors and chess personalities [16,18,20,23,40]. These behaviors proved their effectiveness in many fields including coding binary information utilized in many aspects such as visualization research [17,24,25].

References

1. Al-Samarraie, H., Sarsam, S.M., Alzahrani, A.I., Alalwan, N.: Personality and individual differences: the potential of using preferences for visual stimuli to predict the big five traits. Cognition, Technology & Work 20(3), 337–349 (Aug 2018), https://doi.org/10.1007/s10111-018-0470-6
2. Al-Samarraie, H., Sarsam, S.M., Alzahrani, A.I., Alalwan, N., Masood, M.: The role of personality characteristics in informing our preference for visual presentation: An eye movement study. Journal of Ambient Intelligence and Smart Environments 8(6), 709–719 (2016)
3. American Psychiatric Association: Diagnostic and statistical manual of mental disorders (DSM-5®). American Psychiatric Pub (2013)
4. Ashton, M.C., Lee, K., Perugini, M., Szarota, P., De Vries, R.E., Di Blas, L., Boies, K., De Raad, B.: A six-factor structure of personality-descriptive adjectives: solutions from psycholexical studies in seven languages. Journal of personality and social psychology 86(2), 356–366 (2004)
5. Baranowski, T.: Pokémon go, go, go, gone? Games for Health Journal 5(5), 293–294 (2016)
6. Bartle, R.: Hearts, clubs, diamonds, spades: Players who suit muds. Journal of MUD research 1(1), 19 (1996)
7. Bateman, C., Boon, R.: 21st Century Game Design (Game Development Series). Charles River Media Inc, USA (2005)
8. Bertens, P., Guitart, A., Chen, P.P., Perianez, A.: A machine-learning item recommendation system for video games. In: 2018 IEEE Conference on Computational Intelligence and Games (CIG). pp. 1–4 (2018)
9. Busch, C., Schulte-Nölke, H., Wiewiórowska-Domagalska, A., Zoll, F.: The rise of the platform economy: a new challenge for eu consumer law? Journal of European Consumer and Market Law 5, (2016)
10. Caci, B., Scrima, F., Tabacchi, M.E., Cardaci, M.: The reciprocal influences among motivation, personality traits, and game habits for playing pokémon go. International Journal of Human-Computer Interaction 35(14), 1303–1311 (2018), https://doi.org/10.1080/10447318.2018.1519167
11. Canossa, A., Badler, J.B., El-Nasr, M.S., Tignor, S., Colvin, R.C.: In your face (t) impact of personality and context on gameplay behavior. In: FDG (2015)
12. CeArley, D., Burke, B., Searle, S., Walker, M.J.: Top 10 strategic technology trends for 2018. The Top 10, (2016)
13. Chen, Z., El Nasr, M.S., Canossa, A., Badler, J., Tignor, S., Colvin, R.: Modeling individual differences through frequent pattern mining on role-playing game actions. In: Eleventh Artificial Intelligence and Interactive Digital Entertainment Conference (2015)
14. Corbetta, P.: Social Research: Theory. Methods and Techniques. SAGE Publications, Ltd (2003)
15. Costa, P.T., McCrae, R.R.: Neo personality inventory-revised (NEO PI-R). Psychological Assessment Resources Odessa, FL (1992)
16. Dhou, K., Cruzen, C.: An innovative chain coding technique for compression based on the concept of biological reproduction: an agent-based modeling approach. IEEE Internet Things J. 6(6), 9308–9315 (2019)

17. Dhou, K.: Toward a Better Understanding of Viewers' Perceptions of Tag Clouds: Relative Size Judgment. Ph.D. thesis, USA (2013)
18. Dhou, K.: A novel agent-based modeling approach for image coding and lossless compression based on the wolf-sheep predation model. In: Computational Science - ICCS 2018. pp. 117–128. Springer International Publishing, Cham (2018)
19. Dhou, K.: Towards a better understanding of chess players' personalities: A study using virtual chess players. In: Kurosu, M. (ed.) Human-Computer Interaction. Interaction Technologies. pp. 435–446. Springer International Publishing, Cham (2018)
20. Dhou, K.: An innovative design of a hybrid chain coding algorithm for bi-level image compression using an agent-based modeling approach. Applied Soft Computing 79, 94–110 (2019), http://www.sciencedirect.com/science/article/pii/S1568494619301425
21. Dhou, K.: An innovative employment of virtual humans to explore the chess personalities of garry kasparov and other class-a players. In: Stephanidis, C. (ed.) HCI International 2019 - Late Breaking Papers, pp. 306–319. Springer International Publishing, Cham (2019)
22. Dhou, K.: An exploration of chess personalities in grandmasters and class-A players using virtual humans. International Journal of Entertainment Technology and Management (2020), accepted (to appear)
23. Dhou, K.: A new chain coding mechanism for compression stimulated by a virtual environment of a predator-prey ecosystem. Future Generation Computer Systems 102, 650–669 (2020), http://www.sciencedirect.com/science/article/pii/S0167739X1832630X
24. Dhou, K., Hadzikadic, M., Faust, M.: Typeface size and weight and word location influence on relative size judgments in tag clouds. Journal of Visual Languages & Computing 44, 97–105 (2018), http://www.sciencedirect.com/science/article/pii/S1045926X16300210
25. Dhou, K.K., Kosara, R., Hadzikadic, M., Faust, M.: Size judgment and comparison in tag clouds. IEEE Visualization Poster Proceedings (2013)
26. Fang, X., Zhu, M.: Extraversion and computer game play: Who plays what games? In: Jacko, J.A. (ed.) Human-Computer Interaction. Users and Applications. pp. 659–667. Springer, Berlin Heidelberg, Berlin, Heidelberg (2011)
27. Griffiths, M., King, D., Demetrovics, Z.: Dsm-5 internet gaming disorder needs a unified approach to assessment. Neuropsychiatry 4(1), 1–4 (2014)
28. Karpman, B.: The psychology of chess. Psychoanalytic Review 24(1), 54–69 (1937)
29. Ketola, T.: Corporate states or corporate citizens? chess between corporations, states and citizens with sustainable development at stake. International Journal of Sustainable Economy 3(1), 107–122 (2010)
30. Khalis, A., Mikami, A.Y.: Who's gotta catch 'em all?: Individual differences in pokèmon go gameplay behaviors. Personality and Individual Differences 124, 35–38 (2018), http://www.sciencedirect.com/science/article/pii/S0191886917307067
31. Khodarkovsky, M., Shamkovich, L., Kasparov, G.: New Era: How Garry Kasparov Changed the World of Chess. Ballantine Books, USA (1997)
32. Kim, H., Lee, H.J., Cho, H., Kim, E., Hwang, J.: Replacing self-efficacy in physical activity: unconscious intervention of the ar game, pokémon go. Sustainability 10(6), 1971 (2018)
33. Koo, C., Choi, K., Ham, J., Chung, N.: Empirical study about the pokémongo game and destination engagement. In: Stangl, B., Pesonen, J. (eds.) Information and Communication Technologies in Tourism 2018, pp. 16–28. Springer International Publishing, Cham (2018)

34. Lalot, F., Zerhouni, O., Pinelli, M.: "I wanna be the very best!" agreeableness and perseverance predict sustained playing to pokémon go: A longitudinal study. Games for Health Journal 6(5), 271–278 (2017), https://doi.org/10.1089/g4h.2017.0051, pMID: 28661725

35. van Lankveld, G., Schreurs, S., Spronck, P., van den Herik, J.: Extraversion in games. In: van den Herik, H.J., Iida, H., Plaat, A. (eds.) Computers and Games, pp. 263–275. Springer, Berlin Heidelberg, Berlin, Heidelberg (2011)

36. Larsen, R., Buss, D.M.: Personality Psychology: Domains of Knowledge About Human Nature. McGraw-Hill Publishing (2018)

37. Liszio, S., Masuch, M.: Designing shared virtual reality gaming experiences in local multi-platform games. In: Wallner, G., Kriglstein, S., Hlavacs, H., Malaka, R., Lugmayr, A., Yang, H.S. (eds.) Entertainment Computing - ICEC 2016, pp. 235–240. Springer International Publishing, Cham (2016)

38. Mattheiss, E., Hochleitner, C., Busch, M., Orji, R., Tscheligi, M.: Deconstructing pokémon go - an empirical study on player personality characteristics. In: de Vries, P.W., Oinas-Kukkonen, H., Siemons, L., Beerlage-de Jong, N., van Gemert-Pijnen, L. (eds.) Persuasive Technology: Development and Implementation of Personalized Technologies to Change Attitudes and Behaviors, pp. 83–94. Springer International Publishing, Cham (2017)

39. McCrae, R.R., Costa Jr., P.T.: A Five-Factor Theory of Personality, chap. Handbook of personality: Theory and research, pp. 139–153 (1999)

40. Mouring, M., Dhou, K., Hadzikadic, M.: A Novel Algorithm for Bi-Level Image Coding and Lossless Compression based on Virtual Ant Colonies. In: 3rd International Conference on Complexity, Future Information Systems and Risk. pp. 72–78. Setúbal - Portugal (2018)

41. Ostrom, A.L., Parasuraman, A., Bowen, D.E., Patrício, L., Voss, C.A.: Service research priorities in a rapidly changing context. Journal of Service Research 18(2), 127–159 (2015), https://doi.org/10.1177/1094670515576315

42. Patrício, L., Fisk, R.P., e Cunha, J.F., Constantine, L.: Multilevel service design: From customer value constellation to service experience blueprinting. Journal of Service Research 14(2), 180–200 (2011), https://doi.org/10.1177/1094670511401901

43. Porter, C.E., Donthu, N.: Using the technology acceptance model to explain how attitudes determine internet usage: The role of perceived access barriers and demographics. Journal of Business Research 59(9), 999–1007 (2006), http://www.sciencedirect.com/science/article/pii/S0148296306000993

44. Rasche, P., Schlomann, A., Mertens, A.: Who is still playing pokémon go? a web-based survey. JMIR Serious Games 5(2), e7 (Apr 2017), http://games.jmir.org/2017/2/e7/

45. Ruiz-Ariza, A., Casuso, R.A., Suarez-Manzano, S., Martínez-López, E.J.: Effect of augmented reality game pokémon go on cognitive performance and emotional intelligence in adolescent young. Computers & Education 116, 49–63 (2018), http://www.sciencedirect.com/science/article/pii/S0360131517302002

46. Sarsam, S.M., Al-Samarraie, H.: A first look at the effectiveness of personality dimensions in promoting users' satisfaction with the system. SAGE Open 8(2), 2158244018769125 (2018), https://doi.org/10.1177/2158244018769125

47. Sarsam, S.M., Al-Samarraie, H.: Towards incorporating personality into the design of an interface: a method for facilitating users' interaction with the display. User Modeling and User-Adapted Interaction 28(1), 75–96 (Mar 2018), https://doi.org/10.1007/s11257-018-9201-1

48. Schlickum, M.K., Hedman, L., Enochsson, L., Kjellin, A., Felländer-Tsai, L.: Systematic video game training in surgical novices improves performance in virtual reality endoscopic surgical simulators: A prospective randomized study. World Journal of Surgery 33(11), 2360 (Aug 2009), https://doi.org/10.1007/s00268-009-0151-y

49. Skippon, S., Garwood, M.: Responses to battery electric vehicles: UK consumer attitudes and attributions of symbolic meaning following direct experience to reduce psychological distance. Transportation Research Part D: Transport and Environment 16(7), 525–531 (2011), http://www.sciencedirect.com/science/article/pii/S1361920911000654

50. Statt, N.: How artificial intelligence will revolutionize the way video games are developed and played. The Verge (2019), online from https://www.theverge.com/2019/3/6/18222203/video-game-ai-future-procedural-generation-deep-learning

51. Sverzellati, N., Brillet, P.Y.: When deep blue first defeated kasparov: is a machine stronger than a radiologist at predicting prognosis in idiopathic pulmonary fibrosis? European Respiratory Journal 49(1) (2017), https://erj.ersjournals.com/content/49/1/1602144

52. Tabacchi, M.E., Caci, B., Cardaci, M., Perticone, V.: Early usage of pokémon go and its personality correlates. Computers in Human Behavior 72, 163–169 (2017), http://www.sciencedirect.com/science/article/pii/S0747563217301280

53. Van Lankveld, G., Schreurs, S., Spronck, P.: Psychologically verified player modelling. In: 10th Int. Conf. Intell. Games Simulation (2009)

54. Wise, D.M., Rosqvist, J.: Explanatory style and well-being. Comprehensive handbook of personality and psychopathology p. 285 (2006)

55. Yee, N., Ducheneaut, N., Nelson, L., Likarish, P.: Introverted elves & conscientious gnomes: The expression of personality in world of warcraft. In: Proceedings of the SIGCHI Conference on Human Factors in Computing Systems. pp. 753–762. CHI '11, Association for Computing Machinery, New York, NY, USA (2011), https://doi.org/10.1145/1978942.1979052

Behavlet Analytics for Player Profiling and Churn Prediction

Darryl Charles[1](✉) ⓘ and Benjamin Ultan Cowley[2,3] ⓘ

[1] School of Computing, Engineering, and Intelligent Systems, Ulster University, Newtownabbey, Northern Ireland
dk.charles@ulster.ac.uk
[2] Data Science, Faculty of Educational Sciences, University of Helsinki, Helsinki, Finland
ben.cowley@helsinki.fi
[3] Cognitive Science, Faculty of Arts, University of Helsinki, Helsinki, Finland

Abstract. Players exhibit varying behaviour from each other when playing games. Indeed, a player's own behaviour will change as they learn to play and changing behaviour may also be indicative of when they are prematurely about to quit playing permanently (known as 'churn'). There can be many reasons for player churn including finding a game too easy, too hard, or just not understanding what they must do. The accurate prediction of player churn is important as it allows a publisher or developer to understand and intervene to improve retention and thus increase revenue. Profiling player behaviours through their actions in-game can facilitate personalization, by adapting gameplay for different types of player to enhance player enjoyment and reduce churn rate. Behavlets are data-features that encode short activity sequences ('atoms' of play), which represent an aspect of playing style or player personality traits, e.g. aggressiveness or cautiousness tendencies. Previously we have shown how Behavlets can be used to model variation between players. In this paper, we focus on Behavlet sequences and how process mining and entropy-based analysis can profile evolving behaviour, predict player churn, and adapt play to potentially increase enjoyment.

Keywords: Player modelling · Churn prediction · Entropy · Processing mining · Behavlets

1 Introduction

In the 1980s, when many of the core genres and design patterns were conceived, computer games were often created by one person. Game design at this time was generally based on what the single developer thought would be fun for him/her to create and play. Consequently, a game developer tended to make a game to appeal to people like him/her. The games market is now vastly increased and the demographics and play preferences of players are now much more varied. Games are more complex and expensive to build, and greater attention to detail is required to account for a range of player needs. In the modern era, a game might be more considered more as a service, in which the provider of the game seeks to ensure a quality of service and experience for players

© Springer Nature Switzerland AG 2020
C. Stephanidis et al. (Eds.): HCII 2020, LNCS 12425, pp. 631–643, 2020.
https://doi.org/10.1007/978-3-030-60128-7_46

throughout the lifetime of a game – both inside and outside the game environment. Of course, there are technical requirements to ensure a game is delivered and maintained to run to expectations. However, for a game to be successful it must assist players' learning and mastery and provide them with consistent opportunities to have fun. It is essential that players have a reasonable opportunity to get value from a game (e.g. by completing a narrative arc) given an appropriate amount of focus and effort. In this paper we consider the relationship between the game provider and the player through the medium of gameplay, and how it can be monitored and managed. In [1] we showed how kernels of game behaviour linked to personality/temperament, which we called Behavlets, could be used to profile players based on play preference. Behavlets are data-features that leverage domain-expert knowledge of game design patterns, to encode short activity sequences ('atoms' of play) that represent an aspect of playing style or player personality traits (e.g. aggressive or cautious play), that can be mapped to temperament theory. Behavlets help to understand how recurring patterns of play create meaning for players. For example, for an RTS player, the pattern *"send my units to location X in the early game"* means *"Gather scouting information and forestall a surprise attack"*. These are small steps toward understanding what constitutes 'meaning' to human players, defined in terms of 'semantic units' of play patterns, to ultimately allow analysis of play in the game's own 'language'. To achieve the latter aim requires extending Behavlets, following the state of the art in machine learning [2], by marrying deep learning (or similar) to a domain expert's game knowledge. To facilitate this we propose an extension to our previous work [1] where we consider ordered sequences of Behavlets, which define meaningful player action processes. We label these Behavlet sequences as B-chains due to their relationship to chained skill Atoms from game design theory, which we discuss in more detail later. The extension to our previous approach transforms it into a hierarchical architecture. At the lower level, Behavlets are identified with support from domain knowledge, while higher-level ordered sequences of Behavlets are identified through machine learning to discover common player Behavlet processes. Modelling player behavior based on both Behavlet and B-chains can help develop unique player profiles. Another approach that is used for similar data in other contexts is process mining [3]. Clustering players based on processing mining techniques can help identify underlying variations between players that can be used to personalize games. This approach, along with the potential utility of B-Chains to classify player drop-out, may be used to predict churn and facilitate interventions that improve player retention.

The next section summarises the core concepts of game design, and structural methods for representing game features and patterns of play. Section 3 introduces processing/sequence analytics, an outline of gameplay entropy, and how it relates to behaviour profiling.

2   Game Structure

Though digital and non-digital games have similar core structural elements, we only consider digital games here as players can be given automated feedback, personalized guidance/assistance, and a game may be adapted in real time to enhance player enjoyment.

2.1 Game Fundamentals

A player interacts with the game world via an interface and input mechanism (a game controller) and thus changes the game state; this change in a game state is represented through various forms of aesthetic feedback to a player – visual, audio, haptic. So, a game may be defined in terms of a control loop, in which player actions affect the state of the world and the player learns to take increasing meaningful and skilful actions to effect successful outcomes and progress through a game. Games may be defined as having three core aspects: Mechanics, Dynamics, and Aesthetics [4]. Where dynamics is the interactive gameplay experienced by a player as they use a game controller to alter the state of the game. Aesthetics are the emotions and sensations evoked by the dynamics via players' senses; depending on their preferences, a player's experience can be enhanced significantly by elements within story-based games, or guiding mechanisms, or just-in-time meaningful feedback on player performance. Ultimately, in games it is the mechanics that define the dynamics of gameplay; mechanics define the "rules" a game, its scope, environmental interactions, objectives and the win/loss states. They define player and non-player capabilities, game options, the flow of a story and how game aesthetics are accomplished. A game designer's core objective is to create a system of mechanics that provides players with positive emotional experiences, including fun, enjoyment, pleasure, relaxation, and escapism. Structurally, a modern digital game has some or all of the following 10 'C-word' characteristics, which we playfully name the '**10cc model**':

c1. *Conflict*: a challenge to overcome, either against the game or other players [5].
c2. *Choice*: meaningful player decisions [6].
c3. *Change*: player actions alter the world state [7].
c4. *Consequence*: player actions have positive or negative outcomes [8].
c5. *Contingency*: future game states and outcomes are uncertain [9].
c6. *Community*: social play is crucial in many modern games for retention [10].
c7. *Control*: provide a player with strong feelings of agency and engagement [11].
c8. *Constraint*: deliberate limitation of player choice and actions [12].
c9. *Continuance*: design to support player learning and progression [13].
c10. *Circumstance*: games/levels may have different game aesthetics/mechanics, but still have a goal, rules, a feedback system, and voluntary participation [14].

These characteristics cover similar terms and ideas are commonly found in game definitions and commentaries on game design[1].

2.2 Player Learning and Engagement

Games are designed to engage the player in the process of mastering a challenge that can be difficult, prolonged and complex [15–18]. Games attempt to achieve this primarily by intrinsically motivating players to progress regardless of extrinsic rewards [19].

---

[1] This list may not be exhaustive, but it is comprehensive. Having the words begin with 'c' was initially a coincidence but ultimately sustained as a memory aid.

Kirriemuir et al. consider digital games to be excellent motivational tools and useful educational vehicles that can promote learning and engagement [20–22]. Indeed, Gee recognized that games are inherently good learning machines, and the core features present in game design are what makes games such as popular vehicles for instruction [23]. It is the motivational qualities of games that have led many to argue that games have the potential to motivate, engage and ultimately enhance how students learn [16, 17, 24–28]. Further studies consistently highlight the significant relationship between engagement and learning, reporting that highly motivated students are more likely to engage in the learning process [18, 19, 29–36]. Malone & Lepper [19] proposed a theory of intrinsic motivation in games which suggested that games are rewarding experiences due to a combination of challenge, fantasy and curiosity. These dimensions are further expanded upon by Garris [34], Sweetser & Wyeth [37], Yee [38], and Bostan [39]. Charles [15], distilled and mapped these key motivational characteristics of games to those inherently engaging factors within learning processes. This review uncovered 40 characteristics, which were subsequently condensed into the following engagement factors:

1. *Fun*: Engagement is more likely when an experience is enjoyable. Enjoyment can be attained in a range of ways from experiencing surprise to overcoming difficult challenges.
2. *Structure*: Engagement is also more likely if objectives are clear and constraints have meaning. Contributing game mechanics include choice, control, goals, and rules. Understanding purpose helps people become more intrinsically motivated in a task.
3. *Challenge*: This is central to learning, and the satisfaction of mastering a challenge is critical to engagement and thus enjoyment. Mastery is important for intrinsic motivation.
4. *Feedback*: Engagement is reinforced by explicit and timely achievements. Feedback schemes can be immediate, summative, and can use endogenous or exogenous rewards.
5. *Relationships*: Social features help enhance intrinsic motivation by making achievements more visible and meaningful, so players experience a greater sense of relatedness.
6. *Identity*: Escapism, fantasy, presence, role play (expressiveness) help a player increase their agency within a game. Freedom to express their selves and to explore provides player autonomy, which is essential to intrinsic motivation in tasks. Games generally afford more opportunities for self-expression and free choice without consequence than in real life.
7. *Narrative*: There are two main types of stories in games: a game story as written by the designer, and a player-unique story as the consequence of player actions and experience.

Various authors have recognized learning's importance for engagement within games [27, 30, 40, 41]. For example, several games researchers have related Csikszentmihalyi's Flow theory [42] of optimal experience to learning and challenges within games.

Csikszentmihalyi's idea of Flow is that enjoyment in life is attained by becoming increasingly proficient in any task; even a repetitive and potentially dull tasks at home, such as washing the dishes. Let us consider the exemplar autotelic personality: a person who is best at unlocking enjoyment within life since once they chose a goal to achieve, or a skill to master, they commit to it and are focused its attainment. An autotelic person can apply the flow principle to all parts of their life, and not get distracted by tasks that they have not prioritized. Autotelic people have a unique sense of curiosity and purpose that helps provide them with the structure and drive to be successful in much of what they set out to achieve. Games, as designed and structured entities, can help a person attain more optimal experiences during play by aligning gameplay and challenge closer to their goals and capability [43].

2.3   Game Atoms and Behavlets

Game designers have explored many ways to break down the components of a game, towards building a form of game grammar that would improve the process of analysing game design and enhance the theoretical basis. For example, much of Koster's book A Theory of Fun for Game Design [27] focuses on the inherent fascination that people have for patterns as a motivation to play, outlines how this relates to our desire to learn, and discusses the relationship of learning to our experience of fun. The basic concept is that a game contains patterns of play (Dynamics) that are initially unfamiliar to a player, but as they progress through a game (and become more skilled), an increased understanding of the underlying rules (Mechanics) of the game is gained. Ideas on gameplay patterns can be related to information theory, entropy and uncertainty. For example, Costikyan [9] postulates that uncertainty is a core ingredient of games; we need to be unsure of the outcome of a game for it to be interesting to us. LeBlanc has also discussed the role of uncertainty in the context of Formal Abstract Design Tools (FADTs) [44] to enhance dramatic tension within games [7]. Note that patterns of play are related to game design patterns, which (as mentioned above) are culturally defined objects of play which form the common core of many different games. Design patterns differ to play patterns in that design patterns are often familiar to a player at the beginning of a game. While the pattern consumption that Koster discusses relates to the unique composition of game design patterns (and other novel game mechanics) for each game.

The method that we use here to describe the underlying mechanics of a game is based on the idea of game atoms[2] by Daniel Cook. A skill atom is comprised of a game action, which results in the application of game rules to change game state in the simulation, and the provision of feedback to the player. Based on this, a modelling process occurs in which the player updates their mental model of the game as a system.

Figure 1 provides an illustration of a typical game Atom. Player's prior-belief and knowledge-update icons (head with a brain) are designed to have a colour code associated with them – e.g. the closer the colour is to red (from yellow), the more the skill or knowledge has been mastered by the player. Figure 2 provides an example of an Atom skill chain.

---

[2] http://www.gamasutra.com/view/feature/129948/the_chemistry_of_game_design.php.

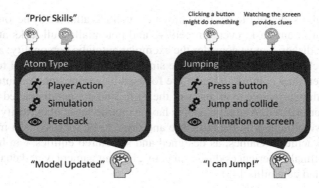

Fig. 1. Game atom prototype (left) and jump Atom example (right) (Color figure online)

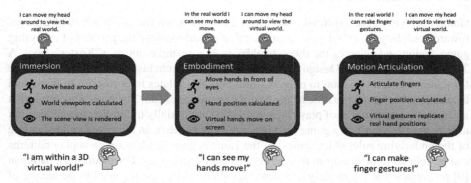

Fig. 2. An Atom skill chain for a natural hand movement game controller in virtual reality

Behavlets might be thought of as short Atom behaviour chains (as opposed to traditional skill-based chains) related to personality/preference-oriented actions in a game or in out of gameplay actions. Behavlets might be categorised in the following areas:

A. In-gameplay environment interactions (Magic Circle [45]):

    a. Reactive play: acting.
    b. Deliberative play: planning.
    c. Social play: text, speech, hanging out.
    d. User Interface: menus, cut scenes.

B. Out-of-gameplay environment interactions (Invisible Playground [8]):

    a. Game system: menus, cut scenes, patching, modding.
    b. Social: forums, social media, friend discussions.
    c. Preparation: reading user guides, software modding, equipment optimization/setup.

Figure 3 illustrates the contrast between contemporary machine learning approaches and the Behavlets approach.

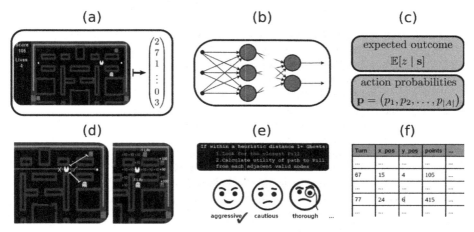

Fig. 3. Quantitative and qualitative ways to derive play patterns. **Top Row**: machine learning applied to games. (a) the game state is converted from the game description language's internal data structures into a vector s; (b) the state vector is given as an input to the LSTM neural network; and (c) the neural network produces both an estimate of the expected outcome of the game and a probability distribution for the possible actions. **Bottom Row**: Behavlet play modelling. (d) a domain expert observes characteristic patterns of play and associated game utilities; (e) then identifies potential rule-based encodings of the observed pattern and labels the pattern with a playing style, e.g. aggressive, cautious; (f) the encoding is expressed as an action-sequence in terms of raw game-log data.

In [1], we identified the core Behavlets within a typical online first person shooter game, focussing only on 1a, 1b, and 1c above (Fig. 3). In that paper we argued that Behavlets are probably best to be identified in this manner as it requires domain knowledge of a game, expertise on game design patterns and patterns of play, and player behaviour.

2.4   Behavlet Chains

A Behavlet Atom defines a simple behaviour, such as waiting. It differs from Skill Atom in that in a Behavlet encodes player behaviour that is correlated to personality or temperament. A Behavlet may be more complex to recognise that a skill Atom in that behavioural facets such as being cautious, aggressive or strategic may require more complex code to recognise than simple actions such as jumping, running, or shooting. A B-chain is a sequence of Behavlets, which define higher order player behaviour processes. A complete set of possible Behavlets define all gameplay actions (or possibility space) within a game, like a behavioural genotype. Each player can be defined by the Behavlets that they typically perform (behavioural phenotype), including the frequency of Behavlet executions and B-chains. Specific Behavlets and B-chains might be expected

Table 1. Behavlets derived from first person shooter genres [1] (e.g. Call of Duty, Destiny)

A. Caution	i. Staying out of range and line of sight of enemies ii. Preferring long range weapons iii. Moving as a group iv. Peeking round corners – being careful of open areas v. Use of sniper rifle scope or binoculars to scout area vi. Takes cover early to regain health vii. Frequent saving viii. Camping
B. Meticulousness	i. Attempt to complete all tasks, gain all achievements ii. Collecting items/weapons iii. Area coverage iv. Area clearing v. Easter egg collecting/uncovering exploits vi. Play precision (precise kills etc.), optimizing kit
C. Impulsiveness	i. Aggressive behaviour (open frequent attacks, less planning/strategy) ii. Weapon choice iii. Less mindful of cover iv. Less cautious about health status
D. Competence	i. Optimized, real-time decision making (e.g. weapon selection) ii. Skill matching and optimized planning (players and quests) iii. Score/accuracy 3 iv. Practice/frequent play
E. Logic	i. Equipment selection ii. Quest/path planning (including team) iii. Battles (actions expose knowledge and planning)
F. Perfectionism	i. Optimized equipment section/set up ii. Perfectionism and repetition (zero deaths, ideal combat stats) iii. Completionism (tasks, equipment, achievements, items)
G. Empathy	i. Playing a support role (reviving, teamwork) ii. Teamwork
H. Morality	i. Team ethic (e.g. sharing loot, not taking kills) ii. Not camping or preying on the weak or showboating iii. Not being disrespectful (e.g. not mocking, no abusive chat)
I. Resourcing	i. Item/weapon searching/collection ii. Managing resources (e.g. in menu system)
J. Speed	i. Completion rate ii. Points/attempts ratio iii. Weapon selection and accuracy
K. Control Skill	i. Ability/weapon choice (particularly real-time) ii. Precise weapon use, shooting accuracy iii. Player character motion (particularly in battle)

to be executed at different times during a player's gameplay life cycle. This temporal ordering and pattern of play will help build a player's profile: for example, their play preference, capability, or risk of churn.

Figure 4 shows an example of three Behavlets within Pac-Man from our experiment within [1] ordered in a typical B-chain. It is important to note that Behavlets are sparse encodings, i.e. one Behavlet will not necessarily occur very often in a game, and a large set of Behavlets will not necessarily cover all of the game's history. After all, not every move is meaningful or emotionally relevant.

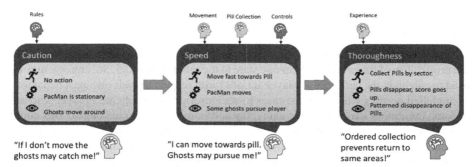

Fig. 4. A B-chain of three ordered Behavlets within Pac-Man gameplay. This B-chain suggests a careful but meticulous player, which might be identified automatically through process mining.

In a modern machine learning approach, a game playing agent can also incorporate information about the sequence of previously encountered states to implement its policy. Such an agent selects the next action based on the observed sequence of states. This is a problem that can be tackled by so called sequence-to-sequence (seq2seq) models [46], that map one sequence of tokens (in our case the game states) to another sequence (in our case the actions chosen by the agent). Such techniques were recently applied in the AlphaStar AI agent for StarCraft 2, equipping it to beat professional players for the first time. These techniques are very similar to language models used in computational linguistics that aim to predict the next word (or action) after observing a sequence of known words (or sequence of game states). To work well, such models must learn a higher-level representation of gameplay from the given state sequence. For example, in Long Short Term Memory (LSTM) models (a type of recurrent artificial neural network [47], this representation is simply a high-dimensional vector (see Fig. 3.a). Thus, it may indeed be possible to learn from low-level game actions to achieve a similar clustering of patterns as Behavlets so. The question remains, how does one interpret the output of the algorithm.

Here we argue that process mining or seq2seq approaches could profitably focus on sequences of Behavlets instead of low-level game actions. Such sequences of Behavlets, or B-chains, contain rich information on patterns of play that are meaningful to players; but the B-chains themselves are certainly best identified through computational intelligence methods, rather than manually.

3 Behavlet Analytics

Statistical methods and entropy calculations can be used to provide information on the variation of Behavlet use by players. However, we hypothesise that player Behavlets occur in a sequenced, patterned order within gameplay, particularly as a player improves (B-chains). Entropy can be considered a measure of uncertainty. Information entropy (H) is the average rate at which information is produced by a stochastic source of data (X) and the standard from is given in (1). Entropy can be used to measure the predictability of player behaviour in terms of Behavlet chain sequences.

$$H(X) = -\sum\nolimits_{i=1}^{n} P(x_i) log_b P(x_i) \tag{1}$$

For example, within a two state stationary graph the most uncertain condition is when the probability of transitioning from one state to the other state is 0.5. So, entropy may be used to calculate the certainty of player actions (with respect to their own past behaviour or modelled norms), where in most cases lower entropy would indicate a player who has become familiar or expert with the gameplay and/or overcoming challenges. This could provide an indicator that a player will soon quit the game. Another scenario that may lead to a player quitting is one in which their behavioural entropy is consistently high, perhaps indicating that they are not adequately learning how to play well.

Entropy rate estimation may be used to calculate Shannon entropy of both stationary and non-stationary processes, and help evaluate player behaviour and performance. For example, we would expect that as a player improves their capability through learning how to play, that a state graph expressing their behaviour would become more stationary. Player Behavlet profiling can be used to identify player behaviour in-game, and this behaviour monitored over time to automatically adapt to player needs or predict player churn. Alternatively, Markov Chains, Decision Trees (as used in [1]), or Reinforcement Learning can be used to model the probabilities of Behavlets being executed by players; given previous behaviour/actions. Kullback–Leibler (D-$_{KL}$) divergence or relative entropy two probability distributions may be used to characterize relative (Shannon) entropy in information systems, randomness in continuous time-series, or information gain when comparing statistical models of inference. D-$_{KL}$ can thus be used to measure similarity between a player's statistical behaviour profile and their previous behaviour or other stored archetypal profiles.

Process mining is another appropriate approach for this type of data and can used to identify common B-chains within full sequences of exhibited Behavlets. Process discovery [3] with approaches such as the α-algorithm [48] or similar may be used to identify B-chains within the logs of many players since it enables the detection of unexpected common sequences as well as expected ones. Petri Nets can be used to help visualize results.

Table 1 shows eleven common Behavlets identified for First Person Shooter (FPS) games, each with a range of behaviours that identify with that Behavlet.

It might be thought that the Behavlets in Table 1 are mutually exclusive, and therefore is Behavlet would be a state – so eleven states. However, it is more realistic to allow for Behavlets to occasionally occur at the same time. Though it would be rare for many Behavlets to be exhibited simultaneously. Thus the data would be quite sparse (See

Table 2 for a representative example). Real values would be generated in the 11D date vector, as shown, and might form the basis of data for a neural network. However, from some methods such as process mining, binning into discrete values is more appropriate as it would reduce the state space substantially.

Table 2. Example of raw data for a compound B-chain (S1–S6) with sparse Behavlet states

	A	B	C	D	E	F	G	H	I	J	K
S1	0.00	0.22	0.00	0.19	0.17	0.00	0.00	0.28	0.00	0.00	0.11
S2	0.32	0.14	0.00	0.14	0.00	0.24	0.00	0.00	0.16	0.00	0.00
S3	0.13	0.41	0.00	0.00	0.00	0.30	0.00	0.00	0.00	0.00	0.00
S4	0.10	0.00	0.00	0.28	0.00	0.00	0.00	0.00	0.28	0.11	0.23
S5	0.00	0.00	0.00	0.00	0.22	0.28	0.25	0.00	0.00	0.11	0.00
S6	0.10	0.00	0.11	0.16	0.22	0.17	0.00	0.13	0.00	0.06	0.00

For example, a player may be cautious, A(i), and stay out of sight so as to choose an appropriate weapon, E(i), and manage resources such as using a health pack I(ii). While the latter two Behavlets cannot be executed simultaneously they would be performed within a short time window. A specific example of a B-chain is shown in Table 3. This particular example would likely be a common gameplay pattern for a careful, meticulous player. Someone who doesn't like to be killed or hurt so optimises equipment and takes time to plan their attack plan. We would expect that as this player learned how to play the game better, that this B-chain would be more evident and thus various measures of patterned play as discussed earlier would support this.

Table 3. B-Chain example for a single player FPS game (binary encoding) – a cautious but successful attack.

	A	B	C	D	E	F	G	H	I	J	K
Caution	1										
Prepare for attack	1	1			1	1			1		
Static Attack	1	1									1
Moving Attack			1						1		
Scavenge		1							1		

4   Conclusion

We have presented a position paper on extending our previous idea of Behavlets to behaviour chains B-chains. Significant player B-chains may be identified through the application of process mining of gameplay logs of player's execution of Behavlets within a game. Furthermore, once identified sequences of B-chains may be modelled using Markov Chain or Reinforcement learning techniques, or by monitoring the entropy of B-chains sequences over time and relative to other sequences. The creation of a game to record appropriate Behavlets in-game logs will be the next stage and the implementation of an experiment with a significant number of participants to provide adequate data for process modelling and information theoretic analysis. The identification of suitable Behavlets for a game and the related tracking code can be time consuming, and so we will investigate ways for automating this activity.

References

1. Cowley, B., Charles, D.: Behavlets: a method for practical player modelling using psychology-based player traits and domain specific features. User Model. User-adapt. Interact. **26** (2016). https://doi.org/10.1007/s11257-016-9170-1
2. Anderson, A., Kleinberg, J., Mullainathan, S.: Assessing human error against a benchmark of perfection. ACM Trans. Knowl. Discov. Data. **11**, 1–25 (2017). https://doi.org/10.1145/304 6947
3. Van der Aalst, W.: Process Mining: Data Science in Action. Springer, Heidelberg (2016). https://doi.org/10.1007/978-3-662-49851-4
4. Hunicke, R., Leblanc, M., Zubek, R.: MDA: a formal approach to game design and game research. In: Game Developers Conference (2001)
5. Suits, B.: Grasshopper: Games, Life and Utopia. David R. Godine, Boston (1990)
6. Costikyan, G.: I have no words and I must design. In: Interactive Fantasy #2. http://www.cos tik.com/nowords.html
7. LeBlanc, M.: Tools for Creating Dramatic Game Dynamics. MIT Press, Cambridge (2006)
8. Salen, K., Zimmerman, E.: Rules of Play-Game Design Fundamentals. MIT Press, Cambridge (2003)
9. Costikyan, G.: Uncertainty in Games. MIT Press, Cambridge (2013)
10. Binmore, K.G.: Game theory and the social contract: playing fair. English **1**, 364 (1994)
11. Avedon, E.M., Sutton-Smith, B.: The Study of Games. Wiley, Hoboken (1971)
12. Suits, B.: What Is a Game? Philos. Sci. **34**, 148–156 (1967). https://doi.org/10.1086/288138
13. Koster, R.: An atomic theory of fun game design. http://www.raphkoster.com/2012/01/24/an-atomic-theory-of-fun-game-design/. Accessed 05 Mar 2014
14. McGonigal, J.: Reality is Broken: Why Games Make Us Better and How They Can Change the World. Vintage Digital (2011)
15. Charles, T.: Enhanced e-Learning Engagement using Game Absorption Techniques ELE-GANT (PhD thesis) (2010)
16. Gee, J.P.: What Video Games Have to Teach Us About Learning and Literacy. Palgrave, Macmillan, London (2003)
17. Oblinger, D., Oblinger, J., Lippincott, J.: Educating the Net Generation (2005)
18. Prensky, M.: Don't bother me, Mom, I'm learning!: How computer and video games are preparing your kids for 21st century success and how you can help!. Paragon House, St. Paul, MN (2006)
19. Malone, T.W., Lepper, M.R., Snow, R., Farr, M.: Making learning fun: a taxonomy of intrinsic motivations for learning. In: Aptitude, Learning and Instruction: III. Conative and Affective Process Analyses, pp. 223–253. Hilsdale, Erlbaum (1987)
20. Kirriemuir, J., McFarlane, A.: Report 8: Literature Review in Games and Learning (2004)
21. Mitchell, A., Savill-Smith, C.: The Use of Computer and Video Games for Learning: A Review of the Literature. Learning and Skills Development Agency, London (2004)

22. de Freitas, S.: Learning in Immersive Worlds: A Review of Games Based Learning, Lonon (2006)
23. Gee, J.P.: Learning by design: good video games as learning machines. E-Learning **2**, 5 (2005)
24. Gallo, D.: Educating for empathy, reason and imagination. J. Creat. Behav. **23**, 98–115 (1989)
25. Prensky, M.: The motivation of gameplay: the real twenty-first century learning revolution. Horiz **10**, 5–11 (2002)
26. Squire, K., Jenkins, H.: Harnessing the power of games in education. Insight **3**, 5–33 (2003)
27. Koster, R.: Theory of Fun for Game Design. Paraglyph Inc., US (2004)
28. Shaffer, D.: How Computer Games Help Children Learn. Palgrave Macmillan, United States of America (2006)
29. Wishart, J.: Cognitive factors related to user involvement with computers and their effects upon learning from an educational computer game. Comput. Educ. **15**, 145–150 (1990)
30. Prensky, M.: Digital Game-Based Learning. McGraw-Hill Education (2001)
31. Klaila, D.: Game-based e-learning gets real (2001)
32. Greenagel, F.: The illusion of e-learning: why we're missing out on the promise of technology (2002). http://www.guidedlearning.com/illusions.pdf
33. Pearce, C.: Story as play space: narrative in games. Game on: the history and culture of videogames (2002)
34. Garris, R., Ahlers, R., Driskell, J.: Games, motivation, and learning: a research and practice model. Simul. Gaming **33**, 441–467 (2002)
35. Mitchell, A.: The use of computer and video games for learning, London (2004)
36. Minsky, M.: The Emotion Machine: Commonsense Thinking, Artificial Intelligence, and the Future of the Human Mind. Simon & Schuster, New York (2006)
37. Sweetser, P., Wyeth, P.: GameFlow: a model for evaluating player enjoyment in games. Comput. Entertain. **3**, 3 (2005)
38. Yee, N.: Motivations for play in online games. CyberPsychol. Behav. **9**, 772–775 (2006)
39. Bostan, B.: Player motivations: a psychological perspective. ACM Comput. Entertain. **7**, 22 (2009)
40. Gee, J.P.: Good Video Games and Good Learning: Collected Essays on Video Games, Learning and Literacy (New Literacies and Digital Epistemologies). Peter Lang, New York (2007)
41. Oblinger, D.: Emerging technologies for learning (2008)
42. Csikszentmihalyi, M.: Flow, The Psychology of Optimal Experience. Harper Perennial, New York (1991)
43. Cowley, B., Charles, D., Black, M., Hickey, R.: Toward an understanding of flow in video games. Comput. Entertain. **6** (2008). https://doi.org/10.1145/1371216.1371223
44. Church, D.: Formal abstract. In: Salen, K., Zimmerman, E. (eds.) The Game Design Reader: A Rules of Play Anthology, pp. 366–380. MIT Press (2006)
45. Huizinga, J.: Homo Ludens: A Study of the Play-Element in Culture. The Beacon Press, Boston (1955)
46. Sutskever, I., Vinyals, O., Le, Q.V.: Sequence to sequence learning with neural networks. Adv. Neural. Inf. Process. Syst. **4**, 3104–3112 (2014)
47. (1997). https://doi.org/10.1162/neco.1997.9.8.1735
48. Van Der Aalst, W., Weijters, T., Maruster, L.: Workflow mining: discovering process models from event logs. IEEE Trans. Knowl. Data Eng. **16**, 1128–1142 (2004). https://doi.org/10.1109/TKDE.2004.47

The Kansei Research on the Manipulation Experience of Mobile Game with Joystick

Hsin-Jung Chen[✉] and Hsi-Jen Chen[✉]

Department of Industrial Design, National Cheng Kung University, No. 1, University Road, East District, Tainan 701, Taiwan
verti0724hhh@gmail.com, hsijen_chen@mail.ncku.edu.tw

Abstract. Nowadays, smartphones have become the largest gaming platform. With the improvement of the performance of smartphones continuously, the manipulation of mobile games has gradually turned to more horizontal and complicated. It also prompted players to pay more attention to the gaming experience; even emerge dedicated joystick for mobile phones. However, the previous literature has rarely discussed the gaming experience and the feelings of the mobile game control process. Therefore, the purpose of this study is to explore the feelings of play mobile games with different joysticks and to find the key Kansei vocabulary that affects players' feelings stronger, to establish the design direction of joysticks which are dedicated to the mobile phone in the future. This research will invite high-involved players of mobile games to conduct Focus group and play mobile games. Through the research results, we can understand the players' expected feelings when playing mobile games, and also provide the future design direction of the joystick, so that players have a better gaming experience, even increase willingness to play mobile games, and make a positive impact on the gaming market. In addition, through this study, we will be able to explore the process of using the Kansei engineering method to understand the users' expected control feelings and apply to the development of future human-computer interactive products and contribute to the field of human-computer interaction.

Keywords: Mobile game · Joystick · Interactivity · Gaming experience · Kansei

1 Introduction

In recent years, with the rapid development of mobile devices and the Internet, the owning rate of smartphones has continued to increase, which has prompted the development of various mobile phone applications (Apps), especially for amusement related apps, among which gaming Apps are the most promising [1]. The high convenience and popularity of smartphones also make players prefer to use their smartphones to play games [2]. In order to meet the needs of the game market, many game companies actively develop various mobile game apps. Mobile devices have become the biggest game platform with the highest market share in the global game market since 2017 [3]. Although the prospect for the mobile game industry is still promising and sales are still growing. A report from

© Springer Nature Switzerland AG 2020
C. Stephanidis et al. (Eds.): HCII 2020, LNCS 12425, pp. 644–657, 2020.
https://doi.org/10.1007/978-3-030-60128-7_47

Flurry Insights considers that the time users spend playing mobile games has plateaued [4]. In addition, the current mobile game market is highly competitive, only a few games will succeed in generating high numbers of downloads where most mobile games fail [3]. Furthermore, research has shown that for most mobile games, users tend to quit games after the first trial [5]. However, the revenue for most of the game developers is created mainly from advertising or from a small number of active users willing to pay for some additional features [6]. Therefore, it is vital to take measures to retain those users.

Yet, Comprehensive research into understanding the behavioral drivers of users' continued use of a product or service is rather limited, even more so in the context of mobile gaming [7]. Besides, researchers have mainly categorized the previous literature on online game adoption into two groups: one focused on the technical side (in terms of realism, animation, scenario, sound, visualization techniques, graphics, etc.); and the other focused on the psychological perspective (the enjoyment of games, flow status, etc.) most of those studies focus on specific games, and do not reveal the correlation between the technical aspects of games and user experience [1]. It is worth noting that the extant literature consistently refers to the relevance of enjoyment to continued use [8–10].

On the other hand, the development trend of mobile games, manufacturers of smart phones continue to produce smartphones with better performance, which promotes the manipulation of mobile games to horizontal, complex and lead contents and storylines more plentiful, even created many new ways of game manipulations [11, 12]. Under this condition, the game control experience has even begun to be valued by players, and there has even been a trend to use the joystick that used to control the console in the past as a mobile game control medium.

From the above background, we can know that the mobile game industry has bright prospects, and it can be speculated that the game control process and the game control medium will have an impact on the gaming experience. In addition, from the literature, you can understand the correlation between gaming experience, enjoyment, and drivers for continued use. Therefore, it is worthwhile to explore the players' expected feelings of gaming experience and to redesign the control mediums that meet their expectations. In order to achieve the research purpose and retain the mobile game players, this study will use Kansei engineering to establish the semantic space of gaming experience, and collect the data of feelings before and after the actual manipulation by subjects, so as to comprehensively explore the user's feelings and preferences during the game control process.

2 Literature Review

2.1 Kansei Engineering and Semantic Space

Kansei. Kansei was proposed by Anitawati Mohd. In the field of cognition, it is defined as the relation between people and objects, and explores the connection between people's perception of objects and motivation for use [13]. In the field of psychology, Kansei images are interpreted as emotional feelings, including the reasons of users' psychological reactions to the object, and it is also a combination of consumer perceptions, judgments, preferences, and attitudes towards objects. Besides, the Kansei image is influenced by the user's culture, life experience, knowledge and growing environment [14].

Kansei Engineering. In the field of engineering, the application of Kansei imagery to product design is called Kansei engineering; it is a consumer-oriented product development technology that mainly explores the relationship between people and objects or products. The purpose is to produce new products based on the emotional needs of consumers. The product contains four key points: how to analyze and collect data about user experience, understand user experience and identify product elements, establish human-centered design and adapting to changes in society and user preferences to modify the direction of product design [15].

Semantic Space. When applying Kansei engineering, it is necessary to establish a semantic space at first. The basic idea is to describe—based on the scope of research area or target product—the idea behind the product from two different perspectives: (1) The semantic description; and (2) The description of product properties or product design elements. These two descriptions span a vector space each. Subsequently, these spaces are merged with each other in the synthesis phase, indicating which of the product properties evokes which semantic impact. When the results from this process are satisfactory, a semantic space can be built describing how the semantic (Kansei vocabulary which describing the target area, mostly adjectives) and the space of application (Product properties or Product design elements) are associated [16].

Furthermore, with the improvement of technology and production process, the product life cycle is shortened. It also makes it difficult for consumers to distinguish the function and value of products when shopping, and makes consumers tend to use subjective feelings to select products. In the past, Kansei engineering was mostly used in product design [15], but many products in the future will be human-computer interactive products that are a combination of physical and virtual parts [16]. Therefore, it is important to apply Kansei engineering to the interaction process between users and products, so that products can be efficiently developed to meet consumer expectations.

2.2 Mobile Games

Types of Mobile Games. Most of the games are designed for entertainment, and few games have educational or other significance in the process of games. In addition, the basic composition of the game includes: specific goals, rules, and the games are played through various media, which can be the props in the game or itself. For the reason that depending on the game medium, different game types are generated [17]. Mobile games, which are transplanted from various platforms in video games or derived from existing games, so that the types of mobile games are quite diverse [12]. In the early stage of the development of game apps, most of the keyboards of mobile phones only have numeric keypads and keys for turning on and hang up. Due to the lack of keys on the phone and the small size of the keys, they are not suitable for many game types of manipulations, making the development direction of mobile games in the past tends to be puzzle games with simple rules, monotonous game screens and easy to manipulate [18]. However, with the improvement of mobile phone performance and the advent of touchscreens, mobile games will take plentiful content, horizontal and complex manipulations as the direction, and game control experience is beginning to be valued by players [12]. Although there are many ways to categorize mobile games, we make a pre-test questionnaire based on the classification in the previous study and App store and then ask the subjects to check the list of game types in the questionnaire based on whether the game type has been downloaded and then ask the subjects to check the list of game types in the questionnaire about whether they have downloaded those types of the mobile game before. Through the pre-test questionnaire, it is found that the download rates of the game types with the above characteristics (plentiful content, horizontal and complex manipulations) are ranked from high to low as follows: MOBA games, shooting games, racing games and sports games, which are the top four. Therefore, this research takes the MOBA games as research objects and selects a game in MOBA games based on factors such as downloads and popularity. Finally, we chose Arena of Valor, a mobile game made by Garena in this study (Fig. 1).

Fig. 1. Arena of Valor (MOBA game)

Manipulating Medium for Mobile Games. A game controller is a device that provides input to a game or entertainment system. It is usually used to control an object or character in the game. In the past, game controllers had to be connected to a game console or computer via a wire [19] until the advent of portable game consoles. Nowadays, smartphones have become the largest gaming platform. However, in the early stage of the development of game apps, mobile games were originally defined as entertainment applications used on small handheld mobile devices with wireless communication capabilities [20]. With the advancement of technology, we can observe changes in their appearance and manipulation, such as the screen becoming larger, the screen resolution improved, the position of the keys moved from below to the sides, and even apply the touchscreen as a manipulation medium [21]. Some scholars consider that the hardware performance of mobile phones is highly related to the development of mobile games. In addition to the simple puzzle games in the past, the emergence of new technologies gives players more choices in manipulation ways and makes the gameplay more diverse and complex [11]. So far, game controllers have been continuously designed and improved, and this phenomenon has made the style of button arrangement various. The components of the joystick may include direction control keys, function keys, mode switching keys, vibration effect switches, start keys and analog joysticks, plus new function buttons on the front and bottom of the joystick. Depending on the type of game, game manufac-turers have also developed components designed for specific types of games, such as steering wheel controllers in racing games or trigger simulators of shooting games [19]. Moreover, many game developers have even actively developed dedicated joysticks for smartphones to meet the needs of players in recent years.

Constituent Elements of Mobile Games. According to previous literature, there are many different definitions of the constituent elements of games. As mentioned above, the basic structure of the game requires props or media, goals, rules and feedback, and the entertainment brought about in the process [17]; some scholars have pointed out that the game itself includes behavioral patterns, rules, conditions, physical and mental entertainment, winning and losing behavior performance [22]. From the perspective of game development and design, some scholars consider that the elements of the game should be novel, challenging, stimulating, harmonious, crisis, and oppressive [23]; other scholars also consider that the elements of the game can be categorized into internal and external. The internal elements of the game are: experience accumulation, competition, challenge, and sense of achievement; the external elements of the game are: goal, level, score, ranking, time limit, limited resources, and rotation [12]. Some scholars have cat-egorized the elements of the game into game design and playability. The game design includes challenge, variety, novelty, and design aesthetic; playability includes perceived ease of use and interactivity [7]. In addition, scholars have found that most of the previ-ous studies have focused on other gaming platforms, such as home consoles, computer games, or online games. Only a few studies have focused on mobile games, and most of the research content is to discuss the elements of game design, not to discuss the gaming experience and game control process of mobile games [1]. We took the interac-tivity (game manipulation experience) as the research direction and conducted a better understanding of the player's feelings when playing four types of games (MOBA games, shooting games, racing games, and sports games) with different manipulation medium (Touch screen and mobile game joysticks) in this paper.

2.3   Interaction Design and User Experience

In the field of interaction design, interaction is completed through the execution of a single or several steps. The steps are considered to be composed of interactive operation images generated by cognitive space, and are divided into input and output: (1) Input is operation Control; (2) Output is feedback and response after manipulation. And Human-computer interaction is the process of being presented in a virtual medium after the user's cognition and actual manipulation; or when people manipulate objects through the interface to interact with the virtual space [24]. Some studies suggest that when consumers use products, interaction behavior has a great impact on user experience. Therefore, understanding the user experience and feelings of an interactive process is an important part of interaction design [25, 26]. Moreover, we can increase enjoyment by satisfying the user's expectations to achieve a better user experience, and enhance the willingness to continue to use the products [27].

2.4 Emotional Cognition and Product Design

Norman [28] believes that emotions are an integral part of user experience in the interaction between users and products. And there are three levels in emotional cognition: visceral level for external design, behavioral level for having pleasure and usability by using products, reflective level for the self-image by users and the significance from products. Huang [29] applied the three levels of emotional cognition to the exploration of smart phones, and explored the elements that users reassemble to re-form mobile phones, which elements users will choose and the reason why, Therefore, this study will be based on the three levels of emotional cognition proposed by Norman. The experience process will be disassembled into analyzable elements and applied to the design of game control medium. For instance, the visceral level includes appearance, color, shape, and size, etc.; the behavioral level includes actions and patterns during manipulation; the reflective level is the aspect of analyzing emotions.

3   Method

In this article, we divide the experimental process into two phases: In the first phase, we collected Kansai vocabulary through the Focus group and made those vocabularies into a questionnaire. By analyzing the results of the questionnaire, we could establish a semantic space for the game experience of the MOBA game; in the second phase, we invite 8 subjects to play MOBA games with different manipulating medium and fill out questionnaires before and after the game. After completing the questionnaire, we interviewed the subjects to find out the relationship between the Kansei vocabulary and the elements of the MOBA game. We hope to contribute to the future design direction of the mobile joystick.

3.1   Phase 1: Establish a Semantic Space for MOBA Games

Focus Group. In this article, we conduct a focus group to collect Kansei vocabulary, and we use the KJ method to classify and name the collected Kansei vocabularies to make the online questionnaire. In addition, we made existing mobile phone joysticks into cards and asked members of focus groups to classify and name those cards through the Card-sorting method. After the Card-sorting method is completed, the existing mobile phone joysticks are divided into three categories, including: (1) suction-type mobile phone joysticks; (2) side-type mobile phone joysticks; (3) hand-held type mobile phone joysticks. Finally, we choose one from each of the three joystick types to experiment based on factors such as compatibility with mobile phones, performance, etc.

In this study, we invite 8 participants in total as Focus group members include: (1) mobile game designers; (2) high-involve mobile game players who play mobile games for an average of more than two hours a day; (3) players with relevant gaming experience, with the purpose of build the semantic space of gaming experience for MOBA games. Referring to the method proposed by Anthropy and Clark [30], we demonstrate screenshots and videos of MOBA games, so that participants can follow the game process and content of MOBA games to explore Kansei vocabulary. Through the focus group interviews, we can: (1) have better communication between participants; (2) direct contact between researchers and research subjects; (3) participants can construct answers and views in their own words (Fig. 2).

Fig. 2. From left to right are joystick in suction-type, side-type, hand-held type

Online Questionnaire. In order to establish the semantic space of the game experience more accurately, we will use the Kansei vocabulary obtained from the focus group to make an online questionnaire, and invite subjects with MOBA game experience to complete the questionnaire. Finally, 122 valid questionnaires have been collected for analysis in this study. After we take SPSS software that was used for reliability analysis and exploratory factor analysis to the result of the online questionnaire, we obtain 19 Kansei vocabularies and categorize those Kansei vocabularies into three factors.

3.2   Phase 2: Game Experience Questionnaire and Interview

In the secondary phase, all subjects are high-involve players who play mobile MOBA games for an average of more than two hours a day. We invite 8 subjects to play MOBA games with different manipulating medium and fill out questionnaires before and after the game. After the questionnaire is completed, we will interview the subject to understand the reasons for the Kansei vocabulary in the questionnaire and link those vocabularies with the elements in the MOBA game. Through the questionnaires which fill out before and after game, we can find out the Kansei vocabularies which have a stronger impact on gaming experience and explore the connection between satisfactions with gaming experience. On the other hand, through the interview with subjects; we can define these three factors of Kansai vocabulary and correspond the factors to three levels of emotional cognition. In addition, we can observe whether each Kansei vocabularies of feelings and each level of emotional cognition have an influence on each other.

3.3 Questionnaire Design

The online questionnaires were divided into two parts. In the first part, participants were asked to fill in their general information, preferences for mobile game types, frequency of playing mobile games, and whether they had used a mobile joystick within a year. The second part is an aim to know how the participants perceive the Kansei vocabulary and their emotions in the MOBA games. Participants fill out a seven-point questionnaire on Likert scales to find out how strong they feel about Kansei vocabulary in the MOBA games. During the filling process, there are game screenshots to assist (See Fig. 3). This questionnaire takes about 10 to 15 min to complete.

Fig. 3. Online questionnaire design

On the other hand, after the result of online questionnaires has been analyzed by reliability analysis and exploratory factor analysis, we can create the game experience questionnaire. The game experience questionnaires were divided into four parts. In the first part, participants were asked to fill in their general information, the satisfaction ranking of the game control media as expected (touchscreen, suction-type, side-type, hand-held type), and whether they had used a mobile joystick within a year. In the second part, participants were asked to fill out questionnaires based on their expectations of four-game manipulating mediums before actually playing the game. During the process, participants were allowed to touch and observe those game manipulating mediums. In the third part, participants actually played the game with different manipulating mediums one after another, and after completing each of them, they filled out the questionnaire immediately. In the last part, participants were asked to write down the reasons for each Kansei vocabulary that emerged on the list of vocabulary which in the questionnaire and to rank four-game manipulating mediums again after the game experience (See Fig. 4). This questionnaire is made in a seven-point questionnaire on Likert scales and takes about 30 min to complete.

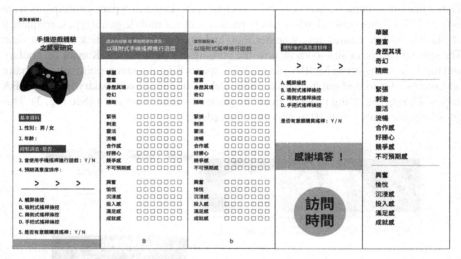

Fig. 4. Game Experience Questionnaire (Partial)

4   Result

After the Focus group completed the discussion, we obtained 65 Kansei vocabularies and reduced them to 26 vocabularies using the KJ method, and used then to create an online questionnaire. According to the questionnaire results, the scores for each question were standardized at the beginning of analysis, and the SPSS software was used for reliability analysis and exploratory factor analysis. First, through the reliability analysis, we removed less relevant vocabularies (Cronbach's Alpha = 0.946; N of Items = 19), and finally obtained 19 Kansei vocabularies. In addition, we had to use KMO (Kaiser-Meyer-Olkin Measure of Sampling Adequacy) and Bartlett's Test of Sphericity to confirm whether the results of the online questionnaire are suitable for exploratory factor analysis. The analysis results indicate that it is highly suitable for exploratory factor analysis (Kaiser-Meyer-Olkin Measure of Sampling Adequacy = 0.912; p = 0.000). Finally, through the exploratory factor analysis, we categorized them into three factors as followed: Factor A contains five words, which are Gorgeous, Plentiful, Sense of presence, Fantasy, and Exquisite; Factor B contains eight words, which are Tense, Exciting, Agile, Smooth, Cooperative, Competitive, Aggressive, Unpredictable; Factor C contains six words, which are Thrilled, Pleasing, Immersive, Engaging, Satisfying, Sense of achievement (Fig. 5).

Factor A	Factor B	Factor C
Gorgeous	Tense	Thrilled
Plentiful	Exciting	Pleasing
Sense of presence	Agile	Immersive
Fantasy	Smooth	Engaging
Exquisite	Cooperative	Satisfying
	Competitive	Sense of achievement
	Aggressive	
	Unpredictable	

Fig. 5. List of Kansei Vocabulary

After interviewing 8 participants, we explored the causes of the Kansei vocabularies in MOBA games and named those three factors by collating and analyzing the content of the interviews. We named factor A as the screen presentation and content of MOBA games; factor B as the process and manipulation of MOBA games; factor C as the overall experience before and after the MOBA games. And we has corresponded three factors to three levels of emotional cognition, namely visceral level, behavioral level, and reflective level. Through interviews with participants, we found that the participants thought that playing with different manipulating mediums affected their feelings about Kansei vocabularies, and some of them were obvious and strong, such as Sense of presence, Tense, Agile, Smooth, Immersive and Engaging. In addition, we also found that the participants' feelings of each Kansei vocabulary also affected each other, such as the connection between Agile and Tense.

In this study, we make a line chart of the scores of each question in the questionnaire, and analyze the results according to the interview content. For the participants, playing MOBA games with different Manipulating mediums affected the feelings of each Kansei vocabulary, and Agile and Smooth were the most obvious. Therefore, we analyzed the results by observing the scores before and after the actual experience of Agile and Smooth in each manipulating medium at first.

4.1 Comparison of Four Manipulating Mediums

First, we conducted the line chart which made from the average scores of each Kansei vocabulary in different manipulating mediums. By observing the scores of Agile and Smooth, we divided the result into two groups: (1) touchscreen and suction-type joysticks; (2) side-type joysticks and hand-held joysticks. If the participants play MOBA games with touchscreens and suction-type joysticks, the feelings of Agile and Smooth could meet the player's expectations, which also increase the scores of visceral and reflective level, including Gorgeous, Plentiful, Sense of presence, Immersive and Engaging; otherwise, if the participants play MOBA games with side-type joysticks and hand-held joysticks, the feelings of Agile and Smooth could not meet the player's expectations, which also decrease the scores of behavior and reflective level, including Tense, Cooperative, Competitive, Immersive, Engaging, Satisfying and Sense of achievement. Through interviews with participants, we found that there are two reasons for this result: (1) participants are used to playing games with touchscreen; (2) the positions of the joystick buttons are different from the buttons on the interface, both of which made them unable to manipulate intuitively. In addition, most of the participants believed that after being familiar with various manipulating media, they could improve the feeling of Agile and Smooth, and hold a positive attitude towards using the joystick to play the game. Secondary, we can observe from the line chart that if the game is played with touchscreen and suction-type joysticks, although it can improve the participants' feeling of the Kansei vocabulary in the visceral level, such as Gorgeous, Plentiful, Sense of presence and Exquisite, those scores were still lower than side-type joysticks and hand-held joysticks to play the game. Through interviews with participants, we can speculate that the reason is that when participants played the game with touchscreen and suction-type joystick, the screen was blocked.

4.2 Connection Between the Kansei Vocabularies

As we interviewed with participants, we found that there are connections between the Kansei vocabularies, especially for the feeling of agile and smooth while they played the MOBA game with different joysticks. For instance, participants' feelings of agile and smooth also affect their feelings about the sense of presence, tense, exciting, immersive, engaging and satisfying; that is, by improving the perception of Kansei vocabulary at the behavioral level will affect the player's perception of Kansei vocabulary in other levels of emotional cognition. In addition, we found that the scores of items that at the reflective level of emotional cognition have a stronger impact on the ranking of satisfaction about joysticks. Therefore, it is important that enhance the feeling of agile and smooth while playing the MOBA game; that is, a better game control medium which can meet players' expectation will lead to a better gaming experience.

5 Discussion

Previous studies indicated that a positive correlation between enjoyment and willingness to continue playing the game. And we can increase enjoyment by satisfying the player's expectations [27, 31]. In this study, we found that the game manipulating medium of the game plays an important role in the gaming experience. Based on the analysis of the questionnaire and interviews, the design directions of three types of joysticks were discussed as follows:

Suction-Type Joysticks. As we can observe from the line chart, both the feeling of agile and smooth can meet the expectation of the player. However, in terms of visceral vocabularies, such as Gorgeous, Plentiful, Sense of presence and Exquisite, those scores were all lower than other types of joysticks, so that there are three suggestions for the design direction of the future after we interviewed with participants: (1) Reduce the scope of covering to the screen to improve the feeling of Gorgeous and Plentiful; (2) In terms of appearance design and material choice, it should improve the feeling of Exquisite; (3) More stable adsorption on the screen to enhance the feeling of Sense of presence and Exquisite.

Side-Type Joysticks and Hand-Held Joysticks. As we can observe from the line chart, both the feeling of agile and smooth fail to meet the expectation of the player. Through interviews with participants, we found that it is critical that players can manipulate more intuitively during the game. Meanwhile, most participants thought that the key position of the joystick unable to correspond to the key position on the interface, and they believed that the habit of playing games with touchscreens is related. However, they still held a positive attitude towards playing games with joysticks and believed that after learning and becoming familiar with the manipulation, they can get better gaming experience. In addition, they thought that types of mobile games play an important role in choosing a mobile joystick; the reason is that the complexity of manipulation is different for different types of mobile games. For example, they tend to use the hand-held joystick for more complex games, such as shooting games and MOBA games; on the other hand, they tend to use suction-type joysticks or side-type joysticks for simple games, such as racing games and sports games. To achieve a better gaming experience, there are four suggestions for the design direction of the future: (1) By collecting the key positions often configured on the mobile game interface and changing the key position of the joystick to match the key position of the game interface, players can perform game operations more intuitively; (2) Because these two types of joysticks have a large contact area with the hand, the choice of surface material and appearance design become important; (3) Lighten the joystick to reduce the burden on players' hands; (4) Be lighter, handier and more portable.

6   Conclusion

In this research, we conducted the Focus group to collect the Kansei Vocabularies about the gaming experience about MOBA games and reduce those Kansei vocabularies to 26 by using the KJ method. We made an online questionnaire to explore how high-involve players feel when playing MOBA games by applying those 26 Kansei vocabularies. Based on the scores of the questionnaire items, Kansei vocabularies can be categorized into three factors and named in accordance with the causes of the Kansei vocabularies in MOBA games eventually: "The screen presentation and content of MOBA games", "The process and manipulation of MOBA games" and "The overall experience before and after the MOBA games". And we found that three factors can correspond to three levels of emotional cognition after we interviewed with participants. Then we invited participants to play the MOBA game with different manipulating medium, and fill out the game experience questionnaire before and after the game. Based on the scores of the questionnaire items, we found that three levels of emotional cognition affected each other, and among that Kansei vocabulary which "Agile" and "Smooth" have the strongest impact on playing MOBA games with different manipulating mediums. Through interviews with participants, we corresponded three levels of emotional cognition to design elements of joysticks, and gave some suggestions for design direction of game joysticks in the future.

In conclusion, past researches have been less focused on the gaming experience and manipulating experience. Since more and more players have a positive attitude toward playing mobile games with joysticks, and we find that improving the game manipulating experience made the overall gaming experience better thus it does worth it to design the joysticks that meet the expectations of players. The findings of the study contribute to HCI Community with the preliminary investigation on game manipulation experience of MOBA games and the way to explore feelings in human-computer interaction, and future research should be further focused on practical experiments and the impact on familiarity with manipulating medium to verify the conclusions of the self-reports.

References

1. Park, H.J., Kim, S.-H.: A Bayesian network approach to examining key success factors of mobile games. J. Bus. Res. **66**(9), 1353–1359 (2013)
2. Hsiao, K.-L., Chen, C.-C.: What drives in-app purchase intention for mobile games? An examination of perceived values and loyalty. Electron. Commer. Res. Appl. **16**, 18–29 (2016)
3. Molinillo, S., Munoz-Leiva, F., Perez-Garcia, F.: The effects of human-game interaction, network externalities, and motivations on players' use of mobile casual games. Ind. Manag. Data Syst. **118**(9), 1766–1786 (2018)
4. Khalaf, S.: Media, productivity & emojis give mobile another stunning growth year. Flurry by Yahoo (2016)
5. Purcell, K., Entner, R., Henderson, N.: The rise of apps culture. Pew Internet & American Life Project, vol. 14 (2010)
6. Brustein, J.: The profitable future of free mobile apps. Hakupäivä 2013, p. 3 (2014). Saatavissa: http://www.businessweek.com/articles/2013-09-19/the-profitablefuture-of-free-mobile-apps
7. Merikivi, J., Tuunainen, V., Nguyen, D.: What makes continued mobile gaming enjoyable? Comput. Hum. Behav. **68**, 411–421 (2017)
8. Moon, J.-W., Kim, Y.-G.: Extending the TAM for a World-Wide-Web context. Inf. Manag. **38**(4), 217–230 (2001)
9. Lin, C.P., Bhattacherjee, A.: Extending technology usage models to interactive hedonic technologies: a theoretical model and empirical test. Inf. Syst. J. **20**(2), 163–181 (2010)
10. Wang, Q., Sun, X.: Investigating gameplay intention of the elderly using an Extended Technology Acceptance Model (ETAM). Technol. Forecast. Soc. Chang. **107**, 59–68 (2016)
11. Uludagli, M.C., Acarturk, C.: User interaction in hands-free gaming: a comparative study of gaze-voice and touchscreen interface control. Turk. J. Electr. Eng. Comput. Sci. **26**(4), 1967–1976 (2018)
12. Chang, L.-Y.: A study of game design elements on smartphone. Master thesis, Tatung University (2016)
13. Lévy, P., Nakamori, S., Yamanaka, T.: Explaining Kansei design studies (2008)
14. Chen, A.-C.: Research of product image in interaction between visual and tactile perception. Master thesis, National Cheng Kung University, pp. 1–68 (2010)
15. Matsubara, Y., Nagamachi, M.: Hybrid Kansei engineering system and design support. Int. J. Ind. Ergon. **19**(2), 81–92 (1997)
16. Schütte, S.T.W., Eklund, J., Axelsson, J.R.C., Nagamachi, M.: Concepts, methods and tools in Kansei engineering. Theor. Issues Ergon. Sci. **5**(3), 214–231 (2004)

17. Choi, D., Kim, J.: Why people continue to play online games: In search of critical design factors to increase customer loyalty to online contents. CyberPsychol. Behav. **7**(1), 11–24 (2004)
18. Kuittinen, J., Kultima, A., Niemelä, J., Paavilainen, J.: Casual games discussion, pp. 105–112. ACM (2007)
19. Lin, H.-Y.: The impact of information systems quality on continous use of app online games. Master thesis, Nanhua University (2015)
20. Lu, W.: Evolution of Video Game Controllers. Prima Publishing, Roseville (2008)
21. Jeong, E.J., Kim, D.J.: Definitions, key characteristics, and generations of mobile games. In: Mobile Computing: Concepts, Methodologies, Tools, and Applications, pp. 289–295. IGI Global (2009)
22. Steinbock, D.: The Mobile Revolution: The Making of Mobile Services Worldwide. Kogan Page Publishers (2005)
23. Hu, J.-M., Wu, T.-M.: Yousi Sheji Gailun. DrMaster Press Co., Ltd. (2015)
24. Adams, E.: Fundamentals of Game Design. Pearson Education (2014)
25. Hwang, G.-L., Chen, G.-S.: A preliminary study on Kansei images and design elements associated with varied sensory channels for the interactive interface of SHD. J. Kansei **1**(2), 4–27 (2013)
26. Svanæs, D.: Interaction design for and with the lived body: some implications of Merleauponty's phenomenology. ACM Trans. Comput.-Hum. Interact. (TOCHI) **20**(1), 8 (2013)
27. Lim, Y., Lee, S.-S., Lee, K.: Interactivity attributes: a new way of thinking and describing interactivity, pp. 105–108. ACM (2009)
28. Babin, B.J., Darden, W.R., Griffin, M.: Work and/or fun: measuring hedonic and utilitarian shopping value. J. Consum. Res. **20**(4), 644–656 (1994)
29. Norman, D.A.: Emotional Design: Why We Love (or Hate) Everyday Things. Basic Civitas Books (2004)
30. Hwang, Y.-S.: An exploratory study on smartphone in three levels of emotional design. Master thesis, National Chiao Tung University, pp. 1–119 (2013)
31. Anthropy, A., Clark, N.: A Game Design Vocabulary: Exploring the Foundational Principles Behind Good Game Design. Pearson Education (2014)
32. Engl, S., Nacke, L.E.: Contextual influences on mobile player experience–a game user experience model. Entertain. Comput. **4**(1), 83–91 (2013)

A Novel Investigation of Attack Strategies via the Involvement of Virtual Humans: A User Study of Josh Waitzkin, a Virtual Chess Grandmaster

Khaldoon Dhou[✉]

College of Business Administration,
Texas A&M University-Central Texas, Killeen, TX, USA
kdhou@tamuct.edu

Abstract. A growing body of evidence suggests that attack is a significant concept that has been explored by researchers from various disciplines such as marketing, psychology, and computing. Additionally, there has been substantial research undertaken on the role of attack in chess, which brought significant contributions to different fields of research. In this paper, the researcher investigates the attack concept in chess, as a strategic game by exploring virtual chess players of different strategies. In particular, the researcher explores the performance of an attacking grandmaster against three other class-A players of different chess personalities that vary in controlling the center of the chessboard. To this end, the researcher collected data from four virtual chess players: a grandmaster and three class-A players. The selected grandmaster is Josh Waitzkin who is known for his fearless attacking style and deep endgame understanding. The class-A players have different personalities: (1) a player who strongly controls the center of the board; (2) a player who ignores the center; and (3) a player who offers traps to control his opponent. The researcher measured different dependent variables including the errors of the players and the moves of the games. The findings show that class-A players of particular chess personalities perform differently. Additionally, the study reveals that there is a positive relationship between the findings and some of the existing real-life scenarios in the business domain.

Keywords: Chess · Chess personality · Virtual humans · Attack · Josh Waitzkin · Grandmaster

1 Introduction

In the last twenty years, the chess world witnessed many interdisciplinary endeavors from the fields of psychology, artificial intelligence, and computer design. This resulted in many significant achievements including a machine being able to defeat Gary Kasparov, the reigning world champion in 1997. Even more,

© Springer Nature Switzerland AG 2020
C. Stephanidis et al. (Eds.): HCII 2020, LNCS 12425, pp. 658–668, 2020.
https://doi.org/10.1007/978-3-030-60128-7_48

current chess applications in the market are very affordable and capable to compete at the level of a grandmaster, the highest rank a chess player can attain. Such applications offer useful features to chess players among which are providing hints, analyzing chess positions, and allowing a player to play against another player or computer opponent.

Computer opponents can come in a variety of ways such as chess engines or virtual humans. They are widely used by chess players for training and they exist in different personalities. Throughout this paper, the term chess personality is defined as the attitude of a chess player during his games such as an attack, defense, or a mixture of both. The personality of a player can shape the direction of a chess game. For example, some grandmasters start attacking at an early stage of a game, and this might cause their opponents to act defensively. Other players like to get their Queen involved during the opening phase.

Investigating the personalities of virtual chess players can play an essential role in addressing many research problems. First, there is evidence that employing software loaded with virtual players with different personalities plays a crucial role in surgical training using a virtual reality simulator [5,32]. Second, existing research suggests that there is a strong association between chess and business in many aspects such as patience, long-term thinking, and perseverance [19,21,23,29,30]. Third, rapid developments in building new chess applications have heightened the need for understanding chess personalities [14]. Virtual chess players helped in investigating different playing styles by allowing researchers to explore games between chess players of various personalities who existed in different eras [12]. Another key thing to remember is that virtual humans made it possible to further examine world champions such as Garry Kasparov and many other top grandmasters [12,14,15]. Additionally, relevant work is not only limited to virtual humans, but it also shows existing studies in virtual environments simulating different types of biological behaviors such as predator-prey ecosystems and ant colonies [9,11,13,16,28]. All these studies showed the effectiveness of simulated behaviors in coding binary information that is widely used in many research activities such as perception and visualization [10,17,18].

In this paper, we explore four virtual players: a grandmaster and three other class-A players. The selected grandmaster is Josh Waitzkin, who is known for being a fearless attacker with a deep endgame understanding. The class-A personalities vary in their skills with regards to traps and controlling the center. This paper builds on previous research in virtual chess players and provides an important opportunity to advance the understanding of chess personalities. The findings should make important contributions to the fields of psychology and computer science. The central question in this paper asks about the errors that virtual players of different personalities make while playing against each other. The main questions addressed in this paper are:

- How does Waitzkin behave while playing against class-A players who vary in their controlling the center and trapping an opponent's personality?
- How are class-A players of various chess personalities related to traps and controlling the center influenced while competing against Waitzkin?

– How is the length of the games played against Waitzkin influenced by the different class-A players employed in the experiment?

The overall structure of this paper takes the form of six sections including this section. Section 2 begins with exploring the related studies and identifying the gaps where further research is needed; Sect. 3 is concerned with the study design; Sect. 4 analyzes the results of the experiment and presents the findings; Sect. 5 provides a general discussion of the research findings based on the existing literature; finally, Sect. 6 concludes the paper, and offers suggestions for future research.

2   Related Work

A large and growing body of the literature has investigated the psychology of chess players. Models were developed over the years to understand a chess player's mind. The first model was offered by Cleveland [7] and it incorporates the most vital aspects in modern chess theory and focuses on chess development. In 1965, de Groot [8] investigated chess players' thinking and memory and how they solve chess problems. De Groot exposed chess players to meaningful chess patterns and asked them to reconstruct them from memory. He found that masters outperformed novice chess players. This was followed up by the study of Chase and Simon [6] who did a similar experiment with random chess positions. They found that chess players of various skills failed to reconstruct them. The previous two experiments show the importance of chess patterns in a chess player's skill.

Chess players vary in their ability and are ranked according to a rating, which is a number that provides an estimation of a chess player's skill measured against other players in the chess community. Many organizations provide chess ratings such as the World Chess Federation and the United States Chess Federation (USCF). For example, according to the USCF [34], the highest title is a Senior Master, which is awarded to a chess player who maintains a rating of 2400 and above. Below that is a Master, for a player who maintains a rating between 2200 and 2399; Expert between 2000 to 2199; class A between 1800 to 1999 and so on.

Chess players are not only characterized by their ratings, but they can also be described by their chess personalities. These personalities are reflected by the playing style of a player during different game phases. For example, Marshall (1942–2017) is a risk-taker who offers sacrifices to gain an advantage during his games [33]. Exploring chess personalities has its roots in psychoanalysis and numerous studies have attempted to investigate it from different angles. For example, Jones [24] explored the personality of grandmaster Paul Murphy and identified many aspects in his playing styles such as attack and piece sacrifice. Similarly, Karpman [25] explored the topic of chess personalities and the conditions at which certain players play the best. He also identified contrasts in personalities among chess grandmasters and the reasons behind some game results. In the same vein, Haran [22] identified five chess personalities depending on the opening variation: normal personality, aggressive personality, defensive personality, semi-open personality, and positional personality.

The rapid developments in Artificial Intelligence and Computing Technology made it possible to include new modern features that enable further exploration of chess personalities. Among these features are the virtual chess players, which are defined as computer programs that simulate real chess players of different levels from beginners to top-rank grandmasters. Virtual humans opened new research horizons and offered alternative prospects on how to analyze chess games and explore the psychology of different players. This began with a study that investigated virtual grandmasters and class-B players that represent actual human chess players [12]. In the study, the author explored the personalities of attacking and defending grandmasters and the outcomes while they compete against less skilled players. They found that an attacker grandmaster tends to have fewer errors than a defensive grandmaster. Similarly, the author found that the class-B players in the study perform better while competing against an attacker grandmaster. These findings have grounds in social sciences as research showed that people instinctively seek to perceive the reasons behind challenging events and how they influence their existence when they face them [36]. This view is also supported by the study conducted in [15] showing that an attacker grandmaster performs better as opposed to a defensive grandmaster while competing against class-A players. What's more, these are not the only studies that investigated virtual chess players. A recent study explored the chess personality of Garry Kasparov and how he is influenced by and influencing class-A players of different personalities [14]. All these studies have emphasized the importance of virtual humans and how they are used to explore the personalities of chess players. It is also important to mention that emulating real chess players is a major area of interest within the game industry. One example is Virtual Kasparov [2], developed by Titus, which incorporates simulated chess players of different personalities. Similarly, Ubisoft developed the Chessmaster and it offers many virtual players representing real players including top grandmasters such as Kasparov and Polgar [33].

Overall, all the studies reviewed here and the tremendous industrial advancements in virtual humans highlight the need to further investigate this field of research. These studies clearly indicate that there is a strong relationship between virtual humans, personalities, and existing real-life scenarios in different fields of research including marketing, management, and psychology. However, there remain several aspects of virtual chess players about which relatively little is known.

3   Method

3.1   Participants

Participants in this study were virtual chess players of different chess personalities. The data for the study was collected from the games between the virtual players participating in the experiment. The virtual players that were chosen for the study simulate Waitzkin, and three other class-A players of different personalities. Below is the description of each of the virtual players in the experiment, as provided by Ubisoft [33]:

- Waitzkin: a well-known chess grandmaster and author who is characterized by being a courageous attacker with a deep comprehension of the endgame.
- Buck: a player who favors openings that include a significant portion of captured pieces. His vulnerability is his almost negligence of dominating the center of the chessboard. His USCF rating is 2355.
- J.T.: he plays specific openings that are outlined to attract his opponent to fall into a prepared trap. His USCF rating is 2330.
- Lili: a player with a comprehensive opening knowledge, however, she favors particular lines of play that can be insignificantly disadvantageous. As opposed to Buck, she has excellent control over the chessboard. Her USCF rating is 2394.

The selection of these players that represent different personalities is influenced by the categories of moves offered by Chase and Simon [6, p. 259] such as opening, exchange, defense, and attack. Additionally, Chase and Simon [6] explored five chess relations between pieces: attack, defense, proximity, color, and type. It is essential to note that the ratings of the class-A players utilized in the experiment were almost identical.

3.2 Materials

The simulations were run using the Chessmaster software offered by Ubisoft [33]. The software is highly praised in the chess community, it plays at the same level as a top-rank grandmaster, and is used in different research projects [12,14,15].

In the design of the current experiment, the researcher manipulated two independent variables: the color of the grandmaster's pieces, and the class-A player's personality. Each class-A player played 78 games against Waitzkin, where half of the games played by each player were with the white pieces and the other half was with the black pieces. The class-A player's personality independent variable has three levels: the personalities of Buck, J.T., and Lili. The description of their personalities was provided in the previous subsection.

The researcher used the Chessmaster for analyzing the games and used the data in the analysis. That is to say, the design involves three dependent variables:

- The agreement percentage of the moves made by the grandmaster
- The agreement percentage of the moves made by a class-A player
- The number of moves in the game: a move is defined as the White player's move followed by the Black player's move

3.3 Procedure

Waitzkin played 78 games against each class-A player utilized in the study. To reduce the chance that the player's color influences the design, each player plays half of the games in the experiment with white color and the other half with black.

4   Results

The researcher conducted a two-way ANOVA to examine the effect of two independent variables (grandmaster's color and class-A player's chess personality) on each of the dependent variables. All the effects were considered statistically significant at $p < 0.05$. There was a significant main effect of the class-A player personality on the number of moves in the games, $F(2, 228) = 5.607$, $p = 0.004$. Pairwise comparisons indicate that the significant main effect reflects a significant difference ($p = 0.003$) between J.T. ($M = 68.410$) and Lili ($M = 57.372$).

There was a significant main effect of the color of the grandmaster on the agreement percentage of the moves made by Waitzkin, $F(1, 228) = 5.919$, $p = 0.016$. This indicates that the Chessmaster agrees more with Waitzkin when he plays with black pieces ($M = 98.111\%$) than when he plays with white pieces ($M = 97.385\%$). Additionally, there was a significant main effect of the color of the grandmaster on the agreement percentage of the moves made by the class-A players, $F(1, 228) = 11.132$, $p = 0.001$. More specifically, the Chessmaster agrees more with the class-A players when Waitzkin plays with the black pieces ($M = 94.410\%$) than white pieces (92.487%). Similarly, there was a significant main effect of a class-A player's personality on the agreement percentage of the moves made by class-A players participating in the experiment, $F(2, 228) = 3.529$, $p = 0.031$. Pairwise comparisons indicate that the significant main effect reflects significant differences ($p = 0.039$) between Buck ($M = 92.744\%$) and Lili ($M = 94.513\%$). Figure 1 shows the Chessmaster's agreement percentages on the moves made by Waitzkin and the other class-A players employed in this study.

5   General Discussion

This study set out with the aim of assessing the importance of chess personality in the errors made by virtual chess players of different personalities. The results of this study indicate that a chess player can perform differently depending on the personality of his opponent. Surprisingly, the findings showed that Waitzkin performed better with black pieces as opposed to when he had white pieces. Likewise, the virtual class-A players performed better with the black pieces than when they had white pieces. It is interesting to note that previous research indicated that the performance of less-skilled chess players, measured by the errors they make is consistent with the performance of their grandmaster opponent. For example, in a former study exploring two groups of chess players: grandmasters and class-B players, the researcher found that class-B players had fewer errors when they played against Anderssen (i.e. an attacker grandmaster), as opposed to when they played against Leko (i.e. defensive grandmaster). Similarly, the same study showed that Anderssen had fewer errors than Leko when they both played against the same class-B players. One possible explanation of why Waitzkin in this experiment performed better with black pieces is related to chess opening. A chess player sometimes tends to perform better when he encounters an opening he is familiar with [14].

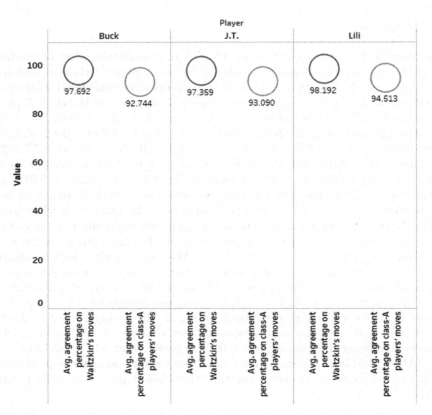

Fig. 1. The Chessmaster's agreement percentages on the moves made by Waitzkin and the other class-A players utilized in the study. As shown in the figure, Waitzkin performed the best while competing against Lili as opposed to the other class-A players. Likewise, Lili did the best among the other class-A players employed in the study.

Openings are not just important in chess, but existing research in the marketing domain showed the importance of carefulness in handling a new product. One example is the purchase of Snapple by Quaker, which owned Gatorade at that time. On the day of declaring that Quaker would purchase Snapple for 1.7 billion dollars, their stock price decreased by about 10%, and three years later, after several attempts to merge Snapple into their environment with Gatorade, Triarc purchased Snapple for 300 million dollars [26]. The example shows that Snapple and Gatorade are different brands and should not be treated as equals without carefulness. Likewise, in chess, openings are different, and not being familiar with a particular opening can result in making more mistakes and probably losing a game. This is further evidenced by the outcomes of the analysis showing that the games against J.T. last the longest (Fig. 2), although he has almost the same rating as the other class-A players utilized in this experiment.

However, J.T. utilizes opening traps while playing, and these can probably make his opponent further resist, especially if not aware of particular opening lines.

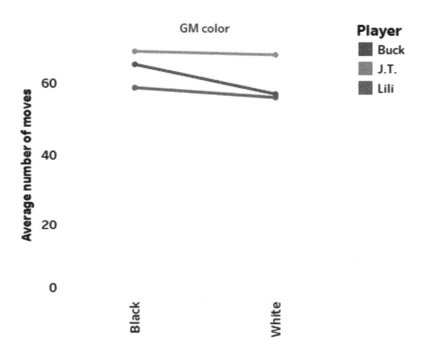

Fig. 2. The average number of moves in the study while competing against Waitzkin. The figure shows that on average, the games involving J.T., a players who considers traps in the openings were the longest

Another important finding was that, although having almost the same rating, the class-A players in the study performed differently while competing against Waitzkin. The experimental results revealed that the Chessmaster significantly agrees more on the moves made by Lili than the moves made by Buck. Controlling the center is an essential chess strategy and for some chess openings, a player sacrifices material to gain more control of the center of the board [4,20,27]. Interestingly, existing research shows that controlling the center, and other activities encountered by students while playing a chess game are analogous to some management principles [4]. In his research, students learn the concept of controlling the center of the board, which leads to controlling the game. Additionally, his research shows that such a concept is comparable to winning the domination in the industry and developing into the performing standard [4].

The findings in this study further support the idea of exploring the personalities of chess players and how players perform while competing against other players. That is to say, the findings of this study are consistent with the findings of other studies involving virtual chess players confirming that players of the same rating perform differently depending on the personalities of the opponents they are competing with. For example, in a previous study that investigates the personality of Garry Kasparov, the findings show that the performance of Kasparov varied while competing against other less-skilled players [14].

6   Conclusion

The purpose of the current study was to determine how a chess grandmaster who considers attacking strategies performs while playing against class-A players of different personalities. For this purpose, the researcher employs virtual players that simulate Waitzkin, as an attacker grandmaster, and other class-A players. Like real players, virtual players have certain characteristics and they follow different game strategies such as attack, defense, and controlling the center. The three class-A players vary in their personalities: a player who tends to capture the opponent's pieces, a player who considers offering traps in the opening phase, and a player with solid center control and comprehensive opening knowledge.

This study has shown that a grandmaster performs differently depending on his opponent's strategy. Likewise, players of the same rating perform differently while competing against the same grandmaster. These findings are consistent with the previous findings exploring grandmasters and less skilled players [12,14, 15]. For example, class-B players of almost the same ratings and different chess personalities had different reactions while competing with two grandmasters of different styles [12]. Likewise, the same study showed that Anderssen, an aggressive grandmaster performed better than Leko while competing against less skilled players of the same rating category.

The findings in this study suggest that in general, chess personality is a crucial factor to consider when evaluating the outcomes of chess games between different players. In other words, although chess players are evaluated based on their chess ratings, this does not seem to be the only way to assess their performance. Additionally, since chess is a fundamentally strategic game, these findings can be extended to be explored in other domains such as psychology, business, and computing. The findings reported here shed new light on the psychology of competition and how the personalities of virtual humans are related to many aspects in domains exploring many attitudes such as aggressiveness and defense. That is to say, the researcher believes that the present study lays the groundwork for future research into exploring how virtual humans can aid in understanding new elements in business strategies. To develop a full picture of the personalities of chess players, additional studies will be needed that explore different aspects of personalities. For example, further studies, which take personality traits into account, will need to be undertaken [1,3,31,35].

References

1. Al-Samarraie, H., Sarsam, S.M., Alzahrani, A.I., Alalwan, N., Masood, M.: The role of personality characteristics in informing our preference for visual presentation: an eye movement study. J. Ambient Intell. Smart Environ. 8(6), 709–719 (2016)

2. Butts, S.: Virtaul Kasparov, April 2002. http://www.ign.com/articles/2002/04/19/virtual-kasparov. Accessed 20 Mar 2017
3. Caci, B., Cardaci, M., Miceli, S.: Autobiographical memory, personality, and Facebook mementos. Eur. J. Psychol. **15**(3), 614–636 (2019). https://ejop.psychopen.eu/index.php/ejop/article/view/1713
4. Cannice, M.V.: The right moves: creating experiential management learning with chess. Int. J. Manag. Educ. **11**(1), 25–33 (2013). http://www.sciencedirect.com/science/article/pii/S1472811712000535
5. Chalhoub, E., et al.: The role of video games in facilitating the psychomotor skills training in laparoscopic surgery. Gynecol. Surg. **13**(4), 419–424 (2016). https://doi.org/10.1007/s10397-016-0986-9
6. Chase, W.G., Simon, H.A.: The mind's eye in chess (1973)
7. Cleveland, A.A.: The psychology of chess and of learning to play it. Am. J. Psychol. **18**(3), 269–308 (1907)
8. De Groot, A.: Thought and choice in chess (1965)
9. Dhou, K., Cruzen, C.: An innovative chain coding technique for compression based on the concept of biological reproduction: an agent-based modeling approach. IEEE Internet of Things J. **6**(6), 9308–9315 (2019)
10. Dhou, K.: Toward a better understanding of viewers' perceptions of tag clouds: relative size judgment. Ph.D. thesis, The University of North Carolina at Charlotte, USA (2013)
11. Dhou, K.: A novel agent-based modeling approach for image coding and lossless compression based on the wolf-sheep predation model. In: Shi, Y., et al. (eds.) ICCS 2018. LNCS, vol. 10861, pp. 117–128. Springer, Cham (2018). https://doi.org/10.1007/978-3-319-93701-4_9
12. Dhou, K.: Towards a better understanding of chess players' personalities: a study using virtual chess players. In: Kurosu, M. (ed.) HCI 2018. LNCS, vol. 10903, pp. 435–446. Springer, Cham (2018). https://doi.org/10.1007/978-3-319-91250-9_34
13. Dhou, K.: An innovative design of a hybrid chain coding algorithm for bi-level image compression using an agent-based modeling approach. Appl. Soft Comput. **79**, 94–110 (2019). http://www.sciencedirect.com/science/article/pii/S1568494619301425
14. Dhou, K.: An innovative employment of virtual humans to explore the chess personalities of Garry Kasparov and other class-A players. In: Stephanidis, C. (ed.) HCII 2019. LNCS, vol. 11786, pp. 306–319. Springer, Cham (2019). https://doi.org/10.1007/978-3-030-30033-3_24
15. Dhou, K.: An exploration of chess personalities in grandmasters and class-a players using virtual humans. Int. J. Entertain. Technol. Manag. (2020, in press)
16. Dhou, K.: A new chain coding mechanism for compression stimulated by a virtual environment of a predator-prey ecosystem. Future Gener. Comput. Syst. **102**, 650–669 (2020). http://www.sciencedirect.com/science/article/pii/S0167739X1832630X
17. Dhou, K., Hadzikadic, M., Faust, M.: Typeface size and weight and word location influence on relative size judgments in tag clouds. J. Vis. Lang. Comput. **44**, 97–105 (2018). http://www.sciencedirect.com/science/article/pii/S1045926X16300210
18. Dhou, K.K., Kosara, R., Hadzikadic, M., Faust, M.: Size judgment and comparison in tag clouds. IEEE Vis. Poster Proc. (2013)
19. Dilmaghani, M.: Gender differences in performance under time constraint: evidence from chess tournaments. J. Behav. Exp. Econ. 101505 (2019). http://www.sciencedirect.com/science/article/pii/S2214804319303052

20. Fischer, R.: A bust to the King's Gambit. Am. Chess Q. 3–9 (2015)
21. Graber, R.S.: Business lessons from chess: a discussion of parallels between chess strategy and business strategy, and how chess can have applications for business education. Acad. Educ. Leadersh. J. **13**(1), 79 (2009)
22. Haran, A.: Collaborative computer personalities in the game of chess. Ph.D. thesis, Dublin City University (2002)
23. Hunt, S., Cangemi, J.: Want to improve your leadership skills? Play chess!. Education **134**(3), 359–368 (2014)
24. Jones, E.: The problem of Paul Morphy: a contribution to the psycho-analysis of chess. Int. J. Psycho-Anal. **12**, 1 (1931)
25. Karpman, B.: The psychology of chess: (Richard Reti). Psychoanal. Rev. (1913–1957) **24**, 54 (1937)
26. Lehn, K.M., Zhao, M.: CEO turnover after acquisitions: are bad bidders fired? J. Finan. **61**(4), 1759–1811 (2006)
27. Montero, B., Evans, C.: Intuitions without concepts lose the game: mindedness in the art of chess. Phenomenol. Cogn. Sci. **10**(2), 175–194 (2011)
28. Mouring, M., Dhou, K., Hadzikadic, M.: A novel algorithm for bi-level image coding and lossless compression based on virtual ant colonies. In: Proceedings of the 3rd International Conference on Complexity, Future Information Systems and Risk - Volume 1: COMPLEXIS, pp. 72–78 (2018)
29. Nielsen, C.: The global chess game ... or is it go? Market-entry strategies for emerging markets. Thunderbird Int. Bus. Rev. **47**(4), 397–427 (2005). https://onlinelibrary.wiley.com/doi/abs/10.1002/tie.20060
30. Rice, B.: Three Moves Ahead: What Chess Can Teach You About Business. Wiley, Hoboken (2010)
31. Sarsam, S.M., Al-Samarraie, H.: Towards incorporating personality into the design of an interface: a method for facilitating users' interaction with the display. User Model. User-Adap. Inter. **28**(1), 75–96 (2018)
32. Schlickum, M.K., Hedman, L., Enochsson, L., Kjellin, A., Felländer-Tsai, L.: Systematic video game training in surgical novices improves performance in virtual reality endoscopic surgical simulators: a prospective randomized study. World J. Surg. **33**(11), 2360–2367 (2009)
33. Ubisoft: Chessmaster grandmaster edition. http://chessmaster.uk.ubi.com/xi/index.php
34. US Chess Federation: USCF Ratings Distribution Charts, October 2015. http://archive.uschess.org/ratings/ratedist.php
35. Vollstädt-Klein, S., Grimm, O., Kirsch, P., Bilalić, M.: Personality of elite male and female chess players and its relation to chess skill. Learn. Ind. Differ. **20**(5), 517–521 (2010). http://www.sciencedirect.com/science/article/pii/S1041608010000403
36. Wise, D.M., Rosqvist, J.: Explanatory style and well-being. In: Comprehensive Handbook of Personality and Psychopathology, p. 285 (2006)

Systems Approach to Designing an Enjoyable Process for Game Designers

Nandhini Giri[✉] and Erik Stolterman

Indiana University, Bloomington, IN 47405, USA
Nandhini.giri@gmail.com

Abstract. The main objective of this paper is to understand game designers' experience of designing games and to come up with a design proposal that can enhance the current game design process to be more enjoyable and game-designer friendly. Our initial motivation for writing this paper was to understand whether the current game design process is enjoyable or not. What are some of the issues that inhibit the game designer's experiences? What can be done to make the process more enjoyable? And how these insights can lead to the design of an enjoyable process that focuses on the game designer's experiences.

Keywords: Game design process · Experience design · Enjoyability

1 Introduction

Game designers create some of the most engaging and enriching experiences for players in the entertainment industry today. Designing games in a fast-paced environment with crucial deadlines and high-quality expectations can lead to very stressful experiences to the game designers. Current research work and methodologies focus a lot on improving the design of games to create better player experiences. However, there is very less focus on designing processes to improve the game designer's experience. A well-designed game improves the quality of the player's experience, but a great design process can improve the quality of the designer's life. Creativity block, lack of ownership, personal issues with health and relationships are some of the problems that emerge in the long run when designers do not enjoy the design process. Employee dissatisfaction and attrition, unexplained delays, major complications in product delivery and additional expenses incurred to sustain the dying process are issues at the organizational level. Game studios adopt best practices and management policies to enhance their employees' satisfaction level. But then, game designers are unique in their own way and it does require some research and effort to create process frameworks that shape the game designers' experiences.

The main objective of this paper is to understand game designer's experience of designing games and to come up with a design proposal that can enhance the current game design process to be more game-designer friendly. Designing a process can be done in innumerable ways and design solutions can get exhaustive. So, this paper focuses on

© Springer Nature Switzerland AG 2020
C. Stephanidis et al. (Eds.): HCII 2020, LNCS 12425, pp. 669–687, 2020.
https://doi.org/10.1007/978-3-030-60128-7_49

the key element of 'enjoyability' in the game design process. It starts with the question of what is enjoyable in the current game design process. What are some of the issues that inhibit the game designer's experiences? How can these insights lead to the design of an enjoyable process that focuses on the game designer's experiences? The scope of the paper is to focus on enjoyability at the 'game designer - design process' interaction level. It can also be applied to the overall studio's design culture, creative vision, company ethics and long-term goals of the designer in terms of career growth and personal factors.

This paper approaches the game design process as a system. A system is defined by the wholes, parts and the relationships between them. A game designer is one of the many components of the whole design process. Designers interact with software tools, team members, creative goals, personal goals, workplace environment and the studio's overall values. All these individual interactions contribute to the whole experience of the design process. The deconstruction of the design process into a system and rebuilding it based on designer experience can help guide designers and game studios to apply the framework to their own workflow and customize it to their needs and employee experience demands. Enjoyability is the aesthetic experience that we aim for in this system's approach. We interviewed game designers and their insights helped us identify the underlying mechanics that form the structural components of this enjoyable design process. These mechanics range from setting common goals or creating a diverse team composition to building a culture of learning and sharing design methodologies. Designers interacting with these established mechanics in the design process experience enjoyable dynamics that can be reinforced through enjoyable factors. Our insights also brought out the factors that inhibit enjoyability that can be watchfully removed from the system for a better designer experience.

2 Related Research

Current literature in gaming research focus on enjoyability in terms of players interaction with games. Malone (1982) in the paper titled "Heuristics for Designing Enjoyable User Interfaces: Lessons from Computer Games", discusses the questions of why computer games are so captivating and how these captivating features can be used to make other user interfaces interesting and enjoyable to use. Elements of challenge, fantasy and curiosity were identified as the major features for analyzing the appeal of computer systems. Wang et al. (2009) synthesized the literature on enjoyment of media entertainment with a focus on digital games. They develop a comprehensive list of game fun factors and proposed a potential "Big Five" of digital game enjoyment that includes technological capacity, game design, aesthetic presentation, game play experience and narrativity. They also conceptualized a three-level threshold model of (1) overcoming playability threshold to pick the game, (2) passing enjoyability threshold for appeal and (3) super fun boosting factors for exceptional entertainment. The authors introduce the topic of enjoyment gaps between game developers and players; that game developers intend to make games fun and use heuristics like game interface, game mechanics, game story and game play as their guiding tools. However, the focus of the paper is on player enjoyability, highlighting the fact that scholarly discussions about game enjoyment come from the uses and gratification perspective (Sherry et al. 2006).

Flow and media enjoyment are another major theme of study in terms of enjoyment and games. Sherry (2004) theorizes on how flow state in media users are facilitated or inhibited by different media experiences along with individual differences in cognitive abilities. Games provide a sensory immersive experience and possess the ideal characteristics to create and maintain flow experiences when the skills of the players are matched with the difficulty level of the game. Sweetser and Wyeth (2005) integrate heuristics into a model that can be used to design, evaluate and understand enjoyment in games that is structured by flow. The proposed game flow model consists of eight elements – concentration, challenge, skills, control, clear goals, feedback, immersion and social interaction. The model was able to distinguish between high-rated and low-rated games and identify why games succeeded or failed.

More recent research work and scholarly literature also focus on the design aspects of playful experiences and the creative process of designing games. Köknar (2019) examines player-centered design philosophy and how it can be suitable to create playful experiences. The author proposes open-ended experiences, a characteristic of sandbox games, to provide players the freedom to interact playfully. Majgaard (2014) in the paper titled "The Playful and Reflective Game Designer", discusses the dynamic relationship between playing games and designing games. The paper documents the progression of students from native consumers of games to becoming reflective game designers. Mastrocola (2019) discusses the creative process in the development of the Brazilian mobile game 'Mind Alone'. The article highlights the main phases of brainstorming, documentation, analyzing the high concept template, production and beta-testing. By discussing the creative process, the paper "demonstrates the strength of the relationship between players and gaming companies in the contemporary digital gaming eco system".

The author who is a game designer also brings Huizinga's thoughts (Huizinga 1955) about people searching for different 'magic circles' in the landscape of daily life. A place where the ordinary rules of the world are suspended, and players can experience meaningful enriching interactions. Thus, enjoyment in games is studied in terms of how players experience the system. The theories and heuristic models are built around the user's experience with computer games. However, game designers are also part of this equation and the magic circle that defines their everyday life of designing games is less talked about. This brings us to the objective of this paper on game designers as players who interact with the design process. There is a gap in the literature when it comes to focusing on the enjoyability of the game design process and designer practices. This builds into the main objective of this paper on designing an enjoyable process for the game designers who are blurred from the literature.

3 Methodology

Our initial motivation for writing this paper was to understand whether the current game design process is enjoyable or not? How much of importance is given to the designers' experience in the game design process? What can be done to make the process more enjoyable?

We decided to contact game designers and talk to them about their experiences with designing games. We were interested in learning more about the design process from the practitioners. We reached out to game design professionals and educators who have industry experience designing games and have played multiple roles in the design process. These game designers are affiliated to Indiana University through the Game design program. We were able to introduce ourselves with the game designers through emails and explain the objective of the research study and schedule one-to-one interviews. Initially, five game designers were interviewed who have played the roles of senior game designer, lead designer, executive producer, creative director, general manager, co-founder and related roles in major game studios. They have 12–23 years of work experience in the game industry (mainstream/indie) and some of them are also affiliated to academic institutions where they lecture courses on game design.

Semi-structured interviews were conducted that lasted for around 45–50 min. In one case we conducted interviews for two-hour long sessions. Interviews were conducted either face to face in the designer's office space or through online video conferencing. Game designers were asked questions about their current experiences of enjoyability in designing games. Details of the questions are provided in the table below (Table 1):

Table 1. Interview questions for game designers

#	Interview question
1	What motivates you in the game design process?
2	What are your design philosophies?
3	What are the factors that sustain interest in the design process?
4	What are some factors that inhibit your creative flow?
5	What are the factors that you find enjoyable and not enjoyable in the design process?
6	Are there ways to improve the process to make it more enjoyable?

The questions were open-ended to focus more on the game designer's personal experiences with the design process. After the first interview that lasted for two sessions of one hour each, the interview questions were cut down to focus mainly on enjoyability and designer experiences with the process. Hand-written notes and audio recordings were then transcribed, coded and interpreted. Both the authors were involved in the coding, analyzing and conceptualization of the constructs. This information and the audio files were stored in a secure online location for storage and retrieval. In order to maintain the anonymity of the interviewees we chose five Pokémon characters based on the authors preferences namely – Bulbasaur, Farfetch'd, Jigglypuff, Pikachu and Togepi. The characters were lined up based on their alphabetic order. These characters were then assigned to the game designers in the order that they were interviewed. All the quotes that appear in this paper are identified by the game character that corresponds to the actual game designer who was interviewed.

A thematic analysis approach helped us analyze the data from the interviews. After every interview, the data was transcribed and added to an online document. This was an iterative process in which we familiarized ourselves with the data and generated initial codes. These initial codes were the enjoyability factors that the designers experienced while designing games. We also found factors that inhibit creativity and grouped them as non-enjoyable factors. After the five interviews were done, we started looking for common patterns, reviewing them and categorizing them into major themes. At this point, we observed that a common pattern emerged on the topic of enjoyability. Game designers frequently referred to their approach in designing player experiences and mentioned that the same design principles apply to their experience with the process as well. Game designers expressed enjoyability in terms of achieving their goals as a team, learning from team members, feeling empowered through challenging design situations, designing through exploring unknown facts and many other factors.

Another common pattern emerged on the topic of enjoyability where game designers felt that their approach to designing player experiences would be a good way to look at their interaction with the design process itself. This insight motivated us to take a step further in designing a process with enjoyable player (designer) experiences. The MDA (acronym for Mechanics Dynamics Aesthetics) framework proposed by Hunicke et al. (2004) provides a formal systems approach in identifying the mechanics, dynamics and aesthetics for designing games. We adopted this framework to design an enjoyable process for the designers as it helps to decompose experiences and map it to implementable mechanics in the design process.

Finally, a sixth game designer (with the anonymous name 'Charmander') was interviewed to broadly understand what is enjoyable, what is not enjoyable and what can be done to make the process more enjoyable. The insights from the final interview reaffirmed the validity of the four subsystems that we had identified earlier. It helped us formulate potential guidelines and make suggestions for a framework to design an enjoyable game design process.

4   Insights from Interviews

In this section of the paper, we elaborate on the four aesthetic experiences as major themes for the design of the enjoyable process. Some of the personal experiences shared by the designers with the design process are highlighted through quotes. It also shows the connection between designer experience and process mechanics that generate run-time enjoyable dynamics. We also present the findings of the initial data analysis process. These findings point to what is enjoyable and what is non-enjoyable, as factors that determine a designer's experience with the game design process.

One of the game designers mentioned the importance of team comradeship in the design process. During the interview, the interviewee recollected some of the memories from high school basketball matches. (Jigglypuff) said "I'm a basketball player from high school. The spirit of team comradeship comes from there". (Jigglypuff) enjoyed working with the team towards common goals and celebrated the accomplishments of the entire team. The fun part was also about learning and mentoring team members. Looking for complementary qualities that are absent in oneself but in abundance from a team member, provides opportunities for learning and mentoring. For example, a person who is not good with documentation can learn these skills from a team member who exhibits these skills. It helps build mutual trust and strengthen each team members' skills. Apart from skill enhancement, it is also about creating a support system. (Bulbasaur) mentioned that during crunch times, the designer who played a managerial role in that project, had a conference room booked and kept the door open for anyone to drop in. Members of the team could come in and ask for support, have a conversation about the challenges or just know that there is someone there to listen to them. This kind of a shared ritual helps foster a feeling of fellowship during difficult situations.

Designers seek new challenges and ways to explore unknown territories. This was evident from the interviews. For instance, (Farfetch'd) indicated that: "And that seems to be most empowering for the team … is to have clear boundaries that gives you a lot of space to still play and explore and self-impress". Real world design experiences, prototyping and inspirations from other mediums like painting, fashion or even architecture gives an opportunity to think beyond the digital space. It brings in fresh perspectives to the medium of game design. An emphasis on the culture of continuous learning and exposure to new ideas can help prevent habituation. One of the designers mentioned the practice of monthly meetups where game designers reviewed existing games and lectured on different topics. (Pikachu) spoke about ambiguity: "All the information should not be immediately accessible; there should be parts of it that are purposefully missing". This kind of a space for exploration, gives designers the courage to explore outside traditional boundaries.

"Everyone feels autonomy, competence and relatedness in different ways" said (Farfetch'd). Self-expression was the next major theme that emerged from the interviews. Designers bring in their own design philosophies to the team and their enjoyability of the process as self-discovery depends on varying degrees of motivational factors. Motivational psychology, self-determination theory in particular, was quoted as a solution to identify different personalities in the team. Knowing designers' motivation helps customize their roles in the design process. Talking about motivation, imposter syndrome was the one major factor designers mentioned as inhibiting their enjoyability of the game design process. Even after years of experience, designers felt that they were still the odd one out in the team or had insecurities about their role. The highly competitive nature of the game industry and job security issues were highlighted as the major reasons for such issues.

Finally, the discussion on the design process as a utopian scenario versus game design as a challenging process of resilience was discussed. (Farfetch'd) continued: "Gain satisfaction from overcoming challenges, struggle, seeing things that are beautifully sad; they give us this feeling of humanity that comes from understanding death, vulnerability… this beautiful array of emotions … I like frustration, sometimes despair and desperation … using that emotion as an enrichment" – this conveyed the various emotions that designers go through, over the process of designing games. It is this mix of experiences that bring enrichment to the design process. A challenging design process not only facilitates learning, but emotionally and socially enriches the designers' experiences. A balanced work pace that includes challenging crunch times followed by some time for decompression is seen as a healthy production process.

Game designers also pointed to some of the main factors that enhance or inhibit the enjoyability of the game design process. The next section discusses these factors that influence the designer's enjoyability of the game design process.

4.1 What Is Enjoyable

Essence of Game Design. "I kept looking for the medium…that was the most expressive, especially the most engaging with people… Games were the one medium where you could get influence from the player and then change the experience literally in real time" said (Pikachu). These lines capture the essence of game design that designers find most enjoyable. The objective of the design process is in maintaining the essence of why designers enjoy the process in the first place. In the overall game design process, there is more flexibility in the beginning of the project, in terms of trying out new things and making mistakes without killing the process. Designers enjoy utilizing this time to try out crazy methods. Prototyping allows room for designers to explore new topics and game genres. Playtesting is one other phase that game designers enjoy. (Togepi) mentioned that "Having people play your game and watching them play can be very motivating…they are playing it in a very …positively naïve sense, so they can really enjoy something that can re-invigorate you". (Charmander) on a similar note commented that "Some of the pleasure is putting games in front of people …You can see them doing verbs, taking action in the games, finding out puzzles, solving things, getting really engaged… addicted to something…wanting to collect something". The final stretch in the game design process is the most challenging phase. Pros complete games and this is what differentiates them from hobbyists. They can take a project in fire and can manage to save the house before it burns down. These challenges posed by the game design process is what makes it enjoyable.

Concept of Unknown. Sometimes it is fun to intentionally not have information immediately accessible. Purposefully missing parts create a symbiotic relationship between the designer and the game design process. Design is a discovery process in itself. It takes a lot of diligence to navigate through the uncertainties and enjoy the ride by filling up the blank spaces. Losing oneself in the process is a way of decompressing and enjoying the process. (Pikachu) mentioned "Zui Hitsu…it's the Japanese technique, needs to follow the brush…this idea that you lose yourself and then… whatever you are doing it just happens…no longer even need to think about what you are doing and then it happens". Sometimes the magical moments from the Zen garden occur when the designer gets lost in the action and just follows the design process.

Team Dynamics. (Pikachu) continued "I'm always trying to glean technique from people". Team dynamics play a major role in the enjoyability of the design process. Mentoring or learning skills from other team members, building mutual trust, comradeship and celebrating achievements as a team are cherishing moments for designers. Also, team composition improves the dynamics at work. (Bulbasaur) said "A large part of doing game design is in the oft-repeated phrase "find the fun". You may start with a cool toy, an intriguing mechanism, or a compelling experience – the parts, loops, and whole of a game – but you will need all three elements plus engaging interactivity to build a fun game." A good design team consists of storytellers who paint a mental picture of the entire experience, inventors who love making complex mechanisms and toymakers with specialized domain knowledge. A studio thrives better when the managers are aware of the different player types and designer personalities in the team.

These are some of the major factors that designers enjoy about the game design process. A right balance between a utopian process that is always in a steady flow state versus one that requires resilience and struggle generates meaningful experiences. Design process should also provide clarity and guide designers to their most effective mental model. This involves an understanding of the objective of the design process, what it takes to reach the end of this process and achieving the sub goals on the way. Design practices like building prototypes and testing out design ideas help validate them. Fresh insights pour into the process when working on real world games like installations and play area designs that involve physical laws and human dynamics. Finally, designing in fractals is a fun-way to observe how top-level changes affect the lower layers of the game design and vice versa. All these factors make game design process enjoyable.

4.2 What Is not Enjoyable

Fear and Threat. Fear and threat are the major inhibitors of creativity, leading to a lack of enjoyability in the game design process. (Farfetch'd) indicated that "You are creative when you have abundance, you are creative when you have room to fail". Financial threat is one major reason why studios are hesitant to experiment with new genres. (Farfetch'd) continued - "I'm threatened, so I'm going to kind of do what I've done before". Designers don't think of new things. They stick with what was done before, doing similar things that have been successful in the past. In this context, "Known is less frightening than the unknown". Studios that run under constant fear, threat and instability have little to no room to try new ideas. In the pursuit of delivering games that have a proven success rate, redundancy often sets into the design process. This process gradually lowers the enjoyability of the game design process.

Clear versus Authoritarian Vision. (Jigglypuff) pointed out that "Designers need to know the big questions first – What is the game you are making; What is the game you don't want to make". Having the vision nailed down and mentioning the scope of the project are great starters. However, when decision making authorities fail to understand the creative process, it leads to confinement and lack of enjoyability in the process. Creative heads need to set the stage for designers. An ideal approach is for the creative heads to provide the pillars/anti-pillars of the project and let the designers come up with the best ideas without going outside these confines. Lack of communicating the vision is also a reason for non-enjoyability in the process. (Farfetch'd) added "It's almost impossible to be creative when you don't know what the vision is. All you are doing is throwing stuff at the wall". (Bulbasaur) added "Also, managers end up micro-managing teams due to their own insecurity". This can lead to a lot of negative effects on the team and process as well.

Habituation. Lack of diversity or contrast in tasks lead to boredom and habituation. (Bulbasaur) mentioned that it is like how a musician gets bored playing repeatedly the same song that was once a big hit and audience expect the same song to be played every time. Designers also felt that flexibility in time leads to more enjoyment compared to an 8am to 5 pm schedule which is too monotonous and suppresses creativity. (Togepi) felt that "Being too tired, being stuck in one place…often you get better ideas when you walk around". Workplace environment and team interaction also contributes to habituation. The designer may be excited about an idea but if the team turns it down, it drains the energy out of the designer. (Togepi) continued "Not being able to give yourself time to think about it…When you approach a deadline that can be tough". Crunch times can be exciting, but designers soon get burnt out if these action-packed episodes are not complemented by a period of decompression and relaxation.

Apart from these major factors that inhibit enjoyability, imposter syndrome was highlighted as one common issue with game designers. Even after years of experience designing games, people still feel out of place. There is an underlying tension of whether the project will get canceled, which prevents the enjoyment of the design process. (Charmander) felt that "Market forces add a lot of stress to the process, particularly if you are making games to be commercially successful". Some of the other factors pointed out were health issues like fatigue and an unhealthy lifestyle. Being disorganized and having too many unfinished tasks can be depressing to the designer. These stress factors are directly related to the level of enjoyability in the process.

Figure 1 summarizes the key design factors for consideration when designing an enjoyable game design process. Enjoyable factors like maintaining the essence of game design throughout the entire process, introducing missing links for exploration, team dynamics, having clarity of vision, handling challenges and novel design practices help enhance the enjoyability of the design process. In order to maintain this enjoyable momentum in the design process, it should be constantly monitored for generation of any undesirable non-enjoyable factors and watchfully eliminated from the design process. These non-enjoyable factors are fear and threat in the work environment, authoritarian vision that inhibits creative flow, habituation due to long exposure to repetitive tasks or work conditions, imposter syndrome due to various sources of insecurity, health issues like fatigue or unhealthy lifestyle and piling up of disorganized, unfinished tasks.

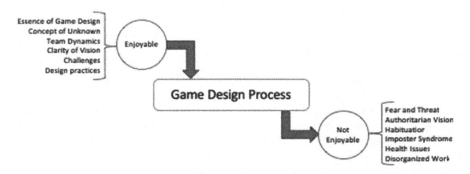

Fig. 1. Enjoyable and non-enjoyable factors

These insights from the interview helped us see the major themes and factors that determine an enjoyable game design process. In the next section, we explore our intention to create an ideal design process that evokes enjoyable experiences for the designers. We approach this design process as a game system that has the necessary subsystems that work towards making the interactions enjoyable. The data from the interview is used as inputs for the initial set up of the game environment. We then identify the dynamics and desired experiences that this system is supposed to provide the designer. We begin with Huizinga's magic circle as the ideal space for designers to experience an enjoyable process.

5 Design Process as a Game System

5.1 Designer Transformation

Johan Huizinga's magic circle consists of a space where the normal rules of the real world are suspended, and the player enters an artificial game world. Experiences of dreams, immersion, narration, catharsis and challenges are encountered in this magic circle. The player leaves the space with an enriched and meaningful experience. On the same lines, game designers entering a new design project encounter a similar situation. Design process starts with an idea conception, pre-production, a production phase and the post-production. Iterations and play testing feedback tighten up the process and shape the initial abstract ideas to working prototypes and final game deliverables. The environment, teams, projects and even the market influences the game designer through the process.

Hunicke et al. (2004) proposed the MDA framework as a formal approach in identifying the mechanics, dynamics and aesthetics in designing games. This systems-based framework for game design motivated us to apply the same approach to the design process. The game design process is the whole system that is experienced within a game studio, constrained by various mechanics like creative and technical goals of the project, time, budget and resources. Designers are part of this whole system and are constantly interacting with subparts and subsystems leading to real time dynamics that evoke different experiences. There are reinforcing and balancing loops that form enjoyable and not enjoyable relationships between the process and the designer.

5.2 Systems Approach to Designing a Process

The four major experiences that were highlighted from the interviews are (1) Fellowship (2) Discovery (3) Expression (4) Challenge. These major experiences correspond to the aesthetic experiences proposed in the MDA framework. We decided to take a systems approach to design an enjoyable game design process using these four key designer emotions. Designer interaction with this design process evokes experiences of fellowship, discovery, expression and challenge leading to enjoyability. Figure 2 depicts the interaction between game designers and the design process.

The design process system includes four subsystems that are each responsible for the desired aesthetic experiences in the game designer. Enjoyable factors are added to the source end of this system, while non-enjoyable factors are removed through the system sink. The subsystems were built based on the data and insights from the interviews. Themes that arose from the data were separated as mechanics and dynamics. This was based on whether the themes are components of the process (mechanics) or runtime

Fig. 2. Game designer interaction with design process

Table 2. Data from Interviews identified as process mechanics and dynamics

Process Mechanics	Process Dynamics	Process Mechanics	Process Dynamics
Common goals	Synergy	Best practices	Mental alignment
Open communication	Trust	Designer philosophy	Identity
Team composition	Learning	Process struggle	Empowerment
Prototypes	Validation	Designer skillset	Enrichment
Missing links	Ambiguity	Production schedule	Healthy
Tracking motivation	Motivation	Process decisions	Ownership

behaviors that require designer inputs (dynamics). Table 2 shows the data that was used to build the mechanics and dynamics.

Based on each aesthetic experience, the dynamics that give rise to these experiences were mapped. Each aesthetic experience had several dynamic factors mapped to them. We then looked at the pool of mechanics that facilitate these runtime dynamics in the process. For example: Synergy is a dynamic interaction at workplace that maps to the aesthetic experience of 'Fellowship'. Common goals in the team is the underlying mechanic that facilitates synergy when the team of designers interact. Similarly, all the themes were mapped to their corresponding aesthetic experience resulting in the four subsystems.

Subsystem: Fellowship as Enjoyability. Our interviews with game designers showed that the experience of fellowship contributes a lot to the enjoyability of a design process. Game design teams often work on cooperative tasks that involves a lot of interaction at the process and individual level. Under the theme of fellowship, we analyzed the interview data to find behaviors and dynamics that contribute to fellowship. The four main sources of enjoyment in this category include:

- Synergy through cooperative tasks
- Sustained interest in process
- Trust building
- Learning and mentoring

These were the key factors that lead to the feeling of fellowship in the game design process. Game designers enjoy comradeship in achieving success together. There is sustained interest in the process when designers work as a team and build mutual trust by solving issues together. They cherish moments of the design process that facilitate skill building and learning among team members.

Having identified the dynamics of this sub-system, we deconstructed the underlying components in the physical world that contribute to these factors.

- Common goals - Synergy is an emergent property that results when a team works towards common goals. Cooperative tasks require teams to strategize and resolve goals as a team and this brings the feeling of fellowship among designers.
- Shared rituals - Goals are further strengthened when the team has sustained interest in the process through shared rituals. The final stretch of the game design process can get very stressful. Cheering rituals motivate designers and bond them to reach the finish line together.
- Open communication - Implementing an open and transparent communication helps designers build trust within the team. Timely support from the management, open feedback and resolving issues together can promote mutual trust.
- Team composition – A healthy team dynamics arises from the composition of the team. Many times, designers are in the wrong place with incompatible people that causes frustration. They do not bond well with the team leading to enjoyability blocks. Identifying the designer's interests and building a diverse team fosters fellowship. Complimenting skills help designers appreciate and learn new skills from each other thus enhancing fellowship.

Figure 3 shows how the 'Fellowship subsystem' works. Designers interact with this subsystem as they work through the entire game design process. The four mechanics mentioned above are to be implemented within this subsystem to generate runtime dynamics that lead to enjoyability through fellowship. The blue rectangular boxes indicate the mechanics to be implemented in the process. The double-sided arrows indicate that this is a reinforcing loop where the game designer and the fellowship subsystem are mutually reinforcing the enjoyable nature of the design process.

Subsystem: Discovery as Enjoyability. Discovery is the next key experience that designers enjoy most in the game design process. The dynamics identified for the experience of discovery include:

- Real-world validity
- Inspiration
- Benign ambiguity

This subsystem focuses on designer's ideas and design practices. The process of discovery is enjoyable, but it also requires real world validity to confirm that designs in the mind can be successfully implemented in the real world. Games are mostly designed for digital platforms. But then inspirations can come from other mediums as well. In fact, it is a good practice for designers to look at other design mediums for fresh ideas. (Charmander) talks about novelty in game design process - "Having some degree of novelty… to some degree it is never seen before… creates a problem space, you need

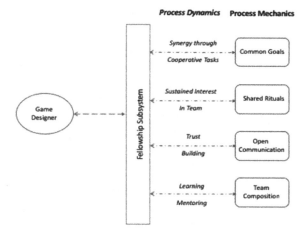

Fig. 3. Fellowship subsystem

problems to solve". Finally, it is not all fun to know exactly what the design process is. Some missing links and ambiguity provide space for exploration and ideas outside the conventional boundaries.

Our interview data for the underlying mechanics corresponding to these interaction dynamics include:

- Prototyping ideas - the design practice of implementing early passes of ideas to test whether they work or not.
- A culture of continuous learning - Lectures on various topics related to game design, exposure to other mediums and studio-level design courses and workshops help designers find inspiration at workplace.
- Intentional missing links in design process for exploration - this is an abstract mechanic that is intentionally provided by the design process. The pre-production phase is also a good time to encourage designers to explore missing links to generate novel ways to game design approaches.

Figure 4 shows this subsystem and how the establishment of the design practices like prototyping, a culture of learning and exploration space lead to interaction dynamics like real-world validity of novel ideas, inspiration and benign ambiguity. This is also a reinforcing loop as depicted by the double arrows between the designer and subsystem interactions leading to discovery as enjoyability in the design process.

Subsystem: Expression as Enjoyability. Expression as enjoyability comes from the designer's identity and ownership in the design process. This subsystem works more at the individual level of the designers and opportunities in the design process for expression. The dynamics identified under this subsystem include:

- Motivation - Designers have different personalities and their levels of motivation are determined by factors of autonomy, relatedness and competence. Designers in the

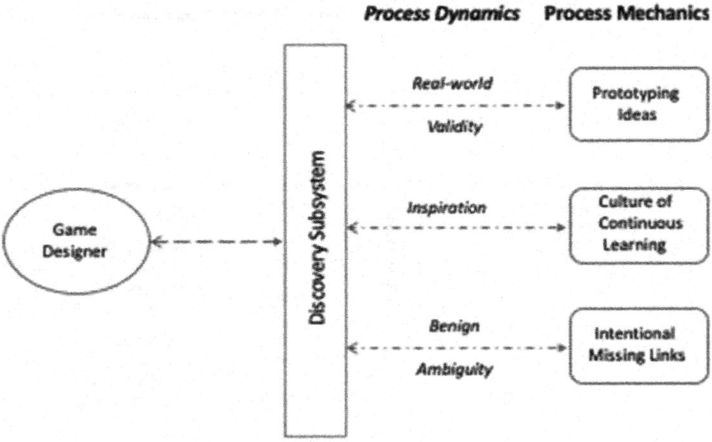

Process Dynamics   **Process Mechanics**

Fig. 4. Discovery subsystem

interview referred to self-determination theory as a source of identifying player types and their intrinsic motivation to pursue goals. An enjoyable design process should acknowledge different designer types and facilitate designers to stay motivated.

- Mental model alignment - Clarity of creative vision was identified by designers as a necessary factor for enjoyability. Design processes are dynamic and constantly changing. While ambiguity can be benign, the process should also help designers reach their most efficient mental model.
- Ownership and Identity – There needs to be a balance between the team's collective vision and the individual designer's ownership and identity in the design process.

The following mechanics can be introduced in the design process to generate opportunities for expression:

- Designer motivation tracker - a management system that can facilitate interaction dynamics of expression, that helps designers stay motivated throughout the entire process. Managers who understand the personalities and player types of their designers can customize team roles and assign tasks based on individual's motivation factors.
- Process decisions - Mental model alignment with the design process is one important factor when it comes to expression. Transparency in the system where the management openly communicates their vision and future goals of the studio can enhance this experience. Acknowledging designer feedback and incorporating changes in the process is another step towards aligning designers with the process.
- Personal design philosophy – The interviewed designers had unique design philosophies that they apply in practice to the game design process. A process that provides a venue for designers to express their own philosophy within the larger framework can foster enjoyability.
- Shared best practices - Team goals take priority in the design process; However, conducting periodic knowledge sharing and best practices sessions can help designers.

They get to know each other's individual approaches to the design process and appreciate the diversity of their design philosophies. This facilitates a sense of ownership and identity in the generic design process. It could also be a team's collective design approach to the process.

Figure 5 shows these mechanics and their runtime dynamics in the designer-process interaction leading to expression as enjoyability. This is again a reinforcing loop represented by double-sided arrows.

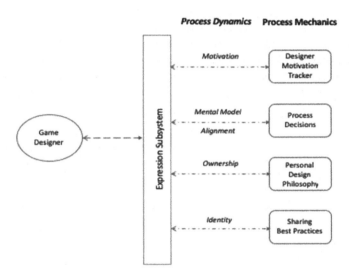

Fig. 5. Expression subsystem

Subsystem: Challenge as Enjoyability. Challenge is the final subsystem that leads to enjoyability in the game design process. This is the most significant component of any game and player experience. No doubt, it is important in the designer's experience of interacting with the process as well. Key interaction dynamics mentioned by the interviewed game designers to design challenging experiences are:

- Empowerment - The process of game design throws many struggles and challenging situations. Conquering these difficult situations empower designers through the process.
- Enrichment - Designers' interaction with the game design process creates cognitive, emotional and social enrichment.
- Healthy production pace - Crunch periods help designers exercise their designer muscles and this makes game design process enjoyable. However, it also requires balance and sensible pacing with periods of relaxation.

The mechanics for this subsystem needs a balancing of dual qualities. The process mechanics should be implemented in a way that it challenges the designer but also ensures that they don't get burnt out in the process.

- Utopian/Struggle - Players lose interest if a game does not provide challenges. The same principle applies to game designing processes; an enjoyable design process should have a good balance between utopian fun phases and periods of struggle. This gives the satisfaction and the feeling of empowerment after overcoming challenging situations.
- Skills Learning - Designer skill set matching with the challenge level makes learning an enriching experience in the design process leading to enjoyability.
- Crunch/Decompress – Similar to the empowering situation, mechanics to schedule the production process with a right balance of power stretches with long working hours followed by an idle phase for decompression make game design process enjoyable. Figure 6 incorporates these mechanics and dynamics into the Challenge subsystem of the design process.

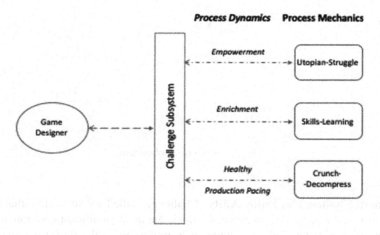

Fig. 6. Challenge subsystem

Thus, the game design process can be deconstructed into a system of various subsystems that the designer can interact with to experience enjoyability. Subsystems are not stand-alone and can interact with one another and have overlapping mechanics and run-time dynamics. Also, some of the enjoyable and not enjoyable factors mentioned earlier can be included within each of these four subsystems as appropriate. These descriptions of the subsystems, the experiences that they evoke and the factors of enjoyability and non-enjoyability helped us build a generic framework for designing an enjoyable game design process. In the following section we develop guidelines to design an enjoyable process.

5.3   Guidelines to Design an Enjoyable Process

The initial objective of the paper was to understand the current game design process, to see if it is enjoyable or not. We decided to interview game designers to get their insights on enjoyability. Through the course of our research work, insights from the interviews showed that the design process can be deconstructed into a system. The key factors that cause enjoyability are experiences of fellowship, discovery, expression and challenge. These four aesthetic experiences evoked by interaction with the design process helped us map it to corresponding process mechanics that generate runtime dynamics which in turn promote enjoyability. Our final step in this study is to bring together all our insights into a framework that serves as a guideline to build enjoyable design processes.

Our framework begins with the vision of designing an enjoyable process. As *(Jigglypuff)* mentioned about clarity in vision: "What is the game you are making; What is the game you don't want to make". Creative designers need clarity in what the design process is about and what it is not about. Providing the pillars and anti-pillars of the design process in advance helps them prepare for what is expected of them in the project. For example: the genre, platform, team size, art style, project duration could define the pillars and anti- pillars of the process. The design process could be defined in terms of the phases of the process, the daily review schedules, client interaction level and others. Post-mortems and designer feedback from previous projects can help define the design process for future projects.

Having defined the scope of the design process, we next move on to building the subsystems of the process. Enjoyability is the genre of this design process. Subsystems can be placed in all the phases of the project or only partially implemented at various levels. For example, at the idea conception phase fellowship and discovery could take up more importance than challenge. Game designers are good at designing levels for players in games. Similarly, subsystems and the corresponding aesthetic experiences can be controlled by implementing the mechanics at appropriate levels of the design process. For example, in the scenario of building a design process that leads to a design culture in an academic game design program at the university level – the first year of education can focus on subsystems of expression and discovery when students are just getting their feet wet into the program. As they form teams in the second or third year of study, subsystems of fellowship and challenge can take precedence.

Subsystems can also be divided further to gain more control over the design process. For example, Challenge subsystem can be further divided into Challenge 1 subsystem that creates a struggle situation for designers while interacting with the process. This could be learning a new skill or going through a crunch tunnel. Challenge 2 subsystem can then balance the struggle effects of Challenge 1 subsystem by providing mentoring support and a decompression phase. The resulting runtime dynamics leads to enrichment and empowerment leading to enjoyability in the design process. Subsystems also focus on certain aspects of the design process. For example, some mechanics require management level implementations whereas others are at the level of designers and their personal motivations. Some rely on the tools and technologies used in the game studio, whereas others depend on building a design culture in the studio with a focus on design philosophies and design practices. Difficulties may arise when the mechanics involve process changes that require multiple departments.

The mechanics identified in this paper are based on the insights from the game designers whom we interviewed. More mechanics can be added to each subsystem based on the process requirements. The enjoyment factors and non-enjoyment factors can themselves be molded into mechanics for subsystems. They can also be used as seasoning to add more fun in the design process. Finally, any design process requires prototyping, playtesting and reiterating. Studios and design teams can iterate several times to find the design process that is most enjoyable to the designers in their teams. They can also generate multiple design processes based on project duration, project genre, gaming platform, business/client operational expectations and other requirements. Themes can be introduced in the design process that align with the game that the designers are working on. A Halloween themed game can have a scary subsystem in the game design process that generates enjoyable chills and thrills!

To summarize the above discussions - game studios, design teams and educators can use the following guidelines to design their own custom design process system based on the project and team requirements.

- Create the Pillars | Anti-Pillars for the design process
- Define what the design process is about + what the design process is NOT about
- Create the subsystems: Fellowship - Discovery - Expression - Challenge
- Source: Add enjoyability factors to the system
- Sink: Remove Non-enjoyability factors from the system
- Prototype, Playtest and Re-iterate

Again, these guidelines are suggestions that are formulated based on the interview insights. They have not been tested on any existing game design process. Integrating these subsystems could be challenging, especially when there are sticky situations where the subsystems may not work as expected. Toxicity in work environments, job insecurity due to frequent layoffs and the influences of negative attitude from the studio management are the major issues trending in gaming industry blog discussions these days. However, the proposed framework here can be a starting point for teams to design enjoyable processes at a team level and then step up to higher levels. Future research work can explore more into the validity of this framework and test the efficiency of the design process guidelines with live game projects in real-world production scenarios.

6   Conclusion and Future Work

Mapping the game design process to a system and de constructing the relations and dynamics of the various parts of the process is a first step in understanding how designers interact with this system. This understanding can then help customize frameworks to each individual or studio level need. Our proposal includes enjoyability as a key component of the design process. There are other experiences that a studio might be interested in providing their designers that enhances designer experiences and workplace productivity. Future work in this area can include case studies of game studios and more in-depth customized process designs. Experiences are very subjective, but a framework that can structure the game design process to shape designer experiences is a handy guide for any organization.

References

Huizinga, J.: Homo Ludens: A Study of the Play-Element in Culture. The Beacon Press, Boston (1955)

Hunicke, R., LeBlanc, M., Zubek, R.: MDA: a formal approach to game design and game research. In: Proceedings of the AAAI Workshop on Challenges in Game AI, vol. 4, no. 1, p. 1722, July 2004

Köknar, C.: Who is at the center?: designing playful experiences by using player-centered approach. In: Fang, X. (ed.) HCII 2019. LNCS, vol. 11595, pp. 11–21. Springer, Cham (2019). https://doi.org/10.1007/978-3-030-22602-2_2

Majgaard, G.: The playful and reflective game designer. Electron. J. E-Learn. **12**(3), 271–280 (2014)

Malone, T.W.: Heuristics for designing enjoyable user interfaces: lessons from computer games. In: Proceedings of the 1982 Conference on Human Factors in Computing Systems, pp. 63–68. ACM, March 1982

Mastrocola, V.M.: The strategic use of smartphone features to create a gaming experience of mystery: the mind alone case. In: Fang, X. (ed.) HCII 2019. LNCS, vol. 11595, pp. 180–190. Springer, Cham (2019). https://doi.org/10.1007/978-3-030-22602-2_15

Sherry, J.L.: Flow and media enjoyment. Commun. Theory **14**(4), 328–347 (2004)

Sherry, J.L., Lucas, K., Greenberg, B.S., Lachlan, K.: Video game uses and gratifications as predictors of use and game preference. Playing Video Games Motives Responses Conseq. **24**(1), 213–224 (2006)

Sweetser, P., Wyeth, P.: Game flow: a model for evaluating player enjoyment in games. Comput. Entertain. (CIE) **3**(3), 3 (2005)

Wang, H., Shen, C., Ritterfeld, U.: Enjoyment of digital games: what makes them "seriously" fun?. In: Serious Games, pp. 47–69. Routledge (2009)

Broader Understanding of Gamification by Addressing Ethics and Diversity

Ole Goethe[1]([✉]) and Adam Palmquist[2]

[1] Kristiania University, Oslo, Norway
`ole.goethe@kristiania.no`
[2] University of Skövde, Skövde, Sweden
`adam.palmquist@his.se`

Abstract. The engagement achieved from gamification is a phenomenon, as gamification is being seen nowadays in a lot of industries. One reason for the massive popularity of gamification is that the use can provide easy access to a sense of engagement and self-efficacy which otherwise may not deliver. By its nature, gamification present users with challenges to overcome and use narrative structure, visuals, strategic elements, and game rules to motivate the users. Gamification is widely applied to increase user engagement, but many empirical studies on effectiveness are inconclusive, and often limited to the integration of tangible game elements such as points, leaderboards or badges. In this article, we will discuss two different perspectives: (i) Ethics: Exploitation, Manipulation, Harms, and Character (ii) Diversity: Culture, Gender and Age. The discussion will lead to opportunities for professionals and researchers to acquire relevant knowledge, assess the mechanisms for the integration of gamification in the context of meaningful engagement, and outline challenges and opportunities for further research.

Keywords: Ethics · Exploitation · Manipulation · Harms · Character · Diversity · Culture · Age · Gender

1 Introduction

Gamification - the use of game elements in non-gaming settings to increase user engagement and improve performance [1] is widely applied to transfer the motivational pull of games and increase user engagement with otherwise monotonous tasks [2]. While there is growing empirical evidence of the general effectiveness of gamification [3], many studies only report small effect size or omit further statistical analysis [4]. Additionally, our understanding of underlying mechanisms remains limited, with recent large-scale studies returning inconclusive results. For example, [5] found that the inclusion of badges, levels and leaderboards influenced user performance, but had no significant effect on perceived competence and intrinsic motivation. Taking a slightly different perspective, [6] included a wider range of game elements and features (e.g., simulated teammates, avatars, and narrative). Results show that aspects such as teammates do not only affect productivity, but also the underlying experience.

© Springer Nature Switzerland AG 2020
C. Stephanidis et al. (Eds.): HCII 2020, LNCS 12425, pp. 688–699, 2020.
https://doi.org/10.1007/978-3-030-60128-7_50

Furthermore, using games as a vehicle to deliver cognitive training may also be advantageous simply because video games appear to have positive effects on a number of outcomes, including working memory, attentional capacity, problem solving, motivation, emotional control, and prosocial behaviors [7]. In essence, delivering targeted cognitive training through a video game medium might provide a range of benefits.

The studies we reviewed were generally enthusiastic about their use of gamified tasks, although given the diversity of study aims, this does not mean that all games worked as expected. The ones that measured intrinsic motivation reported that the use of game like tasks improved motivation, compared with non-gamified versions. For instance, in the study conducted by [8], they identified 21 of 33 studies that compared a game like task directly against a nonqualified counterpart, and these studies can shed light on the specific effects of gamification on testing and training tasks.

2   Related Work

Gamification's promise to bring the motivational and fun characteristics of games to other contexts is very appealing to businesses. Bringing an element of fun to otherwise boring or uninteresting jobs and tasks certainly seems ideal [9]. Critics say that gamification is manipulation; at least that is what many people think [10]. Because gamification is a powerful tool for modifying behaviors, how do we consider ethics specifically for gamification driven engagement?

A prevalent interpretation of Ethics a gamification, was introduced and promoted by the game designer Ian Bogost as exploitationware. The Bogost definition describes gamification sell technique invented only to sell products rather than produce real engagement [11]. Another term used for describing gamification is Pointsification coined by game developer Margret Robertson. Robertson claims that pointsification creates challenges that require time and energy but are not fundamentally satisfying [12]. Bogost [13] are not the only people that have criticized gamification. Critics have questioned of gamification on a variety of reasons [14–17]. Although Werbach and Kim [18] claim the critique of gamification has reacted to behavioral design methods that are often imprecise and declaring that practically all forms of gamification are impermissible or inappropriate. While there exists a discussion the ethical issues of gamification [16, 19, 20] in academia, there is still silence from many professionals. According to Werbach and Kim [18], there have been insufficient serious studies of the ethical issues of gamification given that gamification is one of the fastest developing behavioral tools in both business and information technology.

3   Are Ethics Important in Gamification?

Ok, what's the problem? Gamification has teething just like any other new and disruptive method. To design really engaging gamification it doesn't hurt to make it right from the start. In their research on ethics and gamification Werbach and Kim [18] identifies four distinct areas: exploitation, manipulation, harm, and character of consideration when it comes to designing as well as researching gamification. The areas should in themselves require an article, however, herein they are shortened, summarized and reproduced from this article's perspective (see Fig. 1).

Fig. 1. Understanding ethics using gamification

3.1 Exploitation

The first theme that Werbach and Kim [18] identifies is exploitation. Many organizations ask for loyalty – employers want workers to be loyal, and brands want a reoccurring loyal customer base. Gamification has an impressive past performance regarding producing loyal users. Nevertheless, what if the gamified system gives almost nothing in return, like virtual goods? At least frequent flyer programs or loyal customer systems often give something tangible back to the user. In video games, players sometimes endure boring activities to achieve particular long-term objectives, like picking an endless number of herbs in the MMO (massively multiplayer online) game World of Warcraft, even if the players do not find an endeavor itself rewarding.

But, if the players do not think the task rewarding, why are they doing it? This game element is called grinding and is prevalent in MMO games. To grind in a game means that the players must spend extended periods doing monotonous tasks as a condition to acquire something, often a virtual good, the player desires – like an honorary title, a special badge or even some equipment they can use in the game. One of the ideas behind the grinding element is to make a game feel more prominent without the game developers putting much effort into producing new complex game material - like a new world or another set of scenery. However, doing grinding in a game is optional and can even result in some new equipment for the players to use in the game context.

Conversely, when this game element is applied in, e.g. a gamified work environment, it is often not optional, and there seldom exists a magical work-tool that is rewarded to the employees at the end of the grinding work-session. Getting a virtual badge for taking on an extra shift or working unpaid overtime is not ethical. The employer is capitalizing on the employee´s will to appear respectable and loyal towards the company, and this could be viewed as exploitation if the employees never receive a tangible reward for their extra effort. Correspondingly, social pressure could correspond to exploitation and culture of the company. Individuals, especially newly employed, seek to conform with the work culture, which involves changing their typical behaviors in order to fit in or go along with the new individuals, employees, around you [21]. Creating an "if everyone does it, why shouldn't I?" mentality.

3.2 Manipulation

Gamification is a design technique to affect the user's behavior. Swaying individuals' determination has been a sales trick since humans first barter and have been used ever since with different sell techniques. That salespersons use calculating methods is not new. Grown individuals know this when we are entering a store, and we have time to prepare for an upcoming sales pitch. However, in environments where individuals usually are not prepared for a sale situation, e.g. in nightgowns lying in bed at 10.00 PM playing a social game on the smartphone, should it not be considered more manipulative? Werbach and Kim [18] place in the manipulation category social, mobile games such as Farmville using different game mechanics to manipulate players to a continuous play up to a point then all of a sudden if you want to continue you have to pay with real money. Werbach and Kim [18] reason that these game company's target different intensive and almost obsessive players, called whales, and rely upon them spending heavily for either continuing the game or purchasing different virtual goods. Although not all individuals will become addicted to mobile games, it does not justify behavior that targets vulnerable customers – such as children. Many of these applications have a PEGI 3 nevertheless in, e.g. Candy Crush Saga there are options to buy virtual goods with a price range of 0,7 to 159 euros per object [22]. There exist many explanations of why parents allow this, like indulging the children or to avoid spam [23].

If a gamification design deliberately or negligently applies techniques to promote irrational behavior or even fails to act corrective when some users display such behavior, it falls short of ethical duties regarding manipulation. This category calls for better transparency from the system that uses gamification.

3.3 Harms

Concerning harm, Werbach and Kim [18] divide this theme in two aspects psychical and psychological.

The physical aspect could be connected to exercise, and workplaces were gamification, if it is designed in such a manner, encourages pushing the user of the gamified system to the limit. In a gamified exercise or a diet application, there could exist, certainly kindly meant in the design, push notes, social media functions or competitions that do not concern the user's previous health conditions which could result in exercise injuries or eating disorders. In a gamified work situation, e.g. a call center, there could exist problems with overworking for the employees.

The psychological aspect of harm, the theme has to do with the sensation being watched and measured an information system. Making gamification design work as Jeremy Bentham's Panopticon, a philosophical prison concept with the design to allow all convicts of an institution to be observed by a single guard, without the prisoners being able to know whether they are being watched or not [24]. This could make the gamification design functions as a suppression medium that imposes the interests of managers over the interests of the employees. Similar problems have been identified in previous research concerning socio-technical systems in organizations [25] and can also be found in China's social credit system [26].

The ethical theme of harm could be exemplified by a gamification system that Disney implemented to their cleaning staff in one of the Disneyland hotels in Oregon. In the gamified design, points were awarded to employees when they did different task like finishing cleaning a hotel room. The accumulated points put the different employees on a leaderboard, visual at the staff lunchroom. This competition became so intense it made the employees stop taking lunch breaks or going to the toilet. The reason for this was that the employees thought that they were going to lose their jobs if they did not climb the leaderboard continuously. The employees, in interviews, were calling the gamification implementation the electronic whip [27]. This gamification could be harmful both in a psychological sense - involving stress from the impression that always being watched and measured by your performance, as well as a physical way - involving injury from overworking. Werbach and Kim [18] also a reason that this type of gamification is humiliating for the practitioners.

3.4 Character

Werbach and Kim [18] define this area with the appeal to moral and fundamental of human values.

Gamification could be designed to get the user to make amoral choices regarding human rights which they probably would not have made without the gamified system. Werbach and Kim [18] exemplify these two military examples concerning military organizations such as the U.S. Army and the Israel Defense Force using gamification in civilian society as well as training. The Israel Defense Force used gamification, not in a military training simulation, but in civil society using a gamified blog where readers acquired badges and when they searched for information on the blog and shared the content through social media connections. With the use of social media, this blog became viral [18]. This was made to rally support for military actions conducted by the Israeli Defense Force.

In the case of the U.S Army, gamification was used in a training simulation that rewarded the participants with points and achievements when tapping colleagues' email or finding contraband. This simulation was conducted to exercise the fight against global terrorism [18]. Both gamified cases are questionable regarding the right to privacy or by making civilians spread military propaganda, and the game facilitates the actions. The character theme is referring to the concept of frames that a gamified system purpose – is it a game or is it a reality. Previous research on gamification in higher education purpose that when a learning management system is gamified there exist a possibility that the user does not refer to it as a serious system, even though it is in a serious context. They see it through a more playful frame [28].

4   Situating Diversity in Gamification

Gamification is a double-edged sword. While increasingly pervasive gamified systems create unlimited opportunities for a better quality of life, their domination can cause a negative effect on societies as in; Rewards for achievement, measure progress and provide feedback – strong motivators for behavioral change, learning and growth [29]. This article aims to raise awareness about three distinct diversity elements that will be approached and analyzed; Culture, Gender and Age (see Fig. 2).

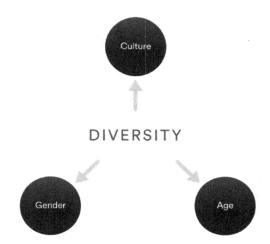

Fig. 2. Situating diversity in gamification.

4.1 Culture

To acquire the meaningful engagement out of gamification and its application in business, learning, and health, both gamification researchers and professionals needs to consider how different cultural manifestations are influenced by the behavioral design that gamification purpose. Al Marshedi, A., Wanick, V., Wills, G. B., & Ranchhod, A. [30] suggest that the cultural context and the cultural environment are of interest for gamification. The individuals and their cultural context need to be considered as well as understood by the gamification researcher and the professional. Correspondingly, Khaled [31] describes the need for cultural models to understand the engagement in gamification better.

However, as of today, there is limited research on the gamification and culture area [30]. If gamification should consider culture as an aspect of the design to engage, there is a need to explore other fields. It should be valuable to explore culture and gamification. The word culture has many definitions, from a social science standpoint Giddens & Griffiths [32] describe it as "the ways of life of the individuals of a society, or of groups within a society. It includes how individuals dress, their marriage customs, language and family life, their patterns of work, religious ceremonies and leisure pursuits".

Giddens & Griffiths definition would be beneficial to understand for gamification professionals and researchers alike. Understanding the client and/or the end-user's culture in gamification means there is a need for consciousness regards to the design and interpreting the outcome of a design based on the cultural context. E.g. if a gamified onboarding program is to be designed and implemented in a global manufacturing company, it needs to consider the different cultural spheres regarding, e.g. work culture, family traditions and/or national norms.

The cultural discussion on engagement and gamification opens for a discussion on how concepts and knowledge from cultural psychology are beneficial for the field of gamification. Cultural psychology takes into consideration a great many things that like cultural collective attributes, cultural emotional attachments, communications understanding and the culture of decision-making [33]. Cultural psychology is beneficial in regard to design gamification avoid, e.g. avoid stereotyping, but also when researching gamification in cultures with high values in either self-enhancement or self-improvement. Actions that affect behavioral change do not happen in a cultural or social vacuum. Many activities that individuals react to in their everyday life have some cultural nuances or are moderated by the home culture or job culture [34].

There are cultural norms that would react opposable on a gamification design in the Scandinavian countries, there is something called the law of Jante (swe: Jantelagen, no/dan Janteloven) which could be described as a code of conduct that portrays not conforming, doing things out of the ordinary, or being overtly personally ambitious as inappropriate. One should never try to be more, try to be different, or consider oneself more valuable than other people [35]. This widespread modesty code could make people react negatively on a gamification design the push a sharing behavior in social media. The law of Jante is unsaid in the Scandinavian societies, but its prevalent in all its stages. Khaled [31] claims that unwritten cultural rules are needed to reflect upon when designing gamification. Here the field of anthropology would be needed to grasp the understanding the law of Jante. This is an example of culture that a gamification professional or researcher need to pay attention to. Additionally, to make the cultural aspect more complex the use of cultural semiotics, metaphors and tropes could play essential roles for engaging a user in gamification design.

4.2 Age

Another diversity aspect in the gamification that needs attention is age. Age has been proven to contribute to the digital divide. But does this compare with gamification? Gamified products on the market has tendency to be designed with a young adult user in mind, and therefore it could be perceived that this user group are more attracted to gamification [36]. However, this assumption may not necessarily be accurate. Studies indicate that the consumer of a gamified product presumed usefulness of gamification decreases over the years, but this does not mean that this is the actual case. In a study of the supposed usefulness of gamification display that gamification appeal more to individuals under the age of 40 [37]. However, in another study, age difference concerning motivation in a gamified exercise software has been assigned insignificant effects [36]. The findings could indicate that gamification has a similar effect, regarding age, on motivation but the difference is determined on how the gamified product presents its use of game mechanics. A gam-y look and feel in the product design makes it more attractable to a younger crowd.

Research on acceptance of serious games could work as a guide for how to navigate in the design field in regard to age. The research field of serious games has studied the well-known factors, such as perceived usefulness, perceived ease-of-use and perceived enjoyment that play a vital role in the acceptance of a system [38]. To consider is that the users' attitudes to gamified products need not be about gamification, but the digital divide between younger and older generations [39, 40]. The knowledge of age diversity is crucial when designing or examining a gamification design. To know the target group that is expected to be engaged is needed, not just for an engaging gamification design but when designing in general. Interesting findings could be examined from the viewpoint of gamification in an e-scape perspective were the viewpoints of environmental psychology is used [41]. A lens that should be used to analyze how gamification work and why it works – there need to be more studies in the area in regard to age.

4.3 Gender

Diversity regarding end-user gender is also a central topic of engagement. Is there a difference between genders when it comes to engagement and gamification?

In the business of game development many of the entertainment games designed, both digital games and analog games, acknowledge that there is a gender difference and therefore the games are designed with a specific gender in mind [42]. Correspondingly, gender has been found to play a role in game-based-learning context [43]. In a study on medical student attitudes toward video games and learning, [44] showed that female students in higher education were about 35% as likely as male students to enjoy the competitive aspects of the games.

However, gender differences concerning the attitude of video games seem to correlate with age of the user [43]. Younger generations are more accepting of video games and do not seem to gender code the gaming activity as much as the older generations [43]. However, boys usually have more positive attitudes towards video games in education than girls [45]. Gender differences have also been observed during gameplay in an educational context, where the different sexes have different player behavior [46]. Does gender attitudes on video games and game-based learning correlate to engagement in gamification? This is a complex problem, with multiple answers.

One of the largest fields of use for gamification is education and the teachers play a vital role in the acceptance of the design. In the higher education context, attitudes towards using gamification in the learning institutions have no significant affected by the teacher's gender [43]. The study indicates that attitude towards using gamification doesn't seem to be affect by gender. Nevertheless, there are indications that in elementary school context, the effect of gamification on the user is affected by gender. The game mechanics, points, badges, levels, was used to boost good behavior in a school class. Pedro et al. [47] found that game mechanics had different effects on the girls and the boys in the class. In their study, the gamification design seemed to have a better effect on the male population than the female [47].

Though, does gender diversity correlate in a more adult gamified context?

In a study observing simulated corporate training show that there is a gender diversity regarding how gamified competition in learning context affects males and females differently. Males are more engaged and have improved learning in a competitive context than females [48]. The finding of this study implicates that gender plays a role in gamification design at least when it comes to the competitive aspects of gamification.

Moreover, a study on university undergraduates, several gamification designs were tested in the relevance of different game mechanics to determine experienced perceived playfulness and if the mechanics was perceived differently by gender. The study shows that there exists a diversity what males and females perceive as playful in a design. Males seem to appreciate points although women report a higher enjoyment in the game mechanic badges [49]. In another study on a gamification framework based on user characteristics, there is an indication that different game design elements apple in a different degree to gender [50]. A conclusion of the above could be that men and women may find different game mechanics and game design techniques more or less appealing which probably affects their engagement in the gamified application.

Diversity in gamification is broad. Here the topics of culture, age and gender are explored to some extent nevertheless there is more topics in this category that can affect the engagement like socioeconomic status or interest. As mentioned, the presented topics deserve a study of their own and should be considered as hypothesis generating rather than hypothesis testing.

In designing gamification, one should also be aware of the fact that variables such as gender, age, and cultural orientations can play a role in variance in the reception of gamified application.

5   Conclusion

The use of gamification can be unethical if the decision-maker loses sight of why their action is desirable. Exploitation can lead users to become enamored with points, badges and leaderboards, rather than the reasons why something is good to do, thereby putting their action at ethical risk. Harms related to how professionals should not to blindly resort to achievements (or points, levels and leaderboards for that matter), because they could stifle users' intrinsic motivation, that is, their desire to engage with a system. Character in terms of "achievements"—recognition for completing minor, secondary or non-essential tasks or goals that do not inherently affect the system's outcome—are a staple tool to reward users for accomplishments and character building.

This article annotates the areas for future work and provides a grounding for the interpretation of proper gamification related to the issues of ethics and diversity. Finally, our perspectives on gamification, suggesting that professionals should refocus on the development of a wider, experience-centered toolbox that move beyond the application of traditional game elements to equip both the researchers and professionals with broader means of creating more meaningful experiences.

References

1. Deterding, S., Dixon, D., Khaled, R., Nacke, L.: From game design elements to gameful-ness: defining gamification. In: Proceedings of the 15th International Academic MindTrek Conference: Envisioning Future Media Environments, pp. 9–15. ACM (2011)
2. Birk, M.V., Mandryk, R.L., Atkins, C.: The motivational push of games: the interplay of intrinsic motivation and external rewards in games for training. In: Proceedings of the 2016 Annual Symposium on Computer-Human Interaction in Play, pp. 291–303. ACM (2016)

3. Denny, P., McDonald, F., Empson, R., Kelly, P., Petersen, A.: Empirical support for a causal relationship between gamification and learning outcomes. In: Proceedings of the 2018 CHI Conference on Human Factors in Computing Systems, p. 311. ACM (2018)

4. Ryan, R.M., Rigby, C.S., Przybylski, A.: The motivational pull of video games: a self-determination theory approach. Motiv. Emot. **30**(4), 344–360 (2006)

5. Mekler, E.D., Bruhlmann, F., Opwis, K., Tuch, A.N.: Do points, levels and leaderboards harm intrinsic motivation? An empirical analysis of common gamification elements. In: Proceedings of the First International Conference on Gameful Design, Research, and Applications, pp. 66–73. ACM (2013)

6. Sailer, M., Hense, J.U., Mayr, S.K., Mandl, H.: How gamification motivates: an experimental study of the effects of specific game design elements on psychological need satisfaction. Comput. Hum. Behav. **69**, 371–380 (2017)

7. Boyle, E., et al.: An update to the systematic literature review of empirical evidence of the impacts and outcomes of computer games and serious games. Comput. Educ. **94**, 178–192 (2016)

8. Lumsden, J., Edwards, E.A., Lawrence, N.S., Coyle, D., Munafò, M.R.: Gamification of Cognitive Assessment and Cognitive Training: A Systematic Review of Applications and Efficacy (2016). https://www.ncbi.nlm.nih.gov/pmc/articles/PMC4967181/

9. Draffan, E.A., et al.: Stepwise approach to accessible MOOC development. Stud. Health Technol. Informat. **217**, 227 (2015)

10. Sicart, M.: The ethics of computer games. The MIT Press. Miguel Sicart is Associate Professor at the Center for Computer Game Research at IT University Copenhagen. He is the author of The Ethics of Computer Games and Beyond Choices: The Design of Ethical Gameplay, both published by the MIT Press (2009)

11. Landers, R.: Gamification Science, Its History and Future: Definitions and a Research Agenda. Simulation & Gaming (2016). https://www.researchgate.net/publication/325297221_Gamifi cation_Science_Its_History_and_Future_Definitions_and_a_Research_Agenda

12. Werbach and Hunter: For the Win: How Game Thinking Can Revolutionize Your Business. Wharton Digital Press (2015). https://www.researchgate.net/publication/266398023_Gamifi cation_in_Theory_and_Action_A_Survey

13. Bogost, I.: Reality is alright. [Web log comment] (2011). http://bogost.com/writing/blog/rea lity_is_broken

14. Kim, T.W.: Gamification ethics: exploitation and manipulation. In: Gamifying Research Workshop Papers, CHI (2015)

15. Rey, P.J.: Gamification, playbor & exploitation, Cyborgology, 15 October 2012. http://thesoc ietypages.org/cyborgology/2012/10/15/gamification-playbor-exploitation-2/

16. Sicart, M.: Playing the good life: gamification and ethics. In: Deterding, S., Waltz, S. (eds.) The Gameful World: Approaches, Issues, Applications, pp. 225–244. MIT Press, Cambridge (2015)

17. Selinger, E., Sadowski, J., Seager, T.: Gamification and morality. In: Deterding, S., Waltz, S. (eds.) The Gameful World: Approaches, Issues, Applications, pp. 371–392. MIT Press, Cambridge (2015)

18. Kim, T.W., Werbach, K.: More than just a game: ethical issues in gamification. Ethics Inf. Technol. **18**(2), 157–173 (2016). https://doi.org/10.1007/s10676-016-9401-5

19. Björk, S.: Dark patterns in the design of games. Presentation. University of Skövde, Skövde (2019)

20. Goethe, O., Salehzadeh Niksirat, K., Hirskyj-Douglas, I., Sun, H., Law, E.L.-C., Ren, X.: From UX to engagement: connecting theory and practice, addressing ethics and diversity. In: Antona, M., Stephanidis, C. (eds.) HCII 2019. LNCS, vol. 11572, pp. 91–99. Springer, Cham (2019). https://doi.org/10.1007/978-3-030-23560-4_7

21. Cialdini, R.B., Goldstein, N.J.: Social influence: compliance and conformity. Annu. Rev. Psychol. **55**, 591–621 (2004)
22. Google Store "Candy Crush Saga" (2020). https://play.google.com/store/apps/details?id=com.king.candycrushsaga&hl=sv
23. Hamari, J., Alha, K., Järvelä, S., Kivikangas, J.M., Koivisto, J., Paavilainen, J.: Why do players buy in-game content? An empirical study on concrete purchase motivations. Comput. Hum. Behav. **68**, 538–546 (2017)
24. Bentham, J.: Panopticon: en ny princip för inrättningar där personer övervakas. Nya Doxa, Nora (2002)
25. Morgan, G.: Images of Organization, 2nd edn. Sage, London (1997)
26. Creemers, R.: China's social credit system: an evolving practice of control. SSRN 3175792 (2018)
27. Lopez, S.: Disney hotel workers try to stay ahead of the "electronic whip." Los Angeles Times, 19 October 2011
28. Palmquist, A., Linderoth, J.: Gamification does not belong at a university. In: Proceedings of the 2020 DiGRA Conference, Tampere (2020, in press)
29. Hicks, K., Dickinson, P., Holopainen, J., Gerling, K.: Good game feel: an empirically grounded framework for juicy design. In: Proceedings of the 2018 DiGRA Conference (2018)
30. AlMarshedi, A., Wanick, V., Wills, G.B., Ranchhod, A.: Gamification and Behaviour. In: Stieglitz, S., Lattemann, C., Robra-Bissantz, S., Zarnekow, R., Brockmann, T. (eds.) Gamification. PI, pp. 19–29. Springer, Cham (2017). https://doi.org/10.1007/978-3-319-455 57-0_2
31. Khaled, R.: Gamification and culture. The gameful world: approaches, issues, applications, p. 301 (2015)
32. Giddens, A., Griffiths, S.: Sociologi. (4, omarb. uppl.) Studentlitteratur, Lund (2007)
33. Britt, S.H.: Consumer Behaviour and the Behavioural Sciences: Theories and Applications. Wiley, Oxford (1966)
34. Usunier, J.C., Lee, J.: Marketing Across Cultures. Pearson Education (2005)
35. Weijo, H.A.: Democracies of taste ruled by the law of jante? Rudiments of a nordic sociology of consumption. In: Askegaard, S., Östberg, J. (eds.) Nordic Consumer Culture. LNCS, pp. 25–47. Springer, Cham (2019). https://doi.org/10.1007/978-3-030-04933-1_2
36. Hamari, J., Koivisto, J.: Why do people use gamification services? Int. J. Inf. Manag. **35**(4), 419–431 (2014)
37. Bittner, J.V., Shipper, J.: Motivational effects and age differences of gamification in product advertising. J. Consum. Mark. (2014)
38. Taylor, A.S.A., Backlund, P., Engstrom, H., Johannesson, M., Lebram, M.: The birth of Elinor: a collaborative development of a game-based system for stroke rehabilitation. In: 2009 Second International Conference in Visualisation, pp. 52–60. IEEE (2009)
39. Morris, M.G., Venkatesh, V.: Age differences in technology adoption decisions: implications for a changing work force. Pers. Psychol. **53**(2), 375–403 (2000)
40. Pfeil, U., Arjan, R., Zaphiris, P.: Age differences in online social networking: a study of user profiles and the social capital divide among teenagers and older users in MySpace. Comput. Hum. Behav. **25**(3), 643–654 (2009)
41. Palmquist, A., Gillberg, D.: Eye of the Beholder: Analyzing a Gamification Design Through a Servicescape Lens (2020)
42. Van Reijmersdal, E.A., Jansz, J., Peters, O., Van Noort, G.: Why girls go pink: game character identification and game-players' motivations. Comput. Hum. Behav. **29**(6), 2640–2649 (2013)
43. Martí-Parreño, J., Seguí-Mas, D., Seguí-Mas, E.: Teachers' attitude towards and actual use of gamification. Procedia-Soc. Behav. Sci. **228**, 682–688 (2016)

44. Kron, F.W., Gjerde, C.L., Sen, A., Fetters, M.D.: Medical student attitudes toward video games and related new media technologies in medical education. BMC Med. Educ. **10**(1), 50 (2010)

45. Bonanno, P., Kommers, P.A.: Exploring the influence of gender and gaming competence on attitudes towards using instructional games. Br. J. Edu. Technol. **39**(1), 97–109 (2008)

46. Bressler, D.M., Bodzin, A.M.: A mixed methods assessment of students' flow experiences during a mobile augmented reality science game. J. Comput. Assist. Learn. **29**(6), 505–517 (2013)

47. Pedro, L.Z., Lopes, A.M., Prates, B.G., Vassileva, J., Isotani, S.: Does gamification work for boys and girls? An exploratory study with a virtual learning environment. In: Proceedings of the 30th Annual ACM Symposium on Applied Computing, pp. 214–219 (2015)

48. Shen, W.-C.M., Liu, D., Santhanam, R., Evans, D.A.: Gamified technology-mediated learning: the role of individual differences recommended citation gamified technology-mediated learning: the role of individual differences. Association for Information System AIS Electron Libr, vol. 47 (2016)

49. Codish, D., Ravid, G.: Gender moderation in gamification: does one size fit all?

50. Toda, A.M., Oliveira, W., Shi, L., Bittencourt, I.I., Isotani, S., Cristea, A.: Planning gamification strategies based on user characteristics and DM: a gender-based case study. arXiv preprint arXiv:1905.09146 (2019)

Game-Based Learning and Instructional Effectiveness in Organizational Communication Classrooms

Dongjing Kang[✉]

Department of Communication and Philosophy, Florida Gulf Coast University,
Fort Myers, FL, USA
dkang@fgcu.edu

Abstract. This study uses an instructional game called "Recreating Assembly Line in a Paper Airplane Factory" to illustrate the effectiveness of game-based learning in higher education. The author describes the game design, its procedures, and the post-game survey. Then, the author uses Lederman and Ruben's [7] *Systematic Assessment of Communication Games criteria* to summarize the insights from game-based instruction and how such instructional methods support undergraduate learning in organizational communication classrooms. Last, the author shares a few insights for using games in higher education.

Keywords: Game-based learning · Organizational communication · Scientific management · Human factors

1 Introduction

The so-called *banking model* of education has been considered problematic by teachers and learners in university classrooms ever since Brazilian humanist and critical theorist Paulo Freire [1] published *The Pedagogy of the Oppressed*. It is, he described traditional education as resembling the operations of a bank. In this model, students were regarded as passive objects of schooling into which "deposits" of knowledge were made and from which withdrawals could also made – by teachers or their colleagues, by peers, employers or the students themselves but without any significant engagement with or transformation of themselves, the world or the knowledge itself.

In contrast to the banking model, games of many sorts can serve as a medium for participation that transforms the student from passive recipient to active learning agent. Historically games have been a source for motivation [2–4], engagement [5], and reinforcement of learning [5] in higher education. The potential of games can be captured in the concept of gamification. Coined by Nick Pelling in 2003, the term *gamification* has been used to describe "educational games," "serious games," and "game-based learning" [6].

To illustrate the effectiveness of game-based teaching and learning, this study introduces a game called "Recreating Assembly Line in a Paper Airplane Factory." It was used

© Springer Nature Switzerland AG 2020
C. Stephanidis et al. (Eds.): HCII 2020, LNCS 12425, pp. 700–707, 2020.
https://doi.org/10.1007/978-3-030-60128-7_51

in five classes of organizational communication behavior to teach scientific management at a public university in southwestern Florida. First, the author described a game used in the course, including the game design, procedures, and a post-game survey. Then, by using Lederman and Ruben's [7] *Systematic Assessment of Communication Games criteria*, the author summarized insights from game-based learning, emphasizing how such instructional methods support undergraduate learning in organizational communication behavior. Last, the author shared a few insights for using games in higher education.

2   A Game-Based Course

The author has designed and implemented a series of interactive games to enhance student learning for five semesters in an upper level course, Organizational Communication Behavior, in a public university in southwestern Florida, United States. The average number of students enrolled in each class was 35. The students are business and communication majors. Eight games are based on eight chapters in scholar Katherine Miller's [8] textbook, *Organizational Communication: Approaches and Processes*. Students receive 5 points for each game in which they participate. As a game-based course, this acuminating reward systems encourage players (students) to continue to participate. Reward mechanisms provide sense of fun by fostering intrinsically rewarding experiences and are equally or more important than the extrinsic rewards that are distributed [9]. The first game plays an important role for stimulating students' interest to play. In the next section, the author introduces the first game by sharing its game design, procedures, and the post-game survey.

2.1   Game Design

In this age of globalization, a large number of manufacturing industries, or key parts of them, have moved out of the United States. College students who self-identify as Generation Z (also known as Post-Millennials or the iGeneration) have limited knowledge and experience with assembly lines. Teaching classic management theory posed a challenge in post-industrial America. Especially in southwestern Florida, many students work in the tourism and service sectors and show very little interest in learning about theoretical models.

The first game, "Recreating Assembly Line in a Paper Airplane Factory," primarily aims to generate student interest in classic organizational theory. Second, the goal of the game is for students to apply the theory in practice. The game is based on Frederick Taylor's *Theory of Scientific Management*, including four major principles: 1) There is one best way to do every job; 2) Proper selection of workers for the job is critical; 3) Workers should be trained in "time-and-motion" studies; and 4) There is an inherent difference between management and workers [8]. A 50-min period is recommended in order to prepare, play and debrief adequately.

The instructor facilitates a pre-game discussion around the key frameworks from the lectures of the previous class: Taylor's scientific management, along with Max Weber's theory of bureaucracy, and Henri Fayol's classic management [8]. Doing so provides a foundation for student understanding of how these concepts played out in organizational life during industrialization.

Following the discussion, the game first casts participants in roles: students are factory workers on an assembly line that mass produces paper airplanes. They formed seven production teams of five students each. The teaching assistant plays the role of middle manager, and the instructor plays the senior manager. The information on production is hierarchically delivered from the senior manager (instructor) to middle manager (teaching assistant), and then disseminated to the workers (students).

Then, the senior manager introduces the procedures of the game: training, producing, and selecting the winner. And the interactions between participants are governed by a series of guidelines; for instance:

1. The senior manager determines the raw materials, 50 pages of recycled A4 papers and the goal the game is to produce as many standardized paper airplanes as possible. A standardized model airplane is given to each student group before the training.
2. The senior manager and the middle manager train teams to produce *one model* of the airplane.
3. Each factory worker must follow the time-and-motion training steps (Fig. 1) to produce the airplanes.
4. The middle manager corrects the mistakes made by the workers during training and supervising the production.
5. The middle manager uses the standardize model to evaluate all groups' products. The winning group is the one to make the largest number of standardized airplanes.

2.2 Procedure

The game starts with 10 to 15 min of training in the five-step fold that makes a classic dart paper airplane. During the training, the senior manager and the middle manager coach all factory workers in folding *one* model of a paper airplane in five steps (motions). Each student has to strictly follow the sequence of each step (Fig. 1 below).

At the end of the training, each production group should form an assembly line. For instance, some groups formed an assembly line (manifest as seat order) based on the steps they were most familiar with. Some groups decided to sit in a random order. Then, the middle-manager checks their product to see if they are ready for mass production. Once the middle manager confirmed each group member's training product is standardized, the group is able to participate in the next module—production.

Following the training, all seven teams are given 10 min to manufacture the airplane (Fig. 2). The middle manager walks around the classroom and supervises the production groups while the senior manager uses the smartphone's stopwatch to time the production. Based on my five-semester observation, students were vitally engaged in the folding of paper airplanes. Often, they became competitive as they observed each other's products. They often motivated each other with, "I've got this!" or, "Let's speed up!" Some more familiar with the game attempted to coach the less familiar members and correct their mistakes.

After the 10-min production, the middle manager checks the quality of each group's production and calculates the numbers. Airplanes that do not fit the "classic dart airplane"

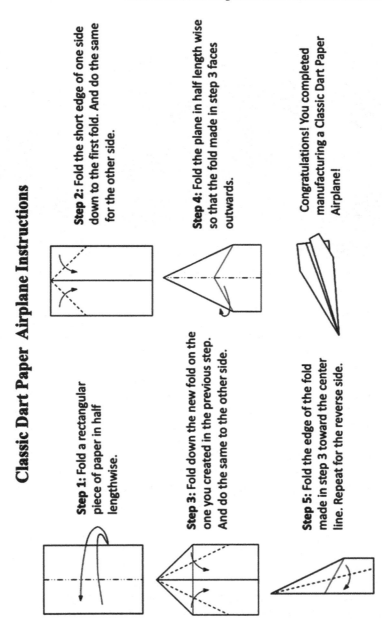

Fig. 1. A standardize guideline to make classic dart paper airplanes.

model are not calculated in the total number. After that, the middle manager writes the amount of each group's production on the whiteboard in front of the classroom. Finally, the senior manager announces the winning group and gives them a bag of chocolates as a reward.

Fig. 2. Students groups are manufacturing paper airplanes in groups.

2.3 Post-game Survey

Right after the game, the instructor hands out a worksheet with which to reflect upon the game and its connection to the instruction material. The worksheet involves two open-ended questions; they are:

1. List a key theory from this chapter that is most applicable to the game.
2. What was the most significant challenge for your group in achieving efficiency and productivity?

Based on two semesters' student responses (n = 66), I conducted a qualitative content analysis [10] to identify the frequencies of key concepts and themes from the data. In the feedback from the first question, 63% of students listed, "Taylor's scientific management theory" as most applicable to: "Recreating Assembly Line in a Paper Airplane Factory," the game. The top two scientific-management principles students mentioned were, "There is one best way to do the job," and "Job training," both of which validated the initial purpose of the game design.

To present the survey results in the second question, I thematized student feedback in order to identify the key challenges in producing paper airplanes on assembly lines. They are: 1) individual differences in expertise and goals; 2) difficulty maintaining good coordination; and 3) maintaining a quality product with speed. In the first theme, most students said it was difficult for every member to stay "on the same page" regarding expertise and goals. Differences in experience folding paper airplanes make the assembly line not run as smoothly as possible. Many students wrote, "Our group had one person stuck on one step" or, "Other members [progressed] at a better pace than one person." In addition, a third of students noted that certain group members had an inconsistent or incomplete grasp of their tasks based on their goals and motivation. One student wrote, "due to a lack of motivation, only three group members did major folding." Groups who won the game often had members who shared a similar understanding of the goals and prior knowledge of folding airplanes.

Second, most of the students believed that the key challenge was to maintain good coordination with one another in different situations. About half of the students said that "finding a good place/location" and "improvising each step with one another [for better coordination]" was absent in their group. Some showed that they slowed down because they had to wait for one another in order to proceed to the next step. Many students also believed it was important to coordinate with each other situationally. One wrote,

> "We originally had a system [assembly line] where each member took the responsibility for one fold, but it backed up production of the planes overall. Therefore, we made an adjustment where each person took care of two folds and the last two people finished the planes, [leading to] rising productivity."

Similar to my observation, it is obvious that the groups that won the game in the past five semesters coordinated with one another, and often supported each other in the process. Improvising coordination between members and self-correction at the group level is the key to an efficient assembly line. Often, members were not completely following the training outlined in Fig. 1.

In the last theme, "maintaining a quality product with speed," students pointed out that the need to speed time of production put pressure on their quality. Based on my observation, some groups produced a large number of airplanes but did not fully meet the standardized model of quality. These non-standardized airplanes always have to be discarded at the end of the game.

In sum, the game "Recreating Assembly Line in a Paper Airplane Factory" validated the scientific management theory and stimulated student interest in learning a theory they had not been exposed to. Based on the post-game survey, students showed that the top three challenges for efficient production were: (1) individual differences in expertise and motivation, (2) members' situational coordination, and (3) time pressure with complex emotions. These challenges indicated human social variables significantly influence their productivity. In the next section, I offer a post-game assessment based on Lederman and Ruben's [7] framework to examine the effectiveness of teaching and learning.

3   Assessment

Lederman and Ruben's [7] proposed a framework to evaluate the effectiveness of game-based learning in the classroom. The three most important components to evaluate whether any gaming activity is a viable methodology for teaching communication concepts are: *validity, reliability, and utility* [7]. First, validity can be understood as face validity and constructive validity. First, face validity means transparent, or face-value. Students had no problem with the first one. Most students were able to provide examples of the first by connecting scientific management to operations at fast food chains like McDonald's and Chipotle in their end-of-semester essays. Second, constructive validity is the deeper, broader validity of the test. Constructive validity criteria include assessing students' long-term identification of the theory and skills at depth. The outcome of this classroom game partially meets the constructive validity criteria. It is clear that most students can articulate scientific management theory in the essays and exams. But it was difficult to measure students' identification of this theory in real life after the semester. How students used the skills taught in the game was not really observable. In the future, maintaining contact with graduates who have taken this course in a longitudinal study could assess constructive validity.

Reliability refers to the replicability of the game including predictability of its outcome. It aims to assess the mastery of learning concepts and theories, especially the "right" way of doing (a task) or the "correct" understanding of something (a concept) [7]. The criteria include assigned roles with low ambiguity, specified channels of information (top-down), fixed rules, and clearly defined goal. The "Recreating Assembly Line in a Paper Airplane Factory" game is highly reliable as it has been practiced in five different classes. The outcome of the game is highly predictable based on observing the game processes.

The final criterion utility is a cost-benefit analysis. This assessment would evaluate the cost including the time, energy, and monetary expenditures associated with the game compared with its results (benefits) [7]. Primarily, the game is low cost by using recycled A4 papers. The benefit outweighs the consumption of time (50 min more than a regular lecture of the theory of scientific management) because participating in the game enhanced students' memory, simulated their interest in the subject, and mastered the application of the theory. Based on five semesters of observation and the post-game survey by the students. more than half of the students could make a direct connection from the game to Taylor's scientific management theory.

4 Future Insights

To conclude, this game-based learning stimulated student interest in organizational communication and enhanced instructional effectiveness. Most importantly, this game also provided space for students to imagine modes of production in industry. During discussions later in the semester, many students showed an interest in human-machine coordination in the assembly lines. Some students bought up the example of Amazon using robots for locating packages for delivery and related it to "Recreating Assembly Line in a Paper Airplane Factory," our game from earlier in the semester. A few students asked, "How do machines coordinate in various situations?" and: "How do they figure out the best way to do the job?" In addition, students pointed out that being attentive to each other's emotion during time pressure is a unique human condition and questioned if programs would be able to do so. Such questions could provide us with a fresh perspective in organizational communication theory regarding technological innovation.

This concern runs parallel to what Morgan says [11]: "21st Century employers not only want workers to be efficient; they must also exhibit flexibility" (p. 29). The tension between efficiency and flexibility (here called *improvisation* but pointing to improvised coordination) can be studied in the human-machine managerial context. Similar games can be designed for stimulating students' interests in developing feedback mechanisms for future human-machine communication. They can enhance our understanding of the human dimension of self-repair and correction and incorporate communication concerns in parallel with other system goals.

References

1. Freire, P.: Pedagogy of the Oppressed. Continuum International Publishing Group (2000)
2. Garris, R., Ahlers, R., Driskell, J.E.: Games, motivation, and learning: a research and practice model. Simul. Gaming **33**(4), 441–467 (2002)
3. Buckley, P., Doyle, E.: Gamification and student motivation. Interact. Learn. Environ. **24**(6), 1162–1175 (2016)
4. Su, C.: The effects of students' motivation, cognitive load and learning anxiety in gamification software engineering education: a structural equation modeling study. Multimed. Tools Appl. **75**, 10013–10036 (2016)
5. Tan Ai Lin, D., Ganapathy, M., Kaur, M.: Kahoot! it: gamification in higher education. Pertanika J. Soc. Sci. Hum. **26**(1), 565–582 (2018)
6. Sera, L.S., Wheeler, E.: Game on: the gamification of the pharmacy classroom. Curr. Pharmacy Teach. Learn. **9**, 155–159 (2017). https://doi.org/10.1016/j.cptl.2016.08.046
7. Lederman, L., Ruben, B.: Systematic assessment of communication games and simulations: an applied framework. Commun. Educ. **33**(2), 152–159 (1984)
8. Miller, K.: Organizational communication: Approaches and processes, 7th edn. Cengage Learning, Stamford (2015)
9. Wang, H., Sun, C.: Game reward systems: Gaming experiences and social meanings. In: DiGRA 2011 CONFERENCE: Think Design Play, vol. 6, pp. 1–15 (2011)
10. Lindlof, T.R., Taylor, B.: Qualitative Communication Research Methods, 3rd edn. Sage, Thousand Oaks (2011)
11. Morgan, G.: Images of Organization. Sage, Thousand Oaks (2006)

Enhancing Social Ties Through Manual Player Matchmaking in Online Multiplayer Games

Md Riyadh[1(✉)], Ali Arya[1], Gerry Chan[1], and Masud Imran[2]

[1] Carleton School of Information Technology, Interactive Media Group, Carleton University,
Ottawa, Canada
{md.riyadh,ali.arya,gerry.chan}@carleton.ca
[2] Department of Software Engineering, Universiti Teknologi Malaysia, Johor Bahru, Malaysia
imasud2@graduate.utm.my

Abstract. Beyond skill and performance, there is a large social aspect to online multiplayer games that contributes to the overall gameplay experience. To complement this experience, player matchmaking techniques in those games have evolved from using only simple skill-based data to integrating multitude of different data such as social data, player personality etc. However, these techniques still lack sensitivity to this social aspect of multiplayer gaming. Modern player matchmaking techniques are dominated by automatic matchmaking algorithms which do not provide a way to the players to manually recommend one friend to another. We identify this as a limitation of the existing player matchmaking techniques which restricts players' ability to leverage their existing ties to enhance their gameplay experience, and perhaps, also deprives them of extending their social ties through online games. We propose that the ability to perform such manual recommendation within online multiplayer games can strengthen the social aspect of online gaming and enhance the overall gameplay experience.

Keywords: Player matchmaking · Recommender system · Online games · Multiplayer games · Social aspect of multiplayer games · Player engagement

1 Introduction

With the rising popularity of multiplayer online games, game developers encounter new challenges. World-renowned games like FIFA are sold million-fold [1] and therefore they must develop and maintain online services for numerous of players attempting to simultaneously. One of these services is player matchmaking, which, typically helps players to find other players who suit their skill level in order to play an enjoyable game [2]. With increasing number of players who are coming from diverse backgrounds, and increasing complexity of the modern online games, effective player matchmaking remains an open challenge.

Due to massive rise in the popularity of online games and the advancement in data collection, storage and analytics capacity, large amounts of data can be recorded during each online multiplayer match. This data provides insights into how players perform in

© Springer Nature Switzerland AG 2020
C. Stephanidis et al. (Eds.): HCII 2020, LNCS 12425, pp. 708–729, 2020.
https://doi.org/10.1007/978-3-030-60128-7_52

different situations and therefore classify the player in terms of skill level and playing style. Researchers have shown that is possible to make use of this data to enhance player matchmaking and eventually increase the player's level of engagement with the game.

Beyond skill and game performance, there is a still large social aspect to multiplayer online games that contributes to overall gameplay experience. Relatively recently, some research has shed light on how we may be able to better design player matchmaking techniques by incorporating personal and social attributes of the users. However, there has been lack of research that focused on leveraging the existing social ties in order to perform player matchmaking and extend the existing social ties through multiplayer gaming.

In early computer games, a player's skill was almost the only influence on the overall gameplay experience. A match played by people with comparable skill is relatively more even and fun, resulting in higher engagement with the game. As a result, a common approach for player matchmaking is leveraging skill ranking systems to find similar skilled players for a match. In course of time, games became more diverse and complex along with the people playing them. For matchmaking purposes, it was no longer possible only to distinguish player by skill. Instead, a variety of other factors became important in matchmaking, such as game-structure [3], individual player's playing behavior (e.g. some players might be highly engaged with their teammates, while others focus solely on their own performance) [4]. However, existing player matchmaking techniques still lack sensitivity to the social aspect of multiplayer gaming. Particularly, a factor that is often neglected in the player matchmaking is playing with someone the users already know and with someone who exists within the player's social circle (i.e. friend of friend). Researchers have repeatedly suggested the impact of existing social ties in multiplayer games. For instance, researchers have found that playing against a friend provide greater engagement and physiological arousal compared to playing against a stranger [5]. Additionally, playing with friends cooperatively is shown to lead to improved team and individual performance [6]. Despite these findings, most current studies on player matchmaking techniques does not emphasize on leveraging people's existing social ties through online gaming.

In order to better understand the player matchmaking technique, which is a form of recommender system, it is important to introduce recommender system in general. For this reason, in the next section, we begin our literature review with studies related to recommendation techniques in general. After that, we review the existing player matchmaking techniques along with an introduction to why matchmaking is important in online multiplayer games. We emphasize on the social aspect of the player matchmaking, which is the primary subject of this research. Section 3 includes research gaps we have identified in the literature. In the subsequent section, we discuss our proposed technique for player matchmaking in online multiplayer games and describe our study design in detail including evaluation criteria, data collection and analysis plans. Section 5 includes discussion on our overall study and what results we expect from our proposed study. Section 6 mentions the limitations of the proposed study. In section 7, we include some closing remarks.

2   Literature Review

2.1   Literature Review Approach

In order to find the publications related to recommendation techniques in general and player matchmaking in online multiplayer games, we started our search in Google Scholar [7], using keywords, such as, recommender system, people recommender system, player matchmaking in multiplayer games, player engagement in multiplayer games, social aspect of player matchmaking, and personal attributes in player matchmaking. The reason why we chose Google Scholar over other similar alternatives (e.g. Microsoft Academic [8]) is that, based on our experience, Google Scholar provided more relevant results. We employed a snowball method [9] where we referred to the bibliography of each paper that we initially collected to enhance our sample. Apart from the relevancy of topic, we primarily focused on peer reviewed publication as one of our inclusion criteria. We attempted to emphasize the studies that claim that their research generalizes to many games, at least of the same genre. Publications that were not cited were excluded from the review.

2.2   Recommender Systems

Recommender Systems are computer algorithms that provide suggestions for items that are presumably of interest to a particular user [10]. These suggestions can come in different forms, typically involving various decision-making processes, such as products to buy or movies to watch. In the most basic terms, personalized recommendations are list of ranked items. This ranking refers to the most suitable products or services for a particular user. In general, recommender systems are based on two broad techniques: content filtering agents and collaborative filtering. **Content-based** approach typically matches the characteristics of the user profile data (e.g. user demographic, preference, history) against the attributes of the items or products, while the basic implementation of this **collaborative filtering** suggests items to the active user based on items that other users with similar taste liked in the past [11].

The advent of social media introduced online services and products where the underlying relationships between users is the primary component [12]. The rapid development within these networks accelerates the advancement of a special category of recommender system named **people recommender system**. In one of the first studies that discussed the people recommender systems in details differentiated people recommender systems from systems that recommend items to people due to their relevancy to factors such as, privacy, trust, reputation, and interpersonal attraction, which typically have negligible influence in item recommendation [13].

In recent decades, different types of social networks have emerged where people recommender systems play a significant role. In regular social networks, users need to explicitly connect to each other (i.e. symmetric and explicit network), for example by sending and accepting invitations (e.g. Facebook) or by following other users (i.e. asymmetric network, e.g. Twitter). In some other networks, for instance, in YouTube, users can form an implicit network by subscribing to the same channel but without explicitly connecting with each other. People recommender systems vary widely based on the type of basic human relationships: familiar people, interesting people, and similar people [12]. Recommendation of familiar people aims at discovering people likely to be already known to each other. This type of recommender system is most widely seen on 'regular' networks. As the nature of an interest relationship is typically unidirectional, interesting people recommendation is primarily applicable for asymmetric networks such as Twitter. On the other hand, similar people recommender system typically aims to connect strangers with a shared interest. Similar people recommendation is especially common in ad-hoc networks. For instance, recommendation of people with similar interests at a conference [14]. Many factors can signal similarity, such as, age, historical activities, or personality.

People recommender systems typically benefit from considering social interaction data in the recommendation model. One study compared the effectiveness of content-based, social and hybrid recommendation algorithms in predicting co-authorship among biomedical scientists. They found that integrating social network information in expert recommendations outperform a purely expertise-based approach [1]. Social behavior data can also indicate 'social trust', which, if integrated in people recommender systems, outperforms social graph based algorithms (such as Friends-Of-A-Friend) [15]. Another study demonstrates that people recommender systems that combine interpersonal relationships and personality similarities of conference participants outperform other state-of-the-art methods, and specifically helps mitigate the 'cold start' problem [16].

2.3   Player Matchmaking in Multiplayer Online Games

To understand player matchmaking in multiplayer online games, we need to understand why matchmaking is important in such games. One of the primary reasons for player matchmaking is to help players find an appropriate challenge, primarily based on the skill and preference of the players, in order to ensure optimum enjoyment and letting players reach the flow state. Consequently, it increases players' engagement with the game, which in turns influences them to buy games from the same developers. Player matchmaking also saves time since with automatic matchmaking, players no longer need to manually go through the list of available players (or matches where other players are waiting more players to join) to find a suitable match. In addition, matchmaking could also bring players together, who, for example share some common interest. If the game allows extensive social interactions between players, this can also positively influence their level of engagement with the game. In the next sections, we describe player engagement, and social context of online gaming and player matchmaking in further details.

Player Engagement. Engagement is one dimension of the experience of playing games [17]. Some researchers define it as a measurement of quality of the experience of playing a video game [18]. A popular concept that is often considered synonymous with player engagement is the "flow model" [19] (Fig. 1). The "flow" is described as the combined effect of challenge a game offer to the players and the gaming skill players bring to the table. In other words, the challenge players' face in a game must align with their skills. If the challenge is negligible compared to player skill, then the player may get bored, whereas, if the challenge surpasses player skill, then it will make the player anxious.

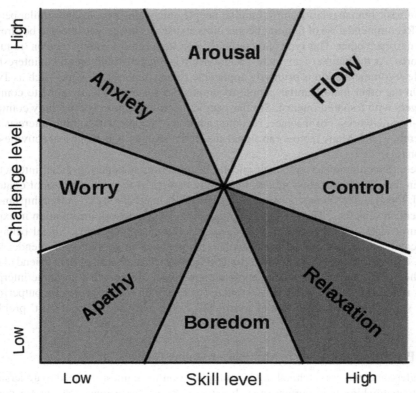

Fig. 1. Model of the Flow zone in relation to challenge and skill level adapted from Csíkszent-mihályi [21].

In the context of player engagement in a single player scenario, the term "balance" refers to how well designed the game is in terms of game mechanics and challenges in order to provide best possible gameplay experience to the players. Researchers found that game balance is strongly correlated with user satisfaction [20]. In order to balance a game for a single player scenario, it may be sufficient to offer different difficulty levels such as, beginner, intermediate and difficult.

However, when it comes to online multiplayer, adjusting the challenge through balance becomes more complicated. The is because every player is unique in their skills and playing behavior, and they expect a different challenge to satisfy themselves [17]. Games that involve the concept of team-play (i.e. as opposed to, for example, two players playing head-to-head) may make this balancing even more complicated, as each player within each unique team is also has unique characteristics. Therefore, in order to enhance the player engagement of online multiplayer games, in addition to game-play balance, it is important to properly match the players and teams in a way that would allow each player to reach the flow state. In multiplayer setting, the difference between the player skills or combined playing abilities is a major factor for balancing the chances of winning for each team or player. Some other important factors in the player engagement include goals, motivation and feedback [22] which are tightly related with each other. The game must have a clearly defined and reachable goal in order to motivate the player to play. In addition, for consistent motivation, players need feedback about their progress towards reach a goal (e.g. score in a game).

Another concept that is often related to player engagement is immersion, which separates the user from the real world by replacing it with a highly realistic simulation [23]. Game developers attempt to create a new world within the game that can potentially immerse the player, with superior graphics, sound or even with "Virtual Reality" apparatus. The aim is to encourage players live in the virtual reality during the game play, with loosening grip of the real surrounding around them. An immersive experience has the capability to encourage player to continue playing a game. Thus, it is one of the important factors of player engagement.

To conclude, player engagement can be described with diverse features such as balance between skill and challenge (i.e. flow model), goal and motivation in the game play, and the ability of the games to immerse the players within the game.

Social Aspect of Gaming. A widely accepted attribute of humans is that we need to feel close with others. Belongingness hypothesis claim that "human beings have a pervasive drive to form and maintain at least a minimum quantity of lasting, positive, and significant personal relationships" [24]. Playing multiplayer games is a potential way to fulfill an individual's need of belongingness. Playing together enables social interactions between players, which contributes to their sense of belonging [25]. Research has shown that multiplayer games can contribute to initiating, enhancing, and maintaining relationships with others [26]. In addition, the need to belong is also considered an essential motivator for player engagement [27].

Researchers have found that social play, compared to play against a computer, causes more engagement and physiological arousal [5]. Multiplayer games can allow creating new and lasting friendships with others and strengthening existing social connections [28]. Researchers also found that playing against a friend can cause greater engagement and physiological arousal compared to playing against a stranger [5]. Another study found that social interaction between players during gameplay positively impacts the player's experience of "flow" [29]. They conclude that while social interaction may not increase flow itself, but it can increase the perceived flow level of players.

Another research suggests that cooperative play with humans can contribute to increased post-play cooperative behavior relative to competitive play [30]. Researchers also found that when playing an online collaborative multiplayer game with their friends, individuals are typically more active in the game compared to when teamed up with strangers [31]. Interestingly though, they also found that this increased activity does not lead to an improvement in players' performance. Their results suggest that playing with friends is beneficial to low skill players, while it negatively affects performance of high skill players. Contrary to this finding, another study found that playing with friends in cooperative games can generally lead to improved team and individual performance [6].

Matchmaking Techniques in Games. A specific application of people recommender system is player matchmaking in games, particularly, in online multiplayer games. These recommender systems typically involve a process of connecting players online so that they can play together with optimum enjoyment [16]. Popular games like FIFA, Battlefield developed automatic matchmaking techniques, which typically offer player matchmaking according to the skill level. Matchmaking in games has become increasingly important in recent years with the exponential increase in number of players, along with the higher complexity of the games, as well as the diversity of players [32]. A body of new research has emerged that focuses exclusively on player matchmaking and goes beyond skill based matchmaking (e.g. using gamers personal attributes [32]). Below we describe several techniques exist today in player matchmaking in online multiplayer games.

Skill-Based Matchmaking. Early player matchmaking tools primarily used skill based ranking systems to find player with similar skills for a match. Arpad Elo developed the first rating system using a skill level with the goal to rate chess players [33]. It updates players' ratings based on the outcome of a match - the winner gains exactly as many skill points as the loser loses. That gain or loss is calculated by the difference between the initial ratings of both players. One thing to note is that if a higher ranked player wins, s/he gains a small portion of the loser's skill points. On the contrary, if the lower ranked player wins, the number of transferred skill points is noticeably higher. In addition, the lower ranked player will gain some points even in the case of draw. Thus, the lower ranked player reasonably gets a higher reward for good performance against a higher ranked player.

Elo rating or the variation of it are not only used in chess but also in a large number of games (e.g. League of Legends [34]). Consequently, these games also leverage the skill to perform the player matchmaking. However, the performance of such matchmaking systems are sometimes criticized as they do not perform well for a large number of players possessing similar skill [2]. To overcome these limitations of these traditional skill-based matchmaking systems, Microsoft developed a new ranking system called TrueSkill [35]. TrueSkill leverages the Bayesian inference technique and conveys the skill in two values: mean and standard deviation, instead of using only a single skill value for every player. The primary value of TrueSkill over traditional skill ranking systems is the additional second update performed on the standard deviations of both players. The more matches a player finishes, the smaller their standard deviations gets, which provides more certainty about a player's true skill.

Game-Structure Sensitive Matchmaking. Due to the sheer diversity of modern computer games and the players who play these games, it has become increasingly difficult to maintain balanced games only based on the skill levels of the players. This is primarily influenced by the fact that modern games introduced variety of ways to dictate the result of a game. For instance, in one of the game modes in Battlefield 4 [36], players can reduce opponents' ticket by either killing opponent game characters or capturing and holding the majority of the control points. Traditional skill rating systems cannot distinguish between these two and hence they also fail to maintain balance in their matchmaking outcome. As a result, for better matchmaking, it is important to consider different structures and modes of the game in addition to player skill. To address this, game developers developed game-structure sensitive matchmaking systems, which primarily involve player clustering and match outcome prediction [17].

Player clustering is about finding a combination of players who can play together and form a perfect team. To achieve this, it is important to have information about different player characteristics, including their skill. In addition, the matchmaking system also needs to determine a feasible opponent team for each team to offer an enjoyable match. The games that offer two players playing head-to-head without the requirement of forming teams does not need to apply the team aspect of the player clustering technique.

Advanced match outcome predictive algorithms take several factors such as player metrics and characteristics into consideration in order to achieve better matchmaking results. In such matchmaking mechanisms, the algorithms may vary widely between games and for different game structures and modes within the game. Due to availability of large datasets regarding games outcomes and player's gameplay behaviors, and enormous computing power, machine learning algorithms can now better predict the outcome of matches in order to find the best suiting match for players.

To summarize, traditional matchmaking systems almost entirely rely on skill ranking systems. Though they have improved over the course of time, such as Microsoft's TrueSkill system, they still largely ignore individual game characteristics. Researchers have shown that considering game-structure in addition to skill can provide better accuracies in predicting match outcomes.

Beyond Skill and Game Structure. Beyond skill and game structure, social aspect of gaming is considered to be an important factor in player enjoyment [37]. Research indicates that, compared to playing against a virtual co-player (i.e. online multiplayer games), a co-located co-player significantly adds to the game enjoyment [37]. One of the reasons for this is that co-location accommodates for more opportunity for social interactions.

While player matchmaking techniques that considers social relationship is widely regarded for its contribution to game enjoyment, they also have significant impact on long term player retention. One study demonstrated that high level of social interactions among exergame players promotes player retention [38].

Evidence shows that personal attributes in addition to skill based player matching can connect gamers in more meaningful ways by considering opportunities for social interactions [32]. Even in adversarial multiplayer games, player matchmaking that considers player behavior and personal preferences in addition to skill balancing adds significantly to the game enjoyment [16]. Integrating gamers' self-described attributes along with other factors in player matchmaking process can also reduce occurrences of perceived bad behavior in online multiplayer games [4].

In addition to player matchmaking, gaming experience can also benefit from providing gaming scenario in accordance with gamers' personality traits. While two players with cooperative personality traits would enjoy playing in cooperative scenario, players with competitive personality traits would enjoy playing in the opposite scenario [39]. Another study suggests that individuals who performs better (longer time spent playing) in multiplayer exergames feels more autonomous and greater enjoyment, which motivates them continue playing in future [40]. Some researchers argue that social exergaming with proper player matchmaking has the potential to help children and adolescents achieve many physiological and psychosocial outcomes [41]. For instance, cooperative play may influence weight loss specifically in overweight/obese adolescents. On the contrary, competitive exergaming, which typically promotes short-term physiological arousal, may also lead to aggression.

A number of services have recently emerged that aim to connect players based on factors other than skill and game structure, such as play style, location, and interests. This has potential for gameplay to facilitate social connectedness and positively impact wellbeing. Horton et al. determined eight such services that have strong social motivation (Table 1) [32]:

Table 1. Matchmaking features of services reviewed by Horton et al. [32] of which 2 are strongly socially motivational (denoted in **bold** text).

Service	Matchmaking feature				
	Skill	Interest	Location	Play Style	Game
Overdog		X			
Leaping Tiger			X		X
Gamerlink	X		X	X	X
Evolve					X
Player Finder			X	X	X
Game Findr			X	X	X
Nearby Gamers			X		
Gamer Seeking Gamer			X	X	X

Player matchmaking in online multiplayer games has come a long way from only relying on skills to considering complex social interactions and personality traits. People recommender system in general has seen significant advancement in recent years, especially due to the prevalence of social media networks and availability of ubiquitous internet connectivity. Researchers have focused on advancing people recommendation techniques for different specific domains of application. As discussed earlier, people recommender systems often leverage established item recommendation techniques. Different domains of people recommender systems such as player matchmaking are yet to investigate people recommender techniques that already exist within other application domains. For instance, there has been no study on how 'serendipitous recommendation' would impact player matchmaking in different gaming scenarios, or how 'cold start' problem can arise and can be addressed in multiplayer online games. There is also a remarkable opportunity to further investigate how 'relationship types' (i.e. familiar, interesting, similar) influence the outcome of player matchmaking in online games. In the next chapter, we discuss few techniques that are worth exploring in player matchmaking for online multiplayer games.

3   Research Gaps

Based on the literature reviewed, we suggest that the following techniques should be investigated in detail in the context of player matchmaking in online multiplayer gaming, which provides a way to leverage the players' existing social connections and attributes:

3.1   Existing Social Interaction Data

Researchers suggest that leveraging existing social interaction is valuable for people recommender systems in regular networks such as social media, and in ad-hoc networks such as academic conferences [42, 43]. However, there is no comprehensive study that investigated the impact of considering interaction metrics from the existing social media sites in player matchmaking for online multiplayer games.

3.2   Existing Personal Attributes and Preferences Data

People recommender systems in various domains have successfully incorporated user preference data from users' existing social networks in order to provide enhanced recommendations [15, 44]. While some player matchmaking techniques utilize personal attributes shared by users exclusively for particular games [32], it is worth investigating how 'preference/attribute' data from users' existing social network can be effectively leveraged to further enhance the player recommendations. It is also worth investigating how accounting for negative user preference in addition to positive user preference can influence the player matchmaking since some research demonstrate that it has the potential to reduce the risk of repeated rejection in other reciprocal social networks [45]. In addition, collaborative filtering methods has been successfully extended for people recommenders in social media by deriving similarity based on similar 'preference' for the users they interact with, or having similar 'attractiveness' for the users who contact them [46]. We suggest this technique should be investigated for player matchmaking as well.

3.3   Manual Recommendation

Research on player matchmaking for online multiplayer games typically focuses on computer generated recommendations based on a variety of factors such as skill, latency, and player attributes etc. Based on our literature review, we did not find any research that studied user initiated manual recommendation for player matchmaking. Manual recommendation is a common phenomenon in everyday life. We rely on manual recommendation, typically from the people we are familiar with, for things like movies, books to employee referrals etc.

Our envisioned manual people recommendation technique in player matchmaking involves at least three parties: the one who sends the recommendation (i.e. recommender), the one who receives the recommendation (i.e. target user), and the one who is being recommended (i.e. recommended user). We also specify that the recommender is the intermediary who is known to both target user and recommended user, and recommended user and target user may or may not be known to each other prior to recommendation but they at least have mutual social connection (i.e. the recommender), and hence they are ought to be part of each other's extended social network. For the case of online multiplayer games, we can consider those players with whom a particular player has played with before, and made a minimum social connection with (e.g. played repeatedly or added the players to user's own social network within the gaming platform) as part of the player's social circle. This consideration is based on the findings by prior studies that multiplayer games can contribute to initiating, enhancing, and maintaining social relationships with others [26].

As discussed in the literature review, researchers found that playing against a person within person's existing social circle can be more engaging and fun compared to playing against a stranger [5]. Our envisioned manual recommendation technique may provide a way to the gamers to leverage their existing social circle in order to find more players within their extended network (e.g. friend of a friend) to play with. It is therefore worth investigating the potential of user initiated manual recommendation in player matchmaking.

4 Study Design

4.1 Proposed Technique

We propose that manual recommendation can be a potential way to leverage users' existing social circle in player matchmaking in online multiplayer games, which, we believe, would eventually make the play more engaging and fun.

As discussed in the previous section, our proposed manual player recommendation involves at least three parties: the one who sends the recommendation, the one who receives the recommendation, and the one who is being recommended. The recommender is known to both target and recommended user, and recommended user and target user may or may not be known to each other prior to the recommendation but they must share a mutual social connection (i.e. the recommender), and hence they are included within each other's extended social network (Fig. 2).

In our proposed recommender system, when a player initiates a manual recommendation, both recommended and target player will be notified about the recommendation through the user interface of the relevant game. We envision that the game UI will accommodate a new list (e.g. Recommended Player or Recommended by Friends) where the recommended players will be visible (Fig. 3). In that list, both the target and the recommended user will be able to see who initiated the recommendation process. In general, the game UI should provide a way to delete the recommendation if users like; in addition, there should also be a way to move the recommended player to the "friends" list so that the "Recommended Player" list can be managed in case there is a large number of recommendation. Ideally, when a recommendation is successful (i.e. the target user and the recommended user played a game together), the game UI should prompt the user to add the recommended / target user to the "friends" list. Adding to "friends" list may follow the existing "friends" acceptance mechanism of the game (i.e. both parties need to accept the friendship request etc.).

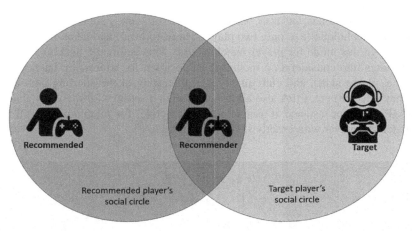

Fig. 2. Two circles depicting target and recommended user's social circle (i.e. existing friends in a gaming platform) and their mutual connection (the recommender).

Fig. 3. An example "Recommended by Friends" list.

It is important to note that there are many genres of games (e.g. action, adventure, strategy, role-playing, sports) and each genre provides different gameplay experience. Games within the same genre can also provide varying gameplay experience. While we would like to generalize our study findings to all kinds of online multiplayer games, it would be difficult to do so by only evaluating the envisioned system with only one game. For this study, we plan to evaluate our proposed solution (i.e. manual recommendation for player matchmaking) in FIFA 2020 by Electronics Arts [47], which falls under the genre of sports game. The primary reason for choosing this game is because the game is one of the most popular online multiplayer games within its category [1]. This game provides many different play modes including team play, one to one play, cooperative and competitive play. For our study, we decided to use one-to-one competitive play as it is one of the popular modes; and also, because this is a sufficiently simple mode to evaluate our proposed technique (e.g. only two players, head-to-head) and there is an automatic counterpart in this mode for player matchmaking. This automatic matchmaking takes several things into consideration including geolocation for addressing latency, player rating (i.e. player skill), and club quality (i.e. the rating of the sporting club that the player has selected) etc. FIFA also allows customizing settings for these matchmaking options (Fig. 4). For instance, if user selects "Restrictive" for "club quality", FIFA will only match the player with exactly same club quality [48].

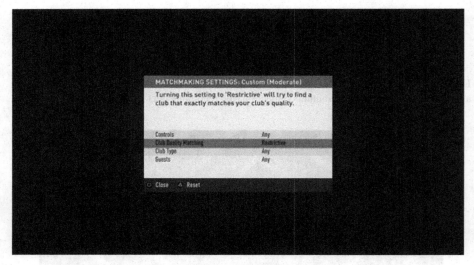

Fig. 4. FIFA matchmaking settings.

FIFA also provides an option to play with friends in this mode instead of being matched with a stranger (Fig. 5). The technique to add friends differ by platforms (e.g. PC, Xbox) [1]. In our evaluation, we are describing the PC mode, in which, FIFA pulls the list of friends from the user's Origin account (i.e. Origin is a digital platform offered by Electronic Arts for gamers that provides variety of services such as digital purchase and adding friends to play with online [49]). Users can select a friend from this list to play an online match.

Since we are evaluating our proposed technique in a specific genre, within a specific game, and a specific game mode, we would like to limit our proposed technique to the following hypothesis:

H1: In one-to-one competitive online sports game, using user initiated manual recommendation for player matchmaking can provide the same or more engaging and fun overall game play experience to the players compared to the typical automatic recommendations which are primarily based on player skill.

Fig. 5. Playing FIFA with friends.

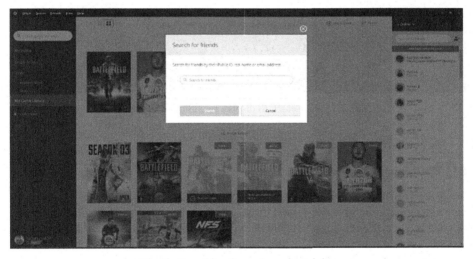

Fig. 6. Searching for a player in Origin.

4.2   System Design

It is important to define how we used manual recommendation for player matchmaking in our specific scenario. The ideal case for our envisioned manual recommendation scenario for FIFA could look like this: a user (i.e. recommender) can select any player (i.e. recommended user) from their friend list (i.e. FIFA or Origin friend list (Fig. 6)) and recommend that player to any other player (i.e. target user) within his/her "friend" list. In addition to the existing friend list, there will be a new list named "Recommended

Players", where all the recommended players will be populated. Once the above recommendation process is done, both the target and recommended users will see each in their "Recommended Players" list by default. They may choose to delete the recommendation if they like. Similar to the existing friend list, users can select any of the available recommended players to start playing an online match.

In our initial study, we plan to present this manual recommendation process to the participants with visual mocks (e.g. Fig. 7) and textual description.

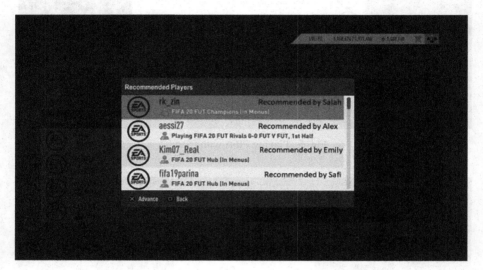

Fig. 7. Visual mock to display recommended players.

4.3   Evaluation Criteria

Our overall objective is to determine whether players have comparable game play experience in online competitive one-to-one FIFA matches when they play with players recommended by their friends (e.g. friends within the gaming network such as FIFA's gaming network) versus when they play with strangers suggested by FIFA's automatic recommendation engine. This can be measured in several ways. In this study, we primarily aim to understand participants' subjective impression of our envisioned manual recommendation process for FIFA compared to the automatic one. This subjective impression will be elicited from the participants' responses in our survey described in Appendix B.

4.4   Data Collection and Analysis Plan

Upon receiving ethical clearance, we will conduct a study for initial evaluation for our hypothesis. In order to conduct the study, we will recruit a minimum of 30 participants who have prior experience with multiplayer FIFA. The session will begin with a short pre-study questionnaire regarding demographics of the participants (see Appendix A).

These participants will then be briefed on our envisioned manual recommendation process for the particular game mode in FIFA. For better representation of the idea, they will be presented with visual mocks along with textual description of the process. They will be asked to take few minutes to imagine playing FIFA using both recommendation techniques. After the introduction to the process, they will be given a survey to complete. The survey primarily aims to understand participants' impression of playing with "recommended players" in contrast with stranger suggested by FIFA's automatic recommendation. The survey consists of a combination of Likert-scale, ordering task, and open-ended questions (Appendix B).

There are three Likert scale questions in the survey, one to understand how the participants enjoy playing with strangers suggested by FIFA automatic recommendation, and the other to understand how the participants would enjoy playing with a player recommended by their existing friends. From the results, we will generate descriptive statistics and frequency histograms to examine the normality of the data. Based on skewness and kurtosis, we will decide on the type of test. To analyze these two questions, based on the shape of the distribution, we will select the appropriate type of statistical test. If the distributions look normal, we will use parametric tests (e.g.: t-test), however, if the distributions are skewed, then we will use non-parametric tests (e.g.: Wilcoxon Signed-Rank test). In this test, the type of recommendation (manual vs. automatic) is the only independent variable while the players' self-reported estimated enjoyment level is the dependent variable.

The third Likert scale question asks the participants to compare their enjoyment level of playing FIFA with players recommended by friends (using the manual player recommendation technique as described in the wireframes) compared to playing with strangers automatically matched by FIFA. Responses for this question will be analyzed with numeric counting and visual graphs. We expect that this third question would provide more insight to users' response to the first two questions and vice versa, as this question somewhat combines the first two questions.

Additionally, we will also ask the participants to share their order of preference regarding how they like to play multiplayer FIFA. In addition to playing using our proposed recommender system and the automatic player matchmaking, we will also add the option for "Playing with friends". This is to encourage the participants to think about their multiplayer FIFA experience holistically while they share their preference instead of confining them to the two primary categories we are dealing with in this study.

We also plan to encourage participants to share if they have any additional thoughts about our proposed technique. We will rely on "Thematic Coding" to identify common patterns in the responses to this part of the survey.

5 Discussion

In this paper, we emphasized on the social aspect of player matchmaking in online multiplayer games. Based on our literature review, we found that there is an opportunity to experiment with manually recommending players to friends within a gaming network as a player matchmaking technique, which has a strong social aspect attached to it as in its core, it encourages leveraging one's social connection in order to have an enjoyable online multiplayer gaming experience. We laid out a detailed a study design to understand how the manual player matchmaking maybe received by the players of a popular online soccer game by using participants' self-reported preference data.

The proposal study will evaluate our hypothesis H1 that "*in one-to-one competitive online sports game, using user initiated manual recommendation for player matchmaking can provide the same or more engaging and fun game play experience to the players compared to the typical automatic recommendations which are primarily based on player skill*". We expect the study to reveal many interesting information in addition to evaluating the hypothesis. Based on our experience with player matchmaking techniques that exist on online multiplayer games and general conversation about the proposed idea of manual player recommendation technique within our research group (several of our researchers play online multiplayer games), we expect the following four outcomes from our proposed study:

(1) The idea of manual player matchmaking will be generally well received within the FIFA players (i.e. study participants), especially because we think that the majority of the participants will express preference for playing with friends of friends (using proposed manual player recommendation technique) over playing with automatically matched strangers. Such finding will validate our hypothesis.

(2) Manual recommendation process itself may become a bottleneck in implementing the technique, as the players may not want to spend time in recommending players; instead they may just go for the automatic matchmaking to save time.

(3) Lack of competitiveness in manually recommended player will not be found to be a major theme. We believe this will indicate the impact of "social" aspect of gaming, as we described in our literature section, which perhaps makes the overall gameplay experience more fun than being in a very competitive gaming scenario with strangers.

(4) Manual player recommendation will enhance players' social circle as it may be regarded by the participants as an effective way for them to strengthen their social circle and existing friendship. Such finding will enable us to argue that the manual player recommendation is superior from automatic player matchmaking since the later provides little opportunity to enhance players' social circle and the sense of belongingness.

Due to the diverse genre of online games and sheer difference of game play experience among those genres, we do not yet anticipate that the result of this proposed study to be generalized to all the gaming genres. However, we do expect that conducting similar studies across different gaming genres would provide us with a clearer idea about the acceptance and efficacy of manual player recommendation among online multiplayer players of different games.

6   Limitation of the Study

We acknowledge the fact that the findings from our proposed study will needed to be established further by incorporating objective data from user study using a functional manual player recommender system in a real game. This objective data can then be correlated with the self-reported participant data after they get a chance to experience playing with manually recommended players. In addition, as mentioned above, we admit that the result of the proposed study cannot be generalized to all gaming genre. Our study design is based on a popular soccer game. As a result, we only anticipate that our results would be relevant for similar sports game.

7 Conclusions

Beyond skill and latency, player matchmaking in online multiplayer games also has a social aspect. Our literature review suggests that online player matchmaking can benefit from manual player recommendation i.e. player can recommend one of their friends in a gaming network to another friend as a potential player to play with. We proposed a detailed study plan to understand the efficacy of such manual player matchmaking in terms of game play enjoyment and enhancing the social aspect of online multiplayer games. We have also discussed potential results we may receive from our proposed study. Along with the proposed study, in the future we would like to conduct similar studies with functional manual player recommender system involving actual game play and by collecting and analyzing both subjective and objective data.

Appendices

Appendix A

Pre-test Questionnaire

1. Age: _____ years old.
2. Gender:

    - Male
    - Female
    - Prefer not to say

3. How do you typically play?

    - Alone
    - With co-located friends
    - With friends online
    - With strangers online

4. What type(s) of video games do you play? (Select all that apply)

☐Action
☐Adventure
☐Role-playing
☐Puzzles
☐Simulations
☐Strategy
☐Sports
☐Board/card game

5. Please list a few of your favourite video games:

   i. _____

   ii. _____

   iii. _____

6. On average, how much time do you spend playing video games?
_____ hours/week.

Appendix B

Survey Questionnaire

1. Automatic player matchmaking in FIFA makes the game more enjoyable

Strongly disagree	Disagree	Neutral	Agree	Strongly agree
○	○	○	○	○

2. It would be enjoyable to play FIFA with players recommended by friends (using the manual player recommendation technique as described in the wireframes)

Strongly disagree	Disagree	Neutral	Agree	Strongly agree
○	○	○	○	○

3. It would be more enjoyable to play FIFA with players recommended by friends (using the manual player recommendation technique as described in the wireframes) compared to playing with strangers automatically matched by FIFA

Strongly disagree	Disagree	Neutral	Agree	Strongly agree
○	○	○	○	○

4. Please rank the following ways of playing multiplayer FIFA in order of your preference. (Indicate the order of preference by using 1, 2, and 3 for each of the following options, where 1 = most preferred, and 3 = least preferred.)

- ___Playing with friends
- ___Playing with players recommended by your friends
- ___Playing with strangers automatically matched by FIFA

Please briefly explain your answer (e.g. why friends over automatic matchmaking?):

_____

_____

_____

_____

_____

5. Finally, please provide any thoughts or comments about manual player recommendation technique in FIFA that you have in the space below.

References

1. FIFA Series. https://en.wikipedia.org/wiki/FIFA_(video_game_series). Accessed 30 Nov 2019
2. Véron, M., Marin, O., Monnet, S.: Matchmaking in multi-player on-line games: studying user traces to improve the user experience (2014). https://doi.org/10.1145/2578260.2578265
3. Myślak, M., Deja, D.: Developing game-structure sensitive matchmaking system for massive-multiplayer online games. In: Aiello, L.M., McFarland, D. (eds.) SocInfo 2014. LNCS, vol. 8852, pp. 200–208. Springer, Cham (2015). https://doi.org/10.1007/978-3-319-15168-7_25
4. Riegelsberger, J., Counts, S., Farnham, S.D., Philips, B.C.: Personality matters: incorporating detailed user attributes and preferences into the matchmaking process. In: Proceedings of the Annual Hawaii International Conference on System Sciences (2007)
5. Ravaja, N., Saari, T., Turpeinen, M., et al.: Spatial Presence and Emotions during Video Game Playing: Does It Matter with Whom You Play? https://doi.org/10.1162/pres.15.4.381

6. Mason, W., Clauset, A.: Friends FTW! Friendship, Collaboration and Competition in Halo: Reach. https://doi.org/10.1145/2441776.2441820
7. Google Scholar. https://scholar.google.ca/
8. Microsoft Academic. https://academic.microsoft.com/home
9. Wohlin, C.: Guidelines for Snowballing in Systematic Literature Studies and a Replication in Software Engineering (2014). https://doi.org/10.1145/2601248.2601268
10. Burke, R.: Hybrid web recommender systems. In: Brusilovsky, P., Kobsa, A., Nejdl, W. (eds.) The Adaptive Web. LNCS, vol. 4321, pp. 377–408. Springer, Heidelberg (2007). https://doi.org/10.1007/978-3-540-72079-9_12
11. Goldberg, D., Nichols, D., Oki, B.M., Terry, D.: Using collaborative filtering to weave an information tapestry. Commun. ACM **35**, 61–70 (1992)
12. Guy, I.: People recommendation on social media. In: Brusilovsky, P., He, D. (eds.) Social Information Access. LNCS, vol. 10100, pp. 570–623. Springer, Cham (2018). https://doi.org/10.1007/978-3-319-90092-6_15
13. Terveen, L., Mcdonald, D.W.: Social Matching: A Framework and Research Agenda (2005)
14. Chin, A., et al.: Using proximity and homophily to connect conference attendees in a mobile social network. In: 2012 32nd International Conference on Distributed Computing Systems Workshops. IEEE (2012)
15. Nepal, S., Paris, C., Pour, A., et al.: A social trust based friend recommender for online communities. In: Collaborative Computing: Networking, Applications and Worksharing (Collaboratecom)
16. Delalleau, O., Contal, E., Thibodeau-Laufer, E., et al.: Beyond skill rating: advanced matchmaking in ghost recon online. IEEE Trans. Comput. Intell. AI Games (2012). https://doi.org/10.1109/TCIAIG.2012.2188833
17. Münnich, S.: Advanced Matchmaking for Online First Person Shooter Games using Machine Learning (2015)
18. Mayes, D.K., Cotton, J.E.: Measuring engagement in video games: a questionnaire. Proc. Hum. Factors Ergon. Soc. Annu. Meet. **45**, 692–696 (2001). https://doi.org/10.1177/154193120104500704
19. Cziksentmihalyi, M.: Flow: The Psychology of Optimal Experience (1990)
20. Andrade, G., Ramalho, G., Gomes, A.S., Corruble, V.: Dynamic Game Balancing: an Evaluation of User Satisfaction (2006)
21. Wikipedia - Flow. https://en.wikipedia.org/wiki/Flow_(psychology). Accessed 3 Jun 2020
22. Prensky, M.: Digital game-based learning. Comput Entertain **1**, 21 (2003). https://doi.org/10.1145/950566.950596
23. Whitson, J., Eaket, C., Greenspan, B., et al.: Neo-immersion: awareness and engagement in gameplay (2008). https://doi.org/10.1145/1496984.1497028
24. Baumeister, R.F., Leary, M.R.: The Need to Belong: Desire for Interpersonal Attachments as a Fundamental Human Motivation (1995)
25. De Kort, Y.A.W., Ijsselsteijn, W.A.: People, places, and play: player experience in a socio-spatial context. Comput. Entertain. **6** (2008). https://doi.org/10.1145/1371216.1371221
26. Harris, J., Hancock, M., Scott, S.D.: Leveraging Asymmetries in Multiplayer Games: Investigating Design Elements of Interdependent Play. https://doi.org/10.1145/2967934.2968113
27. Przybylski, A.K., Rigby, C.S., Ryan, R.M.: A Motivational Model of Video Game Engagement Motivation and Video Games (2010). https://doi.org/10.1037/a0019440
28. Vella, K., Klarkowski, M., Johnson, D., et al.: The Social Context of Video Game Play: Challenges and Strategies. 4–8 (2016). https://doi.org/10.1145/2901790.2901823
29. Choi, D., Kim, J.: Why People Continue to Play Online Games: In Search of Critical Design Factors to Increase Customer Loyalty to Online Contents (2004)

30. Crouse Waddell, J., Peng, W.: Does it matter with whom you slay? The effects of competition, cooperation and relationship type among video game players. Commun. Arts Sci. Build. **429** (2014). https://doi.org/10.1016/j.chb.2014.06.017

31. Zeng, Y., Sapienza, A., Ferrara, E.: The Influence of Social Ties on Performance in Team-based Online Games

32. Horton, E., Johnson, D., Mitchell, J.: Finding and building connections: moving beyond skill- based matchmaking in videogames. In: Proceedings of the 28th Australian Conference on Computer-Human Interaction - OzCHI 2016 (2016)

33. Elo, A.E.: The rating of chess players, past and present. Arco Pub (1978)

34. Welcome to League of Legends. https://play.na.leagueoflegends.com/en_US. Accessed 1 Dec 2019

35. TrueSkill^{TM}: A Bayesian Skill Rating System - MIT Press books. https://ieeexplore.ieee.org/abstract/document/6287323. Accessed 1 Dec 2019

36. Battlefield 4 - Wikipedia. https://en.wikipedia.org/wiki/Battlefield_4. Accessed 1 Dec 2019

37. Gajadhar, B.J., de Kort, Y.A.W., IJsselsteijn, W.A.: Shared fun is doubled fun: player enjoyment as a function of social setting. In: Markopoulos, P., de Ruyter, B., IJsselsteijn, W., Rowland, D. (eds.) Fun and Games 2008. LNCS, vol. 5294, pp. 106–117. Springer, Heidelberg (2008). https://doi.org/10.1007/978-3-540-88322-7_11

38. Chan, G., Arya, A., Whitehead, A.: Keeping players engaged in exergames: a personality matchmaking approach gerry. In: Extended Abstracts of the 2018 CHI Conference on Human Factors in Computing Systems - CHI 2018 (2018)

39. Chan, G., Whitehead, A., Parush, A.: Dynamic player pairing: quantifying the effects of competitive versus cooperative attitudes. In: Korn, O., Lee, N. (eds.) Game Dynamics. LNCS, pp. 71–93. Springer, Cham (2017). https://doi.org/10.1007/978-3-319-53088-8_5

40. Limperos, A.M., Schmierbach, M.: Understanding the relationship between exergame play experiences, enjoyment, and intentions for continued play. Games Health J. (2016). https://doi.org/10.1089/g4h.2015.0042

41. Marker, A.M., Staiano, A.E.: Better together: outcomes of cooperation versus competition in social exergaming. Games Health J. (2015). https://doi.org/10.1089/g4h.2014.0066

42. Roth, M., Ben-David, A., Deutscher, D., et al.: Suggesting friends using the implicit social graph. In: Proceedings of the 16th ACM SIGKDD International Conference on Knowledge Discovery and Data Mining - KDD 2010 (2010)

43. Van Le, T., Nghia Truong, T., Vu Pham, T.: A content-based approach for user profile modeling and matching on social networks. In: Murty, M.N., He, X., Chillarige, R.R., Weng, P. (eds.) MIWAI 2014. LNCS (LNAI), vol. 8875, pp. 232–243. Springer, Cham (2014). https://doi.org/10.1007/978-3-319-13365-2_21

44. Lee, D.H., Brusilovsky, P., Schleyer, T.: Recommending collaborators using social features and MeSH terms. In: Proceedings of the ASIST Annual Meeting (2011)

45. Pizzato, L.A., Rej, T., Yacef, K., Koprinska, I., Kay, J.: Finding someone you will like and who won't reject you. In: Konstan, J.A., Conejo, R., Marzo, J.L., Oliver, N. (eds.) UMAP 2011. LNCS, vol. 6787, pp. 269–280. Springer, Heidelberg (2011). https://doi.org/10.1007/978-3-642-22362-4_23

46. Cai, X., et al.: Collaborative filtering for people to people recommendation in social networks. In: Li, J. (ed.) AI 2010. LNCS (LNAI), vol. 6464, pp. 476–485. Springer, Heidelberg (2010). https://doi.org/10.1007/978-3-642-17432-2_48

47. FIFA 2020. https://en.wikipedia.org/wiki/FIFA_20. Accessed 30 Nov 2019

48. FIFA Matchmaking. https://www.fifplay.com/fifa-19-online-seasons/. Accessed 30 Nov 2019

49. Origin. https://en.wikipedia.org/wiki/Origin_(service). Accessed 30 Nov 2019

A Simulation Game to Acquire Skills on Industry 4.0

Veronica Rossano(✉) 🆔, Rosa Lanzilotti 🆔, and Teresa Roselli 🆔

Department of Computer Science, University of Bari Aldo Moro, via Orabona 4, 70125 Bari, Italy
{veronica.rossano,rosa.lanzilotti,teresa.roselli}@uniba.it

Abstract. The education in Industry 4.0 is a key factor to improve product quality and its efficiency, be competitive, enhance safety, security and sustainability. In this context C-LAB project aims at developing a game-simulation framework able to generate game-based learning tools personalized to the specific business and role of users. The intended users are both company employees and students who will shortly enter into the working market. The first prototype of the game was evaluated by informatics students in terms of perceived usability. The data reveal that the game was appreciated by the students and some improvements were identified.

Keywords: Seirous games · Industry 4.0 · Usability · User study

1 Introduction

C-LAB 4.0 (Competences Lab for Industry 4.0) is a project funded by Apulia Region (Italy). Its final goal is to design and develop an innovative game-based learning solution, able to promote the enhancement of learning processes and to acquire specialized and transversal skills on Industry 4.0 topics, thus producing a significant impact on the construction of Knowledge Communities in the educational and professional field.

One of the main challenges of a knowledge-based digital society is that the using of smart technologies in everyday life requires increasingly digital skills both to work and communicate. The ICT skills are now one of the digital key competences to be able to retrieve, assess, store, produce, present and exchange information, and to communicate and participate in collaborative networks via the Internet [5, 11]. This is particularly true in the working contexts where people have to acquire digital skills essential to be in line with the new digital processes that companies adopt.

The Industry 4.0 is the current industrial revolution, which requires companies using automation of all their productive processes [6]. The adoption of artificial intelligence, cloud computing, internet of things, multi-agent systems, cyber-physical systems in companies of different industrial sectors requires new professional skills and competences, in the automotive sector, for example, this process has been started already ten years ago [4]. Activating educational paths in Industry 4.0 topics is an important requirement, since workers should transform the way they work. In addition, as game-based learning and

© Springer Nature Switzerland AG 2020
C. Stephanidis et al. (Eds.): HCII 2020, LNCS 12425, pp. 730–738, 2020.
https://doi.org/10.1007/978-3-030-60128-7_53

gamification have proven to be effective in supporting learning and teaching activities [1, 3, 9, 12–14, 16], C-LAB 4.0 project aims to develop a game-simulation framework that permits to create game-based learning tools personalized to the specific business and role of users, in order to acquire and enhance their skills related to Industry 4.0 [2]. By adopting the Knowledge Building Community model, the game-simulation framework manages company data and open data in the specific company sector, providing infrastructure and algorithms useful for extracting data and generating case simulations adequate to the company needs. Specifically, the game is customized in accordance with the company's identified themes and specific professional figures in training; game scenarios are simulated to train employees in Industry 4.0 themes. The prototype solution is usable, social and cross-platform, supporting ubiquitous communication and integration of virtual and real world, in order to enhance experiential and social learning in line with today's innovative digital, creative and inclusive learning communities.

Intended users of the framework are workers of small companies, which need to convert their business processes, as well as workers who need to relocate and retrain, and school students who will enter into job market in the short term. For this reason, the project provides for a broad partnership, which includes both private companies and public authorities involved in research for the application of the most innovative methodologies in technology and science.

The implementation of the game-simulation framework has adopted the participatory design methodology [17], operatively managed through the steps of the Progressive Inquiry model. This is an operational strategy to stimulate community of practices among companies, research bodies and final users. They collaborate to conceive and negotiate together the design, development and testing processes of the innovative technological solution.

This article paper describes the C-LAB 4.0 game-simulation framework developed in the contest of automotive companies. The case study is related to the development of a simulation game oriented to the training of CRF (Fiat Research Centre) personnel for the design of car engines. In addition, it presents preliminary results of an experimental study, involving a small group of end users, aimed at evaluating the effectiveness of the game in terms of social and emotional impact on its users as well as the support it provides in motivating and facilitating the learning process in acquiring Industry 4.0 skills.

2 The Game

The mission of the game is to build a car engine that adheres to the objectives defined by the CRF (Fiat Research Centre) company in Bari (Italy). The game learning goal is to teach users to exploit the technical characteristics of different components of a car engine.

According to the storyline of the game, a car manufacturer publishes contests to encourage user to propose new car engine configurations (Fig. 1). Firstly, the minimum requirements for the target client and prizes are published (Fig. 2).

The user has a budget to buy components in the shop. For each component, available in the shop, all technical characteristics can be explored.

Fig. 1. The contest details.

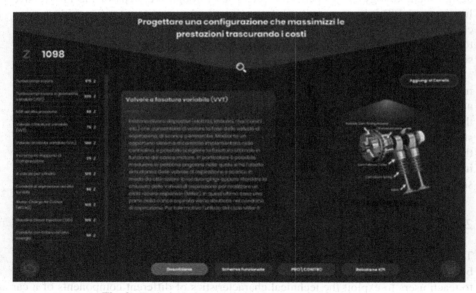

Fig. 2. Technical characteristic of component in the shop

Once a configuration has been produced and confirmed, it will be evaluated by a virtual examiner. The assessment is necessary to exclude those configurations that contain conflicting components. Then a road test is required to test if the engine meets the minimum requirements. The road test consists in carrying out a list of actions to verify the effectiveness of the engine. If the engine passes the test, the company can buy the engine and the user increases his budget with the prize of the contest.

3 Pilot Study

The overall aim of the experimental study of the C-LAB 4.0 project was to evaluate the attractiveness of the developed game in terms of usability and appearance and the user cognitive workload. In this article, the results of the pilot study performed to test the system reliability and research methodology (e.g., time constraints, evaluation instruments, coding techniques, video-recording activities) are reported.

3.1 Instruments

To evaluate the game, different measures were collected. The questionnaire was composed of 6 sections. The first one was devoted to measure the game attractiveness using the Attrackdiff questionnaire [8]. It consists of 28 7-point bipolar items that represent opposites (e.g. good - bad). The items measure the pragmatic quality and the hedonic quality identity. The second section was used to rate perceived workload using the NASA-TLX questionnaire. It is a 6-item survey that investigates 6 subjective dimensions, i.e., mental demand, physical demand, temporal demand, performance, effort and frustration [7].

The third section was aimed at measuring the user engagement using the UES (User Engagement Scale) short form. It is a 12-item survey which measure the user engagement, a quality of user experience characterized by the depth of a user's investment when interacting with a digital system [10]. This tool measures the user engagement by summarizing an index that ranges from 0 to 5. It also provides detailed information about four dimensions of the user engagement, i.e., focused attention (FA), perceived usability (PU), aesthetic appeal (AE) and reward (RW).

The fourth section was used to measure the user-friendliness of the game and the fifth section was the NPS - Net Promoter Score that measure the user loyalty and satisfaction from asking them how likely they will recommend the game to other users. The used scale is 0–10. Respondents can be classified as Promoters (score 9-10), enthusiast users, Passives (score 7–8) satisfied but not enthusiast users, and Detractors (score 0–6) are unhappy users. The NPS score range is between -100 and +100 [15].

Moreover, qualitative data were collected through the notes taken by the observer on significant behaviours or externalized comments of the participants during the study.

3.2 Participants

The pilot study involved 31 students attended the 4th grade of the technical high school "Panetti-Pitagora" in Bari, a city in the south of Italy. The students were all enrolled in the Informatics curriculum of the school. They have deep knowledge and skills in programming and multimedia design.

3.3 Procedure

Initially, all participants filled a demographic questionnaire to let us to interpret correctly the results. Then each student interacted with the game individually for 20 min. They played freely. A researcher observed them during the interaction with the game in order to discover interaction problems or misunderstanding of the content and the functionalities within the game. At the end of the interaction with the game, a brief discussion on different aspects of the game was conducted to gather feedbacks and useful suggestions to improve the game.

4   Analysis and Results

The data gathered were analysed separately according to the questionnaires used. Figure 3 shows the results of the answers the participants gave to the AttrakDiff questionnaire.

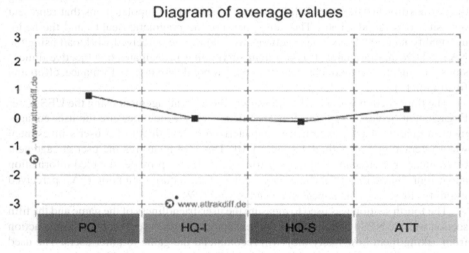

Fig. 3. Diagram of average values of the AttrakDiff questionnaire

The questions related to the *Pragmatic Quality (PQ)* describe the system usability perceived by the users and indicate how successfully users are in achieving their goals using the system. All participants gave a feedback above the mean value. In particular, the game was considered simple to use and practical. The *Hedonic Quality – Identity (HQ-I)* dimension concerning to what extent the system allows users to identify with it and the *Hedonic Quality – Stimulation (HQ-S)* showing to what extent the system supports users in terms of novel, interesting, and stimulating functions, contents and interaction- and presentation-styles obtained in average a neutral score. Finally, the *Attractiveness (ATT)* dimension describing a global value of the system based on the quality perceived by users received an average score above the 0 value. Specifically, the participants found the game very pleasant and likeable. The results showed that the game was considered useful and attractive. In other words, the participants were aware of the fact that the game allowed to them to learn how create a car engine in a pleasant way. However, they did not find the game novel and interesting. This is because the participants are used to play with entertainment games having amazing graphic effects, provide highly exciting challenges etc. While our game is a serious game whose main goal is allow its users to learn about the game car engine configurations.

The workload data revealed that the game is not very hard from a cognitive point of view. In Fig. 4 the arithmetic mean of for each of the 6 questions is represented.

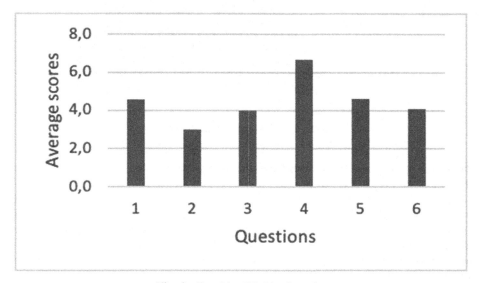

Fig. 4. Cognitive Workload results

The answers are given on a 10-points Likert scale. All the average scores are below the 5 points, in particular the mean for the first question that measures the mental demand (Q1) "How mentally challenging was the task?" the mean is 4.6, like for the question which measures the effort (Q5) "How hard was it to achieve your goal?". The high value of the question that measures the performance "How far have you been able to accomplish what you were asked to do?" (Q4) confirm that the game is easy to understand and use.

Data on the perceived user engagement have been grouped into four measures: focused attention (FA), perceived usability (PU), aesthetic appeal (AE) and reward (RW). For each dimension, the average score of the 5-point Likert scale questions are represented in Fig. 5.

The analysis of the results prove that the game allows to focus attention on the content, the perceived usability (PU) is low, the graphical aspects should be improved (AE). Many problems have been encountered in the final part of the game that require

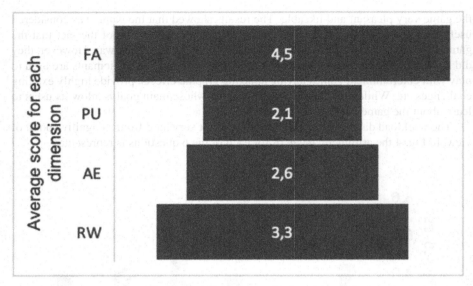

Fig. 5. User Engagement Scale results

the user to drive a car. On the other hand, the user has been interested in the experience (RW).

Unfortunately, the NPS score was −74, this means that not many students will recommend the game to their peers. One of the reasons that could explain this result is that informatics students were not interested in the topic of the game. They were more interested in the software issues, such as the GUI and the user experience of the game. In order to have more realistic results, the game should be tested with workers in the automotive market.

5   Conclusions and Future Works

The life-long learning is one of the main requirements in the current society. This is true also in the industrial world were the processes are rapidly changing, the education in Industry 4.0 is one of the primary objectives for both small and big companies. The C-LAB 4.0 project designed and implemented a simulation game to train users to build new car engine configurations with specific characteristics. A pilot study performed to investigate the usability perceived by the participants. The study revealed that the game was appreciated for allowing users to successfully achieve their learning goals using the system in a very pleasant and likeable way. The participants also found the game easy to understand and use. An emerged drawback of the game is related to its interface graphics, which should be improved in order to better capture the attention of users.

One of the main limits of the pilot study presented in this paper is that the users involved were not properly the typical users of the game. The idea in this first pilot study was to have some technical comments from video-gamer and informatics students. During the discussion, indeed, most of the comments were focused on the GUI. Some of them suggest improving the graphic design, others suggest improving the road test since it was too difficult to drive the car. In the next future, the game is evolving following the users' feedbacks and the next user test will be performed with employees of automotive companies.

Acknowledgment. The authors wish to thank all the young participants to the experiments and their teachers. This work was supported in part by Apulia Region under Grant C-Lab 4.0 - VTGYS52 – POR Puglia FERS-FSE 2014-2020 – Asse Prioritario I – Azione 1.4 - Sub-Azione 1.4.B – Avviso INNOLABS.

References

1. Cassano, F., Piccinno, A., Roselli, T., Rossano, V.: Gamification and learning analytics to improve engagement in university courses. In: Di Mascio, T., et al. (eds.) MIS4TEL 2018. AISC, vol. 804, pp. 156–163. Springer, Cham (2019). https://doi.org/10.1007/978-3-319-98872-6_19
2. Cazzolla, A., Lanzilotti, R., Roselli, T., Rossano, V.: Augmented reality to support education in Industry 4.0. In: 2019 18th International Conference on Information Technology Based Higher Education and Training (ITHET), pp. 1–5. IEEE, September 2019
3. De Freitas, S.I.: Using games and simulations for supporting learning. Learn. Media Technol. **31**(4), 343–358 (2006)
4. Di Bitonto, P., Laterza, M., Roselli, T., Rossano, V.: An evaluation method for multi-agent systems. In: Jędrzejowicz, P., Nguyen, N.T., Howlet, R.J., Jain, L.C. (eds.) KES-AMSTA 2010. LNCS (LNAI), vol. 6070, pp. 32–41. Springer, Heidelberg (2010). https://doi.org/10.1007/978-3-642-13480-7_5
5. Di Bitonto, P., Roselli, T., Rossano, V.: Recommendation in E-learning social networks. In: Leung, H., Popescu, E., Cao, Y., Lau, R.W.H., Nejdl, W. (eds.) ICWL 2011. LNCS, vol. 7048, pp. 327–332. Springer, Heidelberg (2011). https://doi.org/10.1007/978-3-642-25813-8_36
6. Fitsilis, P., Tsoutsa, P., Gerogiannis, V.: Industry 4.0: required personnel competences. Int. Sci. J. Industry 4.0 **3**(3), 130–133 (2018)
7. Hart, S.G., Staveland, L.E.: Development of NASATLX (task load index): results of empirical and theoretical research. Adv. Psychol. **52**, 139–183 (1988)
8. Hassenzahl, M., Wiklund-Engblom, A., Bengs, A., Hägglund, S., Diefenbach, S.: Experience-oriented and product-oriented evaluation: psychological need fulfillment, positive affect, and product perception. Int. J. Hum.-Comput. Interact. **31**(8), 530–544 (2015)
9. Michael, D.R., Chen, S.L.: Serious Games: Games that Educate, Train, and Inform. Muska & Lipman/Premier-Trade (2005)
10. O'Brien, H.L., Cairns, P., Hall, M.: A practical approach to measuring user engagement with the refined user engagement scale (UES) and new UES short form. Int. J. Hum. Comput. Stud. **112**, 28–39 (2018)
11. Punie, Y., Ala-Mutka, K.: Future Learning Spaces: new ways of learning and new digital skills to learn. Nordic J. Digit. Literacy **2**(4), 210–225 (2007)
12. Papastergiou, M.: Digital game-based learning in high school computer science education: Impact on educational effectiveness and student motivation. Comput. Educ. **52**(1), 1–12 (2009)
13. Prensky, M.: Digital game-based learning. Comput. Entertain. (CIE) **1**(1), 21 (2003)
14. Ranchhod, A., Gurău, C., Loukis, E., Trivedi, R.: Evaluating the educational effectiveness of simulation games: a value generation model. Inf. Sci. **264**, 75–90 (2014)

15. Reichheld, F.F.: The one number you need to grow. Harvard Bus. Rev. **81**(12), 46–55 (2003)
16. Rossano, V., Roselli, T., Calvano, G.: A serious game to promote environmental attitude. In: Uskov, V.L., Howlett, R.J., Jain, L.C. (eds.) SEEL 2017. SIST, vol. 75, pp. 48–55. Springer, Cham (2018). https://doi.org/10.1007/978-3-319-59451-4_5
17. Spinuzzi, C.: The methodology of participatory design. Tech. Commun. **52**(2), 163–174 (2005)

Personalised Semantic User Interfaces for Games

Owen Sacco[✉]

Institute of Information and Communication Technology, Malta College of Arts,
Science and Technology (MCAST), Paola, Malta
owensacco@gmail.com
https://iict.mcast.edu.mt/

Abstract. Players interact with games through user interfaces. Although user interfaces are similar in each game, these are manually developed each time for each game. The Web contains vast sources of content that could be reused to reduce the development time and effort to create user interfaces for games. However, most Web content is unstructured and lacks meaning for machines to be able to process and infer new knowledge. In this paper, we present a vocabulary that defines detailed properties used for describing user interfaces for games, and a vocabulary that defines detailed properties used for describing player's user interface preferences. Through these vocabularies, semantically-enriched user interface models can be used for automatically generating personalised user interfaces for games.

Keywords: Digital games · User interfaces · Semantic web · Personalised semantic user interfaces

1 Introduction

User interfaces provide a means for players to interact with games. A successful user interface for games should be user-friendly, provide enough information for users to effortlessly play the game and provide all the necessary behaviour for users to have an immersive experience. User interfaces utilise elements such as text, buttons and images to provide users the means to interact with the game. When designing user interfaces, it is not just about the placement of elements on the screen but most importantly it is about providing the best user experience players could experience in a game and to provide the best interaction between the user and the game. User interfaces should provide: (1) clear interfaces and should avoid ambiguity that might cause confusion to players as to how to navigate through the game; (2) must be concise without overloading the interface with too many user interface elements ending up with interfaces tedious to use; (3) fast responsive interfaces; (4) consistent feel throughout the game; (5) aesthetically attractive to provide players an enjoyable experience; and (6) efficiency by allowing the players to perform tasks in a reasonable time.

© Springer Nature Switzerland AG 2020
C. Stephanidis et al. (Eds.): HCII 2020, LNCS 12425, pp. 739–755, 2020.
https://doi.org/10.1007/978-3-030-60128-7_54

Game User Interfaces can be categorised as follows: (1) diegetic interfaces are those interfaces included in the game world whereby players access such interfaces through their game character; (2) non-diegetic interfaces are those interfaces rendered outside of the game world (i.e. overlaid on top of the game) and is only accessible to the players (rather than accessed through the player's game character); (3) meta interfaces are representations that can exist in the game world such as effects rendered on the screen to indicate low health and are normally represented two dimensionally; and (4) spatial interfaces are three dimensional elements that can exist or not in the game world.

Creating video games that are market competent costs in time, effort and resources which often cannot be afforded by small-medium enterprises, especially by independent game development studios. As designing and developing user interfaces for games are labour and creativity intensive, our vision is to reduce development effort and enhance design creativity by automatically generating novel and semantically-enriched user interfaces for games from Web sources. In this paper we envision a user interface generation that extracts information directly from the Web such as extracts user interface elements or images that are freely available on the Web. Following a semantic-based user interface generation approach not only can reduce the time and cost of user interface creation for games but also directly contribute to web-informed yet unconventional game design.

Web content is dispersed over the Internet in the form of blogs, microblogs, forums, wikis, social networks, review sites, and other Web applications which are currently disconnected from one another. The content and datasets created by these communities all contain information which can be used to generate or reuse user interfaces in games, but are not easily discoverable. For instance, the Web contains many user interface elements that can be reused to generate user interfaces for games but these are dispersed and not easily discoverable. The emerging Web of Data trend [5], where datasets are published in a standard form for easy interlinking, enables to essentially view the whole Web as one massive integrated database. Nevertheless, user interface information is still not enriched with meta-structures that could be used both on the Web and also in games. With such rich meta-structures that add more meaning to content, this would enable Web content to be reused to generate user interfaces for games. Moreover, the representation of *semantically-enriched* and *semantically-interlinked* user interfaces would enable game generators to infer how content can be interacted within the game world without having to rely on software development procedures that require laborious annotation of how each entity can be interacted within the game.

During the last years we have assisted to the growth of Web applications using or collecting data on their users and their behaviour in order to provide adapted and personalised content and services. This caused the need for exchange, reuse, and integration of their data and user models. Games can benefit from these user models to provide a better player experience by tailoring the game according to the player's preferences. Specifically, user interfaces in games such as menus and heads-up displays (HUDs) can be automatically customised based on user preferences without the user having to manually customising these himself/herself. Moreover, having user interface preference models in a standard format, this would enable these models to be interoperable amongst different games such that games would automatically adjust interfaces based on these unified standard user preference models and would not require users to setup their preferences in each game. With semantically-enriched user interfaces, these could be interlinked with user preferences so that games could automatically generate personalised and customised user interfaces for players.

In this paper we present the Game User Interface Ontology (GUIO)[1] – a light-weight vocabulary for formally defining user interfaces in digital games, and the Player User Interface Preference Ontology (PUIPO)[2] – a light-weight vocabulary for formally defining player's user interface preferences in digital games. Through these ontologies, personalised user interfaces could be automatically generated for games.

The remainder of this paper is as follows. Section 2 offers core background information about the Web of data and Sect. 3 reviews current work on semantics in games especially for semantically defining user interfaces for games. Section 4 presents a detailed explanation of the Game User Interface Ontology (GUIO) and Sect. 5 presents a detailed explanation of the Player User Interface Preference Ontology (PUIPO). Section 6 concludes the paper by providing an overall discussion about the future steps of this work.

2   Background: The Web of Data

The *Web of Data* is evolving the Web to be consumed both by machines and humans whereas the traditional Web resulted to be for human consumption only. Indeed, machines cannot process additional meaning from the content found in Web pages since they are simply text and similarly from the non-typed links which do not contain any additional meaning about the relationships amongst the linked pages. Therefore, the *Web of Data* provides various open data formats which have emerged from the Semantic Web.

2.1   The Semantic Web

The Semantic Web [4] provides approaches for structuring information on the Web by using metadata to describe Web data. The advantage of using metadata is that information is added with meaning whereby Web agents or Web enabled devices can process such meaning to carryout complex tasks automatically on behalf of users. Another advantage is that the semantics in metadata improved the way information is presented, for instance merging information

---

[1] Game User Interface Ontology (GUIO) – http://autosemanticgame.eu/ontologies/guio.

[2] Player User Interface Preference Ontology (PUIPO) – http://autosemanticgame.eu/ontologies/puipo.

from heterogeneous sources on the basis of the relationships amongst data, even if the underlying data schemata differ. Therefore, the Semantic Web encouraged the creation of meta-formats to describe metadata that can be processed by machines to infer additional information, to allow for data sharing and to allow for interoperability amongst Web pages. The common format and recommended by W3C for Semantic data representation [3] is the Resource Description Framework (RDF)[3].

2.2 Resource Description Framework (RDF)

RDF is a framework that describes resources on the World Wide Web. Resources can be anything that can be described on the Web; being real-world entities such as a person, real-world objects such as a car and abstract concepts such as defining the concept of game review scores. RDF provides a framework for representing data that can be exchanged without loss of meaning. RDF uniquely identifies resources on the Web by means of Uniform Resource Identifiers (URIs). Resources are described in RDF in the form of triple statements. A triple statement consists of a *subject*, a *predicate* and an *object*. A subject consists of the unique identifier that identifies the resource. A predicate represents the property characteristics of the subject that the resource specifies. An object consists of the property value of that statement. Values can be either literals or other resources. Therefore, the predicate of the RDF statement describes relationships between the subject and the object. If a triple had to be depicted as a graph, the subject and object are the nodes and the predicate connects the subject to the object node. The set of triples describing a particular resource form an RDF graph.

RDF data can be queried by using an RDF query language called SPARQL[4]. SPARQL queries take the form of a set of triple patterns called a basic graph pattern. SPARQL triple patterns are similar to RDF triples with the difference that in a SPARQL triple, each subject, predicate and object can be bound to a variable; the variable's value to be found in the original data graph. When executing a SPARQL query, the resulting RDF data matches to the SPARQL graph pattern.

Moreover, the RDF data may require more meaning to describe its structure and therefore, an RDF vocabulary modelled using the RDF Schema (RDFS)[5] can be used to describe the RDF data's structure. Apart from vocabularies, RDF data may pertain to a specific domain which its structure needs to be explicitly defined using ontologies modelled by RDFS and/or OWL 2[6]. For example, ontologies may describe people such as the Friend of a Friend (FOAF)[7] ontology or may describe information from gaming communities to interlink different

---

[3] RDF—http://www.w3.org/TR/REC-rdf-syntax/.
[4] SPARQL—http://www.w3.org/TR/rdf-sparql-query/.
[5] RDFS—http://www.w3.org/TR/rdf-schema/.
[6] OWL 2—http://www.w3.org/TR/owl2-overview/.
[7] FOAF—http://www.foaf-project.org/.

online communities such as the Semantically-Interlinked Online Communities (SIOC)[8] ontology.

2.3 Linked Data

As mentioned previously, when describing a particular resource within a graph, a URI is assigned to that resource which can be referred to in other graphs using that particular URI. For instance, if a particular resource represents a person within another graph that describes information about that person, the person's (resource) URI can be used for example when describing that s/he is the creator of a game review which is described in another graph. Hence this makes it easy to link data together from different datasets and thus creating *Linked Data*[9]. Datasets which are easily accessible are linked forming the Linking Open Data (LOD) cloud[10] which forms part of the *Web of Data*. In order to publish data in the LOD cloud, it must be structured adhering to the Linked Data principles as stated in [9] and the Data on the Web best practices as stated in [8].

The benefit of linking data is that links amongst data are explicit and try to minimise redundant data as much as possible. Therefore, similar to hyperlinks in the conventional Web that connect documents in a single global information space, Linked Data enables data to be linked from different datasources to form a single global data space [9].

3 Related Work

Semantics in games is still in its infancy and perhaps the closest attempt at using structured real-world data in games is the Data Adventures project [1,2] which uses SPARQL queries on DBpedia to discover links between two or more individuals: the discovered links are transformed into adventure games, with entities of type "Person" becoming Non-Player Characters (NPCs) that the player can converse with, entities of type "City" becoming cities that the player can visit, and entities of type "Category" becoming books that the player can read. The advantages of using rich semantic information to automatically generate games are numerous [15] as more complex, open-world, non-linear, games incorporating very rich forms of interaction are possible (i.e. authentic sandbox games). Current work in using semantics in games focuses on the use of semantic information to generate game worlds or to describe interactions with game worlds such as the work in [10,11,16]. Although these provide useful insights in generic semantic models that describe interactions with game worlds, they do not offer vocabularies for describing game content such as user interfaces and they neither provide a generic approach for reusing Web content to generate user interfaces for games.

---

[8] SIOC—http://sioc-project.org/.
[9] Linked Data—http://linkeddata.org/.
[10] Linking Open Data (LOD) cloud—http://lod-cloud.net.

Attempts in game ontology creation are relevant to our approach, hence, we outline some key game-based ontologies currently existent. The Game Ontology Project [17] is a wiki-based knowledge-base that aims to provide elements of gameplay. However, this project does not take into consideration game user interfaces. Moreover, it does not provide a vocabulary to be consumed by data described in RDF which could make it potentially useful for game user interface generation. The Digital Game Ontology [6] provides a general game ontology by aligning with the Music Ontology, and the Event and Timeline ontology, to provide concepts that describe digital games. However, the vocabulary is not available and in this regard, it is unclear what game concepts this vocabulary provides. The Ludo ontology [13] provides concepts that describe different aspects of serious games, however, it does not provide detailed concepts for describing game user interfaces. The authors in [7] provide a generic ontology for defining RPG games and do not provide detailed concepts to describe user interfaces for games. Finally, the Video Game Ontology (VGO) [12] provides concepts for defining interoperability amongst video games and the Game2Web ontology [14] focuses on linking game events and entities to social data. Although these vocabularies are useful for describing several aspects of game information, the ontologies are still limited to specific features and hence do not provide features for describing detailed user interface information for games.

Our ontology was created since to our knowledge no ontology exists to describe user interfaces for games and no ontology exists to describe preferences for customising user interface in games.

4   Game User Interface Ontology (GUIO)

The Game User Interface Ontology (GUIO)[11] (illustrated in Fig. 1) provides a light-weight vocabulary for formally defining user interfaces in digital games. The process in modelling this ontology involved examining user interfaces in 100 video games from different genres, and common features were extracted resulting in the creation of this ontology.

Game User Interfaces are defined using the main class guio:GameUI. An instance of this class represents formal descriptions of different user interface elements used within a game. These formal descriptions can be used to drive a game engine to generate a game's user interface either at design time or at run time, depending on how the user interface is implemented within the game. These elements can be used or extended by other video game user interface descriptions. Although this ontology is designed for video games, these element descriptions could also be used for generating user interfaces in software artefacts.

Games are made up of different screens each of which have a specific purpose, for example an options screen provides various settings through which a user could configure and setup a game according to his/her preferences, and a map screen shows the location of a player's character within a particular level.

---

[11] Game User Interface Ontology (GUIO) – http://autosemanticgame.eu/ontologies/ guio.

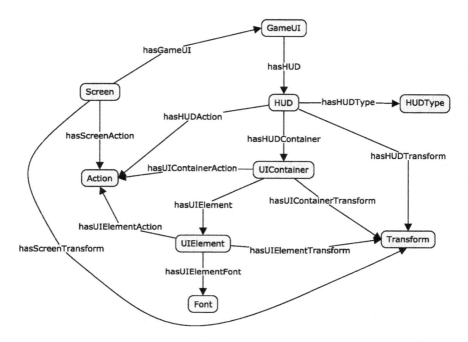

Fig. 1. Overview of the Game User Interface Ontology (GUIO)

Each screen contains game user interface elements that provide contextual information and/or means of interaction through which a player can interact with a game. Screens can formally be defined using the **gvo:Screen** class (described in detail in Subsect. 4.1) and each screen may contain one or more game user interfaces defined by the **guio:GameUI** class. Instances of the **guio:GameUI** class may contain one or several HUD (Heads-Up Display) elements defined by the **guio:HUD** class (explained in Subsect. 4.2) which contain one or several UI containers defined by the **guio:UIContainer** class (explained in Subsect. 4.3). Instances of **guio:UIContainer** contain one or several UI elements defined by the **guio:UIElement** class (explained in Subsect. 4.4). UI elements are linked with actions that define events and methods through which a user could interact with a game. Instances of Actions are defined by the **guio:Action** class (explained in Subsect. 4.5). In summary, games contain screens that may contain one or several game user interfaces that act as containers for HUDs. HUDs serve as placeholders for one or more UI containers that group one or more UI elements through which a player could interact with a game.

This section provides a comprehensive description of classes and properties for defining game user interfaces.

4.1 Screen

Games are made up of several screens each containing different user interface elements that a user could interact with within a game. These screens are defined as instances of the gvo:Screen class and each screen serve a specific purpose within a game. The gvo:Screen class is part of the Game Visual Ontology (GVO)[12]– a light-weight ontology for defining different visual elements within a game. The following are screens (not exhaustive) that are most commonly found in all games and these are defined as subclasses of the gvo:Screen class:

- gvo:License screen provides information about the end-user license of a game, i.e. who owns the copyright of the game and what rights or permissions a buyer of the game has. The user interacts with this screen by reading the license information and agreeing to the license agreement.
- gvo:Splash screen normally contains a poster-like art image of a game, a logo of the publisher and/or developer, and the current version of the game. This screen normally appears when a game is launched.
- gvo:Loading screen provides some type of animated graphic indicating that the game is loading.
- gvo:Title screen appears after the game is loaded and normally contains the title of the game, a graphic art in the background and a player needs to press either a specific key or any key to load the main menu of the game. Some games do not wait for any user input and provide a cutscene instead or even other games go straight to the main menu screen.
- gvo:MainMenu screen provides a player with several options to choose from before commencing the game. This menu typically contains: choose or create a player name, continue or change player, log in, options, tutorials, settings, credits, cutscenes, scores, and any other option the game provides a player to configure, setup and customise the game.
- gvo:Instructions screen normally contain tutorials on how a player can play the game.
- gvo:Options screen provides players to configure or customise the game and normally include: adjust sound, adjust graphics, adjust playing speed, adjust performance, restart the game, change playing modes, change players, access other levels, access tutorials etc.
- gvo:Settings screen is the same as the gvo:Options screen since in some games the gvo:Options screen is called gvo:Settings.
- gvo:Cutscene screen provides an in-game cinematic or short animation or short movie that is not interactive and breaks-up the gameplay. Cutscenes normally adds more context to the narrative of the game.
- gvo:Scene screen represents the environment and a unique level of a game.
- gvo:Map screen displays a map of the current level or a map of the whole game world.
- gvo:Pause screen pauses the game and provides several options to a player such as return to the game, restart the mission or level or game, save the game, load a game, return to the main menu or exit the game.

---

[12] Game Visual Ontology (GVO) – http://autosemanticgame.eu/ontologies/gvo.

- gvo:HighScores screen provides a table with all the high scores achieved in a game by one or several players.
- gvo:Credits screen provides a list of all the cast and crew involved in making the game.
- gvo:Exit screen provides a screen prior to closing the game for example whether the player is sure to exit the game, to save the game before closing etc.

The gvo:Screen class contains the following properties that are related to the classes and properties defined by the Game User Interface Ontology.

- gvo:hasScreenTransform specifies a transform of a screen defined by the guio:Transform class (described in Subsect. 4.6). This defines a position, rotation and scale of a screen relative to the global coordinates of a game.
- gvo:hasScreenAction specifies a generic action defined by the guio:Action class (described in Subsect. 4.5) that can be performed within a screen but are not bound to any UI element actions – i.e. actions over and above the actions bound to UI elements.
- gvo:hasScreenGameUI specifies instances of game user interfaces defined by the guio:GameUI class provided within a specific screen through which a player can interact with a game. Screens can be linked to one or several Game UI instances.
- guio:width specifies a width dimension of a screen in pixels.
- guio:height specifies a height dimension of a screen in pixels.

4.2 HUD (Heads-Up Display)

The HUD (heads-up display) provides a means by which several pieces of information is provided to a player in a visual form as part of the game's user interface. Instances of guio:GameUI class may contain one or several HUDs defined by the guio:HUD class. The guio:GameUI class contains the guio:hasHUD property that specifies a guio:HUD instance. Instances of the guio:HUD class provide several game user interface elements that provide means for a player to interact with a game or provide information about aspects of a game to a player. This information, for instance, includes (but not limited to) the health status of a player's character, the current weapon selected, the amount of ammunition left etc. Each piece of information is defined as an instance of a subclass of the guio:HUD class. The subclasses – the different types of HUD information – include the following (not exhaustive):

- guio:Health displays the current health of a player's character, of other characters such as allies or opponents, or the health of every unit visible on screen in real-time strategy games.
- guio:Lives displays the amount of lives a player's character has left or other characters have left.

- `guio:Time` displays either the time left for a player to complete a task or the time elapsed for a particular task, or the in-game time system in-built within a game.
- `guio:Weapon` displays the current weapon selected and/or the available weapons a player's character can use.
- `guio:Ammunition` displays the available amount of ammunition a player's character has.
- `guio:Inventory` displays the available objects and items which a character carries after the character has either picked up or purchased during the game.
- `guio:Capability` displays available gameplay options that a player can access during gameplay such as spells.
- `guio:Menu` displays a menu with options such as to change settings or exit.
- `guio:GameProgression` displays a player's current gameplay progression for example the current game level.
- `guio:Speedometer` normally a gauge displayed when a player is using a vehicle to measure the speed of a vehicle.
- `guio:Tachometer` normally a gauge displayed when a player is using a vehicle to measure the revolutions per minute.
- `guio:Reticle` displays markings of a sighting device such as a scope.
- `guio:Cursor` displays the mouse pointer in a game.
- `guio:Crosshair` displays an indication where the character is aiming at.
- `guio:Stealthometer` displays the awareness level of enemies towards a player character's presence (normally used in stealth games).
- `guio:Score` the player's current score.
- `guio:Money` the amount of money a player has within the game's economy system.
- `guio:CharacterLevel` displays the current character's level (of experience).
- `guio:ExperiencePoints` displays the amount of experience points the character currently has.
- `guio:Radar` displays a radar that show's a player's surroundings and the positions of objects, vehicles and enemies.
- `guio:Compass` displays a navigational instrument that aligns itself with the game world's magnetic field and indicates where the character is heading. Some games use a compass to guide a player towards the next objective.
- `guio:QuestArrow` are markers that indicate the location of quests.
- `guio:MiniMap` displays a small, simplified version of a larger game map.
- `guio:ContextSensitiveInformation` display important contextual information or messages when required.

The main properties of the `guio:HUD` class include the following:

- `guio:hasHUDAction` this defines a general action bound to an instance of the `guio:HUD` class defined by the `guio:Action` class (described in Subsect. 4.5).
- `guio:hasHUDUIContainer` defines a container for one or more HUD elements and is defined by the `guio:UIContainer` class (described in Subsect. 4.3). HUDs can contain one or several UI containers.

- guio:hasHUDTransform specifies a transform of a HUD defined by the guio: Transform class (described in Subsect. 4.6). This defines a position, rotation and scale of a HUD relative to a screen's local coordinates within a game.
- guio:hasHUDType specifies how a HUD is displayed in a game and is defined by the guio:HUDType class. The guio:HUDType class consists of the following types defined as subclasses: (1) guio:Diegetic specifies that a HUD instance is included in the game world whereby players access HUD instances through their game character; (2) guio:NonDiegetic specifies that a HUD instance is rendered outside of the game world (i.e. overlaid on top of a game) and is only accessible to players (rather than accessed through a player's game character); (3) guio:Meta specifies that a HUD instance is rendered as effects on a screen for instance blood splatter to indicate low health; and (4) guio:Spatial specifies that a HUD instance may appear in a game world but is not part of a narrative or action but are there to provide more information to the player (than a character should be aware of). For example an object a player needs to interact with might glow or jump.
- guio:width specifies a width dimension of a HUD in pixels.
- guio:height specifies a height dimension of a HUD in pixels.

4.3   UI Container

The UI container, defined by the guio:UIContainer class provides a container and placeholder for UI elements defined as instances of the guio:UIElement class (described in Subsect. 4.4). UI containers also serve to group UI elements together so that they could be rendered together. Moreover, any actions bound to the container would be applied to all the UI elements within that specific container. The following are different types of UI containers (not exhaustive) and are defined as subclasses of guio:UIContainer:

- guio:Accordion defines a container that allows players to expand and collapse a group of UI elements.
- guio:Modal defines a small window overlay containing several UI elements that requires the player to interact with before closing the window and returning to the flow of the game.
- guio:Card defines a small rectangle or square container containing several UI elements.
- guio:Carousel defines a container that allows players to browse through and interact with a set of UI elements.
- guio:Sidebar defines a container on the side of a HUD that displays a group of navigational UI elements such as buttons or UI elements that provide information. This container could be visible or collapsed.
- guio:TabBar provides a container with UI elements that allows a player to switch between different modes.
- guio:Toolbar defines a container on which UI elements are placed and grouped together.

- guio:Pagination defines a container whereby UI elements are placed in different containers within the pagination container and allows a user to skip between the inner containers or go through the inner containers sequentially. The pagination containers and the child containers are linked using the guio:partOfUIContainer property described below.
- guio:BentoBox defines a container that organises UI elements in a grid.
- guio:HamburgerMenu defines a container that toggles a menu containing several UI elements. The icon of this container are three horizontal lines on top of each other.
- guio:DonerMenu defines a container that toggles a menu containing several UI elements. The icon of this container are three vertical lines next to each other.
- guio:MeatballsMenu defines a container that toggles a menu containing several UI elements. The icon of this container are three horizontal dots next to each other.
- guio:KebabMenu defines a container that toggles a menu containing several UI elements. The icon of this container are three vertical dots on top of each other.

The main properties of the guio:UIContainer class include the following:

- guio:hasUIElement specifies a UI element defined by the guio:UIElement class (explained in Subsect. 4.4) that is contained within a UI container. UI containers can have one or several UI elements.
- guio:hasUIContainerTransform specifies a transform of a UI container defined by the guio:Transform class (described in Subsect. 4.6). This defines a position, rotation and scale of a UI container relative to a HUD's local coordinates within a screen.
- guio:hasUIContainerAction this defines a general action bound to an instance of the guio:UIContainer class defined by the guio:Action class (described in Subsect. 4.5).
- guio:partOfUIContainer specifies that a UI container is part of another container – i.e. a container within another container.
- guio:width specifies a width dimension of a UI container in pixels.
- guio:height specifies a height dimension of a UI container in pixels.

4.4   UI Element

UI elements, defined by the guio:UIElement class, are visual elements on a computer screen that provide information to users or help users to interact with a game. UI elements are contained within UI containers. The following are different types of UI elements (not exhaustive) and are defined as subclasses of guio:UIElement:

- guio:Checkbox specifies an option that can be selected by a user. Normally, checkboxes are grouped within a set of checkboxes allowing a user to select one or more options. A set of checkboxes can be grouped within a UI container defined using the guio:UIContainer class (explained in Subsect. 4.3).

- guio:Radiobutton specifies an option that can be selected by a user. Normally, radio buttons are grouped within a set of radio buttons and allow users to select only one option from the whole set of radio buttons. A set of radio buttons can be grouped within a UI container defined using the guio:UIContainer class (explained in Subsect. 4.3, and an action bound to a container containing radio buttons would control and ensure that a user selects only one radio button from the whole set.
- guio:Dropdown specifies a list of items that allows users to select only one item at a time. The action bound to a dropdown list would control and ensure that a user selects only one option from the list of items.
- guio:Listbox specifies a list of items that allow users to select more than one item at a time.
- guio:Button specifies a UI element that a user could interact with by clicking or touching. This element typically consists of a label using text, an icon or both. The action bound to a button controls the event, and a method or function bound to the action is executed once the event is triggered by a user.
- guio:Toggle allows a user to change a setting between two states.
- guio:Text specifies a label that can be displayed for information purposes. Text wraps accordingly to the dimensions specified by the UI element in relation to the dimension of the UI controller where the text is contained in.
- guio:TextField allows a user to insert text in a game – for example to provide a name for a character.
- guio:Image specifies an image to be displayed.
- guio:Picker allows users to select a date and time.
- guio:Breadcrumb specifies a trail of links that helps a user figure out where s/he is in a game – for example Main Menu ->Settings ->Display Settings. Each link would be bound to an action that will direct a player to a specific area in the game represented by that link.
- guio:Slider specifies a UI element that allows a user to select a value or a range of values by dragging the slider – for example to adjust the volume, or to adjust the brightness of a screen.
- guio:Stepper specifies a UI element that allows a user to adjust a value in predefined increments.
- guio:Tag defines a label which a user could use to label content.
- guio:Icon defines a simplified image serving as a symbol used to provide visual information to a player or help a player to navigate within a game.
- guio:Tooltip specifies a UI element that allows a player to see hints either when the player hovers over an object or item within a game, or pop-up accordingly as contextual help within a game.
- guio:ProgressBar specifies a UI element that indicates where a player is whilst advancing through a series of tasks or steps.
- guio:Notification specifies a UI element in the form of a message that announces something new for a user to see such as when a task is completed successfully.

- guio:Messagebox specifies a small window that provides information to a user and requires the user to take an action before continuing forward.
- guio:Loader specifies a UI element to inform a player that a game is completing an action in the background and the player should wait until that action is complete.

The main properties of the guio:UIElement class include the following:

- guio:hasUIElementAction this defines an action bound to a UI element defined by the guio:Action class (described in Subsect. 4.5).
- guio:hasUIElementTransform specifies a transform of a UI element defined by the guio:Transform class (described in Subsect. 4.6). This defines a position, rotation and scale of a UI element relative to a UI container's local coordinates within a HUD.
- guio:hasUIElementFont defines a UI element's font details defined by the guio:Font class (described in Subsect. 4.7).
- guio:width specifies a width dimension of a UI element in pixels.
- guio:height specifies a height dimension of a UI container in pixels.

4.5   Action

The guio:Action class defines events such as mouse input, keyboard input, game controller input, motion sensing input, gyroscope input, touch input etc., bound to a specific method or function that a game can execute once the event is triggered by a user. The main properties of the guio:Action class include the following:

- guio:hasActionEvent this defines the event that is triggered by a user using an input device.
- guio:hasActionMethod this defines the method or function the game executes once an event is triggered.
- guio:appliesToDevice this defines to which device or devices the action is bound.

4.6   Transform

The guio:Transform class defines transformation properties that can be applied to Screens, HUDs, UI controllers or UI elements. The properties include the following:

- guio:hasTransformPosition defines the x, y, z position coordinates of an object relative to the parent's coordinates.
- guio:hasTransformRotation defines the x, y, z rotation coordinates of an object relative to the parent's coordinates.
- guio:hasTransformScale defines the x, y, z scale coordinates of an object relative to the parent's coordinates.

4.7 Font

The guio:Font class defines font properties that can be applied to UI elements to visually format the text contained in the elements. The properties include the following:

- guio:hasFontFamily specifies the font family name for an element – for example "arial" or "times".
- guio:hasFontStyle specifies the font style for a text element which could be set to either *normal, italic* or *oblique*.
- guio:hasFontSize specifies the length of an element which could be set to either *centimeters (cm), millimeters (mm), inches (in), pixels (px), points (pt)* or *picas (pc)*.
- guio:hasFontWeight specifies how thick or thin characters in text should be displayed which could be set to either *normal* or *bold*.
- guio:hasFontVariant specifies whether or not text should be displayed in small-caps, which could be set to either *normal* or *small-caps*.

5 Player User Interface Preference Ontology (PUIPO)

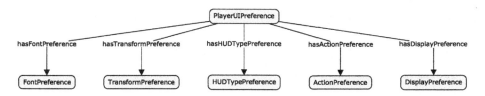

Fig. 2. Overview of the Player User Interface Preference Ontology (PUIPO)

The Player User Interface Preference Ontology (PUIPO)[13] (illustrated in Fig. 2) provides a light-weight vocabulary for formally defining player's user interface preferences in digital games. Preferences are defined on top of formal descriptions defined using the Game User Interface Ontology (GUIO). Using these preferences, games could render user interfaces according to the player's preferences thus enabling personalised user interfaces in games. Preferences are defined as instances of the main class of this ontology – the puipo:PlayerUIPreference class. This following are the properties for defining player's game user interface preferences:

- puipo:hasFontPreference specifies the font preferences of a player that are applied to UI elements. The font preferences are defined as instances of the puipo:FontPrefernce class (which is a subclass of the class guio:Font) and has the puipo:appliesToUIElement property to define to which UI elements the prefernce would be applied to.

---

[13] Player User Interface Preference Ontology (PUIPO) – http://autosemanticgame.eu/ontologies/puipo.

- `puipo:hasTransformPreference` specifies a player's transform preferences for any elements in a game. The transform preferences are defined as instances of the `puipo:TransformPreference` class (which is a subclass of the class `guio:Transform`) and contains the following properties: (1) `puipo:appliesToScreen` specifies to which screen the player's transform preference is applied to; (2) `puipo:appliesToHUD` specifies to which HUD the player's transform preference is applied to; (3) `puipo:appliesToUIContainer` specifies to which UI container the player's transform preference is applied to; and (4) `puipo:appliesToUIElement` specifies to which UI element the player's transform preference is applied to.
- `puipo:hasHUDTypePreference` specifies which HUD type a player prefers (i.e. whether *diegetic*, *meta*, *spatial* or *non-diegetic*). The HUD type preferences are defined as instances of the `puipo:HUDTypePreference` class, which is a subclass of `guio:HUDType` class and contains the property `puipo:appliesToHUD` to define to which HUD this preference applies to.
- `puipo:hasActionPreference` specifies a player's action preferences for example configuration of game controller buttons (i.e. customising which buttons linked to specific events). A player's action preferences are defined as instances of the `puipo:ActionPreference` class, which is a subclass of `guio:Action` and contains the following properties: (1) `puipo:appliesToScreen` specifies to which screen the player's action preference is applied to; (2) `puipo:appliesToHUD` specifies to which HUD the player's action preference is applied to; (3) `puipo:appliesToUIContainer` specifies to which UI container the player's action preference is applied to; and (4) `puipo:appliesToUIElement` specifies to which UI element the player's action preference is applied to.
- `puipo:hasDisplayPreference` specifies a player's display preferences that are applied to screens. The display preferences are defined as instances of the `puipo:DisplayPreference` class that defines preferences such as: (1) resolution, (2) refresh rate, (3) texture quality, (4) anti-aliasing, (5) VSync, (6) tessellation, (7) ambient occlusion, (8) anisotropic filtering, (9) high dynamic range, (10) bloom, (11) motion blur, and (12) field of view.

6   Conclusion

In this paper we presented the Game User Interface Ontology (GUIO) a lightweight vocabulary for formally defining user interfaces in digital games, and Player User Interface Preference Ontology (PUIPO), a light-weight vocabulary for formally defining player's user interface preferences in digital games. Player preferences, defined using PUIPO, link to formal descriptions of user interfaces, defined using GUIO, that can guide games to render user interfaces customised to players' preferences thus enabling personalised semantic user interfaces for games. As future work, we will develop software tools that render automatically user interfaces based on these ontologies.

References

1. Barros, G.A., Liapis, A., Togelius, J.: Playing with data: procedural generation of adventures from open data. In: International Joint Conference of DiGRA and FDG. DiGRA-FDG 2016 (2016)
2. Barros, G.A., Liapis, A., Togelius, J.: Who killed Justin Bieber? Murder mystery generation from open data. In: International Conference on Computational Creativity. ICCC 2016 (2016)
3. Berners-Lee, T.: Semantic Web Road Map, September 1998. http://www.w3.org/DesignIssues/Semantic.html
4. Berners-Lee, T., Hendler, J., Lassila, O.: The semantic web. Sci. Am. **284**, 34–43 (2001)
5. Bizer, C., Heath, T., Idehen, K., Berners-Lee, T.: Linked data on the web (LDOW2008). In: 17th International Conference on World Wide Web. WWW 2008 (2008). https://doi.org/10.1145/1367497.1367760
6. Chan, J.T.C., Yuen, W.Y.F.: Digital game ontology: semantic web approach on enhancing game studies. In: International Conference on Computer-Aided Industrial Design and Conceptual Design. CAID/CD 2008 (2008). https://doi.org/10.1109/CAIDCD.2008.4730603
7. Durić, B.O., Konecki, M.: Specific OWL-based RPG ontology. In: Central European Conference on Information and Intelligent Systems (2015)
8. Farias Lóscio, B., Burle, C., Calegari, N.: W3C. Data on the Web Best Practices. 19 May 2016. W3C Working Draft. http://www.w3.org/TR/dwbp/
9. Heath, T., Bizer, C.: Linked Data: Evolving the Web into a Global Data Space. Morgan and Claypool (2011)
10. Kessing, J., Tutenel, T., Bidarra, R.: Designing semantic game worlds. In: Workshop on Procedural Content Generation in Games. PCG 2012. ACM (2012). https://doi.org/10.1145/2538528.2538530,
11. Lopes, R., Bidarra, R.: A semantic generation framework for enabling adaptive game worlds. In: International Conference on Advances in Computer Entertainment Technology. ACM (2011)
12. Parkkila, J., et al.: An ontology for videogame interoperability. Multimedia Tools Appl. 1–20 (2016). https://doi.org/10.1007/s11042-016-3552-6
13. Rocha, O.R., Faron-Zucker, C.: Ludo: an ontology to create linked data driven serious games. In: ISWC 2015 - Workshop on LINKed EDucation. LINKED 2015 (2015)
14. Sacco, O., Dabrowski, M., Breslin, J.G.: Linking in-game events and entities to social data on the web. In: 2012 IEEE International Games Innovation Conference (IGIC), pp. 1–4, September 2012. https://doi.org/10.1109/IGIC.2012.6329847
15. Tutenel, T., Bidarra, R., Smelik, R.M., Kraker, K.J.D.: The role of semantics in games and simulations. Comput. Entertain. **6**(4), 57:1–57:35 (2008). https://doi.org/10.1145/1461999.1462009
16. Tutenel, T., Smelik, R.M., Bidarra, R., de Kraker, K.J.: Using semantics to improve the design of game worlds. In: Conference on Artificial Intelligence and Interactive Digital Entertainment. AIIDE 2009 (2009)
17. Zagal, J.P., Bruckman, A.: The game ontology project: supporting learning while contributing authentically to game studies. In: 8th International Conference on International Conference for the Learning Sciences. ICLS 2008 (2008). http://dl.acm.org/citation.cfm?id=1599871.1599933

Utilization of Neurophysiological Data to Classify Player Immersion to Distract from Pain

Kellyann Stamp[1]([envelope]) [iD], Chelsea Dobbins[2] [iD], and Stephen Fairclough[3] [iD]

[1] Department of Computer Science, Liverpool John Moores University, Liverpool L3 3AF, UK
K.Stamp@2012.ljmu.ac.uk
[2] School of Information Technology and Electrical Engineering, The University of Queensland, Brisbane, QLD 4072, Australia
C.M.Dobbins@uq.edu.au
[3] School of Natural Sciences and Psychology, Liverpool John Moores University, Liverpool L3 3AF, UK
S.Fairclough@ljmu.ac.uk

Abstract. Painful experiences during clinical procedures can have detrimental effects on the physical and mental health of a patient. Current pain reduction methods can be effective in reducing pain, however these methods are not without fault. Active distraction via computer games have been proven to effectively reduce the experience of pain. However, the potential of this distraction to effectively alleviate pain is dependent on players' engagement with the game, which is determined by the difficulty of the game and the skill of the player. This paper aims to model and classify immersion through increasingly difficult levels of game play, in the presence of pain, using functional Near Infrared Spectroscopy (fNIRS) and heart rate data. Twenty people participated in a study wherein fNIRS data (4 channels located at the prefrontal cortex, four channels located at the somatosensory cortex) and heart rate data were collected whilst participants were subjected to experimental pain, via the Cold Pressor Test (CPT). Participants played a computer game at varying difficultly levels as a distraction. Data were then pre-processed using an Acceleration Based Movement Artefact Reduction Algorithm (AMARA) and Correlation Based Signal Improvement (CBSI). Classification was subsequently undertaken using Linear Discriminant Analysis (LDA), Support Vector Machine (SVM) and Recursive Partitioning (rPart). The results demonstrate a maximum accuracy of 99.2% for the binary detection of immersion in the presence of pain.

Keywords: Functional near infrared spectroscopy · Machine learning · Classification · Immersion · Gaming · Pain

1 Introduction

The experience of pain can have long lasting and detrimental effects on the sufferer, including Post Traumatic Stress Disorder and dissociative experiences [1, 2]. As such, adequately managing pain is crucial to alleviate discomfort. It is common for opioids

© Springer Nature Switzerland AG 2020
C. Stephanidis et al. (Eds.): HCII 2020, LNCS 12425, pp. 756–774, 2020.
https://doi.org/10.1007/978-3-030-60128-7_55

to be administered as a method of pain relief and anxiety reduction in clinical settings. However, this method of pain control is associated with a number of serious adverse effects, including tolerance and withdrawal symptoms from opioid addiction, such as insomnia, vomiting, diarrhoea and tremors [3]. However, distraction techniques are non-pharmaceutical and can be an effective alternative in reducing the perception of pain, due to selective attention. This is especially prevalent in patients whose tendency to catastrophize can affect their perception of pain [4]. Pain is considered to be a threatening form of stimulation that can interrupt attention to other stimuli in the environment [5]. However, directing attention away from painful stimuli, through goal-orientated tasks, can modulate this interruptive function of pain and deliver analgesic relief from painful stimulation [6].

In order to maximize the effectiveness of distraction, the distracting stimuli or task must require a high level of cognitive effort in order to draw attention away from painful stimuli [7]. There are a wide variety of techniques available to distract people from pain, such as watching television or reading a book, however computer games have been proven to be the most effective approach [8–10]. The act of playing a computer game functions as an active distraction, requiring effortful pursuit of game-related goals and focused attention, whereas watching television is relatively passive, in comparison. For a distraction technique to effectively distract from pain, it must require a high degree of attentional focus and mobilization of mental effort. The psychological demands of a computer game can create an immersive experience that actively distracts from pain stimulation [11]. However, achieving this immersive experience is not straightforward. As noted by Fairclough et al. [12], most games are aimed at an 'ideal player', but this ideal player does not exist. Some players will have more or less gaming experience than said 'ideal player' and will therefore find a standard game to be either too easy or too difficult. It is important that the demands or difficulty of the game are optimized and adapted *per* player to engage the individual according to their capabilities. However, adaptive gaming is a method that can be used to enhance immersion by matching game demand to the engagement of the player [13]. In order to create an adaptive game, it is essential to quantify the attentional state of the player.

This paper aims to model and classify immersion of a player using implicit measures of physiological and neurological data, in order to distract from the experience of pain. The platform includes a number of devices to collect various streams of data, including Functional Near Infrared Spectroscopy (fNIRS), which is used to passively record neurovascular data, electrocardiogram (ECG) to collect heart rate and an accelerometer to measure head movement. The hypothesis of this paper is that immersion can be classified using implicit measures, such as fNIRS and heart rate, and that the experience of immersion can reduce the experience of pain. A study was undertaken to determine the effectiveness of using machine learning classifiers to predict the level of immersion. Collecting a subjective measure of immersion and a behavioral measure of pain enables us to understand how the physiology and physicality of a person is affected under such conditions. These data can then be used to verify the effects of pain tolerance, and the effects that a distraction task has on the cortical process.

2 Related Work

Csikszentmihalyi [14] coined the term 'flow' in reference to the psychological state experienced by a person when they are totally involved with a task [15]. The flow model focuses on three cognitive states: boredom, flow and anxiety, in order to describe this optimal realm of engagement and immersion.

Flow is an ideal state for an active distraction from pain, whilst both anxiety and boredom will prevent the player from entering the flow state. However, tailoring the level of game demand in order to achieve this state is difficult, due to the individual differences of players. This theory indicates that monitoring the players in-game performance is not sufficient for determining player state, because it would be unknown as to whether a poorer performance was due to anxiety (as the game is too difficult) or boredom (as the game is not difficult enough) [16]. Using game metrics alone would also not allow the level of cognitive effort that a player was exerting to be determined, as there would be no way to identify whether successful game play was due to high effort or low difficulty. This is especially relevant when considering the previous point that there is no 'ideal player' for a game. The experience of flow is considered to be incredibly delicate and easily broken. This means that outside stimuli are likely to decrease the chances of the player entering (or remaining in) the flow state [15]. For this reason, it would not be suitable for a player to provide a self-score of engagement, as the player would have to attend to this question rather than to the game. In this instance, adaptive gaming would be an ideal solution to enhance immersion by personalizing the game to the player.

Functional Near Infrared Spectroscopy (fNIRS) is a neuroimaging technique designed to measure neurovascular coupling/neuronal activation in the cortex. Neurovascular coupling is characterized by an increase in oxygenated hemoglobin (HbO) and a decrease in deoxygenated hemoglobin (Hbb). One major benefit of fNIRS over other techniques, such as function Magnetic Resonance Imaging (fMRI), is the absence of any need to confine a participant within an apparatus, which enables more flexible data capture to be undertaken [17]. In addition, fNIRS also has a greater spatial resolution than other techniques, such as electroencephalogram (EEG) [18]. fNIRS requires the placement of a montage of sources and detectors, secured to a cap, on a participant's head. The sources emit infrared light, which can penetrate the skull and the outermost 10–15 mm of intracranial space. fNIRS works because skin, bone and tissue have a low absorbency rate for infrared light, whereas HbO and Hbb have a high absorbency rate. Therefore, the amount of light that is returned to the detectors indicates the changes in HbO and Hbb within the cortex. These data can be used to infer psychological concepts, such as attentional state, based on relative level of neuronal activation provoked by a set of stimuli or a specific task [19].

fNIRS has previously been used to monitor attentional state, using machine learning to classify the resulting data [18, 20]. These studies observed maximum classification accuracies of 80% and 90% respectively, in the distinction between high and low attentional states. fNIRS have also been used to observe pain signals in the brain with the intention of demonstrating the feasibility of using the technology as a measure of pain response [21]. One drawback of fNIRS data is that it is highly affected by movement from the participant, especially movement of the head, and physiological changes. For instance, if an individual becomes excited, their heart will beat faster and more blood will circulate [22]. This is true also of a pain response [23]. Both acceleration and physiological data are required to ensure the clearest possible fNIRS signal [24]. Head movement artefacts contained within fNIRS data can lead to false negatives and false positives, where it would appear that a participant is more or less engaged in a task than they actually are. Using filters based on acceleration allows for the removal of head movement artefacts. Acceleration based filters will also enable genuine responses in the brain to be preserved, and not discounted as movement artefacts.

3 Materials and Methods

Our approach focused on collecting fNIRS, heart rate, and head movement (via acceleration) data under three distinct conditions, whereby participants 1) played a computer game, 2) were exposed to a painful stimulus and 3) played a computer game whilst being exposed to a painful stimulus. The study was carried out to determine whether pain tolerance was increased when a distraction task was used (i.e. playing the game) and was conducted as a precursor to the development of a real-time adaptive gaming system. The purpose of this paper is to classify immersion of the player during increasingly difficult levels of game play in order to determine whether immersion can be quantified using objective physiological and neurophysiological measures.

3.1 Participants

Data were collected from 20 participants, of whom 6 were female. Participants were aged between 19 and 29 (M = 22.75 SD = 3.23). Exclusion criteria included being pregnant, history of cardiovascular disease, fainting, seizures, chronic or current pain, Reynaud's disease or diabetes, fractures and open cuts or sores on the feet or calves. Participants were required to confirm that they were not currently taking any medication, with the exception of the contraceptive pill. A full review of the ethics of the experiment was undertaken, and approval was granted by the Liverpool John Moores University Research Ethics Committee. All participants were briefed before their experimental session and were provided with a detailed Participant Information Sheet prior to taking part. Full written consent was provided by each participant involved in this study.

3.2 Design

Participants were exposed to four levels of game difficulty (easy, medium, hard and impossible), which were determined during pre-piloting. After each gaming session, participants completed the subjective Immersive Experience Questionnaire (IEQ), which relates to overall feelings of immersion [15]. The study was designed in this way so that these self-scores could be used to label the physiological data for classification. This would then enable the accuracy of using physiological signals as an indication of immersion to be determined.

Figure 1.1 illustrates the data collection protocol that was undertaken. To ensure that the results collected during each step of this study were independent, a 90 s baseline period was established between each condition. The entire protocol was repeated a total of four times, to enable participants to play each of the four levels of game difficulty (i.e. easy, medium, hard and impossible). Throughout the course of the experiment, all four levels of the game were played in a randomized order. This ensured that the results collected were not influenced by the participant gaining more experience with the game on Easy and Medium levels before they then played Hard and Impossible levels. As such, the participant's response to each level of the game is independent of their level of skill or their familiarity with the game.

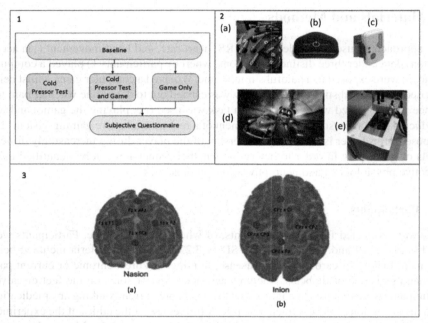

Fig. 1. 1) The data collection protocol, which was repeated four times per participant to correspond to each level of game difficulty. During each cycle, the same level of game difficulty was played for both the Cold Pressor and Game and the Game Only conditions. **2)** Materials that were used to collect raw data during the experimental protocol. (a) fNIRS Equipment (Dancer Design), (b) Bioharness™ ECG Sensor, (c) Shimmer™ Accelerometer, (d) Computer game – Space Ribbon and (e) Cold Pressor Stimulus Tank. fNIRS Optode Placement. **3)** Two light sources (central), and 8 detectors surrounding the light source, with reference to the nasion and inion. (a) Front view. (b) Top view.

3.3 Raw Data Collection

The components, depicted in Fig. 1.2 a–c, were utilized to collect raw physiological and neurological data during the experiment. The platform also consisted of components to distract (via a computer game) and induce (via a Cold Pressor Stimulus Tank) pain (see Fig. 1.2 d–e).

fNIRS data were used to determine changes relating both to game difficulty and the presence of pain. Data was collected using an Artinis™ OxyMon Mk III device, which measured cortical activity (see Fig. 1.2 a). A 2 × 4 cross-channel configuration was used, with a total of 2 sources and 8 detectors. This configuration was created on the fNIRS cap, which was worn on the participants head. Data was collected from 8 channels in total. Four channels were situated at the prefrontal cortex, between Fz and: F1, AFZ, F2 and FCz, and the remaining 4 channels were situated at the somatosensory cortex, between CPZ and: CP1, Cz, CP2 and Pz. This optode layout is illustrated in Fig. 1.3. Source-detector separation was 3 cm and source optodes emitted light at 847 nm and 761 nm wavelengths. The device was configured to record optical density data at a sampling rate of 10 Hz. Data was recorded using the Oxysoft data recording software. Zephyr™ BioHarness monitoring system was used to record electrocardiogram (ECG) data at a sampling rate of 250 Hz (see Fig. 1.2 b). The BioHarness was worn around the torso, underneath the participants clothing. A Shimmer3™ inertial measurement unit (IMU) was also used to record accelerometer data at a sampling rate of 512 Hz (see Fig. 1.2 c). The Shimmer3™ unit was worn around the participants head on an elasticated band. Care was taken to ensure that the band of the Shimmer3™ unit did not disturb the optodes on the fNIRS cap. Accelerometer data was used to influence the pre-processing of fNIRS data.

A racing game was used during the experimental sessions as the distraction (see Fig. 1.2. d). The racing game was a strategy-based game, wherein the goal was to finish the race in first position. Participants had the option to achieve a first-place position via a number of performance boosters, which could be picked up during gameplay. Participants could collect rockets, shields and invisibility boosters by driving over them on the track. Rockets, an offensive weapon, could be fired by the participant at competing vehicles on the track, which would cause the opponent vehicles to be temporarily disrupted. Shields, both an offensive and a defensive weapon, allowed the player to protect themselves from weapons being fired by opponent vehicles, and caused any opponent vehicle that came into contact with the players vehicle to be temporarily disrupted. Invisibility boosters were a defensive weapon that enabled the player to drive through opponent vehicles without causing collisions.

Through pilot testing, four set levels of game difficulty were established: easy, medium, hard, and impossible. Factors within the game were changed to create these four difficulty levels, including the Artificial Intelligence (AI) of the game, the amount of non-playable cars that were also on the track, gravity and race/maneuver speed. Each factor was represented by a number and were manipulated for each level's settings. For instance, during the easy level, the options chosen were set to the minimum, whilst during the impossible level the options were set to the maximum. The options for the Medium and Hard levels were set in-between the minimum and maximum and were determined via pilot testing.

Experimental pain was induced via the Cold Pressor Test (CPT) [22] (see Fig. 1.2 e). Throughout the duration of the experimental session, water was kept at a consistent temperature of 2 degrees centigrade and was not warmed by the participant's foot. During the stages whereby, participants submerged their foot in the CPT and then also played the game, they were instructed to remove their foot from the cold pressor stimuli tank when they felt that the pain they were experiencing was unbearable. Each game condition lasted for 3 min, which is consistent with the recommended maximum duration of the CPT. Over the course of the experiment, participants alternated the foot that was placed in the cold pressor. This was to ensure that repeated immersion of the same foot would not have an effect on pain tolerance. Each CPT was timed, which provided an objective measure of pain tolerance at each difficulty level. This result was kept blind from the participant. Participants played each level of game difficulty with and without the induction of experimental pain. The CPT was used to ensure that the experience of immersion did have an effect on the experience of pain.

In total, 690,028 instances of raw fNIRS data, 16,763,628 instances of raw heart rate data and 26,177,699 instances of raw accelerometer data were collected; thus totalling 43,631,355 instances of raw data overall.

3.4 Data Pre-processing

A data pre-processing pipeline has been created, using a variety of filters and algorithms, which were applied to the raw data (see Fig. 2). These filters were applied to ensure that the signals, which would be used for classification, were free from artefacts, which could affect the classification results.

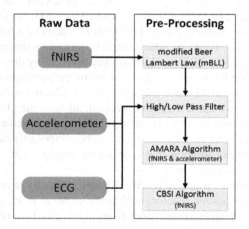

Fig. 2. Data pre-processing pipeline

Firstly, in order to determine activation in the target cortices, the raw Optical Density data that were collected via the fNIRS cap were converted into measures of oxygenated hemoglobin (HbO) and deoxygenated hemoglobin (Hbb), using the modified Beer Lambert Law (mBLL) [25]. In order to ensure that the data related specifically to the condition that the participant was experiencing, and not to unrelated activity within the brain, the baseline and condition data were combined prior to the application of the modified Beer Lambert Law, before the baseline data was again removed. This ensured that the converted Hemoglobin changes reflected only data that was related directly to the condition.

Following this conversion, the fNIRS data was filtered using a 6th Order Chebyshev filter, with passband edge frequencies of 0.5 and 0.1 respectively, for high and low pass filtering. These filters were applied to reduce noise within the signal that related to heart rate and respiration [26], as well as Mayer waves, which occur within the fNIRS signal due to changes in arterial pressure [27]. The same filters were also applied to the ECG and accelerometer data to reduce noise within these signals.

The fNIRS data were then treated with two head movement related filters: Acceleration-Based Movement Artefact Reduction Algorithm (AMARA) and Correlation Based Signal Improvement (CBSI), which were used to ensure the results represented genuine hemodynamic response. Both fNIRS and accelerometer data were firstly processed using the Acceleration-Based Movement Artefact Reduction Algorithm (AMARA) [28]. Artefacts relating to head movement are commonly found in fNIRS signals, which causes a change in blood flow to the brain. These changes can appear to represent changes in activation if they are not removed from the signal. AMARA detects periods of movement within an accelerometer signal and then compares these periods of movement to the fNIRS data. Where it is found that the moving standard deviation (MSD) of the fNIRS signal has changed considerably during the same period of time that movement has been detected within the accelerometer signal, these segments of fNIRS data are marked as 'artefact' segments. Segments where the MSD of both the accelerometer and fNIRS data have no significant deviation are marked as 'acceptable' segments. Reconstruction of artefact segments uses forward and backward baseline adjustments and interpolation to reconstruct the entire signal, with the movement artefacts corrected [28].

A further consequence of head movement artefacts is that they can cause a positive correlation between HbO and Hbb [29]. Usually, these signals are negatively correlated, as a drop in Hbb is expected when HbO rises, and vice versa [29]. Therefore, if the signals illustrate that there isn't a strong negative correlation between HbO and Hbb, it could be an indication that there is remaining noise contained within the signal. Therefore, in order to correct the correlation between the HbO and Hbb signals, the final stage included applying the Correlation Based Signal Improvement (CBSI) algorithm to the fNIRS data [30].

3.5   Experimental Measures and Feature Extraction

Following pre-processing, additional measurements were calculated from the HbO and Hbb data. The first was Total Hemoglobin (HbT), which occurs through addition of the HbO and Hbb signals to provide a signal that details the total cortical activity, as in Eq. (1). The second was Hemoglobin Difference, which is created by finding the difference between HbO and Hbb Hemoglobin, as in Eq. (2).

$$HbT = HbO + Hbb \tag{1}$$

$$HD = Hb0 - Hbb \tag{2}$$

As reported by Xu et al. [31], Hemoglobin Difference can achieve better results than HbO, Hbb and HbT when fNIRS data are being used for machine learning classifications.

The creation of these new measurements provided 32 different features: 8 HbO, 8 Hbb, 8 HbT and 8 Hemoglobin Difference, each relating to the 8 original channels of interest.

In order to determine the heart rate of the participants, ECG data collected from the Bioharness was converted into beats per minute (BPM), as depicted in Eq. (3).

$$BPM = 60000/IBI\,(rPeakECG(n) - rPeakECG(n - 1)) \tag{3}$$

This process involved calculating the inter-beat interval (IBI), which corresponds to the time between consecutive R peaks in an ECG signal, which indicates that the heart has beaten. BPM detection was undertaken by identifying the R peaks in the signal and then finding the difference in milliseconds between two successive beats and then dividing by 60,000 (the number of milliseconds in a minute).

The data were then separated into 8 s windows, which corresponds to the Hemodynamic Delay that is present in fNIRS data. This occurs when the response to the onset of stimuli has a delay of several seconds after the stimuli has been introduced, before changes in the signal reflect this [32]. Within each 8 s epoch, standard descriptive statistics were extracted from the fNIRS data, including: mean, median, range, minimum, maximum and standard deviation. These features were created for each of the 32 original measurements discussed above, to create a feature set comprised of 192 features in total. These descriptive statistics were also extracted from the BPM data, thus totaling 198 features. Following the creation of the feature set, each participant's dataset was normalized using a Standardized Z Score [33] and combined into a single dataset. It should be noted that two participant's data were excluded from this dataset due to short CPT immersion times, where none of their immersions in any condition exceeded 25 s.

3.6 Data Labelling

Subjective levels of immersion were gathered via the Immersive Experience Questionnaire (IEQ), which consists of 32 questions that are scored on a 7-point Likert scale from 1 (*Not at All*) to 7 (*A Lot*). The resulting scores from the IEQ were used as subjective labels for the neurophysiological data. As described above, participants played each level of the game (easy, medium, hard and impossible) under two conditions: 1) game only and 2) experiencing pain whilst playing the game. The average IEQ score was then calculated for each game level, per condition. The data was then labelled such that any participant whose score for each level/condition was a) greater than or equal to the mean was labelled '*immersed*' or b) any score below the mean was labelled '*not immersed*'. As a result of this labelling process, Fig. 3 illustrates the frequency of immersed/not immersed participants for each level during the a) game only condition and b) game and pain condition.

As it can be seen in Fig. 3, the datasets per level, per condition are unbalanced, apart from the medium level of the game only condition, whereby the balance is 50/50. As such, in order to balance the remaining datasets, the majority classes (i.e. those labelled as *immersed*) were randomly undersampled using the *SpreadSubsample* function in Weka [34] in order to create equally labelled data.

a)   b)

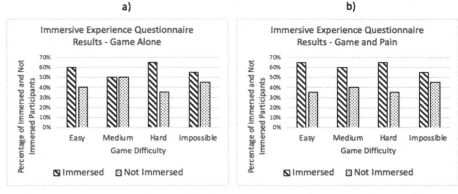

Fig. 3. a) IEQ distribution of *Immersed* and *Non-Immersed* participants during the Game Only condition shown as a percentage and **b)** IEQ distribution of *Immersed* and *Non-Immersed* participants during the Game and Pain condition shown as a percentage.

3.7 Feature Selection

Feature selection was undertaken using the RELIEFF algorithm [35]. RELIEFF uses a k nearest neighbor approach to weight the estimated quality of features. The k value is the value that determines the number of nearest neighbors that should be compared to each data point. This is done in order to determine the nearest values in the same class (hits) and the nearest values in a different class (misses). Each feature is weighted to estimate its quality, based on the amount of hits and misses.

In order to determine how each set of measures (frontal fNIRS sites, central fNIRS sites and heart rate) independently performed during classification, these three sets of measures were separated into individual datasets. The purpose of this separation was to determine the best set of features to use in order to classify immersion. The RELIEFF algorithm was then applied independently to the frontal and central fNIRS data. Due to the heart rate measures only containing six features, feature selection was not performed over this data. The resulting weights were then ordered, from highest to lowest, and plotted on a graph (see Fig. 4). The point in the graph where the "elbow" appears indicates the most relevant features and the feature set is cut down at this point.

The application of the RELIEFF algorithm determined that a total of 15 Frontal and 12 Central fNIRS features were relevant for classification. The features that were selected can be seen in Table 1.

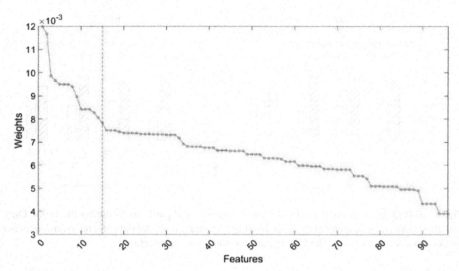

Fig. 4. Example of RELIEFF feature selection of the frontal fNIRS sites. The graph indicates that the elbow, where the relevance of the features becomes obsolete, is at 36 features.

Table 1. Features selected for classification determined by the RELIEFF Algorithm

Frontal features	Weight	Central features	Weight
Fz x AFZ HbT Mean	0.011988036	CPZ x CP2 HbT Mean	0.012807196
Fz x F1 HbT Mean	0.011664447	CPZ x CP2 HbT Median	0.010977391
Fz x F1 HbT Max	0.009856833	CPZ x Cz Oxy Max	0.00930525
Fz x F1 HbT Median	0.00965673	CPZ x Cz Diff Max	0.009305134
Fz x F1 Oxy Max	0.009499116	CPZ x Cz Deoxy Min	0.009305041
Fz x F1 Diff Max	0.009498993	CPZ x CP2 Diff Min	0.009290371
Fz x F1 Deoxy Min	0.009498955	CPZ x CP2 Deoxy Max	0.009290342
Fz x AFZ HbT Median	0.009402018	CPZ x CP2 Oxy Min	0.009290215
Fz x F2 HbT Max	0.008972051	CPZ x CP2 HbT Min	0.009095969
Fz x F2 Oxy Max	0.008418477	CPZ x Cz HbT Mean	0.009075785
Fz x F2 Diff Max	0.008418435	CPZ x Cz HbT Max	0.008980522
Fz x F2 Deoxy Min	0.008418274	CPZ x CP1 HbT Max	0.008715578
Fz x F2 HbT Mean	0.008276955		
Fz x F2 HbT Median	0.008061099		
Fz x FCZ HbT Max	0.007826961		

4   Results

The evaluation uses both parametric and non-parametric machine learning classifiers, including Linear Discriminant Analysis (LDA), Support Vector Machine (SVM) and Recursive Partitioning (rPart), to classify immersion using the selected features in the frontal fNIRS sites, central fNIRS sites and heart rate datasets. These classification algorithms are commonly used in fNIRS studies that involve machine learning [36]. Classification was carried out using RStudio Version 1.1.414 and the Machine Learning in R (MLR) package. The results were validated using k-fold cross validation, where k = 10. Performance measurements that were calculated included:

- *Accuracy* – an overall score of the performance
- *F₁ Score* – the weighted average of the precision and recall of the classifier
- *Balanced Error Rate (BER)* – an average of classification errors that occur in each class

Binary classification was performed for each of the four game levels (Easy, Medium, Hard and Impossible), per condition (i.e. 1) Game and Pain and 2) Game Only). For each condition, data were labelled as *'Immersed'* or *'Not Immersed'* according to the average IEQ score per level (see Sect. 3.6). The aim of this classification was to determine whether immersion could be classified from heart rate and fNIRS data independently, and to identify which type of data was more accurately classified. A combined dataset (fNIRS and heart rate) was also classified, to identify whether this would improve the classification results. Classification was carried out over *Game Only*, and *Game and Pain* conditions independently, to examine the effect of the experience of pain on the classification of immersion.

Each classifier was utilized independently using only the 1) heart rate features, 2) frontal site features, 3) central site features and 4) a merger of 1–3 (i.e. heart rate, frontal and central site features together). The purpose of this was to evaluate each set of features independently to establish the set of features that provided the best results. Data were separated into four difficulty levels for the classification of immersion, to determine whether the level of difficulty would have an effect on the accuracy of the classification. Data were also separated by *Game and Pain* and *Game Only* conditions, to determine whether the inclusion of the CPT has an effect on the accuracy of the classifier. The results of the Heart Rate analysis can be seen in Table 2.

The results in Table 2 report maximum accuracies during both Game and Pain and Game Only conditions during Easy, Medium and Hard games of 86.6%, 80.7% and 77.8%, respectively, whilst the Impossible condition provided adequate results of 62%. The lowest error rates for each level were observed during the Game Only condition, with 45.6% (Easy), 42.6% (Medium) and 44.2% (Hard), whilst the lowest overall BER was observed during the Impossible level at 39.8%. The results illustrate that LDA and SVM outperformed rPart in most cases, with the highest F1 score (92.6%) being observed using SVM during the Game Only/Easy condition. This illustrates that when the game was relatively simple, a linear model using heart rate only features was adequate to distinguish immersion. The results indicate that comparable levels of classification accuracy can be found between the Game and Pain and Game Only conditions of the

Table 2. Heart rate classification results per condition/level

Condition	Performance measure	Game and pain			Game only		
		LDA	SVM	rPart	LDA	SVM	rPart
Easy	Accuracy	85.1%	**85.6%**	84%	86%	***86.6%***	85.6%
	BER	**49.6%**	50%	50.8%	48%	50%	***45.6%***
	F1	91.7%	**92.1%**	91.2%	92.3%	***92.6%***	92%
Medium	Accuracy	***80.7%***	79.8%	71.8%	**70.6%**	68.8%	61.7%
	BER	**50%**	50.5%	53.9%	***42.6%***	45.1%	44.8%
	F1	***89.07%***	88.58%	83.18%	**80.9%**	80.2%	71.6%
Hard	Accuracy	***77.8%***	***77.8%***	68.6%	74.9%	**77.4%**	69.4%
	BER	**48.6%**	50%	50.7%	***44.2%***	50%	50%
	F1	87.1%	***87.4%***	80.5%	85.1%	**86%**	80.4%
Impossible	Accuracy	59.5%	58.9%	***62%***	56%	**58.4%**	49%
	BER	45.5%	47.2%	***39.8%***	**49.5%**	50.5%	52%
	F1	70.4%	**72%**	68.2%	68.7%	**73%**	56.8%

same difficulty levels. Overall, maximum classification accuracy of 86.6% and BER of 92.6% was found in the Game Only/Easy condition, using SVMs. To evaluate whether these results can be improved upon using fNIRS, the results of the frontal fNIRS sites can be seen in Table 3.

Table 3 illustrates that using the frontal fNIRS sites yielded comparable results as the Heart Rate results seen in Table 2. Maximum accuracies of 86.6% (Easy), 80.7% (Medium), 78% (Hard) and 63.8% (Impossible) were reported for each level, across both Game and Pain and Game Only conditions. The lowest overall BER (38%) was observed during the Game and Pain/Impossible condition using rPart. The highest overall accuracy (86.6%) and F1 score (92.7%) were achieved using an SVM classification during the Easy/Game Only condition, which was similar to the HR results. These results illustrate that the classifiers seem to perform best on the Easy level, using the game on its own and when pain is not present. However, when the game increases in complexity, from the Medium – Impossible levels, the presence of pain does not affect the results and produces higher accuracies. To evaluate whether central fNIRS sites can provide further improvement, the results of the central fNIRS sites can be seen in Table 4.

The results presented in Table 4 illustrate that using the central fNIRS sites are an improvement to the results achieved using the frontal sites, especially when an rPart classification is implemented. Maximum accuracies of 88.2% (Easy), 96.9% (Medium), 99.2% (Hard) and 95.3% (Impossible) were reported for each level, across both Game and Pain and Game Only conditions. The highest overall accuracy (99.2%) and F1 score (99.4%) and lowest BER (1.3%) were achieved using the rPart classifier during the Hard/Game and Pain condition. In contrast with previous results, the results from the rPart learner are consistently better than that of LDA and SVM for all measures. We

Table 3. Frontal fNIRS classification results per condition/level

Condition	Performance measure	Game and pain			Game only		
		LDA	SVM	rPart	LDA	SVM	rPart
Easy	Accuracy	**85.6%**	**85.6%**	76.8%	86.1%	***86.6%***	82.1%
	BER	50%	50%	***47.9%***	**48.9%**	50%	52.7%
	F1	92.1%	**92.2%**	86.6%	92.4%	***92.7%***	90%
Medium	Accuracy	***80.7%***	**80.7%**	77.2%	67.6%	**68%**	54%
	BER	50%	50%	***46.7%***	50.5%	**50%**	52.3%
	F1	***89.2%***	89.1%	86.5%	80.2%	**80.8%**	65%
Hard	Accuracy	77.1%	***78%***	63.8%	77%	**77.4%**	69%
	BER	50.5%	***45%***	53.9%	50.3%	50%	**46.7%**
	F1	86.9%	***87.2%***	76.6%	86.8%	**87%**	79.7%
Impossible	Accuracy	56.1%	56.1%	***63.8%***	53.8%	**57.3%**	54.8%
	BER	52.5%	51%	***38%***	54%	51.4%	**46.7%**
	F1	**71.3%**	70.8%	70%	69.4%	***72.3%***	61%

Table 4. Central fNIRS classification results per condition/level

Condition	Performance measure	Game and pain			Game only		
		LDA	SVM	rPart	LDA	SVM	rPart
Easy	Accuracy	85.7%	85.6%	***88.2%***	86.8%	86.7%	**87.1%**
	BER	50%	50%	***27.7%***	40%	50%	**33.1%**
	F1	92%	92.1%	***93%***	**92.7%**	**92.7%**	92.7%
Medium	Accuracy	83.7%	79.3%	***96.9%***	83.3%	80.2%	**90.3%**
	BER	20.9%	40.8%	***7.8%***	19.7%	25.1%	**11%**
	F1	89.3%	87.8%	***98.1%***	88%	86.1%	**92.7%**
Hard	Accuracy	77.8%	77.9%	***99.2%***	74.8%	77.5%	**95.8%**
	BER	50%	50%	***1.3%***	50.9%	50%	**7.5%**
	F1	87.3%	87.4%	***99.4%***	85.3%	87%	**97.2%**
Impossible	Accuracy	54.2%	58%	***95.3%***	60.1%	62%	**88.9%**
	BER	49%	50.3%	***5.7%***	43.3%	44%	**11.5%**
	F1	66.8%	72.3%	***96.2%***	68.4%	72.7%	**90.5%**

were also interested to compare how a combination of the three separate datasets would perform. The results from this combined dataset can be seen in Table 5.

Table 5. Combined dataset (fNIRS and heart rate) classification results per condition/level

Condition	Performance measure	Game and pain			Game only		
		LDA	SVM	rPart	LDA	SVM	rPart
Easy	Accuracy	83.5%	**85.7%**	76.3%	83.1%	**86.6%**	80.6%
	BER	51.3%	**50%**	50.8%	**47.1%**	50%	52.2%
	F1	90.7%	**92.2%**	86.2%	90.5%	**92.7%**	88.8%
Medium	Accuracy	78.5%	**80.7%**	72%	65.4%	**68.4%**	64.1%
	BER	51.3%	**50%**	51.3%	48.8%	45.8%	**43.4%**
	F1	87.8%	**89%**	83.2%	77.4%	**79.9%**	73.9%
Hard	Accuracy	73.2%	**77.9%**	65.5%	74%	**77.4%**	74%
	BER	52.9%	50%	**49.8%**	50.1%	50%	**40.6%**
	F1	84.4%	**87.4%**	77.5%	84.4%	**87.1%**	83.3%
Impossible	Accuracy	51.7%	59.6%	**61%**	47%	**57.6%**	52.5%
	BER	52.5%	49.2%	**40.5%**	58.4%	51.2%	**50.2%**
	F1	63.7%	**73.5%**	65.6%	61.2%	**72.1%**	59.9%

As the results in Table 5 illustrate that the combined dataset does not outperform any individual dataset. Maximum accuracies of 86.6% (Easy), 80.7% (Medium), 77.9% (Hard) and 61% (Impossible) were reported for each level, across both Game and Pain and Game Only conditions. The lowest overall BER (40.5%) was observed during the Game and Pain/Impossible condition using rPart. The highest overall accuracy (86.6%) during the Easy/Game Only condition is comparable to the HR (Table 2) and frontal (Table 3) results. Overall, the results presented in Table 5 indicate that there is no benefit of using the combined data set over the individual datasets. To summarize, the highest accuracy (99.2%) and F1 (99.4%) and lowest BER (1.3%) were achieved using the central dataset, during the Hard/Game and Pain condition and using the rPart classifier. As such, central fNIRS sites, together with rPart, appears to be the most appropriate set of data and classifier to use to detect immersion in the presence of pain.

5 Discussion

It has been established that a computer game is an active distraction task capable of increasing pain tolerance. The rationale of this study was to use fNIRS and heart rate data to differentiate between immersive and non-immersive conditions. Our approach was undertaken in distinct phases, which were utilized to assess the relative contribution of variables derived from fNIRS (frontal and central sites) and heart rate data. Feature selection was undertaken using the RELIEFF algorithm, which indicated that HbT measures were consistently well represented in both the frontal and central sites. It was interesting to note that of the 27 selected features, both from frontal and central sites, 15 of these features (55.5%) were descriptive statistics gathered from the HbT signal. It is also interesting that statistics associated with variation (e.g. min, max) are represented more than measures relating to central tendency (e.g. mean, median). Feature selection has enabled us to determine that measures associated with variation, gathered from the HbT signal, would be the best features derived from fNIRS to utilize for further work. The same pattern, i.e. sensitivity of total hemoglobin in the frontal cortices to the cold pressor test, was observed in earlier studies [3, 5]. Feature selection also indicates that channels Fz x F1, Fz x AFZ, Fz x FCZ, CPZ x CP1, CPZ x Cz and CPZ x CP2 contain the most relevant features. These findings are beneficial for the creation of a real-time system, as the run-time of the real-time data analysis protocol is vital. When a real-time protocol is considered, the removal of channels and measures which did not achieve high weights in this study could improve the run-time of the protocol and enable a more efficient real-time classification.

The classification methodology involved testing heart rate, fNIRS at frontal and central sites independently and then together using LDA, SVM and rPart learners (Tables 2, 3, 4 and 5). The results achieved indicated that the classification accuracies were lowest during the Impossible condition, which could be due to player frustration. However, they may still have been intent on winning the game, and therefore still exhibiting focus towards the task. This indicates that the subjective measures that were gathered are not effectively measuring immersion at the same rate as the objective measures. However, as a real time adaptive game would still need training data, it may be better to label the data using objective measures rather than subjective – the use of conative probing [37] rather than a subjective score would be one example of this.

The results indicate that the effect of pain does not significantly affect the classification of immersion and that the heart rate features produced comparable results to the frontal fNIRS sites but did not outperform the central fNIRS sites. This is a positive result for our study, as it is important to be able to classify immersion in the presence of pain. The results of the HR classification in comparison to fNIRS classification indicate that, although HR can be classified to the same level as frontal fNIRS sites, central fNIRS sites still provide a more accurate classification. The efficacy of fNIRS classification indicates that the application of fNIRS technology is justifiable even considering the more advanced data collection protocol. Although all participants were subjected to the same pain protocol, some participants may have a naturally lower or higher pain tolerance, and therefore feel more or less pain than anticipated at various stages of the study. This means that the signals in the brain relating to pain could have an effect on the classification when a real-time system is used, depending on the level of pain that a participant is feeling. However, as the results between Game and Pain and Game Only conditions were comparable, we hypothesize that the experience of pain should not affect the accuracy of a classification in a real-time system.

The results have important implications for the future development of a neuroadaptive game. In the first instance, the feature selection process identified the metric (HbT) and specific sites that were most responsible for distinguishing levels of game demand. By focusing on these signals and measures in the design of a neuroadaptive game, it is possible to reduce processing time required for classification during a real-time protocol. Using these results, we intend to adapt the methods that have been used this paper into a real-time system. We believe that adapting a game in this way would enable us to create a more immersive game experience, and therefore reduce the perception of pain.

6 Conclusion and Future Work

The purpose of this work was to identify the foundations of a real-time neuroadaptive system to distract people from painful experiences. The results achieved within this paper have enabled us to identify relevant fNIRS sites and measures that could be used in such a system. A maximum classification accuracy of 99.2% was achieved using the rPart classifier for the detection of immersion in the presence of pain.

Alongside the results shown, we accept the limitations of the current study. For instance, short-distance electrodes were not used during the fNIRS measurements. Short distance electrodes are used to record, and later reduce, the amount of noise within a signal that is not related to neurovascular coupling. Signals such as this are recorded from the extracerebral layers, rather than the cerebral tissue layer, and are task-evoked but not related to neurovascular coupling [36]. Further issues in this study may have arisen due to systemic effects contained within the fNIRS signal that have not been removed [29]. Although filters were applied to the fNIRS signal to reduce noise relating to heart rate, respiration and blood pressure, we cannot be certain that all of these features were removed from the signal. In future studies, steps could be taken to reduce the presence of systemic effects such as the use of heart rate, respiration and blood pressure signals by building personalized filters to be applied to each fNIRS signal [38]. We believe that the future use of personalized filters and short-distance channels could improve on the results that have been gathered in this study.

Acknowledgments. The authors would like to thank Onteca Inc., who provided an adapted version of their title *Space Ribbon* for use in this study. The authors would also like to thank all of the participants for agreeing to take part in the study.

References

1. Broad, R.D., Wheeler, K.: An adult with childhood medical trauma treated with psychoanalytic psychotherapy and EMDR: a case study. Perspect. Psychiatr. Care **42**(2), 95–105 (2006)
2. Diseth, T.H.: Dissociation following traumatic medical treatment procedures in childhood: a longitudinal follow-up. Dev. Psychopathol. **18**(1), 233–251 (2006)
3. Anand, K.J., et al.: Tolerance and withdrawal from prolonged opioid use in critically ill children. Pediatrics **125**(5), e1208–e1225 (2010)
4. Greenbaum, S., et al.: The impact of catastrophizing. Anesthesiology **6**, 1292–1301 (2014)
5. Hua, Y., Qiu, R., Yao, W.Y., Zhang, Q., Chen, X.L.: The effect of virtual reality distraction on pain relief during dressing changes in children with chronic wounds on lower limbs. Pain Manag. Nurs. **16**(5), 685–691 (2015)
6. Eccleston, C., Crombez, G.: Pain demands attention: a cognitive-affective model of the interruptive function of pain. Psychol. Bull. **125**(3), 356–366 (1999)

7. Wohlheiter, K.A.: Interactive versus passive distraction for acute pain management in young children: the role of selective attention and development. J. Pediatr. Psychol. **38**(2), 202–212 (2013)

8. Jameson, E., Trevena, J., Swain, N.: Electronic gaming as pain distraction. Pain Res. Manag. **16**(1), 27–32 (2011)

9. Bantick, S.J., Wise, R.G., Ploghaus, A., Clare, S., Smith, S.M., Tracey, I.: Imaging how attention modulates pain in humans using functional MRI. Brain **125**(Pt 2), 310–319 (2002)

10. Legrain, V., Van Damme, S., Eccleston, C., Davis, K.D., Seminowicz, D.A., Crombez, G.: A neurocognitive model of attention to pain: behavioral and neuroimaging evidence. Pain **144**(3), 230–232 (2009)

11. Weiss, K.E., Dahlquist, L.M., Wohlheiter, K.: The effects of interactive and passive distraction on cold pressor pain in preschool-aged children. J. Pediatr. Psychol. **36**(7), 816–826 (2011)

12. Fairclough, S.H., Gilleade, K., Ewing, K.C., Roberts, J.: Capturing user engagement via psychophysiology: measures and mechanisms for biocybernetic adaptation. Int. J. Auton. Adapt. Commun. Syst. **6**(1), 63 (2013)

13. Ewing, K.C., Fairclough, S.H., Gilleade, K.: Evaluation of an adaptive game that uses EEG measures validated during the design process as inputs to a biocybernetic loop. Front. Hum. Neurosci. **10**(May), 1–13 (2016)

14. Nacke, L., Kalyn, M., Lough, C., Mandryk, R.: Biofeedback game design: using direct and indirect physiological control to enhance game interaction. In: Proceedings of the SIGCHI …, pp. 103–112 (2011)

15. Jennett, C., et al.: Measuring and defining the experience of immersion in games. Int. J. Hum Comput Stud. **66**(9), 641–661 (2008)

16. Nacke, L.E., Lindley, C.A.: Flow and immersion in first-person shooters: measuring the player's gameplay experience. In: Proceedings of the 2008 Conference on Future Play: Research Play Share, pp. 81–88 (2008)

17. Harrivel, A.R., Weissman, D.H., Noll, D.C., Peltier, S.J.: Monitoring attentional state with fNIRS. Front. Hum. Neurosci. **7**(December), 861 (2013)

18. Izzetoglu, K., Bunce, S., Izzetoglu, M., Onaral, B., Pourrezaei, K.: fNIR spectroscopy as a measure of cognitive task load. In: Proceedings of 25th Annual International Conference of the IEEE Engineering in Medicine and Biology Society (IEEE Cat. No. 03CH37439), vol. 4, pp. 3431–3434 (2003)

19. Olsson, E., Ahlsén, G., Eriksson, M.: Skin-to-skin contact reduces near-infrared spectroscopy pain responses in premature infants during blood sampling. Acta Paediatr. Int. J. Paediatr. **105**(4), 376–380 (2016)

20. Jennett, C., Cox, A., Cairns, P.: Investigating computer game immersion and the component real world dissociation. In: Proceedings of the 27th International Conference Extend Abstract Human Factors Computer Systems CHI EA 09, no. February 2007, pp. 3407–3412 (2009)

21. Kussman, B.D., et al.: Capturing pain in the cortex during general anesthesia: near infrared spectroscopy measures in patients undergoing catheter ablation of arrhythmias. PLoS ONE **11**(7), 1–13 (2016)

22. Von Baeyer, C.L., Piira, T., Chambers, C.T., Trapanotto, M., Zeltzer, L.K.: Guidelines for the cold pressor task as an experimental pain stimulus for use with children. J. Pain **6**(4), 218–227 (2005)

23. Baker, W.B., Parthasarathy, A.B., Busch, D.R., Mesquita, R.C., Greenberg, J.H., Yodh, A.G.: Modified Beer-Lambert law for blood flow. Biomed. Opt. Express **5**(11), 4053 (2014)

24. Naseer, N., Noori, F.M., Qureshi, N.K., Hong, K.-S.: Determining optimal feature-combination for LDA classification of functional near-infrared spectroscopy signals in brain-computer interface application. Front. Hum. Neurosci. **10**(May), 1–10 (2016)

25. Kocsis, L., Herman, P., Eke, A.: The modified Beer-Lambert law revisited. Phys. Med. Biol. **51**(5) (2006)

26. Bontrager, D., Novak, D., Zimmermann, R., Riener, R., Marchal-crespo, L.: Physiological noise cancellation in fNIRS using an adaptive filter based on mutual information *, Present. In:IEEE International Conference Systems Man, Cybernetics, San Diego, CA, USA, 5–8 October 2014 (2014)
27. Julien, C.: The enigma of Mayer waves: facts and models. Cardiovasc. Res. **70**(1), 12–21 (2006)
28. Metz, A.J., Wolf, M., Achermann, P., Scholkmann, F.: A new approach for automatic removal of movement artifacts in near-infrared spectroscopy time series by means of acceleration data. Algorithms **8**(4), 1052–1075 (2015)
29. Caldwell, M., Scholkmann, F., Wolf, U., Wolf, M., Elwell, C., Tachtsidis, I.: Modelling confounding effects from extracerebral contamination and systemic factors on functional near-infrared spectroscopy. Neuroimage **143**, 91–105 (2016)
30. Cui, X., Bray, S., Reiss, A.L.: Functional near infrared spectroscopy (NIRS) signal improvement based on negative correlation between oxygenated and deoxygenated hemoglobin dynamics. Neuroimage **49**(4), 3039–3046 (2010)
31. Cui, X., Bray, S., Bryant, D.M., Glover, G.H., Reiss, A.L.: A quantitative comparison of NIRS and fMRI across multiple cognitive tasks. Neuroimage **54**(4), 2808–2821 (2011)
32. Schroeter, M.L., et al.: Towards a standard analysis for functional near-infrared imaging. Neuroimage **21**(1), 283–290 (2004)
33. Tsunashima, H., Yanagisawa, K.: Measurement of brain function of car driver using functional near-infrared spectroscopy (fNIRS). Comput. Intell. Neurosci. **2009** (2009)
34. Frank, E., Hall, M.A., Witten, I.H.: The WEKA Workbench Data Mining: Practical Machine Learning Tools and Techniques, Fourth edn., p. 128. Morgan Kaufmann (2016)
35. Kononenko, I., Šimec, E., Robnik-Šikonja, M.: Overcoming the myopia of inductive learning algorithms with RELIEFF. Appl. Intell. **7**(1), 39–55 (1997)
36. Naseer, N., Hong, K.-S.: fNIRS-based brain-computer interfaces: a review. Front. Hum. Neurosci. **9**(January), 1–15 (2015)
37. Krol, L.R., Zander, T.O.: Cognitive and Affective Probing for Neuroergonomics Cognitive and Affective Probing for Neuroergonomics. no. June (2018)
38. Kaiser, V., et al.: Cortical effects of user training in a motor imagery based brain-computer interface measured by fNIRS and EEG. Neuroimage **85**, 432–444 (2014)

Author Index

Abhari, Kaveh 279
Adžgauskaitė, Marta 279
Ahmed, Faruk 507
Ahmed, Salah Uddin 13
Alghabban, Weam Gaoud 519
Almukadi, Wafa 299
Amro, Ahmed 165
Ando, Taisei 3
Andrasik, Frank 507
Arya, Ali 708

Barneche-Naya, Viviana 410
Bercht, Magda 445
Bergen-Cico, Dessa 176
Bernal, Franklin 307
Blankendaal, Romy 586
Boonekamp, Rudy 586

Caci, Barbara 619
Cetinkaya, Deniz 345
Chan, Gerry 708
Charles, Darryl 631
Chauncey, Sarah A. 326
Chen, Hsi-Jen 32, 644
Chen, Hsin-Jung 644
Chen, Weiwen 13
Cheng, Yung-Chueh 32
Corbin, Connor 345
Costa, Mark R. 176
Cowley, Benjamin Ultan 631
Cruciani, Elisa 365

de Fátima Guilhermino, Jislaine 45
de Freitas Guilhermino Trindade, Daniela 45
Dhou, Khaldoon 619, 658
Dhruv, Kaunil 60
Dibitonto, Massimiliano 365
Dobbins, Chelsea 756
Dogan, Huseyin 345
dos Santos Nascimento, Matheus 45
Durkee, Kevin 60

Eliseu, Sérgio 377
Eloy, Lucca 60

Fairclough, Stephen 756
Flett, Agnes 190

Giabbanelli, Philippe J. 538
Giovannetti, Tania 3
Giri, Nandhini 669
Goethe, Ole 688
Goodell, Jim 557
Grant, Trevor 60
Guo, Wenbin 388

Hamam, Doaa 421
Harzalla, Meryem 397
Hayne, Lucas 60
Hendley, Robert 519
Hernández-Ibáñez, Luis 410
Herpich, Fabrício 445
Hirshfield, Leanne 60, 176
Hori, Masaya 255
Horvat, Ana 472
Hoxha, Keti 432
Hu, Xiangen 507, 605
Huang, Jiali 216
Hung, Wei-Hsiang 32
Hysaj, Ajrina 421

Imran, Masud 708
Inch, David 202
Inoue, Hiroaki 255
Izzetoglu, Kurtulus 202

Jiang, Yin 116
Jin, Jiangbo 13

Kang, Dongjing 700
Kanzaki, Sora 78
Kido, Yutaro 78
Kikuchi, Yu 255

Kim, Donghun 105
Kim, Jung Hyup 388
Kiryu, Takuya 255
Knox, Benjamin James 165
Kristo, Saimir 432
Kwon, Jihey 105

Lanzilotti, Rosa 730
Lee, Eunbyul 105
Lee, Sangyup 105
Leszczynska, Katarzyna 365
Liao, Hao-Yu 90
Lim, Chaeyun 105
Lin, Chih-Chang 90
Lindquist, Kristen 216
Lopes, Maria Manuela 377
Loureiro Krassmann, Aliane 445
Lu, Yi 462
Lyons, Joseph B. 266

Maldonado-Mahauad, Jorge 307
Matsuba, Yoshiaki 78
Medaglia, Carlo Maria 365
Mejía, Magali 307
Mendonça Santos, Bruno 45
Mengato, Ronaldo Cesar 45
Merlin, José Reinaldo 45
Miwakeichi, Fumikazu 255

Nakanishi, Miwa 78
Nam, Chang S. 216
Ness, James 574

Ohtsubo, Tomonori 78
Oliveira, Fábio 377
Omheni, Nizar 397

Palmer, Samson 202
Palmquist, Adam 688
Pang, Wei 462
Perna, Valerio 432
Pesavento, Michael 279
Plantak Vukovac, Dijana 472
Pugh, Zachary 216
Pyun, Miran 105

Razza, Rachel 176
Ribeiro, Carlos Eduardo 45
Ribeiro, João Pedro 377

Richards, Dale 202, 227
Riyadh, Md 708
Roselli, Teresa 730
Rossano, Veronica 730

Sacco, Owen 739
Sakamoto, Maiko 3
Schoonderwoerd, Tjeerd 586
Secchi, Davide 240
Sgarbi, Ederson Marcos 45
Shelton-Rayner, Graham 202
Shidujaman, Mohammad 13
Shimizu, Shunji 255
Shubeck, Keith 507, 605
Simpson, Gregory I. 326
Stamp, Kellyann 756
Stapić, Zlatko 472
Stolterman, Erik 669
Su, Yao 127
Sugawara, Daichi 78

Tan, Wei 116
Tarouco, Liane Margarida Rockenbach 445
Tawfik, Andrew A. 538
Thai, Khanh-Phuong (KP) 557
Tung, Fang-Wu 90

van den Bosch, Karel 586
Veintimilla-Reyes, Jaime 307
Villalba-Condori, Klinge 307
Vo, Thy 266

Wang, Junfeng 127
Wang, Lijia 605
Wang, Liying 485
Wang, Qiu 176
Wu, Lei 127
Wu, Xiaoli 138

Xu, Panpan 138

Yamaguchi, Takehiko 3
Yamin, Muhammad Mudassar 165

Zhang, Bo 150
Zhang, Jingyu 150
Zúñiga-Prieto, Miguel 307